R. Gupta's®

Popular Master Guide

Indian Forest Service

MAIN EXAMINATION

BOTANY

PAPER I & II

Conducted by:

UNION PUBLIC SERVICE COMMISSION (UPSC)

RAMESH PUBLISHING HOUSE, NEW DELHI

Published by

O.P. Gupta *for* Ramesh Publishing House

Admin. Office

12-H, New Daryaganj Road, Opp. Officers' Mess,
New Delhi-110002 ✆ 23275224, 23245124

E-mail: info@rameshpublishinghouse.com

For Online Shopping: www.rameshpublishinghouse.com

Showroom

- Balaji Market, Nai Sarak, Delhi-110006 ✆ 23282525 📱 9354373464
- 4457, Nai Sarak, Delhi-110006

Book Code: R-1239

ISBN: 978-81-7812-935-8

Price: ₹ 660

Printed at: J.P. Enterprises, Delhi

CONTENTS

SCHEME OF THE MAIN EXAMINATION

The main examination for the Indian Forest Service comprises:

(A) The written examination consisting of the following papers:

Paper I	General English	300 marks
Paper II	General Knowledge	300 marks
Paper III **Paper IV** **Paper V** **Paper VI**	Any two subjects to be selected from the list of the optional subjects. Each subject will have two papers.	200 Marks for each paper

(B) Interview for Personality Test —Maximum marks: 300

LIST OF OPTIONAL SUBJECTS

1. Agriculture
2. Agricultural Engineering
3. Animal Husbandry & Veterinary Science
4. Botany
5. Chemistry
6. Chemical Engineering
7. Civil Engineering
8. Forestry
9. Geology
10. Mathematics
11. Mechanical Engineering
12. Physics
13. Statistics
14. Zoology

Provided that the candidate will not be allowed to offer the following combination of subjects:

(a) Agriculture and Agricultural Engineering

(b) Agriculture and Animal Husbandry & Veterinary Science

(c) Agriculture and Forestry

(d) Chemistry and Chemical Engineering

(e) Mathematics and Statistics

(f) Of the Engineering subjects viz. Agricultural Engineering, Chemical Engineering, Civil Engineering and Mechanical Engineering not more than one subject.

GENERAL INSTRUCTIONS

1. All the question papers for the examination will be of conventional (Essay) type.
2. All question papers must be answered in English. Question papers will be set in English only.
3. The duration of each of the papers referred to above will be 3 hours.

Previous Years' Paper

Indian Forest Service (Main) Exam, 2025

SUBJECT–BOTANY

(Exam held on 21-11-2025)

PAPER-I

Instructions: *There are EIGHT questions in all, out of which FIVE are to be attempted, question Nos. 1 & 5 are compulsory. Out of the remaining SIX questions, THREE are to be attempted selecting at least ONE question from each of the two Sections A and B. Attempts of questions shall be counted in sequential order. Unless struck off, attempt of a question shall be counted even if attempted partly. Any page or portion of the page left blank in the Question-cum-Answer Booklet must be clearly struck off. All questions carry equal marks. Answers must be written in ENGLISH only.*

SECTION-A

1. (a) What are the major differences between Moss and Liverworts?

(b) What are Biocides? Describe their merits and demerits.

(c) Blue-green algae are also referred to as bacteria. Explain their algal and bacterial features.

(d) Give the scientific name of the organisms used for the production of:

(i) Ethyl alcohol from glucose

(ii) Citric acid

(iii) Bacitracin

(iv) Cellulase

(e) Name the order of Gymnosperms whose members are known as "SEED FERNS". Give its general characteristics.

Ans. (a) Mosses and liverworts are the two principal groups of bryophytes. Although both are non-vascular plants with a dominant gametophyte generation, they differ markedly in their morphology, anatomy, and reproductive organisation. These differences reflect varying levels of structural complexity and ecological adaptation.

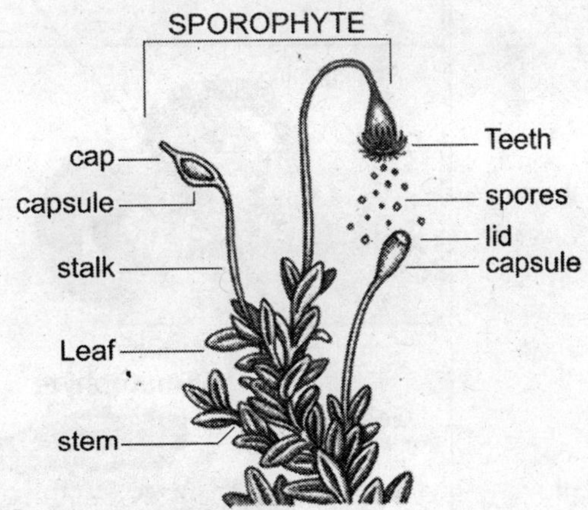

Major differences between Mosses and Liverworts

The plant body in mosses is always leafy. The gametophyte is differentiated into a stem-like axis bearing spirally arranged leaf-like structures. These leaves are usually several cells thick and commonly possess a midrib (costa), indicating a higher degree of tissue differentiation. In liverworts, the gametophyte is commonly **thalloid**, appearing as a flat, dorsiventral, lobed structure closely appressed to the substratum. Even in leafy liverworts, the leaves are thin, arranged in two or three rows, and lack a midrib, showing simpler organisation.

The rhizoids of mosses are multicellular and branched, providing stronger anchorage and more effective absorption of water. In contrast, liverwort rhizoids are unicellular, reflecting a more primitive condition.

A distinct and well-developed protonema stage is a characteristic feature of mosses. It represents an independent juvenile phase from which buds arise to form the leafy gametophyte. In liverworts, the protonema is either extremely short-lived or completely absent, and the gametophyte develops directly.

The sporophyte of mosses is comparatively more complex, consisting of a foot, a long seta, and a capsule with specialised structures such as an operculum and peristome teeth. These structures help in gradual and regulated spore dispersal. In liverworts, the sporophyte is simpler; the capsule lacks peristome teeth, and spore dispersal is aided by elaters, which respond to changes in humidity.

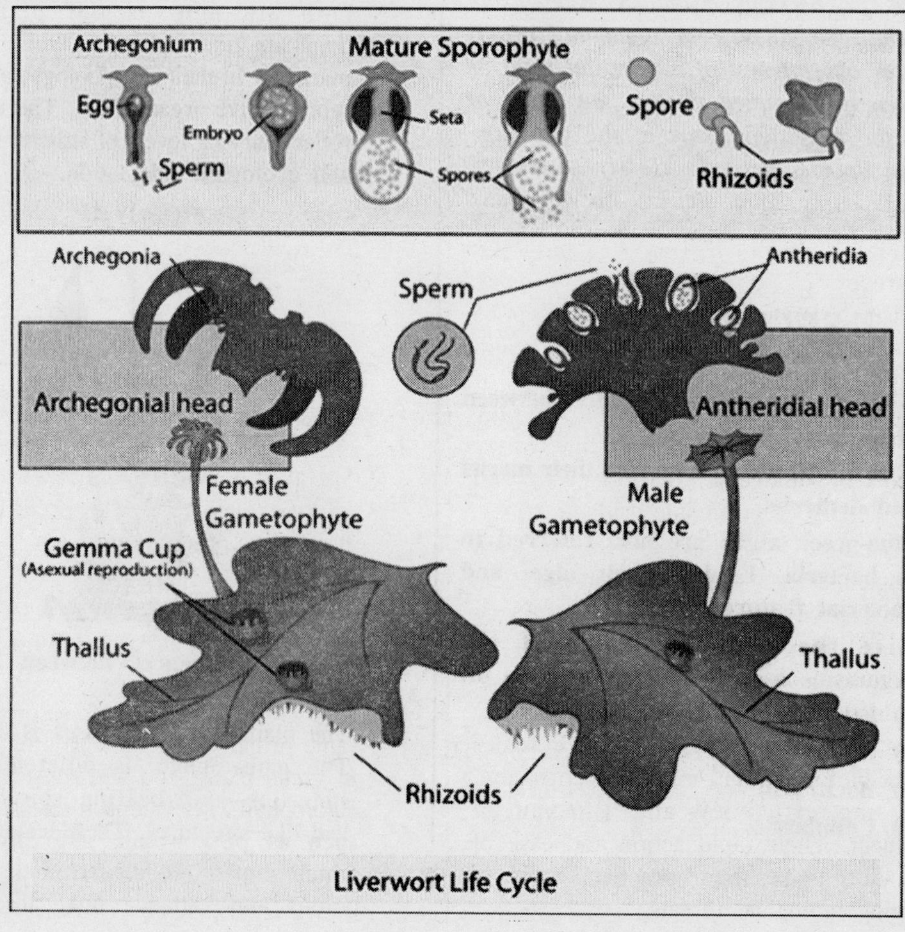

Liverwort Life Cycle

Ecologically, mosses exhibit greater tolerance to desiccation and occupy a wide range of habitats, whereas liverworts are largely confined to moist, shaded environments.

Thus, mosses represent a more advanced level of organisation among bryophytes when compared to liverworts, particularly in terms of structural differentiation and reproductive complexity.

Ans. (*b*) Biocides are chemical substances or formulations designed to kill, control, deter, or render harmless living organisms that are considered harmful to human health, agriculture, industry, or the environment. Unlike pesticides, which are mainly used in agriculture against pests, biocides are used in a much broader context, including public health, household sanitation, industrial systems, and environmental management. They act against a wide range of organisms such as bacteria, fungi, algae, insects, rodents, and other unwanted life forms.

Merits of biocides

One major merit of biocides is their effectiveness in controlling disease-causing organisms. Disinfectants and antiseptics are essential in hospitals and public health systems for preventing the spread of infections and epidemics. Biocides also play a crucial role in water treatment, where they help control pathogenic microorganisms and algae, thereby ensuring safe drinking water. In agriculture and forestry, biocides help in protecting crops, stored products, and materials from damage caused by insects, fungi, and microbes, contributing to higher productivity and reduced economic losses. In industrial systems, such as cooling towers, pipelines, and paints, biocides prevent biofouling and microbial corrosion, increasing efficiency and lifespan of equipment. Their rapid action and ease of application make them practical tools in managing biological threats.

Demerits of biocides

Despite their usefulness, biocides have several serious drawbacks. Many biocides are toxic and non-selective, meaning they may harm non-target organisms, including beneficial microbes, plants, animals, and even humans. Prolonged or excessive use can lead to environmental contamination, affecting soil, water bodies, and food chains.

Another major concern is the development of resistance in target organisms, particularly microbes, which reduces the long-term effectiveness of biocides and creates public health challenges. Some biocides are persistent and bioaccumulative, leading to chronic ecological damage and potential health risks such as endocrine disruption or carcinogenic effects. Improper handling and disposal can further increase occupational and environmental hazards.

Thus, while biocides are indispensable for disease control, sanitation, and industrial protection, their use requires strict regulation, careful selection, and controlled application to balance benefits against ecological and health risks.

Ans. (*c*) Blue-green algae, now scientifically known as cyanobacteria, occupy a unique position in the living world because they exhibit a combination of characteristics typical of both algae and bacteria. This dual nature explains why they were traditionally grouped with algae based on appearance and photosynthetic ability, but later classified as bacteria based on cellular organisation.

Algal features of blue-green algae (cyanobacteria)

Blue-green algae possess chlorophyll-a, the same primary photosynthetic pigment found in green plants and true algae. Along with chlorophyll-a, they contain accessory pigments such as phycocyanin and phycoerythrin, which impart the characteristic blue-green colour and enhance light absorption for photosynthesis. They are autotrophic, capable of synthesising their own food through oxygenic photosynthesis, releasing oxygen as a by-product. Ecologically, they function as primary producers in aquatic and terrestrial ecosystems, similar to algae. Many cyanobacteria occur in filamentous or colonial forms, resembling algal thalli, and several species contribute significantly to biological nitrogen fixation, improving soil fertility in natural ecosystems and rice fields.

Bacterial features of blue-green algae (cyanobacteria)

At the cellular level, blue-green algae are distinctly prokaryotic, a defining bacterial trait. They lack a true nucleus; instead, genetic material is present as naked DNA in a nucleoid region. Membrane-bound organelles such as mitochondria, chloroplasts, endoplasmic reticulum, and Golgi bodies are completely absent. Their cell wall is similar to that of bacteria, containing peptidoglycan. Photosynthetic pigments are not enclosed within chloroplasts but are embedded in thylakoid membranes lying freely in the cytoplasm. Reproduction is exclusively asexual, occurring by binary fission, fragmentation, or formation of specialised cells like hormogonia, with no sexual reproduction. Some cyanobacteria possess heterocysts, specialised thick-walled cells for nitrogen fixation, a feature unique to this group among prokaryotes.

Thus, blue-green algae are termed bacteria because of their prokaryotic cellular organisation, yet they retain algal traits due to their photosynthetic nature and ecological role. This combination places cyanobacteria as an evolutionary bridge between photosynthetic bacteria and higher autotrophic organisms.

Ans. (*d*) The industrial production of several important biochemical substances relies on specific micro-organisms because of their well-established metabolic capabilities and efficiency under controlled conditions. The scientific names of the organisms used are as follows:

(*i*) **Ethyl alcohol from glucose:** Ethyl alcohol is produced by the process of alcoholic fermentation, in which glucose is anaerobically converted into ethanol and carbon dioxide. The organism most commonly employed for this purpose is *Saccharomyces cerevisiae*, a unicellular yeast widely used in brewing, baking, and industrial alcohol production due to its high fermentative efficiency and tolerance to alcohol.

(*ii*) **Citric acid:** Citric acid is produced commercially through microbial fermentation, primarily using the filamentous fungus *Aspergillus niger*. This organism is preferred because it can accumulate large quantities of citric acid in the culture medium when grown under controlled conditions of high sugar concentration and limited nitrogen.

(*iii*) **Bacitracin:** Bacitracin is a polypeptide antibiotic produced by the bacterium *Bacillus licheniformis*. This organism synthesizes bacitracin as a secondary metabolite, which is effective mainly against Gram-positive bacteria and is widely used in topical antibiotic preparations.

(*iv*) **Cellulase:** Cellulase enzymes, which catalyse the breakdown of cellulose into simpler sugars, are commonly produced using the fungus *Trichoderma reesei*. This organism is extensively used in industrial biotechnology for applications in biofuel production, textile processing, and paper industries due to its high cellulase-yielding capacity.

Ans. (*e*) The order of gymnosperms whose members are known as seed ferns is Pteridospermales (also referred to as

Cycadofilicales). This group is entirely extinct and is of great evolutionary significance because it shows a clear combination of fern-like and gymnospermous characters, thereby representing an important transitional stage in the evolution of seed plants.

General characteristics of Seed Ferns (Pterido-spermales)

Seed ferns possessed a fern-like vegetative body. The plants usually had large, pinnately compound leaves resembling true ferns in external appearance. These leaves showed circinate vernation in young stages, a typical fern character. However, unlike true ferns, they did not reproduce by spores.

The stem anatomy exhibited gymnospermous features. The vascular system was well developed, with secondary growth commonly present, indicating the activity of a cambium. The xylem consisted mainly of tracheids, and vessels were absent, as is typical of gymnosperms.

The most striking feature of seed ferns was the presence of seeds borne on leaf-like structures. Ovules were not enclosed within an ovary and were often attached directly to modified pinnules or leaf segments. This open arrangement of ovules clearly places them among gymnosperms, despite their fern-like foliage.

Reproductive organs were not organised into compact cones. Male organs were usually borne on modified leaves, producing pollen, while female organs consisted of exposed ovules, often partially surrounded by cupule-like structures.

Seed ferns flourished mainly during the Late Paleozoic era, especially in the Carboniferous period, and later became extinct. Their mixed characters provide strong evidence for the evolutionary link between pteridophytes and gymnosperms, making them extremely important from a phylogenetic and IFS examination perspective.

2. (*a*) Describe the ecological and horticultural applications of Bryophyta.

(*b*) Draw and label the thallus structure of *Laminaria*. Describe the sexual reproduction in *Laminaria*.

(*c*) Describe the structure of female gametophyte of *Cycas*. Explain the changes in the ovule of *Cycas* after fertilization.

Ans. (*a*) Bryophytes, though small and structurally simple, play a disproportionately important role in both natural ecosystems and human-managed horticultural systems. Their ecological significance arises from their early colonisation of land surfaces and their ability to modify habitats, while their horticultural value lies in their unique physical and physiological properties.

Ecological applications of Bryophyta

Bryophytes are important pioneer plants. They are often the first organisms to colonise bare rocks, volcanic surfaces, and degraded lands. By secreting organic acids, they contribute to rock weathering and the initial stages of soil formation. Their decaying plant bodies add organic matter, gradually creating conditions suitable for higher plants.

They play a crucial role in water regulation. Bryophytes, especially mosses like Sphagnum, have a remarkable capacity to absorb and retain water, acting as natural sponges. This helps in maintaining soil moisture, regulating surface runoff, and reducing soil erosion, particularly in forest ecosystems and wetlands.

Bryophytes significantly contribute to nutrient cycling. They absorb minerals directly from rainwater, dust, and substratum and release these nutrients slowly back into the ecosystem. Some bryophytes associated with cyanobacteria also indirectly aid in nitrogen enrichment of soils.

Ecologically, bryophytes provide micro-habitats for a wide range of organisms such as insects, nematodes, protozoans, and microorganisms. In peatlands, Sphagnum mosses play a dominant role in peat formation, which is an important long-term carbon sink and helps regulate atmospheric carbon dioxide levels.

Horticultural applications of Bryophyta

In horticulture, bryophytes are valued mainly for their water-holding and protective properties. Sphagnum moss is widely used as a packing material for transporting seedlings, bulbs, and live plants because it retains moisture, prevents desiccation, and possesses mild antiseptic properties that reduce microbial infection.

Bryophytes are also used as soil conditioners. Dried and processed *Sphagnum* is added to potting mixes to improve aeration, water retention, and root development, especially in orchids and other epiphytic plants.

In gardening and landscaping, mosses are used for aesthetic purposes, particularly in Japanese gardens, bonsai cultivation, terrariums, and green walls, where they provide a natural, soft green cover and help retain humidity.

Thus, bryophytes, despite their small size and simple structure, have immense ecological importance in maintaining ecosystem stability and practical horticultural value in plant cultivation and landscape management.

Ans. **(*b*)** *Laminaria* is a large brown alga (kelp) showing a high degree of morphological differentiation of the thallus and a well-defined sexual mode of reproduction with heteromorphic alternation of generations.

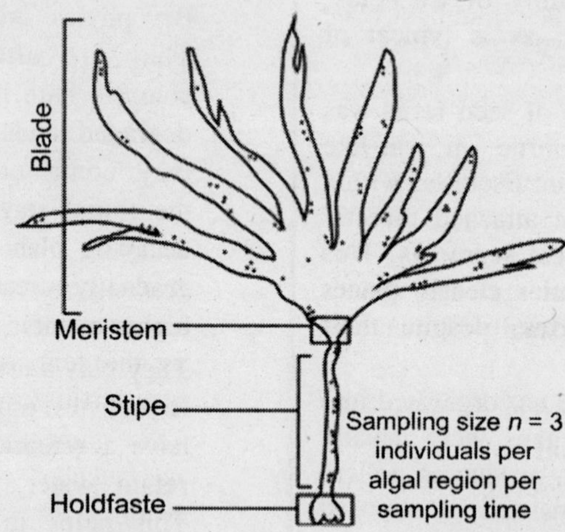

Thallus structure of *Laminaria*

The thallus of *Laminaria* is large, multi-cellular, and parenchymatous, showing clear external differentiation into three distinct regions.

The holdfast is the basal, root-like part that anchors the plant firmly to rocky substrata in marine habitats. It does not absorb nutrients but provides strong mechanical attachment against waves and currents.

Above the holdfast is the stipe, a cylindrical, flexible stalk that elevates the photosynthetic region into better-lit zones of water. Internally, the stipe shows tissue differentiation, including a cortex and a central conducting region that helps in translocation of photosynthates.

The uppermost expanded portion is the blade or lamina, which is broad, flat, and leaf-like. It is the main photosynthetic region and may be entire or divided into segments. Growth occurs from an intercalary meristem located between the stipe and blade, allowing continuous elongation.

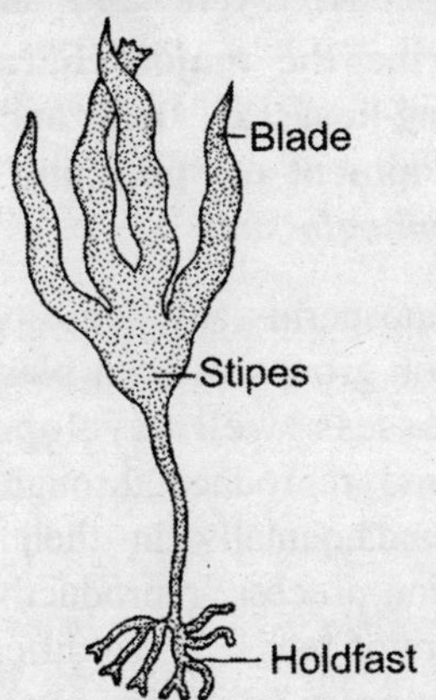

Sexual reproduction in *Laminaria*

Sexual reproduction in *Laminaria* is oogamous and takes place on a microscopic haploid gametophyte generation. The dominant plant body is the diploid sporophyte.

On the sporophyte, specialised fertile regions develop on the blade, bearing sori that contain unilocular sporangia. Meiosis occurs within these sporangia, producing haploid zoospores. These zoospores germinate to form separate male and female gametophytes, which are small, filamentous, and independent.

The male gametophyte produces antheridia, each releasing biflagellate male gametes, while the female gametophyte forms oogonia, each containing a single large, non-motile egg. Fertilisation occurs in water when a male gamete fuses with the egg to form a diploid zygote.

The zygote directly develops into a new diploid sporophyte, completing a heteromorphic alternation of generations, with a large sporophyte and a reduced gametophyte. This reproductive strategy ensures genetic variation and successful survival in marine environments.

Ans. (*c*) In *Cycas*, the female gametophyte is highly developed and represents an important stage in gymnosperm reproduction. It develops within the ovule and later plays a direct role in nourishment of the embryo after fertilisation.

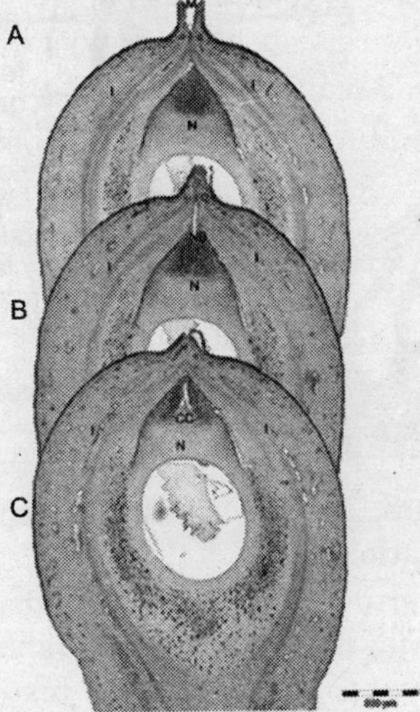

Structure of the female gametophyte of *Cycas*

The female gametophyte of *Cycas* develops from a functional megaspore inside the nucellus of the ovule. The megaspore undergoes repeated free-nuclear divisions followed by wall formation, resulting in a massive, multicellular, haploid tissue known as the female gametophyte or endosperm (pre-fertilisation endosperm).

This gametophytic tissue completely fills the nucellar cavity and serves as a food-storage tissue, rich in starch and other reserve materials. At the micropylar end of the female gametophyte, usually 2 to 8 archegonia are formed. Each archegonium consists of a large egg cell, a short neck, and a neck canal cell. The archegonia are embedded in the gametophytic tissue and open towards the pollen chamber, facilitating fertilisation. The female gametophyte thus performs a dual role: it produces the female sex cells and later nourishes the developing embryo.

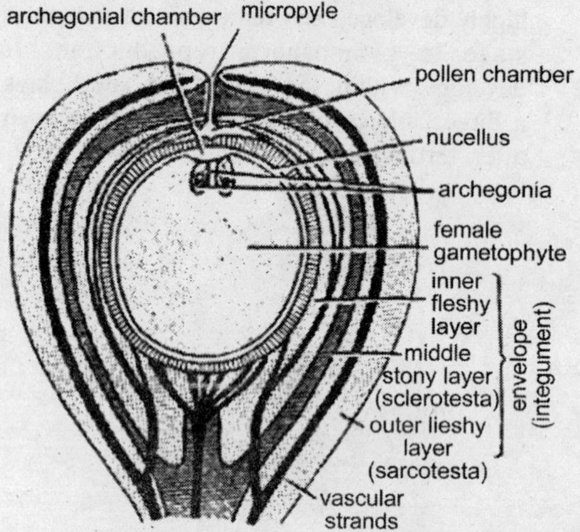

Changes in the ovule of *Cycas* after fertilisation

After fertilisation, one of the male gametes fuses with the egg to form a diploid zygote. The zygote undergoes a resting period followed by embryonic development. The embryo differentiates into radicle, plumule, and two cotyledons, typical of gymnosperms. The female gametophyte persists and enlarges further, becoming the endosperm of the seed, which supplies nourishment to the developing embryo. The nucellus is partially consumed during this process, although a small portion may remain as perisperm. The integument of the ovule undergoes differentiation to form the seed coat, which becomes thick and three-layered, consisting of an outer fleshy layer, a middle hard stony layer, and an inner fleshy layer. The ovule is thus transformed into a seed, containing the embryo, nutritive endosperm, and protective seed coat.

These post-fertilisation changes ensure protection, nourishment, and successful germination of the embryo, reflecting the advanced reproductive adaptations of *Cycas*.

3. (*a*) Differentiate between Gymnosperms and Angio-sperms with reference to their vasculature, fertilization, reproductive structures and seed.

(*b*) Name the causal organism of Leaf spot or Tikka disease of groundnut. What are the symptoms of this disease? Describe its disease cycle and management.

(*c*) Describe the major characteristics of Ophiog-lossaceae. Draw and describe the development of spike and sporangium in *Ophioglossum*.

Ans. (*a*) Gymnosperms and angiosperms are the two major groups of seed plants. Although both possess well-developed vascular tissues and reproduce through seeds, they differ fundamentally in their vasculature, fertilisation process, reproductive structures, and nature of seeds. These differences reflect the evolutionary advancement of angiosperms over gymnosperms.

- **Vasculature:** In gymnosperms, the vascular system is relatively primitive. The xylem is mainly composed of tracheids, and true vessels are generally absent (except in a few cases like Gnetum). The phloem lacks companion cells and consists mainly of sieve cells. In contrast, angiosperms possess a highly advanced vascular system. Their xylem contains vessels, tracheids, fibres, and parenchyma, while the phloem includes sieve tube elements and companion cells, ensuring more efficient transport of water and food.
- **Fertilisation:** Fertilisation in gymnosperms is simple fertilisation. Only one male gamete fuses with the egg to form the zygote. Double fertilisation is absent. In angiosperms, fertilisation is double fertilisation, a unique and defining feature. One male gamete fuses with the egg to form the zygote, while the other fuses with the polar nuclei to form the triploid endosperm, which nourishes the developing embryo.
- **Reproductive structures:** The reproductive structures of gymnosperms are

cones (strobili). Male and female cones bear microsporangia and megasporangia respectively. Ovules are exposed and not enclosed by any ovary. In angiosperms, reproduction occurs through flowers, which are highly specialised structures. Ovules are enclosed within an ovary, providing protection and facilitating efficient pollination mechanisms.

- **Seed:** Seeds of gymnosperms are naked, as they are not enclosed within a fruit. The endosperm is formed before fertilisation and is haploid. In angiosperms, seeds are enclosed within fruits, which develop from the ovary after fertilisation. The endosperm is typically formed after fertilisation and is usually triploid, providing better nourishment to the embryo.

Thus, angiosperms exhibit greater structural, physiological, and reproductive advancement compared to gymnosperms, enabling them to dominate most terrestrial ecosystems.

Ans. **(*b*)** Leaf spot or Tikka disease of groundnut is one of the most destructive fungal diseases of groundnut, causing severe reduction in photosynthetic area and ultimately leading to heavy yield losses if not properly managed.

- **Causal organism:** Tikka disease is caused by two closely related fungal pathogens:
  - ❑ Early leaf spot – Cercospora arachidicola
  - ❑ Late leaf spot – Cercosporidium personatum (syn. Phaeoisariopsis personata)

  Together, these two infections are commonly referred to as Tikka disease.
- **Symptoms of the disease:** The disease primarily affects the leaves, but under severe conditions, petioles and stems may also be infected. In early leaf spot, small, circular to irregular brown spots appear on the upper surface of leaves, surrounded by a conspicuous yellow halo. The centre of the lesion turns dark brown with age.

  In late leaf spot, the lesions are darker, almost black, usually without a prominent yellow halo, and appear mainly on the lower surface of the leaf. As the disease progresses, spots enlarge and coalesce, leading to premature defoliation, which drastically reduces photosynthesis and pod filling.
- **Disease cycle:** The fungus survives between crop seasons mainly in infected crop debris left in the field and occasionally in infected seeds. With the onset of favourable conditions—high humidity, frequent rainfall, and moderate temperatures—the fungus produces conidia, which serve as the primary source of infection.

  These conidia are disseminated by wind, rain splash, insects, and farm operations. Upon landing on susceptible leaf surfaces, they germinate in the presence of moisture, penetrate the host tissue either directly or through stomata, and establish infection. Secondary spread occurs repeatedly during the growing season through newly formed conidia, leading to rapid disease build-up under humid conditions.
- **Disease management:** Effective management of Tikka disease requires an integrated approach. Cultural practices such as crop rotation, deep ploughing to bury infected debris, and removal of plant residues help reduce the initial inoculum. Use of disease-free seeds and resistant or tolerant groundnut varieties is highly recommended.

  Chemical control plays a major role in managing severe infections. Protective fungicides like mancozeb or chlorothalonil and systemic fungicides such as carbendazim or tebuconazole are effective when applied at proper intervals, especially during periods favourable for disease development. Balanced fertilisation and timely irrigation further improve plant vigour and reduce disease severity.

Thus, early detection combined with cultural, genetic, and chemical measures is essential for effective control of Tikka disease and for sustaining groundnut productivity.

Ans. (*c*) The family Ophioglossaceae represents a highly specialised and primitive group of pteridophytes, showing several distinctive morphological and anatomical characters that clearly separate it from other fern families. The genus *Ophioglossum* (adder's tongue fern) is the most characteristic member and is of great evolutionary and systematic importance.

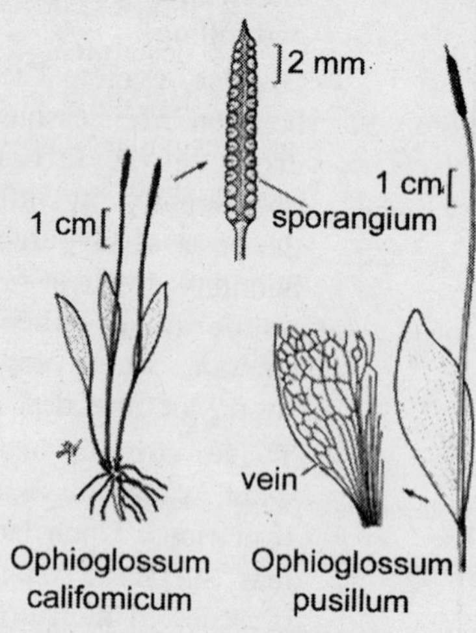

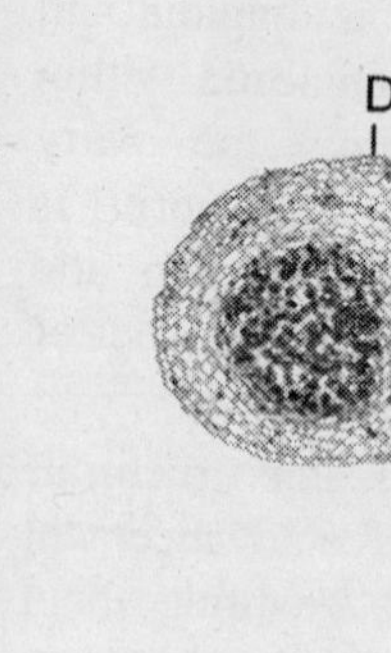

Major characteristics of Ophioglossaceae

Members of Ophioglossaceae are small, perennial, terrestrial ferns commonly found in moist and shady habitats. The sporophyte plant body is simple and consists of an underground rhizome with adventitious roots and a single aerial leaf produced annually. The leaf shows a unique differentiation into two distinct parts: a sterile leaf (trophophyll) and a fertile spike (sporophyll), which arise from a common stalk.

The leaves show simple venation, which may be reticulate or dichotomous, unlike most ferns. Circinate vernation is absent. Anatomically, the vascular system is simple, and secondary growth may be present in the rhizome, which is unusual for ferns. The gametophyte is subterranean, non-green, saprophytic, and associated with mycorrhizal fungi, indicating a primitive condition.

Sporangia are eusporangiate, large, thick-walled, and numerous spores are produced. The family shows homospory, and spores germinate slowly.

Development of spike in *Ophioglossum*

The fertile spike develops as a lateral outgrowth from the base of the sterile leaf blade. It represents a modified fertile segment of the leaf. The spike is usually elongated, unbranched, and erect, bearing sporangia embedded on either side. Each spike contains two vertical rows of sporangia, indicating its leaf origin.

Development of sporangium in *Ophioglossum*

The sporangium is eusporangiate in nature. It develops from a group of superficial initial cells on the fertile spike. These cells divide periclinally to form an outer jacket layer and an inner mass of sporogenous tissue.

The jacket becomes multilayered and forms a thick sporangial wall.

The inner sporogenous tissue differentiates into spore mother cells, each of which undergoes meiosis to produce haploid spores. A single sporangium produces a very large number of spores. At maturity, the sporangium dehisces by a longitudinal slit, releasing spores into the surrounding environment.

Thus, Ophioglossaceae exhibits several primitive features such as eusporangiate sporangia, subterranean gametophyte, and simple leaf organisation, making it an important family for understanding the early evolution of vascular plants.

4. (*a*) Describe the role of fungal enzymes and toxins in the development of plant diseases.

(*b*) What are the salient features of Zygomycetes? With the help of suitable diagrams, describe the sexual reproduction in *Mucor*.

(*c*) What is the difference between Manoxylic and Pycnoxylic wood? Draw well-labelled diagrams of Radial longitudinal section and Tangential longitudinal section of long shoot of *Pinus*.

Ans. (*a*) Fungi cause plant diseases primarily through the production of enzymes and toxins, which play a decisive role in host penetration, tissue colonisation, symptom expression, and disease progression. These biochemical weapons enable pathogenic fungi to overcome plant structural barriers and physiological defence mechanisms.

Role of fungal enzymes in plant disease development

Fungal enzymes are mainly involved in penetration and maceration of host tissues. The plant cell wall is a complex structure composed of cellulose, hemicellulose, pectins, lignin, and proteins. To breach this barrier, pathogenic fungi secrete a range of cell wall–degrading enzymes.

- Cellulases break down cellulose microfibrils, weakening the structural framework of plant cells.
- Pectinases (such as pectin methyl esterase and polygalacturonase) dissolve the middle lamella, causing separation of cells and leading to soft rot symptoms.
- Hemicellulases degrade hemicellulose, further destabilising the cell wall.
- Lignin-degrading enzymes like laccases and peroxidases enable fungi to invade woody tissues.

Proteolytic enzymes degrade structural and defence-related proteins of the host, while cutinases help fungi penetrate the cuticle. Collectively, these enzymes facilitate rapid spread of the pathogen, nutrient acquisition, and extensive tissue destruction.

Role of fungal toxins in plant disease development

Fungal toxins are low-molecular-weight compounds that disrupt normal physiological processes of plants. They may act locally or be translocated within the plant, intensifying disease symptoms. Toxins are broadly classified into host-specific toxins and non-host-specific toxins.

Host-specific toxins affect only particular plant species or cultivars and determine the specificity of the disease. They interfere with vital cellular functions such as membrane integrity, ion transport, or enzyme activity, leading to rapid cell death. Non-host-specific toxins act on a wide range of plants and cause general symptoms like chlorosis, necrosis, wilting, and growth inhibition.

Toxins may inhibit photosynthesis, respiration, or protein synthesis, alter membrane permeability, and disturb hormonal balance. Some toxins induce excessive production of reactive oxygen species, resulting in oxidative stress and tissue damage.

Integrated role in disease expression

Enzymes and toxins act synergistically. Enzymes facilitate entry and spread of the pathogen, while toxins kill host cells or suppress defence responses, creating a favourable environment for fungal growth. Together, they determine the severity, speed, and characteristic symptoms of fungal plant diseases.

Thus, fungal enzymes and toxins are central to pathogenesis, transforming a healthy plant into a diseased one through biochemical disruption and structural degradation, and their understanding is crucial for effective disease management strategies.

Ans. **(*b*)** Zygomycetes represent a primitive group of fungi characterised by simple thallus organisation and a distinctive mode of sexual reproduction. *Mucor* is a typical genus used to explain the reproductive features of this group.

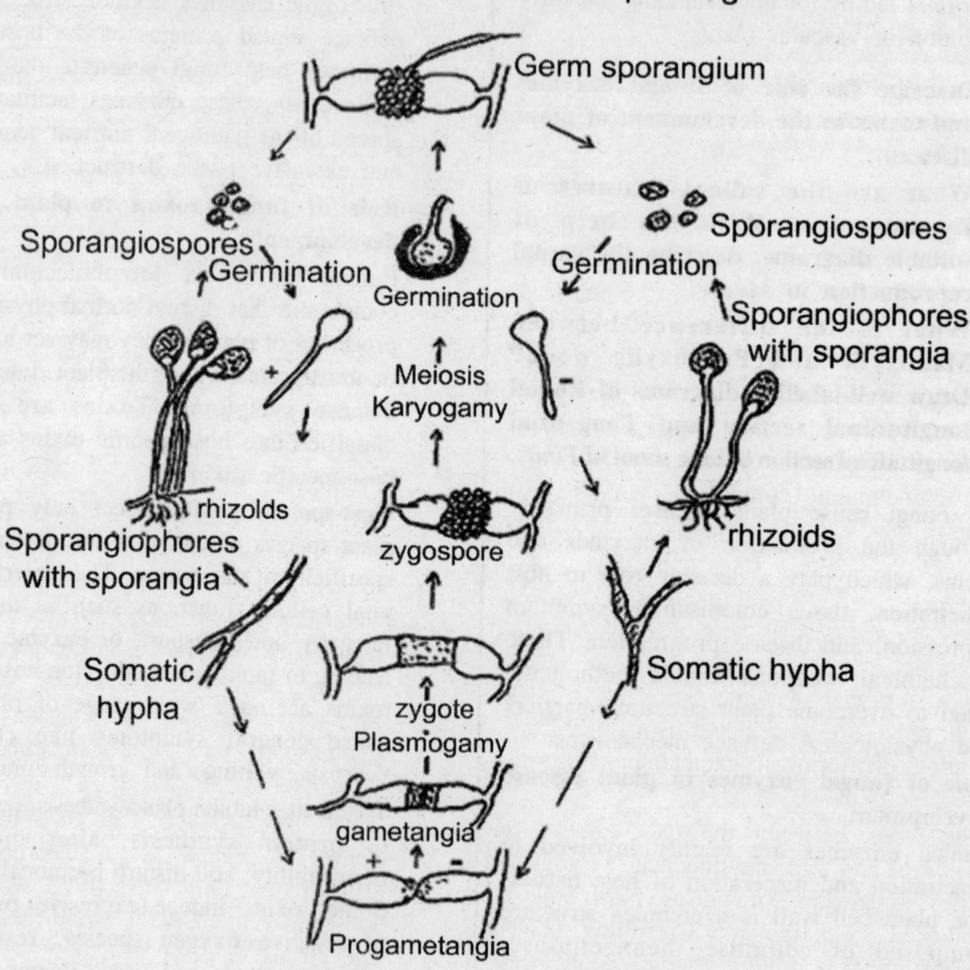

Salient features of Zygomycetes

Members of Zygomycetes are mostly terrestrial fungi, commonly found growing as saprophytes on decaying organic matter such as bread, fruits, and dung. Some members are parasitic. The mycelium is well developed, coenocytic, and aseptate, meaning it lacks cross-walls and contains multinucleate cytoplasm. Septa appear only to delimit reproductive structures or in old hyphae.

The cell wall is mainly composed of chitin and chitosan. Zygomycetes reproduce asexually by means of non-motile sporangiospores, which are produced endogenously inside sporangia borne on sporangiophores. Under unfavourable conditions, they reproduce sexually, forming a thick-walled resting structure known as a zygospore, which is characteristic of the group.

Sexual reproduction is generally gametangial copulation, and species may be homothallic or heterothallic. The life cycle does not show alternation of generations, and meiosis occurs during zygospore germination.

Sexual reproduction in *Mucor*

Sexual reproduction in *Mucor* takes place under unfavourable environmental conditions and is isogamous in nature. It occurs by gametangial copulation between two compatible hyphae, usually designated as + and – strains.

Initially, two hyphae of opposite strains grow towards each other and develop swollen terminal portions called progametangia. These terminal swellings come into contact, and septa are laid down near their tips, cutting off terminal gametangia from the basal suspensors.

The walls between the two gametangia dissolve, and their multinucleate protoplasts fuse, a process known as plasmogamy, followed by karyogamy, resulting in the formation of a diploid zygote. Soon after, a thick, dark, ornamented wall is formed around the zygote, producing a resistant zygospore.

The zygospore undergoes a resting period and helps the fungus survive adverse conditions. When favourable conditions return, the zygospore germinates. During germination, meiosis occurs, and a short sporangiophore emerges, bearing a germ sporangium that produces haploid spores. These spores are released and germinate to form new mycelia, completing the life cycle.

Thus, sexual reproduction in *Mucor* ensures genetic recombination and survival through the formation of a resistant zygospore, a defining feature of Zygomycetes.

Ans. (*c*) Difference between Manoxylic and Pycnoxylic wood

Manoxylic wood is characterised by a large amount of parenchymatous tissue and comparatively less compact xylem. As a result, the wood is soft, loose, and spongy. Vascular tissues are widely spaced, and mechanical strength is relatively low. This type of wood is typically found in Cycads, where the stem is thick but mechanically weak due to abundant ground tissue.

Pycnoxylic wood, on the other hand, is dense, compact, and hard because it contains very little parenchyma and a predominance of tracheids. The xylem elements are closely packed, providing greater mechanical strength and efficiency in conduction. This type of wood is characteristic of conifers such as *Pinus* and represents an advanced gymnospermous condition adapted for tall growth and support.

Thus, the essential difference lies in the degree of compactness and proportion of parenchyma, with manoxylic wood being loose and pycnoxylic wood being dense and strong.

Radial Longitudinal Section (RLS) of long shoot of *Pinus*

In the radial longitudinal section, the cut is made parallel to the radius of the stem. The wood shows long, vertically arranged tracheids with prominent bordered pits on their radial walls. Medullary rays appear as elongated vertical bands running radially and help in lateral conduction of water and food. Resin canals, lined by epithelial cells, are clearly visible and run longitudinally, serving in secretion and defence. Annual rings can be identified by the difference between early wood and late wood tracheids.

RADIAL LONGITUDINAL SECTION (RLS)

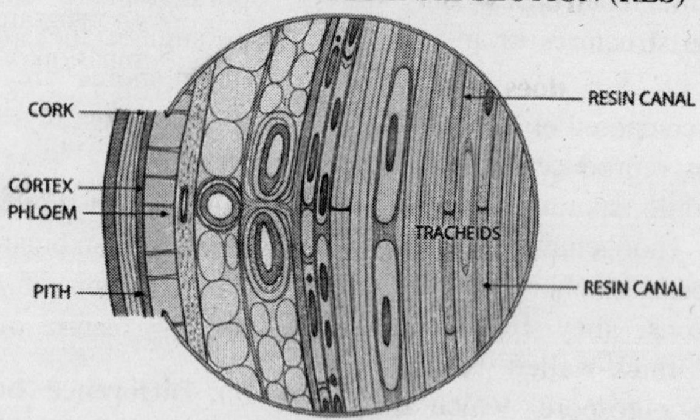

TANGENTIAL LONGITUDINAL SECTION (TLS)

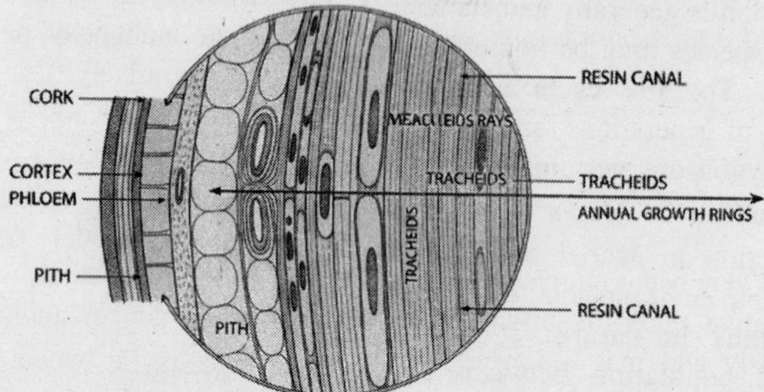

Tangential Longitudinal Section (TLS) of long shoot of *Pinus*

In the tangential longitudinal section, the cut is made tangential to the growth rings. The medullary rays appear as narrow, spindle-shaped or lens-shaped structures because they are cut across their width. Longitudinally arranged tracheids are seen running parallel to the axis of the stem, though bordered pits are less distinct than in RLS. Resin canals appear as elongated oval or circular cavities in this section, again lined by epithelial cells.

These two longitudinal sections together reveal the pycnoxylic nature of Pinus wood, highlighting its compact tracheid-based structure, efficient conduction system, and strong mechanical support.

SECTION-B

5. (*a*) Write short notes on the following:

(*i*) Adventive embryony

(*ii*) Haploid parthenogenesis

(*b*) Explain successive stages in the development of male gametophyte in angiosperms.

(*c*) Explain the concept of cellular totipotency in plants. How is this property utilized in plant tissue culture?

(*d*) Write the botanical names of any two dye-yielding plants with family and mention the plant parts from where the dyes are obtained.

(*e*) What is Herbarium? How does it act as a source of information for plants? Differentiate between herbarium and virtual herbarium.

Ans. (*a*)

(*i*) **Adventive embryony:** Adventive embryony is a special type of apomixis in which the embryo develops directly from somatic (diploid) cells of the ovule, such as the nucellus or integuments, without the formation or participation of the egg cell. As a result, fertilisation is not involved in embryo formation, and the embryo produced is genetically identical to the parent plant.

In adventive embryony, the normal sexual process may occur simultaneously, but the adventive embryos often grow more vigorously and may suppress the sexually produced embryo. Consequently, a single seed may contain more than one embryo, a condition known as polyembryony. However, the embryos formed adventively are true clones of the mother plant because they originate from diploid somatic tissue.

This phenomenon is commonly observed in plants such as Citrus, Mangifera (mango), and Opuntia. In Citrus, for example, nucellar cells surrounding the embryo sac divide and give rise to multiple embryos, leading to the production of uniform seedlings.

Adventive embryony has significant agricultural and horticultural importance. It helps in maintaining desirable traits over successive generations, as there is no genetic variation. It is widely used for producing disease-free, true-to-type plants, especially in fruit crops. At the same time, it limits variability, which may be a disadvantage for breeding programmes that rely on genetic recombination.

Thus, adventive embryony represents an important natural mechanism of asexual seed formation, combining the advantages of seed propagation with clonal uniformity.

(*ii*) **Haploid parthenogenesis:** Haploid parthenogenesis is a type of parthenogenesis in which an embryo develops from an unfertilised egg, and the resulting individual is haploid, containing only a single set of chromosomes. Since fertilisation does not occur, there is no fusion of male and female gametes, and the genetic contribution comes exclusively from the mother.

In this process, the egg cell undergoes mitotic divisions without prior syngamy and directly develops into an embryo. Because the egg is haploid, the organism formed is also haploid. Haploid parthenogenesis is most commonly observed in certain insects, particularly in members of Hymenoptera such as bees, wasps, and ants.

A classic example is seen in the honeybee, where male drones develop from unfertilised eggs by haploid parthenogenesis, while females (workers and queens) develop from fertilised diploid eggs. This system of sex determination is known as haplodiploidy. Haploid males produce sperm by mitosis rather than meiosis, as they possess only one set of chromosomes.

Haploid parthenogenesis has important biological and evolutionary significance. It allows rapid population increase without mating and ensures expression of recessive genes, which can be advantageous for natural selection. In plant breeding and genetics, artificial induction of haploid parthenogenesis is valuable because haploid plants help in producing pure homozygous lines in a short time.

Thus, haploid parthenogenesis represents an efficient reproductive strategy in certain organisms and a useful tool in genetic and breeding studies.

Ans. (*b*) The development of the male gametophyte in angiosperms takes place within the anther and proceeds through a series of well-defined and successive stages, ultimately leading to the formation of a functional pollen grain capable of fertilisation.

The process begins with the differentiation of microspore mother cells (MMCs) in the pollen sacs (microsporangia) of the anther. Each microspore mother cell is diploid and undergoes meiosis, resulting in the formation of a tetrad of four haploid microspores. This stage is known as microsporogenesis. The microspores are initially held together by a callose wall, which later dissolves, releasing individual microspores.

Each free microspore enlarges and undergoes structural differentiation to form a pollen grain. The pollen wall differentiates into two distinct layers: the outer thick and sculptured exine, made of sporopollenin, and the inner thin intine, composed mainly of cellulose and pectin. At this stage, the microspore nucleus enlarges and migrates to one side of the cell.

The microspore then undergoes its first mitotic division, which is unequal, producing two cells: a large vegetative (tube) cell and a small generative cell. This marks the formation of a two-celled pollen grain, which is the stage at which pollen is usually shed in most angiosperms.

The generative cell becomes spindle-shaped and is enclosed within the cytoplasm of the vegetative cell. It later undergoes a second mitotic division to produce two male gametes (sperm cells). This division may occur either within the pollen grain before pollination or within the pollen tube after pollination, depending on the species.

The fully developed male gametophyte thus consists of a vegetative cell, which forms the pollen tube during germination, and two male gametes, which participate in double fertilisation. The vegetative nucleus controls pollen tube growth, while the male gametes are responsible for syngamy and triple fusion.

Thus, the male gametophyte of angiosperms is highly reduced, consisting of only two or three cells, and its stepwise development ensures efficient fertilisation within the enclosed reproductive system of flowering plants.

Ans. (*c*) *Cellular totipotency* is the inherent capacity of a single living plant cell to regenerate into a complete plant, provided it is placed under suitable environmental and nutritional conditions. This concept is based on the fact that almost all plant cells retain their entire genetic information, even after they have differentiated structurally and functionally.

In plants, differentiation does not usually involve loss of genetic material but only selective gene expression. When a differentiated cell is isolated and exposed to appropriate external conditions, it can undergo dedifferentiation, regain its capacity to divide, and then redifferentiate into various tissues and organs. This ability of plant cells to reverse their developmental fate forms the biological basis of cellular totipotency.

Utilisation of cellular totipotency in plant tissue culture

Plant tissue culture is a practical application of cellular totipotency under in vitro conditions. In this technique, small pieces of plant tissue called explants (such as leaf, stem, root, or meristem) are cultured aseptically on a nutrient medium containing minerals, vitamins, carbohydrates, and growth regulators.

Under suitable conditions, explant cells divide actively to form an unorganised mass of cells known as callus, representing dedifferentiation. By manipulating the concentration and ratio of plant growth regulators, especially auxins and cytokinins, the callus can be induced to undergo organogenesis (formation of shoots and roots) or somatic embryogenesis (formation of embryo-like structures). These structures eventually develop into complete plantlets.

Cellular totipotency is extensively utilised for mass clonal propagation (micropropagation) of elite plant varieties, ensuring uniformity and rapid multiplication. It is also used for producing disease-free plants, particularly through meristem culture, as meristematic regions are often virus-free. In plant breeding, totipotency enables the development of haploid plants, somatic hybrids, and genetically transformed plants.

Thus, cellular totipotency forms the fundamental biological principle behind plant tissue culture, transforming a single cell into a whole plant and playing a crucial role in modern agriculture, horticulture, and biotechnology.

Ans. (*d*) Dye-yielding plants have been used since ancient times for colouring textiles, food, and other materials. Two important dye-yielding plants are given below along with their families and dye-producing parts.

Indigofera tinctoria (Family: Fabaceae)

This plant is the chief natural source of the blue dye indigo. The dye is obtained from the leaves, which contain the glucoside indican. During processing, indican is converted into indigo through fermentation and oxidation. Indigo has been extensively used for dyeing cotton and other fabrics.

Rubia cordifolia (Family: Rubiaceae)

This plant yields the red dye known as madder. The dye is extracted mainly from the roots, which contain colouring substances such as alizarin and purpurin. Madder has been traditionally used for dyeing wool, silk, and cotton and also holds medicinal importance.

Thus, different plant parts such as leaves and roots serve as sources of natural dyes, highlighting the economic and cultural significance of dye-yielding plants.

Ans. (*e*) **Herbarium:** A herbarium is a systematically organised collection of preserved plant specimens that are dried, pressed, mounted on herbarium sheets, and properly labelled. Each specimen is accompanied by essential information such as the scientific name, family, locality, habitat, date of collection, and name of the collector. Herbaria are usually maintained in botanical institutions, universities, and research centres and serve as permanent records of plant diversity.

Herbarium as a source of information for plants

A herbarium acts as an authoritative source of botanical information in several ways. It provides authentic reference material for identification and classification of plants, enabling accurate comparison with newly collected specimens. Type specimens preserved in herbaria are crucial for taxonomic verification and nomenclature, as they form the basis for naming plant species.

Herbarium specimens also offer valuable data on plant distribution, habitat preferences, flowering and fruiting periods, and historical changes in vegetation over time. They support studies in plant ecology, evolution, conservation biology, pharmacognosy, and ethnobotany. In addition, herbaria are used in teaching to familiarise students with plant diversity and diagnostic characters.

Difference between herbarium and virtual herbarium

A conventional herbarium consists of physically preserved plant specimens stored in cabinets under controlled conditions. It allows direct examination of morphological features such as texture, venation, and reproductive structures, but access is limited to the location where it is housed, and specimens are prone to damage by pests, humidity, and handling.

A virtual herbarium, on the other hand, is a digital collection of high-resolution images and data of herbarium specimens made available through online platforms. It enables global access, rapid data retrieval, and easy sharing of information without risking damage to original specimens. However, it does not allow physical examination of plant parts and depends on image quality and accurate digitisation.

Thus, while traditional herbaria provide physical authenticity and taxonomic reliability, virtual herbaria enhance accessibility and information dissemination, and together they complement each other in modern botanical research and education.

6. (*a*) **Draw and explain anomalous secondary growth in *Boerhavia diffusa* and *Salvadora sp.***

(*b*) **Describe the floral characters, and draw floral diagrams and floral formulae of subfamilies Papilionaceae, Caesalpinieae and Mimoseae of family Fabaceae.**

(*c*) **Mention the botanical name, family with morphology of the parts used for the following:**

(*i*) **Fig** (*ii*) **Tea**
(*iii*) **Oats** (*iv*) **Oil palm**
(*v*) **Clove**

Ans. (*a*) *Anomalous secondary growth* refers to any deviation from the normal dicotyledonous pattern of secondary growth due to abnormal behaviour of the cambium or formation of additional cambia. *Boerhavia diffusa* and *Salvadora* show two distinct and classical types of anomalous secondary growth, often asked in IFS and university examinations.

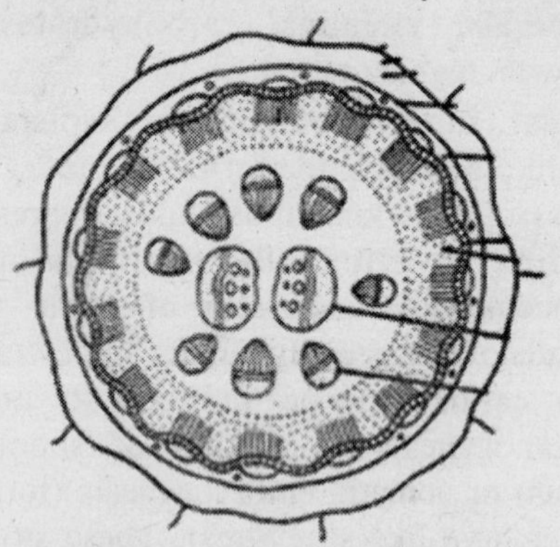

Anomalous Secondary Thickening
In Boerhavia Stem (Diagrammatic)

Anomalous secondary growth in *Boerhavia diffusa*

In *Boerhavia diffusa*, anomalous secondary growth occurs due to the formation of successive accessory cambia. Initially, the stem shows normal secondary growth through the activity of a normal vascular cambium, which produces secondary xylem towards the inside and secondary phloem towards the outside.

After a short period, the normal cambium becomes inactive. Subsequently, new cambia arise from the parenchymatous cells of the pericycle or outer cortical region. Each newly formed cambium ring functions independently and cuts off secondary xylem internally and secondary phloem externally. This process is repeated several times, resulting in the formation of many concentric rings of vascular tissues. Between these vascular rings, conjunctive tissue composed mainly of parenchyma is present. Thus, the stem shows alternating rings of xylem, phloem, and parenchyma, giving it a characteristic ringed or polystelic appearance.

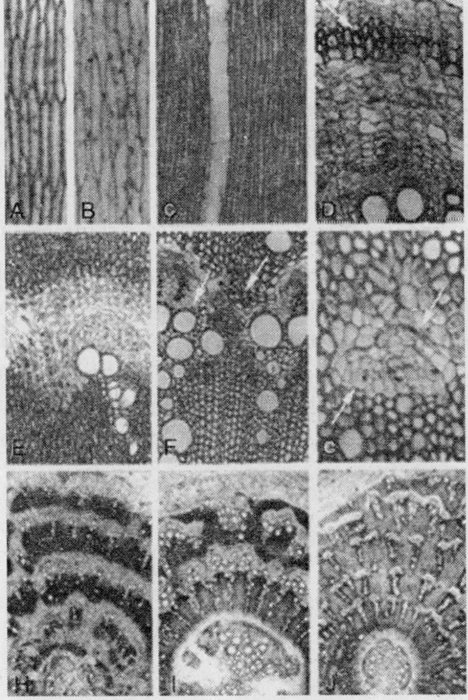

This type of anomalous secondary growth increases the conducting surface and storage capacity of the stem and is considered an adaptation related to the herbaceous and prostrate habit of Boerhavia diffusa.

Anomalous secondary growth in *Salvadora sp.*

In Salvadora, anomalous secondary growth arises due to the irregular activity of a single vascular cambium, not because of successive cambial rings. The cambium does not function uniformly along its circumference.

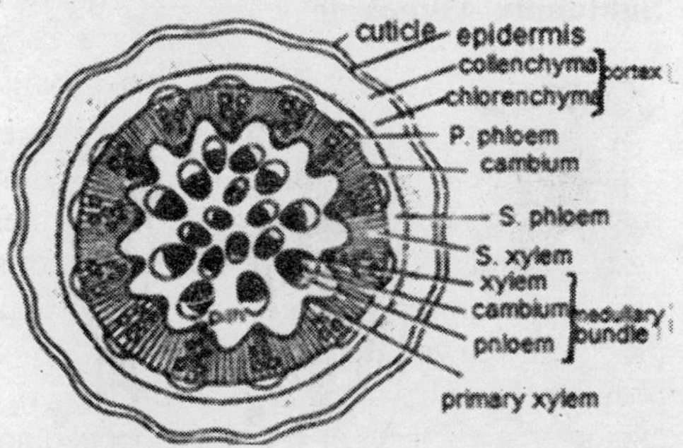

As a result of this uneven activity, certain regions of the cambium produce phloem on the inner side instead of xylem. These phloem patches later become completely surrounded by secondary xylem and are known as included phloem or interxylary phloem.

The included phloem appears as isolated phloem islands embedded within the xylem mass. This arrangement ensures continued translocation of food even when the outer phloem becomes crushed or non-functional during extensive secondary growth.

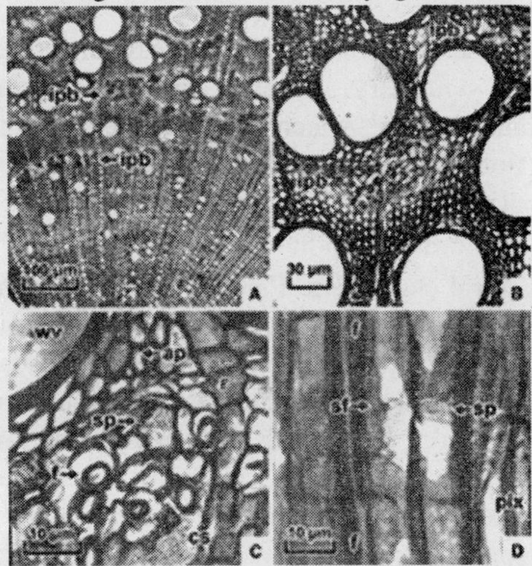

Such anomalous growth is commonly associated with plants growing under xerophytic or halophytic conditions, like *Salvadora*, and is considered an adaptive feature for survival in stressful environments.

Thus, *Boerhavia diffusa* shows anomalous secondary growth due to successive accessory cambia, whereas *Salvadora* exhibits anomaly through the formation of included phloem within secondary xylem, representing two fundamentally different mechanisms of anomalous secondary growth in dicot stems.

Ans. (*b*) The family Fabaceae (Leguminosae) is a large and economically important family of angiosperms. On the basis of floral structure, it is traditionally divided into three subfamilies: Papilionaceae, Caesalpinieae, and Mimoseae.

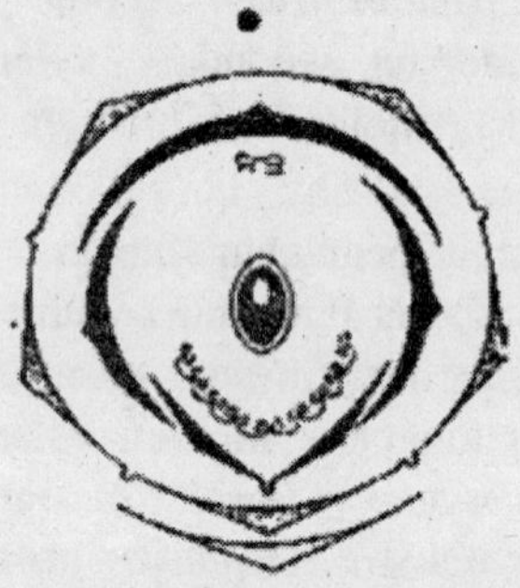

These subfamilies show clear differences in symmetry, corolla arrangement, and androecium, which are reflected in their floral characters, floral formulae, and floral diagrams.

Subfamily Papilionaceae

Floral characters: Flowers are zygomorphic, bisexual, complete, and hypogynous. The calyx consists of 5 sepals, usually gamosepalous. The corolla is papilionaceous, consisting of 5 petals arranged as one large posterior standard (vexillum), two lateral wings, and two anterior petals fused to form a keel.

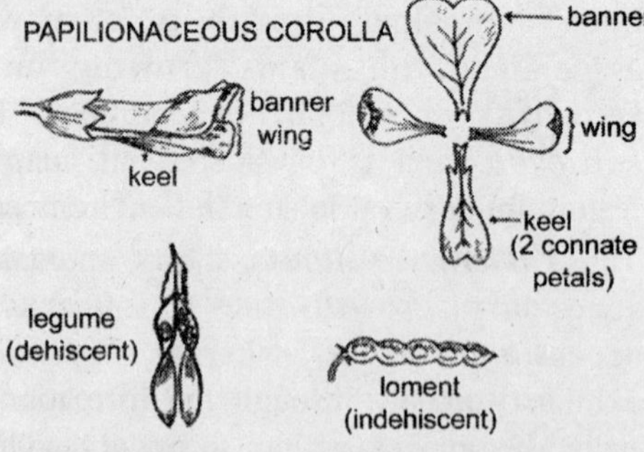

The androecium typically has 10 stamens, most commonly diadelphous (9 + 1). The gynoecium is monocarpellary, with a superior ovary, unilocular, bearing marginal placentation. The fruit is a legume.

Floral formula:

⚥ % $K_{(5)}$ $C_{1+2+(2)}$ $A_{(9)+1}$ G_1

Subfamily Caesalpinieae

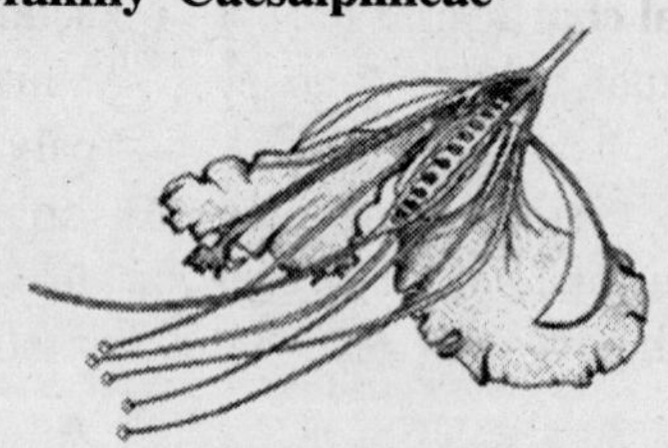

Floral characters: Flowers are zygomorphic or sometimes weakly actinomorphic, bisexual, complete, and hypogynous. The calyx consists of 5 free or partially fused sepals. The corolla has 5 free petals, but unlike Papilionaceae, the posterior petal is innermost in aestivation.

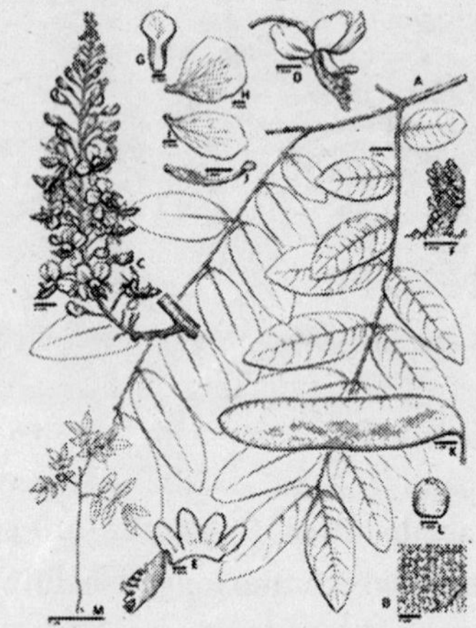

The androecium usually consists of 10 free stamens, though the number may vary. The gynoecium is monocarpellary, with a superior ovary and marginal placentation. The fruit is generally a legume.

Floral formula: ⚥ % K_5 C_5 A_{10} G_1

Subfamily Mimoseae

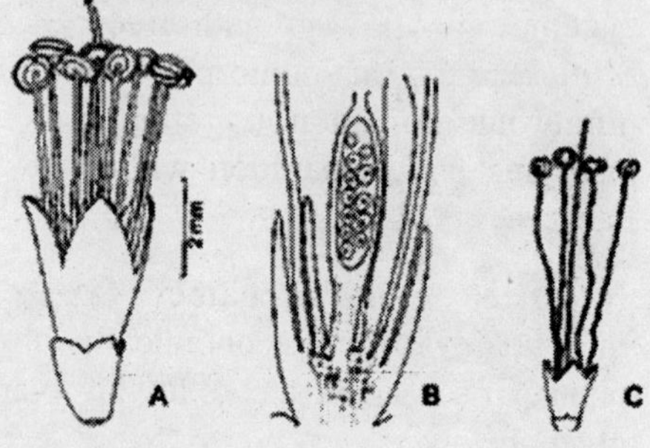

Floral characters: Flowers are actinomorphic, bisexual, small, and usually arranged in dense heads or spikes. The calyx consists of 5 sepals, often gamosepalous and inconspicuous. The corolla has 5 small, fused petals forming a tubular structure.

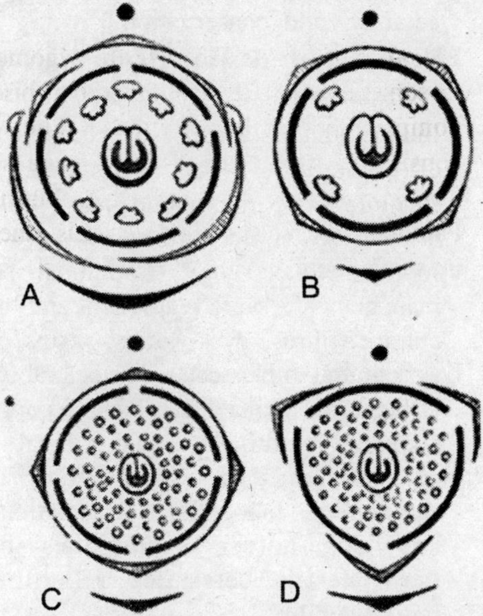

The androecium is the most conspicuous part of the flower, consisting of numerous stamens, which are long, brightly coloured, and exserted, giving a fluffy appearance. The gynoecium is monocarpellary, with a superior ovary and marginal placentation. The fruit is a legume.

Floral formula: ⚥ $\oplus$ $K_{(5)}$ $C_{(5)}$ A_{∞} G_1

Thus, Papilionaceae is characterised by a papilionaceous corolla and diadelphous stamens, Caesalpinieae by less specialised zygomorphic flowers with free petals, and Mimoseae by actinomorphic flowers with numerous conspicuous stamens, clearly justifying their separation within the family Fabaceae.

Ans. (*c*) The botanical name, family, and morphology of the economically important plant parts used in the following plants are given below.

(*i*) **Fig**

Botanical name: *Ficus carica*

Family: *Moraceae*

Part used and morphology: The edible part of fig is a syconus, which is a special type of fleshy, hollow inflorescence. It has a pear-shaped structure with a small apical opening called the ostiole. Numerous tiny unisexual flowers are borne on the inner wall of the hollow receptacle. After fertilisation, the entire inflorescence becomes fleshy, and the true fruits inside are achenes, giving the fig its characteristic granular texture.

(*ii*) **Tea**

Botanical name: *Camellia sinensis*

Family: *Theaceae*

Part used and morphology: The commercially important part of tea consists of the young leaves and terminal buds. The leaves are simple, alternate, leathery, and lanceolate with serrated margins. They possess numerous oil glands and are rich in caffeine and tannins. Young leaves are preferred because they contain higher concentrations of flavour-producing compounds.

(*iii*) **Oats**

Botanical name: *Avena sativa*

Family: *Poaceae*

Part used and morphology: The edible part of oats is the caryopsis (grain). It is a dry, one-seeded fruit in which the pericarp is fused with the seed coat. The grain contains a large endosperm rich in starch and proteins, and a lateral embryo. The fruit is usually enclosed by persistent glumes and lemma-palea in harvested form.

(*iv*) **Oil palm**

Botanical name: *Elaeis guineensis*

Family: *Arecaceae*

Part used and morphology: Oil is obtained from the fruit, specifically from the mesocarp and endosperm. The fruit is a drupe, consisting of an outer exocarp, a thick oily mesocarp yielding palm oil, and a hard endocarp enclosing the seed. The seed endosperm yields palm kernel oil. Thus, oil palm provides two distinct edible oils from different fruit tissues.

(*v*) **Clove**

Botanical name: *Syzygium aromaticum*

Family: *Myrtaceae*

Part used and morphology: Clove is the dried unopened flower bud. The bud is elongated and nail-shaped, consisting of a long calyx tube ending in four calyx teeth, enclosing undeveloped petals and stamens. The buds are rich in essential oil, mainly eugenol, which gives clove its strong aroma and medicinal value.

Thus, in these plants, different morphological structures such as inflorescence (fig), leaves (tea), fruit (oats and oil palm), and flower buds (clove) are economically utilised.

7. (*a*) Write an account on ethnobotanical research in India.

(*b*) Describe the androecium of the following families and give their floral formulae:

(*i*) Malvaceae

(*ii*) Brassicaceae

(*iii*) Orchidaceae

(*iv*) Asclepiadaceae

(*v*) Verbenaceae

(*c*) "Plant tissue culture technology can be utilized to save endangered and threatened plants." Substantiate the statement.

Ans. (*a*) *Ethnobotanical research* in India deals with the systematic study, documentation, validation, and application of traditional knowledge about plants used by India's diverse ethnic and indigenous communities for medicine, food, fibres, dyes, tools, rituals, and other daily needs. Because India has very high cultural diversity and biodiversity, ethnobotany has developed here as a major interdisciplinary field linking botany, anthropology, pharmacology, ecology, and conservation.

Scope and major themes in Indian ethnobotany

Indian ethnobotanical work broadly covers ethnomedicine (folk remedies, herbal formulations, ethnoveterinary practices), ethnofood (wild edible plants, famine foods), ethnoecology (traditional resource management, sacred groves), and material culture (fibres, dyes, gums, resins, timber, agricultural implements). The central objective is not only listing "uses" but recording the complete traditional context—local names, part used, method of preparation, dosage, seasonality, taboo/ritual associations, and knowledge-holder communities—because these details determine reliability and reproducibility.

How ethnobotanical research is conducted

Field research typically includes surveys in tribal/rural areas, interviews with traditional healers and elders, participatory observation, preparation of herbarium vouchers, and botanical authentication (so that the "same plant" is not confused across regions). Modern approaches increasingly include phytochemical screening, pharmacological validation, DNA barcoding/quality control, and GIS-based mapping of medicinal plant populations to link traditional claims with scientific evidence and conservation needs (e.g., quality standards and documentation activities promoted through national medicinal plant programmes).

Institutional and programmatic development in India

Ethnobotany became more organised in India through national-level efforts, especially the All India Coordinated Research Project on

Ethnobiology launched by the Government of India (MoEF-related initiative), which aimed at large-scale, multidisciplinary documentation of ethnobiological knowledge across regions.

The Botanical Survey of India (BSI) has also had ethnobotany as a core objective, focusing on survey and documentation of traditional plant knowledge along with botanical authentication.

Legal-ethical framework and benefit sharing

A major shift in Indian ethnobotanical research has been the emphasis on ethical documentation, protection of community knowledge, and access-and-benefit sharing. The Biological Diversity Act, 2002 provides a national framework to regulate access to biological resources and associated knowledge, and supports documentation mechanisms linked to local institutions.

In practice, documentation initiatives such as People's Biodiversity Registers (PBRs)—prepared through local biodiversity bodies—are important tools for recording local biological resources and related traditional knowledge in a structured way for conservation and governance.

Applied value: conservation, healthcare, and rural livelihoods

Ethnobotanical research in India supports:

- Drug discovery and standardised herbal medicine (leads for pharmacology, safer formulations, authentication of raw drugs).
- Conservation planning by identifying high-use species, pressure points, and sustainable harvest practices, and by supporting cultivation of medicinal plants to reduce wild extraction.
- Livelihood strengthening through value chains in medicinal plants, non-timber forest products, and community-based enterprise—when coupled with fair benefit sharing and sustainable collection.

Current direction and challenges

Modern Indian ethnobotany increasingly focuses on moving from "lists of plants" to evidence-backed, ethically sourced, community-partnered knowledge. Key challenges remain: incomplete recording of preparation/dose details in some studies, erosion of oral traditions, overharvesting of high-demand species, misidentification/adulteration in trade, and ensuring that communities receive recognition and equitable benefits when their knowledge contributes to products or patents.

Overall, ethnobotanical research in India has evolved from descriptive documentation to a more rigorous and responsible discipline that supports biodiversity conservation, public health, and sustainable development, while increasingly recognising the rights and roles of knowledge-holding communities.

Ans. (*b*) The **androecium** (male reproductive whorl) shows distinct structural modifications in different angiosperm families, which are of high diagnostic and taxonomic value. The androecial characters of the given families, along with their floral formulae, are described below.

(*i*) **Family:** *Malvaceae*

Androecium: The androecium consists of numerous stamens (A_∞). The filaments of all stamens are fused together to form a staminal tube surrounding the style, a condition known as monadelphous. The anthers are monothecous (single-lobed) and reniform, which is a characteristic feature of this family.

Floral formula: ⚥ ⊕ $K_{(5)}$ C_5 A_∞ $G_{(5)}$

(*ii*) **Family:** *Brassicaceae (Cruciferae)*

Androecium: The androecium typically consists of six stamens arranged in a characteristic tetradynamous condition. Out of these, four stamens are long and two are short. All stamens are free. The anthers are dithecous and introrse.

Floral formula:

⚥ ⊕ K_{2+2} C_4 A_{2+4} $G_{(2)}$

(*iii*) **Family:** *Orchidaceae*

Androecium: The androecium is highly modified and reduced. Usually, only one stamen is fertile (rarely two), while the others are reduced to staminodes. The filament and style are fused to form a complex structure called the column or gynostemium. The pollen grains are aggregated into compact masses known as pollinia, which are characteristic of orchids.

Floral formula: ⚥ % P_{3+3} A_1 $G_{(3)}$

(*iv*) **Family:** *Asclepiadaceae*

Androecium: The androecium consists of five stamens, which are epipetalous (attached to petals). The anthers are fused with the stigma and style head to form a complex structure called the gynostegium. Pollen grains are not free; they are grouped into pollinia, which are connected by translator arms, an advanced feature related to specialised pollination.

Floral formula: ⚥ ⊕ K_5 $C_{(5)}$ A_5 $G_{(2)}$

(*v*) **Family:** *Verbenaceae*

Androecium: The androecium usually consists of four stamens, arranged in a didynamous condition (two long and two short). Occasionally, only two stamens may be present. Stamens are epipetalous, attached to the corolla tube. The anthers are dithecous.

Floral formula: ⚥ % $K_{(5)}$ $C_{(5)}$ A_4 $G_{(2)}$

Thus, variations in number, fusion, and arrangement of stamens—such as monadelphous, tetradynamous, pollinia-bearing, and didynamous conditions—clearly distinguish these families and are of great importance in systematic botany.

Ans. (*c*) Plant tissue culture technology provides powerful and practical tools for the conservation of endangered and threatened plant species, especially when conventional methods of propagation and conservation are inadequate or ineffective. Many threatened plants face problems such as low seed viability, poor germination, slow growth, habitat destruction, overexploitation, and limited natural regeneration. Tissue culture helps overcome these limitations by enabling rapid, controlled, and large-scale multiplication under laboratory conditions.

One of the most important applications is in vitro clonal propagation (micropropagation). From a very small amount of starting material such as shoot tips, nodal segments, or meristems, a large number of genetically identical plantlets can be produced in a short time. This is particularly useful for rare species with small or declining populations, as it avoids destructive harvesting from the wild while ensuring population recovery.

Plant tissue culture is also crucial in germplasm conservation. Endangered plants can be maintained in vitro for long periods using slow-growth techniques, where reduced temperature, light, or nutrient levels slow down metabolism. This allows safe preservation of valuable genetic material in minimal space and under controlled conditions, reducing the risk of extinction due to natural calamities or habitat loss.

Another major contribution is through cryopreservation, where tissues such as shoot tips, embryos, or pollen are stored at ultra-low temperatures ($-196°C$) in liquid nitrogen. At this temperature, all metabolic activities stop, allowing long-term storage of plant genetic resources without genetic alteration. This method is especially valuable for species with recalcitrant seeds that cannot be stored using conventional seed banks.

Tissue culture also supports reintroduction and restoration programmes. Plantlets produced in vitro can be hardened and successfully transferred to natural habitats or botanical gardens, helping restore dwindling populations. Additionally, disease-free plants can be produced through meristem culture, which is vital for conserving threatened species affected by viral or microbial infections.

Thus, plant tissue culture technology plays a vital role in *ex situ* conservation, complements *in situ* conservation efforts, and provides a scientifically sound, efficient, and sustainable approach to saving endangered and threatened plant species for future generations.

8. (*a*) Why are botanical gardens considered as "outdoor laboratories"?

(*b*) Write an account on cell suspension culture. What are its applications?

(*c*) How are protoplasts utilized to obtain hybrids with potential agronomic value? Give two examples.

Ans. (*a*) Botanical gardens are described as "outdoor laboratories" because they provide a living, organised, and accessible collection of plants that supports education, research, conservation, and public awareness under natural or semi-natural conditions. Unlike indoor laboratories, botanical gardens allow direct observation and experimentation on living plants in real environmental settings.

One of the primary reasons botanical gardens function as outdoor laboratories is their role in taxonomic and systematic studies. Plants from different regions and habitats are grown, labelled, and maintained systematically, enabling students and researchers to study morphological variations, diagnostic characters, phenology, and classification through direct comparison of living specimens.

Botanical gardens also facilitate experimental research. Scientists can conduct studies on plant physiology, ecology, pollination biology, hybridisation, acclimatisation, and growth responses under controlled yet natural conditions. Long-term observations on flowering, fruiting, and seasonal behaviour are possible, which are difficult to achieve in indoor laboratories.

Another important aspect is their role in conservation biology. Botanical gardens act as centres for *ex situ* conservation of rare, endemic, and endangered plant species. They allow experimentation on propagation techniques, tissue culture, and reintroduction strategies, thereby serving as practical research sites for biodiversity conservation.

Botanical gardens further function as training grounds for horticulture and landscaping. Techniques such as pruning, grafting, layering, nursery management, and plant introduction are demonstrated and practiced, providing hands-on learning experiences.

Thus, by combining living collections, research facilities, conservation efforts, and educational activities in an open environment, botanical gardens effectively function as outdoor laboratories, bridging theoretical knowledge with practical botanical science.

Ans. (*b*) **Cell suspension culture** is an important in vitro technique in plant biotechnology in which isolated plant cells or small cell aggregates are grown in a liquid nutrient medium under sterile conditions. It is usually established from friable callus tissue and represents a highly useful system for studying cellular behaviour and for large-scale production of valuable plant products.

Account of cell suspension culture

Cell suspension cultures are initiated by transferring small pieces of friable callus into a liquid nutrient medium containing appropriate mineral salts, vitamins, carbon source, and plant growth regulators, usually auxins. The culture is maintained in conical flasks or bioreactors on a rotary shaker, which keeps the cells uniformly suspended, ensures proper aeration, and facilitates nutrient uptake.

Depending on the nature of the callus, the suspension may consist of single cells or small clusters of cells. Regular subculturing is required to maintain active growth and prevent nutrient depletion. Growth in suspension culture follows a characteristic pattern comprising lag phase, exponential (log) phase, linear phase, and stationary phase. Cells are usually harvested during the exponential phase when metabolic activity is highest.

Cell suspension cultures can be of two main types:

- Batch cultures, where fresh medium is added only during subculturing
- Continuous cultures, where fresh medium is continuously supplied and spent medium is removed, maintaining cells in an active growth phase

Applications of cell suspension culture

One of the most important applications is the commercial production of secondary metabolites such as alkaloids, glycosides, flavonoids, pigments, and pharmaceuticals. Examples include production of shikonin, ajmalicine, and anthocyanins under controlled conditions, independent of climate and seasonal variations.

Cell suspension cultures are widely used in plant physiology and biochemical studies. They provide a uniform population of cells, making them ideal for studying cell division, differentiation, metabolism, enzyme activity, and responses to hormones or stress factors.

They are also valuable in genetic and molecular studies, including mutation research, somaclonal variation, gene expression analysis, and genetic transformation. Suspension cultures facilitate the isolation of protoplasts, which are essential for somatic hybridisation and genetic engineering.

In addition, cell suspension cultures play a role in synthetic seed production, cryopreservation, and scaling up plant tissue culture systems using bioreactors for industrial applications.

Thus, cell suspension culture is a versatile and powerful technique that bridges basic plant cell biology with applied biotechnology, contributing significantly to research, industry, and agriculture.

Ans. (*c*) **Protoplasts** are plant cells from which the cell wall has been completely removed, usually by enzymatic treatment with cellulase and pectinase. Because the rigid cell wall is absent, protoplasts from different plant species—even those that cannot be crossed sexually—can be fused artificially. This property is exploited to obtain somatic hybrids with potential agronomic value, a technique known as somatic hybridisation.

Utilisation of protoplasts for obtaining agronomically useful hybrids

The process begins with the isolation of protoplasts from selected plant tissues, commonly mesophyll cells or cell suspension cultures. Protoplasts from two genetically distinct plants are then induced to fuse using chemical agents such as polyethylene glycol (PEG), high pH and calcium ions, or by electrofusion. Fusion results in the formation of a heterokaryon, a cell containing nuclei from both parental protoplasts.

Following fusion, the hybrid protoplast regenerates a new cell wall and undergoes mitotic divisions to form a hybrid callus. By culturing this callus on suitable nutrient media with appropriate growth regulators, it can be induced to regenerate shoots and roots, ultimately developing into a complete somatic hybrid plant.

Somatic hybridisation allows the combination of desirable traits from two different species or genera that are sexually incompatible. Traits such as disease resistance, abiotic stress tolerance, improved yield, and cytoplasmic characters (e.g., male sterility) can be transferred efficiently. In some cases, only the cytoplasm of one parent is retained along with the nucleus of the other, producing cybrids, which are useful for transferring mitochondrial or chloroplast traits.

Examples of agronomically useful somatic hybrids

One classic example is the somatic hybrid between potato (Solanum tuberosum) and tomato (Solanum lycopersicum), commonly referred to as pomato. This hybrid was developed to combine the tuber-producing ability of potato with the aerial fruiting habit of tomato, demonstrating the feasibility of interspecific somatic hybridisation.

Another important example is the somatic hybrid between cultivated potato (Solanum tuberosum) and wild potato species such as Solanum brevidens. This hybrid has been used to transfer viral disease resistance and stress tolerance from wild species into cultivated potato varieties, contributing to crop improvement.

Thus, protoplast technology enables the creation of novel hybrids beyond the limits of sexual reproduction, making it a powerful tool in modern plant breeding for developing crops with enhanced agronomic performance.

PAPER-II

Instructions: *There are EIGHT questions in all, out of which FIVE are to be attempted, question Nos. 1 & 5 are compulsory. Out of the remaining SIX questions, THREE are to be attempted selecting at least ONE question from each of the two Sections A and B. Attempts of questions shall be counted in sequential order. Unless struck off, attempt of a question shall be counted even if attempted partly. Any page or portion of the page left blank in the Question-cum-Answer Booklet must be clearly struck off. All questions carry equal marks. Answers must be written in ENGLISH only.*

SECTION-A

1. Write short notes on the following:

(*a*) Cell adhesion

(*b*) Structure of mitochondria and their role in the production of ATPs

(*c*) Sex-linked inheritance

(*d*) Tests of significance and their uses

(*e*) Male sterility and its role in plant breeding

Ans. (*a*) **Cell adhesion** refers to the ability of cells to attach to one another or to the extracellular matrix (ECM) through specialised molecular interactions. It is a fundamental property of multicellular organisms and plays a crucial role in tissue formation, structural integrity, communication between cells, development, and regulation of physiological processes.

Cell adhesion is mediated by specific molecules known as cell adhesion molecules (CAMs), which are present on the cell surface. These molecules bind either to identical molecules on neighbouring cells (cell–cell adhesion) or to components of the extracellular matrix (cell–matrix adhesion). Major classes of CAMs include cadherins, integrins, selectins, and immunoglobulin superfamily proteins. Each class has a distinct structure and function but collectively ensures proper organisation of cells within tissues.

Cadherins are calcium-dependent adhesion molecules that are especially important in maintaining tissue architecture and establishing cell polarity. Integrins mainly mediate cell–matrix adhesion and link the cytoskeleton of the cell to extracellular components such as collagen and fibronectin, thereby providing mechanical stability and enabling signal transmission. Selectins are involved in transient cell adhesion, particularly in immune responses, while immunoglobulin-like CAMs play roles in cell recognition and signalling.

Cell adhesion is essential during embryonic development, where it guides cell migration, differentiation, and organ formation. It also regulates cell growth and survival, as loss of adhesion can trigger programmed cell death (anoikis). In plants, cell adhesion is maintained largely through the middle lamella, rich in pectic substances, which cements adjacent cells together and maintains tissue cohesion.

Defects in cell adhesion can lead to serious consequences such as developmental abnormalities, cancer metastasis, and tissue disintegration. Thus, cell adhesion is a key biological mechanism that ensures coordinated cellular behaviour, structural stability, and proper functioning of multicellular organisms.

Ans. (*b*) **Structure of mitochondria and their role in the production of ATPs**

Structure of mitochondria

Mitochondria are double-membrane-bound, semi-autonomous organelles commonly known as the *powerhouses of the cell*. Each mitochondrion is bounded externally by a smooth outer membrane, which is freely permeable to small molecules and ions due to the presence of porin proteins.

Inside this lies the inner membrane, which is highly selective and impermeable to most ions. The inner membrane is thrown into numerous inward folds called cristae, which greatly increase the surface area available for enzymatic reactions. Embedded in the inner membrane are the electron transport chain (ETC) complexes and ATP synthase particles (F_0 – F_1 particles or oxysomes).

The space between the outer and inner membranes is called the intermembrane space, which plays a key role in proton accumulation during respiration. The inner membrane encloses the mitochondrial matrix, a dense fluid-filled region containing enzymes of the Krebs cycle, circular mitochondrial DNA, RNA, ribosomes (70S type), and various metabolites, reflecting the semi-autonomous nature of mitochondria.

Role of mitochondria in ATP production

Mitochondria are the primary sites of aerobic respiration and ATP synthesis in eukaryotic cells. The process begins in the matrix with the Krebs cycle, where acetyl-CoA is oxidised to carbon dioxide, generating reduced coenzymes NADH and $FADH_2$.

These reduced coenzymes donate electrons to the electron transport chain located on the inner mitochondrial membrane. As electrons move through a series of carriers, energy is released and used to pump protons (H^+ ions) from the matrix into the intermembrane space, creating an electrochemical proton gradient.

ATP is synthesised through oxidative phosphorylation when protons flow back into the matrix through ATP synthase complexes. The energy released during this proton movement drives the phosphorylation of ADP to ATP. This mechanism is explained by the chemiosmotic hypothesis proposed by Peter Mitchell.

Thus, the unique structural organisation of mitochondria—especially the cristae and inner membrane—directly supports efficient ATP production, making mitochondria indispensable for cellular energy metabolism.

Ans. (*c*) **Sex-linked inheritance** refers to the transmission of genetic traits that are controlled by genes located on the sex chromosomes, particularly the X chromosome. Because males and females differ in their sex chromosome composition, sex-linked traits show distinct inheritance patterns compared to autosomal traits.

In humans and many other organisms, females possess two X chromosomes (XX), while males possess one X and one Y chromosome (XY). Genes present on the X chromosome but absent on the Y chromosome are called X-linked genes. As males have only one X chromosome, they are hemizygous for X-linked genes, meaning that a single recessive allele on the X chromosome is sufficient to express the trait. In contrast, females must possess two recessive alleles to express the same trait.

Most sex-linked traits are X-linked recessive. Such traits typically appear more frequently in males than in females. Affected males transmit the trait to all their daughters (as carriers) but not to their sons, since sons inherit the Y chromosome from the father. Carrier females can transmit the trait to both sons (who may be affected) and daughters (who may become carriers).

Common examples of X-linked recessive disorders in humans include haemophilia, colour blindness, and Duchenne muscular dystrophy. Y-linked inheritance, also called holandric inheritance, is rare and involves genes present only on the Y chromosome; such traits are transmitted exclusively from father to son.

Sex-linked inheritance is important in understanding genetic diseases, population genetics, and evolutionary biology, as it explains characteristic patterns of inheritance that deviate from Mendelian autosomal ratios.

Ans. (*d*) Tests of significance and their uses

Tests of significance are statistical procedures used to determine whether an observed difference, relationship, or effect in a set of data is real (statistically significant) or has occurred merely by chance. They form the core of inferential statistics, enabling researchers to draw valid conclusions about a population based on sample data.

In any test of significance, a null hypothesis (H_0) is first formulated, which assumes that there is no significant difference or relationship between the variables under study. An alternative hypothesis (H_1) is then proposed, suggesting the presence of a real effect. The test compares calculated statistical values with critical (tabulated) values at a chosen level of significance (commonly 5% or 1%). If the calculated value exceeds the critical value, the null hypothesis is rejected.

Commonly used tests of significance include the t-test, z-test, chi-square (χ^2) test, F-test, and analysis of variance (ANOVA). The t-test is used to compare means between two small samples, the z-test for large samples, the chi-square test for testing association or goodness of fit, and ANOVA for comparing means of more than two groups simultaneously.

Uses of tests of significance

Tests of significance are widely used to validate experimental results in biological, agricultural, medical, and social science research. In biology and biotechnology, they help determine whether differences in growth, yield, treatment effects, or genetic ratios are meaningful. In genetics, they are used to test Mendelian inheritance ratios using the chi-square test.

They also help in decision-making, such as evaluating the effectiveness of drugs, fertilisers, or treatments, and in assessing relationships between variables. Overall, tests of significance ensure that conclusions are objective, reliable, and scientifically sound, reducing the risk of errors due to random variation.

Ans. (*e*) Male sterility and its role in plant breeding

Male sterility is a condition in which a plant is unable to produce functional pollen grains, while the female reproductive organs remain normal and fertile. As a result, such plants cannot self-pollinate but can be fertilised by pollen from other plants. Male sterility occurs naturally or can be induced artificially and is of great importance in plant breeding programmes, especially for hybrid seed production.

Male sterility may arise due to genetic, cytoplasmic, or cytoplasmic–genetic factors. In genetic male sterility (GMS), sterility is controlled by nuclear genes, usually recessive.

In cytoplasmic male sterility (CMS), sterility is governed by mitochondrial genes present in the cytoplasm and is maternally inherited.

In cytoplasmic–genetic male sterility (CGMS), interaction between sterile cytoplasm and nuclear genes determines fertility or sterility, making it the most widely used system in crop improvement.

Role of male sterility in plant breeding

Male sterility plays a crucial role in the commercial production of hybrid seeds. It eliminates the need for manual emasculation, which is laborious, time-consuming, and expensive, especially in crops with small flowers. By ensuring that a male-sterile plant can only receive pollen from a selected male parent, it guarantees controlled cross-pollination and genetic purity of hybrids.

The use of male sterility facilitates exploitation of heterosis (hybrid vigour), leading to hybrids with higher yield, better quality, disease resistance, and stress tolerance. It is extensively used in crops such as rice, maize, sorghum, pearl millet, sunflower, and onion.

Thus, male sterility is a powerful biological tool that enhances efficiency, economy, and precision in plant breeding, making large-scale hybrid seed production feasible and reliable.

2. (*a*) Give a brief account of numerical and structural variations in chromosomes and their significance.

(*b*) Give a brief account of multigene families.

(*c*) Describe in detail the backcross and pedigree methods of plant breeding.

Ans. (*a*) Numerical and structural variations in chromosomes and their significance

Chromosomal variations are alterations in the number or structure of chromosomes and represent an important source of genetic variation in organisms. Such variations arise due to errors during cell division or chromosome breakage and rejoining. They play a significant role in evolution, speciation, adaptation, and genetic disorders.

Numerical variations in chromosomes

Numerical variations involve a change in the chromosome number and are broadly classified into euploidy and aneuploidy.

Euploidy refers to variations in whole sets of chromosomes. When the chromosome number is an exact multiple of the basic set, the condition is called polyploidy (e.g., $3n$, $4n$, $6n$). Polyploidy is extremely common in plants and may arise naturally or be induced artificially. Examples include wheat (hexaploid) and cotton (tetraploid).

Aneuploidy involves the loss or gain of one or a few chromosomes, resulting in chromosome numbers such as $2n - 1$ (monosomy) or $2n + 1$ (trisomy). Aneuploidy usually arises due to non-disjunction during meiosis and is more common in animals than polyploidy. In humans, trisomy 21 causes Down's syndrome.

Significance of numerical variations

Numerical changes, especially polyploidy, contribute to increased vigour, adaptability, and speciation in plants. Many crop plants are polyploids and show improved yield, larger organ size, and tolerance to environmental stress. Aneuploidy, though often harmful, has been valuable in gene mapping and genetic analysis.

Structural variations in chromosomes

Structural variations occur due to breakage and rearrangement of chromosomes, followed by abnormal rejoining. The major types include deletion, duplication, inversion, and translocation.

Deletion involves loss of a chromosome segment, leading to loss of genes and often severe phenotypic effects.

Duplication is the repetition of a chromosome segment, increasing gene dosage and sometimes creating raw material for evolution.

Inversion occurs when a chromosome segment breaks and reinserts in reversed orientation, either including the centromere (pericentric) or excluding it (paracentric).

Translocation involves transfer of a chromosome segment to a non-homologous chromosome, which may be reciprocal or non-reciprocal.

Significance of structural variations

Structural changes alter gene arrangement and expression and may cause abnormal segregation, reduced fertility, or genetic disorders. At the same time, they play a major role in chromosomal evolution and speciation by creating reproductive isolation. Structurál variations are also important tools in cytogenetics, helping in chromosome identification, gene localisation, and breeding programmes.

Thus, numerical and structural chromosomal variations are fundamental genetic phenomena that influence development, heredity, evolution, and practical applications in plant and animal improvement.

Ans. (*b*) **Multigene families** are groups of structurally similar genes present within the same genome that have arisen through gene duplication events and have subsequently diverged to perform related or specialised functions. The genes in a multigene family usually show similar DNA sequences, indicating a common evolutionary origin, but they may differ in expression pattern, regulation, or specific function.

Multigene families are formed mainly by duplication of an ancestral gene, followed by accumulation of mutations over evolutionary time. These duplications may occur due to unequal crossing over, replication errors, or chromosomal rearrangements. Once duplicated, some gene copies may retain the original function, others may acquire new functions (neofunctionalisation), or divide the original function among themselves (subfunctionalisation).

Multigene families can be of two main types. In clustered multigene families, the related genes occur close together on the same chromosome, often arranged in tandem repeats, as seen in the globin gene family. In contrast, dispersed multigene families have gene members spread across different chromosomes, as seen in genes encoding ribosomal proteins.

These gene families are of great biological significance. They allow organisms to produce large quantities of essential proteins, enable fine regulation of gene expression in different tissues or developmental stages, and provide raw material for evolutionary innovation. In plants and animals, multigene families contribute to adaptability, complexity, and survival under varying environmental conditions.

Thus, multigene families represent an important genetic strategy by which organisms expand functional diversity while retaining essential biological roles.

Ans. (*c*) **Backcross and pedigree methods of plant breeding**

Plant breeding employs several systematic methods to develop improved crop varieties.

Among these, the backcross method and the pedigree method are two classical and widely used approaches, each serving distinct breeding objectives.

Backcross method

The backcross method is primarily used to transfer one or a few specific desirable genes (such as disease resistance, pest resistance, or quality traits) from a donor parent into an otherwise superior and well-adapted variety called the recurrent parent. The key objective is to improve a single trait without altering the overall genetic makeup of the elite variety.

In this method, the recurrent parent is first crossed with a donor parent possessing the desired trait. The resulting F_1 hybrid is then repeatedly backcrossed to the recurrent parent for several generations (usually 5–6 backcrosses). In each backcross generation, plants showing the desired trait are selected and again crossed with the recurrent parent. With successive backcrosses, the genetic contribution of the recurrent parent increases, while only the target gene from the donor parent is retained.

After completing the required number of backcrosses, selected plants are selfed for a few generations to achieve homozygosity of the transferred gene. The final product is a variety that is almost identical to the recurrent parent but with the added desirable character.

Significance of the backcross method

This method is highly efficient for improving well-established varieties, especially for simply inherited traits. It is extensively used for incorporating disease resistance, insect resistance, and male sterility genes. The method is rapid, precise, and causes minimal disturbance to the genetic background of the original variety.

Pedigree method

The pedigree method is one of the most commonly used methods for breeding self-pollinated crops and is designed to improve complex traits such as yield, plant type, and quality that are governed by many genes. In this method, two genetically diverse parents with complementary desirable traits are crossed to produce the F_1 generation. The F_1 plants are selfed to produce the F_2 generation, where a high degree of genetic variability appears. Individual plants are selected in each generation, starting from F_2 onward, based on desirable phenotypic characters.

A unique feature of the pedigree method is that the ancestry (pedigree) of each selected plant is carefully recorded in every generation. Selected plants are grown as progeny rows in the next generation, and superior families and individuals are continuously identified and advanced. Selection and selfing are repeated through successive generations until homozygous and uniform lines are obtained, usually by the F_6 or F_7 generation.

Significance of the pedigree method

The pedigree method allows continuous selection and evaluation, enabling the breeder to discard inferior lines early and focus on promising ones. It is particularly suitable for improving quantitative traits and developing varieties with a new combination of characters. However, it requires detailed record-keeping, skilled selection, and considerable time and labour.

Conclusion: The backcross method is best suited for introducing specific traits into elite varieties, while the pedigree method is ideal for developing entirely new, superior varieties through systematic selection. Together, these methods form the foundation of classical plant breeding and continue to play a vital role in crop improvement programmes worldwide.

3. (a) Give a detailed account of regulation of gene expression.

(b) Explain the structure and significance of polytene and B chromosomes.

(c) Comment on the role of RNA in origin and evolution.

Ans. (a) Regulation of gene expression

Gene expression refers to the process by which the information encoded in a gene is used to synthesise a functional product, usually a protein or functional RNA. Regulation of gene expression is the precise control of the timing, location, and amount of gene product formed. It is essential for cell differentiation, development, adaptation to environment, metabolic efficiency, and survival of organisms. Although the basic genetic code is the same in all cells of an organism, differential gene expression leads to structural and functional diversity.

Levels of regulation of gene expression

Gene expression can be regulated at several levels, from DNA to functional protein.

1. **Transcriptional regulation:** This is the most important and common level of gene regulation. It controls whether a gene is transcribed into RNA.

   In prokaryotes, regulation is mainly achieved through the operon model. An operon consists of structural genes, an operator, a promoter, and a regulatory gene. The classic example is the lac operon of E. coli.

   - In the absence of lactose, a repressor protein binds to the operator and prevents transcription.
   - In the presence of lactose (inducer), the repressor is inactivated, allowing RNA polymerase to transcribe the structural genes.

   In eukaryotes, transcriptional regulation is more complex. It involves:

   - Promoters (e.g., TATA box)
   - Enhancers and silencers, which may be located far from the gene
   - Transcription factors, which bind to regulatory DNA sequences and either activate or repress transcription

   Only when the correct combination of transcription factors is present does transcription occur.

2. **Post-transcriptional regulation:** After trans-cription, gene expression can be regulated by controlling the processing and stability of RNA.

   In eukaryotes, the primary transcript (hnRNA) undergoes capping, polyadenylation, and splicing. Regulation may occur through:

   - Alternative splicing, where different combi-nations of exons are joined to produce different proteins from the same gene
   - RNA stability, where some mRNAs are rapidly degraded while others are stable and translated repeatedly
   - RNA interference (RNAi), where small RNAs (miRNA, siRNA) bind to mRNA and block translation or cause degradation

   This level allows fine-tuning of gene expression without altering transcription.

3. **Translational regulation:** Gene express-ion can also be controlled at the level of translation, determining how efficiently an mRNA is translated into protein.

   This involves regulation of:

   - Initiation factors
   - Ribosome binding
   - Availability of tRNA and amino acids

   In some cases, mRNA may be stored in an inactive form and translated only when required, such as during early embryonic development.

4. **Post-translational regulation:** Even after a protein is synthesised, its activity can be regulated. This includes:

- Protein folding and assembly
- Chemical modifications such as phosphorylation, methylation, acetylation, or glycosylation
- Proteolytic cleavage to activate inactive precursors
- Protein degradation via proteasomes or lysosomes

These mechanisms control the activity, stability, and localisation of proteins.

5. **Epigenetic regulation:** Epigenetic regulation involves heritable changes in gene expression without alteration of DNA sequence.

   Major epigenetic mechanisms include:
   - DNA methylation, which generally suppresses gene expression
   - Histone modification, which alters chromatin structure
   - Chromatin remodelling, controlling accessibility of DNA to transcription machinery

   Epigenetic regulation is crucial in development, imprinting, X-chromosome inactivation, and environmental responses.

Significance of regulation of gene expression

Regulation of gene expression ensures:

- Cellular differentiation and development
- Metabolic efficiency, preventing unnecessary protein synthesis
- Adaptive responses to environmental changes
- Maintenance of homeostasis

Defects in gene regulation can lead to diseases such as cancer, genetic disorders, and metabolic abnormalities.

Thus, regulation of gene expression is a multilevel, highly coordinated process that allows organisms to utilise genetic information efficiently, ensuring proper growth, development, and survival.

Ans. (*b*) Structure and significance of polytene and B chromosomes

Chromosomes show remarkable structural variations in different organisms and tissues. Among these, polytene chromosomes and B chromosomes are special types that differ from normal (A) chromosomes in structure, origin, and biological significance.

Polytene chromosomes

Structure: Polytene chromosomes are giant chromosomes formed due to repeated rounds of DNA replication without cell division, a process known as endoreduplication. As a result, many sister chromatids remain aligned side by side, giving rise to a thick, conspicuously large chromosome.

They are most characteristically found in the salivary gland cells of dipteran insects, such as Drosophila. Polytene chromosomes show a distinct pattern of alternating dark bands and light interbands, which are constant and species-specific. These bands represent regions of tightly packed DNA, while interbands correspond to less condensed, transcriptionally active regions.

A prominent feature of polytene chromosomes is the presence of chromosome puffs or Balbiani rings. These are localised swellings formed due to active transcription and represent sites of intense RNA synthesis.

Significance: Polytene chromosomes are extremely important in cytogenetic and molecular studies. Their large size and clear banding pattern allow precise gene mapping and chromosomal identification. Chromosome puffs provide direct visual evidence of gene activity and regulation, making polytene chromosomes valuable tools for studying transcriptional control. They have also contributed significantly to understanding chromosome organisation and gene expression in eukaryotes.

B chromosomes

Structure: B chromosomes, also known as accessory or supernumerary chromosomes, are extra chromosomes present in addition to the normal diploid set (A chromosomes). Their number is variable, even among individuals of the same species, and they are usually smaller, heterochromatic, and structurally simple compared to A chromosomes.

B chromosomes do not pair regularly with the normal chromosomes during meiosis and often show irregular inheritance patterns. They may originate from fragments of A chromosomes or through chromosomal rearrangements during evolution.

Significance: B chromosomes are generally non-èssential for normal growth and development, as organisms can survive without them. In many cases, they are considered genetically inert or contain mostly repetitive DNA. However, in some species, B chromosomes may influence phenotypic traits, fertility, vigour, or adaptability, especially when present in low numbers.

From an evolutionary perspective, B chromosomes are important because they illustrate chromosomal polymorphism and genome flexibility. They provide insights into chromosome behaviour, inheritance mechanisms, and the evolutionary dynamics of genomes.

Conclusion: Polytene chromosomes represent an extreme form of chromosomal amplification associated with high transcriptional activity, while B chromosomes are dispensable, variable chromosomes with potential evolutionary significance. Both types contribute greatly to our understanding of chromosome structure, function, and genome organisation.

Ans. (*c*) Role of RNA in origin and evolution of life

RNA is believed to have played a central and primordial role in the origin and early evolution of life on Earth. The concept that RNA preceded DNA and proteins in biological systems is embodied in the widely accepted RNA world hypothesis, which proposes that early life forms were based primarily on RNA molecules.

RNA as the first genetic material

RNA is considered the earliest genetic material because it uniquely combines two essential properties required for life:

1. Ability to store genetic information, like DNA
2. Ability to catalyse biochemical reactions, like proteins

Unlike DNA, RNA can function both as an information carrier and as a catalyst. Certain RNA molecules, known as ribozymes, possess enzymatic activity and can catalyse reactions such as RNA splicing, peptide bond formation, and self-replication. This dual capability supports the idea that early life did not require separate molecules for heredity and catalysis.

Role in early self-replication and metabolism

In primitive pre-cellular systems, RNA molecules could have acted as self-replicating entities, capable of templated replication using complementary base pairing. Such self-replicating RNAs would have undergone variation and natural selection, leading to increased complexity. RNA-based catalytic systems likely drove early metabolic pathways, forming the foundation for biochemical networks.

RNA as a precursor to DNA and proteins

During evolution, DNA gradually replaced RNA as the primary genetic material because DNA is more chemically stable, making it better suited for long-term information storage. Proteins, composed of 20 different amino acids, eventually replaced RNA as the main catalytic molecules due to their greater structural and functional diversity. However,

RNA retained its essential intermediary role, linking DNA and proteins.

RNA in modern biological systems: evolutionary evidence

The continued presence of RNA at the core of fundamental cellular processes provides strong evolutionary evidence for its ancient role. The ribosome, the site of protein synthesis, is a ribozyme in which ribosomal RNA (rRNA), not protein, catalyses peptide bond formation. Transfer RNA (tRNA) and messenger RNA (mRNA) are indispensable for decoding genetic information.

Additionally, RNA primers are required for DNA replication, and many coenzymes (e.g., NAD^+, FAD, ATP) contain ribonucleotide components, reflecting remnants of an RNA-based world.

RNA and evolutionary innovation

RNA molecules such as microRNAs and small interfering RNAs play regulatory roles in gene expression, influencing development and evolution. RNA viruses, which use RNA as their genetic material, demonstrate RNA's capacity for rapid mutation and evolution, providing insight into early evolutionary dynamics.

Conclusion: RNA represents a crucial evolutionary bridge between non-living chemistry and modern cellular life. Its ability to act as both genetic material and catalyst strongly supports its role in the origin of life, while its continued central functions in present-day organisms highlight its enduring evolutionary significance. Thus, RNA is not merely an intermediary molecule but a key driver in the origin and evolution of biological systems.

4. (*a*) What is cell signalling? Give a brief account of cell receptors.

(*b*) Explain the structure and functions of extracellular matrix.

(*c*) Write a note on different methods of gene mapping.

Ans. (*a*) Cell signalling and cell receptors

Cell signalling is the process by which cells communicate with one another to coordinate physiological activities and respond appropriately to internal and external stimuli. It involves the transmission of information in the form of chemical signals from one cell (signalling cell) to another (target cell), leading to a specific cellular response. Cell signalling is essential for growth, development, metabolism, immune responses, homeostasis, and adaptation in multicellular organisms.

Cell signalling generally occurs in three main stages:

1. Reception of the signal by the target cell
2. Transduction of the signal through a cascade of intracellular events.
3. Response, such as gene expression, enzyme activation, or changes in cell behaviour

Depending on the distance between signalling and target cells, signalling may be autocrine, paracrine, endocrine, or juxtacrine.

Cell receptors: Cell receptors are specialised protein molecules located on the cell surface or inside the cell that specifically recognise and bind signalling molecules known as ligands (e.g., hormones, neurotransmitters, growth factors). The binding of a ligand to its receptor triggers a conformational change in the receptor, initiating signal transduction pathways inside the cell.

Types of cell receptors

1. **Cell surface (membrane-bound) receptors:** These receptors are embedded in the plasma membrane and bind to hydrophilic ligands that cannot cross the lipid bilayer.
   - Ion channel-linked receptors open or close ion channels upon ligand binding, altering membrane potential.

- G-protein–coupled receptors (GPCRs) activate G-proteins, leading to the generation of second messengers such as cAMP, IP_3, and Ca^{2+}.
- Enzyme-linked receptors, such as receptor tyrosine kinases, possess intrinsic enzymatic activity and initiate phosphorylation cascades.

2. **Intracellular receptors:** These receptors are located in the cytoplasm or nucleus and bind lipophilic ligands like steroid hormones and thyroid hormones that can diffuse across the cell membrane. The receptor–ligand complex directly interacts with DNA to regulate gene transcription.

Significance of cell signalling and receptors

Cell signalling ensures precise coordination among cells, allowing organisms to function as integrated systems. Receptors provide specificity and sensitivity, enabling cells to respond selectively to particular signals even at very low concentrations. Any defect in signalling pathways or receptor function can lead to disorders such as cancer, diabetes, immune dysfunctions, and developmental abnormalities.

Thus, cell signalling and cell receptors together form a fundamental communication network that governs cellular behaviour and organismal integrity.

Ans. ***(b)* Structure and functions of extracellular matrix (ECM)**

The extracellular matrix (ECM) is a complex, non-living network of macromolecules secreted by cells into the extracellular space. It provides structural, mechanical, and biochemical support to surrounding cells and plays a vital role in tissue organisation, cell behaviour, and intercellular communication, especially in animal tissues.

Structure of extracellular matrix: The ECM is mainly composed of three major components:

1. **Fibrous proteins:** These proteins provide strength, elasticity, and structural integrity to tissues.
   - Collagen is the most abundant ECM protein and provides tensile strength to tissues such as skin, bone, and tendons.
   - Elastin imparts elasticity, allowing tissues like lungs and blood vessels to stretch and recoil.
   - Fibronectin and laminin are adhesive glycoproteins that link cells to the ECM and help organise ECM components.
2. **Proteoglycans and glycosaminoglycans (GAGs):** Proteoglycans consist of a core protein attached to long carbohydrate chains called GAGs (e.g., chondroitin sulfate, heparan sulfate, hyaluronic acid). These molecules form a hydrated gel-like matrix that resists compression and allows diffusion of nutrients and metabolites.
3. **Adhesive molecules:** These molecules, such as fibronectin and laminin, connect ECM components to cell surface receptors (integrins). They act as molecular bridges between the ECM and the cytoskeleton of cells, enabling mechanical and signalling interactions.

Functions of extracellular matrix

The ECM provides mechanical support and tissue integrity, holding cells together and determining the shape and strength of tissues and organs. In bones and cartilage, it forms a rigid framework, while in connective tissues it provides flexibility and resilience.

It plays a crucial role in cell adhesion and anchorage, ensuring that cells remain attached at appropriate locations. Through integrin-mediated interactions, the ECM influences cell shape, polarity, migration, and differentiation.

The ECM also functions in cell signalling and regulation of gene expression. By binding growth factors and interacting with cell receptors, it regulates cell proliferation, survival, and differentiation. Thus, ECM is not merely structural but actively participates in controlling cellular behaviour.

During development, wound healing, and tissue repair, ECM components guide cell migration and organisation. In pathological conditions, abnormal ECM composition or remodelling is associated with diseases such as cancer metastasis, fibrosis, and arthritis.

Ans. (*c*) Methods of gene mapping

Gene mapping refers to the determination of the relative positions of genes on a chromosome and the distances between them. It is an essential tool in genetics, helping to understand genome organisation, inheritance patterns, and the genetic basis of traits and diseases. Several complementary methods are used for gene mapping, depending on the organism and the level of resolution required.

1. **Linkage (genetic) mapping:** Linkage mapping is based on the principle that genes located close together on the same chromosome tend to be inherited together and show less recombination during meiosis. The frequency of recombination between two genes is used to estimate the distance between them.

   Recombination frequency is expressed in map units or centimorgans (cM), where 1 cM represents a 1% chance of recombination between two genes. By analysing progeny from controlled crosses and calculating recombination frequencies, genes can be arranged linearly on a chromosome. This method was first developed by Thomas Hunt Morgan and his colleagues using Drosophila.

   Significance: Linkage mapping is useful for locating genes controlling qualitative and quantitative traits, especially in plant and animal breeding.

2. **Cytological mapping:** Cytological mapping correlates genetic maps with visible chromosome structures. It involves locating genes on specific regions of chromosomes by observing chromosomal features under a microscope.

   This method makes use of:
   - Banding patterns (e.g., G-banding, Q-banding)
   - Deletion and duplication analysis, where loss of a chromosome segment reveals the approximate position of a gene
   - Polytene chromosomes, especially in Drosophila, where genes can be mapped directly to specific bands

   Significance: Cytological mapping provides a physical framework for genetic maps and helps in identifying chromosomal aberrations associated with genes.

3. **Physical mapping:** Physical mapping determines the actual physical distance between genes, measured in base pairs (bp), kilobases (kb), or megabases (Mb). It does not rely on recombination frequencies.

   Techniques used include:
   - Restriction mapping, based on restriction enzyme cutting sites
   - Fluorescence *in situ* hybridisation (FISH), where labelled DNA probes hybridise to specific chromosome regions
   - Clone-based mapping using BACs and YACs

   Significance: Physical maps provide high-resolution gene localisation and are essential for genome sequencing projects.

4. **Molecular marker-based mapping:** This method uses DNA markers such as RFLPs, RAPDs, AFLPs, SSRs, and SNPs to map genes. Markers closely linked to genes of interest are identified by analysing their co-segregation in mapping populations.

   Significance: Marker-based mapping is widely used in modern plant and animal breeding, enabling marker-assisted selection and rapid gene identification.

5. **Comparative mapping:** Comparative mapping involves comparing gene order and arrangement between different species to identify conserved chromosomal regions. It is based on the concept of synteny.

   Significance: This method helps in transferring genetic information from model organisms to related species and understanding genome evolution.

SECTION-B

5. Write short notes on the following:

(*a*) Role of apospory and diplospory in plant breeding

(*b*) Photoperiodism

(*c*) RuBisCO

(*d*) Sovereign Rights and Intellectual Property Rights

(*e*) Phosphorus and nitrogen cycles

Ans. (*a*) Role of apospory and diplospory in plant breeding

Apospory and diplospory are two important forms of apomixis, in which seeds are formed without meiosis and fertilisation. In both cases, the resulting progeny are genetically identical to the mother plant, a feature of great significance in plant breeding.

Apospory is a condition in which the female gametophyte (embryo sac) develops directly from somatic cells of the nucellus or integument, without the formation of a megaspore mother cell or meiosis. The embryo sac is diploid, and the embryo develops either parthenogenetically or after pseudogamy.

In plant breeding, apospory helps in the fixation of heterosis, as superior hybrid genotypes can be perpetuated unchanged through seeds. It allows rapid multiplication of elite genotypes and ensures uniformity and genetic stability in crop populations.

Diplospory occurs when the megaspore mother cell itself forms the embryo sac without undergoing meiosis. As a result, the embryo sac remains diploid, and the embryo develops without fertilisation. Diplospory is genetically more stable than apospory because the embryo sac originates from the normal reproductive cell.

In breeding programmes, diplospory is valuable for maintaining true-to-type varieties over generations and for producing uniform **seed** progeny without repeated hybridisation.

Significance in plant breeding

Both apospory and diplospory eliminate segregation and recombination, making them powerful tools for preserving desirable gene combinations. They reduce the cost and effort involved in hybrid seed production, ensure genetic purity, and are particularly useful in crops where conventional breeding is difficult.

Thus, apospory and diplospory have immense potential in modern plant breeding for stabilising superior genotypes and improving crop productivity.

Ans. (***b***) Photoperiodism is the physiological response of plants to the relative length of day and night, particularly in relation to flowering. It enables plants to synchronise their reproductive phase with favourable seasonal conditions, ensuring successful pollination and seed formation.

Based on photoperiodic response, plants are classified into short-day plants, long-day plants, and day-neutral plants. Short-day plants flower when the day length is shorter than a critical photoperiod, requiring a long uninterrupted dark period; examples include rice and chrysanthemum. Long-day plants flower when the day length exceeds a critical photoperiod, such as wheat and spinach. Day-neutral plants flower independently of day length, as seen in tomato and sunflower.

Photoperiodic perception occurs mainly in the leaves, where the light-sensitive pigment phytochrome plays a central role. Phytochrome exists in two interconvertible forms, Pr and Pfr, and acts as a molecular switch that measures night length. The floral stimulus produced in leaves is transported to the shoot apex, where it initiates floral development.

Photoperiodism has significant importance in agriculture and plant breeding. Understanding photoperiodic responses helps breeders develop photoperiod-insensitive varieties, allowing crops to be grown across different latitudes and seasons. It also enables manipulation of flowering time through artificial lighting or darkening, which is widely practiced in horticulture.

Thus, photoperiodism is a crucial adaptive mechanism that regulates flowering and seasonal behaviour in plants.

Ans. (*c*) RuBisCO (Ribulose-1,5-bisphosphate carboxylase/oxygenase) is the most abundant and one of the most important enzymes in the biosphere, playing a central role in photosynthetic carbon fixation. It is located in the stroma of chloroplasts and is the key enzyme of the Calvin cycle.

RuBisCO catalyses the carboxylation of ribulose-1,5-bisphosphate (RuBP) by incorporating atmospheric carbon dioxide to form two molecules of 3-phosphoglycerate (3-PGA), which subsequently enter the Calvin cycle for carbohydrate synthesis. Through this reaction, RuBisCO is responsible for the primary entry of inorganic carbon into the organic world, sustaining almost all life on Earth.

Structurally, RuBisCO is a large, complex enzyme composed of eight large subunits (L_8) and eight small subunits (S_8). The large subunits are encoded by chloroplast DNA, while the small subunits are encoded by nuclear DNA, reflecting its dual genetic control. For activation, RuBisCO requires Mg^{2+} ions and CO_2 (carbamylation).

RuBisCO also exhibits oxygenase activity, whereby it reacts with oxygen instead of carbon dioxide, leading to photorespiration. This process results in the loss of previously fixed carbon and reduces photosynthetic efficiency, especially under high temperature and low CO_2 conditions. The dual activity of RuBisCO is a major limitation of C_3 photosynthesis.

Despite being relatively slow and inefficient, RuBisCO is produced in very large quantities by plants to compensate for its low catalytic rate. In C_4 and CAM plants, specialised mechanisms concentrate CO_2 around RuBisCO to minimise photorespiration.

Thus, RuBisCO is a pivotal enzyme in photosynthesis, global carbon cycling, and plant productivity, making it a central focus of research in plant physiology, ecology, and crop improvement.

Ans. (*d*) **Sovereign Rights and Intellectual Property Rights**

Sovereign Rights

Sovereign rights refer to the inherent authority of a nation over its natural resources, including biological resources and associated traditional knowledge, within its territorial boundaries. In the context of biology and biodiversity, sovereign rights were internationally recognised through the Convention on Biological Diversity (CBD), 1992, which affirmed that countries have the right to regulate access to their genetic resources.

Under sovereign rights, a country can control access, use, conservation, and benefit-sharing related to its biological resources. This principle aims to prevent biopiracy, ensure equitable sharing of benefits, and protect the interests of indigenous and local communities who have conserved and used biological resources over generations.

In India, sovereign rights over biological resources are implemented through the Biological Diversity Act, 2002, which regulates access and promotes conservation and sustainable use.

Intellectual Property Rights (IPR)

Intellectual Property Rights are legal rights granted to creators or inventors to protect their intellectual creations such as inventions, plant varieties, designs, trademarks, and traditional knowledge. In the biological and agricultural context, IPR includes patents, plant breeders' rights, geographical indications, and protection of traditional knowledge.

IPR encourages innovation and research by granting exclusive rights for a limited period, allowing inventors to commercially exploit their creations. In plant sciences, IPR is particularly relevant in crop improvement, biotechnology, genetic engineering, and pharmaceutical research. International agreements such as TRIPS (Trade-Related Aspects of Intellectual Property Rights) govern IPR standards globally.

Relationship and significance

Sovereign rights and IPR are closely linked. While sovereign rights protect a nation's control over its biological resources, IPR governs how innovations derived from those resources are legally protected. A balance between the two ensures that countries and local communities benefit fairly from commercial utilisation of biological resources while still promoting scientific advancement and innovation.

Thus, sovereign rights safeguard national and community interests over biodiversity, whereas intellectual property rights protect and promote creativity, innovation, and technological progress in a regulated and ethical manner.

Ans. (*e*) Phosphorus and nitrogen cycles

Phosphorus cycle

The phosphorus cycle describes the movement of phosphorus through lithosphere, hydrosphere, and biosphere, and is unique because it lacks a significant gaseous phase. Phosphorus occurs mainly as phosphate ions (PO_4^{3-}) in rocks, especially apatite. Through weathering and erosion, phosphates are released into soil and water.

Plants absorb inorganic phosphates from the soil and incorporate them into nucleic acids, ATP, phospholipids, and coenzymes. Animals obtain phosphorus by feeding on plants or other animals. When plants and animals die, decomposers mineralise organic phosphorus back into inorganic phosphate, returning it to the soil.

Some phosphates are lost to aquatic systems, where they settle as sediments and, over geological time, form new rocks. Human activities such as excessive use of phosphate fertilisers and detergents disturb the cycle and often cause eutrophication of water bodies.

Nitrogen cycle

The nitrogen cycle involves the continuous circulation of nitrogen between atmosphere, soil, and living organisms. Atmospheric nitrogen (N_2) is abundant but biologically inert and must be converted into usable forms.

Nitrogen fixation converts atmospheric nitrogen into ammonia or nitrates, carried out by nitrogen-fixing bacteria (e.g., *Rhizobium*, *Azotobacter*), cyanobacteria, lightning, and industrial processes. Ammonia is converted into nitrites and nitrates by nitrifying bacteria through nitrification.

Plants absorb nitrates and ammonia to synthesise amino acids, proteins, nucleic acids, and chlorophyll. Animals obtain nitrogen by consuming plants or other animals. On death and excretion, organic nitrogen is decomposed into ammonia by ammonifying bacteria.

Finally, denitrifying bacteria convert nitrates back into atmospheric nitrogen, completing the cycle. Human activities such as fertiliser use and fossil fuel burning significantly influence the nitrogen cycle, often leading to soil and water pollution.

Both phosphorus and nitrogen cycles are essential for ecosystem productivity, nutrient balance, and sustainability of life on Earth.

6. (*a*) Give a brief account of direct and indirect methods of gene transfer in plants.

(*b*) What are enzymes and coenzymes? Describe their mechanism of action.

(*c*) What are the various threats to plant diversity? Give a detailed account of *in situ* and *ex situ* methods of its conservation.

Ans. (*a*) Direct and indirect methods of gene transfer in plants

Gene transfer in plants involves the introduction of a foreign or desired gene into the plant genome to produce genetically modified plants with improved traits such as disease resistance, stress tolerance, or enhanced nutritional quality. Gene transfer methods are broadly classified into direct and indirect methods based on whether a biological vector is involved.

Direct methods of gene transfer

In direct methods, the foreign DNA is introduced into plant cells without the use of a biological vector. These methods rely on physical or chemical means to facilitate DNA entry into the cell.

The most widely used direct method is biolistics or gene gun method, where DNA-coated microscopic particles of gold or tungsten are shot at high velocity into plant tissues. Some particles penetrate the cell wall and membrane, allowing the DNA to integrate into the plant genome. This method is especially useful for monocots such as rice, wheat, and maize, which are less susceptible to bacterial infection.

Another method is electroporation, where plant protoplasts are exposed to a brief electric pulse that creates temporary pores in the plasma membrane, allowing DNA to enter. Polyethylene glycol (PEG)-mediated gene transfer is also used with protoplasts, where PEG facilitates DNA uptake by destabilising the cell membrane. Other methods include microinjection, where DNA is directly injected into the nucleus, and silicon carbide fibre-mediated transfer, though these are less commonly used.

Direct methods are versatile and can transfer genes across species barriers, but they often result in random integration and multiple gene copies, which may cause gene silencing.

Indirect methods of gene transfer

Indirect methods use a biological vector, most commonly a bacterium or virus, to transfer the desired gene into plant cells.

The most important indirect method involves Agrobacterium tumefaciens, a soil bacterium that naturally transfers a segment of its Ti plasmid (T-DNA) into plant cells. In genetic engineering, the tumour-inducing genes are removed and replaced with the desired gene. The modified T-DNA integrates into the plant genome, leading to stable gene expression. This method is highly efficient, precise, and widely used for dicot plants, though monocot transformation is also now possible with improved protocols.

Plant viruses can also be used as vectors for transient gene expression, especially in research studies, though they are less commonly used for stable transformation.

Direct methods are preferred when host range is a limitation, while indirect methods are favoured for their efficiency, stability, and lower copy number insertion. Together, these approaches form the foundation of modern plant genetic engineering and crop improvement.

Ans. (*b*) Enzymes and coenzymes and their mechanism of action

Enzymes are biological catalysts, mostly protein in nature, that increase the rate of biochemical reactions without being consumed in the process. They are highly specific, acting on particular substrates, and function efficiently under mild conditions of temperature, pH, and pressure found in living cells. Some enzymes may be composed entirely of protein, while others require additional non-protein components for activity.

Coenzymes are organic, non-protein molecules that associate temporarily with enzymes and are essential for their catalytic activity. Many coenzymes are derived from vitamins. Common examples include NAD^+, $NADP^+$, FAD, coenzyme A, and ATP. When a coenzyme binds tightly to an enzyme, it is called a prosthetic group; when it binds loosely, it functions as a cosubstrate.

Mechanism of enzyme action: The mechanism of enzyme action involves the formation of an enzyme–substrate (ES) complex, which lowers the activation energy of the reaction, thereby speeding it up.

1. **Formation of enzyme–substrate complex:** The substrate binds to a specific region of the enzyme called the active site, forming the ES complex. This interaction is highly specific.

   Two main models explain this interaction:

   - Lock-and-key model: The active site is rigid and pre-shaped to fit the substrate exactly.
   - Induced-fit model: The active site undergoes a conformational change upon substrate binding, resulting in a better fit and more effective catalysis.

2. **Catalysis:** Once the ES complex is formed, the enzyme facilitates the reaction by:

   - Bringing substrates into close proximity and correct orientation
   - Straining or weakening specific bonds of the substrate
   - Providing an alternative reaction pathway with lower activation energy

   During this step, coenzymes often participate by transferring electrons, hydrogen atoms, acyl groups, or phosphate groups between molecules. For example, NAD^+ acts as an electron carrier in oxidation–reduction reactions.

3. **Formation and release of products:** The substrate is converted into products, forming an enzyme–product (EP) complex. The products are then released, and the enzyme is free to catalyse another reaction.

Role of coenzymes in enzyme action

Coenzymes act as temporary carriers of specific chemical groups or electrons that enzymes alone cannot transfer. They complement the enzyme's protein part (apoenzyme), together forming the holoenzyme. Without coenzymes, many enzymes remain inactive.

Thus, enzymes accelerate metabolic reactions by forming transient complexes with substrates, while coenzymes assist by carrying functional groups or electrons, ensuring smooth and efficient functioning of cellular metabolism.

Ans. **(*c*) Threats to plant diversity and methods of its conservation**

Threats to plant diversity

Plant diversity across the world is facing severe decline due to a combination of natural and human-induced factors. The most serious threat is habitat destruction and fragmentation, mainly caused by deforestation, expansion of agriculture, urbanisation, mining, and industrial development. When natural habitats are destroyed or broken into small isolated patches, plant populations decline and genetic diversity is lost.

Overexploitation of plant resources for timber, fuel, medicines, fodder, and ornamental trade has led to the depletion of many species, particularly slow-growing and endemic plants. Invasive alien species pose another major threat by competing with native plants for space, nutrients, and light, often leading to displacement of indigenous flora.

Climate change has emerged as a growing threat, altering temperature and rainfall patterns and affecting flowering time, pollination, seed set, and survival of plants. Pollution, including industrial effluents, pesticides, and excessive fertiliser use, degrades soil and water quality, adversely affecting plant growth. In addition, overgrazing, forest fires, and shifting cultivation further accelerate loss of plant diversity.

***In situ* conservation of plant diversity**

In situ conservation refers to the protection and maintenance of plant species in their natural habitats, where they continue to evolve and adapt under natural ecological conditions. This is considered the most effective and long-term method of conservation.

The major *in situ* conservation measures include the establishment of biosphere reserves, national parks, wildlife sanctuaries, and conservation reserves. These protected areas conserve entire ecosystems along with their associated plant diversity. Sacred groves, traditionally protected forest patches maintained by local communities, are important examples of community-based *in situ* conservation in India.

In situ conservation helps preserve genetic diversity, ecological interactions, and evolutionary processes. It also allows plants to adapt naturally to environmental changes and supports conservation of rare, endemic, and threatened species in their native range.

***Ex situ* conservation of plant diversity**

Ex situ conservation involves the preservation of plant species outside their natural habitats under controlled conditions. This approach is especially important for species that are critically endangered, have very small populations, or face immediate risk of extinction in the wild.

Common *ex situ* methods include botanical gardens, arboreta, seed banks, field gene banks, tissue culture repositories, and cryopreservation. Botanical gardens maintain living plant collections for conservation, research, and education. Seed banks store viable seeds under controlled temperature and humidity for long-term preservation. For plants with recalcitrant seeds or poor seed viability, tissue culture and cryopreservation of embryos, meristems, or cells are used. *Ex situ* conservation provides a backup against extinction, facilitates research, multiplication, and reintroduction programmes, and supports breeding and restoration efforts. However, it complements rather than replaces *in situ* conservation, as it does not fully preserve ecological interactions.

Both *in situ* and *ex situ* conservation methods are essential and complementary. Together, they provide a comprehensive strategy to protect plant diversity, ensure sustainable use of plant resources, and maintain ecological balance for present and future generations.

7. (*a*) Describe the patterns and trends of ecological succession. Discuss its significance.

(*b*) What are secondary metabolites? Discuss their importance.

(*c*) What are the various applications of micro-propagation?

Ans. (*a*) Patterns, trends, and significance of ecological succession

Ecological succession is the natural, orderly, and directional process by which one biological community gradually replaces another over time, leading to the development of a relatively stable and self-sustaining ecosystem. Succession reflects progressive changes in species composition, structure, and functioning of an ecosystem in response to environmental conditions and biological interactions.

Patterns of ecological succession: Ecological succession shows different patterns based on habitat conditions and initiating factors.

1. **Primary succession:** Primary succession occurs on bare, lifeless substrates where no previous life existed, such as newly exposed rocks, lava flows, sand dunes, or glacial moraines. The first colonisers are pioneer species, usually lichens, algae, or mosses, which can tolerate extreme conditions. These organisms gradually modify the environment by accumulating organic matter and weathering the substrate, making it suitable for higher plants. Over time, grasses, shrubs, and finally trees establish, leading to a mature community.
2. **Secondary succession:** Secondary succession takes place in areas where a pre-existing community has been disturbed or destroyed by events such as fire, floods, cultivation, or deforestation, but where soil and seeds remain intact. Succession here proceeds faster than primary succession. Early stages are dominated by herbs and grasses, followed by shrubs and trees, eventually restoring a stable ecosystem.
3. **Hydrosere and xerosere:** Based on moisture conditions, succession may follow specific sequences such as hydrosere (starting in aquatic habitats like ponds and lakes) or xerosere (starting in dry habitats like rocks or sand). These series illustrate predictable changes in vegetation and habitat conditions.

Trends of ecological succession: Ecological succession exhibits several well-defined trends as the ecosystem matures.

There is a gradual increase in species diversity and biomass, as more complex plant and animal communities establish. The structure of vegetation changes from simple, low-growing forms to stratified, complex communities with trees, shrubs, and ground vegetation.

The soil becomes deeper and richer, with increased organic matter, improved nutrient cycling, and greater microbial activity. Energy flow becomes more efficient, with longer food chains and better utilisation of resources. Succession also shows a shift from r-selected species (fast-growing, short-lived pioneers) to K-selected species (slow-growing, long-lived climax species). Community interactions become more stable, and the ecosystem develops greater resistance to environmental fluctuations.

Significance of ecological succession

Ecological succession plays a vital role in ecosystem development and stability. It enables the gradual recovery of ecosystems after disturbances and ensures natural regeneration of vegetation and wildlife. Succession contributes to soil formation, nutrient cycling, and improvement of habitat conditions.

It helps in maintaining biodiversity by creating a variety of habitats over time and supports ecosystem services such as water regulation, carbon sequestration, and climate moderation. Understanding succession is essential for ecosystem management, restoration ecology, forestry, and conservation planning, as it guides reforestation, reclamation of degraded lands, and sustainable land-use practices.

Thus, ecological succession represents a fundamental ecological process that shapes the structure, function, and long-term sustainability of ecosystems.

Ans. (*b*) Secondary metabolites and their importance

Secondary metabolites are organic compounds produced by plants, microorganisms, and some animals that are not directly involved in normal growth, development, or reproduction, unlike primary metabolites such as carbohydrates, proteins, and lipids. Although they are not essential for basic metabolic functions, secondary metabolites play a crucial role in the interaction of organisms with their environment and in survival under biotic and abiotic stresses.

Secondary metabolites are usually species-specific or group-specific and are synthesised in small quantities during particular stages of growth or under specific environmental conditions. In plants, they are commonly classified into three major groups:

- Alkaloids (e.g., morphine, quinine, nicotine)
- Terpenoids (e.g., essential oils, rubber, carotenoids)
- Phenolic compounds (e.g., tannins, flavonoids, lignin)

Importance of secondary metabolites

Secondary metabolites play a vital role in plant defence. Many compounds protect plants against herbivores, insects, and pathogens by acting as toxins, repellents, or anti-feedants. Alkaloids and phenolics, for example, deter grazing and inhibit microbial growth.

They are important in ecological interactions. Pigments such as flavonoids and anthocyanins attract pollinators and seed dispersers, while volatile terpenoids aid in plant–plant and plant–insect communication. Some secondary metabolites also help plants tolerate environmental stresses like UV radiation, drought, and salinity.

Secondary metabolites have immense economic and medicinal value. Many pharmaceuticals are derived from plant secondary metabolites, including anticancer drugs (vincristine), analgesics (morphine), antimalarials (quinine), and antibiotics. They are also used in the preparation of spices, flavouring agents, perfumes, dyes, pesticides, and beverages.

In agriculture, secondary metabolites contribute to natural pest resistance and are exploited in developing eco-friendly biopesticides. In industry, compounds like rubber, resins, and essential oils are commercially important.

Thus, secondary metabolites, though not essential for basic metabolism, are of great ecological, medicinal, agricultural, and industrial importance, making them indispensable for both natural ecosystems and human welfare.

Ans. (*c*) Applications of Micropropagation: Micro-propagation is the in vitro clonal multiplication of plants using tissue culture techniques under sterile conditions. It exploits the principle of cellular totipotency and has wide applications in agriculture, horticulture, forestry, and conservation biology.

One of the most important applications of micro-propagation is rapid mass multiplication of elite plant varieties. From a small piece of plant tissue, thousands of genetically identical plantlets can be produced within a short time and limited space. This is especially useful for crops with slow or poor natural propagation, such as banana, sugarcane, potato, orchids, and many ornamental plants.

Micropropagation is extensively used for the production of disease-free and virus-free plants. Through meristem culture, plants free from systemic pathogens can be obtained, which is crucial for vegetatively propagated crops like potato, citrus, and banana. This improves crop yield and quality.

Another major application is in the conservation of rare, endangered, and threatened plant species. Plants that have low seed viability, poor germination, or are on the verge of extinction can be multiplied and preserved through tissue culture, supporting both *ex situ* conservation and reintroduction programmes.

Micropropagation ensures uniformity and true-to-type propagation, which is essential in commercial horticulture and plantation crops. Since plants are clones of the parent, desirable traits such as yield, quality, and flowering behaviour are maintained without genetic variation.

It is also valuable in plant breeding and biotechnology. Micropropagation helps in rapid multiplication of newly developed hybrids, transgenic plants, and plants produced through somatic hybridisation. It supports germplasm exchange and storage using in vitro conservation techniques.

Thus, micropropagation is a powerful and versatile technology that enhances plant production, improves crop health, conserves biodiversity, and supports modern plant breeding and biotechnology.

8. (*a*) Give an account of the causes and consequences of global warming. Write down the different measures to control this phenomenon.

(*b*) What are Nif genes? Describe their role in the regulation of nitrogenase enzyme.

(*c*) Discuss pentose phosphate pathway and its significance. How does it differ from glycolytic pathway?

Ans. (*a*) Causes, consequences, and control measures of global warming

Global warming refers to the long-term rise in the average temperature of the Earth's atmosphere and surface, primarily due to the enhanced greenhouse effect caused by human activities. It is one of the most serious environmental challenges facing the world today, affecting climate systems, ecosystems, and human societies.

Causes of global warming

The principal cause of global warming is the increased concentration of greenhouse gases in the atmosphere, which trap outgoing infrared radiation and raise global temperatures.

The most important greenhouse gas is carbon dioxide (CO_2), released mainly through the burning of fossil fuels such as coal, petroleum, and natural gas for energy, transport, and industrial activities. Large-scale deforestation further aggravates the problem by reducing carbon sequestration and increasing atmospheric CO_2 levels.

Methane (CH_4), another potent greenhouse gas, is emitted from rice fields, landfills, ruminant livestock, and natural gas leakage. Nitrous oxide (N_2O) is released from excessive use of nitrogen fertilisers and industrial processes. Chlorofluorocarbons

(CFCs) and other industrial gases, though present in smaller quantities, have very high global warming potential.

Rapid industrialisation, urbanisation, population growth, and unsustainable consumption patterns collectively intensify greenhouse gas emissions, driving global warming.

Consequences of global warming

Global warming has wide-ranging and serious consequences for natural and human systems. One of the most visible effects is climate change, manifested as rising global temperatures, altered rainfall patterns, and increased frequency of extreme events such as heat waves, floods, droughts, cyclones, and wildfires.

Melting of glaciers and polar ice caps has led to sea-level rise, threatening coastal ecosystems, islands, and low-lying human settlements with submergence and saltwater intrusion. Changes in temperature and precipitation adversely affect agriculture, reducing crop productivity and food security in many regions.

Global warming also poses severe threats to biodiversity. Many plant and animal species face habitat loss, altered phenology, and increased extinction risk. Coral bleaching, forest dieback, and shifts in species distribution are direct ecological impacts.

Human health is affected through heat stress, spread of vector-borne diseases, malnutrition, and water scarcity. Economic losses due to climate-related disasters are increasing worldwide.

Measures to control global warming

Controlling global warming requires global, national, and individual-level efforts.

A key measure is the reduction of greenhouse gas emissions by shifting from fossil fuels to renewable energy sources such as solar, wind, hydro, and biomass. Improving energy efficiency in industries, buildings, and transportation significantly lowers emissions.

Afforestation and reforestation help absorb atmospheric CO_2 and restore ecological balance. Conservation of existing forests is equally important. Sustainable agricultural practices, including reduced fertiliser use and improved livestock management, can lower methane and nitrous oxide emissions. International agreements and policies aimed at climate mitigation, along with public awareness, lifestyle changes, waste reduction, and adoption of cleaner technologies, are essential for long-term control.

Global warming is a complex, human-induced phenomenon with profound environmental, social, and economic consequences. Effective mitigation depends on collective responsibility, sustainable development, and timely action to protect the Earth's climate system for future generations.

Ans. (*b*) Nif genes and their role in regulation of nitrogenase enzyme

Nif genes (nitrogen fixation genes) are a specific group of genes found mainly in nitrogen-fixing prokaryotes such as *Rhizobium*, *Azotobacter*, *Clostridium*, and cyanobacteria. These genes are responsible for the synthesis, assembly, regulation, and functioning of the nitrogenase enzyme system, which catalyses the biological fixation of atmospheric nitrogen (N_2) into ammonia (NH_3).

The nif genes usually occur as a cluster on the bacterial chromosome or plasmid (for example, the symbiotic plasmid in Rhizobium). They are designated as nifH, nifD, nifK, nifA, nifL, and several accessory nif genes.

Role of nif genes in nitrogenase synthesis

The nitrogenase enzyme consists of two protein components:

- Dinitrogenase reductase (Fe-protein)
- Dinitrogenase (MoFe-protein)

The nifH gene codes for the Fe-protein, while nifD and nifK genes code for the two subunits of the MoFe-protein. These structural nif genes are directly involved in forming the active nitrogenase complex.

Several other nif genes (such as nifE, nifN, nifB, nifV) are involved in the biosynthesis and insertion of metal cofactors like molybdenum, iron, and sulfur, which are essential for nitrogenase activity.

Regulation of nitrogenase by nif genes

Nitrogenase is an oxygen-sensitive and energy-intensive enzyme, so its synthesis and activity are tightly regulated by nif genes.

The key regulatory genes are nifA and nifL:

- nifA encodes a transcriptional activator protein that activates the expression of structural nif genes by binding to promoter regions when conditions are favourable.
- nifL encodes a regulatory protein that inhibits nifA activity under unfavourable conditions.

The regulation depends mainly on oxygen concentra-tion and availability of fixed nitrogen (ammonia or nitrate).

Under low oxygen and nitrogen-deficient conditions, nifL becomes inactive, allowing nifA to activate transcription of nif structural genes, leading to nitrogenase synthesis.

Under high oxygen or sufficient fixed nitrogen, nifL inhibits nifA, preventing unnecessary nitrogenase production.

In symbiotic systems like Rhizobium–legume association, the plant helps maintain a low-oxygen environment in root nodules using leghaemoglobin, enabling nif gene expression and nitrogenase activity.

Significance

Through coordinated action and regulation, nif genes ensure that nitrogenase is produced only when required and under suitable conditions, conserving cellular energy and protecting the enzyme from oxygen damage. Thus, nif genes play a central role in biological nitrogen fixation, contributing significantly to soil fertility, agricultural productivity, and the global nitrogen cycle.

Ans. (*c*) Pentose phosphate pathway, its significance, and differences from glycolysis

The pentose phosphate pathway (PPP), also known as the hexose monophosphate (HMP) shunt, is an alternative pathway of glucose oxidation that operates in the cytoplasm of cells. Unlike glycolysis, it does not primarily function to produce ATP but plays a crucial role in generating reducing power and metabolic intermediates required for biosynthetic reactions.

Pentose phosphate pathway: The pentose phosphate pathway begins with glucose-6-phosphate, a glycolytic intermediate, and proceeds through two distinct phases:

1. **Oxidative phase:** In this phase, glucose-6-phosphate undergoes a series of oxidation reactions, resulting in the formation of ribulose-5-phosphate, along with the release of carbon dioxide. The most important outcome of this phase is the production of NADPH, a reduced coenzyme. Two molecules of NADPH are generated per molecule of glucose-6-phosphate oxidised.
2. **Non-oxidative phase:** In this phase, ribulose-5-phosphate is converted into various five-carbon sugars, including ribose-5-phosphate, which is essential for the synthesis of nucleotides and nucleic acids. Through a series of reversible reactions, pentose sugars are also converted into glycolytic intermediates such as fructose-6-phosphate and glyceraldehyde-3-phosphate, linking the pathway with glycolysis.

Significance of the pentose phosphate pathway

The most important function of the pentose phosphate pathway is the generation of NADPH, which is essential for reductive biosynthesis. NADPH provides reducing power for the synthesis of fatty acids, steroids, amino acids, and nucleotides. It is also crucial for maintaining reduced glutathione, which protects cells against oxidative damage, especially in red blood cells.

The pathway supplies ribose-5-phosphate, required for the synthesis of DNA, RNA, ATP, NAD^+, and FAD. In photosynthetic tissues and rapidly dividing cells, this function is particularly important.

The pentose phosphate pathway also provides metabolic flexibility, allowing cells to balance their needs for NADPH, ribose sugars, and glycolytic intermediates depending on physiological conditions.

Differences between pentose phosphate pathway and glycolytic pathway

The pentose phosphate pathway differs from glycolysis in several fundamental aspects. Glycolysis is primarily an energy-yielding pathway, producing ATP and NADH through the breakdown of glucose into pyruvate, whereas the pentose phosphate pathway does not produce ATP directly.

Glycolysis generates NADH, which is mainly used in ATP production through oxidative phosphorylation, while the pentose phosphate pathway produces NADPH, which is used in biosynthetic and protective reactions.

Carbon dioxide is released in the oxidative phase of the pentose phosphate pathway, whereas glycolysis does not involve decarboxylation steps. Glycolysis occurs in almost all living cells as a central metabolic pathway, while the pentose phosphate pathway is especially active in tissues involved in biosynthesis, such as liver, adipose tissue, adrenal cortex, and actively dividing cells.

Thus, the pentose phosphate pathway complements glycolysis by supplying reducing power and biosynthetic precursors, while glycolysis mainly fulfils the energy requirements of the cell. Together, these pathways ensure efficient utilisation of glucose according to cellular needs.

YOUR SPACE

YOUR SPACE

Previous Years' Paper

Indian Forest Service (Main) Exam, 2024

SUBJECT–BOTANY

(Exam held on 27-11-2024)

PAPER-I

Instructions: *There are EIGHT questions in all, out of which FIVE are to be attempted. Question Nos. 1 & 5 are compulsory. Out of the remaining SIX questions, THREE are to be attempted selecting at least ONE question from each of the two Sections A and B. Attempts of questions shall be counted in sequential order. Unless struck off, attempt of a question shall be counted even if attempted partly. Any page or portion of the page left blank in the Question-cum-Answer Booklet must be clearly struck off. All questions carry equal marks. Answers must be written in ENGLISH only.*

SECTION-A

1. (*a*) What is a systemic fungicide? Describe the characteristics of an ideal fungicide.

(*b*) Describe Hfr strains of bacteria. How do they mediate bacterial recombination?

(*c*) What are mycoplasmas? Compare mycoplasma with protoplasts and spheroplasts.

(*d*) Describe the various elementary processes associated with the telome theory. Explain the origin of reproductive structures in ferns.

(*e*) Highlight the salient features of progymnosperms, and discuss their affinities with pteridophytes and gymnosperms.

2. (*a*) Describe streptococci, staphylococci and sarcinae arrangements of cocci forms of bacteria. Explain homo- and hetero-polysaccharides found in bacterial cell wall. Draw and label the peptidoglycan structure of a typical Gram +ve bacteria.

(*b*) Discuss the various anatomical features of gametophyte and sporophyte of a member of Polytrichaceae. Comment on the significance of these features in relation to environmental conditions.

(*c*) Give an account of reserve food material found in various classes of algae. Add a note on the algae in medicine.

3. (*a*) What are the different types of interactions among microbes in soil? Discuss their role in soil ecosystem.

(*b*) Explain the xerophytic and hydrophytic characters of *Equisetum*. Give a comparative account of spore-bearing structures of *Selaginella* and *Equisetum*.

(*c*) "Gnetales are considered as a highly advanced group among gymnosperms." Justify the statement by commenting on the vegetative and reproductive characters.

4. (*a*) What are the symptoms of sheath blight of rice? Name its causal organism, and describe the disease cycle and its management.

(*b*) Discuss the general characteristics, range of thallus organization, and asexual and sexual mode of reproduction in Chlorophyceae.

(*c*) Explain coralloid roots with suitable diagram. How do they differ from the normal roots of *Cycas*?

SECTION-B

5. (*a*) Differentiate between the floral characters of Magnoliaceae and Euphorbiaceae. Name two species of each of these families with their economic importance.

(*b*) Distinguish between artificial and natural system of classification. What are their merits and demerits?

(*c*) Discuss the importance of ethnobotany in the evolution of modern medicine. How have the cultural and religious practices in India been helpful in ethnobotanical studies?

(*d*) What is gynogenesis? How is it different from androgenesis?

(*e*) Comment on the importance of botanical gardens in India.

6. (*a*) Distinguish between diplospory and apospory with suitable examples.

(*b*) Write short notes on the following:

(*i*) Supportive evidences from palynology in taxonomy

(*ii*) Principles of ICN

(*iii*) Importance of herbaria in taxonomy

(*c*) What are protoplasts? Describe briefly the protocol for enzymatic isolation of protoplasts.

7. (*a*) Write the botanical name, family and the uses of the plants from where the following products are obtained :

(*i*) Resin (*ii*) Jute

(*iii*) Cassava (*iv*) Long pepper

(*v*) Pyrethrum

(*b*) (*i*) In a plant, both direct and indirect shoot regenerations are possible. Which method will you prefer and why?

(*ii*) Give an example for cybrids produced through cell fusion and their importance.

(*c*) Describe the various events during fertilization starting from pollen germination to fertilization in angiosperms.

8. (*a*) Give a detailed account of centres of origin of cultivated plants with reference to Vavilovian concept. Differentiate between the primary and secondary centres of origin. Name two plants of New World, presently cultivated in the Old World at large scale.

(*b*) Describe the various stages of micro-propagation. How can you use this technology to reduce pressure on natural populations of endangered and threatened plants?

(*c*) Describe the structure of stomata with a labelled diagram. Distinguish between haplocheilic and syndetocheilic stomata.

PAPER-II

Instructions: *There are EIGHT questions in all, out of which FIVE are to be attempted. Question Nos. 1 & 5 are compulsory. Out of the remaining SIX questions, THREE are to be attempted selecting at least ONE question from each of the two Sections A and B. Attempts of questions shall be counted in sequential order. Unless struck off, attempt of a question shall be counted even if attempted partly. Any page or portion of the page left blank in the Question-cum-Answer Booklet must be clearly struck off. All questions carry equal marks. Answers must be written in ENGLISH only.*

SECTION-A

1. (*a*) Explain different kinds of Endoplasmic reticulum and give a brief account on Endomembrane system.

(*b*) Discuss cAMP-mediated regulation of signal transduction.

(*c*) Give a brief account on theories of organic evolution.

(*d*) Explain different kinds of plastids with reference to their structure and functions.

(*e*) Briefly describe the properties of genetic code with examples. Explain, in short, the degeneracy of the code by Wobble hypothesis.

2. (*a*) What is mutation breeding? Discuss different methods of mutation breeding along with their applications and limitations.

(*b*) Discuss briefly *Agrobacterium*-mediated gene transfer method in plants with special emphasis on T-DNA processing.

(*c*) If a red coloured Four-o'clock plant is crossed with a white flowered one, what will be the flower colours of the F_1; of the F_2; of the offspring of a cross between F_1 with its red parent, and also with its white parent? (In Four-o'clock plant red flower colour (R) is incompletely dominant over white (r); while heterozygous plants (Rr) being pink flowered).

3. (*a*) Discuss the control points and explain various molecular factors involved in cell cycle regulation.

(*b*) Write notes on the following:

(*i*) Hardy-Weinberg equilibrium

(*ii*) A normal woman, whose father had hemophilia, married a normal man. What is the chance of hemophilia in their children? Explain with suitable reasons.

(*c*) Name two diseases caused by prion in humans. Mention the ways by which prions can infect humans. Enumerate the steps by which prions can cause disease.

4. (*a*) Describe the process of DNA replication in eukaryotic organism mentioning the role of specific enzymes at different stages.

(*b*) Describe heterosis and inbreeding depression along with their genetic bases.

(*c*) Explain origin and induction of polyploidy. Justify the importance of polyploidy in relation to crop improvement.

SECTION-B

5. (*a*) What are the characteristics of "triple response" induced by ethylene in etiolated seedlings?

(*b*) With reference to soil-water relationship, differentiate between field capacity and permanent wilting percentage.

(*c*) State the specific applications of regression analysis and correlation analysis in assessing the relationship between variables.

(*d*) Enumerate any four species each of endemic and threatened plants with the help of botanical name, family and their distribution in India.

(*e*) Explain different types of vegetation in India along with their geographical distributions.

6. (*a*) Define water potential. Discuss the major factors influencing the water potential in plants.

(*b*) Give a critical account on ecological succession. Discuss the concept of 'climax'.

(*c*) "Crassulacean acid metabolism is an adaptation to desert life of plants." Comment and discuss.

7. (*a*) Discuss the structure-function relationship of phloem tissues with reference to translocation of photoassimilates.

(*b*) Write a note on the inhibitors of photosynthetic electron transport as effective herbicides.

(*c*) Compare the applications of standard deviation and coefficient of variation in data analysis.

8. (*a*) Discuss the biotechnical approaches used in the conservation of biodiversity with special reference to endangered species.

(*b*) "Phytochrome-mediated responses can be grouped according to their fluence requirements." Comment.

(*c*) Give a critical account on biogeochemical cycles with reference to any terrestrial ecosystem.

ANSWERS

PAPER-I

1. (*a*): A systemic fungicide is a chemical substance that, upon entering a plant, moves internally through its vascular tissues to protect against fungal infections. Unlike contact fungicides, which remain on the surface and provide only localized protection, systemic fungicides are absorbed and transported through the plant's xylem or phloem, allowing them to combat pathogens both at the site of infection and in other parts of the plant.

This movement within the plant can be categorized as follows:

- **Locally systemic** fungicides travel a short distance from the application site, protecting neighboring tissue.
- **Translaminar** fungicides penetrate through the leaf blade from one side to the other, ensuring coverage of both surfaces.
- **Xylem-mobile (acropetal)** fungicides are absorbed and transported upward through the xylem from the roots or lower leaves to the growing tips.
- **Highly systemic** fungicides circulate through both xylem and phloem, moving upward and downward, offering comprehensive protection.

These movements allow systemic fungicides to target early-stage infections and prevent future fungal attacks, making them both preventive and curative.

Movement of Systemic Fungicides

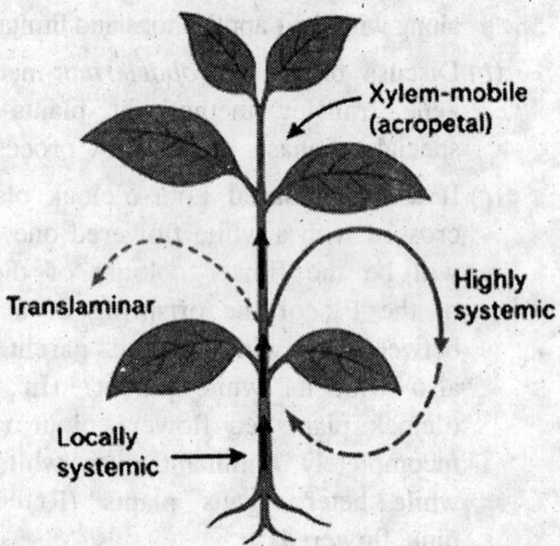

The characteristics of an ideal systemic fungicide include:

- **Effective systemic mobility:** It should move effciently within the plant, protecting both treated and newly formed tissues.
- **Broad-spectrum action:** It must act against a wide variety of fungi including both biotrophic and necrotrophic species.
- **Low phytotoxicity:** It should not cause any harm or stress to the plant even when applied in slightly higher doses or under different climatic conditions.

- **Environmental safety:** It should degrade into harmless products and should not adversely affect soil microbes, aquatic systems, pollinators, or other non-target organisms.
- **Resistance management:** It should have a novel or combined mode of action that minimizes the risk of fungal resistance. It should be usable in rotation with other fungicides.
- **Good residual activity:** It should remain active within the plant for an adequate duration, reducing the need for frequent reapplication.
- **Ease of application and compatibility:** It should mix well with other agrochemicals and be easy to apply by common methods such as foliar sprays or soil drenches.
- **Cost-effectiveness and availability:** It should be affordable for farmers and available in stable formulations with adequate shelf life.

Systemic fungicides are essential in modern agriculture because they can suppress infections that are not visible or have already penetrated plant surfaces. Their internal action also reduces the need for repeated spraying and improves disease control under unfavorable weather conditions. Thus, an ideal systemic fungicide must integrate efficacy, safety, longevity, and economic viability.

1. (***b***): Hfr strains (High-frequency recombination strains) are specialized bacterial cells, typically *Escherichia coli*, that have the F (fertility) plasmid integrated into their chromosomal DNA. This integration transforms the F plasmid from an independent circular DNA molecule into an episome, enabling the bacterium to transfer chromosomal genes to a recipient cell during conjugation.

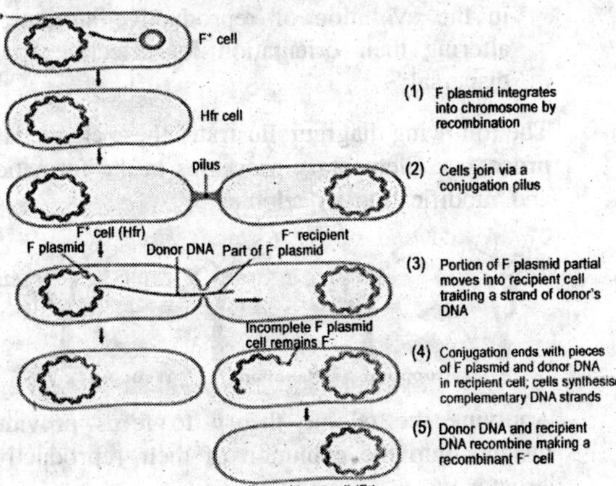

The integration of the F plasmid occurs at specific sites on the bacterial chromosome through homologous recombination. Once integrated, the F plasmid's origin of transfer (oriT) initiates the transfer of DNA during conjugation. However, unlike F^+ cells that transfer only the F plasmid, Hfr cells transfer part of their chromosomal DNA along with a portion of the F plasmid.

The process of conjugation begins when the Hfr cell forms a pilus to establish contact with an F^- recipient cell. A single strand of the donor's DNA, starting from the oriT, is transferred to the recipient. Due to the size of the bacterial chromosome and the fragility of the mating bridge, the entire chromosome is rarely transferred. Consequently, the recipient cell remains F^- but acquires new genetic material from the donor.

The transferred DNA can undergo homologous recombination with the recipient's chromosome, leading to genetic variation. This mechanism has been instrumental in mapping bacterial genes by determining the sequence in which genes are transferred during conjugation.

In summary, Hfr strains facilitate the transfer of chromosomal genes between bacteria, promoting genetic diversity and enabling detailed genetic studies.

1. (***c***): Mycoplasmas are a unique group of bacteria characterized by the absence of a cell wall. This feature imparts them with a high degree of flexibility and pleomorphism, allowing them to adopt various shapes. Due to the lack of a rigid cell wall, they are inherently resistant to antibiotics that target cell wall synthesis, such as beta-lactam antibiotics. Mycoplasmas are among the smallest self-replicating organisms, typically measuring between 0.1 to 0.3 micrometers in diameter. Their plasma membrane contains sterols, which provide structural stability and are uncommon in most bacteria. These organisms are often parasitic, relying on host organisms for essential nutrients, and are known to cause various diseases in humans, animals, and plants.

In contrast, protoplasts and spheroplasts are forms of bacterial cells that have undergone artificial removal of their cell walls. Protoplasts result from the complete removal of the cell wall, typically from Gram-positive bacteria, leaving the plasma membrane as the sole boundary. Spheroplasts, on the other hand, are derived from Gram-negative bacteria and retain portions of their outer membrane after partial removal of the cell wall. Both forms are osmotically fragile and require isotonic conditions to maintain integrity. Unlike mycoplasmas, protoplasts and spheroplasts are not naturally occurring and are often used in laboratory settings for genetic manipulation and studies involving membrane biology.

The key distinctions among mycoplasmas, protoplasts, and spheroplasts are summarized below:

Feature	Mycoplasmas	Protoplasts	Spheroplasts
Origin	Naturally occurring	Artificially induced	Artificially induced
Cell wall presence	Absent	Completely removed	Partially removed
Membrane composition	Single membrane with sterols	Single membrane	Inner and outer membranes
Stability	Stable in various environments	Osmotically fragile	Osmotically fragile
Occurrence	Found in nature	Laboratory-generated	Laboratory-generated
Antibiotic resistance	Resistant to cell wall-targeting drugs	No inherent resistance	No inherent resistance

In summary, while mycoplasmas are naturally occurring, wall-less bacteria with unique adaptations for survival, protoplasts and spheroplasts are laboratory-generated forms used primarily for research purposes. Understanding these differences is crucial in microbiology, especially in contexts involving antibiotic resistance and genetic engineering.

1. (***d***): The telome theory, proposed by Walter Zimmermann, elucidates the evolution of complex plant structures from simple, dichotomously branched axes known as telomes. These primitive units, either fertile (bearing sporangia) or sterile, underwent specific evolutionary processes leading to the diverse morphology observed in modern vascular plants.

Elementary Processes of Telome Theory: Zimmermann identified five fundamental processes that transformed telomes into intricate plant organs:

- **Overtopping:** In this process, among two equally growing branches, one becomes dominant, growing more vigorously than the other. This dominance leads to the formation of a main axis with lateral branches, setting the foundation for differentiated structures like stems and leaves.
- **Planation:** Here, the three-dimensional arrangement of branches becomes flattened into a single plane. This planar configuration is a precursor to the development of leaf-like structures.
- **Syngenesis (Webbing):** Adjacent telomes and mesomes fuse through the development of parenchymatous tissue, forming a continuous surface. This fusion results in the formation of laminae, contributing to the evolution of complex leaves.
- **Reduction:** This involves the simplification or loss of certain structures, leading to more streamlined organs. For instance, complex branching systems may reduce to simpler forms, aiding in the development of microphyllous leaves.
- **Curvation (Recurvation):** Fertile telomes bearing sporangia bend or curve, repositioning the sporangia. This bending is significant in the evolution of reproductive structures, altering their orientation for effective spore dispersal.

The following diagram illustrates these elementary processes: Elementary processes in the formation and modification of telomes

Applying the telome theory to ferns provides insights into the evolution of their reproductive structures:

Sporangia: Initially terminal on fertile telomes, sporangia underwent curvation, repositioning to the abaxial (underside) surface of leaves. This repositioning is evident in the sori of modern ferns.

Sporophylls: Through overtopping and planation, certain branches became specialized for reproduction, evolving into sporophylls—leaves bearing sporangia. Syngenesis further facilitated the development of a continuous lamina, enhancing spore production and dispersal.

This evolutionary pathway underscores the transformation from simple branched systems to the complex reproductive organs observed in contemporary ferns.

1. **(*e*):** Progymnosperms represent an extinct group of vascular plants that bridge the evolutionary gap between pteridophytes (ferns and their allies) and gymnosperms (seed-producing plants). Emerging during the Middle to Late Devonian period, they exhibit a combination of characteristics from both ancestral and derived plant groups.

Salient Features of Progymnosperms:

- **Woody Structure:** Progymnosperms were among the first plants to develop true wood, characterized by secondary xylem produced by a vascular cambium. This adaptation allowed for increased structural support and the potential for greater height.
- **Reproductive Strategy:** Unlike gymnosperms, progym-nosperms reproduced via spores. Early members were homosporous, producing one type of spore, while later forms exhibited heterospory, producing distinct microspores and megaspores—a precursor to seed development.
- **Leaf Morphology:** Their foliage often resembled that of ferns, with large, dissected fronds. This similarity initially led to misclassification as ferns.
- **Branching Patterns:** They exhibited both dichotomous and lateral branching, contributing to a complex canopy structure.
- **Notable Genera:** *Archaeopteris* is a well-known genus within this group, recognized for its tree-like stature and fern-like leaves.

Affinities with Pteridophytes:

- **Spore-Based Reproduction:** Like pteridophytes, progym-nosperms reproduced via spores, lacking seeds.
- **Leaf Structure:** The frond-like leaves of progymnosperms closely resemble those of ferns.
- **Vascular Organization:** Both groups possess vascular tissues, though progymnosperms exhibit more advanced secondary growth.

Affinities with Gymnosperms:

- **Wood Formation:** The presence of a vascular cambium and secondary xylem aligns progymnosperms with gymnosperms, indicating an evolutionary step towards seed plants.
- **Heterospory:** The development of distinct spore types in later progymnosperms mirrors the reproductive strategy of gymnosperms.
- **Growth Habit:** Their arborescent form and extensive root systems are characteristic of gymnospermous trees.

In summary, progymnosperms exhibit a mosaic of features linking them to both pteridophytes and gymnosperms. Their structural and reproductive adaptations mark a significant evolutionary transition from spore-bearing to seed-bearing plants.

2. **(*a*):** Cocci are spherical bacteria that exhibit various arrangements based on their division planes and the tendency of daughter cells to remain attached post-division.

Streptococci: Streptococci are chains of cocci resulting from cell divisions occurring in a single plane, with daughter cells remaining attached. This arrangement is characteristic of the genus *Streptococcus*, which includes species like *Streptococcus pyogenes*.

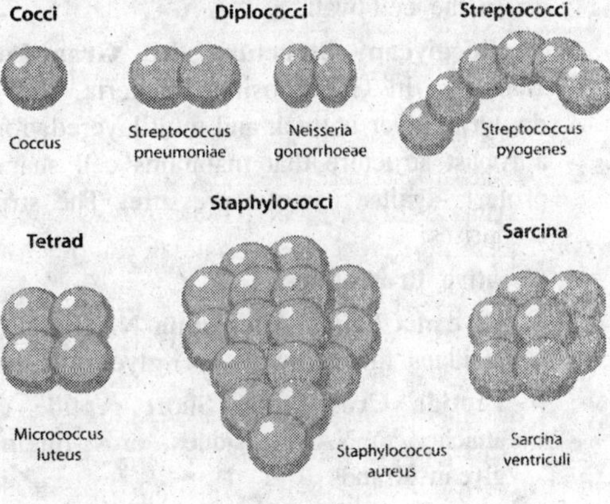

Staphylococci: Staphylococci form irregular, grape-like clusters due to cell divisions occurring in multiple planes, with cells remaining attached in a random fashion. This arrangement is typical of the genus *Staphylococcus*, such as *Staphylococcus aureus*.

Sarcinae: Sarcinae are cocci arranged in cubical packets of eight or more cells, resulting from cell divisions in three perpendicular planes. This arrangement is seen in the genus *Sarcina*, like *Sarcina ventriculi*.

Polysaccharides in Bacterial Cell Walls: Polysaccharides are essential components of bacterial cell walls, contributing to structural integrity and protection. They are categorized into:

Homopolysaccharides: These consist of repeating units of a single type of monosaccharide. In bacteria, examples include:

- **Dextran:** Composed of glucose units; produced by *Leuconostoc* and *Streptococcus* species.
- **Levan:** Made up of fructose units; synthesized by various bacterial species. Homopolysaccharides primarily serve as energy reserves and contribute to biofilm formation.

Heteropolysaccharides: These are composed of different types of monosaccharide units. In bacterial cell walls, the most notable heteropolysaccharide is peptidoglycan, which consists of alternating units of:

- N-acetylglucosamine (NAG) N-acetylmuramic acid (NAM)
- These sugar chains are cross-linked by short peptide chains, providing rigidity and strength to the cell wall.

Peptidoglycan Structure in Gram-Positive Bacteria: In Gram-positive bacteria, the peptidoglycan layer is thick and multilayered, forming a robust structure that maintains cell shape and protects against osmotic pressure. The structure comprises:

Creative Proteomics:

- **Glycan Chains:** Alternating NAG and NAM residues linked by β-(1,4)-glycosidic bonds.
- **Peptide Cross-links:** Short peptide chains attached to NAM residues, cross-linking the glycan strands.
- **Teichoic Acids:** Polymers of glycerol or ribitol phosphate that are covalently linked to the peptidoglycan, contributing to cell wall maintenance and ion regulation.

This complex structure provides the necessary strength and rigidity for the bacterial cell wall, enabling it to withstand environmental stresses.

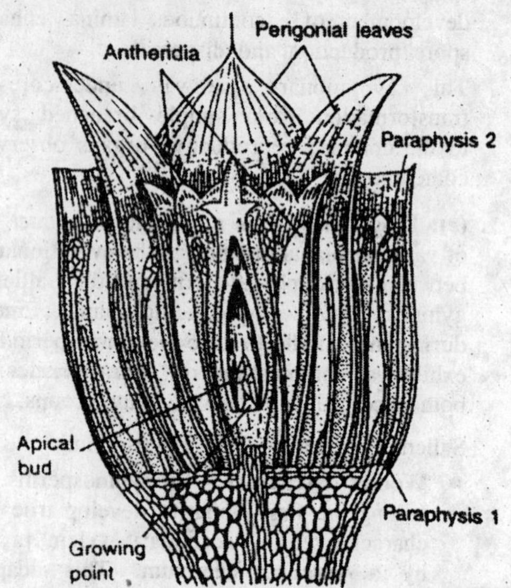

2. (***b***): Members of the family Polytrichaceae, such as *Polytrichum* and *Polytrichastrum*, are mosses that exhibit distinct anatomical features in both their gametophyte and sporophyte generations. These features are adaptations to their terrestrial environments, aiding in water conduction, photosynthesis, and reproduction.

Gametophyte Anatomy: The gametophyte is the dominant, photosynthetic phase of the life cycle.

- **Stem and Rhizoids:** The erect stem contains a central conducting strand composed of hydroids (water-conducting cells) and leptoids (sugar-conducting cells), analogous to xylem and phloem in vascular plants. Rhizoids anchor the plant and assist in water absorption.
- **Leaves:** Leaves are spirally arranged and possess a prominent midrib (costa) that supports parallel photosynthetic lamellae on the upper surface. These lamellae increase surface area for photosynthesis and help retain moisture.

- **Reproductive Structures:** Species are typically dioicous, with separate male and female plants. Male gametophytes bear antheridia at the apex, surrounded by perigonial leaves forming a splash-cup structure that aids in sperm dispersal. Female gametophytes have archegonia at the apex, surrounded by perichaetial leaves.

Sporophyte Anatomy: The sporophyte is dependent on the gametophyte for nutrition and consists of:

- **Foot:** Embedded in the gametophyte tissue, it facilitates nutrient transfer.
- **Seta:** A stalk that elevates the capsule, containing conducting tissues similar to those in the gametophyte stem.
- **Capsule (Sporangium):** Contains spores and features a peristome with nematodontous teeth (composed of whole cells) and an epiphragm (a membrane covering the capsule mouth), regulating spore release.
- **Calyptra:** A hairy, protective cap derived from gametophyte tissue that covers the developing capsule.

Environmental Significance: These anatomical features confer several advantages:

- **Water Conduction:** The presence of hydroids and leptoids allows efficient internal water and nutrient transport, enabling growth in drier habitats.
- **Photosynthetic Effciency:** Lamellae increase photosynthetic surface area and help retain moisture, allowing survival in high light and low humidity conditions.
- **Reproductive Adaptations:** The splash-cup mechanism enhances sperm dispersal in the absence of free-standing water, and the elevated capsule aids in effective spore distribution.

In summary, the anatomical adaptations of Polytrichaceae gametophytes and sporophytes are crucial for their survival and reproduction in terrestrial environments, reflecting an evolutionary advancement among mosses.

2. (*c*): Algae, a diverse group of photosynthetic organisms, exhibit varying types of reserve food materials across different classes. These storage compounds not only reflect their evolutionary adaptations but also have significant implications in medicine due to their bioactive properties.

Reserve Food Materials in Various Classes of Algae

Chlorophyceae (Green Algae):

Reserve Material: Starch

- **Characteristics:** Stored within chloroplasts, similar to higher plants, facilitating energy storage for metabolic processes.

Phaeophyceae (Brown Algae):

- **Reserve Materials:** Laminarin and Mannitol
- **Characteristics:** Laminarin is a β-glucan stored in vacuoles, while mannitol serves as both a storage compound and osmoprotectant, aiding in stress tolerance.

Rhodophyceae (Red Algae):

- **Reserve Material:** Floridean Starch
- **Characteristics:** A highly branched polysaccharide stored in the cytoplasm, distinct from plant starch, supporting energy needs.

Bacillariophyceae (Diatoms):

- **Reserve Materials:** Chrysolaminarin and Oil
- **Characteristics:** Chrysolaminarin is a soluble β-glucan stored in vacuoles; oils provide buoyancy and energy reserves.
- **Xanthophyceae (Yellow-Green Algae):** Reserve Materials: Oil and Leucosin.
- **Characteristics:** Leucosin (similar to chrysolaminarin) is a carbohydrate reserve; oils serve as energy storage
- **Cyanophyceae (Blue-Green Algae/Cyanobacteria):** Reserve Material: Cyanophycean Starch
- **Characteristics:** A glycogen-like polysaccharide stored in the cytoplasm, providing energy during unfavorable conditions.

Medicinal Applications of Algae: Algae have been recognized for their therapeutic potential, contributing to various medical applications:

- **Antioxidant Properties:** Compounds like phycobiliproteins and carotenoids scavenge free radicals, reducing oxidative stress.
- **Antiviral and Antibacterial Agents:** Sulfated poly-saccharides from red and brown algae inhibit viral replication and bacterial growth.

- **Anti-inflammatory Effects:** Algal extracts modulate inflammatory pathways, offering relief in conditions like arthritis.
- **Anticancer Potential:** Certain algal metabolites induce apoptosis in cancer cells and inhibit tumor growth.
- **Cholesterol Management:** Algal sterols and fibers aid in lowering blood cholesterol levels.
- **Immune System Enhancement:** Polysaccharides from algae stimulate immune responses, enhancing the body's defense mechanisms.
- **Wound Healing:** Alginates from brown algae are used in wound dressings for their moisture-retentive and healing properties.

In summary, the diverse reserve food materials in algae not only reflect their adaptability but also underpin their significant role in medical science, offering a reservoir of bioactive compounds for therapeutic applications.

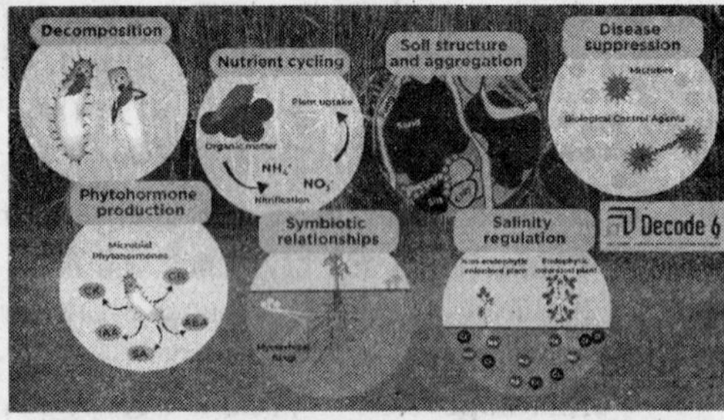

3. **(*a*):** Soil ecosystems are dynamic environments where diverse microbial communities interact in various ways, infuencing soil health, fertility, and plant growth. These interactions can be categorized based on the nature of the relationships among microorganisms:

Types of Microbial Interactions in Soil

Mutualism (Symbiosis): Both organisms benefit from the association.

Example: Rhizobium bacteria form nodules on legume roots, fixing atmospheric nitrogen into forms usable by plants, while receiving carbohydrates and a protective niche from the host plant.

Commensalism: One organism benefits, and the other is neither harmed nor benefited.

Example: Certain bacteria utilize organic acids produced by fungi during decomposition, without affecting the fungi.

Parasitism: One organism benefits at the expense of the other.

Example: Pathogenic fungi or bacteria invade plant roots, extracting nutrients and causing diseases.

Predation: One organism preys upon another.

Example: Protozoa consume bacteria, regulating bacterial populations and nutrient cycling.

Amensalism: One organism is inhibited or destroyed while the other remains unaffected.

Example: Production of antibiotics by certain soil bacteria suppresses the growth of competing microorganisms.

Competition: Organisms for the same resources, such as nutrients or space, which can limit the growth of one or both parties.

Example: Different microbial species competing for limited organic substrates in the soil.

Neutralism: Co-existing organisms do not significantly affect each other.

Example: Two microbial species occupying the same soil niche without interacting.

Role of Microbial Interactions in the Soil Ecosystem:

- **Nutrient Cycling:** Microbial interactions facilitate the decomposition of organic matter, releasing essential nutrients like nitrogen, phosphorus, and sulphur back into the soil, making them available for plant uptake.
- **Soil Structure Maintenance:** Microorganisms produce extracellular polysaccharides that help in the aggregation of soil particles, improving soil structure, aeration, and water retention.
- **Plant Growth Promotion:** Beneficial microbes, such as mycorrhizal fungi and plant growth-promoting rhizobacteria (PGPR), enhance nutrient uptake, produce growth hormones, and protect plants from pathogens.
- **Disease Suppression:** Certain soil microbes can inhibit or outcompete pathogenic organisms through the production of antibiotics, siderophores, or by inducing systemic resistance in plants.
- **Detoxification of Pollutants:** Some soil microorganisms can degrade or immobilize harmful substances, contributing to soil remediation and health.

- **Carbon Sequestration:** Through the decomposition of organic matter and formation of stable humic substances, microbes play a role in carbon storage within the soil, impacting global carbon cycles.

In summary, the intricate web of microbial interactions in soil ecosystems is fundamental to maintaining soil health, fertility, and productivity. Understanding these relationships is crucial for sustainable agriculture and environmental conservation.

3. **(*b*):** *Equisetum*, commonly known as horsetail, exhibits a combination of xerophytic and hydrophytic adaptations, enabling it to thrive in diverse environmental conditions.

Xerophytic Characters of *Equisetum*: These features enable *Equisetum* to survive in dry habitats:

- **Silica Deposition:** The epidermal cells of the stem are impregnated with silica, providing rigidity and reducing water loss.
- **Sunken Stomata:** Stomata are located in grooves between ridges on the stem surface, minimizing transpiration.
- **Sclerenchymatous Hypodermis:** Beneath the epidermis, a layer of sclerenchyma offers mechanical support and reduces water loss.
- **Reduced Leaves:** Leaves are small, scale-like, and non-photosynthetic, reducing surface area for transpiration.
- **Photosynthetic Stem:** The green stem carries out photosynthesis, compensating for the reduced leaf area.

Hydrophytic Characters of *Equisetum*: These adaptations allow *Equisetum* to thrive in moist environments:

- **Vallecular Canals:** Large air spaces in the cortex facilitate gas exchange and buoyancy.
- **Carinal Canals:** Located near the vascular bundles, these canals aid in water conduction.
- **Central Pith Cavity:** A hollow central cavity reduces stem weight and aids in aeration.
- **Reduced Vascular Tissue:** The xylem is less developed, reflecting adaptation to water-abundant habitats.

Comparative Account of Spore-Bearing Structures: *Selaginella* and *Equisetum* differ in their reproductive structures:

Sporangia Arrangement:

Selaginella: Sporangia are borne on specialized leaves called sporophylls, arranged in strobili.

Equisetum: Sporangia are borne on umbrella-like structures called sporangiophores, forming a terminal strobilus.

Spore Type:

Selaginella: Heterosporous, producing distinct microspores and megaspores.

Equisetum: Homosporous, producing one type of spore.

Elaters:

Selaginella: Spores lack elaters.

Equisetum: Spores possess hygroscopic elaters that aid in spore dispersal.

These differences highlight the evolutionary adaptations of each genus to their respective environments and reproductive strategies.

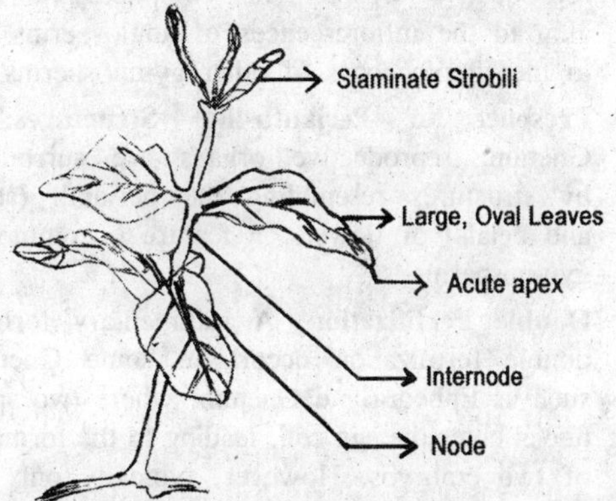

3. **(*c*):** Gnetales, encompassing the genera *Gnetum*, *Ephedra*, and *Welwitschia*, are considered highly advanced among gymnosperms due to a suite of unique vegetative and reproductive features that exhibit notable parallels with angiosperms.

Vegetative Characters

Presence of Vessel Elements in Xylem: Unlike most gymnosperms, which possess only tracheids for water conduction, members of Gnetales have vessel elements in their xylem tissue. This feature, characteristic of angiosperms, enhances the efficiency of water transport within the plant.

Leaf Morphology:

Gnetum: Exhibits broad, flat leaves with reticulate (net-like) venation, closely resembling those of dicotyledonous angiosperms.

Ephedra: Possesses small, scale-like leaves, with photosynthesis primarily occurring in the green stems.

Welwitschia: Features only two large, strap-like leaves that grow continuously from the base throughout the plant's life.

Growth Habit: Gnetales display diverse growth forms, including trees, shrubs, and lianas (Gnetum), as well as ground-hugging forms (Welwitschia), reflecting a wide range of ecological adaptations.

Opposite Phyllotaxy: Leaves are arranged in opposite pairs, a trait common in angiosperms but rare among gymnosperms.

Reproductive Characters

Compound Strobili: The reproductive structures of Gnetales are organized into compound strobili (cones), composed of multiple units that bear reproductive organs. This complexity is more akin to the inflorescences of angiosperms than to the simple cones of other gymnosperms.

Presence of Perianth-like Structures: In Gnetum, reproductive organs are surrounded by structures resembling the perianth (sepals and petals) of flowers, a feature uncommon in gymnosperms.

Double Fertilization: A rudimentary form of double fertilization occurs in some Gnetales, such as Ephedra and Gnetum, where two sperm nuclei enter the egg cell, leading to the formation of two embryos. However, typically only one embryo develops fully. This phenomenon is reminiscent of the double fertilization seen in angiosperms, though the outcomes differ.

Non-Motile Sperm and Pollen Tubes: Gnetales produce non-flagellated sperm that are delivered to the egg via a pollen tube, similar to the mechanism in angiosperms and differing from the motile sperm found in some other gymnosperms like cycads and ginkgo.

Reduced Gametophyte: The female gametophyte in Gnetales is highly reduced and lacks archegonia, paralleling the condition found in angiosperms and indicating an advanced reproductive strategy among gymnosperms.

In summary, the advanced vegetative features such as vessel elements and angiosperm-like leaves, combined with reproductive traits like compound strobili, perianth-like structures, and double fertilization, position Gnetales as a highly evolved group within gymnosperms. These characteristics not only highlight their unique evolutionary path but also underscore their significance in understanding the transition from gymnosperms to angiosperms.

4. **(*a*):** Sheath blight of rice is a significant disease affecting rice cultivation, leading to substantial yield losses.

Symptoms:

- **Initial Lesions:** Appear as oblong, water-soaked spots on the leaf sheaths near the water line.
- **Lesion Progression:** Lesions enlarge, becoming grayish-white with dark brown margins, and may coalesce to cover large areas.
- **Leaf Blades:** Infection can spread to leaf blades, causing irregular lesions and potential dieback.
- **Plant Lodging:** Severe infections weaken the plant, leading to lodging (falling over).

Causal Organism

Pathogen: *Rhizoctonia solani* AG1-IA, a soil-borne fungus.

Disease Cycle

Survival: The fungus survives in soil and plant debris as sclerotia or mycelium.

Infection: Sclerotia germinate under favorable conditions, producing hyphae that infect rice sheaths.

Spread: The fungus spreads through contact between infected and healthy plants, especially in dense canopies.

Reproduction: New sclerotia form on infected tissues, returning to the soil to continue the cycle.

Management

Cultural Practices: Use wider plant spacing to reduce humidity.

Apply balanced fertilization; avoid excessive nitrogen. Remove and destroy infected plant residues.

Chemical Control: Apply fungicides like azoxystrobin or propiconazole at early disease stages. Follow recommended application timings and dosages.

Biological Control: Utilize antagonistic organisms such as *Trichoderma* spp. to suppress the pathogen.

Resistant Varieties: Plant rice varieties that show tolerance or resistance to sheath blight.

Implementing an integrated disease management approach combining these strategies can effectively control sheath blight in rice.

4. (*b*): Chlorophyceae, commonly known as green algae, represent a diverse class of photosynthetic organisms predominantly found in freshwater environments. They exhibit a wide range of morphological forms and reproductive strategies, contributing significantly to aquatic ecosystems.

General Characteristics:

- **Pigmentation:** Possess chlorophylls *a* and *b*, imparting a characteristic green color.
- **Storage Product:** Store carbohydrates in the form of starch within chloroplasts.
- **Cell Wall Composition:** Primarily composed of cellulose, with some species exhibiting additional polysaccharides.
- **Habitat:** Predominantly freshwater, though some species inhabit marine and terrestrial environments.
- **Flagella:** When present, flagella are typically equal in length and inserted apically.

Range of Thallus Organization: Chlorophyceae exhibit a remarkable diversity in thallus (plant body) structures, ranging from unicellular to complex multicellular forms:

- **Unicellular Motile Forms:** Single-celled organisms with flagella, e.g., *Chlamydomonas*.
- **Unicellular Non-Motile Forms:** Single-celled organisms without flagella, e.g., *Chlorella*.

Colonial Forms:

- **Motile Colonies:** Aggregates of flagellated cells functioning together, e.g., *Volvox*.
- **Non-Motile Colonies:** Groups of non-flagellated cells embedded in mucilage, e.g., *Hydrodictyon*.
- **Palmelloid Forms:** Non-motile cells embedded in a gelatinous matrix, often a temporary stage under unfavorable conditions.

Filamentous Forms:

- **Unbranched Filaments:** Linear chains of cells, e.g., *Ulothrix*.
- **Branched Filaments:** Filaments with lateral branches, e.g., *Cladophora*.
- **Heterotrichous Forms:** Thalli exhibiting both prostrate (creeping) and erect systems, e.g., *Stigeoclonium*.
- **Siphonous Forms:** Multinucleate, tubular thalli without cross-walls, e.g., *Caulerpa*.

Modes of Reproduction: Chlorophyceae reproduce through vegetative, asexual, and sexual means:

Vegetative Reproduction

- **Fragmentation:** Thallus breaks into fragments, each developing into a new individual.
- **Asexual Reproduction:** Zoospores: Motile, flagellated spores produced within sporangia; common in unicellular and filamentous forms.
- **Aplanospores:** Non-motile spores formed under unfavorable conditions.
- **Autospores:** Non-motile spores resembling the parent cell in shape and size.

Sexual Reproduction: Sexual reproduction in Chlorophyceae exhibits diversity in gamete morphology:

- **Isogamy:** Fusion of morphologically similar gametes; e.g., *Chlamydomonas*.
- **Anisogamy:** Fusion of *dissimilar gametes*, differing in size or motility; e.g., *Eudorina*.
- **Oogamy:** Fusion of a large, non-motile egg with a small, motile sperm; e.g., *Volvox*.

The life cycle is typically *haplontic*, with the zygote being the only diploid stage, undergoing meiosis to produce haploid spores.

In summary, Chlorophyceae demonstrate a vast array of structural and reproductive adaptations, enabling them to occupy diverse ecological niches and play a vital role in aquatic ecosystems.

4. (*c*): Coralloid roots are specialized structures found in *Cycas*, exhibiting unique morphological and anatomical features that distinguish them from normal roots.

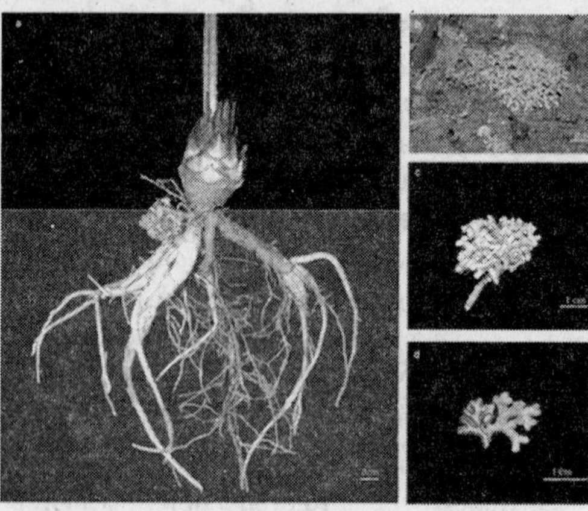

Coralloid Roots in *Cycas*: Coralloid roots are short, dichotomously branched roots that emerge near the soil surface. They are negatively geotropic, growing upwards, and often protrude above the ground, resembling coral structures. These roots harbor symbiotic cyanobacteria, such as Nostoc and Anabaena, within their cortical cells, facilitating nitrogen fixation.

Diagram of Coralloid Root: The following diagram illustrates the structure of a coralloid root in *Cycas*:

Differences Between Coralloid and Normal Roots in *Cycas*

Feature	Coralloid Roots	Normal Roots
Origin	Develop from lateral branches of normal roots	Originate from the radicle during seed germination
Growth Direction	Negatively geotropic (grow upwards)	Positively geotropic (grow downwards)
Branching Pattern	Dichotomously branched, forming coral-like structures	Irregular branching pattern
Color	Greenish due to presence of cyanobacteria	Brownish
Symbiotic Association	Contain cyanobacteria (Nostoc, Anabaena) for nitrogen fixation	Generally lack symbiotic cyanobacteria
Function	Nitrogen fixation, aiding in nutrient acquisition	Anchorage and absorption of water and minerals
Anatomical Features	Presence of an algal zone in the cortex; reduced vascular tissues	Well-developed vascular tissues; absence of algal zone

In summary, coralloid roots in *Cycas* are specialized adaptations that facilitate symbiotic nitrogen fixation, distinguishing them from the typical absorptive and anchoring functions of normal roots.

5. (*a*): Floral characters of Magnoliaceae vs Euphorbiaceae:

Character	Magnoliaceae	Euphorbiaceae
Habit	Mostly trees or shrubs	Herbs, shrubs, or trees, some xerophytes
Floral symmetry	Actinomorphic (radial symmetry)	Mostly actinomorphic; some zygomorphic
Inflore-scence	Solitary or rarely in clusters	Usually cymose or racemose, or flowers may be solitary
Sexuality	Bisexual flowers (perfect)	Often unisexual (monoecious or dioecious plants)
Perianth	Undifferentiated tepals, arranged in whorls or spirally	Distinct calyx and corolla, or perianth absent
Androecium	Numerous stamens, spirally arranged	Few to many stamens, sometimes in complex arrangements

Character	Magnoliaceae	Euphorbiaceae
Gynoecium	Apocarpous, many carpels, superior ovary	Syncarpous, 3-carpellary, trilocular ovary, superior
Ovary position	Superior	Superior
Fruit	Aggregate of follicles or berries	Mostly schizocarpic (e.g., regma), capsule, or drupe
Pollination	Mainly entomophilous (insect-pollinated)	Also entomophilous, sometimes anemophilous
Floral formula (typical)	⚥ ⊕ P ∞ A ∞ G ∞ (free)	♂ ⊕ K5 C5 A∞; ♀ ⊕ K5 C5 G(3)

Examples and Economic Importance:

Magnoliaceae:

1. *Magnolia grandiflora* – Cultivated as an ornamental tree for its large fragrant flowers.
2. *Michelia champaca* (Champak) – Valued for its fragrant yellow flowers used in perfumery and worship.

Euphorbiaceae:

1. *Ricinus communis* (Castor plant) – Produces castor oil, used in medicine, cosmetics, and industry.
2. *Hevea brasiliensis* (Rubber tree) – Source of natural rubber extracted from latex, critical for tyre and industrial goods manufacturing.

5. (*b*): Artificial vs Natural System of Classification:

Feature	Artificial System	Natural System
Basis of classification	One or a few superficial or convenient characters (e.g., habit, number of stamens)	Many morphological and structural characters (e.g., floral, vegetative, anatomical)
Developed by	Early taxonomists like Linnaeus	Later taxonomists like Bentham and Hooker
Scientific accuracy	Less accurate, non-evolutionary	More accurate and reflects natural affinities
Grouping	Often places unrelated plants together based on similar features	Groups plants with similar overall morphology and structure
Ease of use	Easy and quick to use	Comparatively complex and time-consuming
Examples	Linnaeus' Sexual System (based on number of stamens)	Bentham and Hooker's system (based on a range of natural characters)

Merits and Demerits:

Artificial System:

- **Merits:**
  - ❑ Simple and easy to understand.
  - ❑ Useful for quick identification.
  - ❑ Useful during early botanical studies when knowledge of plant morphology was limited.
- **Demerits:**
  - ❑ Often unnatural groupings.
  - ❑ Ignores evolutionary relationships.
  - ❑ Can be misleading in terms of plant affinity and genetic relationship.

Natural System:

- **Merits:**
  - ❑ More reliable and scientific.
  - ❑ Reflects natural similarities and dissimilarities.
  - ❑ Helps in understanding evolutionary and phylogenetic relationships.
- **Demerits:**
  - ❑ Requires extensive knowledge and observation.
  - ❑ More time-consuming and complex.
  - ❑ Sometimes based on subjective interpretation of characters.

Thus, while artificial systems were stepping stones in taxonomy, natural systems offer a more holistic and biologically meaningful grouping of plants.

5. (*c*): Ethnobotany is the scientific study of the relationship between people and plants in traditional cultural contexts. It investigates how indigenous communities use plants for medicine, food, rituals, and shelter. This knowledge has played a crucial role in shaping modern pharmacology and medicine.

Role in Modern Medicine:

1. **Source of Medicinal Compounds:**
   - ❑ Many modern drugs have their origins in traditional plant-based remedies. For example:
     - ❖ *Morphine from Papaver somniferum (opium poppy)*
     - ❖ *Quinine from Cinchona bark*
     - ❖ *Aspirin from Salix alba (willow bark)*
     - ❖ *Artemisinin from Artemisia annua*
   - ❑ Over 25% of modern drugs are derived from plant sources traditionally used in ethnomedicine.
2. **Drug Discovery Pipeline:** Ethnobotanical leads reduce the time and cost of screening by directly targeting plants known for specific therapeutic effects.
3. **Preservation of Traditional Knowledge:** Documentation of indigenous practices preserves knowledge that might otherwise be lost with modernization.
4. **Holistic Health Understanding:** Traditional systems like Ayurveda and Unani emphasize balance and holistic healing, concepts now integrated into modern complementary and alternative medicine.

Cultural and Religious Practices in India and Their Contribution: India is exceptionally rich in ethnobotanical tradition due to its diverse ecosystems and multi-ethnic, multi-lingual society.

1. **Ayurveda and Other Traditional Systems:**
   - ❑ Ancient scriptures like the Charaka Samhita and Sushruta Samhita document the use of over 600 medicinal plants.
   - ❑ Practices like Panchakarma and Rasayana utilize herbal formulations that continue to influence modern nutraceuticals and wellness therapies.
2. **Religious Associations:**
   - ❑ Plants like Tulsi (*Ocimum sanctum*), Neem (*Azadirachta indica*), and Peepal (*Ficus religiosa*) are considered sacred and used for health, reflecting deep-rooted ethnobotanical wisdom.
   - ❑ Ritualistic offerings, sacred groves, and festivals (e.g., Vanamahotsava) promote conservation of medicinal plants.
3. **Tribal Knowledge:** India's tribal populations (e.g., Gonds, Bhils, Santhals) use plants for healing wounds, fever, fertility, etc., providing critical data for ethnopharmacological studies.
4. **Sacred Groves and Biodiversity Hotspots:** These culturally protected areas have preserved rare medicinal species and serve as natural laboratories for ethnobotanical research.

   In conclusion, ethnobotany bridges tradition and science, offering sustainable pathways for drug discovery and conservation, with India standing as a global reservoir of ethnobotanical wealth.

5. (*d*): Gynogenesis: Gynogenesis is a type of asexual reproduction or haploid development where the embryo develops from the female gamete (egg cell) without any genetic contribution from the male gamete. However, activation of the egg requires stimulation by a male gamete, but the male nucleus does not fuse with the egg nucleus or participate in embryogenesis.

- It results in the formation of a haploid individual carrying only the maternal genome.
- It occurs naturally in some fishes and amphibians and can be induced artificially in plants and animals.
- Gynogenesis is used in plant breeding, haploid production, and genetic studies to fix desirable traits.

Androgenesis: Androgenesis is the counterpart of gynogenesis. In this process, the embryo develops from the male gamete (pollen or sperm), while the female nucleus either degenerates or does not participate in development.

- It leads to a haploid organism with only paternal genetic material.

- In plants, it can be induced via anther or pollen culture, producing haploid plants useful for creating doubled haploid lines.

Key Differences:

Feature	Gynogenesis	Androgenesis
Genetic Source	Only from the female (egg)	Only from the male (sperm or pollen)
Activation	Male gamete stimulates egg, but doesn't contribute	Female gamete is present but non-functional
Resulting Offspring	Haploid with maternal genome only	Haploid with paternal genome only
Common in	Fish, amphibians, some induced plants	Mostly induced in plants (e.g., anther culture)
Application	Fixing maternal traits, haploid production	Development of male haploids, breeding lines

Both processes are important tools in genetic engineering, plant biotechnology, and breeding programs for generating pure lines and studying gene expression.

5. (*e*): Importance of Botanical Gardens in India: Botanical gardens are institutions that maintain documented collections of living plants for the purposes of scientific research, conservation, education, and public display. In India, botanical gardens play a vital role in the study and preservation of plant diversity, both native and exotic.

Key Importance of Botanical Gardens in India:

1. **Conservation of Plant Biodiversity:**
   - ❑ Botanical gardens act as ex-situ conservation centers where rare, endangered, and endemic species are cultivated and protected.
   - ❑ They help prevent extinction of plant species by maintaining living gene banks.
2. **Research and Education:**
   - ❑ Serve as research hubs for taxonomists, geneticists, and botanists.
   - ❑ Used for education and training of students, researchers, and the public on plant identification, ecology, and taxonomy.
3. **Introduction and Acclimatization of Exotic Species:**
   - ❑ Botanical gardens have historically served to introduce and acclimatize foreign plants (e.g., tea, rubber, and quinine in colonial India).
   - ❑ Help evaluate the adaptability of economically useful plants to Indian conditions.
4. **Environmental Awareness and Recreation:**
   - ❑ Promote public interest in nature and environment, playing a vital role in ecological education and recreational tourism.
   - ❑ Often host events like flower shows, tree walks, and awareness campaigns.
5. **Support to Herbal and Medicinal Plant Studies:** Many Indian gardens maintain dedicated sections for medicinal plants, supporting Ayurvedic and ethnobotanical research.
6. **Climate Change Mitigation and Urban Greening:** By maintaining a wide range of plant species, they contribute to urban biodiversity, reduce carbon footprint, and improve microclimatic conditions.

Major Botanical Gardens in India:

- Acharya Jagadish Chandra Bose Indian Botanical Garden, Howrah – One of the oldest and largest in Asia.
- Lalbagh Botanical Garden, Bengaluru – Known for scientific horticulture and rare plant collections.
- National Botanical Research Institute (NBRI), Lucknow – A leading center for plant research.
- Tropical Botanic Garden and Research Institute (TBGRI), Kerala – Focused on tropical biodiversity and tribal plant knowledge.

In sum, botanical gardens in India are not just plant repositories but are essential for scientific innovation, biodiversity conservation, public education, and cultural heritage preservation.

6. (*a*): Distinction between Diplospory and Apospory with Examples: Both diplospory and apospory are types of apomixis, a form of asexual reproduction in plants where seeds are formed without fertilization, and meiosis is either absent or bypassed. However, they differ in the origin and development of the embryo sac.

1. **Diplospory:**
   - Definition: Diplospory is a type of gametophytic apomixis where the embryo sac develops directly from the megaspore mother cell (MMC) or archesporial cell without undergoing meiosis.
   - As meiosis is skipped or modified, the resulting embryo sac is diploid, genetically identical to the parent plant.
   - The diploid egg develops into an embryo without fertilization (parthenogenesis).
   - Example: Eupatorium, Taraxacum (dandelion), and Erigeron.

2. **Apospory:**
   - Definition: Apospory is also a type of gametophytic apomixis, but here, the embryo sac arises from a somatic (nucellar or integumentary) cell of the ovule instead of the megaspore mother cell.
   - The MMC either degenerates or is non-functional, and the somatic cell bypasses meiosis and directly forms a diploid embryo sac.
   - The embryo again develops parthenogenetically or via pseudogamy.
   - Example: Hieracium, Parthenium, and Ranunculus.

Key Differences:

Feature	Diplospory	Apospory
Origin of embryo sac	Megaspore mother cell (archesporial cell)	Somatic cell of nucellus or integuments
Role of meiosis	Meiosis is suppressed or altered	Meiosis does not occur
Functional MMC	Yes, it forms embryo sac directly	No, it degenerates or is non-functional
Genetic nature of embryo sac	Diploid (same as mother plant)	Diploid (same as mother plant)
Example species	*Taraxacum, Erigeron*	*Hieracium, Parthenium*

Both mechanisms ensure clonal reproduction through seeds, maintaining the genetic fidelity of the parent plant, and are valuable in crop improvement, especially in fixing heterosis.

6. (*b*): (*i*) Supportive Evidences from Palynology in Taxonomy: Palynology is the study of pollen grains and spores, both living and fossilized. It provides important taxonomic evidence, especially in angiosperms, by examining the morphology, structure, and ornamentation of pollen grains.

Key Contributions of Palynology to Taxonomy:

1. **Species Identification:**
   - ❑ Pollen grain size, shape, number of apertures (colpi or pores), and surface sculpturing are often unique to genera or species, aiding in precise classification.
   - ❑ Example: Asteraceae have tricolporate pollen; Poaceae show monoporate pollen.
2. **Taxonomic Delimitation:**
   - ❑ Differences in pollen morphology support separation or grouping of taxa.
   - ❑ Helps in resolving complex genera or cryptic species by highlighting micromorphological distinctions.
3. **Phylogenetic Relationships:** Palynological traits, being relatively stable, serve as conservative characters, reflecting evolutionary relationships and helping in cladistic classification.
4. **Fossil Evidence and Evolution:** Fossilized pollen helps trace the evolutionary history and origin of plant families and supports taxonomic revisions.
5. **Pollination Mechanism Correlation:** Pollen structure relates to pollination type (e.g., smooth pollen for wind pollination, sticky and sculptured for insect pollination), aiding in ecological classification.
6. **Support for Artificial vs. Natural Classification:** Palynological evidence often supports natural and phylogenetic systems over artificial ones by providing micromorphological validation.

Example Applications:

- Used to differentiate species in *Solanum*, *Brassica*, and *Cyperaceae*.

- Supported the separation of *Caryophyllaceae* and *Chenopodiaceae* based on differences in aperture patterns.

In sum, palynology offers microscopic yet powerful data to reinforce and refine plant taxonomy and systematics.

6. (*b*): (*ii*) Principles of ICN (International Code of Nomenclature): The International Code of Nomenclature (ICN) for algae, fungi, and plants is the globally accepted set of rules and recommendations that govern the scientific naming of plant taxa. It ensures uniformity, stability, and universality in plant nomenclature.

Main Principles of ICN:

1. **Principle I – Botanical Nomenclature is Independent:** The nomenclature of plants is independent of zoological and bacteriological nomenclature, though some rules may be similar.
2. **Principle II – Type Concept:**
   - ❑ Each name of a taxon is based on a type specimen. This type (holotype) acts as a permanent reference point for the application of the name.
   - ❑ For example, a species name is anchored to a type specimen, and a genus to a type species.
3. **Principle III – Priority of Publication:** The earliest validly published name has priority and must be adopted (principle of priority), except in some officially conserved or rejected names to promote stability.
4. **Principle IV – Only One Correct Name:** A taxon can bear only one correct scientific name, the one that is validly published, legitimate, and in accordance with the rules.
5. **Principle V – Names Must Be Latin or Latinized:** Scientific names must be in Latin or treated as Latin, regardless of their derivation or origin.
6. **Principle VI – Rules are Retroactive:** Unless explicitly limited, the rules of nomenclature are retroactive, meaning they apply to all names, including those published in the past.

Purpose of ICN:

- To promote nomenclatural stability.
- To avoid duplication or ambiguity in naming.
- To provide a standardized system for global scientific communication.

The ICN is revised and updated during the International Botanical Congress (IBC), held every six years—the latest being the Shenzhen Code (2017), and the upcoming 2023 Code (Rio Code) will reflect further updates.

6. (*b*): (*iii*) Importance of Herbaria in Taxonomy: A herbarium is a systematically arranged collection of preserved plant specimens, usually dried, mounted on sheets, and labeled with essential data such as species name, date and place of collection, habitat, and collector's name. It serves as a permanent reference and research resource for taxonomists and botanists.

Importance of Herbaria in Taxonomy:

1. **Reference for Plant Identification:** Herbaria house authenticated specimens that help researchers accurately identify unknown plant species by comparison.
2. **Type Specimen Repository:** Herbaria preserve type specimens (holotype, isotype, syntype, etc.), which are nomenclatural standards for species descriptions.
3. **Taxonomic Revision and Research:** Useful for revising genera and families, clarifying synonymy, and updating classification based on historical and modern specimens.
4. **Documentation of Flora:** Herbaria serve as records of plant biodiversity from various geographical regions, including extinct or endangered species.
5. **Historical and Geographical Data:** Each specimen is associated with collection data that provides insights into the plant's original habitat, distribution, and seasonal behavior.
6. **Support in Molecular Taxonomy:** DNA can be extracted from herbarium specimens, making them valuable in molecular phylogenetics and barcoding studies.
7. **Education and Training:** Act as learning centers for students and researchers to study plant morphology, diversity, and classification.
8. **Global Networking and Digitization:** Digitized herbaria enable global sharing of plant data, facilitating international taxonomic collaboration and conservation planning.

Major Herbaria in India:

- Central National Herbarium (CNH), Howrah – Maintained by Botanical Survey of India.

- Herbarium of Forest Research Institute (FRI), Dehradun
- Madras Herbarium, Coimbatore

In conclusion, herbaria are indispensable tools for plant taxonomy, contributing to scientific research, conservation, and biodiversity management.

6. (*c*): Protoplasts are plant cells without their cell walls, enclosed only by the plasma membrane. They represent the living portion of a plant cell, and are capable of performing vital cellular functions such as respiration, metabolism, and division. Protoplasts are commonly used in plant genetic engineering, somatic hybridization, and cell fusion studies.

Protocol for Enzymatic Isolation of Protoplasts: Protoplasts are typically isolated from plant tissues (e.g., leaf mesophyll) by enzymatic digestion of the cell wall using a combination of cellulase and pectinase.

1. **Selection and Preparation of Material:**
   - Choose young, healthy leaves (usually from sterile in vitro grown plants).
   - Surface-sterilize with 70% ethanol (1–2 min) followed by 0.1% $HgCl_2$ or 1% sodium hypochlorite (5–10 min).
   - Wash thoroughly with sterile distilled water.
2. **Plasmolysis (Optional):** Leaves may be pre-treated in an osmoticum solution (e.g., 0.4–0.6 M mannitol or sorbitol) for 30 minutes to stabilize the plasma membrane before digestion.
3. **Enzymatic Digestion:**
   - Cut leaves into small strips (1–2 mm wide).
   - Incubate in an enzyme solution containing:
     - ❑ Cellulase (e.g., 1–2%) – to degrade cellulose
     - ❑ Pectinase or macerozyme (0.5–1%) – to degrade pectic substances
     - ❑ Osmoticum (mannitol/sorbitol) – to maintain osmotic balance
     - ❑ pH adjusted to ~5.5 with MES buffer
   - Incubate in the dark at 25–28°C for 3–16 hours with gentle shaking.
4. **Filtration and Collection:**
   - Filter the digest through nylon mesh (40–100 μm) to remove debris.
   - Centrifuge the filtrate at low speed (100×g) for 5 minutes.
   - Discard supernatant and resuspend the pellet in osmotic solution.
5. **Purification of Protoplasts:**
   - Use a density gradient (e.g., sucrose or Percoll) to separate intact protoplasts from broken cells and debris.
   - Centrifuge and collect the viable, floating protoplast layer.
6. **Viability Check:** Assess protoplast viability using fluorescein diacetate (FDA) staining or Evans Blue exclusion method.

Applications:

- Somatic hybridization
- Genetic transformation
- Single-cell culture and regeneration
- Functional genomics

Protoplasts provide a versatile tool in plant biotechnology and developmental biology, allowing direct access to the plant genome and cellular machinery.

7. (*a*): **Botanical Name, Family, and Uses of Plants Producing Specific Products:**

Product	Botanical Name	Family	Uses
(*i*) Resin	*Pinus roxburghii*	Pinaceae	Resin is used in making varnishes, paints, sealing wax, and adhesives.
(*ii*) Jute	*Corchorus capsularis / C. olitorius*	Tiliaceae (or Malvaceae as per APG)	Fibres used for making sacks, ropes, mats, and gunny bags.
(*iii*) Cassava	*Manihot esculenta*	Euphorbiaceae	Roots are used as a source of starch and food; also used in industrial alcohol production.
(*iv*) Long pepper	*Piper longum*	Piperaceae	Used as a spice and in traditional medicine (Ayurveda) for respiratory and digestive ailments.
(*v*) Pyrethrum	*Chrysanthemum cinerariifolium*	Asteraceae	Flower extracts used as a natural insecticide (pyrethrins), safe for humans and pets.

These plants hold significant value in agriculture, industry, and medicine, reflecting the economic and ethnobotanical richness of plant resources.

7. (*b*): (*i*) Preferred Method: Direct Shoot Regeneration: When both direct and indirect shoot regeneration are possible in a plant, direct regeneration is usually preferred over indirect regeneration.

Reasons for Preferring Direct Shoot Regeneration:

1. **Genetic Stability:**
   - ❑ Direct regeneration involves organ formation from pre-existing meristematic tissues (e.g., nodes, shoot tips) without callus formation.
   - ❑ This reduces the risk of somaclonal variation, ensuring that regenerated plants are genetically true-to-type.
2. **Faster Process:** It is a quicker method since it bypasses the intermediate callus phase, leading to rapid shoot development.
3. **Less Contamination and Mutation Risk:** Fewer subcultures and shorter culture duration reduce chances of microbial contamination and unintended genetic changes.
4. **Higher Efficiency in Micropropagation:** Direct organogenesis allows high-frequency regeneration with high fidelity, ideal for clonal propagation of elite genotypes.
5. **Better for Commercial Applications:** Widely preferred in tissue culture industries (e.g., for banana, sugarcane, orchids) where genetic uniformity and speed are critical.

When Indirect Method May Be Used:

- Indirect shoot regeneration (via callus) is useful for genetic engineering, mutagenesis, or when explant does not directly form shoots.
- However, it requires careful monitoring due to greater variability.

Thus, direct shoot regeneration is the method of choice for routine propagation and maintaining genetic integrity, especially in commercial and conservation programs.

7. (*b*): (*ii*) Example of Cybrids and Their Importance:

Example: Cybrid: *Nicotiana tabacum* (tobacco) cybrid developed by fusing:

- Protoplast of albino tobacco (lacking chloroplasts) and
- Irradiated protoplast of green tobacco (having chloroplasts but inactivated nucleus)

This fusion produces a cytoplasmic hybrid (cybrid) with the nucleus of one parent and cytoplasmic organelles (e.g., mitochondria and chloroplasts) from both parents.

What are Cybrids?

Cybrids, or cytoplasmic hybrids, are cells resulting from the fusion of:

- One enucleated protoplast (cytoplasm donor) and
- One intact protoplast (nuclear and partial cytoplasmic donor)

Importance of Cybrids:

1. **Transfer of Cytoplasmic Traits:** Useful in transferring cytoplasmic male sterility (CMS), which is critical for hybrid seed production in crops like rice, sunflower, and tobacco.
2. **Organelle Genetics Studies:** Help in studying mitochondrial and chloroplast inheritance independently from nuclear DNA.
3. **Creation of Novel Traits:** Enable combining desirable nuclear genome from one species with mitochondria or chloroplasts from another, facilitating traits like disease resistance or herbicide tolerance.
4. **Overcoming Sexual Barriers:** Useful in asexual gene transfer where traditional crossing is not possible due to sexual incompatibility.

Thus, cybrids are valuable in plant biotechnology, breeding, and cytoplasmic gene transfer, offering unique combinations of nuclear and cytoplasmic genomes.

7. (*c*): Fertilization in angiosperms is a highly specialized and coordinated process involving several sequential events, starting from the germination of pollen on the stigma to the fusion of gametes within the ovule. The entire process ensures successful formation of a zygote and endosperm.

1. **Pollen Germination:**
   - When a mature pollen grain lands on a compatible stigma, it germinates in response to stigmatic secretions.

- The pollen tube emerges from the germ pore and penetrates the stigmatic tissue.

2. **Pollen Tube Growth:**
   - The pollen tube grows through the style, guided by chemotropic signals (e.g., calcium ions, LURE peptides) from the ovule.
   - The tube is nourished by style tissues and grows towards the ovary, carrying two male gametes (sperm cells) in its cytoplasm.
3. **Entry into Ovule (Pollen Tube Entry):**
   - The pollen tube enters the ovule through the micropyle – this mode is called porogamy (most common).
   - It can also enter through the chalaza (chalazogamy) or integuments (mesogamy) in rare cases.
4. **Entry into Embryo Sac:**
   - The pollen tube penetrates one of the synergids of the egg apparatus in the embryo sac (located in the ovule).
   - The synergid disintegrates, allowing release of the two male gametes into the embryo sac.
5. **Double Fertilization:** Unique to angiosperms, double fertilization involves two fusion events:

   (*a*) **Syngamy:** One male gamete fuses with the egg cell to form the diploid (2*n*) zygote, which develops into the embryo.

   (*b*) **Triple Fusion:** The second male gamete fuses with the two polar nuclei (or secondary nucleus) to form a triploid (3*n*) primary endosperm nucleus, which gives rise to the endosperm (nutritive tissue).
6. **Post-Fertilization Events:**
   - Zygote → Embryo
   - Primary endosperm nucleus → Endosperm
   - Ovule → Seed
   - Ovary → Fruit

Significance:

- Double fertilization ensures coordinated development of embryo and endosperm.
- Endosperm provides nutrition for the developing embryo and seedling.

This process highlights the evolutionary advancement of angiosperms, enhancing reproductive success and efficiency.

8. (*a*): **Centres of Origin of Cultivated Plants: Vavilovian Concept:** The concept of centres of origin of cultivated plants was introduced by Russian botanist Nikolai I. Vavilov in the early 20th century. He studied the geographical distribution of crop plants and their wild relatives, proposing that domestication began in specific regions where maximum genetic diversity of a crop is found.

Vavilovian Concept:

- Vavilov identified eight major geographical centres of origin (later expanded to more), known as Vavilovian Centres.
- These are regions where domesticated plants first evolved and were selected by early human societies for desirable traits.
- According to him, genetic diversity is greatest in a crop's original home, which makes these centres important for plant breeding and conservation.

Major Centres of Origin (Vavilov's Original List):

1. Chinese Centre
2. Indian Centre (Hindustan)
3. Central Asiatic Centre
4. Near Eastern Centre
5. Mediterranean Centre
6. Abyssinian (Ethiopian) Centre
7. South American Centre
8. Central American and Mexican Centre

Modern studies have identified even more secondary or minor centres due to later introductions, hybridizations, and selection events.

Primary vs. Secondary Centres of Origin:

Feature	Primary Centre	Secondary Centre
Definition	Original site of domestication of a crop	Regions where a crop spread later and developed diversity
Genetic Diversity	Very high (genetic reservoir)	Moderate to high, but derived from primary centre
Presence of Wild Relatives	Common	Often absent
Importance	Source of landraces, wild types, and breeding material	Source of adapted cultivars or varietal diversification

Examples of Plants from the New World Cultivated in the Old World:

1. **Maize (*Zea mays*):**
   - Origin: Mexico (Central America)
   - Now widely grown in Asia, Africa, and Europe.
2. **Potato (*Solanum tuberosum*):**
   - Origin: South America (Peru-Bolivia region)
   - Now cultivated extensively in Europe, India, and China.

Significance:

- Understanding centres of origin helps in crop improvement, conservation of plant genetic resources, and discovery of resistance genes.
- These centres are now a focus for biodiversity protection due to increasing genetic erosion.

Vavilov's work remains foundational in agricultural science and plant breeding.

8. (*b*): Stages of Micropropagation and Its Role in Conservation of Endangered Plants:

Micropropagation: Micropropagation is the technique of propagating plants in vitro using tissue culture methods under sterile conditions. It allows rapid multiplication of genetically identical (clonal) plants from small tissue explants and is particularly valuable for conserving rare, endangered, or medicinal species.

Stages of Micropropagation:

1. **Stage I – Initiation:**
   - A small tissue (explant) such as a shoot tip, leaf, or node is excised from the donor plant.
   - Surface-sterilized and placed on a nutrient medium (like Murashige and Skoog medium) containing suitable hormones (e.g., cytokinins and auxins).
   - Aseptic conditions are critical at this stage.
2. **Stage II – Multiplication:**
   - The initial shoot or meristem proliferates into multiple shoots due to the presence of high cytokinin concentration.
   - Subculturing is repeated several times to multiply the shoots exponentially.
3. **Stage III – Rooting:**
   - The microshoots are transferred to a root-inducing medium containing auxins (e.g., IAA, IBA, NAA) to promote root formation.
   - Rooted plantlets are then considered complete microplants.
4. **Stage IV – Acclimatization (Hardening):**
   - In vitro plantlets are gradually acclimatized to outside conditions by transferring to soil or vermiculite in a greenhouse or shade house.
   - Plants adapt to lower humidity, non-sterile environ-ments, and natural light.

Use of Micropropagation in Conservation of Endangered Plants:

1. **Mass Propagation of Rare Species:** Micro-propagation enables rapid production of large numbers of individuals from a single endangered plant, helping in reforestation and habitat restoration.
2. **Reduction of Wild Harvesting:** Commercial demand for medicinal and ornamental plants often leads to overexploitation. Tissue culture can supply these species in large numbers without disturbing natural populations.
3. **Germplasm Preservation:** In vitro cultures can be cryo-preserved or maintained long-term as living libraries, acting as genetic reservoirs for future restoration efforts.
4. **Propagation of Difficult-to-Seed Plants:** Some endan-gered species have low seed viability or dormancy. Micropropagation bypasses the need for seed and ensures better survival.
5. **Pathogen-Free Plants:** Micropropagated plants are often disease-free, which enhances survival and helps in maintaining healthy restored populations.

Examples of Conservation through Micro-propagation: *Rauwolfia serpentina, Saussurea lappa, Podophyllum hexandrum*, and *Vanilla planifolia* have been successfully micropropagated and reintroduced into natural habitats.

Micropropagation thus serves as a powerful tool for biodiversity conservation, ensuring that threatened species are propagated efficiently and safeguarded for future generations without further depleting wild stocks.

8. (*c*): **Structure of Stomata:** A stoma (plural: stomata) is a microscopic pore found on the epidermis of leaves, stems, and other aerial parts of plants. It facilitates gas exchange and transpiration. Each stoma is bordered by two guard cells that control its opening and closing.

Main Components:

1. **Guard Cells:**
   - ❑ Kidney-shaped (in dicots) or dumbbell-shaped (in monocots).
   - ❑ Contain chloroplasts (unlike most epidermal cells).
   - ❑ Regulate the opening and closing of the stoma by changing turgor pressure.
2. **Stomatal Pore:** The gap between guard cells through which gas exchange occurs.
3. **Subsidiary Cells (if present):**
   - ❑ Surround guard cells.
   - ❑ Provide mechanical support and assist in stomatal movement.

Labelled Diagram of Stoma (Dicot Type):

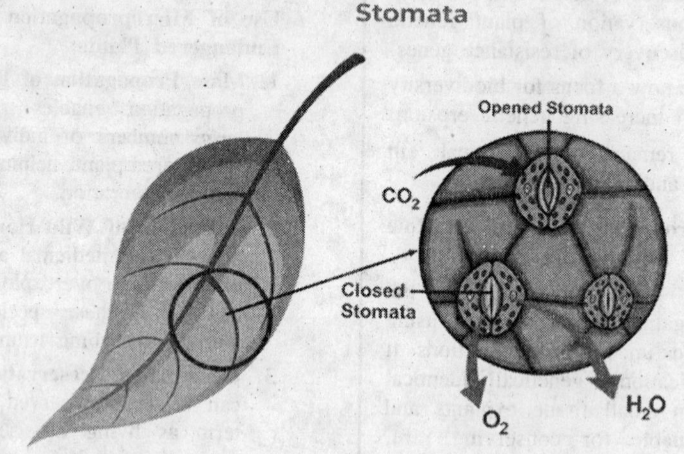

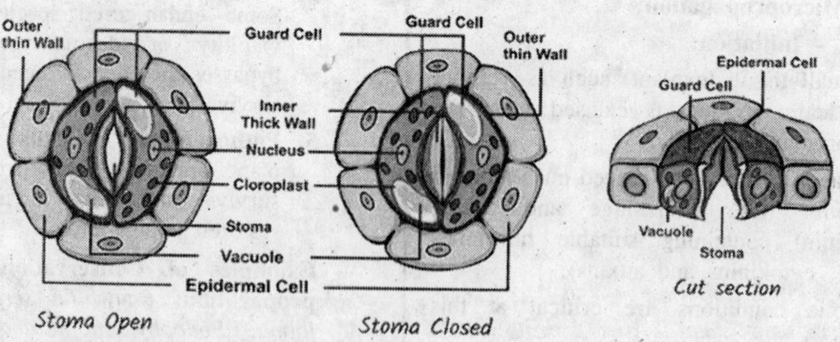

Types of Stomata Based on Development:

1. **Haplocheilic Stomata (Mesogenous Type):**
   - Also called monocot-type.
   - Guard cells arise directly from a single initial meristematic cell.
   - Subsidiary cells (if present) originate from neighboring epidermal cells independently.

- Found in gymnosperms, ferns, and many dicots.
- Considered primitive.

Example: Cycas, Pinus

2. Syndetocheilic Stomata (Perigenous Type):

- Guard cells and subsidiary cells originate from the same mother cell (stomatal initial).
- All associated cells form a coordinated developmental unit.
- Typically found in fossil plants and some living ferns and Gnetales.
- Considered advanced and more complex.

Example: Gnetum

Comparison Table:

Feature	Haplocheilic	Syndetocheilic
Origin of Guard Cells	From a single initial cell	From a single initial cell
Origin of Subsidiary Cells	From surrounding epidermal cells	From the same initial cell as guard cells
Developmental Simplicity	Simple, independent	Complex, coordinated
Found in	Gymnosperms, ferns, many dicots	Fossil plants, Gnetum, Bennettitales

Thus, stomata not only serve essential physiological functions but also reflect evolutionary adaptations and phylogenetic relationships.

PAPER-II

1. (*a*): Endoplasmic Reticulum (ER):

ER is a membranous organelle forming a network of cisternae, tubules, and vesicles in the cytoplasm. It is continuous with the outer membrane of the nuclear envelope and exists in two main forms:

Types of Endoplasmic Reticulum:

1. Rough Endoplasmic Reticulum (RER):

- **Structure:** Studded with ribosomes on the cytosolic surface, giving it a 'rough' appearance under the microscope.
- **Function:** Primarily involved in the synthesis of proteins that are either secreted from the cell, inserted into the plasma membrane, or delivered to lysosomes.
- **Special Role:** Post-translational modification of proteins (folding, glycosylation) and packaging into vesicles for transport.

2. Smooth Endoplasmic Reticulum (SER):

- **Structure:** Lacks ribosomes, appears smooth.
- **Function:** Involved in lipid synthesis, metabolism of carbohydrates, detoxification of drugs and poisons (especially in liver cells), and storage of calcium ions (notably in muscle cells—sarcoplasmic reticulum).
- **Special Role:** In steroid-secreting cells (e.g., adrenal cortex, testes), SER is abundant for hormone synthesis.

Diagram – Types of Endoplasmic Reticulum

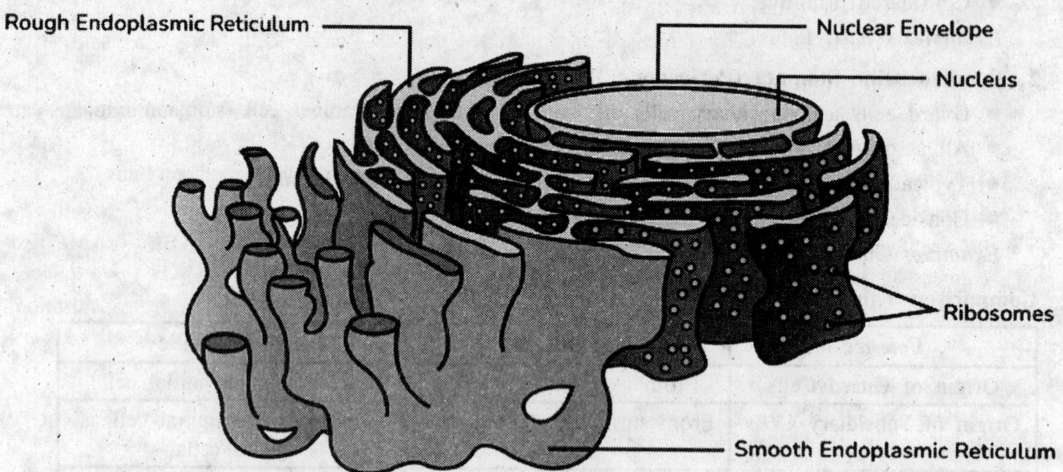

Endomembrane System: The endomembrane system is a group of interconnected organelles that function in the synthesis, modification, and transport of biomolecules within the cell.

Components of the Endomembrane System:

1. **Nuclear Envelope:** Encloses the nucleus, continuous with RER.
2. **Endoplasmic Reticulum (RER and SER):** Site of protein and lipid synthesis.
3. **Golgi Apparatus:** Modifies, sorts, and packages proteins and lipids received from ER.
4. **Transport Vesicles:** Small membrane-bound carriers that shuttle materials between organelles.
5. **Lysosomes:** Contain hydrolytic enzymes for intracellular digestion.
6. **Plasma Membrane:** Part of the system as it receives secretory vesicles.

Functional Significance:

- Provides compartmentalization in eukaryotic cells.
- Ensures directional flow of materials (nucleus → ER → Golgi → vesicles → membrane or lysosome).
- Critical for cellular communication, secretion, and membrane biogenesis.

Together, the ER and endomembrane system are essential for the dynamic processing and transport of macromolecules vital for cellular structure and function.

1. (*b*): **cAMP-mediated regulation of signal transduction**

Overview: Cyclic AMP (cAMP) is a second messenger involved in transducing extracellular signals into intracellular responses. The process is crucial for regulating cellular activities like metabolism, gene expression, and cell growth. It operates through G-protein coupled receptors (GPCRs) and the enzyme adenylyl cyclase.

Steps in cAMP-Mediated Signal Transduction:

1. **Signal Reception:** A first messenger (e.g., hormone like epinephrine or glucagon) binds to a G-protein coupled receptor (GPCR) located on the plasma membrane.
2. **Activation of G-Protein:**
   - The receptor undergoes conformational change and activates a heterotrimeric G-protein.
   - Gαs subunit binds GTP and dissociates from β and γ subunits.
3. **Activation of Adenylyl Cyclase:** GTP-bound Gαs activates the enzyme adenylyl cyclase, which is membrane-bound.

4. **Synthesis of cAMP:**
   - Adenylyl cyclase catalyzes ATP → cAMP.
   - cAMP now acts as a second messenger within the cell.
5. **Activation of Protein Kinase A (PKA):**
   - cAMP binds to the regulatory subunits of Protein Kinase A, causing them to release the catalytic subunits.
   - The free catalytic subunits are now active and phosphorylate specific target proteins.
6. **Cellular Response:**
   - PKA phosphorylates enzymes, ion channels, and transcription factors (e.g., CREB – cAMP response element-binding protein).
   - Leads to a cascade of reactions: glycogen breakdown, increased heart rate, gene transcription, etc.
7. **Termination of Signal:**
   - Phosphodiesterase (PDE) breaks down cAMP to AMP.
   - Gαs hydrolyzes GTP → GDP and re-associates with $\beta\gamma$, ending the signal.

Diagram – cAMP Signal Transduction Pathway

Significance:

- cAMP mediates rapid and reversible cellular responses.
- Amplifies the original extracellular signal: one receptor can activate multiple G-proteins → many cAMP molecules → extensive cellular response.

- Plays a role in glucose metabolism, cardiac stimulation, learning and memory, and hormone action.

Thus, cAMP is a pivotal intracellular messenger that regulates diverse physiological processes via a well-orchestrated signal transduction cascade.

1. (*c*): **Theories of Organic Evolution:** Organic evolution refers to the gradual development of complex organisms from simpler ancestral forms over geological time. Several theories have been proposed to explain the mechanisms behind this process. Below is a brief account of the major theories:

1. Lamarck's Theory of Inheritance of Acquired Characters (1809):

- Proposed by Jean Baptiste de Lamarck.
- Suggested that traits acquired during an organism's lifetime are passed to offspring.
- Example: Giraffes stretching their necks to reach higher leaves → long neck inherited by next generation.
- Key Concepts:
  - ❑ Use and disuse of organs.
  - ❑ Inheritance of acquired traits.
- Criticism: No experimental evidence; later disproven by genetics.

2. Darwin's Theory of Natural Selection (1859):

- Proposed by Charles Darwin in "*On the Origin of Species*".
- Evolution occurs through natural selection where organisms with favorable variations survive and reproduce.
- Key Principles:
  - ❑ Overproduction and struggle for existence.
  - ❑ Variation exists among individuals.
  - ❑ Survival of the fittest.
  - ❑ Favorable traits are inherited.
- Limitation: Lacked mechanism of heredity (genetics was unknown at the time).

3. Mutation Theory (1901):

- Proposed by Hugo de Vries based on work with *Oenothera lamarckiana* (evening primrose).
- Stated that sudden large mutations (not gradual variations) are responsible for evolution.
- New species arise in single steps, not gradual processes.
- Criticism: Most mutations are harmful, and evolution is rarely abrupt.

4. Modern Synthetic Theory of Evolution (Neo-Darwinism):

- Combines Darwin's natural selection with Mendelian genetics, population genetics, mutation, gene flow, and genetic drift.
- Contributors: Dobzhansky, Fisher, Haldane, Wright, and Mayr.
- Key Features:
  - ❑ Variation arises via mutation and recombination.
  - ❑ Genetic variation is acted upon by natural selection.
  - ❑ Evolution occurs in populations, not individuals.
  - ❑ Gradual accumulation of changes leads to speciation.

5. Other Supporting Theories:

- Punctuated Equilibrium (Eldredge & Gould): Evolution proceeds with long periods of stasis interrupted by short bursts of rapid change.
- Neutral Theory (Kimura): Most genetic mutations are neutral and spread by genetic drift, not selection.

These theories collectively provide a comprehensive understanding of how life evolved on Earth. The modern synthetic theory is currently the most widely accepted explanation of organic evolution.

1. (*d*): **Different kinds of plastids with reference to their structure and functions:** Plastids are double-membrane-bound organelles found in plant cells and some algae. They arise from proplastids and perform various functions such as photosynthesis, storage, and pigment synthesis. Based on structure and function, plastids are broadly classified into three main types:

1. Chloroplasts (Green Plastids)

- **Structure:**
  - ❑ Surrounded by an outer and inner membrane.
  - ❑ Inner membrane encloses a fluid-filled stroma containing enzymes, circular DNA, and ribosomes.
  - ❑ Contains a system of thylakoids arranged in stacks called grana connected by stromal lamellae.
  - ❑ Thylakoid membranes contain chlorophyll *a*, chlorophyll *b*, and other pigments.

- **Function:**
  - ❑ Site of photosynthesis – converts light energy into chemical energy (glucose).
  - ❑ Produces oxygen and stores energy in ATP and NADPH.
  - ❑ Synthesizes some amino acids and fatty acids.

2. Chromoplasts (Coloured Plastids except Green)

- **Structure:**
  - ❑ Contain lipid-soluble pigments such as carotenoids (orange-red-yellow colors).
  - ❑ Lack thylakoid membranes.
  - ❑ Irregular shape and smaller than chloroplasts.
- **Function:**
  - ❑ Responsible for the bright coloration in fruits, flowers, and aging leaves to attract pollinators and aid in seed dispersal.
  - ❑ May synthesize or store pigments like carotenes and xanthophylls.

3. Leucoplasts (Colorless Plastids)

- **Structure:**
  - ❑ Non-pigmented plastids with a simple internal structure.
  - ❑ Typically found in non-photosynthetic tissues such as roots, tubers, and seeds.
- **Types and Functions:**
  - ❑ Amyloplasts–store starch (e.g., potato tubers).
  - ❑ Elaioplasts–store lipids or oils.
  - ❑ Aleuroplasts–store proteins (e.g., in seeds).

Diagram – Types of Plastids

Plastids

Etioplast Proplastid

Chromoplast Chloroplast Leucoplast

Interconversion of Plastids: Plastids are interconvertible depending on environmental and cellular needs:

- Proplastids → Chloroplasts (in light),
- Chloroplasts → Chromoplasts (during fruit ripening),
- Leucoplasts ↔ Chloroplasts (e.g., potato tuber exposed to light).

Thus, plastids are essential organelles contributing to the metabolic, storage, and pigment-related functions critical to plant growth, reproduction, and adaptation.

1. (*e*): Properties of Genetic Code with examples and Wobble Hypothesis: The genetic code is a set of rules by which the information in nucleic acid sequences (mRNA) is translated into amino acid sequences of proteins. It is universal for almost all organisms and composed of codons (triplets of nucleotides).

Properties of Genetic Code:

1. Triplet Nature:

- Each codon consists of three nucleotides.
- Example: AUG codes for methionine.

2. Degeneracy:

- More than one codon can code for the same amino acid.
- Example: Leucine is coded by UUA, UUG, CUU, CUC, CUA, and CUG (6 codons).

3. Non-overlapping and Commaless:

- The code is read in a continuous sequence of triplets without overlap or punctuation.
- Example: In mRNA sequence AUGGCU, it's read as AUG – GCU, not AUG – UGC.

4. Unambiguous:

- Each codon specifies only one amino acid.
- Example: UUU always codes for phenylalanine.

5. Universal:

- With few exceptions, the code is the same in viruses, bacteria, plants, and animals.
- Example: UGA is a stop codon in most organisms.

6. Start and Stop Codons:

- Start codon: AUG (codes for methionine; signals the beginning of translation).
- Stop codons: UAA, UAG, UGA (do not code for amino acids; signal termination).

Degeneracy of the Code & Wobble Hypothesis:

Degeneracy:

- Since 64 codons code for only 20 amino acids, multiple codons specify the same amino acid.
- Provides redundancy that reduces the impact of mutations.

Wobble Hypothesis (Crick, 1966):

- Explains why a single tRNA can recognize multiple codons.
- The third base of the codon (3') and the first base of the anticodon (5') have flexible pairing.
- This "wobble" allows tRNAs to pair with more than one codon, hence contributing to degeneracy.

  Example:
- tRNA with anticodon 3′-GCI-5′ (I = inosine) can pair with codons 5′-CGU, CGC, CGA – all coding for arginine.

Thus, the genetic code is a highly efficient, error-tolerant system ensuring accurate translation, with degeneracy explained structurally by the Wobble Hypothesis.

2. (*a*): Mutation Breeding – Definition: Mutation breeding is the process of exposing plant seeds, tissues, or cells to physical or chemical mutagens to induce heritable mutations, followed by selection of desirable mutants. It accelerates genetic variation and helps develop new crop varieties with beneficial traits.

It was first systematically applied by L. J. Stadler in the 1920s using X-rays in barley and maize.

Methods of Mutation Breeding:

1. **Physical Mutagenesis:** Uses ionizing radiation to induce mutations in plant genetic material.

- Gamma rays: Most widely used (from Cobalt-60).
- X-rays: Also used, but less penetrating than gamma rays.
- Fast neutrons, alpha particles, beta rays: Used in some specific cases.

Procedure: Dry or wet seeds are irradiated → grown in M1 generation → desirable mutants selected in M2 and further generations.

2. **Chemical Mutagenesis:** Uses chemical agents to cause point mutations.

- EMS (Ethyl Methane Sulphonate): Induces alkylation, causes GC → AT transitions.
- Sodium azide, nitrosoguanidine, nitrous acid: Commonly used for treating seeds or explants.

Procedure: Seeds soaked in aqueous solution of mutagen → washed and germinated → mutant selection in later generations.

Applications of Mutation Breeding:

- Crop improvement: Enhanced yield, disease resistance, early maturity, dwarfism, flower color, and stress tolerance.
- Overcoming genetic uniformity: Introduces variability in asexually propagated crops.
- Improvement of vegetative traits where hybridization is difficult.

Examples of Success:

- 'Sharbati Sonora' (semi-dwarf wheat) – India
- 'Pusa Lal Meeruti' (improved bold-seeded cowpea)
- 'Aruna' (castor mutant with determinate growth)
- 'Jagannath' (high-yielding mutant rice variety)

Limitations of Mutation Breeding:

- Random nature of mutations: Most are undesirable or lethal; large populations must be screened.
- Low frequency of beneficial mutations.
- Requires multi-generational testing to stabilize traits.
- May not always be reproducible.
- Induced mutations often involve only single gene traits; complex traits (e.g., yield) are harder to improve.

Mutation breeding remains a valuable tool in plant biotechnology, particularly when hybridization is not feasible. It is now also integrated with molecular marker-assisted selection for improved precision.

2. (*b*): Agrobacterium-mediated gene transfer in plants with emphasis on T-DNA processing: *Agrobacterium tumefaciens* is a soil-borne bacterium that naturally transfers a segment of its DNA into the genome of dicotyledonous plants. This ability is harnessed in genetic engineering to introduce desirable genes into plants.

Mechanism of Agrobacterium-Mediated Gene Transfer: Agrobacterium carries a large Ti (tumor-inducing) plasmid, which contains a region called T-DNA (Transfer DNA) and vir (virulence) genes. T-DNA is the segment that gets transferred into the plant genome during infection.

Key Steps of Gene Transfer and T-DNA Processing:

1. Signal Induction:

- Wounded plant tissues release phenolic compounds (e.g., acetosyringone), which are sensed by the bacterium.
- These signals activate vir genes on the Ti plasmid.

2. T-DNA Border Recognition:

- T-DNA is flanked by 25 bp direct repeat border sequences (Right and Left Borders).
- VirD1 and VirD2 proteins recognize and nick the T-DNA at the right border.
- VirD2 attaches to the 5′ end of the nicked strand and helps guide T-DNA into the plant cell.

3. Formation of T-strand:

- The nicked single-stranded DNA (T-strand) is generated from the T-DNA region.
- VirD2 remains attached to the 5′ end of the T-strand; this complex is essential for T-DNA protection and integration.

4. Transport into Plant Cell:

- T-strand is coated with VirE2 protein, which protects it from nucleases.
- The entire complex (T-strand + VirD2 + VirE2) is transferred into the plant cell via a Type IV secretion system.

5. Nuclear Import and Integration:

- T-strand is imported into the plant nucleus, guided by nuclear localization signals in VirD2 and VirE2.
- It integrates into the plant genome by illegitimate (non-homologous) recombination.

Engineering with Ti Plasmid:

- In genetic engineering, tumor-inducing genes are removed from T-DNA and replaced with desired genes (e.g., insect resistance, herbicide tolerance).
- Binary vector systems are used, where T-DNA and vir genes are separated on two different plasmids (one for gene of interest, one for virulence).

Applications:

- Widely used for creating transgenic plants (e.g., Bt cotton, Golden Rice).
- Suitable for dicots; monocot transformation is now also possible with optimized protocols.

Agrobacterium-mediated gene transfer is preferred for its high efficiency, low transgene copy number, and stable integration, making it a powerful tool in plant genetic engineering.

2. (*c*): Inheritance of Flower Colour in Four-o'clock Plant (*Mirabilis jalapa*): This question is based on incomplete dominance, where the heterozygous genotype exhibits a blended phenotype. In the Four-o'clock plant:

- RR = Red flowers
- Rr = Pink flowers (intermediate)
- rr = White flowers

Cross 1: Red (RR) × White (rr)

Parents: RR × rr

Gametes: R and r

F_1 Generation:

All offspring are Rr → Pink flowers

Cross 2: F_1 × F_1 (Rr × Rr)

Gametes: R and r from both parents

F_2 Generation (Punnett Square):

	R	r
R	RR (Red)	Rr (Pink)
r	Rr (Pink)	rr (White)

Genotypic ratio: 1 RR : 2 Rr : 1 rr

Phenotypic ratio: 1 Red : 2 Pink : 1 White

Cross 3: F_1 (Rr) × Red Parent (RR)

Gametes: R and r from Rr; R from RR

Offspring Genotypes:

- 50% RR (Red)
- 50% Rr (Pink)

Phenotypes: 1 Red : 1 Pink

Cross 4: F_1 (Rr) × White Parent (rr)

Gametes: R and r from Rr; r from rr

Offspring Genotypes:

- 50% Rr (Pink)
- 50% rr (White)

Phenotypes: 1 Pink : 1 White

Summary:

Cross Type	Genotypes	Phenotypes
RR × rr	All Rr	All Pink
Rr × Rr	1 RR : 2 Rr : 1 rr	1 Red : 2 Pink : 1 White
Rr × RR	1 RR : 1 Rr	1 Red : 1 Pink
Rr × rr	1 Rr : 1 rr	1 Pink : 1 White

This clearly illustrates incomplete dominance; where heterozygotes express an intermediate trait instead of dominant masking recessive.

3. (*a*): Control Points and Molecular Factors in Cell Cycle Regulation: The cell cycle is a tightly regulated sequence of events that ensures accurate replication and division of a cell. It is divided into four main phases: G_1 (gap 1), S (synthesis), G_1 (gap 2), and M (mitosis). Progression through the cell cycle is regulated at specific checkpoints by a network of proteins that sense internal and external cues.

Major Cell Cycle Checkpoints:

1. G_1 Checkpoint (Restriction Point):

- Occurs at the end of G_1 phase.
- Determines whether the cell will proceed to S phase or enter G_0 (quiescence).
- Checks for:
  - ❑ DNA integrity
  - ❑ Adequate nutrients
  - ❑ Growth signals (mitogens)

2. G_2/M Checkpoint:

- Occurs at the end of G_2 phase before mitosis begins.
- Checks for:
  - ❑ DNA replication completeness
  - ❑ DNA damage
  - ❑ Cell size

3. Metaphase (Spindle Assembly) Checkpoint:

- Occurs during mitosis (at metaphase).
- Ensures all chromosomes are properly attached to the mitotic spindle before anaphase begins.
- Prevents unequal chromosome segregation.

Key Molecular Factors Involved:

1. Cyclins and Cyclin-dependent Kinases (Cdks):

- Core components of the cell cycle control system.
- Cdks are serine/threonine kinases activated only when bound to specific cyclins.
- Different cyclin-Cdk complexes act at specific phases:
  - ❑ Cyclin D–Cdk4/6: G_1 phase
  - ❑ Cyclin E–Cdk2: G_1/S transition
  - ❑ Cyclin A–Cdk2: S phase
  - ❑ Cyclin B–Cdk1 (MPF): G_2/M transition

2. Cdk Inhibitors (CKIs):

- *p*21, *p*27, *p*16 bind to cyclin-Cdk complexes and inhibit their activity.
- Prevent uncontrolled progression under stress or DNA damage.

3. Retinoblastoma Protein (Rb):

- In its hypophosphorylated form, Rb binds to E2F transcription factors and blocks S-phase gene expression.
- Phosphorylated by Cyclin D–Cdk4/6 → releases E2F → transcription of S-phase genes.

4. *p*53 Tumor Suppressor Protein:

- Activated in response to DNA damage.
- Induces *p*21 expression → inhibits Cyclin E–Cdk2 → arrests cell cycle in G_1.
- If damage is irreparable, p53 triggers apoptosis.

5. Anaphase Promoting Complex (APC/C):

- A ubiquitin ligase that degrades securin and cyclin B during metaphase-anaphase transition.
- Triggers chromatid separation and exit from mitosis.

3. (*b*) (*i*): Hardy–Weinberg Equilibrium: The Hardy–Weinberg equilibrium is a fundamental principle in population genetics that describes a theoretical state where allele and genotype frequencies remain constant from one generation to the next, provided certain conditions are met.

Statement: In a large, randomly mating population with no mutation, migration, selection, or genetic drift, the frequencies of alleles and genotypes remain in equilibrium.

If:

p = frequency of allele A
q = frequency of allele a

Then,

$p + q = 1$ (allele frequency)

Genotype frequencies,

$AA = p^2$
$Aa = 2pq$
$aa = q^2$

Thus, the Hardy–Weinberg equation is:

$$p^2 + 2pq + q^2 = 1$$

Conditions for Equilibrium:

1. Large population size (no genetic drift)
2. Random mating
3. No mutation altering allele frequencies
4. No migration (no gene flow in/out)
5. No natural selection

Applications:

- Acts as a null model in population genetics.
- Used to calculate carrier frequency of recessive genetic disorders (e.g., cystic fibrosis, sickle cell anemia).
- Helps detect evolutionary forces (if actual frequencies deviate from expected ones).

  Example: If 9% of a population shows a recessive trait (*aa*), then:

- $q^2 = 0.09 \rightarrow q = 0.3 \rightarrow p = 0.7$
- Heterozygotes (A*a*) $= 2pq = 2 \times 0.7 \times 0.3 = 0.42$ (42%)

In essence, Hardy–Weinberg equilibrium provides a mathematical framework to assess whether a population is evolving at a particular genetic locus.

3. (*b*) (*ii*): Probability of Hemophilia in Children when Mother is Carrier and Father is Normal:

Background: Hemophilia is an X-linked recessive disorder, meaning the defective gene is carried on the X chromosome. Since males have only one X chromosome (XY), a single defective gene causes disease. Females have two X chromosomes (XX), so they must inherit two defective copies to be affected; otherwise, they are carriers.

Given,

- The woman is normal, but her father had hemophilia.
- Therefore, her genotype is X^HX^h (carrier), as she inherited one defective X (X^H) from her hemophilic father and one normal X (X^H) from her normal mother.
- The man is normal → genotype: X^HY

Cross:

Mother (X^HX^h) × Father (X^HY)

	X^H (Father)	**Y (Father)**
X^H (Mother)	X^HX^H (Normal daughter)	X^HY (Normal son)
X^h (Mother)	X^HX^h (Carrier daughter)	X^hY (Hemophilic son)

Probabilities:

- 50% daughters:
  - ❑ 25% X^HX^H (normal)
  - ❑ 25% X^HX^h (carrier)
- 50% sons:
  - ❑ 25% X^HY (normal)
  - ❑ 25% X^hY (hemophilic)

3. (*c*): Prion Diseases in Humans, Modes of Infection, and Disease Mechanism:

Prion Diseases in Humans: Prions are misfolded, infectious proteinaceous agents that cause neurodegenerative diseases by inducing abnormal folding of normal proteins in the brain.

Two major prion diseases in humans are:

1. **Creutzfeldt–Jakob Disease (CJD)**
2. **Kuru:** Other examples include Gerstmann–Sträussler–Scheinker syndrome (GSS) and Fatal Familial Insomnia (FFI).

Modes of Prion Infection in Humans:

1. **Inherited (Familial):** Mutations in the PRNP gene coding for the prion protein (PrP) are inherited in an autosomal dominant manner (e.g., familial CJD, FFI).
2. **Sporadic:** Most common form; occurs without known cause or risk factors due to spontaneous misfolding of PrP proteins.
3. **Acquired:**
   - Contaminated surgical instruments, organ transplants, or infected food (e.g., consuming beef from cattle with BSE, or "mad cow disease", which causes variant CJD).

- Ritual cannibalism led to Kuru among the Fore people in Papua New Guinea.

Steps of Prion Disease Mechanism:

1. **Misfolded Prion Formation (PrP^{Sc}):** The normal cellular prion protein (PrP^{C}) is converted into an abnormal, beta-sheet-rich form (PrP^{Sc}) upon contact.
2. **Template-Directed Conversion:** PrP^{Sc} acts as a template, inducing misfolding of PrP^{C} into more PrP^{Sc}, creating a self-propagating cycle.
3. **Aggregation and Accumulation:** PrP^{Sc} is resistant to protease degradation and accumulates in the central nervous system, forming amyloid plaques.
4. **Neuronal Damage:** Leads to neurodegeneration, vacuolation (spongiform changes), and death of nerve cells without inflammation.
5. **Clinical Symptoms:** Rapidly progressive dementia, ataxia, muscle stiffness, and ultimately coma and death.

Prion diseases are fatal, untreatable, and uniquely infectious, as they do not involve nucleic acids—only protein misfolding and propagation.

4. **(*a*): DNA Replication in Eukaryotic Organisms with Enzyme Roles:** DNA replication is a semi-conservative process in which each daughter DNA molecule contains one parental and one newly synthesized strand. In eukaryotes, replication occurs during the S phase of the cell cycle and is tightly regulated.

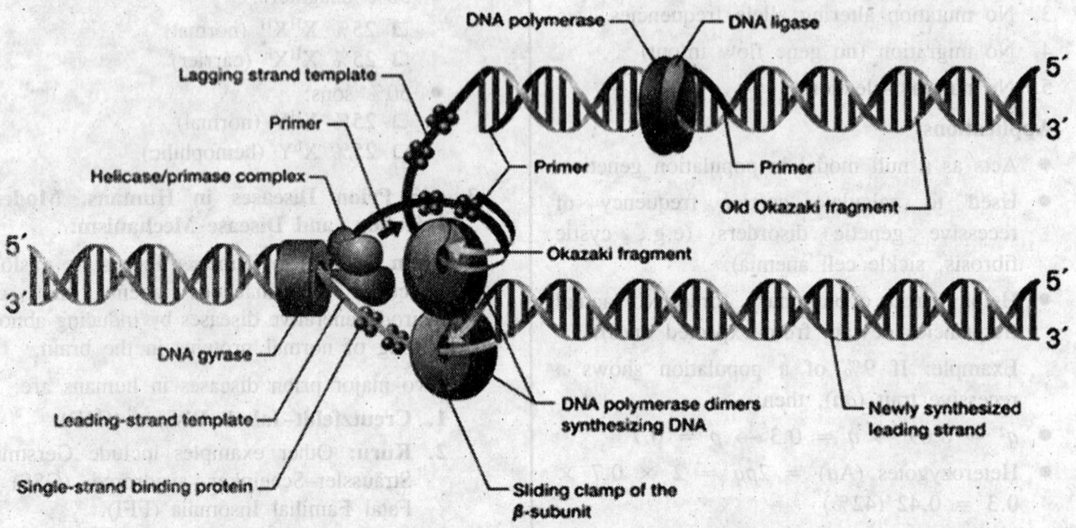

This Diagram provides a comprehensive visual representation of the eukaryotic DNA replication process, highlighting key components.

Steps of DNA Replication and Role of Enzymes:

1. **Origin Recognition and Initiation:**
   - Replication begins at multiple origins of replication (replicons) due to the large size of eukaryotic genomes.
   - Origin Recognition Complex (ORC): Binds to origin sites and recruits other proteins.
   - Helicase Loader (Cdc6, Cdt1) helps load helicase.

2. **DNA Unwinding:**
   - Helicase (MCM complex): Unwinds the double helix by breaking hydrogen bonds between base pairs.
   - Single-Strand Binding Proteins (RPA in eukaryotes): Prevent reannealing of separated strands.
   - Topoisomerase I & II: Relieve supercoiling ahead of the replication fork.

3. **Primer Synthesis:** Primase (part of DNA Pol α complex): Synthesizes short RNA primers

(~10 nt) to provide a free 3′-OH group for DNA polymerase.

4. Elongation of DNA Strands:

- DNA Polymerase α: Extends the RNA primer with a short stretch of DNA (~20–30 nt), then dissociates.
- DNA Polymerase δ and ε: Carry out bulk DNA synthesis.
  - ❑ Pol δ → synthesizes the lagging strand.
  - ❑ Pol ε → synthesizes the leading strand.
- Sliding Clamp (PCNA): Encircles DNA and tethers polymerase for high processivity.
- Clamp Loader (RFC): Loads PCNA onto DNA.

5. Okazaki Fragment Processing (Lagging Strand):

- RNA primers are removed by RNase H and FEN1 (Flap Endonuclease 1).
- DNA Polymerase δ fills the gaps.
- DNA Ligase I seals nicks between adjacent fragments to complete the strand.

6. End Replication Problem:

- At chromosome ends, conventional polymerases can't replicate the 3′ end of the lagging strand.
- Telomerase, a ribonucleoprotein enzyme, extends telomeres using an internal RNA template.

4. (*b*): Heterosis and Inbreeding Depression with Genetic Bases

1. Heterosis (Hybrid Vigour):

Definition: Heterosis refers to the phenomenon where F_1 hybrids resulting from a cross between genetically diverse parents show superior traits such as increased yield, growth rate, fertility, or resistance compared to both parents.

Example: Hybrid maize (e.g., 'Double Cross Hybrids') shows higher yield than either inbred parent.

Genetic Basis of Heterosis: There are three main hypotheses:

(*i*) Dominance Hypothesis:

- Suggests that deleterious recessive alleles present in homozygous condition in inbreds are masked by dominant alleles in the hybrid.
- Thus, hybrid performance is due to the accumulation of favorable dominant alleles.

(*ii*) Overdominance Hypothesis:

- States that the heterozygous condition itself is superior to either homozygous condition.
- Certain gene combinations at specific loci exhibit overdominance in hybrids (e.g., Aa is more vigorous than AA or aa).

(*iii*) Epistasis:

- Interaction between non-allelic genes across loci contributes to hybrid superiority.

2. Inbreeding Depression:

Definition: Inbreeding depression is the reduction in biological fitness and vigor of a population due to mating between closely related individuals, which increases homozygosity.

Effects:

- Decreased yield, fertility, disease resistance, and vigor.
- More pronounced in cross-pollinated species like maize, sugar beet, etc.

Example: Inbred maize lines show reduced vigor and yield compared to their hybrids.

Genetic Basis of Inbreeding Depression:

- Increased homozygosity leads to expression of harmful recessive alleles that are otherwise masked in heterozygous condition.
- Loss of heterozygote advantage → decline in overall fitness.
- Reduces genetic buffering against environmental stress and mutations.

4. (*c*): Origin, Induction, and Importance of Polyploidy in Crop Improvement:

Definition of Polyploidy: Polyploidy is a condition where an organism possesses more than two complete sets of chromosomes. It is common in plants and plays a vital role in evolution and crop improvement.

- Diploid ($2n$) – Normal condition
- Triploid ($3n$), Tetraploid ($4n$), Hexaploid ($6n$) – Polyploid conditions

Types of Polyploidy:

1. Autopolyploidy:

- Chromosome duplication within a single species.

- Arises through somatic doubling or meiotic errors.
- Example: Autotetraploid potato ($4n = 48$)

2. **Allopolyploidy:**

- Chromosome doubling occurs in a hybrid between two species, making it fertile.
- Example: Triticale (hybrid of wheat and rye), Raphanobrassica (radish × cabbage hybrid)

Origin of Polyploidy (Natural and Spontaneous):

- Unreduced gametes ($2n$ instead of n) formed during meiosis due to spindle failure.
- Somatic doubling in meristematic cells by chromosome replication without cell division.
- Common in nature, especially among angiosperms like wheat, cotton, tobacco.

Induction of Polyploidy (Artificial Methods):

1. **Chemical Induction:**

- Colchicine (a mitotic inhibitor) blocks spindle fiber formation → chromosomes replicate but don't separate → chromosome doubling.
- Other chemicals: oryzalin, nitrous oxide.

2. **Physical Methods:** Heat shock or cold shock during mitosis/meiosis can lead to polyploidy in rare cases.

3. **Tissue Culture Techniques:** In vitro colchicine treatment of shoot apices or callus cultures.

Importance of Polyploidy in Crop Improvement:

1. **Increased Vigor and Size:**

- Polyploids often show gigantism – larger leaves, flowers, and fruits.
- Example: Autotetraploid grapes, bananas, apples.

2. **Fertility Restoration in Hybrids:**

- Allopolyploidy makes sterile hybrids fertile by providing homologous chromosome pairing.
- Example: Triticale (fertile hybrid of wheat and rye).

3. **Buffer Against Recessive Mutations:** Multiple gene copies reduce the effect of harmful mutations.

4. **Adaptation and Evolution:** Polyploids are often more tolerant to environmental stress, salinity, and drought.

5. **Seedless Varieties:** Triploids are sterile and used to produce seedless fruits like banana and watermelon.

5. **(*a*): Triple Response Induced by Ethylene in Etiolated Seedlings:** In etiolated (dark-grown) dicot seedlings, ethylene induces a well-characterized physiological syndrome known as the "triple response". This response is a classic hallmark of ethylene action and plays a key role in seedling development under soil. The triple response consists of the following three main features:

1. **Inhibition of hypocotyl elongation:** Ethylene suppresses the longitudinal cell expansion in the hypocotyl, resulting in shorter, thicker stems. This inhibition helps the seedling resist mechanical damage as it pushes through the soil.

2. **Radial swelling (thickening) of the hypocotyl:** Due to inhibition of elongation and stimulation of lateral cell expansion, the hypocotyl becomes swollen. This is caused by increased cell width and cortical cell division, providing mechanical strength.

3. **Exaggerated curvature or horizontal growth of the apical hook:** Ethylene promotes differential growth on one side of the apical region, resulting in a tighter or exaggerated apical hook. This protects the delicate shoot apex as the seedling emerges through the soil.

These responses are particularly important in underground seedling development, allowing the seedling to navigate around obstacles and reduce mechanical injury. Ethylene's role in coordinating these responses was confirmed through experiments using ethylene-insensitive mutants and ethylene biosynthesis inhibitors, which fail to show the triple response.

This physiological effect is also used in bioassays for ethylene sensitivity, such as the Arabidopsis triple response assay, where seedlings are grown in the dark on ethylene-supplemented media.

5. **(*b*): Difference between Field Capacity and Permanent Wilting Percentage (PWP) with Reference to Soil-Water Relationship:** In the context of soil-water relationships, field capacity and permanent wilting percentage represent two

important moisture content levels that define the availability of water to plants. They are described below:

1. **Field Capacity (FC):**

- Definition: It is the amount of water retained in the soil after excess gravitational water has drained away, usually 1–3 days after irrigation or heavy rainfall.
- Soil water condition: Water is held in soil pores against gravity but is still readily available to plant roots.
- Tension or suction: Water is held at a soil matric potential of about –0.01 to –0.03 MPa (or 0.1 to 0.3 bars).
- Availability: Water is easily available to plants at field capacity.
- Visual appearance: Soil appears moist but not saturated; no water drains out if squeezed.

2. **Permanent Wilting Percentage (PWP):**

- Definition: It is the soil moisture content at which plants permanently wilt and cannot recover even if water is supplied later.
- Soil water condition: Water is present in the soil but is held so tightly by soil particles that plant roots cannot absorb it.
- Tension or suction: Water is held at a soil matric potential of about –1.5 MPa (or 15 bars).
- Availability: Water is unavailable to plants at this stage.
- Visual appearance: Soil feels dry and crumbly.

Comparison Table:

Feature	Field Capacity (FC)	Permanent Wilting Percentage (PWP)
Definition	Water left after gravitational drainage	Point where plants permanently wilt
Water availability	Easily available to plants	Unavailable to plants
Soil water potential	–0.01 to –0.03 MPa	–1.5 MPa
Visual condition	Moist soil	Dry, crumbly soil
Biological implication	Ideal for root uptake and plant growth	Causes plant death due to dehydration

The difference between FC and PWP represents the "available water capacity" of soil, which determines how much water plants can actually use for growth.

5. (*c*): **Specific Applications of Regression Analysis and Correlation Analysis in Assessing the Relationship Between Variables:** Both regression and correlation are key statistical tools used to analyze the relationship between variables. Though they are related, they serve different specific applications in research and data analysis.

1. **Regression Analysis**

Purpose: To model the dependence of one variable (dependent or response variable) on one or more independent (predictor) variables, and to predict or estimate the value of the dependent variable.

Specific Applications:

- **Prediction and Forecasting:** Used extensively in agriculture, economics, and environmental science to predict outcomes (e.g., crop yield prediction based on rainfall and fertilizer input).
- **Quantifying Impact:** Helps determine how much an independent variable (like soil nitrogen) influences a dependent variable (like plant growth).
- **Model Building:** Used to construct empirical models (e.g., linear, multiple regression models) for complex biological and ecological systems.
- **Trend Analysis:** In climatology or botany, regression helps assess long-term changes such as increase in temperature over years and its effect on plant phenology.
- **Control Variables:** In experimental design, regression adjusts for the effect of confounding variables.

2. **Correlation Analysis**

Purpose: To measure the degree and direction (positive or negative) of linear association between two variables, without implying causation.

Specific Applications:

- **Identifying Strength of Association:** Used to check how strongly two biological variables (e.g., leaf area and transpiration rate) are related.
- **Preliminary Analysis:** Often used before regression to test whether any meaningful relationship exists between variables.
- **Ecological and Environmental Studies:** Helps in assessing whether variables such as humidity and disease incidence are correlated.
- **Selection in Plant Breeding:** Correlation between yield and contributing traits (like number of tillers, panicle size) helps breeders choose desirable genotypes.
- **Economic Botany and Market Analysis:** Correlation between consumer demand and plant product availability, or between price and supply.

Summary of Difference in Applications:

Aspect	Regression Analysis	Correlation Analysis
Purpose	Predict or explain one variable using others	Measure strength and direction of association
Causation	Implies directional influence	Does not imply causation
Output	Regression equation and coefficients	Correlation coefficient (r)
Use	Predictive modeling, control, optimization	Association assessment, feature selection

Both methods complement each other and are widely used in botany, environmental science, agronomy, and ecological modeling.

5. (*d*): Four Endemic and Four Threatened Plant Species – Botanical Name, Family, and Distribution in India:

I. Endemic Plant Species in India: These are species that are native to and restricted within a particular geographical region, often due to unique ecological conditions.

Botanical Name	Family	Distribution in India
Impatiens denisonii	Balsaminaceae	Nilgiri Hills, Western Ghats (Tamil Nadu)
Cycas beddomei	Cycadaceae	Eastern Ghats, Andhra Pradesh
Primula boveana	Primulaceae	Western Himalayas (limited to Kashmir Valley)
Vateria indica	Dipterocarpaceae	Western Ghats (Kerala, Karnataka)

II. Threatened Plant Species in India: These are species that face risk of extinction, categorized by IUCN as Critically Endangered (CR), Endangered (EN), or Vulnerable (VU).

Botanical Name	Family	Distribution in India
Rauvolfia serpentina	Apocynaceae	Himalayan foothills, Northeast India
Saussurea costus	Asteraceae	Alpine Himalayas (Himachal Pradesh, J&K)
Nepenthes khasiana	Nepenthaceae	Khasi Hills, Meghalaya (only Indian pitcher plant)
Pterocarpus santalinus	Fabaceae	Southern Eastern Ghats (Andhra Pradesh)

These examples highlight India's rich biodiversity and the urgent need for conservation of endemic and threatened flora, especially in biodiversity hotspots like the Western Ghats, Eastern Himalayas, and Northeast India.

5. (*e*): Types of Vegetation in India and Their Geographical Distribution: India's vast geographic and climatic diversity has given rise to multiple types of natural vegetation, ranging from tropical rainforests to alpine meadows. The classification is generally based on climate, altitude, soil, and rainfall.

1. Tropical Evergreen Forests

- **Rainfall:** Above 200 cm annually
- **Characteristics:** Dense, multilayered forests with tall trees, evergreen species, and high biodiversity
- **Dominant Trees:** Dipterocarpus, Hopea, Mesua, Canarium
- **Geographical Distribution:**
  - ❑ Western Ghats (Kerala, Karnataka)
  - ❑ Andaman & Nicobar Islands
  - ❑ Northeastern states (Assam, Meghalaya, Arunachal Pradesh)

2. Tropical Deciduous Forests (Monsoon Forests)

Divided into:

(a) Moist Deciduous Forests

- **Rainfall:** 100–200 cm
- **Trees:** Shorea robusta (Sal), *Terminalia*, *Toona*, *Lagerstroemia*
- **Areas:** Eastern India (Jharkhand, Odisha), Western Ghats, Uttar Pradesh

(b) Dry Deciduous Forests

- **Rainfall:** 70–100 cm
- **Trees:** *Tectona grandis* (Teak), *Anogeissus*, *Boswellia*
- **Areas:** Central India (Madhya Pradesh, Maharashtra), Rain-shadow regions

3. Thorn and Scrub Forests

- **Rainfall:** Less than 70 cm
- **Vegetation:** Xerophytic shrubs, thorny trees like *Acacia, Zizyphus, Euphorbia*
- **Distribution:** Rajasthan, Gujarat, parts of Haryana and Deccan Plateau

4. Montane Forests: These vary with altitude and are found in Himalayan and Nilgiri regions:

(a) Temperate Forests (1000–3000 m)

- **Trees:** Oak, Chestnut, Maple, Conifers (Pine, Fir, Deodar)
- **Areas:** Western and Eastern Himalayas

(b) Alpine Vegetation (Above 3000 m)

- **Vegetation:** Shrubs, grasses, and herbaceous plants
- **Areas:** Higher reaches of Jammu & Kashmir, Himachal Pradesh, Sikkim

5. Tidal or Mangrove Forests

- **Location:** Deltaic regions, saline coastal swamps
- **Dominant Plants:** *Rhizophora, Avicennia, Sonneratia*
- **Distribution:** Sundarbans (West Bengal), Mahanadi and Godavari deltas, Andaman coast

6. Semi-Desert and Desert Vegetation

- **Rainfall:** Less than 25 cm
- **Flora:** *Cactus, Prosopis, Capparis*
- **Regions:** Thar Desert in Rajasthan, parts of Kutch in Gujarat

India's vegetation reflects a transition from equatorial rainforest in the south to alpine tundra in the north, showcasing one of the richest floral diversities globally.

6. (a): Definition of Water Potential: Water potential (Ψ) is defined as the potential energy of water per unit volume relative to pure water under standard conditions. It represents the tendency of water to move from one region to another and is a key concept in plant water relations.

- Water always moves from a region of higher water potential to a region of lower water potential.
- It is measured in pressure units such as Megapascals (MPa) or bars.
- For pure water at standard conditions, the water potential is zero ($\Psi = 0$).

Formula:

$$\Psi = \Psi s + \Psi p + \Psi g + \Psi m$$

Where:

Ψs: Solute potential (osmotic potential)

Ψp: Pressure potential (turgor pressure)

Ψg: Gravitational potential (important in tall plants)

Ψm: Matric potential (relevant in dry soils or seeds)

Major Factors Influencing Water Potential in Plants:

1. Solute Potential (Ψs)

- Always negative in plant cells.

- Adding solutes decreases water potential by reducing free water molecules.
- More solutes → more negative Ψs → lower overall Ψ.
- Plays a major role in osmosis and water absorption from soil.

2. **Pressure Potential (Ψp)**
   - The physical pressure exerted by the cell wall on the cytoplasm (turgor pressure).
   - Can be positive (in turgid cells) or negative (in xylem under tension).
   - Increases water potential when positive, aiding in cell expansion and growth.
3. **Gravitational Potential (Ψg)**
   - Becomes significant in tall plants, influencing vertical water movement.
   - Depends on height and density of water column.
   - Often considered in whole-plant water transport models.
4. **Matric Potential (Ψm)**
   - Results from the adhesion of water molecules to surfaces (e.g., soil particles or seed coats).
   - Important in dry soils or seeds where water is tightly bound.
   - Reduces water potential by restricting free movement of water.

6. (*b*): Critical Account on Ecological Succession and the Concept of Climax:

Ecological Succession: Ecological succession is the gradual and sequential process of change in the structure and composition of a biological community over time, leading to the development of a stable ecosystem. It involves replacement of one community by another in a given area until a relatively stable climax community is established.

Types of Succession:

1. **Primary Succession:**
   - ❑ Occurs in lifeless areas where no previous community existed (e.g., lava fields, bare rocks).
   - ❑ Begins with pioneer species like lichens and mosses that initiate soil formation.
2. **Secondary Succession:**
   - ❑ Takes place in areas where a community previously existed but was disturbed (e.g., after fire, flood, or human activity).
   - ❑ Soil and seeds are usually present, so succession is faster than primary.
3. **Autogenic Succession:** Driven by internal changes in the community (e.g., organic matter accumulation or shading).
4. **Allogenic Succession:** Triggered by external environ-mental factors (e.g., climate change, erosion).
5. **Hydrosere, Xerosere, Lithosere:** These are successions occurring in water bodies, dry areas, and bare rocks respectively.

Stages of Succession:

1. Nudation – Formation of bare area
2. Invasion – Migration and establishment of pioneer species
3. Competition and Coaction – Interaction among species
4. Reaction – Modification of the environment by organisms
5. Stabilization or Climax – Formation of a stable, self-sustaining community

Concept of 'Climax': A climax community is the final, stable stage in ecological succession. It is in equilibrium with the environment, and barring disturbances, it remains relatively unchanged over time.

Key Features of Climax Community:

- Stability: Composition remains stable over time.
- Self-regulation: Balanced nutrient cycling and energy flow.
- High biodiversity: Complex food webs and stratified vegetation.
- Maximum biomass: Greater productivity and species interactions.

Climax Theories:

1. **Monoclimax Theory (Clements):** Every region has one climax determined by climate.
2. **Polyclimax Theory (Tansley):** Multiple climax communities can exist due to edaphic, biotic, or topographic factors.

3. **Climax Pattern Hypothesis (Whittaker):** A continuum of climax types based on gradients of environmental conditions.

Critical Viewpoint:

- While classical views consider climax communities as static, modern ecology recognizes them as dynamic, affected by disturbances and environmental change.
- Human activities and climate change often interrupt or reset succession, preventing true climax from being reached.

Ecological succession illustrates how ecosystems recover, evolve, and maintain balance. The concept of climax provides a model for the potential end-point, but real-world ecosystems often remain in flux due to natural and anthropogenic factors.

6. **(*c*): "Crassulacean Acid Metabolism is an Adaptation to Desert Life of Plants":** Crassulacean Acid Metabolism (CAM) is a specialized photosynthetic adaptation found in many desert and semi-arid plants. It enables plants to minimize water loss in hot, arid environments while still maintaining carbon fixation for photosynthesis. This adaptation is especially common in succulent plants such as species from the families Crassulaceae, Cactaceae, Euphorbiaceae, and Orchidaceae.

Key Features of CAM Adaptation:

1. **Temporal Separation of Gas Exchange and Photosynthesis:**
   - Stomata open at night when the temperature is lower and humidity is higher, reducing water loss.
   - CO_2 is taken in at night and stored in the form of malic acid in vacuoles.
   - Stomata remain closed during the day, preventing transpiration.
   - During daytime, CO_2 is released internally from malic acid and used in the Calvin cycle for photosynthesis.
2. **Metabolic Pathway:**
   - Night (Dark Phase):

     CO_2 + PEP $\rightarrow$ Oxaloacetate $\rightarrow$ Malate (stored as malic acid)
   - Day (Light Phase):

     Malic acid $\rightarrow$ CO_2 + Pyruvate $\rightarrow$ Calvin Cycle

This day-night partitioning of CO_2 assimilation enables survival under extreme water-stressed conditions.

Examples of CAM Plants:

- *Opuntia* (prickly pear cactus)
- *Kalanchoe* (Crassulaceae)
- *Agave*
- *Aloe*
- *Vanilla planifolia* (an orchid)

Ecological and Physiological Significance:

- **Water Use Efficiency (WUE):** CAM plants have the highest WUE among all photosynthetic types, essential for desert survival.
- **Survival in Nutrient-Poor Soils:** Their slow growth and metabolism are suited for environments with limited soil nutrients and organic matter.
- **Succulence and Storage:** Many CAM plants are succulents, storing water in leaves or stems to complement CAM physiology.

Commentary: The evolution of CAM is a strategic adaptation to arid and semi-arid environments where evapotranspiration risk is high and daytime stomatal opening would be fatal due to massive water loss. By modifying the timing of CO_2 uptake and internalizing the carbon pool, CAM plants maintain photosynthesis while preserving precious water resources, ensuring survival in otherwise inhospitable ecosystems.

Thus, CAM is a classic example of physiological adaptation to desert life, enabling plants to thrive under extreme drought stress.

7. **(*a*): Structure–Function Relationship of Phloem Tissues with Reference to Translocation of Photoassimilates**: The phloem is a complex permanent tissue in vascular plants specialized for the translocation of photoassimilates, primarily sugars (mainly sucrose), from source (e.g., mature leaves) to sink (e.g., roots, fruits, young leaves). This transport occurs through a process called translocation, which is an energy-dependent and bidirectional movement.

Main Components of Phloem and Their Functional Roles:

1. Sieve Tube Elements (STEs):

- **Structure:**
  - ❑ Elongated, living cells arranged end to end forming sieve tubes.
  - ❑ End walls have sieve plates with pores allowing cytoplasmic continuity.
  - ❑ Lack nucleus and have reduced organelles to facilitate mass flow.
- **Function:**
  - ❑ Serve as the main conducting channels for translocation of sugars and other solutes.
  - ❑ Their low resistance structure allows efficient movement of photoassimilates.

2. Companion Cells:

- **Structure:**
  - ❑ Narrow, nucleated cells closely associated with STEs.
  - ❑ Have numerous mitochondria, dense cytoplasm, and plasmodesmata connecting them to STEs.
- **Function:**
  - ❑ Regulate and maintain STEs by performing metabolic functions for them.
  - ❑ Actively participate in phloem loading and unloading of assimilates via proton-sucrose symporters.

3. Phloem Parenchyma:

- **Structure:**
  - ❑ Living parenchymatous cells found around sieve tubes.
- **Function:**
  - ❑ Store food materials such as starch.
  - ❑ Help in lateral transport and temporary storage of solutes.

4. Phloem Fibres (Bast Fibres):

- **Structure:**
  - ❑ Dead, lignified cells providing mechanical strength.
- **Function:**
  - ❑ Structural support to the phloem tissue, not directly involved in transport.

Mechanism of Phloem Translocation (Pressure Flow Hypothesis):

1. Phloem Loading (at Source):

- ❑ Sucrose is actively loaded into sieve tubes by companion cells.
- ❑ This decreases water potential in sieve tubes; water enters osmotically from xylem.
- ❑ Turgor pressure builds up at the source end.

2. Mass Flow through Sieve Tubes:

- ❑ The pressure difference between source and sink drives bulk flow of sap through sieve tubes.

3. Phloem Unloading (at Sink):

- ❑ Sucrose is removed actively or passively at sink tissues (e.g., root tips).
- ❑ Water exits the sieve tubes, reducing pressure.

Structure–Function Correlation:

Phloem Component	Structural Specialization	Function in Translocation
Sieve Tube Elements	Perforated sieve plates, reduced organelles	Long-distance flow of photoassimilates
Companion Cells	Dense cytoplasm, connected via plasmodesmata	Assist in loading/ unloading and metabolic regulation
Phloem Parenchyma	Storage capacity and lateral connections	Temporary storage and lateral transport
Phloem Fibres	Thick-walled, lignified	Provide mechanical strength

The intricate structural specialization of phloem tissues ensures functional efficiency, enabling plants to distribute photosynthates quickly and precisely to where they are needed for growth, storage, or metabolism.

7. (*b*): Inhibitors of Photosynthetic Electron Transport as Effective Herbicides: Photosynthetic electron transport is a critical component of the light-dependent reactions of photosynthesis. Certain chemicals act as inhibitors of this electron transport chain (ETC), thereby disrupting photosynthesis and killing the plant. Many such inhibitors have been commercially developed into herbicides due to their targeted action on photosynthetic machinery.

Mechanism of Action: The photosynthetic electron transport chain operates between Photosystem II (PSII), cytochrome b6f complex, and Photosystem I (PSI). Inhibitors block specific steps in this chain, leading to:

- Disruption of ATP and NADPH synthesis
- Accumulation of reactive oxygen species (ROS)
- Cellular damage and plant death

Key Classes of Electron Transport Inhibitors Used as Herbicides:

1. PSII Inhibitors:

- Target: Bind to the QB site of the D1 protein in PSII, blocking electron transfer from QA to plastoquinone.
- Examples:
  - ❑ Atrazine (a triazine): Commonly used in maize and sorghum fields
  - ❑ Diuron (a substituted urea)
  - ❑ Simazine
- Effect: Chlorosis and necrosis due to failure in photophosphorylation and ROS generation.

2. PSI Inhibitors:

- Target: Accept electrons from PSI and transfer them to oxygen, producing toxic superoxide radicals.
- Example: Paraquat (Methyl viologen)
- Effect: Membrane damage due to oxidative stress, leading to rapid desiccation of tissues.

3. Inhibitors of Cytochrome b6f Complex:

- Target: Block electron flow between PSII and PSI.
- Example: Antimycin A (used experimentally)
- Effect: Inhibits proton gradient formation, disrupting ATP synthesis.

Why They Are Effective as Herbicides:

- Selectivity: Can be tailored to target specific crops or weeds.
- Rapid Action: Visible symptoms (wilting, bleaching) occur quickly.
- Mode of Application: Can be applied pre-emergence or post-emergence.
- Persistence: Some compounds remain active in soil, preventing regrowth.

Environmental Considerations:

- Excessive use can lead to soil and water contamination.
- Development of resistance in weeds (especially to triazines like atrazine).
- Harmful to non-target plants and aquatic organisms.

These inhibitors, by targeting the highly specific and vital electron transport system, serve as potent chemical tools in weed management, but require judicious and regulated use to prevent ecological damage.

7. (*c*): Comparison of Applications of Standard Deviation and Coefficient of Variation in Data Analysis:

1. **Standard Deviation (SD):** Definition: Standard deviation measures the absolute variability or dispersion of data points around the mean in the same units as the original data.

Formula:

$$SD = \sum (xi - x^{-})_2 n$$

Applications:

- Absolute Measure of Dispersion: Helps understand the spread of values in raw data.
- Risk Assessment: In fields like agriculture or finance, SD shows fluctuation in yield or stock prices.
- Precision Indicator: Used to assess repeatability or consistency of experimental results.
- Control Charts in Quality Analysis: Helps detect variation from process norms.
- Confidence Intervals and Hypothesis Testing: SD is used in constructing confidence limits and in t-tests or z-tests.

Limitation: Cannot be used for comparing datasets with different units or means.

2. **Coefficient of Variation (CV):** Definition: CV is the relative measure of dispersion, expressing standard deviation as a percentage of the mean.

Formula:

$$CV = (SD\bar{x}) \times 100$$

Applications:

- Comparative Analysis: Useful for comparing variability of two or more datasets with different units or scales.
- Assessing Relative Stability: In agronomy or ecology, CV helps identify the most stable crop genotype or environmental response.
- Experimental Design: Lower CV indicates higher experimental precision.
- Benchmarking Variability: Used to standardize variation across traits or treatments.

Limitation:

- Not meaningful when the mean is near zero (can produce very high or misleading CV values).

Comparison Table:

Aspect	Standard Deviation (SD)	Coefficient of Variation (CV)
Nature	Absolute measure of dispersion	Relative measure of dispersion
Units	Same as data	Unitless (% expression)
Best Use	When comparing variation within same dataset	When comparing across datasets or variables
Sensitivity to Scale	Sensitive to scale of measurement	Independent of scale or unit
Comparative Value	Cannot compare across datasets directly	Enables meaningful comparison between datasets

8. (*a*): Biotechnical Approaches Used in the Conservation of Biodiversity with Special Reference to Endangered Species: The conservation of biodiversity, especially endangered species, is a pressing global priority. Biotechnical approaches, which use modern biotechnological tools and techniques, provide innovative and effective methods for in situ (within natural habitat) and ex situ (outside natural habitat) conservation.

1. In Vitro Conservation Techniques

(*i*) Micropropagation (Tissue Culture)

- Enables mass propagation of rare or endangered plant species from small tissue samples.
- Useful for species with low seed viability or slow growth.
- Example: *Saussurea obvallata* (Brahma Kamal) and *Rauvolfia serpentina* have been propagated through tissue culture.

(*ii*) Somatic Embryogenesis

- Produces plantlets from somatic (non-reproductive) cells.
- Allows production of genetically uniform and disease-free individuals.

(*iii*) In Vitro Germplasm Storage

- Tissue cultures are stored under low temperatures for long-term preservation (slow-growth conditions).
- Protects endangered genotypes from extinction due to habitat loss.

2. Cryopreservation

- Ultra-low temperature preservation of seeds, embryos, pollen, or tissues in liquid nitrogen (–196°C).
- Maintains genetic integrity over extended periods.
- Useful for long-term storage of recalcitrant seeds (which cannot be dried) like those of mango, jackfruit, and endangered orchids.

3. Molecular Marker-Assisted Conservation

- DNA fingerprinting and molecular markers (RAPD, AFLP, SSR) help assess genetic diversity and identity of threatened species.
- Facilitates monitoring of population structure and avoids inbreeding in breeding programs.

4. **Genetic Engineering and Transgenics**
    - Introduces genes for disease resistance, stress tolerance, or enhanced growth into endangered species.
    - Experimental use in conserving tree species like Populus or rare crop relatives.
5. **Synthetic Seed Technology**
    - Somatic embryos or shoot buds are encapsulated in a gel-like matrix to form "synthetic seeds."
    - Can be stored, transported, and grown like true seeds.
    - Applicable to endangered orchids and medicinal plants.
6. **DNA Banks and Genomic Libraries**
    - Conservation of genetic material in the form of DNA sequences.
    - Used to preserve rare alleles and to restore extinct genotypes through genome editing or cloning in the future.
7. **Clonal Propagation of Rare Species**
    - Vegetative propagation methods used to conserve species with low seed production.
    - Example: Endangered medicinal plants like *Withania somnifera* and *Nothapodytes nimmoniana.*

Examples of Endangered Species Conserved Biotechnically:

- *Nepenthes khasiana* (Indian pitcher plant)
- *Vanda coerulea* (blue orchid)
- *Taxus wallichiana* (Himalayan yew)
- *Podophyllum hexandrum* (Himalayan mayapple)

8. (*b*): **"Phytochrome-mediated responses can be grouped according to their fluence requirements":** Phytochrome is a photoreceptor protein in plants that detects red (R) and far-red (FR) light and regulates various aspects of plant development in response to light signals. The activity of phytochrome depends on the quantity and quality of light, and the physiological responses it mediates can be grouped based on the fluence (*i.e.*, light intensity or dose) required to trigger them.

Types of Phytochrome-Mediated Responses Based on Fluence Requirement:

1. **Very Low Fluence Responses (VLFRs)**
    - Light Requirement: Extremely low fluence (as little as 0.0001 μmol m^{-2}).
    - Saturation: Do not require red light saturation and are not reversible by far-red light.
    - Sensitivity: Triggered even by brief or weak light exposure, such as moonlight or scattered sunlight.
    - Example Responses:
        - ❑ Seed germination in light-sensitive seeds (e.g., Arabidopsis)
        - ❑ Initial stages of de-etiolation
        - ❑ Cotyledon unfolding
2. **Low Fluence Responses (LFRs)**
    - Light Requirement: 1 to 1000 μmol m^{-2}.
    - Saturation: Reversible by far-red light; shows red/far-red reversibility, a hallmark of classic phytochrome action.
    - Example Responses:
        - ❑ Lettuce (*Lactuca sativa*) seed germination
        - ❑ Hypocotyl elongation inhibition
        - ❑ Chlorophyll synthesis initiation

These responses are used extensively in experimental photobiology to characterize phytochrome behavior.

3. **High Irradiance Responses (HIRs)**
    - Light Requirement: Continuous exposure to high light intensity, regardless of R/FR ratio.
    - Saturation: Not reversible by far-red light.
    - Dependence: Requires prolonged light exposure; usually involves Pfr accumulation over time.
    - Example Responses:
        - ❑ Inhibition of stem elongation under continuous red or blue light
        - ❑ Anthocyanin synthesis
        - ❑ Cotyledon expansion in continuous light

HIRs often involve multiple photoreceptors including phytochrome and cryptochrome.

Commentary: Grouping phytochrome-mediated responses based on fluence requirement is important for understanding how plants sense and respond to different light environments:

- VLFRs are crucial for seeds buried in soil or shaded environments.
- LFRs allow plants to make reversible decisions based on light quality.
- HIRs enable plants to sustain developmental responses under prolonged light, such as during long days.

Thus, fluence-based classification helps distinguish between the sensitivity and reversibility of different phytochrome responses and highlights the adaptability of plants to variable light conditions in their environment.

8. (*c*): Critical Account on Biogeochemical Cycles with Reference to a Terrestrial Ecosystem:

Biogeochemical Cycles – Overview: Biogeochemical cycles refer to the movement and recycling of elements and compounds (like carbon, nitrogen, phosphorus, and water) between the biotic (living) and abiotic (non-living) components of an ecosystem. These cycles ensure nutrient availability, ecosystem productivity, and ecological stability.

In any terrestrial ecosystem, such as a tropical forest or grassland, these cycles operate in an interconnected manner to regulate life-supporting processes.

1. Carbon Cycle (Example from Tropical Forest Ecosystem):

- Input: CO_2 from the atmosphere is fixed by plants via photosynthesis.
- Transfer: Carbon moves to herbivores and carnivores through the food chain.
- Return:
  - ❑ Respiration by plants, animals, and microbes releases CO_2 back to the atmosphere.
  - ❑ Decomposition of dead biomass by microbes returns carbon to the soil as humus and to the atmosphere as CO_2.
- Storage: Forests act as carbon sinks, storing carbon in biomass and soil.

Critical Role: Tropical forests regulate global carbon balance and climate. Deforestation leads to CO_2 release and climate destabilization.

2. Nitrogen Cycle:

- Fixation: Atmospheric N_2 is converted into ammonium (NH_4^+) by nitrogen-fixing bacteria (e.g., *Rhizobium* in legume roots).
- Nitrification: NH_4^+ is oxidized to nitrite (NO_2^-) and then nitrate (NO_3^-) by soil bacteria (*Nitrosomonas*, *Nitrobacter*).
- Assimilation: Plants absorb NO_3^- and synthesize amino acids and proteins.
- Ammonification: Organic nitrogen from dead organisms is decomposed into NH_4^+.
- Denitrification: Nitrates are converted back into N_2 by anaerobic bacteria, returning it to the atmosphere.

Terrestrial Significance: Nitrogen is crucial for plant productivity. Intensive agriculture alters nitrogen cycling, causing soil degradation and eutrophication.

3. Phosphorus Cycle:

- Source: Phosphorus originates from rock weathering, entering soil as phosphate (PO_4^{3-}).
- Uptake: Absorbed by plants and passed to animals via the food chain.
- Return: Through decay and excretion, phosphate returns to the soil.
- No gaseous phase: It is sedimentary, making it slower than other cycles.

Ecological Note: In forest ecosystems, mycorrhizal fungi enhance phosphorus uptake. Phosphorus limitation is a major constraint in tropical soils.

4. Water Cycle (Hydrological Cycle):

- Evaporation from soil and plant surfaces (transpiration) moves water to the atmosphere.
- Condensation and precipitation return water to land.

- Infiltration and percolation recharge groundwater, supporting plant roots.

Role: Maintains soil moisture, regulates plant physiology, and controls nutrient transport.

Critical Observations in Terrestrial Ecosystems:

- Biogeochemical cycles are interdependent—carbon and nitrogen cycling are coupled via plant growth and microbial activity.
- Human activities (deforestation, fertilizer use, fossil fuel combustion) have intensified nutrient imbalances.
- Soil microorganisms are key players in nutrient transformation and stability.
- Disturbances (e.g., forest fires, overgrazing) disrupt nutrient fluxes, reduce productivity, and increase greenhouse gas emissions.

YOUR SPACE

Previous Years' Paper

Indian Forest Service (Main) Exam, 2023

SUBJECT–BOTANY

(Exam held on 29-11-2023)

PAPER-I

Note: *There are EIGHT questions in all, out of which FIVE are to be attempted, questions Nos. 1 & 5 are compulsory. Out of the remaining SIX questions, THREE are to be attempted selecting at least ONE question from each of the two Sections A and B. Attempts of questions shall be counted in sequential order. Unless struck off, attempt of a question shall be counted even if attempted partly. Any page or portion of the page left blank in the Question-cum-Answer Booklet must be clearly struck off. All questions carry equal marks. Answers must be written in ENGLISH only.*

SECTION-A

1. (*a*) How does bacteria acquire resistance to any antibiotic? Explain.

(*b*) Compare the symptoms of wart disease of potato and late blight of potato and name their causal organisms.

(*c*) Compare the important features of Sporophytes of Anthoceros and Funaria with suitable diagrams.

(*d*) Describe heterospory and seed habit. Discuss their significance in the evolution of plants.

(*e*) Describe female fructifications of Cordaitales and discuss its affinities with Cycads.

2. (*a*) Draw and describe the major differences in the cell wall compositions of Gram-positive and Gram-negative bacteria.

(*b*) Give an account of economic importance of algae with special reference to their uses in:

(*i*) *Food*

(*ii*) *Industry, and*

(*iii*) *Biofertilizers.*

(*c*) Discuss the general characters that evolved in Bryophytes for terrestrial habitats.

3. (*a*) What are the major objectives behind studying plant pathology?

Describe the different types of classification of plant diseases.

(*b*) Give a comparative account of the development of female gametophytes of *Pinus* and *Gnetum*. Comment on the affinities of *Gnetum* with Conifers and Angiosperms.

(*c*) Discuss the significance of heterothallism in fungi. Differentiate between morphological and physiological heterothallism.

4. (*a*) Describe the symptoms, causal organism, disease cycle and management of ergot disease of pearl millet.

(*b*) Describe the various stages of evolution of sporophyte in Bryophytes with reference to the progressive sterilization of potential sporophytic tissue.

(*c*) Draw and label the flagellum of a Gram-negative bacteria. Describe the different types of arrangements of flagella.

SECTION-B

5. (*a*) Describe the merits and demerits of Hutchinson's system of classification.

(*b*) What is Periderm? Discuss the major components of periderm.

(*c*) What are the important agents which help plants in their pollination?

(*d*) Give four examples of old world plant species with their botanical names, which have been cultivated for:

(*i*) over 4000 years.

(*ii*) over 2000 years.

(*e*) Explain somaclonal and gametoclonal variants and their applications.

6. (*a*) Differentiate between the following:

(*i*) Liliaceae and Orchidaceae

(*ii*) Cucurbitaceae and Euphorbiaceae

(*b*) Mention the botanical name, family and the parts used of two plants of each of the following categories:

(*i*) Timber

(*ii*) Millets

(*iii*) Spices obtained from below ground parts

(*c*) Differentiate between Intraxylary phloem and Interxylary phloem with the help of suitable diagram and examples.

7. (*a*) Describe the floral features of the family Asteraceae with floral formula and floral diagrams. Explain why this family is considered as highly evolved among Angiosperms.

(*b*) Distinguish between bisporic embryo sac and tetrasporic embryo sac. Explain with suitable diagrams the various types of tetrasporic embryo sacs.

(*c*) What are the factors that affect the yield and viability of protoplast during protoplast culture?

8. (*a*) Classify fibers with examples based on:

(*i*) origin and structure.

(*ii*) their commercial uses.

(*b*) What are the different methods of micro-propagation? Discuss the advantages and disadvantages of *in vivo* and *in vitro* micropropagation.

(*c*) What are hallucinogens? Explain giving examples of Marijuana and its bioactive compounds.

PAPER-II

Note: *There are EIGHT questions in all, out of which FIVE are to be attempted, questions Nos. 1 & 5 are compulsory. Out of the remaining SIX questions, THREE are to be attempted selecting at least ONE question from each of the two Sections A and B. Attempts of questions shall be counted in sequential order. Unless struck off, attempt of a question shall be counted even if attempted partly. Any page or portion of the page left blank in the Question-cum-Answer Booklet must be clearly struck off. All questions carry equal marks. Answers must be written in ENGLISH only.*

SECTION-A

1. Write short notes on the following:

(*a*) Nuclear pore complex

(*b*) Microtubule binding proteins

(*c*) Substitution mutation

(*d*) Functions of ribosomes and subunits

(*e*) Nuclear male sterile lines for hybrid seed production

2. (*a*) What are the processes of membrane transport? How do carrier molecules transport materials across a cell membrane?

(*b*) Explain extranuclear inheritance citing examples from two different organelles.

(*c*) What are the different stages involved in micropropagation?

3. (*a*) Describe the mechanism of meiotic crossing-over and the theories related to the process.

(*b*) "Mitochondria are semi-autonomous organelles." Justify.

(*c*) What are cell cycle regulators? Discuss their different types. Why are these important?

4. (*a*) Give a detailed account of direct gene transfer methods.

(*b*) Is heterochromatin genetically inactive? Explain. Discuss the function and features of heterochromatin.

(*c*) Give the difference between dominance and epistasis. Explain different kinds of epistatic interactions.

SECTION-B

5. Write short notes on the following:

(*a*) Effects of global warming

(*b*) Z-test

(*c*) Red Data Book

(*d*) Heat shock proteins and their functions

(*e*) GS-GOGAT pathway

6. (*a*) Describe different types of biogeochemical cycles. Discuss their importance.

(*b*) Describe the key features of enzyme active sites.

(*c*) What are the different types and attributes of biodiversity? Discuss various causes for the loss of biodiversity.

7. (*a*) Explain CO_2 concentrating mechanisms in plants. What are the benefits of CO_2 concentrating mechanisms?

(*b*) Discuss various hot spots of diversity and their role in conservation.

(*c*) Discuss probability and the types of probability distributions.

8. (*a*) (*i*) Describe phytochrome and its involvement in the photoperiodic induction of flowering in plants.

(*ii*) Describe the molecular basis of vernalization.

(*b*) Write a detailed note on the Convention on Biological Diversity.

(*c*) Give the key features of chemiosmotic theory.

ANSWERS

PAPER-I

1. (*a*) Bacteria can acquire resistance to antibiotics through various mechanisms, a process often driven by evolutionary pressures and natural selection. Here are some common ways in which bacteria develop antibiotic resistance:

- ***Mutation:*** Bacteria reproduce rapidly, and during each replication, there is a chance that genetic mutations may occur. Some of these mutations can confer resistance to antibiotics. If an antibiotic is present, bacteria without the mutation may be killed, while those with the mutation survive and reproduce. Over time, the population becomes dominated by resistant strains.

- ***Horizontal Gene Transfer (HGT):*** Bacteria have the ability to transfer genetic material horizontally, not only to their offspring but also to other bacteria in the same environment. This can happen through processes such as conjugation (direct transfer of DNA between bacterial cells), transformation (uptake of foreign DNA from the environment), and transduction (transfer of genetic material via bacteriophages). If a bacterium carrying antibiotic resistance genes shares genetic material with a susceptible bacterium, the latter can become resistant.
- ***Plasmids and Mobile Genetic Elements:*** Resistance genes are often carried on mobile genetic elements, such as plasmids. These small, circular pieces of DNA can easily transfer between bacteria, spreading resistance. Bacteria can acquire plasmids carrying multiple resistance genes, making them resistant to multiple antibiotics simultaneously.
- ***Efflux Pumps:*** Bacteria can develop mechanisms to pump out antibiotics before they can exert their effect. Efflux pumps are proteins that actively transport antibiotics out of bacterial cells, reducing their concentration inside the cell and rendering the antibiotic ineffective.
- ***Altering Antibiotic Targets:*** Some bacteria can modify the target sites of antibiotics. For example, they may change the structure of the protein that the antibiotic normally targets, making the antibiotic unable to bind and inhibit its function.
- ***Biofilm Formation:*** Bacteria within biofilms (thin layers of microorganisms encased in a protective matrix) can exhibit increased resistance to antibiotics. The matrix can physically shield the bacteria from the action of antibiotics, and the slow growth of bacteria within biofilms may reduce their susceptibility to certain drugs.

The overuse and misuse of antibiotics in medicine, agriculture, and aquaculture have accelerated the development of antibiotic resistance. This global concern highlights the importance of responsible antibiotic use, the development of new antibiotics, and alternative approaches to combat bacterial infections.

1. (***b***) Wart disease of potato (Synchytrium endobioticum) and late blight of potato (Phytophthora infestans) are two distinct diseases that affect potatoes. Here's a comparison of the symptoms associated with each:

Wart Disease of Potato with causal organism Synchytrium endobioticum:

- ***Galls or Warts:*** The hallmark symptom of wart disease is the development of warts or galls on the tubers. These galls are irregularly shaped, warty outgrowths that vary in size and can deform the affected potatoes.
- ***Color Changes:*** Infected tubers may exhibit color changes, often becoming darker than healthy potatoes.
- ***Reduction in Yield:*** Wart disease can lead to a significant reduction in the yield of affected potato plants.
- ***Aerial Symptoms:*** While the disease primarily affects the tubers, there may be no conspicuous symptoms on the aerial parts of the plant. However, in some cases, there might be mild leaf distortions.

Late Blight of Potato with causal organism Phytophthora infestans:

Foliage Symptoms:

- ***Leaf Lesions:*** Late blight typically starts with the appearance of dark green to black lesions on the leaves. These lesions often have a water-soaked appearance.
- ***White Fungal Growth:*** Under humid conditions, a white, downy fungal growth may be observed on the undersides of the leaves.

Tuber Symptoms:

- ***Dark Lesions:*** Late blight can also affect the tubers, causing dark, often irregular lesions.
- ***Rapid Decay:*** Tubers may undergo rapid decay, especially in warm and humid conditions.

Stem Symptoms:

- ***Stem Lesions:*** Lesions can develop on the stems, leading to a collapse of the entire plant in severe cases.
- ***Rapid Spread:*** Late blight is known for its rapid spread, especially under favorable environmental conditions. It can cause significant damage to potato crops if not managed promptly.
- ***Favorable Conditions:*** The disease thrives in cool, wet conditions, and its spread is facilitated by rain and wind.

While wart disease primarily affects the tubers and leads to the development of warts, late blight affects both the foliage and tubers, causing lesions, decay, and potential plant collapse. Both diseases can result in significant economic losses if not effectively managed through proper agricultural practices and, in some cases, the use of resistant potato varieties.

1. (*c*) Compare the Important Features of Sporophytes of Anthoceros and Funaria with suitable diagram

Anthoceros and Funaria are both examples of bryophytes, which are non-vascular plants characterized by a life cycle that includes a dominant gametophyte stage. Here are some key features comparing the sporophytes of Anthoceros (a hornwort) and Funaria (a moss):

Anthoceros (Hornwort):

- ***Sporophyte Structure:*** Anthoceros sporophytes are elongated, horn-shaped structures.
- They lack a seta (stalk) and are directly attached to the gametophyte.
- ***Capsule Characteristics:*** The capsule of Anthoceros is simple and elongated, resembling a horn.
- It typically splits open along one side to release spores.
- ***Stomata:*** Anthoceros sporophytes possess stomata, which are minute pores that allow gas exchange.
- ***Photosynthetic Tissues:*** The sporophytes of Anthoceros may contain photosynthetic tissues, contributing to their ability to photosynthesize.

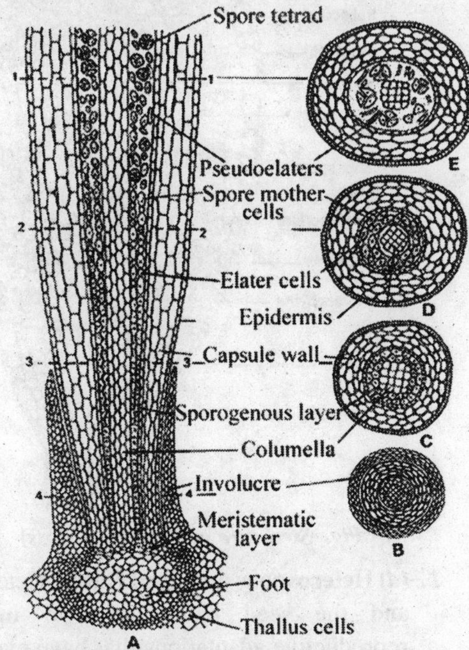

Fig. Anthoceros: (A) L.S. of sporangium; (B-E) Cross section of sporophyte

Funaria (Moss):

- ***Sporophyte Structure:*** Funaria sporophytes consist of a foot, seta (stalk), and capsule. The seta elevates the capsule above the gametophyte.
- ***Capsule Characteristics:*** The capsule of Funaria is often pear-shaped and is borne at the end of a seta. It has a peristome, which is a ring of tooth-like structures that control the release of spores.
- ***Stomata:*** Funaria sporophytes also possess stomata, allowing for gas exchange.
- ***Calyptra:*** A calyptra, a protective structure derived from the archegonium, covers the developing capsule of Funaria.
- ***Peristome Teeth:*** The peristome teeth in the capsule of Funaria play a role in spore dispersal. They can move in response to humidity changes, aiding in the controlled release of spores.

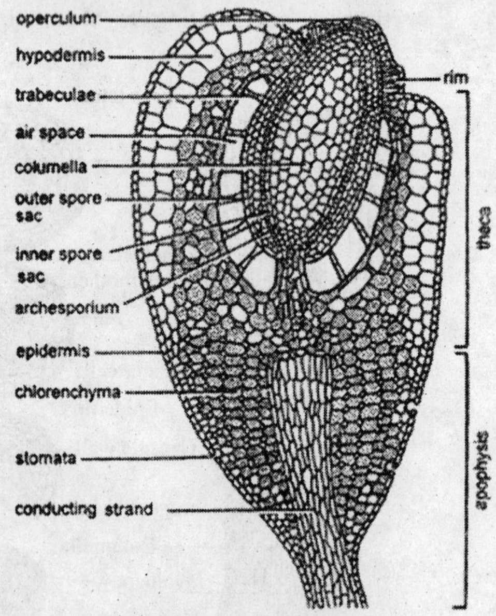

Fig. Structure of Funaria (Moss)

1. **(*d*) Heterospory and Seed Habit:** Heterospory and the seed habit are two important reproductive adaptations that have evolved in certain plant groups, conferring advantages for survival, dispersal, and reproductive success.

Heterospory:

Definition: Heterospory is a reproductive strategy in which a plant species produces two distinct types of spores—microspores and megaspores—each giving rise to different types of gametophytes.

Microspores: Microspores develop into male gametophytes (microgametophytes) that produce male gametes (sperm cells).

Megaspores: Megaspores develop into female gametophytes (megagametophytes) that produce female gametes (egg cells).

Examples: Heterospory is commonly found in seed plants (gymnosperms and angiosperms).

Seed Habit:

Definition: The seed habit is a reproductive adaptation in which plants produce seeds as part of their life cycle.

Seed Structure: A seed is a mature ovule containing a plant embryo, stored nutrients, and a protective seed coat.

Advantages:

- Seeds provide protection to the developing embryo, shielding it from desiccation, predation, and environmental stresses.
- Seeds can remain dormant until conditions are favorable for germination, allowing for better timing of germination and seedling establishment.
- Seeds facilitate dispersal, as they often have adaptations for wind, water, or animal dispersal, promoting the colonization of new habitats.

Examples: Seed plants, including gymnosperms (e.g., pine trees) and angiosperms (flowering plants), exhibit the seed habit.

Significance in the Evolution of Plants

- Heterospory and the seed habit are pivotal adaptations in the evolutionary history of plants, representing key innovations that have significantly influenced their success and diversification in terrestrial environments. Heterospory, the production of distinct types of spores (microspores and megaspores) with specialized reproductive roles, enhanced reproductive efficiency and allowed plants to adapt more effectively to life on land. This innovation facilitated the development of separate male and female gametophytes, minimizing the risk of self-fertilization and contributing to the complexity of plant life cycles.

- Complementing heterospory, the seed habit further revolutionized plant evolution. Seeds, consisting of a protective coat surrounding a developing embryo and stored nutrients, provide a multifaceted advantage. Firstly, the seed habit offered a remarkable solution to the challenges of terrestrial life by protecting the embryo from desiccation, mechanical damage, and predation. Secondly, seeds allowed for dormancy, delaying germination until environmental conditions were optimal, ensuring the strategic timing of plant establishment.
- Together, these adaptations facilitated the colonization of diverse habitats and the exploitation of ecological niches. The ability of seeds to disperse through various mechanisms, including wind, water, and animals, significantly contributed to the spatial expansion of plant populations. Additionally, the temporal control afforded by both heterospory and the seed habit enabled plants to synchronize their reproductive processes with environmental cues, enhancing their overall fitness and adaptability.
- In summary, the evolution of heterospory and the seed habit represents a remarkable trajectory in plant adaptation. These innovations provided plants with sophisticated mechanisms for reproduction, dispersal, and survival, contributing to their resilience and proliferation across diverse ecosystems throughout evolutionary history.

1. (*e*) Female Fructifications of Cordaitales and Discuss its Affinities with Cycads:

Cordaitales is an extinct order of gymnosperms that existed from the Carboniferous to the Permian periods. The female fructifications of Cordaitales were structures associated with reproductive organs, specifically the cones or seed cones. These cones bore seeds and played a crucial role in the reproduction of Cordaitales plants. Here are some characteristics of the female fructifications in Cordaitales:

- ***Seed Cones:*** Cordaitales produced seed cones, which were the reproductive structures containing the female reproductive organs and seeds. These cones were generally larger and more complex than the male cones, reflecting the importance of seed production in the life cycle of these plants.
- ***Organization:*** The female fructifications of Cordaitales were organized into cone structures similar to those seen in modern conifers. The cones consisted of scales or bracts that protected the reproductive organs and seeds.
- ***Ovules and Seeds:*** The scales of the female cones housed ovules, which were the structures containing the female gametophyte and later developed into seeds upon fertilization. The seeds had a protective seed coat, aiding in their dispersal and survival.
- ***Fertilization:*** Fertilization in Cordaitales involved the transfer of pollen (carrying male gametes) to the female cone. Once fertilized, the ovules within the female fructifications developed into seeds.
- ***Reproductive Adaptations:*** The evolution of complex cones with differentiated male and female fructifications in Cordaitales

represented an adaptation for efficient seed production and dispersal. The development of seeds with protective coats enhanced the success of these plants in colonizing various habitats.

It's important to note that while Cordaitales share some similarities with modern conifers, they are not direct ancestors of the conifers we see today. Instead, they represent a distinct and now-extinct group of gymnosperms that played a significant role in ancient ecosystems during the Paleozoic era. The study of their reproductive structures, including female fructifications, provides valuable insights into the evolutionary history of seed plants.

2. (*a*) Draw and Describe the Major Differences in the Cell Wall Compositions of Gram-positive and Gram-negative Bacteria:

Gram-Positive Cell Wall	Gram-Negative Cell Wall
Layers	
Single layered	Double layered
Composition	
Consisting of several layers of peptidoglycan	Consisting of a single layer of peptidoglycan
Thickness	
15 to 80 nanometers	10 nanometers
Periplasmic space	
Small	Large
Outer membrane	
Absent	Present
Teichoic Acid	
Present	Absent
Porins	
Absent	Present
Lipid Content	
Very low (2 – 5 per cent)	High (15-20 per cent)
Lipopolysaccharides	
Absent	Present
Gram staining Pro-cedure	
Retains the crystal violet dye and appears purple in colour	It does not retain the crystal violet dye and appears pink in colour

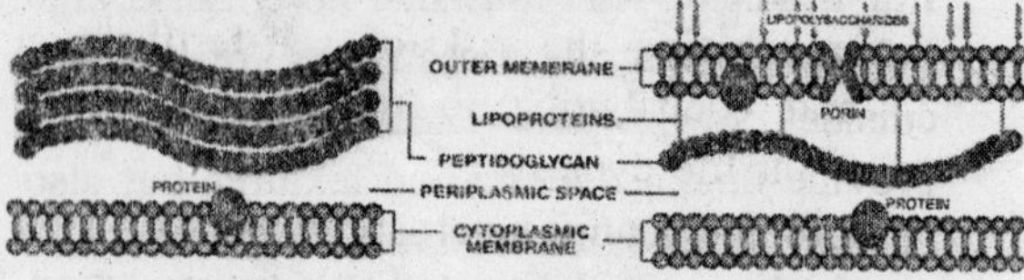

Gram-positive and Gram-negative Bacteria

2. (*b*) Algae possess remarkable economic significance across diverse industries, playing a pivotal role in addressing global challenges and meeting human needs. From a biological standpoint, algae contribute significantly to atmospheric oxygen levels through photosynthesis and act as essential carbon sinks, aiding in climate change mitigation. In the realm of nutrition, certain algae species serve as valuable sources of essential nutrients, finding applications in human diets and aquaculture, supporting the production of seafood. Moreover, algae exhibit promise as a renewable energy source, with lipid-rich species being utilized in the production of biodiesel. The pharmaceutical and nutraceutical industries benefit from the bioactive compounds present in algae, offering potential solutions for various health-related applications. Algae contribute to wastewater treatment by absorbing nutrients, and their extracts are used in cosmetics, personal care products, and the food industry as stabilizers and thickeners. Additionally, algae play crucial roles in agriculture, providing livestock feed supplements and serving as natural fertilizers. With ongoing research and technological advancements, the economic importance of algae is poised to expand further, offering sustainable solutions across multiple sectors.

(*i*) **Economic Importance of Algae with Special Reference to Food:** Algae hold significant economic importance, particularly in the realm of food, offering diverse applications that contribute to both human nutrition and the agricultural sector. Certain species of algae are directly consumed by humans and are rich in essential nutrients. For instance, seaweeds like nori, dulse, and kelp are integral components of various cuisines worldwide. These algae not only provide unique flavors and textures but also deliver essential vitamins, minerals, and proteins. Moreover, algae play a vital role in supporting aquaculture by serving as a primary food source for fish and shellfish. The cultivation of algae as feed in aquaculture systems enhances the growth and nutritional profile of farmed seafood, contributing to the overall productivity of the industry. This practice not only ensures the sustainability of aquaculture operations but also addresses the increasing global demand for high-quality seafood. In addition to direct consumption and aquaculture, certain types of algae contribute to the food industry through the extraction of valuable compounds. Agar and carrageenan, derived from red algae, are widely used as gelling agents and stabilizers in the production of various processed foods, including desserts, dairy products, and meat products. These algae-derived additives enhance the texture and quality of food products while also providing functional benefits in terms of stability and shelf life.The economic importance of algae in the food sector extends to their potential as functional ingredients. Algal extracts and compounds, known for their health-promoting properties, are increasingly incorporated into functional foods and nutraceuticals. This includes products such as algae-based supplements and fortified foods, catering to the growing demand for health-conscious and sustainable dietary choices. In conclusion, algae contribute significantly to the economic landscape of the food industry. Whether directly consumed, used as feed in aquaculture, or as valuable additives and functional ingredients, algae play a crucial role in ensuring food security, nutrition, and the development of innovative food products with environmental sustainability in mind.

(*ii*) **Economic Importance of Algae with Special Reference to Industry:** Algae hold substantial economic importance in various industries, contributing to sustainable practices, resource diversification, and the development of innovative technologies. One of the primary industrial applications of algae lies in biofuel production. Certain algae species are rich in lipids, which can be converted into biodiesel through a process known as transesterification. Algae-based biofuels offer a renewable and potentially more sustainable alternative to traditional fossil fuels, helping to reduce greenhouse gas emissions and dependence on finite resources. In the field of bioremediation, algae play a crucial role in wastewater treatment and pollution control. Algae have the ability to absorb and metabolize pollutants, such as heavy metals and nutrients, from industrial effluents and agricultural runoff. This not only helps in maintaining water quality but also provides a cost-effective and environmentally friendly solution to mitigate the impact of industrial activities on aquatic ecosystems. Algae are extensively used in the production of high-value compounds for the pharmaceutical and nutraceutical industries. The bioactive compounds present in certain algae, including antioxidants, pigments, and polysaccharides, have applications in the development of pharmaceutical drugs, dietary supplements, and health-pro-moting products. This contributes to advancements in medical research and fosters the creation of value-added products with potential therapeutic benefits. In the agricultural sector, algae serve as a source of sustainable fertilizers and soil conditioners. Algae-based fertilizers provide essential nutrients to crops, enhancing soil fertility and promoting healthier plant growth. Additionally, some algae species can form symbiotic relationships with plants, facilitating nutrient uptake and improving overall crop yield. The cosmetic and personal care industry also benefits from the economic contributions of algae. Extracts from various algae species are incorporated into skincare and cosmetic products for their moisturizing, anti-aging, and skin-conditioning properties. Algal compounds such as alginates and carrageenan are used as thickeners and stabilizers in cosmetic formulations. As a source of biomass, algae are utilized in the production of bioplastics, offering a renewable alternative to traditional petroleum-based plastics. Algae-derived bioplastics have the potential to reduce environmental impacts and contribute to the circular economy. In conclusion, the economic importance of algae in industry is multifaceted. From biofuel production and bioremediation to pharmaceuticals, agriculture, cosmetics, and sustainable materials, algae play a pivotal role in driving innovation and sustainability across various industrial sectors. Continued research and technological advancements are likely to uncover new applications, further expanding the economic contributions of algae to industry.

(*iii*) Economic Importance of Algae with Special Reference to Biofertilizers: Algae contribute significantly to agriculture and the production of biofertilizers, playing a vital role in enhancing soil fertility and promoting sustainable farming practices. Algal biofertilizers offer several economic and environmental benefits:

- ***Nutrient Enrichment:*** Algae, particularly blue-green algae (cyanobacteria) and green algae, fix atmospheric nitrogen and convert it into forms that are readily available to plants. This natural nitrogen-fixing ability is crucial for enriching soil with nitrogen, an essential nutrient for plant growth.
- ***Phosphorus Uptake:*** Some algae have the ability to solubilize phosphorus in the soil, making it more accessible to plants. This is significant because phosphorus is a key nutrient required for various physiological processes in plants.
- ***Micronutrient Supply:*** Algae contain a range of micronutrients, including vitamins, minerals, and trace elements. When used as biofertilizers, algae contribute to the overall nutritional content of the soil, supporting plant health and productivity.
- ***Improved Soil Structure:*** The organic matter produced by algae helps improve soil structure, water retention, and drainage. This is especially beneficial in regions with poor soil quality, as it enhances the soil's ability to support plant growth.
- ***Sustainable Agriculture:*** Algal biofertilizers promote sustainable agricultural practices by reducing the reliance on synthetic fertilizers. The use of algae in agriculture aligns with the principles of organic and environmentally friendly farming, leading to cost savings for farmers in the long term.
- ***Environmental Impact:*** Algal biofertilizers contribute to reducing the environmental impact associated with traditional fertilizers. Runoff from synthetic fertilizers can lead to water pollution, whereas algal biofertilizers are more environmentally friendly and have a lower risk of causing harm to aquatic ecosystems.

- ***Biodiversity Support:*** The use of algal biofertilizers can enhance the biodiversity of soil microorganisms, creating a healthier and more balanced soil ecosystem. This, in turn, contributes to improved nutrient cycling and plant resilience.
- ***Adaptability to Various Crops:*** Algal biofertilizers can be adapted to a variety of crops, making them versatile for different agricultural systems and practices. This adaptability contributes to their widespread application in diverse farming environments.

The economic importance of algae in the context of biofertilizers lies in their ability to provide sustainable and cost-effective solutions to enhance soil fertility and crop productivity. As agriculture faces challenges related to environmental sustainability and resource efficiency, the use of algal biofertilizers represents a promising avenue for addressing these concerns while supporting the economic well-being of farmers.

2. (*c*) General Characters that Evolved in Bryophytes for Terrestrial Habitats: Bryophytes, which include mosses, liverworts, and hornworts, represent a group of non-vascular plants that were among the earliest land-dwelling organisms. The transition of plants from aquatic to terrestrial habitats involved the evolution of several key characters in bryophytes to adapt to life on land. Here are some general characteristics that evolved in bryophytes for terrestrial habitats:

- ***Non-Vascular Tissue:*** Bryophytes lack vascular tissues, such as xylem and phloem, which are present in more advanced plants. This limits their ability to transport water and nutrients over long distances. However, it is an adaptation that allowed them to colonize terrestrial environments, as it helped prevent desiccation in a less water-saturated environment.
- ***Rhizoids:*** Bryophytes have simple, unicellular or multicellular structures called rhizoids that anchor the plants to the substrate. These structures also aid in water absorption from the soil, contributing to the plant's overall water balance.
- ***Dominant Gametophyte Phase:*** The life cycle of bryophytes is characterized by a dominant gametophyte (haploid) phase. The gametophyte is the structure that produces gametes (sperm and egg). This adaptation is thought to be advantageous in the retention of water and nutrients, as the gametophyte forms a mat-like structure on the substrate.
- ***Spore Dispersal:*** Bryophytes reproduce through spores rather than seeds. Spores are produced in sporangia, which are capsules located on the tips of specialized structures. The release of spores allows bryophytes to disperse and colonize new areas, aiding in their adaptation to diverse terrestrial environments.
- ***Cuticle:*** A waxy cuticle covers the surface of bryophytes, reducing water loss through evaporation. While this adaptation helps prevent desiccation, it also limits the exchange of gases (such as carbon dioxide and oxygen) with the surrounding environment.
- ***Simple Tissues:*** Bryophytes have simple tissues with no true leaves, stems, or roots. These structures contribute to their low stature and are adapted for efficient nutrient absorption and water retention.
- ***Stomata-Like Structures:*** Some bryophytes possess stomata-like structures on their surfaces. These openings allow for gas exchange, crucial for photosynthesis and respiration. Stomata-like structures are typically surrounded by specialized cells that control their opening and closing.
- ***Symbiotic Associations:*** Bryophytes often form symbiotic associations with fungi

(mycorrhizae) that assist in nutrient absorption, particularly phosphorus. This mutualistic relationship enhances the plant's ability to extract essential nutrients from the soil.

- ***Asexual Reproduction:*** Bryophytes can reproduce asexually through fragmentation and the formation of specialized structures called gemmae. Gemmae are small, multicellular structures that can develop into new plants under suitable conditions.
- ***Tolerance to Desiccation:*** Bryophytes exhibit a high tolerance to desiccation, allowing them to survive in periods of drought or when water availability is limited. This adaptation is facilitated by their ability to quickly rehydrate when water becomes available.

These general characteristics collectively represent the suite of adaptations that allowed bryophytes to thrive in terrestrial habitats, paving the way for the subsequent evolution of more complex plant forms.

3. **(*a*) Major Objectives behind Studying Plant Pathology:** The science that deals with the study of diseases of plants, their development and control is called Plant Pathology. Plant diseases are caused by biotic agents like fungi, bacteria, actinomycets, Mycoplasma, viruses, nematodes, and flowering parasites or by abiotic like unfavorable environmental conditions or nutritional deficiencies. Study of plant pathology includes the study of sciences viz, Microbiology, Bacteriology, Virology, Mycology, Nematology, protozology, phycology, unfavorable, environmental factors, nutritional deficiencies and flowering plant parasites.The study of plant pathology is driven by several key objectives, each aimed at ensuring the health, productivity, and sustainability of plant populations essential for human survival. Firstly, plant pathology seeks to understand and mitigate the impact of plant diseases, caused by pathogens such as fungi, bacteria, viruses, and nematodes, which can lead to significant crop losses. By unraveling the complexities of these diseases, researchers can develop effective strategies for disease management, including the development of resistant plant varieties and environmentally friendly control measures.

Secondly, plant pathology plays a crucial role in safeguarding global food security. As the world's population continues to grow, the demand for food increases, making it imperative to identify and address threats to crop production. Plant pathologists contribute to the development of sustainable agricultural practices that enhance crop resilience and reduce the reliance on chemical inputs, thereby promoting long-term food security.

Furthermore, the study of plant pathology contributes to advancements in biotechnology and genetic engineering. By understanding the molecular mechanisms underlying plant-pathogen interactions, scientists can manipulate plant genomes to confer resistance against specific diseases. This knowledge also aids in the development of innovative technologies for early disease detection and rapid response, minimizing the economic and environmental impact of plant diseases.

In summary, the objectives of studying plant pathology are multifaceted, encompassing the protection of global food supplies, the development of sustainable agriculture, and the advancement of scientific knowledge to address current and future challenges in plant health. Through these objectives, plant pathology not only contributes to the well-being of crops but also plays a pivotal role in ensuring the overall health of ecosystems and the human population.

Plant Pathology is one among the branches of agricultural science that deals with cases, etilogy, resulting losses and management of plant diseases with four major objectives.

- Study the diseases (s) or disorders caused by biotic and abiotic agent.
- Study of mechanism of disease development by pathogens.
- Study of interaction between plant and pathogen in relation to the overall environment.
- Develop suitable management strategies for managing the diseases and losses caused by them.

Different Types of Classification of Plant Diseases

Plant disease is classified on the basis of various parameters:

I. ON THE BASIS OF THE NATURE OF THE CAUSAL AGENT:

1. Non-infectious disease\non parasitic disease:

- This type of diseases is caused by non-living organisms.
- Could not be spread to others.
- They are induced by unfavorable environmental condition of soil or air such as mineral deficiencies or excesses in the soil, low or high temperatures, improper water, oxygen and light relation.
- May also be caused by air pollution, nutrient deficiency, mineral toxicity, etc.
- These diseases may also be caused by mechanical injuries.
- Example—blossom and rot of potatoes, blank heart of potatoes, scald of apples.

2. Infectious disease\Parasitic disease:

- These are caused by the attack of some living agents called pathogens. The causal agents may be a plant or an animal or a virus.
- It can spread from diseased to healthy plants.
- In the case of a disease caused by a parasitic organism the diseased plant is called a host.
- The pathogen may subsist in whole or in part upon the living tissue of the host.
- Biotic factors like fungi, bacteria, algae, nematodes, viruses etc. are the causing agents.

II. ON THE BASIS OF HOST PLANT

- Cereal disease
- Vegetable disease
- Fruit disease
- Forest disease
- Ornamental disease

III. ON THE BASIS OF PERPETUATION OF SPREAD

- Soil-borne diseases-pathogen survive in soil or on infested plant debris present on the soil either as their resting spores or as mycelial strands and rhizomorphs. E.g. Root rot, wilt and seedling blight.
- Seed-borne diseases-the microorganisms are carried along with seeds. E.g. damping off.
- Airborne diseases- the microorganisms are spread through air. e.g. blight, rust, powdery mildew.

IV. ON THE BASIS OF OCCURRENCE AND GEOGRAPHIC DISTRIBUTION

1. Endemic disease:

- A disease which is regularly present in a certain region or a part of a region (district) in a moderate to severe from is referred to as endemic
- E.g. wart disease in potato.

2. Epidemic [Epiphytotic] disease:

- Epiphytotic is term applied to the infectious plant disease which spread widely but occur periodically.
- The causal agent may be regularly present in the locality but the environment favorable for its rapid development occurs only periodically.

- The epiphytotic diseases are thus very responsive to variation in the environment.
- E.g. rust, late blight, mildews.

3. **Sporadic disease:**
   - They are plant disease which occur only here or there at irregular intervals and in relatively few instances.
   - A given disease may be endemic in one region and epidemic in another.
   - E.g. leaf blight, wilt.

V. ON THE BASIS OF EXTENT OF INFECTION

- Localized diseases: affecting only a part of the plant, limited to a definite area.
- Systemic diseases: pathogen spreads throughout the plant body and is associated with almost every stage of plants life cycle.

VI. ON THE BASIS OF PATHOGEN GENERATIONS

- Monocyclic disease\Simple interest disease : those diseases which have only generation in one cropping season E.g. loose smut of wheat.
- Polycyclic disease\Compound interest disease : those diseases which have, more than one generation in a cropping season
- E.g. late blight of potato.
- Polyetic disease: these are also polycyclic disease but complete their disease cycle in more than one year or above. E.g. Cedar apple rust.

VII. ON THE BASIS OF ORGAN THE PATHOGENS ATTACK

- Root disease.
- Shoot disease.
- Fruit disease.
- Foliage disease.

VIII. ON THE BASIS OF SYMPTOMS

- Rust-caused by Basidiomycetes of the order Uredinales. e.g. stem rust of wheat, caused by Puccinia graminis.
- Smuts-caused by a fungus of the order Ustilaginales e.g. loose smut of wheat, caused by Ustilago nuda tritici.
- Rots- disease that infect underground part, caused by bacteria, fungi, or nematodes, Rhizoctonia is root rot.
- Blight- It is a rapid and complete chlorosis and death of plant tissue, e.g. late blight disease of potato by Phytopthora infestans.
- Leaf spot-caused by fungi and bacteria, e.g. Bacterial leaf spot is commonly caused by Xanthomonas compestris.
- Canker- It is a dead area, e.g. citrus canker.
- Wilt-it affects vascular system of plants, e.g. Bacterial wilt of cucurbits caused by Erwinia tracheiphila.
- Powdery mildew-causes foliage of stems, flowers, and fruits, e.g. grapes, cucumber, etc.
- Downy mildew-caused by family Peronosporaceae. E.g. Rose and lettuce.

3. (*b*) Comparative Account of the Development Female Gametophytes of Pinus and Gnetum:

Female Gametophyte of Pinus:

- Megaspore is the first cell of the female gametophyte and germinates inside the mega-sporangium, which is never shed.
- Megaspore becomes larger and by free nuclear division produces numerous nuclei, round each of which cytoplasm collects and cell-wall is formed and thus a tissue, known as endosperm, is formed. The endosperm represents the female gametophyte and is formed before fertilization.
- Endosperm is solid and consists of two regions:
  - ❑ A region of small cells towards the top and
  - ❑ A region of large cells towards the base.
- In the former region 2 or 3 archegonia develop and these are separated from one another.

- Archegonium consists of a neck composed of 8 cells in two tiers of 4, a ventral canal cell and a very large cavity surrounded by a layer of jacket cells and containing ovum or egg.

Female Gametophyte of Gnetum :

- Megaspore or cenomegaspore is the first cell of the female gametophyte and germinates inside the mega-sporangium.
- Cenomegaspore produces numerous nucleus by free nuclear division which lie in the cytoplasm. Surrounding a large vacuole. Wall formation begins around the free nuclei, from base upwards but it is not complete. This tissue represents the female gametophyte. Sometimes 2-4 accessory female gametophytes are formed above the main gametophyte but these undergo degeneration.
- Endosperm is formed after fertilization.
- No formation of archegonia.
- One or two free nuclei situated towards the microstyle are covered by cytoplasma and form one or two ova or eggs.

Affinities of Gnetum with Conifers and Angiosperms: Gnetum is a unique and intriguing group of gymnosperms that exhibits affinities with both conifers and angiosperms. It belongs to the division Gnetophyta, which consists of three genera: Gnetum, Welwitschia, and Ephedra. Among these, Gnetum is of particular interest due to its morphological and reproductive features that show similarities with both conifers (another group of gymnosperms) and angiosperms (flowering plants).

Here are some key points highlighting the affinities of Gnetum with conifers and angiosperms:

Reproductive Structures:

- **Conifer-Like Seed Cones:** Gnetum produces seed cones that are reminiscent of those found in conifers. These cones are typically woody and bear seeds, which is a characteristic feature shared with many conifers.
- **Angiosperm-Like Seed Coat:** On the other hand, Gnetum seeds have a fleshy outer layer, resembling the seed coat of some angiosperms. This is in contrast to the typically hard seed coat seen in most gymnosperms.

Vascular Tissue:

- **Angiosperm-Like Vessels:** The vascular tissue in Gnetum includes vessels, which are also present in angiosperms. Conifers, in contrast, lack vessels in their xylem.

Leaf Morphology:

- **Angiosperm-Like Leaves:** The leaves of Gnetum are broad and often have reticulate venation, a feature more commonly associated with angiosperms than with typical conifer leaves.

Double Fertilization:

- **Angiosperm-Like Reproductive Mechanism:** Gnetum is unique among gymnosperms because it employs a form of double fertilization, a process typically associated with angiosperms. In double fertilization, one sperm cell fertilizes the egg to form the embryo, while the other combines with other cells to produce nutrient tissue.

Ecological Traits:

- **Tropical Habitats:** Gnetum is primarily found in tropical regions, which is a departure from the typical coniferous habitats. Angiosperms are diverse and dominant in tropical ecosystems, so Gnetum's ecological preference adds to its connection with angiosperms.

Genetic Evidence:

- **Molecular Similarities:** Genetic studies have shown molecular similarities between Gnetum and angiosperms, further supporting the idea of a closer relationship between the two groups.

The affinities of Gnetum with both conifers and angiosperms raise interesting questions about the evolutionary relationships among these plant groups. Gnetum appears to represent a bridge between gymnosperms and angiosperms, providing valuable insights into the complex evolutionary history of seed plants.

3. **(*c*) Significance of Heterothallism in Fungi:** Heterothallism is a significant reproductive strategy observed in certain fungi, and it plays a crucial role in their genetic diversity and adaptation. In heterothallic fungi, sexual reproduction requires the presence of two different mating types, usually referred to as "+" (plus) and "−" (minus). Individuals of the same mating type are unable to undergo sexual reproduction with each other, promoting outcrossing and genetic recombination. This mechanism stands in contrast to homothallism, where a single individual is self-fertile, possessing both mating types and capable of self-fertilization. One of the key advantages of heterothallism is the promotion of genetic diversity within fungal populations. By necessitating the interaction between different mating types, heterothallism enhances the likelihood of outcrossing during sexual reproduction. This genetic recombination introduces novel combinations of genetic material, leading to increased variability in the offspring. This genetic diversity is crucial for fungi in adapting to changing environmental conditions, combating diseases, and responding to selective pressures.

Heterothallism also serves as a mechanism to prevent inbreeding depression, a phenomenon characterized by the accumulation of deleterious recessive alleles in a population due to mating between closely related individuals. By requiring the presence of distinct mating types for sexual reproduction, heterothallic fungi reduce the risk of inbreeding, contributing to the overall health and fitness of the population. Furthermore, heterothallism enhances the adaptability of fungi to diverse ecological niches. Fungi are essential components of ecosystems, participating in nutrient cycling, symbiotic relationships, and decomposition. The ability to generate diverse genetic combinations through sexual reproduction allows heterothallic fungi to explore a broader range of environmental conditions and ecological interactions. This adaptability is particularly important in the face of environmental changes and challenges. The study of heterothallism in fungi has practical implications as well, especially in industries such as agriculture and medicine. Understanding the reproductive strategies of fungi is crucial for the development of effective strategies to control fungal diseases in crops and to harness fungi for beneficial applications, such as the production of antibiotics or enzymes.

In summary, the significance of heterothallism in fungi lies in its role in promoting genetic diversity, preventing inbreeding depression, and enhancing adaptability to changing environments. This reproductive strategy contributes to the overall success and resilience of fungal populations, highlighting the intricate ways in which fungi have evolved to ensure their survival and ecological relevance.

Differentiate between Morphological and Physiological Heterothallism:

Heterothallism is a reproductive strategy found in certain fungi where sexual reproduction involves the fusion of specialized sexual structures from two different mating types. There are two main types of heterothallism: morphological heterothallism and physiological heterothallism. Let's differentiate between these two:

Morphological Heterothallism:

- ***Definition:*** In morphological heterothallism, the two mating types are distinguishable based on observable morphological differences in sexual structures. These structures are often macroscopic and can be easily identified.
- ***Morphological Structures:*** Fungi exhibiting morphological heterothallism typically produce sexual structures like different types of fruiting bodies or reproductive organs that are visibly distinct between the two mating types. For example, different types of spore-bearing structures may be produced by each mating type.
- ***Example:*** The classic example of morphological heterothallism is found in some species of the fungus Neurospora, where one mating type produces large, flask-shaped perithecia, and the other produces smaller, more spherical perithecia.

Physiological Heterothallism:

- ***Definition:*** Physiological heterothallism is characterized by the absence of macroscopic morphological differences between the two mating types. Instead, the distinction between mating types is based on physiological or biochemical differences.
- ***Physiological Characteristics:*** The physiological differences may involve the production of specific biochemical signals or recognition factors that allow mating to occur. These differences are often at the cellular or molecular level and may not be visibly apparent.
- ***Example:*** Candida albicans, a yeast species that can cause infections in humans, exhibits physiological heterothallism. The two mating types are not visibly distinct, but they differ in the expression of specific genes and the release of chemical signals that enable mating.

In summary, the primary difference between morphological and physiological heterothallism lies in the nature of the characteristics that distinguish the mating types:

Morphological Heterothallism involves visible, macroscopic differences in sexual structures between mating types.

Physiological Heterothallism involves subtle, often microscopic, differences at the physiological or molecular level without obvious morphological distinctions.

Both types of heterothallism contribute to genetic diversity in fungal populations by promoting outcrossing, which involves the fusion of genetic material from different individuals and enhances adaptability to changing environmental conditions.

5. (*a*) Merits and Demerits of Hutchinson's System of Classification:

Merits:

- Hutchinson's system is a Phylogenetic one based on evolutionary trends which deals with the trends of evolution in all the parts of the plant.
- Hutchinson has described 411 angiosperm families which is comparatively more than the earlier systematists. However, the number increased due to rearrangements also.
- He has put Gymnosperms before Angiosperms, which is logical and true on the basis of evolution.
- Dicotyledones has been placed before Monocotyledones. Dicots have been divided into two groups Lignosae and Herbaceae on the basis of habit. He has considered two different lines of evolution, one in the tree (arboreal) habit and the other with the herbaceous habit. His basic Phylogenetic principle is paralleled those of Bessey with certain exceptions.

- He has included gross morphological characters along with anatomical as well as embryological parameters in his principles of classification, which seems logical.

Demerits:

- Though Hutchinson's system is Phylogenetic one, it could not be accepted universally due to certain controversies.
- Hutchinson's fundamental principle that Dicots have evolved in two directions, one from herbaceous Ranales and the other from woody Magnoliales has not been adopted by many.
- According to Benson (1957), Hutchinson's Phylogenetic studies gained populance for the brilliance of clarity on hypothetical Phylogenetic concepts. Hutchinson's system could not find an adoption till date (Lawrence, 1964) although revision of monocots has been accepted. Failure of explanatory notes on disposition of orders comprises reasons for non-adoption of Hutchinson's system in certain quarters despite its merits.

5. **(b) Periderm:** Periderm is the outer layer of the bark of a tree. Let us know about the composition and formation of periderm.

Composition of Periderm: Phellogen, phellem, and phelloderm, all together make up the periderm. Non-technically, the secondary phloem and periderm are collectively called the bark of a tree.

Formation of Periderm: In woody plants, cork cambium is the outermost lateral meristem. Cork cambium, also called phellogen, is another meristematic tissue developed in the cortex region. Due to the cambial ring activity, the outer layers such as cortex cells and epidermis get crushed. This is the time when the cork cambium develops as a new protective layer. Cork cambium starts to differentiate cells and form outer cork (phellem) and inner secondary cortex (phelloderm).

Major Components of Periderm: Structurally, the periderm is composed of three specialized cell types: phellem, phellogen, and phelloderm. The phellem, or cork, forms a series of cell layers at the outermost level of the periderm and is derived from the underlying meristematic phellogen layer (cork cambium).

Three components of periderm:

- ***Cork cambium or phellogen:*** It is made up of narrow, thin walled, rectangular cells. It produces cells on both sides. Outer cells differentiate into cork and inner into secondary cortex.
- ***Cork or phellem:*** Cock is impervious to water due to deposition of suberin in the cell walls.
- ***Secondary cortex of phelloderm:*** These cells are parenchymatous in nature, it contains chloroplasts and synthesize and store food.

5. **(*c*)** Pollination, a crucial process in plant reproduction, involves the transfer of pollen from the male reproductive organs (anthers) to the female reproductive organs (stigmas) of flowers. Several agents contribute to pollination, ensuring the genetic diversity and reproduction of plant species. Some important agents include:

Insects (Entomophily):

- ***Bees:*** Most plants rely heavily on bees for pollination. Bees are attracted to flowers by nectar and collect pollen as they move from one flower to another.
- ***Butterflies:*** These insects are particularly effective pollinators for brightly colored, fragrant flowers. They have a long proboscis for feeding on nectar.
- ***Flies:*** Various fly species, including hoverflies and bee flies, assist in pollination by visiting flowers for nectar.

Birds (Ornithophily):

- ***Hummingbirds:*** Particularly in the Americas, hummingbirds play a crucial role in pollination. Their long bills and specialized tongues allow them to feed on nectar and inadvertently transfer pollen.

Wind (Anemophily):

- ***Wind:*** In wind-pollinated plants, such as many grasses and some trees (e.g., pine and oak), pollen is lightweight and produced in large quantities. The wind carries the pollen to nearby plants for pollination.

Water (Hydrophily):

- ***Water:*** In aquatic plants, pollen is released into the water, and currents aid in its transport to female reproductive organs.

Mammals:

- ***Bats:*** In some regions, bats are important pollinators. They are attracted to night-blooming flowers with a strong odor and consume nectar while transferring pollen.

Other Insects:

- ***Beetles:*** Although not as efficient as bees, some beetles play a role in pollination, particularly in plants with large, bowl-shaped flowers.

Human Activities (Anthropophily):

- ***Humans:*** In agricultural settings, humans play a role in pollination, especially in the cultivation of crops such as fruits and vegetables. Controlled pollination by humans can enhance crop yield and quality.

Each of these pollination agents has unique characteristics that influence the type of flowers they visit, the distance they travel, and the effectiveness of pollen transfer. The diversity of pollination strategies reflects the adaptability of plants to their environments and the co-evolution with their respective pollinators.

5. (*d*) Four Examples of Old-World Plant Species with Their Botanical Names, which have been Cultivated for:

(*i*) Over 4000 years:

- Emmer Wheat (Triticum dicoccum): Botanical Name: Triticum dicoccum

  Cultivation Duration: Emmer wheat is one of the earliest cultivated wheat varieties and has been grown for over 4000 years. It was a staple crop in ancient civilizations and played a significant role in early agriculture.

- Barley (Hordeum vulgare):

Botanical Name: Hordeum vulgare

Cultivation Duration: Barley, one of the oldest cultivated grains, has been grown for over 4000 years. It was a crucial food source in ancient civilizations and continues to be used for food, fodder, and malt production.

- **Flax (Linum usitatissimum):**

  Botanical Name: Linum usitatissimum

Cultivation Duration: Flax has a history of cultivation that spans over 4000 years. It is primarily grown for its fibers, which are used to produce linen, and its seeds, which yield flaxseed oil.

- **Olive (Olea europaea):**

  Botanical Name: Olea europaea

Cultivation Duration: Olives have been cultivated for over 4000 years in the Mediterranean region. The trees are valued for their fruit, which is pressed to produce olive oil, and they hold cultural and symbolic significance.

(*ii*) Over 2000 years:

- **Rice (Oryza sativa):**

  Botanical Name: Oryza sativa

  Cultivation Duration: Rice has been cultivated for over 2000 years, particularly in Asia. It is a staple food for a large portion of the world's population and has played a crucial role in the development of various ancient civilizations.

- **Grapes (Vitis vinifera):**
  Botanical Name: Vitis vinifera
  Cultivation Duration: Grapes have a history of cultivation exceeding 2000 years. They are primarily grown for the production of wine, raisins, and table grapes. Vitis vinifera is the principal species used in winemaking.
- **Sesame (Sesamum indicum):**
  Botanical Name: Sesamum indicum
  Cultivation Duration: Sesame has been cultivated for over 2000 years and is valued for its seeds, which yield sesame oil. It is used in culinary applications and has historical significance in various cultures.
- **Figs (Ficus carica):**
  Botanical Name: Ficus carica
  Cultivation Duration: Figs have been cultivated for over 2000 years, with evidence of their consumption dating back to ancient times. The fruit is consumed fresh or dried and has been part of traditional diets in many regions.

These plant species have a rich history of cultivation, contributing not only to food but also to cultural practices and economies. Their resilience and adaptability have made them enduring components of human agriculture and diet over the course of centuries.

5. (*e*) **Somaclonal and Gametoclonal Variants and their Applications:** Somaclonal and gametoclonal variants represent fascinating avenues within the realm of plant biotechnology, offering innovative approaches to harness genetic diversity and manipulate plant traits. Somaclonal variation arises from the tissue culture of somatic cells, leading to genetic modifications that can be advantageous for crop improvement and stress resilience. On the other hand, gametoclonal variation involves the selection and regeneration of plants from gametic cells, providing opportunities for rapid generation advancement and the creation of novel genetic combinations. These distinct variants hold significant promise for applications in agriculture, enabling advancements in crop breeding, stress tolerance, and the understanding of plant genetics. This exploration of somaclonal and gametoclonal variants underscores their pivotal roles in shaping the future of sustainable and resilient crop production.

Somaclonal Variants: Somaclonal variation refers to genetic variations that arise in plants derived from somatic tissues, typically through tissue culture methods such as callus or cell culture.

Applications:

- ***Crop Improvement:*** Somaclonal variation can lead to the development of plants with desirable traits, such as resistance to diseases, improved stress tolerance, or altered growth habits. This variation can be exploited for crop improvement through the selection and propagation of superior somaclonal variants.
- ***Stress Tolerance:*** Somaclonal variants may exhibit enhanced tolerance to environmental stresses, such as drought, salinity, or temperature extremes. This can be valuable in developing crops with increased resilience to challenging growing conditions.
- ***Disease Resistance:*** Somaclonal variation can result in plants with increased resistance to specific pathogens. This can be crucial in developing cultivars with improved disease resistance, reducing the need for chemical treatments.
- ***Genetic Studies:*** Somaclonal variation provides a platform for studying the genetic and epigenetic mechanisms underlying variation. It can be used to investigate the role of specific genes in plant

development, stress response, and other physiological processes.

Gametoclonal Variants: Gametoclonal variation refers to genetic variations that arise in plants through the selection and regeneration of plants from gametic cells, such as pollen or ovules.

Applications:

- ***Haploid Production:*** Gametoclonal variants can be used to produce haploid plants, which are plants with a single set of chromosomes. Haploid plants are valuable in plant breeding as they can be used to produce doubled haploid lines with homozygous genotypes.
- ***Genetic Manipulation:*** Gametoclonal variation allows for the manipulation of genetic material at the gametic level. This can be exploited for introducing specific genes or traits into a plant population.
- ***Rapid Generation Advancement:*** Gametoclonal variants can be used to accelerate the generation advancement process in plant breeding. By selecting and propagating plants with desirable traits directly from gametic cells, breeding cycles can be shortened.
- ***Genetic Diversity:*** Gametoclonal variation can contribute to the generation of genetic diversity within a breeding program. This diversity can be harnessed for the development of new crop varieties with improved traits.

6. (a) Differentiate between the following:

(*i*) Liliaceae And Orchidaceae: Liliaceae and Orchidaceae are two distinct plant families, each characterized by unique features. Here are some key differences between the two:

Morphology:

- ***Liliaceae (Lily Family):*** Plants in the Liliaceae family typically have simple, linear leaves with parallel venation. The flowers are often large and showy, with six petal-like tepals arranged in two whorls of three.
- ***Orchidaceae (Orchid Family):*** Orchids exhibit a wide range of morphological diversity. Their leaves can be simple or compound, and they often have a distinctive bilateral symmetry. Orchid flowers are often complex and showy, with unique structures such as a modified lip (labellum) and a specialized column.

Flower Structure:

- ***Liliaceae:*** Flowers usually have six petal-like tepals (undifferentiated petals and sepals). The floral parts are typically in multiples of three.
- ***Orchidaceae:*** Orchid flowers are bilaterally symmetrical and consist of three sepals and three petals, but one petal is highly modified into a lip (labellum). The specialized reproductive column is a distinctive feature.

Inflorescence:

- ***Liliaceae:*** Inflorescences are often racemes or spikes, with flowers arranged along a central stem.
- ***Orchidaceae:*** Orchids exhibit various types of inflorescences, including spikes, racemes, and panicles. The arrangement of flowers depends on the orchid species.

Pollination Mechanism:

- ***Liliaceae:*** Lilies and related plants are often pollinated by bees and other insects. They typically produce nectar to attract pollinators.
- ***Orchidaceae:*** Orchids employ diverse pollination mechanisms, including mimicry of female insects to attract pollinators, or the production of attractants like scent and visual cues.

Habitat:

- ***Liliaceae:*** Lilies and related plants are found in a variety of habitats, including meadows, woodlands, and gardens.

- ***Orchidaceae:*** Orchids exhibit a wide range of ecological adaptations and are found in diverse habitats such as tropical rainforests, temperate woodlands, and even deserts.

Economic Importance:

- ***Liliaceae:*** Some members, like onions and garlic, are economically important as food crops.
- ***Orchidaceae:*** Orchids are often prized for their ornamental value, and some species are used in the production of vanilla and traditional medicines.

While both Liliaceae and Orchidaceae encompass diverse plant species, these differences highlight the distinct characteristics that set them apart in terms of morphology, floral structure, and ecological adaptations.

(ii) **Cucurbitaceae and Euphorbiaceae:** Cucurbitaceae and Euphorbiaceae are two distinct plant families with notable differences in terms of morphology, habitat, and economic importance. Here are some key distinctions between the two:

Morphology:

- ***Cucurbitaceae (Gourd or Cucumber Family):*** Plants in the Cucurbitaceae family are often vines with tendrils. Leaves are typically simple and palmately lobed or compound. Flowers are usually unisexual, and the fruits are often fleshy, with a hard outer rind or a pepo-type fruit (like in pumpkins and cucumbers).
- ***Euphorbiaceae (Spurge Family):*** Euphorbiaceae includes a diverse range of plants, some of which are trees, shrubs, or herbs. The leaves vary widely in shape, and the flowers are typically unisexual. Many species in this family have a unique glandular structure called a cyathium, which is a modified inflorescence.

Latex Production:

- ***Cucurbitaceae*:** Generally, members of this family do not produce latex.
- ***Euphorbiaceae:*** Many plants in this family produce latex, a milky sap that can be toxic or irritating to the skin. The presence of latex is a characteristic feature of Euphorbiaceae.

Floral Structure:

- ***Cucurbitaceae:*** Flowers are often large, and the plants are monoecious or dioecious, meaning individual plants have either male or female flowers.
- ***Euphorbiaceae:*** Flowers are small and often inconspicuous, arranged in cyathia. These inflorescences may have both male and female flowers.

Economic Importance:

- ***Cucurbitaceae:*** Economically important members include cucumbers (Cucumis sativus), pumpkins (Cucurbita pepo), watermelons (Citrullus lanatus), and melons (Cucumis melo).
- ***Euphorbiaceae:*** Some members of this family have economic importance, such as the rubber tree (Hevea brasiliensis) for latex production, castor bean (Ricinus communis) for castor oil, and Jatropha curcas for biodiesel production.

Distribution:

- ***Cucurbitaceae:*** Found in various habitats, including tropical and subtropical regions, and often cultivated for food.
- ***Euphorbiaceae:*** Widespread family with members found in diverse habitats, including tropical and subtropical regions, as well as temperate zones.

In summary, while both Cucurbitaceae and Euphorbiaceae are plant families with economic significance, they differ in terms of morphology, latex production, floral structure, and the types of plants they include. Cucurbitaceae is known for its vining plants with fleshy fruits, while Euphorbiaceae encompasses a diverse range of plants, some of which produce latex and have unique inflorescences.

6. (*b*) (*i*) Timber: Two timber-yielding plants along with their botanical names, family, and parts commonly used:

Teak:

Botanical Name: *Tectona grandis*

Family: Lamiaceae (formerly placed in Verbenaceae)

Parts Used: The primary timber-yielding part is the hardwood from the trunk. Teak wood is highly valued for its durability, strength, and resistance to decay. It is commonly used in the construction of furniture, boats, flooring, and outdoor structures.

Mahogany:

Botanical Name: *Swietenia macrophylla* (also Swietenia mahagoni for American or West Indian mahogany)

Family: Meliaceae

Parts Used: The timber comes from the heartwood of the trunk. Mahogany wood is known for its rich reddish-brown colour, durability, and fine grain. It is widely used in high-quality furniture, cabinetry, musical instruments, and boat construction.

Both teak and mahogany are prized for their excellent timber qualities, making them valuable resources in the woodworking industry. They are known for their durability, resistance to decay, and attractive appearance, which makes them preferred choices for various applications in construction and craftsmanship.

6. (*b*) (*ii*) Millets: Two millets-yielding plants along with their botanical names, family, and parts commonly used:

Pearl Millet:

Botanical Name: *Pennisetum glaucum*

Family: Poaceae (Grass family)

Parts Used: The seeds, or grains, of pearl millet are the primary edible part. Pearl millet is a major cereal crop in arid and semi-arid regions, and its grains are used for human consumption, as well as for fodder.

Foxtail Millet:

Botanical Name: *Setaria italica*

Family: Poaceae (Grass family)

Parts Used: The seeds of foxtail millet are the primary part used for consumption. The grains are rich in carbohydrates and are commonly used in various culinary preparations, including porridge, flatbreads, and as a rice substitute.

Both pearl millet and foxtail millet are important food crops, especially in regions with challenging growing conditions. They are valued for their nutritional content, resilience to drought, and versatility in culinary applications. The seeds of these millets serve as staple foods for many communities and contribute to global food security.

6. (*c*) (*iii*) Two spices obtained from below-ground parts yielding plants along with their botanical names, family, and commonly used parts:

Turmeric:

Botanical Name: *Curcuma longa*

Family: Zingiberaceae (Ginger family)

Parts Used: The rhizomes (underground stems) of turmeric are the primary part used. These rhizomes are harvested, dried, and ground to produce the bright yellow spice commonly used in culinary and medicinal applications.

Ginger:

Botanical Name: *Zingiber officinale*

Family: Zingiberaceae (Ginger family)

Parts Used: The rhizomes of ginger are the commonly used part. Similar to turmeric, ginger rhizomes are harvested and used either fresh or dried. Ginger is a versatile spice used in cooking, baking, and for its medicinal properties.

Both turmeric and ginger belong to the Zingiberaceae family and are renowned for their distinct flavors, aromatic qualities, and various health benefits. These spices are integral to many cuisines worldwide and are used in a range of dishes, from savory to sweet. Additionally, they have been traditionally used for their medicinal properties in different cultures.

6. (*c*) Differentiation between Intraxylary Phloem and Interxylary Phloem with the help of Suitable Diagram and Examples:

Interxylary phloem is defined as strands or bands of phloem embedded within the secondary xylem of a stem or root of a plant that has a single vascular cambium. In this definition, interxylary phloem differs from intraxylary phloem, bicollateral bundles, pith bundles, and successive cambia.

Intraxylary Phloem: The intraxylary phloem involves the production of phloem in the pith's periphery. In Combretum Loefl. (Combretaceae) intraxylary phloem (internal phloem) and/or interxylary phloem (included phloem) may be present. The occurrence of intraxylary phloem is a synapomorphy of the order Myrtales, to which the Combretaceae belong.

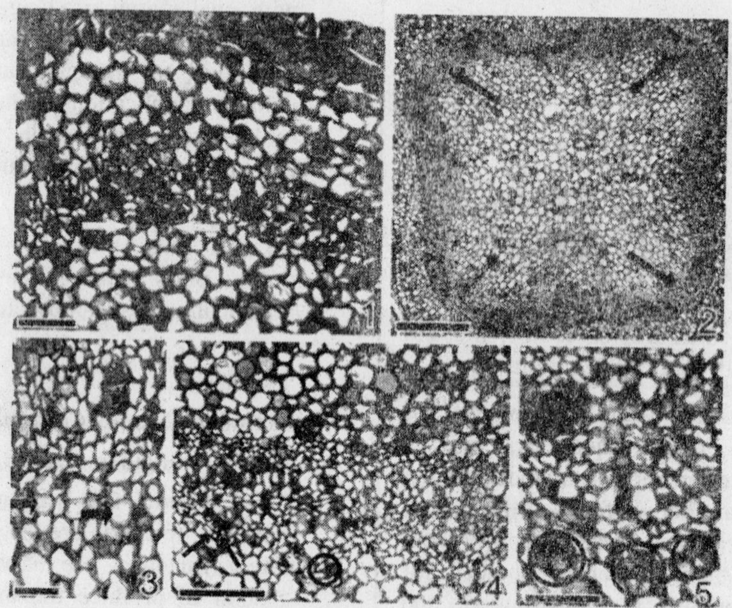

Fig.: *Transverse sections of young stem showing development of perimedullary procambium and intraxylary phloem in Combretum rotundifolium. 1. First visible protoxylem elements (arrow) and parenchyma cells bordering the protoxylem. 2. Overview of third internode with depressed areas lacking perimedullary procambium (arrows) in the vascular system. 3. Detail of figure 2, showing a depressed area without perimedullary procambium, with protoxylem (arrows) and parenchyma cells right below. 4. Detail of figure 2, with collateral bundles and perimedullary procambium (arrows) with low activity, producing the first phloem cells (circle). 5. Isolated strands of intraxylary phloem (circles) from perimedullary procambium. Scale bar for 1, 3 & 5 = 25 μm; for 2 & 4 = 50 μm.*

Interxylary Phloem: Interxylary phloem is the presence of phloem strands embedded within the secondary xylem (wood), and produced by the activity of a single cambium. Stems with this cambial variant are also referred to as foraminate, due to the conspicuous interxylary phloem strands in the shape of dots scattered within the wood. (Fig.1A). However, the presence of interxylary phloem is sometimes less evident and can only be confirmed by microscopy.

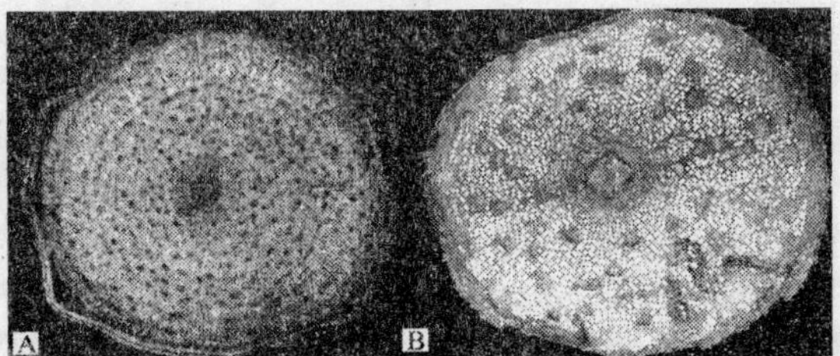

Fig. Stem cross-section of Strychnos (Loganiaceae). **A.** *S. guianensis, macroscopic view.* **B.** *S. millepunctata, microscopic view.*

PAPER-II

1. (*a*) Nuclear Pore Complex: The Nuclear Pore Complex (NPC) is a remarkable cellular structure that serves as the gateway between the nucleus and the cytoplasm in eukaryotic cells. Composed of a multitude of proteins known as nucleoporins, the NPC forms a large channel within the nuclear envelope, facilitating the selective transport of macromolecules such as proteins and RNA. This complex and dynamic assembly is essential for maintaining cellular function, gene expression, and overall homeostasis. Functionally, the NPC acts as a selective barrier, regulating the movement of molecules based on size, charge, and specific transport signals. It allows small molecules to diffuse passively while requiring active transport facilitated by transport receptors for larger macromolecules. The intricate interplay of nucleoporins and the regulation of nucleocytoplasmic transport are vital for cellular health.

Disruptions in NPC function have been associated with various diseases, including certain cancers and neurodegenerative disorders, underscoring the importance of understanding its molecular intricacies. Research on the NPC not only sheds light on fundamental cellular processes but also holds potential for identifying therapeutic targets. In essence, the Nuclear Pore Complex stands as a testament to the elegance of cellular architecture and the intricacies of molecular regulation, embodying the sophistication of eukaryotic cell biology. Its study continues to unravel the mysteries of cellular function and has far-reaching implications for both basic science and medical research.

1. (*b*) Microtubule Binding Proteins: Microtubule binding proteins (MBPs) play critical roles in the dynamic and versatile functions of microtubules, which are essential components of the eukaryotic cytoskeleton. Microtubules are dynamic polymers of tubulin subunits that form a network of tracks within cells, influencing cellular shape, providing structural support, and participating in intracellular transport. MBPs interact with microtubules, modulating their stability, organization, and dynamics. Here are key notes on microtubule binding proteins:

- ***Stabilizing Microtubules:*** Some MBPs act as microtubule stabilizers by binding to and protecting microtubules from depolymerization. Tau and MAP2 (microtubule-associated proteins) are examples of stabilizing MBPs. These proteins are crucial for maintaining the structural integrity of neuronal processes.
- ***Motor Proteins:*** Motor proteins, such as kinesins and dyneins, are MBPs that utilize the energy derived from ATP hydrolysis

to move along microtubules. Kinesins generally move towards the microtubule's plus end, while dyneins move towards the minus end. These motor proteins are vital for intracellular transport of organelles, vesicles, and other cellular cargo.

- ***Regulating Dynamics:*** Microtubule dynamics, including polymerization and depolymerization, are finely tuned by MBPs. Proteins like stathmin and EB (end-binding proteins) modulate microtubule dynamics by promoting depolymerization or capping growing microtubule ends, respectively.
- ***Cell Division:*** MBPs are integral to cell division processes. Centrosomes, organizing centers for microtubules, contain γ-tubulin ring complexes that nucleate microtubules. Motor proteins assist in chromosome segregation during mitosis.
- ***Cell Signaling:*** MBPs also participate in cell signaling pathways. For instance, the adenomatous polyposis coli (APC) protein serves a dual role by regulating both microtubule dynamics and acting as a tumor suppressor involved in Wnt signaling.
- ***Neuronal Function:*** In neurons, microtubule-associated proteins like MAP2 and Tau contribute to the organization of microtubules in axons and dendrites. Dysregulation of these proteins has been linked to neurodegenerative disorders, such as Alzheimer's disease.
- ***Cancer and Therapeutic Targets:*** Aberrant expression or mutations in MBPs are associated with various cancers. Targeting microtubules and their binding proteins is a common strategy in cancer chemotherapy, exemplified by taxanes like paclitaxel.

Understanding the intricate interactions between microtubules and their binding proteins is crucial for unraveling the complexities of cellular structure, function, and dynamics. The diverse roles of MBPs highlight their significance in both normal cellular physiology and pathological conditions, making them attractive targets for therapeutic interventions in various diseases.

1. (*c*) Substitution Mutation: A substitution mutation is a type of genetic mutation in which one nucleotide in a DNA sequence is replaced by another. This alteration can result in various outcomes, depending on the specific nucleotide substitution and its location within a gene. Substitution mutations can be classified into two main types: transitions and transversions.

- ***Transitions***: Transitions involve the replacement of a purine base (adenine or guanine) with another purine or a pyrimidine base (thymine or cytosine) with another pyrimidine. This type of substitution maintains the overall size and structure of the DNA molecule. For example, an adenine-thymine (A-T) base pair may be replaced by a guanine-cytosine (G-C) pair.
- ***Transversions:*** Transversions, on the other hand, involve the substitution of a purine base with a pyrimidine or vice versa. This type of substitution results in a change in the overall shape of the DNA molecule. An example of a transversion is the replacement of an adenine-thymine (A-T) pair with a cytosine-guanine (C-G) pair.

Substitution mutations can have different consequences at the protein level, as the sequence of nucleotides in DNA determines the sequence of amino acids in a protein. Silent mutations may occur when the substitution does not lead to a change in the amino acid sequence due to the redundancy of the genetic code. Missense mutations result in the replacement of one amino acid with another, potentially altering the protein's function. Nonsense mutations introduce a premature stop codon, leading to the production of a truncated and often nonfunctional protein.

Substitution mutations can arise spontaneously or be induced by various factors such as exposure to mutagenic substances or errors during DNA replication. The impact of these mutations on an organism depends on the specific gene affected and the functional significance of the altered protein. Understanding substitution mutations is crucial in the study of genetics, evolution, and the development of genetic diseases.

1. (*d*) Functions of Ribosomes and Subunits: Ribosomes are essential cellular structures responsible for protein synthesis, a fundamental process in all living cells. They are composed of two subunits—large and small—that work in concert to carry out the intricate task of translating genetic information from messenger RNA (mRNA) into functional proteins. Here are the functions of ribosomes and their subunits:

- ***Protein Synthesis:*** The primary and most crucial function of ribosomes is to synthesize proteins by reading the information encoded in the mRNA. This process, known as translation, occurs in two main steps: initiation, elongation, and termination. The small subunit is responsible for recognizing and binding to the mRNA, while the large subunit catalyzes the formation of peptide bonds between amino acids, leading to the synthesis of a polypeptide chain.
- ***Initiation of Protein Synthesis:*** The small ribosomal subunit binds to the mRNA's start codon, and initiator tRNA carrying the amino acid methionine associates with this complex. The large subunit then joins, forming a functional ribosome that is ready to commence protein synthesis.
- ***Elongation of Polypeptide Chain:*** During elongation, the ribosome moves along the mRNA, reading the codons and facilitating the binding of appropriate tRNA molecules carrying complementary amino acids. The large subunit catalyzes the formation of peptide bonds between adjacent amino acids, leading to the extension of the growing polypeptide chain.
- ***Termination of Protein Synthesis:*** The process concludes when the ribosome encounters a stop codon on the mRNA. Release factors aid in the termination process, causing the release of the newly synthesized protein from the ribosome. The ribosomal subunits then dissociate, ready to engage in another round of protein synthesis.
- ***Subunit Interactions:*** The interaction between the small and large subunits is crucial for the proper functioning of ribosomes. The small subunit is responsible for mRNA recognition and binding, while the large subunit facilitates the peptidyl transferase activity required for peptide bond formation. Together, they create a functional ribosome that orchestrates protein synthesis.
- ***Regulation of Gene Expression:*** Ribosomes can influence gene expression by selectively translating specific mRNAs based on regulatory signals. The availability and interaction of ribosomal subunits contribute to the regulation of protein production in response to cellular needs and environmental cues.

In summary, ribosomes, composed of small and large subunits, are central to the synthesis of proteins in cells. Their coordinated actions during initiation, elongation, and termination of protein synthesis highlight their pivotal role in maintaining cellular function and integrity. Understanding the functions of ribosomes and their subunits is crucial for unraveling the complexities of cellular processes and molecular biology.

1. ***(e)* Nuclear Male Sterile Lines for Hybrid Seed Production:** Nuclear Male Sterile Lines (NMSLs) play a pivotal role in modern agriculture, particularly in the context of hybrid seed production. Male sterility, the inability of a plant to produce viable pollen, is a trait that has been harnessed and controlled through nuclear genes to create these specialized lines. The significance of NMSLs in hybrid seed production lies in their ability to enhance heterosis, leading to improved crop performance and yield. The resulting F1 hybrid plants exhibit heightened vigor and uniformity, contributing to more reliable and desirable agricultural outcomes. The mechanism underlying nuclear male sterility involves the interaction of specific genes within the nuclear genome. Researchers have made significant strides in identifying and isolating these genes, unraveling the molecular basis of male sterility. The intricate interplay between cytoplasmic and nuclear genomes adds another layer of complexity to this phenomenon. Developing NMSLs involves careful selection of sterility genes, employing breeding strategies such as backcrossing with fertile lines and pedigree breeding for stability. Marker-assisted selection, utilizing molecular markers, has emerged as an efficient tool in this process, facilitating the identification and tracking of desired traits. Despite the advantages NMSLs offer in hybrid seed production, their maintenance poses challenges. The development of restorer lines, which possess genes capable of restoring fertility in the hybrid progeny, is a critical aspect. Environmental factors can also influence the expression of male sterility, requiring careful consideration and management. Genetic drift, the gradual changes in allele frequencies over generations, necessitates vigilant efforts to maintain the genetic purity of NMSLs. Applications of NMSLs extend across various crop species, including cereals like rice, wheat, and maize, vegetables such as tomato, pepper, and eggplant, as well as oilseeds like canola and sunflower. Ongoing research and technological advancements, particularly in gene editing technologies like CRISPR/Cas, hold promise for refining and expanding the utility of NMSLs. Integrating these developments with genomic tools enhances the precision and efficiency of breeding programs.

2. **(*a*) Process of Membrane Transport:** Membrane transport refers to the movement of substances across cell membranes. There are two main types of membrane transport: passive transport and active transport.

(*a*) Passive Transport:

Diffusion:

- ***Simple Diffusion:*** This is the movement of molecules from an area of higher concentration to an area of lower concentration. It occurs through the lipid bilayer of the membrane for small, nonpolar molecules.
- ***Facilitated Diffusion:*** This process involves the movement of substances across the membrane with the help of transport proteins. Channel proteins and carrier proteins facilitate the passage of specific ions and molecules.

Osmosis: Osmosis is the passive movement of water molecules across a selectively permeable membrane from an area of lower solute concentration to an area of higher solute concentration. The movement of water is driven by the concentration gradient of solutes.

Filtration: Filtration involves the movement of water and solutes through a membrane due to a mechanical force, such as pressure. It is common in processes like kidney filtration, where blood pressure forces water and small molecules through capillary walls.

(*b*) Active Transport:

Primary Active Transport: In primary active transport, energy derived from the hydrolysis of ATP (adenosine triphosphate) is directly used to pump ions or molecules against their concentration gradient. Examples include the sodium-potassium pump, which actively transports sodium ions out of the cell and potassium ions into the cell.

Secondary Active Transport (Coupled Transport): Secondary active transport utilizes the energy stored in an ion concentration gradient (established by primary active transport) to drive the transport of other substances against their concentration gradient. There are two types:

- ***Symport:*** Two substances are transported in the same direction.
- ***Antiport:*** Two substances are transported in opposite directions.

Bulk Transport:

Endocytosis: The cell engulfs substances by wrapping its membrane around them, forming vesicles. There are two main types:

- ***Phagocytosis:*** Cell "eating", where solid particles are engulfed.
- ***Pinocytosis:*** Cell "drinking", where small droplets of extracellular fluid are taken in.

Exocytosis: Intracellular vesicles fuse with the cell membrane, releasing their contents outside the cell.

The processes of membrane transport are crucial for maintaining cellular homeostasis, regulating the internal environment, and allowing cells to interact with their surroundings.

How do carrier molecules transport across a cell membrane: Carrier molecules play a pivotal role in the facilitated diffusion and active transport of substances across cell membranes. These specialized proteins are integral to the selective and controlled movement of ions, molecules, and other essential compounds into and out of cells. The process involves the binding of the specific substance to the carrier protein, which undergoes conformational changes to facilitate the transport across the membrane.

In facilitated diffusion, carrier proteins assist the movement of specific molecules across the membrane down their concentration gradient. The substrate, often a larger or polar molecule, binds to the carrier protein at a specific binding site. This binding induces a conformational change in the carrier protein, allowing the molecule to be transported across the membrane to the side with a lower concentration. Importantly, facilitated diffusion does not require energy input, as it relies on the existing concentration gradient.

Active transport, on the other hand, utilizes carrier proteins to move substances against their concentration gradient, necessitating the expenditure of energy, typically derived from adenosine triphosphate (ATP). In primary active transport, the carrier protein directly utilizes energy from ATP to pump ions or molecules across the membrane. For instance, the sodium-potassium pump actively transports sodium ions out of the cell and potassium ions into the cell, maintaining the cell's electrochemical gradient. Secondary active transport, also known as coupled transport, involves carrier proteins that utilize the energy generated by the primary active transport of ions. This energy is harnessed to transport other substances against their concentration gradients. Symporters transport two different substances in the same direction, while antiporters move two substances in opposite directions. This coordinated movement ensures efficient nutrient uptake and waste removal, contributing to cellular function and homeostasis. In summary, carrier molecules are integral to the dynamic processes of facilitated diffusion and active transport, ensuring the controlled and selective movement of substances across cell membranes. These proteins exhibit specificity for certain molecules, undergo conformational changes upon binding, and play a crucial role in maintaining the delicate balance of cellular environments essential for proper cell function.

2. (*b*) Extranuclear Inheritance Citing Examples from Two Different Organelles: Extranuclear inheritance refers to the unique transmission of genetic information through organelles outside the cell nucleus. Two primary examples of extranuclear inheritance are mitochondrial DNA (mtDNA) and chloroplast DNA (cpDNA). Mitochondria, the energy-producing organelles in eukaryotic cells, contain their own small circular DNA distinct from nuclear DNA. The inheritance of mtDNA follows a maternal pattern, with mitochondria typically passed down from the mother due to the degradation of paternal mitochondria during fertilization. Chloroplasts, responsible for photosynthesis in plants and certain algae, also possess circular DNA and exhibit maternal inheritance. During plant fertilization, chloroplasts from pollen are typically excluded, resulting in the inheritance of cpDNA exclusively from the mother. Understanding extranuclear inheritance is crucial for unraveling evolutionary relationships and has significant implications for studying genetic diversity, maternal lineages, and the role of organelles in cellular function and adaptation. [Extranuclear inheritance refers to the transmission of genetic information through non-nuclear genetic elements, specifically from organelles outside the cell nucleus. While the majority of an organism's genetic material is located in the cell nucleus, there are genetic elements in other cellular structures, such as mitochondria and chloroplasts, that also play a crucial role in inheritance]. The two main examples of extranuclear inheritance are mitochondrial DNA (mtDNA) and chloroplast DNA (cpDNA). Let's explore these in detail:

Mitochondrial DNA (mtDNA):

- *Location:* Mitochondria are membrane-bound organelles found in the cytoplasm of eukaryotic cells.
- *Genetic Material:* Mitochondria have their own small circular DNA molecules, separate from the nuclear DNA.
- *Inheritance Pattern:* Maternal Inheritance—In most animals, mitochondria are inherited exclusively from the mother. This is because the mitochondria in the sperm are usually degraded during fertilization, while the mitochondria in the egg are retained.
- *Mutation Accumulation:* Due to the high rate of oxidative metabolism occurring in mitochondria, and the lack of sophisticated DNA repair mechanisms, mtDNA is more prone to mutations. These mutations can lead to various mitochondrial diseases.

Chloroplast DNA (cpDNA):

- *Location:* Chloroplasts are present in plant cells and some algae, where they are responsible for photosynthesis.
- *Genetic Material:* Chloroplasts, like mitochondria, have their own circular DNA.
- *Inheritance Pattern: Maternal Inheritance*—Similar to mitochondria, chloroplasts are usually inherited from the mother in plants. During fertilization, the chloroplasts in the pollen are generally excluded from the fertilized egg.
- *Genetic Variation:* Chloroplast DNA is often used in studies related to plant evolution and taxonomy due to its maternal inheritance and slower mutation rates compared to nuclear DNA.

Significance: Extranuclear inheritance has implications for the study of evolutionary relationships and phylogenetic analysis, especially in plants. The maternal inheritance pattern of extranuclear DNA allows researchers to trace maternal lineages over generations.

Challenges: Extranuclear DNA has a higher mutation rate compared to nuclear DNA, which can lead to the accumulation of genetic changes over time.

The uniparental inheritance pattern (maternal inheritance) makes it challenging to create genetic hybrids with specific combinations of nuclear and extranuclear genes.

In summary, extranuclear inheritance involves the transmission of genetic information from organelles outside the cell nucleus, with mitochondrial DNA and chloroplast DNA being prominent examples. The maternal inheritance pattern is a key feature, impacting the study of evolution, genetics, and lineage tracing in various organisms.

2. (*c*) Different Stages Involved in Micropropagation: Micropropagation, also known as plant tissue culture, is an advanced plant propagation technique that enables the rapid and precise reproduction of plants under sterile laboratory conditions. The process begins with the careful selection of a suitable plant species and the collection of small plant parts, known as explants, from a donor plant. These explants undergo rigorous surface sterilization to eliminate contaminants. The aseptic explants are then placed in a nutrient-rich culture medium containing specific plant growth regulators to stimulate cell division and differentiation. Through successive stages of multiplication, shoot initiation, shoot multiplication, and rooting, a large number of genetically identical plantlets can be produced from a single explant. The developed plantlets are acclimatized to *ex vitro* conditions before being transplanted into the natural environment. Micropropagation offers several advantages, including the production of disease-free plants, rapid multiplication, and the preservation of desirable genetic traits. This technique has significant applications in agriculture, horticulture, and conservation efforts for rare and endangered plant species.

Micropropagation is a method used to propagate plants asexually using small plant parts, such as shoot tips or nodal segments, under sterile conditions. The process involves several stages to achieve successful propagation. Here are the typical stages involved in micropropagation:

- ***Initiation or Explant Selection:*** Selection of a suitable plant species and cultivar. Collection of explants (small plant parts) from the selected donor plant. Common explants include shoot tips, nodal segments, or meristematic tissue.
- ***Surface Sterilization:*** The collected explants are subjected to surface sterilization to eliminate any contaminants. This is usually done using a combination of disinfectants like bleach or ethanol.
- ***Establishment of Aseptic Culture:*** The sterile explants are placed in a culture medium containing nutrients, vitamins, and plant growth regulators (hormones) under aseptic conditions. This culture medium is designed to support the growth of plant cells and tissues.
- ***Multiplication or Proliferation:*** The explants start to multiply and form a mass of undifferentiated cells called a callus. This callus is then subcultured onto fresh media to promote further cell division.
- ***Shoot Initiation:*** From the callus, shoot buds or shoots are induced by manipulating the concentration of plant growth regulators in the culture medium.
- ***Shoot Multiplication:*** The developed shoots are subcultured onto a new medium

to encourage further multiplication. This stage helps in obtaining a large number of shoots from a single explant.

- ***Rooting:*** The multiplied shoots are transferred to a rooting medium, which contains a different hormonal composition to stimulate the development of roots.
- ***Acclimatization:*** Once rooted, the plantlets are gradually acclimatized to *ex vitro* conditions (outside the culture vessel) by exposing them to ambient humidity and light. This is a critical step for the survival of the plants when transferred to the natural environment.
- ***Transplantation***: Finally, the successfully acclimatized plantlets are ready for transplantation to the field or greenhouse, where they can grow into mature plants.

Throughout these stages, strict aseptic techniques are maintained to prevent contamination by microorganisms. The composition of the culture media is adjusted at each stage to promote the specific growth and development required for the next phase in the micropropagation process.

4. (*a*) Detailed Account of Direct Gene Transfer Methods: Direct gene transfer methods are techniques used to introduce foreign genetic material into the cells of an organism without relying on conventional methods such as sexual reproduction. Among these methods, electroporation is a commonly employed technique. In electroporation, electric pulses create temporary pores in the cell membrane, allowing DNA to enter the cell. Another method is microinjection, where a fine needle injects genetic material directly into the nucleus or cytoplasm of the target cells. Particle bombardment, or biolistics, is a unique approach in which DNA-coated microprojectiles are shot into the target cells using high-velocity particles. Additionally, liposome-mediated gene transfer involves encapsulating genetic material within lipid vesicles that fuse with the cell membrane, releasing the DNA into the cell. These direct gene transfer methods are pivotal in genetic engineering, biotechnology, and gene therapy, enabling precise control over the modification of an organism's genetic makeup for various purposes, including the development of genetically modified crops, the creation of transgenic animals, and the potential treatment of genetic disorders in humans. The term direct transfer of gene is used when the foreign DNA is directly introduced into the plant genome. Direct DNA transfer methods rely on the delivery of naked DNA into the plant cells. The direct gene transfer can be broadly divided into two categories.

A. Physical gene transfer methods—electroporation, microinjection, particle bombardment.

B. Chemical gene transfer methods—Poly-ethylene glycol (PEG)-mediated, diethyl amino ethyl (DEAE) dextran-mediated, calcium phosphate precipitation.

(A) Physical Gene Transfer Methods:

- ***Electroporation:*** This method involves suspension of plant protoplasts in a suitable ionic solution containing linearized recombinant plasmid DNA. This mixture is then exposed to low voltage-long pulses or high voltage short pulses for the desired number of cycles. The electrical pulses are thought to induce transient pores in the plasma lemma through which the DNA molecules are incorporated. Treated protoplasts are then cultured to obtain cell colonies and plants. This method is called electroporation (i.e. introduction of DNA into plant cells by making minute pores in the plant cell membrane).
- ***Microinjection:*** Microinjection is a direct physical method involving the mechanical insertion of the desirable DNA into a target cell. The target cell may be the one identified from intact cells, protoplasts,

callus, embryos, meristems, etc. Microinjection is used for the transfer of cellular organelles and for the manipulation of chromosomes. The technique of microinjection involves the transfer of the gene through a micropipette (0.5-10.0 pm tip) into the cytoplasm/nucleus of a plant cell or protoplast. While the gene transfer is done, the recipient cells are kept immobilized in agarose embedding, and held by a suction holding pipette. As the process of microinjection is complete, the transformed cell is cultured and grown to develop into a transgenic plant. In fact, transgenic tobacco and Brassica napus have been developed by this approach. The major limitations of microinjection are that it is slow, expensive, and has to be performed by trained and skilled personnel.

- **Particle Bombardment Gun Method (Biolistics):** Particle bombardment is the most effective method for gene transfer, and creation of transgenic plants. This method is versatile due to the fact that it can be successfully used for the DNA transfer in mammalian cells and microorganisms. The micro projectile bombardment method was initially named as biolistics by its inventor Sanford (1987). Biolistics is a combination of biological and ballistics. In this method, 1-2 μm gold or tungsten particles coated with DNA are shot into the plant cells using a helium pressure particle gun device. Important crop plants like, wheat, rice and maize have now been transformed by this method.

(B) Chemical Gene Transfer Methods: Polyethylene glycol (PEG)-mediated transfer: DNA molecules can be forced to enter into the host genome only in those cells which do not possess cell walls. The naked plant protoplasts are mixed with molecules of linearized plasmid DNA containing the foreign gene. The two are mixed in a transformation medium rich in Mg^{2+} ions in place of Ca^{2+} ions, following which 20% polyethylene glycol (PEG) solution is added. After the treatment, the PEG concentration is reduced and Ca^{2+} concentration is enhanced. It promotes the frequency of transformation.

The chemical method involving transformation in presence of polyethylene glycol is convenient and simple but there are, however, some disadvantages:

- Many cells are so sensitive that the chemical method cannot be applied whereas some cells die during the treatment.
- This method is not perfect because many treated cells do not contain any transfer DNA.
- Sometimes the foreign DNA is degraded in the cytoplasm before reaching the nucleus.

4. (*b*) Heterochromatin Genetically Active: Heterochromatin and euchromatin are two distinct types of chromatins, the complex of DNA and proteins that makes up chromosomes within a cell nucleus. While euchromatin is considered genetically active and involved in gene expression, heterochromatin is generally associated with gene silencing and inactivity. However, it's important to note that the relationship between chromatin structure and gene activity is more nuanced. Heterochromatin is a densely packed form of chromatin, and it is characterized by a tight, condensed structure that limits access to the underlying DNA. This condensed state is often associated with transcriptional repression, meaning that genes located within heterochromatin regions are less likely to be transcribed and expressed. Heterochromatin is typically found at the periphery of the nucleus and around the centromeres and telomeres of chromosomes. In contrast, euchromatin has a more open and relaxed structure, allowing for greater accessibility of the DNA. This open configuration facilitates the binding of transcriptional machinery, making it more conducive to gene expression. Euchromatin is often found in regions of the genome where active transcription and gene activity occur. However, the relationship between chromatin structure and gene activity is dynamic, and the distinction between heterochromatin and euchromatin is not absolute. Heterochromatin can undergo changes in response to cellular signals or developmental cues, leading to a loosening of its structure and increased gene activity. Additionally, certain modifications to the histone proteins associated with chromatin (epigenetic modifications) can influence whether a particular region is in a transcriptionally active or inactive state.

In summary, while heterochromatin is generally associated with transcriptional repression and inactivity, the regulation of gene expression is a complex interplay of various factors, and there are instances where heterochromatin regions can become transcriptionally active under specific conditions.

Functions and Features of Heterochromatin: Heterochromatin is a tightly packed form of DNA or condensed DNA, which comes in multiple varieties. These varieties lie on a continuum between the two extremes of constitutive heterochromatin and facultative heterochromatin. Both play a role in the expression of genes. Because it is tightly packed, it was thought to be inaccessible to polymerases and therefore not transcribed; however, according to Volpe et al. (2002), and many other papers since, much of this DNA is in fact transcribed, but it is continuously turned over via RNA-induced transcriptional silencing (RITS). Recent studies with electron microscopy and OsO_4 staining reveal that the dense packing is not due to the chromatin. Constitutive heterochromatin can affect the genes near itself (e.g. position-effect variegation). It is usually repetitive and forms structural functions such as centromeres or telomeres, in addition to acting as an attractor for other gene-expression or repression signals. Facultative heterochromatin is the result of genes that are silenced through a mechanism such as histone deacetylation or Píwi-interacting RNA (piRNA) through RNAi. It is not repetitive and shares the compact structure of constitutive heterochromatin. However, under specific developmental or environmental signaling cues, it can lose its condensed structure and become transcriptionally active. Heterochromatin has been associated with the di- and tri -methylation of H3K9 in certain portions of the human genome. H3K9me3-related methyltransferases appear to have a pivotal role in modifying heterochromatin during lineage commitment at the onset of organogenesis and in maintaining lineage fidelity. Chromatin is found in two varieties: euchromatin and heterochromatin. Originally, the two forms were distinguished cytologically by how intensely they get stained – the euchromatin is less intense, while heterochromatin stains intensely, indicating tighter packing. Heterochromatin is usually localized to the periphery of the nucleus. Despite this early dichotomy, recent evidence in both animals and plants has suggested that there are more than two distinct heterochromatin states, and it may in fact exist in four or five 'states', each marked by different combinations of epigenetic marks. Heterochromatin mainly consists of genetically inactive satellite sequences, and many genes are repressed to various extents, although some cannot be expressed in euchromatin at all. Both centromeres and telomeres are heterochromatic, as is the Barr body of the second, inactivated X-chromosome in a female.

Here are some features of heterochromatin:

- ***Condensed Structure:*** Heterochromatin is characterized by a highly compact and condensed structure. The DNA in heterochromatin is tightly wound around histone proteins, making it less accessible to the cellular machinery involved in transcription.
- ***Transcriptional Repression:*** Heterochromatin is generally associated with transcriptional repression. The condensed structure limits the access of transcriptional machinery to the DNA, leading to reduced or silenced gene expression.
- ***Late Replication:*** Heterochromatin tends to replicate later in the cell cycle compared to euchromatin. This timing difference in replication is one of the factors contributing to the maintenance of its condensed state.
- ***Location at Specific Chromosomal Regions:*** Heterochromatin is often found in specific regions of the chromosomes, including near the centromeres and telomeres. These regions are important for chromosome structure and stability.
- ***Enrichment in Repetitive Sequences:*** Heterochromatin is often enriched in repetitive DNA sequences, such as satellite DNA and transposons. These repetitive elements contribute to the overall compactness of heterochromatin.
- ***Binding of Heterochromatin Proteins:*** Heterochromatin is associated with specific proteins, including heterochromatin protein 1 (HP1). These proteins play a role in maintaining the condensed structure and are involved in gene silencing.
- ***Epigenetic Modifications:*** Heterochromatin is marked by specific epigenetic modifications to histone proteins, such as histone methylation and histone deacetylation. These modifications contribute to the stable and repressive nature of heterochromatin.
- ***Nuclear Periphery Association:*** Heterochromatin is often localized near the nuclear periphery. This positioning may play a role in the organization of the nucleus and the regulation of gene expression.

4. (*c*) Difference Between Dominance and Epistasis: Dominance and epistasis are both concepts related to the interaction of genes, but they refer to different aspects of genetic inheritance.

Dominance:

- ***Definition:*** Dominance refers to the relationship between alleles of a single gene, where one allele (the dominant allele) masks or suppresses the expression of the other allele (the recessive allele) in a heterozygous individual.
- ***Phenotypic Expression:*** In a heterozygous genotype (Aa), the dominant allele (A) determines the phenotype, and the recessive allele (a) remains hidden. Both homozygous dominant (AA) and heterozygous (Aa) individuals exhibit the same dominant phenotype.
- ***Example:*** In Mendelian genetics, if a pea plant has a genotype of AA or Aa for the seed color gene (where A represents the dominant allele for yellow seeds and a represents the recessive allele for green seeds), the plant will have yellow seeds because the dominant allele (A) masks the expression of the recessive allele (a).

Epistasis:

- ***Definition:*** Epistasis involves the interaction between genes at different loci (gene locations) where the alleles of one gene mask or modify the expression of alleles of another gene.
- ***Multiple Genes:*** Unlike dominance, epistasis involves the interaction of alleles from different genes. It may occur in pathways where the product of one gene affects the expression of genes at subsequent steps.

- ***Complementary and Duplicate Epistasis:*** There are different types of epistasis, including complementary epistasis (where two dominant alleles are required for the expression of a particular trait) and duplicate epistasis (where either of two dominant alleles at different loci can produce the same phenotype).
- ***Example:*** In coat colour in Labrador Retrievers, the expression of the B gene determines whether the dog has black or brown fur. However, the E gene at a different locus control whether pigment is produced. If a dog is homozygous recessive (ee) for the E gene, it will have a yellow coat, regardless of the genotype at the B locus.

Dominance pertains to the relationship between alleles of a single gene, while epistasis involves the interaction of genes at different loci, where the alleles of one gene influence the expression of alleles at another gene. Both concepts contribute to the complexity and diversity of genetic traits observed in organisms.

Different Kinds of Epistatic Interactions: Epistasis, a term derived from the Greek word meaning "standing upon", refers to the intricate interplay between genes at different loci, where the expression of one gene influences or masks the phenotypic outcome of another. This phenomenon adds layers of complexity to the understanding of genetic interactions beyond simple Mendelian inheritance. Various kinds of epistatic interactions illustrate the nuanced ways in which genes collaborate or compete to shape the observable traits of an organism. From complementary epistasis, where the presence of specific alleles at one locus is indispensable for a particular phenotype, to suppressive epistasis, where certain alleles inhibit the expression of genes at other loci, these interactions provide insights into the intricate dance of genetic factors. In this genetic choreography, different types of epistasis contribute to the rich tapestry of inheritance patterns, adding depth to our comprehension of how genes collectively orchestrate the diverse characteristics observed in living organisms. Epistasis is a phenomenon in genetics where the effect of one gene masks or modifies the effect of another gene. There are several types of epistatic interactions, each describing a specific way in which genes at different loci can interact. Here are some common kinds of epistatic interactions:

- ***Complementary Epistasis:*** In complementary epistasis, the presence of at least one dominant allele at one locus is required for the expression of a particular phenotype. If an individual has two recessive alleles at the interacting locus, the phenotype will be different.
- ***Example:*** The flower color in some plants may be determined by two genes, A and B. The presence of at least one dominant allele at both loci (A_B_ or A_bb or aaB_) produces the colored phenotype, while the recessive alleles at both loci (aabb) result in a different phenotype.
- ***Duplicate (Redundant) Epistasis:*** In duplicate epistasis, there are multiple genes that can independently influence the same phenotype. The presence of dominant alleles at any one of these loci is sufficient to produce a particular phenotype.
- ***Example:*** The control of hair color in some mammals may involve multiple genes. The presence of dominant alleles at any one of these genes can result in the same hair color phenotype.
- ***Recessive Epistasis:*** Recessive epistasis occurs when the presence of homozygous recessive alleles at one gene locus masks the expression of another gene at a different locus, regardless of the genotype at the second locus.

- ***Example:*** Coat color in Labrador Retrievers is determined by two gene loci, B and E. The presence of homozygous recessive alleles (ee) at the E locus masks the expression of the B locus, leading to a yellow coat color regardless of the genotype at the B locus.
- ***Dominant Epistasis:*** Dominant epistasis occurs when the presence of at least one dominant allele at one gene locus masks the expression of another gene at a different locus.
- ***Example:*** In some cases of flower color determination, the presence of at least one dominant allele at a gene locus (let's call it gene C) masks the expression of another gene at a different locus (gene D), leading to a specific flower color.
- ***Suppressive Epistasis (Antagonistic Epistasis):*** In suppressive epistasis, the presence of a particular allele at one locus suppresses the expression of a gene at another locus, resulting in the inhibition of a specific phenotype.
- ***Example:*** The interaction between the Rb gene (which controls retinoblastoma) and the E2F gene is an example of suppressive epistasis. The Rb gene product inhibits the action of the E2F transcription factor.

These types of epistatic interactions highlight the complexity and variety of genetic relationships that contribute to the expression of phenotypes in organisms. Epistasis plays a crucial role in shaping the inheritance patterns observed in different traits.

5. (*a*) **Effects of Global Warming:** Global warming, driven primarily by human activities such as the burning of fossil fuels and deforestation, has profound and far-reaching effects on the Earth's climate and ecosystems. One of the most noticeable consequences is the rise in average global temperatures. As the planet warms, a cascade of interconnected impacts unfolds, affecting the environment, weather patterns, sea levels, and biodiversity.

Firstly, the warming climate contributes to the melting of glaciers and polar ice caps, leading to rising sea levels. This poses a significant threat to coastal areas and low-lying island nations, increasing the risk of flooding, erosion, and saltwater intrusion into freshwater sources. Small island nations and densely populated coastal regions face displacement and loss of habitat, exacerbating the challenge of climate-induced migration.

Secondly, changes in temperature and precipitation patterns have profound implications for ecosystems and biodiversity. Species may face challenges in adapting or migrating to more suitable habitats as their current environments undergo alterations. Coral reefs, vital marine ecosystems, are particularly vulnerable to temperature increases, leading to coral bleaching and a decline in marine biodiversity. Shifts in ecosystems can also affect the availability of resources for human populations, impacting agriculture, fisheries, and water supply.

Extreme weather events, including hurricanes, droughts, heatwaves, and wildfires, are becoming more frequent and intense due to global warming. These events pose direct threats to human safety, food security, and infrastructure. Disruptions in agricultural production, water scarcity, and increased vulnerability to natural disasters can result in economic losses and exacerbate social inequalities.

The warming of oceans contributes to changes in ocean currents and acidity levels. Ocean acidification, caused by the absorption of excess carbon dioxide, poses a threat to marine life, particularly organisms with calcium carbonate shells, such as corals, mollusks, and some plankton species. This has implications for the entire marine food web and can affect global fisheries and the livelihoods of communities dependent on them.

Global warming also influences the spread of infectious diseases. Warmer temperatures and altered precipitation patterns can expand the geographical range of disease vectors like mosquitoes, affecting the prevalence of diseases such as malaria, dengue fever, and Zika virus.

Mitigating the impacts of global warming requires international cooperation and concerted efforts to reduce greenhouse gas emissions, transition to renewable energy sources, and enhance resilience in vulnerable communities. The effects of global warming are a stark reminder of the urgent need for sustainable practices and a collective commitment to address climate change to safeguard the health of the planet and future generations.

5. (*b*) *z*-Test: A z test is conducted on a population that follows a normal distribution with independent data points and has a sample size that is greater than or equal to 30. It is used to check whether the means of two populations are equal to each other when the population variance is known. The null hypothesis of a z test can be rejected if the z test statistic is statistically significant when compared with the critical value.

The z test formula compares the z statistic with the z critical value to test whether there is a difference in the means of two populations. In hypothesis testing, the z critical value divides the distribution graph into the acceptance and the rejection regions. If the test statistic falls in the rejection region, then the null hypothesis can be rejected otherwise it cannot be rejected. The z test formula to set up the required hypothesis tests for a one sample is given below.

One-Sample *z* Test: A one-sample z test is used to check if there is a difference between the sample mean and the population mean when the population standard deviation is known. The formula for the z test statistic is given as follows:

$z = \dfrac{\overline{x}-\mu}{\dfrac{\sigma}{\sqrt{n}}}$. $\overline{X}$ is the sample mean, μ is the population mean, σ is the population standard deviation and n is the sample size.

The algorithm to set a one sample z test based on the z test statistic is given as follows:

Left Tailed Test:

Null Hypothesis : $H_0 : \mu = \mu_0$

Alternate Hypothesis : $H_1 : \mu < \mu_0$

Decision Criteria: If the z statistic $< z$ critical value then reject the null hypothesis.

Two Tailed Test:

Null Hypothesis : $H_0 : \mu = \mu_0$

Alternate Hypothesis : $H_1 : \mu \neq \mu_0$

Decision Criteria: If the z statistic $> z$ critical value then reject the null hypothesis.

5. (*c*) Red Data Book: The Red Data Book is a public document that is created for recording endangered and rare species of plants, animals, fungi as well as some local subspecies that are present in a particular region. The Red Data Book helps us in providing complete information for research, studies and also for monitoring the programs on rare and endangered species and their habitats. This book is mainly created to identify and protect those species which are on the verge of extinction.

The name of this book has its origins in Russia, it was originally known as the Red Data Book of the Russian Federation or the RDBRF. The book was based on research conducted between 1961 and 1964 by biologists in Russia. Hence, it is also called the Russian Red Data Book.

Currently, the International Union for Conservation of Nature maintains the Red

Data Book. IUCN is the world's most detailed inventory centre of the global conservation status of biological species. The International Union for Conservation of Nature (IUCN) was founded in 1948 with an aim to maintain a complete record of every species that ever lived.

The Red Data Book contains the complete list of threatened species. The main aim behind this documentation is to provide complete information for research and analysis of different species.

The Red Data Book contains colour-coded information sheets, which are arranged according to the extinction risk of many species and subspecies.

- Black represents species that are confirmed to be extinct.
- Red represents species that are endangered
- Amber for those species whose status is considered to be vulnerable
- White is assigned for species that are rare
- Green for species that were formerly endangered, but their numbers have started to recover
- Grey coloured for the species that are classified as vulnerable, endangered, or rare but sufficient information is not available to be properly classified.

In a nutshell, the Red Data Book indexes species as:

- Threatened
- Not threatened
- Unknown

Furthermore, The Red Data Book also has information as to why a species has become extinct along with the population trends and the extent of its range (distribution).

5. (*d*) Heat Shock Proteins and their Functions: Heat shock proteins (HSPs), also known as stress proteins, are a group of highly conserved proteins that play crucial roles in cellular protection and homeostasis, particularly during stressful conditions such as exposure to elevated temperatures (heat shock). The primary function of heat shock proteins is to assist in the folding and unfolding of proteins, preventing protein aggregation and maintaining cellular integrity under various stressors. Here are some key functions of heat shock proteins:

- ***Protein Folding and Unfolding:*** Heat shock proteins act as molecular chaperones, assisting in the correct folding of newly synthesized proteins and facilitating the refolding of denatured or misfolded proteins under stress conditions. This helps prevent the aggregation of unfolded proteins, which can be detrimental to cellular function.
- ***Cellular Stress Response:*** Heat shock proteins are part of the cellular stress response, activated in response to various stressors, including heat, oxidative stress, exposure to toxins, and other environmental challenges. Their increased expression helps cells adapt to and survive these stress conditions.
- ***Proteasomal Degradation Regulation:*** Heat shock proteins play a role in regulating the degradation of proteins through the proteasome. They can target misfolded or damaged proteins for degradation, ensuring the removal of potentially harmful molecules from the cell.
- ***Prevention of Apoptosis (Programmed Cell Death):*** Some heat shock proteins, particularly those in the HSP70 family, have anti-apoptotic functions. They can inhibit the initiation of apoptosis by interacting with key components of the apoptotic machinery, promoting cell survival during stress.
- ***Transport of Proteins Across Cell Membranes:*** Heat shock proteins are involved in the translocation of proteins across cell membranes. For example, HSP70 facilitates the translocation of proteins into organelles such as the mitochondria and endoplasmic reticulum.

- ***Immune System Modulation:*** Heat shock proteins can modulate the immune response. Certain heat shock proteins, when released from stressed or damaged cells, can act as "danger signals", activating immune responses and promoting the clearance of damaged cells.
- ***Developmental Regulation:*** Heat shock proteins are involved in the regulation of embryonic development and differentiation. They play essential roles in ensuring proper protein folding during development, contributing to the formation of functional tissues and organs.
- ***Neuroprotection:*** Heat shock proteins have neuroprotective functions, especially in response to conditions that induce cellular stress in the nervous system. They help prevent protein misfolding and aggregation, which are associated with neurodegenerative diseases.

Understanding the functions of heat shock proteins is essential in various fields, including cell biology, medicine, and biotechnology. Research on these proteins continues to uncover their diverse roles in maintaining cellular homeostasis and protecting cells from the detrimental effects of stress.

5. (*e*) **GS-GOGAT Pathway:** The GS-GOGAT pathway, or the glutamine synthetase-glutamate synthase pathway, plays a pivotal role in nitrogen assimilation in plants. As an essential element, nitrogen is acquired by plant roots primarily in the form of ammonium from the soil. The GS-GOGAT pathway operates as a two-step process, starting with the enzyme glutamine synthetase (GS), which catalyzes the condensation of ammonium with glutamate to produce glutamine. Subsequently, the enzyme glutamate synthase (GOGAT) facilitates the conversion of 2-oxoglutarate and glutamine into two molecules of glutamate. The synthesized glutamate serves as a central amino acid precursor, contributing to the formation of various nitrogen-containing compounds, including other amino acids and proteins crucial for plant growth and development. The GS-GOGAT pathway is particularly significant under conditions where ammonium is the primary nitrogen source, showcasing its importance in efficient nitrogen assimilation and the synthesis of essential biomolecules in plants. The regulation of this pathway is intricate, responding to factors such as nitrogen availability, developmental stage, and environmental cues, and its understanding is essential for enhancing nitrogen use efficiency in agriculture and ensuring optimal plant productivity.

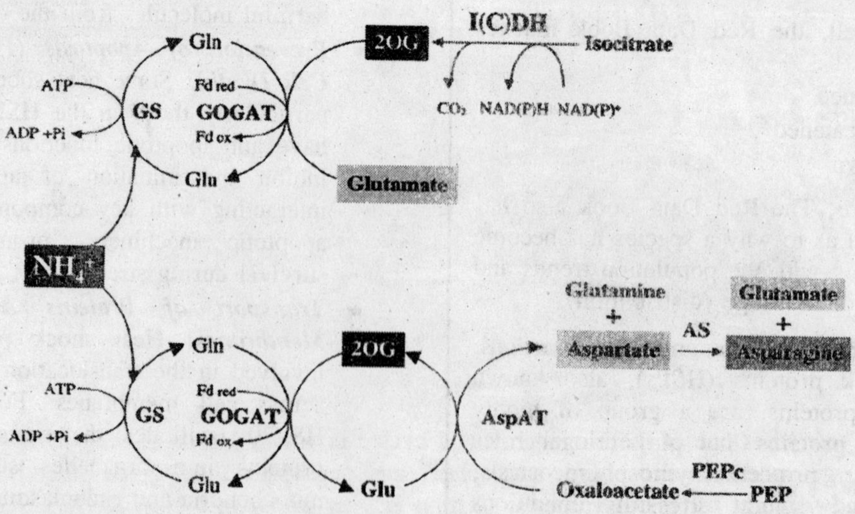

Primary amino acid synthesis by the GS/GOGAT cycle in plants. Ammonium is almost exclusively assimilated by the GS/GOGAT pathway. This requires energy, reductant, and C skeletons in the form of 2OG. This organic acid can be synthesized either by an isocitrate dehydrogenase, I(C) DH, or an AspAT. The I(C)DH origin allows for a direct net synthesis of Glu. On the other hand, the AspAT origin produces 2OG at the expense of Glu (no net synthesis) leading to the production of Asp from OAA synthesized via PEPc. The Asp can be used to produce Asn in a reaction carried out by Asn synthase (AS).

6. ***(a) Different Types of Biogeochemical Cycles:*** The matter on Earth is conserved and present in the form of atoms. Since matter can neither be created nor destroyed, it is recycled in the earth's system in various forms.

The earth obtains energy from the sun which is radiated back as heat, rest all other elements are present in a closed system. The major elements include:

- Carbon
- Hydrogen
- Nitrogen
- Oxygen
- Phosphorus
- Sulphur

These elements are recycled through the biotic and abiotic components of the ecosystem. The atmosphere, hydrosphere and lithosphere are the abiotic components of the ecosystem.

Types of Biogeochemical Cycles

Biogeochemical cycles are basically divided into two types:

- **Gaseous Cycles** – Includes Carbon, Oxygen, Nitrogen, and the Water cycle.
- **Sedimentary Cycles** – Includes Sulphur, Phosphorus, Rock cycle, etc.

Let us have a look at each of these biogeochemical cycles in brief:

- ***Water Cycle:*** The water from the different water bodies evaporates, cools, condenses and falls back to the earth as rain. This biogeochemical cycle is responsible for maintaining weather conditions. The water in its various forms interacts with the surroundings and changes the temperature and pressure of the atmosphere. There's another process called Evapotranspiration (*i.e.* vapour produced from leaves) which aids this process. It is the evaporation of water from the leaves, soil and water bodies to the atmosphere which again condenses and falls as rain.

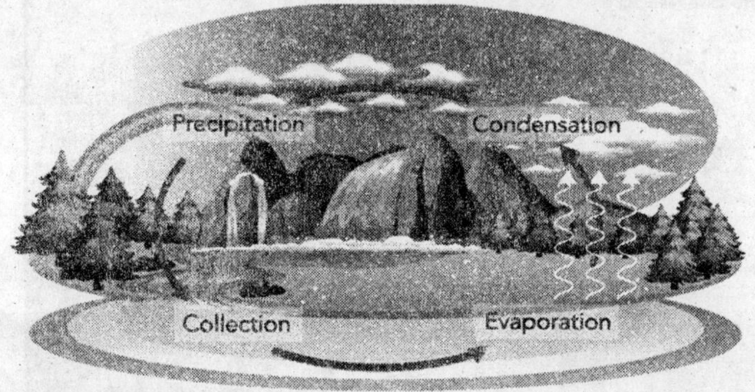

- ***Carbon Cycle:*** It is one of the biogeochemical cycles in which carbon is exchanged among the biosphere, geosphere, hydrosphere, atmosphere and pedosphere. All green plants use carbon dioxide and sunlight for photosynthesis. Carbon is thus stored in the plant. The green plants, when dead, are buried into the soil that gets converted into fossil fuels made from carbon. These fossil fuels when burnt, release carbon dioxide into the atmosphere. Also, the animals that consume plants, obtain the carbon stored in the plants. This carbon is returned to the atmosphere when these animals decompose after death. The carbon also returns to the environment through cellular respiration by animals. Huge carbon content in the form of carbon dioxide is produced that is stored in the form of fossil fuel (coal & oil) and can be extracted for various commercial and non-commercial purposes. When factories use these fuels, the carbon is again released back in the atmosphere during combustion.

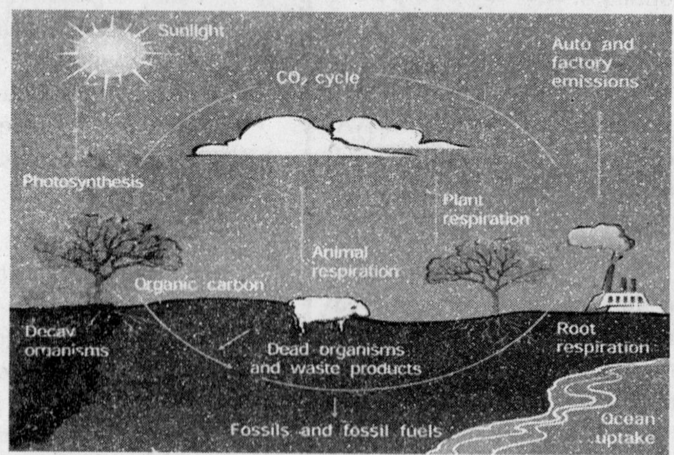

- ***Nitrogen Cycle:*** It is the biogeochemical cycle by which nitrogen is converted into several forms and it gets circulated through the atmosphere and various ecosystems such as terrestrial and marine ecosystems. Nitrogen is an essential element of life. The nitrogen in the atmosphere is fixed by the nitrogen-fixing bacteria present in the root nodules of the leguminous plants and made available to the soil and plants. The bacteria present in the roots of the plants convert this nitrogen gas into a usable compound called ammonia. Ammonia is also supplied to plants in the form of fertilizers. This ammonia is converted into nitrites and nitrates. The denitrifying bacteria reduce the nitrates into nitrogen and return it into the atmosphere.

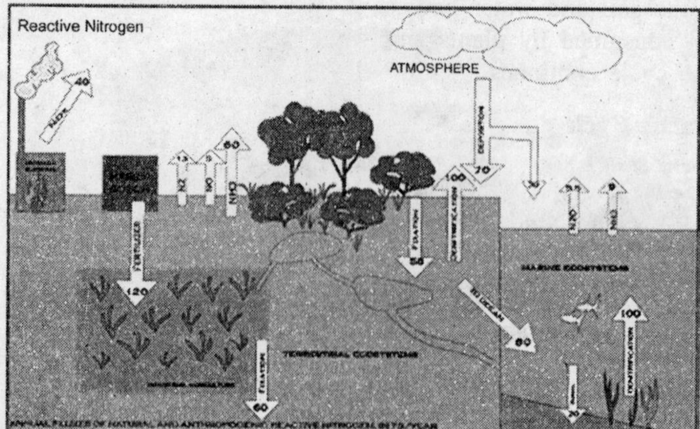

- ***Oxygen Cycle:*** This biogeochemical cycle moves through the atmosphere, the lithosphere and the biosphere. Oxygen is an abundant element on our Earth. It is found in the elemental form in the atmosphere to the extent of 21%.Oxygen is released by the plants during photosynthesis. Humans and other animals inhale the oxygen exhale carbon dioxide which is again taken up by the plants. They utilise this carbon dioxide in photosynthesis to produce oxygen, and the cycle continues.

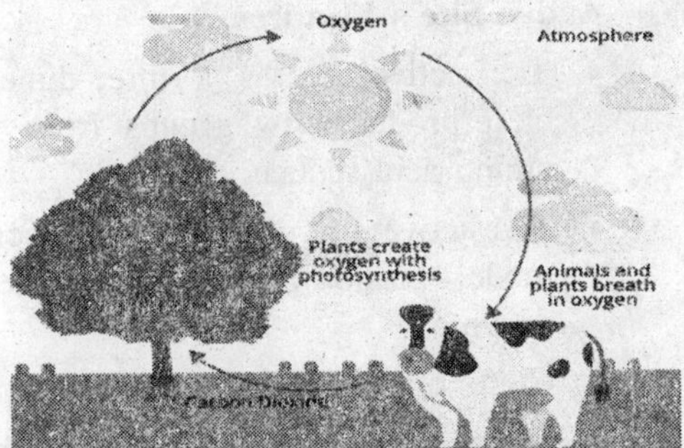

- *Phosphorous Cycle:* In this biogeochemical cycle, phosphorus moves through the hydrosphere, lithosphere and biosphere. Phosphorus is extracted by the weathering of rocks. Due to rains and erosion phosphorus is washed away in the soil and water bodies. Plants and animals obtain this phosphorus through the soil and water and grow. Microorganisms also require phosphorus for their growth. When the plants and animals die, they decompose, and the stored phosphorus is returned to the soil and water bodies which is again consumed by plants and animals and the cycle continues.

Phosphorus Cycle

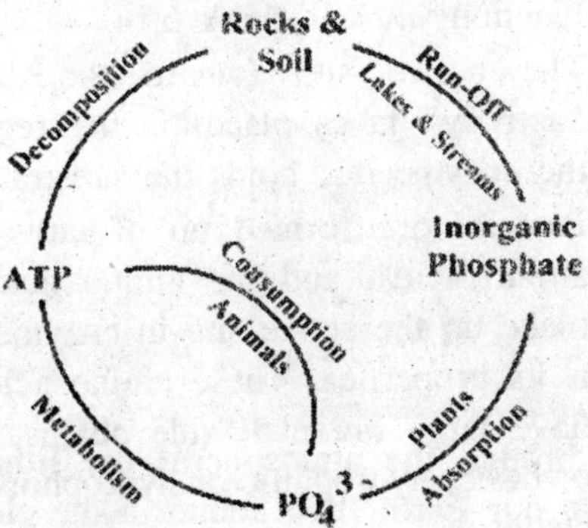

- *Sulphur Cycle:* This biogeochemical cycle moves through the rocks, water bodies and living systems. Sulphur is released into the atmosphere by the weathering of rocks and is converted into sulphates. These sulphates are taken up by the microorganisms and plants and converted into organic forms. Organic sulphur is consumed by animals through food. When the animals die and decompose, sulphur is returned to the soil, which is again obtained by the plants and microbes, and the cycle continues.

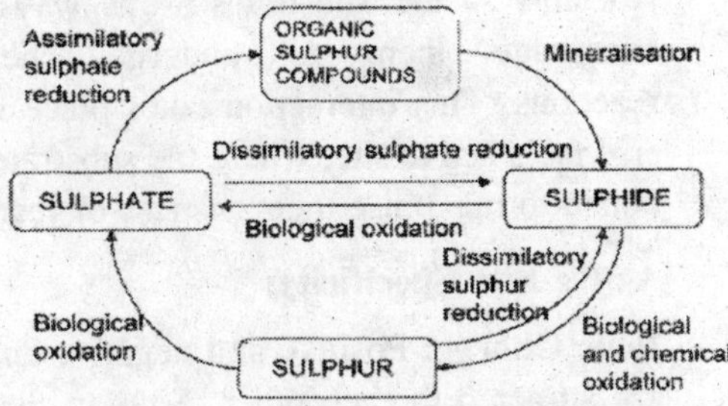

Importance of Biogeochemical Cycles

- These cycles demonstrate the way in which the energy is used. Through the ecosystem, these cycles move the essential elements for life to sustain. They are vital as they recycle elements and store them too, and regulate the vital elements through the physical facets. These cycles depict the association between living and non-living things in the ecosystems and enable the continuous survival of ecosystems.
- It is important to comprehend these cycles to learn their effect on living entities. Some activities of humans disturb a few of these natural cycles and thereby affecting related ecosystems. A closer look at these mechanisms can help us restrict and stop their dangerous impact.

6. (*b*) Key Features of Enzyme Active Sites: The active site of an enzyme is the part of the enzyme where substrate molecules bind and a chemical reaction takes place. The active site is made up of amino acid residues that establish temporary bonds with the substrate (binding site) as well as residues that catalyse that substrate's reaction (catalytic site).

The portion of an enzyme that binds substrate molecules is known as the active site. This is critical for the catalytic activity of the enzyme. Enzymes are proteins that reduce the activation energy of chemical reactions, allowing them to move much faster. They accomplish this by interacting with chemical reactants – the substrates – in ways that encourage them to undergo chemical reactions. This interaction takes place in the enzyme's active site, where the substrates are bound to maximise their chances of reacting.

Active Site Specificity:

Ionic Charge: Positive and negative charges are attracted to each other. Similar charges, such as two positive charges, repel each other actively. Another way an enzyme active site might attract substrates or parts of substrates while rejecting others to obtain the perfect fit is through a mechanism known as repulsion.

- ***Polarity:*** Non-polar molecules prefer other non-polar molecules, whereas polar molecules prefer other polar ones. Certain amino acids in the active site might therefore attract or repel different sections of the substrate, resulting in a better match.
- ***Hydrophobicity or hydrophilicity:*** Opposites do not attract in this scenario. Instead, what attracts what draws. Hydrophilic amino acids attract hydrophilic substrates, while hydrophobic amino acids attract other hydrophobic compounds.
- ***Size and shape of the active site:*** The active sites of enzymes are structured in such a way that they can only 'fit' with specific substrates.

Some vitamins and minerals are necessary because they act as cofactors, assisting enzymes in binding to their substrates. Enzymes involved in energy production, for example, utilise various B vitamins as cofactors. That's why B vitamins are found in many energy "shots" and supplements.

Active Site's Features

- The active site is a three-dimensional cleft produced by groups from various amino acid sequences.
- The active site of an enzyme occupies a modest portion of the total volume of the enzyme.
- Clefts or crevices are active locations.
- Multiple weak attractions bind substrates to enzymes.
- Binding specificity is determined by the precise arrangement of atoms in an active site.

The Process:

- An enzyme will bind to one or more reactant molecules in order to catalyse a process. The enzyme's substrates are those compounds.
- One substrate can be broken down into a number of products in some reactions. In other cases, two substrates are combined to form a bigger molecule or portions are swapped. In fact, there is most likely an enzyme to speed up any biological reaction you can think of!
- The active site (where the catalytic "activity" takes place) is the region of the enzyme that binds the substrate.
- Proteins are formed up of units called amino acids, and the amino acids that make up the active site in enzymes give it its properties. These amino acids can have large or small side chains, acidic or basic, hydrophilic or hydrophobic side chains.

- The active site's amino acid composition, as well as their relative placements in 3D space, give it a distinct size, shape, and chemical behaviour. An enzyme's active site is specifically designed to bind to a specific target—the enzyme's substrate or substrates—and assist them in undergoing a chemical reaction thanks to these amino acids.

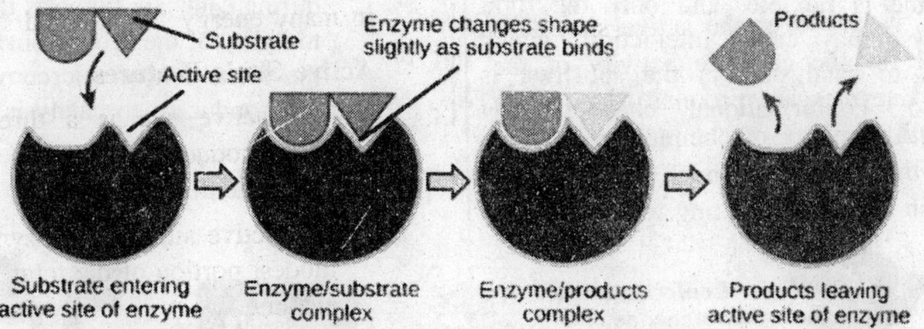

BINDING THEORIES:

- **Lock and Key Model:** Emil Fischer, a 19th-century chemist, proposed this concept. He claimed that the active site and substrate are two stable structures that, like a key and a lock, fit together properly without any further change. The interactions between substrates will be strongest if one perfectly binds to its active site, resulting in high catalytic efficiency. As time passed, the model's shortcomings became apparent. The competitive enzyme inhibitor methylglucoside, for example, can bind tightly and precisely to the active site of 4-alpha-glucanotransferase. On methylglucoside, however, 4-alpha-glucanotransferase is inactive, and no glycosyl transfer occurs. Because of its strong binding, the Lock and Key hypothesis cannot explain this, as it would predict a high efficiency of methylglucoside glycosyl transfer. Apart from competitive inhibition, this theory is unable to explain the mechanism of non-competitive inhibitors, which do not bind to the active site yet nonetheless influence catalytic activity.

The Lock and Key Mechanism

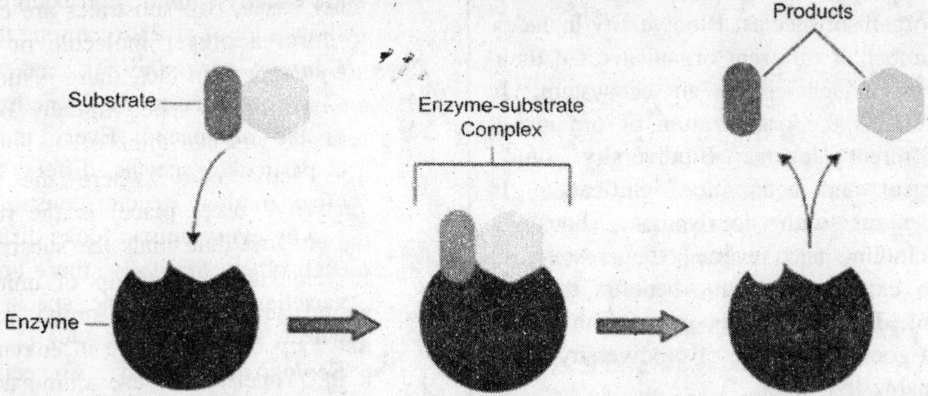

- **Induced Fit:** The active site and the binding part of the substrate are not exactly complementary, according to Daniel Koshland's theory of enzyme-substrate binding. The induced fit model is a variation on the lock-and-key model, in which an active site is flexible and changes form until the substrate is completely bound. This model works in the same way that a glove does: the glove changes shape to fit the hand. The enzyme's shape attracts its substrate at first. The surface of an enzyme is flexible, and only the right catalyst may cause interaction, which leads to catalysis. As the substrate is bound, conformational changes may occur. The reaction products will move away from the enzyme after the reaction, and the active site will revert to its original structure. The fact that the entire protein domain can migrate several nanometers during catalysis supports this notion. This mobility of the protein surface can lead to the formation of microenvironments that are conducive to catalysis.

Induced Fit Model

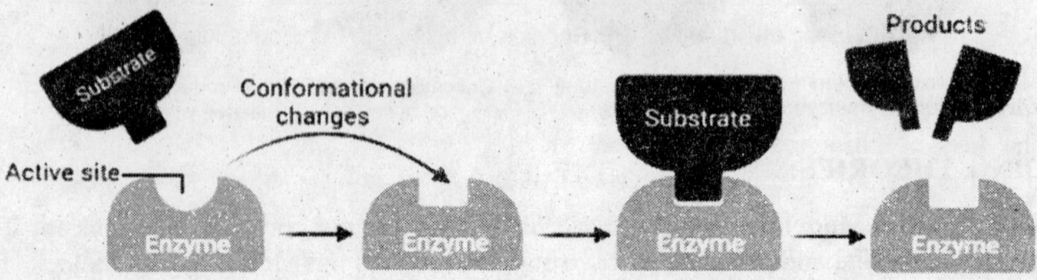

6. (*c*) **Different Types and Attributes of Biodiversity:** Biodiversity describes the richness and variety of life on earth. It is the most complex and important feature of our planet. Without biodiversity, life would not sustain. The term biodiversity was coined in 1985. It is important in natural as well as artificial ecosystems. It deals with nature's variety, the biosphere. It refers to variabilities among plants, animals and microorganism species. Biodiversity includes the number of different organisms and their relative frequencies in an ecosystem. It also reflects the organization of organisms at different levels. Biodiversity holds ecological and economic significance. It provides us with nourishment, housing, fuel, clothing and several other resources. It also extracts monetary benefits through tourism. Therefore, it is very important to have a good knowledge of biodiversity for a sustainable livelihood.

Types of Biodiversity: There are the following three different types of biodiversity:

- Species Biodiversity
- Genetic Biodiversity
- Ecological Biodiversity
- ***Species diversity:*** Species diversity refers to the variety of different types of species found in a particular area. It is the biodiversity at the most basic level. It includes all the species ranging from plants to different microorganisms. No two individuals of the same species are exactly similar. For example, humans show a lot of diversity among themselves.
- ***Genetic diversity:*** It refers to the variations among the genetic resources of the organisms. Every individual of a particular species differs from each other in their genetic constitution. That is why every human looks different from each other. Similarly, there are different varieties in the same species of rice, wheat, maize, barley, etc.
- ***Ecological diversity:*** An ecosystem is a collection of living and non-living organisms and their interaction with each other. Ecological biodiversity refers to the variations in the plant and animal species

living together and connected by food chains and food webs. It is the diversity observed among the different ecosystems in a region. Diversity in different ecosystems like deserts, rainforests, mangroves, etc., include ecological diversity.

1 Genetic diversity | 2 Species diversity | 3 Ecological diversity

Various Causes for the Loss of Biodiversity: The loss of biodiversity, often referred to as biodiversity decline or biodiversity loss, is a critical environmental issue with far-reaching consequences. Several interconnected factors contribute to the ongoing loss of biodiversity worldwide. Here are various causes for the decline in biodiversity:

- ***Habitat Destruction and Fragmentation:*** Clearing of land for agriculture, urbanization, logging, and infrastructure development leads to the destruction and fragmentation of natural habitats. Fragmentation isolates populations, disrupts ecological processes, and reduces the availability of suitable habitats for many species.
- ***Climate Change:*** Changes in global climate patterns, driven by human activities such as the burning of fossil fuels, deforestation, and industrial processes, impact ecosystems and disrupt the distribution and behaviour of many species. Temperature changes, altered precipitation patterns, and extreme weather events can affect the survival and reproduction of various organisms.
- ***Pollution:*** Pollution from industrial, agricultural, and urban sources introduces harmful substances into air, water, and soil. Pesticides, fertilizers, heavy metals, and pollutants can have detrimental effects on the health of ecosystems, leading to declines in species populations.
- ***Overexploitation:*** Unsustainable harvesting of resources, such as overfishing, hunting, and logging, can deplete populations of economically valuable species and disrupt ecosystems. Overexploitation often occurs due to high demand for products derived from these species, leading to declines in their numbers and sometimes even extinction.
- ***Invasive Species:*** Introduction of non-native species to new environments, whether intentionally or accidentally, can lead to the displacement of native species. Invasive species can outcompete, prey upon, or introduce diseases to native species, contributing to population declines and loss of biodiversity.
- ***Disease:*** Emerging diseases, often facilitated by factors like global travel and trade, can have devastating effects on wildlife populations. Diseases introduced by humans or spread through anthropogenic activities can lead to outbreaks that decimate vulnerable species.
- ***Population Growth and Urbanization:*** Human population growth and the associated expansion of urban areas

can put tremendous pressure on natural habitats. Increased resource consumption, pollution, and habitat conversion for agriculture and infrastructure contribute to biodiversity loss.

- ***Lack of Conservation Measures:*** Insufficient or ineffective conservation efforts and lack of protected areas can leave species vulnerable to various threats. Adequate conservation measures are crucial for safeguarding habitats and implementing strategies for sustainable resource use.
- ***Land Use Changes:*** Changes in land use, including shifts in agricultural practices and the conversion of natural landscapes to other uses, can negatively impact biodiversity. Monoculture agriculture, for example, often leads to the loss of diverse ecosystems and reduces habitat availability for many species.

Addressing the loss of biodiversity requires comprehensive conservation strategies, sustainable resource management, and global cooperation. Efforts to protect and restore natural habitats, mitigate climate change, and promote sustainable development are essential for preserving the Earth's rich biological diversity.

Previous Years' Paper (Solved)

Indian Forest Service (Main) Exam, 2022

SUBJECT–BOTANY

(Exam held on 22-11-2022)

PAPER-I

INSTRUCTIONS: *There are EIGHT questions in all, out of which FIVE are to be attempted. Questions Nos. 1 & 5 are compulsory. Out of the remaining SIX questions, THREE are to be attempted selecting at least ONE question from each of the two Sections A and B. Attempts of questions shall be counted in sequential order. Unless struck off, attempt of a question shall be counted even if attempted partly. Any page or portion of the page left blank in the Question-cum-Answer Booklet must be clearly struck off. All questions carry equal marks. Answers must be written in ENGLISH only. Neat sketches may be drawn, wherever required.*

SECTION–A

1. (*a*) What are plasmids? Describe their role in bacterial genetic recombination.

(*b*) Explain how algae play harmful role in spoiling the water bodies.

(*c*) Draw and describe the structure and function of haustorium in *Phytophthora*.

(*d*) Write down the Koch's postulates.

(*e*) List five features in which the Bennettitales differ from the Cycads, and three in which they resemble.

2. (*a*) What is transduction? Describe in brief generalized and specialized transduction.

(*b*) What are the common features of *Anthoceros* and Chlorophyceae? Describe the development of sporophyte of *Anthoceros*.

(*c*) Describe the development of ascus in *Neurospora*. Why is *Neurospora* considered as a model for genetic studies?

3. (*a*) Describe the economical and ecological importance of *Sphagnum*.

(*b*) Describe and illustrate the development of female gametophyte in *Pinus*. Trace the pathway of pollen tube in the ovule leading to the formation of zygote.

(*c*) Explain with examples how bacteria improve soil fertility.

4. (*a*) Give an account of classification of gymnosperms as proposed by Takhtajan, Cronquist and Zimmermann. Where do we find gymnosperms distributed in India?

(*b*) Describe the life cycle of *Ustilago*. How can you differentiate loose smut and covered smut?

(*c*) Draw and describe the structure of strobilus in *Lycopodium* and discuss the development of sporangium.

SECTION–B

5. (*a*) State the salient features of Brassicaceae. Give the botanical names of any three economically important plants belonging to the family.

(*b*) What are the pollen characters of taxonomic importance?

(*c*) Mention the scientific name, family and economically important part of two beverage-yielding plants.

(*d*) Distinguish between:

(*i*) Redifferentiation and Dedifferentiation

(*ii*) Indirect organogenesis and Direct organogenesis

(*e*) What are the merits and demerits of Rolf Dahlgren's system of classification?

6. (*a*) What are the structural features of stomata that help in their opening and closing mechanism? Mention the four common types of stomata with their diagnostic features.

(*b*) With the help of suitable diagrams, describe the development of nuclear endosperm. How does the process of its cellularization take place?

(*c*) How are cybrids different from somatic hybrids? Describe the methodology of somatic hybrid production.

7. (*a*) Describe in detail about the production of haploid plants from anther culture.

(*b*) Write down the scientific name, family and commercially important plant part of the following:

(*i*) Hemp

(*ii*) Nutmeg

(*iii*) Indigo

(*iv*) Ergot

(*v*) Jatropha

(*c*) Define polyembryony. What are the various ways in which it may arise in angiosperms? State the practical value of polyembryony.

8. (*a*) Discuss the role of ethnobotany with two examples in health care and treatment of diseases in India.

(*b*) What are the adaptations among angiosperms for cross-pollination? State the advantages and disadvantages of self-pollination.

(*c*) What do you mean by centre of origin of crops? Describe the concept of centre of origin of cultivated crops according to Vavilov.

PAPER-II

INSTRUCTIONS: *There are EIGHT questions in all, out of which FIVE are to be attempted. Questions Nos. 1 & 5 are compulsory. Out of the remaining SIX questions, THREE are to be attempted selecting at least ONE question from each of the two Sections A and B. Attempts of questions shall be counted in sequential order. Unless struck off, attempt of a question shall be counted even if attempted partly. Any page or portion of the page left blank in the Question-cum-Answer Booklet must be clearly struck off. All questions carry equal marks. Answers must be written in ENGLISH only. Neat sketches may be drawn, wherever required.*

SECTION–A

1. Wrtie short notes on the following:

(*a*) Membrane lipids

(*b*) Cyclins and cyclin-dependent kinases

(*c*) Homologous recombination

(*d*) Characteristics of cytoplasmic inheritance

(*e*) Usage of backcrossing in plant breeding

2. (*a*) What is the basic structure of G-protein-coupled receptors? Where are they located in the cell? Explain their mechanism of action and functions.

(*b*) Explain the sex-linked pattern of inheritance with an example.

(*c*) (*i*) Explain how the hybrid plants express heterosis.

(*ii*) State the role of apomixis in crop plant improvement.

3. (*a*) Explain the process of regulation of *lac* operon in *E. coli.*

(*b*) "Peroxisomes play a key role in the oxidation of biomolecules." Elaborate the statement.

(*c*) Give a critical account of the role of molecular markers in plant breeding.

4. (*a*) What are lampbrush chromosomes? Draw a diagram and describe their structure. Are lampbrush chromosomes significant? Explain.

(*b*) Explain the important features of a genetic code.

(*c*) State the conditions to apply the Poisson probability distribution. Add a brief note on the importance of binomial distribution.

SECTION–B

5. Write short notes on the following:

(*a*) Phytochromes and their role in gene expression

(*b*) Micronutrients essential for plant growth and their uptake mechanism

(*c*) Processes of phytoremediation

(*d*) Major consequences of global warming

(*e*) Student's '*t*'-test.

6. (*a*) How is ATP synthesized in plants? Discuss the role of ATP in photosynthesis.

(*b*) Give a comparative account of Hydrosere and Xerosere.

(*c*) Explain with an example how coefficient of variation helps to compare the dispersion of two different characters in the same population.

7. (*a*) Describe the different hypotheses of endemism. Mention the criteria for identifying biodiversity hotspots.

(*b*) "Complete oxidation of pyruvate to CO_2 and water occurs through a series of reactions." What are these reactions collectively called?

Draw the cycle with the name of the intermediates and the enzymes.

(*c*) Describe *Agrobacterium tumefaciens* mediated gene transfer technique in plants.

8. (*a*) What is fruit ripening?

Briefly discuss the biochemical and physiological changes during this process. Add a note on molecular mechanism of fruit ripening.

(*b*) Give an idea of different categories of Intellectual Property Rights (IPR). Add a brief note on the application of IPR in protecting issues related to biodiversity conservation and traditional knowledge.

(*c*) How do auxins control the growth of axillary buds? Explain.

Add a note on the applications of auxins in agriculture.

ANSWERS

PAPER-I

1. (*a*) Plasmids: Plasmid refers to the separated DNA molecule from chromosomal DNA, which has the ability to replicate on its own.

Plasmids are known to be small, circular molecules of DNA that have the ability to replicate independently, as they do not depend on the organism's chromosomal DNA for replication. Due to this, plasmids are also known as extrachromosomal DNA. Plasmids are vital tools in genetic engineering as they help in gene cloning and gene therapy. Plasmids are found in bacterial cells and certain eukaryotes. A plasmid measures up to 1 to 200 kb in size and produces enzymes that can degrade antibiotics or heavy metals. There are five main types of plasmids namely, fertility F-plasmids, resistance plasmids, virulence plasmids, degradative plasmids and Col plasmids.

Role of Plasmids in Bacterial Genetic Recombina-tion: Researchers can insert DNA fragments or genes into a plasmid vector, creating a so-called recombinant plasmid. This plasmid can be introduced into a bacterium by way of the process called transformation. Then, because bacteria divide rapidly, they can be used as factories to copy DNA fragments in large quantities.

1. (*b*) **Algae Play Harmful Role in Spoiling the Water Bodies:** The overgrowth of algae consumes oxygen and blocks sunlight from underwater plants. When the algae eventually dies, the oxygen in the water is consumed. The lack of oxygen makes it impossible for aquatic life to survive. Excessive algal growth consumes high amounts of dissolved oxygen and deprives the aquatic life of oxygen. It blocks the sunlight from entering the water and disrupts photosynthesis. Some algal blooms are considered harmful as they produce toxins that are detrimental to aquatic life.

1. (*c*) **Structure and Function of Haustorium in Phytophthora:** The simplest forms of haustoria are small spheres. The largest are complex formations adding significant mass to a cell, expanding between the cell wall and cell membrane. The intracellular haustorium is connected with the intercellular hypha by a neck-like constriction at the penetration site.

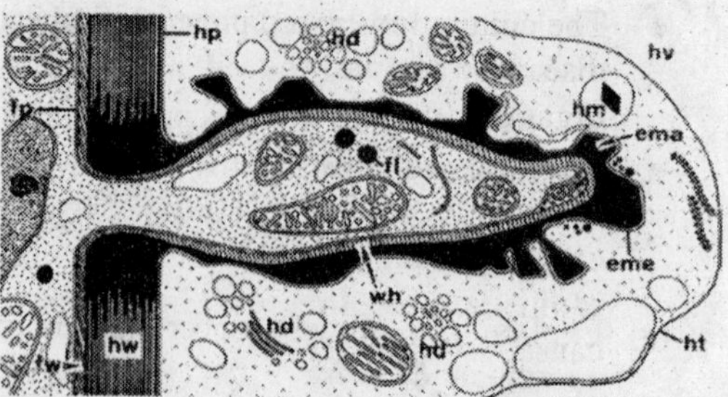

Phytophthora* : *Ultrastructure of Haustorium

Haustoria create an intimate association with the host cell for molecular exchange, such as nutrient uptake in fungi. In addition, haustoria are sites for secretion of fungal and oomycete effectors.

1. (*d*) **Koch's Postulates:** Koch's postulates are four criteria designed to establish a causal relationship between a microbe and a disease. The postulates were formulated by Robert Koch and Friedrich Loeffler in 1884, based on earlier concepts described by Jakob Henle, and the statements were refined and published by Koch in 1890. Koch applied the postulates to describe the etiology of cholera and tuberculosis, both of which are now ascribed to bacteria. The postulates have been controversially generalized to other diseases. More modern concepts in microbial pathogenesis cannot be examined using Koch's postulates, including viruses (which are obligate intracellular parasites) and asymptomatic carriers. They have largely been supplanted by other criteria such as the Bradford Hill criteria for infectious disease causality in modern public health and the Molecular Koch's postulates for microbial pathogenesis. Koch's four postulates are:

- The microorganism must be found in abundance in all organisms suffering from the disease but should not be found in healthy organisms.
- The microorganism must be isolated from a diseased organism and grown in pure culture.

- The cultured microorganism should cause disease when introduced into a healthy organism.
- The microorganism must be re-isolated from the inoculated, diseased experimental host and identified as being identical to the original specific causative agent.

1. (*e*) The Bennettitales and Cycads are both ancient groups of plants that share some similarities but also have distinct features that set them apart. Here are five features in which the Bennettitales differ from the Cycads and three features in which they resemble each other:

Five features in which the Bennettitales differ from the Cycads:

- **Reproductive Structures:** The reproductive structures of Bennettitales differ significantly from those of Cycads. Bennettitales have complex flower-like structures with both male and female reproductive parts organized in a cone-like arrangement. In contrast, Cycads have separate male and female cones.
- **Leaf Morphology:** Bennettitales have large, compound leaves that are highly divided into leaflets, resembling fern fronds or palm leaves. Cycads, on the other hand, have simple leaves that are often pinnately compound or palm-like but less divided than those of Bennettitales.
- **Growth Habit:** Bennettitales were primarily herbaceous or small shrubs, with some forms reaching tree-like proportions. Cycads, in contrast, are typically larger and have a woody trunk, resembling small palm trees.
- **Geologic Age:** Bennettitales were a dominant group during the Mesozoic Era, particularly in the Jurassic and Cretaceous periods, and became extinct by the end of the Cretaceous. Cycads, although ancient, have persisted through time and still exist today.
- **Fossil Evidence:** Fossil evidence of Bennettitales consists of well-preserved flowers, leaves, and stems, making their identification and classification relatively straightforward. Cycads also have a rich fossil record, but their identification can sometimes be challenging due to limited preservation of their reproductive structures.

Three features in which the Bennettitales resemble the Cycads:

- **Gymnosperm Nature:** Both Bennettitales and Cycads are gymnosperms, meaning they produce seeds without enclosing them in a fruit. This is in contrast to angiosperms (flowering plants) that enclose their seeds in fruits.
- **Pollination by Insects:** Both Bennettitales and Cycads have been hypothesized to have relied on insects for pollination. Some species of Cycads, as well as certain interpretations of Bennettitales reproductive structures, suggest an ancient association with specific pollinators.
- **Strobili or Cones:** Both groups produce cone-like structures for reproduction. Although the structure and arrangement of the cones differ between Bennettitales and Cycads, they both serve as reproductive structures containing the male and female gametes.

2. (*a*) **Transduction:** Transduction is a mode of genetic transfer from one bacteria to another through a virus. There is no direct contact between the bacterial cells. The other ways of genetic recombination in bacteria include transformation and conjugation. In this process, bacteriophages, which infect bacteria, use host cells to multiplicate and while assembling they sometimes pack the bacterial DNA with them. Later, when these viruses infect new bacterial cells, the bacterial genome that they carry may get inserted into the host genome. Transduction is commonly used in genetic engineering for inserting foreign DNA into the host cell. Transduction was discovered by Zinder and Lederberg in Salmonella. Hershey and Chase used transduction as a tool to confirm that DNA is the genetic material.

Types of Transduction: Transduction is common in both virulent and temperate phages, i.e. by lytic or lysogenic cycle. Transduction is of two types:

- **Generalized Transduction**: In this, the phage can carry any part of DNA.
- **Specialized Transduction:** In this, the phage carries only the specific part of DNA.

Generalized Transduction: Generalized transduction can occur by both lytic or lysogenic cycle. Here, any random part of DNA gets packed in bacteriophages by mistake along with the viral genome. It occurs at the lytic stage of the phage life cycle. When the virus-containing bacterial DNA infects another cell, it can get inserted into the host genome or if it was a plasmid, then it can reform the plasmid. Generalized transduction is used to study linkage information, gene mapping, comparing genomes of two different bacteria, mutagenesis, etc.

Example of generalized transduction includes *E.coli* transduction by P1 phage.

Specialized Transduction: Specialized transduction can occur only through the lysogenic cycle, i.e. by temperate phage. Here, only the specific part of the bacterial DNA is packed into the virus. It occurs when the prophage, i.e. viral DNA, which gets inserted into the bacterial genome in the lysogenic cycle excises. When prophage excises from bacterial DNA, some parts of bacterial DNA, which are flanked on both sides of the prophage are also excised. Here, the newly packed phage genome consists of both bacterial and viral genome. Later, when the virus with the recombinant genome infects a new bacterial cell, the bacterial gene also gets inserted into the host genome with the viral genome through lysogeny. The recipient cell now shows the newly acquired characteristics. Specialized transduction is commonly used for isolation and insertion of genes of choice.

Example of specialized transduction includes *E.coli* transduction by λ phage.

2. (*b*) Common Features of Anthoceros: Anthoceros is a hornwort that belongs to the family Anthocerotaceae. It is the largest genus of hornworts and is found inhabiting globally. It occurs in moist and shaded sub-tropical and temperate regions. They have a small or medium-sized green thallus that has lobed margins.

Common Features of Chlorophyceae: The Chloro-phyceae includes many familiar phytoplanktonic green algae such as Chlamydomonas, Scenedesmus and Pediastrum. Most chlorophycean algae are photosynthetic, but colourless heterotrophic species are also known (Polytoma, Polytomella etc.).

Development of Sporophyte of Anthoceros: The first division of the zygote is vertical. In other Bryophytes the first division of the zygote is transverse. This is the important difference in the development of sporophyte of Hornworts and rest of the Bryophytes. The second division is transverse and is so oriented that the upper two cells are usually longer than the lower two (quadrant stage). All the four cells divide by vertical walls to produce eight cells (octant stage). The eight cells are arranged in two tiers of four cells each. Further development of the sporophyte varies in different species. In *A. erectus* the lower tier of four cells of octant stage form the foot while the seta and capsule are formed from the upper tier of four cells. In majority of the species like *A. fusiformis*, *A. pearsoni* and *A. himalayensis* upper tier of four cells divide by transverse division to form three tiers of four cells each. The lowermost tier forms the foot, the middle tier forms the meristematic zone or intermediate zone and uppermost tier develops into the capsule. The four cells of the lower tier divide by irregular divisions to form broad, bulbous foot, made up of parenchymatous cells. In some species (e.g., *A. punctatus*) the superficial cells of the foot form a palisade layer of cells while in some species (e.g., *A. laevis*, *A. himalayensis*) the superficial layer grows into haustoria like projections.

The uppermost tier of four cells which forms the capsule divide by one to two transverse divisions to form two to three tiers of cells. It is followed by periclinal division to form an outer layer of amphithecium and the central mass of cells called endothecium. The entire endothecium develops into the sterile columella. In young sporophyte it is made of four cells but in mature sporophyte it is made of sixteen vertical rows of cells (4 × 4). The amphithecium divides by a periclinal division to differentiate into an outer sterile layer of jacket initials and inner fertile layer. The cells of the jacket initials divide by anticlinal and periclinal divisions to form four to six layered capsule wall. The outermost layer of the capsule wall is called epidermis. It is characterised by the presence of stomata. The cells of the inner layers of capsule wall have chloroplast. In young sporophyte the archesporium over archs the columella. The archesporium may single layered in thickness throughout in its further development (e.g., *A. erectus*) or become two layered (e.g., *A. pearsoni*) or two to four layered (e.g., *A. hallii*).

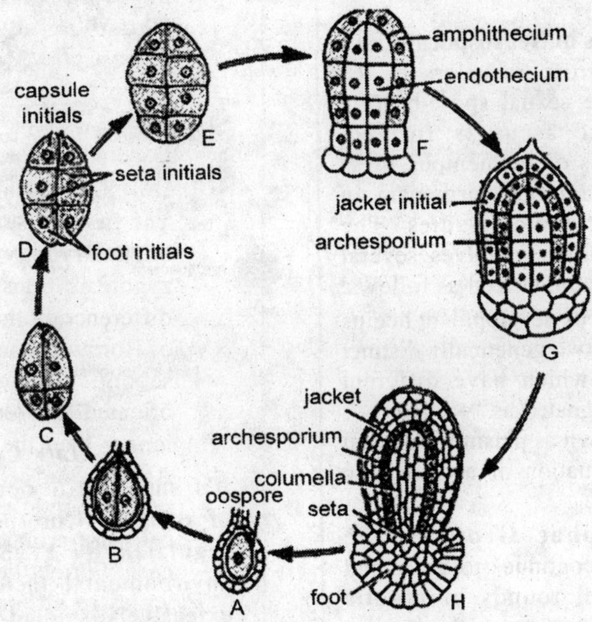

(A-H) : Anthoceros. Successive stages in the development of sporophyte

On maturity the archesporium gives rise to two types of cells: spore mother cells and elater mother cells. These cells are arranged in alternate manner one above the another. Spore mother cells are spherical or oval with dense cytoplasm and large nuclei. These cells divide by meiotic divisions to form spore tetrads. Elater mother cells are elliptical with small nuclei. These cells divide mitotically to form four celled elaters. The four cells of the elaters may remain attached to each other or may break into 1-celled, 2-celled or 3-celled units. The broken units are called pseudo elaters. (The elaters are without thickening bands and therefore, called pseudo elaters). By the activity of the meristematic zone various tissues of the capsule are continuously produced so that it becomes elongated. The young sporophyte of the Anthoceros is surrounded by a fleshy covering or sheath. It is called involucre. It is developed partly from the tissue of the archegonium and partly from the tissue of the gametophytic thallus. In young stages the sporophyte is completely surrounded by involucre.

2. (*c*) **Development of Ascus in Neurospora:** Ascus development in Neurospora refers to the process by which the sexual spore-bearing structure called the ascus is formed. Neurospora is a genus of filamentous fungi commonly used as a model organism in genetic and developmental studies. The development of the ascus involves several stages, which can be summarized as follows:

- **Plasmogamy:** Ascus development begins with the fusion of two genetically distinct haploid hyphae, which have different mating types, designated as "+" and "–". This fusion is known as plasmogamy and results in the formation of a dikaryotic hypha.
- **Dikaryotic Hyphae Growth:** The dikaryotic hypha continues to grow and undergoes several rounds of mitotic divisions. During this stage, the hyphae extend and branch, forming a complex network.
- **Pre-ascus Formation:** As the dikaryotic hyphae grow, certain regions within the network differentiate into pre-asci. Pre-asci are elongated structures that will eventually give rise to ascospores.
- **Ascus Development:** The pre-asci undergo further differentiation and morphological changes to form mature asci. The nuclei within the pre-asci undergo a series of mitotic divisions, resulting in the formation of eight haploid nuclei.
- **Ascospore Formation:** Each haploid nucleus migrates into a specialized compartment within the ascus called an ascospore, where it becomes surrounded by a protective membrane. Each ascus typically contains eight ascospores.
- **Ascus Discharge:** Once the ascospores are fully formed, the ascus becomes pressurized, leading to the discharge of the ascospores. The ascospores are released into the surrounding environment, where they can germinate and give rise to new fungal colonies.

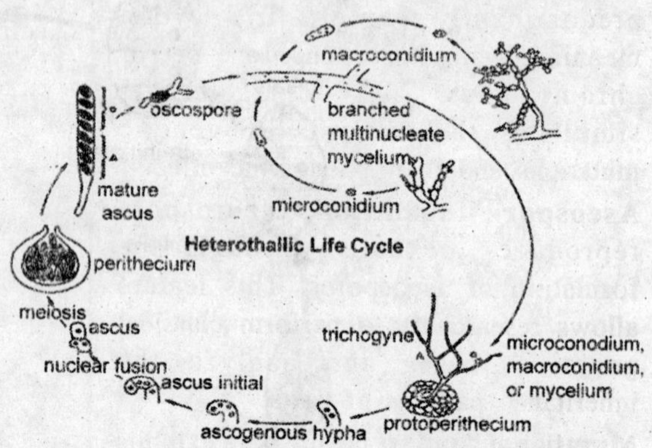

Life Cycle

It's important to note that the development of ascus in Neurospora, like other fungi, is regulated by a variety of genetic and environmental factors. Researchers have extensively studied ascus development in Neurospora to gain insights into the genetic control of sexual reproduction and the underlying molecular mechanisms involved in fungal development.

Neurospora is Considered as a Model for Genetic Studies: *Neurospora crassa*, often referred to as "Neurospora," is a model organism extensively used in genetic and biochemical studies. Neurospora is a filamentous fungus that belongs to the division Ascomycota and is commonly found growing on decaying plant material. There are several reasons why Neurospora is considered a valuable model organism for genetic research:

- **Easy cultivation:** Neurospora grows quickly on simple and inexpensive media, making it easy to cultivate and maintain in the laboratory.
- **Compact genome:** The genome of Neurospora is relatively small and well-characterized, consisting of seven chromosomes. This simplicity allows researchers to study the organism's genetic makeup and manipulate it effectively.
- **Haploid life cycle:** Neurospora has a predominantly haploid life cycle, meaning it possesses only one set of chromosomes. This characteristic simplifies the analysis of genetic mutations and their phenotypic effects.
- **Ascospore formation:** Neurospora reproduces sexually through the formation of ascospores. This feature allows researchers to perform classical genetic crosses and analyze the inheritance patterns of traits.
- **Mutational studies:** Neurospora exhibits a high frequency of spontaneous mutations, which has facilitated the discovery of numerous genes and their functions. The ease of generating and analyzing mutants in Neurospora has contributed significantly to our understanding of gene function, mutation, recombination, and other genetic processes.
- **Biochemical studies:** Neurospora has been extensively studied in biochemical research, particularly in understanding metabolic pathways, enzyme functions, and cellular processes. It has provided valuable insights into various biological processes, including the metabolism of carbohydrates, amino acids, vitamins, and lipids.
- **Research history:** Neurospora has a rich history of research dating back to the early 20th century when it was used by George Beadle and Edward Tatum to establish the "one gene, one enzyme" hypothesis. This groundbreaking work earned them the Nobel Prize in Physiology or Medicine in 1958.

3. (*a*) Economical and Ecological importance of *Sphagnum*:

Economic Importance of *Sphagnum*: *Sphagnum* is a bryophyte which is of great economic importance in plant genera. It is commonly known as *sphagnum moss* or *peat moss*. It inhibits bacterial and fungal growth by acidifying its surroundings. The economic importance of *Sphagnum moss* is derived from its applications in horticulture, floriculture, soil conditioning, wound dressing, water filtration, and its role in supporting research in various fields. The commercial utilization of *Sphagnum moss* contributes to economic activities, employment opportunities, and the growth of industries that rely on its unique properties. Some of the uses showing the economic importance of Sphagnum are listed below:

- **Horticulture and gardening:** *Sphagnum moss* is widely used in the horticulture and gardening industry. It is valued for its exceptional water-holding capacity, air porosity, and ability to retain nutrients. *Sphagnum moss* is used as a component in potting mixes, seed starting media, and as a top dressing for potted plants. It provides excellent moisture retention and promotes healthy root development, making it a preferred choice for growing a wide range of plants, including ornamentals, vegetables, and herbs.

- **Floriculture:** *Sphagnum moss* is commonly used in the floral industry for floral arrangements, wreaths, and hanging baskets. It is prized for its natural beauty, moisture retention, and ability to extend the lifespan of cut flowers and foliage. *Sphagnum moss* helps keep the plant materials hydrated and enhances their presentation, making it a valuable material for floral designers and florists.
- **Soil conditioners:** Due to its high organic matter content and unique physical properties, *Sphagnum moss* is used as a soil conditioner to improve soil structure and fertility. It can be added to garden beds, agricultural fields, and landscapes to enhance moisture retention, promote aeration, and increase nutrient availability. *Sphagnum moss* can improve soil quality in sandy or clayey soils, thereby enhancing crop yields and overall plant health.
- **Wound dressings and medical applications:** *Sphagnum moss* has natural antiseptic properties and high absorbency, making it suitable for wound dressing materials. It has been traditionally used as a wound dressing in some cultures and is still employed in certain medical applications. *Sphagnum moss* has been found to exhibit antibacterial and antifungal properties, and its ability to absorb fluids helps in wound healing processes.
- **Water filtration and purification:** *Sphagnum moss* has been utilized in water filtration systems and as a natural filtration medium. Its dense structure and acidic nature enable it to remove impurities, suspended solids, and certain contaminants from water. *Sphagnum moss* can be employed in both residential and industrial settings for water treatment, helping to improve water quality.
- **Archaeological and paleontological research:** Sphagnum mosses are often found in peat bogs, which preserve organic materials exceptionally well. *Peat bogs* with *Sphagnum moss* have been valuable sources of information for archaeological and paleontological studies. The preserved plant and animal remains found in peat bogs can provide insights into past environments, human history, and climate change.

Ecological Importance of Sphagnum: *Sphagnum moss*, commonly known as peat moss, is a key component of many wetland ecosystems and plays a vital role in the environment. Sphagnum mosses are ecologically important for their contribution to carbon sequestration, water regulation, habitat creation, nutrient cycling, and erosion control in wetland ecosystems. Preserving and restoring Sphagnum-dominated habitats is crucial for maintaining biodiversity, mitigating climate change, and ensuring the health and functioning of these valuable ecosystems. Here are some of the ecological importance of Sphagnum:

- **Carbon sequestration:** Sphagnum mosses have a unique ability to capture and store large amounts of carbon dioxide (CO_2) from the atmosphere through photosynthesis. They accumulate and retain organic matter, creating deep layers of peat. Peatlands, which are dominated by Sphagnum, are among the most efficient carbon sinks on the planet, helping to mitigate climate change by reducing the concentration of greenhouse gases.
- **Water regulation:** *Sphagnum mosses* have exceptional water-holding capacity due to their structure and ability to retain moisture. They can hold up to 20 times their weight in water. This characteristic helps regulate water levels in wetlands by storing water during periods of excess rainfall and slowly releasing it during dry periods. *Sphagnum* also acts as a natural water filter, removing pollutants

and excess nutrients from water, thus improving water quality.

- **Habitat and biodiversity:** *Sphagnum mosses* provide a unique habitat for a wide range of plant and animal species. Their thick, waterlogged carpets create a specialized environment that supports a diverse array of organisms. Many rare and specialized species, such as insect larvae, frogs, and orchids, rely on Sphagnum-dominated wetlands for their survival. The moss also serves as a nursery for various plant species by providing a suitable substrate for germination and growth.
- **Acidification and nutrient cycling:** *Sphagnum mosses* create an acidic environment in peatlands due to the release of organic acids. This acidic condition inhibits the decomposition of organic matter, resulting in the accumulation of peat over time. The low pH conditions favour the growth of Sphagnum while limiting the growth of other plant species. Sphagnum mosses also play a crucial role in nutrient cycling by absorbing and retaining nutrients like nitrogen and phosphorus, thus preventing their release into surrounding water bodies.
- **Erosion control:** *Sphagnum mosses* form dense mats that stabilize the soil and prevent erosion. Their intricate growth pattern and water-holding capacity help to bind and retain soil particles, reducing the risk of erosion caused by wind and water. This is particularly important in wetland areas where the fragile peat layers can be easily eroded if not protected by Sphagnum.

3. (*b*) Gametophytes of Pinus: The initial stage of gametophyte formation is the spore phase. The male gametophyte is represented by the pollen grain or microspore, whereas the female gametophyte, or the initial stage of it, is represented by the megaspore.

Development of Female Gametophyte: The female gametophyte of Pinus develops from the functional megaspore which enlarges considerably. The nucleus of the megaspore divides mitotically forming a large number of nuclei unaccompanied by wall formation. The number of free nuclei is constant for a particular species, say for example, it is 2,000 for *P. gerardiana* and 2,500 for *P. roxburghii* and *P. wallichiana*. With the increase in size, the megaspore develops a vacuole at the centre which forces by cytoplasm along with nuclei towards the periphery. Thus, the nuclei lie in a thin film of cytoplasm around the vacuole. Thereafter, the cell wall formation starts in a centripetal fashion, from periphery inwards. At this stage, numerous radially elongated multinucleate tube-like cells called alveoli are formed and the wall formation takes place through alveoli. Each alveolus containing a nucleus at its mouth directs its growth.

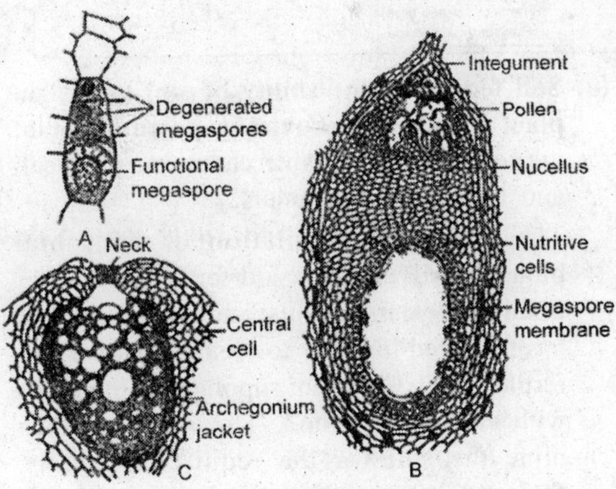

Pinus: A. Linear tetrad showing large functional megaspore.
B. Free nuclear stage of female gametophyte,
C. An archegonium.

Then, cross-walls are laid down on each alveolus to form uninucleate cells. In this way, the entire gametophyte becomes cellular and the tissue thus formed represents endosperm or female prothallus.

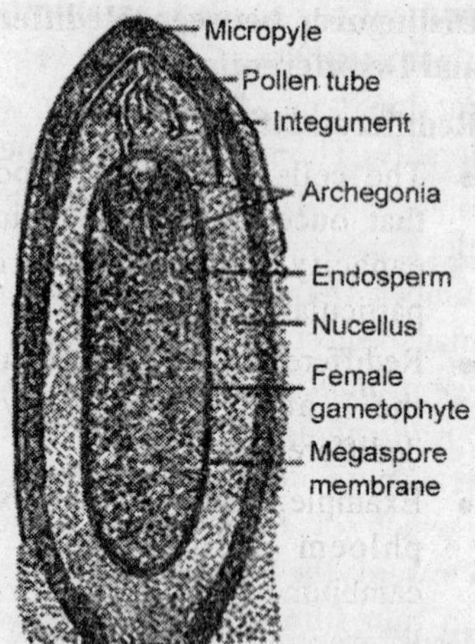

***Pinus*: Median L.S. of a mature ovule**

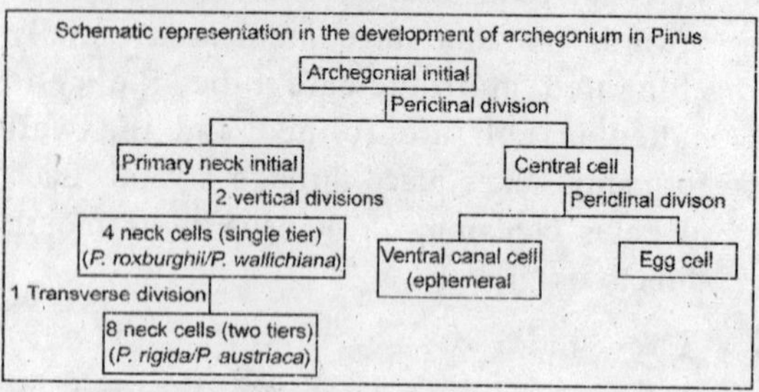

3. (*c*) Soil fertility is the ability of soil to sustain plant growth by providing essential plant nutrients and favourable chemical, physical, and biological parameters.

The microbial population or microbial biomass (MB) reflects soil fertility. For over 2 million years, plants and soil microbes have worked together to create what we call fertile "soil". The plant supplies the microbes with carbon rich food. The microbes then mine the soil for the required minerals. Microbes can actually manufacture nitrogen and antibiotics that protect the plant from pathogens in return creating carbon stores that build soil structure and sequester carbon. Like all good partners, what is good for one is good for the other, i.e., a healthy MB predicts a healthy plant. Therefore, supplying NPK directly to plants disrupts the plant microbe relationship - plants no longer feed the microbes and the MB decreases accordingly. Soils with low MB suffer from erosion, compaction, and poor structure. Sadly, this is how we have lost 50% of the earth's soil.

Soil microbes, like all living things, need food. They need to be fed carbon and nitrogen from plants or organic matter so they can mine the minerals, P, K, Mg, Cu, S etc. from the soil. If there is not enough of any nutrient, including the minerals that should be in the soil, it negatively affects the number of microbes; just as humans do not thrive when we are deficient in a critical nutrient.

Role of bacteria in increasing soil fertility:

- Bacteria increase soil fertility through nutrient recycling such as carbon, nitrogen, sulphur, and phosphorus.
- Bacteria decompose dead organic matter and release simple compounds in the soil, which can be taken up by plants.
- Nitrogen-fixing bacteria fix atmospheric nitrogen and increase the nitrogen content of the soil, which can be readily absorbed by plants. They also improve soil structure and increase the water-holding capacity of the soil.

Example: Rhizobium is an example of a symbiotic bacterium that attaches to the roots of leguminous plants and it increases soil fertility by converting atmospheric nitrogen into organic compounds.

5. (*a*) Salient Features of Brassicaceae: Following are the important characteristics of the family

- These are generally herbs, annuals, biennials, or shrubs.
- The taproots are swollen due to food storage.
- The stem is erect, herbaceous, and rarely woody.
- Leaves are alternate, opposite, simple and exstipulate

Economically Important of Three Plants of Brassicaceae Family:

Cotton: **Botanical Name:** *Gossypium barbadense*

Wheat: **Botanical Name:** *Triticum aestivum*

Black pepper: **Botanical Name:** *Piper nigrum*

5. (*b*) Pollen Characters of Taxonomic Importance: Pollen morphology is conducted as an aid to the morphological study and a significant tool for modern taxonomist for the delimitation of species. Mature pollen grain size, exine sculpturing, and number of pores are the most distinctive features. Pollen characters are useful in solving complicated problems of interrelationships between various taxa and assessment of their status in the classification, particularly with reference to the families, subfamilies, tribes, genera, species, and subspecies. Pollen morphology is conducted as an aid to the morphological study and a significant tool for modern taxonomist for the delimitation of species. Mature pollen grain size, exine sculpturing, and number of pores are the most distinctive features. Palynological data has been useful at generic and specific level.

5. (*c*) Scientific Name, Family and Economically Important Part of Two Beverage Yielding Plants: Beverage crops are those crops through which we get liquids other than water. Any portable liquid is known as a beverage. It is a liquid that is intended for drinking. It is a less formal word for a drink. It plays an important role in human life. It provides energy and freshness to our bodies.

1. Tea

Botanical Name: *Camellia sinensis* (L).

Family: Theaceae

Economically Important Part: *Leaves*

2. Coffee (Hindi - Kafi):

Botanical Name: *Coffea arabica*

Family: *Rubiaceae*

Economically Important Part: *Berries*

5. (*d*) (*i*) Distinguish between Redifferentiation and Dedifferentiation:

Redifferentiation:

- The cells divide and produce cells that once again lose their dividing capacity but mature to carry out particular tasks.
- Redifferentiation is the event of losing the ability to divide by dedifferentiated cells.
- Example: The secondary xylem and phloem formation in vascular cambium.

Dedifferentiation:

- The cells that have lost their capability to divide and attain a specific function is known as differentiation.
- When certain conditions are met, cells that have lost the ability to divide regain it.
- Dedifferentiation is the process through which mature cells revert to their pluripotent state.
- The cork cambium and interfascicular cambium are examples of dedifferentiated tissues.

(*ii*) Distinguish between Indirect Organogenesis and Direct Organogenesis: Indirect organogenesis and direct organogenesis are two different pathways involved in the process of plant tissue culture, specifically in the regeneration of new plant organs from explants (small pieces of plant tissue). Here's how they differ:

Indirect Organogenesis:

- In indirect organogenesis, the regeneration of new plant organs occurs through an intermediate callus phase.
- Callus is a mass of undifferentiated, rapidly dividing cells that forms at the cut or wounded surface of the explant.

- Initially, the explant is cultured on a nutrient medium containing plant growth regulators such as auxins (e.g., 2, 4-dichlorophenoxyacetic acid or 2, 4-D) to induce callus formation.
- The callus tissue can then be subcultured onto a medium with different growth regulators to promote the development of specific organs such as shoots or roots.
- Eventually, shoots or roots develop from the callus tissue, leading to the formation of new plantlets.
- Indirect organogenesis involves a sequence of cellular changes, including dedifferentiation of the explant cells into a callus, followed by redifferentiation into new organs.

Direct Organogenesis:

- In direct organogenesis, the regeneration of new plant organs occurs directly from the explant without an intermediate callus phase.
- The explant is cultured on a nutrient medium containing specific plant growth regulators, typically cytokinins, which promote the direct formation of shoots or roots.
- The presence of cytokinins in the culture medium stimulates the growth of buds or shoots from the preexisting meristematic cells present in the explant.
- These buds or shoots elongate and develop into complete plantlets with shoots and roots.
- Direct organogenesis bypasses the callus formation step and directly induces the formation of specific organs, hence the name.

5. (*e*) **Merits and Demerits of Rolf Dahlgren's System of Classification:** Rolf Dahlgren was a Swedish botanist known for his contributions to plant taxonomy and classification. He proposed a system of classification known as the Dahlgren system, which was based on the principles of evolutionary relationships and shared characteristics among plants. While the Dahlgren system had its merits, it also faced certain limitations. Let's explore the merits and demerits of Rolf Dahlgren's system of classification:

Merits of the Dahlgren System:

- **Phylogenetic Basis:** The Dahlgren system aimed to reflect the evolutionary relationships among plants by considering their shared characteristics. It focused on grouping plants based on their genetic relatedness and common ancestry, providing a framework for understanding plant evolution.
- **Comparative Approach:** Dahlgren emphasized the importance of comparing various plant structures, including reproductive organs, vegetative characteristics, and embryological features, to determine relationships and classify plants. This approach allowed for a more comprehensive understanding of plant diversity.
- **Emphasis on Key Features:** The Dahlgren system focused on certain key features, such as the nature of the embryo, presence or absence of vascular bundles, and floral characteristics, which played a crucial role in plant classification. This allowed for a more detailed and nuanced categorization of plants.
- **Utilization of Modern Techniques:** Dahlgren incorporated modern techniques, such as electron microscopy and phytochemistry, into his classification system. These techniques provided additional information about plant structure and composition, enhancing the accuracy and precision of the system.

Demerits of the Dahlgren System:

- **Lack of Universality:** The Dahlgren system was primarily designed for flowering plants (angiosperms) and did not cover other plant groups comprehensively. It had limited applicability to non-flowering plants like ferns, mosses, and algae, which required separate classification systems.

- **Overemphasis on Certain Characteristics:** The Dahlgren system relied heavily on certain characteristics, such as floral structure, which led to an overemphasis on these features. This could result in misclassification or inadequate representation of plant diversity, especially in groups with unique evolutionary traits.
- **Incomplete Representation of Evolutionary Relationships:** While the Dahlgren system aimed to represent evolutionary relationships, it faced challenges in accurately depicting complex evolutionary patterns. The system was based on available knowledge and technology at the time and may not have accounted for recent discoveries or advancements in molecular biology.
- **Subjectivity and Subject to Revision:** Classification systems, including the Dahlgren system, are subjective to some extent, as they rely on the interpretation and judgment of the taxonomist. Additionally, as scientific knowledge advances, new evidence may require revisions or modifications to the system, potentially altering the classification of certain plant groups.

7. (*a*) The term haploid refers to those plants which contains gametophytic number of chromosomes. Anther/pollen culture mediated production of haploid plants approves the concept of totipotency. Guha and Maheshwari in 1964 reported direct development of haploid embryo from pollen of Datura innoxia by anther culture. In an extended work, Bourgin and Nitsch in 1967 were able to accomplish complete haploid plants in Nicotiana tobacco. Since then there have been upsurge interest in the production of haploids due to their considerable potential for plant breeding. One of the bases for haploid productions vitro is due to application in cell biology, genetics of higher plants and haploid breeding. Haploids can be exploited to detect and recover mutants in the plants. In plant mutation breeding, mutants are recessive and are difficult to recover due to heterozygous nature of plant. However, haploid exhibit only one set of alleles and facilitates easy detection of mutants. In addition, doubling of haploid chromosomes leads to the production of homozygous plants in short span of time. The time taken for haploid production using conventional breeding requires several years. Therefore, anther culture offers a novel tool for the production of haploid.

- **Anther Culture Technique:** The sterilization of flower buds is initiated by sterilizing agents such as sodium hypochlorite (2%) or calcium hypochlorite (5%). After repeated rinse with sterile distilled water to remove all tracers of mercuric chloride, flower buds are carefully inscised under aseptic environment and sepals and petals are completely removed. The anthers are then dissected out and cultured on agar medium. Anther filaments are cut off carefully to avoid damaging of anther. The damaged portion in the anther may tend to develop callus. Generally 6-10 anthers are placed in the culture vessel. Observation in tobacco anther culture shows that anthers cultured on media turn brownish within 12-15 days (2 weeks). After 2-3 weeks in culture, small callus like protruberance is seen and entire callus mass is emerged or burst out from the anther or embryo emerged out and develops into plantlet. The callus may also differentiate to plantlets. The plantlets emerged out of the anthers in

4-5 weeks. In the case of microspore or pollen culture, anthers are excised and about 10-15 numbers (anthers) are transferred into sterilized beaker. The anthers are then crushed against wall of the beaker using glass rod. Pollens are squeezed out to collect at the bottom of the beaker containing suitable aqueous media. The anther extract are selected for centrifugation (100-150 g) and collected the pellet of pollen grains. The isolated pollen is washed and subjected to culture.

- **Microspore Culture:** Certain culture method like nurse culture is generally followed by isolated microspore culture. In this method, anther of mother plant is placed horizontally in the container supplied with shallow layer of liquid media. A filter paper disc is placed above the anther and about ten pollen grains are placed on the filter paper disc. The proliferation of microspore results in cluster of parenchymatous cells within 1 to 2 weeks. These clones were then transferred to agar culture media for successful induction of androgenesis.
- **Diploitization:** Haploid plants can produce flower, but they are sterile. In order to ensure the production of fertile haploid plants, diploitization process is required. Diploitization is accomplished by treating plantlet obtained by anthers directly in colchicine solution for 24 hrs. In another method colchicine paste can be prepared and applied directly on the axils of in vitro haploid plantlets. After colchicine treatment, homozygous diploid plants are obtained due to the duplication of chromosomes. These homozygous diploid plants are fertile.
- **Plant Regeneration:** Regeneration from embryo is a simple procedure and can take place on the induction medium. While most of the media containing growth regulators and high sucrose levels, plantlets development fail to occur unless the embryos are shifted to embryo culture media, which is free from hormones and low sucrose concentration. When callus is produced from microspore, regeneration is accomplished on hormones free or low level of auxin with increased level of cytokinin. When auxin is essential, certain auxins like IAA is often employed. Benzyl adenine and kinetins are the commonly used cytokinin in the medium. In cereals, regeneration frequencies occur at less frequency and still decreases with increasing callus age. Appearance of albinos due to the 2, 4-D, is another serious problems in regeneration of cereals.
- **Characteristics of Microspore Derived Plants:** The majority of microspore derived plants are haploids, but in some cases, both diploid and polyploids may be present as in case of tobacco. Aneuploids and mixaploid chimeras have also been sighted commonly in vitro. Several occasions, evidence for homozygous natures of anther derived diploids are seen from genetic is biochemical analysis. Convincing evidence based on cytological studies reveals that diploids and polyploids problem arise due to the nuclear fusion or endureduplication in microspore during culture. In addition, culture temperature is also added to the problem in vitro.

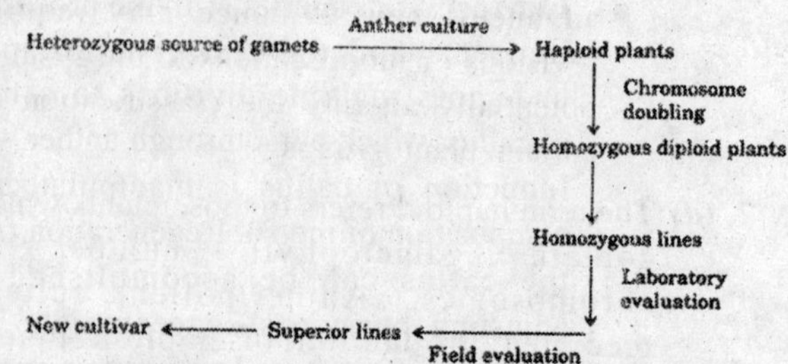

- **Ontogeny of Androgenesis:** Anther culture shows various modes of microspore development leading to androgenesis. They are direct and indirect androgenesis.

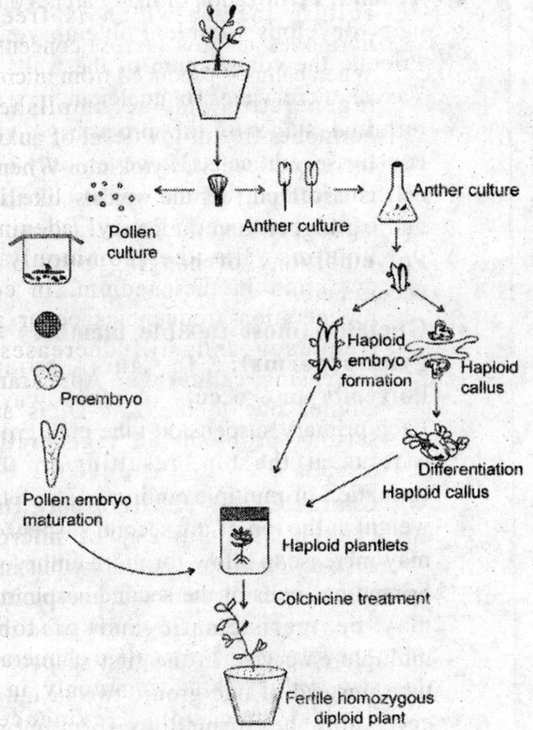

***In vitro* Haploid Production — an overview**

- **Direct Androgenesis:** During microspore development, various stages of embryogenesis are followed due to the behaviour of microspore like zygote. The embryo is released at globular stage from exine and continues to develop further and finally cotyledons are transformed into plantlets.
- **Indirect Androgenesis:** In the process of indirect androgenesis, microspore undergoes multiple divisions to a mass of callus, which burst through anther wall. Induction of callus is manipulated by composition of media. Regeneration from the callus can be accomplished by adjusting hormones concentration. The callus is differentiated to form embryo or shoots and further transformed into plantlets.

7. (*b*) Scientific name, family and commercially important plant parts:

***(i)* Hemp:**

Scientific Name: *Cannabis sativa*

Family: *Cannabaceae*

Commercially Important Plant Parts: The flowers and leaves of the female hemp plant are used for various purposes, such as the production of CBD (cannabidiol) oil, fiber, and seeds. Hemp fibers are used in textiles, paper, and construction materials, while hemp seeds are consumed as a nutritional food source and used for oil extraction.

***(ii)* Nutmeg:**

Scientific Name: *Myristica fragrans*

Family: *Myristicaceae*

Commercially Important Plant Parts: The seed of the nutmeg plant is the commercially valuable part. It is used as a spice and flavoring agent in culinary applications, including baking, cooking, and beverages. Nutmeg is also used in the production of essential oils and is known for its medicinal properties.

***(iii)* Indigo:**

Scientific Name: *Indigofera tinctoria* (common indigo)

Family: *Fabaceae* (Leguminosae)

Commercially Important Plant Parts: The leaves of the indigo plant are primarily used for their dyeing properties. They contain a blue pigment called indigo, which is used to produce a natural blue dye. Indigo dye has been used historically for coloring textiles, especially in the production of blue denim.

***(iv)* Ergot:**

Scientific Name: *Claviceps purpurea*

Family: *Clavicipitaceae*

Commercially Important Plant Parts: Ergot is a fungal disease that affects various grasses, including rye, wheat, barley, and oats. The fungal sclerotia, also known as ergot bodies, are the commercially important part. They contain alkaloids with pharmaceutical properties and have been historically used to produce ergotamine, a medication used for treating migraines.

(*v*) **Jatropha:**

Scientific Name: *Jatropha curcas*

Family: *Euphorbiaceae*

Commercially Important Plant Parts: The seeds of the jatropha plant are commercially valuable. They are used for the extraction of jatropha oil, which is a potential biofuel source. Jatropha oil can be processed into biodiesel and used as a renewable energy alternative to fossil fuels. Additionally, jatropha seeds contain a toxic compound called curcin, which has potential applications in pest control.

7. (*c*) **Polyembryony:** The production of two or more than two embryos from a single seed or fertilized egg is termed as Polyembryony. In plants, this phenomenon is caused either due to the fertilization of one or more than one embryonic sac or due to the origination of embryos outside of the embryonic sac.

Polyembryony with Different Types of Gymnosperms

- **Cycadales (living organs and bones):** Although rare, this group exhibits Simple Polyembryony. It was first spotted by A.N. Rao at Cycas Circinalis. Two connected arches of the same ovule sometimes grow independently into two embryos and rarely have two seedlings.
- **Coniferales (found in cooler regions and incorporating both extinct and living forms):** This section presents both Polyembryony Simple and Cleavage. Cleavage embryos have been reported in Pine, Cedrus, Tsuga, Sciadopitys, Sequoia, Thuja, Juniperus and Podocarpus. However, both are common in the Pressressus.
- **Texales:** Fertilization of many archegonia eggs develops Simple Polyembryony. Prior to the construction of the walls at Taxus, there were 16 nuclei in it. The terminal stage of the proembryo can contain several cells. However, only one cell cuts off part of the apical cell thus gaining higher than the others. Cleavage Polyembryony of hanging cells also occurs here.
- **Gnetales (most flexible members of gymnosperms):** In this group, Polyembryony occurs in many ways. Each primary suspension tube may grow a fetus at the top, resulting in the formation of multiple embryos. The fetal weight at the top of the second suspensor may increase to allow for more embryos. Sometimes cells of the second suspensor may be meristematic and produce multiple embryos. In the first suspensor tube, instead of one group, two or more cells may be formed to form more embryos at the top.

Practical Value of Polyembryony: In the past, polyembryony was considered a rare ingredient but is now regarded as a desirable ingredient in citrus fruits, mangoes, jams, roses, apples, almonds, and so on, to find products of real value. It is therefore a very important part of Horticulture and in particular, Nucellar adventive polyembryony is very important to it. It helps to maintain the similarity between parent and offspring. Nucellar plants show energy recovery. In addition, nucellar embryos are disease-free. There is a lot of practical importance in polyembryony. It is particularly useful for the propagation of certain species of plants. For instance, adventive embryos, which retain characteristics of the parent plant, are used to create genetically uniform seedlings of citrus and mango. Moreover, in the case of citrus, grafts from other types are also used in orchard stock.

PAPER-II

1. (*a*) Membrane Lipids: Membrane lipids are an essential component of plant cell membranes. In botany, the most common membrane lipids are phospholipids, glycolipids, and sphingolipids. Phospholipids are the most abundant membrane lipids in plants. They consist of a polar head group, usually phosphoric acid, and two hydrophobic fatty acid tails. Phospholipids play a crucial role in the formation of the lipid bilayer, which forms the structural basis of cell membranes. Phosphatidylcholine, phosphatidylethanolamine, and phosphatidylserine are some of the most common phospholipids found in plant cell membranes. Glycolipids are another important class of membrane lipids in plants. They consist of a hydrophilic carbohydrate head group and a hydrophobic fatty acid tail. Glycolipids are important for cell-to-cell communication and the formation of plant cell walls. One example of a glycolipid found in plant cell membranes is monogalactosyldiacylglycerol (MGDG). Sphingolipids are a third class of membrane lipids found in plant cells. They are structurally similar to phospholipids but have a sphingosine backbone instead of a glycerol backbone. Sphingolipids are important for cell signaling and cell recognition. One example of a sphingolipid found in plant cell membranes is ceramide. Membrane lipids play a critical role in the structure and function of plant cell membranes. They are essential for maintaining the integrity of the cell, regulating the movement of molecules into and out of the cell, and mediating cell signaling and communication.

1. (*b*) Cyclin and Cyclin-dependent Kinases: Cyclins are among the most important core cell cycle regulators. Cyclins are a group of related proteins, and there are four basic types found in humans and most other eukaryotes: G_1/S cyclins, and M cyclins. As the names suggest, each cyclin is associated with a particular phase, transition, or set of phases in the cell cycle and helps drive the events of that phase or period. For instance, M cyclin promotes the events of M phase, such as nuclear envelope breakdown and chromosome condensation.

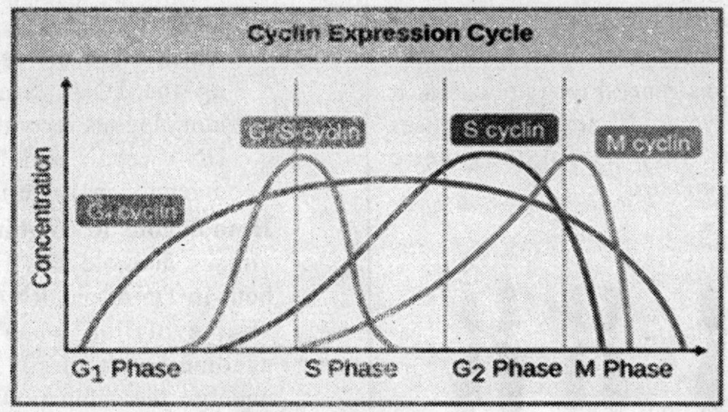

Control of the Cell Cycle

The levels of the different cyclins vary considerably across the cell cycle, as shown in the diagram at right. A typical cyclin is present at low levels for most of the cycle, but increases strongly at the stage where it's needed. M cyclin, for example, peaks dramatically at the transition from G_2 to M phase. G_1 cyclins are unusual in that they are needed for much of the cell cycle.

Cyclin-dependent kinases: In order to drive the cell cycle forward, a cyclin must activate or inactivate many target proteins inside of the cell. Cyclins drive the events of the cell cycle by partnering with a family of enzymes called the Cyclin-dependent kinases (Cdks). A lone Cdk is inactive, but the binding of a cyclin activates it, making it a functional enzyme and allowing it to modify target proteins. Cdks are kinases, enzymes that phosphorylate (attach phosphate groups to) specific target proteins. The attached phosphate group acts like a switch, making the target protein more or less active. When a cyclin attaches to a Cdk, it has two important effects: it activates the Cdk as a kinase, but it also directs the Cdk to a specific set of target proteins, ones appropriate to the cell cycle period controlled by the cyclin. For instance, G_1/ S cyclins send Cdks to S phase targets (e.g., promoting DNA replication), while M cyclins send Cdks to M phase targets (e.g., making the nuclear membrane break down).

1. (*c*) Homologous Recombination: "Homologous recombi-nation is the exchange of genetic information between two similar or identical strands of a double-stranded DNA molecule." It is also known as general recombination. It occurs in eukaryotes, bacteria and viruses naturally. It is very useful in genetic engineering techniques.

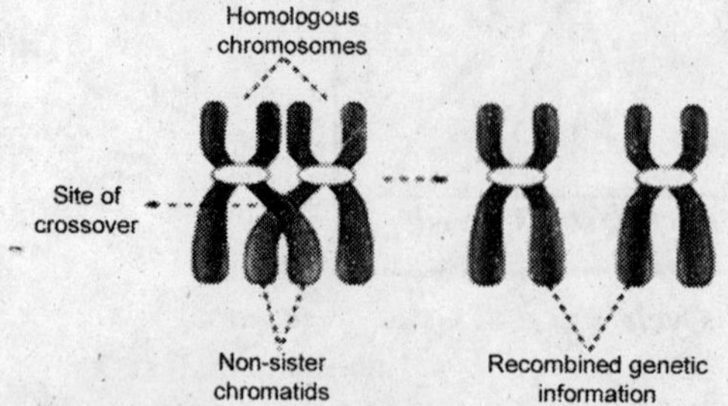

Homologous Recombination in Eukaryotes

- **DNA Repair:** Homologous recombination plays an important role in repairing damaged DNA. DNA strands that are damaged by ionizing radiation or chemicals undergo recombination during mitosis to overcome the injury. If left unrepaired, these broken DNA can go on to amplify and cause mutations in the genome.
- **Genetic Diversity:** The sex cells undergo meiosis to produce specialised cells called ovum and sperm. During the process of meiosis, chromosomal crossover takes place which is the exchange of genetic material between homologous chromosomes. This event of recombination brings genetic diversity every time an organism reproduces.

Homologous Recombination in Bacteria:

- Horizontal gene transfer is the phenomenon of transferring foreign DNA into another organism without being related to it. The incoming DNA is highly similar to the receiver's DNA, and they undergo homologous recombination to incorporate the foreign DNA.
- It is the process of the transfer of DNA from one organism to another within the same species. They undergo homologous recombination to incorporate the donor DNA by binding to several proteins, which make the cells competent to take up the DNA. Similar to eukaryotes, homologous recombination also helps in DNA repair and brings about genetic diversity in bacteria.

Homologous Recombination in Viruses: In viruses, homologous recombination occurs both in DNA and RNA strands. It helps in viral evolution when two separate viral genomes with disadvantageous mutations undergo recombination and produce a fully functional genome. Homologous recombination is also a primary phenomenon in the incorporation of human herpesvirus - 6 in human telomeres causing rashes, fever and in infants and children. Covid-19 caused by the SARS-Cov-2 virus is also a result of viral evolution by homologous recombination.

1. (*d*) Characteristics of Cytoplasmic Inheritance: Cyto-plasmic inheritance refers to the inheritance of genetic material that is located outside the nucleus of the cell, specifically in the cytoplasm. This type of inheritance is typically found in organisms that have cells with both a nucleus and other organelles, such as mitochondria and chloroplasts. Here are some key characteristics of cytoplasmic inheritance:

- **Uniparental inheritance:** In cytoplasmic inheritance, the genetic material is passed down from only one parent, usually the mother. This is because the cytoplasmic organelles, such as mitochondria, are usually inherited exclusively from the mother's egg.
- **Maternal inheritance:** The inheritance pattern for cytoplasmic genes is often called maternal inheritance, as the maternal parent's cytoplasm provides the majority of the cytoplasmic organelles to the offspring.
- **Non-Mendelian inheritance:** Cyto-plasmic inheritance does not follow the classic Mendelian inheritance pattern of dominant and recessive alleles. Instead, it typically shows a more complex pattern of inheritance, with traits being influenced by the presence or absence of multiple cytoplasmic genes.
- **Mitochondrial DNA:** The most well-known example of cytoplasmic inheritance is the inheritance of mitochondrial DNA, which is responsible for energy production in the cell. Mitochondrial DNA is typically maternally inherited and has its own unique characteristics compared to nuclear DNA.
- **Chloroplast inheritance:** In plants, chloroplasts are also inherited via the cytoplasm, and the genes that they contain can influence traits such as leaf colour and shape.

1. (*e*) Uses of Backcrossing in Plant Breeding: Backcross breeding enables breeders to transfer a desired trait such as a transgene from one variety (donor parent, DP) into the favoured genetic background of another (recurrent parent, RP). If the trait of interest is produced by a dominant gene, this process involves four rounds of backcrossing within seven seasons. If the gene is recessive, this process requires more generations of selfing and thus nine or more seasons are needed. The rate at which the DP genes are removed and the RP genes are recovered in the genetic makeup of the plant can be calculated using the number of backcross generations utilized. This rate is dramatically increased with the recent advances in marker technology which allow breeders to control the gene of interest and control the genetic background.

Backcrossing can be used to introduce a wide range of traits, such as disease resistance, insect resistance, yield potential, and quality attributes, among others. It is especially useful when the trait of interest is controlled by a single gene, as it allows for efficient transfer of the trait from the donor parent to the recurrent parent. Backcrossing is a powerful tool in plant breeding that allows breeders to combine desirable traits from different plant varieties to create new cultivars with improved characteristics.

3. (*a*) Process of Regulation of *lac* operon in *E. coli*: Gene expression is basically the synthesis of the polypeptide chain encoded by a particular gene. Therefore, we can say that the expression of the gene can be quantified in terms of the amount of protein synthesised by the genes.

Regulation of Gene Expression: We can infer that the gene regulation can take place at various steps of gene expression which includes the following:

- **Replication level:** Any error in copying the DNA may result in an altered expression.
- **Transcriptional level:** During transcription, any error in the polymerization may again lead to a change in expression of the gene.
- **Post-transcriptional level:** During the post-transcriptional modification i.e., RNA splicing, there may be some changes.
- **Translational level:** During translation, if there is an error in the attachment of *m*RNA to the *t*RNA molecules, there may arise some changes.

The regulation of the expression of the gene can be explained with the example of an enzyme, say peroxidase in bacteria. This enzyme catalyzes the hydrolysis of hydrogen peroxide to water and oxygen. Now, if the bacteria are moved to another environment where they fail to manufacture hydrogen peroxide, the enzyme no longer plays its role. In such a situation, the bacteria will not synthesize the enzyme anymore. Thus, we can say that the environmental, metabolic and physiological condition regulates the expression of genes.

Gene Regulation in *E. coli*: Gene regulation in prokaryotes is most extensively observed at the initiation of transciption. Thus, the gene expression during transcription initiation is affected by regulation. The regulation usually takes place in the expression of the RNA polymerase at the promoter site. This affects the accessory proteins which bind to the recognition sites. These accessory proteins can regulate the promoter site in two ways:

- Positive regulation by activators
- Negative regulation by repressors

In Operons, the operator is situated right next to the promoter where the regulator binds to control its entire functioning.

Lac Operon: Lac operon is an operon or a group of genes with a single promoter that encode genes for the transport and metabolism of lactose in *E. coli* and other bacteria.

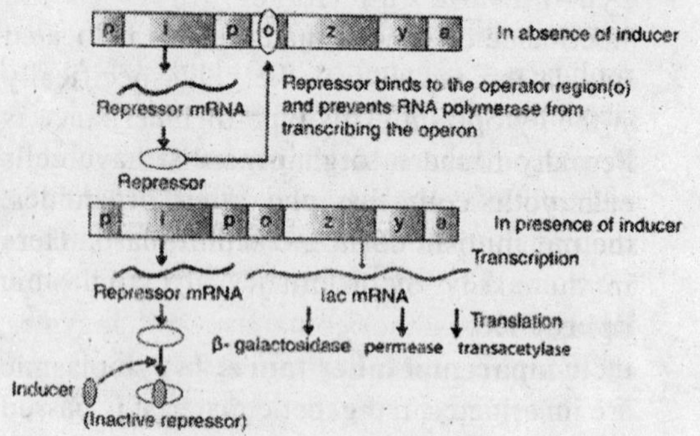

Lac Operon

Gene regulation in prokaryotes can be explained with the help of the Lac Operon model. Here the alteration in physiological and environmental conditions can be observed leading to an alteration in expression in prokaryotes. It was observed by Jacob and Monod. The lac operon consists of:

- **Regulatory gene *i*:** It codes for the repressor protein.
- ***z* gene:** It codes for beta-galactosidase which catalyzes the hydrolysis of lactose into glucose and galactose.
- ***y* gene:** It codes for permease which regulates the lactose permeability in the cell.
- ***a* gene:** It codes for transacetylase which assists the enzyme beta-galactosidase.

3. (*b*) Peroxisomes are eukaryotic cells' membrane-bound organelles present in the cytoplasm. The oxidation of biomolecules is carried out by these organelles. Peroxisome reticulum is a type of peroxisome present in the liver cells of mammals and plants. Peroxisomes are small spherical organelles that are mostly found in eukaryotic cells and are surrounded by cell membranes. Peroxisomes include digestive enzymes as well as oxidative enzymes. These are also known as peroxisome reticulum and are found in the liver cells of mammals and plants. Peroxisomes are necessary for the production of phospholipids, which are necessary for nerve cell myelination. They are self-replicating organelles that lack DNA and ribosomes and are found in eukaryotic cells. Peroxisomes are small organelles found in eukaryotic cells that play a crucial role in the metabolism of biomolecules, particularly in the oxidation of fatty acids and other lipids. Peroxisomes contain several enzymes, including catalase and various oxidases, that are involved in the breakdown of various biomolecules. The primary function of peroxisomes is the breakdown of fatty acids, which is accomplished through a series of oxidation reactions. The fatty acids are first activated by the addition of coenzyme A, which allows them to be transported into the peroxisome. Once inside the peroxisome, the fatty acids are oxidized by various enzymes, producing acetyl-CoA, which can be used by the cell for energy production. In addition to fatty acid oxidation, peroxisomes are also involved in the breakdown of other biomolecules, such as amino acids, and the detoxification of harmful substances, such as hydrogen peroxide. Overall, peroxisomes play a critical role in maintaining cellular homeostasis and are essential for the proper functioning of many tissues and organs in the body.

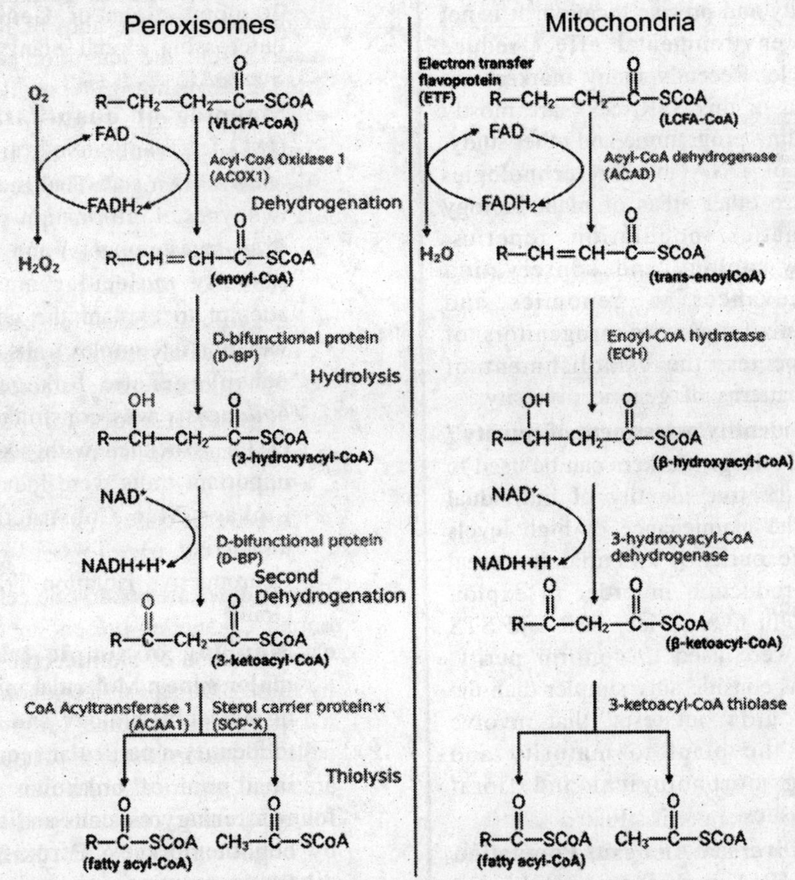

The process of peroxisomal β-oxidation

3. (*c*) Role of Molecular Markers in Plant Breeding: Molecular marker may be defined as any site (locus) in the genome of an organism at which the DNA base sequence varies among the different individuals of a population. Such markers generally have no apparent effect on the phenotype of the individual. Genetic markers represent genetic differences between individual organisms or species. Generally, they do not represent the target genes themselves but act as 'signs' or 'flags'. Genetic markers that are located in close proximity to genes (i.e. tightly linked) may be referred to as gene 'tags'. DNA (or molecular) markers a type of genetic markers, which reveal sites of variation in DNA.

Molecular markers are widely used in crop improvement due to its simplicity, reproducibility and precise location. It is not affected to environmental effect reduce breeding cycle. Recently many markers are available, out of this SSR, SNP are mostly used in breeding programme and other study. Application of DNA marker technologies molecular also other areas of plant biology like systematics, population genetics, evolutionary biology and conservation genetics, advances in genomics and identification of the wild progenitors of domestic species, the establishment of geographic patterns of genetic diversity.

- **Cultivar identity/assessment of 'purity'/ Hybrid Testing:** Markers can be used to confirm the true identity of individual plants. The maintenance of high levels of genetic purity is essential in cereal hybrid production in order to exploit heterosis. In hybrid rice, SSR and STS markers were used to confirm purity, which was considerably simpler than the standard 'grow-out tests' that involve growing the plant to maturity and assessing morphological and floral characteristics.
- **Genetic Diversity Analysis/ Population genetics:** DNA markers are useful in the assessment of genetic diversity in germplasm, cultivars and advanced breeding material using several techniques, such as restriction fragment length polymorphism (RFLP), random amplified polymorphic DNA (RAPD), amplified fragment length polymorphism (AFLP) and microsatellites. In general, type II markers such as RAPDs, microsatellites, and AFLPs are considered to be non-coding. Such markers have found widespread use in population genetic studies. SSR marker based genetic diversity analysis of modern rice varities and coastal landraces. RAPD-PCR (randomly amplified polymorphic DNA polymerase chain reaction) for a study of the genetic diversity within and among 20 populations of Geum reptans, an outcrossing clonal plant species in the Swiss Alps.
- **Mapping of quantitative trait loci (QTL):** Quantitative trait locus (QTL) analysis is a statistical method that links two types of information-phenotypic data (trait measurements) and genotypic data (usually molecular markers)- in an attempt to explain the genetic basis of variation in complex traits. The first high-density genetic linkage map for *P. haitanensis* was constructed and fifteen QTLs associated with six economically important traits were identified. Genetic Linkage Map Construction and QTL analysis of Two Inter specific Reproductive Isolation Traits in Sponge Gourd .
- **Mapping of simple traits/Mapping major genes:** Molecular markers are used in molecular biology and biotechnology to identify a particular sequence of DNA in a pool of unknown DNA. Genes conferring resistance to the bacterial blight e.g. xa5 , Xa2 , X*a*25(*b*) and Rice Blast resistance genes e.g. Pi24 .

- **Mapping of mutations:** Genetic mapping of a mutation-defined gene is the first step toward isolating and cloning the corresponding normal gene and ultimately identifying its encoded protein. Genetic mapping using next-generation sequencing that combines single nucleotide polymorphism discovery, mutation localization and potential identification of causal sequence variants. CandiSNP is a user-friendly application that will aid in novel discoveries from forward-genetic mutant screens.
- **Marker-assisted selection (MAS):** Once tightly linked markers have been identified to the genes or QTLs, they should be used for MAS. DNA markers are used in the marker assisted or marker aided selection. MAS have several advantages over straight selection.
- **Marker-assisted pyramiding:** Pyramiding is the simultaneous integration of multiple genes/QTLs into a single genotype. DNA markers may facilitate selection, without phenotyping. The most widely application of pyramiding is the integration of multiple disease resistance genes into a plant to develop "durable" or stable resistance to a disease.
- **Marker assisted back cross breeding (MAB):** Backcrossing is a plant breeding method most commonly used to incorporate one or a few genes into an adapted or elite variety. The use of DNA markers in backcrossing greatly increases the efficiency of selection.
- **Molecular taxonomy and evolution:** DNA markers are useful in the study of crop evolution. The development of increasingly informative molecular markers has allowed for detailed investigations of the evolution of a number of crops e.g. identification of crop progenitors.
- **Identification of individuals:** More recently molecular markers, such as SNPs and simple sequence repeats (SSRs) have been developed for the selection of fragrant rice.

4. (*a*) Lampbrush chromosomes: These are the largest known chromosomes found in the yolk rich oocytic nuclei of certain vertebrates such as fishes, amphibians, reptiles and birds. They can be seen with naked eye and are characterized by fine lateral loops, arising from the chromomeres, during first prophase (diplotene) of meiosis.

These loops give it a brush-like appearance; that is why these are called lampbrush chromosomes first discovered by Flemming in 1882 and were described in shark oocytes by Ruckert (1892). Lampbrush chromosomes of certain urodele oocytes may reach upto 5900μ in length.

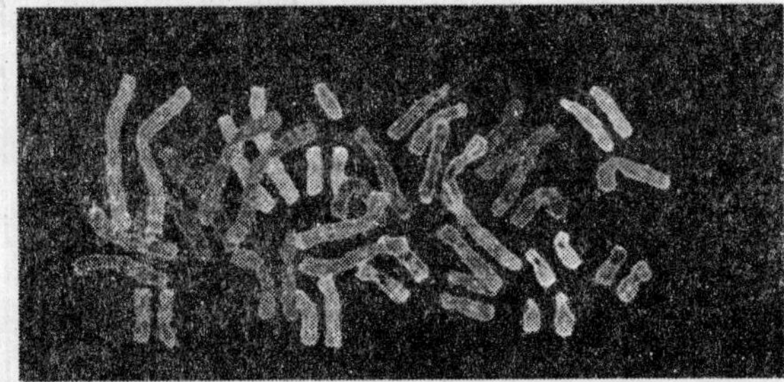

It consists of longitudinal axis formed by a single DNA molecule along which several hundred bead-like chromomeres are distributed in a linear fashion. From each chromomere there emerge two symmetrical lateral loops (one for each chromatid), which are able to expand or contract in response to various environmental conditions.

About 5 to 10% of the DNA is in the lateral loops. Loop formation reduces the mass of the corresponding chromomeres, implying a spinning out of chromomere material into the lateral strands. The centromeres also have the appearance of elongate Feulgen-positive chromomeres but they characteristically lack lateral loops.

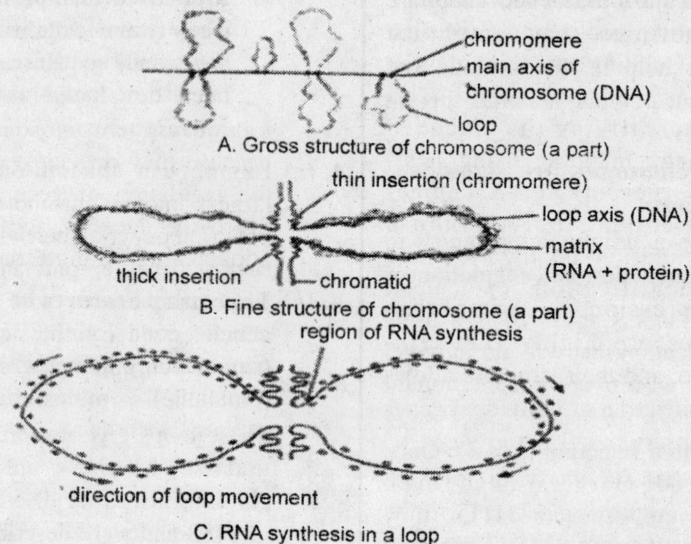

Lampbrush Chromosomes

Lampbrush chromosomes can be dissected in (toto) from oocyte nucleus. Individual chromosomes are liable to stretching. With extreme stretching, chromomeres begin to separate transversely into two halves, so that the paired loops form double stranded bridges. The axis between chromomeres is also double, which can be seen in certain special regions where two elements separate longitudinally and bear single loops (Callan, 1955).

These experiments indicate that each chromomere possesses four quadrants separated by both a transverse and a longitudinal line of division. Callan (1963) regards it as that the entire chromatid pair is made up of two continuous strands, which lie parallel to one another in the interchromomere regions, are tightly folded in the chromomeres, and separate as single, unfolded fibres in the loops. Each of the two fibres would correspond to one conventional metaphase chromatid.

There is fundamental similarity in the organization of amphibian lampbrush chromosomes and dipteran giant polytene chromosomes: in both cases, very long single fibres correspond to single chromatids and are partly but not completely extended. The substructure of the salivary chromosome 'puffs' also bear some similarity to that of the lampbrush lateral loops.

Lateral loops are formed of DNA, in chromomeres regions DNA is tightly folded and transcriptionally inactive. In lateral loops RNA synthesis is intense. Each loop in turn has an axis formed by a single DNA molecule, which is coated by a matrix of nascent RNA and proteins. The matrix is asymmetrical, being thicker at one end of the loop. RNA synthesis starts at the thinner end and progresses toward the thicker end.

Functions of Lampbrush chromosomes

- **Synthesis of RNA:** Functions of lampbrush chromosomes involve synthesis of RNA and protein by their loops. RNA is synthesized only at the thin insertion and then carried around the loops to the thick insertion. There it may be either destroyed or released into nucleus.

- **Formation of yolk material:** There are some probabilities that lampbrush chromosomes help in the formation of certain amount of yolk material for the egg.

Lampbrush chromosomes are significant for several reasons:

- They provide a unique opportunity to study the organization and regulation of gene expression. Lampbrush chromosomes are highly transcriptionally active, and their structure allows for easy visualization of individual genes and their transcriptional activity.
- They are useful for studying meiosis. Lampbrush chromosomes are formed during meiotic prophase I, and their extended structure provides an excellent model for studying the pairing and recombination of homologous chromosomes during this stage.
- Chromosomes for gene editing and gene therapy, as their extended structure makes it easier to manipulate individual genes. They have potential applications in biotechnology. Researchers are exploring the use of lampbrush.

Lampbrush chromosomes are significant because they provide valuable insights into the regulation of gene expression and the process of meiosis, and they have potential applications in biotechnology.

4. (*b*) Important Features of Genetic Code: The genetic code can be defined as the set of certain rules using which the living cells translate the information encoded within genetic material (DNA or mRNA sequences). The ribosomes are responsible to accomplish the process of translation. They link the amino acids in an mRNA-specified (messenger RNA) order using tRNA (transfer RNA) molecules to carry amino acids and to read the mRNA three nucleotides at a time.

Genetic Code Table: The complete set of relationships among amino acids and codons is said to be a genetic code which is often summarized in a table.

SECOND LETTER

FIRST LETTER	U	C	A	G	THIRD LETTER
U	UUU Phe	UCU Ser	UAU Tyr	UGU Cys	U
	UUC Phe	UCC Ser	UAC Tyr	UGC Cys	C
	UUA Leu	UCA Ser	UAA Stop	UGA Stop	A
	UUG Leu	UCG Ser	UAG Stop	UGG Trp	G
C	CUU Leu	CCU Pro	CAU His	CGU Arg	U
	CUC Leu	CCC Pro	CAC His	CGC Arg	C
	CUA Leu	CCA Pro	CAA Gln	CGA Arg	A
	CUG Leu	CCG Pro	CAG Gln	CGG Arg	G
A	AUU Ile	ACU Thr	AAU Asn	AGU Ser	U
	AUC Ile	ACC Thr	AAC Asn	AGC Ser	C
	AUA Ile	ACA Thr	AAA Lys	AGA Arg	A
	AUG Met	ACG Thr	AAG Lys	AGG Arg	G
G	GUU Val	GCU Ala	GAU Asp	GGU Gly	U
	GUC Val	GCC Ala	GAC Asp	GGC Gly	C
	GUA Val	GCA Ala	GAA Glu	GGA Gly	A
	GUG Val	GCG Ala	GAG Glu	GGG Gly	G

Genetic Code Table

It can be seen that many amino acids are shown in the table by more than one codon. For example, there are six ways to write leucine in mRNA language.

Note: A codon is a sequence of three nucleotides which together form a unit of genetic code in a DNA or RNA molecule.

A key point of the genetic code is its universal nature. This indicates that virtually all species with minor exceptions use the genetic code for protein synthesis.

In other words, genetic code is defined as the nucleotide sequence of the base on DNA which is translated into a sequence of amino acids of the protein to be synthesized.

Properties of Genetic Code

- **Triplet code:** A codon or a code word is defined as a group of bases that specify an amino acid. There is strong evidence, which proves that a sequence of three nucleotides codes for an amino acid in the protein, i.e., the code is a triplet. The four bases of nucleotide i.e, (A, G, C, and U) are used to produce three-base codons. The 64 codons involve sense codons (that specify amino acids). Hence, there are 64 codons for 20 amino acids since every codon for one amino acid means that there exist more than code for the same amino acid.
- **Commaless code:** No room for punctuation in between which indicates that every codon is adjacent to the previous one without any nucleotides between them.
- **Nonoverlapping code:** The code is read sequen-tially in a group of three and a nucleotide which becomes a part of triplet never becomes part of the next triplet.

  For example

  5′-UCU-3′ codes for Serine

  5′-AUG-3′ codes for methionine
- **Polarity:** Each triplet is read from 5′ → 3′ direction and the beginning base is 5′ followed by the base in the middle then the last base which is 3′. This implies that the codons have a fixed polarity and if the codon is read in the reverse direction, the base sequence of the codon would reverse and would specify two different proteins.
- **Degenerate code:** Every amino acid except tryptophan (UGG) and methionine (AUG) is coded by various codons, i.e, a few codons are synonyms and this aspect is known as the degeneracy of genetic code.
- **Start and Stop Codons:** Generally, AUG codon is the initiating or start codon. The polypeptide chain starts either with eukaryotes (methionine) or prokaryotes (N- formylmethionine). On the other hand, UAG, UAA and UGA are called as termination codons or stop codons. These are not read by any tRNA molecules and they never code for any amino acids.

4. (*c*) Poisson distribution definition is used to model a discrete probability of an event where independent events are occurring in a fixed interval of time and have a known constant mean rate. In other words, Poisson distribution is used to estimate how many times an event is likely to occur within the given period of time. λ is the Poisson rate parameter that indicates the expected value of the average number of events in the fixed time interval. Poisson distribution has wide use in the fields of business as well as in biology.

Poisson Distribution Formula: Poisson distribution formula is used to find the probability of an event that happens independently, discretely over a fixed time period, when the mean rate of occurrence is constant over time. The Poisson distribution formula is applied when there is a large number of possible outcomes. For a random discrete variable X that follows the Poisson distribution, and λ is the average rate of value, then the probability of x is given by:

$$f(x) = P(X = x) = (e^{-\lambda} \lambda^x)/x!$$

Where

$x = 0, 1, 2, 3...$

e is the Euler's number ($e = 2.718$)

λ is an average rate of the expected value and λ = variance, also λ > 0

Poisson Distribution Mean and Variance: For Poisson distribution, which has λ as the average rate, for a fixed interval of time, then the mean of the Poisson distribution and the value of variance will be the same. So for X following Poisson distribution, we can say that λ is the mean as well as the variance of the distribution.

Hence: E(X) = V(X) = λ

where

E(X) is the expected mean

V(X) is the variance

λ > 0

Properties of Poisson Distribution: The Poisson distribution is applicable in events that have a large number of rare and independent possible events. The following are the properties of the Poisson Distribution. In the Poisson distribution,

- The events are independent.
- The average number of successes in the given period of time alone can occur. No two events can occur at the same time.
- The Poisson distribution is limited when the number of trials *n* is indefinitely large.
- mean = variance = λ
- $np = \lambda$ is finite, where λ is constant.
- The standard deviation is always equal to the square root of the mean μ.
- The exact probability that the random variable X with mean $\mu = a$ is given by $P(X = a) = \mu^a/a!\ e^{-\mu}$
- If the mean is large, then the Poisson distribution is approximately a normal distribution.

Applications of Poisson Distribution: There are various applications of the Poisson distribution. The random variables that follow a Poisson distribution are as follows:

- To count the number of defects of a finished product
- To count the number of deaths in a country by any disease or natural calamity
- To count the number of infected plants in the field
- To count the number of bacteria in the organisms or the radioactive decay in atoms
- To calculate the waiting time between the events.

Importance of Binomial Distribution: The binomial distribution is a fundamental probability distribution that describes the number of successes in a fixed number of independent Bernoulli trials, where each trial has two possible outcomes: success or failure. The binomial distribution is important because it provides a simple and versatile model for calculating the probability of successes or failures in a fixed number of trials with two possible outcomes.

The importance of the binomial distribution lies in its wide applicability in real-world scenarios, such as in genetics, quality control, finance, and polling. Some examples of its applications are:

- **Genetics:** The binomial distribution is used to model the probability of inheriting a particular gene from each parent, which can lead to the development of certain genetic diseases.
- **Quality control:** The binomial distribution is used to determine the probability of a certain number of defective products in a batch of manufactured goods.
- **Finance:** The binomial distribution is used in options pricing models, where the underlying asset can either go up or down in value.
- **Polling:** The binomial distribution is used to estimate the proportion of voters who support a particular candidate in an election.

5. (a) Phytohormones and Their Role in Gene Expression: Phytohormones or plant hormones are the organic compounds that control growth and development. The five main plants hormones synthesized and secreted by plants are auxins, gibberellins, cytokinins, abscisic acid and ethylene. Phytohormones, also known as plant hormones, are chemical messengers that play crucial roles in regulating various physiological processes in plants, including growth, development, and response to environmental stimuli. These hormones act by binding to specific receptors on the cell surface or inside the cell, which trigger a cascade of biochemical reactions that ultimately lead to changes in gene expression.

Phytohormones, play an essential role in regulating gene expression in plants. They act as signaling molecules that coordinate various physiological processes, including growth, development, and responses to environmental stimuli. Phytohormones bind to specific receptors located on the surface of plant cells or within the cell, triggering a cascade of biochemical reactions that ultimately lead to changes in gene expression. These changes in gene expression can result in a wide range of effects on plant growth and development, including changes in cell division, differentiation, and elongation.

For example, auxins, a type of phytohormone, are involved in promoting cell elongation and division and root and shoot growth. They achieve this by activating specific genes that are involved in these processes and regulating the expression of other genes involved in cell growth and differentiation.

Overall, plant hormones are critical regulators of gene expression in plants, and their specific functions and mechanisms of action vary depending on the hormone and the physiological process being regulated.

5. (b) Micronutrients, including iron, zinc, manganese, and copper, are required in very small amounts. Micronutrients are often required as cofactors for enzyme activity. Mineral nutrients are usually obtained from the soil through plant roots, but many factors can affect the efficiency of nutrient acquisition.

Plant micronutrient uptake mechanisms involve both passive and active transport processes. Passive transport occurs through diffusion, which is the movement of molecules from areas of high concentration to areas of low concentration. This is the primary mechanism for the uptake of micronutrients that are present in the soil solution in sufficient quantities, such as zinc and manganese.

Active transport, on the other hand, is the movement of molecules across the cell membrane against a concentration gradient, requiring energy input from the plant. This is the primary mechanism for the uptake of micronutrients that are present in the soil solution in low concentrations, such as iron and copper. The active transport of micronutrients involves specific transporters located in the root cells of plants. These transporters are selective and only allow the uptake of specific micronutrients. For example, the transporter IRT1 is responsible for the uptake of iron in plants. In addition, some plants can form symbiotic relationships with beneficial soil microorganisms, such as mycorrhizal fungi, which can improve the uptake of micronutrients. The fungi can increase the surface area of the root system and release enzymes that help break down soil minerals, releasing micronutrients for uptake by the plant. The mechanisms of plant micronutrient uptake are complex and involve both passive and active transport processes, as well as interactions with soil microorganisms.

5. (c) Processes of Phytoremediation: Living plants are used in phytoremediation technologies to clean up soil, air, and water that have been contaminated with dangerous pollutants. It's defined as "the employment of green plants and associated microbes, as well as appropriate soil amendments and agronomic techniques, to either contain, remove, or render harmful environmental toxins harmless." Many plants, including mustard, alpine pennycress, hemp, and pigweed, have demonstrated their ability to hyperaccumulate toxins at toxic waste sites. Phytoremediation has been used successfully to recover abandoned metal mine workings, sites where polychlorinated biphenyls were deposited during manufacturing, and mitigation of continuing coal mine discharges, decreasing pollutants in soils, water, and air. Phytoremediation is a plant-based method of extracting and removing elemental contaminants from the environment or lowering their bioavailability in soil. Plants have the ability to absorb ionic substances from the soil through their root system, even at low concentrations.

5. (*d*) Major Consequences of Global Warming: Global warming, also known as climate change, is the long-term increase in the Earth's average surface temperature due to human activities, primarily the burning of fossil fuels. The consequences of global warming can have far-reaching and severe effects on the planet and its inhabitants. Here are some major consequences of global warming:

- **Rising sea levels:** As the planet warms, glaciers and ice sheets are melting at an increasing rate, causing sea levels to rise. This could lead to flooding of low-lying areas and displacement of millions of people.
- **Extreme weather events:** Global warming can cause more frequent and severe extreme weather events, such as hurricanes, droughts, floods, and heatwaves, which can cause widespread damage to infrastructure and loss of life.
- **Loss of biodiversity:** Many plant and animal species are unable to adapt to the rapid changes caused by global warming, resulting in habitat loss, extinction, and changes to ecosystems.
- **Food insecurity:** Changes in temperature and rainfall patterns can lead to crop failures and food shortages, especially in regions already vulnerable to food insecurity.
- **Health impacts:** Increased temperatures can lead to an increase in heat-related illnesses and diseases such as asthma, and changes in rainfall patterns can increase the spread of vector-borne diseases like malaria and dengue fever.
- **Economic impacts:** The economic impacts of global warming are vast, including damage to infrastructure, loss of productivity, and increased costs due to mitigation and adaptation measures.

5. (*e*) Student's 't' test: In the area of statistics, a student's t-test is mentioned as a method of testing the theory about the mean of a small sample drawn from a normally distributed population where the standard deviation of the given population is unknown.

We can define the Student t-test as a method that tells you how significant the differences can be between different groups. A Student t-test is defined as a statistic and this is used to compare the means of two different populations.

It is a method that is often used in hypothesis testing to find out whether a process or whether a given treatment actually has any effect on the population of interest, or whether or not two populations are different from each other. You wish to know whether the mean petal length of iris flowers differs according to their distinct species. You find two different species of iris flowers growing in a garden and they measure 25 petals of each species. You can test the difference between these two groups with the help of the Student *t*-test.

- The null hypothesis (H_0) is one that tells the true difference between these groups.
- The alternate hypothesis (Ha) is one that tells the true difference is different from zero.

The formula for the two-sample *t*-test (*a.k.a.* the Student's *t*-test) is shown below.

Student *t* test formula, $t = \dfrac{\overline{x}_1 - \overline{x}_2}{\sqrt{\left(s_2\left(\dfrac{1}{n_1} + \dfrac{1}{n_2}\right)\right)}}$

In the formula given above, *t* is equal to the *t*-value, x_1 and x_2 are the means of the two groups being compared, s_2 is the pooled standard error of the two groups, and n_1 and n_2 are the numbers of observations in each of the groups.

A larger *t*-value denotes the difference between group means is greater than the pooled standard error, indicating a more significant difference between the groups.

8. (*a*) **Fruit Ripening:** Ripening is the process by which fruits attain their desirable flavour, quality, colour, palatable nature and other textural properties. Ripening is associated with change in composition i.e. conversion of starch to sugar. On the basis of ripening behaviour, fruits are classified as climacteric and non-climacteric fruits.

Climacteric: Climacteric fruits are defined as fruits that enter 'climacteric phase' after harvest i.e. they continue to ripen. During the ripening process the fruits emit ethylene along with increased rate of respiration. Ripe fruits are soft and delicate and generally cannot withstand rigours of transport and repeated handling. These fruits are harvested hard and green, but fully mature and are ripened near consumption areas. Small dose of ethylene is used to induce ripening process under controlled conditions of temperature and humidity.

Climacteric fruits are: Mango, Banana, Papaya, Guava, Sapota, Kiwi, Fig, Apple, Passion fruit, Apricot, Plum and Pear.

These fruit in fully ripe state are too delicate to withstand transportation over long distances and should preferably be ripened near the consumption area.

Non-Climacteric: Non-climacteric fruits once harvested do not ripen further. Nonclimacteric fruits produce very small amount of ethylene and do not respond to ethylene treatment. There is no characteristic increased rate of respiration or production of carbon dioxide.

Non-climacteric fruits are: Orange, Mousambi, Kinnow, Grapefruit, Grapes, Pomegranate, Litchi, watermelon, Cherry, Raspberry, Blackberry and Strawberry.

Biochemical and Physiological Changes during the Fruit Ripening Process: The fruit ripening process involves a series of biochemical and physiological changes that occur as the fruit reaches its mature and edible stage. These changes are regulated by various hormones, enzymes, and signaling pathways. It's important to note that the ripening process is influenced by various factors such as temperature, humidity, and the fruit's genetic makeup. Different fruits have different ripening patterns and responses to external stimuli, so the specific changes may vary. While the specific changes can vary among different fruit species, here are some general processes that take place during fruit ripening:

- **Ethylene Production:** Ethylene is a key hormone involved in fruit ripening. As the fruit matures, it begins to produce ethylene, which acts as a signal for the initiation and coordination of ripening processes. Ethylene production increases dramatically during the later stages of ripening.
- **Softening:** One of the prominent changes during fruit ripening is the softening of the fruit's flesh. This softening is primarily caused by the breakdown of cell wall components, such as pectin, cellulose, and hemicellulose. Enzymes

called cell wall-modifying enzymes, including pectinases and cellulases, are responsible for the degradation of these structural components.

- **Colour Changes:** Fruits often undergo colour changes during ripening. This is due to the degradation of chlorophyll, which gives green fruits their colour, and the synthesis of pigments such as carotenoids and anthocyanins. Carotenoids are responsible for the yellow, orange, and red colours in many fruits, while anthocyanins contribute to purple, blue, and red hues.
- **Flavour Development:** Ripening is also associated with the development of desirable flavours in fruits. As the fruit ripens, there is a conversion of starches to sugars, resulting in increased sweetness. The breakdown of organic acids contributes to a decrease in tartness. Additionally, volatile compounds, such as esters and alcohols, are synthesized, contributing to the characteristic aroma of ripe fruits.
- **Aroma Production:** Fruits often release specific aromatic compounds during ripening, which attract animals for seed dispersal. These compounds are synthesized through various pathways, including the lipoxygenase pathway and the shikimate pathway. The production of volatile compounds contributes to the fruity and floral aromas associated with ripe fruits.
- **Changes in Texture:** Besides softening, fruit ripening may involve changes in texture. This can include the development of juiciness, increased water content, and changes in the texture of the fruit's skin.
- **Seed Maturation:** As the fruit ripens, the seeds within it undergo maturation. This often involves changes in seed colour, hardening of the seed coat, and accumulation of energy reserves in the form of starches and oils. These changes prepare the seeds for dispersal and subsequent germination.

Molecular Mechanism of Fruit Ripening: Fruit ripening is a highly coordinated developmental process that coincides with seed maturation. The ripening process is regulated by thousands of genes that control progressive softening and/or lignification of pericarp layers, accumulation of sugars, acids, pigments, and release of volatiles. Key to crop improvement is a deeper understanding of the processes underlying fruit ripening. In tomato, mutations blocking the transition to ripe fruits have provided insights into the role of ethylene and its associated molecular networks involved in the control of ripening. However, the role of other plant hormones is still poorly understood. In this review, we describe how plant hormones, transcription factors, and epigenetic changes are intimately related to provide a tight control of the ripening process.

The molecular mechanism of fruit ripening is a complex process that involves the interplay of various signaling pathways, hormones, and gene expression. While the specific molecular events can vary among different fruit species, the following are some key components and processes involved in fruit ripening:

- Ethylene Signaling
- Transcriptional Regulation
- Cell Wall Modification
- Pigment Biosynthesis
- Sugar Metabolism
- Aroma Volatile Production
- Hormonal Crosstalk

It's important to note that fruit ripening is a highly coordinated and tightly regulated process. The molecular mechanisms involved can vary among different fruit species and even within different stages of ripening for a particular fruit.

8. (*b*) Intellectual Property Rights (IPR) are legal rights that provide creators protection for original works, inventions, or the appearance of products, artistic works, scientific developments, and so on.The definition of intellectual property rights is any and all rights associated with intangible assets owned by a person or company and protected against use without consent. Intangible assets refer to non-physical property, including right of ownership in intellectual property. Examples of intellectual property rights include:

- Patents
- Domain names
- Industrial design
- Confidential information
- Inventions
- Moral rights
- Database rights
- Works of authorship
- Service marks
- Logos
- Trademarks
- Design rights
- Business or trade names
- Commercial secrets
- Computer software

Types of Intellectual Property

There are four main types of intellectual property rights, including patents, trademarks, copyrights, and trade secrets. Owners of intellectual property frequently use more than one of these types of intellectual property law to protect the same intangible assets. For instance, trademark law protects a product's name, whereas copyright law covers its tagline.

1. **Patents:** The U.S. Patent and Trademark Office grants property rights to original inventions, from processes to machines. Patent law protects inventions from use by others and gives exclusive rights to one or more inventors. Technology companies commonly use patents, as seen in the patent for the first computer to protect their investment in creating new and innovative products. The three types of patents consist of:
   - **Design patents:** Protection for the aesthetics of a device or invention. Ornamental design patents include a product's shape (Coca-Cola bottle), emojis, fonts, or any other distinct visual traits.
   - **Plant patents:** Safeguards for new varieties of plants. An example of a plant patent is pest-free versions of fruit trees. But inventors may also want a design patient if the tree has unique visual properties.
   - **Utility patents:** Protection for a product that serves a practical purpose and is useful. IP examples include vehicle safety systems, software, and pharmaceuticals. This was the first, and is still the largest, area of patent law.
2. **Trademarks:** Trademarks protect logos, sounds, words, colours, or symbols used by a company to distinguish its service or product. Trademark examples include the Twitter logo, McDonald's golden arches, and the font used by Dunkin. Although patents protect one product, trademarks may cover a group of products. The Lanham Act, also called the Trademark Act of 1946, governs trademarks, infringement, and service marks.
3. **Copyrights:** Copyright law protects the rights of the original creator of original works of intellectual property. Unlike patents, copyrights must be tangible. For instance, you can't copyright an idea. But you can write down an original speech, poem, or song and get a copyright. Once someone creates an original work of authorship (OWA), the author automatically owns the copyright. But, registering with the U.S. Copyright Office gives owners a head-start in the legal system.

4. **Trade Secrets:** Trade secrets are a company's intellectual property that isn't public, has economic value, and carries information. They may be a formula, recipe, or process used to gain a competitive advantage.

To qualify as a trade secret, companies must work to protect proprietary information actively. Once the information is public knowledge, then it's no longer protected under trade secrets laws. According to 18 USC § 1839(3), assets may be tangible or intangible, and a trade secret can involve information that's:

- Business
- Financial
- Technical
- Economic
- Scientific
- Engineering

Intellectual Property Rights (IPR) can play a significant role in protecting issues related to biodiversity conservation and traditional knowledge. Here are some applications of IPR in this context:

- **Patents:** Patents can be used to protect inventions and technologies that contribute to biodiversity conservation and traditional knowledge. This includes innovations in the field of biotechnology, genetic engineering, and pharmaceuticals derived from natural resources. By obtaining patents, individuals and organizations can gain exclusive rights to their inventions, which can incentivize further research and development in these areas.
- **Plant Variety Protection:** Plant variety protection (PVP) systems grant breeders exclusive rights over new plant varieties they have developed. PVP can be used to protect traditional and indigenous plant varieties, preventing unauthorized use, commercial exploitation, or misappropriation of such resources. This provides an incentive for the conservation and sustainable use of traditional crops and plants.
- **Traditional Knowledge Documentation:** Intellectual property tools such as copyrights and database rights can be used to protect the documentation of traditional knowledge. This helps safeguard traditional knowledge from misappropriation, unauthorized use, or exploitation by third parties. By establishing ownership and control over the documentation, indigenous communities can ensure that their knowledge is respected and preserved.
- **Traditional Cultural Expressions:** Intellectual property laws, such as copyrights and related rights, can be utilized to protect traditional cultural expressions, including traditional music, dances, stories, and art. This allows indigenous communities to control the use of their cultural expressions, prevent unauthorized commercialization, and maintain the integrity and authenticity of their cultural heritage.
- **Access and Benefit-Sharing:** Intellectual property systems can be linked to access and benefit-sharing mechanisms, which aim to ensure fair and equitable sharing of benefits derived from the utilization of genetic resources and traditional knowledge. By requiring users to obtain prior informed consent and negotiate mutually agreed terms, IPR can help protect traditional knowledge holders' rights and provide them with economic benefits.

8. (*c*) Auxin control the Growth of Auxillary Buds: Auxin is a class of plant hormones that plays a crucial role in regulating various aspects of plant growth and development. One of the key functions of auxin is to control the growth and development of auxiliary buds in plants. Auxiliary buds, also known as axillary buds, are located in the leaf axils, which are the angles formed between the stem and the base of the leaves. These buds

have the potential to develop into branches or flowers. However, their growth and activation are tightly regulated by the plant hormone auxin. When auxin levels are high in the main stem, it inhibits the growth and activation of the auxiliary buds. This phenomenon is known as apical dominance. The apical bud, located at the top of the stem, produces high levels of auxin, which move downward through the stem. This downward movement of auxin inhibits the growth and development of the auxiliary buds along the stem. However, when the apical bud is removed or its auxin production is reduced, the auxin levels in the main stem decrease. This reduction in auxin concentration releases the inhibition on the auxiliary buds, allowing them to grow and develop into branches. This is often observed when pruning plants, where the removal of the apical bud promotes branching. Furthermore, the redistribution of auxin within the plant also influences the growth of auxiliary buds. If auxin is applied to a specific area of the stem or if it accumulates in the lower side of a tilted stem, it promotes the growth and development of auxiliary buds in those regions. Auxin controls the growth of auxiliary buds by regulating their activation and development. High levels of auxin in the main stem inhibit the growth of auxiliary buds, while a decrease in auxin concentration or its redistribution promotes their growth and branching.

Applications of Auxins in Agriculture: The following points highlight the six practical applications of auxins. The applications are:

- **Rooting:** Besides indole acetic acid, some other synthetic auxins especially naphthalene acetic acid and indole butryic acid are widely employed in initiating early and vigorous rooting in plants which are propagated by cuttings.
- **Prevention of Pre-Harvest Drop of Fruits:** Premature falling of the fruits can be checked by the application of auxins such as 2, 4-D and 2, 4 6 trichloro-phenoxy acetic acid which delay the formation of the abscission layer.
- **Parthenocarpy:** Parthenocarpic seedless fruits are obtained on commercial scale by the application of auxins in many plants.
- **Inhibition of Buds to Prevent Sprouting:** Auxins like a-naphthalene acetic acid prolong the dormancy of buds in potato tubers and thus are very useful in preventing the eyes of potato tubers to sprout during storage.
- **Shortening of Internodes:** In apples and pear the fruits are developed on dwarf spurs. Treatment of the other terminal shoots with a-naphthalene acetic acid prevents the elongation of their internodes so that they also become dwarf. The latter may also bear the fruits.
- **Selective Weed Killers:** At higher concentrations the auxins may have profound herbicidal properties and are utilised in the eradication of the weeds. The significance of their activity lies in their selective toxic action on plants. For instance 2, 4-dichloro phenoxyacetic acid. (2, 4-D) is a potent weed killer and most of the broad-leaved dicotyledonous plants which occur as weeds are killed by this synthetic auxin, but usually the cereals (which are monocotyledonous) remain unaffected.

Previous Years' Paper (Solved)

Indian Forest Service (Main) Exam, 2021

SUBJECT–BOTANY

(Exam held on 06-03-2022)

PAPER-I

INSTRUCTIONS: *There are EIGHT questions in all, out of which FIVE are to be attempted. Questions Nos. 1 & 5 are compulsory. Out of the remaining SIX questions, THREE are to be attempted selecting at least ONE question from each of the two Sections A and B. Attempts of questions shall be counted in sequential order. Unless struck off, attempt of a question shall be counted even if attempted partly. Any page or portion of the page left blank in the Question-cum-Answer Booklet must be clearly struck off. All questions carry equal marks. Answers must be written in ENGLISH only. Neat sketches may be drawn, wherever required.*

SECTION–A

1. (*a*) Give two examples where microbes have helped in controlling soil and water pollution and mention how.

(*b*) What are phytotoxins and phytoalexins? Discuss the role they play in plant pathogenesis.

(*c*) Give a brief account of structure and function of heterocyst.

(*d*) Briefly discuss the morphological and anatomical features of sporogonium of *Marchantia*.

(*e*) List five angiosperm-like features of *Gnetum*. However, justify its inclusion in gymnosperms.

2. (*a*) Describe with the help of labelled diagrams the structure of *Funaria* capsule.

(*b*) Briefly discuss the stelar system in Pteridophytes.

(*c*) (*i*) Elaborate with two examples, one each from bacteria and fungi, where they have helped in establishing a pharma industry.

(*ii*) What are mycoplasma and how are these different from bacteria and fungi?

3. (*a*) Discuss with one example of each, how plants acquire resistance against plant pathogens:

(*i*) Artificial inoculation with microbes

(*ii*) Treatment with chemicals

(*iii*) Genetically engineered disease-resistance

(*b*) Describe the structure and development of male gametophyte in *Cycas* with the help of diagrams. Put an explanatory note on its unique features.

(*c*) Discuss in brief, with one example of each, haplo-diplontic and triphasic life cycle in Algae.

4. (*a*) (*i*) What are plantibodies and what is their role in immunization of plants against plant pathogens?

(*ii*) Explain the role of at least two enzymes in the development of plant diseases.

(*b*) (*i*) Describe with the help of diagram, the disease cycle of *Phytophthora infestans*.

(*ii*) Briefly discuss the fruiting bodies of *Agaricus*.

(*iii*) Comment on the structure and composition of lichen thallus.

(*c*) Describe the features of Bennettitalean flower with the help of diagram.

SECTION–B

5. (*a*) State five salient features of Poaceae. Give the binomial of any three economically important plants belonging to this family.

(*b*) Discuss the types of tapetum found in anther and explain its functions.

(*c*) Mention the botanical name, family, and morphology of the useful part in any four fibre producing plants.

(*d*) What is symmetry? Discuss briefly the various types of symmetries found in plants.

(*e*) Discuss APG IV system of classification.

6. (*a*) Anatomical data of plants are useful in solving many taxonomic problems. Elucidate with at least three examples.

(*b*) With suitable example and diagram, explain abnormal secondary growth due to the formation of accessory cambial rings.

(*c*) Describe in brief various procedures for isolation and fusion of protoplasts in plants. Comment on the usefulness of this technology in plant development.

7. (*a*) Compare the androecium in Orchidaceae and Asclepiadaceae.

(*b*) Differentiate between gums, resins and dyes. Give the binomial, family and morphology of the useful parts of two plants from each of the above categories.

(*c*) Define apomixis and discuss in brief the types, causes and its significance.

8. (*a*) With the help of diagrams, describe the leaf anatomy of C_4 plants. How does the anatomy of C_4 plants differ from the anatomy of C_3 plants?

(*b*) How many types of embryo development occur in dicot plants? Discuss in detail the embryo development in *Capsella bursa-pastoris*.

(*c*) (*i*) Give a brief account of usefulness of biofuels as compared to fossil fuels.

(*ii*) Discuss in brief any two energy plants. How will they be useful in the economy of a country?

PAPER-II

INSTRUCTIONS: *There are EIGHT questions in all, out of which FIVE are to be attempted. Questions Nos. 1 & 5 are compulsory. Out of the remaining SIX questions, THREE are to be attempted selecting at least ONE question from each of the two Sections A and B. Attempts of questions shall be counted in sequential order. Unless struck off, attempt of a question shall be counted even if attempted partly. Any page or portion of the page left blank in the Question-cum-Answer Booklet must be clearly struck off. All questions carry equal marks. Answers must be written in ENGLISH only. Neat sketches may be drawn, wherever required.*

SECTION–A

1. Write short notes on the following:

(*a*) Chi-square test

(*b*) Polyribosomes

(*c*) Crossing over

(*d*) Non-coding RNA

(*e*) Cell signalling

2. (*a*) Define monohaploids. How can haploids be produced artificially? Describe.

(*b*) How can genetically uniform plants be produced through micropropagation technique?

(*c*) What is the utility of test cross in plant breeding?

3. (*a*) Describe the structure of heterochromatin and euchromatin. How is constitutive heterochromatin different from facultative heterochromatin?

(*b*) What are lysosomes? Discuss various functions of lysosomes.

(*c*) Discuss the biogenesis of chloroplast.

4. (*a*) Write a detailed note on direct evidences of organic evolution.

(*b*) Describe in brief the molecular map of Ti plasmid.

(*c*) Write a note on linear regression. What are 'residuals' and why are they important for statistical analysis?

SECTION–B

5. Write short notes on the following:

(*a*) Convention on Biological Diversity

(*b*) Role of Cytokinin in leaf senescence

(*c*) Active ion transport in plants

(*d*) Polarity of water and its significance

(*e*) Inter-relationship between nitrogen and carbon assimilation in plants

6. (*a*) How is ethylene, 'as a phytohormone', different from other hormones? Explain its mechanism of action and physiological effects.

(*b*) What is enzyme inhibition? Describe reversible enzyme inhibition and its types, giving suitable examples.

(*c*) Explain the mechanism and factors causing dormancy of seeds.

7. (*a*) Name the complexes and their composition associated with electron transport chain in plant mitochondria. Describe the role of ubiquinone in ATP synthesis in mitochondria.

(*b*) "Calvin cycle is autocatalytic."—Justify the statement.

(*c*) Explain that C_2 cycle returns to the C_3 cycle, three-quarters of the carbon that would have been lost as glycolate.

8. (*a*) Write a detailed note on secondary succession sequence of a forest, post clear felling. Explain the importance of soil seed bank and vegetation diversity in adjacent areas of clear-felled area on the diversity of regenerated ecosystem.

(*b*) What are point and non-point sources of pollution? Describe the role of gaseous emissions from a thermal power plant on the atnospheric pollution loads of the area where these thermal power plants are functional.

(*c*) Write a detailed note on biodiversity hotspots of India. Why is endemism high in such areas?

ANSWERS

PAPER-I

1. (*a*) In simple terms, bioremediation is a system of sewage treatment where microbes are used to degrade flowing sewage into carbon dioxide and water. The process also reduces the stench from raw sewage. The microbes simply eat up contaminants such as oil and organic matter (*e.g.,* waste food), convert them and then let off carbon dioxide and water. The process uses naturally occurring bacteria, fungi or plants to degrade substances that are hazardous to human health or the environment. Bioremediation technology includes phytoremediation (plants) and rhizoremediation (plant and microbe interaction). At present, the process is used to check contamination in soil, groundwater and surface water. The system does not require construction or any major modification of drains or diversion of flow. It takes place in open drains without displacement of sewage. The process also does not require any additional land or power, making it a simple and easy system. It is cheaper than conventional treatment methods, easy to handle and, importantly, does not require skilled manpower.

Under the process, bacteria are cultured in bulk and applied to the flowing sewage. Then, the microbes are activated and they multiply—with or without oxygen and food available in the form of organic matter present in sewage. Sometimes, enzymes are also added to activate the microbes. However, bioremediation can be effective only in places where environmental conditions permit microbial growth and activity. Where the conditions are not favourable for their growth, manipulation of environmental parameters is carried out to allow microbial growth and allow degradation at a faster rate. These microbes consume the organic mass of the waste water and utilize the nutrients from sewage for their growth, ultimately enhancing the cleaning action of waste water.

The Cleaning Process : The Microbes eat up contaminants such as oil and organic matter, letting off carbon dioxide and water.

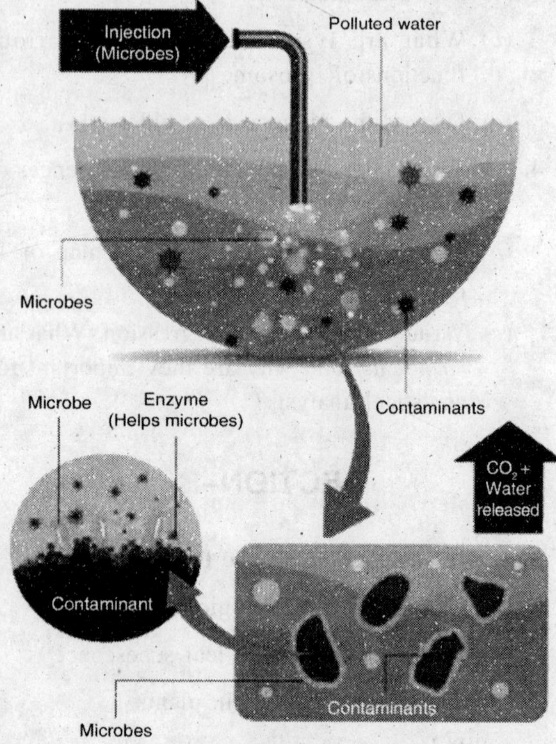

Fig. *The Cleaning Process*

The treatment can restore water quality and increases the self-cleansing capacity of the water body. The process also helps reduce biochemical oxygen demand (BOD) in sewage and reduces odour. Waste water often contains organic materials that are decomposed by microorganisms, which use oxygen in the process, and BOD is the amount of oxygen that is used by such organisms in breaking down the waste matter. The microorganisms that are used already exist in nature and this prevents any harm to the environment. Sometimes, they are indigenous to a contaminated area, otherwise, they need to be brought in to the targeted site. It has been found that as a result of this process, heavy metals and toxic chemicals are also reduced. It also leads to the suppression and elimination of harmful pathogenic bacteria such as *E. coli* from the treated water.

1. (*b*) Phytotoxins: Phytotoxins are poisonous substances synthesized by plants or plant pathogens through naturally occurring biochemical reactions. Plants use them as defensive agents against predators (pests, insects, stress, etc.) and diseases.

Phytoalexins: Phytoalexins are toxic antimicrobial substances synthesized 'de novo' in the plants in response to injury, infectious agents or their products and physiological stimuli. The term phytoalexin was first used by the two phytopathologists Muller and Borger (1940) for fungi static compounds produced by plants in response to mechanical or chemical injury or infection.

Role, They Play in Plant Pathogenesis

Bacterial and fungal plant pathogens are known to produce toxic substance in infectected plants, which are named as phytotoxins. Phytotoxins are small molecules and have a variety of structures including sesquiterpenoids, sesterterpenoids, diketo-piperazines, peptides, spirocyclic lactams, isocoumarins, polyketides, tetramic acids and perylenequinones. Phytotoxins may be classified as host specific toxins (HST) and non-host specific toxins (NHST). Host specific toxins affect only plants of a genotype susceptible to the pathogens. On the other hand, non-host specific toxins affect a lot of plants. The term phytotoxins is used to describe toxic chemicals produced by plants themselves, which function as defensive agents against their predators. Most examples pertaining to this definition of phytotoxin are members of various classes of specialized or secondary metabolites, including alkaloids, terpenes, and especially phenolics, though not all such compounds are toxic or serve defensive purposes. Phytotoxins may also be toxic to humans. Toxins are potent molecules produced by a large variety of bacterial pathogens that target host cells and play key roles in the host–pathogen dialog. They are major virulence factors often sufficient to determine the outcome of the infection.

Phytoalexins are lipophilic compounds and were first detected after a study of late blight of potato caused by Phytophthora infesting. Phytoalexins are believed to be synthesized in living cells but surprisingly necrosis follows very quickly. According to Bill (1981), peak concentration of phytoalexins almost always coincides with necrosis. Although the exact mechanism of production of phytoalexin has not been properly understood, it is considered that a metabolite of the host plant interacts with specific receptor on the pathogen's membrane resulting in the secretion of "phytoalexin elicitor" which enters the host plant cells and stimulates the phytoalexin synthesis. Phytoalexins are considered to stop the growth of pathogens by altering the plasma membrane and inhibiting the oxidative phosphorylation. Some common phytoalexins are Ipomeamarone, Orchinol, Pistatin, Phaseolin, Medicarpin, Rishitin, Isocoumarin, 'Gossypol' Cicerin, Glyceolin, Capisidiol etc.

1. (*c*) Structure and Function of Heterocyst: Heterocysts are found in many species of filamentous blue-green algae. They are cells of slightly larger size and with a more thickened wall than the vegetative cells. Structural details of the heterocyst are: the presence of three additional wall layers, the absence of granules, sparse thylakoid network throughout, except at the poles where a dense coiling of membranes occurs. Other characters include the two pores at opposite poles 'plugged' with refractive material called the polar granule. They are cells of slightly larger size and with a more thickened wall than the vegetative cells. Structural details of the heterocyst are: the presence of three additional wall layers, the absence of granules, sparse thylakoid network throughout, except at the poles where a dense coiling of membranes occurs.

Various functions have been assigned to the heterocyst from time to time. Their role in akinete formation is suggested by

(*i*) the formation of akinetes adjacent to the heterocysts and

(*ii*) prevention of sporulation by detachment of the heterocysts from the vegetative cells (potential akinetes).

Despite substantial evidence for such a role, it is not applicable to all akinete-forming genera. Heterocysts are now widely believed to be the site of nitrogen fixation in blue-green algae.

The main facts in favour of such a role are:

(*i*) fixation of nitrogen by all heterocystous algae,

(*ii*) inhibition of heterocyst formation by combined nitrogen and

(*iii*) direct observations on acetylene reduction by isolated heterocysts.

1. (*d*) Morphological and Anatomical Features of Sporogonium of Marchantia:

After fertilization the diploid zygote or oospore enlarges and it completely fills the cavity of the archegonium. It first divides by transverse division (at right angle to the archegonium axis) to form an outer epibasal cell and inner hypo basal cell. The second division is at right angle to the first and results in the formation of four cells. This represents the quadrant stage.

The epibasal cell forms the capsule and hypo basal cells form the foot and seta. Since the capsule is developed from the epibasal cell and forms the apex of the sporogonium, the type of embryogeny is known as exoscopic. The next division is also vertical and it results in formation of eight celled stage or octant stage.

Now the divisions are irregular and globular embryo is formed. The lower cells divide to form a massive and bulbous foot.

The cells of the seta divide in one plane to form vertical rows of cells. In upper region of capsule (when the young sporogonium is about a dozen or more cells in circumference) periclinal division occurs and it differentiates it into outer single layered amphithecium and multilayered endothecium. The cells of the endothecium divide only by anticlinal divisions to form a single layered sterile jacket or capsule wall. The endothecium forms the archesporium. Its cells divide and re-divide to form a mass of sporogenous cells (sporocytes). Half of the sporogenous cells become narrow and elongate to form the elater mother cells.

In *M. polymorpha* sporogenous cells divide by five successive divisions to form thirty-two spore mother cells while in *M. domingensis* sporogenous cells divide only by three to four divisions to form eight or sixteen spore mother cells.

The elater mother cells elongate considerably to form long, slender diploid cells called elaters. Elaters are pointed at both the ends and have two spiral bands or thickenings on the surface of the wall. These are hygroscopic in nature and help in dispersal of spores. (Fig.)

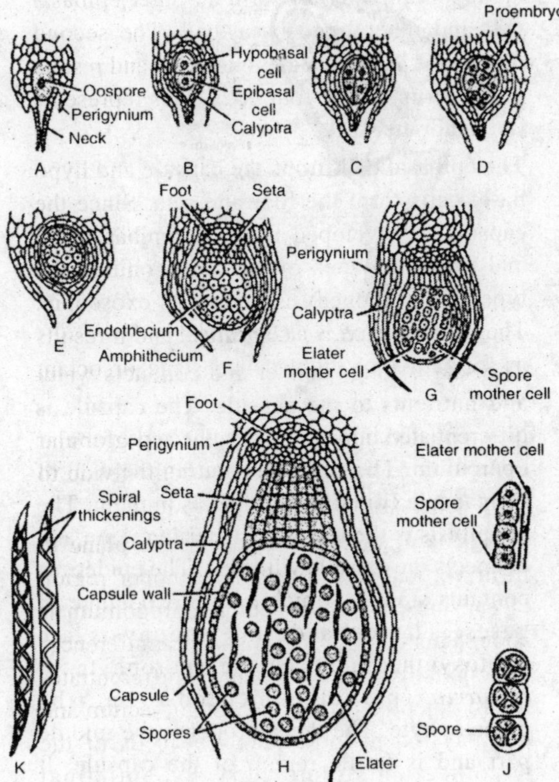

Fig. : *Marchanita. Development of sporophyte. (A-J). Successive stages in the development of sporogonium, (H). L.S. of mature sporogonium, (J) Spores tetred, (K) Two elaters.*

The quadrant type of development of sporogonium is quite common in many species of Marchantia (*e.g.*, M. polymorpha) but in a few species zygote divides by two transverse divisions to form the 3-celled filamentous embryo. A mature sporogonium can be differentiated into three parts, viz., the foot, seta and capsule. Foot is bulbous and multicellular. It is composed of parenchymatous cells. It acts as anchoring and absorbing organ. It absorbs the food from the adjoining gametophytic cells for the developing sporophyte. Seta connects the foot and the capsule. At maturity, due to many transverse divisions it elongates and pushes the capsule through three protective layers viz., calyptra, perigynium and perichaetium. Capsule is oval in shape and has a single layered wall which encloses spores and elaters. It has been estimated that as many as 3,00,000 spores may be produced in single sporogonium and there are 128 spores in relation to one elater.

1. (*e*) Five Angiosperm-like Features of Gnetum

- The general habit of the sporophyte of many species of Gnetum resembles with angiosperms.
- Reticulate venation in the leaves of Gnetum is an angiospermic character.
- Presence of vessels in xylem is again an angiospermic character.
- Clear tunica and corpus configuration of shoot apices is a character of both Gnetum and angiosperms.
- Tetrasporic development of the female gametophyte is again a character which brings Gnetum close to angiosperms.

Justification of its inclusion in Gymnosperms: Gnetum shows several resemblances with gymnosperms and has, therefore, been finally included under this group. Some of the characteristics common in both Gnetum and other gymnosperms are under mentioned:

- Wood having tracheids with bordered pits.
- No sieve tubes and companion cells are present.
- Presence of naked ovules.
- Absence of fruit formation because of the absence of ovary.
- Anemophilous type of pollination.
- Development of prothallial cell.
- Cleavage polyembryony.
- Resemblance of the vascular supply of the peduncle of the cone of Cycadeoidea-wielandii with that of a single flower of Gnetum.
- Resemblance of the structure of basal part of the ovule in Gnetum and Bennettites.

2. (*a*) Structure of Funaria Capsule:

Funária is commonly called 'cord moss'. It is distributed throughout the world. *Funaria hygrometrica* is the common species. It grows in close tufts on rocks, trunks of trees, damp walls and damp soils. They help in the process of soil formation (Pedogenesis).

The plant body is a gametophyte. It is small, 1 to 3 cm high and consists of slender erect radial stem covered with small, simple leaf like structures arranged in a spiral manner. The gametophyte is attached to the substratum by means of multicellular rhizoids. They are characterized by the presence of oblique septa. The leaves are simple, sessile ovate and have broad membranous base and pointed apex.

The lateral 'wing' or lamina is made up of single layer of thin-walled cells which are rich in chloroplasts. Midrib contains small strands of slightly thickened narrow cells which help in conduction.

Structure of Sporophyte or capsule: The structure of mature sporophyte of *Funaria* is complex. The sporophyte is differentiated into foot, seta and capsule. The foot is small, conical and is embedded in the gametophyte.

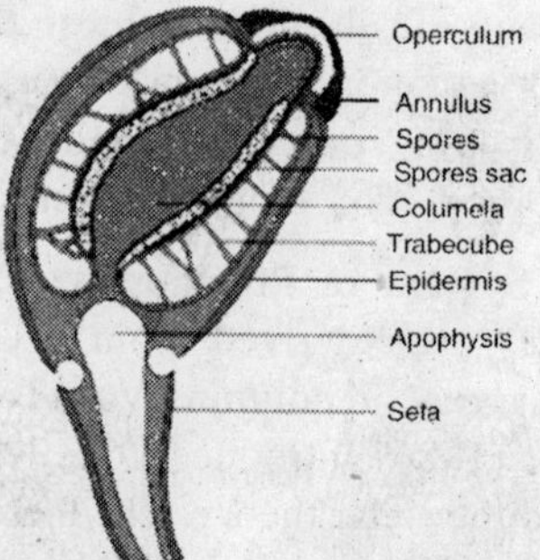

Fig. *L.S. of Capsule*

The seta is long, slender and conducts water and nutrients to the capsule. The capsule is differentiated into apophysis, theca proper and operculum. The cells constituting the wall of the capsule contain chloroplasts in them. The apophysis is the lowermost sterile region and connects the capsule with seta. The epidermis contains stomata which help in exchange of gases. The cells of the apophysis are photosynthetic, hence the sporophyte of *Funaria* partially depends on the gametophyte. The theca proper is the middle part and is fertile region of the capsule. It consists of a central columella surrounded by spore sac. The spore sac is surrounded by a single cylindrical air sac traversed by delicate filaments made up of parenchyma cells called trabeculae. The trabeculae extend from the outer wall of the spore sac to the innermost layer of the capsule wall. The spore sac contains spore mother cells which undergo meiotic division to produce haploid spores. The apical region consists of the operculum and peristome. The operculum is the lid of the capsule and comes out as a circular cup shaped lid after the dehiscence of the capsule. The peristome has one or two rows of thickened, tooth like projections found on the top of the capsule. They are hygroscopic and help in the dispersal of the spores. During favourble conditions the spores germinate to produce thread like green branched structure called protonema. It produces rhizoids and number of lateral buds which develop into new plants. In the life cycle of *Funaria* the haploid gametophytic phase (n) alternates with diploid sporophytic phase ($2n$) and shows alternation of generation.

2. **(b) Stelar System in Pteridophytes:** The term stele has been derived from a Greek word meaning rod or column. Van Tieghem and Douliot (1886) introduced this term and put forward the stelar theory. The theory suggests that the cortex and the stele are the two fundamental parts of a shoot system. Both these components (stele and cortex) separated by endodermis.

There are several types of stele found in pteridophytes which are: Protostele, Siphonostele, Solenostele, Dictyostele, Polycyclic stele, Eustele and Polystele.

1. **Protostele:** Jeffrey (1898), for the first time pointed out the stelar theory from the point of view of the phylogeny. According to him, the primitive type of stele is protostele. In protostele, the vascular tissue is a solid mass and the central core of the xylem is completely surrounded by the strand of phloem. This is the most primitive and simplest type of stele.
   - Pith is absent in protostele *i.e.,* it is non-medullated.
   - Majority of the pteridophytes show protostelic conditions in their rhizome, stem or roots.

There are five forms of protostele

1. Haplostele
2. Actinostele
3. Plectostele
4. Mixed Protostele
5. Mixed Protostele with pith

(a) Haplostele: This is the most primitive type of protostele. Here the central solid smooth core of xylem remains surrounded by uniform layers of phloem (*e.g.,* in Selaginella spp., Gleichenia, Lycopodium).

- Named by Brebner in 1902.
- Usually present in fossil genera like Rhynia and Horneophyton.

(b) Actinostele: This is the modification of the haplostele and somewhat more advanced in having the central xylem core with radiating ribs or arms (*e.g.,* in Psilotum spp., Asteroxylon, Lycopodium serratum).

- Xylem is star shaped or stellat, hence the name.
- The phloem is not present in continuous manner.
- Phloem occurs as separate patches between arms of the xylem.
- Named by Brebner in 1902.

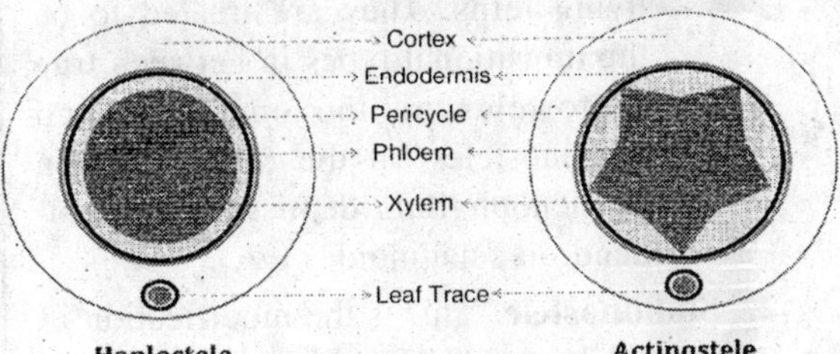

(c) Plectostele: This is the most advanced type of protostele. Here the central core of xylem is divided into number of plates arranged parallel to each other. The phloem alternates the xylem (*e.g.,* in Lycopodium clavatum).

- Named by Zimmerman in 1930.

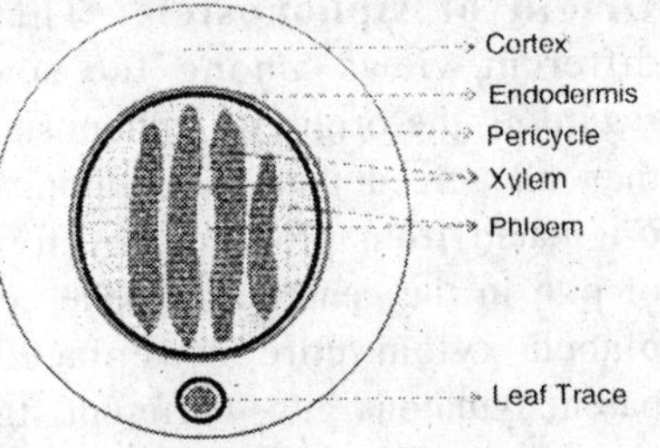

Plectostele

(d) Mixed protostele: Xylem is divided into several units or groups. Each xylem units are scatteredly arranged inside the ground mass of phloem. Example: Lycopodium cernuum.

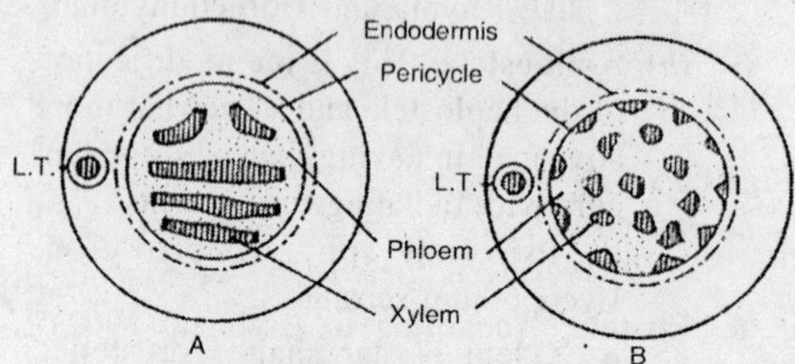

Fig. *Stelar system in terms. A. plectostele; B. mixed*

(*e*) **Mixed protostele with pith:** Here the xylem elements (*i.e.*, tracheids) are mixed with the small patches of parenchymatous cells of the pith. This type is found in primitive fossils and living ferns. They are treated to be the transitional types in between true protosteles on the one hand and siphonosteles on the other (*e.g.*, in Hymenophyllum demissum, Lepidodendron selaginoides *etc.*).

2. **Siphonostele:** This is the modification of protostele. A stele in which the protostele is medullated or with pith at the centre is known as siphonostele. Such stele contains a tubular vascular region and a parenchymatous central region *i.e.*, the central core of pith is surrounded by the xylem.

- It is advanced than protostele.

Origin of siphonostele: There are different views among the scientists regarding the origin of siphonostele. But they all agreed that, the siphonostele is originated from protostele by formation of pith in the center. Here, the centrally placed xylem core is replaced with parenchymatous pith. Different stages of changing protostele to siphonostele can be observed in the T. S at different levels in Gleichenia, Osmunda and Anemia. There are two views regarding the origin of pith in the siphonostele.

According to this theory, the pith is formed as a result of the invasion of cortical parenchymatous cells into the stele. The invasion of pith occurs through the leaf gap or branch gap.

Thus pith and cortex are homogeneous structures according to this theory.

This theory is not accepted by most of the authors since in many pteridophytes there is stele without leaf gaps but having siphonostele.

Boodle's theory: According to the theory proposed by Boodle (1901), and Gwynne Vaughan, the siphonostele has been evolved from the protostele by a transformation of the inner vascular tissue into parenchyma.

A siphonostele may be of the following types

(*a*) **Ectophloic:** In this type of siphonostele, the pith is surrounded by concentric xylem cylinder and next to xylem the concentric phloem cylinder.

(*b*) **Amphiphloic:** In this type of siphonostele the pith is surrounded by the vascular tissue. The concentric inner phloem cylinder surrounds the central pith. Next to the inner phloem is the concentric xylem cylinder which is immediately surrounded by outer phloem cylinder (*e.g.*, in Marsilea rhizome).

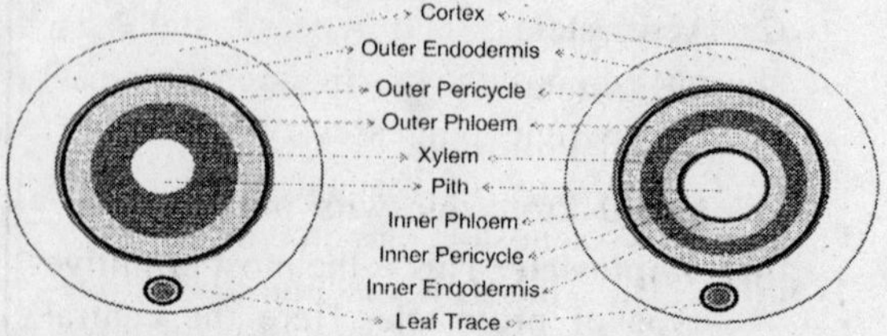

3. **Solenostele:** In solenostele, pith is found with one leaf gap. It may be ectophloic or amphiphloic-solenostele.

(*a*) **Ectophloic:** Xylem is surrounded by only on the outer side by phloem. E.g. in Osmunda.

(*b*) **Amphiphloic:** In center, pith is found. Xylem is surrounded on both sides by phloem. e.g. Marsilea rhizome.

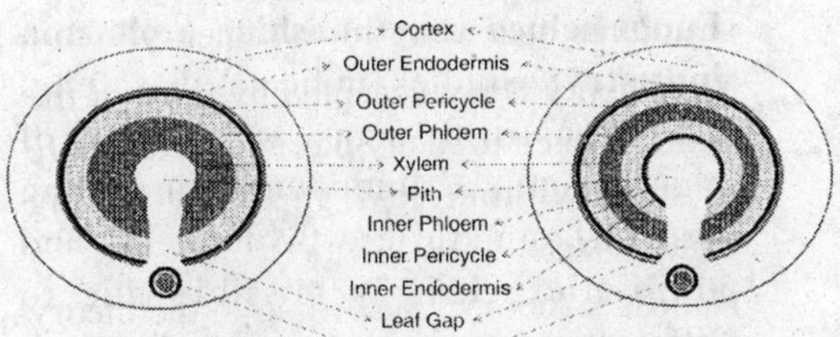

4. **Dictyostele:** Solenostele that is broken into a network of separate vascular strands are called dictyostele. This breaking up of stelar core is due to the presence of large number of leaf gaps. Each such separate vascular strands is called meristele. Each meristele is of protostelic type. The dictyostele with many meristeles looks like a cylindrical meshwork.

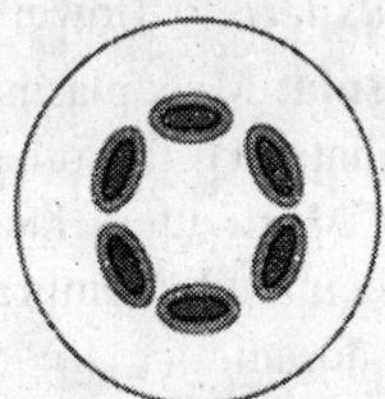

Examples: *Pteris, Adiantum capillus-veneris.*

5. **Polycyclic Stele:** This type of stelar organization is the most complex one amongst all vascular cryptogams (pteridophytes). Such type of steles is always siphonostelic in structure. A typical polycyclic stele possesses two or more concentric rings of vascular tissue. This may be a solenostele or a dictyostele. Two concentric rings of vascular tissue are found in Pteridium aquilinum and three in Matonia pectinata.

(*a*) Polycyclic solenostele

(*b*) Polycyclic dictyostele

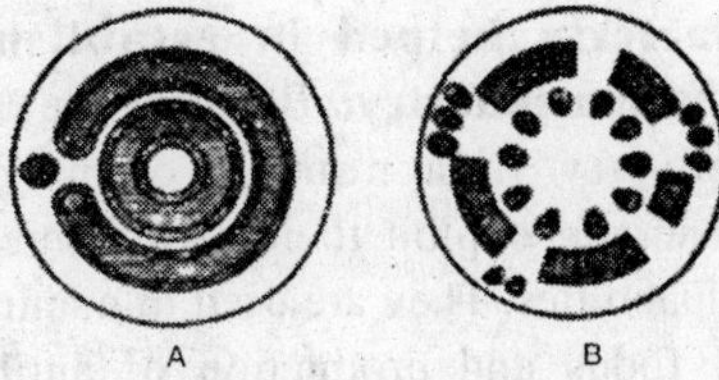

Fig. *Polycyclic stele—types (diagrammatic, sectional views). A. Polycyclic solenestele. B. Polycyclic dictyostele.*

6. **Eustele:** According to Brebner (1902), there is one more modification of the siphonostele known as eustele. Here the vascular system consists of a ring of collateral or bicollateral vascular bundles situated on the periphery of the pith. The example of this type is internode of Equisetum.

- It is the modification of ectophloic siphonostele.
- Splitting takes place because of the overlapping leaf gaps.

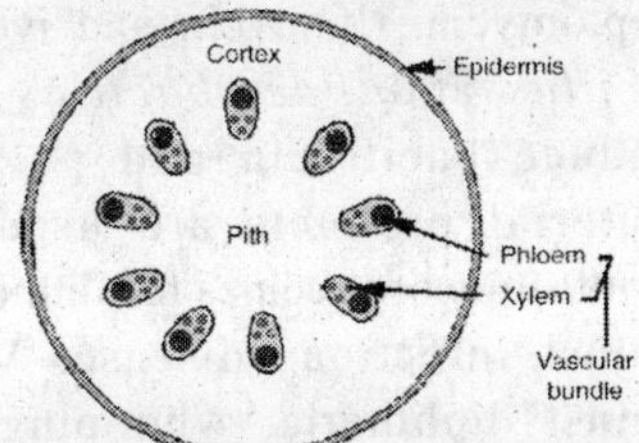

7. **Polystele:** More than one stele in the axis of pteridophytes is present known as polystele. It is a type that must have derived from protostele because each such stele shows protostelic condition. In *Selaginella kraussiana* generally two stele presents. But in *Selaginella laevigata* as many as 16 steles are present.

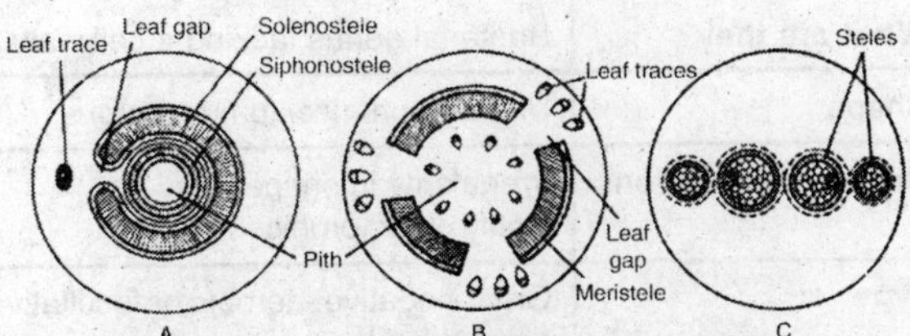

Fig. *(A–C). Stelar System: A. Polycyclic solenostele, B. Polycyclic dictyostele, C. Polystele*

2. (*c*) (*i*) **Bacteria helped in establishing a pharma industry:** Bacteria are used in industry in a number of ways that generally exploit their natural metabolic capabilities. They are used in manufacture of foods and production of antibiotics, probiotics, drugs, vaccines, starter cultures, insecticides, enzymes, fuels and solvents.

In addition, with genetic engineering technology, bacteria can be programmed to make various substances used in food science, agriculture and medicine. In the pharmaceutical industry, bacteria are used to produce antibiotics, vaccines, and medically-useful enzymes. Most antibiotics are made by bacteria that live in soil.

Actinomycetes such as *Streptomyces* produce tetracyclines, erythromycin, streptomycin, rifamycin and ivermectin. *Bacillus* and *Paenibacillus* species produce bacitracin and polymyxin. Bacterial products are used in the manufacture of vaccines for immunization against infectious disease. Vaccines against diphtheria, whooping cough, tetanus, typhoid fever and cholera are made from components of the bacteria that cause the respective diseases. It is significant to note here that the use of antibiotics against infectious disease and the widespread practice of vaccination (immunization) against infectious disease are two twentieth-century developments that have drastically increased the quality of life and the average life expectancy of individuals in developed countries.

Fungi helped in establishing a pharma industry: Studies indicate that fungi can transform many structures of pharmaceutical compounds, including anti-inflammatories, β-blockers, and antibiotics. This is possible due to different mechanisms in combination with the extracellular and intracellular enzymes, which have broad of biotechnological applications.

Penicillin, which fights bacterial infection, is released by strains of the mould Penicillium. Other medicine that come from fungi include cyclosporine from *Tolypocladium inflatum* (enables organ transplants) and lovastatin from *Aspergillus terreus* (lowers cholesterol).

(*ii*) **Mycoplasma:** Mycoplasma is a genus of bacteria that, like the other members of the class Mollicutes, lack a cell wall around their cell membranes. Peptidoglycan is absent.

This characteristic makes them naturally resistant to antibiotics that target cell wall synthesis. They can be parasitic or saprotrophic.

The table below depicts the differences between Mycoplasma and Bacteria.

	Mycoplasma	Bacteria
What are they?	Bacterial genus lacking a cell wall	Microscopic entities that are ubiquitous
Shape	Usually spherical to filamentous	Spiral, coccus, bacillus
Shape modifications	Irregularity in shape, they are highly pleomorphic	Due to the presence of a rigid cell wall, their shape is definite
Type	Gram-negative, aerobic or facultative aerobic bacteria	It can be of any type
Genome	It has a low molecular weight	The genome of bacterial species varies

Difference between Bacteria and Fungi:

- Bacteria do not contain membrane-bound organelles but fungi contain membrane-bound organelles.
- Bacteria contain 70S ribosomes but Fungi contain 80S ribosomes.
- Fungi are Immobile organisms (they do not move) but some bacteria use flagella to move.
- Fungi can be seen by human eyes too (fungi such as yeast and mushroom) but bacteria can only be seen by a microscope.

4. (*a*) (*i*) **Plantibodies and Their Role in Immunization of Plants against Plant Pathogens:** A plantibody is an antibody that is produced by plants that have been genetically engineered with animal DNA encoding a specific human antibody known to neutralize a particular pathogen or toxin. The transgenic plants produce antibodies that are similar to their human counterparts, and following purification, plantibodies can be administered therapeutically to acutely ill patients or prophylactically to at-risk individuals (such as healthcare workers). The term plantibody and the concept are trade marked by the company Biolex.

Transgenic plants offer an attractive method for large-scale production of antibodies for immunotherapy. Antibodies produced in plants have many advantage that are beneficial to humans, plants, and the economy as well. They can be purified cheaply and in large numbers. The many seeds of plants allow for ample storage, and they have no risk of transmitting diseases to humans because the antibodies are produced without the need of the antigen or infectious microorganisms. Plants could be engineered to produce antibodies which fight off their own plant diseases and pests, for example, nematodes, and eliminate the need for toxic pesticides. Antibodies generated by plants are cheaper, easier to manage, and safer to use than those obtained from animals. The applications are increasing because recombinant DNA is very useful in creating proteins that are identical when exposed into a plant. A recombinant DNA is an artificial DNA that is created by combining two or more sequences that would not normally come together. In this way, DNA injected into a plant is turned into recombinant DNA and manipulated. The favorable properties of plants are likely to make the plant systems a useful alternative for small, medium and large-scale production throughout the development of new antibody-based pharmaceuticals.

(*ii*) **Role of Enzymes in the Development of Plant Diseases:** Enzymes secreted by microorganism play a key role in disease development. These break down plant substances into smaller molecules which pathogen easily absorb and utilize for its growth and energy. Hydrolases is most important enzymes involved in the production of disease by plant pathogens. Important classes of enzyme involved in the Development of Plant Diseases are:

- **Cutinases:** These degrade cutin. Cuticle is made up of cutin which is admixed with waxes at upper part and in the lower part it is admixed with pectin and cellulose.
- **Pectinases:** Pectinases are also known as pectolytic or pectinolytic enzymes. These enzymes degrade pectic substances. Pectic substances are polysaccharides consisting mostly of chains of galacturonan molecules interspersed with a much smaller number of rhamnose and a small side chains of galacturonan, xylan and some other pentose sugars.

- **Cellulases (Cellulolytic enzymes):** These enzymes degrade cellulose, the chief constituent of cell walls. These are produced by many phytopathogens such as fungi, bacteria and nematodes. Saprophytic fungi and bacteria break down most of the cellulose in nature. Cellulases degrade cellulose to facilitate penetration and spread of the pathogen into the host tissue. They degrade cellulose in a series of steps, which are catalysed by series of enzymes, known as cellulose complex.
- **Hemicellulases:** Hemicelluloses are complex mixtures of polysaccharide polymers. They constitute primary cell wall as a major constituent. They are also constituent in varying level in middle lamella and secondary cell wall. Many pathogens are known to secrete hemicellulases which degrade hemi-celluloses to monomer units.
- **Ligninases:** These are lignin degrading enzymes. Lignin is found in the middle lamella as well as in the secondary wall of xylem vessels and the fibers. Lignin gives hard texture to the wood and it is impervious to water and air. It is composed of phenylpropanoid units. Ligninases re-produced in many basidiomycetous fungi, particularly wood rotting fungi. They degrade wood by dissolving lignin of wood making their food available and degrading the wooden logs. Most of lignin in the world is degraded and utilized by a group of basidiomycete fungi known as white rot fungi.

4. (*b*) (*i*) Disease Cycle of *Phytophthora infestans:*

The asexual life cycle of *Phytophthora infestans* is characterized by alternating phases of hyphal growth, sporulation, sporangia germination (either through zoospore release or direct germination, *i.e.* germ tube emergence from the sporangium), and the re-establishment of hyphal growth. There is also a sexual cycle, which occurs when isolates of opposite mating type meet. Hormonal communication triggers the formation of the sexual spores, called oospores. The different types of spores play major roles in the dissemination and survival of *P. infestans.*

Sporangia are spread by wind or water and enable the movement of *P. infestans* between different host plants. The zoospores released from sporangia are biflagellated and chemotactic, allowing further movement of *P. infestans* on water films found on leaves or soils. Both sporangia and zoospores are short-lived, in contrast to oospores which can persist in a viable form for many years.

People can observe *Phytophthora infestans* produce dark green, then brown then black spots on the surface of potato leaves and stems, often near the tips or edges, where water or dew collects. The sporangia and sporangiophores appear white on the lower surface of the foliage. As for tuber blight, the white mycelium often shows on the tubers' surface. Under ideal conditions, *P. infestans* completes its life cycle on potato or tomato foliage in about five days.

Sporangia develop on the leaves, spreading through the crop when temperatures are above 10 °C (50 °F) and humidity is over 75–80% for 2 days or more. Rain can wash spores into the soil where they infect young tubers, and the spores can also travel long distances on the wind. The early stages of blight are easily missed. Symptoms include the appearance of dark blotches on leaf tips and plant stems. White mold will appear under the leaves in humid conditions and the whole plant may quickly collapse. Infected tubers develop grey or dark patches that are reddish brown beneath the skin, and quickly decay to a foul-smelling mush caused by the infestation of secondary soft bacterial rots. Seemingly healthy tubers may rot later when in store. *P. infestans* survives poorly in nature apart from its plant hosts. Under most conditions, the hyphae and asexual sporangia can survive for only brief periods in plant debris or soil, and are generally killed off during frosts or very warm weather. The exceptions involve oospores, and hyphae present within tubers. The persistence of viable pathogen within tubers, such as those that are left in the ground after the previous year's harvest or left in cull piles is a major problem in disease management.

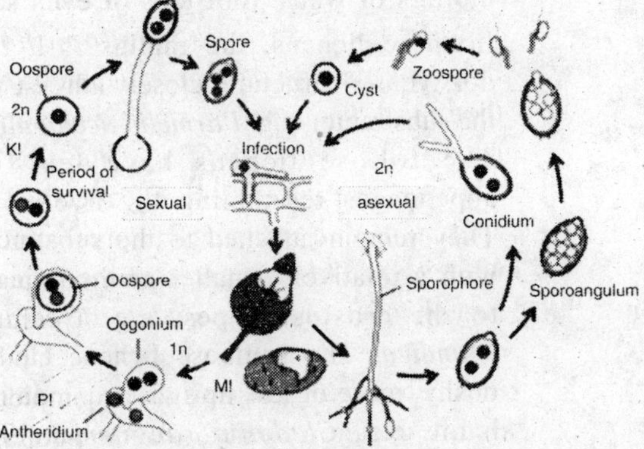

Fig. *Disease Cycle of Phytophthora infestans*

(ii) **Fruiting Body of *Agaricus*:** Agaricus is an edible fungus and is commonly known as mushroom. In old literature it is known by the generic name Psalliota. It is a saprophytic fungus found growing on soil humus, decaying litter on forest floors, in the fields and lawns, wood logs and manure piles. It grows best in moist and shady places and is commonly seen during rainy season. It is cosmopolitan in distribution.

Development of the Basidiocarp or Sporophore: The development of the basidiocarp takes place from the subterranean mycelial strand known as rhizomorph. After absorbing sufficient food material mycelium produces fruiting bodies, which are very small in size and remain underground. These tiny, pin head structures come above the soil under favourable conditions (*i.e.,* after rain or when enough moisture is present in the soil). These are the primodia of basidiocarp.

These primordia enlarge into round or ovoid structures and represent the 'button stage' of the basidiocarp (Fig). A longitudinal section of button stage shows that it can be differentiated into a bulbous basal portion representing the stalk region and an upper, hemispherical part which at maturity forms the cap or pileus region. A ring like cavity (gill chamber) develops at the junction of stalk and pileus region (Fig.).

At this stage the basidiocarp is not fully open but the young pileus is connected with stalk by a membrane known as partial or inner veil or velum. Due to rapid absorption of water and food material, the stalk further elongates.

The button projects above the soil and elongates considerably. The growth is very slow at the lower portion of the button while it is very rapid at the upper portion. As a result of such growth the button develops into umbrella like cup (Fig.). Velum gets broken due to enlargement of the cap and elongation of the stalk. It exposes the hymenium or the gills. Atkins (1906) described the development of basidiocarp as hemi-angiocarpic *i.e.,* the hymenium is at first enclosed but becomes exposed at maturity. Simultaneously, the development also takes place in the gill region.

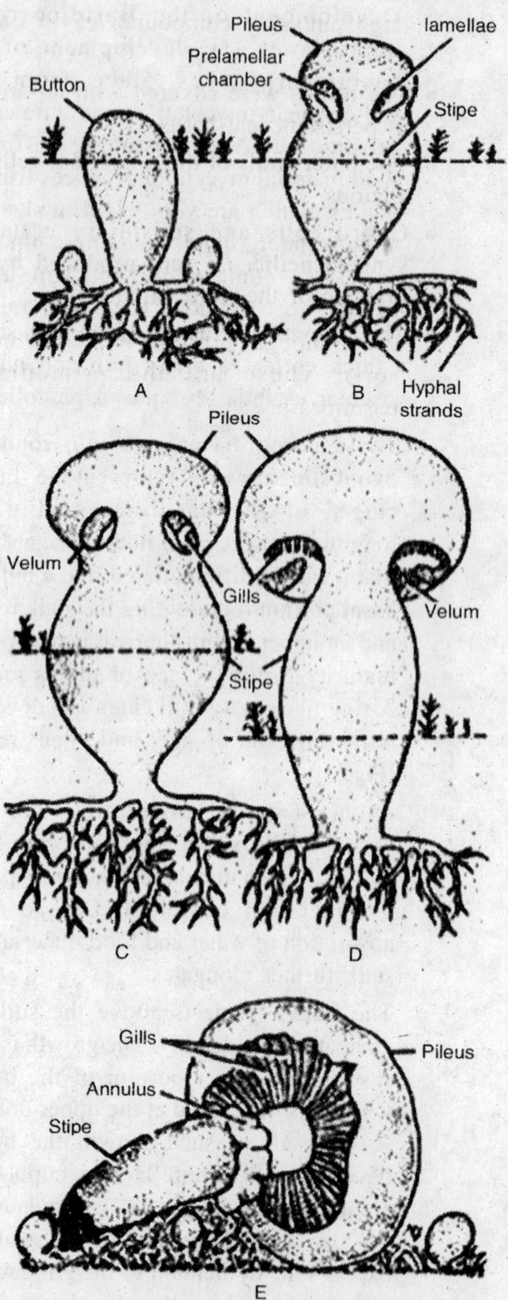

Fig. *Agaricus: Development of Fruiting Body (Basidiocarp) A-D: Vertical sections of developing basidiocarp showing various stages of development.*
E- A mature basidiocarp

The tissue of the upper region of the gill chamber differentiates into slow and fast-growing alternate bands called primordium of gills. Gills or lamellae are of three types *i.e.,* long gills, half-length gills, quarter length gills (Fig.). Simultaneously, the development also takes place in the gill region. The tissue of the upper region of the gill chamber differentiates into slow and fast-growing alternate bands called primordium of gills.

(*iii*) Structure and Composition of Lichen Thallus: In a lichen thallus, the phyco-symbiont and the myco-symbiont are intimately associated, but their identity is maintained. On the basis of gross morphology, lichens are distinguished into three types — crustose, foliose and fruticose. The crustose lichens grow as a crust adhering closely to a substratum which may be a rock, bark of trees, mortars of walls, roof-tops or even soil. In these lichens, the thallus is a flat, dorsiventral structure, closely adressed to the substratum, e.g. *Parmelia acetabulum.* The foliose lichens have leaf-like appendages resembling the liverworts. They remain attached to the substratum with a relatively smaller area compared to the crustose types, e.g. *Cetraria islandica.* The fruticose lichens have a bushy, more or less upright or pendulous habit, e.g. *Cladonia rangiferina.* The basidiolichens have a quite different type of thallus. They resemble the basidiocarps of thin bracket- fungi projecting from the branch of trees which serves as the substratum, e.g. *Cora pavonica.* The internal structure of most lichen thalli shows differentiation into several layers of fungal tissues with interlocked algal or cyanobacterial cells or filaments. In the foliose thalli, these layers are more or less well-defined and arranged dorsiventrally. In crustose forms, the layers are not so well demarcated. In fruticose lichens, the dorsiventrality is absent.

The different forms of lichen thalli are shown in Fig.

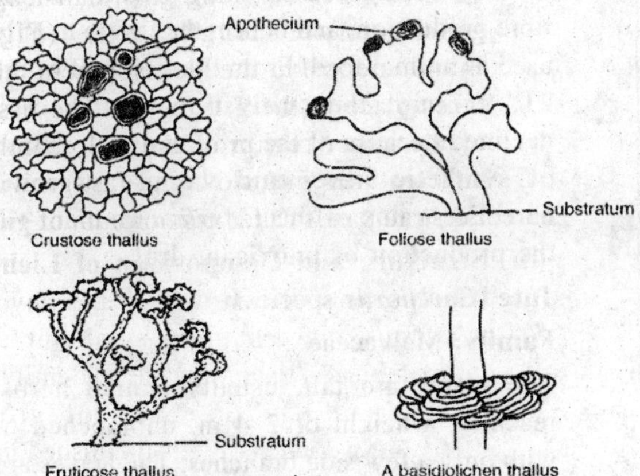

Fig. *Different types of lichen thalli*

4. (c) Features of Bennettitalean Flower: Bennettites (Bennettitales) are extinct seed plants with a habit resembling that of the cycads both in the Stature and in the morphology of leaves. Bennettites are reconstructed as small, sparsely branched or unbranched trees or small shrubs. The trunk is slender or in some bennettites barrel-shaped.

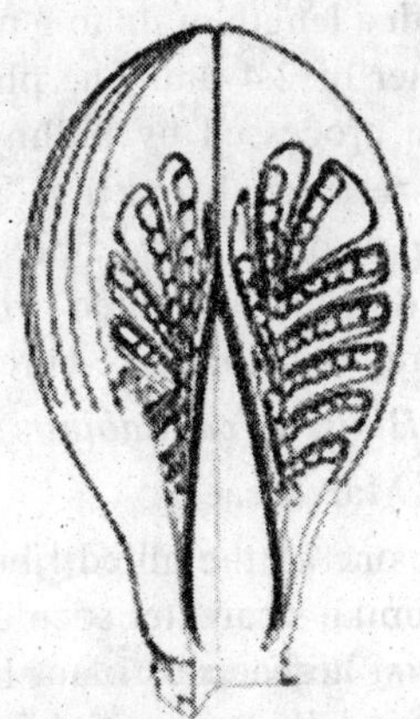

Vegetative Organs:

- Plants were un-branched trees, usually 1-2 metres in height, with compressed internodes and ramentum, bearing a crown of large pinnately compound leaves on the top.
- The trunks were covered with an armour of persistent leaf-bases.
- The outer walls of the epidermal cells are sinuous.
- Guard cells and subsidiary cells are syndetocheilic, *i.e.,* are produced by the division of the same initial.
- The anatomical structure of the stem shows a thick cortex, a broad pith and narrow vascular cylinder composed of collateral bundles with exarch xylem.

Spore-Producing Organs:

- Flowers unisexual or bisexual in strobili.
- Microsporophylls frond-like forming a loose cone.
- Megasporophylls are not leaf-like, but found in specialised cone-like structure.

5. (a) Five Salient Features of Poaceae

- A few plants arboreal in habit.
- All florets in a spikelet are fertile.
- Glumes are persistent.
- Lemmas are herbaceous and leafy.
- Stigmas are three.

Binomial of Three Economically Important Plants

- *Triticum aestivum,*
- *Oryza sativa,*
- *Zea mays* (Maize),

5. (b) Types of Tapetum found in Anther and its Functions

Tapetum is the innermost layer of cells found in the anther. It plays a nutritive role for the microspores present in the anther. It is also known to contribute to the synthesis of sporopollenin, which is the material required for pollen grain wall formation.

Two types of Tapetum

- **Secretory Tapetum:** It is also known as the Glandular tapetum. This type of anther remains surrounded to the anther locule.

- **Amoeboid Tapetum:** It is also known as Plasmodial tapetum. In this type, a multinucleate plasmodium is formed after the dissolution of the tapetal cell walls.

Functions of Tapetum

- It helps in pollen wall formation.
- It transports nutrients to the inside of anthers.
- It synthesises callase enzymes for the separation of the microspore tetrads.
- Development of Orbicules.
- It also synthesises pollenkitt and tryphine, which bind pollen grain together and also help in effective pollination.

5. (*c*) Fibre Producing Plants

Flax (*Linum usitatissimum*)

Family: Linaceae

Flax is also grown for the fiber produced from the stem of the plant. The fiber is processed to make the finest paper and linen products. High-quality flax line fibers are used in applications where strength and fineness are desired. Such uses include fine linens, clothing, draperies, furniture, lace and thread. Coarser grades are used where strength is important, but where fabric fineness is not as crucial, such as twine, canvas and bags. Flax is obtained from the stem of the flax plant. This material is then put to use in order to make linen and fabric yarn. These flax seeds are obtained from a blue flowered plant that is generally known as the linen flax. It is also commonly known as the Linum Usitatissimum.

Hemp (*Cannabis sativa*)

Family: Cannabaceae

Cannabis sativa is an annual herbaceous flowering plant indigenous to Eastern Asia, but now of cosmopolitan distribution due to widespread cultivation. It has been cultivated throughout recorded history, used as a source of industrial fiber, seed oil, food, recreation, religious and spiritual moods and medicine. Traditionally, *C. sativa* L. plants were cultivated primarily as a fibre crop for the production of textiles and ropes, especially in the western world. Despite their high nutritional value, the seeds of this plant were initially considered as a by-product of the fibre production, and hence, they were mainly used as animal feed. From the first half of the 21st century, the cultivation of this crop declined because of the progressive diffusion of synthetic fibres and the use of some narcotic strains of the *C. sativa* L. plant for the production of intoxicant drugs.

Jute (*Corchorus* species)

Family: Malvaceae

The plants are tall, usually annual herbs, reaching a height of 2–4 m, unbranched or with only a few side branches. The leaves are alternate, simple, lanceolate, 5–15 cm long, with an acuminate tip and a finely serrated or lobed margin. The flowers are small (2–3 cm diameter) and yellow, with five petals; the fruit is a many-seeded capsule.

Jute fibre is made from the bark tissue of *C. olitorius* and *C. capsularis*, especially in South Asian countries, though fibre made from *C. olitorius* is considered to be of lesser quality. Finished fibres appear golden and silky with a length of up to 3 metres and with a diameter of 2.4 μm. The plant stalk is cut and then processed by pulling up, rippling, partial retting, breaking, spinning and combing to obtain fine fibres that are well separated from unwanted woody material. Afterwards the fibres are cured and dried.

Kenaf (***Hibiscus cannabinus***)

Family: Malvaceae

Kenaf is one of the allied fibres of jute and shows similar characteristics. It is an annual or biennial herbaceous plant (rarely a short-lived perennial) growing to 1.5-3.5 m tall with a woody base. The stems are 1-2 cm diameter, often but not always branched. The leaves are 10-15 cm long, variable in shape, with leaves near the base of the stems being deeply lobed with 3-7 lobes, while leaves near the top of the stem are shallowly lobed or unlobed lanceshaped. The flowers are 8-15 cm diameter, white, yellow, or purple; when white or yellow, the centre is still dark purple. The fruit is a capsule 2 cm diameter, containing several seeds. The leaves are cooked and eaten in Manipur, and are called sougri.

5. (*d*) **Symmetry:** A flower is considered symmetrical when each whorl consists of an equal number of parts or when the parts of any one whorl are multiples of that preceding it. Thus, a symmetrical flower may have five sepals, five petals, five stamens, and five carpels, or the number of any of these parts may be a multiple of five.

Two main types of symmetry occur: Bilateral symmetry, where structures can be divided into two mirror halves, and radial symmetry, with multiple planes of symmetry. Different organ arrangements or phyllotactic patterns produce different types of symmetry, which may vary within a plant's life span.

5. (*e*) **APG IV System of Classification:** The APG system (Angiosperm Phylogeny Group system) of plant classification is the first version of a modern, mostly molecular-based, system of plant taxonomy. Published in 1998 by the Angiosperm Phylogeny Group, it was replaced by the improved APG II in 2003, APG III system in 2009 and APG IV system in 2016.

The APG IV system of flowering plant classification is the fourth version of a modern, mostly molecular-based, system of plant taxonomy for flowering plants (angiosperms) being developed by the Angiosperm Phylogeny Group (APG). It was published in 2016, seven years after its predecessor the APG III system was published in 2009, and 18 years after the first APG system was published in 1998. In 2009, a linear arrangement of the system was published separately; the APG IV paper includes such an arrangement, cross-referenced to the 2009 one.

Compared to the APG III system, the APG IV system recognizes five new orders (Boraginales, Dilleniales, Icacinales, Metteniusales and Vahliales), along with some new families, making a total of 64 angiosperm orders and 416 families. In general, the authors describe their philosophy as "conservative", based on making changes from APG III only where "a well-supported need" has been demonstrated. This has sometimes resulted in placements that are not compatible with published studies, but where further research is needed before the classification can be changed.

8. (*a*) **Leaf Anatomy of C_4 Plants:** In C_4 photosynthesis, where a four-carbon compound is produced, unique leaf anatomy allows carbon dioxide to concentrate in 'bundle sheath' cells around Rubisco. This structure delivers carbon dioxide straight to Rubisco, effectively removing its contact with oxygen and the need for photorespiration.

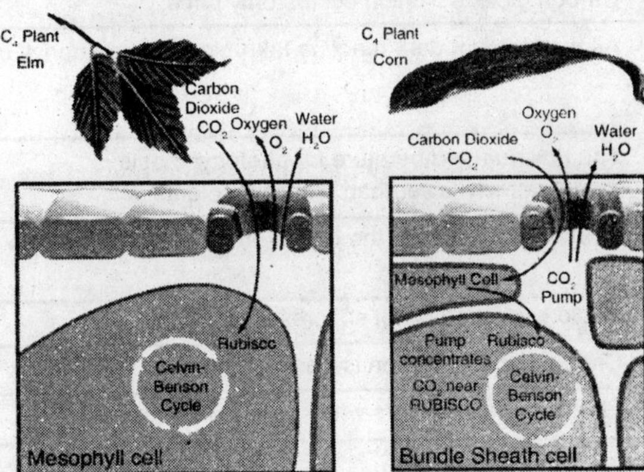

C_4 plants inhabit dry, tropical areas. They have a high productivity of biomass possessing a different type of leaf anatomy, Kranz anatomy. The bundle sheath cells, in this anatomy, form many layers around vascular bundles. This is distinguished by the presence of many chloroplasts, the presence of thick walls impermeable to exchange of gases and exhibits no intercellular spaces.

Difference Between Anatomy of C_3 and C_4 Plants

- C_3 plants are defined as plants that exhibit the C_3 pathway. These plants use the Calvin cycle in the dark reaction of photosynthesis. The leaves of C_3 plants do not show Kranz anatomy. Here the photosynthesis process takes place only when the stomata are open. Approximately 95% of the shrubs, trees, and plants are C_3 plants.
- On the other hand, C_4 plants are defined as the plants that use the C_4 pathway or Hatch-Slack pathway during the dark reaction. The leaves possess kranz anatomy, and the chloroplasts of these plants are dimorphic. About 5% of plants on earth are C_4 plants.

C_3 Plants	C_4 Plants
The first stable intermediate product is 3-carbon acid -phosphoglyceric acid.	The first stable intermediate product is a 4 carbon acid:- oxaloacetate (which is then reduced to malate)
Photosynthetic functions occur only in mesophyll cells – on the surface of the leaves	Photosynthetic functions occur in mesophyll and bundle sheath cells.
C_3 requires cool and wet environments.	C_4 requires tropical and dry environments.
95% of the green plants are C_3 plants.	5% of the green plants are C_4 plants.
Examples include rice, wheat, oats, barley, cotton, peanuts, tobacco, sugar beets, soybeans and spinach	Examples include Maize, Sugarcane, pearl millet, sorghum.
Leaves of these plants DO NOT show Kranz anatomy.	Leaves of these plants show Kranz anatomy.
C_3 Plants are common in temperate climates.	C_4 plants are common in tropical climates.
C_3 plants exhibit only granal type of chloroplast	C_4 plants exhibit granal as well as agranal type of chloroplast
Carbon dioxide fixation occurs only once.	Carbon dioxide fixation occurs twice.
All the steps of dark reaction take place in mesophyll cells.	The initial steps are carried out in mesophyll cells and the subsequent steps are carried out in bundle-sheath cells.
The optimum temperature for photosynthesis is comparatively lower than that of C_4 plants	The optimum temperature for photosynthesis is comparatively higher than C_3 plants
C_3 photosynthesis is the oldest and the most common	C_4 photosynthesis is a recent phenomenon, emerging after C_3 photosynthesis
Photorespiration is not suppressed	Photorespiration is suppressed
Carbon dioxide fixation is slow.	Carbon dioxide fixation is faster.
Photosynthesis occurs when stomata are open	Photosynthesis occurs even when stomata are closed.

8. (*b*) Types of Embryo Development in Dicot: According to Soueges, the mode of origin of the four-celled pro-embryo and the contribution made by each of these cells makes the base for the classification of the embryonal type. However, Schnarf (1929), Johansen (1945) and Maheshwari (1950) have recognized five main types of embryos in dicotyledons.

They are as follows:

I. The terminal cell of the two-celled pro-embryo divides by longitudinal wall.

(*i*) **Crucifer type:** Basal cell plays little or no role in the development of the embryo.

(*ii*) **Asterad type:** Basal and terminal cells play an important role in the development of the embryo.

II. The terminal cell of the two-celled proembryo divides by a transverse wall, Basal cell plays a little or no role in the development of the embryo.

III. Solanad type: Basal cell usually forms a suspensor of two or more cells.

IV. Caryophyllod type: Basal cell does divide further.

V. Chenopodiad type: Both basal and terminal cells take part in the development of the embryo.

Here citing the example of *Capsella bursa-pastoris* (Shepherd's purse), the detailed study of Crucifer type of the development of the embryo has been given.

Development of dicot embryo in *Capsella bursapastoris* (Crucifer type):

For the first time Hanstein (1870) worked out the details of the development of embryo in *Capsella bursapastoris,* a member of Crucifeae.

The oospore divides transversely forming two cells, a terminal cell and basal cell. The cell towards the micropylar end of the embryo sac is the suspensor cell and the other one makes to the embryo cell. The terminal cell by subsequent divisions gives rise to the embryo while the basal cell contributes the formation of suspensor.

The terminal cell divides by a vertical division forming a 4-celled 1-shaped embryo. In certain plants the basal cell also forms the hypocotyl in addition of suspensor. The terminal cells of the four-celled pro-embryo divide vertically at right angle to the first vertical wall forming four cells. Now each of the four cells divides transversely forming the octant stage (8-celled) of the embryo.

The four cells next to the suspensor are termed the hypo-basal or posterior octants while the remaining four cells make the epibasal or anterior octants.

The epibasal octants give rise to plumule and the cotyledons, whereas the hybobasal octants

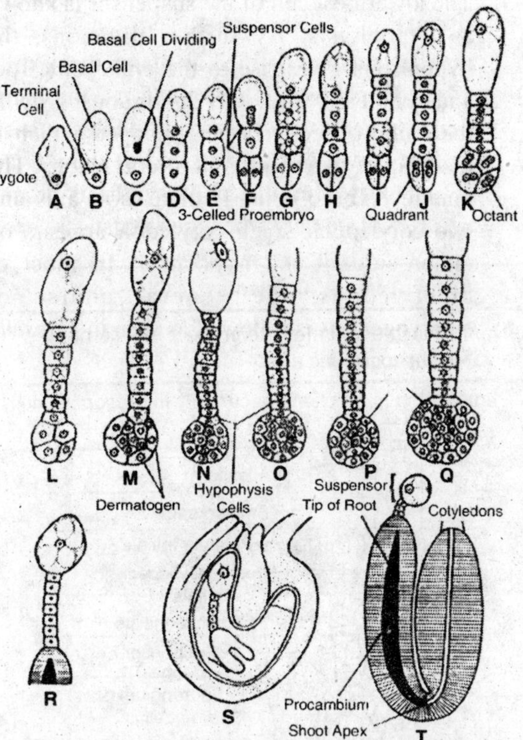

Fig. *Stages in the development of a typical dicot embryo in Capsella bursapastoris.*

give rise to the hypocotyl with the exception of its tip. Now all the eight cells of the octant divide periclinally forming outer and inner cells. The outer cells divide further by anticlinal division forming a peripheral layer of epidermal cells, the dermatogen. The inner cells divide by longitudinal and transverse divisions forming periblem beneath the dermatogen and plerome in the central region. The cells of periblem give rise to the cortex while that of plerome form the stele.

At the time of the development of the octant stage of embryo the two basal cells divide transversely forming a 6-10 celled filament, the suspensor which attains its maximum development by the time embryo attains globular stage. The suspensor pushes the embryo cells down into the endosperm. The distal cell of the suspensor is much larger than the other cells and acts as a haustorium.

The lowermost cell of the suspensor is known as hypophysis. By further divisions, the hypophysis gives rise to the embryonic root and root cap. With the continuous growth, the embryo becomes heart-shaped which is made up of two primordia of cotyledons. The mature embryo consists of a short axis and two cotyledons. Each cotyledon appears on either side of the hypocotyl. In most of dicotyledons, the general course of embryogenesis is followed as seen in *Capsella bursapastoris.*

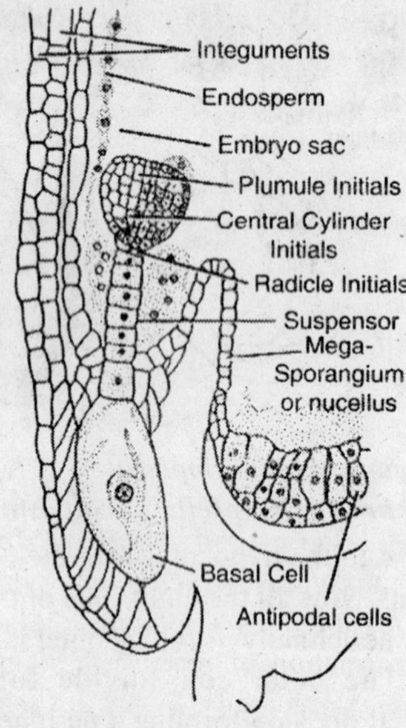

Fig. *The embryo, L.S. showing differentiation of embryo in Capsella.*

8. (*c*) (*i*) Usefulness of Biofuels as Compared to Fossil Fuels

Biofuels help reduce the carbon footprint of transportation and other industries, by making the most of our planet's carbon cycle. Every gallon of biofuel that replaces a gallon of fossil fuel helps reduce greenhouse-gas emissions.

The advantages of biofuels compared to fossil fuels; the carbon intensity can be drastically reduced. This is a key consideration, since the historic impact of infrastructure investment and delivery systems for petro-based fuels are based on delivering fossil carbon.

Various Advantages of Biofuels

1. **Efficient Fuel**: Biofuel is made from renewable resources and relatively less-flammable compared to fossil diesel. It has significantly better lubricating properties. It causes less harmful carbon emission compared to standard diesel. Biofuels can be manufactured from a wide range of materials. The overall cost-benefit of using them is much higher.
2. **Cost-Benefit:** As of now, biofuels cost the same in the market as gasoline does. However, the overall cost-benefit of using them is much higher. They are cleaner fuels, which means they produce fewer emissions on burning. With the increased demand for biofuels, they have the potential of becoming cheaper in the future as well.
3. **Durability of Vehicles' Engine:** Biofuels are adaptable to current engine designs and perform very well in most conditions. It has higher cetane and better lubricating properties. When biodiesel is used as a combustible fuel, the durability of the engine increases.
4. **Easy to Source:** Gasoline is refined from crude oil, which happens to be a non-renewable resource. Although current reservoirs of gas will sustain for many years, they will end sometime in the near future. Biofuels are made from many different sources such as manure, waste from crops, other byproducts, algae and plants grown specifically for the fuel.
5. **Renewable:** Most of the fossil fuels will expire and end up in smoke one day. Since most of the sources like manure, corn, switchgrass, soybeans,

waste from crops and plants are renewable and are not likely to run out any time soon, it makes the use of biofuels efficient in nature. Also, these crops can be replanted again and again.

6. **Reduce Greenhouse Gases:** Studies suggest that biofuels reduce greenhouse gases up to 65 per cent. Fossil fuels, when burnt, produce large amounts of greenhouse gases *i.e.*, carbon dioxide in the atmosphere. These greenhouse gases trap sunlight and cause the planet to warm. Besides, the burning of coal and oil increases the temperature and causes global warming. To reduce the impact of greenhouse gases, people around the world are using biofuels.
7. **Economic Security:** Not every country has large reserves of crude oil. For them, having to import the oil puts a huge dent in the economy. If more people start shifting towards biofuels, a country can reduce its dependence on fossil fuels.
8. **Reduce Dependence on Foreign Oil:** While locally grown crops have reduced the nation's dependence on fossil fuels, many experts believe that it will take a long time to solve our energy needs. As prices of crude oil are touching sky high, we need some more alternative energy solutions to reduce our dependence on fossil fuels.
9. **Lower Levels of Pollution:** Since biofuels can be made from renewable resources, they cause less pollution to the planet. However, that is not the only reason why the use of biofuels is being encouraged. They release lower levels of carbon dioxide and other emissions when burnt compared to standard diesel. Its use also results in a significant reduction of PM emissions.

Disadvantages of Fossil Fuels: The disadvantages of fossil fuels are:

1. The burning of coal and petroleum produces a lot of pollutants, causing air pollution.
2. Fossil fuels release oxides of carbon, nitrogen, sulphur, etc., that cause acid rain, affecting soil fertility and potable water.
3. The burning of fossil fuels produces gases such as carbon dioxide that causes global warming.

8. (*c*) (*ii*) Energy Plants: Energy crops are low-cost and low-maintenance crops grown solely for energy production by combustion (not for food). The crops are processed into solid, liquid or gaseous fuels, such as pellets, bioethanol or biogas. The fuels are burned to generate electrical power or heat. Energy crops include maize or sweet sorghum and herbaceous and woody plants, such as miscanthus (*Miscanthus giganteus*), switchgrass (*Panicum virgatum*), kenaf (*Hibiscus cannabinus*), reed canary grass (*Phalaris arundinacea*) or giant reed (*Arundo donax*), and eucalyptus (*Eucalyptus globulus*), are regarded as appropriate plants for the formation of renewable bioenergy, such as biohydrogen. Mixed or single microbial culture can be employed for transformation of energy crops into biohydrogen. For the production of biohydrogen from energy crops, mostly batch mode bioreactors are widely used in past years; however, in recent times, continuous mode of biohydrogen production is followed extensively.

Jatropha: Another major source of biofuel since it has features that can help the world become less reliant on crude oil. When water is scarce, the Jatropha shrub grows swiftly and lives without much difficulty. Furthermore, Jatropha seeds contain 40 per cent oil. The Jatropha bush has a 50-year lifespan, and it can thrive even if the area is infested with pests or suffers from drought. Surprisingly, this plant is the focus of India's biodiesel business, which finally benefits the farming community financially. Scientific estimates indicate that roughly 2.47 acres (1 hectare) of Jatropha can produce around 0.83 tons or 752 kilograms to 2.20 tons, *i.e.,* 1995. 81 kilograms of oil.

Rapeseed - Rapeseed oil is utilized in the production of biofuels. Rapeseed is crushed or treated first for this. Rapeseed oil is a popular biodiesel fuel nowadays. Canola, in fact, has a competitive edge over. Rapeseed also comes in the form of Canola. Canola, unlike other rapeseed strains, has a reduced Uric acid concentration, making it better to eat for both animals and people. In general, biodiesel manufactured from vegetable oil does not function well in cold areas since most vegetable oils have a higher saturated fat percentage, which causes crystals to form and reduces the efficiency of a car's engine. But due to lower saturated fat content in canola oil, it is harder for ice to form, in colder temperatures.

Energy Plants Useful in the Economy of a Country: The biofuel policy aims to promote the use in transport of fuels made from biomass, as well as other renewable fuels. Biofuels provide the prospect of new economic opportunities for people in rural areas in oil importer and developing countries. The central policy of biofuel concerns job creation, greater efficiency in the general business environment, and protection of the environment. Projections are important tools for long-term planning and policy settings. Renewable energy sources that use indigenous resources have the potential to provide energy services with zero or almost zero emissions of both air pollutants and greenhouse gases. Biofuels are expected to reduce dependence on imported petroleum with associated political and economic vulnerability, reduce greenhouse gas emissions and other pollutants, and revitalize the economy by increasing demand and prices for agricultural products.

PAPER-II

1. (*a*) **Chi-square Test:** A chi-squared test (also chi-square or **χ^2 test**) is a statistical hypothesis test that is valid to perform when the test statistic is chi-squared distributed under the null hypothesis, specifically Pearson's chi-squared test and variants thereof. Pearson's chi-squared test is used to determine whether there is a statistically significant difference between the expected frequencies and the observed frequencies in one or more categories of a contingency table.

In the standard applications of this test, the observations are classified into mutually exclusive classes. If the null hypothesis that there are no differences between the classes in the population is true, the test statistic computed from the observations follows a χ^2 frequency distribution. The purpose of the test is to evaluate how likely the observed frequencies would be assuming the null hypothesis is true.

Test statistics that follow a χ^2 distribution occur when the observations are independent. There are also χ^2 tests for testing the null hypothesis of independence of a pair of random variables based on observations of the pairs.

Chi-squared tests often refers to tests for which the distribution of the test statistic approaches the χ^2 distribution asymptotically, meaning that the sampling distribution (if the null hypothesis is true) of the test statistic approximates a chi-squared distribution more and more closely as sample sizes increase.

1. (*b*) Polyribosomes: A polyribosome (or polysome or ergosome) is a group of ribosomes bound to an mRNA molecule like "beads" on a "thread". It consists of a complex of an mRNA molecule and two or more ribosomes that act to translate mRNA instructions into polypeptides. Originally coined "ergosomes" in 1963, they were further characterized by Jonathan Warner, Paul M. Knopf, and Alex Rich.

Polysomes are formed during the elongation phase when ribosomes and elongation factors synthesize the encoded polypeptide. Multiple ribosomes move along the coding region of mRNA, creating a polysome. The ability of multiple ribosomes to function on an mRNA molecule explains the limited abundance of mRNA in the cell. Polyribosome structure differs between prokaryotic polysomes, eukaryotic polysomes, and membrane bound polysomes. Polysome activity can be used to measure the level of gene expression through a technique called polysomal profiling.

1. (*c*) Crossing Over: Crossing over refers to the interchange of parts between non-sister chromatids of homologus chromosomes during meiotic prophase (pachytene). In other words, crossing over results from exchange of genetic material between non-sister chromatids involving breakage and reunion at precise point. The term crossing over was first used by Morgan and Cattell in 1912.

The features of crossing over are given below:

1. Crossing over takes place during meiotic prophase, *i.e.*, during pachytene. Each pair of chromosome has four chromatids at that time.
2. Crossing over occurs between non-sister chromatids. Thus one chromatid from each of the two homologus chromosomes is involved in crossing over.
3. It is universally accepted that crossing over takes place at four strand stage.
4. Each crossing over involves only two of the four chromatids of two homologus chromosomes. However, double or multiple crossing over may involve all four, three or two of the four chromatids, which is very rare.
5. Crossing over leads to re-combinations or new combinations between linked genes. Crossing over generally yields two recombinant types or crossover types and two parental types or non-crossover types.
6. Crossing over generally leads to exchange of equal segments or genes and recombination is always reciprocal. However, unequal crossing over has also been reported.
7. The value of crossover or recombinants may vary from 0-50%.
8. The frequency of recombinants can be worked out from the test cross progeny. It is expressed as the percentage ratio of recombinants to the total population (recombinants + parental types). Thus,

Crossing over frequency (%)

$$= \frac{\text{Number of recombinants}}{\text{Total progeny}} \times 100$$

1. (*d*) Non-coding RNA: A non-coding RNA (ncRNA) is an RNA molecule that is not translated into a protein. The DNA sequence from which a functional non-coding RNA is transcribed is often called an RNA gene. Abundant and functionally important types of non-coding RNAs include transfer RNAs (tRNAs) and ribosomal RNAs (rRNAs), as well as small RNAs such as microRNAs, siRNAs, piRNAs, snoRNAs, snRNAs, exRNAs, scaRNAs and the long ncRNAs such as Xist and HOTAIR. The number of non-coding RNAs within the human genome is unknown; however, recent transcriptomic and bioinformatic studies suggest that there are thousands of them.

Many of the newly identified ncRNAs have not been validated for their function. It is also likely that many ncRNAs are non-functional (sometimes referred to as junk RNA), and are the product of spurious transcription.

Noncoding RNAs belong to several groups and are involved in many cellular processes. These range from ncRNAs of central importance that are conserved across all or most cellular life through to more transient ncRNAs specific to one or a few closely related species. The more conserved ncRNAs are thought to be molecular fossils or relics from the last universal common ancestor and the RNA world, and their current roles remain mostly in regulation of information flow from DNA to protein.

1. (*e*) Cell signalling: Cell signalling is the process by which cells communicate with other cells within their body or with the external environment. Cell signalling occurs by several distinct pathways. Multicellular organisms need cell signalling to regulate different functions. *e.g.*, nerve cells in coordinate with muscle cells to help in body movement. Cell signalling can be intercellular as well as intracellular.

Intracellular signals are produced by the same cells that receive the signal. Intercellular signals travel throughout the body. This permits specific glands to produce signals that act on different tissues. Cell signalling molecules are of the following types:

- **Intracrine ligands:** These are produced by the target cell and bind to the receptor within the cell.
- **Autocrine ligands:** They function internally and on other target cells. For *e.g.*, immune cells.
- **Juxtacrine ligand:** These target the adjacent cells.
- **Paracrine ligands:** These target the cells in the vicinity of the original cells. For *e.g.*, neurotransmitters.
- **Endocrine ligands:** These produce hormones.

3. (*a*) Heterochromatin: Heterochromatin are a tightly packed form of DNA in the nucleus. They are so compactly organized that they are inaccessible to the protein involved in gene expression. Even the crossing over cannot take place. These are of two types – facultative heterochromatin and constitutive heterochromatin.

Constitutive heterochromatin can affect the genes near itself (*e.g.*, position-effect variegation). It is usually repetitive and forms structural functions such as centromeres or telomeres, in addition to acting as an attractor for other gene-expression or repression signals.

Facultative heterochromatin is the result of genes that are silenced through a mechanism such as histone deacetylation or Piwi-interacting RNA (piRNA) through RNAi. It is not repetitive and shares the compact structure of constitutive heterochromatin.

Heterochromatin is usually localized to the periphery of the nucleus. Despite this early dichotomy, recent evidence in both animals and plants has suggested that there are more than two distinct heterochromatin states, and it may in fact exist in four or five 'states', each marked by different combinations of epigenetic marks. Heterochromatin mainly consists of genetically inactive satellite sequences, and many genes are repressed to various extents, although some cannot be expressed in euchromatin at all.

Both centromeres and telomeres are heterochromatic, as is the Barr body of the second, inactivated X-chromosome in a female.

Euchromatin: Euchromatin are loosely packed form of chromatin. These are active during transcription. It contains 90% of the entire human genome. Housekeeping genes are one of the forms of euchromatin. Euchromatin is a lightly packed form of chromatin (DNA, RNA, and protein) that is enriched in genes, and is often (but not always) under active transcription. Euchromatin stands in contrast to heterochromatin, which is tightly packed and less accessible for transcription. 92% of the human genome is euchromatic. In eukaryotes, euchromatin comprises the most active portion of the genome within the cell nucleus. In prokaryotes, euchromatin is the *only* form of chromatin present; this indicates that the heterochromatin structure evolved later along with the nucleus, possibly as a mechanism to handle increasing genome size.

Euchromatin is composed of repeating subunits known as nucleosomes, reminiscent of an unfolded set of beads on a string, that are approximately 11 nm in diameter. At the core of these nucleosomes are a set of four histone protein pairs: H3, H4, H2A, and H2B. Approximately 147 base pairs of DNA are wound around the histone octamers, or a little less than 2 turns of the helix. Nucleosomes along the strand are linked together via the histone, H1, and a short space of open linker DNA, ranging from around 0-80 base pairs. The key distinction between the structure of euchromatin and heterochromatin is that the nucleosomes in euchromatin are much more widely spaced, which allows for easier access of different protein complexes to the DNA strand and thus increased gene transcription.

Difference between Constitutive Heterochromatin and Facultative Heterochromatin

Constitutive Heterochromatin	Facultative Heterochromatin
The regions of chromosomes, which are invariably heterochromatic, containing highly repetitive sequence of DNA, which are genetically-inactive and serves as a structural element of the chromosome.	The regions of the chromosomes, which become heterochromatic in certain cells and tissues; as an example, it makes up the inactive X chromosome in female somatic cells.
A permanent factor to a particular cell type	Not a permanent character of each cell of particular cell types
Stable	Reversible
Made up of satellite DNA	Made up of LINE-sequences
Contains polymorphism	Does not contain polymorphism

3. (*b*) Lysosomes: A lysosome is a membrane-bound cell organelle that contains digestive enzymes. Lysosomes are involved with various cell processes. They break down excess or worn-out cell parts. They may be used to destroy invading viruses and bacteria. If the cell is damaged beyond repair, lysosomes can help it to self-destruct in a process called programmed cell death, or apoptosis.

Various Functions of Lysosomes

- The key function of lysosomes is digestion and removal of waste. Cellular debris or foreign particles are pulled in to the cell through the process of endocytosis. The process of endocytosis happens when the cell membrane falls in on itself (invagination), creating a vacuole or a pouch around the external contents and then bringing those contents into the cell.

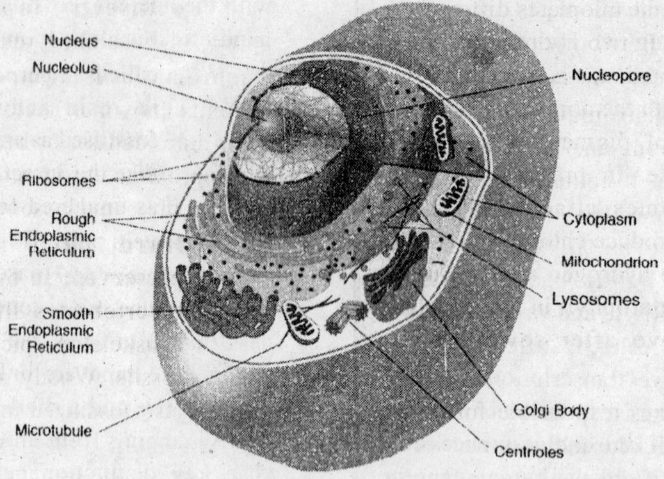

- On the other hand, discarded wastes and other substances originating from within the cell is digested by the process of autophagocytosis or autophagy. The process of autophagy involves disassembly or degradation of the cellular components through a natural, regulated mechanism.

3. (*c*) **Biogenesis of Chloroplast:** Chloroplast biogenesis is a multistage process leading to fully differentiated and functionally mature plastids. Complex analysis of chloroplast biogenesis was performed on the structural and functional level of its organization during the photoperiodic plant growth after initial growth of seedlings in the darkness.

Chloroplast also arises by division from the existing ones. This is very clear in algae, where one chloroplast divides into two during cell division. In higher plants, the division of chloroplasts is very difficult to observe as, the number of chloroplasts is very high. Still, sometimes the dividing chloroplast is seen under the phase contrast microscope as in Spinach. In case of meristematic cells, chloroplasts are not found. But these cells contain numerous small vesicles of about 1 μm in diameter which are known as Pro-plastids. These pro-plastids contain chloroplast DNA.

According to the nature of the cell, these pro-plastids differentiate into either amyloplasts (starch containing particles) or lipoplasts (filled with lipids) or proteinoplasts (filled with proteins). These are all colourless, hence they are also called Leukoplasts.

In presence of light, the pro-plastids differentiate into chloroplast (containing the green pigment chlorophyll):

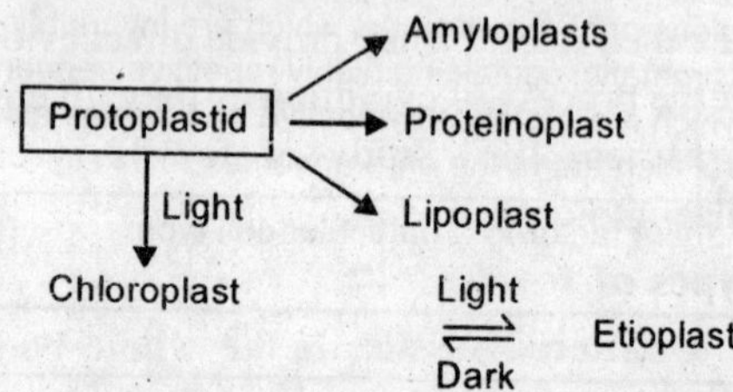

In presence of light, pro-plastids are transformed into chloroplasts, with the enlargement and formation of tubules and invagination of the inner membranes. These tubules are finally formed as grana. But under etiolated conditions, invaginations of the inner membrane occur but they remain contracted into a compact structure known as Pro-lamellar body. This stage of pro-plastid is known as etioplast.

The conversion of these etioplasts to chloroplasts under light gives an excellent tool for the study of chloroplast biogenesis. The pigment present in the etioplasts differs from chlorophyll in having two hydrogen's less in the porphyrin ring and, again, the phytol ring was not attached with the porphyrin ring. This altered structure of pigment is known as Protochlorophyllide. In presence of light, phytol ring becomes attached with the porphyrin ring to produce chlorophyll as with the addition of two hydrogen atoms. But the bulk quantity of chlorophyll in the etioplasts is formed de novo after several hours of illumination.

The enzyme which is responsible for the de novo synthesis of the chloroplast is 5-aminolevulinate synthetase (ALA synthetase). Again, it has been noted that the induction of enzyme for the synthesis of chlorophyll occurs through activation of Phytochrome, the light-receptor pigment.

This stimulation of enzymes requires a short exposure to red light.

4. (*a*) Direct Evidences of Organic Evolution:

Fossils: The preserved remains or prints of organisms which were buried in remote past are called fossils. They provide direct evidence for the process of evolution as they give proof of ancient life. Study of fossils is called palaeontology.

Types of fossils:

1. **Unaltered fossils:** If the whole body or body part of the organism is found to be preserved as if that was in live form, such fossils are called as unaltered fossils.

   (*a*) **Entire organism preservation:** Complete body of organism get preserved in this type. Examples are:

   - **Wooly Mammoths:** In the ice of Siberia elephant like wooly mammoths were found buried. These were about 25000 years old, perfectly preserved with intact eyes, skin, blood, flesh and partially digested food in stomach.
   - **Insects tapped in amber:** Fossilised resins of conifers are called amber. If insect get trapped in resin and if such resin gets fossilised as amber, then along with that the insect get fossilised intact as unaltered fossil.

   (*b*) **Hard parts of invertebrates preserved:** In this case hard part of invertebrates like shell, chitinous exoskeleton, spicules get preserved as fossils. Woody part of plants can be also fossilized in the same way.

2. **Altered fossils:** If certain changes or alterations have taken place in the morphology or anatomy of the original organism. Those are of following types:

   (*a*) ***Petrified fossils:*** Petrifaction means conversion in to rocks. These fossils are hard, rock like. Those are formed by replacement of organic matter of dead organisms by mineral matter. The replacement takes place molecule by molecules. This process is very fine and even cellular structures also remained preserved. Replica of the organism is formed. Such fossils are called pseudomorphs. About 20 minerals are known to cause purification. Common are silica, calcite, pyrites etc. *e.g.,* woody tissue of some plants, calcareous skeleton of corals and certain sponges, limy molluscan shells etc.

   (*b*) ***Carbonisation:*** Occasionally the soft part of a body leaves a thin film of carbon while decaying. Thus exact body outline of organisms can be obtained. During this process it loses nitrogen oxygen and hydrogen results in abundance of carbon. *e.g.,* Extinct swimming reptile Icthyosaurus and other organisms like jelly fish, worms, leaves etc.

3. **Traces of organisms preserved:** Sometimes only certains impressions or marks on hard media get preserved as a fossil.

(*a*) ***Moulds and Casts:*** Sometimes a dead organism gets buried in mud which gradually gets converted into hard rock. Meanwhile the organic part of the dead organism disintegrated and a cavity remains. This cavity gives exact idea about the external appearance of the organism. This is called a mould. Cast is similar to moulds but the cavity of mould gets filled with some mineral. This material is hardened and a cast is formed. *e.g.,* soft bodied animals, shells, skulls etc.

(*b*) ***Tracks and trails:*** Tracks are the footprints that are formed over the dryland or sea bottom or in muddy environments. Wet sand or mud receive impressions of feet of passing animals and get covered by the sediments before they are disturbed or eroded.

(*c*) ***Burrows and borings:*** Some animals live in burrows, tubes and holes in the ground wood or rocks. The presence of such burrows in sedimentary rocks of past are called fossil burrows. Borings are holes made by animals. Such fossil holes occur on fossil shells, wood and organic objects.

(*d*) ***Gastrolites and coprolites***: Gastrolites are the hard stony pieces found from stomachs of ancient reptiles and fishes. Coprolites are fossilised faeces of ancient animals.

Incompleteness of fossil record: All organisms that die cannot be fossilised. This is because the conditions required for fossil formation are very rare. Many groups of animals never leave fossils. Many fossils cannot be searched by human. The number of species known about through the fossil record is less than 5% of the number of species alive today. Fossilised species may represent less than 1% of all the species that have ever lived.

Conditions required for fossilisation:

- If the organism has some hard body part like bone, teeth or shell etc. then there are more chances of fossil formation. As the harder parts decompose slowly.
- There are more chances of formation of fossils of aquatic animals than terrestrial animals.
- The regions which undergoing erosion are not suitable for fossil formation but the regions where deposition is going on are suitable for fossilisation.
- High concentration of minerals is required for the process of mineralisation or petrifaction.
- For the beginning of the fossilisation the organisms should be prevented from decomposition. Many organisms decompose before they undergo fossilisation.
- For the beginning of fossilisation the dead organism should get covered by sediments before they undergo decomposition and can be remain protected from erosion and environmental damage.
- The organisms with soft body part rarely fossilised if they somehow get oxygen deficient environment so that they can remain protected from scavengers. It may possible if it get buried in mud with little seepage of oxygen rich water or there are some other organic things in that mud which consume the available oxygen more rapidly.
- And after all the fossil if formed, it should be properly excavated or should be within the reach of human. E.g. a fossil buried thousands of feet below the ice of Antarctica cannot be found by human.

Dating of fossils: The dating of fossils is mainly carried out by radiometry method. This is the most sensitive and universally accepted method. The age of the fossil is calculated using radioactive isotopes and their half life. Many rocks are having one or other radioactive element which undergo decay and converted into a stable element. Each radioactive element is having its own specific half life period *i.e.,* the time in which half amount of the element decayed. Many radiometric methods such as Uranium lead method, Potassium Argon Method, Rubidium Strontium Method and Carbon Method are using different radioisotopes available for calculating the age of fossil.

4. (*b*) Molecular Map of Ti Plasmid:

The Tumour inducing or Ti plasmid is present in the bacterium *Agrobacterium tumifaciens.* It is widely used now as a cloning vector to deliver desirable genes to the host plant to get transgenic plants. The main characteristics of Ti plasmid are:

- Size of the plasmid is ~ 250 kbp
- There are different kinds of Ti plasmids based on the different genes they possess, which code for different opines, *e.g.* leucinopine, nopaline, octopine, etc.
- It is a pathogenic species to many dicotyledonous plants. It causes crown gall disease in plants.
- It contains one or more T-DNA region.
- *Agrobacterium tumifaciens* has the ability to transform the normal cells into tumour cells by inserting a DNA piece known as T-DNA and it starts producing chemicals, that are required by the bacterium.
- After inserting the desired gene into Ti plasmid, it loses its pathogenic ability but is still able to insert the desired gene into the plant cell.
- It contains *vir* or virulence genes, which transfer T-DNA region to plant cells and gets integrated into the plant genome.
- Ti plasmid can be modified as per the requirement to insert the desired genes.
- *Agrobacterium tumifaciens* is called "nature's genetic engineer"

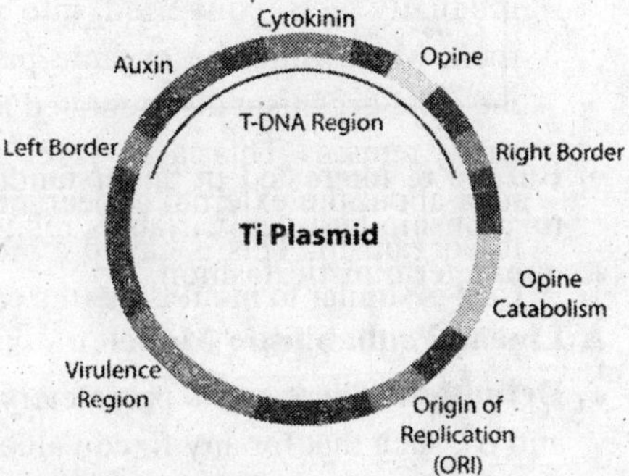

4. (*c*) Linear Regression:

Regression

- Technique used for the modeling and analysis of numerical data.
- Exploits the relationship between two or more variables so that we can gain information about one of them through knowing values of the other.
- Regression can be used for prediction, estimation, hypothesis testing, and modeling causal relationship.

Why Linear Regression?

- Suppose we want to model the dependent variable Y in terms of three predictors, X_1, X_2, X_3

  $Y = f(X_1, X_2, X_3)$
- Typically it will not have enough data to try and directly estimate f
- Therefore, we usually have to assume that it has some restricted form, such as linear.

  $Y = X_1 + X_2 + X_3$

Linear Regression is a Probabilistic Model

- Much of mathematics is devoted to studying variables that are deterministically related to one another.

  $y = \beta_0 + \beta_1 x$

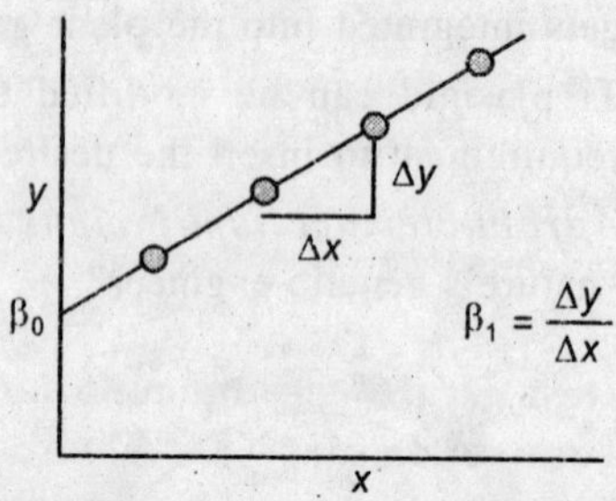

- But we're interested in understanding the relationship between variables related in a non-deterministic fashion.

A Linear Probabilistic Model

- **Definition:** There exists parameters β_0, β_1 and σ^2, such that for any fixed value of the independent variable *x*, the dependent variable is related to *x* through the model equation

$$y = \beta_0 + \beta_1 x + \varepsilon$$

- ε is a *rv* assumed to be $N(0, \sigma^2)$

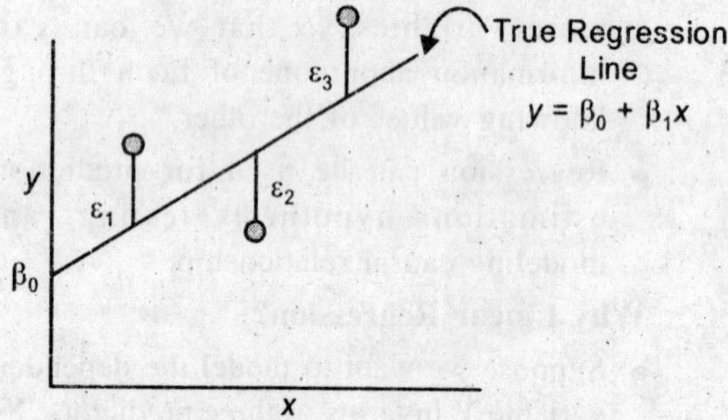

Implications

- The expected value of Y is a linear function of X, but for fixed *x*, the variable Y differs from its expected value by a random amount.
- Formally, let x^* denote a particular value of the independent variable *x*, then our linear probabilistic model says:

$E(Y \mid x^*) = \mu_{Y \mid x^*}$

= mean value of Y when *x* is x^*

$V(Y \mid x^*) = \sigma^2_{Y \mid x^*}$

= variance of Y when *x* is x^*

Graphical Interpretation

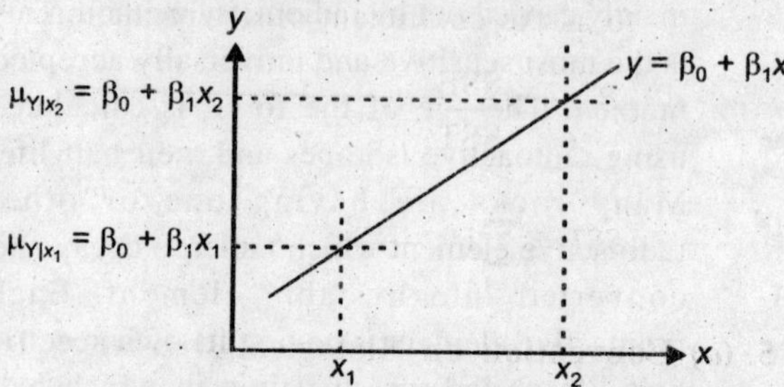

- For example, if *x* = height and *y* = weight then $\mu_{Y \mid x = 60}$ is the average weight for all individuals 60 inches tall in the population.

Residual Values:

- Predicted, or fitted, values are values of *y* predicted by the least-squares regression line obtained by plugging in $x_1, x_2, ..., x_n$ into the estimated regession line

$$\hat{y}_1 = \hat{\beta}_0 - \hat{\beta}_1 x_1$$

$$\hat{y}_2 = \hat{\beta}_0 - \hat{\beta}_1 x_2$$

- **Residuals** are the deviations of observed and predicted values

$$e_1 = y_1 - \hat{y}_1 \qquad e_2 = y_2 - \hat{y}_2$$

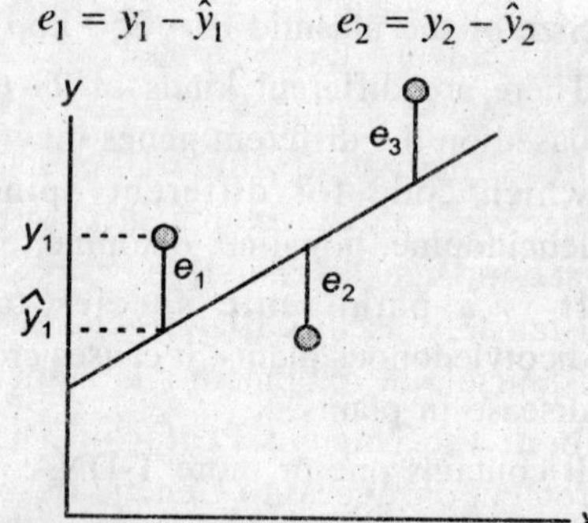

Residuals are Important for Statistical Analysis:

- They allow us to calculate the error sum of squares (SSE):

$$SSE = \sum_{i=1}^{n} (e_i)^2 = \sum_{i=1}^{n} (y_1 - \hat{y}_1)^2$$

- Which in turn allows us to estimate σ^2:

$$\hat{\sigma}^2 = \frac{SSE}{n-2}$$

- As well as an important statistic referred to as the coefficient of determination:

$$r^2 = 1 - \frac{SSE}{SST};$$

$$SST = \sum_{i=1}^{n} (y_1 - \bar{y})^2$$

5. (*a*) Convention on Biological Diversity: The Convention on Biological Diversity (CBD) is a multilateral treaty and has three goals which are biological diversity conservation; the components are being used sustainably; and the equitable and fair sharing of benefits that arise from the genetic resources.

Overview:

- At the Earth Summit that was held in Rio De Janeiro in 1992, the CBD was opened for signature.
- In the year 1993, the CBD came into force.
- The only UN member state that has not ratified this convention is the United States.
- The CBD has two supplementary agreements, the Nagoya Protocol and the Cartagena Protocol.

The objective of the CBD: The CBD's objective is the development of strategies so that biological diversity can be conserved and sustainably used. CBD is generally seen as sustainable development's key document.

About the Nagoya Protocol: The Nagoya Protocol on Access to Genetic Resources is a supplementary agreement of the CBD. Under this protocol, a transparent legal framework has been set for the implementation of one of CBD's three objectives which is the equitable and fair sharing of benefits that arise from genetic resources. In 2010, in Nagoya, Japan, this protocol was adopted and in 2014 it came into force.

About the Cartagena Protocol: The Cartagena Protocol on Biosafety to the Convention on Biological Diversity governs the movements from one country to another of all the living modified organisms (LMOs) that result from modern biotechnology. In 2000 this protocol was adopted as CBD's supplementary agreement and in 2003 it came into force.

Latest Draft recommendation: A draft recommendation was released recently focusing on health and biodiversity. The draft called for a unifying and integrated approach so that the health of people, ecosystems, and animals is sustainably optimized and balanced. COVID-19 pandemic's impact on well-being, health, and biodiversity was also addressed by the draft. Also, ways were outlined to reduce infection outbreaks and pathogen spillover. Early warning surveillance and information sharing were also focused upon so that pandemics can be prevented. It also stated the need for addressing the inequities in global health such as access to medicines, diagnostics, vaccines, and medical equipment. The governments were also encouraged to implement the One Health approach in their respective COVID-19 recovery plan.

5. (*b*) Role of Cytokinin in Leaf Senescence: Cytokinins modulate a number of important developmental processes, including the last phase of leaf development, known as senescence, which is associated with chlorophyll breakdown, photosynthetic apparatus disintegration and oxidative damage. Cytokinins delay the senescence of leaves and other organs by controlling protein synthesis and mobilisation of resources. Leaf senescence can be delayed by plant hormones such as cytokinin.

5. (*c*) Active Ion Transport in Plants: Active transport always leads to accumulation of molecules are ions towards one side of the membrane. This mode of transportation in plants is carried out by membrane proteins and transports the substance from the lower concentration to higher concentration.

Active transport is a mode of transportation in plants, which uses stored energy to move the particles against the concentration gradient. In a plant cell, it takes place in the root cells by absorbing water and minerals.

5. (*d*) Polarity of Water and its Significance: Although the net charge of a water molecule is zero, water is polar because of its shape. The hydrogen ends of the molecule are positive and the oxygen end is negative. This causes water molecules to attract each other and other polar molecules. Water (H_2O) is polar because of the bent shape of the molecule. The shape means most of the negative charge from the oxygen on side of the molecule and the positive charge of the hydrogen atoms is on the other side of the molecule. This is an example of polar covalent chemical bonding.

More important, the polarity of water is responsible for effectively dissolving other polar molecules, such as sugars and ionic compounds such as salt. Ionic compounds dissolve in water to form ions. This is important to remember because for most biological reactions to occur, the reactants must be dissolved in water.

5. (*e*) Inter-relationship between Nitrogen and Carbon Assimilation in Plants: Improved understanding of crop production systems in relation to N-supply has come from a knowledge of basic plant biochemistry and physiology. Gene expression leads to protein synthesis and the formation of metabolic systems; the ensuing metabolism determines the capacity for growth, development and yield production. This constitutes the genetic-potential. These processes set the requirements for the supply of resources. The interactions between carbon dioxide (CO_2) and nitrate (NO_3) assimilation and their dynamics are of key importance for crop production. In particular, an adequate supply of NO_3, its assimilation to amino acids (for which photo-synthesized carbon compounds are required) and their availability for protein synthesis, are essential for metabolism. An adequate supply of NO_3 stimulates leaf growth and photosynthesis, the former via cell growth and division, the latter by larger contents of components of the light reactions, and those of CO_2 assimilation and related processes. If the supply of resources exceeds the demand set by the genetic potential then production is maximal, but if it is less then potential is not reached; matching resources to potential is the aim of agriculture. However, the connection between metabolism and yield is poorly quantified.

Biochemical characteristics and simulation models must be better used and combined to improve fertiliser-N application, efficiency of N-use, and yields. Increasing N-uptake at inadequate N-supply by increasing rooting volume and density is feasible, increasing affinity is less so. It would increase biomass and NuC ratio. With adequate N, at full genetic potential, more C-assimilation per unit N would increase biomass, but energy would be limiting at full canopy. Increasing C-assimilation per unit N would increase biomass but decrease N-C at both large and small N-supply. Increasing production of all biochemical components would increase biomass and demand for N, and maintain N-C ratio. Changing C- or N-assimilation requires modifications to many processes to effect improvements in the whole system; genetic engineering molecular bio-logical alterations to single steps in the central metabolism are unlikely to achieve this, because targets are unclear, and also because of the complex interactions between processes and environment. Achievement of the long-term objectives of improving crop N-use and yield with fewer inputs and less pollution, by agronomy, breeding or genetic engineering, requires a better understanding of the whole system, from genes via metabolism to yield.

6. (*a*) Ethylene as Phytohormone: Different from Other Hormone: Ethylene is a group of plant growth regulators which are widely used for ripening fruits and for the production of more flowers and fruits. Ethylene is a small hydrocarbon, the colourless flammable gas which is denoted by a formula C_2H_4 or $H_2C=CH_2$. Ethene is the IUPAC name for ethylene. It has a "sweet and musky" odour when it is pure. It is the simplest alkene and also the second simplest unsaturated hydrocarbon C_2H_2. Ethylene is abundantly used in the chemical industry, and the polyethene is extremely produced using ethylene. Further, ethylene is also used in agricultural practices to ripen fruits, germination of the seed, etc. Ethylene is best known for its effect on fruit ripening and organ abscission, and thus has great commercial importance in agriculture.

Mechanism of Action: The ethylene in a plant growth regulator that acts as a trace level of entire plant life by regulating and stimulating the opening of flowers, fruit ripening and shedding of leaves. During the ancient days, Egyptians used this technique with gash figs to stimulate ripening. The action of ethylene on leaf growth may be auxin-dependent or auxin-independent. Hormonal coordination is an important aspect, which regulates leaf growth processes. Auxin induces ethylene production, and many effects of exogenous auxins are, in fact, ethylene responses.

Mechanism of ethylene action

- **Membrane permeability:**
  - Ethylene acts by changing permeability of the cell membrane.
  - Ethylene is lipid soluble, hence it gets dissolved in lipid membrane and alters the permeability of membrane.
- **Nucleic acid and protein metabolism:** Some responses like fruit ripening & abscission are due to gene expression and protein synthesis. Synthesises specific mRNA and enzymes.
- **Regulation of auxin metabolism:** Reduces biosynthesis of auxins and inhibits its transport.

The Physiological Effects of Ethylene - Plant Hormone: The physiological effects of ethylene are:

- Ethylene breaks seed and bud dormancy.
- Ethylene is highly effective in fruit ripening.
- Ethylene enhances the rate of respiration during fruit ripening.
- Ethylene promotes senescence and abscission of leaves and flowers.
- Ethylene initiates flowering and regulates so many physiological processes.
- Ethylene initiates germination in peanut seeds and sprouting of potato tubers.
- Ethylene also promotes root growth and root hair formation, thus helping the plants to increase their absorption surface.

6. (*b*) Enzyme Inhibition: Enzyme inhibitors can block the binding site, preventing the substrate from attaching to the active site, and decreasing the enzyme's catalytic activity. Reversible inhibitors attach to enzymes via non-covalent interactions like hydrogen bonds, hydrophobic contacts, and ionic bonds. In the pharmaceutical and medical industries, enzyme inhibitors are essential. Pharmacologists benefit from a basic grasp of inhibitor activity during the development of new therapeutic medicines. Insecticides such as malathion, herbicides such as glyphosate, and disinfectants such as triclosan are all examples of artificial inhibitors. Other synthetic enzyme inhibitors inhibit acetylcholinesterase, an enzyme that breaks down acetylcholine, and are utilised in chemical warfare as nerve agents.

Reversible Enzyme Inhibition: Reversible inhibitors attach to enzymes with non-covalent interactions such as hydrogen bonds, hydrophobic interactions and ionic bonds. Multiple weak bonds between the inhibitor and the enzyme active site combine to produce strong and specific binding. In contrast to irreversible inhibitors, reversible inhibitors generally do not undergo chemical reactions when bound to the enzyme and can be easily removed by dilution or dialysis.

Types of Reversible Enzyme Inhibition: Reversible inhibitors are generally categorised into four types, as introduced by Cleland in 1963. They are classified according to the effect of the inhibitor on the V_{max} (maximum reaction rate catalyzed by the enzyme) and K_m (the concentration of substrate resulting in half maximal enzyme activity) as the concentration of the enzyme's substrate is varied.

Examples of reversible inhibition:

- competitive inhibition (Raises K_m only)
- uncompetitive inhibition (Lowers V_{max} and K_m)
- non-competitive inhibition (Lowers V_{max} only).

6. (*c*) Mechanism and Factors Causing Dormancy of Seeds: In several species seeds germinate as soon as they have undergone maturation and provided proper conditions for germination. To this category belong the seeds of bean, pea, maize, etc. In some species the seeds may germinate while being attached to the parent plant or enclosed inside the fruit. This is called the process of vivipary. In many species seeds are incapable of germinating because of some inhibitory factor(s). Such seeds even placed under suitable environments of germination are unable to germinate. This is called process of seed dormancy. Sometimes the seeds are quiescent. Such seeds do not germinate because of the lack of favourable environmental conditions.

The physiological inability of a seed to germinate even under favourable condition is called seed dormancy. Many kinds of seeds can germinate immediately after maturation. The seeds in some species of citrus may germinate in the fruit. But in some cases, seed passes a period of rest or inactivity before germination. Hormonal regulation may be a highly conserved mechanism of seed dormancy among seed plants. Induction and maintenance of seed dormancy by abscisic acid (ABA) and dormancy release by gibberellin (GA) are observed in many species.

There are certain major causes for the seed dormancy. Listed below are the few reasons for the seed dormancy.

- Light
- Temperature
- Hard Seed Coat
- Period after ripening
- Germination inhibitors
- Immaturity of the seed embryo
- Impermeability of seed coat to water
- Impermeability of seed coat to oxygen
- Mechanically resistant seed coat
- Presence of high concentrate solutes.

Previous Years' Paper (Solved)

Indian Forest Service

IFS–Botany Main Examination, 2020

(Exam held on 07-03-2021)

PAPER-I

INSTRUCTIONS: *There are EIGHT questions in all, out of which FIVE are to be attempted. Questions Nos. 1 & 5 are compulsory. Out of the remaining SIX questions, THREE are to be attempted selecting at least ONE question from each of the two Sections A and B. Attempts of questions shall be counted in sequential order. Unless struck off, attempt of a question shall be counted even if attempted partly. Any page or portion of the page left blank in the Question-cum-Answer Booklet must be clearly struck off. All questions carry equal marks. Answers must be written in ENGLISH only. Neat sketches may be drawn, wherever required.*

SECTION–A

1. Answer the following questions keeping your answers brief and to the point.

(*a*) How can algae be used in sewage treatment?

(*b*) With a labelled sketch describe the ultra-structure of bacterial flagella. Describe its mechanism of movement.

(*c*) Explain in detail the process of fertilization in Angiosperms.

(*d*) Describe and differentiate heterocyst cell from blue-green algal cell.

(*e*) Deuteromycotina has been called "Waste Basket Assemblage."— Substantiate.

2. (*a*) Describe the stelar organization and evolution in Pteridophytes.

(*b*) Describe the life cycle of the pathogen causing damping-off of seedlings of tobacco and tomato.

(*c*) Describe the mechanism and benefits of parasexuality.

3. (*a*) Discuss the three kinds of mycelia encountered in Basidiomycetes. With suitable diagrams bring out the significance of clamp connection.

(*b*) Trace the evolution of sporophytes in Bryophytes with neat labelled sketches only.

(*c*) What are Antibiotics? Describe the mode of action of aminoglycosides.

4. (*a*) Name the organisms causing black, yellow and brown rust of wheat. Describe the symptoms of black rust of wheat and the life cycle of the pathogen causing it.

(*b*) What do you mean by genetic recombination? Describe different methods of bacterial recombination.

(*c*) What is dissemination of disease? Describe methods of plant virus dissemination in brief.

SECTION–B

5. Answer the following questions keeping your answers brief and to the point.

(*a*) Comment on

(*i*) Totipotency

(*ii*) Somatic hybrids vs. Cybrids.

(*b*) What are Petrocrops? Name 4 (four) promising petrocrop species with family.

(*c*) Enumerate the applications of palynology.

(*d*) What is plant defence? Explain different mechanisms of plant defence.

(*e*) 'Petrified fossils are the marvels of paleo-botanical studies."— Substantiate.

6. (*a*) Define Fumitories and Masticatories. Describe in detail the origin, botanical characteristics and cultivation of one representative each of the above categories.

(*b*) Illustrate the floral characters of the family Arecaceae with floral formula and floral diagram. Why is this family economically important?

(*c*) What is tissue culture? How can this technique help in reviving the endangered plant species?

7. (*a*) Differentiate Heterospory from Homospory. How does heterospory lead to seed habit? Discuss the biological significance of heterospory with reference to *Selaginella*.

(*b*) Enlist the botanical names of five plants yielding drugs and mention the plant parts from where the drugs are obtained.

(*c*) Describe successive stages of development of cellular endosperm.

8. (*a*) Describe the methods of cultivation of rubber plants. Describe how the latex is processed to get rubber. What precautions are taken while tapping rubber?

(*b*) What are the differences between Dicot and Monocot roots? With suitable diagrams explain secondary growth in dicot roots.

(*c*) Mention the botanical name with family of plants yielding the following, with the morphology of the part used:

(*i*) Spices (*ii*) Perfumery

(*iii*) Gums (*iv*) Sugar

(*v*) Beverages

PAPER-II

INSTRUCTIONS: *There are EIGHT questions in all, out of which FIVE are to be attempted. Questions Nos. 1 & 5 are compulsory. Out of the remaining SIX questions, THREE are to be attempted selecting at least ONE question from each of the two Sections A and B. Attempts of questions shall be counted in sequential order. Unless struck off, attempt of a question shall be counted even if attempted partly. Any page or portion of the page left blank in the Question-cum-Answer Booklet must be clearly struck off. All questions carry equal marks. Answers must be written in ENGLISH only. Neat sketches may be drawn, wherever required.*

SECTION–A

1. Write short notes on the following:

(*a*) Membrane proteins—structure and function

(*b*) Chromosomal sex determination in higher plants

(*c*) Origin and cytological behaviour of trisomics

(*d*) Male sterility and its significance in plant hybrid production

(*e*) Pearson's correlation coefficient.

2. (*a*) Describe briefly the role of allopolyploidy in the evolution and speciation of plants.

(*b*) In what ways is a plant vacuole similar to a lysosome? What are lysosomal storage diseases?

(*c*) Describe various mechanisms of transport of molecules across the cell membrane.

3. (*a*) What are the criteria for cytoplasmic inheritance? Describe the plastid inheritance in *Mirabilis jalapa* (four o'clock plant).

(*b*) Describe briefly the prophase I of meiosis. What are recombination nodules?

(*c*) What is the significance of normal, binomial and Poisson distributions of data?

4. (*a*) How was gene linkage discovered? Describe gene mapping by three-point test cross.

(*b*) What are autocrine, paracrine and endocrine types of intercellular signaling?

(c) "Genetic code is triplet, degenerate and universal." Explain.

SECTION–B

5. Write short notes on the following:

(*a*) Oxidative phosphorylation

(*b*) Vernalization

(*c*) Seed dormancy

(*d*) Global warming

(*e*) Biodiversity hotspots

6. (*a*) What is meant by biodiversity? What are alpha, beta and gamma diversity? Why is conservation of biodiversity essential for future of mankind?

(*b*) What is the concept of climax community? How does succession progress in tropical forest ecosystem after extensive damage?

(*c*) What are the abiotic and biotic components of an ecosystem?

7. (*a*) What are the steps of nitrogen cycle? Describe the processes and factors involved in nodule formation of legumes.

(*b*) Explain the Z-scheme of light reaction of photosynthesis.

(*c*) Give a concise account of Krebs cycle.

8. (*a*) What is plant stress physiology? Explain developmental and physiological mechanisms against environmental stresses.

(*b*) What are the differences among afforestation, reforestation and social forestry? Why are these important for environmental protection and ecosystem functions required for the human society?

(*c*) Write an elaborate note on the phytogeographical zones (regions) of India.

ANSWERS

PAPER-I

1. (*a*) Algae in wastewater range in size from tiny single cells to branched forms of visible length. Unicellular green algae such as Chlorella and Scenedesmus have been widely used in waste-water treatment because they often colonize the ponds naturally, and they have fast growth rates and high nutrient uptake capabilities per unit biomass due to their small size.

Classes of algae that are commonly found in wastewater treatment plants are:

- **Green (chlorophyta):** These are fresh-water species, can be unicellular or multicellular. Motile green (euglenophyta).
- **Yellow-green (chrysophyta):** Most forms are unicellular. In this group, the most important are diatoms which have shells composed mainly of silica.
- **Blue-green (cyanophyta):** These are unicellular, usually enclosed in a sheath and have no flagella. An important characteristic is their ability to use nitrogen in cell synthesis, from the atmosphere as nutrient.

Some of algae strains that can grow well in municipal wastewater and their roles in treating the waste water are given below:

- ***Chlorella***: Chlorella is used for the removal of lead (II) ions from wastewater. It is also used to remove nutrients (N and P) from domestic wastewater.
- ***Pithophora sp.***: It is used for the removal of the malachite green dye from wastewater.
- ***Scenedesmus abundans***: It is used to eliminate cadmium and copper present in contaminated water and also in the process of detoxification of cyanide from wastewater.
- ***Sargassum muticum***: It is used for the removal of Methylene Blue dye from wastewater.
- ***Spirulina sp.***: It can also be used for the biosorption of heavy metals like antimony and chromium present in wastewater.
- ***Botryococcus braunii***: It is used for the removal of nitrogen, phosphorus and other simple inorganic compounds from industrial wastewater, most commonly in piggery wastewater.
- ***Dunaliella salina***: It is used for the removal of heavy metals like Cu, Cd, Co and Zn and also in the treatment of hypersaline wastewater.
- ***Ankistrodesmus sp.***: It has immense capability to absorb metals, and there is considerable potential for using them to treat wastewaters.
- ***Actinastrum sp.***: Removes copper from wastewater.
- ***Microactinium sp.***: Removal of zinc and cadmium from wastewater.
- ***Pediastrum sp.***: Indicators of organic compounds in wastewater. The process occurs through biosorption.

1. (***b***) Flagella are microscopic hair-like structures involved in the locomotion of a cell. The word "flagellum" means "whip". The flagella have a whip-like appearance that helps to propel a cell through the liquid. They are filamentous structures found in archaea, bacteria, and eukaryotes.

1. Archaeal flagella are nonhomologous.
2. Bacterial flagella are a coiled, thread-like structure, sharp bent, consisting of a rotary motor at its base and are composed of the protein flagellin.
3. Eukaryotic flagella are complicated cellular projections that pummel backwards and forward and are found in protist cells, gametes of plants, and animals. It is made up of a protein called tubulin.

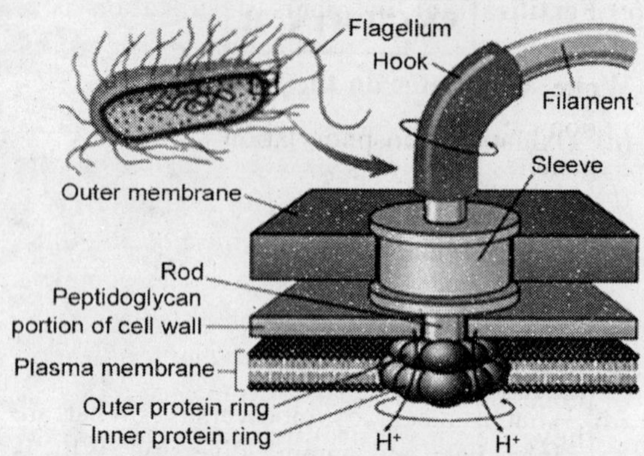

Figure: *Ultra-Structure of Bacterial Flagella*

Mechanism of Movement: The most common mechanism used by bacteria to swim through liquid media is the flagellum. The bacterial flagellum consists of 3 major domains: an ion driven motor, which can provide a torque in either direction; the hook, a universal joint which transmits motor torque even if it is curved; and the filament, a very long structure which acts as a propeller, and behaves differently depending on which way the motor turns. When the bacterial flagellum is rotated by the motor, the filament forms a supercoil, giving it an overall corkscrew-like shape. Flagellated bacteria are able to undergo directed movement through changes in the rotary behaviour of the flagellum. When the flagellum rotates clockwise, the filament forms a long pitch supercoil, allowing several flagella on a single cell to form a large bundle, which propels the bacterium along a straight line in a single direction. When the filament is rotated in the opposite direction, it forms a shorter pitch supercoil; this causes the flagellar bundle to disassemble, and the independent motion of several flagella on the cell cause it to tumble randomly. Using these two modes of motion, bacteria can move up or down a stimulus gradient by decreasing their tumbling frequency or increasing their tumbling frequency), allowing them to undergo a biased random walk.

1. (*c*) **Fertilization:** In plants, fertilization is a process of sexual reproduction, which occurs after pollination and germination. Fertilization can be defined as the fusion of the male gametes (pollen) with the female gametes (ovum) to form a diploid zygote. It is a physicochemical process which occurs after the pollination of the carpel. The complete series of this process takes place in the zygote to develop into a seed. In the fertilization process, flowers play a significant role as they are the reproductive structures of angiosperms (flowering plants). The method of fertilization in plants occurs when gametes in haploid conditions fuse to produce a diploid zygote. In the course of fertilization, male gametes get transferred into the female reproductive organs through pollinators (honey bees, birds, bats, butterflies, flower beetles) and the final product will be the formation of the embryo in a seed.

Fertilization Process: In flowers, the pollen grain germinates after the pollination of the carpel and grows into the style by creating the pathway for the pollen grain to move down to the ovary. The pollen tube opens into the ovule through the micropyle and bursts into the embryo sac. Here, the male nucleus unites with the nucleus of an egg inside the ovule forming a diploid zygote, which later swells up and develops into a fruit.

Types of Fertilization: Fertilization process can be grouped into three types and are classified mainly based on the entry of the pollen tube into the ovule.

Porogamy: It is the common type of fertilization carried out in all angiosperms or flowering plants. In this type of fertilization, the pollen tube enters the ovule through the micropyle.

Chalazogamy: This type of fertilization is carried out on all *Casuarina* species of plants.

Mesogamy: This type of fertiiization is seen in all Cucurbit plants, such as pumpkin, ridge gourds, bitter gourd and other gourd plants.

Double Fertilization: Double fertilization is a process of fertilization characterized by the fusion of a female gametophyte with two male gametes. In this mechanism, one sperm cell fuses with the egg-producing zygote, and the other fuses with the two polar nuclei to make the endosperm. All angiosperm plants undergo double fertilization process.

1. (*d*) **Heterocysts cell:** These are specialized cells of the filament distinguished from others by their thick wall, polar nodule(s) and homogenous contents. Heterocysts are commonly found in the members of Stigonematales and Nostocales (except *Oscillatoriaceae*). They grow in the filament either terminally (*Gloeotrichia*) or intercalary (*Nostoc*) or both terminal and intercalary (*Anabaena desikacharyiensis*).

Structure: Pale yellow, thick-walled specialized cells, larger than vegetative cells are called heterocysts. The wall of the heterocyst is differentiated into three regions, an outer fibrous, middle homogenous and inner lamellar layer. It has pore(s) at the pole(s) where it remains attached with the vegetative cell. The pores are plugged with polar nodule(s) or polar granules. The wall of the heterocyst is thicker towards the polar regions.

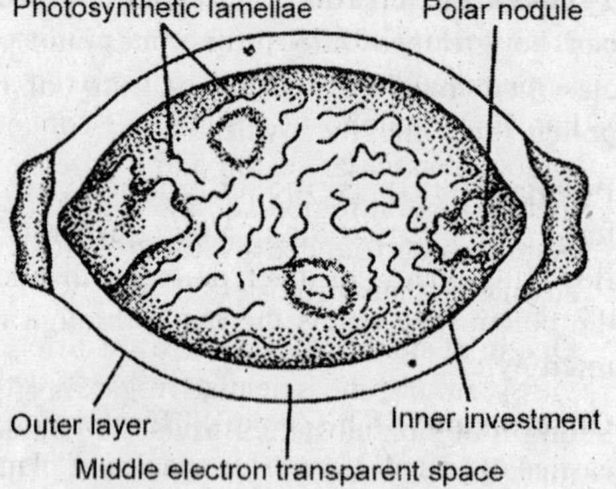

Figure: *Structure of Heterocyst*

Blue Green Algae Cell: According to two kingdom system BGA were included in class Cyanophyceae or Myxophyceae of Algae. But now they are included in Kingdom Monera, because of their prokaryotic nature.

Structure of BGA: It is similar to Gram (–ve) eubacteria. BGA is surrounded by a mucilagenous sheath. This sheath is made up of mucopolysaccharides [Pectic acid]. The cell wall of BGA is also bilayered. Outer wall is made up of lipopolysaccharides and the inner wall is made up of peptidoglycan.

The cytoplasm of BGA is divided into two parts:

Peripheral cytoplasm: It is known as chromoplasm. In this part gas vacuoles and photosynthetic thylakoids are found.

Central cytoplasm: This is known as centroplasm. In this region nucleoid is present. Ribosomes are of 70s type, and are scattered in both chromoplasm and centroplasm.

A special type of cell is found for nitrogen fixation in BGA which is known as heterocyst. Heterocysts is thick walled, non-green cell. Heterocysts don't perform the photosynthesis like other vegetative cells. Nitrogenase enzyme is necessary for nitrogen fixation. For the synthesis of this enzyme, there is a special type of gene present in BGA, which is known as nif-gene. This gene stimulates the production of nitrogenase enzyme.

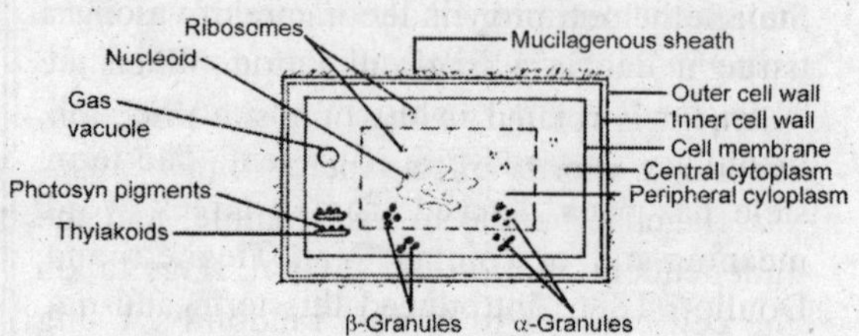

1. (*e*) Deuteromycetes is also known as fungal waste basket because it lacks perfect sexual stage or its sexual stage is yet to be discovered. Until then the fungus is placed in deuteromycetes, once the sexual phase is discovered its accordingly placed into its respective class. Deuteromycetes are an artificial group of fungi, of which there exist approximately fifteen thousand species, often referred to as "fungi imperfecti" because their only known reproductive mechanism is asexual. Deuteromycetes—also known as Deuteromycota, Deuteromycotina, fungi imperfecti, and mitosporic fungi—are fungi that are unable to produce sexual spores and are therefore placed in their own separate phylum. The deuteromycetes are commonly called fungi imperfecti, that is, "imperfect fungi," a term accepted by many mycologists.

Reproduction in the deuteromycetes occurs in several different forms. Spores, or conidia, may be produced directly on the mycelium (the mass of hyphae, or tubular filaments, forming the body of a fungus) or on a structure of specialized mycelial cell called a condiophore. Some of these fungi do not produce spores. Nonsporulating fungi are able to propagate themselves by fragmenting the hyphae or by producing a mass of hyphae called a sclerotium. Sclerotia can be microscopic in size or as large as several millimeters in diameter. Conidia can vary in size and shape from small (2-3 microns long) to large (250-300 microns long). Colours can range from clear (hyaline) to a variety of earth tones. Conidia may consist of one to several cells.

2. (*a*) Stelar Organization & Its Evolution in Pteridophytes

Stele is the central cylinder or core of vascular tissue in higher plants and Pteridophytes. It consists of xylem, phloem, pericycle and medullary rays and pith if present. The term stele has been derived from a Greek word meaning rod or column. Van Tieghem and Douliot (1886) introduced this term and put forward the stelar theory. The theory suggests that the cortex and the stele are the two fundamental parts of a shoot system. Both these components (stele and cortex) separated by endodermis. Tieghem and Duoliot recognized only three types of steles. They also thought that the monostelic shoot were rare in comparison of polystelic shoots. But now it is an established fact that most shoots are monostelic and polystelic condition rarely occurs. The stele of the stem remains connected with that of leaf by a vascular connection known as the leaf supply.

There are several types of stele found in pteridophytes which are:

1. Protostele
2. Siphonostele
3. Solenostele
4. Dictyostele
5. Polycyclic stele
6. Eustele
7. Polystele

1. **Protostele:** Jeffrey (1898), for the first time pointed out the stelar theory from the point of view of the phylogeny. According to him, the primitive type of stele is protostele. In protostele, the vascular tissue is a solid mass and the central core of the xylem is completely surrounded by the strand of phloem. This is the most primitive and simplest type of stele. Pith is absent in protostele *i.e.* it is non-medullated. Majority of the pteridophytes show protostelic conditions in their rhizome, stem or roots. There are five forms of protostele.

   - Haplostele
   - Actinostele
   - Plectostele
   - Mixed Protostele
   - Mixed Protostele with pith

2. **Siphonostele:** This is the modification of protostele. A stele in which the protostele is medullated or with pith at the centre is known as siphonostele. Such stele contains a tubular vascular region and a parenchymatous central region *i.e.,* the central core of pith is surrounded by the xylem. It is advanced than protostele.

   Origin of siphonostele: There are different views among the scientists regarding the origin of siphonostele. But they all agreed that, the siphonostele is originated from protostele by formation of pith in the center. Here, the centrally placed xylem core is replaced with parenchymatous pith.

   - Different stages of changing protostele to siphonostele can be observed in the T.S at different levels in Gleichenia, Osmunda and Anemia.
   - There are two views regarding the origin of pith in the siphonostele.

   Jeffrey's theory: According to this theory, the pith is formed as a result of the invasion of cortical parenchymatous cells into the stele. The invasion of pith occurs through the leaf gap or branch gap. Thus, pith and cortex are homogeneous structures according to this theory. This theory is not accepted by most of the authors since in many pteridophytes there is stele without leaf gaps but having siphonostele.

   Boodle's theory: According to the theory proposed by Boodle (1901), and Gwynne Vaughan, the siphonostele has been evolved from the protostele by a transformation of the inner vascular tissue into parenchyma.

   A siphonostele may be of the following types:

   (*a*) **Ectophloic:** In this type of siphonostele, the pith is surrounded by concentric xylem cylinder and next to xylem the concentric phloem cylinder.

(*b*) **Amphiphloic:** In this type of siphonostele the pith is surrounded by the vascular tissue. The concentric inner phloem cylinder surrounds the central pith. Next to the inner phloem is the concentric xylem cylinder which is immediately surrounded by outer phloem cylinder (e.g., in *Marsilea rhizome*).

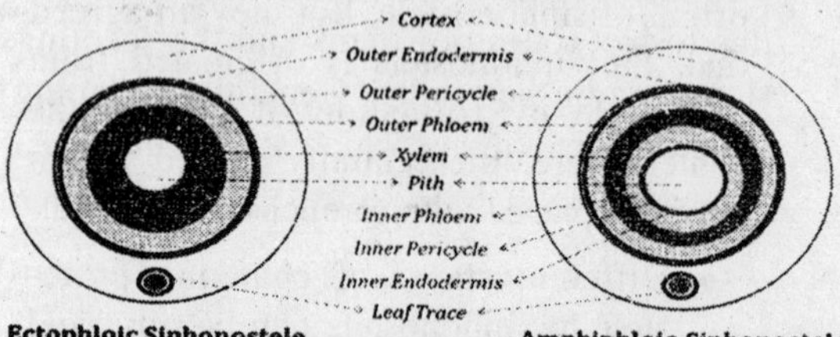

3. **Solenostele:** In solenostele, pith is found with one leaf gap. It may be ectophloic or amphiphloic solenostele.

(*a*) **Ectophloic:** Xylem is surrounded by only on the outer side by phloem. e.g., in Osmunda.

(*b*) **Amphiphloic:** In center, pith is found. Xylem is surrounded on both sides by phloem. e.g. Marsilea rhizome.

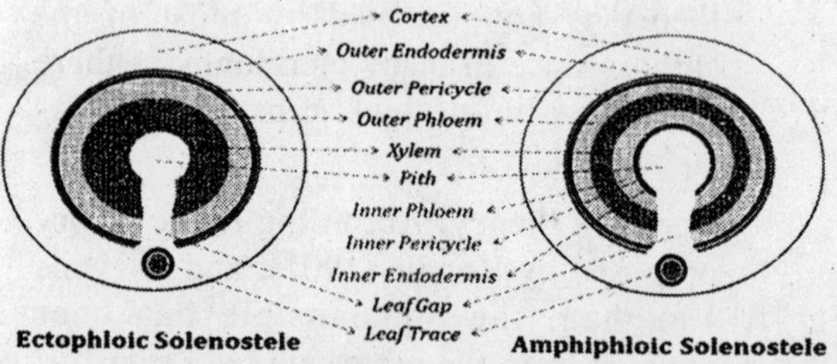

4. **Dictyostele:** Solenostele that is broken into a network of separate vascular strands are called dictyostele. This breaking up of stelar core is due to the presence of large number of leaf gaps. Each such separate vascular strands are called meristele. Each meristele is of protostelic type. The dictyostele with many meristeles looks like a cylindrical meshwork.

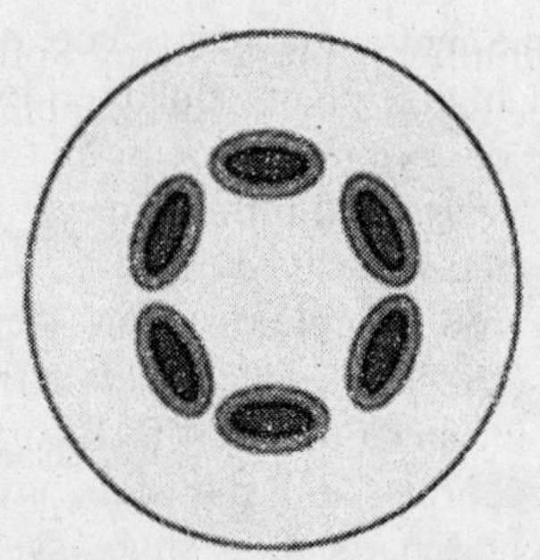

Examples: Pteris, Adiantum capillus-veneris.

5. **Polycyclic Stele:** This type of stelar organization is the most complex one amongst all vascular cryptogams (pteridophytes). Such type of steles is always siphonostelic in structure. A typical polycyclic stele possesses two or more concentric rings of vascular tissue. This may be a solenostele or a dictyostele. Two concentric rings of vascular tissue are found in *Pteridium aquilinum* and three in *Matonia pectinata*.

(*a*) *Polycyclic solenostele*

(*b*) *Polycyclic dictyostele*

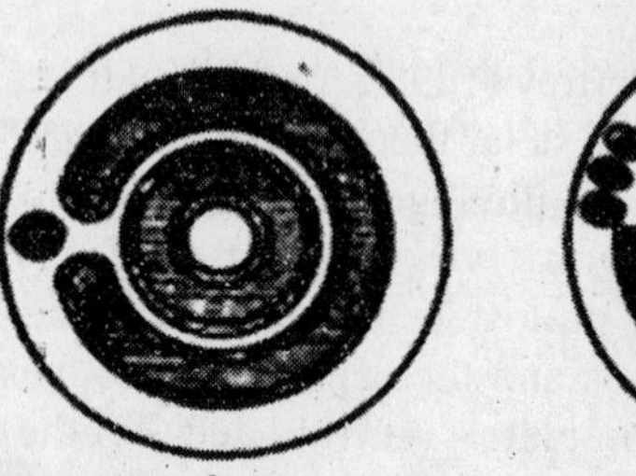

Figure: *Polycyclic stele—types (diagrammatic. sectional views). A. Polycyclic solenostele; B. Polycyclic dictyostele.*

6. **Eustele:** According to Brebner (1902), there is one more modification of the siphonostele known as eustele. Here the vascular system consists of a ring of collateral or bicollateral vascular bundles situated on the periphery of the pith. The example of this type is internode of Equisetum. It is the modification of

ectophloic siphonostele. Splitting takes place because of the overlapping leaf gaps.

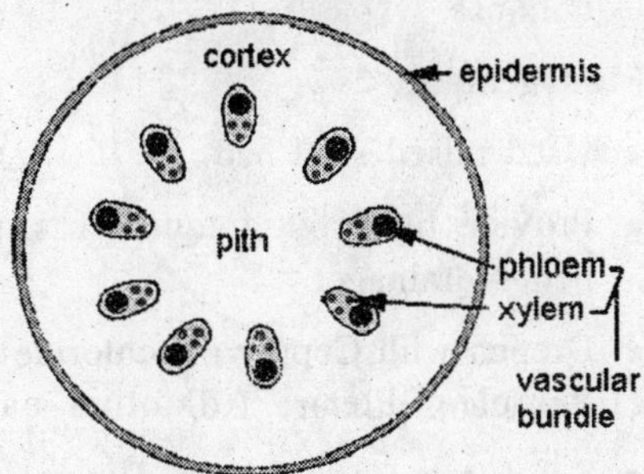

7. **Polystele:** More than one stele in the axis of pteridophytes is present known as polystele. It is a type that must have derived from protostele because each such stele shows protostelic condition. In *Selaginella kraussiana* generally two stele presents. But in *Selaginella laevigata* as many as 16 steles are present.

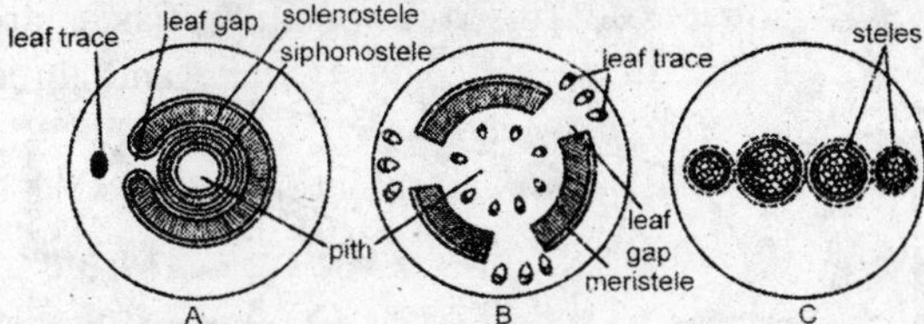

Figure: *(A-C). Stelar System: A. Polycyclic solenostele; B. Polycyclic dictyostele; C. Polystele*

2. (*b*) Damping off Seedling of Tobacco

Damping Off: *Pythium aphanidermatum, Pythium debaryanum*

- Damping off is a serious problem in tobacco nurseries both in heavy clay soils and light sandy soils.
- It is caused by several soil inhabiting fungi predominant being *Pythium aphanidermatum, Pythium debaryanum, Phytophthora sp.* and sometimes *Rhizoctonia solani* are also involved.
- The disease may appear at any stage of the seedlings but maximum damage is observed 5-6 weeks after sowing.

Symptoms: Disease is noticed in two phases, viz.

- Pre-emergence damping-off
- Post-emergence damping-off

Pre-emergence damping-off: Seedlings are infected which die before emergence from the soil resulting in poor and uneven stand of the seedlings.

Post-emergence damping-off: Post emergence damping-off is the most destructive phase. The tiny two leaved seedlings may disappear due to wet rotting of stems and the seedlings stand diminishes daily. Generally damping-off occurs in patches which spread quickly if unchecked. The older seedlings show shriveling and brown discolouration of the stems near the soils and start rotting under wet soil conditions.

Pythium Oospores

- The decayed stems collapse and seedlings topple over leaving parchment like brown crest over the soil.
- The wet rotting and sudden collapse of seedlings starts in circular patches and under wet weather conditions may extend over the whole seedbed causing near total loss.

Life cycle

- Oospores and chlamydospores in soil act as initial source of infection.
- Under favourable wet conditions oospores germinate liberating zoospores which infect the seedlings at soil level or just below.

Epidemiology

- High humidity, high soil moisture, cloudiness and low temperatures below 24°C for few days are ideal for infection and development of disease.
- Crowded seedlings, dampness due to high rainfall, poor drainage and excess of soil solutes hamper plant growth and increase the pathogenic damping-off.

Damping-off Seedling of Tomato

Damping-off: *Pythium aphanidermatum*

"Damping-off" is a general term for the death of seedlings, either before or after emergence, under damp conditions. It is mainly an early season problem, causing the greatest losses in cool, wet soils. Fungi that cause damping-off occur in all soils where tomatoes are grown and they infect tomatoes when the soil is wet. Infection is most common under cool conditions, although both *Phytophthora* and *Rhizoctonia* can also infect seedlings in warmer soils. Once tomato seedlings reach the 2- or 3-leaf stage, they are no longer susceptible to infection by *Pythium* or *Rhizoctonia*; however, *Phytophthora* can infect tomato plants at any stage. Damping-off due to *Pythium* may increase where green manures such as volunteer grain are worked into the soil just before planting.

Favourable conditions

- High humidity, high soil moisture, cloudiness and low temperatures below 24°C for few days are ideal for infection and development of disease.
- Crowded seedlings, dampness due to high rainfall, poor drainage and excess of soil solutes hamper plant growth and increase the pathogenic damping-off.

Symptoms

- Damping-off of tomato occurs in two stages, *i.e.*, the pre-emergence and the post-emergence phase.
- In the pre-emergence the phase the seedlings are killed just before they reach the soil surface.
- The young radical and the plumule are killed and there is complete rotting of the seedlings.
- The post-emergence phase is characterized by the infection of the young, juvenile tissues of the collar at the ground level.
- The infected tissues become soft and water soaked. The seedlings topple over or collapse.

Management

- Used raised seed bed.
- Provide light, but frequent irrigation for better drainage.
- Drench with Copper oxychloride 0.2% or Bordeaux mixture 1%.
- Seed treatment with fungal culture *Trichoderma viride* (4 g/kg of seed) or Thiram (3 g/kg of seed) is the only preventive measure to control the pre-emergence damping off.
- Spray 0.2% Metalaxyl when there is cloudy weather.

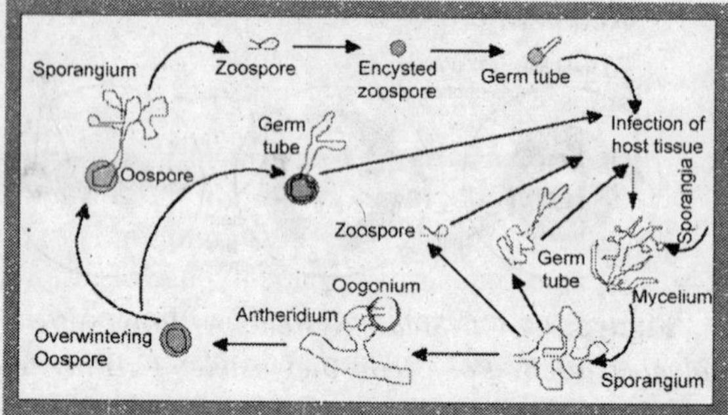

Figure: *Life cycle of Pythium aphanidermatum*

2. (*c*) Mechanism of Parasexuality

- In some fungi, true sexual cycle comprising of nuclear fusion and meiosis is absent. These fungi derive the benefits of sexuality through a cycle known as parasexual cycle. First Reported by Gudio Pontecorvo and J.A. Roper (1952). Parasexual cycle was reported in *Aspergillus nidulans*, the imperfect stage of *Emericella nidulans*. Since then, parasexual cycle has been discovered not only in several members of Deuteromycetes but also in fungi belonging to Ascomycetes and Basidiomycetes.

- Parasexuality is defined as a cycle in which Plasmogamy, Karyogamy and Meiosis [Haploidization] take place in sequence but not at a specified time or at specified points in the life cycle of an organism. Generally parasexual cycle occurs in those fungi in which true sexual cycle does not take place.
- Generally, parasexual cycle occurs in those fungi in which true sexual cycle does not take place. The members of class Deuteromycetes (Deuteromycotina) in which sexual cycle does not occur, exhibit parasexual cycle generally. Parasexual cycle was first discovered by Pontecarvo and Roper of University of Glasgow in 1952 in *Aspergillus nidulans*, the imperfect stage of *Emericella nidulans.*

Steps Involved in Parasexual Cycle: According to Pontecarvo (1958), parasexual cycle in *A. nidulans* involves the following steps:

(i) **Formation of heterokaryotic mycelium:** Heterokaryotic mycelium is formed in several ways. The most common is by the anastomosis of somatic hyphae of different genetic combinations. The foreign nucleus or nuclei introduced into a mycelium multiplies and its progeny spreads through the mycelium rendering it heterokaryotic. Mutation in one or more nuclei of a homokaryotic mycelium also makes it heterokaryotic. It happens in some of the fungi belonging to Ascomycetes. Still a third way is by the fusion of some of the nuclei and their subsequent multiplication and spread among the haploid nuclei. In this type of heterokaryotic mycelium, a fixture of haploid and diploid nuclei occurs.

(ii) **Fusion between two nuclei (Karyogamy):** The fusion of nuclei in the mycelium has been demonstrated. The nucelar fusion may be of two types:

- fusion between like nuclei and
- fusion between unlike nuclei.

The nuclear fusion results in the formation of homozygous or heterozygous diploid nucleus respectively. If the genotype of unlike nuclei present in the heterokaryotic mycelium is A and B, then five types of nuclei can be formed by their fusion: two types of haploid nuclei (A and B), two types of homozygous diploid nuclei (AA and BB) and one type of heterozygous diploid nucleus (AB).

(iii) **Multiplication of diploid nuclei:** The above mentioned five types of nuclei multiply at about the same rate but the diploid nuclei are present in much smaller number than the haploid nuclei. Portecarvo (1958) estimates a proportion of one diploid heterozygous nucleus to 1000 haploid nuclei.

(iv) **Occasional mitotic crossing over:** During multiplication of diploid nuclei, mitotic crossing over may take place. This results in the formation of new gene combinations. These recombinations, which are dependent on the existence of heterokaryosis, give the fungus some of the advantages of sexuality within the parasexual cycle. According to Pontecarvo's (1958) estimates, the amount of recombinations which may be expected to occur in an ascomycete through its parasexual cycle is 500 times smaller than through its sexual cycle.

(v) **Sorting out of Diploid nuclei:** In those fungi which produce uninucleate conidia, sorting out of the diploid nucleus occurs by their incorporation into conidia which germinate to produce diploid mycelia. Diploid strains of several important imperfect fungi have been isolated. Roper (1952) first synthesized and isolated diploid strains of *Aspergillus nidulans.* The conidia of diploid strains are somewhat larger than those of haploid strains.

(vi) **Occasional haploidisation of the diploid nuclei:** Occasionally, some hyphae of diploid mycelium form haploid conidia which form haploid mycelia on germination. The formation of haploid conidia by diploid mycelium indicates that haploidisation occurs in some diploid nuclei.

(vii) **Sorting of new haploid strains:** Some diploid nuclei undergo haploidisation in the mycelium and are sorted out by incorporation of haploid nuclei in the uninucleate conidia. Some of these haploid strains are genotypically different from their parents because of their mitotic recombinations.

Benefits of Parasexuality

- Parasexual cycle is of importance in industrial processes. Several fungi which are used in various industrial processes belong to fungi imperfecti or Deuteromycetes and in these fungi only parasexual cycle operates.
- New and better strains of these fungi are obtained by mutation through parasexual cycle. The strains of desirable characters can be developed through mitotic recombinations.
- Parasexuality can also be applied in the analysis of genetic and physiological processes of perfect and imperfect fungi. Parasexual cycle has also been successfully employed in genetic control of pathogenicity and host-range in several species of Fusarium.

3. (*a*) The well-developed, filamentous mycelium consists of a mass of branched, septate hyphae generally spreading in a fan-shaped manner. The cell wall is chitinous in nature. Within the cell wall is the plasma membrane. The cytoplast contains a complement of usual cell organelles except the chloroplasts. The septum, as in the Ascomycetes, originates as an annular outgrowth on the inside of the tubular wall.

It grows inwards like a narrow shelf reducing diameter of the pore. The hyphae ramify in the substratum and absorb food. The mycelium generally is a weft of interlacing and anastomosing hyphae. In a few genera, however, the mycelial hyphae run parallel to one another and get bundled together to form definite and conspicuous thick cords of macroscopic size. These are the rhizomorphs. The rhizomorph is covered by a sheath (cortex) and behaves like a unit. The mycelium in different species varies in colour and may be white, yellow or orange. It is generally perennial. The mycelium of Basidiomycetes passes through three distinct stages namely, the primary, the secondary and the tertiary before the fungus completes its life cycle. The first stage is represented by the primary mycelium or homokaryon (B) which is formed by the germination of a basidiospore (A). The latter, finding conditions of temperature, food supply and moisture congenial for growth, germinates to form a hypha consisting of uninucleate cells. It represents the primary mycelium and constitutes the hapiophase. It does not bear any sex organs—a feature in sharp contrast to the Phycomycetes and Ascomycetes, nor does it bear any basidia or basidiospores. The primary mycelium may multiply by conidia or sometimes by oidia.

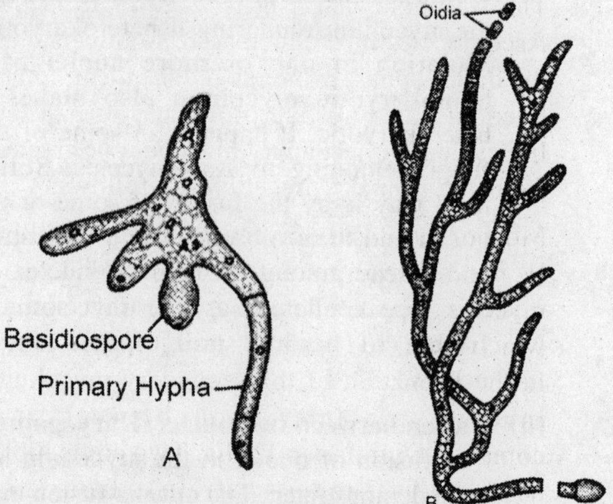

Figure: *Basidiomycetes. A.-Germinating basidiospores B.-Primary mycelium with one of the hyphae breaking into oidia.*

The second stage is the secondary mycelium (Fig.). The cells of the secondary mycelium are binucleate. It represents the dikaryophase in the life cycle.

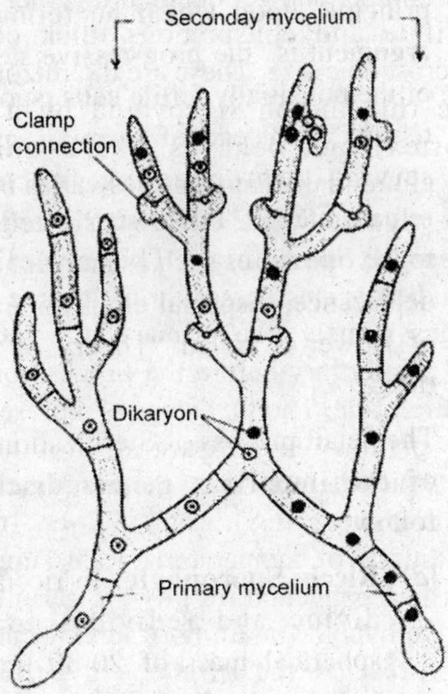

Figure: *Basidiomycetes. Sketch showing the formation of a secondary mycelium from a dikaryotised cell produced by somatogamous copulation between two uninucleate cells of primary mycelia of opposite strains.*

The Basidiomycetes, in fact, differ from the Ascomycetes in the increased prominence of the dikaryophase which is independent, long-lived and thus plays a prominent role in the life cycle. The secondary mycelium originates from the primary mycelium as follows:

Most of the Basidiomycetes are heterothallic. It means the primary or homokaryotic mycelium in them is of two distinct strains which are called + and – strain. The first step in the formation of the secondary mycelium involves the interaction between two compatible primary mycelia. Two compatible hyphae (+ and – strain) from the neighbouring mycelia meet. The intervening walls between the two adjacent cells at the point of contact dissolve. The protoplasts of the uninucleate cells intermingle in the fusion cell (plasmogamy). The two nuclei in the fusion cell do not fuse. They lie side by side constituting a dikaryon. One of these is of + strain and the other of – strain. The binucleate cell thus established is known as the dikaryotised cell. Both the uninucleate and binucleate cells may be found in the same mycelium. The first formed portions of a mycelium may be uninucleate and the later formed portions binucleate. The dikaryotic cell divides repeatedly by conjugate divisions to give rise to a secondary or dikaryotic mycelium. It consists of binucleate cells. During nuclear divisions of the dikaryotic cell special structures called the clamp connections are formed. These clamp connections ensure that the sister nuclei of the dikaryon, at each division, separate into daughter cells.

The secondary mycelium differs from the primary mycelium in being long-lived, presence of clamp connections, vigorous growth, mode of branching, binucleate condition of cells, and development of fructifications in the Homobasidiomycetidae and teleutospores or brand spores (probasidia) in the Heterobasidiomycetidae.

Clamp Connections: When the dikaryotic cell (A) is ready to divide a pouch-like outgrowth arises from its wall (B), it arises midway between the two nuclei of the dikaryon. The two closely associated nuclei of the cell now divide simultaneously. This is called conjugate division. One of the four daughter nuclei, generally the lower one of the upper pair, passes into the pouch (C). A septum appears at the base of the pouch (D). As a result, the pouch is cut off from the main cell. It may now be called a clamp cell. The clamp cell grows into hook like structure. Its tip bends over and finally fuses with the lateral wall (E) of the parent cell. The clamp cell now forms a bridge. It is called the clamp connection.

The presence of hook like clamp connections is a safe criterion for distinguishing a secondary or dikaryotic mycelium from the primary or monokaryotic mycelium. The clamp connections by some mycologists are considered homologous to the hooks of the ascogenous hyphae of the Ascomycetes. This view is supported by the general occurrence of a clamp connection at the base of a basidium. Moore and Mclear (1962) studied the fine structure of septa of the dikaryotic hyphae of Basidiomycetes.

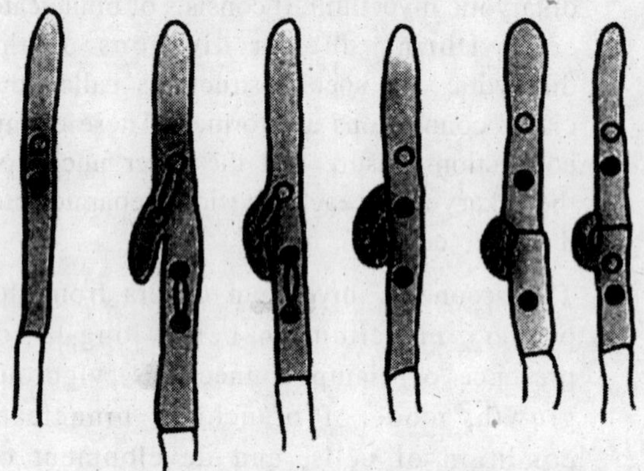

Figure: *Basidiomycetes showing the formation of Clamp Connections*

3. (*b*) Evolution of Sporophytes in Bryophytes: According to the complexity of structure, the sporophye of bryophytes may be arranged in a series between the simple and the most elaborate. The series start with the simple sporophyte of riccia, runs through that of sphaerocarpos, anthoceros, marchantia and finally ends in a highly complex sporophye of funaria and pogonatum. However, the evolution of sporophytes has been explained with the help of two theories put forward by botanist—

(*a*) Theory of Sterilization

(*b*) Reduction Theory

1. **Theory of Sterilization:** This theory was put forward by BOWER and supported by Cavers, Campbell and Smith. This theory illustrates that a natural advance in the progressive elaboration and complexity of the sporophyte. The fundamental of principle upon which he formulated his argument is "the prog-ressive sterilization of the potentially fertile cells (sporogenous tissue)" . Instead of forming spores and serving a propagating function they remain sterile. These sterile cells are put to the other uses such as nutrition, support, dehiscence, dispersal etc. This hypothesis of Bower is called "Theory of Sterilization".

The detail process of Sterilization of some of the important genera discussed as follow:

(*a*) **Riccia Sporophyte:** In riccia, zygote divide and redivides to farm a spherical mass of 20-30 undifferentiated cell. Periclinal segmentation forms an inner mass of cell called endothecium and outer single layer amohithecium. The amohithecium forms the single layered capsule wall. The endothecium forms the central mass of sporogenous tissue. Practically, all the sporogenous cells are fertile and develop into spores. However, few of them undergo degeneration to form the nurse cells. The sporophye of riccia is simplest among all of the bryophytes and has least amount of sterile cells. The entire embryo froms the spore producing capsule. There is not foot and Seta. It is just a spore producing organ without any distributing function.

(*b*) **Marchantia Sporophyte:** Sterilization of fertile cells is more advanced in the genus. Half of the embryo divided from the hypobasal regions remains sterile. It forms the foot and Seta. The upper epibasal half is fertile and forms the spore producing capsule. The sterile cell elongates, develop spirally thickened walls and become the elators. A few of the cells of sporogenous cells at the top may be differentiated into sterile, apical cell. The capsule of Marchantia has both spore producing and spore distributing body. It illustrates a step further in the progressive sterilization of the sporogenous tissue.

(*c*) **Anthoceros Sporophyte:** It illustrates a step further than riccia and Marchantia in the progressive sterilization of the potentially of fertile tissue. The endothecium cells become completely sterile and forms a group of cells known as columella. The sporogenous cells arise from the innermost layer of the amohithecium. It surrounds the columella. The sporogenous cells become differentiated into spore mother cell and pseudo-elaters. The archegonium of anthoceros is extremely reduced. The outer amohithecium develops into several cells layer thick capsule wall. The capsule wall develops a well-ventilated photosynthetic tissue protected by the Epidermis.

(*d*) **Funaria Sporophyte:** In funaria major portion of the Sporophyte remain sterile to form the foot and Seta. The capsule is differentiated into central column of andothecium surrounded by many layered amphithecium. The inner layer of the endothecium forms the sterile columella and the superficial cell form the sporogenous tissue. Thus, the archesporium arise from the outermost layer of cells of the endothecium.

It is thus extremely reduced and consists of single layer of fertile tissues. The amohithecium become differentiated into the Epidermis, photosynthetic tissue of the capsule wall and the outer spore sac.

The Bower theory of sterilization gives a clear explanation of the evolution of sporophye into upward direction.

2. **Reduction Theory:** This theory was put forward by kashyap, church, Goebal and Evans. They hold that the evolution of sporophyte has been in downward direction. They hold the fact that evolution of Sporophyte is retrogressive evolution. They mainly based their theory on the reduction of different organs which result in the simplification of Structure of Sporophyte. On the basis of this view the simplest type of Sporophyte of riccia is considered as the most advance one.

The significant steps in the reduction series are:

- Simplification of dehiscence apparatus.
- Reduction of the green photosynthetic tissue in the capsule wall.
- Disappearance of stomata and intercellular spaces.
- Increase in the thickness of capsule wall.
- The gradual elimination of foot and Seta.

Evidence from comparative morpho-logy and experimental genetics support the view that the simple Sporophyte of riccia is an advanced but a reduced structure.

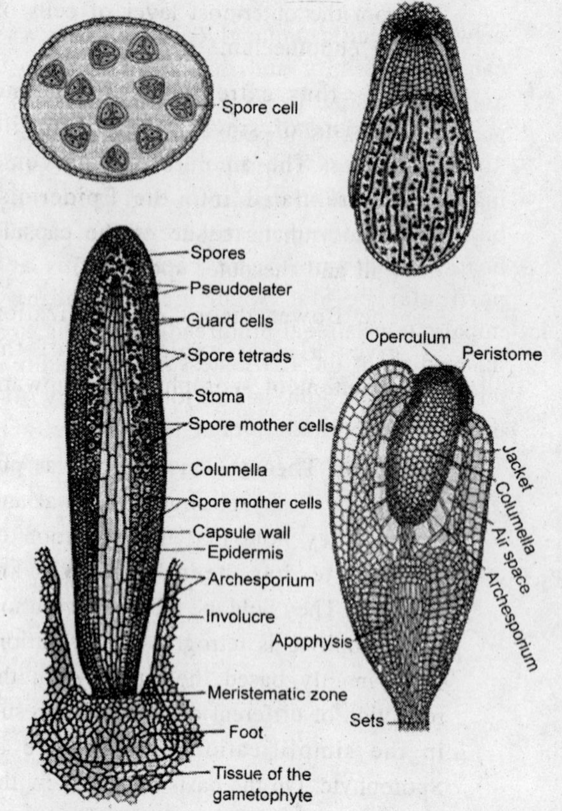

Figure: *Evolution of Sporophytes in Bryophytes.*

3. (*c*) Antibiotics: Any substance that inhibits the growth and replication of a bacterium or kills it outright can be called an antibiotic. Antibiotics are a type of antimicrobial designed to target bacterial infections within (or on) the body. This makes antibiotics subtly different from the other main kinds of antimicrobials widely used today:

- Antiseptics are used to sterilise surfaces of living tissue when the risk of infection is high, such as during surgery.
- Disinfectants are non-selective antimicrobials, killing a wide range of micro-organisms including bacteria. They are used on non-living surfaces, for example in hospitals.

Of course, bacteria are not the only microbes that can be harmful to us. Fungi and viruses can also be a danger to humans, and they are targeted by antifungals and antivirals, respectively. Only substances that target bacteria are called antibiotics, while the name antimicrobial is an umbrella term for anything that inhibits or kills microbial cells including antibiotics, antifungals, antivirals and chemicals such as antiseptics.

Most antibiotics used today are produced in laboratories, but they are often based on compounds scientists have found in nature. Some microbes, for example, produce substances specifically to kill other nearby bacteria in order to gain an advantage when competing for food, water or other limited resources. However, some microbes only produce antibiotics in the laboratory.

Antibiotics are used to treat bacterial infections. Some are highly specialised and are only effective against certain bacteria. Others, known as broad-spectrum antibiotics, attack a wide range of bacteria, including ones that are beneficial to us.

There are two main ways in which antibiotics target bacteria. They either prevent the reproduction of bacteria, or they kill the bacteria, for example by stopping the mechanism responsible for building their cell walls.

The introduction of antibiotics into medicine revolutionised the way infectious diseases were treated. Between 1945 and 1972, average human life expectancy jumped by eight years, with antibiotics used to treat infections that were previously likely to kill patients. Today, antibiotics are one of the most common classes of drugs used in medicine and make possible many of the complex surgeries that have become routine around the world.

Mode of Action of Aminoglycosides: Aminoglycoside is a medicinal and bacteriologic category of traditional Gram-negative antibacterial medications that inhibit protein synthesis and contain as a portion of the molecule an amino-modified glycoside (sugar). The term can also refer more generally to any organic molecule that contains amino sugar substructures. Aminoglycoside antibiotics display bactericidal activity against Gram-negative aerobes and some anaerobic bacilli where resistance has not yet arisen but generally not against Gram-positive and anaerobic Gram-negative bacteria.

Streptomycin is the first-in-class aminoglycoside antibiotic. It is derived from *Streptomyces griseus* and is the earliest modern agent used against tuberculosis. Streptomycin lacks the common 2-deoxystreptamine moiety (image right, below) present in most other members of this class. Other examples of aminoglycosides include the deoxystreptamine-containing agents kanamycin, tobramycin, gentamicin, and neomycin.

Mechanism: Aminoglycosides display concentration-dependent bactericidal activity against "most gram-negative aerobic and facultative anaerobic bacilli" but not against gram-negative anaerobes and most gram-positive bacteria. They require only short contact time, and are most effective against susceptible bacterial populations that are rapidly multiplying. These activities are attributed to a primary mode of action as protein synthesis inhibitors, though additional mechanisms are implicated for some specific agents, and/or thorough mechanistic descriptions are as yet unavailable. The inhibition of protein synthesis is mediated through aminoglycosides' energy-dependent, sometimes irreversible binding, to the cytosolic, membrane-associated bacterial ribosome (image at right). (Aminoglycosides first cross bacterial cell walls—lipopolysaccharide in gram-negative bacteria—and cell membranes, where they are actively transported. While specific steps in protein synthesis affected may vary somewhat between specific aminoglycoside agents, as can their affinity and degree of binding, aminoglycoside presence in the cytosol generally disturbs peptide elongation at the 30S ribosomal subunit, giving rise to inaccurate mRNA translation and therefore biosynthesis of proteins that are truncated, or bear altered amino acid compositions at particular points. Specifically, binding impairs translational proofreading leading to misreading of the RNA message, premature termination, or both, and so to inaccuracy of the translated protein product. The subset of aberrant proteins that are incorporated into the bacterial cell membrane may then lead to changes in its permeability and then to "further stimulation of aminoglycoside transport". The amino sugar portion of this class of molecules (e.g., the 2-deoxystreptamine in kanamycins, gentamicins, and tobramycin, see above) are implicated in the association of the small molecule with ribosomal structures that lead to the infidelities in translation (ibid.). Inhibition of ribosomal translocation—*i.e.*, movement of the peptidyl-tRNA from the A- to the P-site—has also been suggested. Recent single-molecule tracking experiments in live *E. coli* showed an ongoing but slower protein synthesis upon treatment with different aminoglycoside drugs. (Spectinomycin, a related but distinct chemical structure class often discussed with aminoglycosides, does not induce mRNA misreading and is generally not bactericidal.) Finally, a further "cell-membrane effect" also occurs with aminoglycosides; "functional integrity of the bacterial cell membrane" can be lost, later in time courses of aminoglycoside exposure and transport.

- **Pharmacokinetics and pharmacodynamics:** There are a significant variability in the relationship between the dose adminis-tered and the resultant plasma level in blood. (TDM) is necessary to obtain the correct dose. These agents exhibit a post-antibiotic effect in which there is no or very little drug level detectable in blood, but there still seems to be inhibition of bacterial re-growth.

- **Indications:** Aminoglycosides are useful primarily in infections involving aerobic, Gram-negative bacteria, such as Pseudomonas, Acinetobacter, and Enterobacter. In addition, some Mycobacteria, including the bacteria that cause tuberculosis, are susceptible to aminoglycosides. Streptomycin was the first effective drug in the treatment of tuberculosis, though the role of aminoglycosides such as streptomycin and amikacin has been eclipsed (because of their toxicity and inconvenient route of administration) except for multiple-drug-resistant strains. The most frequent use of aminoglycosides is empiric therapy for serious infections such as sepsis, complicated intra-abdominal infections, complicated urinary tract infections, and nosocomial respiratory tract infections.
- **Nonsense suppression:** The interference with mRNA proofreading has been exploited to treat genetic diseases that result from premature stop codons (leading to early termination of protein synthesis and truncated proteins). Aminoglycosides can cause the cell to overcome the stop codons, insert a random amino acid, and express a full-length protein. The aminoglycoside gentamicin has been used to treat cystic fibrosis (CF) cells in the laboratory to induce them to grow full-length proteins. CF is caused by a mutation in the gene coding for the cystic fibrosis transmembrane conductance regulator (CFTR) protein. In approximately 10% of CF cases, the mutation in this gene causes its early termination during translation, leading to the formation of a truncated and non-functional CFTR protein. It is believed that gentamicin distorts the structure of the ribosome-RNA complex, leading to a mis-reading of the termination codon, causing the ribosome to "skip" over the stop sequence and to continue with the normal elongation and production of the CFTR protein.

5. (*a*) (*i*) **Totipotency:** Totipotency is the genetic potential of a plant cell to produce the entire plant. In other words, totipotency is the cell characteristic in which the potential for forming all the cell types in the adult organism is retained. The basis of tissue culture is to grow large number of cells in a sterile controlled environment. The cells are obtained from stem, root or other plant parts and are allowed to grow in culture medium containing mineral nutrients, vitamins and hormones to encourage cell division and growth. As a result, the cells in culture will produce an unorganised proliferative mass of cells which is known as callus tissue. The cells that comprise the callus mass are totipotent. Thus, a callus tissue may be in a broader sense totipotent, *i.e.*, it may be able to regenerated back to normal plant given certain manipulations of the medium and the cultural environment. Truly speaking, totipotency of the cell is manifested through the process of differentiation and the hormones in this process play the major role than any other manipulations.

The ultimate objective in plant protoplast, cell and tissue culture is the reconstruction of plants from the totipotent cell. Although the process of differentiation is still mysterious in general, the expression of totipotent cell in culture has provided a lot of information's. On the other hand, the totipotentiality of somatic cells has been exploited in vegetative propagation of many economical, medicinal as well as agriculturally important plant species. Therefore, from fundamental to applied aspect of plant biology, cellular totipotency is highly important.

(ii) Somatic Hybrids Vs. Cybrids:

- The somatic hybridization involves three aspects. The three aspects are: (A) Fusion of Protoplasts, (B) Selection of Hybrid Cells and (C) Identification of Hybrid Plants.
- Somatic hybrid: protoplasts from the cells of two species are taken and fused together.
- Cybrid: a complete cell of a species is fused with the anucleated cytoplasm.
- Somatic hybrids don't have species barrier, whereas cybrids are bound to species barrier.
- Cybrids contain nucleus of one species but cytoplasm of both the parents (has genetic material of only one parent), whereas somatic hybrids contain genetic material of both the parents.
- The cytoplasmic hybrids where the nucleus is derived from only one parent and the cytoplasm is derived from both the parents are referred to as cybrids. The phenomenon of formation of cybrids is regarded as cybridization. Normally, cybrids are produced when protoplasts from two phytogenetically distinct species are fused. Genetically, cybrids are hybrids only for cytoplasmic traits.

5. (b) Petro-crops are the plants that produce petroleum compound as a supplement to petrol. Some plants or algae produce hydrocarbons, ethanol and so on, that can serve as an actual and potential source of energy. Such plants are known as petro-crops. Petroplants are the plants which provide liquid hydrocarbons as a substitute of liquid fuels. The hydrocarbons present in these plants can be converted to petroleum hydrocarbons. Petroplants include the members Euphorbiaceae, Apocyanaceae, Urticaceae, Asclepiaceae.

The oil crisis during World War II had led the Italians and the French to switch over to petroplants for petroleum production. The thick milky latex, extracted from Euphorbia Abyssinica was used in gasoline refinery. In 1970, Melvin Calvin showed the feasibility of procuring petroleum substitutes from certain specific groups of plants which are rich in hydrocarbons. Gopher plant (*Euphorbia lathyris*), milk bush (*Euphorbia tirucalli*) and milk weed (*Calotrophis procera*) are important petroplants. One advantage with the Euphoria plants is that they can grow even in semiarid lands and do not require irrigation and fertilizers for their growth.

Examples:

Pedillanthus macrocarpus	Family: Euphorbiaceae
Calotropis procera	Family: Apocynaceae
Jatropha curcas	Family: Euphorbiaceae
Copaifera langsdorffii.	Family: Fabaceae

5. (c) Botanists use living pollen and spores (actuopalynology) in the study of plant relationships and evolution, while geologists (palynologists) may use fossil pollen and spores (paleopalynology) to study past environments, stratigraphy (the analysis of strata or layered rock) historical geology and paleontology.

- The oil industry is credited with demonstrating the usefulness of palynomorphs in the study of stratigraphic sequences of rocks and the potential for oil and gas exploration. Because palyno-morphs are resistant to decomposition and are produced in great abundance, their recovery from rocks and sediments via special and careful chemical treatments is possible and provides scientists with information needed to describe plant life of past ages. By describing the sequence of selected palynomorphs through the rock layers of Earth, stratigraphers (scientists who study the rock layers of the earth) are able to correlate rocks of the same age and may therefore locate and correlate layers that contain oil or natural gas.

- Palynomorphs recovered from the gut or intestinal tract of early humans, and those associated with artifacts (pots, tools, or other cultural objects) found at their grave sites have been used to understand the diets and hunting practices of these early people. For instance, the pollen and spores found in the feces recovered from the mummies of humans living seven thousand years ago, allowed scientists to describe the changes in diets through several generations of native people in northern Chile.
- Melissopalynology is the study of pollen in honey, with the purpose of identifying the source plants used by bees in the production of honey. This is important to honey producers because honey produced by pollen and nectar from certain plants as mesquite, buckwheat, tupelo or citrus trees demand a higher price on the market than that produced by other plant sources. Some plants may produce nectar and pollen that is harmful to human health. A careful monitoring of the pollen types found in honey may identify these toxic sources and the honey produced may be kept out of the commercial market.
- Palynology is a useful tool in many applications, including a survey of atmospheric pollen and spore production and dispersal (aerobiology), in the study of human allergies, the archaeological excavation of shipwrecks, and detailed analysis of animal diets. Entomopalynology is the study of pollen found on the body or in the gut of insects. It is useful for determining insect feeding and migratory habits, especially as it involves economically important insects (as the boll weevil, or earwigs).

5. (*d*) **Plant Defense:** Plant defense describes a range of adaptations evolved by plants which improve their survival and reproduction by reducing the impact of herbivores. Plants can sense being touched, and they can use several strategies to defend against damage caused by herbivores. Many plants produce secondary metabolites, known as allelochemicals, that influence the behaviour, growth, or survival of herbivores. These chemical defenses can act as repellents or toxins to herbivores, or reduce plant digestibility.

- Other defensive strategies used by plants include escaping or avoiding herbivores in any time and/or any place, for example by growing in a location where plants are not easily found or accessed by herbivores, or by changing seasonal growth patterns. Another approach diverts herbivores toward eating non-essential parts, or enhances the ability of a plant to recover from the damage caused by herbivory. Some plants encourage the presence of natural enemies of herbivores, which in turn protect the plant. Each type of defense can be either constitutive (always present in the plant), or induced (produced in reaction to damage or stress caused by herbivores).
- Historically, insects have been the most significant herbivores, and the evolution of land plants is closely associated with the evolution of insects. While most plant defenses are directed against insects, other defenses have evolved that are aimed at vertebrate herbivores, such as birds and mammals. The study of plant defenses against herbivory is important, not only from an evolutionary view point, but also in the direct impact that these defenses have on agriculture, including human and livestock food sources; as beneficial 'biological control agents' in biological pest control programs; as well as in the search for plants of medical importance.

Mechanism of Plant Defense: Plants defend themselves against pathogens by a combination of two structural and biochemical defence mechanism.

- Structural characteristics that act as physical barriers and inhibit the pathogen from gaining entrance and spreading through the plant.
- Biochemical reactions that take place in the cells and tissues of the plant and produce substances that are either toxic to the pathogen or create conditions that inhibit growth of the pathogen in the plant.

Pre-existing Structural and Chemical Defenses

- The main defense of a plant against pathogens is its surface, which the pathogen must adhere to and penetrate if it is to cause infection. This is also called passive defence mechanism. Some structural defenses are present in the plant even before the pathogen comes in contact with the plant. Such structures include the amount and quality of wax and cuticle that cover the epidermal cells, the structure of the epidermal cell walls, the size, location, and shapes of stomata and lenticels, and the presence of tissues made of thick-walled cells that hinder the advance of the pathogen on the plant.
- Waxes on leaf and fruit surfaces form a water-repellent surface, thereby preventing the formation of a film of water on which pathogens might be deposited and germinate (fungi) or multiply (bacteria). A thick mat of hairs on a plant surface may also exert a similar water repelling effect and may reduce infection. A thick cuticle may increase resistance to infection in diseases in which the pathogen enters its host only through direct penetration. Cuticle thickness, however, is not always correlated with resistance, and many plant varieties with cuticles of considerable thickness are invaded easily by directly penetrating pathogens. The thickness and toughness of the outer wall of epidermal cells are apparently important factors in the resistance of some plants to certain pathogens. Thick, tough walls of epidermal cells make direct penetration by fungal pathogens difficult or impossible. Plants with such walls are often resistant, although if the pathogen is introduced beyond the epidermis of the same plants by means of a wound, the inner tissues of the plant are invaded easily by the pathogen.
- Many pathogenic fungi and bacteria enter plants only through stomata. Although the majority of pathogens can force their way through closed stomata, some wheat varieties, in which the stomata open late in the day, are resistant because the germ tubes of spores germinating in the night dew desiccate due to evaporation of the dew before the stomata begin to open. The structure of the stomata, e.g., a very narrow entrance and broad, elevated guard cells, may also confer resistance to some varieties against certain of their bacterial pathogens. The cell walls of the tissues being invaded vary in thickness and toughness and may sometimes inhibit the advance of the pathogen. Lenticels are opening in outer walls involved in gaseous exchange. They are weak points in defence unless the cork cells within them are suberized. After suberization and periderm formation, lenticels are more resistant to invasion by pathogens.

Pre-Existing Biochemical Defence: Plants liberate different chemicals, which interfere with activities of the pathogen and pathogenesis, thereby preventing or reduce infection. These chemicals and the biochemical conditions that develop may act either directly through toxic or lytic effect on the invader or indirectly through stimulating antagonistic plant surface microflora. The compounds pre-existing in plants as constitutive antibiotics. Plants liberate different chemicals, which interfere with activities of the pathogen and pathogenesis, thereby preventing or reduce infection. These chemicals and the biochemical conditions that develop may act either directly through toxic or lytic effect on the invader or indirectly through stimulating antagonistic plant surface microflora. The compounds pre-existing in plants as constitutive antibiotics and those, which are formed in response to wounds as wounds antibiotics'.

- **Release of Anti-Microbial Compounds:** Plants while growing and developing release gases as well as organic substances, from leaves and roots (leaf and root exudates), containing sugars, amino acid, organic acids, enzymes, glycoside etc. These materials have profound effect on the nature of surrounding environment. Theses inhibitory substances directly affect the micro-organism, or encourage certain groups to dominate the environment and function as antagonists of the pathogen.
- **Inhibitors Present in The Plant Cells:** In many host-parasite interactions, pre-existing toxic substances in the cells form the basis of resistance. Several phenolic compounds, tannins and some fatty acid like compounds such as dienes pre-existing in high concentrations in cells have been implicated for the resistance or young tissues to parasitic fungi. Several other types of preformed compounds such as saponins (glycosylated steroidal or triterpenoid compound) tomatine in tomato and avenacin in oats, have antifungal membranolytic activity. Plants surface cells also contain variable amounts of hydrolytic enzymes such as glucanases and chitinases, which may cause break-down of pathogen cell wall components.

5. (*e*) The word petrifaction means turning into stones. The fossils form when minerals replace all or the parts of the organisms. Water is full of dissolved minerals. It seeps through the layer of sediments to reach the dead organism. When water evaporates only the hardened, materials are left behind. There is molecule by molecule replacement of plant parts by minerals such as iron, pyrites, silicates, carbonates, sulphates etc. These minerals get deposited and impregnated inside the cells and the tissues of the plant. This type of fossil can be studied by preparing the sections and are most suitable for the study of structural details. Petrified plant organs roughly spherical in shape are known as coal balls.

Petrified fossils can be found near volcanic deposits and sedimentary rocks in many locations worldwide. Petrified wood is the most common type of petrified fossil, but all living organisms can be petrified. One of the most common petrified animal fossils are bone and teeth. However, these types of petrified fossils are less common than petrified wood because they can easily decompose.

Using petrified fossils, paleontologists can explain the gradual change of relatively complex life forms, also in the process called biological evolution. With biological evolution, scientists have the ability to explain life's diversity and specific adaptations. Phylogeny is the study of how organisms are related through evolution. Information from petrified fossils allow scientists to build a picture of how a certain variation of species are related. Depending on the species found in the fossil, scientists can use the data to understand how adaptations caused the species to evolve, or become extinct. The petrification of fossils is a very rare form of fossilization and isn't completely understood by scientists.

7. (*a*) **Difference Between Homospory and Heterospory**

- The main difference between homospory and heterospory is that the homospory is the production of a single type of spores with the same size whereas the heterospory is the production of two types of spores, megaspores and microspores, with different sizes. Furthermore, most seedless vascular plants and bryophytes are homosporous while all seed plants and some pteridophytes are heterosporous.

- Homospory and heterospory are two conditions of spore production. Heterospory is one of the adaptations of plants that ensure their success to the land.
- Homospory refers to the production of a single kind of spore, neither microspore nor megaspore, while heterospory refers to the production of two types of spores differing in size and sex, the male microspore and the female megaspore. Thus, this is the main difference between homospory and heterospory.
- Furthermore, another important difference between homospory and heterospory is that the homospory occurs in seedless, vascular plants and bryophytes while heterospory occurs in seed plants and some pteridophytes.
- The sex differentiation occurs at the gametophytic stage in homosporous plants while the sex differentiation occurs at the sporophytic stage in heterosporous plants. Hence, this is also a difference between homospory and heterospory.
- The germination of the homospore produces a single type of gametophyte, which is bisexual, while the germination of the megaspore produces female gametophyte and the germination of the microspore produces the male gametophyte. Therefore, we can take this as another difference between homospory and heterospory.
- Also, self-fertilization is prominent in homosporous plants while cross-fertilization is prominent in heterosporous plants.
- Furthermore, the embryo of homosporous plants obtains nutrients from the green prothallus while the embryo of heterosporous plants obtains nutrients from the endosperm in angiosperms and from the female gametophyte in gymnosperms.
- Homospory is the production of a single type of spores. It occurs in seedless, vascular plants. The homospore germinates to produce a bisexual gametophyte. On the other hand, heterospory is the production of two types of spores different in size as well as in sex. They are megaspores, which germinates to produce the female gametophyte and the microspores, which germinates to produce the male gametophyte. Heterospory mainly occurs in seed plants. However, the main difference between homospory and heterospory is the size and the sex of the spores produced by plants.

Heterospory lead to Seed Habit: Heterospory or anisospory is the production of two distinct types of spores: megaspores and microspores. These spores vary both in size and sex. The megaspores are large in size and produce the female gametophyte upon germination. In contrast, microspores are small in size and produce the male gametophyte upon germination. Here, the production of these two types of spores occurs in two types of sporangia known as megasporangia and microsporangia, respectively. Also, plants that produce both types of sporangia in the same sporophyte are called monoecious. Besides, plants that produce each type of sporangia in separate sporophytes are called dioecious. Then, the germinated female gametophyte produces archegonia to produce egg cells. Most importantly, the microspore is carried to the female gametophyte either through the wind, water currents or by means of animals. Microspores germinate on the female gametophyte to produce sperm cells. Moreover, fertilization of the male and female gametes occurs on the female gametophyte. Furthermore, heterospory facilitates cross-fertilization. Nevertheless, heterospory mainly occurs in angiosperms and gymnosperms that produce seeds.

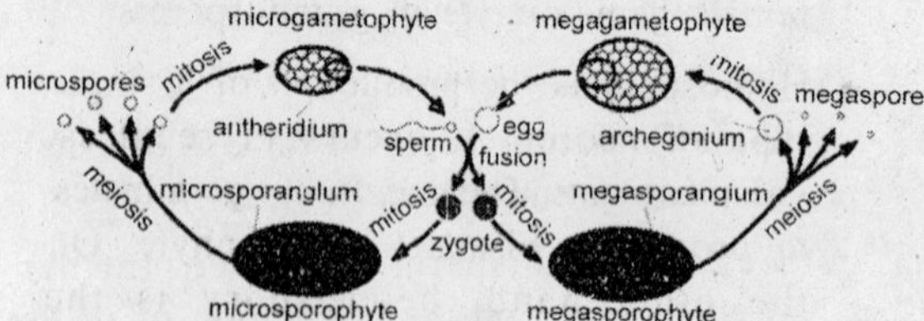

Figure: *Heterospory life cycle*

Biological Significance of Heterospory with Reference to Selaginella

The occurrence of two kinds of spores in the same plant is called the heterospory. Of the two kind spores, the smaller are called micro-spores, and the larger called megaspores. Microspore produces within microsporangia and megaspore produced in megasporangia. Microspore develops into male gametophyte and megaspore develops into female game-tophytes, thus heterospory associated with sexual differentiation of gametophyte. The phenomenon of heterospory is common in eight genera of pteridophytes. These are Selaginella, Isoetes, Stylites, Marsilea, Pilularia, Regnellidium, Salvinia and Azolla.

Biological Significance of Heterospory: In homosporous pteridophyte, the spores germinate on the soil to produce game-tophytes that are independent of the sporo-phytic plant. In doing so, the gametophyte of the homospores pteridophyte with much vegetative tissue has to manufacture not only its own food but also for the developing embryo which is dependent upon it. In heterosporous pteridophytes, spore germinate within the sporangium and gives rise to a prothallus. Reduced gametophyte retained within the spore wall, depending entirely upon the food deposited in the spores. These pteridophyte (heterosporous) obtained their nourishment from the parent sporophyte, they are independent of external conditions than are free living gametophyte of homosporous pteridophytes. In Selaginella two types of spores, microspore and megaspore are present which are depend on parent sporophyte for the nutrition. This feature *i.e.*, two type of spore have been considered as pre-requisites for the formation of seeds. It is generally agreed that seed plants arose from the heterosporous vascular plants that instead of discharging the megaspore acquired the habit of retaining it within the megasporangium. In the seed-bearing plants, there are two kinds of spores: microspores and megaspores, which grow to form male and female gametophytes respectively. In these plants, the single megaspore (embryo sac) is not shed from the megasporangium but retained within it while still attached to the mother plant. It germinates inside the megasporangium (nucellus) producing the much-reduced female gametophytes bearing the archegonia. After fertilization, the zygote within the ovule gives rise to an embryo, the rest of the game-tophytic tissue to nutritive tissue or endo-sperm and the integument thickness to form a seed coat. This entire structure, *i.e.*, the integumented ovule is known as seed. It is detached from the parent plant and germinates to form a new plant.

So, we can say that for the production of seed following character are essential:

1. Two types of spores. 2. Megasporangium does not open and single megaspore within it germinates to form a female gametophyte. 3. Nucellus becomes invested by covering or integument which later forms a seed-coat. 4. Inside the nucellus, linear tetrad of four haploid megaspores as a result of the reduction division of the functional megaspore mother cell. In these four cells, lower one give rise to female gametophyte rest degenerate. 5. Male gametes reach the egg by means of tubular outgrowth of the male gametophytes known as the pollen-tube.

Selaginella exhibits a remarkable approach to the seed habit characteristic of the spermatophytes because if following feature:

- Heterospory occurs in almost all the species of Selaginella
- Only one functional megaspore mother cell produced which by reduction division produce 4 haploid megaspores.
- The fertilization and development of embryo in both the species take place while the megaspore is enclosed within megasporangium.

Although Selaginella are advanced just because of the above features, but its approach to the true seed is not complete due to the following features:

- There is integument or covering.
- The retention of megaspore permanently within the megasporangium has not become established.
- After the development of the embryo there is lack of resting period.

7. (*b*) Botanical names of 5 plants yielding drugs and plant parts where the drug obtained.

- Belladona (*Atropa belladonna*): Drugs obtained from roots.
- Turmeric (*Curcuma longa*): Drugs obtained from underground stems.
- Quinine (*Cinchona officinalis*): Drugs obtained from barks.
- Ephedrine (*Ephedra gerardiana*): Drugs obtained from stems and woods.
- Emblic (*Gooseberry*): Drugs obtained from fruits.

7. (*c*) Successive Cellular Endosperms: This type is the opposite of the nuclear endosperm. In this type, Cell wall formation follows each cell division. Thus, the endosperm divides into many segments. There might not be coherency in the divisions and they can happen along different planes. Cellular divisions of the endosperm consequently lead to the formation of the coconut meat. Plants like Petunia and Dhatura have this kind of endosperm.

Characteristics of Cellular Endosperm

- Found in 25% families, generally in dicots.
- No free nuclear phase at any stage.
- Wall formation begins with 1st division of primary endosperm nucleus.
- Cellular endosperm has been further divided based on the orientation of walls following the first two or three divisions:
  - Orientation of wall formed after the 1st nuclear division in vertical *i.e.*, longitudinal to embryo sac. The second wall is also vertical but at right angles to the first. The subsequent wall formation is restricted to the micropylar end only. Example— *Adoxa, Cetranthus*
  - Orientation of the 1st wall is transverse and one or both cells then divided vertically. Example— *Scutellaria, Verbascum*
  - First 2-3 division are transverse. Example— *Ericaceae and Annonaceae.*
  - Orientation of the 1st wall is oblique, and the two cells thus formed may be of equal or unequal size. Example— *Myosytis arvensis*
  - Orientation of the first wall is indefinite. Example— *Senecia, Gunnera*

Endosperm Haustoria

- Characteristic feature of cellular endosperm.
- One or more cells becomes specialized to function as haustoria.
- The haustoria are formed at micropylar or chalazal or at both the ends and penetrate the nucellar tissue to absorb nutrition.
- Some secondary haustoria are also formed in addition to micropylar and chalazal haustoria. Example— *Alectra*
- Multinucleated chalazal endosperm haustorium occurs in *Magnolia obovata.*

PAPER-II

1. (*a*) Structure and Functions of Membrane Protein: Membrane proteins are common proteins that are part of, or interact with, biological membranes. Membrane proteins fall into several broad categories depending on their location. Integral membrane proteins are a permanent part of a cell membrane and can either penetrate the membrane (transmembrane) or associate with one or the other side of a membrane (integral monotopic). Peripheral membrane proteins are transiently associated with the cell membrane. Membrane proteins are common, and medically important—about a third of all human proteins are membrane proteins, and these are targets for more than half of all drugs.

Structure of Membrane Proteins: The amino acids of a membrane protein are localised according to polarity:

- Non-polar (hydrophobic) amino acids associate directly with the lipid bilayer.
- Polar (hydrophilic) amino acids are located internally and face aqueous solutions.

Transmembrane proteins typically adopt one of two tertiary structures:

- Single helices/helical bundles
- Beta barrels (common in channel proteins).

Functions of Membrane Proteins: Membrane proteins can serve a variety of key functions:

- Junctions: Serve to connect and join two cells together.
- Enzymes: Fixing to membranes localises metabolic pathways.
- Transport: Responsible for facilitated diffusion and active transport.
- Recognition: May function as markers for cellular identification.
- Anchorage: Attachment points for cytoskeleton and extracellular matrix.
- Transduction: Function as receptors for peptide hormones.

1. (*b*) In higher plants, individuals are classified as males, females or hermaphrodites, on the basis of whether the flower possesses only anthers, or only ovary or both. It is believed that the primitive type of floral condition in these plants was hermaphroditism, where flowers are bisexual. A range of types from these hermaphrodites to those having unisexual flowers with no trace of other sex are known in higher plants. These variations in higher plants are listed in Table given below. Of the eight types listed in Table, we have relatively better information on dioecious plant species and mechanism of sex determination in only these dioecious plant species will be discussed.

***Table:* Different types of sex expression in higher plants**

	Type of sex expression	*Flowers of different types*
1.	Hermaphrodites	All perfect (⚥) flowers
2.	Monoecious	Separate ♀ and ♂ flowers, but on the same plant
3.	Dioecious	Separate ♀ and ♂ flower on differnt plants
4.	Andromonoecious	Perfect (⚥) and ♂ flowers on the same plant
5.	Gynomonoecious	Perfect (⚥) and ♀ flowers on the same plant
6.	Trimonoecious	Perfect (⚥), ♀ and ♂ flowers on the same plant

7.	Androdioecious	Perfect (⚥) and ♂ flowers on separate plants
8.	Gynodioecious	Perfect ⚥ and ♀ flowers on separate plants

Allen (1940) gave a list of plant species in which sex chromosomes had been reported. Subsequently Wastergaard (1950) prepared a list of plant species where the presence of a pair of heteromorphic sex chromosomes was well established and also of those where it was not so well established. For some dioecious plant species, the different types of chromosome constitutions involving heteromorphic sex chromosomes in one sex are listed in Table given below:

Table: *Chromosome constitution of two sexes in some dioecious plant species.*

	Mechanism	*Examples*
1.	Male heterogametic (♀ XX; ♂ YY)	*Humulus lupulus* *Melandrium album, M. rubrum*
	less well established	*Rumex angiocarpus* *Populs spp., Salix, Smilax & Cannabis.*
2.	Male heterogametic (♀ XX; ♂ XO)	*Vallisneria spiralis* *Dioscorea sinuata*
3.	Male heterogametic (♂ with an extra chromosome)	*Phoradendron flavescens, P. villosum.*
4.	Female heterogametic (♀ XY; ♂ XX)	*Fragaria elatior & other Fragaria species*
5.	Compound chromosomes (e.g. ♀ XX; ♂ Y_1XY_2)	*Rumex acetosa* *Humulus japonicus*
6.	No sex chromosomes (perhaps gene controlled)	*Spinacia oleracea* *Ribes alpinum* *Vitis cinerea, V. rupestris, V. vinifera*
		Carica papaya *Asparagus officinalis* *Bryonia dioica*
7.	No. sex chromosomes (in male, translocation heterozygosity)	*Viscum fischeri*

1. (*c*) Trisomics are aneuploids, carrying an extra chromosome to the normal somatic complement. The nature of this additional chromosome determines its types; normal in primary, isochromosome in secondary, and translocated in tertiary or interchange types. The extra chromosome causes meiotic irregularities manifested by its abnormal associations at metaphase-I and unequal separation of chromosomes, laggard and bridge formation at anaphase-I. This leads to the formation of unbalanced gametes ($n + 1$) in trisomic individuals. Poor viability and vigor of $n + 1$ gametes severely reduce the transmission rate of trisomics through the disturbances in prezygotic, zygotic, and postzygotic stages. Since the trisomics carry an extra chromosome, the modified segregation ratios have immense significance in comprehensive genome mapping using both classical and molecular markers. A trisomic has an extra chromosome which is homologous to one of the chromosomes of the complement. Therefore, it forms a trivalent. This trivalent may take a variety of shapes in primary and secondary trisomics. In a tertiary trisomic a characteristic pentavalent is observed.

1. (*d*) Male sterility refers to the absence of functional pollen grains in otherwise hermaphrodite flowers. Male sterility is of great value in the production of hybrid seed. Male sterility is of two types: Genetic and Cytoplasmic. There are several natural mechanisms that control the mode of pollination in crop plants. Two of these mechanisms, self-incompatibility and male sterility are of special significance because of their utilization in hybrid seed production. Male sterility is characterized by nonfunctional pollen grains, while female gametes function normally.

Male sterility is classified into three groups:

- Genetic
- Cytoplasmic
- Cytoplasmic genetic

Genetic male sterility: Genetic male sterility is ordinarily governed by a single recessive gene, *ms*, but dominant genes governing male sterility are also known, e.g., in safflower. Male sterility alleles arise spontaneously or may be artificially induced. A male sterile line may be maintained by crossing it with heterozygous male fertile plants. Such a mating produces 1 : 1 male sterile and male fertile plants.

- **Utilization in plant breeding:** Genetic male sterility may be used in hybrid seed production. The progeny from **ms ms × Ms ms** crosses are used as female, and are interplanted with a homozygous male fertile **(Ms Ms)** pollinator. The genotypes of the msms and **Ms ms** lines are identical except for the **ms** locus, *i.e.*, they are isogenic and are known as male sterile **(A)** and maintainer **(B)** lines, respectively. The female line would, therefore, contain both male sterile and male fertile plants; the latter must be identified and removed before fertile plants; the latter must be identified and removed before pollen shedding. Pollen dispersal from the male (pollinator) line should be good for a satisfactory seed set in the female line. In India, it is being used for hybrid seed production of arhar (*C. catan*) by some private seed companies.

Cytoplasmic Male Sterility: This type of male sterility is determined by the cytoplasm. Since the cytoplasm of a zygote comes primarily from egg cell, the progeny of such male sterile plants would always be male sterile. The male sterile line is maintained by crossing it with the pollinator strain used as the recurrent parent in the backcross programme since its nuclear genotype is identical with that of the male sterile line. Such a male fertile line is known as the maintainer line or B line as it is used to maintain the male sterile line. The male sterile line is also known as A line. It is observe in some important plant crops viz. Maize, (*Zea mays*), *Nicotiama tabacum, Triticum aestivum, Gossypium hrisutum, Sorghum bicolor, Helianthus annus, Oryza sativa.*

- **Utilization in plant breeding:** Cytoplasmic male sterility may be utilized for producing hybrid seed in certain ornamental species, or in species where a vegetative part is of economic value. But in those crop plants where seed is the economic part, it is of no use because the hybrid progeny would be male sterile.

Cytoplasmic-Genetic male sterility: This is a case of cytoplasmic male sterility where a nuclear gene for restoring fertility in the male sterile line is known. The fertility restorer gene R, is dominant and is found in certain strains of the species, or may be transferred from a related species e.g., in wheat. This gene restores male fertility in the male sterile line, hence it is known as restorer gene. The cases of cytoplasmic male sterility would be included in the cytoplasmic genetic system as and when restorer genes for them would be discovered. This system is known in maize, jowar, bajra, sunflower, rice and wheat.

The plants would be male sterile in the presence of male sterile cytoplasm if the nuclear genotype were rr, but would be male fertile if the nucleus were Rr or RR. The development of new restorer strains is somewhat indirect. First a restorer strain (R) is crossed with a male sterile line (A), the resulting male fertile plants are used as the female parent in repeated backcrosses with the strain (C), used as the recurrent parent, to which the transfer of restorer gene is desired. In each generation, male sterile plants are discarded, and the male fertile plants are used as females for backcrossing to the strain C. This acts as a selection device for the restorer gene R during the backcross programme. At the end of the backcross programme, a restorer line isogenic to the strain C would be recovered.

- **Utilization in plant breeding:** The cytoplasmic-genetic male sterility is used commercially to produce hybrid seed in maize, bajra and jowar.

Origin of Male Sterile Cytoplasm

- **Spontaneous mutation:** Mutant male sterile cytoplasms arise spontaneously in low frequencies. Mutant cytoplasms have been isolated in maize, bajra and sunflower.
- **Interspecific hybridization:** Transfer of the full somatic chromosome complement of a crop species, through repeated back-crossing into the cytoplasm of a related wild species often leads to cytoplasmic male sterility.
- **Induction through Ethidium bromide:** Ethidium bromide is a potent mutagen for cytoplasmic genes or plasmagenes. Male sterile cytoplasm may be induced by seed treatment with Ethidium bromide e.g., Petunia.

1. (*e*) Coefficient of Correlation: A coefficient of correlation is generally applied in statistics to calculate a relationship between two variables. The correlation shows a specific value of the degree of a linear relationship between the X and Y variables, say X and Y. There are various types of correlation coefficients. However, Pearson's correlation (also known as Pearson's R) is the correlation coefficient that is frequently used in linear regression.

Pearson's Coefficient Correlation: Karl Pearson's coefficient of correlation is an extensively used mathematical method in which the numerical representation is applied to measure the level of relation between linearly related variables. The coefficient of correlation is expressed by "*r*".

Karl Pearson Correlation Coefficient Formula

$$r = \frac{\Sigma\left(X-\overline{X}\right)\left(Y-\overline{Y}\right)}{\sqrt{\Sigma\left(X-\overline{X}\right)^2}\sqrt{\left(Y-\overline{Y}\right)^2}}$$

Where, $\overline{X}$ = mean of X variable

$\overline{Y}$ = mean of Y variable

Alternative Formula (covariance formula)

$$\text{Cov(X.Y)} = \frac{\Sigma\left(X-\overline{X}\right)\left(Y-\overline{Y}\right)}{N} = \frac{\Sigma XY}{N}$$

Pearson correlation example

1. When a correlation coefficient is (1), that means for every increase in one variable, there is a positive increase in the other fixed proportion. For example, shoe sizes change according to the length of the feet and are perfect (almost) correlations.
2. When a correlation coefficient is (–1), that means for every positive increase in one variable, there is a negative decrease in the other fixed proportion. For example, the decrease in the quantity of gas in a gas tank shows a perfect (almost) inverse correlation with speed.
3. When a correlation coefficient is (0) for every increase, that means there is no positive or negative increase, and the two variables are not related.

4. (*a*) Genetic linkage is the tendency of DNA sequences that are close together on a chromosome to be inherited together during the meiosis phase of sexual reproduction. Two genetic markers that are physically near to each other are unlikely to be separated onto different chromatids during chromosomal crossover, and are therefore said to be more *linked* than markers that are far apart. In other words, the nearer two genes are on a chromosome, the lower the chance of recombination between them, and the more likely they are to be inherited together. Markers on different chromosomes are perfectly *unlinked*. Genetic linkage is the most pro Genetic linkage is the tendency of DNA sequences that are close together on a chromosome to be inherited together during the meiosis phase of sexual reproduction. Two genetic markers that are physically near to each other are unlikely to be separated onto different chromatids during chromosomal crossover, and are therefore said to be more linked than markers that are far apart. In other words, the nearer two genes are on a chromosome, the lower the chance of recombination between them, and the more likely they are to be inherited together. Markers on different chromosomes are perfectly unlinked. Genetic linkage is the most prominent exception to Gregor Mendel's Law of Independent Assortment. The first experiment to demonstrate linkage was carried out in 1905. At the time, the reason why certain traits tend to be inherited together was unknown. Later work revealed that genes are physical structures related by physical distance.

The typical unit of genetic linkage is the centimorgan (cM). A distance of 1 cM between two markers means that the markers are separated to different chromosomes on average once per 100 meiotic products, thus once per 50 meioses. Gregor Mendel's Law of Independent Assortment states that every trait is inherited independently of every other trait. But shortly after Mendel's work was rediscovered, exceptions to this rule were found. In 1905, the British geneticists William Bateson, Edith Rebecca Saunders and Reginald Punnett cross-bred pea plants in experiments similar to Mendel's. They were interested in trait inheritance in the sweet pea and were studying two genes—the gene for flower colour (*P*, purple, and *p*, red) and the gene affecting the shape of pollen grains (*L*, long, and *l*, round). They crossed the pure lines *PPLL* and *ppll* and then self-crossed the resulting *PpLl* lines. According to Mendelian genetics, the expected phenotypes would occur in a 9 : 3 : 3 : 1 ratio of PL : Pl : pL : pl. To their surprise, they observed an increased frequency of PL and pl and a decreased frequency of Pl and pL : prise, they observed an increased frequency of PL and pl and a decreased frequency of Pl and pL:

Bateson, Saunders, and Punnett experiment

Phenotype and genotype	**Observed**	**Expected from 9:3:3:1 ratio**
Purple, long (P_L_)	284	216
Purple, round (P_ll)	21	72
Red, long (ppL_)	21	72
Red, round (ppll)	55	24

Their experiment revealed linkage between the P and L alleles and the p and l alleles. The frequency of P occurring together with L and p occurring together with l is greater than that of the recombinant Pl and pL. The recombination frequency is more difficult to compute in an F2 cross than a backcross, but the lack of fit between observed and expected numbers of progeny in the above table indicate it is less than 50%. This indicated that two factors interacted in some way to create this difference by masking the appearance of the other two phenotypes. This led to the conclusion that some traits are related to each other because of their near proximity to each other on a chromosome. The understanding of linkage was expanded by the work of Thomas Hunt Morgan. Morgan's observation that the amount of crossing over between linked genes differs led to the idea that crossover frequency might indicate the distance separating genes on the chromosome. The centimorgan, which expresses the frequency of crossing over, is named in his honour.

Three Point Cross

- During meiosis, chromosomes are replicated and form a tetrad (see arrow). While the chromosomes are lined up close to one another, they have the opportunity to interact with one another, get tangled, and recombine to form new combinations of alleles.
- Three-point cross refers to using 3 points (genes) to determine the order and distance between the genes.

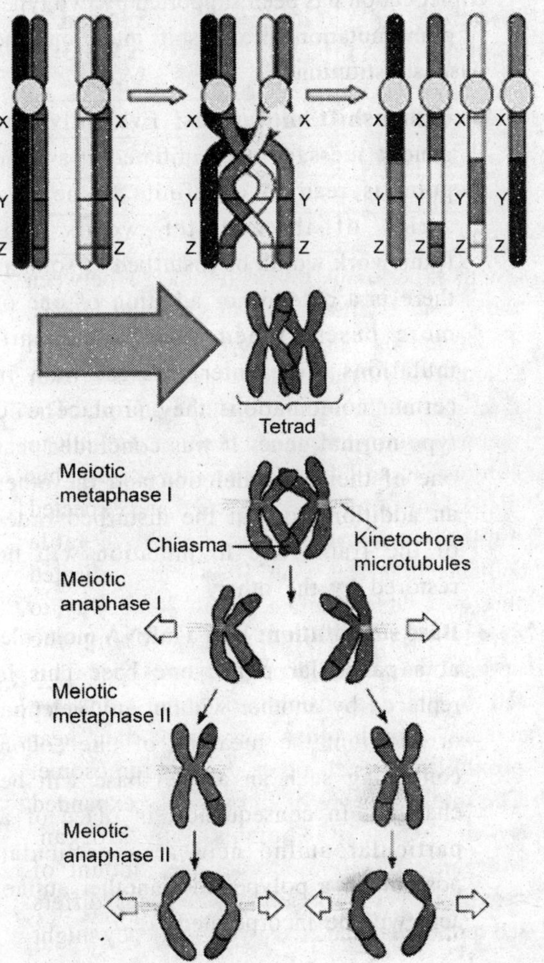

4. (*b*) **Autocrine Signaling:** Autocrine signals are produced by signaling cells that can also bind to the ligand that is released. This means the signaling cell and the target cell can be the same or a similar cell (the prefix auto- means self, a reminder that the signaling cell sends a signal to itself). This type of signaling often occurs during the early development of an organism to ensure that cells develop into the correct tissues and take on the proper function. Autocrine signaling also regulates pain sensation and inflammatory responses. Further, if a cell is infected with a virus, the cell can signal itself to undergo programmed cell death, killing the virus in the process. In some cases, neighbouring cells of the same type are also influenced by the released ligand. In embryological development, this process of stimulating a group of neigh-bouring cells may help to direct the differen-tiation of identical cells into the same cell type, thus ensuring the proper developmental outcome.

Paracrine Signaling: Signals that act locally between cells that are close together are called paracrine signals. Paracrine signals move by diffusion through the extracellular matrix. These types of signals usually elicit quick responses that last only a short amount of time. In order to keep the response localized, paracrine ligand molecules are normally quickly degraded by enzymes or removed by neighbouring cells. Removing the signals will re-establish the concentration gradient for the signal, allowing them to quickly diffuse through the intracellular space if released again.

One example of paracrine signaling is the transfer of signals across synapses between nerve cells. A nerve cell consists of a cell body, several short, branched extensions called dendrites that receive stimuli, and a long extension called an axon, which transmits signals to other nerve cells or muscle cells. The junction between nerve cells where signal transmission occurs is called a synapse. A synaptic signal is a chemical signal that travels between nerve cells. Signals within the nerve cells are propagated by fast-moving electrical impulses. When these impulses reach the end of the axon, the signal continues on to a dendrite of the next cell by the release of chemical ligands called neurotransmitters by the presynaptic cell (the cell emitting the signal). The neurotransmitters are transported across the very small distances between nerve cells, which are called chemical synapses. The small distance between nerve cells allows the signal to travel quickly; this enables an immediate response, such as, Take your hand off the stove! When the neurotransmitter binds the receptor on the surface of the postsynaptic cell, the electro-chemical potential of the target cell changes, and the next electrical impulse is launched. The neurotransmitters that are released into the chemical synapse are degraded quickly or get reabsorbed by the presynaptic cell so that the recipient nerve cell can recover quickly and be prepared to respond rapidly to the next synaptic signal.

Endocrine Signaling: Signals from distant cells are called endocrine signals, and they originate from endocrine cells. (In the body, many endocrine cells are located in endocrine glands, such as the thyroid gland, the hypothalamus, and the pituitary gland.) These types of signals usually produce a slower response but have a longer-lasting effect. The ligands released in endocrine signaling are called hormones, signaling molecules that are produced in one part of the body but affect other body regions some distance away. Hormones travel the large distances between endocrine cells and their target cells via the bloodstream, which is a relatively slow way to move throughout the body. Because of their form of transport, hormones get diluted and are present in low concentrations when they act on their target cells. This is different from paracrine signaling, in which local concen-trations of ligands can be very high.

4. (*c*) The Code is a Triplet Codon: The nucleotides of mRNA are arranged as a linear sequence of codons, each codon consisting of three successive nitrogenous bases, *i.e.*, the code is a triplet codon. The concept of triplet codon has been supported by two types of point mutations: frame shift mutations and base substitutions.

- **Frameshift mutations:** Evidently, the genetic message once initiated at a fixed point is read in a definite frame in a series of three letter words. The framework would be disturbed as soon as there is a deletion or addition of one or more bases. When such frame shift mutations were inter-crossed, then in certain combinations they produce wild type normal gene. It was concluded that one of them was deletion and the other an addition, so that the disturbed order of the frame due to mutation will be restored by the other.
- **Base substitution:** If in a mRNA molecule at a particular point, one base pair is replaced by another without any deletion or addition, the meaning of one codon containing such an altered base will be changed. In consequence, in place of a particular amino acid at a particular position in a polypeptide, another amino acid will be incorporated.

***Table*: The genetic dictionary. The trinucleotide codons are written in the 5'-3' direction**

First base	Second base U		Second base C		Second base A		Second base G		Third base
U	UUA	Phe	UCU	Ser	UAU	Tyr	UGU	Cys	U
	UUC		UCC		UAC		UGC		C
	UUA	Leu	UCA		UAA	Non-sense codon	UGA}	Non-sense codon	A
	UUG		UCG		UAG		UGG}	Trp	G
C	CUU	Leu	CCU	Pro	CAU	His	CGU	Arg	U
	CUC		CCC		CAC		CGC		C
	CUA		CCA		CAA	Gln	CGA		A
	CUG		CCG		CAG		CGG		G
A	AUU	Ileu	ACU	Thr	AAU	Asn	AGU	Ser	U
	AUC		ACC		AAC		AGC		C
	AUA		ACA		AAA	Lys	AGA	Arg	A
	AUG*	Met	ACG		AAG		AGG		G
G	GUU	Val	GUC	Ala	GAU	Asp	GGU	Gly	U
	GUC		GCC		GAC		GGC		C
	GUA		GCA		GAA	Glu	GGA		A
	GUG		GCG		GAG		GGG		G

*AUG – Met or chain initiation codon.

***Table:* Amino acids and their messenger RNA codons**

Alanine –	GCA	Glycine –	GGA	Leucine –	CUA	Threonine –	ACA
(Ala)	GCG	(Gly)	GGC	(Leu)	CUG	(Thr)	ACG
	GCC		GGC		CUC		ACC
	GCU		GGU		CUU		ACU
Arginine –	AGA	Glutamine –	CAA		UUA		
(Arg)	AGG	(Gln; Glun)	CAG		UUG	Tryptophan –	UGG
	CGA	Glutamic		Methionine –	AUG	(Trp)	
	CGG	acid –	GAA	(Met)		Tyrosine –	UAC
	CGC	(Glu)	GAG	(Starting		(Tyr)	UAU
	CGU	Histidine –	CAC	codon)		Valine –	GUA
Aspartic		(His)	CAU	Phenylalanine –	UUC	(Val)	GUG*
acid –	GAC	(Isoleucine –	AUC	(Phe)	UUU		GUC
(Asp)	GAU	(Ile)	AUU				GUU
Asparagine–	AAC		AUA	Proline –	CCA		
(Asn; Aspn)	AAU			(Pro)	CCG	Terminator –	UAA
Cysteine –	UGC	Lysine –	AAA		CCC	(Nonsense	(ocher)
(Cys)	UGU	(Lys)	AAG		CCU	codons)	UAG
				Serine –	AGC		(amber)
				(Ser)	AGU		UGA
					UCA		(opal)
					UCG		
					UCC		
					ICU		

*GUC is also used as a start codon for some proteins.

The Genetic Code is Degenerate: More than one codon may specify the same amino acid; this is called degeneracy of the code. For example, except for tryptophan and methionine, which have a single codon each, all other 18 amino acids have more than one codon. Thus, nine amino acids, namely phenylalanine, tyrosine, histidine, glutamine, asparagine, lysine, aspartic acid, glutamic acid and cysteine, have two codons each. Isoleucine has three codons. Five amino acids, namely valine, proline, threonine, alanine and glycine, have four codons each. Three amino acids, namely leucine, arginine and serine, have six codons each. The code degeneracy is basically of two types: partial and complete. Partial degeneracy occurs when first two nucleotides are identical but the third (*i.e.*, 3′ base) nucleotide of the degenerate codons differs, e.g., CUU and CUC code for leucine, Complete degeneracy occurs when any of the four bases can take third position and still code for the same amino acid (e.g., UCU, UCC, UCA and UCG code for serine).

The Genetic Code is (Nearly) Universal: With some minor exceptions, all living organisms on Earth use the same genetic code. This means that the codons specifying the 202020 amino acids in your cells are the same as those used by the bacteria inhabiting hydrothermal vents at the bottom of the Pacific Ocean. Even in organisms that don't use the "standard" code, the differences are relatively small, such as a change in the amino acid encoded by a particular codon. A genetic code shared by diverse organisms provides important evidence for the common origin of life on Earth. That is, the many species on Earth today likely evolved from an ancestral organism in which the genetic code was already present. Because the code is essential to the function of cells, it would tend to remain unchanged in species across generations, as individuals with significant changes might be unable to survive. This type of evolutionary process can explain the remarkable similarity of the genetic code across present-day organisms.

5. (*a*) Oxidative Phosphorylation: Oxidative phosphorylation is the final step in cellular respiration. It occurs in the mitochondria. It is linked to a process known as electron transport chain. The electron transport system is located in the inner mitochondrial membrane. The electrons are transferred from one member of the transport chain to another through a series of redox reactions. Oxidative phosphorylation is a highly efficient method of producing large amounts of ATP, the basic unit of energy for metabolic processes. During this process electrons are exchanged between molecules, which creates a chemical gradient that allows for the production of ATP.

Metabolic pathway in which cells use enzymes to oxidize nutrients, thereby releasing the chemical energy stored within in order to produce adenosine triphosphate (ATP) is called oxidative phosphorylation. This process takes place inside the mitochondria of the cell. Oxidative phosphorylation is carried out by almost all aerobic organisms. During the process of oxidative phosphorylation, the transfer of electrons takes place from electron donors to electron acceptors such as oxygen in redox reactions. Energy stored in the relatively weak double bond of oxygen is released during the process of redox reaction which is used to form ATP. A series of protein complexes catalyze these redox reactions within the inner membrane of the mitochondria in eukaryotes. In prokaryotes, these protein complexes are located in the cell's intermembrane space. Adenosine diphosphate (ADP) is converted into adenosine triphosphate using enzyme ATP synthase in a phosphorylation reaction. ATP synthase is also called complex V. It is the final enzyme used in the process of oxidative phosphorylation. Three ATPs are produced by oxidation of one NADH through the process of electron transfer chain.

Oxidative Phosphorylation Steps: The major steps of oxidative phosphorylation in mitochondria include:

Delivery of Electrons by NADH and $FADH_2$: Reduced NADH and $FADH_2$ transfer their electrons to molecules near the beginning of the transport chain. After transferring the electrons, they get oxidised to NAD^+ and FAD and are utilised in other steps of cellular respiration.

Electron Transport and Proton Pumping: The electrons move from a higher energy level to a lower energy level, thereby releasing energy. Some of the energy is used to move the electrons from the matrix to the intermembrane space. Thus, an electrochemical gradient is established.

Splitting of Oxygen to form Water: The electrons are then transferred to the oxygen molecule which splits into half and uptakes H^+ to form water.

ATP Synthesis: The H^+ ions pass through an enzyme called ATP synthase while flowing back into the matrix. This controls the flow of protons to synthesize ATP.

Chemiosmosis: Oxidative phosphorylation uses the chemical reactions that release energy to drive a chemical reaction that requires energy. These 2 sets of reactions are coupled and interrelated.

The electrons that flow through electron transport chain is an exergonic process and the synthesis of ATP is an endergonic process. These two processes are ingrained within a membrane. As a result, energy will be transmitted from the electron transport chain to ATP synthase by the movement of proteins. This process is termed as chemiosmosis.

Endergonic Process is a chemical reaction in which energy is absorbed. There will be a change in free energy and it is always positive. Exergonic Process is a chemical reaction in which there will be a positive flow of energy from the system to the surrounding environment. Chemical reactions are also considered exergonic when they are spontaneous.

Electron Transport Chain

- Most of the biochemical catabolic processes like the citric acid cycle, glycolysis, beta-oxidation, etc. produce the coenzyme NADH. It consists of electrons having high transfer potential.
- These reactions release a huge amount of energy on oxidation. These reactions are also known to be the uncontrollable reactions since the energy within the cells is not released at once.
- The electrons are separated from the NADH and then passed to the oxygen with a series of enzymes releasing a small amount of energy. All these series of enzymes having complexes is known as electron transport chain.
- This chain can be seen in the inner layer or membrane of mitochondria. The salts of succinic acid are also oxidized by this electron chain transport system.
- In the case of eukaryotes, the enzymes make use of energy that has been released in the electron transport system from the oxidation of NADH that pumps protons across the inner membrane of the mitochondria. This results in the generation of the electrochemical gradient across the membrane. This can be considered as one of the best examples to understand the concept of oxidative phosphorylation.

5. (*b*) **Vernalization:** Many plants do not come to flower before they experience a low temperature. These plants remain vegetative during the warm season, receive low temperature during winter, grow further and then bear flowers and fruits. Requirement of low temperature prevents precocious reproductive development in autumn. It allows the plant to reach vegetative maturity before reproduction can occur. The condition occurs in winter varieties of some annual food plants (e.g., Wheat, Barley, and Rye), some biennial (e.g., Cabbage, Sugar beet, Carrot) and perennial plants (e.g., Chrysanthemum).

Site for Vernalization: The stimulus of vernalization is perceived only by the meristematic cells, e.g., shoot tip, embryo tips, root apex, developing leaves, etc.

Mechanism of Vernalization: The stimulus received by the actively dividing cells of shoot or embryo tip travels to all parts of the plant and prepare it to flower. The stimulus has been named as vernalin. It can be passed from one plant to another through grafting in case of Henbane but not in others. However, the chemical has not been separated. In some plants cold treatment can be replaced by gibberellins. Vernalization prepares the plant to flower. The induction of flowering depends upon the presence of other favourable conditions. Photoperiodism, however, not only prepares the plant to flower but also brings about flowering. Thus, Henbane is a long-day plant which also requires cold treatment. Unless and until both are provided the plant will not come to flower (Fig.).

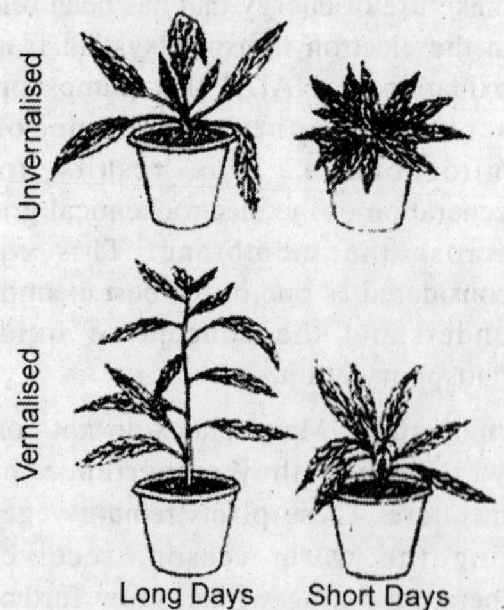

Figure: *Effect of Vernalization and Photoperiods on Henbane*

Importance of Vernalization:

- Vernalization can help in shortening the juvenile or vegetative period of plant and bring about early flowering. It is not only applicable to temperate plants but also to some tropical plants, e.g., Wheat, Rice, Millets, Cotton.
- It increases yield, resistance to cold and diseases, and
- Kernel wrinkles of Triticale can be removed by vernalization.

5. (*c*) **Seed Dormancy:** Seed dormancy can be defined as the state or a condition in which seeds are prevented from germinating even under the favourable environmental conditions for germination including, temperature, water, light, gas, seed coats, and other mechanical restrictions. The main reason behind these conditions is that they require a period of rest before being capable of germination. These conditions may vary from days to months and even years. These conditions are the combination of light, water, heat, gases, seed coats and hormone structures.

There are certain major causes for the seed dormancy. Listed below are the few reasons for the seed dormancy.

- Light
- Temperature
- Hard Seed Coat
- Period after ripening
- Germination inhibitors
- Immaturity of the seed embryo
- Impermeability of seed coat to water
- Impermeability of seed coat to oxygen
- Mechanically resistant seed coat
- Presence of high concentrate solutes

Types of Seed Dormancy: The seed dormancy is of following types:

- **Innate dormancy:** It is the condition of seeds which is incapable of germination even if conditions suitable for seedling growth are supplied.

- **Enforced dormancy:** It is the condition of seeds which is incapable of germination due to an environmental restraint which includes, an adequate amount of moisture, oxygen, light and a suitable temperature.
- **Induced dormancy:** This type of seed dormancy occurs when the seed has imbibed water, but has been placed under extremely unfavourable conditions for germination. Finally, seed fails to germinate even under more favourable conditions.

Methods of Breaking Seed Dormancy: The different methods of breaking dormancy are mentioned below:

The natural breaking of Seed Dormancy: Nature of dormancy stops when the embryo gets appropriate environment such as adaptive moisture and temperature. The seed coat that exists in many species becomes permeable due to the rupturing of smoothing action of natural agents like microorganism, temperature, and abrasion by the digestive tract of birds and animals that feed on these seeds.

Artificial Overcoming of Seed Dormancy: Some of the artificial methods used for breaking seed dormancy are listed below:

- Action with hot water for termination of waxes, surface inhibitors, etc.
- Rupturing of seed coats by filing, chipping, or threshing through machines.
- Exposure to heat, cold or light, depending upon the type of seed dormancy.
- By applying Hydraulic pressure for 5 to 20 minutes in order to weaken the tough seed coats.
- Seed coats are treated with concentrated Sulphuric acid for removing all traces of the mineral acid.

Treatment to Break Dormancy in Seeds: There are separate treatments to overcome dormancy, and they are further divided into the following groups:

Seed coat treatment: These treatments make a hard seed coat permeable to water or gases either by softening or cracking. This process is called scarification. The treatment can be either chemical or physical in nature.

Embryo treatments:

- **Stratification:** The incubation of seeds at an appropriate low temperature over a moist layer before transferring to a temperature suitable for germination.
- **High-temperature treatment:** Incubation at 40-50 °C for a few hours to a few days may have an effect in overcoming dormancy in some species. For instance, rice seeds treated with hot water at 40°C for at least 4 hours.
- **Chemical treatments:** Plant growth regulators or other chemicals can be used in induced germination growth regulators.

Importance of Seed Dormancy

- It follows the storage of seeds for later use by animals and man.
- It helps in the dispersal of the seeds through the unfavourable environment.
- Dormancy induced by the inhibitors present in the seed coats is highly useful to desert plants.
- Allows the seeds to continue to be in suspended animation without any harm during cold or high summer temperature and even under drought conditions.
- Dormancy helps seeds to remain alive in the soil for several years and provides a continuous source of new plants, even when all the mature plants of the area have died down due to natural disasters.

5. (*d*) **Global Warming:** Global warming is a phenomenon where the earth's average temperature rises due to increased amounts of greenhouse gases. Greenhouse gases such as carbon dioxide, methane and ozone trap the incoming radiation from the sun. This effect creates a natural "blanket" which

prevents the heat from escaping back into the atmosphere. This effect is called a greenhouse effect.

Contrary to popular belief, greenhouse gases are not inherently bad. In fact, the greenhouse effect is quite important for life on earth. Without this effect, the sun's radiation would be reflected back into the atmosphere, freezing the surface and making life impossible. However, when greenhouse gasses in excess amounts get trapped, serious repercussions begin to appear. The polar ice caps begin to melt, leading to the rise in sea levels. Furthermore, the greenhouse effect is accelerated when polar ice caps and sea ice melts. This is due to the fact the ice reflects 50% to 70% of the sun's rays back into space; but without ice, the solar radiation gets absorbed. Seawater reflects only 6% of the sun's radiation back into space. What's more frightening is the fact that the poles contain large amounts of carbon dioxide trapped within the ice. If this ice melts, it will significantly contribute to global warming.

Global warming can be stopped when combined efforts are put in. For that, individuals and governments, both have to take steps towards achieving it. We must begin with the reduction of greenhouse gas. Furthermore, they need to monitor the consumption of gasoline. Switch to a hybrid car and reduce the release of carbon dioxide. Moreover, citizens can choose public transport or carpool together. Subsequently, recycling must also be encouraged for instance, when you go shopping, carry your own cloth bag. Another step you can take is to limit the use of electricity which will prevent the release of carbon dioxide. On the government's part, they must regulate industrial waste and ban them from emitting harmful gases in the air. Deforestation must be stopped immediately and planting of trees must be encouraged. In short, all of us must realize the fact that our earth is not well. It needs to treatment and we can help it heal.

5. (*e*) **Biodiversity Hotspots:** Biodiversity is referred to as the variation of plant and animal species in a particular habitat. Species evenness and species richness form the major components of biodiversity. India is known for its rich biodiversity and has around 24.46% of the geographical area covered by forests and trees. Coined by Norman Myers, the term "Biodiversity hotspots" can be defined as the regions which are known for their high species richness and endemism.

Biodiversity Hotspots - 2 Main Qualifying Criteria: According to Conservation International, a region must fulfil the following two criteria to qualify as a hotspot:

- The region should have at least 1500 species of vascular plants *i.e.*, it should have a high degree of endemism.
- It must contain 30% (or less) of its original habitat, *i.e.*, it must be threatened.

Following the criteria must for an area to be declared as Biodiversity Hotspot, there are major four biodiversity hotspots in India:

- ***The Himalayas*:** Considered the highest in the world, the Himalayas (overall) comprises North-East India, Bhutan, Central and Eastern parts of Nepal. This region (NE Himalayas) holds a record of having 163 endangered species which includes the Wild Asian Water Buffalo, One-horned Rhino; and as many as 10,000 plant species, of which 3160 are endemic. This mountain range covers nearly 750,000 km^2.
- ***Indo–Burma Region*:** The Indo-Burma Region is stretched over a distance of 2,373,000 km^2. In the last 12 years, 6 large mammal species have been discovered in this region: The Large-antlered Muntjac, the Annamite Muntjac, the Grey-shanked Douc, the Annamite Striped Rabbit, the Leaf Deer, and the Saola. This hotspot is also known for the endemic freshwater turtle species, most of which are threatened

with extinction, due to over-harvesting and extensive habitat loss. There are also 1,300 different bird species, including the threatened White-eared Night-heron, the Grey-crowned Crocias, and the Orange-necked Partridge.

- ***The Western Ghats***: The Western Ghats are present along the western edge of peninsular India and covers most of the deciduous forests and rain forests. As per UNESCO, it is home to at least 325 globally threatened flora, fauna, bird, amphibian, reptile and fish species. Originally, the vegetation in this region was spread over 190,000 km^2 but has been now reduced to 43,000 km^2. The region is also known for the globally threatened flora and fauna represented by 229 plant species, 31 mammal species, 15 bird species, 43 amphibian species, 5 reptile species and 1 fish species. UNESCO mentions that "Of the total 325 globally threatened species in the Western Ghats, 129 are classified as Vulnerable, 145 as Endangered and 51 as Critically Endangered."
- ***Sundaland***: The Sundaland hotspot lies in South-East Asia and covers Singapore, Thailand, Indonesia, Brunei, and Malaysia. In the year 2013, the Sundaland was declared as a World Biosphere Reserve by the United Nations. This region is famous for its rich terrestrial and marine ecosystem. Sundaland is one of the biologically richest hotspots in the world which comprises 25,000 species of vascular plants, of which 15,000 are found only in this region.

6. (*a*) **Biodiversity:** The term biodiversity (from "biological diversity") refers to the variety of life on Earth at all its levels, from genes to ecosystems, and can encompass the evolutionary, ecological, and cultural processes that sustain life.

Alpha, Beta and Gamma Biodiversity:

- **Alpha diversity:** Alpha diversity describes the species diversity within a community at a small scale or local scale, generally the size of one ecosystem.
- **Beta diversity:** Beta diversity describes the species diversity between two communities or ecosystems.
- **Gamma diversity:** Gamma diversity is studied at a very large scale—a biome—where species diversity is compared between many ecosystems.

Biodiversity is Essential for Future Mankind: Biodiversity is important to most aspects of our lives. We value biodiversity for many reasons, some utilitarian, some intrinsic. This means we value biodiversity both for what it provides to humans, and for the value it has in its own right. Utilitarian values include the many basic needs humans obtain from biodiversity such as food, fuel, shelter, and medicine. Further, ecosystems provide crucial services such as pollination, seed dispersal, climate regulation, water purification, nutrient cycling, and control of agricultural pests. Biodiversity also holds value for potential benefits not yet recognized, such as new medicines and other possible unknown services. Biodiversity has cultural value to humans as well, for spiritual or religious reasons for instance. The intrinsic value of biodiversity refers to its inherent worth, which is independent of its value to anyone or anything else. This is more of a philosophical concept, which can be thought of as the inalienable right to exist. Finally, the value of biodiversity can also be understood through the lens of the relationships we form and strive for with each other and the rest of nature. We may value biodiversity because of how it shapes who we are, our relationships to each other, and social norms. These relational values are part of peoples' individual or collective sense of wellbeing, responsibility for, and connection with the environment.

6. (*b*) According to classical ecological theory, succession stops when the sere has arrived at an equilibrium or steady state with the physical and biotic environment. Excluding prime disturbances, it will persist indefinitely. This end point of succession is called climax.

The final or terminal and more or less stabilised community in succession that is able to established equilibrium with the environment condition of that area, was termed climax by Clements (1916).

It is self-perpetuating and in equilibrium with the physical and biotic environment and represent a steady state of species composition, community structure and energy flow.

The final or stable community in a sere is the climax community or climatic vegetation. The final community is not replaced.

According to Clements (1916, 1935), Climax has the following Three Principal Characteristics:

- **Unity:** Climax is a unit. All the species are not taken as an organized unit. Life or growth forms of plants indicate the climate type. In other words, climax is a unit, which acts as the index of climate of an area.
- **Stability:** The form of climax community is more or less stable with the climate.. This climax community cannot replace through competition. In other words, according to the Clements in a particular climate area there may be develop climax community only with a few characteristic dominant species.
- **Origin and Phylogenetic Relations:** Climax community is treated as an equivalent to an organism, like which it takes birth, grows and develops and become mature. Clements designated it a Super-organism. In any climatic region, the developmental stages of the climax community have their own characteristics, which reflect the type of climate.

Characteristics of a Climax Community:

- The vegetation is tolerant of environmental conditions.
- The vegetation of the climax community will have high ecological amplitude.
- They show rich diversity in species composition and a well-drained spatial structure.
- The community possesses a complex food chain system.
- Individuals in the climax stage are replaced by others of the same kind. Thus, the species composition maintains equilibrium.
- The ecosystem will be balanced and self-sustainable.
- There is equilibrium between gross primary production and total respiration.
- The energy used from the sunlight and energy released after decomposition will be balanced.
- The uptake of nutrients from the soil and the release of nutrients back to the soil by decomposition will be balanced.
- It is an index of the climate of the area. The life or growth forms indicate the climatic type.

Succession Progress in Tropical Ecosystem After Excessive Damage: When you see an older forest, it's easy to picture that the forest has been there forever. This is not the case. Ecosystems are "dynamic." This means that ecosystems change over time. That forest may lie on land that was once covered by an ocean millions of years ago. Lightning may have sparked a fire in a forest, destroying much of the plant life there. Or the forest may have been cut down at one point for agricultural use, then abandoned and allowed to re-grow over time. During the ice ages, glaciers once covered areas that are tropical rainforests today. Both natural forces and human actions cause ecosystems to change. If there is a big ecosystem change caused by natural forces or human actions, the plants and animals that live there may be destroyed. Or they may be forced to leave. Over time, a new community will develop, and then that community may be replaced by another. You may see several changes in the plant and animal composition of the community over time. Ecological succession is the constant replacement of one community by another. It happens after a big change in the ecosystem. And, of course, succession occurs on brand new land.

Primary succession is the type of ecological succession that happens on new lands—lands where life has not yet existed. Primary succession can take place after lava flow cools and hardens into new land, or a glacier recedes exposing new land. Since the land that results from these processes is completely new land, soil must first be produced. How is soil produced? Primary succession always starts with a pioneer species. This is the species that first lives in the habitat. If life is to begin on barren rock, which is typical of new land, the pioneer species would be an organism such as a lichen. A lichen is actually an organism formed from two species. It results from a symbiotic relationship between a fungus and an algae or cyanobacteria. The lichen is able to thrive as both the fungus and the algae or bacteria contribute to the relationship. The fungus is able to absorb minerals and nutrients from the rock, while algae supplies the fungus with sugars through photosynthesis. Since lichens can photosynthesize and do not rely on soil, they can live in environments where other organisms cannot. As a lichen grows, it breaks down the rock, which is the first step of soil formation.

The pioneer species is soon replaced by other populations. Abiotic factors such as soil quality, water, and climate will determine the species that continue the process of succession. Mosses and grasses will be able to grow in the newly created soil. During early succession, plant species like grasses that grow and reproduce quickly will take over the landscape. Over time, these plants improve the soil and a few shrubs can begin to grow. Slowly, the shrubs are replaced by small trees. Small trees then are succeeded by larger trees. Since trees are more successful at competing for resources than shrubs and grasses, a forest may be the end result of primary succession.

Secondary Succession: Sometimes ecological succession occurs in areas where life has already existed. These areas already have soil full of nutrients. Secondary succession is the type of succession that happens after something destroys the habitat, such as a flood or other natural disaster. Abandoning a field that was once used for agriculture can also lead to secondary succession. In this case, the pioneer species would be the grasses that first appear. Lichen would not be necessary as there is already nutrient-rich soil. Slowly, the field would return to its natural state. A forest fire can alter a habitat such that secondary succession occurs. Although the area will look devastated at first, the seeds of new plants are underground. They are waiting for their chance to grow. Just like primary succession, the burned forest will go through a series of communities, starting with small grasses, then shrubs, and finally bigger trees.

6. (*c*) Biotic and Abiotic Components of an Ecosystem: An ecosystem is a group or community composed of living and non-living things and their interactions with each other. They can be natural as well as artificial. Every ecosystem has two components, namely, biotic components and abiotic components. Biotic components refer to all living organisms in an ecology while abiotically refers to the non-living things. These biotic and abiotic interactions maintain the equilibrium in the environment.

Components of Ecosystem

- Biotic components are the living things that have a direct or indirect influence on other organisms in an environment. For example, plants, animals, and microorganisms and their waste materials.
- Abiotic components of an ecosystem include all chemical and physical elements *i.e.* non-living components. Abiotic components can vary from region to region, from one ecosystem to another. They mainly take up the role of life supporter. They determine and restrict the population growth, number, and diversity of biotic factors in an ecosystem. Hence, they are called limiting factors.
- A terrestrial ecosystem consists of abiotic factors like climate, type of soil or rock, altitude, temperature, nutrients, and minerals, whereas abiotic components in an aquatic ecosystem include dissolved gases, depth of water, salinity, pH of water, light intensity etc.

Biotic components can be classified into three categories:

Producers: These include all the autotrophs. They use light energy and synthesize food on their own, e.g., plants, green algae, etc.

Consumers: These include all the heterotrophs that directly or indirectly depend on producers for their food. Consumers are further categorized as herbivores, carnivores, omnivores and parasites.

Decomposers: These include saprophytes which act on dead matter and decay them for their nutrition.

The relevance of biotic and abiotic components in an environment appears when they start interacting with each other. For example, biotic elements like plants provide food for other organisms. The soil is the abiotic element which supports the growth of the plants by providing nutrients and other essential elements. Biotic components depend on abiotic components for their survival and help in the formation of abiotic factors like soil, nutrients, etc.

Food Chains and Webs: A food chain is a chain which shows how organisms are linked to each other through food. A food web shows how two food chains are connected. A single food web consists of many food chains. Every food chain begins with producers and ends with top carnivores.

7. (*a*) Nitrogen Cycle: Nitrogen cycle is a biogeochemical process through which nitrogen is converted into many forms, consecutively passing from the atmosphere to the soil to organism and back into the atmosphere. It involves several processes such as nitrogen fixation, nitrification, denitrification, decay and putrefaction. The nitrogen gas exists in both organic and inorganic forms. Organic nitrogen exists in living organisms, and they get passed through the food chain by the consumption of other living organisms. Inorganic forms of nitrogen are found in abundance in the atmosphere. This nitrogen is made available to plants by symbiotic bacteria which can convert the inert nitrogen into a usable form—such as nitrites and nitrates. Nitrogen undergoes various types of transformation to maintain a balance in the ecosystem. Furthermore, this process extends to various biomes, with the marine nitrogen cycle being one of the most complicated biogeochemical cycles.

Stages of Nitrogen Cycle: Process of Nitrogen Cycle consists of the following steps:—Nitrogen fixation, Nitrification, Assimilation, Ammonification and Denitrification. These processes take place in several stages and are explained below:

Nitrogen fixation: It is the initial step of the nitrogen cycle. Here, Atmospheric nitrogen (N_2) which is primarily available in an inert form, is converted into the usable form—ammonia (NH_3).

During the process of Nitrogen fixation, the inert form of nitrogen gas is deposited into soils from the atmosphere and surface waters, mainly through precipitation. Later, the nitrogen undergoes a set of changes, in which two nitrogen atoms get separated and combine with hydrogen to form ammonia (NH_4^+).

The entire process of Nitrogen fixation is completed by symbiotic bacteria which are known as Diazotrophs. Azotobacter and Rhizobium also have a major role in this process. These bacteria consist of a nitrogenase enzyme which has the capability to combine gaseous nitrogen with hydrogen to form ammonia.

Types of Nitrogen Fixation

- **Atmospheric fixation:** A natural phenomenon where the energy of lightning breaks the nitrogen into nitrogen oxides and is then used by plants.
- **Industrial nitrogen fixation:** Is a man-made alternative that aids in nitrogen fixation by the use of ammonia. Ammonia is produced by the direct combination of nitrogen and hydrogen and later, it is converted into various fertilisers such as urea.
- **Biological nitrogen fixation:** We already know that nitrogen is not usable directly from the air for plants and animals. Bacteria like Rhizobium and blue-green algae transform the unusable form of nitrogen into other compounds that are more readily usable. These nitrogen compounds get fixed in the soil by these microbes.

Nitrification: In this process, the ammonia is converted into nitrate by the presence of bacteria in the soil. Nitrites are formed by the oxidation of Ammonia with the help of *Nitrosomonas bacterium* species. Later, the produced nitrites are converted into nitrates by Nitrobacter. This conversion is very important as ammonia gas is toxic for plants.

The reaction involved in the process of Nitrification is as follows:

$$2NH_4^+ + 3O_2 \rightarrow 2NO_2^- + 4H^+ + 2H_2O$$

$$2NO_2^- + O_2 \rightarrow 2NO_3^-$$

Assimilation: Primary producers—plants take in the nitrogen compounds from the soil with the help of their roots, which are available in the form of ammonia, nitrite ions, nitrate ions or ammonium ions and are used in the formation of the plant and animal proteins. This way, it enters the food web when the primary consumers eat the plants.

Ammonification: When plants or animals die, the nitrogen present in the organic matter is released back into the soil. The decomposers, namely bacteria or fungi present in the soil, convert the organic matter back into ammonium.

Denitrification: Denitrification is the process in which the nitrogen compounds make its way back into the atmosphere by converting nitrate (NO_3^-) into gaseous nitrogen (N). This process of the nitrogen cycle is the final stage and occurs in the absence of oxygen. Denitrification is carried out by the denitrifying bacterial species—Clostridium and Pseudomonas, which will process nitrate to gain oxygen and gives out free nitrogen gas as a byproduct.

Factors Affecting Nodule Formation: Nodulation is affected by both external and internal factors.

- External factors include heat, acidity, nitrate content of the soil, etc.
- If soil is rich in nitrogen content, it interferes with the nodule formation and symbiotic association as plants already have enough nitrogen and they do not need more.
- Nitrogen fixation is an oxygen-sensitive process. The root nodules contain a heme pigment called leghaemoglobin, which facilitates the diffusion of oxygen.
- Nodule formation is autoregulated by leaf tissues. Plants have evolved defense mechanisms to check the infection.
- Ethylene also regulates nodule formation internally.

7. (*b*) **Z-Scheme of Light Reaction in Photosynthesis:** The "Z-scheme" describes the oxidation/reduction changes during the light reactions of photosynthesis. The vertical axis in the figure represents the reduction potential of a particular species—the higher the position of a molecular species, the more negative its reduction potential, and the more easily it donates electrons. The electron transport chain of photosynthesis is often put in a diagram called the z-scheme, because the redox diagram from P680 to P700 resembles the letter Z to NADPH. Activities of the electron transport chain, especially from cytochrome b_6f, lead to pumping of protons from the stroma to the lumen.

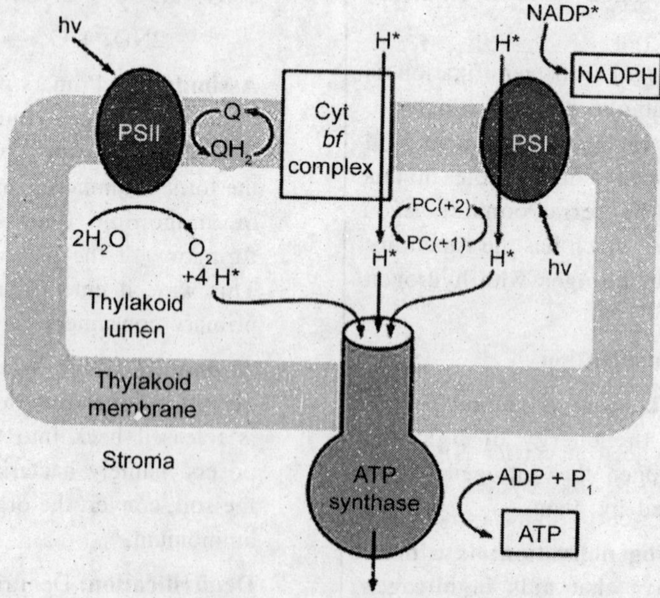

Figure: *Z-scheme of Photosynthesis*

In the Z-scheme, electrons are removed from water (to the left) and then donated to the lower (non-excited) oxidized form of P680. Absorption of a photon excites P680 to P680*, which "jumps" to a more actively reducing species. P680* donates its electron to the quinone-cytochrome *bf* chain, with proton pumping. The electron from cytochrome *bf* is donated to PSI, converting P700 to P700*. This electron, along with others, is transferred to NADP, forming NADPH. Alternatively, this electron can go back to cytochrome *bf* in cyclic electron flow.

7. (*c*) The Krebs Cycle, also called the citric acid cycle, is the second major step in oxidative phosphorylation. After glycolysis breaks glucose into smaller 3-carbon molecules, the Krebs cycle transfers the energy from these molecules to electron carriers, which will be used in the electron transport chain to produce ATP.

Krebs Cycle Products: The first step of utilizing glucose, glycolysis, produces a few ATP as well as the molecules which will be processed with the Krebs cycle. During glycolysis, a single glucose molecule is split into two smaller, three-carbon molecules called pyruvate. Pyruvate is then converted to acetyl CoA. Acetyl CoA is then utilized within the Krebs cycle to produce several major products. In turn, these products then drive the formation of ATP, the cell's main energy source.

Before the first stages of the Krebs cycle, pyruvate is converted into acetyl CoA. During this process, one molecule of CO_2 and one molecule of the electron carrier NADH are produced. The Krebs cycle involves converting this acetyl CoA into carbon dioxide. During the steps of the cycle, two molecules of CO_2 are released, in addition to 3 more molecules of NADH, one of $FADH_2$, and one of GTP.

So, for every 1 pyruvate molecule added, the Krebs cycle will produce:

2 molecules of CO_2
3 molecules of NADH
1 molecule of $FADH_2$
1 molecule of GTP

A molecule of glucose contains 2 pyruvate molecules, so 1 glucose molecule will produce double the amount of products listed above as it moves through the Krebs cycle. These products will then be converted to ATP in later stages of aerobic respiration. Carbon dioxide is the only "waste" product and must be removed from the cell. Large organisms must remove carbon dioxide from all their cells. In these animals, carbon dioxide is typically exchanged in the gills or lungs for oxygen, which helps drive the final stages of aerobic respiration.

The Krebs cycle happens only within the mitochondrial matrix. Pyruvate is formed in the cytosol of the cell, then imported into the mitochondria. Here, it is converted to acetyl CoA and imported into the mitochondrial matrix. The mitochondrial matrix is the innermost part of the mitochon-dria. The mitochondrial matrix has the required enzymes and environment for the complex reactions of the Krebs cycle to take place. Further, the products of the Krebs cycle drive the electron transport chain and oxidative phosphorylation, both of which occur in the inner mitochondrial membrane. The electron carriers will dump their electrons and protons into the chain, which ultimately drives the production of ATP. This molecule is then exported from the mitochondria as the main energy source for the cell. Mitochondria are found in almost all organi-sms, especially multicellular organisms. Plants, animals, and fungi all use the Krebs cycle as an indispensable part of aerobic respiration.

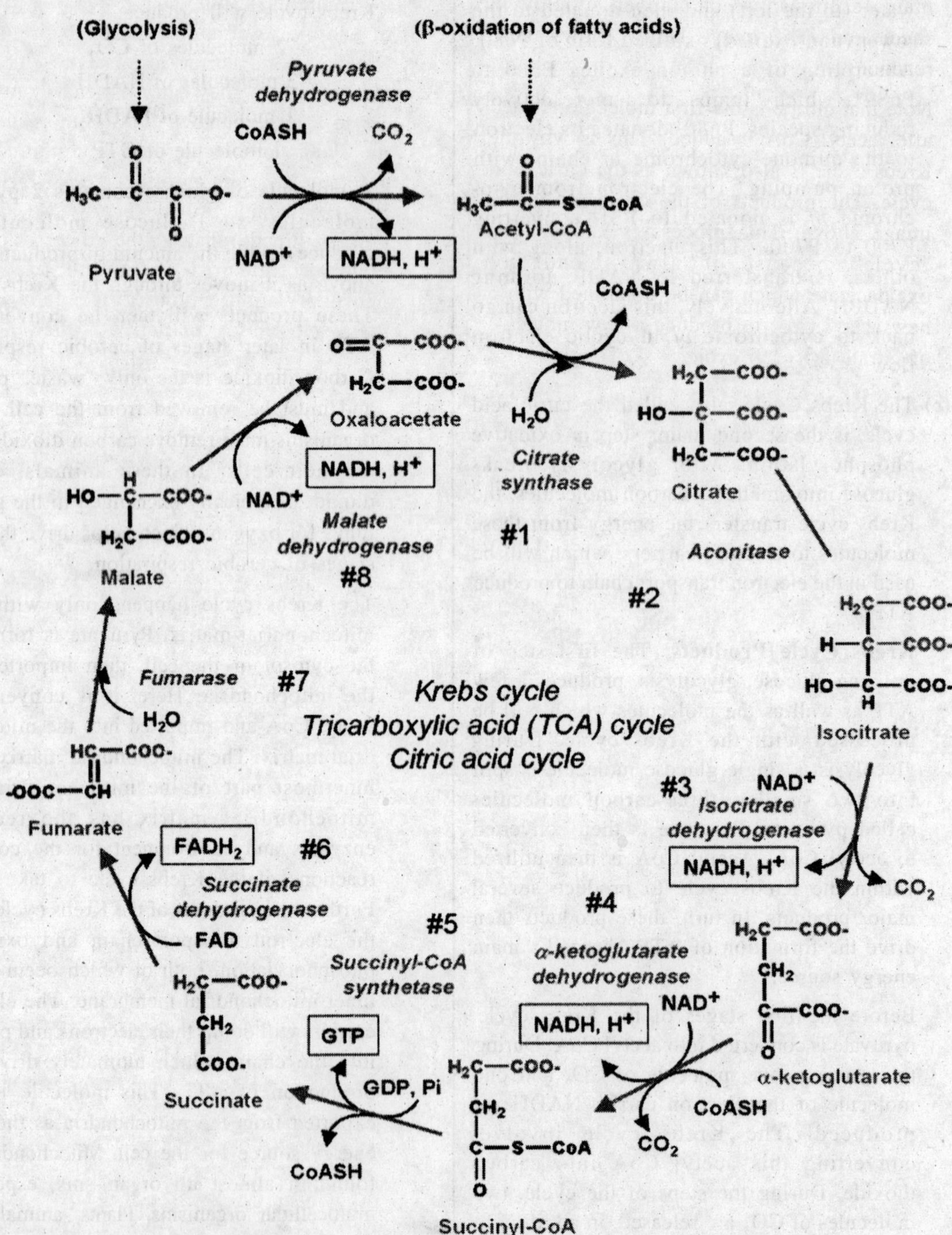
(Glycolysis)
(β-oxidation of fatty acids)
Pyruvate dehydrogenase
CoASH
CO2
NAD+
NADH, H+
Pyruvate
Acetyl-CoA
CoASH
Oxaloacetate
H2O
Citrate synthase
Citrate
#1
NADH, H+
NAD+
Malate dehydrogenase
Malate
#8
Aconitase
#2
Isocitrate
Fumarase
#7
H2O
Krebs cycle
Tricarboxylic acid (TCA) cycle
Citric acid cycle
Fumarate
FADH2
#6
Succinate dehydrogenase
FAD
#3
NAD+
Isocitrate dehydrogenase
NADH, H+
CO2
#4
#5
Succinyl-CoA synthetase
α-ketoglutarate dehydrogenase
NAD+
NADH, H+
GTP
GDP, Pi
Succinate
CoASH
α-ketoglutarate
CoASH
CO2
Succinyl-CoA

Krebs Cycle Steps: The Krebs cycle has 9 main reactions, which happen quickly in succession. The image below shows these reactions.

Note that citrate is the first molecule created after acetyl CoA is added. This is why the Krebs cycle is also known as the citric acid cycle. The products of the cycle are in the image above. This process is known as a "cycle" because it always ends on oxaloacetate which can be combined with a new acetyl CoA to produce a new molecule of citrate for each cycle.

Krebs Cycle Functions: The Krebs cycle is likely the most important part of the process of aerobic respiration because it drives the formation of electron carriers. These carriers are important. They carry the energy used to create a large number of ATP molecules in the final steps of aerobic respiration. The electron carriers produced (NADH and $FADH_2$) cannot provide energy to cellular process directly. Instead, the processes of the electron transport chain and oxidative phosphorylation will use the energy from these molecules to activate the enzyme complex ATP synthase, which produces ATP.

Previous Years' Paper (Solved)

Indian Forest Service

IFS–Botany Main Examination, 2019

PAPER-I

INSTRUCTIONS: *There are EIGHT questions in all, out of which FIVE are to be attempted. Questions Nos. 1 & 5 are compulsory. Out of the remaining SIX questions, THREE are to be attempted selecting at least ONE question from each of the two Sections A and B. Attempts of questions shall be counted in sequential order. Unless struck off, attempt of a question shall be counted even if attempted partly. Any page or portion of the page left blank in the Question-cum-Answer Booklet must be clearly struck off. All questions carry equal marks. Answers must be written in ENGLISH only. Neat sketches may be drawn, wherever required.*

SECTION–A

1. (*a*) Explain the role of bacterial cell wall in protecting against lysis and how this role may be experimentally demonstrated.

(*b*) Define mycoplasma. Explain its structure. Give symptomatology and control measures of little leaf disease of brinjal.

(*c*) What are cyanobacteria? Write an account on their cell structure. How do they contribute to the soil fertility?

(*d*) Describe the I.S. of male cone of Pinus. Add a note on the germiantion of its pollen grains.

(*e*) Describe each of the following plasmids and their importance:

(*i*) F-factor

(*ii*) R-fator

(*iii*) Col plasmid

2. (*a*) Explain the process of infection by pathogenic fungi.

(*b*) Define the term 'contagium vivum fluidum'. Who coined this term? Differentiate TMV from that of T_4 phage in terms of morphology and nuclear content.

(*c*) Differentiate a rust fungus from that of smut fungus in their symptoms and spore morphology.

3. (*a*) Give an account on the sporocarp of Marsilea. Explain the laminar or leaf segment hypothesis of its evolution.

(*b*) Differentiate between the enzymes and toxins produced by phytopathogenic microorganisms. Write an account on industrial production of penicillin.

(*c*) Gnetales is considered to be the most advanced among gymnosperms. Substantiate.

4. (*a*) What is an ovule? Describe its structure and types.

(*b*) How would you differentiate between the early and late blight diseases of potato? Mention the pathogens involved and the control measures practiced.

(*c*) Define mycorrhiza. Differentiate between ecto-and endo-mycorrhiza. Elaborate the significance of ecto-mycorrhiza in coniferous forestry programmes.

SECTION–B

5. (*a*) Give an account of Bentham and Hooker system of classification. In spite of so many latest classifications, why do people still prefer to use this system of classification?

(*b*) How are protoplasts isolated? Describe the methods of protoplast culture.

(*c*) Define endosperm. With suitable diagrams, describe various types of endosperms based on development.

(*d*) What is self-incompatibility? Discuss its importance in seed formation.

(*e*) Illustrate the floral characters of Cucurbitaceae family. Give floral diagram and floral formula.

6. (*a*) What is ethnobotany? Highlight its relevance to rural population in India.

(*b*) Distinguish among differentiation, dedifferentiation and redifferentiation.

(*c*) What are mycotoxins? How do the aflatoxins affect cattle, popultry and human beings?

7. (*a*) Summarize the role of protoplast fusion in somatic hybridization.

(*b*) Write the botanical names, family and uses of the following:

(*i*) Asafoetida

(*ii*) Black pepper

(*iii*) Ginger

(*iv*) Coriander

(*v*) Fennel

(*c*) Enumerate the process of herbarium preparation and add a note on its significance. Mention any two Indian herbaria of national importance.

8. (*a*) Illustrate the anatomy of C_4 plants. How do they differ from C_3 plants?

(*b*) Mention the botanical names with family of plants yielding the following. For each product, give examples of two plants:

(*i*) Narcotics

(*ii*) Insecticides

(*iii*) Dyes

(*iv*) Timber

(*v*) Fibre

(*c*) How would you distinguish the anomalous secondary thickening from normal secondary thickening? Describe the anomalous secondary thickening in Dracaena.

PAPER-II

INSTRUCTIONS: *There are EIGHT questions in all, out of which FIVE are to be attempted. Questions Nos. 1 & 5 are compulsory. Out of the remaining SIX questions, THREE are to be attempted selecting at least ONE question from each of the two Sections A and B. Attempts of questions shall be counted in sequential order. Unless struck off, attempt of a question shall be counted even if attempted partly. Any page or portion of the page left blank in the Question-cum-Answer Booklet must be clearly struck off. All questions carry equal marks. Answers must be written in ENGLISH only. Neat sketches may be drawn, wherever required.*

SECTION–A

1. Write short notes on the following:

(*a*) Nucleosome modification and its significance.

(*b*) Behaviour and significance of B-chromosome in genetic variation.

(*c*) Importance of RNA molecule and its role in the origin and evolution of living organisms.

(*d*) Types and applications of molecular markers.

(*e*) Calculate the mean, standard error and coefficient of variation from the following data:

Number of flowers/plants (x)	4	6	5	8	7	9
Number of plants (y)	3	6	5	5	9	4

2. (*a*) Discuss the structure and function of synaptonemal complex, mentioning its location. State the different structural types of DNA with outline sketches.

(*b*) Describe *lac* operon and its negative as well as positive controls, with suitable diagrms.

(*c*) Discuss the molecular mechanism of base analogue incorporation and its effects.

3. (*a*) Describe the steps involved in T-DNA processing and transfer from *Agrobacterium* cell to the host plant nuclear genome, with suitable diagram. Add a note on the types and advantages of apomixis.

(*b*) Distinguish between paracentric and pericentric inversions with diagrams. Explain with sketches the different meiotic products resulting from a single crossover within a paracentric and pericentric loop.

(*c*) Explain the molecular mechanism of point mutation.

4. (*a*) What are prions and where do they exist? Explain the process of prion replication and role of cofactors in prion infectivity.

(*b*) Discuss the meiotic configurations in a translocation heterozygote (considering 2 pairs of chromosomes involved in translocation), with diagrams, and its subsequent effects on pollen fertility.

(c) Write an account on the applications of 'z' and chi-square tests in plant breeding programme.

SECTION–B

5. Write short notes on the following:

(*a*) Roles of abscisic acid and cytokinin in the regulation of seed dormancy.

(*b*) How can longitudinal growth of the seedlings be manipulated by plant growth regulators?

(*c*) Alpha – Beta – Gamma biodiversity and its relation with different spatial scales of ecosystem.

(*d*) IUCN's classification scheme for the conservation status of species.

(*e*) Types of intellectual property rights and justify the role of a particular IPR in biological resources accessibility.

6. (*a*) How is phytochrome associated with flowering?

(*b*) How do photoperiodic response and photoinductive cycles influence flowering?

(*c*) Give a detailed account of 'Fire' as an ecological factor controlling structural and functional integrity of an ecosystem. How does it affect carbon and energy balances in tropical forests?

7. (*a*) Describe the role of cytochromes in electron transport chain during photosynthesis.

(*b*) Write an account on photolysis of water during photochemical reaction.

(*c*) What is meant by biodiversity conservation? Discuss the methods of *ex-situ* and *in-situ* conservations.

8. (*a*) What are the most important criteria to classify if an element of nutrient belongs to 'gaseous' or 'sedimentary' cycle? Draw the global sulphur cycle.

(*b*) Write an account on nitrate reductase and factors regulating its activity. How is ammonium assimilated into various metabolities?

(*c*) Define leaft senescence. Describe the important biochemical and physiological changes during this process.

ANSWERS

PAPER-I

1. (*a*) **Function of bacterial cell walls = prevent osmotic lysis**

- **Osmosis**: The diffusion of water from an area of high water concentration to an area of low water concentration across a semi-permeable membrane.
- Because solutes (ions, molecules) take up space, there is an inverse relationship between solute concentration and water concentration:
  - If high solute concentration = low water concentration
  - If low solute concentration = high water concentration

Because we are interested in what happens to cells, we need to describe the environment in which the cell is living.

Hypoosmotic/hypotonic environments: solute concentration of environment is less than within cell.

Hyperosmotic/hypertonic environments: solute concentration of environment is higher than within cell.

Isoosmotic/Isotonic environments: solute concentration of environment is equal to that within cell.

If a compartment (for example a cell) has a higher solute concentration than its environment (outside of cell), the water concentration inside the cell will be less than outside the cell. Consequently there will be net movement/osmosis of water into the cell from the environment. As water moves in, pressure builds up inside the cell and eventually the cytoplasmic membrane will break in a process called ***osmotic lysis*** (similar to explosion of a water balloon). ***Osmotic lysis always kills a cell.***

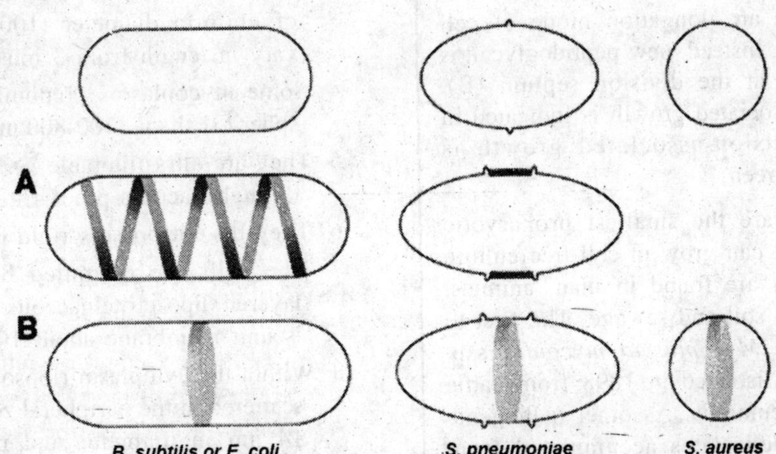

Bacteria cell wall peptidoglycan prevents osmotic lysis: Most bacteria grow in hypo-osmotic environments. How do bacteria prevent osmotic lysis? Most bacteria synthesize a strong cell wall made of cross-linked peptidoglycan. The cell wall is outside the cytoplasmic membrane similar to a "boiler plate" or suit of armor. The cell wall peptidoglycan is similar to cross-linked wire. The peptidoglycan of the cell wall prevents osmotic lysis when water moves into the cell, but ONLY if the cell wall peptidoglycan is cross-linked. Anything which prevents the cross links from forming or which cuts the cross-links will weaken the peptidoglycan so that it no longer can prevent osmotic lysis.

Incorporation of new cell wall in differently shaped bacteria. Rod-shaped bacteria such as *B. subtilis* or *E. coli* have two modes of cell wall synthesis: new peptidoglycan is inserted along a helical path (A), leading to elongation of the lateral wall, and is inserted in a closing ring around the future division site, leading to the formation of the division septum (B). *S. pneumoniae* cells have the shape of a rugby ball and elongate by inserting new cell wall material at the so called equatorial rings (A), which correspond to an outgrowth of the cell wall that encircles the cell. An initial ring is duplicated, and the two resultant rings are progressively separated, marking the future division sites of the daughter cells. The division septum is then synthesized in the middle of the cell (B). Round cells such as *S. aureus* do not seem to have an elongation mode of cell wall synthesis. Instead, new peptidoglycan is inserted only at the division septum (B). Elongation-associated growth is indicated in red, and division-associated growth is indicated in green.

1. (*b*) Mycoplasmas are the smallest prokaryotic organisms that can grow in cell-free culture medium. They are found in man, animals, plants, insects, soil and sewage. The first to be recognized, *Mycoplasma mycoides* ssp. *mycoides*, was isolated in 1898 from cattle with pleuropneumonia. As other pathogenic and saprophytic isolates accumulated from veterinary and human sources they became known as pleuropneumonia-like organisms (PPLO), a term long superseded by 'mycoplasmas'.

Mycoplasma (Greek: *mykes*, fungus; *plasma*, something moulded) refers to the filamentous (fungus-like) nature of the organisms of some species and to the plasticity of the outer membrane resulting in pleomorphism.

1. They are unicellular, smallest, non-motile and prokaryotic organisms forming fried egg shaped colonies (Fig.)

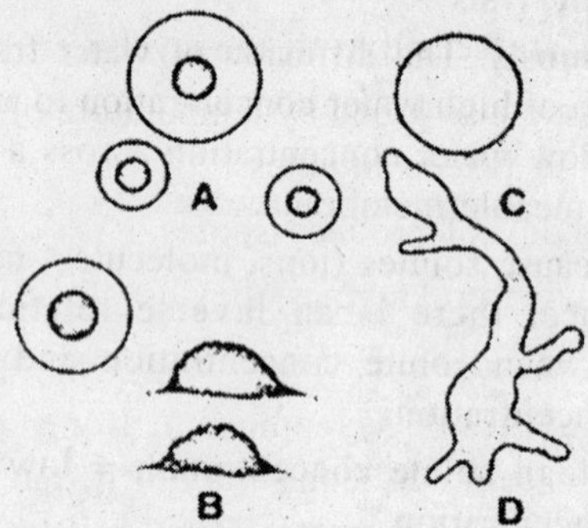

Figure: *(A–D). Mycoplasma ; Colony morphology and cell shape. (A) Entire colony, (B) Longitudinal section of colony, (C) Spherical form, (D) Irregular filamentous form*

2. They are pleomorphic *i.e.*, able to change their shape depending upon culture media.
3. They may be rod like, ring like, globoid or filamentous (Fig. C, D). The filaments are of uniform diameter (100-300 nm) and vary in length from 3 nm to 150 nm.
4. Some mycoplasma predominantly assume spherical shape (300-800 nm in diameter).
5. They are ultra-filterable *i.e.*, they can pass through bacteria-proof filters.
6. They do not possess rigid cell wall.
7. The cells are delimited by soft tripple layered lipo-proteinaceous membrane. It is unit membrane about 10 nm thick.
8. Within the cytoplasm ribosomes are found scattered in the peripheral zone. These are 14 nm in diameter and resemble with bacteria in sedimentation characteristic of both the nucleoprotein and nucleic acid.
9. The ribosomes are 72S type.

10. Within the cytoplasm fine fibrillar DNA is present. It is double stranded helix.
11. Mycoplasma generally grow more slowly than bacteria.
12. They require sterol for their nutrition.
13. They are usually resistant to antibiotics like penicillin, cephaloridine, vencomycin etc. which action cell wall.
14. They are sensitive to tetracycline.
15. They are also killed by temperature of 40-55°C in fifteen minutes.
16. They do not produce spores.
17. Like other prokaryotes, they usually divide by binary fission.

Cell Structure of Mycoplasma: In mycoplasma, the cells are small varying from 300 nm to 800 nm in diameter. Rigid cell wall is absent. Cells are surrounded by a triple layered lipo-proteinaceous unit membrane (Fig.). It is about 10 nm thick. Unit membrane encloses the cytoplasm. Within the cytoplasm RNA (ribosomes) and DNA are present. The ribosomes are 14 nm in diameter and 72 S type. DNA is double stranded helix. It can be distinguished from bacterial DNA by its low guanine and cytosine content. The DNA is up to four per cent and RNA is about eight per cent and it is less than half that usually occurs in other protoplasm's. The guanine and cytosine (G and C) contents in DNA range from 23-46 per cent. In some species *e.g.*, M. gallisepticum some polar bodies protrude out from one or the other end of the cell. These are called bleb and are considered to be the site of enzymatic activities and attachment during infection.

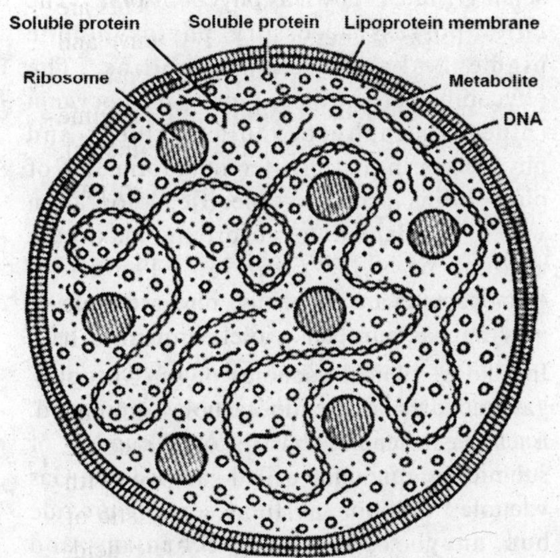

Figure: *Mycoplasma, Structure of a typical cell*

Symptoms of Little Leaf Disease: The main symptom of the disease is the production of very short leaves by affected plant. The petioles are so much reduced in size that leaves appear sticking to the stem. Such leaves are narrow, soft, smooth and yellowish in colour. Newly formed leaves are further reduced in size. The internodes are shortened and at the same time large number of axillary buds are stimulated to grow into short branches with small leaves. This gives whole plant a bushy appearance. Usually such plant unable to form flowers. Fruiting is very rare.

Causal Organism: Mycoplasma like organism (MLO).

Disease Cycle: The disease is transmitted through by the vector Cestius phycitis. Artificially the disease has been transmitted successfully to tomato, potato and tobacco. Probably during the season of Brinjal crop, the causal agent survives on weed hosts and from there it is transmitted to main crop by its insect vector.

Control Measures of Little Leaf Disease: Since no effective control measure is found it is better to eradicate the weed host and remove the diseased Brinjal plants. Tetra-cycline has been reported to control the disease.

1. (*c*) Cyanobacteria: Cyanobacteria (blue-green algae) are microorganisms that structurally resemble bacteria (they lack a nucleus and organelles). However, unlike other bacteria, cyanobacteria contain chlorophyll *a* and conduct oxygenic photosynthesis. Cyanobacteria are approximately 2.5 billion years old and thus are the oldest oxygenic phototrophs on Earth. The early evolution of Earth's oxygen-rich atmosphere is most likely due to cyanobacterial photosynthesis. Cyanobacteria are morphologically and physiologically diverse and broadly distributed in terrestrial and aquatic environments. Morphological groups include coccoid, filamentous nonheterocystous, and heterocystous genera. Heterocysts are specialized cells harboring nitrogen fixation, a process by which atmospheric nitrogen (N_2) is converted to a biologically useful form (NH_3). All heterocystous and some coccoid/filamentous cyanobacteria fix nitrogen. This enables cyanobacteria to exploit ecosystems devoid of nitrogen compounds, including those located in polar, open ocean, and desert regions. Cyanobacterial nitrogen fixation can be a significant source of biologically available nitrogen in these ecosystems.

Cyanobacteria move by gliding, using mucilaginous excretions as propellant, or, in the case of planktonic genera, by altering buoyancy through gas vesicle formation and collapse. Cyanobacteria exhibit remarkable ecophysiological adaptations to global change. They tolerate desiccation, hypersalinity, hyperthermal, and high ultraviolet light conditions, often for many years. Over their long evolutionary history, they have formed numerous endosymbiotic and mutualistic associations with microorganisms, higher plants, and animals, including lichens (fungi), ferns, cycads, diatoms, seagrasses, sponges, and even polar bears. Cyanobacteria have also exploited man-made pollution of aquatic environments, especially nutrient-stimulated primary productivity or eutrophication.

Cell Structure and Contribution to Soil Fertility: Cyanobacterial cells are larger and more elaborate than bacteria. Cell structure is typically prokaryotic—one envelope organisation with peptidogly can wall, naked DNA, 70S ribosomes and absence of membrane bound structures like endoplasmic reticulum, mitochondria, Golgi bodies, plastids, lysosomes, sap vacuoles. The cell wall is four layered with peptidoglycan present in the second layer. The outer part of the protoplast contains a number of photosynthetic thylakoids. It is called chromoplasm. The thylakoids lie freely in the cytoplasm. Their membranes contain chlorophyll a, carotenes and xanthophyll's. Chlorophyll *b* is absent.

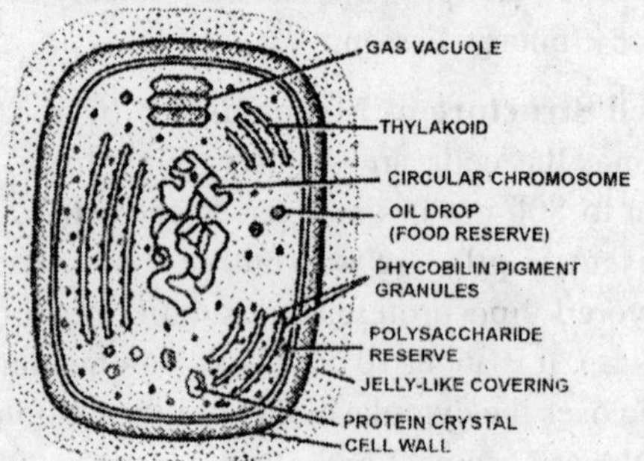

Figure: *Ultrastructure of a cyanophycean cell*

Attached to the thylakoid membranes are small granules known as phycobilisomes. The latter possess accessory photosynthetic pigments known as phycobilins. The phycobilins are of three types—phycocyanin (blue), allophycocyanin (blue) and phycoerythrin (red). Differential formation of phycobilins produces specific colouration which is adapted to absorbing maximum amount of solar radiation. Therefore, cyanobacteria are not always blue green. They may appear purplish, violet, brownish, etc.

Instead of typical vacuoles or sap vacuoles, gas vacuoles or pseudo-vacuoles are found. Each gas vacuole consists of a number of submicroscopic units called gas vesicles. Gas vacuoles function as light screen; provide buoyancy regulating mechanism and pneumatic strength. A naked, circular, double stranded DNA lies coiled generally in the central part of the cytoplasm known as centroplasm. The coiled up DNA is equivalent to a single chromosome of higher organisms. It is often called nucleoid. Like bacteria, small circular DNA segments may also occur in addition to nucleoid. They are known as plasmids or transposons. 70S ribosomes occur here and there. Semicircular group of coiled membranes often attaches the plasma membrane with the nucleoid. It is known as lamella some. Four types of inclusions occur in the cells. They are α-granules (cyanophycean starch), β-granules (lipid droplets), volutin granules and polyhedral bodies (ribulose biphosphate carboxylase).

Inoculation with cyanobacteria had positively affected the soil fertility through enhancing rice rhizosphere soil biological activity in terms of total count bacteria, carbon dioxide evolution, dehydrogenase activity and nitrogenase activity.

1. (*d*)

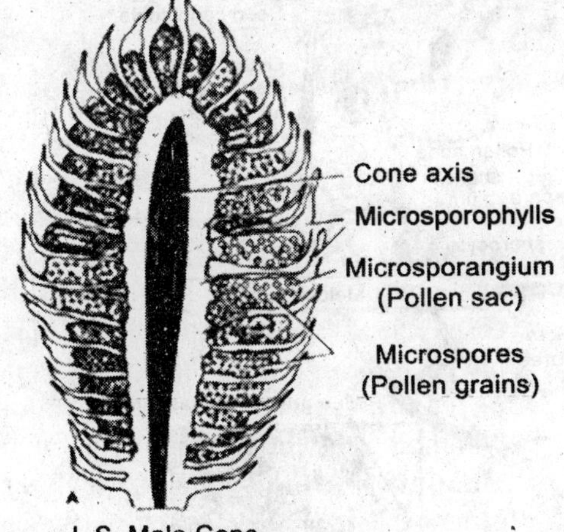

Figure: *L.S Male Cone*

Germination of Pollen Grains: Each ovule secretes a mucilaginous drop at the micropylar end. A gap is produced between the ends of the ovuliferous scales. It forms a passage for the entry of pollen grains. Wind carried pollen grains. The mucilage drop entangles the pollen grain. Pollen grain is carried through the micropyle to the surface of the nucellus.

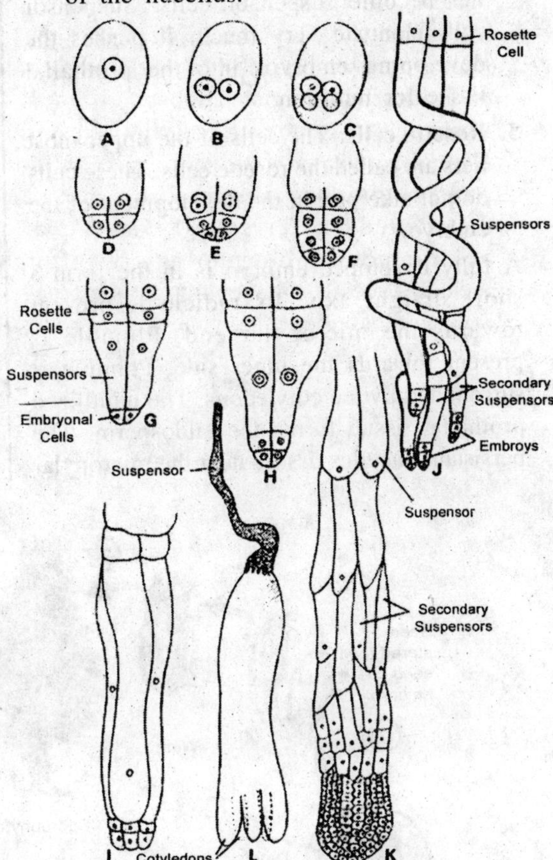

Figure: *Germination of Pollen grains*

Formation of Embryo and Seed: Diploid nucleus divides thrice to form eight cells. The lower four cells becomes proembryonal cells. The upper four nuclei are separated by incomplete cell walls. Four proembryonal divides to produce three tiers of cells:

1. **Embryonal cell:** The cells of the lower tier become embryonal cells. The four embryonal cells separate from each other. Each develops into a separate embryo independently. Each embryonal cell forms secondary suspensor cells. The formation of more than one embryo from a single fertilized oosphere is called polyembryony. Only one embryo reaches maturity. The rest are aborted.

2. **Suspensor cells:** The cells of the middle tier become suspensor cells. Suspensor cells elongate very much. It pushes the developing embryos into the prothalial tissue for nutrition.

3. **Rosette cells:** The cells of the upper most tiers are called the rosette cells. These cells do not take part in the development of the embryo.

A fully developed embryo is in the form a short straight axis. Its radicle is present towards the micropylar end. Plumule is present towards the inner side. Plumule is surrounded by ten cotyledons. The unutilized prothalial tissue forms the endosperm. The persistant nucellus tissues near the micropylar end form the perisperm. The integument becomes hard testa. Some part of the ovuliferous scale fuses with the developing seed. It makes a large wing for dispersal of seed. The axis of the female cone rapidly increases. It produces gaps in ovuliferous scales. The cone becomes woody for the dispersal of seeds.

Germination of Seed: The radicle grows out. It splits the testa at the micropylar end. This radicle grows down into the soil and forms the **primary root.** The hypocotyl elongates to form a loop. Then it becomes straight. It carries with it the plumule and the cotyledons. The testa is also carried up with the cotyledons.

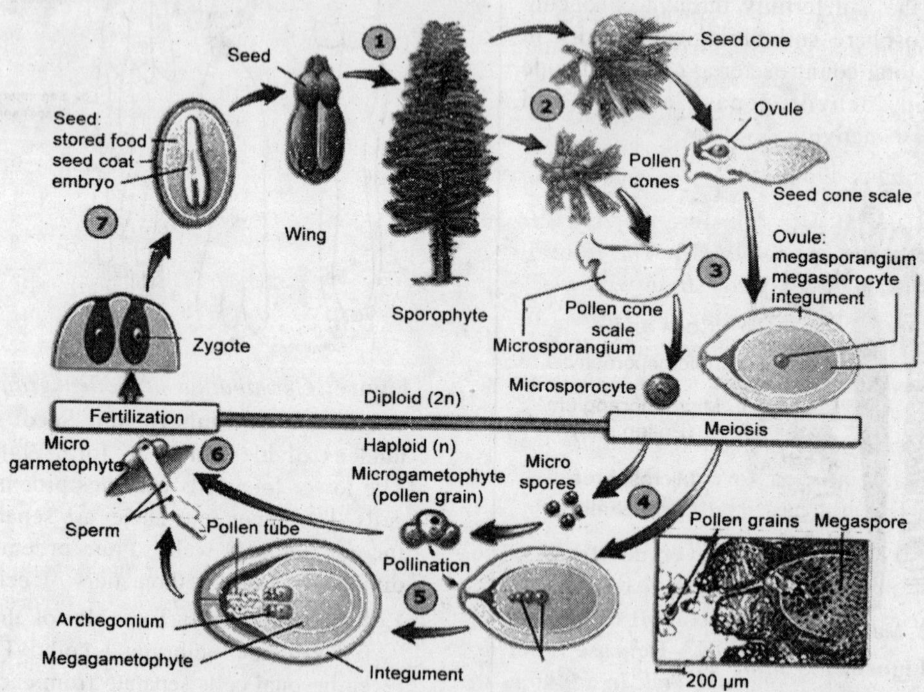

1. (*e*) (*i*) **F- Factor:** The fertility factor (first named F by one of its discoverers Esther Lederberg; also called the sex factor in *E. coli* or the F sex factor; also called F-plasmid) allows genes to be transferred from one bacterium carrying the factor to another bacterium lacking the factor by conjugation. The F factor is carried on the F episome, the first episome to be discovered. Unlike other plasmids, F factor is constitutive for transfer proteins due to a mutation in the gene *finO*. The F plasmid belongs to a class of

conjugative plasmids that control sexual functions of bacteria with a fertility inhibition (Fin) system.

The F-plasmid belongs to a class of conjugative plasmids that control sexual functions of bacteria with a fertility inhibition (Fin) system. In this system, a trans-acting factor, FinO, and antisense RNAs, FinP, combine to repress the expression of the activator gene TraJ. TraJ is a transcription factor that upregulates the *tra* operon. The *tra* operon includes genes required for conjugation and plasmid transfer. This means that an F$^+$ bacteria can always act as a donor cell. The *finO* gene of the original F plasmid (in E. coli K12) is interrupted by an IS3 insertion, resulting in constitutive tra operon expression. F$^+$ cells also have the surface exclusion proteins TraS and TraT on the bacterial surface. These proteins prevent secondary mating events involving plasmids belonging to the same incompatibility (Inc) group. Thus, each F$^+$ bacterium can host only a single plasmid type of any given incompatibility group.

In the case of Hfr transfer, the resulting transconjugates are rarely Hfr. The result of Hfr/F$^-$ conjugation is a F$^-$ strain with a new genotype. When F-prime plasmids are transferred to a recipient bacterial cell, they carry pieces of the donor's DNA that can become important in recombination. Bioengineers have created F plasmids that can contain inserted foreign DNA; this is called a bacterial artificial chromosome.

The first DNA helicase ever described is encoded on the F-plasmid and is responsible for initiating plasmid transfer. It was originally called E. coli DNA Helicase I, but is now known as F-plasmid TraI. In addition to being a helicase, the 1756 amino acid (one of the largest in *E. coli*) F-plasmid TraI protein is also responsible for both specific and non-specific single-stranded DNA binding as well as catalyzing the nicking of single-stranded DNA at the origin of transfer.

(*ii*) **R-factor:**

Resistance Plasmids: The R-Factor also called as the resistance factors or resistance plasmids. They are self-replicating, small, circular DNA elements, that codes for antibiotic resistance. These were first discovered in Japan in the year 1959 when the strains of Shigella (a genus of Gram-negative, aerobic, non-spore-forming, non-motile, rod-shaped bacteria) were found to become resistant to several antibiotics used during a dysentery epidemic. The R factor by itself is non-transmissible.

Structure of Resistance Plasmid

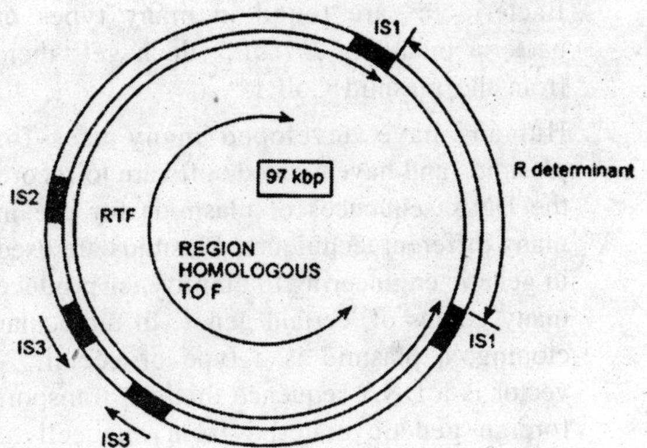

The structure of resistance plasmid can be generally described as a circular piece of DNA, its length ranging between 80 - 95 kb and constitutes the major portion of the R-RTF (Resistance Transfer Factor) molecules. This plasmid is largely homologous to the F factor and contains similar genes. It also contains a fin 0 gene that represses the function of transfer operon. The R factors vary in their size and in the content of genes for drug resistance. The R determinant is smaller than the RTF. Both the RTF and R determinant combine to form one unit and are separated from each other by one IS 1 element on either side. The IS 1 elements help in the exchange of R determinant between the different types of R-RTF units.

The importance of resistance plasmid are as follows:

- The resistance plasmids play an important role in the transmission of MDR genes in bacteria.
- They are also involved in the gene carrier for the autonomous replica-tion, conjugation, and resistance to ampicillin.
- The resistance plasmids contain genes that can build resistance against the antibiotics and help bacteria in producing Pilli.

(*iii*) **Col plasmid:** Col plasmids contain genes that make bacteriocins (also known as colicins), which are proteins that kill other bacteria and thus defend the host bacterium. Bacteriocins are found in many types of bacteria including *E. coli*, which gets them from the plasmid ColE1.

Humans have developed many uses for plasmids and have created software to record the DNA sequences of plasmids for use in many different techniques. Plasmids are used in genetic engineering to amplify, or produce many copies of, certain genes. In molecular cloning, a plasmid is a type of vector. A vector is a DNA sequence that can transport foreign genetic material from one cell to another cell, where the genes can be further expressed and replicated. Plasmids are useful in cloning short segments of DNA. Also, plasmids can be used to replicate proteins, such as the protein that codes for insulin, in large amounts. Additionally, plasmids are being investigated as a way to transfer genes into human cells as part of gene therapy. Cells may lack a specific protein if the patient has a hereditary disorder involving a gene mutation. Inserting a plasmid into DNA would allow cells to express a protein that they are lacking.

3. (*a*) Sporocarp of Marsilea:

- Marselia is heterosporous and Leptosporangiate: It bears two kinds of spores; microspores and megaspores produced inside microsporangium and megasporangium.
- Sporangia are formed inside specialized structures called sporocarps.
- Sporocarps are formed from the petiole of the leaf.
- When young it is green and soft with hairs. On maturity becomes hard and turns brown.
- Each sporocarp is attached to the petiole by means of stalk called pedicel.

Origin of Sporocarp of Marsilea: Two views

- Laminar concept by Bower: Sporocarp is formed by the fusion of one or more leaflets or pinnae.
- 'Whole leaf concept' by Johnson: Sporocarp is formed by the whole leaf.

Morphology of Sporocarp:

- Each sporocarp is oval or oblong body or bean seed shaped.
- The portion where the sporocarp attaches with the pedicel is called the raphe.
- Above Raphe the sporocarp has two horn shaped parts called tubercles.

The laminar or leaf segment hypothesis: According to the supporters of this hypothesis the sporocarp is a lateral modified fertile segment of the leaf but their interpretations are different which are given below:

- Russow (1872) and Busgen (1890) regarded the sporocarp to be made up of 2 leaflets with ventral surface facing each other.
- Goebel (1882, 1905, 1930) considered the sporocarp as a fertile leaflet (pinna), comparable with one or more leaflets.
- Campbell (1893, 1928, 1940) regarded the sporocarp as a folded pinnate leaf formed by the fusion of several pairs of pinnae.
- Bower (1926) stated "the hypothesis seems to be tenable that the sporocarp consists of rachis, bearing 2 rows of pinnules, this is indicated by the veination.
- Eames (1936) compared it to the tip of the leaf with 4 leaflets. He was of the opinion that the body of the sporocarp represents the two distal leaf-lefts and the region of 1st and 2nd protuberance represent the remaining 2 proximal.

- Smith (1938, 1955) considered the sporocarp as a modified pinna with one midrib and several lateral branches.
- Takhtajan (1953) considered the sporocarp as a more specialised fertile segment of a leaf as in Schizaeaceae.
- Puri and Garg (1953) regarded the sporocarp equivalent to a single leaflet which consists of as many pinnules as the number of lateral bundles.
- Gupta K. M. (1962) regarded the sporocarp to be leaflet with as many lobes as the number of lateral bundles. The sori are situated marignally in the depressions of the lobes.

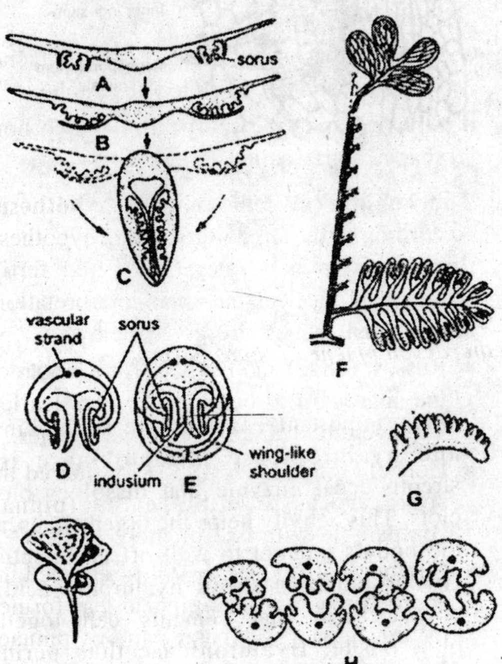

Figure: *(A–I) Marsilea, Morphological nature of sporocarp A–C, Smith's view, D, E. Eames' view, F. Purl and Garg's interpretation, G.H. Bower's interpretation. I. Busgen's interpretation.*

The following evidences support the above hypothesis:

- The sporocarp initial and the leaf initial both are two sided apical cells and they behave in the same way during early segmentation.
- In M. polycarpa, 10-15 sporocarps arise acropetally on one side of the petiole.
- In M. quadrifolia, branching of peduncle is similar to the formation of pinnules.
- The vascular supply of the sporocarp is similar to that of the sterile leaflets.
- Presence of epidermis with stomata, hypodermis and parenchyma with air spaces also supports the laminar hypothesis of sporocarp.

Petiolar or whole leaf hypothesis:

- Johnson (1898, 1933) proposed this hypothesis and regarded the sporocarp as homologous to the swollen end of the petiole. The marginal cells here develop sporangia instead of lamina. The evidence in support of this theory is that sometimes the primary sporocarp gives rise to secondary sporocarp which develops from the initial arising from the marginal cells of the stalk of primary sporocarp.

Development of Sporocarp:

- The development of sporocarp is described by Johnson (1898) in M. quadrifolia. According to him the leaf arises from a bifacial apical leaf cell. It cuts off a pair of segments. When the leaf primordium is 6-7 cells high, the sporocarp initial develops at its base.
- This cell behaves as a two sided apical leaf cell and cuts off segments on either side. The second sporocarp initial appears in the same way as the first sporocarp initial appears. Similarly, the third sporocarp initial arises. This means that these sporocarps are the branches of the leaf.
- The sporocarp initial forms a mass of undifferentiated cells by cutting segments on both lateral sides. It grows into sporocarp. Two rows of soral mother cells appears on ventral side of the young sporocarp.
- Formation of inoculations takes place due

to undifferentiated growth of soral mother cells and their derivatives. These soral mother cells form two alternating rows of canals. These are called soral. Each soral canal is lined on its inner surface by a two layered tissue called. The receptacle of the sorus faces the indusium in each canal and the sporangia arise upon the receptacle in basipetal manner.

- The first sporangial initial appears at the tip of the receptacle and develops into megasporangia. Subsequently the two initials develop on the lateral side of the megasporangium.

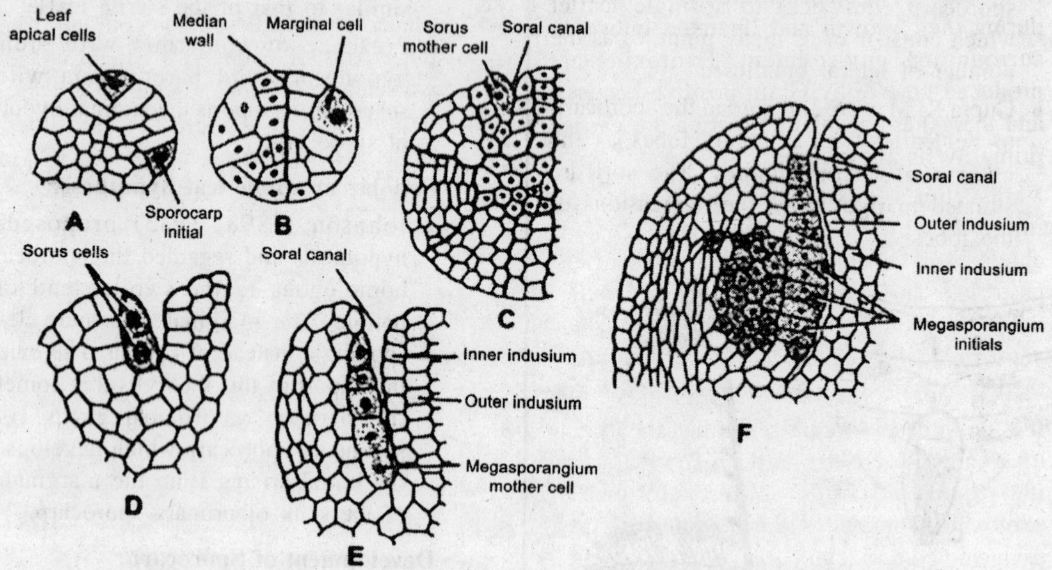

Figure: *Marsilea, Successive stages in the development of sporocarp.*

3. (*b*) Enzymes: Many pathogens produce a series of enzymes to help overcome body defenses and establish themselves in the host. One example is leukocidins, a group of enzymes that destroy white blood cells. This destruction lessens the body's ability to perform phagocytosis.

Other bacterial enzymes are hemolysins. These enzymes destroy red blood cells. Streptococci, staphylococci, and certain *Clostridium* species produce hemolysins.

Coagulases are bacterial enzymes that clot the blood. These enzymes convert fibrinogen into fibrin, which forms the threads of a blood clot. The clot helps staphylococci avoid the body's phagocytes and contributes to its pathogenicity.

Other important enzymes are streptokinase and hyaluronidase. Streptokinase is a streptococcal enzyme that dissolves blood clots. This activity helps the organism escape the body's attempt to wall off an infection. Hyaluronidase destroys hyaluronic acid, a polysaccharide that "cements" cells together in a tissue. Hyaluronidase thus permits organisms to spread through tissues and establish themselves at sites distant from that of the intial infection. Another enzyme, called collagenase, breaks down collagen in the connective tissues of muscles. It thereby encourages the spread of infection.

Toxin: Many bacteria are able to produce poisonous substances called toxins. Toxins act on the body's cells, tissues, and organs and interfere with important body processes, thereby interrupting normal body functions. Those microorganisms that produce toxins are said to be toxigenic. The condition in which toxins are produced is called toxemia.

Two important types of toxins are exotoxins and endotoxins.

Exotoxins are proteins produced by bacteria during their growth and liberated into their surrounding environment. Exotoxins are produced chiefly by Gram-positive bacteria, and the genes for this production are carried primarily on the plasmids.

Various types of exotoxins exist. Neurotoxins interfere with the nervous system, while enterotoxins interfere with activities of the gastrointestinal tract. In response to toxins, the body produces special antibodies called antitoxins, which unite with and neutralize the toxins, providing defense against disease.

It is possible to immunize against the effects of exotoxins by injecting toxoids into individuals. Toxoids are preparations of exotoxins chemically treated to destroy their toxigenicity but retain their ability to elicit antibody formation in the body. Toxoids are currently available to protect against diphtheria and tetanus (the DT injection).

Endotoxins are portions of the cell wall of Gram-negative bacteria. They consist primarily of lipopolysaccharides and are released when bacteria break apart during the process of lysis. Since lysis occurs during antibiotic therapy, the effects of endotoxins can bring about a worsening of symptoms during the recovery period. This condition is called endotoxin shock. It is accompanied by fever, chills, aches, and cardiovascular collapse.

Industrial Production of Penicillin: Commercial production of penicillin is depicted in Fig. The commercial production of most of the antibiotics follows a similar plan. The major differences relate to the microorganism, media composition, and extraction procedure. For penicillin production, inoculum of a high yielding strain of P. chrysogenum is prepared as follows: inoculum is first cultured in flasks in wheat bran nutrient solution for 1 week at 24°C.

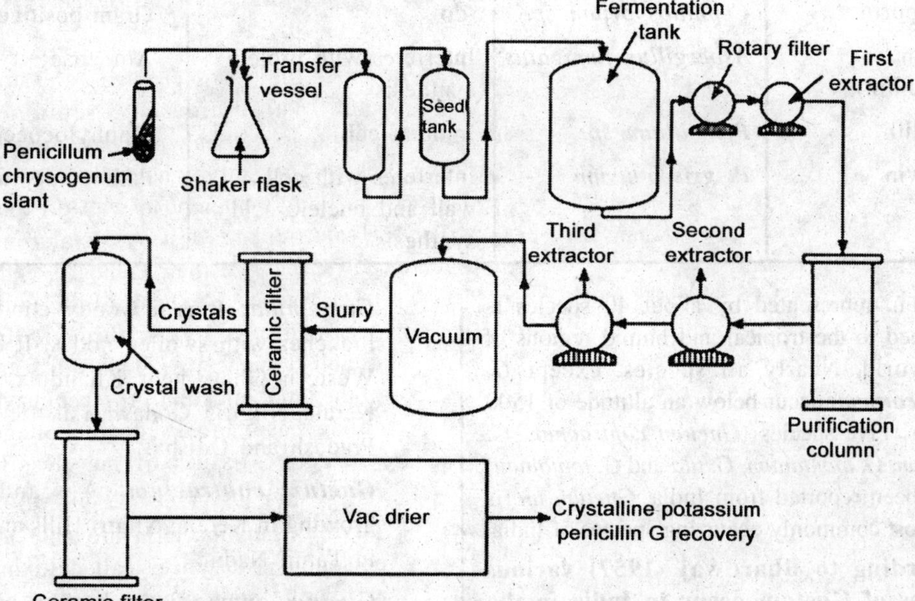

Figure: *Commercial production of penicillin*

The culture is then transferred to inoculum tanks, and grown for 1-2 days under aeration; this supports heavy mycelial growth. The inoculum is now added to very large fermentors containing the production medium, which consists of 10 per cent total glucose/molasses, 4-5% corn-steep liquor solids, 0.5-0.8 per cent phenylacetic acid and 0.5% vegetable oil; pH is adjusted to 6.0 and temperature is regulated at 25- 26°C. Earlier media contained lactose, but it is no longer used. The fermentation is carried out under aerobic conditions, and nutrient supply is maintained by regular feeding (fed-batch culture). The fungus grows in a submerged culture mostly as mycelial balls.

The fermentation is carried out for 7 days. Initially, mycelial growth occurs, and carbohydrates are used up. This reduces the carbohydrate level in the medium; this favours penicillin production, which begins from the second day of fermentation. The pH of medium rises to 8.0 by the 7th day, and penicillin production stops at this stage. Phenylacetic acid is the precursor for the benzene ring side chain of Penicillin G. The presence of precursor promotes the production of Penicillin G. At the end of fermentation period, the fungal biomass is separated by filtration and used as animal feed supplement. Penicillin G is present in the broth, and is extracted using an organic solvent. Penicillin G is finally purified as potassium salt; it is converted to 6-aminopenicillanic acid (6-APA) either chemically or biologically. The side chain of 6-APA is variously modified to obtain a variety of derivatives of penicillin, which are used in medicine. In addition, several other fungal metabolites are used as antibiotics (Table).

Table: Some other fungal metabolites used as antibiotics

Antibiotic (Product)	Microbial source	Mode of action	Primary spectrum
Ampicillin (a penicillin derivative)	*Penicillium sp.*	Inhabits cell-wall synthesis	Gram-positive and Gram-negative bacteria
Cephalosporin	*Cephalosporium sp.*	-do-	Gram-positive bacteria
Fumagillin (Amoebacillin)	*Aspergillus fumigatus*	Interferes with protein synthesis	Amoebae
Methichillin	*Penicillium sp.*	Inhibits cell	Staphylococci
Griseofulvin	*P. griseofulvum*	Interferes with cell wall and nucleic acid synthesis	Pathogenic fungi

3. (*c*) Gnetum, represented by about 40 species is confined to the tropical and humid regions of the world. Nearly all species, except *G. microcarpum*, occur below an altitude of 1500 metres. Five species (*Gnetum contractum, G. gnemon, G. montanum, G. ula* and *G. latifolium*) have been reported from India. *Gnetum ula* is the most commonly occurring species of India.

According to Bhardwaj (1957) various species of Gnetum occur in India in the following regions:

***Gnetumula*:** It is a woody climber having branches with swollen nodes. It is found in Western Ghats near Khandala, forests of Kerala, Nilgiris, Godawari district of Andhra Pradesh and Odisha.

***Gnetum contractum*:** A scandent shrub growing in Kerala, Nilgiri Hills and Coonoor in Tamil Nadu.

***Gnetum gnemon*:** A shrubby plant found in Assam (Naga-Hills, Golaghat and Sibsagar).

***Gnetum montanum*:** A climber with smooth, slender branches, swollen at the nodes. It is found in Assam, Sikkim and parts of Odisha.

***Gnetum latifolium*:** A climber found in Andaman and Nicobar Islands.

Gnetales, believed by some botanists to be the ancestors of flowering plants or angiosperms, are the highly evolved members of gymnosperms and show following characteristics:

1. These are woody plants, of which some species are trees (*Gnetum gnemon*), many are lianes or shrubs and a few are stumpy turnip-like (e.g. *Welwitschia mirabilis*).
2. Leaves are simple elliptical or strap-shaped or sometimes reduced to minute scales. They are generally opposite or whorled.
3. Vessels are present in the secondary wood.
4. 'Flowers' are unisexual, usually dioecious and only rarely monoecious as in some species of Gnetum.
5. 'Flowers' are arranged in compound strobili or 'inflorescences'.
6. The male flowers are surrounded by a perianth. Each male flower contains an antherophore with one to eight synangia.
7. A single erect orthotropous ovule is present in each female flower.
8. Nucellus of the ovule remains surrounded by two or three envelopes.
9. The micropyle of each ovule remains projected in the form of a long bristle-like tube.
10. At the time of fertilization the pollen tube contains two male nuclei.
11. A unicellular primary suspensor is present in the embryo.
12. Two cotyledons are present in the embryo.

Sporne (1965) divided Gnetales into following three unigeneric families:

(*i*) Gnetaceae: Gnetum

(*ii*) Ephedraceae: Ephedra

(*iii*) Welwitschiaceae: Welwitschia

4. (*a*) Ovule: The ovule is part of the makeup of the female reproductive organ in seed plants. It's the place where female reproductive cells are made and contained, and it is what eventually develops into a seed after *fertilization*, only for the seed to then ripen and produce a complete adult plant. Ovules are contained in ovaries at the bottom of a vase-like structure, the carpel, which has a neck called a style and an opening at the top, called a stigma.

After fertilization the ovule starts to swell and its wall starts to toughen up in preparation to become a seed, while the ovary starts to grow around it and becomes the fruit. Keep in mind that some plants, like the avocado, have a single ovule in their ovary, while others, like the kiwifruit, have many, which develop into many seeds in the fruit. Another way that plants differ with regards to their ovules is the place where the ovules are found. Specifically, in *gymnosperms*, such as conifers, the ovules are found on the scales of female cones, while in *angiosperms*, which are flowering plants, the ovules are found inside of the ovary within the carpel.

Structure of Ovule: The ovule is made up of the nucellus, the integuments that form the outermost layer, and the female gametophyte (called an embryo sac in flowering plants), which are found at the very center.

The Nucellus: The nucellus is the largest part of the ovule. It houses the embryo sac as well as nutritive tissue and actually remains present in some flowering plants after fertilization as a source of nutrients for the embyo.

The Integuments: The integument is the tough outer protective layer of the ovule. In the diagrams below we can see that gymnosperms, such as pine trees and spruce trees, usually have one integument in an ovule, so we call them unitegmic. On the other hand, angiosperms, like maples and daisies, typically have two integuments, and we call them bitegmic. The integument encloses the nucellus except for a small gap, which is called the *micropyle*.

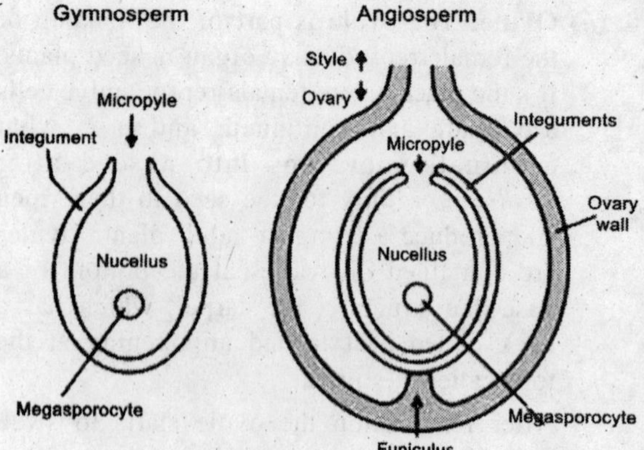

Figure: *Plant ovules*

The Female Gametophyte: This is the part of the ovules that contains the gamete-producing sex organs, which are critical for sexual reproduction. The female gametophyte contains a single set of unpaired chromosomes, meaning that it's haploid. Note that it is commonly called the embryo sac or *megagametophyte*.

Types of Ovules: Ovules have been separated into six categories based on their shapes:

Orthotropous (Atropous): This is where the body of these ovules is straight so that the chalaza, where the nucellus and integuments merge, the *funicle,* which attaches the ovule to the placenta, and the *micropyle* are all aligned.

Anatropous: In this case, the ovules become completely inverted during development so that the micropyle lies close to the hilum. The hilum is a scar that marks the point where the seed was attached to the fruit wall by the funicle.

Hemi-anatropous: The body of these ovules becomes at a right angle in relation to the funicle, so it looks like the ovule is lying on its side.

Campylotropous: The body of this type is bent and the alignment between the chalaza and micropyle is lost. The embryo sac is only slightly curved.

Amphitropous: The body of the ovule is very much curved that the embryo sac and the ovule itself take the shape of a horseshoe.

Circinotropous: The funicle in this case is especially long that it creates a nearly full circle around the ovule whose micropyle is ultimately pointing upwards.

4. (*b*) Differentiate between Early and Late bilght Disease of Potato

Different Causes: Early blight is caused by two different closely related fungi, Alternaria tomatophila, and Alternaria solani, which lives in soil and plant debris.

Late blight is caused by Phytophthora infestans, a microorganism which prefer moist and cool environments.

Different Symptoms: Early blight mainly affects the stems, leaves, and fruits of vegetables, and is most susceptible to disease at the branches of leaves and stems. At the seedling stage, the base of the stem of the seedlings is dark brown lesions, slightly sunken, and has a ring pattern. The onset of adulthood generally develops from the lower leaves to the upper part. The leaves are infected, the primary brown necrotic small points, and then expanded into a round to nearly round, dark brown, with concentric wheel pattern, the wheel surface has a thorny hair, and some varieties have a yellow-green halo around the lesion.

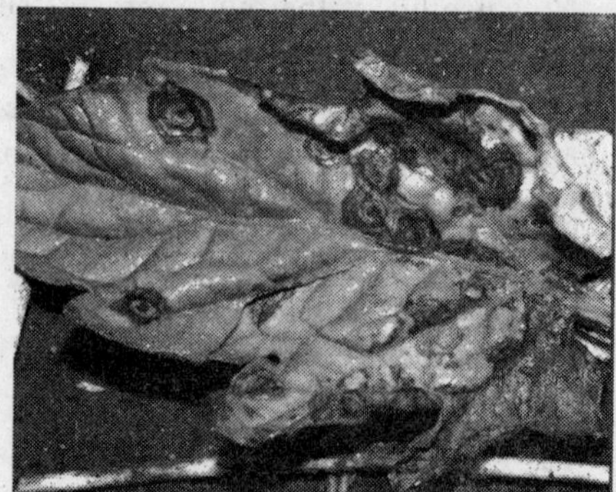

Figure: *Early blight*

The disease of the fruit begins in the vicinity of the flower buds. It is mostly elliptical to amorphous brown to black lesions, dip, hard, and dense black mold layer in the later stage. The center of the lesion has a concentric pattern. When it is wet, the black mold layer is the main recognition symptom of the disease.

When the late blight occurs, the plants often die in the short term. The disease can occur in the seedling stage and the adult stage. In the seedling stage, the leaves are dark green water-stained lesions, and the lesions spread from the leaves to the main stem, causing the stems to become thin and dark brown, causing the seedlings to wilt or folding.

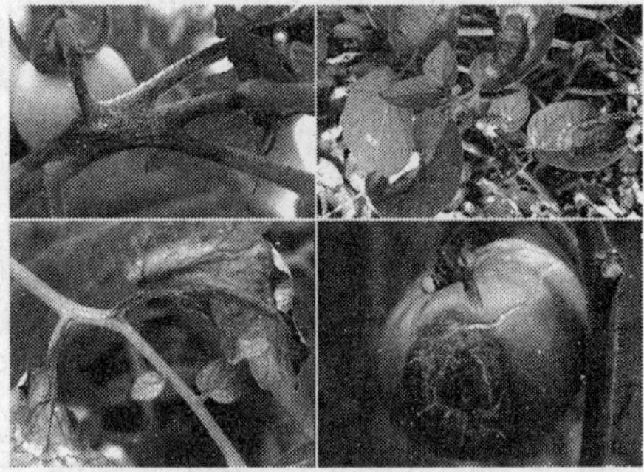

Figure: *late blight*

When infected in adulthood, it is often the simultaneous onset of stems, leaves, and fruits. The stems become dark brown and rot-like. There are water-soaked irregular lesions on the leaves. White mold is found in the disease-health junction on the back of the leaves. The fruit, especially the green fruit, has oil-stained lesions.

Early Blight and Late Blight of Potato

Early Blight: Early blight and late blight, two serious diseases of potato, are widely distributed. Both are found everywhere potatoes are grown. The terms "early" and "late" refer to the relative time of their appearance in the field, although both diseases can occur at the same time.

Early blight of potato is caused by the fungus, *Alternaria solani*, which can cause disease in potato, tomato, other members of the potato family, and some mustards. This disease, also known as target spot, rarely affects young, vigorously growing plants. It is found on older leaves first. Early blight is favoured by warm temperatures and high humidity.

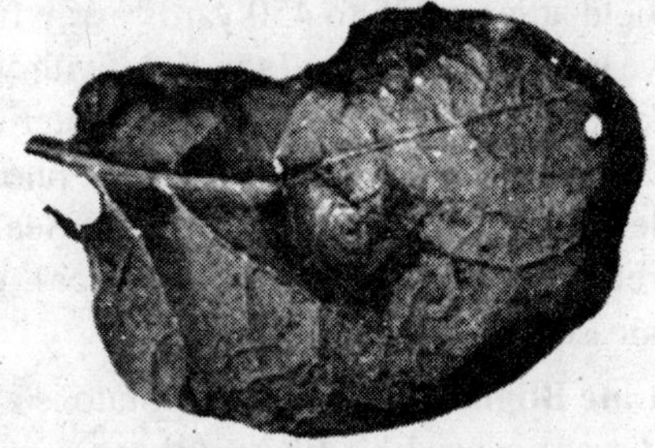

***Symptoms*:** Spots begin as small, dark, dry, papery flecks, which grow to become brown-black, circular-to-oval areas. The spots are often bordered by veins that make them angular. The spots usually have a target appearance, caused by concentric rings of raised and depressed dead tissue. A yellowish or greenish-yellow ring is often seen bordering the growing spots. As the spots become very large, they often cause the entire leaf to become yellow and die. This is especially true on the lower leaves, where spots usually occur first and can be very abundant. The dead leaves do not usually fall off. Dark brown to black spots can occur on stems.

Tubers are affected, as well, with dark, circular to irregular spots. The edges of the spots are often raised and purple to dark metallic gray in colour. When the tuber is sliced open, the flesh under the spots is usually brown, dry, and leathery or corky in texture. As the disease advances, the potato flesh often becomes water soaked and yellow to greenish yellow. Early blight spots are less likely to become rotted by secondary organisms than the other tuber rots.

***Prevention*:** Varieties resistant to this disease are available. In general, late maturing varieties are more resistant than the earlier maturing varieties. Keep plants healthy; stressed plants are more predisposed to early blight. Avoid overhead irrigation. Do not dig tubers until they are fully mature in order to prevent damage. Do not use a field for potatoes that was used for potatoes or tomatoes the previous year. Keep this year's field at least 225 to 450 yards away from last year's field. Surround the field with wheat to keep wind-blown spores from entering. Use adequate nitrogen levels and low phosphorus levels to reduce disease severity. See current recommendations for chemical control measures.

Late Blight: Late blight of potato is a serious disease caused by *Phytophthora infestans*. It affects potato, tomato and, occasionally, eggplant and other members of the potato family. Late blight is the worst potato disease. It was first reported in the 1830s in Europe and in the US. It is famous for being the cause of the 1840s Irish Potato Famine, when a million people starved and a million and a half people emigrated. Late blight continued to be a devastating problem until the 1880s when the first fungicide was discovered. In recent years, it has reemerged as a problem. It is favoured by cool, moist weather and can kill plants within two weeks if conditions are right.

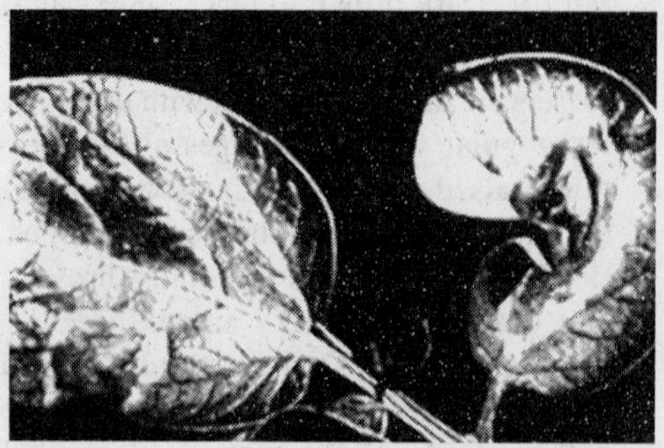

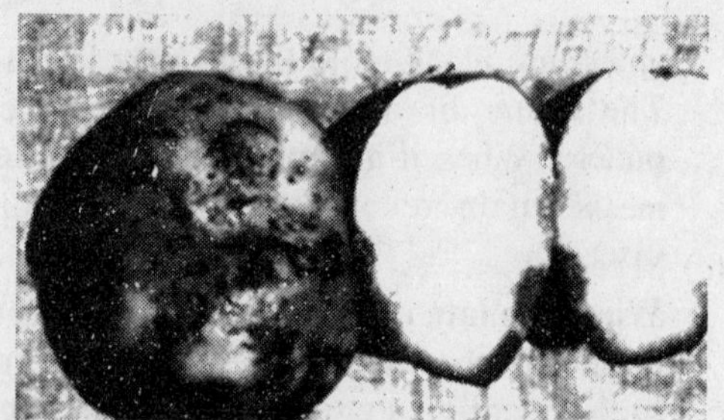

***Symptoms*:** Leaf spots begin as small, pale to dark green, irregularly shaped spots. The spots often have pale green to yellow rings surrounding them. The spots are not bordered by veins but can grow across them. In cool, moist weather, the spots grow rapidly into large brown to purplish black areas. The disease may kill entire leaflets or grow down the petioles and into the stem, killing the plant above it. When the weather is moist, a white fungal growth appears on the edges of the dead areas, usually on the undersides of the leaves. In the field, plants often give off a distinctive fetid or decaying odour.

On susceptible potato varieties, the tubers can become infected. Small to large, slightly depressed areas of brown to purplish skin can be seen on the outside of the tuber. When the tuber is cut open, there is a tan-brown, dry, granular rot, which extends ½" to ¾" into the tuber. The border of this area is indistinct. If potatoes are stored under warm or humid conditions, the rot will continue to progress. Often secondary rot organisms set in and completely destroy the tubers.

***Disease Identification*:** White, fluffy fungal growth is present on the bottoms of leaves in moist weather. Leaf spots are not bordered by veins.

***Prevention*:** Use disease-free seed potatoes. Keep cull/compost piles away from potato growing areas. Destroy any volunteer potato plants. Keep tubers covered with soil throughout the season to prevent tuber infection. Remove infected tubers before storing to prevent the spread of disease in storage. Kill vines completely before harvest to avoid inoculation of the tubers during harvest. Resistant varieties are available, although some fungicides must still be applied to resistant cultivars. See current recommendations for chemical control measures.

4. (*c*) **Mycorrhiza:** A mycorrhiza is a symbiotic association between a green plant and a fungus. The plant makes organic molecules such as sugars by photosynthesis and supplies them to the fungus, and the fungus supplies to the plant water and mineral nutrients, such as phosphorus, taken from the soil. Mycorrhizas are located in the roots of vascular plants, but mycorrhiza-like associations also occur in bryophytes and there is fossil evidence that early land plants that lacked roots formed arbuscular mycorrhizal associations. Most plant species form mycorrhizal associations, though some families like Brassicaceae and Chenopodiaceae cannot. Different forms for the association are detailed in the next section. The most common is the arbuscular type that is present in 70% of plant species, including many crop plants such as wheat and rice.

Differentiate between Ectomycorrhizae and Endomycorrhizae:

Ectomycorrhizae and endomycorrhizae are two types of mycorrhizae. Fungal hyphae of ectomycorrhizae do not penetrate into the cortical cells of the plant root while fungal hyphae of endomycorrhizae penetrate inside the cortical cells of the plants. Therefore, this is the key difference between ectomycorrhizae and endomycorrhizae. Furthermore, ectomycorrhizae are less common while endomycorrhizae occur in more than 85% of vascular plants. Hence, this is also a difference between ectomycorrhizae and endomycorrhizae.

Moreover, a further difference between ectomycorrhizae and endomycorrhizae is that ectomycorrhizae form a hyphae mantle while endomycorrhizae do not produce a hyphae mantle. Additionally, endomycorrhizae form vesicles and arbuscules. But, ectomycorrhizae do not form vesicles and arbuscules. Therefore, this is a significant difference between ectomycorrhizae and endomycorrhizae.

Ectomycorrhizae vs Endomycorrhiza

	Ectomycorrhizae	Endomycorrhiza
Definition	Ectomycorrhizae is a type of mycorrhizal association in which fungal hyphae do not penetrate the cortical cells of the plant root	Endomycorrhizae is a type of mycorrhizal association in which fungal hyphae penetrate the cortical cells of the plant root and form vesicles and arbuscules
Abundance	Less abundant (only 4%)	Highly abundant (80%)
Hyphae Mantle	Produce a hyphae mantle	Do not produce a hyphae mantle
Hartig Net	Produce a hartig net	Do not produce a hartig net
Arbuscules and Vesicles	Arbuscules and vesicles are absent	Arbuscules and vesicles are present
Fungi involved	Ascomycota and Basidiomycota	Glomeromycota
Penetration into Cortical Cells	Do not penetrate into cortical cells of the roots	Penetrate into cortical cells of the plant roots
Plants	Conifers like Pinus, Cedrus, Abies and deciduous non-conifers, like oak, beech, birch etc.	About 85% of vascular plants including orchids, shrubs and foliage plants, nut trees etc.

Ectomycorrhizae vs Endomycorrhizae: Mycorrhizae is one of the important symbiotic relationships that occur between plant and fungi. Ectomycorrhizae and endomycorrhizae are two types of mycorrhizae. Ectomycorrhizae characteristically form a hyphae mantle and hartig net. The fungal hyphae do not penetrate inside the cortical cells of the plant roots. On the other hand, endomycorrhizae do not produce a hyphae mantle. They form vesicles and arbuscules. Moreover, their hyphae penetrate inside the cortical cells of the plant roots. Ectomycorrhizae can be seen in pine trees while endomycorrhizae are found in orchids. Thus, this is the difference between ectomycorrhizae and endomycorrhizae.

Significance of Ecto-mycorrhiza in Coniferous Forestry Programme: Ectomycorrhizal (ECM) associations involve the most diverse category of myocrrhizae. The diversity derives from the fungal partners; more than 5,000 species of fungi, mainly Basidiomycetes, with a limited number of Ascomycetes and Zygomycetes, make the relationship very diverse. On the contrary, however, relatively few families of plants such as Fagaceae, Pinaceae, Betulaceae, and Dipterocarpaceae are involved in the ECM associations. These plants, however, are distributed over wide areas of temperate and boreal forests, and are therefore economically important. ECM fungi make associations with plants by forming a sheath (mantle) around fine root tips with hyphae that grow inward between root cells of the cortex and make Hartig net, and emanate outward through the soil, increasing the surface area to absorb nutrients and water. Thus, the mycorrhizal fungi gain photosynthates and other essential substances from the plant and in return help the plant take up water and minerals. Pine wilt disease (PWD) is a globally serious forest disease, and also shows the importance of ectomycorrhizal relationships. Pine trees planted on a mountain slope were killed by PWD, but some trees survived at the top of the slope, where mycorrhizal associations developed far better than on lower slopes. ECM associations, beside fertilization, also increase the supply of water to the pines, and elevate host resistance against disease and parasites. Moreover, inoculation of pine seedlings with ECM fungi under laboratory conditions confirmed the increase in their resistance to PWD. Pine seedlings can tolerate the adverse effects of environmental stress such as acid mist when infected with ECM fungi. These fungi can also make a significant contribution to forest ecosystems by increasing biomass and creating a network among trees through which nutrients may transported. ECM fungi also improve the growth of host plants at the seedling stage. Many pioneer plants in wastelands are facilitated in their establishment by ECM. This association has been successfully applied to reforestation programs in tropical forests by inoculating mycorrhizae on to nursery seedlings.

5. (*a*) **Bentham and Hooker system of classification:** A widely followed natural system of classification considered the best was proposed by two English botanist **George Bentham** (1800 - 1884) and **Joseph Dalton Hooker** (1817-1911). The classification was published in a three volume work as "*Genera Plantarum*" (1862-1883) describing 202 families and 7569 genera and 97, 205 species. In this system the seeded plants were classified into 3 major classes such as Dicotyledonae, Gymnospermae and Monocotyledonae.

Class I Dicotyledonae: Plants contain two cotyledons in their seed, leaves with reticulate venation, tap root system and tetramerous or pentamerous flowers come under this class It includes three sub-classes—**Polypetalae, Gamopetalae** and **Monochlamydeae.**

Sub-class 1: Polypetalae: Plants with free petals and dichlamydeous flowers come under polypetalae. It is further divided into three series—**Thalamiflorae, Disciflorae** and **Calyciflorae.**

Series (i) Thalamiflorae: Plants having flowers with dome or conical shaped thalamus and superior ovary are included in this series. It includes 6 orders and 34 families.

Series (ii) Disciflorae: Flowers having prominent disc shaped thalamus with superior ovary come under this series. It includes 4 orders and 23 families.

Series (iii) Calyciflorae: It includes plants having flowers with cup shaped thalamus and with inferior or sometimes with half inferior ovary. Calyciflorae includes 5 orders and 27 families.

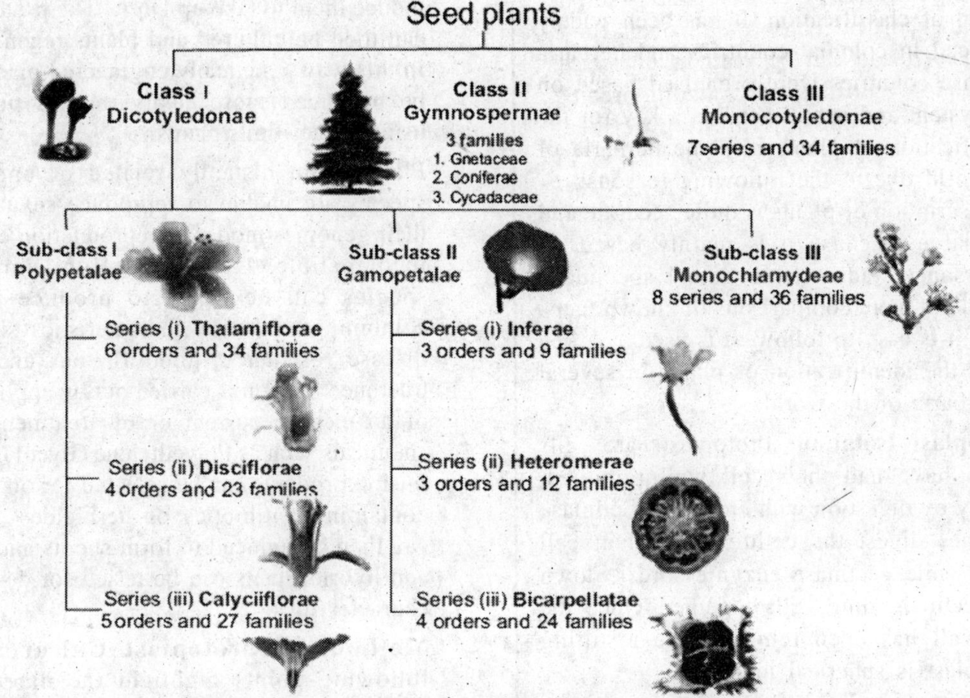

Figure: *Bentham and Hooker system of classification*

Sub-class 2. Gamopetalae: Plants with united petals, which are either partially or completely fused to one another and dichlamydeous are placed under Gamopetalae. It is further divided into three series—Inferae, Heteromerae and Bicarpellatae.

Series (i) Inferae: The flowers are epigynous and with inferior ovary. Inferae includes 3 orders and 9 families.

Series (ii) Heteromerae: The flowers are hypogynous, superior ovary and with more than two carpels. Heteromerae includes 3 orders and 12 families.

Series (iii) Bicarpellatae: The flowers are hypogynous, superior ovary and with two carpels. Bicarpellatae includes 4 orders and 24 families.

Sub-class 3. Monochlamydeae: Plants with incomplete flowers either apetalous or with undifferenciated calyx and corolla are placed under Monochlamydeae. The sepals and petals are not distinguished and they are called perianth. Sometimes both the whorls are absent. Monochlamydeae includes 8 series and 36 families.

Class II Gymnospermae: Plants that contain naked seeds come under this class. Gymnospermae includes three families—Gnetaceae, Coniferae and Cycadaceae.

Class III Monocotyledonae: Plants contain only one cotyledon in their seed, leaves with parallel venation, fibrous root system and trimerous flowers come under this class. The Monocotyledonae has 7 series and 34 families.

The Bentham and Hooker system of classification is still supposed to be the best system of classification. It has been widely practiced in colonial countries and herbaria of those countries were organised based on this system and is still used as a key for the identification of plants in some herbaria of the world due to the following reasons:

- Description of plants is quite accurate and reliable, because it is mainly based on personal studies from actual specimens and not mere comparisons of known facts.
- As it is easy to follow, it is used as a key for the identification of plants in several herbaria of the world.

5. (*b*) **Protoplast Isolation:** Protoplasts are cells which have had their cell wall removed, usually by digestion with enzymes. Cellulase enzymes digest the cellulose in plant cell walls while pectinase enzymes break down the pectin holding cells together. Once the cell wall has been removed the resulting protoplast is spherical in shape.

Digestion is usually carried out after incubation in an osmoticum (a solution of higher concentration than the cell contents which causes the cells to plasmolyse). This makes the cell walls easier to digest. Debris is filtered and/or centrifuged out of the suspension and the protoplasts are then centrifuged to form a pellet. On resuspension the protoplasts can be cultured on media which induce cell division and differentiation. A large number of plants can be regenerated from a single experiment—a gram of potato leaf tissue can produce more than a million protoplasts, for example.

Protoplasts can be isolated from a range of plant tissues: leaves, stems, roots, flowers, anthers and even pollen. The isolation and culture media used vary with the species and with the tissue from which the protoplasts were isolated. Protoplasts are used in a number of ways for research and for plant improvement. They can be treated in a variety of ways (electroporation, incubation with bacteria, heat shock, high pH treatment) to induce them to take up DNA. The protoplasts can then be cultured and plants regenerated. In this way genetically engineered plants can be produced more easily than is possible using intact cells/plants.

Plants from distantly related or unrelated species are unable to reproduce sexually as their genomes/modes of reproduction etc. are incompatible. Protoplasts from unrelated species can be fused to produce plants combining desirable characteristics such as disease resistance, good flavour and cold tolerance. Fusion is carried out by application of an electric current or by treatment with chemicals such as Polyethylene Glycol (PEG). Fusion products can be selected for on media containing antibiotics or herbicides. These can then be induced to form shoots and roots and hybrid plants can be tested for desirable characteristics.

Methods of Protoplast Culture: The following points highlight the nine main techniques of protoplast culture. The techniques are: 1. Agar Plating Method 2. Micro-Chamber 3. Nurse Culture 4. Immobilization of Protoplast 5. Nutrient Requirement 6. Growth Regulators 7. Cultural Conditions 8. Cell Wall Regeneration 9. Regeneration.

Agar Plating Method: Protoplast can be cultured conveniently by using agar plating method. Two millilitres of protoplast suspension in culture medium is mixed with same amount of molten agar medium of the same composition in petri dish. The temperature of the medium is maintained at 4°C before mixing with protoplast suspension, which is then incubated in inverted position at 27°C. The petri dish is then sealed with paraffin to avoid desiccation.

5. (*c*) **Endosperm:** The endosperm is a tissue produced inside the seeds of most of the flowering plants following fertilization. It is triploid in most species. It surrounds the embryo and provides nutrition in the form of starch, though it can also contain oils and protein. This can make endosperm a source of nutrition in animal diet. For example, wheat endosperm is ground into flour for bread (the rest of the grain is included as well in whole wheat flour), while barley endosperm is the main source of sugars for beer production. Other examples of endosperm that forms the bulk of the edible portion are coconut "meat" and coconut "water", and corn. Some plants, such as orchids, lack endosperm in their seeds.

Various Types of Endosperms based on Development: Three main types of endosperm development in flowering plants are: (i) Nuclear type (ii) Cellular type and (iii) Helobial type. The formation of endosperm is initiated by mitotic divisions of the primary endosperm nucleus (3N). The formation of endosperm occurs usually prior to the zygotic division. Endosperm accumulates food reserves and functions as the nutritive tissue for the developing embryo.

(*i*) **Nuclear type:** In nuclear type of endosperm the first division of primary endosperm nucleus and few subsequent nuclear divisions are not accompanied by wall formation. The nuclei produced are free in the cytoplasm of the embryo sac and they may remain free indefinitely or wall formation takes place later. In the coconut, cell wall formation of endosperm is never found complete. In Areca and Phoenix the endosperm becomes very hard.

(*ii*) **Cellular type:** In this case, there is cytokinesis after each nuclear division of endosperm nucleus. The endosperm, thus, has a cellular form, from the very beginning because first and subsequent divisions are all accompanied by wall formation e.g. Petunia, Datura, Adoxa, etc.

(*iii*) **Helobial type:** It is an intermediate type between the nuclear and cellular types. The first division is accompanied by cytokinesis but the subsequent ones are free nuclear. The chamber towards micropylar end of embryo sac is usually much larger than the chamber towards chalazal end.

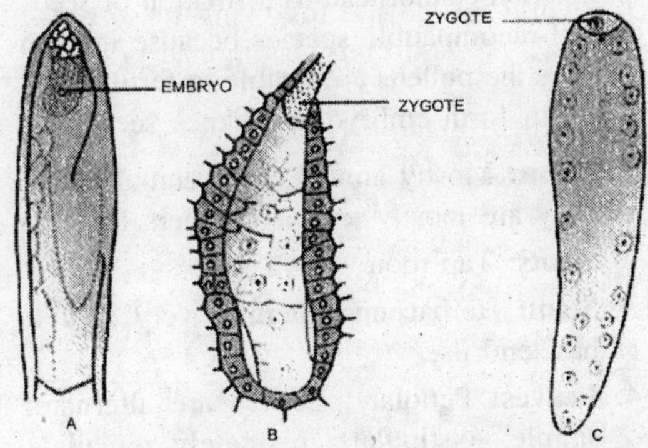

Figure: *Types of endosperm development. A. Nuclear, B. Helobial and C. Cellular*

A large number of nuclei are formed in the micropylar chamber by free nuclear divisions while the nucleus of the chamber towards chalazal end divides to form a fewer free nuclei or may not divide at all.

5. (*d*) **Self-incompatibility:** Self-incompatibility (SI) is a general name for several genetic mechanisms in angiosperms, which prevent self-fertilization and thus encourage outcross and allogamy. It should not be confused with genetically controlled physical or temporal mechanisms that prevent self-pollination, such as heterostyly and sequential hermaphroditism (dichogamy). In plants with SI, when a pollen grain produced in a plant reaches a stigma of the same plant or another plant with a similar genotype, the process of pollen germination, pollen-tube growth, ovule fertilization and embryo development is halted at one of its stages and consequently

no seeds are produced. SI is one of the most important means of preventing inbreeding and promoting the generation of new genotypes in plants, and it is considered as one of the causes for the spread and success of angiosperms on the earth.

Importance in Seed Formation: When inspite of viable pollens they are unable to germinate on the stigma of the same flower it is called self incompatibility and this leads to cross pollination e.g., radish. Self-pollination cannot lead to formation of seeds in self-incompatible species because in such flowers the pollens are unable to fertilize the ovule to form embryo and hence seeds.

5. (*e*) 1. **Habit:** Mostly annual or perennial herbs. They are mostly tendril climbers.

2. **Roots:** Tap root
3. **Stem:** Herbaceous. Stem is very soli. It has tendrils.
4. **Leaves:** Petiolate; Leaves are alternate; simple; exstipulate; palmately reticulate venation. Sonic leaves bear tendrils in their axils.
5. **Inflorescence:** The flowers are solitary but some have Racemose or cymose clusters.
6. **Flower:** Pedicilate; ebracteate; actinomorphic; Regular; complete or incomplete; unisexual or hermaphrodite; plant may be monoecious or dioecious; epigenous;
7. **Calyx:** 5 sepals; united; campanula e; grem
8. **Corolla:** 5 petals; united at base or free; yellow or white.
9. **Stamens in male flowers:** 3 to 5 sy mens; united by various degree; anther are very long. Stamens are borne on calyx tube.
10. **Carpels in female flowers:** 3 fused carp 'Is; syncarpous; inferior ovary; Parietal placentation.
11. **Fruits:** Fleshy berry
12. **Seed:** Non-endospermic seed.

Floral formula and floral diagram

Floral Formula:

Male Flower: $\oplus$ ⚥ $K_{(5)}\ C_5\ Or_{(5)}\ A_{(3\text{-}5)}\ G_0$

Female Flower: $\oplus$ ⚥ $K_{(5)}\ C_5\ Or_{(5)}\ A_0\ G_{(3)}$

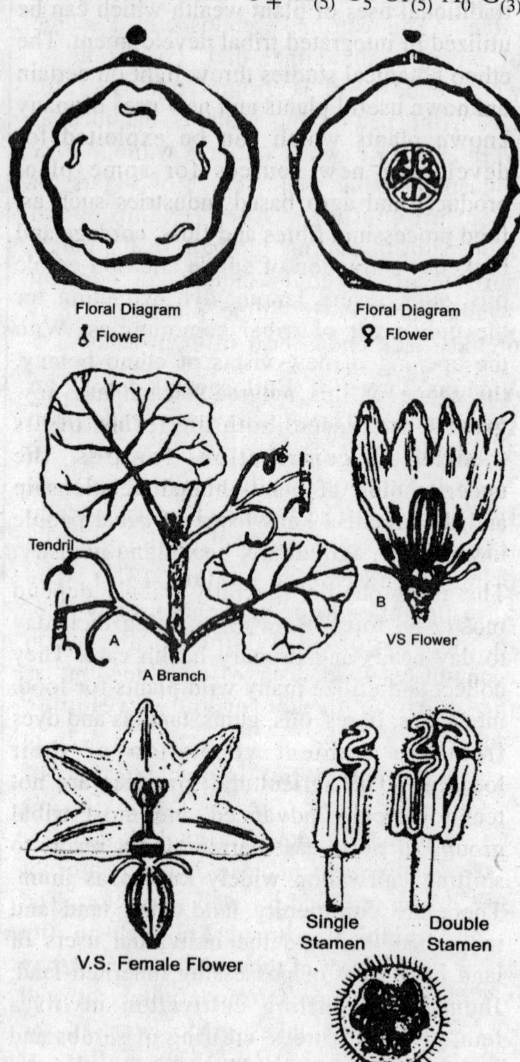

Figure: *Cucurbita Maxima.*

6. (*a*) **Ethnobotany and its Relevance to Rural Population in India:** Ethnobotany is the study of a region's plants and their practical uses through the traditional knowledge of a local culture and people. An ethnobotanist thus strives to document the local customs involving the practical uses of local flora for many aspects of life, such as plants as medicines, foods, intoxicants and clothing.

Ethno botanical knowledge is very ancient. It provides information regarding the traditional uses of plant wealth which can be utilized in integrated tribal development. The ethno botanical studies throw light on certain unknown useful plants and new uses of many known plants which can be exploited for developing new sources for some plant products and agro based industries such as, food processing, fibres and floss, cordage and basketry, extraction of edible and non-edible oils, gum, resins, tannin, dye extraction for the upliftment of tribal communities. With the opening of new vistas of ethno botany, the scope of this natural science has now greatly increased both in terms of its theoretical contribution towards the understanding of plant- human relationship and the practical knowledge of tribal people in medicine, agriculture, health and industry.

The rural people specially tribals depend mostly on forest flora for meeting their day to day needs and primary health care. They collect and utilize many wild plants for food, medicines, fibres, oils, gums, tannins and dyes from the ambient vegetation of their localities. The agricultural practices are not technologically advanced and most tribal groups in north-east part of India resort to shifting cultivation widely known as jhum. There are community land, clan land and individual land and the individual users of land have right of possessing inherited land. Jhuming or shifting cultivation involves felling of forest trees, clearing of shrubs and undergrowth in limited area and turning of soil for sowing crops.

The cleared land is used for agriculture for short time and when the fertility of the soil decreases, the area is abandoned by tribals and then they shift to new area and clear the forest vegetation for agricultural purpose. Jhuming has caused deforestation and soil erosion. Thus the existing land use and its unscientific management have aggravated the problems of soil erosion, floods, depletion of water resources and overall productivity. Therefore, it has now become essential for botanists, agricultural scientists, anthropologists and government agencies to take stock of the problems of the tribal communities and make coordinated efforts in this direction. It requires proper management of settlements of tribal population because the migration of tribal communities compels them for shifting cultivation.

Rural peoples have knowledge about the utility of many plant species which are unknown to modern society, it is for the botanists to collect information regarding the traditional uses of such wild plants from them. The rural culture is changing rapidly due to urbanization, rapid industrialization and changing pattern of life. The medicinal plants are almost the exclusive source of drugs for the majority of world population even today. Plant products constitute approximately 25% of the total prescribed medicines even in most advanced countries like U.S.A. The record of use of herbal medicines in India is very old. India with diverse ethnic groups and rich biodiversity has a century old heritage of medicinal phototherapy for the treatment of various diseases and promotion of health. The branch of ethno botany which deals with the traditional systems of medicine or folk lore medicines is called medico-ethno botany.

Tribal communities utilize ethno medicinal plants for the treatment of diseases and disorders like diarrhoea, dysentery, fever, headache, skin diseases, boils and blisters, rheumatism and gout, piles, jaundice, ophthalmic diseases, toothache, bone fracture, snake bite, helminthic or worm infection, cuts and wounds, cough, cold, asthma, leprosy etc. The ethno medicinal data will serve as a useful source of information for the chemists, pharmacologists and practitioners of herbal medicines for detection and isolation of bioactive compounds used in modern medicines.

During the last few decades, a succession of the so called Wonder drugs e.g. reserpine quinine, ephedrine, cocaine, emetine, khelline, colchicine, digitoxin, artemisin, podophyllotoxin' guguhpid, taxol etc. have been discovered from plants with rich ethno botanical lore in tribal societies. The isolation of these alkaloids from plants heralded a new era in the use of plant products in modern medicines. The last thirty years or so witnessed a resurgence of interest in the traditional medicines and drugs obtained from plants all over the world. The tranquilizers rescinnamine and reserpine have been isolated from the roots of Rauvolffia serpentina which has been in use in India for more than thousand years in folk medicine for the treatment of snake bite insanity, epilepsy, fever and high blood pressure.

The native of Madagascar used Catharanthus roseus (Sadaa bahar) as an oral hypoglycemic agent. It yielded two important drugs; Vinblastine and Vincristine which are known to be effective in leukemia (blood cancer). Out of 120 active compounds currently isolated from higher plants and used in modern medicines 75% show a positive correlation between their modern therapeutic use and the traditional use of plants from which they are derived. The efficacies of a number of phytopharmaceuticals derived from plants such as atropine (pupil dialator), berberin (used in gastrointestinal disorders), caffeine (a stimulant), digitoxin (a cardiac tonic), emetine (antiamoebic), ephedrine (anti asthmatic), morphine (analgesic), papain (protein digestant and anthelmintic), quinine (antimalarial), reserpine (tranquilizer), Vinblastine and Vincnstme (antileukaemic), Camptothecin, (antitumour), forskoline (hypotensive and antispasmodic) with rich folk-lore have been discovered.

The primitive societies in India have been dependent on herbal medicines from the time immemorial. In fact, all traditional systems of medicine had their roots and origin in folk medicines or ethno medicines. The knowledge of ethno botany plays a vital role in the primary health care and economy of the rural population of our country and has potential for the discovery of new herbal drugs and new sources of nutraceuticals etc.

6. (*b*) **Differentiation:** Plants cells are derived from meristems of shoot apex, root apex, and cambium by a process known as differentiation where cells get differentiated into different structures in order to perform different functions in the plant body. Major structural changes take place in the plant cell wall and the protoplasm during this process. Tracheary elements of the xylem of vascular plants undergo differentiation. The cells lose the contents of its protoplasm, and the cellulose cell walls get lignified into secondary cell walls, which increase its elasticity and allow the cell walls to withstand extreme pressure conditions during transportation of water to longer distances.

Dedifferentiation: Under certain conditions, plants cells that are already differentiated and lost the ability of further division regain the capacity of division and differentiation. This process is known as dedifferentiation. The fully differentiated parenchyma cells undergo dedifferentiation, which leads to the formation of cork cambium and inter-fascicular cambium. A dedifferentiated tissue has the ability to act as meristem that could give rise to a different set of cells. The ability of those cells for further differentiation depends on different parameters such as genetic and epigenetic variations. This concept is used in plant tissue culture to develop a callus.

Redifferentiation: Once new cells are formed from the dedifferentiated tissues that act as meristems, the cells lose their ability for further division and differentiation.

Eventually, they get mature in order to accomplish specific functions of the plant body. Secondary xylem and secondary phloem are the best examples to describe the process of redifferentiation. Dedifferentiated vascular cambium divides further to give rise to the secondary xylem in the inside and secondary phloem on the outside. The secondary phloem and secondary xylem cells lose their ability for further division; instead, they become mature to fulfill specific functions of the plant body, which include transportation of food and water, respectively. Phelloderm is a layer of secondary tissues that is produced by the dedifferentiated cork cambium. Similar to secondary xylem and phloem, phelloderm's cells lose their ability for further differentiation but become mature in order to perform specific functions such as limitation of dehydration and prevention of the entry of pathogens into the plant body due to the destruction of the epidermis.

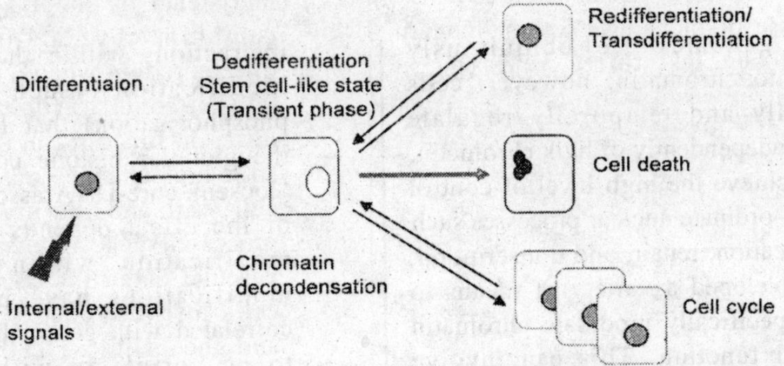

Figure: *Differentiation and Redifferentiation*

6. (*c*) Mycotoxins are toxic compounds that are naturally produced by certain types of moulds (fungi). Moulds that can produce mycotoxins grow on numerous foodstuffs such as cereals, dried fruits, nuts and spices. Mould growth can occur either before harvest or after harvest, during storage, on/in the food itself often under warm, damp and humid conditions. Most mycotoxins are chemically stable and survive food processing.

Several hundred different mycotoxins have been identified, but the most commonly observed mycotoxins that present a concern to human health and livestock include aflatoxins, ochratoxin A, patulin, fumonisins, zearalenone and nivalenol/deoxynivalenol. Mycotoxins appear in the food chain as a result of mould infection of crops both before and after harvest. Exposure to mycotoxins can happen either directly by eating infected food or indirectly from animals that are fed contaminated feed, in particular from milk. In chickens, the effects of aflatoxins include liver damage, impaired productivity and reproductive efficiency, decreased egg production, inferior eggshell quality, inferior carcass quality and increased susceptibility to disease. Pigs are also highly affected by aflatoxins, with the chronic effects largely apparent as liver damage. In cattle, the primary symptoms are reduced weight gain as well as liver and kidney damage; where milk production is also reduced. Different forms of the enzymes that metabolize aflatoxins (e.g. cytochrome P450s, glutathione S-transferases) are considered responsible for the different susceptibilities of different animals to the toxic effects of aflatoxins.

The worldwide contamination of foods and feeds with aflatoxins is a significant problem. Occurrence of aflatoxins is influenced by certain environmental factors. The extent of feed and food contamination with aflatoxins vary with geographic location, agricultural and agronomic practices, and the susceptibility of commodities to fungal invasion during preharvest, storage, and/or processing periods. The high toxicity and carcinogenicity of these compounds and their ability to cause various pathological conditions in human and animals has led to widespread screening of foods and feeds potentially contaminated with them. Crop contamination with aflatoxins causes significant economic loss for producers, marketers, and processors of diverse susceptible crops.

PAPER-II

1. (*a*) Eukaryotic genomes are ubiquitously associated into chromatin; however, cells must spatially and temporally regulate specific loci independently of bulk chromatin. In order to achieve the high level of control required to co-ordinate nuclear processes such as DNA replication, repair, and transcription, cells have developed a variety of means to locally and specifically modulate chromatin structure and function. This can involve covalent modification of histones, the incorporation of histone variants, and non-covalent remodelling by ATP-dependent remodelling enzymes.

Since they were discovered in the mid-1960s, histone modifications have been predicted to affect transcription. The fact that most of the early post-translational modifications found were concentrated within the tail extensions that protrude from the nucleosome core lead to two main theories regarding the mechanism of histone modification. The first of the theories suggested that they may affect electrostatic interactions between the histone tails and DNA to "loosen" chromatin structure. Later it was proposed that combinations of these modifications may create binding epitopes with which to recruit other proteins. Recently, given that more modifications have been found in the structured regions of histones, it has been put forward that these modifications may affect histone-DNA and histone-histone interactions within the nucleosome core. Modifications (such as acetylation or phosphorylation) that lower the charge of the globular histone core are predicted to "loosen" core-DNA association; the strength of the effect depends on location of the modification within the core. Some modifications have been shown to be correlated with gene silencing; others seem to be correlated with gene activation. Common modifications include acetylation, methylation, or ubiquitination of lysine; methylation of arginine; and phosphorylation of serine. The information stored in this way is considered epigenetic, since it is not encoded in the DNA but is still inherited to daughter cells. The maintenance of a repressed or activated status of a gene is often necessary for cellular differentiation.

Modifications to these proteins affect different processes in the cell such as the activation/inactivation of transcription, chromosome packaging, DNA damage and DNA repair. The modification of histones is an important post-translational process that plays a key role in gene expression.

Histone variants: Although histones are remarkably conserved throughout evolution, several variant forms have been identified. This diversification of histone function is restricted to H2A and H3, with H2B and H4 being mostly invariant. H2A can be replaced by H2AZ (which leads to reduced nucleosome stability) or H2AX (which is associated with DNA repair and T cell differentiation), whereas the inactive X chromosomes in mammals are enriched in macroH2A. H3 can be replaced by H3.3 (which correlates with activate genes and regulatory elements) and in centromeres H3 is replaced by CENPA.

ATP-dependent nucleosome remodelling: A number of distinct reactions are associated with the term ATP-dependent chromatin remodelling. Remodelling enzymes have been shown to slide nucleosomes along DNA, disrupt histone-DNA contacts to the extent of destabilizing the H2A/H2B dimer and to generate negative superhelical torsion in DNA and chromatin.

Dynamic nucleosome remodelling across the Yeast genome: Studies in 2007 have catalogued nucleosome positions in yeast and shown that nucleosomes are depleted in promoter regions and origins of replication. About 80% of the yeast genome appears to be covered by nucleosomes and the pattern of nucleosome positioning clearly relates to DNA regions that regulate transcription, regions that are transcribed and regions that initiate DNA replication.

Disulphide crosslinked nucleosome core particles: A recent advance in the production of nucleosome core particles with enhanced stability involves site-specific disulphide crosslinks. Two different crosslinks can be introduced into the nucleosome core particle. A first one crosslinks the two copies of H2A via an introduced cysteine (N38C) resulting in histone octamer which is stable against H2A/H2B dimer loss during nucleosome reconstitution. A second crosslink can be introduced between the H3 N-terminal histone tail and the nucleosome DNA ends via an incorporated convertible nucleotide. The DNA-histone octamer crosslink stabilizes the nucleosome core particle against DNA dissociation at very low particle concentrations and at elevated salt concentrations.

The surface of nucleosomes is studded with a multiplicity of modifications. At least eight different classes have been characterized to date and many different sites have been identified for each class. Operationally, modifications function either by disrupting chromatin contacts or by affecting the recruitment of nonhistone proteins to chromatin. Their presence on histones can dictate the higher-order chromatin structure in which DNA is packaged and can orchestrate the ordered recruitment of enzyme complexes to manipulate DNA. In this way, histone modifications have the potential to influence many fundamental biological processes, some of which may be epigenetically inherited.

Modifications to these proteins affect different processes in the cell such as the activation/inactivation of transcription, chromosome packaging, DNA damage and DNA repair. The modification of histones is an important post-translational process that plays a key role in gene expression.

1. (*b*) The behaviour of B chromosomes during mitosis differs from species to species. For example, in rye B chromosomes occupy central position at metaphase while in maize, they occupy peripheral position at metaphase. The meiotic behaviour of B chromosomes is studied during pachytene stage. They have been observed to behave in four different ways as given below:

(*i*) They do not pair with 'A' chromosome.

(*ii*) Lower degree of pairing is observed among 'B' chromosomes. Whenever they pair long B will pair with long B and short B with short B.

(*iii*) When single B chromosome is present, it remains univalent during pachytene. When two B chromosomes are present, they pair at pachytene but at metaphase remain as univalent. When more number of B chromosomes are present, they result in clumping of chromosomes at early stages of meiosis, but these chromosomes act as univalent at diakinesis and metaphase I.

(*iv*) Sometimes they show preferential non-disjunction during meiosis and post meiotic divisions as in case of Lilium and Trillium.

Effects of B-Chromosomes: B chromosomes are not essential for the normal growth and reproduction of plants and thus have no beneficial effects. However, effects of B chromosomes differ from species to species. In maize, B chromosomes lead to:

(*i*) Reduction in vigour and fertility,

(*ii*) Production of defective seeds with partially developed endosperm, and

(*iii*) Increase in the percentage of abortive pollens.

In Festuca, 1 or 2 B chromosomes have beneficial effect on vegetative growth. B chromosomes were found to have deleterious effects in rye and positive effects in wheat. B chromosomes are believed to originate from A chromosomes. Breakage of A chromosome and subsequent hetero chromatization leads to formation of B chromosomes.

1. (*c*) RNA, in one form or another, touches nearly everything in a cell. RNA carries out a broad range of functions, from translating genetic information into the molecular machines and structures of the cell to regulating the activity of genes during development, cellular differentiation, and changing environments. RNA is a unique polymer. Like DNA, it can bind with great specificity to either DNA or another RNA through complementary base pairing. It can also bind specific proteins or small molecules, and, remarkably, RNA can catalyze chemical reactions, including joining amino acids to make proteins. All the RNA in cells are themselves copies of DNA sequences contained in the genes of a cell's chromosomes. Genes that are copied-"transcribed"—into the instructions for making individual proteins are often referred to as "coding genes." The genes that produce RNAs used for other purposes are therefore called "noncoding RNA" genes.

RNA-based evolution is a theory that posits that RNA is not merely an intermediate between Watson and Crick model of the DNA molecule and proteins, but rather a far more dynamic and independent role-player in determining phenotype. By regulating the transcription in DNA sequences, the stability of RNA, and the capability of messenger RNA to be translated, RNA processing events allow for a diverse array of proteins to be synthesized from a single gene. Since RNA processing is heritable, it is subject to natural selection suggested by Darwin and contributes to the evolution and diversity of most eukaryotic organisms.

In accordance with the central dogma of molecular biology, RNA passes information between the DNA of a genome and the proteins expressed within an organism. Therefore, from an evolutionary standpoint, a mutation within the DNA bases results in an alteration of the RNA transcripts, which in turn leads to a direct difference in phenotype. RNA is also believed to have been the genetic material of the first life on Earth. The role of RNA in the origin of life is best supported by the ease of forming RNA from basic chemical building blocks (such as amino acids, sugars, and hydroxyl acids) that were likely present 4 billion years ago. Molecules of RNA have also been shown to effectively self-replicate, catalyze basic reactions, and store heritable information. As life progressed and evolved over time only DNA, which is much more chemically stable than RNA, could support large genomes and eventually took over the role as the major carrier of genetic information.

Most RNA processing events work in concert with one another and produce networks of regulating processes that allow a greater variety of proteins to be expressed than those strictly directed by the genome. These RNA processing events can also be passed on from generation to generation via reverse transcription into the genome. Over time, RNA networks that produce the fittest phenotypes will be more likely to be maintained in a population, contributing to evolution. Studies have shown that RNA processing events have especially been critical with the fast phenotypic evolution of vertebrates—large jumps in phenotype explained by changes in RNA processing events. Human genome searches have also revealed RNA processing events that have provided significant "sequence space for more variability". On the whole, RNA processing expands the possible phenotypes of a given genotype and contributes to the evolution and diversity of life.

1. (*d*) Types and Applications of Molecular Markers: For many years, gene mapping was limited to identifying organisms by traditional phenotype markers. This included genes that encoded easily observable characteristics such as blood types or seed shapes. The insufficient number of these types of characteristics in several organisms limited the mapping efforts that could be done. This prompted the development of gene markers which could identify genetic characteristics that are not readily observable in organisms (such as protein variation).

Some commonly used types of molecular markers are:

- RFLP (or Restriction fragment length polymorphism)
- SSLP (or Simple sequence length polymorphism)
- AFLP (or Amplified fragment length polymorphism)
- RAPD (or Random amplification of polymorphic DNA)
- VNTR (or Variable number tandem repeat)
- SSR Microsatellite polymorphism, (or Simple sequence repeat)
- SNP (or Single nucleotide polymorphism)
- STR (or Short tandem repeat)
- SFP (or Single feature polymorphism)
- DArT (or Diversity Arrays Technology)
- RAD markers (or Restriction site associated DNA markers)

Molecular genetic markers can be divided into two classes (a) biochemical markers which detect variation at the gene product level such as changes in proteins and amino acids and (b) molecular markers which detect variation at the DNA level such as nucleotide changes: deletion, duplication, inversion and/ or insertion. Markers can exhibit two modes of inheritance, *i.e.* dominant/recessive or co-dominant. If the genetic pattern of homo-zygotes can be distinguished from that of hetero-zygotes, then a marker is said to be co-dominant. Generally co-dominant markers are more informative than the dominant markers.

Genetic markers can be used to study the relationship between an inherited disease and its genetic cause (for example, a particular mutation of a gene that results in a defective protein). It is known that pieces of DNA that lie near each other on a chromosome tend to be inherited together. This property enables the use of a marker, which can then be used to determine the precise inheritance pattern of the gene that has not yet been exactly localized.

Application of Molecular Markers: Molecular markers are employed in genealogical DNA testing for genetic genealogy to determine genetic distance between individuals or populations. Uniparental markers (on mitochondrial or Y chromosomal DNA) are studied for assessing maternal or paternal lineages. Autosomal markers are used for all ancestry.

Molecular markers have to be easily identifiable, associated with a specific locus, and highly polymorphic, because homozygotes do not provide any information. Detection of the marker can be direct by RNA sequencing, or indirect using allozymes.

Some of the methods used to study the genome or phylogenetics are RFLP, AFLP, RAPD, SSR. They can be used to create genetic maps of whatever organism is being studied.

There was a debate over what the transmissible agent of CTVT (canine transmissible venereal tumor) was. Many researchers hypothesized that virus like particles were responsible for transforming the cell, while others thought that the cell itself was able to infect other canines as an allograft. With the aid of genetic markers, researchers were able to provide conclusive evidence that the cancerous tumor cell evolved into a transmissible parasite. Furthermore, molecular genetic markers were used to resolve the issue of natural transmission, the breed of origin (phylogenetics), and the age of the canine tumor.

Molecular markers have also been used to measure the genomic response to selection in livestock. Natural and artificial selection leads to a change in the genetic makeup of the cell. The presence of different alleles due to a distorted segregation at the genetic markers is indicative of the difference between selected and non-selected livestock.

2. (*a*) The synaptonemal complex (SC) is a protein structure that forms between homologous chromosomes (two pairs of sister chromatids) during meiosis and is thought to mediate synapsis and recombination during meiosis I in eukaryotes. It is currently thought that the SC functions primarily as a scaffold to allow interacting chromatids to complete their crossover activities.

Structure and Function of Synaptonemal complex: In the last post we discussed the process of crossing over. In the post DNA packaging, we discussed how complex is the packaging mechanism? In the process of crossing over three major happenings takes place first breakage, then movement of these segments (transposition) and fusion by ligase in correct position. In the sea of genetic material, a process like crossing over to take place there should be a framework or a mechanism with all the necessary enzymes to carry out the process effectively. I once again want to tell you when we move deep down into the cell to explain the happenings in this minute system I often think these words are not powerful enough to convey the reality. It is incredibly amazing. Synaptonemal complex is the structure assigned with the duty of carrying out the process "crossing over".

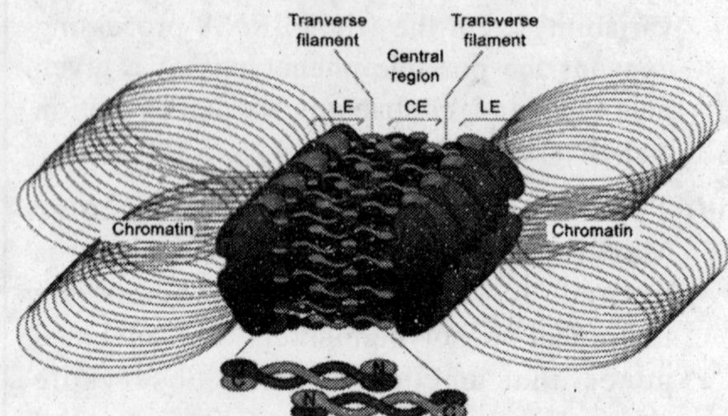

Figure: *Synaptonemal complex*

Synaptonemal complex is a highly organised structure of filaments seen between synapsed chromosome during zygotene and pachytene stages of prophase I of meiosis I. The structure is complex and we got the detail only with an electron microscope.

Synaptonemal complex consists of three parallel dense lines that are equally spaced or it is a tripartite ribbon like structure. It is a 0.2 uM thick protein rich frame work. These lateral lines are flanked by chromatin. The two lateral lines are denser than the central line. Each lateral line is attached to the inner side of the homologous chromosome. The central and lateral elements are joined by LC fibres (L lateral to C cental fibres). The ends of lateral elements are attached to the inner surface of nuclear membrane. Lateral lines are rich in DNA, RNA and protein whereas central line has RNA and protein with little DNA. Synaptonemal complex is essential for chiasma formation and crossing over. Recombination process is carried out by a large protein assembly of 90 nm diameter called Recombination nodule (RNs) seen on the central element of Synaptonemal complex.

The major functions of Synaptonemal complex:

1. Maintenance of synapsis in fixed state for an extended period for crossing over to occur.
2. To provide a structural framework within which exchange of segments takes place.
3. To segregate recombination DNA from the rest of other chromosomal DNA.

Different Structural Types of DNA: Pictures of the double helix of deoxyribonucleic acid (DNA) have become so common that everyone is familiar with its overall shape and structure (Figure 1a). This structure is known as B-DNA, and represents an average conformation of DNA, based on fibre diffraction studies. However, this average shape of DNA is very unlikely to exist within the cells of living organisms, for several reasons. First, there is simply not enough room for the DNA to be stretched out in a perfect, linear B-DNA conformation. In nearly all cells, from simple bacteria through complex eukaryotes, the DNA must be compacted by more than a thousandfold in order even to fit inside the cell or nucleus. Furthermore, refined resolution of the structure of DNA, based on X-ray crystallography of short synthetic pieces of DNA, has shown that there is considerable variance of the helical structure of DNA, based on the sequence. For example, a 200-bp piece of DNA can run as if it were more than 1000 bp on an acrylamide gel, if it has the right sequence. The double helix is not the same uniform structure. The structure (and function) of DNA depends on the sequence of the DNA. There are three families of DNA helices: A-DNA, which can readily form within certain stretches of purines (e.g. GAGGGA); B-DNA, which is favoured by mixed sequences (although the exact conformation depends on the particular nucleotide sequence, as described below); and Z-DNA, which is favoured by alternating pyrimidine—purine steps (e.g. CGCGCG). The A- and B-DNA families are right-handed helices, while the Z-DNA family has a left-handed orientation of the helix, as shown in Figure 1b. These different conformations of the DNA helix have important biological functions.

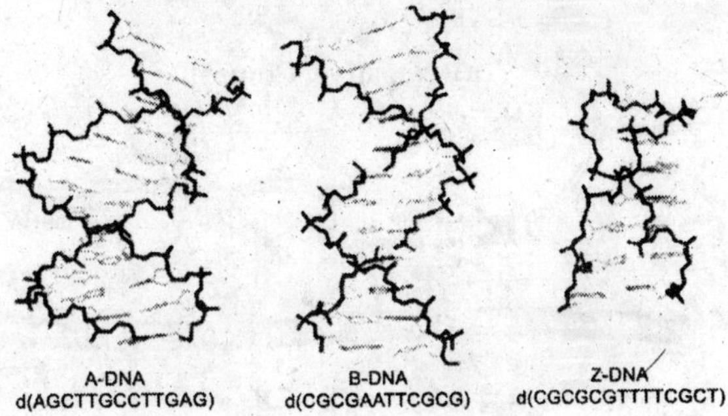

2. (*b*) Lac Operon: "Lac operon is an operon or a group of genes with a single promoter that encode genes for the transport and metabolism of lactose in E.coli and other bacteria."

Gene regulation in prokaryotes can be explained with the help of Lac Operon model. Here the alteration in physiological and environmental conditions can be observed leading to an alteration in expression in prokaryotes. It was observed by Jacob and Monod. The lac operon consists of:

- Regulatory gene *i*: It codes for the repressor protein.
- *z* gene: It codes for beta-galactosidase which catalyzes the hydrolysis of lactose into glucose and galactose.
- *y* gene: It codes for permease which regulates the lactose permeability in the cell.

- *a* gene - It codes for transacetylase which assists the enzyme beta-galactosidase.

Hence, all these genes help in the lactose metabolism. In lac operon, lactose acts as an inducer. If lactose is provided in the medium for the bacteria, the regulatory gene is activated. The inducer will bind to the repressor protein and render it inactive which allows transcription of the operon. Thus, lac operon is negatively regulated in this case.

Gene regulation in eukaryotes is regulated by transcriptional activators and repressors. The repressors bind to specific DNA sequences and inhibit transcription. In eukaryotes, transcription involves several steps. It occurs in both, nucleus (transcription) and cytoplasm (translation).

Negative and Positive Control of Lac Operon: The lac operon exhibits both systems. It is a negative control system because expression is typically blocked by an active repressor (the lac repressor) that turns off transcription. The lac repressor binds to the operator region and negatively controls (prevents) transcription. However, when CAP (catabolite gene activating protein) binds upstream of this operator region near the promoter and transcription increases, this is an example of a positive control system. We see this positive control of transcription happen when glucose levels decline.

(a) Negative Control

Inducer
Inactive repressor
Transcription
mRNA
R
P O
A B C
Active repressor
No transcription

(b) Positive Control

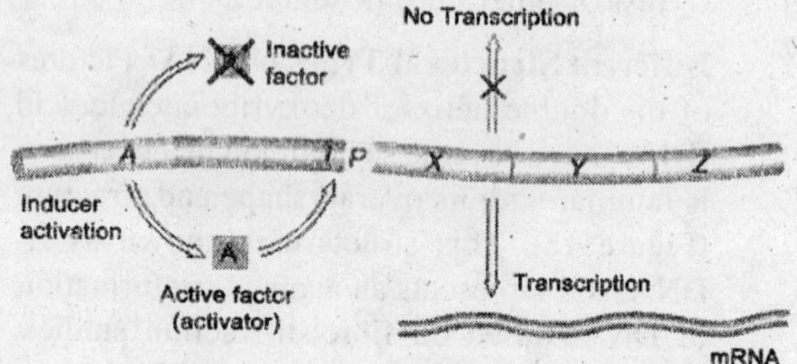

2. (*c*) Base analogs are molecules which have a very similar structure to one of the four nitrogenous bases which are used in DNA (adenine, guanine, cytosine or thymine). They form a structure similar to one of the DNA nucleotides and then can be used to form the new strand in semi conservative replication. This means that the base analog is now incorporated into the DNA double helix. Once in the DNA helix, some base analogs change shape. This means if used as a template strand during replication, they will pair with a different base and cause a base change mutation.

An example of a base analog which can be mutagenic is 5-bromouracil which has a similar structure to Thymine so will form hydrogen bonds with Adenine in the template strand. It can then change shape so it is complementary to guanine. This means the base change would be thymine-adenine to guanine-cytosine.

Mutations are also caused by compounds that substitue for normal bases (base analogs) or slip between the bases (intercalating agents) to cause errors in replication. Base analogs are structurally similar to proper bases but differ in ways that make them treacherous to the cell. Thus base analogs are similar enough to the proper base to get taken by cells, converted in to nucleoside triphosphates, and incoporated into DNA during replication. But, because of the structural difference between these analogues and the proper bases, the analogues base-pair inaccurately, leading to frequent mistakes during the replication process. One of the most mutagenic base analogs is 5-bromouracil, an analog of thymine. The presence of bromo substituent allows the base to mispair with guanine via enol tautomer.

5-bromouracil (5-BU) is a derivative of uracil and behaves as a thymine analog, which increases the probability of a tautomeric shift from the normal keto form to the enol form, mis-pairing with guanine instead of adenine. After one round of replication, an A – T to G – C transition mutation results.

Intercalating agents are flat molecules containing several polycyclic rings that bind to the equally flat purine or pyrimidine bases of DNA. Intercalating agents are compounds, such as proflavin, acridine and ethidium, that can bind to the major and minor grooves of DNA and cause addition or deletion of bases during replication. They may result in a frameshift mutation, which can alter the codon reading frame and result in aberrant DNA transcription and replication.

Thymine | 5-Bromouracil (keto form) | 5-Bromouracil (enol form)

5-BU (keto form) | Adenine | 5-BU (enol form) | Guanine

5. (*a*) Seed dormancy can be defined as the state or a condition in which seeds are prevented from germinating even under the favourable environmental conditions for germination including, temperature, water, light, gas, seed coats, and other mechanical restrictions.The main reason behind these conditions is that they require a period of rest before being capable of germination. This conditions may vary from days to months and even years. These conditions are the combination of light, water, heat, gases, seed coats and hormone structures. Plant growth regulators or other chemicals can be used in induced germination growth regulators.

Role of Abscisic acid (Plant Growth Inhibitors) in the Regulation of Seed Dormancy

It is a growth inhibitor which was discovered in the 1960s. It was initially called dormant. Later another compound abscisin-II was discovered and are commonly called as abscisic acid. This growth inhibitor is synthesized within the stem, leaves, fruits, and seeds of the plant. Abscisic acid mostly acts as an antagonist to Gibberellic acid. It is also known as the stress hormone as it helps by increasing the tolerance of plants to different kinds of stress.

Functions of Abscisic acid

1. Stimulates closing of stomata in the epidermis.

2. Helps in the development and maturation of seeds.
3. Inhibits plant metabolism and seed germination.
4. It is involved in regulating abscission and dormancy.
5. It is widely used as a spraying agent on trees to regulate dropping of fruits.
6. Induces dormancy in seeds and helps in withstanding desiccation and other unfavourable growth factors.

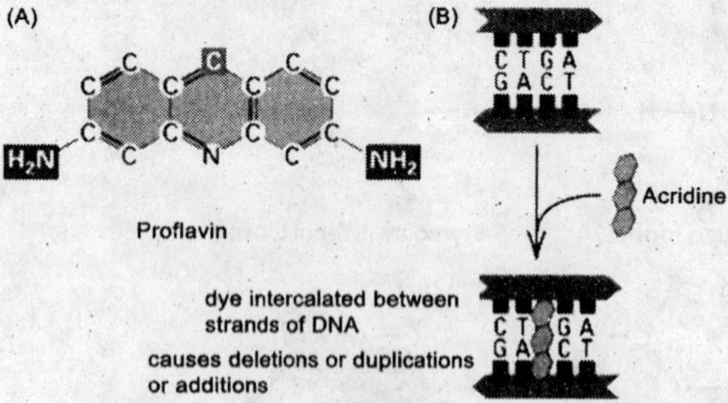

Role of Cytokinin in the Regulation of Seed Dormancy

These are produced in the regions where cell division occurs; mostly in the roots and shoots. They help in the production of new leaves, lateral shoot growth, chloroplasts in leaves etc. They help in overcoming apical dominance and delay ageing of leaves.

Functions of Cytokinins

1. Break bud and seed dormancy.
2. Promotes the growth of the lateral bud.
3. Promotes cell division and apical dominance.
4. They are used to keep flowers fresh for a longer time.
5. Used in tissue culture to induce cell division in mature tissues.
6. Promote lateral shoot growth and adventitious shoot formation.
7. Promote nutrient mobilization which in turn helps delay leaf senescence.
8. Helps in delaying the process of ageing (senescence) in fresh leaf crops like cabbage and lettuce.
9. Involved in the formation of new leaves and chloroplast organelles within the plant cell.
10. Used to induce the development of shoot and roots along with auxin, depending on the ratio.

5. (*b*) Plant growth regulators (also called plant hormones) are numerous chemical substances that profoundly influence the growth and differentiation of plant cells, tissues and organs. Plant growth regulators function as chemical messengers for intercellular communication.

Auxins: Auxins (Gk. *auxein* = to grow) are weakly acidic growth hormones having an unsaturated ring structure and capable of promoting cell elongation, especially of shoots (more pronounced in decapitated shoots and shoot segments) at a concentration of less than 100 ppm which is inhibitory to the roots. Among the growth regulators, auxins were the first to be discovered.

Types of auxins: There are two major categories of auxins: natural auxins and synthetic auxins:

- **Natural auxins:** These are naturally occurring auxins in plants and therefore, regarded as **phytohormones**. Indole 3-acetic acid (IAA) is the best known and universal auxin. It is found in all plants and fungi.
- **Synthetic auxins:** These are synthetic compounds which cause various physiological responses common to IAA. Some of the important synthetic auxins are 2,

4-D (2, 4-dichlorophenoxy acetic acid) is the weedicide. IBA is both natural and synthetic auxin.

Functions of auxins: Auxins control several kinds of plant growth processes. These are as follows:

- **Cell elongation:** Auxins promote elongations and growth of stems and roots and enlargement of many fruits by stimulating elongation of cells in all directions.
- **Apical dominance:** In many plants, the apical bud grows and the lower axillary buds are suppressed. Removal of apical bud results in the growth of lower buds. The auxin (IAA) of the terminal bud inhibits the growth of lateral buds. This phenomenon is known as apical dominance.
- **Weed control:** Weeds are undesirable in a field with a crop. By the spray of 2, 4-D, broad-leaved weeds can be destroyed but 2, 4-D does not affect mature monocotyledonous plants.
- **Root differentiation**
- **Control of lodging**
- **Parthenocarpy:** Parthenocarpy can be induced by application of IAA in a paste form to the stigma of a flower or by spraying the flowers with a dilute solution of IAA.

Gibberellins: Gibberellins are weakly acidic hormones having gibbane ring structure which cause cell elongation of intact plants in general and increased internodal length of genetically dwarfed plants (*i.e.*, corn, pea) in particular.

Functions of gibberellin

- **Stem elongation:** The gibberellins induce elongation of the internodes.
- **Leaf expansion:** In many plants leaves become broader and elongated when treated with gibberellic acid.
- **Reversal of dwarfism:** One of the most striking effects of gibberellins is the elongation of genetic dwarf (mutant) varieties of plants like corn and pea.
- **Bolting and Flowering:** Gibberellins induce stem elongation in 'rosette plants' e.g., cabbage, henbane, etc. Such plants show retarded internodal growth and profuse leaf development. In these plants just prior to the reproductive phase, the internodes elongate enormously causing a marked increase in stem height. This is called bolting.
- **Enzyme formation:** One of the most dramatic effects of GA is its induction of hydrolytic enzymes in the aleurone layer of endosperm of germinating barley seeds and cereal grains. GA stimulates the production of digestive enzymes like proteases, a-amylases, lipases which help to mobilise stored nutrients.

Cytokinins (Phytokinins): Cytokinins are plant growth hormones which are basic in nature, either aminopurine or phenyl urea derivatives that promote cell division (cytokinesis) either alone or in conjugation with auxin.

Functions of cytokinins

- **Cell division:** Cytokinins are essential for cytokinesis and thus promote cell division. In presence of auxin, cytokinins stimulate cell division even in non-meristematic tissues.
- **Cell enlargement and Differentiation:** Under some conditions cytokinins enhance the expansion of leaf cells in leaf discs and cotyledons. These cells considered to be mature and under normal conditions do not expand.
- **Delay in senescence:** Cytokinin delay the senescence (ageing) of leaves and other organs by controlling protein synthesis and mobilization of resources (Disappearance of chlorophyll). It is called Richmond Lang effect.

- **Counteraction of apical dominance:** Auxins and cytokinins act antagonistically in the control of apical dominance. Auxins are responsible for stimulating growth of apical bud.
- **Breaking of dormancy:** Cytokinins breaks seeds dormancy of various types and thus help in their germination.
- **Accumulation and Translocation of solutes**

5. (*c*) • Alpha diversity refers to the average species diversity in a habitat.
   - Beta diversity refers to the differences in species composition.
   - Gamma diversity is the measure of the overall number of species.

The terms alpha, beta, and gamma diversity are used to describe the spatial component of biodiversity.

Alpha diversity: Alpha diversity is just the diversity of each site (local species pool). It refers to the average species diversity in a habitat or specific area. Alpha diversity is a local measure, the number of species found in a particular area or ecosystem. For example; Habitat X has 5 species of ants—Therefore, the alpha diversity for ants in this place is 5.

Beta diversity: Beta diversity represents the differences in species composition among sites. It refers to the ratio between local or alpha diversity and regional diversity. This is the diversity of species between two habitats or regions. It is the variation of the species composition between two habitats or regions. It considers the alpha diversity of the habitats and the number of unique species on each habitat. It is calculated by the following equation; (number species in habitat 1- number of species habitat 2&1 have in common) + (number of sp in H2- number of sp H1&2 have in common).

Gamma diversity: Gamma diversity is the diversity of the entire landscape (regional species pool). It is the total diversity of a landscape and is a combination of both alpha and beta diversity. It is a measure of the overall number of species (the diversity) within a region. It is basically the sum of all the species of all habitats within the region of interest.

Alpha, Beta and Gamma Biodiversity and it relation with different spatial scales of Ecosystem: Scale is absolutely critical in ecological studies. Everything, and I mean everything, depends on the scale at which it is defined. This is true for species diversity as well. Diversity of species (sometimes communities) in a landscape is generally observed in three different scales.

Alpha diversity is the diversity within a community at a particular site. When we casually speak of diversity in an area, more often than not it refers to alpha diversity. This diversity is on a small scale, generally of the size of one ecosystem. Beta diversity is the diversity of species between two communities (or ecosystems). It is at a larger scale, and looks to compare the diversity between two separate entities that are often divided by a clear geographical barrier like a river or a mountain ridge. Gamma diversity is a very large scale, where diversity is compared between many ecosystems, at the level of a biome. It could range over areas like the entire slope of a mountain, the entire littoral zone of a sea shore etc.

5. (*d*) The International Union for Conservation of Nature (IUCN) is the world's oldest and largest global environmental organisation. Founded in 1948, today IUCN the largest professional global conservation network. IUCN has more than 1,200 member organizations including 200+ government and 900+ non-government organizations. The Union's headquarters are located in Gland, near Geneva, in Switzerland. Conserving biodiversity is central to the mission of IUCN. The main areas of function are:

1. Science—the IUCN Red List of Threatened Species™.
2. Action—hundreds of conservation projects all over the world.
3. Influence—through the collective strength of more than 1,200 government and non-governmental member organizations.

IUCN Red Data Book : Threatened Species classification: Threatened species are any species which are vulnerable to extinction in the near future. International Union for Conservation of Nature treats threatened species not as a single category, but as a group of three categories: vulnerable, endangered, and critically endangered, depending on the degree to which they are threatened.

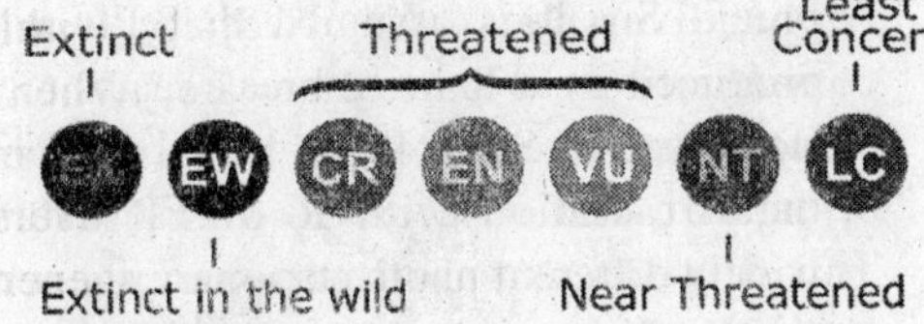

Critically Endangered Species: Critically Endangered (Cr) is the highest risk category assigned by the IUCN for wild species. Critically endangered species means a species numbers have decreased, or will decrease by 80% within three generations. It is therefore considered to be facing an extremely high risk of extinction in the wild.

Endangered (EN) species: Endangered (EN) species is a population of organisms which is at risk of becoming extinct because it is either few in numbers, or threatened by changing environmental or predation parameters. Also it could mean that due to deforestation there may be a lack of food and/or water. It is therefore considered to be facing a very high risk of extinction in the wild.

Vulnerable (VU) species: Vulnerable (VU) species is a species which has been categorised by the IUCN as likely to become endangered unless the circumstances threatening its survival and reproduction improve. It is therefore considered to be facing a high risk of extinction in the wild.

Other divisions: Extinct, Functionally Extinct and Extinct in the wild: A species becomes extinct when the last existing member of that species dies. Extinction therefore becomes a certainty when there are no surviving individuals that are able to reproduce and create a new generation. A species may become functionally extinct when only a handful of individuals survive, which are unable to reproduce due to poor health, age, sparse distribution over a large range, a lack of individuals of both sexes (in sexually reproducing species), or other reasons.

Status of Plants and Animals : 2012 list

Of the total 63,837 species globally assessed plants and animals, the IUCN classified the numbers as below in 2012.

1. 81 as Extinct.
2. 63 as Extinct in the Wild.
3. 3,947 as Critically Endangered.
4. 5766 species in Endangered.
5. 10,104 in Vulnerable.
6. 4,467 in Near Threatened.
7. 10,497 species - Data Deficient.

List of Extinct Plants in India: Extinct plants are enlisted in Red Data book of Botanical Survey of India. As per the Red Data book of Botanical Survey of India (BSI), 17 plants have been recorded as extinct. However, during recent exploration by BSI in some of the previously unexplored areas, numbers of such reported extinct species of plants have been rediscovered.

5. (*e*) The four types of intellectual property include: 1. Trade Secrets, 2. Trademarks, 3. Copyrights, and 4. Patents.

The first type of intellectual property right is a trade secret. All inventions generally start out as a trade secret of the inventor. Inventors have an instinctual desire to keep their ideas secret. To market your invention, you should protect your idea with one or more of the other types of intellectual property rights: patents, trademarks, and copyrights.

4 types of intellectual property to protect your idea:

Trade Secrets

- Protects secret information
- E.g., New invention, Coke formula

Trade Marks

- Protects brands
- E.g., Apple for cell phones

Copy Rights

- Protects works of authorship
- E.g., books, movies, drawings

Patents

- Protects functional or ornamental features
- E.g., swipe feature or iPhone design

The Indian Patent Act is being amended, in part, because of our commitments under General Agreement on Trade and Tariff (GATT). Similar considerations have prompted us to formulate a Protected Plant Varieties Act. At the same time, a National Biological Diversity Act is also on the anvil in response to our commitments to the Convention on Biological Diversity (CBD). The CBD has advanced beyond the conventional intellectual property rights (IPR) regime to accept the sovereign rights of nations over their biodiversity resources, and the need thereof to share benefits of commercial applications of traditional knowledge of sustainable uses of biodiversity resources with local communities. It is important for India to benefit from these provisions and create a legislative framework that would be a model for other developing countries as well. Intellectual Property Rights (IPR) are now being extended to biological resources, beyond the conventional domain of mechanical and chemical innovations. On this new biological frontier, considerable pertinent knowledge and resources already exist in the public domain, and CBD has clearly accepted the need to respect and share its benefits with these public-domain resources. These considerations must be reflected in the Amended Patent Act. It is also vital that we ensure a proper harmonization of the provisions of the new Patent Act, Protected Plant Varieties Act, and the Biological Diversity Act.

6. (*a*) **Phytochrome associated with Flowering**

In Short-Day Plants (SDP): In several SDP like Xanthium, soybean, Amaranthus, Chrysanthemum, Pharbitis and Chenopodium, night break by R inhibits flowering and FR is effective in reversing a red light (R) night break. So, it is assumed that Pfr which is produced by a R night break reacts to inhibit flowering in SDP. It has also been observed that irradiation with R or FR establishes widely different photo stationary states of 0.75 and 0.03, respectively, yet both when applied singly prevent flowering. Thus it is clear that inhibition of flowering is not proportional to the amount of Pfr. but it depends on the maintenance of the Pfr level for sufficient time above some threshold level. A relatively short exposure with R is effective in preventing flowering in SDP because it induces a high photo stationary state (Pfr/P = 0.75). Thus, when the plants are returned to darkness, it takes a relatively long time for Pfr to decay below the threshold level.

There is evidence that phytochrome controls flowering response in SDP not only in the dark period, but also during the day period. In Xanthium and Pharbitis, the light quality during a light period intervening between a subcritical dark period and an inductive dark period strongly favour flower formation. Action spectra indicate that the maximum promotion is at 660 nm and inhibition at 730 nm. It is likely that phytochrome is the photoreceptor since there is evidence of R/FR reversibility. Again, in dark-grown a seedling of Pharbitis, a prior exposure to light with either long or brief R irradiation is required if a single inductive dark period is to be effective for flowering. The effect of R irradiation is reversible with FR, hence it indicates that phytochrome is the photoreceptor.

In Long-Day Plants (LDP): It is generally believed that phytochrome controls opposite reactions in SDP and LDP. This means that light interruptions of long nights which inhibit flowering in SDP should promote flowering in LDP. Basically this is true but very brief interruptions of long nights do not always promote flowering in many LDP. Generally, a long night break is effective for LDP. The light quality during prolonged night breaks shows that either FR or R and sometimes a mixture of R and FR is effective in promoting flowering in LDP. It has further been demonstrated that flowering in various LDP is more enhanced with incandescent lamp with a high proportion of FR energy than with fluorescent lamps having less FR energy. In crucifers, neither R nor FR shows marked acceleration of flowering. Here blue light is most effective either as night interruption or as day extension.

The exact identity of the blue light photoreceptor is not yet known hence the name crypto chrome has been given which implies a "**hidden pigment**". In view of the similarity between the absorption spectra of β-carotene and riboflavin and the action spectrum for phototropism. It has been proposed that carotenoids and flavins are the probable photoreceptors or crypto chrome for blue light responses. Carotenoid zeaxanthin has recently been implicated as a blue light photoreceptor. It has photo-protective role and a role in signal transduction. Absorption spectrum of zeaxanthin closely matches the action spectrum for blue light stimulated stomatal opening. The most common flavins occurring widely in living organisms are riboflavin and its two nucleotide derivatives, flavin mononucleotide (FMN) and flavin adenine dinucleotide (FAD). Blue light has been shown to regulate gene expression. The gene that codes for the enzyme chalcone synthase (for flavonoid biosynthesis) is blue light regulated, while the gene for the small subunit of Rubisco and for the, proteins that bind chlorophylls *a* and *b* are not only sensitive to red light (*i.e.*, phytochrome response), but also sensitive to blue light. Another enzyme, glutamyl semi-aldehyde-amino-transferase, a key enzyme in chlorophyll biosynthetic pathway, is encoded by GSA gene which is sensitive to blue light. Recently, a gene has been isolated from Arabidopsis, which has been shown to encode the blue photoreceptor that causes inhibition of hypocotyl elongation. The gene and the corresponding protein have been named CRY 1 (for crypto chrome 1). Two chromophores are likely to be associated with CRY 1. One of them is a flavin (FAD) and the other is possibly a pterin. In view of the above observations, several hypotheses have been put forward to account for the promotive effect of FR and the requirement of prolonged exposure to light in LDP. It has been argued whether phytochrome is the only photoreceptor involved in photo induction in LDP.

6. (*b*) Significance of Photo-inductive Cycles: The concept of photo-inductive cycle suggest that some factor involved in flowering is accumulated during the inductive cycle. In some plants, e.g., Xanthium enough of this factor is accumulated after only one cycle to promote flowering. In other plants, more than one inductive cycle is needed. In long-day plants the non-inductive cycle as in Plantago lanceolata. However, in short-day plants non-inductive cycle appears to be inhibitory. It inhibits the effect of previous inductive cycle.

A plant, if subjected to certain length of day period and night period in 24-36 hours duration, then it is called one photoperiodic cycle. Such periodic cycle responsible for inducing flower formation, is referred to as 'photo inductive cycle'. The required number of photo inductive cycles varies from species to species; this is because of inherent genetic makeup of the said plant. For example, Cockleburr needs just one photo inductive cycle but plants like *Plantago lanceolata* or *Salvia accidentales* require at least 17-25 cycles for 100% flowering. If the provided inductive cycles are less than what is required, the number of flowers produced in such plants will be less than 100%. This suggests that during the inductive cycles some flower inducing material gets accumulated and if such a substance produced reaches a threshold value the flower production is maximal.

It is important to know that the photoperiodic response is 'all or none' phenomenon. Once the provided stimulus produces a proper impact on the genome, the flowering is initiated and once it is initiated it cannot be reverted to vegetative condition under normal circumstances.

Using different lengths of light and dark period, it is noticed that the dark period is important for short day plants for flowering. Shortening of photoperiod has profound influence on the quantitative yield of flowers. The importance of photoperiod, *i.e.* Day period on short day plants is very interesting. For example Xanthium requires 15½ of continuous dark period and 8½ hours of day period for 100% flowering. If such a plant that is maintained with 15½ long dark period and the day period is shorted by 2 or 3 hours, the total number of flowers produced will be significantly lower than the plant that is exposed to 8½ hours of day period. This suggests that the photoperiod affects flowering ability in quantitative terms, it means that proper dark period is essential for flowering but one cannot expect the plant to grow and produce flowers in continuous dark. This is because light is required for photosynthesis for it provides energy rich and components for the development of floral primordia. If the photosynthate supply is not adequate the total growth of the floral axis is affected. In fact, in one of the experiments, a short day plant which is kept in continuous dark conditions is induced to produce flowers by providing sugar solution to the leaves.

6. (*c*) Fire ecology is a scientific discipline concerned with natural processes involving fire in a ecosystem and the ecological effects, the interactions between fire and the abiotic and biotic components of an ecosystem, and the role as an ecosystem process.

Many ecosystems, particularly praire, savanna, chaparral and coniferous forests, have evolved with fire as an essential contributor to habitat vitality and renewal.

Tropical forest ecosystems are capable of storing large quantities of carbon in tree, other organic matter, and soil. Forests may add to the pool of carbon dioxide in the atmosphere through fire in tropical forests. Tropical forest may also reduce the amount of carbon dioxide in the atmosphere through increases in biomass and organic matter accumulation. Because of the relation between forests and atmosphere carbon dioxide would result in storage of additional carbon and thus reduce atmospheric CO_2. Changes in the surface energy budget of the forest following fire give a good indication of the changes that occur in the surface characteristics of a tropical forests as it recovers from disturbance. It can also observe the impacts that climate will have on the energy balance in years of drought and in extremely wet conditions. Latent heat flux recovering vegetation effects the energy balance by controlling how much water is transpired from the plants.

7. (*a*) Cytochromes are iron-containing proteins that facilitate the movement of electrons in a wide variety of metabolic processes. Cytochromes are widely distributed throughout nature. They are found in all eukaryotes and in most, but not all, prokaryotes.

An electron transport chain (ETC) is a series of complexes that transfer electrons from electron donors to electron acceptors via redox (both reduction and oxidation occurring simultaneously) reactions, and couples this electron transfer with the transfer of protons (H^+ ions) across a membrane. This creates an electrochemical proton gradient that drives the synthesis of adenosine triphosphate (ATP), a molecule that stores energy chemically in the form of highly strained bonds. The molecules of the chain include peptides, enzymes (which are proteins or protein complexes), and others. The final acceptor of electrons in the electron transport chain during aerobic respiration is molecular oxygen although a variety of acceptors other than oxygen such as sulphate exist in anaerobic respiration. Electron transport chains are used for extracting energy via redox reactions from sunlight in photosynthesis or, such as in the case of the oxidation of sugars, cellular respiration. In eukaryotes, an important electron transport chain is found in the inner mitochondrial membrane where it serves as the site of oxidative phosphorylation through the action of ATP synthase. It is also found in the thylakoid membrane of the chloroplast in photosynthetic eukaryotes. In bacteria, the electron transport chain is located in their cell membrane.

In chloroplasts, light drives the conversion of water to oxygen and $NADP^+$ to NADPH with transfer of H^+ ions across chloroplast membranes. In mitochondria, it is the conversion of oxygen to water, NADH to NAD^+ and succinate to fumarate that are required to generate the proton gradient.

Electron transport chains are major sites of premature electron leakage to oxygen, generating superoxide and potentially resulting in increased oxidative stress.

The electron transport chain consists of a spatially separated series of redox reactions in which electrons are transferred from a donor molecule to an acceptor molecule. The underlying force driving these reactions is the Gibbs free energy of the reactants and products. The Gibbs free energy is the energy available ("free") to do work. Any reaction that decreases the overall Gibbs free energy of a system is thermodynamically spontaneous.

The function of the electron transport chain is to produce a transmembrane proton electrochemical gradient as a result of the redox reactions. If protons flow back through the membrane, they enable mechanical work, such as rotating bacterial flagella. ATP synthase, an enzyme highly conserved among all domains of life, converts this mechanical work into chemical energy by producing ATP, which powers most cellular reactions. A small amount of ATP is available from the substrate-level phosphorylation, for example, in glycolysis. In most organisms the majority of ATP is generated in electron transport chains.

In oxidative phosphorylation, electrons are transferred from a low-energy electron donor (e.g., NADH) to an acceptor (e.g., O_2) through an electron transport chain. In photo-phosphorylation, the energy of sunlight is used to *create* a high-energy electron donor and an electron acceptor. Electrons are then transferred from the donor to the acceptor through another electron transport chain.

Photosynthetic electron transport chains, like the mitochondrial chain, can be considered as a special case of the bacterial systems. They use mobile, lipid-soluble quinone carriers (phylloquinone and plastoquinone) and mobile, water-soluble carriers (cytochromes, etc.). They also contain a proton pump. It is remarkable that the proton pump in all photosynthetic chains resembles mitochondrial *Complex III.*

Photosynthetic electron transport chains are discussed in greater detail in the articles Light-dependent reaction.

Electron transport chains are redox reactions that transfer electrons from an electron donor to an electron acceptor. The transfer of electrons is coupled to the translocation of protons across a membrane, producing a proton gradient. The proton gradient is used to produce useful work. About 30 work units are produced per electron transport.

7. (*b*) Photolysis of Water: Photodissociation, photolysis, or photodecomposition is a chemical reaction in which a chemical compound is broken down by photons. It is defined as the interaction of one or more photons with one target molecule. Photodissociation is not limited to visible light. Any photon with sufficient energy can affect the chemical bonds of a chemical compound. Since a photon's energy is inversely proportional to its wavelength, electromagnetic waves with the energy of visible light or higher, such as ultraviolet light, x-rays and gamma rays are usually involved in such reactions.

It is the process of breakdown of water molecule into hydrogen and oxygen under the influence of light during the light reaction of photosynthesis. In photosynthesis, chemical process by which molecules are broken down into smaller units through the absorption of light.

Significance of Photolysis of Water

(*a*) The photochemical phase is Hill reaction. It occurs in presence of light. It includes excitation of chlorophyll, photolysis of water molecule, photophosphorylation and reduction of NADP to 15 $NADPH_2$.

(*b*) The excited chlorophyll transfers an electron from chlorophyll in many steps. Chlorophyll loses an electron from the water molecule in E.T.C. system. Water splits into H^+ and OH^- ions. Oz is released in it.

$4H_2O$ Light $\rightarrow 4H^+ + 4OH$-Mn^{++}, Cl_4OH^- $\rightarrow 2H_2O + O_2$

(*c*) The formation of ATP by linking ADP and Pi is called photophosphorylation in photosynthetic E.T.C. ADP + Pi $\rightarrow$ ATP. It includes two sets of photochemical reactions catalysed in pigment systems PS-I and PS-II. NADP is then reduced is $NADPH_2$.

Photolysis of Water during Photosynthesis

Photolysis is part of the light-dependent reaction or light phase or photochemical phase or Hill's reaction of photosynthesis. The general reaction of photosynthetic photolysis can be given as

H_2A + 2 photons (light) $\rightarrow 2\ e^- + 2\ H^+ + A$

The chemical nature of "A" depends on the type of organism. In purple sulphur bacteria, hydrogen sulphide (H_2S) is oxidized to sulphur (S). In oxygenic photosynthesis, water (H_2O) serves as a substrate for photolysis resulting in the generation of diatomic oxygen (O_2). This is the process which returns oxygen to Earth's atmosphere. Photolysis of water occurs in the thylakoids of cyanobacteria and the chloroplasts of green algae and plants.

7. (*c*) **Biodiversity Conservation:** Biodiversity conservation refers to the protection, upliftment, and management of biodiversity in order to derive sustainable benefits for present and future generations.

It is believed that an area with higher species abundance has a more stable environment compared to an area with lower species abundance. We can further claim the necessity of biodiversity by considering our degree of dependency on the environment. We depend directly on various species of plant for our various needs. Similarly, we depend on various species of animals and microbes for different reasons.

Biodiversity is being lost due to the loss of habitat, over-exploitation of resources, climatic changes, pollution, invasive exotic species, diseases, hunting, etc. Since it provides us with several economic and ethical benefits and adds aesthetic value, it is very important to conserve biodiversity.

Following are the important strategies for biodiversity conservation:

- All the varieties of food, timber plants, livestock, microbes and agricultural animals should be conserved.
- All the economically important organisms should be identified and conserved.
- Unique ecosystems should be preserved first.
- The resources should be utilised efficiently.
- Poaching and hunting of wild animals should be prevented.
- The reserves and protected areas should be developed carefully.
- The levels of pollutants should be reduced in the environment.
- Deforestation should be strictly prohibited.
- Environmental laws should be followed strictly.
- The useful and endangered species of plants and animals should be conserved in their nature as well as artificial habitats.
- Public awareness should be created regarding biodiversity conservation and its importance.

Biodiversity conservation is the protection and management of biodiversity to obtain resources for sustainable development.

Biodiversity conservation has three main objectives:

- To preserve the diversity of species.
- To maintain life-supporting systems and essential ecological processes.
- Sustainable utilization of species and ecosystem.

***Ex-situ* Conservation:** *Ex-situ* conservation of biodiversity involves the breeding and maintenance of endangered species in artificial ecosystems such as zoos, nurseries, botanical gardens, gene banks, etc. There is less competition for food, water and space among the organisms.

Ex-situ conservation has the following advantages:

1. The animals are provided with a longer time and breeding activity.
2. The species bred in captivity can be reintroduced in the wild.
3. Genetic techniques can be used for the preservation of endangered species.

***In-situ* Conservation:** *In-situ* conservation of biodiversity is the conservation of species within their natural habitat. In this method, the natural ecosystem is maintained and protected.

The *in-situ* conservation has several advantages. Following are the important advantages of *in-situ* conservation:

1. It is a cost-effective and convenient method of conserving biodiversity.
2. A large number of living organisms can be conserved simultaneously.
3. Since the organisms are in a natural ecosystem, they can evolve better and can easily adjust to different environmental conditions.

Certain protected areas where in-situ conservation takes place include national parks, wildlife sanctuaries and biosphere reserves.

National Parks: These are small reserves maintained by the government. Its boundaries are well demarcated and human activities such as grazing, forestry, habitat and cultivation are prohibited. For *e.g.*, Kanha National Park, Bandipur National Park.

Wildlife Sanctuaries: These are the regions where only wild animals are found. Human activities such as timber harvesting, cultivation, collection of woods and other forest products are allowed here as long as they do not interfere with the conservation project. Also, tourists visit these places for recreation.

Biosphere Reserves: Biosphere reserves are multi-purpose protected areas where the wildlife, traditional lifestyle of the inhabitants, and domesticated plants and animals are protected. Tourist and research activities are permitted here.

Previous Years' Paper (Solved)

Indian Forest Service

IFS–Botany Main Examination, 2018

PAPER-I

INSTRUCTIONS: *There are EIGHT questions in all, out of which FIVE are to be attempted. Question Nos. 1 & 5 are compulsory. Out of the remaining SIX questions, THREE are to be attempted selecting at least ONE question from each of the two Sections A and B. Attempts of questions shall be counted in sequential order. Unless struck off, attempt of a question shall be counted even if attempted partly. Any page or portion of the page left blank in the Question-cum-Answer Booklet must be clearly struck off. All questions carry equal marks. Answers must be written in ENGLISH only. Neat sketches may be drawn, wherever required.*

SECTION–A

1. Answer the following keeping your answers brief and to the point.

(*a*) Distinguish between Bacteria and Archaea.

(*b*) Comment on why *Albugo candida* and *Phytophthora infestans* are not considered as fungi.

(*c*) Distinguish between Chlorophyta and Rhodophyta.

(*d*) What is Peristome? Describe its formation and role.

(*e*) What are coralloid roots? Where are these found and what important role do they play?

2. (*a*) Compare loose smut with covered smut of wheat plants on the basis of symptoms, casual organism, disease cycle and disease management.

(*b*) Describe the evolutionary significance of various stellar structures found in Pteridophytes. Give one suitable example in each case.

(*c*) Describe the diversity of photosynthetic pigments found in the major classes of Algae.

3. (*a*) What are the recent developments in the use of microbes in industrial products? Why do microbes serve as most ideal organisms in industrial applications?

(*b*) Explain the progressive sterilization of potentially sporogenous tissue found in Bryophyta. Add a note on the role of elaters.

(*c*) Describe the structure and chemical composition of TMV. How does it infect the host?

4. (*a*) Describe the organization of female cone in *Pinus.* Discuss on the morphological nature of ovuliferous scale.

(*b*) Comment on how far *Selaginella* advances towards seed habit.

(*c*) What is Systemic Acquired Resistance (SAR)? Discuss the role of salicylic acid in SAR.

SECTION–B

5. Answer the following keeping your answers brief and to the point.

(*a*) How do you justify *Asteraceae* as a phylogenetically advanced family in dicotyledons?

(*b*) Explain 'Nemec phenomenon' and its significance.

(*c*) What are cortical vascular bundles? How are they formed?

(*d*) Discuss the role of Botanical Gardens in conservation of plants.

(*e*) What is haploid cell culture? How is this technique useful in agriculture?

6. (*a*) Give an account of Cronquist's classification of flowering plants. Add a note on merits and demerits of this system of classification.

(*b*) What is totipotency? Give an experimental evidence to demonstrate it.

(*c*) What is Helobial type of endosperm? Describe the process of its development.

7. (*a*) What is polyembryony? How is it induced? Discuss its applications.

(*b*) Write the botanical name of the plants, their family, economically important plant parts and uses for the following:

(*i*) Cinnamon
(*ii*) Clove
(*iii*) Saffron
(*iv*) Nutmeg
(*v*) Lesser Cardamom

(*c*) Compare the floral characters of *Malvaceae* and *Solanaceae*. Give the floral diagrams of the two families.

8. (*a*) Name the four types of tea recognized in the trade. What are their properties and methods of processing?

(*b*) Describe the organization of essential organs of *Asclepiadaceae* family. Discuss the pollination mechanism in it.

(*c*) Give an account on hydrocarbon plants and their potential as a source of sustainable energy.

PAPER-II

INSTRUCTIONS: *There are EIGHT questions in all, out of which FIVE are to be attempted. Question Nos. 1 & 5 are compulsory. Out of the remaining SIX questions, THREE are to be attempted selecting at least ONE question from each of the two Sections A and B. Attempts of questions shall be counted in sequential order. Unless struck off, attempt of a question shall be counted even if attempted partly. Any page or portion of the page left blank in the Question-cum-Answer Booklet must be clearly struck off. All questions carry equal marks. Answers must be written in ENGLISH only. Neat sketches may be drawn, wherever required.*

SECTION—A

1. Write a short note on each of the following:

(*a*) Packaging of DNA in chromatin

(*b*) Chloroplast dimorphism

(*c*) Post-transcriptional modifications of mRNA

(*d*) Role of endoplasmic reticulum in protein sorting and targeting

(*e*) Objectives and properties of probability

2. (*a*) Describe the molecular basis of cell cycle transitions with suitable illustrations. Explain the role of CDKs in controlling transitions between cell cycle stages.

(*b*) Discuss the mechanism of transport of molecules across the cell membrane by uniport, symport and antiport. Add a note on co-transport by symporter and uniporter.

3. (*a*) Describe the molecular mechanism of gene linkage and crossing-over. Explain how gene mapping is constructed using gene linkage with suitable diagrams.

(*b*) Describe different methods of selection and hybridization in plant breeding. Give a note on heterosis breeding.

4. (*a*) Describe different stages of micropropagation in detail, mentioning the significances of each stage. Give a brief account on commercial micropropagation.

(*b*) Describe the initiation of translation process in prokaryotes with suitable illustrations. How does it differ from eukaryotes?

SECTION—B

5. Write a brief note on each of the following:

(*a*) Role of Rubisco in carbon metabolism

(*b*) Importance of different types of secondary metabolites in plant defense and as pharmaceuticals

(*c*) Endemism and endangered plant species

(*d*) Hot spots in India : Characteristics and conservations

(*e*) Allosteric enzymes and metabolic control

6. (*a*) Illustrate the structure of ATP synthase and discuss the mechanism of ATP synthesis in higher plants.

(*b*) Explain elaborately the molecular basis of fruit ripening. How can this process be manipulated?

7. (*a*) Discuss the mechanism of nitrogen fixation associated with legumes and elaborate the factors controlling the process.

(*b*) Describe the adaptive responses at the morphological and physiological levels in higher plants to water deficit stress conditions.

8. (*a*) Explain the ecological characteristics of different types of forests found in India. Describe briefly about the dominance of vegetation types of tropical and alpine forests.

(*b*) Discuss the concept of climax community. Write a note on succession of estuarine ecosystem.

ANSWERS

PAPER-I

SECTION-A

1. (*a*) Distinguish between Bacteria and Archaea

Basis for Comparison	*Archaea*	*Bacteria*
Meaning	Archaea are single-cell, simple micro-organisms and are capable of surviving under extreme condition. They are considered as the most primitive cells, which originated on the earth 4 billion years ago.	Bacteria are also single-cell but have the complex structure. All types of bacteria except archaea falls under this category.
Found in	Archaea are found in unusual environment like in hot spring, ocean depth, salt brine.	They are found everywhere like in the soil, water, living and non-living organisms.
Cell Wall	The cell wall is said to be as pseudopeptidoglycan.	The cell wall is made up of peptidoglycan with muramic acid or lipopolysaccharide.

Basis for Comparison	***Archaea***	***Bacteria***
Lipid membrane	Archaea have ether bonds with the branching of aliphatic acids in their lipid membrane.	Eubacteria or bacteria have lipid membrane of ester bonds with fatty acids.
Metabolic pathway	Archaea do not follow glycolysis or Krebs cycle but uses similar pathway.	Follow glycolysis pathway and Kreb's cycle to break down glucose.
Types	Methanogens, Halophiles, Thermoacidophiles.	Gram-positive and gram-negative.
Reproduction	Archaea reproduce asexually by binary fission, fragmentation, or by the budding process.	Bacteria can produce spores which allow them to live in unfavourable condition.
Other features	Thymine is absent in the tRNA (transferase RNA). Introns are present. RNA polymerase is complex and contains 10 subunits. Archaea are non-pathogens.	Thymine is present in the tRNA. Introns are absent. RNA polymerase is simple and contains 4 subunits. Some bacteria are pathogens.
Examples	1. *Pyrolobus fumarii.* 2. *Sulfolobus acidocaldarius.* 3. *Pyrococcus furiosus.* 4. *Methanobacterium formicum.*	1. *Streptococcus pneumoniae.* 2. *Yersinia pestis.* 3. *Escherichia coli (E.coli).* 4. *Salmonella enterica.*

1. (*b*) *Albugo candida* and *Phytophthora infestans* are not to be considered as fungi:

Albugo candida is an obligate parasite on a number of flowering plants. It is a common species responsible for the disease "white rust" on the members of family cruciferae. It is commonly known as white rust, is a species of oomycete in the family Albuginaceal. It is some times called a fungus, but infact forms part of a distinct lineage of fungus like microorganisms oomycetes, commonly known as water moulds.

Phytophthora infestans is a genus of micro-organisms in the stramenopile kindom which includes water molds, diatoms and brown algae. *Phytophthora infestans* unlike true fungi because their cell wall contain cellulose instead of chitin, their hyphae lack cross walls, and diploid phase, rather than haploid phase, dominates their life cycle. Another striking feature of *Phytophthora* is that it produces swimming spores called zoospores, during one phase of its life cycle, a vestige of its evolutionary origin in water, so on the basis of above characteristics *Albugo candida* and *Phytophthora infestans* are not to be considered as true fungi.

1. (*c*) Distinguish between Chlorophyta and Rhodophyta

Chlorophyta

- common name: Green algae
- major pigment: chlorophyll a and b
- stored food: starch
- cell wall: cellulose
- habitat: fresh water, brackish water, salt water.
- flagellar number and position of insertions: 2-8 equal, apical.

Rhodophyta

- common name: Red algae

- major pigment: chlorophyll a and d, phycoerythrin.
- stored food: Floridean starch
- cell wall: cellulose, pectin and polysulphate esters.
- habitat: fresh water (some), brackish water, salt water (most).
- flagellar number and position of insertions: absent.

1. (*d*) **Peristome** is an anatomical feature that surrounds an opening to an organ or structure. Some plants, fungi, and shelled gastropods have peristomes.

In mosses, the peristome is a specialized structure in the sporangium that allows for gradual spore discharge, instead of releasing them all at once.

Most mosses produce a capsule with a lid which falls off when the spores inside are mature and thus ready to be dispersed. The opening thus revealed is called the stoma and is surrounded by one or two peristomes. Each peristome is a ring of triangular "teeth" formed from the remnants of dead cells with thickened cell walls. There are usually 16 such teeth in a single peristome, separate from each other and able to both fold in to cover the stoma as well as fold back to open the stoma. This articulation of the teeth is termed arthrodontous and is found in the moss subclass Bryopsida. In other groups of mosses, the capsule is either nematodontous with an attached operculum (as in the Polytrichopsida), or else splits open without operculum or teeth.

There are two subtypes of arthrodontous peristome.

1. The first is termed **haplolepidous** and consists of a single circle of 16 peristome teeth.
2. The second type is the diplolepidous peristome found in subclass *Bryidae*. In this type, there are two rings of peristome teeth—an inner endostome (short for endoperistome) and an exostome. The endostome is a more delicate membrane, and its teeth are aligned between the teeth of the exostome. There are a few mosses in the Bryopsida that have no peristome in their capsules. These mosses still undergo the same cell division patterns in capsule development, but the teeth do not fully develop.

In pitcher plants, the peristome is a reflexed ring (or partial ring) of tissue that surrounds the entrance to the digestive tube in these plants. It often (for example in Cephalotus and Nepenthes) possesses sharp, overhanging 'teeth' which aid in prey retention. It is often studded with nectar secreting glands, hence its popular name, nectar roll.

In fungi the basidiocarps of some gasteroid fungi—such as puffballs and earthstars—release spores through an apical opening that is termed a peristome and is variously delimited, its features often being diagnostic when distinguishing closely related species.

Peristome teeth serve as a valve that allows the spores to exit the capsule. The peristome teeth open and splay outward during times of low humidity, allowing the spores to float away and disperse. One layer readily absorbs and releases water, while the other layer does not react very much to varying humidity levels. This causes the teeth to bend outward during times of low humidity.

Some peristome teeth work in other ways; example, Funaria mosses have slits between the teeth that expand during dry periods. In other mosses, such as Polystrichum mosses, the peristome teeth do not respond to moisture.

1. (*e*) Coralloid root is developed in Cycas. It is produced in clusters at the base of the stem and protrudes out over the ground. It is dichotomously branched and greenish brown in colour. It contains an algal zone in the cortex. This algal zone contains blue green like Nostoc and Anabaena, which grow in

symbiotic association with coralloid root. The coralloid roots contain symbiotic cyanobacteria (blue-green algae), which fix nitrogen and, in association with root tissues, produce such beneficial amino acids as asparagine and citrulline.

Coralloid roots are negatively geotropic roots found in Cycads. The middle cortex of coralloid roots contains nitrogen fixing species of cyanobacterium named *Anabaenacycadae*. Thus coralloid roots play important role in supplying nitrogen to plants.

4. (*a*) Organisation of female cone of pinus and 1st year, 2nd year and 3rd year female cones.

1. Female cone develops either solitary or in groups of 2 to 4.
2. They also develop in the axil of scaly leaves on long shoots like male cones.
3. Each female cone is an ovoid, structure when young but becomes elongated or cylindrical at maturity.

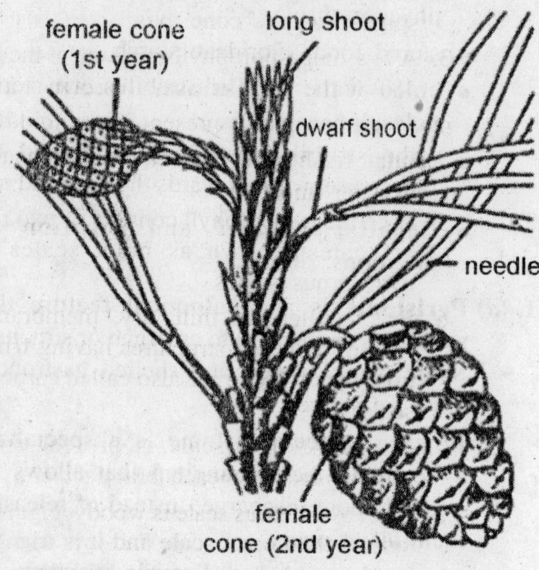

Figure: *Pinus. A fertile long shoot bearing 1st and 2nd year female cones.*

L.S. Female Cone:

1. In the centre is present a cone axis.

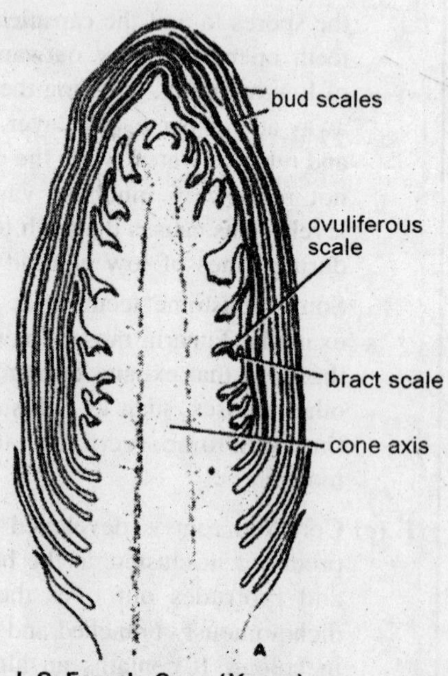

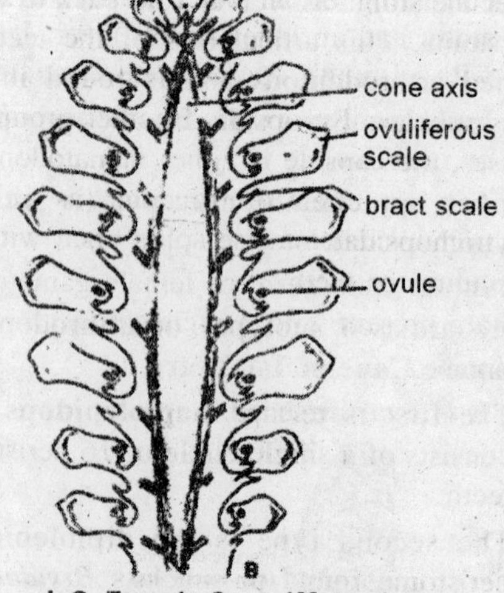

Figure: *Pinus. A, L.S. female cone (young); B, L.S. female cone (old).*

2. Many megasporophylls are arranged spirally on the cone axis.
3. A few megasporophylls, present at the base and at the apex of strobilus, are sterile.
4. Megasporophylls present in the middle of the strobilus are very large and they decrease in size towards the base and apex.
5. Each megasporophyll consists of two types of scales, known as bract scales and ovuliferous scales.
6. Bract scales are thin, dry, membranous, brown- coloured structures having fringed upper part. These are also called carpellary scales.
7. An ovuliferous scale is present on the upper surface of each bract scale.
8. Each ovuliferous scale is woody, bigger and stouter than bract scale and it is triangular in shape. A broad sterile structure, with pointed tip, is present at the apex of these scales. This is called apophysis.
9. At the base of upper surface of each ovuliferous scale are present two sessile and naked ovules.
10. Micropyle of each ovule faces towards the cone axis.
11. Each ovule is orthotropous, and it remains surrounded by a single integument, consisting of an outer fleshy, a middle stony and an inner fleshy layer. It opens with a mouth opening called micropyle.
12. Integument surrounds the megasporangium or nucellus.
13. Just opposite the micropyle is present a pollen chamber.
14. In the endosperm or female gametophyte are present 2 to 5 archegonia.

Female Cone of 1st Year:

1. It is oval in shape.

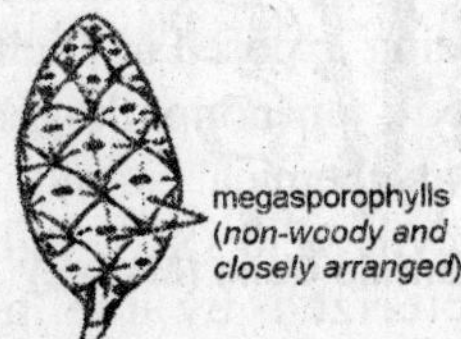

Figure: *Pinus. A 1st Year female cone.*

2. It ranges from 1 to 4 cm. in length.
3. It is green to reddish-green in colour.
4. It is attached with the help of a short stalk on the long shoot.
5. Megasporophylls are arranged very close to each other, and so the cone is a compact structure.

Female Cone of 2nd Year:

1. It is elongated and larger than the first year cone.
2. It ranges from 5 to 15 cm. or more in length.
3. It is red-coloured structure.
4. It is woody in nature.
5. Megasporophylls are compactly arranged but not so compact as in 1st year cone.
6. Seeds are present inside in the later stages.

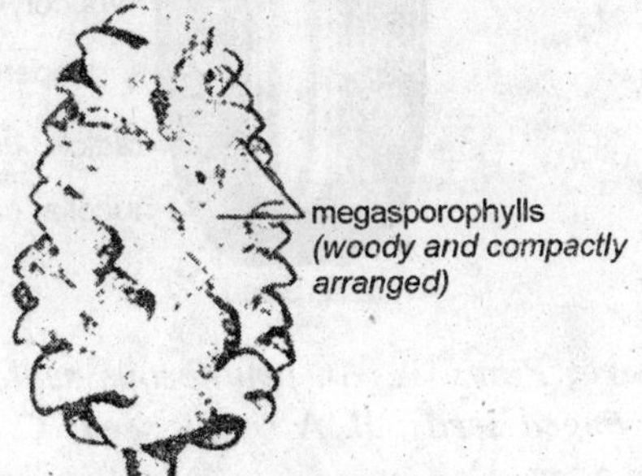

Figure: *Pinus. A 2nd Year female cone.*

Female Cone of 3rd Year:

1. It is elongated or roughly rounded in shape.
2. It is also woody in nature like the 2nd year cone.
3. Megasporophylls are loosely arranged.
4. Seeds are dispersed from 3rd year cone.

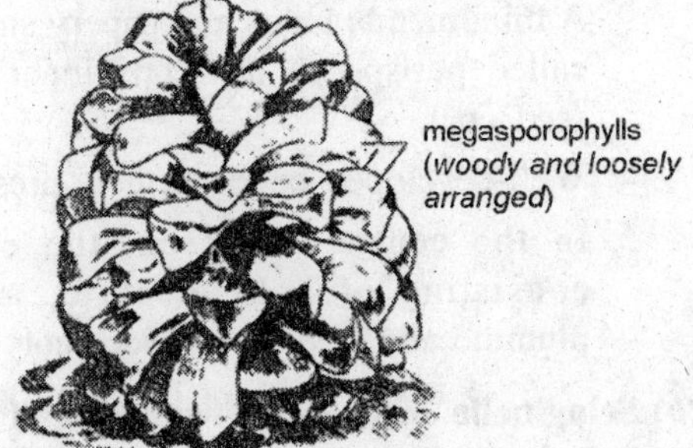

Figure: *Pinus. A 3rd Year female cone.*

Seed:

1. Both the ovules of each ovuliferous scale develop into seeds.

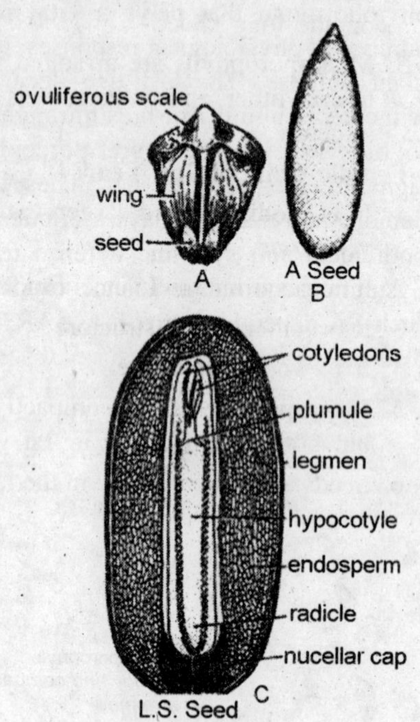

Figure: *Pinus. A, An ovuliferous scale bearing two winged seeds; B, A single seed; C, L.S. seed.*

2. Each seed contains a large membranous wing formed from the ovuliferous scale.

Anatomy of seed shows:

1. It is enveloped by a seed coat developed from the middle stony layer of the ovule.
2. Inner fleshy layer may survive in the form a thin membrane. Outer fleshy layer disappears.
3. A thin, membranous and papery structure, called perisperm, develops inner to the seed coat.
4. Well-developed endosperm is present.
5. In the centre is present the embryo consisting of a hypocotyle, radicle, plumule and 2 to 14 or more cotyledons.

4. (*b*) Selaginella advances towards seed habit: Selaginella is a tropical plant. It has world wide distribution. It grows in damp forests. Some species occur in temperate regions. They grow in moist shady places. The plant body is **sporophyte.** The body is divided into root, stem and leaves.

(*i*) It is a heterosporous pteridophyte.

(*ii*) In some species of Selaginella, viz., *S. rupestris* and *S. monospora,* the megaspore number is reduced to one.

(*iii*) In *S. rupestris,* the megaspore is retained within the megasporangium and the development of female gametophyte and subsequent fertilisation takes place in situ and even the young sporophyte can be seen developing on the parent plant.

(*iv*) Therefore, it becomes evident that the heterosporous vascular cryptogam, Selaginella, has considerably advanced towards seed habit in some species but its approach to the true seed is not complete due to the following reasons:

(*a*) The megasporangium wall is dehiscent and is not covered with the protective integuments,

(*b*) The retention of the megaspore permanently within the megasporangium has not become established,

(*c*) The absence of complete histological fusion between the megasporangium wall and the megaspore,

(*d*) The direct access of sperms to the egg,

(*e*) There is lack of resting period after the development of embryo.

4. (*c*) Systemic Acquired Resistance: Systemic acquired resistance (SAR) is a form of induced resistance that is activated throughout a plant after being exposed to elicitors from virulent, avirulent, or nonpathogenic microbes, or artificial chemical stimuli such as chitosan or salicylic acid (SA). Induction of SAR is characterized by the accumulation of salicylic acid to stimulate defense mechanisms, often resulting in a localized hypersensitive response. SA is not a mobile signal agent, but is proposed to be the first chemical in the induction of pathogenesis-related (PR) genes, especially PR-1. PR genes code for proteins such as chitinases and β-1,3-glucanases among others, and play a role in either preventing or slowing colonization of pathogens in the host.

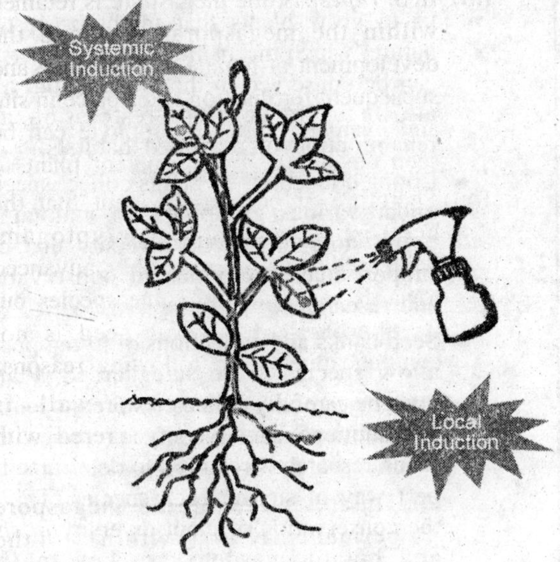

Figure: *Simple schematic representation of how local induced resistance triggered by exogenous application of chemical elicitors (red (dark gray in print versions) arrows) or microbial communities in the soil (blue (light gray in print versions) arrows) induce systemic resistance (purple (gray in print versions) arrows).*

Induction of SAR has increased disease resistance to a number of pathogens and pests, including *Ascochyta fabae* and *Uromyces viciae-fabae* on faba beans and *Meloidogyne incognita* and *Ralstonia solanacearum* on tomatoes. It has been suggested that SAR is most effective against biotrophic and hemibiotrophic pathogens and not against necrotrophic pathogens since it stimulates the SA pathway. Repeated inoculations can increase the level of resistance, but it can take several days for SAR to develop throughout the host plant.

Salicylic acid (SA) is an important phytohormone that plays a vital role in a number of physiological responses, including plant defense. The last two decades have witnessed a number of breakthroughs related to biosynthesis, transport, perception and signaling mediated by SA. These findings demonstrate that SA plays a crictical role in both local and systemic defense responses. Systemic acquired resistance (SAR) is one such SA-dependent response. SAR is a long distance signaling mechanism that provides broad spectrum and long-lasting resistance to secondary infections throughout the plant. This unique feature makes SAR a highly desirable trait in crop production.

SECTION-B

5. (*a*) The family Asteraceae (Compositae) is regarded as the phylogenetically most advanced and highly evolved and is considered to occupy the highest position in the plant kingdom.

1. It includes maximum number of genera (950) and species (20000).
2. The members of this family are worldwide in distribution.
3. Plants mostly herbaceous annuals, biennials or perennials.
4. Leaves exstipulate, opposite or whorled.
5. Floral buds are well protected by involucral bracts.
6. Flowers sessile, small, inconspicuous.
7. Flowers arranged to form capitulum inflorescence.
8. Flowers epigynous and in many species zygomorphic.
9. Calyx reduced to pappus or scales.
10. Corolla gamopetalous and tubular.
11. Reduction in the number of stamens.
12. Stamens epipetalous and syngenesious.

13. Gynoecium bicarpellary, syncarpous, inferior, unilocular.
14. Single ovule.
15. Basal placentation.
16. Fruit simple, in some mechanism of wind dispersal (parachute).
17. Some plants are wind pollinated.
18. Seed non-endospermic.
19. Due to small flowers much of the material is saved.

5. (*b*) Botanist, Bohumil Nemec had made researches with the anthers of the flowering plant species named *Hyacinthus orientalis*. The Nemec-phenomenon is an expression of the dominance of the female potency over the male in microspore. Under normal conditions, dominance of male potency was observed in the petaloid. Here, a male gametophyte was usually two or three nucleated. But under abnormal conditions (due to nechrohormones), dominance of female potency was observed. Here, a male gametophyte was 8 nucleated and he had named it as pollen embyrosacs. This female dominancy resulted in embryosac like male gametophytes. This phenomenon is called as Nemec-phenomenon.

5. (*c*) The cortical vascular bundle is a vascular system which allows the transportation of water and nutrients through the voluminous cortex of the cactus. This system is unique to cacti, and helps to replace the water lost to the dry desert air. The cortical bundle emerges radially from the xylem and produces shoots that run tangentially to the cortex, branching extensively and vascularizing every part of the cortex. The size of the cortical bundle can vary greatly from species to species. Because cacti live a long time, the cortical bundles have to function for many years. In every cactus species, the cortical bundles produce secondary phloems. In very old cortical bundles located at the base of very old shoots, the secondary phloem may attain a thickness of several millimeters.

5. (*d*) Role of Botanical Garden in Conservation of Plants: Botanic gardens have collectively accumulated centuries of resources and expertise that now means they play a key role in plant conservation. Many of these activities contribute to *ex situ* conservation, but botanic gardens also play an important role in *in situ* conservation. Botanic garden activities that are used for plant conservation:

- Horticulture and cultivation skills allow us to grow plants that might be lost in nature, which means that species diversity can be conserved in the gardens, but also allows us to consider restoration and rehabilitation of degraded habitats.
- Living collections of plants collect species under various groupings, to maintain a living store of genetic diversity that can support many activities in conservation and research.
- Seed banks and collections of living plants allow species to be safeguarded. Plants must be carefully collected stored to ensure maximum genetic diversity is retained, and much research is required to determine the best way of storing each species. This is the conservation of plant diversity *in situ,* and botanic gardens are key to this strategy's capacity and success.
- Research and development into plant taxonomy and genetics, phytochemistry, useful properties, informing selection of plants that can withstand degraded and changing environments (especially important in face of the threats posed by climate change).
- Education is a strength of botanic gardens that allows them to communicate the importance of conserving plants, reaching out to diverse audiences, and also to communicate how this may be achieved.
- Linking plants with the well-being of people, and also helping conserve indigenous and local knowledge, to encourage the sustainable use of plant resources for the benefit of all, as part of sustainable development.

5. (*e*) Haploids were first discovered back in 1921, when plant breeders and botanists conducted in-depth research to develop haploid cells. It wasn't until 1967 that scientists Hitsch and Bourgin were finally able to obtain haploid plants derived from the Nicotiana tabacum. Plants such as algae develop at least one haploid cell during their lifetime. In some plants like canola, sunflowers, cotton, rye, barley, oats, rice, and corn, haploids are deliberately obtained to encourage breeding.

In vitro production of haploids is of great significance in plant breeding programmes. Some of them are listed below:

1. Development of homozygous lines
2. Generation of exclusive male plants
3. Induction of mutations
4. Production of disease resistance plants
5. Production of insect resistance plants
6. Production of salt tolerance plants
7. Cytogenetic research

Haploids are useful in several areas of cytogenetic research. These include

(*i*) Production of aneuploids
(*ii*) Determination of the nature of ploidy
(*iii*) Determination of basic chromosome number
(*iv*) Evaluation of origin of chromosomes.

8. Induction of genetic variability
9. Doubled haploids in genome mapping
10. Evolutionary studies

Crops Developed Through Anther Cultures: Anther culture has made it possible to develop many new varieties of plants. In general, the new crops are high-yielding varieties with disease resistance. Some of them are resistance to cold, salt etc. Many plant breeders these days use anther cultures in their regular breeding programmes.

6. (*a*) **Cronquist's System Classification of Flowering Plants:** Arthur Cronquist (1919) of U.S.A presented a comprehensive system of classification in 1968 and thereafter its revised version in 1981. His system is parallel to that of Takhtajan's system in so many respects. He divided the angiosperms in two classes—Magnoliopsida (= Dicotyledons) and Liliopsida (= Monocotyledons). Magnoliopsida is further divided into six sub-classes, viz., Magnoliidae, Hamamelidae, Caryophyllidae, Dilleniidae, Rosidae and Asteridae; Liliopsida has five sub-classes, viz., Alismatidae, Arecidae, Commelinidae, Zingiberidae and Liliidae.

The division Magnoliophyta has two classes, *viz.,* Magnoliopsida (= Dicotyledons) and Liliopsida (= Monocotyledons). There are six sub-classes, sixty four orders, 318 families, and about 165,000 species in Magnoliopsida (= Dicotyledons) whereas in Liliopsida (= Monocotyledons) there are five sub-classes, nineteen orders, 65 families and about 50,000 species.

The outline of Cronquist's (1981) system of classification is as follows:

Class A. Magnoliopsida (= Dicotyledones)

Sub-class I.	***Magnoliidae***
Order	1. Magnoliales
" "	2. Laurales
" "	3. Piperales
" "	4. Aristolochiales
" "	5. Illiciales
" "	6. Nymphaeales
" "	7. Ranunculales
" "	8. Papaverales
Sub-Class II.	***Hamamelidae***
Order	1. Trochodendrales
" "	2. Hamamelidales
" "	3. Daphnophyllales
" "	4. Dedymelales
" "	5. Eucommiales
" "	6. Urticales
" "	7. Leitneriales
" "	8. Juglandales

,, ,,	9. Myricales
,, ,,	10. Fagales
,, ,,	11. Casuarinales
Sub-Class III.	***Caryophyllidae***
Order	1. Caryophyllales
,, ,,	2. Polygonales
,, ,,	3. Plumbaginales
Sub-Class IV.	***Dilleniidae***
Order	1. Dilleniales
,, ,,	2. Theales
,, ,,	3. Malvales
,, ,,	4. Lecythidales
,, ,,	5. Nepenthales
,, ,,	6. Violales
,, ,,	7. Salicales
,, ,,	8. Capparales
,, ,,	9. Batales
,, ,,	10. Ericales
,, ,,	11. Diapensiales
,, ,,	12. Ebenales
,, ,,	13. Primulales
Sub-Class V.	***Rosidae***
Order	1. Rosales
,, ,,	2. Fabales
,, ,,	3. Proteales
,, ,,	4. Podostemales
,, ,,	5. Haloragales
,, ,,	6. Myrtales
,, ,,	7. Rhizophorales
,, ,,	8. Cornales
,, ,,	9. Santalales
,, ,,	10. Rafflesiales
,, ,,	11. Celastrales
,, ,,	12. Euphorbiales
,, ,,	13. Rhamnales
,, ,,	14. Linales
,, ,,	15. Polygalales
,, ,,	16. Sapindales
,, ,,	17. Apiales

Sub-class VI.	***Asteridae***
Order	1. Gentianales
,, ,,	2. Solanales
,, ,,	3. Lamiales
,, ,,	4. Callitrichales
,, ,,	5. Plantaginales
,, ,,	6. Scrophulariales
,, ,,	7. Campanulales
,, ,,	8. Rubiales
,, ,,	9. Dipsacales
,, ,,	10. Calycerales
,, ,,	11. Asterales

Class B. Liliopsida (= Monocotyledons)

Sub-class I.	***Alismatidae***
Order	1. Alismatales
,, ,,	2. Hydrocharitales
,, ,,	3. Najadales
,, ,,	4. Triuridales
Sub-class II.	***Arecidae***
Order	1. Arecales
,, ,,	2. Cyclanthales
,, ,,	3. Pandanales
,, ,,	4. Arales
Sub-class III.	***Commelinidae***
Order	1. Commelinales
,, ,,	2. Eriocaulales
,, ,,	3. Restionales
,, ,,	4. Juncales
,, ,,	5. Cyperales
,, ,,	6. Hydatallales
,, ,,	7. Typhales
Sub-class IV.	***Zingiberidae***
Order	1. Bromeliales
,, ,,	2. Zingiberales
Sub-class V.	***Liliidae***
Order	1. Liliales
,, ,,	2. Orchidales

Merits of Cronquist's System of Classification:

(*a*) Cronquist system of plant classification is completely a phylogenetic classification.

(*b*) Conquist has taken vast literature from different fields of science into consideration. His system is based on morphological, anatomical, embryological, palynological, serological, cytological, chemical as well as ultrastructural evidences.

(*c*) Synoptical keys for each group up to the family level are very much useful.

Demerits of Cronquist's System of Classification:

(*a*) Cronquist system of classification at some level has shown too much reliance on single characters like centrifugal stamens, free-central placentation, etc.

(*b*) The arrangement of certain Families in Liliales has been strongly criticized, particularly the submergence of Amaryllidaceae into Liliaceae.

6. (*b*) Totipotency: Totipotency is the ability of a living cell to express all of its genes to regenerate a whole new individual. Totipotent cells from plants have been used in tissue-culture techniques to produce improved plant materials that are pathogen-free and disease-resistant. Totipotent cells from animals are now being used to clone mammals, although ethical questions remain over whether cloning a human should be done.

Steward Experimental Evidence to Demonstrate Totipotency: The ability or capacity of the mature living cells when free from the plant body develop into a new organism in controlled condition is known as Totipotency. (Lotus = entire, potential = power). Haberlandt in 1902 (German botanist) has first given the concept of cellular totipotency in plant body.

He stated that ever living cell of the plant body able to regenerate the whole plant body because it is derived from the fertilized egg and contain hereditary information. He tried to grow isolated green cells of leaves but failed to achieve the success. Later in 1950 F.E. Steward got success in proving the cellular totipotency. Cellular totipotency is a property of plant cell because a differentiated plant cell retain its capacity to give rise to a whole plant but in animal cell it losses the capacity of regeneration after differentiation.

Steward Experiment: Steward et al took the 2 mg. slices of phloem tissue of carrot (Daucus carrotd) and grown in a liquid nutrient medium containing coconut water. The part of the plant is taken for tissue culture is known as Explants (Ex. Phloem tissue of Carrot root). The liquid nutrient medium containing explants was allowed some hours for shaking.

Then the culture cell divide continuously to form mass of undifferentiated tissue known as callus. Some of these cell cluster started differentiating the initial of root. When it transfer to semi solid medium then it develop shoot system and give rise new plant. These plant then transfer to pot/soil where they develop in to flowering plant.

Steward experiment shows that in plant even mature (fully differentiated cells) can dedifferentiate, divide, come together re-differentiate and produced a new plant. Plant tissue derived form foot, stem, leaf, vegetative bud, floral bud, anther & embryo can exhibit cellular totipotency.

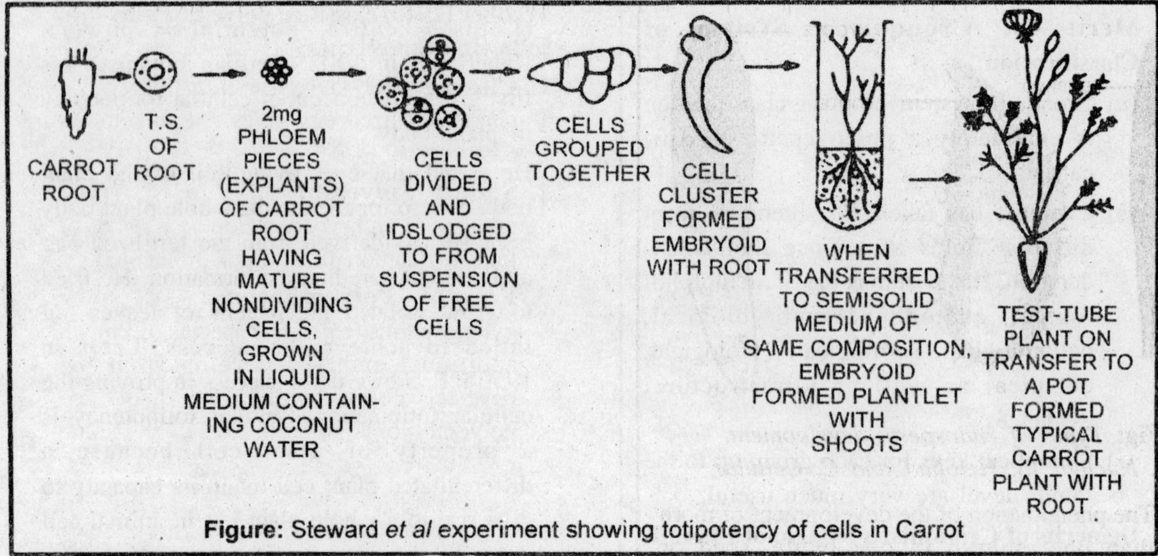

Figure: Steward *et al* experiment showing totipotency of cells in Carrot

6. (*c*) **Helobial Type of Endosperm:** This type is frequently found in the members of the order Helobiales. This type is intermediate between the nuclear and the cellular types. In this type the first division is followed by a transverse wall resulting in a micropylar and chalazal chamber. Further divisions are generally free nuclear and may be formed by the micropylar chamber only. Eremurus is an example of a typical Helobial endosperm. Here the primary endosperm nucleus divides transversely forming two chambers, a large micropylar and a small chalazal. Free nuclear divisions occur in both but are more rapid in micropylar chamber. Thus, when four nuclei are formed in the chalazal chamber, eight nuclei are produced in the micropylar chamber. When the chalazal chamber has eight nuclei, the micropylar chamber contains sixteen nuclei, and when there are 30 to 32 nuclei in chalazal chamber the micropylar chamber has considerably a large number of nuclei. In older ovules, the chalazal chamber begins to degenerate. Finally, when cell formation takes place in the micropylar chamber, the chalazal chamber is almost crushed and shows only a few disorganized nuclei.

Three main types of endosperm development in flowering plants are:

(*i*) Nuclear type

(*ii*) Cellular type and

(*iii*) Helobial type.

The formation of endosperm is initiated by mitotic divisions of the primary endosperm nucleus (3N). The formation of endosperm occurs usually prior to the zygotic division. Endosperm accumulates food reserves and functions as the nutritive tissue for the developing embryo.

The Helobial type is an intermediate type between the nuclear and cellular types. The first division is accompanied by cytokinesis but the subsequent ones are free nuclear. The chamber towards micropylar end of embryo sac is usually much larger than the chamber towards chalazal end. A large number of nuclei are formed in the micropylar chamber by free nuclear divisions while the nucleus of the chamber towards chalazal end divides to form a fewer free nuclei or may not divide at all.

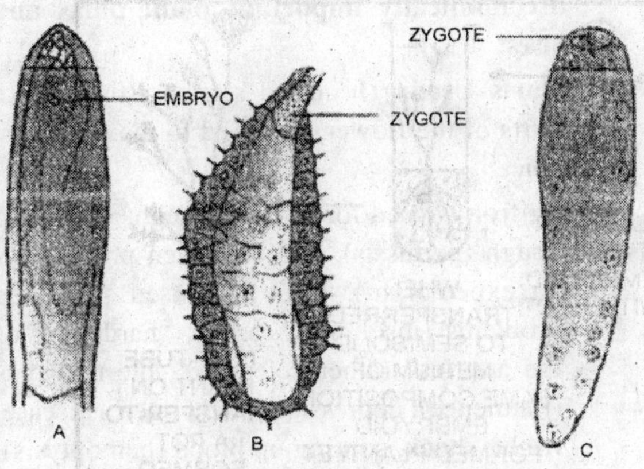

Fig: *Types of endosperm development. A. Nuclear, B. Helobial and C. Cellular*

7. (*a*) The phenomenon of the development of more than one embryo in one ovule, seed or fertilized ovum is called polyembryony. It occurs in both animals as well as plants. Most striking cases of polyembryony are seen in certain animals (*e.g.* parasitic Hymenoptera), where up to 2,000 embryos may spring from one zygote.

In plants, this phenomenon was first reported by Antoni van Leeuwenhoek (1719) in orange seeds. In several gymnosperms, the polyembryony is so common that it might be regarded as an important character of this group. In majority of the gymnosperms showing polyembryony, usually two or more archegonia develop in a female gametophyte. And as each archegonium contains an egg, two or more eggs may be fertilized and thus two or more potential embryos may be created. Only one embryo, however, survives usually, and all the others perish during the course of the development.

Types of Polyembryony: Polyembryony may be of following two types:

1. **Induced Polyembryony:** It includes cases of experimentally induced polyembryony.
2. **Spontaneous Polyembryony:** It includes all cases of naturally occurring polyembryony.

Webber (1940) classified polyembryony into following three types:

1. **Cleavage Polyembryony:** In this type a single fertilized egg gives rise to number of embryos.
2. **Simple Polyembryony:** In this type number of embryos develop as a result of the fertilization of several archegonia.
3. **Rosette Polyembryony:** In some gymnosperms (e.g. a few species of Pinus), additional embryos develop from the rosette cells, and this type of polyembryony has been termed as rosette polyembryony.

Induced polyembryony includes instances of experimentally used cases.

Application of Polyembryony

- The adventives embryos develop from nucellar embryo provide uniform seedlings for root stocks which yield consistent results in fruit production.
- The nucellar seedling as a root stock has a tap root and, therefore develops a better root system.
- The nucellar seedlings show a restoration of the vigour lost after repeat vegetative propagation.
- Polyembryony has ecological significance as it increases the probability of survival under varied conditions.
- Nucellar polyembryony is the only practical approach to raise virus-free clones of polyembryonatic citrus species in nature.
- Disease-free plants can also be obtained through nucellar embryo culture.

7. (*b*) (*i*) Cinnamon

Botanical Name: Cinnamon *(Cinnamomum verum)*

Family: Lauraceae

Economically important plant parts and uses:

Part Used: Bark

Cinnamon has many common everyday uses and some not so common uses. Everybody has probably used cinnamon for some reason, whether for cooking purposes or medicinal purposes. Despite being widely used in food and pharmacy it is also important in the cosmetic and perfumery industries . In some areas cinnamon has been known to be used for religious purposes. It is no wonder cinnamon is an important economic plant with all these possible uses for its products.

(*ii*) Clove

Botanical Name: *Syzygium aromaticum.*

Family: Myrtaceae

Economically important plant parts and uses:

Parts Used: The dried immature flower buds are mostly used as a spice but also as an herbal medicine.

Cloves have a unique flavor which can be best described as is fruity, crisp and rather bitter. The distinctive flavor is mainly because of the eugenol content found in the essential oil. It has been used traditionally to prevent nausea, for bad digestion, enhance blood circulation, to relieve hiccups and enhance liver function. One of its uses in folk medicine was to put two whole cloves in the mouth, without chewing or swallowing, to help to suppress the desire for alcohol.

The clove has antiseptic properties and has been used as a remedy for ailments associated with the respiratory system, infections of the digestive system and urinary tract infections. It is considered to be useful for infections of both bacterial and viral nature. In aromatherapy, the clove essential oil is considered to be both warming and stimulating.

(*iii*) Saffron

Botanical Name: *Coccus sativus*

Family: Iridaceae

Economically important plant parts and uses:

Parts Used: The dried stigmas (thread-like parts of the flower) are used to make saffron spice.

Saffron is used for asthma, cough, whooping cough (pertussis), and to loosen phlegm (as an expectorant). It is also used for sleep problems (insomnia), cancer, "hardening of the arteries" (atherosclerosis), intestinal gas (flatulence), depression, Alzheimer's disease, fright, shock, spitting up blood (hemoptysis), pain, heartburn, and dry skin. Women use saffron for menstrual cramps and premenstrual syndrome (PMS). Men use it to prevent early orgasm (premature ejaculation) and infertility.

Saffron is also used for to increase interest in sex (as an aphrodisiac) and to induce sweating. Some people apply saffron directly to the scalp for baldness (alopecia). In foods, saffron is used as a spice, yellow food colouring, and as a flavoring agent. In manufacturing, saffron extracts are used as fragrance in perfumes and as a dye for cloth.

(*iv*) Nutmeg

Botanical Name: *Myristica fragrans*

Family: Myristiacaceae

Economically important plant parts and uses:

Parts Used: The pericarp (fruit covering) is used to make jam, or is finely sliced, cooked with sugar, and crystallised to make a fragrant candy.

Nutmeg and mace are used for diarrhea, nausea, stomach spasms and pain, and intestinal gas. They are also used for treating cancer, kidney disease, and trouble sleeping (insomnia); increasing menstrual flow; causing a miscarriage; as a hallucinogen; and as a general tonic. Nutmeg and mace are applied to the skin to kill pain, especially pain caused by achy joints (rheumatism), mouth sores, and toothache.

In foods, nutmeg and mace are used as spices and flavorings. In manufacturing, nutmeg oil is used as a fragrance in soaps and cosmetics. Nutmeg oil is distilled from worm-eaten nutmeg seeds. The worms remove much of the starch and fat, leaving the portions of the seed that are rich in oil.

(*v*) Lesser Cardamom

Botanical Name: *Elettaria cardamomum*

Family: Zingiberaceae

Economically important plant parts and uses:

Parts Used: Fruit and seeds.

Lesser cardamom are used to add flavor to both food and drink, as cooking spices and as a medicine. *Elettaria cardamomum* is used as a spice and in medicine; it is also smoked sometimes; it is used as a food plant by the larva of the moth *Endoclita hosei.*

7. (*c*) Floral Characters of Malvaceae

Inflorescence: Solitary axillary (Hibiscus, Urena), solitary terminal (Abutilon), raceme (Althaea), panicle (Kydia).

Flower: Pedicellate, bracteate, bracteolate in the form of epicalyx, hermaphrodite rarely unisexual (Napaea), complete, actinomorphic, pentamerous, hypogynous.

Epicalyx: Epicalyx 3 (Gossypium), 7 to 9 (Althaea) and in a few totally absent (Abutilon, Sida).

Calyx: Sepals five, connate at the base, persistent, sometimes forming a tube (Urena), valvate aestivation.

Corolla: Petals 5, polypetalous sometimes slightly connate at the base with the staminal tube-thus epipetalous, large showy, twisted. Prominent veins can be observed on the petals.

Androecium: Stamens indefinite, monadelphous, forming a staminal tube; epipetalous staminal tube united with the corolla, anthers monothecous, reniform, basifixed, filament short, introrse.

Gynoecium: Multicarpellary usually five (Hibiscus) or ten (Althaea) indefinite (Abutilon) or 3 (Kydia); syncarpous, ovary superior, penta or multilocular with axile placentation, ovules one to many in each loculus; style one, long, passing through the staminal tube; stigma correspond to the number of carpels.

Fruit: Schizocarpic carcerulus (Abutilon, Malva, Sida), capsule (Hibiscus, Gossypium), berry (Malvaviscus).

Seed: Non-endospermic, in some genera seed coat is densely tomentose (Gossypium).

Pollination: Entomophilous. Insects are attracted for nectar, showy nature of corolla and protandrous flowers.

Floral formula:

⊕ ⚥ Epi 3–7 K (5) $\widehat{C5\ \ A}$ (α) G (5–α).

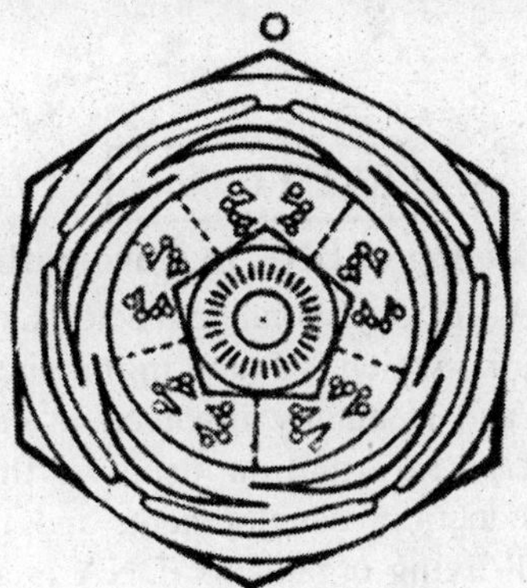

Floral diagram of *Althaea* (after Eichler).

Floral Characters of Solanaceae

Inflorescence: Solitary axillary, umbellate cyme, or helicoid cyme in Solanum.

Flower: Bracteate or ebracteate, pedicellate, complete, hermaphrodite, actinomorphic, pentamerous, hypogynous.

Calyx: Sepals 5, gamosepalous, tubular or campanulate, valvate or imbricate, persistent, green or coloured, hairy, inferior.

Corolla: Petals 5, gamopetalous, tubular or infundibuliform, valvate or imbricate aestivation, scale or hair-like outgrowth may arise from the throat of the corolla tube, coloured, inferior.

Androecium: Stamens 5, epipetalous, polyandrous, alternipetalous, filaments inserted deep in the corolla tube, anthers dithecous, usually basifixed or dorsifixed, introrse, inferior.

Gynoecium: Bicarpellary, syncarpous, ovary superior, bilocular, unilocular in Henoonia, axile placentation placentae swollen, many ovules in each loculus, ovary obliquely placed; in some cases nectariferous disc is present; style simple; stigma bifid or capitate.

Fruit: A capsule or beery.

Seed: Endospermic.

Pollination: Entomophilous.

Floral formula:

$Br \oplus ⚥ K_{(5)} \overbrace{C_{(5)} A_5} G_{(\underline{2})}$

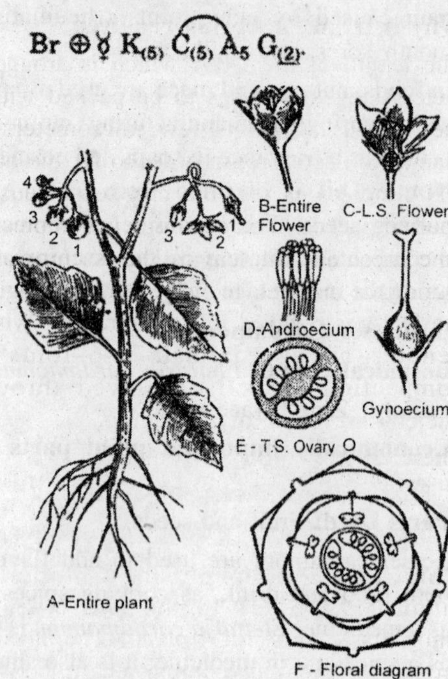

Fig: *Solanum nigrum*

PAPER-II

SECTION-A

1. (*a*) Packaging of DNA in Chromatin:

DNA - Deoxyribonucleic acid is a hereditary material which is found in the nucleus of the cell and is mainly involved in carrying the genetic information used in the growth, reproduction, development, and functioning of all living organisms. DNA is an organic, complex, molecular structure, found in both prokaryotic and eukaryotic cells and also in many viruses. In the year 1953, the DNA structure was suggested by Watson and Crick. According to their discovery, the DNA is a double helix, the long molecule made up of a double helical structure of two polynucleotide chains or strands running anti-parallel to each other. The two strands are connected by Hydrogen bonds between the complementary nitrogenous bases. The Adenine pairs up with Thymidine with the help of two H-Bonds and Guanine pairs up with Cytosine with the help of three H-bonds. DNA is a polymer of nucleotides, namely the deoxyribonucleotides. The term deoxyribonu-cleotides can be divided into two words *i.e.,* deoxyribose + nucleotides, where deoxyri-bose is a sugar and nucleotide is made up of a nitrogenous base, a sugar molecule, and phosphate group.

DNA Packaging

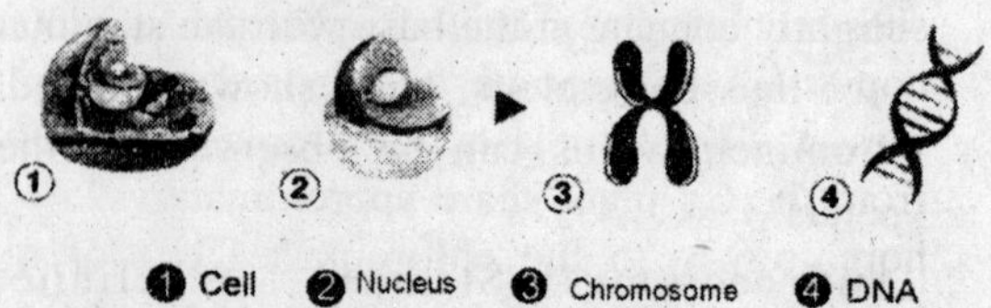

Why is DNA Packaging required?

The length of the DNA which is around 3 meters long and it has to be packed within the nucleus which is few micrometers in diameter. Therefore, in order to fix the huge DNA molecules into the minute nucleus, it need be packed into an extremely compressed or compacted structure called as chromatin. During the initial stage of the DNA packaging, the DNA is reduced into 11 nm fiber which denotes an approximate 5-6–folds of compaction. This is achieved through nucleosome order of packaging.

There are two order of packaging:

1. First order of packaging–Nucleosome.
2. Second order of packaging–Solenoid.

1. (*b*) Chloroplast dimorphism: Chloroplast dimorphism refers to the two types of chloroplast found in C4 plants. The physical properties, including contour length, buoyant density and Tm, of chloroplast DNA isolated from purified mesophyll (MC) and bundle sheath chloroplasts (BSC) of a C4 plant are identical. DNA renaturation measurements indicate that both DNAs have a complexity of 9.1×10^7 daltons. BSC and MC chloroplast are homologous as measured using 203 Hg-labeled DNA hybridized as a tracer with an excess of the second DNA type, retention of heteroduplexes on a sulfhydryl affinity column and testing for mismatch by measuring the release of 203 Hg-C after digestion with S_1 single-strand-specific nuclease. The Sal restriction endonuclease patterns determined by electron microscopic measurement of DNA fragment lengths of the two DNA types are identical. The only detectable difference between the two chloroplasts is the DNA content: bundle sheath chloroplasts contain approximately 50 copies of the genome as opposed to 20 in mesophyll chloroplasts. Chloroplasts DNAs from the C4 plant share approximately 95% homology with the chloroplast DNA of a C3 (Calvin cycle pathway) plant of the same genus. Thus the significant differences in physiology and morphology between mesophyll and bundle sheath chloroplasts of C4 plants and between the plastids of C3 and C4 plants are not due to major differences in the genetic complement of mature plastids.

1. (*c*) Post-transcriptional Modification of mRNA

- The nascent RNA, also known as primary transcript, needs to be modified to become functional tRNAs, rRNAs, and mRNAs.
- The modification is very much essential to eukaryotic systems.
- Post transcriptional modification includes
  → Capping at the 5'- end.
  → Tailing at the 3'- end.
  → mRNA splicing.

Capping at the 5'- End:

- 7-methyl guanosine is added at the 5' end of almost all eukaryotic RNAs by a 5'-5' triphosphate linkage.
- The capping process occurs in **nuclei, prior** to the splicing. **m^7GpppGp----**
- The 5'cap protects the RNA from ribonucleases.
- The cap structure of mRNA will be recognized by the cap-binding protein required for translation.
- The cap binds to cap binding complex of proteins which promotes binding of the mRNA to the ribosome to initiate the process of translation.
- Generation of the 5' cap occurs in a series of three to four steps shown below.

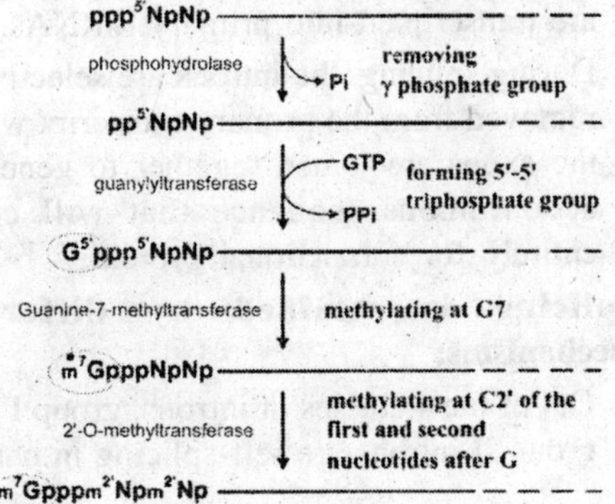

Poly-A Tail at 3' -End

- Eukaryotic RNAs posses a string of 80 to 250 A residues at the 3' end.
- This poly-A tail protects mRNA from enzymatic destruction, also acts as binding site for many proteins.
- There is no poly-T sequence on the DNA template from which the RNA is transcribed. The tailing process dose not depend on the template.
- The tailing process occurs in the **nuclei,** prior to the splicing.
- The tailing process takes place in multiple steps with the help of the enzyme polyadenylate polymerase.
- RNA + nATP → RNA-(AMP)n + nPPi (n = 80 - 250).
- The enzyme uses the cleaved mRNA as a primer; does not require any template.

mRNA Splicing:

- The matured mRNAs are much shorter than the DNA templates.
- The mRNA which has been transcribed contains sequences encompassing one gene. However, the structural genes are composed of **coding** and **non-coding** regions that are alternatively separated. Hence, these are also termed as **"split genes".**
- **Exons** are the **coding** sequences that appear on split genes and primary transcripts, and will be expressed to matured mRNA.
- **Introns** are the **non-coding** sequences that are transcripted into primary mRNAs.
- During splicing, the introns are selectively removed from the primary transcript while the exons are joined together to generate a continuous sequence that will code entirely for a functional protein.

Splicing is attained by different mechanisms:

1. Out of the 4 classes of introns, group I and group II introns are self-splicing in nature wherein no enzymes, or energy source (ATP) is needed. Splicing occurs by two simple trans-esterification steps.
2. The next class of introns are not self-splicing in nature but require involvement of a large protein complex called spliceosome. They are hence called **spliceosomal introns.** The **spliceosome** is responsible for removing introns and splicing exons together. It is made up of small ribonucleoprotein particles (snRNPs) which recognize the intron-exon boundaries.
3. The fourth category of introns differ from the other three in the requirement of energy as ATP and an endonuclease. The endonuclease is functional in cleaving the phosphodiester bonds at the two ends of the intron while the two exons are joined by a reaction similar to that followed by DNA ligases.

1. (*d*) The endoplasmic reticulum is a network of membrane-enclosed tubules and sacs, called *cisternae.* This network extends from the nuclear envelope throughout the cytoplasm (remember that the outer membrane of the nuclear envelope is continuous with the rough endoplasmic reticulum). There are two types of endoplasmic reticulum (ER) - *smooth* and *rough.* The rough kind is covered with ribosomes on its outer surface and is involved in protein processing and sorting. The smooth ER is not associated with ribosomes and functions in lipid metabolism.The rough ER is a sort of mail room for proteins- proteins that get sent to the ER, are sorted according to their destinations, then forwarded to the appropriate cellular compartment (for some proteins, further sorting occurs in the Golgi apparatus, as well).

Because of the complex internal organization of eukaryotic cells, the sorting and targeting of proteins to their appropriate destinations are considerable tasks. The first step of protein sorting takes place while translation is still in progress. Many proteins destined for the endoplasmic reticulum, the Golgi apparatus, lysosomes, the plasma membrane, and secretion from the cell are synthesized on ribosomes that are bound to the membrane of the endoplasmic reticulum. As translation proceeds, the polypeptide chains are transported into the endoplasmic reticulum, where protein folding and processing take place. From the endoplasmic reticulum, proteins are transported in vesicles to the Golgi apparatus, where they are further processed and sorted for transport to lysosomes, the plasma membrane, or secretion from the cell. The endoplasmic reticulum, Golgi apparatus, and lysosomes are thus distinguished from other cytoplasmic organelles by their common involvement in protein processing and connection by vesicular transport.

1. (*e*) Objective probability is the probability that an event will occur based on an analysis in which each measure is based on a recorded observation or a long history of collected data. The concept of subjective probability can be contrasted with the idea subjective estimate. Objective probabilities are a more accurate way to determine the probability of a given outcome than subjective measurements. An objective probability will examine past data and use mathematical equations involving the data to determine the likelihood of an independent event occurring. An independent event is an event whose outcome is not influenced by prior events. Subjective probability, by contrast, may utilize some method of data analysis but is largely based on a person's estimate or intuition about a situation and the likely outcome.

Objective probability allows the observer to gain insight from historical data to gain insight into the likelihood of a given outcome. In contrast, subjective probability allows the observer to gain insight by referencing things they have learned and their own experience. Objective probability is based on empirical evidence using statistics, experiments, and mathematical measurements rather than relying on things like on anecdotes, personal experience, educated guesses, or hunches. In the financial world, using objective probability is particularly important in order to avoid making emotional decisions when investing. People often rely on hunches, rules of thumb, or old wive's tales to justify making the particular investment that too much relies on subjective matters and emotional influence. Objective probability rids you of all of that emotion and anecdotal nonsense.

- Objective probability is the probability that an event will occur based on an analysis in which each measure is based on a recorded observation or a long history of collected data.
- In contrast, subjective probability allows the observer to gain insight by referencing things they have learned and their own experience.
- In finance, people ought to use objective probabilities to make decisions instead of relying on subjective stories, personal experience, or anecdotal evidence.

4. (*a*) **Different Stages of Micro-Propagation with their Significance**

According to Murashige of California University, micro-propagation is distinctly divided into five stages.

Stage 0—Mother Plant Selection: Before initiation of micro-propagation, selection of suitable mother plant is crucial in the whole exercise of propagation. Generally, disease free mother explant is selected for the micro-propagation to reduce contamination of cultures. Certain growth parameters of mother plant can be improved by pretreatment of mother explant before initiation of cultures.

Stage I—Establishment of Aseptic Culture: Micro-propagation begins with successful establishment of cultures of selected plant material. The initial steps of micro-propagation are generally associated with several hurdles such as rate of contamination and phenolic exudation. Plant tissues are commonly associated with bacteria and fungus.

In tissue culture media, presence of sucrose as a carbon source encourages their growth and consequently kills inoculated tissues. Therefore, adequate sterilization methods are employed to eliminate microorganisms from explant. Several sterilizing agents or surface disinfectants such as sodium hypochlorite (2%), calcium hypochlorite and saturated chlorine water are used.

Sodium hypochlorite is often used as 5-6% commercial bleach. Examples are chlorox or javex. The plant segments are presoaked in 10-15% commercial bleach for 10-12 minutes. High concentration is minimised to avoid tissue damage or cell death. To increase wettability, a small amount of (0.1%) of surfactents such as tween 20, or teepol is added to the disinfecting chlorite (0.1 to 1%) treatment.

In addition, a quick dipping (5-30 sec) of explant in 70% ethanol is frequently performed prior to bleach soaking. In certain cases, ethanol dipping may be followed by brief flaming. In the final treatment, sterile water is employed to remove traces of mercuric chloride before inoculating explant.

Beginning of micro-propagation encounters another barrier—phenolic exudation. During propagation of explant, high polyphenol oxidases are responsible for synthesis and release of phenolics, which can eventually kill plant tissues. Several chemicals can be employed to check exudation of phenolics. Adsorption property of activated charcoal can effectively reduce the problem.

The most potential antioxidant chemical polyphenyl pyrrolidine (PVP) can effectively check phenolics exudation. Adding some other antioxidants like ascorbic acid into culture media and incubating the initial period of primary culture in citric acid, reduced light or dark incubation of culture can minimize the damage. In addition, liquid media and frequent sub culturing in liquid media are some of the promising methods in controlling phenolics.

Stage II—Multiplication of shoots: The main objective of the stage II is the multiplication of organs like shoot and increasing their numbers considerably. They are able to give rise to new individual plant.

Multiplication of shoots through tissue culture involves four routinely used methods like:

(*a*) Callus mediated multiplication

(*b*) Adventitious shoots mediated multiplication

(*c*) By apical or axillary shoots

(*d*) Direct or indirect embryogenesis.

Stage III—*In Vitro* Rooting: Shoots or plantlets obtained during stage II are very small and do not contain roots enable to grow in soil, even fails to utilize soil nutrients. Therefore, adequate steps are taken in stage III to grow individual plantlets that can carry out photosynthesis and survive without external supply of carbohydrate. Therefore, *in vitro* grown shoots must be transferred to a rooting media.

There is a clear distinction between rooting media from shooting media. In vitro rooting can be accomplished by adding auxins to the culture media. Generally, addition of cytokinin is totally restricted due to its total inhibition role. Root induction takes place readily in many herbaceous species, but it can be very difficult or recalcitrant in most woody species.

In vitro rooting can be both in vivo and in vitro. In addition to the favourable role of auxins in root induction, strength of media is very important. Media containing half or quarter strength of the salts can be useful in the induction of roots in vitro. Supplying riboflavin and other adjuvants enhances root induction process in stage III.

Further, even in high value ornamentals, prices are high for the buyers and existing prices are not remunerative to producers due to high cost of production.

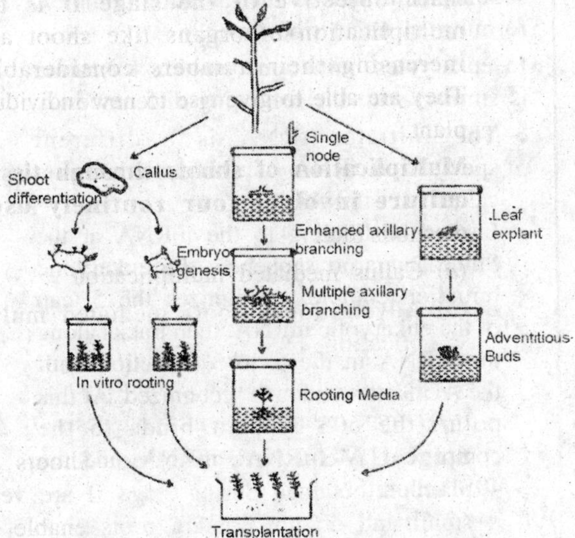

Fig: *Overview of micropropagation*

Stage IV—Transplantation or Hardening: Once in vitro rooting process completes, plantlets are ready to be transferred from the aseptic tissue culture container into the soil. Immediate transfer of tissue culture plants into soil is detrimental for survival of regenerated plants due to desiccation, infection, and light temperature shock.

Tissue culture plants generally lack protective cuticle layer and hairy roots, therefore are subjected for light and temperature shock. Excess of water loss was noticed from the leaves of plants immediately after transplantation. High rate of water loss due to lack of protective cuticle layer and root hairs, therefore every chances of exposure of seedlings to light and temperature shock. Plantlets are not developed on their own. The photosynthetic minimum period (7 days) is required for them to be capable of producing their own source of carbon. In addition to these problems, invitro grown roots are highly tender and their vascular systems are poorly developed. In order to compound these problems regenerated plants are subjected to hardening and is carried out by removing test tube grown plantlets and washed under distilled water to remove media sticking to the basal portion of the shoots, plantlets are then placed in sterilized soil or humus soil plus sand (1 : 1) or vermiculate soil. These are completely covered by plastic sheet or directly placed in green house to provide 90 to 100 per cent humidity for upto 15 days. Humidity is gradually reduced to 90% then to 80% and finally to 70%. The acclimatized plants are then transferred to the field.

Commercial Micropropagation: Commercial micropropagation industry is considered as relevant to agribusiness as tissue culture has the capability to break the plateau in yield improvements reached by green revolution and has several exclusive practical applications leading to improvement in crop productivity which are not possible in conventional science. Agricultural crops offer potentially very high volume demand. Sugarcane, banana and potato are three crops capable of offering high volume market. Potential demand from teak, eucalyptus, bamboo, coffee, tea etc. will be a bonus and will further stabilize the foundations of commercial micropropagation. All this market has remained unresponsive to plantlets from "State-of-art" technology. Regarding Global Trade in Commercial Micropropagation too, use of sophisticated facility for production of plants has not proven to be a guarantee of smooth trade between buyer and producer. Unreliability in supply and unpredictability of quality are still two main issues which are awaiting practical solution. Further, even in high value ornamentals, prices are high for the buyers and existing prices are not remunerative to producers due to high cost of production.

4. (*b*) Initiation of Translation Process in Prokaryotes: Translation is similar in prokaryotes and eukaryotes. Here we will explore how translation occurs in *E. coli*, a representative prokaryote, and specify any differences between bacterial and eukaryotic translation.

Initiation: The initiation of protein synthesis begins with the formation of an initiation complex. In *E. coli*, this complex involves the small 30S ribosome, the mRNA template, three initiation factors that help the ribosome assemble correctly, guanosine triphosphate (GTP) that acts as an energy source, and a special initiator tRNA carrying *N-formyl-methionine* (fMettRNA^{fMet}) (Figure 1). The initiator tRNA interacts with the start codon AUG of the mRNA and carries a formylated methionine (fMet). Because of its involvement in initiation, fMet is inserted at the beginning (N terminus) of every polypeptide chain synthesized by *E. coli*. In *E. coli* mRNA, a leader sequence upstream of the first AUG codon, called the *Shine-Dalgarno sequence* (also known as the ribosomal binding site AGGAGG), interacts through complementary base pairing with the rRNA molecules that compose the ribosome. This interaction anchors the 30S ribosomal subunit at the correct location on the mRNA template. At this point, the 50S ribosomal subunit then binds to the initiation complex, forming an intact ribosome.

In eukaryotes, initiation complex formation is similar, with the following differences:

- The initiator tRNA is a different specialized tRNA carrying methionine, called Met-tRNAi.
- Instead of binding to the mRNA at the Shine-Dalgarno sequence, the eukaryotic initiation complex recognizes the 5' cap of the eukaryotic mRNA, then tracks along the mRNA in the 5' to 3' direction until the AUG start codon is recognized. At this point, the 60S subunit binds to the complex of Met-tRNAi, mRNA, and the 40S subunit.

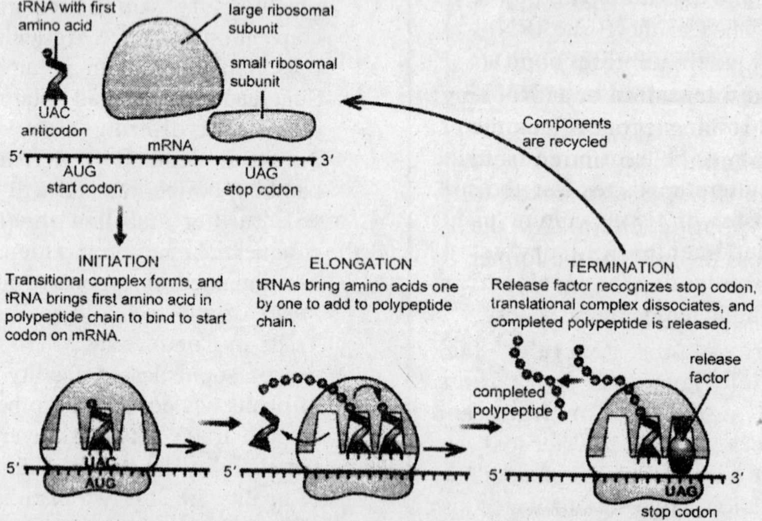

Fig. 1: *Translation in bacteria begins with the formation of the initiation complex, which includes the small ribosomal subunit, the mRNA, the initiator tRNA carrying N-formyl-methionine, and initiation factors. Then the 50S subunit binds, forming an intact ribosome.*

Elongation: In prokaryotes and eukaryotes, the basics of elongation of translation are the same. In *E. coli,* the binding of the 50S ribosomal subunit to produce the intact ribosome forms three functionally important ribosomal sites: The **A (aminoacyl)** site binds incoming charged aminoacyl tRNAs. The **P (peptidyl)** site binds charged tRNAs carrying amino acids that have formed peptide bonds with the growing polypeptide chain but have not yet dissociated from their corresponding tRNA. The **E (exit)** site releases dissociated tRNAs so that they can be recharged with free amino acids. There is one notable exception to this assembly line of tRNAs: During initiation complex formation, bacterial fMet-tRNA^{fMet} or eukaryotic Met-tRNAi enters the P site directly without first entering the A site, providing a free A site ready to accept the tRNA corresponding to the first codon after the AUG.

Elongation proceeds with single-codon movements of the ribosome each called a translocation event. During each translocation event, the charged tRNAs enter at the A site, then shift to the P site, and then finally to the E site for removal. Ribosomal movements, or steps, are induced by conformational changes that advance the ribosome by three bases in the 3' direction. Peptide bonds form between the amino group of the amino acid attached to the A-site tRNA and the carboxyl group of the amino acid attached to the P-site tRNA. The formation of each peptide bond is catalyzed by **peptidyl transferase,** an RNA-based ribozyme that is integrated into the 50S ribosomal subunit. The amino acid bound to the P-site tRNA is also linked to the growing polypeptide chain. As the ribosome steps across the mRNA, the former P-site tRNA enters the E site, detaches from the amino acid, and is expelled. Several of the steps during elongation, including binding of a charged aminoacyl tRNA to the A site and translocation, require energy derived from GTP hydrolysis, which is catalyzed by specific elongation factors. Amazingly, the *E. coli* translation apparatus takes only 0.05 seconds to add each amino acid, meaning that a 200 amino-acid protein can be translated in just 10 seconds.

Termination: The termination of translation occurs when a nonsense codon (UAA, UAG, or UGA) is encountered for which there is no complementary tRNA. On aligning with the A site, these nonsense codons are recognized by release factors in prokaryotes and eukaryotes that result in the P-site amino acid detaching from its tRNA, releasing the newly made polypeptide. The small and large ribosomal subunits dissociate from the mRNA and from each other; they are recruited almost immediately into another translation initiation complex.

In summary, there are several key features that distinguish prokaryotic gene expression from that seen in eukaryotes. These are illustrated in Figure 2.

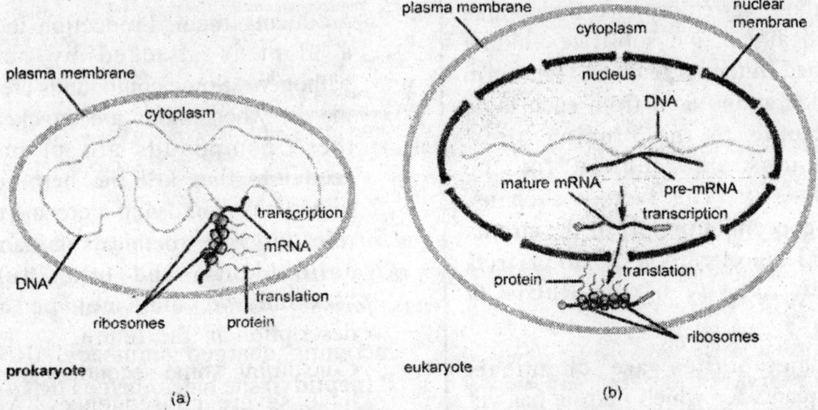

Fig. 2: *(a) In prokaryotes, the processes of transcription and translation occur simultaneously in the cytoplasm, allowing for a rapid cellular response to an environmental cue. (b) In eukaryotes, transcription is localized to the nucleus and translation is localized to the cytoplasm, separating these processes and necessitating RNA processing for stability.*

SECTION-B

5. (*a*) The vast variety of plant species fixes atmospheric carbon dioxide using the enzyme RuBisCO in Calvin-Benson cycle. The oxygenation reaction directs the flow of carbon through the photorespiratory pathway and this results in loss of 25-30% of the fixed carbon. The oxygenation reaction can be enhanced by temperature, drought and other environmental factors. Thus, the reduction in Rubisco-oxygenase reaction increases the carbon assimilation significantly. Thats why, currently scientists are trying their best to genetically engineer the crop plant so as to have more efficient Rubisco. Ribulose-1,5-Bisphosphate Carboxylase Oxygenase (RuBisCO) is an enzyme involved in the Calvin cycle that catalyzes the first major step of carbon fixation. It catalyzes either the carboxylation or the oxygenation of Ribulose-1,5-Bisphosphate (RuBP) with carbon dioxide or oxygen. The enzyme usually consists of the large and small chain subunits. The large chain is a part of chloroplast DNA molecule and there is several small related small chain genes in the nucleus of the plant cell. The small chains are imported to the stromal compartment of chloroplast from the cytosol by crossing the outer chloroplast membrane. The enzymatically active substrate binding sites are located in the large chains that form dimer in which amino acid from each large chain contribute to the binding sites. Magnesium ions are required for the enzymatic activity. The factors such as, temperature, concentration, pH of the stroma cells, and the level of carbon dioxide affects the enzymatic activity of the RuBisCO enzyme.

5. (*b*) Secondary metabolites are chemicals produced by plants for which no role has yet been found in growth, photosynthesis, reproduction, or other "primary" functions. These chemicals are extremely diverse; many thousands have been identified in several major classes. Each plant family, genus, and species produces a characteristic mix of these chemicals, and they can sometimes be used as taxonomic characters in classifying plants. Humans use some of these compounds as medicines, flavorings, or recreational drugs. Secondary metabolites can be classified on the basis of chemical structure (for example, having rings, containing a sugar), composition (containing nitrogen or not), their solubility in various solvents, or the pathway by which they are synthesized (e.g., phenylpropanoid, which produces tannins). A simple classification includes three main groups: the terpenes (made from mevalonic acid, composed almost entirely of carbon and hydrogen), phenolics (made from simple sugars, containing benzene rings, hydrogen, and oxygen), and nitrogen-containing compounds (extremely diverse, may also contain sulphur).

The apparent lack of primary function in the plant, combined with the observation that many secondary metabolites have specific negative impacts on other organisms such as herbivores and pathogens, leads to the hypothesis that they have evolved because of their protective value. Many secondary metabolites are toxic or repellant to herbivores and microbes and help defend plants producing them. Production increases when a plant is attacked by herbivores or pathogens. Some compounds are released into the air when plants are attacked by insects; these compounds attract parasites and predators that kill the herbivores. Recent research is identifying more and more primary roles for these chemicals in plants as signals, antioxidants, and other functions, so "secondary" may not be an accurate description in the future.

Consuming some secondary metabolites can have severe consequences. Alkaloids can block ion channels, inhibit enzymes, or interfere with neurotransmission, producing hallucinations, loss of coordination, convulsions, vomiting, and death. Some phenolics interfere with digestion, slow growth, block enzyme activity and cell division, or just taste awful.

Most herbivores and plant pathogens possess mechanisms that ameliorate the impacts of plant metabolites, leading to evolutionary associations between particular groups of pests and plants. Some herbivores (for example, the monarch butterfly) can store (sequester) plant toxins and gain protection against their enemies. Secondary metabolites may also inhibit the growth of competitor plants (allelopathy). Pigments (such as terpenoid carotenes, phenolics, and flavonoids) colour flowers and, together with terpene and phenolic odours, attract pollinators.

5. (*c*) Endemism is the ecological state of a species being unique to a defined geographic location, such as an island, nation, country or other defined zone, or habitat type; organisms that are indigenous to a place are not endemic to it if they are also found elsewhere. The extreme opposite of endemism is cosmopolitan distribution. An alternative term for a species that is endemic is precinctive, which applies to species (and subspecific categories) that are restricted to a defined geographical area.

An endangered species is a species which has been categorized as very likely to become extinct. Endangered (EN), as categorized by the International Union for Conservation of Nature (IUCN) Red List, is the second most severe conservation status for wild populations in the IUCN's schema after Critically Endangered (CR). In 2012, the IUCN Red List featured 3,079 animal and 2,655 plant species as endangered (EN) worldwide. The figures for 1998 were, respectively, 1,102 and 1,197. Many nations have laws that protect conservation-reliant species: for example, forbidding hunting, restricting land development or creating protected areas.

5. (*d*) The term 'hot spot' was introduced by N. Myers in 1988 for those geographical regions particularly rich in 'endemic', 'rare' and 'threatened' species found in relatively small areas but facing significant threats to habitat loss. To qualify a hot spot the area must contain 0.5 % (*i.e.* 1500) of the world's 300,000 plant species and should have lost 70% or more of its primary vegetation.

Of the 34 globally identified biodiversity hot spots, India harbour four of them, which are as follows:

1. Eastern Himalaya
2. Indo-Burma
3. Western Ghats and Sri Lanka; and
4. Sundaland (Andman & Nicobar)

Efforts have been initiated to save biodiversity both by ex-situ and in-situ conservation.

International Biodiversity day is celebrated across the globe on 22nd May every year.

The Biological Diversity Act, 2002 is a federal legislation enacted by the Parliament of India for preservation of biological diversity in India, and provides mechanism for equitable sharing of benefits arising out of use of traditional biological resources and knowledge. The Act was enacted to meet the obligations under Convention on Biological Diversity (CBD), to which India is a party. **The National Biodiversity Authority (NBA)** was established in 2003 to implement India's Biological Diversity Act (2002). The NBA is a Statutory, Autonomous Body and it performs facilitative, regulatory and advisory function for the Government of India on issues of conservation, sustainable use of biological resources and fair and equitable sharing of benefits arising out of the use of biological resources.

Convention on International Trade in Endangered Species of Wild Fauna and Flora (CITES) was signed in Washington, DC, on 3 March 1973. In August 2000, 152 States were parties to this Convention. The aim of CITES is to put a ban on international trade in wildlife. **The World Conservation Union IUCN** brings together States, government agencies and a diverse range of non-governmental organizations in a unique world partnership. IUCN seeks to influence, encourage and assist societies throughout the world to conserve the integrity and diversity of nature and sustainable use of natural resources. **International Treaty on Plant Genetic Resources for Food and Agriculture** was adopted in Rome in November 2001 to create a legally binding framework for the protection and sustainable use of all plant genetic resources for food and agriculture. **The United Nations Convention on Biological Diversity (CBD), 1992** known informally as the Biodiversity Convention, is a multilateral treaty. The Convention has three main goals like conservation of biological diversity (or biodiversity); sustainable use of its components; and fair and equitable sharing of benefits arising from genetic resources. The most significant feature of **1972 World heritage Convention** is that it links together in a single document the concepts of nature conservation and preservation of cultural properties. The Convention recognises the way in which people interact with nature and fundamental need to preserve the balance between the two. The law of sea 1982, envisaged by UNO aims at protecting marine biodiversity and to control marine pollution.

5. (*e*) An allosteric enzyme is an enzyme that contains a region to which small, regulatory molecules ("effectors") may bind in addition to and separate from the substrate binding site and thereby affect the catalytic activity. On binding the effector, the catalytic activity of the enzyme towards the substrate may be enhanced, in which case the effector is an activator, or reduced, in which case it is a de-activator or inhibitor.

Allosteric enzymes playa pivotal role in cells because they have two functions — they not only catalyze reactions in metabolic pathways, but also control the rates of these pathways. Regulation by allosteric enzymes involves the binding of signaling molecules to specific regulatory sites, and this binding induces conformational changes which result in alterations in catalytic activity.

The control of metabolic pathways by allosteric enzymes is analogous to a molecular value which has "on" and "off" positions. In the "off" position flow through the pathway is severely hindered, while in the "on" position the flow is normal. Koshland has recently said that *"this type of cooperativity, which has since been shown in many enzymes, receptors, and ion channels, is of critical importance to both evolution and the field of proteomics because it can serve as a general model for the way in which the networks of interacting enzymes of metabolic pathways are regulated."*

6. (*a*) **ATP Synthase:** ATP synthase is an enzyme that directly generates adenosine triphosphate (ATP) during the process of cellular respiration. ATP is the main energy molecule used in cells. ATP synthase forms ATP from adenosine diphosphate (ADP) and an inorganic phosphate (Pi) through oxidative phosphorylation, which is a process in which enzymes oxidize nutrients to form ATP. ATP synthase is found in all lifeforms and powers all cellular activities.

The function of ATP synthase is to produce ATP. ATP is necessary to power all cellular processes, so it is constantly being used by cells and constantly needs to be produced. Each ATP synthase can produce about 100 molecules of ATP every second. Eukaryotes, such as plants, animals, and fungi, have organelles called mitochondria that mainly function as ATP producers. Plants also have chloroplasts that contain ATP synthase and can produce ATP from sunlight and carbon dioxide. Bacteria and archaea, which make up the prokaryotes, do not have mitochondria but produce ATP through similar cellular respiration processes in their plasma membrane. Across all forms of life, ATP synthase has basically the same structure and function. Therefore, it is thought to have evolved early on in the evolution of life, and would have been found in the last common ancestor of all life on Earth.

Structure of ATP Synthase: ATP Synthase has two parts. The part embedded within the membrane of the mitochondria (in eukaryotes), thylakoid membrane of the chloroplast (only in plants), or plasma membrane (in prokaryotes) is called Fo. This is a motor that is powered by H^+ ions flowing across the membrane. The part within the mitochondria, stroma of the chloroplast, or inside the bacterial or archaeal cell is called F1-ATPase. This is another motor that is used to generate ATP. These two parts are thought to have been two separate structures with two different functions that eventually evolved into ATP synthase. The Fo region is similar to DNA helicases (enzymes that unzip DNA so that it can be used as a template for reproduction), while the F_1-ATPase region is similar to the H^+ motors that allow flagella, arm-like appendages on some bacteria, to move. F_1-ATPase has a central stalk and rotor that, when turned, converts ADP and Pi into ATP.

This is a rendering of the structure of ATP synthase. Fo is shown in blue and purple, while F_1-ATPase is shown in red.

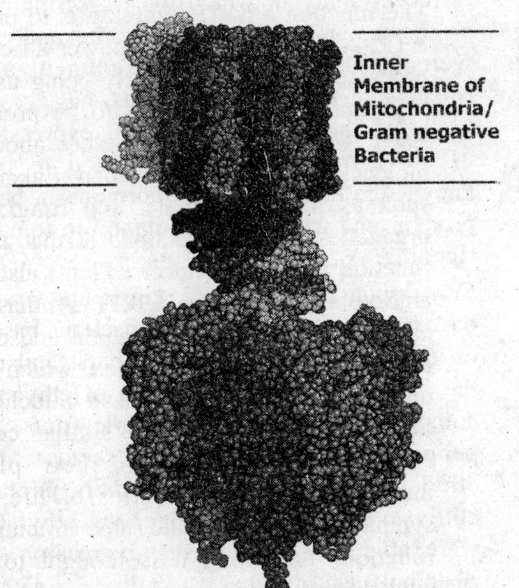

Mechanism of ATP Synthesis in higher Plants: ATP is produced through different methods: through cellular respiration in the mitochondria, during photosynthesis in the chloroplasts of plants, and across the inner membrane of bacteria and archaea, which do not have mitochondria. Although the methods of ATP production vary across different types of organisms, they all follow a similar basic procedure.

In the mitochondria of eukaryotes, the molecules NADH and $FADH_2$, which are products of the citric acid cycle, pass electrons down an electron transport chain, where they travel through three different protein complexes. This process releases energy, and this energy allows protons (H^+ ions) to travel down a proton gradient through the protein complexes, which act as proton pumps. The flow of these protons down the gradient turns the rotor and stalk of the ATP synthase, which makes it possible for a phosphate group to join with adenosine diphosphate (ADP), forming ATP. In chloroplasts, the process is similar, except light energy is the type of energy that excites electrons, causing them to flow down the electron transport chain and enable H^+ ions to travel through a membrane in the chloroplast. These methods are similar in very different organisms since the ability to generate ATP existed in the common ancestor of all living organisms.

6. (*b*) **Molecular basis of Fruit Ripening:** Fruit ripening is a highly coordinated developmental process that coincides with seed maturation. The ripening process is regulated by thousands of genes that control progressive softening and/or lignification of pericarp layers, accumulation of sugars, acids, pigments, and release of volatiles. Key to crop improvement is a deeper understanding of the processes underlying fruit ripening. In tomato, mutations blocking the transition to ripe fruits have provided insights into the role of ethylene and its associated molecular

networks involved in the control of ripening.

Fruits are a distinctive characteristic of Angiosperms. They occur today in a 'wide variety of forms and types. The ancestral fruit, dry and dehiscent, probably emerged in the early Cretaceous period; fleshy fruits appeared later in the Cretaceous or early Tertiary. The diversification of fruits from a dry dehiscent form to a fleshy drupe or berry, correlated with the rise of vertebrates, main agents of seed dispersal. The maturation of fruits is a complex and highly coordinated developmental process.

In fleshy fruits, ripening results in the production of succulent, flavorful, and soft pericarp that attract animals and facilitate seed dispersal. In addition to softening, fruits normally exhibit increased accumulation of sugars, acids, pigments, and volatiles that increase interest and palatability to animals. Moreover, fruits are an important source of supplementary diet, providing minerals, vitamins, fibers, and antioxidants for humans. From an agronomical point of view, nutritional value, flavour, processing qualities, and shelf-life determine the quality of fruits.

The main changes associated with ripening include colour (loss of green colour and increase in non-photosynthetic pigments that vary depending on species and cultivar), taste (increase in sugar and decline in organic acids), and flavour (production of volatile compounds providing the characteristic aroma).

Analytical tools that allow comprehensive phenotyping at the level of transcriptome, proteorne, and metabolome facilitate an overview of the metabolic network; whilst network analysis is beginning to yield a detailed understanding of the systems regulation underlying fruit development.

Hormonal and Transcriptional Regulation During Ripening: Fruits are generally classified into two physiological groups, climacteric and non-climacteric, according to their respiratory activity and associated ethylene biosynthesis profiles during ripening. Ethylene synthesis in climacteric fruits such as tomato, apple, and banana, is essential for normal fruit ripening and blocking either synthesis or perception of this hormone prevents ripening.

Efforts to uncover the transcriptional regulation underlying carpel and fruit development were first focused on the dry dehiscent siliques of the model plant *Arabidopsis*.

A number of important advances in our understanding of mechanisms that regulate ripening have also come from the characterization of monogenic tomato mutants, including ripening-inhibitor *(rin)*, non-ripening *(nor)*, colourless non-ripening *(Cnr)*, green-ripe *(Gr)*, green flesh *(gf)*, high pigment 1 *(hp1)*, high pigment 2 *(hp2)*, and never-ripe.

The *rin* mutant encodes a partially deleted MADS-box protein of the SEPALLATA. clade, whereas *Cnr* is an epigenetic change which alters the promoter methylation of SQUAMOSA promoter binding (SPB) protein. NOR is a member of the NAC-domain transcription factor family.

A recent study in which the transcriptome, proteome, and targeted metabolite analysis were combined during development and ripening of *nor* and *rin* mutants, has helped to refine the ethylene-regulated expression of downstream genes and added to our knowledge the role of this hormone in both protein- and metabolite regulation in tomato ripening.

Fruits such as strawberry, citrus and grape have been classified as non-climacteric, based on the lack of the respiratory burst and on the low endogenous production of ethylene compared to standard climacteric fruits. In pepper fruits, some cultivars seem to be ethylene-insensitive, while others pepper cultivars treated with exogenous ethylene were able to stimulate the expression of ripening-specific genes.

In strawberry, which has emerged as a prime model of non-climacteric fruit ripening, ethylene is relatively high in green fruits, decreases in white fruits, and finally increases again at the red stage of ripening. Interestingly, this last increase is accompanied by an enhanced respiration rate that resembles the one that occurs in climacteric fruits at the onset of ripening.

Recent comparative transcriptome and metabolome studies during the maturation processes of climacteric and non-climacteric fruits (tomato and pepper, respectively) suggest that both species have similar ethylene-mediated signaling components. In pepper, the regulation of these genes is, however, clearly different and may reflect altered ethylene sensitivity or regulators other than ethylene than in tomato. Unlike the situation described in tomato the ethylene biosynthesis genes, aminocyclopropane-1-carboxylic acid (ACC) synthase, and ACC oxidase, are not induced in pepper. However, genes downstream of ethylene perception, such as cell wall-related genes, ethylene response factor 3 (ERF3), and carotenoid biosynthesis genes, are up-regulated during pepper fruit ripening.

Genetic manipulation of fruit ripening: This involves antisense RNA approach. Few examples are:-

1. Manipulation of enzyme polygalacturonase
2. Manipulation of ethylene biosynthesis.

1. Manipulation of enzyme polygalacturonase (development of flavr Savr tomato): Softening of fruits is largely due to degradation of cell wall (pectin) by enzyme polygalacturonase (PG). The gene encoding PG has been isolated and cloned (pTOM6).

Procedure involves:

1. Isolation of DNA from tomato plant that encodes the enzyme polygalacturonase (PG).
2. Transfer of PG gene to a vector bacteria and production of complementary DNA (cDNA) molecules.
3. Introduction of cDNA into a fresh tomato plant to produce transgenic plant.

Mechanism of PG antisense RNA approach: In normal plants, PG gene encodes a normal or sense mRNA that produce the enzyme PG and it is actively involved in fruit ripening. The cDNA of PG encodes for antisense mRNA, which is complementary to sense mRNA. The hybridization between sense and anti-sense mRNA render the sense mRNA ineffective. Consequently, no poly-galacturonase is produced hence fruit ripening is delayed.

Rise and fall of flavr savr tomato: Genetically engineered tomato known as flavr savr was approved by US Food and Drug Administration on 18th may 1994. FDA ruled that flavr savr tomatoes are as safe as normal tomatoes. The new tomatoes could be shipped without refrigeration too far off places as it was capable of resisting rot for more than 3 weeks (double the time of a conventional tomato). But there are some limitations:

1. Transgenic tomatoes could not be grown properly in different parts of United States of America.
2. Yield of tomatoes was low.
3. Cost was high.

Therefore unfortunately, within a year after its entry, flavr savr was withdrawn and it is now almost forgotten.

2. Manipulation of ethylene biosynthesis: Ethylene plays a key role in ripening of fruits. Ethylene is synthesized from S-adenosyl methionine via the formation of an intermediate namely 1-amino-cyclopropane 1-carboxylic acid (ACC) catalyzed by ACC synthase. Next step is conversion of ACC to ethylene by ACC oxidase. Three different strategies have been developed to block ethylene biosynthesis. These are:

1. ***Antisense gene of ACC oxidase:*** Transgenic plants with antisense gene of ACC oxidase have been developed. In these plants production of ethylene was reduced by about 97%.
2. ***Antisense gene of ACC synthase:*** Ethylene biosynthesis was inhibited to an extent of 99.5% by inserting antisense gene of ACC synthase and the tomato ripening was markedly delayed.
3. ***Insertion of ACC deaminase gene:*** ACC deaminase is a bacterial enzyme. It acts on ACC group and consequently substrate availability for ethylene biosynthesis is reduced. Bacterial gene encoding ACC deaminase has been transferred and expressed in tomato plants. Ethylene biosynthesis is inhibited up to 90% in these plants. Fruit ripening is delayed about 6 week.

7. (*a*) Mechanism of Nitrogen Fixation associated with Legumes and Factor Controlling the Process: Nitrogen fixation is a process by which nitrogen (N_2) in the atmosphere is converted into ammonia (NH_3). Atmospheric nitrogen or molecular nitrogen (N_2) is relatively inert: it does not easily react with other chemicals to form new compounds. Fixation processes free up the nitrogen atoms from their diatomic form (N_2) to be used in other ways.

Nitrogen fixation is essential for all forms of life because nitrogen is required to biosynthesize basic building blocks of plants, animals and other life forms, *e.g.*, nucleotides for DNA and RNA and amino acids for proteins. Therefore nitrogen fixation is essential for agriculture and the manufacture of fertilizer.

Rhizobia Bacteria: The first Rhizobia were isolated from root nodules by M. Beijerinck, and shown to have the ability to re-infect their legume hosts, and to fix N_2 in symbiosis. *Rhizobium leguminosarum* is a species of gram-negative, aerobic, rod shaped bacteria that is found in soil and which causes formation of root nodules on some, but not all, types of field pea, lentil, kidney bean, and clover.

Leguminous plants: Leguminous plants are included under the family Fabaceae or Leguminosae, most of them have symbiotic nitrogen-fixing bacteria, Rhizobia in structures called root nodules.

Symbiotic Nitrogen Fixation: Biological nitrogen fixation was discovered by the German agronomist Hermann Hellriegel and Dutch microbiologist Martinus Beijerinck. Biological nitrogen fixation can be represented by the following equation, in which two moles of ammonia are produced from one mole of nitrogen gas, at the expense of 16 moles of ATP and a supply of electrons and protons (hydrogen ions):

$$N_2 + 8H^+ + 8e^- + 16\ ATP = 2NH_3 + H_2 + 16ADP + 16\ Pi$$

This reaction is performed exclusively by prokaryotes (the bacteria and related organisms), using an enzyme complex termed Nitrogenase. This enzyme consists of two proteins - an iron protein and a molybdenum-iron protein. The reactions occur while N_2 is bound to the nitrogenase enzyme complex. The Fe protein is first reduced by electrons donated by ferredoxin. Then the reduced Fe protein binds ATP and reduces the molybdenum-iron protein, which donates electrons to N_2, producing HN = NH. In two further cycles of this process (each requiring electrons donated by ferredoxin) HN = NH is reduced to $H_2N\text{-}NH_2$, and this in turn is reduced to $2NH_3$.

In free-living diazotrophs, the nitrogenase-generated ammonium is assimilated into glutamate through the glutamine synthetase/ glutamate synthase pathway.

Biological nitrogen fixation is of two types: Symbiotic nitrogen fixation and Non-symbiotic nitrogen fixation.

The best-studied example is the association between legumes and bacteria in the genus Rhizobium. A symbiotic relationship in which both partners benefits is called mutualism. A mutualistic symbiosis is an association between two organisms from which each derives benefit. It is usually a longer-term relationship, and with symbiotic nitrogen (N_2) fixation, often involves a special structure to house the microbial partner. Each N_2-fixing symbiotic association involves an N_2-fixing prokaryotic organism, the microsymbiont (*e.g.*, Rhizobium, Symbiotic nitrogen fixation occurs in plants that harbour nitrogen-fixing bacteria within their Klebsiella, Nostoc or Frankia) and a eukaryotic, usually photosynthetic, host (e.g., leguminous or non-leguminous plant, water fern or Fiverwort).

Mechanism of Symbiotic Nitrogen Fixation:

Root Nodule Formation: Rhizobia can infect their hosts and induce root nodule formation using following mechanisms:

- Root hair penetration and infection thread formation, as occurs in clovers and beans.
- Entry via wounds or sites of lateral root emergence, as found in peanut and the pasture legume *Stylosanthes.*
- Penetration of root primordia found on the stem of plants such as *Sesbania.*

Function of Root Nodule: In the context of the whole plant, the root nodule functions as a nitrogen source and a carbon sink.

Oxygen Protection of Bacterial Nitrogen Fixation: Nitrogenase is highly oxygen sensitive because one of its components, the Mo Fe cofactor, is irreversibly denatured by oxygen. On the other hand, the large amount of energy required for this reaction has to be generated by oxidative processes; thus, there is a high demand for oxygen in nodules. Different strategies are used in different symbiotic interactions to cope with this paradox. In legume nodules, a low oxygen tension in the central part of the nodule is achieved—Symbiotic Nitrogen Fixation by a combination of a high metabolic activity of the microsymbiont and an oxygen diffusion barrier in the periphery of the nodule, that is, in the nodule parenchyma. Because oxygen diffuses -104 times faster through air than through water, it is generally assumed that oxygen diffusion in nodules occurs via the intercellular spaces. The nodule parenchyma contains very few and small intercellular spaces, and this morphology is thought to be responsible for the block in oxygen diffusion. In the infected cells of the central part of the nodule, high levels of the oxygen carrier protein leg hemoglobin facilitate oxygen diffusion. In this way, the microsymbiont is provided with sufficient oxygen to generate energy within a low overall oxygen concentration. In contrast to Rhizobium, Frankia bacteria can form specialized vesicles in which nitrogenase is protected from oxygen.

Gene Regulation in Root Nodules: To obtain nitrogen-fixing root nodules, several genes of both symbionts are specifically induced or repressed during nodule development. The use of reporter genes as well as in situ hybridization studies has provided detailed insights into the spatial and temporal regulation of such genes in indeterminate nodules. In such nodules, major, sudden developmental changes occur at the transition of the prefixation zone to the interzone: starch is deposited in the plastids of the infected cells, and the bacteroid morphology alters. These events are accompanied by changes in bacterial gene expression: transcription of bacterial nif genes, which encode enzymes involved in the nitrogen fixation process, is induced, whereas expression of the bacterial outer membrane protein gene ropA is dramatically reduced.

Factors Controlling the Biological Nitrogen Fixation in Legumes: The factors are:

1. **Environmental Factor:** Usually, the factors which favour photosynthesis such as adequate moisture, warm temperatures, bright sunlight and higher CO_2 levels, also enhance biological nitrogen fixation. Rate of biological nitrogen fixation is usually maximum in early afternoon when carbohydrates (mainly as sucrose) are rapidly trans-located from shoots to root nodules through phloem. At this time, transpiration is also rapid which facilitates translocation of fixed nitrogen from root nodules and roots to shoots through xylem.
2. **Stage of Plant Growth:** In leguminous crop plants such as soybean, pigeon pea and peanut, maximum nitrogen fixation occurs after flowering when demand for nitrogen increases for developing fruits and seeds. These legumes have especially rich protein content in their seeds. In soybean, the seeds may contain up to 40% protein which is highest known protein content in any plant. In such legumes, about 90% of nitrogen fixation occurs during reproductive stage and only about 10% of it occurs in first two months of vegetative stage.

   Rate of nitrogen fixation is higher in perennial legumes such as alfalfa in comparison to annual legumes such as soybeans, peas and beans. It is because in annual legumes, root nodules are to be formed a fresh every year while in perennial legumes, the nodules are formed in the very first year of their growth which persist in subsequent years and therefore, they fix more N_2.
3. **Fertilizers in the Soil:** Increased amounts of NO_3^- and NH_4^+ in the soil suppress formation of root nodules and cause more rapid senescence of already established nodules. Consequently, nitrogen fixation is markedly inhibited under such conditions.
4. **Genetic Factors:** Many genetic factors control nitrogen fixation and yields of leguminous crop plants:
   (*i*) As has been mentioned earlier, there are host plant specific nodulin or Nod genes and rhizobial nodulation or nod genes that are involved in the formation of root nodules. Scientists are attempting to increase the efficiency of nodules formation by altering the rhizobial genes and selecting more compatible varieties of host plants.
   (*ii*) Reduction of N_2 to two molecules of NH_3 by nitrogen fixing organisms is coupled with the production of one H_2 molecule also causing wastage of energy. Active hydrogenase enzyme found in some rhizobia and free living bacteria can split this H_2 to electrons and protons ($H_2 <=> 2H^+ + 2e^-$). Efficiency of such organisms in nitrogen fixation is obviously more than those organisms which lack this enzyme. Through genetic engineering techniques, bacterial strains can be developed with active hydrogenase enzyme and consequently, rate of nitrogen fixation can be enhanced.

7. (*b*) Water, comprising 80-90% of the biomass of non-woody plants, is the central molecule in all physiological processes of plants by being the major medium for transporting metabolites and nutrients. Drought is a situation that lowers plant water potential and turgor to the extent that plants face difficulties in executing normal physiological functions. However, a few groups of animals and a wide variety of plants are known for their tolerance to desiccation during the adult stages of their life cycle. Though our knowledge on plant's drought tolerance is ancient, the modern scientific study of drought tolerance started in 1702 with Anthony von Leeuwenhoek's discovery of the survival of rotifers without water for months.

We describe the adaptive responses at the morpho-physiological levels in higher plants to water deficit stress conditions.

Photosynthesis: Drought stress is known to reduce photosynthesis by decreasing both leaf area and photosynthetic rate per unit leaf area. Reduced photosynthetic rate is mainly through stomatal closure or metabolic impairment. Continued photosynthetic light reactions during drought stress under limited intercellular CO_2 concentration results in the accumulation of reduced photosynthetic electron transport components, which can potentially reduce molecular oxygen, resulting in the production of reactive oxygen species (ROS). ROS can cause severe damage to the photosynthetic apparatus. The adaptive responses that plants have developed to reduce drought-induced damage to photosynthesis include thermal dissipation of light energy, the xanthophyll cycle, the water-water cycle, and dissociation of the light-harvesting complexes from photosynthetic reaction centers. The metabolic impairment during drought stress is mainly caused by changes in photosynthetic carbon metabolism. The biochemical efficiency of photosynthesis under drought stress mainly depends on ribulose-1, 5-bisphosphate (RuBP) regeneration and the activity of ribulose-l, 5-bisphosphate carboxylase/oxygenase (RuBisCO). Considerable progress has been made in improving the stomatal components for CO_2 diffusion, photosynthetic light reaction, and metabolic changes, including the expression of photosynthesis-related genes to regulate photosynthesis under drought towards the improvement of grain yield.

The C4 pathway of carbon assimilation has been suggested to be the major adaptation of the C3 pathway to limit water loss, reduce photorespiration, and improve photosynthetic efficiency under drought stress. However, many important crops—induding rice, wheat, soybean, and potato—use the C3 pathway of photosynthesis. Although the transfer of the C4 pathway into C3 crops is underway, so far its contribution to increased grain yield is very limited. Photosynthetic adaptation of plants to drought stress involves a complex interaction of hormones, ROS, sugars, and other metabolic events. Combinations of computational models, which integrate the physiological and metabolic processes with gene expression data, along with modern breeding and transgenic technologies hold promise in improving photosynthesis and hence crop yield under normal as well as drought stress conditions.

Hormonal regulation: Major phytohormones, such as abscisic acid (ABA), cytokinin (CK), gibberellic acid (GA), auxin, and ethylene, regulate diverse processes which enable plant adaptation to drought stress. Upon exposure of plants to drought stress, ABA is the major hormone synthesized in roots and translocated to leaves to initiate adaptation of plants to drought stress through stomatal closure and reduced plant growth.

Transpiration and stomatal conductance: The immediate response of plants on being exposed to drought stress is stomatal closure. However, stomatal closure not only diminishes water loss through transpiration but also reduces CO_2 and nutrient uptake, and hence alters metabolic pathways such as photosynthesis 55. Plants growing in dry areas have developed xeromorphic traits to reduce transpiration under drought stress. Reduction in transpiration under drought stress conditions can also be achieved through leaf shedding (i.e. deciduous species in drought) as well as decrease in leaf number, leaf size, and branching. Another adaptation to counter drought stress is sclerophylly, where plants form hard leaves that will not suffer permanent damage due to wilting and can be restored to full functionality when normal conditions resume 56. Recent research has shown that decreased stomatal conductance in response to drought stress is related not only to reduced expression of aquaporin genes but also to anatomical traits leading to reduction of chloroplast surface area exposed to intercellular space per unit leaf area. Several other factors, including leaf developmental stage and light availability, are also known to interact with drought in modulating mesophyll and chloroplast differentiation, ultimately affecting conductance and photosynthetic capacity. Reduction in stomatal size and number on exposure to drought is another adaptation for survival under drought conditions. Previous studies have shown that while there is an increase in stomatal density under mild drought stress, there is a decrease during severe drought. Thus, all these adaptations in plants reduce the negative impacts of drought stress on photosynthesis and thereby have a positive effect on water use efficiency (WUE), which in turn will result in high yield potential and high yield. Such an adaptation was shown in rice by over expression of the Arabidopsis AP2/ERF TFHARDY that improved WUE (the ratio of biomass produced to water used) by enhancing photosynthesis and reducing transpiration. The above reported traits therefore exemplify adaptive mechanisms in plants to survive under drought stress without loss of productivity or yield.

Root morphology: In many agriculturally important crops, drought stress is perceived first by the root system, which continues to grow underneath the soil even though shoot growth is inhibited under these conditions. Although the growth of the primary root is not affected by drought stress, the growth of lateral roots is significantly reduced, mainly by suppression of the activation of the lateral root meristems . The Arabidopsis R2R3-type MYB TF MYB96 has been shown to regulate activation of lateral root meristem through an ABA signaling cascade, with an activation-tagged mutant showing enhanced DR with reduced lateral root formation. The plant microRNA miR393 has also been shown to play a role in root-mediated adaptation to drought stress response through attenuation of auxin signaling. In addition to the lateral roots, the presence of small roots is also considered as an adaptive strategy to increase water uptake by providing more absorptive surface. Presence of specialized tissues like rhizodermis, with a thickened outer cell wall or suberized exodermis, or reduction in the number of cortical layers are considered an adaptive advantage for drought stress survival. Hydrotropism is another adaptive measure taken by plants to counter stress, where studies have shown that degradation of amyloplasts in the columella cells of plant roots on exposure to drought stress increases hydrotropism.

Osmotic adjustment: Osmotic adjustment (OA) is defined as a process of solute accumulation in dividing cells when the water potential is reduced, and thereby helps in maintaining the turgor. Cell enlargement and growth in plants is highly dependent on water availability and helps in maintaining the turgor. Turgor measurement in growing regions of plants, especially the leaves and stems, shows little or no reduction, though cell enlargement is inhibited during drought stress and is believed to be due to OA. Under conditions of drought stress, OA has been implicated in maintaining stomatal conductance, photosynthesis, leaf water volume, and growth.

Previous Years' Paper (Solved)

Indian Forest Service
IFS–Botany Main Examination, 2017

PAPER-I

INSTRUCTIONS: *There are EIGHT questions in all, out of which FIVE are to be attempted. Question Nos. 1 & 5 are compulsory. Out of the remaining SIX questions, THREE are to be attempted selecting at least ONE question from each of the two Sections A and B. Attempts of questions shall be counted in sequential order. Unless struck off, attempt of a question shall be counted even if attempted partly. Any page or portion of the page left blank in the Question-cum-Answer Booklet must be clearly struck off. All questions carry equal marks. Answers must be written in ENGLISH only. Neat sketches may be drawn, wherever required.*

SECTION—A

1. *Write short notes on each of the following:*

(*a*) Distinguish between Prokaryotes and Eukaryotes.

(*b*) What is Aflatoxin? State its importance.

(*c*) Explain the pigments observed in Rhodophyceae.

(*d*) Discuss Ammonification, Nitrification and Denitrification, starting the names of bacteria responsible for each step.

(*e*) Explain the development stages of *Pinus* male gametophyte.

2. (*a*) Describe Algal Phylogeny.

(*b*) Describe sporophyte development in bryophytes with suitable illustrations.

(*c*) Discuss the molecular basis of plant-pathogen interaction, with examples.

(*d*) Describe the role of bacteria in pharmaceuticals, agriculture and industry.

3. (*a*) Distinguish between Simple and Cleavage Polyembryony. With the help of labelled diagram, compare the embryogeny of *Pinus* and *Cycas*.

(*b*) Enumerate the sporophytic and gametophytic feature of *Psilotum*. Comment on its systematic position.

(*c*) Discuss the role of transduction in genetic recombination in bacteria.

(*d*) Characterize the different types of Mycorrhiza with examples. Discuss its role in agriculture and forestry.

4. (*a*) Define Telome. Discuss Zimmermann's telome concept citing examples from major pteridophytic groups.

(*b*) Describe briefly the symptoms and control measure of black stem rust of wheat. Name the causal organism. Why is it known as macrocyclic rust?

(*c*) Distinguish between Lytic and Lysogenic cycles. Explain briefly the steps of multiplication process of T4-bacteriophage by lytic cycle.

(*d*) Discuss the role of amphibious plants in the evolution of land plants.

SECTION—B

5. *Answer the following keeping your answers brief and to the point:*

(*a*) Explain with examples, the different provisions of author citations.

(*b*) Discuss Vavilove's Centres of diversity.

(*c*) Give five botanical names of fibre yielding plants and mention the parts from where fibres are obtained.

(*d*) Discuss in brief, the distinctive flora of the Mesozoic Era.

(*e*) Give a concept on the Inflorescence of Musaceae.

6. (*a*) Discuss the basic outline of classification according to the principles of Bentham and Hooker. State its merits and demerits.

(*b*) Compare the floral characteristics of Fabaceae and Asclepiadaceae. Give floral diagrams and name an economically important plant of each of these families.

(*c*) What do you mean by Palynology? Give an account of application of palynology.

(*d*) Define Ethnobotany. Describe the role of ethnobotany in the discovery of modern drugs, citing examples.

7. (*a*) Write the botanical name, active constituents and uses of five plants of economics importance belonging to each of the families Fabaceae, Rosaceae and Brassicaceae.

(*b*) Discuss the different levels of biodiversity. Comment briefly on *in situ* and *ex situ* conservation of biodiversity. State the role of cryopreservation in the conservation of plant biodiversity.

(*c*) What is Apomixis? Discuss different apomictic developmental pathways with suitable illustrations. Give a note on genetics of apomixis.

8. (*a*) What is meant by Anomalous Secondary Growth? Give a descriptive account on comparison of normal and anomalous secondary growth in dicot with examples and illustrations, wherever necessary.

(*b*) Define botanical Garden and state how it differs from other gardens. Name two internationally reputed botanical gardens. Discuss the role of an ideal botanical garden in education.

(*c*) Write notes on the following:

(*i*) Micropropagation : Definition, stages and application.

(*ii*) Callus Culture : Origin and application.

(*iii*) Protoplast Fusion : Origin, merits and demerits.

PAPER-II

INSTRUCTIONS: *There are EIGHT questions in all, out of which FIVE are to be attempted. Question Nos. 1 & 5 are compulsory. Out of the remaining SIX questions, THREE are to be attempted selecting at least ONE question from each of the two Sections A and B. Attempts of questions shall be counted in sequential order. Unless struck off, attempt of a question shall be counted even if attempted partly. Any page or portion of the page left blank in the answer book must be clearly struck off. All questions carry equal marks. Answers must be written in ENGLISH only. Neat sketches may be drawn, wherever required.*

SECTION—A

1. *Write a short note on each of the following:*

(*a*) Complexes in electron transport chain of mitochondria.

(*b*) Molecular basis of sex determination.

(*c*) Significance of accessory chromosomes.

(*d*) Merits and demerits of GM plants in India.

(*e*) Chi-square test.

2. (*a*) Describe the number and structural variations in chromosome. Add a note on their significance.

(*b*) Describe with illustrations about chromosomal behaviour during meisis with translocation, inversion and duplication.

3. (*a*) Elucidate the role of RNA in the origin and evolution of living organisms.

(*b*) With suitable example, explain the tripartite sex-determination.

4. (*a*) Explain the bio-chemical and molecular basis of mutations.

(b) Narrate briefly the various methods of gene transfer in plants.

SECTION—B

5. *Write brief notes on each of the following:*

(a) Allelopathy.

(b) Intellectual property rights.

(c) Molecular markers in plant breeding.

(d) Role of carotenoids in plants.

(e) Evidences of organic evolution.

6. (a) "Calvin cycle is said to be autocatalytic"– Justify the statement. Compare the mode of CO_2 assimilation in C_3 and C_4 plants. How does C_4 pathway differ from C_3 pathway in terms of efficiency?

(b) Describe the role of phytohormones in agri-horticulutre.

7. (a) With illustration describe the structure of phytochrome. Explain the role of phytochrome in flower development process.

(b) Describe the methods of breaking seed dormancy. Trace the physiological changes involved during seed germinations.

8. (a) Phytoremediation is not an ultimate solution to all the maladies of air and water. Explain details with specific examples.

(b) Describe the various phytogeographical zones met within India and add their salient features. In an ideal situation, there will be a high temperature and rainfall with restricted snowfall plus *Rhododendron*, Oaks, Orchids and Ferns– what is your inference?

ANSWERS

PAPER-I

1. (a) The distinction between prokaryotes and eukaryotes is considered to be the most important distinction among groups of organisms. Eukaryotic cells contain membrane-bound organelles, such as the nucleus, while prokaryotic cells do not. Differences in cellular structure of prokaryotes and eukaryotes include the presence of mitochondria and chloroplasts, the cell wall, and the structure of chromosomal DNA.

Prokaryotes were the only form of life on Earth for millions of years until more complicated eukaryotic cells came into being through the process of evolution.

Eukaryotic Cell versus Prokaryotic Cell comparison chart

	Eukaryotic Cell	Prokaryotic Cell
Nucleus	Present	Absent
Number of chromosomes	More than one	One—but not true chromosome: Plasmids
Cell Type	Usually multicellular	Usually unicellular (some cyanobacteria may be multicellular)
True Membrane bound Nucleus	Present	Absent
Example	Animals and Plants	Bacteria and Archaea
Genetic Recombination	Meiosis and fusion of gametes	Partial, undirectional transfers DNA

	Eukaryotic Cell	Prokaryotic Cell
Lysosomes and peroxisomes	Present	Absent
Microtubules	Present	Absent or rare
Endoplasmic reticulum	Present	Absent
Mitochondria	Present	Absent
Cytoskeleton	Present	May be absent
DNA wrapping on proteins	Eukaryotes wrap their DNA around proteins called histones.	Multiple proteins act together to fold and condense prokaryotic DNA. Folded DNA is then organized into a variety of conformations that are supercoiled and wound around tetramers of the HU protein.
Ribosomes	larger	smaller
Vesicles	Present	Present
Golgi apparatus	Present	Absent

Eukaryotic Cell versus Prokaryotic Cell Comparison Chart

	Eukaryotic Cell	Prokaryotic Cell
Chloroplasts	Present (in plants)	Absent; chlorophyll scattered in the cytoplasm
Flagella	Microscopic in size; membrane bound; usually arranged as nine doublets surrounding two singlets	Submicroscopic in size, composed of only one fiber
Permeability of Nuclear Membrane	Selective	Not present
Plasma membrane with steroid	Yes	Usually no
Cell wall	Only in plant cells and fungi (chemically simpler)	Usually chemically complexed
Vacuoles	Present	Present
Cell size	10-100um	1-10um

1. (*b*) Aflatoxins are poisonous carcinogens that are produced by certain molds (*Aspergillus flavus* and *Aspergillus parasiticus*) which grow in soil, decaying vegetation, hay, and grains. They are regularly found in improperly stored staple commodities such as cassava, chili peppers, corn, cotton seed, millet, peanuts, rice, sesame seeds, sorghum, sunflower seeds, tree nuts, wheat, and a variety of spices. When contaminated food is processed, aflatoxins enter the general food supply where they have been found in both pet and human foods, as well as in feed stocks for agricultural animals. Animals fed contaminated food can pass aflatoxin transformation products into eggs, milk products, and meat.

   Aspergilli belong to the class of imperfect filamentous fungi. Among the approximately

250 known species, many are producers of beneficial secondary metabolites, such as antibiotics and other pharmaceuticals. For example, *Aspergillus terreus*, produces lovastatin, a potent cholesterol-lowering drug. Other *Aspergilli* secrete antibiotics (penicillin and cephalosporin), antifungals (griseofulvin), and anti-tumor drugs (terrequinone A). Many uncharacterized compounds are produced by *Aspergilli* through various metabolic pathways. These compounds include pathway end products and pathway intermediates or shunt metabolites formed along these pathways and may also have beneficial pharmaceutical properties that can be a potential source of new drugs. However, there are many secondary metabolites produced by *Aspergillus* species, however, they are not always beneficial. Some of them are even toxic and/or carcinogenic and called mycotoxins. Mycotoxins are structurally very diverse chemical compounds with diverse toxic effects and a variety of biological activities.

Within the genus *Aspergillus*, *Aspergillus flavus* and *Aspergillus parasiticus* is the most important economically and most notorious because it produces aflatoxins. *A. flavus fungus*, one of the most abundant soil-borne molds on earth, is a saprobe that is capable of surviving on many organic nutrient sources like plant debris, animal fodder, cotton, compost piles, dead insects and animal carcasses, stored grains, and even immunocompromised humans and animals.

1. (*c*) The Rhodophyceae or the Red algae is probably the oldest group of Eukaryotic Algae encompassing about 4000 species of mostly multicellular and predominantly marine algae. It is the only class in the division Rhodophyta.

The members Rhodophyceae along with some members of Chlorophyceae and Phaeophyceae form a group of macro algae commonly called as seaweeds. They owe their red colour to the photosynthetic pigment phycoerythrin. Despite their name, not all Rhodophyceae are red. These algae may also be purple, brown or black because of presence of the additional pigments. The pigments present are chlorophyll a, chlorophyll–d, carotenes, phycoerythrins and phycocyanins.

The unique photosynthetic pigments include-chlorophyll–d, phycobilins: r-phycoerythrin and r-phycocyanin and the xanthophyll-taraxanthin besides the general chlorophyll-α and the α and β-carotene, lutein, zeaxanthin, neoxanthin.

1. (*d*) Ammonification is the process by which the organically bound nitrogen of microbial, plant, and animal biomass is recycled after their death. Ammonification is carried out by a diverse array of microorganisms that perform ecological decay services, and its product is ammonia or ammonium ion. Ammonium is a suitable source of nutrition for many species of plants, especially those living in acidic soils. However, most plants cannot utilize ammonium effectively, and they require nitrate as their essential source of nitrogen nutrition.

Nitrate is synthesized from ammonium by an important bacterial process known as nitrification. The first step in nitrification is the oxidation of ammonium to nitrite (NO_2^-), a function carried out by bacteria in the genus *Nitrosomonas*. Once formed, the nitrite is rapidly oxidized further to nitrate, by bacteria in the genus Nitrobacter. The bacteria responsible for nitrification are very sensitive to acidity, so this process does not occur at significant rates in acidic soil or water. This is the reason why plants of acidic habitats must be capable of utilizing ammonium as their source of nitrogen nutrition.

Denitrification is a microbially facilitated process where nitrate is reduced and ultimately produces molecular nitrogen (N_2) through a series of intermediate gaseous nitrogen oxide products. Facultative anaerobic bacteria perform denitrification as a type of respiration that reduces oxidized forms of nitrogen in response to the oxidation of an electron donor such as organic matter. The preferred nitrogen electron acceptors in order of most to least thermodynamically favourable include nitrate (NO_3), nitrite (NO_2), nitric oxide (NO), nitrous oxide (N_2O) finally resulting in the production of dinitrogen (N_2) completing the nitrogen cycle. Denitrifying microbes require a very low oxygen concentration of less than 10%, as well as organic C for energy. Since denitrification can remove NO_3, reducing its leaching to groundwater, it can be strategically used to treat sewage or animal residues of high nitrogen content.

Denitrifying bacteria, microorganisms whose action results in the conversion of nitrates in soil to free atmospheric nitrogen, thus depleting soil fertility and reducing agricultural productivity. *Thiobacillus denitrificans, Micrococcus denitrificans*, and some species of *Serratia, Pseudomonas*, and *Achromobacter* are implicated as denitrifiers.

1. (*e*) The spore is the first phase of gametophyte generation. The microspore or pollen grain represents the male gametophyte, while the megaspore represents the first stage of female gametophyte which develops into a female gametophyte.

Development of Male Gametophyte before Pollination:

The basic pattern of the development of male gametophyte of Pinus is similar to that of Ginkgo. The pollen grains undergo endosporic development. The pollen nucleus divides mitotically to produce a small lens-shaped first prothallial cell towards the proximal end and a large central cell on the distal end.

The central cell again cuts off a second prothallial cell and an antheridial initial. Both the prothallial cells are ephemeral and the second prothallial cell remains attached to the first prothallial cell.

The antheridial initial divides to form a small antheridial cell and a large tube cell. The pollen grains are released from the microsporangium at the 4-celled stage (2 prothallial cells, an antheridial cell and a tube cell).

Development of Male Gametophyte after Pollination:

After pollination, the 4-celled pollen stores in the pollen chamber and remains ungerminated for about 11 months. The pollen develops the next spring. The tube cell of the pollen comes out through the pollen aperture in the form of a pollen tube. The pollen tube proceeds towards the archegonium, penetrating the nuclear tissue of the ovule. The antheridial cell within the pollen tube divides to form a stalk cell and a spermatogenous (body) cell.

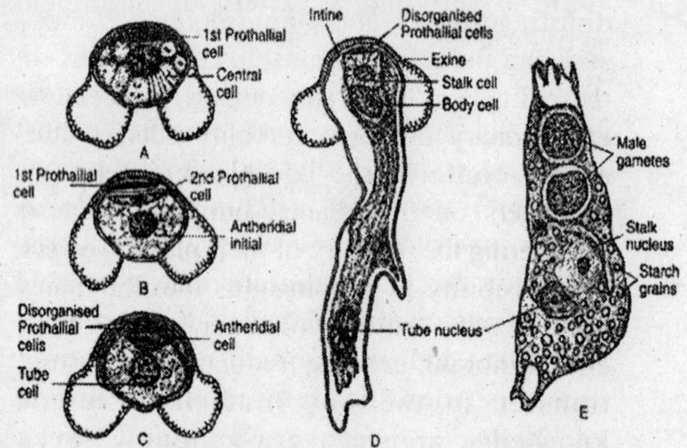

Fig.: *A–E, The stages in the development of male gametophyte*

The spermatogenous cell divides to form two male nuclei just prior to fertilisation. The male nuclei are actually the male gametes which are non-motile and ephemeral.

2. (*a*) The green algae and land plants form a monophyletic lineage (the chlorophytes) that contains both protistan and higher taxa. An important issue regarding the evolution of this green lineage that still remains in question is the identity of the green algal (*i.e.,* flagellate) ancestor of land plants. Modern molecular phylogenetic data provide the framework for reconstructing this evolutionary history and for asking deeper questions about the origin of the genetic inventions that have played a role in the radiation of the green lineage, a group that contains nearly all levels of vegetative morphology, from single cells to filaments to well-organized colonies to complex terrestrial plants.

The green lineageos, however, only one example of photosynthetic taxa that have successfully colonized our planet. A much greater diversity of plastid-containing organisms is defined by the various other forms of algae. The algae include the green algae relatives of land plants and a diverse collection of single-celled and multicellular taxa such as the heterokonts, rhodophytes (red algae), cryptophytes, chlorarachniophytes, dinoflagellates, and haptophytes. Understanding the interrelationships and origins of these lineages is an interesting problem in evolutionary biology, not only because the algae contain the dominant primary producers on this planet, but also because uncovering the ancestry of their plastids offers the possibility to gain insights into the many facets of endosymbiosis, such as endosymbiont genome reduction and gene transfer to the host nucleus. Present knowledge argues overwhelmingly for a cyanobacterial origin of all algal plastids, with stable incorporation of many of the endosymbiont's genes in the host genome. These and other recent data concerning the origins of algae and their plastids form.

2. (*b*) A sporophyte develops from an egg, held within a flask-like archegonium, that has been fertilized. The fertilized egg grows by the formation of additional cells. In the great majority of species the embryonic sporophyte elongates and one part becomes a foot that penetrates the gametophyte and anchors the embryonic sporophyte to the gametophyte. The opposite end will develop into the spore-bearing capsule (and also the supporting stalk, or seta, in species in which the mature capsule is stalked). The embryonic sporophyte is often protected by a calyptra, a covering that develops from the wall of the archegonium. The calyptra is therefore a very close covering over the embryonic sporophyte. This photo shows an intact, reddish calyptra over an embryonic sporophyte of the moss Dawsonia longiseta. In addition to the calyptra there is often some additional protective covering though in a number of genera the tissue of the calyptra fuses with other tissue to form a composite protective covering.

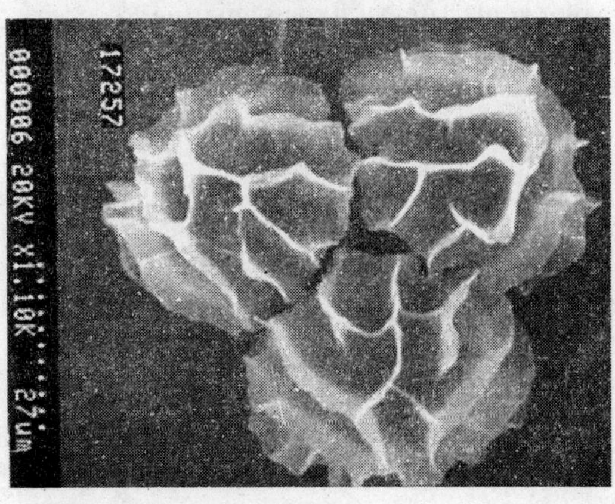

2. (*c*) During the contact between plant and pathogenic microorganism, a particular chain of events is produced in the plant organism. The interaction between plant and pathogen may develop by two ways given below.

1. The plant is provided by a receptor that interacts with bacterial protein. As a result, quick protective reaction is being developed. In such a situation, the bacteria is called avirulent for a given plant genotype.
2. The proteins of the pathogenic organism are virulent for the given plant genotype. The plant is affected by the pathogen, whereas protective mechanisms are being activated more slowly.

In both cases, with the start of pathogenesis gene transcription, the cell walls strengthen. Then in the place of pathogen penetration, the active forms of oxygen are formed, causing the death of infected cells.

At the present moment, the best studied are the molecular mechanisms providing hypersensitive response (HR). In this case, the plant receptor interacts with the pathogen molecule. In order such interaction could occur, the plant and bacteria of a certain genotype should meet, *i.e.*, a bacteria carrying the avirulence gene (avr) interacts with a plant, which has the corresponding R-gene. Such process is called an incompatible combination and leads to quick progressing of events, or to hypersensitive response. Receptors activate the passes of signal transduction and launch several protective systems. In the place of pathogen penetration, the strong oxidants are being synthesized such as H_2O_2, O_2, OH. Then the oxidative burst is being developed, followed by the death of infected cells according to the mechanism similar to apoptosis known in vertebrates. Hypersensitive response is being developed in the place of pathogen penetration into the neighbouring cells. Rapidly developing local process produces signal molecules spreading along vascular system of a plant.

The scheme of molecular events occurring during pathogenesis of plants. SA - salicylic acid; JA - jasmonic acid; H_2O_2 reactive oxygen species; PR - pathogenesis-related genes; SAR - systemic acquired resistance; ISR - induced systemic resistance; PCD-programmed cell death; PTGC-post-transcriptional gene silencing. By thin arrows are given direct involvement of a substance of gene product in a reaction. Empty arrows denote the events that need additional elements for signal transduction.

In dependence of local events, the set of signal molecules is being organized, which in turn, forms this or that generalized response. In the whole plant organism, the pathogenesis-related genes (PR-genes) are activated, the cell walls strengthen, and the plant accumulates some amount of protective substances, which are more effective in the struggle with this definite pathogenic form. In the plant cells, the salicylic acid (SA) is produced in considerable amounts and causes activation of SA-induced genes. The integrity of these events is named as systemic acquired resistance (SAR). The other systemic, or referring to the whole organism, response to pathogen infection is an induced systemic resistance (ISR). It differs from SAR by activation of some differing set of pathogenesis genes and by other ways of signal transduction (without participance of salicylic acid) .

2. (*d*) Role of bacteria in Pharmaceuticals

Antibiotics: Antibiotics are compounds produced by microorganisms which either kill the target pathogen or inhibit its growth. The first antibiotic was discovered by Alexander Fleming in 1929. He accidentally discovered that Pencillium notatum inhibited the growth of gram positive bacterium staphylococcus. Antibiotics are secondary metabolites, mostly produced by streptomyces, a bacterial genus belonging to actinomycetes.

Erythromycin, an antibiotic synthesized by Streptomyces erythraeus is bacteriostatic and acts by interfering with protein synthesis. This antibiotic is also broad spectrum and used in treatment of diphtheria, mycoplasmal infections, whooping cough, etc.

Tetracycline, another antibiotic produced by Streptomyces inhibits protein synthesis of pathogens. It is active against bacteria, mycoplasma, rickettsia and Chlamydia.

Vaccines

A vaccine is a preparation of either the altered whole microorganism or its specific components, that is used to induce immunity in host. Bacteria can be thus used for preparation of vaccines which evoke hormonal and cell mediated responses to ward off pathogens during active infection. Attenuated bacterial vaccines include vaccine against tuberculosis (*Mycobacterium tuberculosis*) and typhoid (*Salmonella* species) bacteria. Inactivated whole agent bacterial vaccines have been formulated for *Vibrio cholera, Pneumococcus, Bordetella* and *Salmonella*. Bacterial vaccines prepared from bacterium Clostridium tetani and *Corynebacterium diptheriae* are the toxoid vaccines, *i.e.*, they contain the inactivated toxins of these bacteria.

Steroid Biotransformation

Plant sterols like stigma sterol, Sapogenins are abundant in nature and can be converted into animal steroids using microorganisms. Few bacterial can alter the plant sterols, *e.g.*, Corynebacterium simplex is used for production of prednisolone.

Role of Bacteria in Agriculture and Industry

The benefits done by bacteria to the agriculture and industries are listed below:

1. Agriculture: Many species of saprophytic and symbiotic bacteria add to the fertility of the soil and provide nitrogen to the plants.

(*a*) **Ammonifying bacteria:** *Bacillus subtilis, B. mycoides, B. ramosus*, etc., act upon the dead animal and plant tissues and decompose their complex organic compounds like proteins into ammonium compounds. They are also known as putrefying bacteria.

(*b*) **Nitrifying bacteria:** Nitrosomonas oxidise the ammonium compounds into nitrites in the presence of free oxygen and Nitrobacter oxidise nitrites into nitrates in the presence of free oxygen. Thus ammonifying and nitrifying bacteria increase the amount of nitrogenous compounds in the soil. Dead plants, animals and dung, etc., are converted into humus by the action of putrefying bacteria. This humus itself acts as fertilizer for plants.

(*c*) **Nitrogen fixing bacteria:** They are Azotobacter, *Clostridium* and *Rhizobium* species. They fix free nitrogen of the soil and make it available to the plants. The first two bacteria live freely in soil and fix the atmospheric nitrogen in the form of nitrogenous compounds in the soil.

Azotobacter is also found in the soil; this fixes the nitrogen gas of the atmosphere in the presence of carbohydrates. This fixation of free nitrogen from the atmosphere through ammonia into free nitrates and again their conversion into ammonia and free nitrogen takes place by means of nitrifying and denitrifying bacteria, along with other organisms. This process is termed nitrogen cycle.

2. Industry: A large number of saprophytic bacteria are employed in the manufacture of various industrial products.

(*a*) **Butter making industry:** Saprophytic bacteria such as Lacto bacilli popularly known as starters, make the milk sour and produce various flavours. These bacteria are largely employed in butter industry for ripening milk and producing flavours in butter.

(*b*) **Cheese making industry:** Bacteria are employed in this industry. First the casein of milk is coagulated and then it is ripened by certain bacteria. Bacteria make the case in spongy, soft and give it characteristic taste and flavour.

(*c*) **Vinegar making industry:** Bacillus aceti convert the sugar solution into vinegar.

(*d*) **Alcohol and acetone manufacture:** Butyl alcohol and acetone are manufactured by the action of bacteria on molasses.

(*e*) **Tobacco curing:** Crude dry tobacco leaves pass through curing and ripening processes before they are ready for use. Bacteria are employed in both these processes and the peculiar taste and smell in the tobacco is due to the bacterial activity. For this purpose molasses and alcohol are added to tobacco.

(*f*) **Tea curing:** Crude tea leaves are acted upon by certain bacteria. The process is known as curing, which is employed to impart a peculiar taste and flavour to the leaves. For this purpose alcohol is added to tea leaves.

(*g*) **Leather tanning:** The hides and skins after drying, salting and clearing are steeped in fluids containing specific bacteria. The process of fermentation goes on for some time and then they are transferred to tan-pits and are further allowed to be fermented. This whole process is known as tanning and the bacteria employed in the process are obtained from cow dung and the excreta of dogs and poultry.

(*h*) **Fibre retting:** Retting is the process of separating fibres from the plant tissues. Bacteria are employed in this industry, which cause decay of the softer tissues and render fibres easily separable mechanically. Fibres of flax, hemp, jute, coconut and other fibrous plants are obtained by immersing the specific plant organs in stagnant pond water where bacteria develop and cause retting.

(*i*) **The sewage work:** In order to remove solid and semi-solid constituents of sewage it is allowed to putrify. Putrifying bacteria are allowed to act upon sewage under anaerobic conditions. It gets decayed and liquefied. It is now filtered and the liquid is either drained out to the river or used as manure in fields. For this purpose, in the soak pits the horse dung is filled up.

5. (*a*) In botanical nomenclature, author citation refers to citing the person or group of people who validly published a botanical name, *i.e.*, who first published the name while fulfilling the formal requirements as specified by the International Code of Nomenclature for algae, fungi, and plants (ICN). In cases where a species is no longer in its original generic placement (*i.e.*, a new combination of genus and specific epithet), both the author(s) of the original genus placement and those of the new combination are given (the former in parentheses).

In botany, it is customary (though not obligatory) to abbreviate author names according to a recognised list of standard abbreviations.

There are differences between the botanical code and the normal practice in zoology. In zoology, the publication year is given following the author name(s) and the authorship of a new combination is normally omitted. A small number of more specialized practices also vary between the recommendations of the botanical and zoological codes.

In biological works, particularly those dealing with taxonomy and nomenclature but also in ecological surveys, it has long been the custom that full citations to the place where a scientific name was published are omitted, but a short-hand is used to cite the author of the name, at least the first time this is mentioned. The author name is frequently not sufficient information, but can help to resolve some difficulties. Problems include:

- The name of a taxon being referred to is ambiguous, as in the case of homonyms such as Ficus L., the fig tree genus, vs. Ficus Riding, 1798, a genus of mollusc's.
- The publication of the name may be in a little-known journal or book. The author name may sometimes help to resolve this.
- The name may not have been validly published, but the supposed author name may be helpful to locate the publication or manuscript in which it was listed.

Rules and recommendations for author citations in botany are covered by Articles 46-50 of the International Code of Nomenclature (ICN). As stated in Article 46 of the botanical Code, in botany it is normal to cite only the author of the taxon name as indicated in the published work, even though this may differ from the stated authorship of the publication itself.

The simplest form of author citation in botany applies when the name is cited in its original rank and its original genus placement (for binomial names and below), where the original author (or authors) are the only name cited, and no parentheses are included.

The Latin term "et" or the ampersand symbol "&" can be used when two authors jointly publish a name.

In many cases the author citation will consist of two parts, the first in parentheses, *e.g.*:

- *Helianthemum coridifolium* (Vill.) Cout.

This form of author citation indicates that the epithet was originally published in another genus (in this case as Cistus coridifolius) by the first author, Dominique Villars (indicated by the enclosing parentheses), but moved to the present genus Helianthemum by the second (revising) author (António Xavier Pereira Coutinho). Alternatively, the revising author changed the rank o1 the taxon, *e.g.,* raising it from subspecies to species (or vice versa), from subgenus to Section, etc.

When citing a botanical name including its author, the author's name is often abbreviated. To encourage consistency, the International Code of Nomenclature for algae, fungi, and plants ICN recommends—

- Recommendation 46A, Note 1 the use of Brummitt & Powell's Authors of Plant Names (1992), where each author of a botanical name has been assigned a unique abbreviation.
- These standard abbreviations can be found at the International Plant Names Index.

For example, in:

Rubus ursinus Cham. & Schldl.

the abbreviation "Cham." refers to the botanist Adelbert von Chamisso and "Schldl." to the botanist Diederich Franz Leonhard von Schlechtendal; these authors jointly described this species (and placed it in the genus Rubus) in 1827.

When "ex" is a component of the author citation, it denotes the fact that an initial description did not satisfy the rules for valid publication, but that the same name was subsequently validly published by a second author or authors (or by the same author in a subsequent publication). Article 46.4 However, if the subsequent author makes clear that the description was due to the earlier author (and that the earlier author accepted the name), then no "ex" is used, and the earlier author is listed alone. For example:

Andropogon aromaticus Sieber ex Schult.

Indicates that Josef Schultes validly published this name (in 1824 in this instance), but his description was based on an earlier description by Franz Sieber. (Note that in botany, the author of the earlier name precedes the later, valid one; in zoology, this sequence (where present) is reversed).

The following forms of citation are all equally correct:

- Rubus ursinus Cham. & Schldl.
- Rubus ursinus Cham. et Schldl.
- Rubus ursinus von Chamisso & von Schlechtendal
- Rubus ursinus von Chamisso et von Schlechtendal

As indicated above, either the original or the revising author may involve multiple words, as per the following examples from the same genus:

- Helianthemum sect. Atlanthemum (Raynaud) G.López, Ortega Oliv. & Romero García
- Helianthemum apenninum Mill. subsp. rothmaleri (Villar ex Rothm.) M.Mayor & Fern.Benito
- Helianthemum conquense (Borja & Rivas Goday ex G.López) Mateo & V.J.Arán Resó

The ancillary term "in" is sometimes employed to indicate that the authorship of the published work is different from that of the name itself, for example:

- Verrucaria aethiobola Wahlenb. in Acharius, Methodus, Suppl.: 17. 1803

5. (*b*) Vavilov Centres of Diversity

(1) Mexico-Guatemala, (2) Peru-Ecuador-Bolivia, (2A) Southern Chile, (2B) Paraguay-Southern Brazil, (3) Mediterranean, (4) Middle East, (5) Ethiopia, (6) Central Asia, (7) Indo-Burma, (7A) Siam-Malaya-Java, (8) China and Korea.

A Vavilov Center (of Diversity) is a region of the world first indicated by Nikolai Vavilov to be an original center for the domestication of plants. Vavilov developed a theory on the centers of origin of cultivated plants. He stated that plants were not domesticated somewhere in the world at random but there are regions where the domestication started. The center of origin is also considered the center of diversity.

Vavilov centers are regions where a high diversity of crop wild relatives can be found, representing the natural relatives of domesticated crop plants. Later in 1935 Vavilov divided the centers into 12, giving the following list:

1. Chinese center
2. Indian (Hindustan) center
3. Indo-Malayan center
4. Central Asiatic center
5. Persian center
6. Mediterranean center
7. Abyssinian center
8. South American center
9. Central American center
10. Chilean center
11. Brazilian-Paraguayan center
12. North American center

Center	***Plants***
1. South Mexican and Central American Center	Includes southern sections of Mexico, Guatemala, Honduras and Costa Rica. • **Grains and Legumes:** maize, common bean, lima bean, tepary bean, jack bean, grain amaranth • **Melon Plants:** malabar gourd, winter pumpkin, chayote • **Fiber Plants:** upland cotton, bourbon cotton, henequen (sisal) • **Miscellaneous:** sweetpotato, arrowroot, pepper, papaya, guava, cashew, wild black cherry, chochenial, cherry tomato, cacao.

Center	Plants
2. South American Center	62 plants listed; three sub-centers Peruvian, Ecuadorean, Bolivian Center: • **Root Tubers:** Andean potato, Other endemic cultivated potato species. Fourteen or more species with chromosome numbers varying from 24 to 60, Edible nasturtium • **Grains and Legumes:** starchy maize, lima bean, common bean • **Root Tubers:** edible canna, potato • **Vegetable Crops:** pepino, tomato, ground cherry, pumpkin, pepper • **Fiber Plants:** Egyptian cotton • **Fruit and Miscellaneous:** cocoa, passion flower, guava, heilborn, quinine tree, tobacco, cherimoya, coca • 2A) Chiloe Center (Island near the coast of southern Chile) • Common potato (48 chromosomes), Chilean strawberry • 2B) Brazilian-Paraguayan Center • Manioc, peanut, rubber tree, pineapple, Brazil nut, cashew, Erva-mate, purple granadilla.
3. Mediterranean Center	Includes the borders of the Mediterranean Sea. 84 listed plants • **Cereals and Legumes:** durum wheat, emmer, Polish wheat, spelt, Mediterranean oats, sand oats, canarygrass, grass pea, pea, lupine • **Forage Plants:** Egyptian clover, white clover, crimson clover, serradella • **Oil and Fiber Plants:** flax, rape, black mustard, olive • **Vegetables:** garden beet, cabbage, turnip, lettuce, asparagus, celery, chicory, parsnip, rhubarb, • Ethereal Oil and Spice Plants: caraway, anise, thyme, peppermint, sage, hop.
4. Middle East	Includes interior of Asia Minor, all of Transcaucasia, Iran, and the highlands of Turkmenistan. 83 species • **Grains and Legumes:** einkorn wheat, durum wheat, poulard wheat, common wheat, oriental wheat, Persian wheat, two-row barley, rye, Mediterranean oats, common oats, lentil, lupine • **Forage Plants:** alfalfa, Persian clover, fenugreek, vetch, hairy vetch • **Fruits:** pomegranate, apple, pear, quince, cherry, hawthorn.
5. Ethiopia	Includes Abyssinia, Eritrea, and part of Somaliland. 38 species listed; rich in wheat and barley. • **Grains and Legumes:** Abyssinian hard wheat, poulard wheat, emmer, Polish wheat, barley, grain sorghum, pearl millet, African millet, cowpea, flax, teff • **Miscellaneous:** sesame, castor bean, garden cress, coffee, okra, myrrh, indigo.
6. Central Asiatic Center	Includes Northwest India (Punjab, Northwest Frontier Provinces and Kashmir), Afghanistan, Tajikistan, Uzbekistan, and western Tian-Shan. 43 plants • **Grains and Legumes:** common wheat, club wheat, shot wheat, peas, lentil, horse bean, chickpea, mung bean, mustard, flax, sesame

Center	Plants
	• **Fiber Plants:** hemp, cotton. • **Vegetables:** onion, garlic, spinach, carrot. • **Fruits:** pistacio, pear, almond, grape, apple.
7. Indian Center	Two subcenters **Indo-Burma:** Main Center (India): Includes Assam and Burma, but not Northwest India, Punjab, nor Northwest Frontier Provinces, 117 plants • **Cereals and Legumes:** rice, chickpea, pigeon pea, urd bean, mung bean, rice bean, cowpea. • **Vegetables and Tubers:** eggplant, cucumber, radish, taro, yam. • **Fruits:** mango, orange, tangerine, citron, tamarind. • **Sugar, Oil, and Fiber Plants:** sugarcane, coconut palm, sesame, safflower, tree cotton, oriental cotton, jute, crotalaria, kenaf. • **Spices, Stimulants, Dyes, and Miscellaneous:** hemp, black pepper, gum arabic, sandalwood, indigo, cinnamon tree, croton, bamboo. • **7A) Siam-Malaya-Java:** statt Indo-Malayan Center: Includes Indo-China and the Malay Archipelago, 55 plants. • **Cereals and Legumes:** Job's tears, velvet bean. • **Fruits:** pummelo, banana, breadfruit, mangosteen. • **Oil, Sugar, Spice, and Fiber Plants:** candlenut, coconut palm, sugarcane, clove, nutmeg, black pepper, manila hemp.

5. (*c*) Five botanical names of fibre yielding plants and parts from where fibre is obtained.

1. *Abroma augusta* L. (Perrenial Indian hemp)

   Part used : Bast fibre (stem and branches)

2. *Coco nucifera* L. (Coconut fibre, coir)

   Part used: Coir, fibre from husk of the coconut

3. *Cannabis sativa* L. (Hemp fibre) Hemp fibre from hemp stalk

4. *Crotalaria juncea* L. (Sunnhemp)

   Fibre from stem and branches

5. *Gossypium arboreum* L. (Cotton).

   Cotton fibre obtained from seeds

5. (*d*) In geologic time, the Mesozoic Era, the second era in the Phanerozoic Eon, spans the time between roughly 250 million years ago (mya) and 65 mya.

The Mesozoic Era contains three geologic time periods including the Triassic Period (250 mya to approximately 206 mya), Jurassic Period (206 mya to approximately 144 mya), and the Cretaceous Period (144 mya to 65 mya).

Flora: Conifers were the dominant terrestrial plants for most of the Mesozoic. Flowering plants appeared late in the era but did not become widespread until the Cenozoic. The dominant land plant species of the time were gymnosperms, which are vascular, cone-bearing, non-flowering plants such as conifers that produce seeds without a coating. This is opposed to the earth's current flora, in which the dominant land plants in terms of number of species are angiosperms. One particular plant genus, Ginkgo, is thought to have evolved at this time and is represented today by a single species, Ginkgo biloba. As well, the extant genus Sequoia is believed to have evolved in the Mesozoic. Some plant species had distributions that were markedly different from succeeding periods; *e.g.*, the Schizeales, a fern order, were skewed to the Northern Hemisphere in the Mesozoic, but are now better represented in the Southern Hemisphere.

Fauna: Dinosaurs were the dominant terrestrial vertebrates throughout much of the Mesozoic.

The extinction of nearly all animal species at the end of the Permian Period allowed for the radiation of many new lifeforms. In particular, the extinction of the large herbivorous pareiasaurs and carnivorous gorgonopsians left those ecological niches empty. Some were filled by the surviving cynodonts and dicynodonts, the latter of which subsequently became extinct.

Recent research indicates that the specialized animals that formed complex ecosystems, with high biodiversity, complex food webs and a variety of niches, took much longer to reestablish, recovery did not begin until the start of the mid-Triassic, 4M to 6M years after the extinction and was not complete until 30M years after the Permian–Triassic extinction event. Animal life was then dominated by various archosaurs: dinosaurs, pterosaurs, and aquatic reptiles such as ichthyosaurs, plesiosaurs, and mosasaurs.

The climatic changes of the late Jurassic and Cretaceous provided for further adaptive radiation. The Jurassic was the height of archosaur diversity, and the first birds and eutherian mammals also appeared. Angiosperms radiated sometime in the early Cretaceous, first in the tropics, but the even temperature gradient allowed them to spread toward the poles throughout the period. By the end of the Cretaceous, angiosperms dominated tree floras in many areas, although some evidence suggests that biomass was still dominated by cycad and ferns until after the Cretaceous–Paleogene extinction.

Some have argued that insects diversified with angiosperms because insect anatomy, especially the mouth parts, seems particularly well-suited for flowering plants.

6. (*a*) Outline of Bentham and Hooker System of Classification

Phanerogams or seed plants

Class 1: Dicotyledons
(14 series,
25 orders and 165 families)

Subclass 1 : Polypetalae
Series 1: Thalamiflorae (6 orders)
Series 2: Disciflorae (4 orders)
Series 3: Calyciflorae (5 orders)

Subclass 2: Gamopetalae
Series 1: Inferae (3 orders)
Series 2: Heteromerae (3 orders)
Series 3: Bicarpellatae (4 orders)

Class 2 : Gymospermae
3 families

Class 3 Monocotyledons
(7 series, 34 families)

Series 1: Microspermae
Series 2: Epigynae
Series 3: Coronarieae
Series 4: Calycineae
Series 5: Nudiflorae
Series 6: Apocarpae
Series 7: Glumaceae

Outline of Bentham and Hooker System of Classification

Subclass 3: Monochlamydeae

Series 1: Curvembryeae

Series 2: Multiovulatae aquaticae

Series 3: Multiovulatae terretris

Series 4: Microembryeae

Series 5: Daphnales

Series 6: Achlamydosporae

Series 7: Unisexuales

Series 8: Ordines anomali.

Merits of Bentham and Hooker System of Classification

(*i*) It is a natural system of classification with immense practical utility. It is very popular in many countries and used for arrangement of plant species in Kew Herbarium, and in many countries including India.

(*ii*) The descriptions of the taxa are based on an actual study, thus making the system detailed, authentic and highly practical. The accuracy of Latin descriptions is unparallel.

(*iii*) The larger genera are divided into subgenera with definite number of species which helps in easy identification of plants.

(*iv*) The keys for the identification of genera and families are precise and useful.

(*v*) It includes geographical distribution of genera and species.

(*vi*) Dicots start with Ranales which is considered as most primitive amongst the angiosperms by many taxonomists.

(*vii*) The gymnosperms are placed as a separate independent group and not along with dicots as had been done by de Candolle.

(*viii*) The monocots are placed after dicots which is accepted by present day taxonomists.

(*ix*) The position of gamopetalae after polypetalae is accepted as fused petals are considered an advanced character over free petals.

(*x*) The sequence adopted in the classification suggests an evolutionary pattern.

Demerits of Bentham and Hooker System of Classification

1. The classification does not include any information about the origin of angiosperms even when it was published after Darwin theory of evolution.

2. The position of gymnosperms between dicots and monocots is inappropriate according to the accepted evolutionary sequence. The gymnosperms constitute an independent group considered as equivalent to the angiosperms and are placed before them in most classifications.

3. The grouping of Monochlamydeae is artificial as it is based on single character and has separated some closely related families. For example:

   (*i*) Chenopodiaceae, Illecebraceae (placed in Monochlamydeae) are related to Caryophyllaceae (placed in Polypetalae), and placed in same order by modern taxonomists.

   (*ii*) Podestemaceae (belonging to Multiovulatae aquaticae, Monochlamydeae) is regarded closely related to Saxifragaceae or Crassulaceae of Rosales (placed in Polypetalae).

   (*iii*) Lauraceae (belonging to Daphnales, Monochlamydeae) is considered related to Magnoliaceae of Ranales (belonging to Polypetalae).

   (*iv*) Nepenthacaeae (belonging to Multiovulatae terrestris, Monochlamydeae) is related to Saracenniaceae (placed in Parietales, Polypetalae).

4. Advanced family like Orchidaceae with inferior ovary and zygomorphic flowers has been considered primitive by placing it in the beginning of Monocots.

5. The arrangement of Monocots is unnatural and un-phylogenetic.
6. Compositae or Asteraceae has been placed in the beginning of Gamopetalae which is unnatural.
7. Families Liliaceae (placed in Coronarieae) and Amaryllidaceae (placed in Epigynae) are closely related but have been separated on the basis of ovary characteristics.
8. The position of Series Inferae with inferior ovary before the series Heteromerae and Bicarpellatae with superior ovaries, is not accepted as the inferior ovary is derived from the superior ovary.

6. (*b*) Floral Characteristics of fabaceae

Inflorescence: *Racemose*.

Flower: Complete, bisexual, zygomorphic, perigynous, bracteate/ebracteate.

Calyx: Five sepals, gamosepalous; imbricate aestivation.

Corolla: Five petals, polypetalous, papilionaceous, vexillary aestivation.

Androecium: Ten stamens (9+1), diadelphous, anther dithecous.

Gynoecium: Superior ovary, monocarpellary, unilocular, marginal placentation, single, sort -style and flat, hairy-stigma.

Fruit: Legume.

Seed: One or more, non-endospermic.

Floral formula:

Fabaceae floral formula

% ⚥ $K_{(5)}C_1 + (2) + 2A_{(9)} + 1G_1$

Floral diagram:

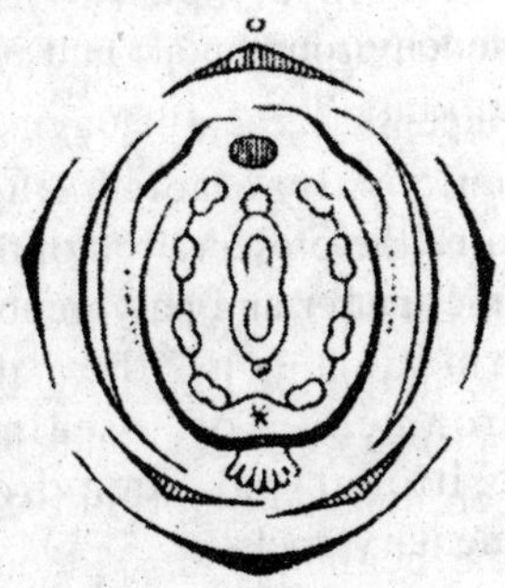

Economic importance:

- Pulses (gram, moong, soya bean)
- Medicine (muliathi)
- Edible oil (soya bean, groundnut)
- Fibres (sun hemp)
- Dye (Indigofera)
- Fodder (Sesbania, Trifolium)
- Ornamentals (lupin, sweet pea)

Floral Characteristics of Asclepiadaceae

Floral characters:

Inflorescence: Mostly umbellate cymes (Calotropis) or dichasial cyme ending in monochasial cyme.

Flower: Bracteate or ebracteate, pedicellate, complete, hermaphrodite, actinomorphic, rarely zygomorphic (Ceropegia), pentamerous, hypogynous.

Calyx: Sepals 5, polysepalous or gamosepalous-fused near the base, quincuncial aestivation, sometimes valvate.

Corolla: Petals 5, gamopetalous, 5 lobed, twisted aestivation or valvate, corona may be scaly or hairy out growth from petals – corolline corona in Cryptostegia, Cryptolepis or form staminal tube, *i.e.*, staminal corona in Calotropis and Asciepias.

Androecium: Stamens 5, synandrous, gynostegium (stamens fused with stigmatic disc to form gynostegium), anthers dithecous, epipetalous, coherent; the pollen grains of each half anther usually agglutinated into granular mass of tetrads or waxy pollen called pollinium (Asclepias, Calotropis). Thus each stamen has two pollinia.

The pollinia of two adjacent anther halves are connected together at the black, dot-like gland called corpusculum by appendages called – retinacula. The two pollinia (of adjacent anther halves), two retinacula and a corpusculum together form a single translator. So in all there are 5 translators.

Gynoecium: Bicarpellary, syncarpous, ovaries free, superior, enclosed in staminal tube, ovules many on marginal placentation, each carpel is unilocular; style 2, free, distinct; stigmas united to form a pentangular disc with which anthers are fused to form gynostegium.

Fruit: An etaerio of two, often widely divergent follicles; in some one follicle is abortive.

Seed: Many small, compressed with long silky hairs.

Pollination: Entomophilous, translator mechanism.

Floral formula:

$$\oplus ☿ K_{5 \text{ or } (5)} \widehat{C_{(5)} A_{(5)}} \widehat{G_{(2)}}.$$

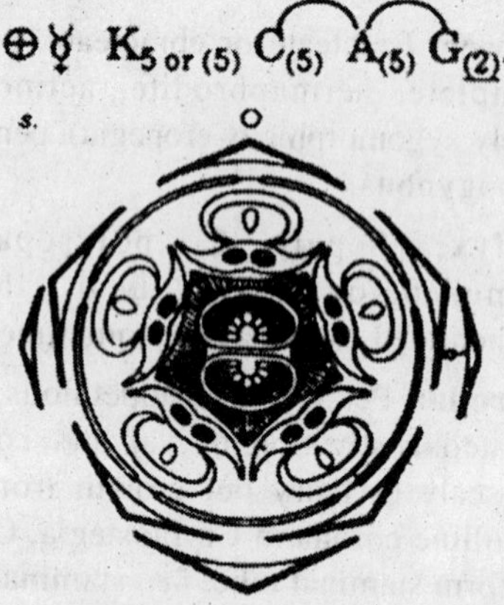

Fig.: *Floral diagram of Asclepias incarnata, the gynostegium along with the coronary structures can be observed inside the petals. (after Eichler)*

Economic Importance of Asclepiadaceae:

1. **Food:** Gymnema lactiferum yields latex which is used as food in Ceylon.
2. **Fibres:** Some plants like Daemia extensa, Calotropis procera, C. gigantea, Marsdenia and Leptadenia, etc., yield silky fibres which are used for making ropes, mat, stuffing pillows, etc.
3. **Medicinal:** The source of medicine in the family is latex from which alkaloids are extracted. The roots of Oxystelma esculentum are specific for jaundice. This roots of Pentatropis are used in gonorrhoea. Hemidesmus indicus is used in leucorrhoea, rheumatism and in snake bites. Daemia extensa is used in cough; asthma and diarrhoea.
4. **Rubber:** *Cryptostegia grandiflora* is a natural source of rubber in India.
5. **Poison:** Some species of Asclepias are important as live-stock poison. The sap of Matelea has been used as an arrow poison.
6. **Ornamental:** Asclepias, Cryptostegia, Hoya, Huernia, Ceropegia, Periploca etc., are cultivated for ornamental purposes.

6. (*c*) Palynology is the branch of biology that studies tiny particles like pollen and spores. Studying the pollen and spores produced by plants tells us a lot about the plants themselves, but that's not all that palynology can do! Pollen and spores also give us clues that we use to understand what life was like in the past, help people who suffer from allergies, track the migration of insects, and even solve crimes!

Palynology is used for a diverse range of applications, related to many scientific disciplines:

Biostratigraphy and geochronology. Geologists use palynological studies in biostratigraphy to correlate strata and determine the relative age of a given bed, horizon, formation or stratigraphical sequence.

- **Palaeoecology and climate change:** Palynology can be used to reconstruct past vegetation (land plants) and marine and freshwater phytoplankton communities, and so infer past environmental (palaeoenvironmental) and palaeoclimatic conditions.
- Organic palynofacies studies, which examine the preservation of the particulate organic matter and palynomorphs provide information on the depositional environment of sediments and depositional palaeoenvironments of sedimentary rocks.

- Geothermal alteration studies examine the colour of palynomorphs extracted from rocks to give the thermal alteration and maturation of sedimentary sequences, which provide estimates of maximum palaeotemperatures.
- **Limnology studies:** Freshwater palynomorphs and animal and plant fragments, including the prasinophytes and desmids (green algae) can be used to study past lake levels and long term climate change.
- Taxonomy and evolutionary studies.
- **Forensic palynology:** The study of pollen and other palynomorphs for evidence at a crime scene.
- **Allergy studies:** Studies of the geographic distribution and seasonal production of pollen, can help sufferers of allergies such as hay fever.
- **Melissopalynology:** The study of pollen and spores found in honey.
- Archaeological palynology examines human uses of plants in the past. This can help determine seasonality of site occupation, presence or absence of agricultural practices or products, and 'plant-related activity areas' within an archaeological context. Bonfire Shelter is one such example of this application.

6. (*d*) Ethnobotany is the study of the relationship between people and plants. This interdisciplinary field includes studying plants as wild foods and as agricultural crops; as constructs for houses and modes of transportation; as baskets, pottery, and art; as clothing and types of weaving; as medicines and alternative methods for healing; and in the context of cultural myths and religious ceremonies. Research topics address more complex issues, including the cultural consequences of the extinction of a particular plant species on the diet of a culture, impacts of acculturation on a culture's uses of plants, and the transmission of ethnobotanical knowledge from one generation to the next.

Role of medicinal plants in modern medicines

The use of natural products with therapeutic properties is as ancient as human civilization and, for a long time, mineral, plant and animal products were the main sources of drugs. Primitive peoples throughout the world made use of their indigenous flora as a source of medicines. Through the process of trial and error, these cultures examined and discovered many plants that produce unique molecular entities with valuable biological properties such as aspirin from willow bark (Salix alba), the anticancer alkaloid vincristine from the Madagascar periwinkle (Catharanthus roseus), and cardiac glycoside digitoxin from Digitalis species. Galegine, an active antihyperglycemic agent isolated from the plant Galega officinalis L. provided the template for the synthesis of metformin and opened up interest in the synthesis of other biguanidine-type antidiabetic drugs.

Recently, Butler *et al.* (2015) 19 have reported that a total of 25 natural product (NP) based drugs were approved for marketing worldwide during 2008 to Introduction Chemical and Biological Screening of Selected Medicinal Plants m3 2013, among which 5 are classified as NP, 10 as semi-synthetic NPs, and 10 as NP derived drugs.

7. (*a*) FAMILY: FABACEAE

1. Clovers

Botanical Name: *Triolium* species

Active Constituents: Isoflavones

Uses: Used as natural remedies to alleviate the symptoms of menopause such as hot flashes, headaches and skin problems.

2. Sunnhemp

Botanical Name: *Crotalaria juncea*

Active Constituents: Fibre

Uses: Used as fodder and much used in the traditional manufacture of ropes stings, twins, floormat and finishing nets.

3. Alfaalfa

Botanical Name: *Medicago sativa*

Active constituents: Saponin glycosides

Uses: Used for grazing, hay, silage as well as green manure and cover crop.

4. Silk Tree

Botanical Name: *Albizia* species

Active Constituents: Natural protein fibre

Uses: Used in clothing, furniture, industry, medicine and biomaterial.

5. Hyacinth bean

Botanical Name: *Lablab purpureus*

Active Constituents: Cyanogenic glycosides.

Uses: The hyacinth bean is an old domesticated pulse and multipurpose crop. Due to seed availabilities of one forage cultivar, it is often green as forage for livestock and as an ornamental plants.

FAMILY: ROSACEAE

1. Apple

Botanical Name: *Malus pumila*

Active Constituents: Vitamins, Minerals, Proteins, Carbohydrates, Threonine, Isoleucine, Leucine, Lycine, Methionine, Cystine, etc.

Uses: Apples are the second most popular fruit in the country. We eat in average 46 pounds of apples and apple products per person annually.

2. Pear

Botanical Name: *Pyrus commumis*

Active Constituents: Arbutin and chlorogenic acid

Uses: Pears are a mild, sweet fruit with a fibros center. They are rich in important antioxidants, flavonniods and dietary fiber and pack all of these nutrients in a fat free cholesterol-free, 100, caloric package.

3. Plums

Botanical Name: *Prunus* species

Active Constituents: Phenolic Compounds sorbitol and isatin.

Uses: Plums are known for their laxative effect, which has been attributed to the various compounds present in the fruits, such as dietary fibre, sorbitol and isatin. Because it aids the digestive system, prunes and prune juice are often used to help regulate the functioning of the digestive system.

4. Almonds

Botanical Name: *Prunus dulcis*

Active Constituents: Mono-unsaturated oleic acid, Linoleic acid and saturated fatty acid.

Uses: It is Ayurvedic healing for its sattvic values. Almond and its nourishing oil has been prescribed in Ayurvedic medication for treating loss of memory frigidity, premature ejaculation, mood fluctuation, Alzeimer's disease, psoriasis, dark complexion, debility, muscular pain and dry skin conditions.

5. Roses

Botanical Name: *Rosa* species

Active Constituents: French rose contains about 0.03% the volatile oil, mainly phenylethanol, citronellol, Nerol, Geraniol, Eugenol.

Uses: Basic uses of rose flower like cooking, cosmetics, gardening, medicines, etc.

The volatile oil content to promote the role of bile secretion. Rose tea helps to fight against infection in the digestive tract and intestines.

FAMILY: BRASSICACEAE

1. Cabage

Botanical Name: *Brassica oleracea* var. *capitata*

Active Constituents: Sterols, triglycericles and essential fatty acids.

Uses: Commonly eaten as a vegetable. People also use the leaves for medicine.

2. Cauliflower

Botanical Name: *Brassica oleracea* var. *botrytis*

Active Constituents: Vitamins, phenol, flavonoid and free sugar, fatty acid and antioxidants.

Uses: Commonly eaten as vegetable. It helps reduce cancer risk, fight in inflammation, decrease risk of heart disease and brain disorders, provide high levels of vitamins and minerals. It also improves digestion and detoxification. It helps balance hormone and preserve eye health.

3. Turnip

Botanical Name: *Brassica rapa* Subsp. *rapa*

Active Constituents: Starch, sugar, ascorbic acid and glucosinolates

Uses: Though a healthy vegetable overall, the turnip greens are the part that house the majority of antioxidants. The leafy greens offer vitamins A, C, Xanthin and lutein. These antioxidants work together with phytochemicals to combat disease causing toxins in the body.

4. Radish

Botanical Name: *Raphnus raphanistrum* subsp. *sativus*

Active Constituents: Alkaloids and Nitrogen compounds Coumarins, enzymes, Gibberellins, glucosinolates, organic acids, Phenolic compounds, etc.

Uses: The root is used as food and also as medicines. It is used for stomach and intestinal disorders, bile-ducts problems, loss of appetite and swelling of the mouth and throat inflammation or excessive mucus of the respiratory tract, bronchitis, colds and cough.

5. Rapseed

Botanical Name: *Brassica napus*

Uses: Glucosinolate, sinapine, phytics acid, erucic acid

Active Constituents: Rapeseed oil is used as a vegetable oil. It is a good source of Vitamin E and it is safe to cook at high temperatures with a burning point of 230ºC much higher than olive oil.

7. (*b*) Different Levels of Biodiversity

1. **Species diversity:** It is the effective number of different species that are represented in a collection of individuals (a dataset). The effective number of species refers to the number of equally-abundant species needed to obtain the same mean proportional species abundance as that observed in the dataset of interest (where all species may not be equally abundant). Species diversity consists of two components, species richness and species evenness. Species richness is a simple count of species, whereas species evenness quantifies how equal the abundances of the species are.

2. **Genetic Diversity:** The level of biodiversity, refers to the total number of genetic characteristics in the genetic makeup of a species. It is distinguished from genetic variability,which describes the tendency of genetic characteristics to vary. Genetic diversity serves as a way for populations to adapt to changing environments. With more variation, it is more likely that some individuals in a population will possess variations of alleles that are suited for the environment. Those individuals are more likely to survive to produce offspring bearing that allele. The population will continue for more generations because of the success of these individuals.

3. **Ecosystem diversity:** Refers to the diversity of a place at the level of ecosystems. The term differs from biodiversity, which refers to variation in species rather than ecosystems. Ecosystem

diversity can also refer to the variety of ecosystems present in a biosphere, the variety of species and ecological processes that occur in different physical settings.

***In-situ* Conservation Methods:** *In-situ* conservation, the conservation of species in their natural habitats, is considered the most appropriate way of conserving biodiversity.

Conserving the areas where populations of species exist naturally is an underlying condition for the conservation of biodiversity. That's why protected areas form a central element of any national strategy to conserve biodiversity.

***Ex-situ* Conservation Methods:** *Ex-situ* conservation is the preservation of components of biological diversity outside their natural habitats. This involves conservation of genetic resources, as well as wild and cultivated or species, and draws on a diverse body of techniques and facilities. Some of these include:

Gene banks, *e.g.*, seed banks, sperm and ova banks, field banks.

Role of Cryopreservation in the Conservation of Plant Biodiversity: According to some sources there are approximately 250,000 higher plant species in the world today, but of these many thousands are endangered. Between 40-100000 plants have been used by mankind over the years, but only approximately 7000 plant species are cultivated today, of which about 30 form the basis of the world's agriculture. Of these, three crops - maize, wheat and rice - provide over half of humans' calorific and protein requirements. However, their diversity is declining, and, for example over the last century the number of varieties of maize grown in America has fallen by over 90%. Such narrowing of the diversity of crop varieties makes staple food supply vulnerable to interruption by the effects of pests, diseases and global climate change. To maintain food security mankind must keep the diversity of plants and crop plants to allow for the breeding of plants for future needs.

Many plant species are traditionally and effectively conserved by conventional seed storage techniques, which involve drying seeds to approximately 5% moisture content and maintaining them at 18°C (the temperature of a domestic freezer). Seeds that can be conserved this way are known as orthodox seeds. However, many plants, particularly tropical species, do not produce orthodox seeds; rather their seeds rapidly lose viability and cannot survive desiccation and/ or cold storage. Such seeds are known as recalcitrant. For plants, which produce recalcitrant seeds or that are propagated vegetatively, *e.g.*, banana and potato, traditional conservation involves maintenance in field collections. However, such collections remain vulnerable to loss due to the effects of extreme weather conditions, pests and diseases, and increasing maintenance costs. Plant biotechnology provides alternative approaches that can be used to safeguard the survival of such plant species.

7. (*c*) In botany, apomixis was defined by Hans Winkler as replacement of the normal sexual reproduction by asexual reproduction, without fertilization. Its etymology is Greek for "away from" + "mixing". This definition notably does not mention meiosis. Thus "normal asexual reproduction" of plants, such as propagation from cuttings or leaves, has never been considered to be apomixis, but replacement of the seed by a plantlet or replacement of the flower by bulbils were categorized as types of apomixis. Apomictically produced offspring are genetically identical to the parent plant.

Schematic of sexual and apomictic developmental pathways. The sexual pathway is depicted in the center: a somatic cell undergoes a reductional division and eventually forms an embryo sac with reduced polar nuclei in the central cell and a reduced egg cell, both of which participate in double fertilization. The fertilized egg gives rise to a sexually derived embryo and the fertilized central cell forms the endosperm. In apomicts, key developmental steps are deregulated such that an unreduced cell lineage gives rise to the embryo sac containing unreduced polar nuclei in the central cell and an unreduced egg (gametophytic apomixis). Alternatively, an unreduced somatic cell gives rise directly to an embryo (sporophytic apomixis). In gametophytic apomixis, the embryo results from parthenogenetic development of the unreduced egg cell. The unreduced embryo sac can originate from an aberrant or missing meiosis (diplospory) or from an unreduced (nonmeiotic) somatic cell that directly develops into an embryo sac (apospory). In gametophytic apomicts, the central cell either develops autonomously or, as in the majority of apomicts, requires fertilization to initiate endosperm development (pseudogamy), whereas in sporophytic apomicts, embryos are usually reliant on the presence of a sexually derived endosperm.

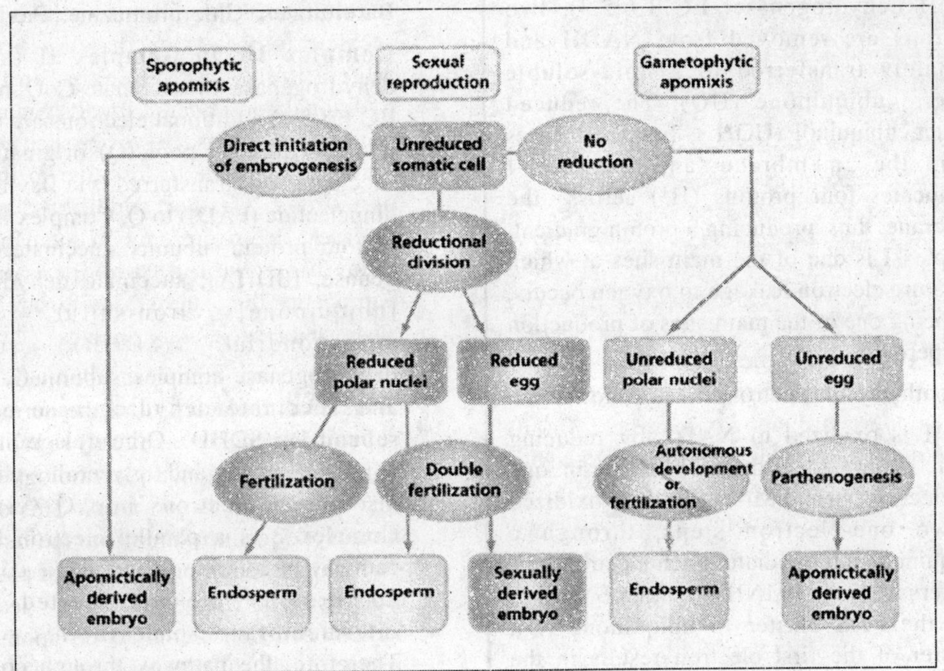

Genetics of Apomixis: Apomixis, asexual reproduction through seeds, has the potential to revolutionize agriculture if its genetic basis can be elucidated. However, the genetic control of natural apomixis has remained obscure until quite recently, owing to all the complications of Mendelian genetics, such as epistatic gene interactions, components that are expressed sporophytically and gametophytically, expression modifiers, polyploidy, aneuploidy, segregation distortion, suppressed recombination, etc., that seem to have accumulated during the evolution of apomixis. In this review we show how molecular markers and superior phenotypic methods have been used to clarify the genetics of apomixis in monocots as well as dicots during the past 15 years. Many of the complexities in the genetics of apomixis are likely secondary and have evolved as a consequence of the reproductive process. New mapping techniques, such as comparative mapping, linkage disequilibrium mapping, and deletion mapping, and new high-throughput sequencing methods, will help to penetrate the core of apomixis chromosomal regions. If the evolutionary genetic load can be exposed and removed, the apomixis genes may be used in agriculture as a tool to fix elite genotypes.

PAPER-II

1. (*a*) Complexes in Electron Transport Chain of Mitochondria

Complex I: In Complex I (NADH: ubiquinone oxidoreductase, NADH-CoQ reductase, or NADH dehydrogenase; EC 1.6.5.3), two electrons are removed from NADH and ultimately transferred to a lipid-soluble carrier, ubiquinone (UQ). The reduced product, ubiquinol (UQH_2), freely diffuses within the membrane, and Complex I translocates four protons (H^+) across the membrane, thus producing a proton gradient. Complex I is one of the main sites at which premature electron leakage to oxygen occurs, thus being one of the main sites of production of superoxide.

The pathway of electrons is as follows:

NADH is oxidized to NAD^+, by reducing Flavin mononucleotide to $FMNH_2$ in one two-electron step. $FMNH_2$ is then oxidized in two one-electron steps, through a semiquinone intermediate. Each electron thus transfers from the $FMNH_2$ to an Fe-S cluster, from the Fe-S cluster to ubiquinone (Q). Transfer of the first electron results in the free-radical (semiquinone) form of Q, and transfer of the second electron reduces the semiquinone form to the ubiquinol form, QH_2. During this process, four protons are translocated from the mitochondrial matrix to the intermembrane space. As the electrons become continuously oxidized and reduced throughout the complex an electron current is produced along the 180 Angstrom width of the complex within the membrane. This current powers the active transport of four protons to the intermembrane space per two electrons from NADH.

This complex is inhibited by Alkylguanides (Example: Guanethidine), Rotenone, Barbiturates, Chlorpromazine, Piericidin.

Complex II: In Complex II (succinate dehydrogenase or succinate-CoQ reductase; EC 1.3.5.1) additional electrons are delivered into the quinone pool (Q) originating from succinate and transferred (via flavin adenine dinucleotide (FAD)) to Q. Complex II consists of four protein subunits: succinate dehydrogenase, (SDHA); succinate dehydrogenase [ubiquinone] iron-sulfur subunit, mitochondrial, (SDHB); succinate dehydrogenase complex subunit C, (SDHC) and succinate dehydrogenase complex, subunit D, (SDHD). Other electron donors (*e.g.*, fatty acids and glycerol 3-phosphate) also direct electrons into Q (via FAD). Complex 2 is a parallel electron transport pathway to complex 1, but unlike complex 1, no protons are transported to the intermembrane space in this pathway. Therefore, the pathway through complex 2 contributes less energy to the overall electron transport chain process.

This complex is inhibited by Carboxin.

Complex III: In Complex III (cytochrome bc1 complex or $CoQH_2$-cytochrome complex reductase; EC 1.10.2.2), the Q-cycle contributes to the proton gradient by an asymmetric absorption/release of protons. Two electrons are removed from QH_2 at the QO site and sequentially transferred to two molecules of cytochrome c, a water-soluble electron carrier located within the inter membrane space. The two other electrons sequentially pass across the protein to the Qi site where the quinone part of ubiquinone is reduced to quinol. A proton gradient is formed by one quinol ($2H+2e^-$) oxidations at the Qo site to form one quinone ($2H+2e^-$) at the Qi site. (in total four protons are translocated: two protons reduce quinone to quinol and two protons are released from two ubiquinol molecules).

QH_2 + 2 cytochrome c (FeIII) + 2 H+in
Q + 2 cytochrome c (FeII) + 4 H+out.

When electron transfer is reduced (by a high membrane potential or respiratory inhibitors such as antimycin A), Complex III may leak electrons to molecular oxygen, resulting in superoxide formation.

This complex is inhibited by British Antilewisite(BAL), Napthoquinone and Antimycin.

Complex IV: In Complex IV (cytochrome c oxidase; EC 1.9.3.1), sometimes called cytochrome AA3, four electrons are removed from four molecules of cytochrome c and transferred to molecular oxygen (O_2), producing two molecules of water. At the same time, eight protons are removed from the mitochondrial matrix (although only four are translocated across the membrane), contributing to the proton gradient. The activity of cytochrome c oxidase is inhibited by cyanide, carbon monoxide, azide, hydrogen sulphide(H_2S).

1. (*b*) **Molecular Basis of Sex Determination:** Sex determination is a process that leads to the physical separation of male and female gamete-producing structures to different individuals of a species. Even though sexually reproducing species have only three possible options—to relegate the two sexes to separate individuals, to keep them together on the same individual, or to have a combination of both—plants in particular display a great variety of sexual phenotypes. In angiosperms, a sex-determining process is manifest in species that are monoecious, in which at least some flowers are unisexual but the individual is not, or dioecious, in which unisexual plants produce flowers of one sex type. In plants that produce no flowers and are homosporous, sex determination is manifest in the gametophyte generation with the production of egg- and sperm-forming gametangia on separate individual gametophytes.

1. (*c*) **Significance of Accessory Chromosome:** An unpaired sex chromosome. Either of a pair of chromosomes in diploid cells, or a single chromosome in haploid cells, carrying genes that determine the sex and sex-linked characteristics of an organism. Most mammals, including humans, have one pair of sex chromosomes in diploid cells, designated XX in females and XY in males.

1. (*d*) The process of genetic modification involves inserting a gene from bacteria or a virus (or a gene that helps plants survive the application of highly toxic pesticides) into an organism where it would normally not be found.

The purpose is to alter the genetic code in plants and animals to make them more productive or resistant to pests or farming techniques, like being doused with chemicals that would ordinarily kill them.

Merits of GM Plants in India: Growing GMO plants is supposed to allow farmers to:

(*i*) Spend less money producing more food.

(*ii*) **Use fewer pesticides and herbicides:** The amount of pesticide chemicals used on the plants are reduced, so their exposure to dangerous pesticides are also reduced.

(*iii*) Do less tilling to remove weeds, thereby protecting the soil.

(*iv*) Foods with better texture, flavour and nutritional value.

(*v*) Foods with a longer shelf life for easier shipping.

Demerits of GM Plants in India

(*i*) Creating "super weeds" that have evolved a resistance to glyphosate, a common herbicide in GMO food production.

(*ii*) **Allergic Reactions:** It states that genetic modification often adds or mixes proteins that were not indigenous to the original animal or plant, which might cause new allergic reactions in our body.

(*iii*) **Raise of Super pest:** The chance in evolution of pest is more.

(*iv*) **Cross-Pollination:** Cross-pollination can cover quite large distances, where new genes can be included in the offspring of organic, traditional plants or crops that are miles away. This can result in difficulty in distinguishing which crop fields are organic and which are not, posing a problem to the task of properly labelling non-GMO food products.

1. (*e*) Chi-square test: A chi-squared test, also written as $\chi 2$ test, is any statistical hypothesis test where the sampling distribution of the test statistic is a chi-squared distribution when the null hypothesis is true. Without other qualification, 'chi-squared test' often is used as short for Pearson's chi-squared test. The chi-squared test is used to determine whether there is a significant difference between the expected frequencies and the observed frequencies in one or more categories.

In the standard applications of the test, the observations are classified into mutually exclusive classes, and there is some theory, or say null hypothesis, which gives the probability that any observation falls into the corresponding class. The purpose of the test is to evaluate how likely it is that the null hypothesis is true, given the observations.

Chi-squared tests are often constructed from a sum of squared errors, or through the sample variance. Test statistics that follow a chi-squared distribution arise from an assumption of independent normally distributed data, which is valid in many cases due to the central limit theorem. A chi-squared test can be used to attempt rejection of the null hypothesis that the data are independent.

2. (*a*) Changes in the number and structure of the chromosomes may occur spontaneously or experimentally by the action of radiation or chemicals. The number of chromosomes is generally constant for plant and animal species.

'Chromosomal change' in number are of two main kinds: (1) Euploids : a change in the number of chromosome sets, the set being kept balanced (2) Aneuploids: there is a loss or gain of one or more chromosomes. In exceptional cases there are haploid organisms. In plants, polyploids (triploid, tetraploid) are rather common. They originate by reduplication without cytokinesis.

In animals, polyploids are scarce, because sex is frequently determined by a pair of different chromosomes (XY). Polyploidy can be induced by colchicine, this substance in used in agriculture to improve certain plant species. Allopolyploidy consists of the formation of a hybrid with different sets of chromosomes. Sometimes a diploid gamete fertilizes a normal haploid gamete, producing a new species with a triploid number. Thus there are two main kinds of change in the number of chromosomes.

In euploids the change is in the haploid number but the entire set of chromosome is kept balanced, whereas, in aneuploids there is a loss or gain of one or more chromosome(s) causing the set to become unbalanced. In humans aneuploidy may cause severe alterations of the phenotype. Polyploidy and allopolyploidy are expamples of euploidy.

Among the aneuploid organisms there are the trisomic (*i.e.*, with three similar chromosomes instead of a normal pair) and the nionosomic (missing one member of a pair of homologous chromosomes) conditions. There two conditions are important in humans and may arise by nondisjunctional division.

Chromosomal aberrations: Also called 'structural alterations' involve a change in the molecular organization of the chromosome. One or two breaks are produced at the level of the chromatin fiber, and the effect depends on whether it occurs in the G, phase (one chromatid) or in the G, (two chromatids).

Chromosomal aberration should be differentiated from gene or point mutations, which occur at molecular level. Ionizing radiations X-rays, y-rays, p-rays, fast neutrons, slow neutrons and ultraviolet light can produce point mutations or chromosomal aberrations.

The number of mutations increases proportionally with the dose of X-radiation. The effect of radiation is cumulative. An exposure of culture cells to 2DR (roentgen units) is sufficient to produce one chromosome break per cell. In contrast to mutations which increase proportionally with the dose, chromosomal aberrations increase exponentially with the dose. Breakage can be followed by "healing" of the broken end (the breaks may be at the chromosome or the chromatid level).

Chromatid breaks are produced in cells irradiated after the S-phase. If two breaks are produced, translocation, inversions, and large deletions may be induced. Dicentric chromosomes may be produced, which form a bridge at anaphase. In the human, heavy medical radiation, nuclear accidents or radioactive substances may produce chromosomal aberrations. In the production of new antibiotics and plants, irradiation is being used to economic advantage. Somatic mutations are not transmitted from one generation to another, whereas, germ cell mutations may be passed to the offsprings.

Significance: Cytogenetic studies have provided excellent methods for establishing taxonomic interrelationships and have, thereby, contributed to studies of evolution and systematics. One of the most frequent causes of evolution is a change in the order of genes as a result of chromosomal aberrations. In plants, aneuploids and polyploidy are frequent sources of variations, where as in mammals and birds, speciation depends more on chromosomal rearrangement and point mutations.

In the study of evolution, the number of chromosomes, the characteristics of the karyotype, the total chromosomal area, and the content of DNA are investigated. The presence of metacentric chromosomes may, in some cases, result from fusion of two acrocentric chromosomes.

The contrasting phenomenon (*i.e.*, dissociation) may lead to an increase in chromosome number. The problem of evolution is very complex. Knowledge of cytogenetics is most fundamental to the understanding of this problem of evolution. One example of importance of cytogenetics in evolution is given in a comparison of the chromosome pairs of the primates and humans. Primates have 48 chromosomes (24 pairs) while human have 23 pairs instead of 24 pairs of primates. There comparative studies have demonstrated that:

- 13 pairs of chromosome in humans are identical with 13 pairs in the chimpanzee.
- Chromosome number 2 in humans has resulted from centric fusion (or Robertsonion translocation) of two chromosomes present in hominoid apes.
- The other chromosomes differ in the occurrence of nine pericentric inversions and two additions of chromatin material.

2. (*b*) The behaviour of the chromosomes in the phases of meiosis: Chromosomal rearrangements encompass several different classes of events: deletions, duplications, inversions; and translocations. Each of these events can be caused by breakage of DNA double helices in the genome at two different locations, followed by a rejoining of the broken ends to produce a new chromosomal arrangement of genes, different from the gene order of the chromosomes before they were broken. Consistent with the origin of chromosomal rearrangements by breakage, rearrangements can be induced artificially by using ionizing radiation.

This kind of radiation, of which X rays and gamma rays are the most commonly used, is highly energetic and causes numerous double-stranded breaks in DNA.

To understand how chromosomal rearrangements are produced by breakage, several points should be kept in mind:

(*i*) Each chromosome is a single double-stranded DNA molecule.

(*ii*) The first event in the production of a chromosomal rearrangement is the generation of two or more double-strand breaks in the chromosomes of a cell.

(*iii*) Double-strand breaks in a cell are potentially lethal, unless they are repaired.

(*iv*) Repair systems in the cell correct the double-stranded breaks by joining broken ends back together.

(*v*) If the two ends of the same break are rejoined, the original DNA order is restored. If ends of two different breaks are joined together, then a chromosomal rearrangement is produced.

(*vi*) However, the only recoverable chromosomal rearrangements are those that produce DNA molecules that have one centromere and two telomeres. If a chromosome lacks a centromere, it will not be dragged to either pole at anaphase of mitosis and meiosis and will end up not being incorporated into the progeny nucleus. Such acentric chromosomes are not inherited. If a chromosome is dicentric (has two centromeres), it will often be simultaneously dragged to opposite poles at anaphase. This will cause an anaphase bridge to form. These anaphase bridge chromosomes will typically not be incorporated into either progeny cell, depending on the organism under consideration. Telo-meres are special DNA sequences at each end of the linear DNA molecule of a eukaryotic chromosome. Telomeres are needed to prime proper DNA replication at the ends. Broken (nontelomeric) ends cannot replicate properly.

(*vii*) There cannot be "too large" a segment of DNA lost or duplicated in the rearrangement. If a rearrangement duplicates or deletes a segment of a chromosome, the rules governing gene balance apply. The larger the segment of a chromosome lost or duplicated, the more likely will it cause phenotypic abnormalities.

In organisms with repetitive DNA, homologous repetitive segments within one chromosome or on different chromosomes can act as sites for illegitimate crossing-over. Deletions, duplications, inversions, and translocations can all be produced by such crossing-over; thus crossing-over probably constitutes a significant source of these rearrangements.

There are two general types of rearrangements, balanced and imbalanced. Balanced rearrangements change the chromosomal gene order but do not remove or duplicate any of the DNA of the chromosomes. The two simple classes of balanced rearrangements are inversions and reciprocal translocations.

INVERSION: An inversion is a rearrangement in which an internal segment of a chromosome has been broken twice, flipped 180 degrees, and rejoined:

A reciprocal translocation is a rearrangement in which acentric fragments of two nonhomologous chromosomes trade places, as follows:

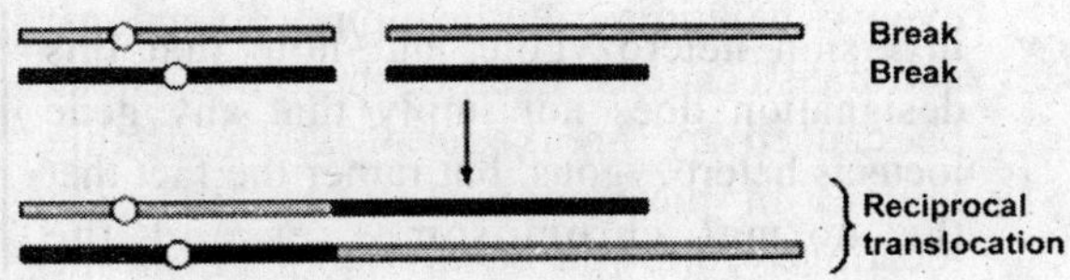

Note that, for both inversions and translocations, no chromosomal material is gained or lost—there is simply a change in the relative locations of genes on the rearranged chromosomes. In addition to the effects of the rearrangement itself, it is important to realize that the DNA molecules are disrupted at each of the two breaks that are rejoined abnormally to produce the inversion or the translocation. Sometimes these breaks will occur within genes. When they do, they will generally disrupt gene function. In addition, the DNA sequences on either side of the translocation junction points are not normally juxtaposed. Sometimes the junction occurs in such a way that a novel gene fusion is produced.

Imbalanced rearrangements change the gene dosage of a part of the affected chromosomes. As with aneuploidy for whole chromosomes, the loss of one copy or the addition of an extra copy of a segment of a chromosome can disrupt normal gene balance. The two simple classes of imbalanced rearrangements are deletions and duplications. A deletion is the loss of a segment within one chromosome arm and the juxtaposition of the two segments on either side of the deleted segment:

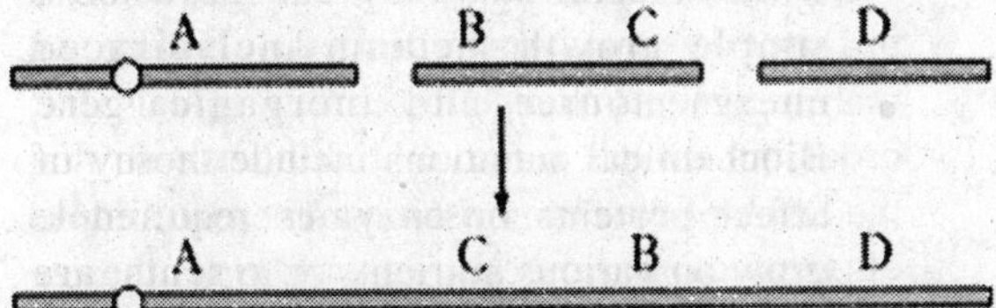

A duplication is a repetition of a segment of a chromosome arm. In the simplest type of duplication, the two segments are adjacent to one another (a tandem duplication):

The following sections consider the properties of these balanced and imbalanced aberrations.

Inversions: Inversions are of two basic types. If the centromere is outside the inversion, then the inversion is said to be paracentric, whereas inversions spanning the centromere are pericentric.

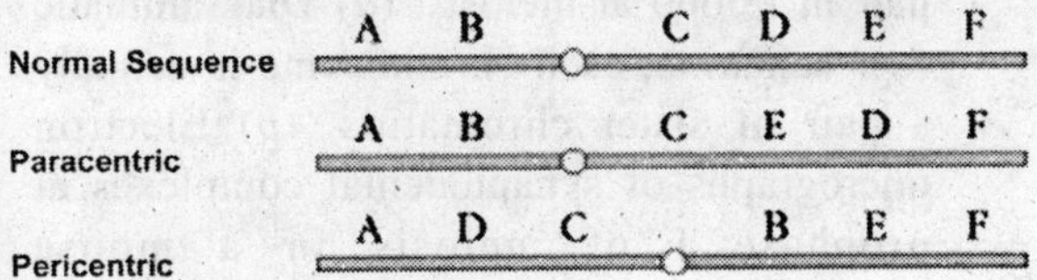

Because inversions are balanced rearrangements, they do not change the overall amount of the genetic material, so they are generally viable and show no particular abnormalities at the phenotypic level. In some cases, one of the chromosome breaks is within a gene of essential function, and then that breakpoint acts as a lethal gene mutation linked to the inversion. In such a case, the inversion could not be bred to homozygosity. However, many inversions can be made homozygous, and, furthermore, inversions can be detected in haploid organisms; so, in these cases, the breakpoint is clearly not in an essential region.

Effects of inversions at the DNA level. Genes are represented by A, B, C, and D. Template strand is dark green; nontemplate strand is light green; jagged lines indicate break in DNA. The letter P stands for promoter; thick arrow indicates the position.

Most analyses of inversions are carried out on cells that contain one normal haploid chromosome set plus one set carrying the inversion. This type of cell is called an inversion heterozygote, but note that this designation does not imply that any gene locus is heterozygous, but rather the fact that the normal chromosome set and the chromosomal rearrangement are present. Microscopic observation of meioses in inversion heterozygotes reveals the location of the inverted segment because one chromosome twists once at the ends of the inversion to pair with the other, untwisted chromosome; in this way the paired homologs form an inversion loop.

The chromosomes of inversion heterozygotes pair in a loop at meiosis. (*a*) Diagrammatic representation; each chromosome is actually a pair of sister chromatids. (*b*) Electron micrographs of synaptonemal complexes at prophase I of meiosis in a mouse heterozygous.

At meiosis, crossing-over within the inversion loop of a heterozygous paracentric inversion connects homologous centromeres in a dicentric bridge while also producing an acentric fragment—one without a centromere. Then, as the chromosomes separate during anaphase I, the centromeres remain linked by the bridge. The acentric fragment cannot align itself or move, and consequently it is lost. Tension eventually breaks the dicentric bridge, forming two chromosomes with terminal deletions. The gametes containing such deleted chromosomes may be inviable, but, even if viable, the zygotes that they eventually form will probably be inviable. Hence, a crossover event, which normally generates the recombinant class of meiotic products, instead produces lethal products. The overall result is a lower recombinant frequency. In fact, for genes within the inversion, the RF is zero. For genes flanking the inversion, the RF is reduced in proportion to the relative size of the inversion.

Meiotic products resulting from a single crossover within a paracentric inversion loop. Two nonsister chromatids crossover within the loop.

Inversions affect recombination in another way, too. Inversion heterozygotes often have mechanical pairing problems in the region of the inversion, which reduces the opportunity for crossing-over in the region.

The net genetic effect of a heterozygous pericentric inversion is the same as that of a paracentric—crossover products are not recovered—but the reasons are different. In a pericentric inversion, because the centromeres are contained within the inverted region, the chromosomes that have engaged in crossing-over separate in the normal fashion, without the creation of a bridge. However, the crossover produces chromatids that contain a duplication and a deletion for different parts of the chromosome. In this case, if a nucleus carrying a crossover chromosome is fertilized, the zygote dies because of its genetic imbalance. Again, the result is the selective recovery of noncrossover chromatids in viable progeny.

Meiotic products resulting from a meiosis with a single crossover within a pericentric inversion loop.

4. (*a*) Biochemical Basis of Mutations: Biochemical mutations are mutations that may not be visible or affect a specific morphological characteristic but may have a general affect on the ability to grow or proliferate.

(*a*) Most microorganisms are prototrophs which means that they can grow on a simple growth medium including an energy source and inorganic salts. Biochemical mutations include those that affect proteins or enzymes required to grow on various nutrients or to synthesize various components. Thus, these mutations cause the microorganisms to become auxotrophs (they must be supplied with additional nutrients if they are to grow). For example, the bacterium Escherichia coli does not require the amino acid tryptophan for growth because they can synthesize tryptophan. However, there are E. coli mutants that have mutations in the trp genes. These mutants are auxotrophic for tryptophan, and tryptophan must be added to the nutrient medium for growth.

(*b*) Humans can also have biochemical mutations (also called inborn errors in metabolism). Such examples include hemophilia, phenylketonuria, and galactosemia.

Molecular Basis of Mutations: Gene mutations can arise spontaneously or they can be induced. Spontaneous mutations are naturally occurring mutations and arise in all cells. Induced mutations are produced when an organism is exposed to a mutagenic agent, or mutagen; such mutations typically occur at much higher frequencies than spontaneous mutations do.

To understand the mechanisms of gene mutation requires analysis at the level of DNA and protein molecules. Preceding chapters have described models for DNA and protein structure and have considered the nature of mutations that alter these structures. Molecular genetics techniques can be used to determine the sequence of large segments of DNA and the sequence changes resulting from mutations. Sequencing has greatly increased our understanding of the pathways that lead to mutagenesis and has even helped to unravel the mysteries of mutational hot spots—genetic sites with a penchant for mutating.

Much work on the molecular basis of mutation has been carried out in single-celled bacteria and their viruses. However, many mutations leading to inherited diseases in humans also have been analyzed. We shall review some of the findings of these studies. We shall also consider biological repair mechanisms, because repair systems play a key role in mutagenesis, operating to lower the final observed mutation rates. For example, in Escherichia coli, with all repair systems functioning, base substitutions occur at rates of $10^{-10}10$ to 10^{-9} per base pair per cell per generation. As a general principle, base substitutions arise by a perturbation of the normal pairing of complementary bases.

4. (*b*) Various Methods of Gene Transfer in Plants: Gene transfer is one of the most recent areas of plant cell and tissue culture. It has brought a revolution in agriculture for the improvement of several genetic traits. Even in India voice of cotton sown in Andhra Pradesh and Gujarat was raised in Parliament.

Indian plant biotechnologists have made impressive progress in transformation of crops like mustard, rice, potato, tomato, and brinjal. Efforts are being made to transform the other crops too.

1. Direct Gene Transfer Methods: There are five different methods that transfer foreign DNA of desired function into plant cells. These methods are briefly discussed herewith.

(*a*) **Stimulation by Chemical Helpers:** In 1977, Lurquin and Kado demonstrated the stimulation by poly-L-ornithine in uptake of plasmid DNA by cowpea protoplasts. In the presence of calcium ions, polyethylene glycol (PEG) also enhances DNA uptake by the protoplasts in the range 10^{-2} and 10^{-5}.

(*b*) **Liposome-entrapped Plasmid Transfer:** Liposomes are microscopic lipid molecules. These are produced when phospholipids are dispersed in aqueous phase. Charges can be developed on liposomes as desired. Liposomes entrap DNA and interact with many cells in such a way that plasmid will be transferred into plant genome. For example, unilamellar liposomes have been used for transformation and expression of a cloned cDNA copy of potato spindle tuber viroid (PSTV) and a chimeric DNA of E. coli plasmid into protoplasts.

(c) **Electroporation:** Introduction of foreign DNA into the living cells (as protoplasts) by exposure of brief electric pulse (250-350 V) is known as electroporation. Minimum manipulation of protoplasts ensures their high survival rates. Using electroporation, transient expression of foreign DNA has been demonstrated in maize, wheat and rice.

(d) **Microinjection:** In 1986, Crossway and co-workers used microinjection technique for direct gene transfer into plant cells. Animal cells can be transformed at high frequency by microinjection than the plant cells.

In this technique protoplasts are surface attached on a slide by embedding in agarose using a holding pipette. DNA is transferred by injecting a microneedle or a glass micropipette having fine tip (0.5 – 1μm) diameter). The microinjected protoplasts are cultured as described earlier.

(e) **Particle (Microprojectile) Bombardment Gun:** It is also called as particle gun, shot gun, microprojectile gun and biolistic missile. In this method foreign DNA containing desired genes are coated onto the surface of tungusten or gold particles (4 micrometer diameter).

These particles are bombarded to a high velocity (by particle gun) onto plant cells or tissues. The particles pierce cell walls and membrane.

2. Vector-mediated Gene Transfer in Plant Cells: Agrobacterium consists of Ti-plasmid which is directly responsible for tumour induction. Transfer of small DNA segment (T-DNA) from Ti-plasmid and its integration into host genome induces tumour formation in plants. T-DNA region of Ti-plasmid is essential for Agrobacterium-mediated transformation of plants.

The Ti-plasmid is taken out from Agrobacterium (A.) tumifaciens and a foreign DNA of desired function is inserted into T-DNA region by using restriction enzyme. The recombinant T-plasmid is incorporated into A. tumifaciens cells. The steps of Agrobacterium-mediated gene transfer in a plant.

(a) **Co-cultivation with Protoplasts:** Freshly isolated protoplasts are co-cultivated with transformed A. tumifaciens for a few days. Then the protoplasts are washed and cultured in medium containing antibiotic. The regenerated protoplasts are transferred onto culture medium that enables the development of transformed callus and plants.

(b) **Leaf-disc Infection Method:** In this approach leaves (of tomato, tobacco, Petunia, etc.) are surface sterilised and inoculated with a genetically modified A. tumifaciens cells. Then the leaves are cultured for two days. During this time infection takes place.

The leaf discs containing infection are transferred to a selection cum regeneration medium containing kanamycin. Kanamycin selectively eliminates the non-transformed cell/tissues. Within 2-4 weeks, these cultures regenerate into transformed plantlets.

Then, the genetically modified plantlets are transferred into soil after hardening of regenerated plant so that they can be acclimatised with the new environment. Presence and function of foreign gene in transgenic plant are found out by molecular techniques as given in transgene analysis.

3. Transgene Analysis: In plant transformation experiments selection of transformed cells from the mixed populations of both transformed and untransformed cells is an important event. A marker gene (*e.g.*, antibiotic resistance or herbicide resistance) is also introduced along with foreign DNA into the host cells.

A selection medium is prepared into which antibiotics or herbicide (for which marker gene has been introduced) is mixed. The transformed cells/tissues are cultured on selection medium.

Only those cells will grow on such medium which contains marker gene such cells are said to be transformed. The untransformed cells will not grow because they lack marker gene.

After selection subsequent maintenance of marker in transgenic plant is not necessary. Since the herbicide-resistance gene may be transformed to bacterium or herbicide-resistance gene may be transferred to weeds, the marker genes must be eliminated. The removal of marker enables the transgene to function and express properly.

Integration and expression of transgenes are further studied following molecular techniques like PCR, Southern blot, Northern blot, Western blot, etc.

5. (*a*) Allelopathy: Allelopathy is a process by which a plant releases chemicals that can either inhibit or competitors. Allelopathic plants do sometimes pose obstacles that are hard to overcome, however. Soil sickness, a general term for a problem that may well be caused by residues of allelochemicals that persist in the soil after the plant is gone, may make some sites unsuitable for growing other plants.

Allelopaths are plants that have an advanced weapon in their arsenal. The allelopathic plant competes with other species through "chemical warfare" by releasing chemicals that inhibit the growth of its neighbouring plants.

The word allelopathy derives from two separate words. They are allelon which means "of each other", and pathos which means "to suffer". Allelopathy refers to the chemical inhibition of one species by another. The "inhibitory" chemical is released into the environment where it affects the development and growth of neighbouring plants.

Allelopathic chemicals can be present in any part of the plant. They can be found in leaves, flowers, roots, fruits, or stems. They can also be found in the surrounding soil. Target species are affected by these toxins in many different ways. The toxic chemicals may inhibit shoot/root growth, they may inhibit nutrient uptake, or they may attack a naturally occurring symbiotic relationship thereby destroying the plant's usable source of a nutrient.

Not all plants have allelopathic tendencies. Some, though they exhibit these tendencies, may actually be displaying aggressive competition of a non-chemical form. Much of the controversy surrounding allelopathy is in trying to distinguish the type of competition being displayed. In general, if it is of a chemical nature, then the plant is considered allelopathic. There have been some recent links to plant allelotoxins directed at animals, but data is scarce.

5. (*b*) IPR-Intellectual Property Rights: Intellectual property (IP) is a legal field that refers to creations of the mind such as musical, literary, and artistic works; inventions; and symbols, names, images, and designs used in commerce, including copyrights, trademarks, patents, and related rights. Under intellectual property law, the holder of one of these abstract "properties" has certain exclusive rights to the creative work, commercial symbol, or invention by which it is covered.

Intellectual property rights are a bundle of exclusive rights over creations of the mind, both artistic and commercial. The former is covered by copyright laws, which protect creative works such as books, movies, music, paintings, photographs, and software and gives the copyright holder exclusive right to control reproduction or adaptation of such works for a certain period of time.

The second category is collectively known as "industrial properties", as they are typically created and used for industrial or commercial purposes. A patent may be granted for a new, useful, and non-obvious invention, and gives the patent holder a right to prevent others from practising the invention without a license from the inventor for a certain period of time. A trademark is a distinctive sign which is used to prevent confusion among products in the marketplace.

An industrial design right protects the form of appearance, style or design of an industrial object from infringement. A trade secret is an item of non-public information concerning the commercial practices or proprietary knowledge of a business. Public disclosure of trade secrets may sometimes be illegal.

The term "intellectual property" denotes the specific legal rights described above, and not the intellectual work itself.

The importance of intellectual property in India is well established at all levels—statutory, administrative and judicial. India ratified the agreement establishing the World Trade Organization (WTO). This Agreement, inter-alia, contains an Agreement on Trade Related Aspects of Intellectual Property Rights (TRIPS) which came into force from 1st January 1995. It lays down minimum standards for protection and enforcement of intellectual property rights in member countries which are required to promote effective and adequate protection of intellectual property rights with a view to reducing distortions and impediments to international trade. The obligations under the TRIPS Agreement relate to provision of minimum standard of protection within the member countries legal systems and practices.

The Agreement provides for norms and standards in respect of following areas of intellectual property:

(*i*) Copyrights and related rights

(*ii*) Trade Marks

(*iii*) Geographical Indications

(*iv*) Industrial Designs

(*v*) Lay out Designs of Integrated Circuits

(*vi*) Protection of Undisclosed Information (Trade Secrets)

(*vii*) Patents

(*viii*) Plant varieties

5. (*c*) Molecular Markers in Plant Breeding: A molecular marker is a molecule contained within a sample taken from an organism (biological markers) or other matter. It can be used to reveal certain characteristics about the respective source. DNA, for example, is a molecular marker containing information about genetic disorders, genealogy and the evolutionary history of life. Specific regions of the DNA (genetic markers) is are used to diagnose the autosomal recessive genetic disorder cystic fibrosis, taxonomic affinity (phylogenetics) and identity (DNA Barcoding). Further, life forms are known to shed unique chemicals, including DNA, into the environment as evidence of their presence in a particular location. Other biological markers, like proteins, are used in diagnostic tests for complex neurodegenerative disorders, such as Alzheimer's disease. Non-biological molecular markers are also used, for example, in environmental studies.

When using molecular markers to study the genetics of a particular crop, it must be remembered that markers have restrictions. It should first be assessed what the genetic variability is within the organism being studied. Analyze how identifiable particular genomic sequence, near or in candidate genes. Maps can be created to determine distances between genes and differentiation between species. Genetic markers can aid in the development of new novel traits that can be put into mass production. These novel traits can be identified using molecular markers and maps. Particular traits such as colour, may be controlled by just a few genes. Qualitative traits (requires less that 2 genes) such as colour, can be identified using MAS (marker assisted selection). Once a desired marker is found, it is able to be followed within different filial generations. An identifiable marker may help follow particular traits of interest when crossing between different genus or species, with the hopes of transferring particular traits to offspring.

5. (*d*) Role of Carotenoids in Plants

Carotenoids also called tetraterpenoids, are organic pigments that are produced by plants and algae, as well as several bacteria and fungi. Carotenoids can be produced from fats and other basic organic metabolic building blocks by all these organisms. The only animals known to produce carotenoids are aphids and spider mites, which acquired the ability and genes from fungi or it is produced by endosymbiotic bacteria in whiteflies.

Establishment of an orchard is a long term investment and deserves a very critical planning. The selection of proper location and site, planting system and planting distance, choosing the varieties and the nursery plants have to be considered carefully to ensure maximum production.

Carotenoids in photosynthesis

Carotenoids, in the early stages of the emergence of single-celled photosynthetic organisms, are probably been used for light harvesting at wavelengths different from those covered by chlorophyll. Therefore carotenoids, acting as light absorbing accessory pigments, have allowed to expand the range of solar radiation absorbed and so utilized for photosynthesis, energy that is then transferred to chlorophyll itself.

The major carotenoids involved in light harvesting, that accumulate in green plant tissues, are beta-carotene, lutein, neoxanthin, and violaxanthin, that absorb light energy in the 400 – 500 nm range.

Moreover, they protect chlorophyll from photooxidation (in humans, they may contribute to the protection of photo-oxidative damage caused by UV rays, thus acting as a endogenous photo-protective agents).

Carotenoids and autumn leaf colour

Leaf colour of deciduous plants in different seasons, green, yellow, orange or red, is due to the presence in them of natural pigments. In spring and summer, the predominant pigment present in the leaf is chlorophyll, and therefore the colour is green.

During the fall, the colour changes from green to yellow, orange or red, depending on the type of plant: this is a consequence of the change, both qualitative and quantitative, in the pigment content.

In fact, as a result of the decrease of the temperature and daylight hours, the production of chlorophyll is interrupted and that already present is demolished into colourless metabolites. In this way the predominant pigments become carotenoids (yellow-orange), molecules much more stable than the chlorophyll, which remain in the leaf colouring it (it do not seem to be synthesized de novo), and anthocyanins (red-purple), which, unlike carotenoids, are not present during the growing season, but are synthesized in autumn, just before leaf fall. Therefore, it can be concluded that the red-purple colour assumed from the leaves of certain plants is not a side effect of leaf senescence but results from anthocyanins de-novo synthesis.

Depending on the prevalence of carotenoids or anthocyanins, leaf colour changes from green to yellow/orange, as in Ginkgo biloba (yellow), or red-purple as in some maples.

Plants with non green leaves

Their colour is not due to the absence of chlorophyll but the presence of very high amounts of other pigments, typically carotenoids and anthocyanins, that "cover" the chlorophyll, determining the colour of the leaf.

Apocarotenoids in plants

These oxygenated carotenoids, containing fewer than 40 carbon atoms, have many functions in plants and animals and are also important for the aroma and flavour of foods.

Some of their main functions include the following.

- Apocarotenoids have significant roles in the response signals involved in the development and in the response to the environment (for example abscisic acid).
- They can act as visual or volatile signals to attract pollinators.
- They are important in the defense mechanisms of plants.
- They have a role in regulating plant architecture.
- An apocarotenal, trans-beta-apo-8-carotenal, found in citrus fruits and spinach, with a low provitamin A activity, is used in pharmaceuticals and cosmetics, and is also a food additive (E160e) legalized by the European Commission for human consumption.
- Apocarotenoids make an important contribution to the nutritional quality and flavour of many types of foods such as fruits, wine and tea. Two natural apocarotenoids, crocetin and bixina, have economic importance as they are used as pigments.

5. (*e*) **Evidences of Organic Evolution:** The term evolution is derived from Latin word evolve which means unfolding or unrolling which implies the process of gradual and orderly change from one condition to another through succession or a series of changing events.

By organic evolution it is understood that the gradual and orderly changes are taking place in all life forms on the earth's crust, since the origin of first life.

Evolution in plants is different from animal evolution. During prehistoric period of life the divergency of plants from animals takes place from ancestral prophytes collectively called "protista" plants show adaptive responses and specialization just as animals but line of evolution differs. Organic evolution in plants is a truthful event and a fact. It is supported by following evidences.

(I) Evidences from palaeobotany: The story of evolution of plants is written in rocks in the alphabets of fossils. Thus the fossil history of plants shows the following procession of plant's life through the ages.

(*i*) Algae are the primitive group of plants originated in autic habitat as the age of fossil algae "Stromatolites" was trace back to pre-cambrian period.

(*ii*) Nematophyton are the first true vascular plants invading and evolved from algae in paleozoic rock.

(*iii*) Psilophytopsida are common indevonian rock fossil lycopods are the next steps of evolution.

(*iv*) Proto lepidodendron, follows the lepidodendron are the huge tree like ferns ancestors of gymnosperms and angiosperm.

(*v*) Pteridosperms of caboniferous rock provided evidence for first seed plant with frond like leaves and seeds bornne in sporophyll.

(*vi*) Nymphaeaceae is the angiospermic family which has close relation with fossil ancestors of jurassic rock.

(*vii*) The wood fossil ancestors of Jurassic rock.

(*viii*) The wood fossil of homoxylon from rajmahal hills of India is Jurassic fossil resemble the xylem with gymnosperms and pollen grains resemble nelumbo of angiosperms.

(II) Evidences from comparative morphology: There is marked morphological resemblances in body form of different plant taxo show evolutionary tendencies.

Homology and analogy: Organs which similar in structure and differs in the development are homologous but the organs which are differs embryologically in development and similar in function but differs in morphology are analogous organs.

The phylloclade of ruscus and claades of asparagus are similar in function and origin and homologous in nature. But both phylloclade and cladodes are anlogous to the normal leaves. Flowers are homologous to vegetative to the normal leaves. Flowers are homologous to vegetative shoot.

Vestigel organs: The structures in the body of plants which are reduced in structure and less used are called vestigial. In course of evolution these organs reduce retroessively and become vestigeal.

Staminodes in flowers, specialization of stamens into nectaries, rudimentary leaflets in apricot, reduction of leaflets into glands in apricot are the signs & evolution.

(III) Evidences from comparative anatomy:

(*a*) Cambium comparatively less active in herbaceous stem than the woody stem.

(*b*) Limited secondary growth in herbaceous plants than woody plants.

(*c*) Absence of heart wood in herbs and more heart wood in woody stems.

(*d*) Lack of definite arrangement of vascular bundles in monocots and in ring in monocots and dicots.

(*e*) Polyrach stele of monocot is advanced over diarch or triarch stele of dicot.

(IV) Evidences from comparative physiology: Photosynhesis in the fundamental natural process in green plants, respiration is the common feature of all life forms. Physiological similarity among simplest plants to complex form indicates their common origine from chlorella to higher trees.

(V) Evidences from comparative biochemistry: Presence of characteristic chemical substance like aromatic oils, alkaloids, carbohydrates, viz, aromatic ail in labiata, aljaloids in solanceae, oily seeds of eurherbiaceai, resins in pinaceae, establishes relationship among different group of plants.

(VI) Evidences from developmental biology: According to biogenetic law or theory of recapitulation by haeckel developmental pattern of different group of plants establish the phylogenetic relations.

(*a*) Protonema stage of moss resembles algae indicating the evolution of moss from algae.

(*b*) Filamentous prothallus of ferns found close relation with algae.

(*c*) Cilliated sperm in modern cycads shows pteridophytean ancestry and recalled broyphytes.

(VII) Evidence from plant geography: Similar species occupying different geographical area likes to develop divergent lines of evolution longer period of isolation of one region from other the greater is the degree of difference which brought about evolution of new character.

(VIII) Evidences from ecology: From ecological succession studies it is evident that, hydric or hydrophytic is primitive over the mesophytic and mesophytic is primitive over xerophyte habit Hospitalized Patients.

7. (*a*) Structure of Phytochrome: Phytochrome is a soluble chromoprotein with a molecular mass of 250 kDa. It occurs as a dimer made up of two subunits, each of 125 kDa. Each subunit consists of two components — light-absorbing pigment molecule, chromophore and a polypeptide chain, Apo protein. The Apo protein monomer has a molecular mass of 125 kDa.

Apo protein and chromophore together make up the holochrome. The chromophore is a linear tetrapyrrole similar to phycocyanin termed phytochromobilin and it is a ring attached to the protein through thioether-linkage to a cysteine residue.

Role of Phytochrome in Flower Development Process: There are experimental evidence (Hendricks and Borthwick) that only red light (wavelength 660 mμ) is effective in inhibiting flower initiation in short-day plants, when the dark period towards midnight is interrupted with this illumination. This wavelength of light at the same time accelerates the growth of stem and root and formation of anthocyanin pigment.

It is more interesting to note that this inhibition of flowering in short day plants can be reversed by treating the plants with far-red light (wavelength 730 mμ). This suggests the existence of a single compound, phytochrome, responsible for photoperiodic action. The phytochrome (probably) exists in two inter convertible forms P730 and P660. When P660 is illuminated with red light (660 mμ) it is transformed to the P730 form.

The P730 form can be converted into the P660 form by far red light (730 mμ). During night P730 is converted into P660 form and hence at the end of day period the predominent form of phytochrome is P730 because sun light contains more red light of 660 mμ) wavelength.

In short day plants flowering is initiated when there is sufficient accumulation of P660 and that is the reason why flowering is inhibited in these plants when dark period is interrupted by red light of 660 mμ wavelength which converts P660 form into P730 form.

Fig.: Structure of the phytochrome chromophore and its binding to the apoprotein. The chromophore is covalently linked to the protein at cysteine residue via a thioether bond. The chromophore undergoes *cis-trans* isomerization at carbon 15 in response to red and far-red light.

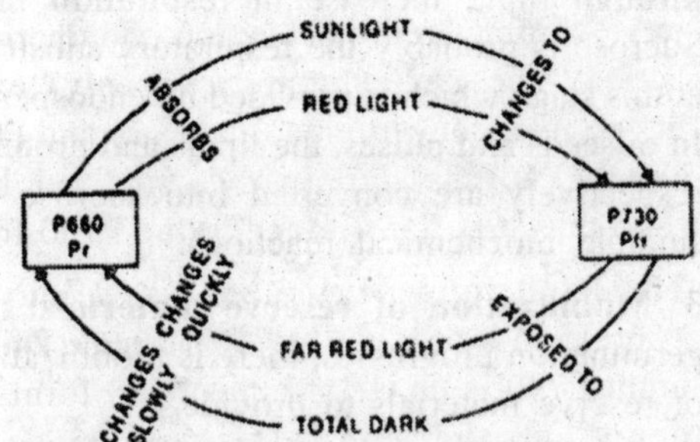

Fig.: Diagram to depict the phytochrome concept.

7. (*b*) Methods of Breaking Seed Dormancy: Various methods have been used by seed scientist and technologists to break the dormancy of seed.

Simple and widely used methods are

A. Scarification: Any treatment *i.e.*, physical or chemical that weakness the seed coat, is known as scarification.

Scarification method is applied, when dormancy is imposed by hard seen coat *e.g.*, in legumes- cajanus cajan, (tur), gram etc.

In this method there are various way to break hard seed coat such as:

(*i*) Seeds are either rubbed on a sand paper manually. At the time of rubbing care should be taken that not to damage the axis of the seed *e.g.*, Green gram & subabool.

(*ii*) When seed coat is too hard *i.e.*, of woody nature, the seed coat has to be removing completely by breaking it. E.g. Rubber (Havea app) seed India teak wood seed.

(*iii*) Soaking treatment: Soaking hard seed coat in concentrated or diluted solution of sulphuric acid for 1 to 60 minutes, it remove seed coat impermeability, *e.g.*, cotton seeds, India teak wood seeds etc.

B. Temperature Treatments:

(*i*) When the dormancy is due to embryo factor *i.e.*, the seed is incubating at low temp. (0 – 5°C) over a substratum for 3 to 10 days placing it at optimum temp. Required for germination. E.g. mustard. – (Brassica campestrits)

(*ii*) Some seeds required a brief period of incubation (from a few hours to one to five days) at 40 to 50°C before germinating at required temp. (in this method care should be taken that moisture content of the seed is not more than 15% *e.g.*, paddy (Oryza Sativa)

(*iii*) Hot water treatment is also an effective method of breaking hard-seedness in legumes. In this method the seeds are soaked in water at 80°C temp. For 1–5 minutes (depending up on the type of seed) before putting for germination.

C. Light Treatments: Same seeds do not germinate in dark thus it provides continuous or periodic exposure of light is essential *e.g.*, Lettuce (Lactuca Sativa) required red light (660 nm) or white light is essential for germination to occur.

D. Treatments with growth regulators & other Chemicals: Endogenous dormancy may be due to presence of germination inhibitors. Application of low level of growth regulators (*i.e.*, Gibberellins, Cytokinins and Ethylene etc) may break the seed dormancy.

Most widely used growth regulators are gibberellins and kinetics *e.g.*, seeds of sorghum crop presoaking seed treatment with GA3 at the conc. of 100 ppm have been used for breaking seed dormancy.

Among other chemicals potassium nitrate (0.2%) and thio–urea (0.5 to 3%) are widely used for breaking seed dormancy in oat (Avena Sativa), barley (Hordeum vulgare), tomato (Lycopersicon spp).

(For prepare 100 ppm solution of GA3, weigh 100 mg of GA3 & dissolve in a few drops of alcohol and make up the final volume (1000 ml) by adding distilled water).

(50 ppm kinetin 5 mg dissolved in few drops of alkaline made with sodium hydroxide and makes the final volume 100 ml, it gives to final conc. of 50 ppm).

Physiological changes

1. Water uptake: Seed germination starts with the imbibition of water by dry seed coat. Due to imbibition of water the seed coat becomes more permeable to O_2 and water and less resistant to outward growth of embryo. After imbibition, the inner contents of the seed increase in volume, thereby exerting pressure on the seed coat leading to rupture of the seed coat. The plumule and radical emerge thereafter.

2. Respiration: After initiation of germination process, enormous energy is required for various biochemical changes which are met through rapid increase in respiration rate. Sucrose is probably the respiratory substrate at this stage which is provided by endosperm. In oilseeds and pulses, the lipids and proteins respectively are converted into sucrose by suitable biochemical reactions.

3. Mobilization of reserve materials: As germination progresses, there is mobilization of reserve materials to provide.

(*i*) Building blocks for the development of embryo

(*ii*) Energy for the biosynthetic process

(*iii*) Nucleic acids for protein synthesis and embryonic development.

Physiological changes during Seed Germination

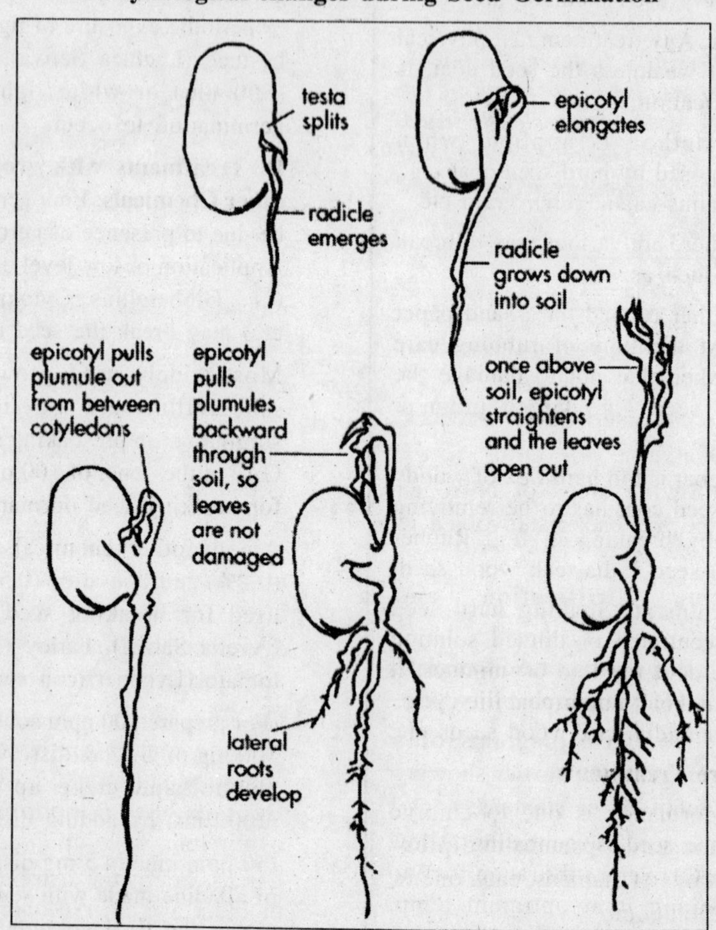

Previous Years' Paper (Solved)

Indian Forest Service

IFS–Botany Main Examination, 2016

PAPER-I

INSTRUCTIONS: *There are EIGHT questions in all, out of which FIVE are to be attempted. Question Nos. 1 & 5 are compulsory. Out of the remaining SIX questions, THREE are to be attempted selecting at least ONE question from each of the two Sections A and B. Attempts of questions shall be counted in sequential order. Unless struck off, attempt of a question shall be counted even if attempted partly. Any page or portion of the page left blank in the Question-cum-Answer Booklet must be clearly struck off. All questions carry equal marks. Answers must be written in ENGLISH only. Neat sketches may be drawn, wherever required.*

SECTION—A

1. *Answer the following keeping your answers brief and to the point:*

(*a*) Comment on the characteristics of Archaea, Bacteria and Eukarya.

(*b*) Explain the following steps of Nitrogen fixation and name the bacteria involved in each process:

Ammonification, Nitrification and Denitrification

(*c*) With the help of graphic presentation, explain the Isomorphic and Heteromorphic life cycle.

(*d*) Draw well-labelled floral diagrams of a pentamerous actinomorphic flower showing the following conditions of stamens:

Obdiplostemonous and pseudo-obdiplostemonous conditions of stamens, each one in a separate floral diagram.

(*e*) Discuss briefly the *Inter situ*, *Ex situ* and *In situ* conservation.

(*f*) "India is top megadiverse country with 2 hottest Hot spots out of 25 Hot spots." Justify the statement.

(*g*) Describe the economic importance of Gymnosperms.

(*h*) Discuss the morphological nature of sporocarp of *Marsilea*.

2. (*a*) Write a detailed note on sustainable utilization of Bioresources and ecosystem research.

(*b*) Explain the mode of virus infection in T-even phage and Lambda (λ) phage.

(*c*) Explain the main steps of "Telome theory".

3. (*a*) Describe the role of bacteria in agriculture, medicine and industry.

(*b*) "Vessels of *Gnetum* are different from the vessels of Angiosperms in origin." Explain critically.

(*c*) "All viruses are constructed according to geometrical rules of symmetry." Explain critically.

(*d*) Give the name of the casual organism, symptoms and measures to control a plant disease caused by a bacterium.

4. (*a*) Describe the range of thallus structures in Lichens. Lichens are rare or absent in cities. What conclusion can be drawn from this?

(*b*) Explain the morphological nature of ovuliferous scale of *Pinus*.

(*c*) Discuss briefly the distribution of Cryptogams in India and their economic potential.

SECTION—B

5. *Answer the following keeping your answer brief and to the point:*

(*a*) Distinguish between the following:

(*i*) Rust and Smut

(*ii*) Cladode and Phyllode

(*b*) Differentiate between the following:

(*i*) Isokont and Heterokont

(*ii*) Centric and Eccentric growth rings

(*c*) Draw well-labelled diagrams of the following:

(*i*) Flower showing androphore and gynophore

(*ii*) Winged pollen of *Pinus*

(*d*) Distinguish between the following:

(*i*) Monoxylic and Pycnoxylic stem

(*ii*) Medullary and Cortical vascular bundles

(*e*) Differentiate between the following:

(*i*) Descending and Ascending imbricate aestivation

(*ii*) Hypanthium and Hypanthodium

(*f*) Draw well-labelled diagrams of the following:

(*i*) Male flower of *Euphorbia*

(*ii*) Tyloses

(*g*) Discuss briefly the following:

(*i*) Taxonomic position of Caytoniales

(*ii*) Peristome teeth of *Funaria*

(*h*) Explain briefly the following:

(*i*) Coenocytic mycelium

(*ii*) Parasitism in fungi

6. Write about the following:

(*a*) Explain the progressive sterilization of the sporogenous tissue in Bryophytes.

(*b*) Theory of Endemism

(*c*) Taxonomic Hierarchy

7. (*a*) 'Ranalisma' forms a connective link between Dicotyledons and Monocotyledons. Discuss it critically.

(*b*) Describe the various stages of development of exine of pollen wall. Add a note on the importance of sporopollenin.

(*c*) South Pacific Ocean is considered as the "Cradle home of primitive vesselless Angiosperms". Write the names of such plants.

8. (*a*) Draw the ultrastructural diagram of Heterocyst.

(*b*) Draw the floral diagram of *Orchid* of Monandrae group.

(*c*) Write short notes on the following:

(*i*) Totipotency

(*ii*) Cybrids

(*iii*) Symmetry and differentiation

(*iv*) Apomixis

PAPER-II

INSTRUCTIONS: *There are EIGHT questions in all, out of which FIVE are to be attempted. Question Nos. 1 & 5 are compulsory. Out of the remaining SIX questions, THREE are to be attempted selecting at least ONE question from each of the two Sections A and B. Attempts of questions shall be counted in sequential order. Unless struck off, attempt of a question shall be counted even if attempted partly. Any page or portion of the page left blank in the answer book must be clearly struck off. All questions carry equal marks. Answers must be written in ENGLISH only. Neat sketches may be drawn, wherever required.*

SECTION—A

1. Write a short note on each of the following:

(*a*) How are the membranes arranged in chloroplast to suit its functions?

(*b*) How is cell signal transduction affected?

(*c*) Explain the basis of molecular sex differentiation.

(*d*) Comment on nuclear pore complex.

(*e*) What are the check points affected during the cell cycle?

2. (*a*) How does a genetic code regulate gene expression? Describe the molecular method of gene mapping.

(*b*) Comment on cytoplasmic genes and explain the cytoplasmic inheritance with different examples.

3. (*a*) Describe different methods of gene transfer in plants. Explain the advantages and disadvantages of transgenic plants.

(*b*) Explain the applications of *t* and *z* tests. Discuss the significance of normal, bionomial and Poison distributions of biological data.

4. (*a*) Discuss the role of RNA in evolution. Describe the various modifications that an RNA undergoes ever since its synthesis until it reaches the stages of translation.

(*b*) What is the significance of polytene and lampbrush chromosomes? Describe different species of RNA with a note on their functions.

SECTION—B

5. Write brief notes on each of the following:

(*a*) Describe the methods of conservation of endangered species.

(*b*) Describe the structure of ATPase. How is it suited to phosphorylation?

(*c*) Enumerate the roles of Fe, Mg, Mn and K in plants.

(*d*) Describe the functional roles of plastidial pigments.

(*e*) Describe the structure of N_2ase.

6. (*a*) Discuss the significance of different carbon fixation pathways in plants.

(*b*) Describe different processes involved in the molecular basis of fruit ripening.

7. (*a*) Explain the role of different co-enzymes in plants with suitable examples.

(*b*) Discuss the roles of different hormones and enzymes involved in seed germination.

8. (*a*) Describe different eco-systems. Comment on forest management program.

(*b*) Discuss the role of phytoremediation in the treatment of heavy metal polluted soil. Explain the bioremediation of hydrocarbon.

ANSWERS

PAPER-I

1. (*a*) **Characteristics of Archaea, Bacteria and Eukarya**

All archaebacteria have cell walls, but the structure of walls varies depending on the species. Archaebacteria lack peptidoglycan, which distinguishes them from closely related organisms in the kingdom Bacteria. Archaebacteria have membrane lipids comprised of fatty acids and have complex RNA polymerase to transcribe and copy DNA templates into RNA products. Archae also digest using a system of internal metabolism, which takes place in several stages. That is the biggest thing that distinguishes it from the other domains.

Eukarya have eukaryotic cells. They have membranes composed of unbranched fatty acid chains attached to glycerol by ester linkages. Not all Eukarya possess cells with a cell wall, but for those Eukarya having a cell wall, that wall contains no peptidoglycan. Eukarya are resistant to traditional antibacterial antibiotics but are sensitive to most antibiotics that affect eukaryotic cells. Eukarya contain rRNA that is unique to the Eukarya as indicated by the presence of molecular regions distinctly different from the rRNA of Archaea and Bacteria. Eukarya is divided into four kingdoms (or more, depending on whether or not you consider protists to be multiple kingdoms): Plantae, Animalia, Protista, and Fungi.

The protista are the one-celled eukaryotic organisms. As eukaryotes, they have nuclear membranes and linear chromosomes (with associated proteins) that can undergo meiosis and mitosis. The first eukaryotes were unicellular protists, some of which gave rise to the fungi, animals and plants that do not occur on earth today. Modern protists show modes of life that closely resemble higher eukaryotes. Some being photosynthetic, some ingestive, and some absorptive, some motile, some nonmotile, some with cell walls and some without all combinations of these characteristics are represented in various members of this group.

Unlike other eukaryotic cell, bacterial cell is the only cell which lacks prominent nucleus within. This feature has led to the scientists to consider bacteria as primitive organisms, *i.e.*, earliest forms of life on earth. Bacteria have a cell wall which is distinct from other cells having cell wall. The wall is made of different substances. The cell membrane in plants and animals is mostly lipid bilayer and a single layer. But bacteria especially the gram negative ones have an outer membrane called periplasm which lies below cell wall but above cell membrane. Pilli are the organelles of reproduction seen in bacteria. These help in sexual reproduction of bacteria. They are pipe like structures on the surface of bacteria. All the organisms either live by their own or on other resources. But bacteria have different modes of food procurement. Some of them synthesize their own food like plants by use of sunlight. Others derive food energy from chemical sources around them (chemotrops). Sulfur bacteria, hydrogen bacteria, iron bacteria, etc. Few of them are parasites which live on alive plants and animals. They cause diseases to the host in doing so. Many bacteria are saprophytes which means, they live on dead and decaying matter. They live in a give and take relationships with other animals. Ex: rhizobium in roots, E-coli in intestine. Most organisms have one or two methods of reproduction. But bacteria have many.

1. (*b*) Ammonification, Nitrification & Denitrification

Bacteria remove nitrogen from wastewater by a two-step biological process: nitrification followed by denitrification. Technically, it is a three step-process: ammonification precedes nitrification and denitrification.

Ammonification: While travelling through sewer pipes, the majority of the nitrogen contained in raw sewage (urea and faecal material) is converted from organic-nitrogen to ammonia through a process called hydrolysis. Technically, in the majority of situations, more ammonium than ammonia is created during ammonification. The actual ratio is influenced by pH and temperature.

Nitrification: The biological conversion of ammonium to nitrate nitrogen is called Nitrification. Nitrification is a two-step process. Bacterium known as Nitrosomonas converts ammonia and ammonium to nitrite. Next, bacterium called Nitrobacter finishes the conversion of nitrite to nitrate. The reactions are generally coupled and proceed rapidly to the nitrate form; therefore, nitrite levels at any given time are usually low.

These bacteria known as "nitrifiers" are strict "aerobes," meaning they must have free dissolved oxygen to perform their work. Nitrification occurs only under aerobic conditions at dissolved oxygen levels of 1.0 mg/L or more. At dissolved oxygen (DO) concentrations less than 0.5 mg/L, the growth rate is minimal. Nitrification requires a long retention time, a low food to microorganism ratio (F:M), a high mean cell residence time (measured as MCRT or Sludge Age), and adequate buffering (alkalinity). A plug-flow, extended aeration tank is ideal. Temperature, as discussed below, is also important, but not really.

Denitrification: The biological reduction of nitrate (NO_3) to nitrogen gas (N_2) by facultative heterotrophic bacteria is called Denitrification. "Heterotrophic" bacteria need a carbon source as food to live. "Facultative" bacteria can get their oxygen by taking dissolved oxygen out of the water or by taking it off of nitrate molecules. Denitrification occurs when oxygen levels are depleted and nitrate becomes the primary oxygen source for microorganisms. The process is performed under anoxic conditions, when the dissolved oxygen concentration is less than 0.5 mg/L, ideally less than 0.2. When bacteria break apart nitrate (NO_3^-) to gain the oxygen (O_2), the nitrate is reduced to nitrous oxide (N_2O), and, in turn, nitrogen gas (N_2). Since nitrogen gas has low water solubility, it escapes into the atmosphere as gas bubbles. Free nitrogen is the major component of air, thus its release does not cause any environmental concern.

The nitrification process produces acid. This acid formation lowers the pH of the biological population in the aeration tank and can cause a reduction of the growth rate of nitrifying bacteria. The optimum pH for Nitrosomonas and Nitrobacter is between 7.5 and 8.5; most treatment plants are able to effectively nitrify with a pH of 6.5 to 7.0. Nitrification stops at a pH below 6.0. The nitrification reaction (that is, the conversion of ammonia to nitrate) consumes 7.1 mg/L of alkalinity as CaCO for each mg/L of ammonia nitrogen oxidized. An alkalinity of no less than 50-100 mg/L is required to insure adequate buffering. Water temperature also affects the rate of nitrification. Nitrification reaches a maximum rate at temperatures between 30 and 35 degrees C (86°F and 95°F). At temperatures of 40°C (104°F) and higher, nitrification rates fall to near zero. At temperatures below 20 degrees C, nitrification proceeds at a slower rate, but will continue at temperatures of 10 degrees C and less. However, if nitrification is lost, it will not resume until the temperature increases to well over 10°C.

1. (*c*) Alternation of generations (also known as metagenesis) is a term used to describe the type of life cycle that occurs in those plants and algae in the Archaeplastida and the Heterokontophyta that have distinct sexual haploid and asexual diploid stages. In these groups, a multicellular gametophyte, which is haploid with *n* chromosomes, alternates with a multicellular sporophyte, which is diploid with 2*n* chromosomes, made up of *n* pairs. A mature sporophyte produces spores by meiosis, a process which reduces the number of chromosomes to half, from 2*n* to *n*.

Relative importance of the sporophyte and the gametophyte.

Equal (homomorphy or isomorphy)

- Filamentous algae of the genus Cladophora, which are predominantly found in fresh water, have diploid sporophytes and haploid gametophytes which are externally indistinguishable. No living land plant has equally dominant sporophytes and gametophytes, although some theories of the evolution of alternation of generations suggest that ancestral land plants did.

Unequal (heteromorphy or anisomorphy).

- **Dominant gametophyte (gametophytic):** In liverworts, mosses and hornworts, the dominant form is the haploid gametophyte. The diploid sporophyte is not capable of an independent existence, gaining most of its nutrition from the parent gametophyte, and having no chlorophyll when mature.
- **Dominant sporophyte (sporophytic):** In ferns, both sporophyte and gametophyte are capable of living independently, but the dominant form is the diploid sporophyte. The haploid gametophyte is much smaller and simpler in structure. In seed plants, the gametophyte is even more reduced (at the minimum to only three cells), gaining all its nutrition from the sporophyte. The extreme reduction in the size of the gametophyte and its retention within the sporophyte means that when

applied to seed plants the term 'alternation of generations' is somewhat misleading: "[s]porophyte and gametophyte effectively function as a single organism". Some authors have preferred the term 'alternation of phases'.

Differentiation of the gametes

- **Both gametes are same (isogamy):** Like other species of Cladophora, *C. callicoma* has flagellated gametes which are identical in appearance and ability to move.

Antheridia and archegonia occur on different gametophytes, which are then called dioicous.

- The moss *Mnium hornum* has the gametophyte as the dominant generation. It is dioicous: male plants produce only antheridia in terminal rosettes, female plants produce only archegonia in the form of stalked capsules. Seed plant gametophytes are also dioicous. However, the parent sporophyte may be monoecious, producing both male and female gametophytes or dioecious, producing gametophytes of one gender only. Seed plant gametophytes are extremely reduced in size; the archegonium consists only of a small number of cells, and the entire male gametophyte may be represented by only two cells.

Differentiation of the spores

- **All spores the same size (homospory or isospory):** Horsetails (species of Equisetum) have spores which are all of the same size.
- **Spores of two distinct sizes (heterospory or anisospory):** Larger megaspores and smaller microspores. When the two kinds of spore are produced in different kinds of sporangia, these are called megasporangia and microsporangia. A megaspore often (but not always) develops at the expense of the other three cells resulting from meiosis, which abort.
- Megasporangia and microsporangia occur on the same sporophyte, which is then called monoecious.
- Most flowering plants fall into this category. Thus the flower of a lily contains six stamens (the microsporangia) which produce microspores which develop into pollen grains (the microgametophytes), and three fused carpels which produce integumented megasporangia (ovules) each of which produces a megaspore which develops inside the megasporangium to produce the megagametophyte. In other plants, such as hazel, some flowers have only stamens, others only carpels, but the same plant (*i.e.*, sporophyte) has both kinds of flower and so is monoecious.
- **Flowers of European Holly, a dioecious species:** Male above, female below (leaves cut to show flowers more clearly)
- Megasporangia and microsporangia occur on different sporophytes, which are then called dioecious.
- An individual tree of the European holly (Ilex aquifolium) produces either 'male' flowers which have only functional stamens (microsporangia) producing microspores which develop into pollen grains (microgametophytes) or 'female' flowers which have only functional carpels producing integumented megasporangia (ovules) that contain a megaspore that develops into a multicellular megagametophyte.

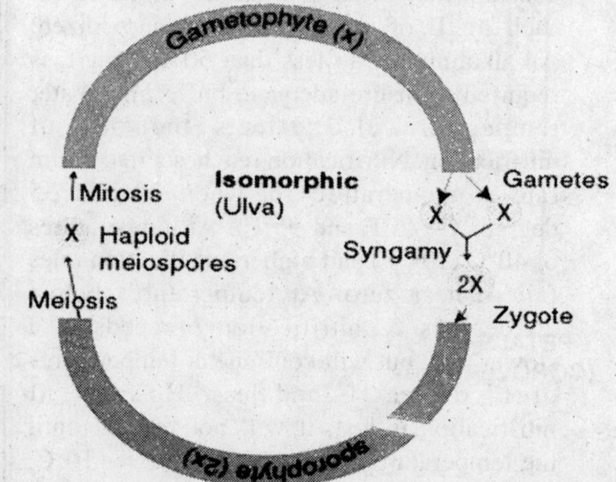

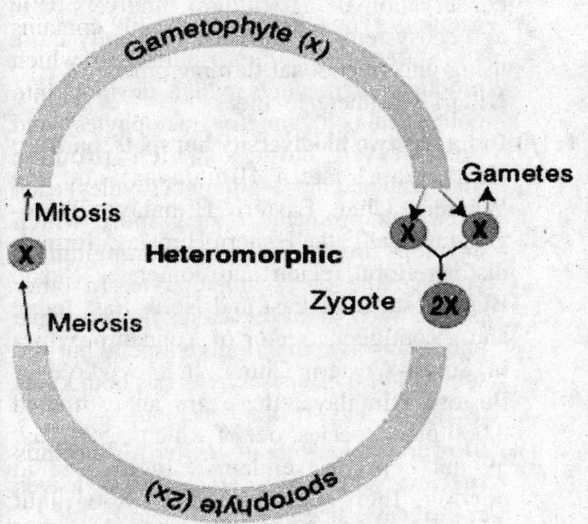

1. (*d*) Well labelled floral diagrams of pentamerous actinomorphic flower showing the (*i*) Obdiplostemonous and (*ii*) Pseudo-Obdiplostemonous conditions of stamens.

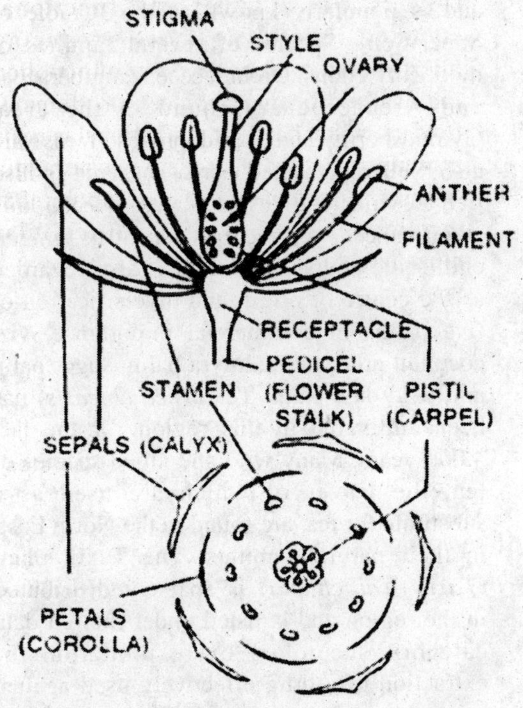

Fig. 1

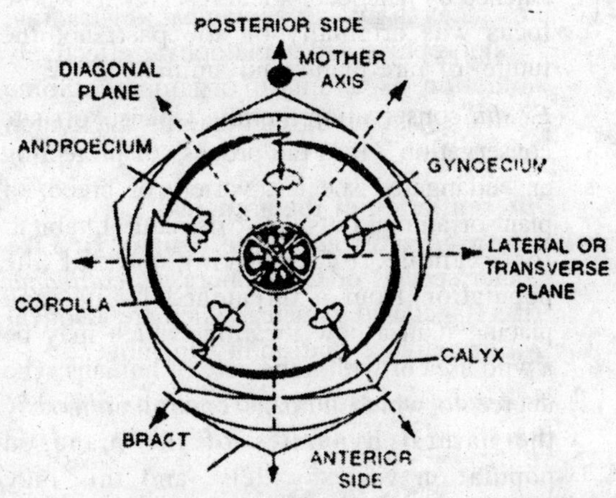

Fig. 2

1. (*e*) Inter situ, Ex situ and In situ conservation

Anyone who has taken a course in conservation biology, or even read a book on the subject, knows that there are fundamentally two kinds of conservation: *in situ* and *ex situ*. The former, aimed at preserving species where they presently occur naturally, will perhaps always rightly be the front line of conservation. The latter, however, has become increasingly important as botanical gardens, zoos, and other cultural institutions strive to save the rarest species by growing them under intensive care in living collections and backing this effort with seed banks, tissue culture, and other relatively expensive high-tech methods.

Each strategy has its advantages and disadvantages. In places like Hawaii, where approximately half the native flora is considered at risk of extinction in the next few decades, scientists and conservationists have begun asking themselves how they can do more for these roughly 500 species, through innovative and more cost-effective strategies that aim to bridge the gap between these two methodologies. Although the term has been around for over a decade, the concept of "*inter situ*" conservation first came to the attention of the public in Hawaii through a radical experimental plan that was hatched by paleoecological researchers whose focus was originally on the past, not the future, of rare plants and animals.

Ex situ conservation literally means, "off-site conservation". It is the process of protecting an endangered species, variety or breed, of plant or animal outside of its natural habitat; for example, by removing part of the population from a threatened habitat and placing it in a new location, which may be a wild area or within the care of humans. The degree to which humans control or modify the natural dynamics of the managed population varies widely, and this may include alteration of living environments, reproductive patterns, access to resources, and protection from predation and mortality. *Ex situ* management can occur within or outside a species' natural geographic range. Individuals maintained *ex situ* exist outside of an ecological niche. This means that they are not under the same selection pressures as wild populations, and they may undergo artificial selection if maintained *ex situ* for multiple generations.

Agricultural biodiversity is also conserved in *ex situ* collections. This is primarily in the form of gene banks where samples are stored in order to conserve the genetic resources of major crop plants and their wild relatives. (That means *ex situ* conservation is a process of conserving endangered plants or animals in the human care by giving them their own environment). Intex of Nepal some example are (one horned rhinoceros, golden michelia).

In situ conservation is the on-site conservation or the conservation of genetic resources in natural populations of plant or animal species, such as forest genetic resources in natural populations of tree species. It is the process of protecting an endangered plant or animal species in its natural habitat, either by protecting or cleaning up the habitat itself, or by defending the species from predators. It is applied to conservation of agricultural biodiversity in agroecosystems by farmers, especially those using unconventional farming practices, *e.g.*, Nilgiri biosphere in India.

1. (*f*) India has two biodiversity hot spots, namely: Himalaya (Eastern Himalayas) and the Western Ghat. Eastern Himalaya Phyto-geographically, the Eastern Himalaya forms a distinct floral region and comprises Nepal, Bhutan, states of East and North-East India, and a contiguous sector of Yunnan province in South-Western China. In the whole of Eastern Himalaya, there are an estimated 9,000 plant species, out of which 3,500 (*i.e.*, 39 per cent) are endemic. In the Indian portion, there occurs some 5,800 plant species, roughly 2,000 (*i.e.*, 36 per cent) of which are endemic. At least 55 flowering plants endemic to this area are recognized as rare, *e.g.*, the Pitcher Plant (*Nepenthes khasiana*). The area has long been recognized as a rich centre of primitive flowering plants and is popularly known as the 'Çradle of Speciation'. Species of several families of monocotyledons, Orchidaceae, Zingiberaceae and Arecaceae are found in the area. Gymnosperms and Pteridophytes (ferns) are also well represented here. The area is also rich in wild relatives of plants of economic significance, *e.g.*, rice, banana, citrus, ginger, chilli, jute and sugarcane. It is also regarded as the centre of origin and diversification of five palms of commercial importance, viz, coconut, arecanut, palmyra palm, sugar palm and wild date palm. Tea (*Thea sinensis*) has been cultivated in this region for the last 4,000 years. Many wild and allied species of tea, the leaves of which are used as a substitute for tea, are found in the North East, in their natural habitats. The Taxol plant (*Taxus wallichiana*) is sparsely distributed in the region and is listed under the red data category due to its overexploitation for extraction of a drug effectively used against cancer. As regards faunal diversity, 63 per cent of the genera of land mammals in India are found in this region. During the last four decades, two new mammals have been discovered in the region – Golden Langur from Assam-Bhutan region, and Namdapha Flying Squirrel from Arunachal Pradesh, indicating the species richness of the region. The region is also a rich centre of avian diversity – more than 60 per cent of the bird species found in India have been recorded in the North East. The region also hosts two endemic genera of lizards, and 35 endemic reptilian species, including two turtles. Of the 240 Indian amphibian species, at least 68 species are known to occur in the North East, 20 of which are endemic. From Namdapha National Park itself, a new genus of mammal, a new subspecies of a bird, six new amphibians' species, four new species of fish, at least 15 new species of beetles and six new species of flies have been discovered.

Western Ghats: The Western Ghats region, which is spread into 6 states of India, is considered to be one of the most important bio-geographic zones of India, as it is one of the richest centres of endemism. Due to varied topography and microclimatic regimes, some areas within the region are considered to be active zones of speciation. The region has 490 arborescent taxa, of which as many as 308 are endemic. About 1,500 endemic species of dicotyledonous plants are reported from the Western Ghats. 245 species of orchids belonging to 75 genera are found here, of which 112 species in ten genera are endemic to the region. As regards the fauna, as many as 315 species of vertebrates belonging to 22 genera are endemic, including 12 species of mammals, 13 species of birds, 89 species of reptiles, 87 species of amphibians and 104 species of fish. The extent of endemism is high amongst amphibian and reptile species. There occur 117 species of amphibians in the region, of which 89 species (76 per cent) are endemic. Of the 165 species of reptiles found in Western Ghats, 88 species are endemic. Many of the endemic and other species are listed as threatened.

1. (*g*) Economic importance of gymnosperm

Gymnosperms are the group of plants whose seeds have no covering or they are not covered by fruit or ovary. Gymnosperms are found in the temperate zones as well as higher tropics. Gymnosperm trees find a variety of use especially for timber used in construction, obtaining resins as well as in paper manufacturing. Many Gymnosperm trees also have medicinal properties and yield essential oils.

Some of the Important Uses of Gymnosperms are:

1. These plants are very useful in making furniture and for other construction purposes.
2. They are the sources of food to animals and humans.
3. The strong roots of gymnosperm prevent from soil erosion.
4. Gymnosperm plants are also scientifically important because they provide lots of evidences about the past.
5. Beside these points, gymnosperm is also used as lumber.
6. They are also used to make perfume, oil, nail polish and many more.

1. (*h*) The Marsileaceae are a small family of heterosporous aquatic and semi-aquatic ferns, though at first sight they do not physically resemble other ferns. The group is commonly known as the "pepperwort family" or as the "water-clover family" because the leaves of the genus Marsilea superficially resemble the leaves of a four-leaf clover (a flowering plant). Leaves of this fern have sometimes been used to substitute for clover leaves on Saint Patrick's Day. In all, the family contains 3 genera and 50 to 80 species with most of those belonging to Marsilea.

Like other ferns, members of the Marsileaceae produce spores, but not seeds when they reproduce. Unlike other ferns, the spores in this family are produced inside sporocarps. These are hairy, short-stalked, bean-shaped structures usually 3 to 8 mm in diameter with a hardened outer covering. This outer covering is tough and resistant to drying out, allowing the spores inside to survive unfavourable conditions such as winter frost or summer desiccation.

Despite this toughness, the sporocarps will open readily in water if conditions are favourable, and specimens have been successfully germinated after being stored for more than 130 years. Each growing season, only one - orocarp typically develops per node along to rhizome near the base of the other leaf-stalks, though in some species of Marsilea there may be two or occasionally as many as twenty.

The resemblance of the sporocarps to peppercorns gives the family its common name of pepperwort like other ferns, members of the Marsileaceae produce spores, but not seeds when they reproduce. Unlike other ferns, the spores in this family are produced inside sporocarps. These are hairy, short-stalked, bean-shaped structures usually 3 to 8 mm in diameter with a hardened outer covering. This outer covering is tough and resistant to drying out, allowing the spores inside to survive unfavourable conditions such as winter frost or summer desiccation.

The sporocarps are functionally and developmentally modified leaflets, although they have much shorter stalks than the vegetative leaflets. Inside the sporocarp, the modified leaflets bear several sori, each of which consists of several sporangia covered with a thin hood of tissue (the indusium). Each sorus includes a mix of two types of sporangium, each type producing only one of two kinds of spores. Towards the centre of each sorus and developing first are the megasporangia, each of which will produce a single large female megaspore. Surrounding them at the edge of the sorus and developing later are the microsporangia, each of which will produce many small male microspores. Because the Marsileaceae produce two kinds of spore (and thus two kinds of gametophyte), they are called heterosporous. While heterospory is the norm among all plants with seeds, such as the flowering plants and conifers, it is very rare among other groups of plants. Also, most heterosporous plants produce their two kinds of sporangia in different places on the plant. Since the Marsileaceae grow both kinds together in a single cluster, they differ from other plants in this regard as well. The spores remain dormant inside the sporocarp through unfavourable conditions, but when conditions are suitable and wet, the sporocarp will germinate. It splits into halves, allowing the tissue coiled inside to become hydrated. As this internal tissue swells with water, it pushes the halves of the hard outer covering apart, and emerges as a long gelatinous worm-like sorophore. The sorophore is a sorus-bearing structure unique to the Marsileaceae; it may extend to more than ten times the length of the sporocarp inside which it was coiled. This extension carries the numerous spore-producing sori attached along each side of the sorophore out into the water.

2. (*a*) Sustainable Utilization of Bioresources and Ecosystem Research

Department (DASB) - Tomorrow's world depends on today's investments. With an ever-increasing human population and consumption of resources at record highs, the future for our fragile Earth depends on protection of the remaining natural environment and sustainable use of our bio-resources. In order to design and develop systems, which can sustain human welfare and the preservation of natural capital for future generations, the knowledge of the complex relationships and interactions in the ecosystem and the interpretation of their reactions to disturbances are crucial.

The objective of the Department is the promotion of a sustainable use of the natural and agricultural ecosystems to link the needs of modern society and the protection of the environment. Research focuses on innovative technologies based on low impact processes to answer to the standard of quality and production of the modern society. Thanks to the most innovative approaches in chemistry, physiology and molecular biology, a careful planning of resources use can be achieved and, in case of disequilibria in the ecosystems caused by anthropic activity counter-balancing actions can be put on place. The understanding of the mechanisms regulating the stability of ecosystems will help in their protection and in a sustainable development of agriculture.

2. (*b*) T-even phages, also known as the E. coli phages, are a group of double-stranded bacteriophages from the family Myoviridae. Bacteriophage means to "eat bacteria", and phages are well known for being obligate intracellular parasites that reproduce within the host cell and are released when the host is destroyed by lysis. Containing about 160 genes, these virulent viruses are among the largest, most complex viruses that are known and one of the best studied model organisms. They have played a key role in the development of virology and molecular biology.

Bacteriophages were first discovered by the English scientist Frederick Twort in 1915 and Félix d'Hérelle in 1917. In the late 1930s, T.L. Rakieten proposed either a mixture of raw sewerage or a lysate from E.coli infected with raw sewerage to the two researchers Milislav Demerac and Ugo Fano. These two researchers isolated T3, T4, T5, and T6 from E.coli. Also, in 1932, the researcher J.Bronfenbrenner had studied and worked on the T2 phage, at which the T2 phage was isolated from the virus. This isolation was made from a fecal material rather than from sewerage. At any rate, Delbruck was involved in the discovery of the T even phages. His part was naming the bacteriophages into Type 1(T1), Type 2 (T2),Type 3 (T3), etc.

Phages have multiple factors contributing to their structure. It consists of the head, collar, helical sheath, the core or tube, hexagonal base plate, tail fibres (not all) and finally tail pins. The head's job is to enfold or surround nucleic acids. The tail fibres help in attaching the phage to a bacterial cell. The tail acts as a duct through which the nucleic acid goes through during an infection. The collar helps support the head (to stay in place). Bacteriophages in general (including T-even bacteriophages) contain a head structure, which can vary in size and shape. The head enfolds nucleic acid and acts as the protective covering. Certain phages have tails attached to the phage head. The tail is a hollow duct through which the nucleic acid passes during infection. T-even Bacteriophages have genomes that code for phage-specific DNA replication, recombination, and DNA repair functions. Also, they offer well branded genes and proteins. Similar to all viruses, they depend on many of their hosts important makeups and roles or functions (transcription and translation, membranes, breakdown of energy, etc.), for their reproduction.

Diagram of the DNA injection process

Penetration is also a value characteristic of phage-host infection that involves the injection of the phages genetic material inside the bacterium. Penetration of nucleic acid takes place after the irreversible adsorption phase. Mechanisms involving penetration of the phages nucleic acid are specific for each phage. This penetration mechanism can involve electrochemical membrane potential, ATP molecules, enzymatic splitting of peptidoglycan layer, or all of these three factors can be vital for the penetration of the nucleic acid inside the bacterial cell. Studies have been done on the T2 bacteriophage (T4-like phage) mechanism of penetration and it has shown that the phages tail does not penetrate inside the bacterial cell wall and penetration of this phage involves electrochemical membrane potential on the inner membrane.

Enterobacteria phage λ (lambda phage, coliphage λ) is a bacterial virus, or bacteriophage, that infects the bacterial species Escherichia coli (E. coli). It was discovered by Esther Lederberg in 1950 when she noticed that streaks of mixtures of two E. coli strains, one of which treated with ultraviolet light, was "nibbled and plaqued". This virus has a temperate lifecycle that allows it to either reside within the genome of its host through lysogeny or enter into a lytic phase (during which it kills and lyses the cell to produce offspring).

The phage particle consists of a head (also known as a capsid), a tail, and tail fibres. The head contains the phage's double-strand linear DNA genome. During infection, the phage particle recognizes and binds to its host, E. coli, causing DNA in the head of the phage to be ejected through the tail into the cytoplasm of the bacterial cell. Usually, a "lytic cycle" ensues, where the lambda DNA is replicated and new phage particles are produced within the cell. This is followed by cell lysis, releasing the cell contents, including virions that have been assembled, into the environment. However, under certain conditions, the phage DNA may integrate itself into the host cell chromosome in the lysogenic pathway. In this state, the λ DNA is called a prophage and stays resident within the host's genome without apparent harm to the host. The host is termed a lysogen when a prophage is present. This prophage may enter the lytic cycle when the lysogen enters a stressed condition.

The virus particle consists of a head and a tail that can have tail fibres. The whole particle consists of 12–14 different proteins with more than 1000 protein molecules total and one DNA molecule located in the phage head. However, it is still not entirely clear whether the L and M proteins are part of the virion.

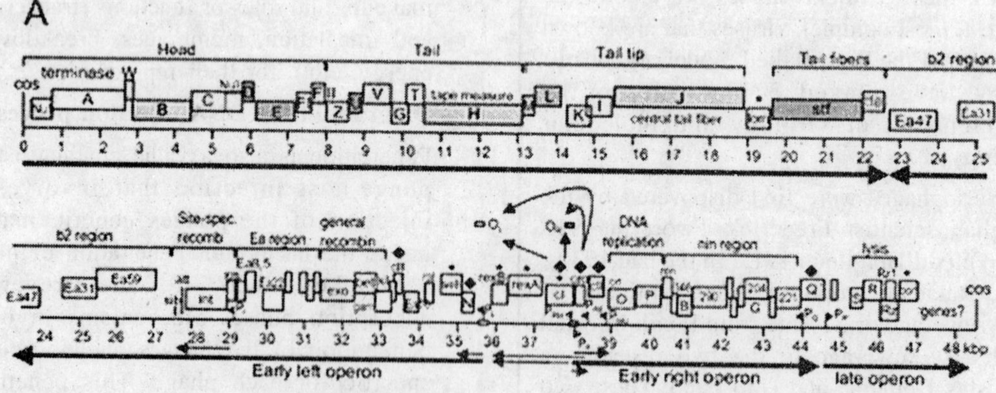

Fig. *Linear layout of lambda phage genome with major operons, promoter regions and capsid coding genes.*

The genome contains 48,490 base pairs of double-stranded, linear DNA, with 12-base single-strand segments at both 5' ends. These two single-stranded segments are the "sticky ends" of what is called the cos site. The cos site circularizes the DNA in the host cytoplasm. In its circular form, the phage genome, therefore, is 48,502 base pairs in length. The lambda genome can be inserted into the E. coli chromosome and is then called a prophage.

Life cycle

Infection

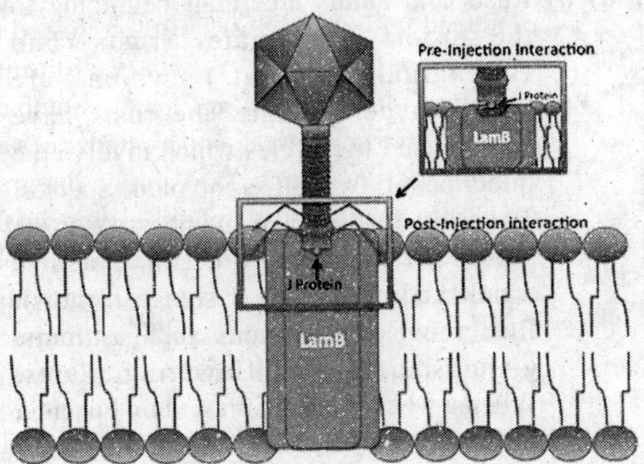

Lambda phage is a non-contractile tailed phage, meaning during an infection event it cannot 'force' its DNA through a bacterial cell membrane. It must instead use an existing pathway to invade the host cell, having evolved the tip of its tail to interact with a specific pore to allow entry of its DNA to the hosts.

Bacteriophage Lambda binds to an E. coli cell by means of its J protein in the tail tip. The J protein interacts with the maltose outer membrane porin (the product of the lamB gene) of E. coli, a porin molecule, which is a part of the maltose operon.

2. (*c*) Telome Theory

It is now widely accepted (on the basis of overwhelming amount of evidence) that the land-dwelling plants evolved from aquatic ancestors. All organisms known in the Precambrian, Cambrian and Ordovician periods of Paleozoic Era lived in aquatic environment. The evolutionary conquest of land probably occurred sometimes between the late Cambrian and early Silurian. The concrete evidence of early vascular land plants came from the Silurian in the form of fossil plant Cooksonia of Rhynia group of plants. A number of theories on land-plant evolution exists of which the Telome theory of Walter Zimmermann (1930, 1952) is the most comprehensive. This theory is based on fossil record and synthesises the major steps in the evolution of vascular plants.

According to this theory, all vascular plants evolved —either directly or indirectly — from a simple leafless Rhynia type ancestral form made up of sterile and fertile axes (the telomes). Evolutionary modification of its parts produces more advanced vascular plants with roots, stems, leaves, more complex vascular systems and protected sporangia. According to Zimmermann, these telomes or telome trusses of primitive Rhynia type of vascular plants have been subjected to certain evolutionary processes in varying degrees among the various taxonomic groups.

These evolutionary processes are:

(*i*) Overtopping

(*ii*) Reduction,

(*iii*) Plantation,

(*iv*) Syngenesis or webbing, and

(*v*) Curvation.

(*i*) **Overtopping:** In this process, one of the two dichotomising branches of the primitive axis produced by the apical meristem outgrows or overgrows the other. The larger axis thus produced becomes the stem, while the shorter or overtopped branches represent the beginnings of lateral branches or leaves. Now the earlier dichotomy will be transformed to pseudomonopodial branch.

(*ii*) **Reduction:** In this process, the activity of terminal meristem of each telome of the truss becomes suppressed resulting into much shorter branches by decreasing the length of telomes and mesomes. This process is responsible for the formation of microphyllous leaves of the Lycopsida and Sphenopsida as well as the needle-like leaves of conifers.

(*iii*) **Plantation:** The process of plantation caused the telomes and mesomes of the truss to shift from a three-dimensional pattern (cruciate dichotomy) to a single plane (fan-shaped dichotomy).

The process of infilling with photosynthetic and other tissues between the planted branches is called webbing which have led to the evolution of flattened leaf-like structure with a dichotomously veined lamina.

(*iv*) **Syngenesis:** This is an evolutionary process where tangential fusion of mesomes and telomes takes place. The lateral fusion of sterile vegetative telomes and mesomes resulted into complex anastomosing vascular systems in stem (*e.g.*, polystelic condition in Selaginella).

The fusion of fertile trusses with their terminal sporangia resulted in the formation of synangia of Psilotum. The closed or reticulate venation pattern of some ferns, gymnosperm and many flowering plants are the result of syngenesis of the dichotomising veins of the primitive leaf.

(*v*) **Curvation:** This evolutionary process is caused due to the unequal growth of the tissues on two opposite flanks of the telome.

It has two sub-processes:

(*i*) **Recurvation:** In this sub-process the telome bends inward towards an axis. The inward-projecting sporangia on a sporangiophore of Equisetum (Sphenopsida) is the result of this sub-process.

(*ii*) **Incurvation:** In this sub-process, the fertile telome bends downward resulting in the downward shifting of the sporangia from terminal to the ventral surface of the leaf. This sub-process is responsible for the formation of ventral position of the sporangia in fern (Pteropsida) leaf.

5. (*a*) (*i*) Rusts and smuts are fungi belonging to the orders Urediniales (rusts) and Ustilaginales (smuts) which are basidiomycete fungi. The rusts have complicated life cycles which involve the infection of two different plant species. The most well-known members of these groups are wheat rust (Puccinia graminis tritici) and corn smut (Ustilago myadis). Rust fungi attack plants such as ferns, gymnosperms, and flowering plants. When a wheat plant is infested by Puccinia graminis tritici, the infestation may become obvious during the summer growing season when rust coloured growth appears on the stems of infected plants. Fungal hyphae are composed of groups of spore generating structures (sporangia) called uredinia that rupture the stem and become visible. It is the spores released from the uredinia (called urediniospores) that infect new wheat plants and spread the disease. In the fall, Puccinia produces black sporangia (called telia) and the infected wheat plants have distinct black patches on their stems. Spores from the telia (called teliospores) do not attack other wheat plants but instead infect barberry plants. Teliospores which land on barberry leaves germinate and form small cup-shaped structures called spermagonia. Each spermagonium produces long filaments called receptive hyphae which extend above the spermagonium and spermatia, which are sexual gametes. The spermagonium also produces a nectar-like substance which is attractive to flies. Spermatia are mixed with this nectar and flies transfer the spermatia from adjacent spermagonia as they feed. New fungal mycelia, resulting from the union of the spermatia with the receptive hyphae of spermagonia of different genetic strains, grow on the underside of the barberry leaf. There, the mycelium produces a larger bell-shaped sporangium called an aecium, which generates aeciospores which in turn infect new wheat plants.

Smut fungi differ from rust fungi in several ways. While rust fungi require two different hosts to complete their life cycle, smut fungi may complete their life cycle on only one host, which is always a flowering plant. Another difference between rust and smut fungi is seen in the way that they infect their host plants. Infections from rust fungi are localized to that part of the plant close to where a germinated urediniospore, aeciospore, or teliospore becomes established. Smut fungi spread to infest the entire plant from a single initial infection site, often targeting specific organs.

(*ii*) A Cladode is a stem which is modified into a leaf-like structure for photosynthesis. A Phylloclade is a branch which is modified into a leaf-like structure for photosynthesis.

Simply put, a phylloclade is a type of cladode. Both structures are modified into flat, leaf-like structures. The flatness is designed to maximize surface area, for photosynthesis. Furthermore, phylloclades have several internodes functioning like a leaf, while cladodes only have one or two.

Generally, the simplest way to distinguish a phylloclade or cladode form a true leaf is by examining the roots, while the leaves are still small, underdeveloped, and very short-lived, or ephemeral.

Two examples for a phylloclade are:

Muehlenbeckia - Also called wire vine; a very rugged, flower-like plant.

Opuntia - Also called prickly pear; an edible cactus.

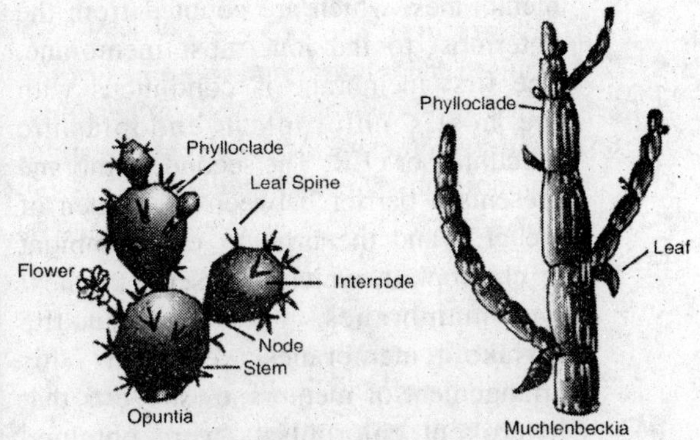

Two examples for a cladode are:

Ruscus - a genus of flowering plants

Asparagus - a commonly eaten, flowering perennial plant

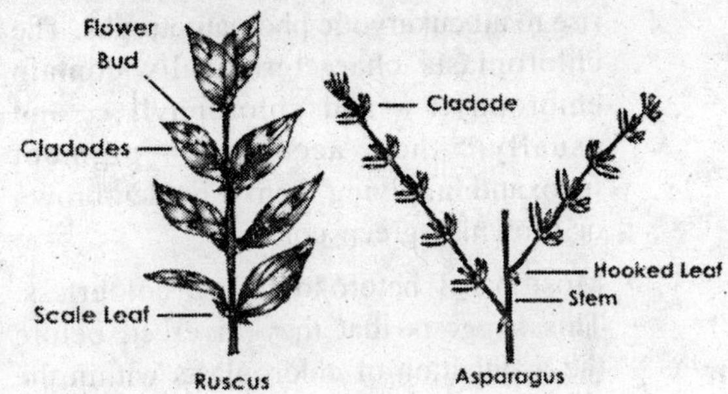

5. (*b*) (*i*) The heterokonts or stramenopiles (formally, Heterokonta or Stramenopiles) are a major line of eukaryotes currently containing more than 25,000 known species. Most are algae, ranging from the giant multicellular kelp to the unicellular diatoms, which are a primary component of plankton. Other notable members of the Stramenopiles include the (generally) parasitic oomycetes, including Phytophthora of Irish potato famine infamy and Pythium which causes seed rot and damping off.

The name "heterokont" refers to the type of motile lifecycle stage, in which the flagellated cells possess two differently shaped flagella.

Many heterokonts are algae with chloroplasts surrounded by four membranes, which are counted from the outermost to the innermost membrane. The first membrane is continuous with the host's chloroplast endoplasmic reticulum, or cER. The second membrane presents a barrier between the lumen of the cER and the primary endosymbiont or chloroplast, which represents the next two membranes, within which the thylakoid membranes are found. This arrangement of membranes suggests that heterokont chloroplasts were obtained from the reduction of a symbiotic red algal eukaryote, which had arisen by evolutionary divergence from the monophyletic primary endosymbiotic ancestor that is thought to have given rise to all eukaryotic photoautotrophs. The chloroplasts characteristically contain chlorophyll a and chlorophyll c, and usually the accessory pigment fucoxanthin, giving them a golden-brown or brownish-green colour.

Most basal heterokonts are colourless. This suggests that they diverged before the acquisition of chloroplasts within the group.

(ii) Eccentric growth rings: A layer of wood formed in a plant during a single period of growth is known as Eccentric Growth. Growth rings are visible as Eccentric Circles of varying width when a tree cut cross wise. They represent layers of cells produced by vascular cambium.

Centric growth rings: Centric growth rings became larger and larger in diameter outward from the centre of the stump. Because a single tree is usually formed each year, the age of the tree at the time it was cut can be determined by simply counting the rings.

If the year of cutting is known, the year during which each ring was formed can be determined by counting backwards from the outside ring. Such dating of rings may reveal that rings formed during certain extreme drought years are unusually narrow. This has led to speculation that tree ring characteristics may indicate a number of things about past water and climatic conditions.

5. (c) (i) Flower showing Androphore and Gynophore

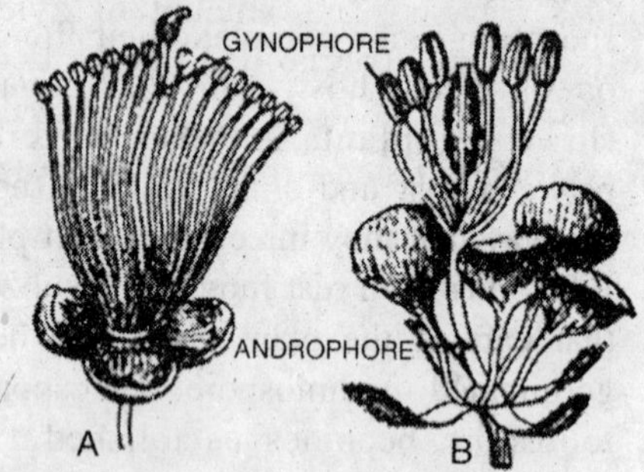

(ii) Winged pollen of *Pinus*

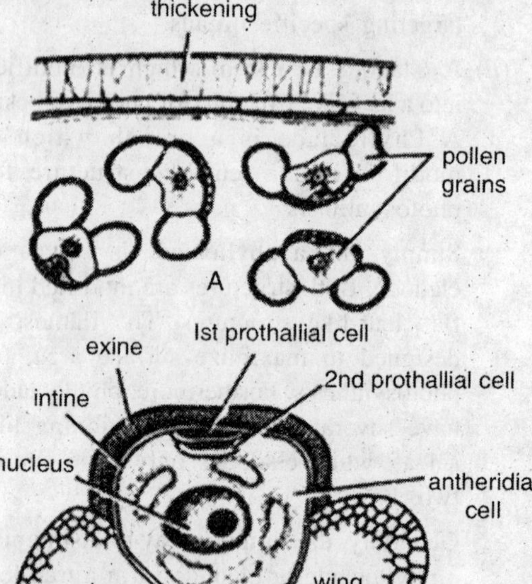

5. (d) (i) Manoxylic wood: Secondary vascular tissues with large amounts of softer storage cells (*i.e.*, parenchyma) mixed with the wood or xylem cells (*e.g.*, tracheids). The stems of these plants are softer than the wood of trees we use for lumber.

Examples of plants with manoxylic wood are sago palms or cycads, the spurs or short shoots of Ginkgo trees, as well as many extinct seed fern groups including Callistophytes, Lyginopterids, Medullosids, Calamopityales and Buteoxylonales.

Pycnoxylic wood: Secondary vascular tissues with copious amount of xylem cells (*e.g.*, tracheids) and little parenchyma.

This wood is much stronger and durable.

Examples of plants with pycnoxylic wood are conifers or cone-bearing trees, the long shoots of Ginkgo, and angiosperms.

Conifers (mostly evergreen cone-bearing trees such as pines) have wood that is light-weight, light in colour, and strong in tension, but weak in shear (along the grains). Therefore, this is called "soft wood", which is usually cheaper and used for building inexpensive furniture or used for paper pulp.

Flowering plants (mostly deciduous trees such as oak/maple) have wood that is darker in colour, heavier in weight, and strong in compression, tension, and shear. Therefore, this is called "hard wood", which is used to make durable furniture, flooring, and building structures.

(ii) **Medullary Vascular Bundle:** There are numerous vascular Lundes in the pith known as medullary bundles. Medullary bundles are absent from the pith of the leafy, redictual cacti. Medullary bundles may be found in the cortex of certain plants in the melastomaceae, caly conth aceae, etc., in the pith in members of piperaceae, cucurbitaceae, etc., or even in Medullary rays, as in transmedullary bundles of *Citrullus vulgaris, Lagenaria valgaris* and other cucurbits.

Cortical Vascular bundle: The cortical bundle is a vascular system which allows the transportation of water and nutrients through the voluminous cortex of the cactus. This system is unique to cacti, and helps to replace the water lost to the dry desert air. The cortical bundle emerges radially from the xylem and produces shoots that run tangentially to the cortex, branching extensively and vascularizing every part of the cortex. The size of the cortical bundle can vary greatly from species to species. Because cacti live a long time, the cortical bundles have to function for many years. In every cactus species, the cortical bundles produce secondary phloems. In very old cortical bundles located at the base of very old shoots, the secondary phloem may attain a thickness of several millimeters.

5. (*e*) (*i*) Imbricate Aestivation: In this kind, one petal or sepal is internal or being overlapped on both the margins and one petal or sepal is external with both of its margins overlapping. Out of the remaining sepals or petals, one margin is overlapping and another margin is overlapped.

There are two forms of imbricate aestivation, viz., descendingly imbricate and ascendingly imbricate.

(*a*) Descendingly Imbricate or Vexillary Aestivation: In this form of aestivation the posterior petal overlaps one margin of the two lateral petals. Another margin of such two lateral petals overlaps the two anterior petals that are united. Therefore, the overlapping is in descending order and therefore the name. Example: Corolla of Fabaceae.

(*b*) Ascendingly imbricate aestivation: In this form the posterior odd petal is the innermost being overlapped by one margin of the two lateral petals. Another margin of the two lateral petals is overlapped by the two anterior petals. In this, the overlapping of petals starts from the anterior side proceeding towards the posterior side. This is just reverse of descendingly imbricate aestivation. Example: Petals of Caesalpiniaceae

5. (*e*) (*ii*) **Hypanthium:** In a pomegranate flower, Punica granatum, the petals, except for their fused bases, soon fall. The hypanthium with sepal lobes and stamens still attached develops to form the outer layer of the fruit.

In angiosperms, a hypanthium or floral cup is a structure where basal portions of the calyx, the corolla, and the stamens form a cup-shaped tube. It is sometimes called a floral tube, a term that is also used for corolla tube and calyx tube. It often contains the nectaries of the plant. It is present in most flowering species, although varies in structural dimensions and appearance. This differentiation between the hypanthium in particular species is useful with identification. Some geometric forms are obconic shapes as in toyon, whereas some are saucer-shaped as in Mitella caulescens.

Its presence is diagnostic of many families, including the Rosaceae, Grossulariaceae, and Fabaceae. In some cases, it can be so deep, with such a narrow top, that the flower can appear to have an inferior ovary — the ovary is below the other attached floral parts. The hypanthium is known by different common names in differing species. In the eucalypts, it is referred to as the gum nut; in roses it is called the hip.

Hypanthodium is a special type of inflorescence. The penducle becomes fleshy, flattened and forms a hollow cup with a small opening at the top. The male and female flowers are borne on the inner wall of the cup or receptacles with male flowers are the base of receptacle. The flowers are usually sessile, example. Rubber.

5. (*f*) (*i*) **Male flower of Euphorbia**

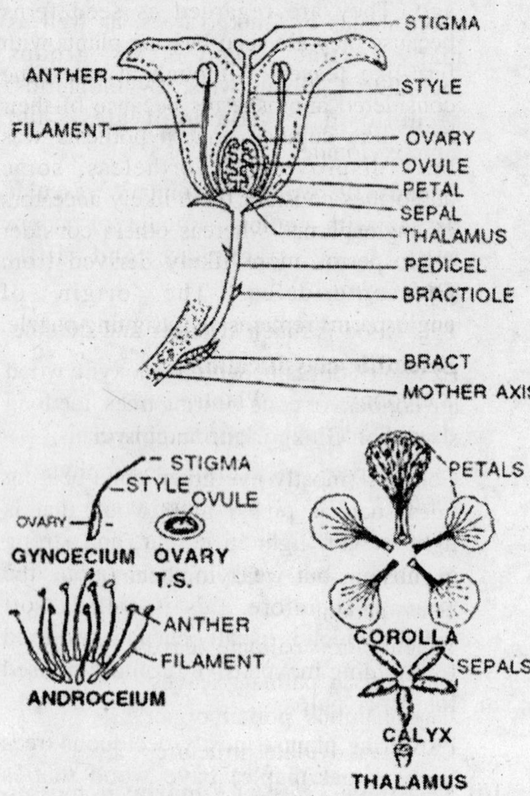

(*ii*) **Tyloses**

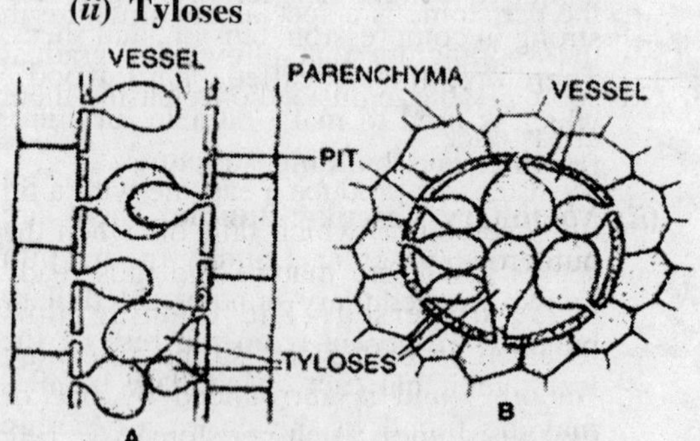

Formation of Tyloses in heartwood

A. L.S. vessel showing tyloses.

B. T.S. vessel showing tyloses.

5. (*g*) (*i*) **Taxonomic Position of Caytoniales:** The Caytoniales are an extinct order of seed plants known from fossils collected throughout the Mesozoic Era, specifically in the late Triassic to Maastrichtian

period, around 250 to 70 million years ago. They are regarded as seed ferns because they are seed-bearing plants with fern-like leaves. Although at one time considered angiosperms because of their berry-like cupules, that hypothesis was later disproven. Nevertheless, some authorities consider them likely ancestors of angiosperms, whereas others consider angiosperms more likely derived from Glossopteridales. The origin of angiosperms remains an intriguing puzzle.

Scientific classification

Kingdom:	Plantae
(unranked):	Spermatophyta
Division:	Pteridospermophyta
Order:	Caytoniales
Gothan 1932	
Family:	Caytoniaceae

Form genera

Sagenopteris palmate leaves

Mexiglossa palmate leaves

Caytonanthus pollen organ

Caytonia ovulate structure

(ii) **Peristome Teeth of Funaria:** In mosses, the peristome is a specialized structure in the sporangium that allows for gradual spore discharge, instead of releasing them all at once.

Most mosses produce a capsule with a lid (the operculum) which falls off when the spores inside are mature and thus ready to be dispersed. The opening thus revealed is called the stoma (meaning "mouth") and is surrounded by one or two peristomes. Each peristome is a ring of triangular "teeth" formed from the remnants of dead cells with thickened cell walls. There are usually 16 such teeth in a single peristome, separate from each other and able to both fold in to cover the stoma as well as fold back to open the stoma. This articulation of the teeth is termed arthrodontous and is found in the moss subclass Bryopsida. In other groups of mosses, the capsule is either nematodontous with an attached operculum (as in the Polytrichopsida), or else splits open without operculum or teeth.

Arthrodontous capsule of the moss *Dicranella varia*

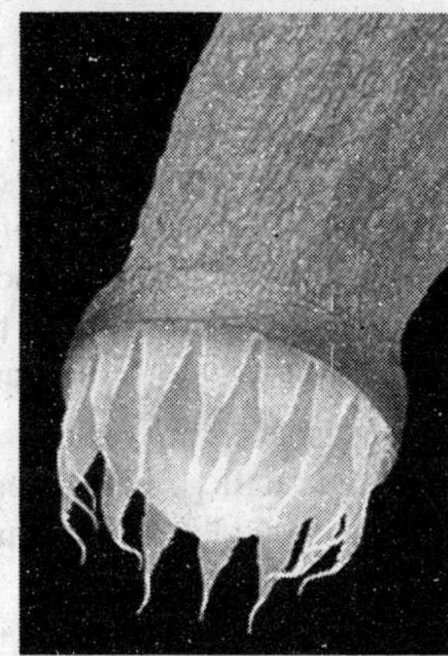

Peristoma of *Bryum capillare*

There are two subtypes of arthrodontous peristome. The first is termed haplolepidous and consists of a single circle of 16 peristome teeth. The second type is the diplolepidous peristome found in subclass Bryidae.

5. (*h*) (*ii*) Coenocytic Mycelium: Filamentous fungi could contain more than one nuclei in a coenocytic mycelium. A coenocyte capability as a single coordinated unit is composed of a couple of cells linked structurally and functionally, *i.e.*, through gap junctions. Fungal mycelia where hyphae lack septa are often called "aseptate" or "coenocytic". Filamentous fungi may contain multiple nuclei in a coenocytic mycelium. A coenocyte functions as a single coordinated unit composed of multiple cells linked structurally and functionally, *i.e.*, through gap junctions. Fungal mycelia in which hyphae lack septa are known as "aseptate" or "coenocytic".

(*ii*) Parasitism in Fungi: A parasite is an organism that lives on or in another organism, known as that parasite's host. The parasite gains nourishment from the host, but the host is either harmed by the parasite's presence or unaffected by it. There are parasitic plants, animals and fungi.

The parasitic fungus that causes oak wilt is spread from tree to tree via insects, which carry the fungal spores on their legs. Oak wilt is a serious problem in many forests and urban areas, since it spreads easily and almost always leads to defoliation and tree death within several years. Symptoms of oak wilt include the formation of large spore mats on the tree's trunk and rapid loss of discoloured leaves.

Blackpoint disease can be caused by a number of parasitic fungal species. It causes black smudges to appear on the heads of wheat and other grains. Blackpoint disease occurs most often in fields that are overly moist and when levels of humidity are high.

One example of a parasitic fungus is Ceratocystis fagacearum, a fungus that causes the disease oak wilt.

6. (*a*) Progressive Sterilization of the Sporogenous Tissue: The process of the sterilization of sporogenous tissue is very conspicuous in bryophytes. According to Bower the more complex sporophytes have been evolved from the simpler ones by the progressive sterilization of potentially sporogenous tissue. The evolution may be traced from the simplest sporophyte found in Riccia (Hepaticopsida) to the more complex sporophyte found in Funaria (Bryosida). There is ever increasing sterilization of sporogenous tissue. The so formed sterile tissues function in different ways, *e.g.*, the foot may absorb the food and perform the function of anchorage; chlorophyllous tissue, stomata and inter-cellular spaces are meant for food manufacture; elaters, operculum and peristome help in the dehiscence of the spores somehow or the other; columella of Funaria acts as storage tissue for food and water whereas the columella of Anthoceros is quite mechanical in function and helps in the dispersal of spores.

The simplest type of sporophyte is found in Riccia. The zygote divides transversely giving rise to two cells. These two cells divide vertically and a four celled embryo is formed. This is followed by several irregular divisions and a 20 to 30 celled embryo is formed. At this stage there are periclinal divisions and the embryo is differentiated into amphithecium and endothecium.

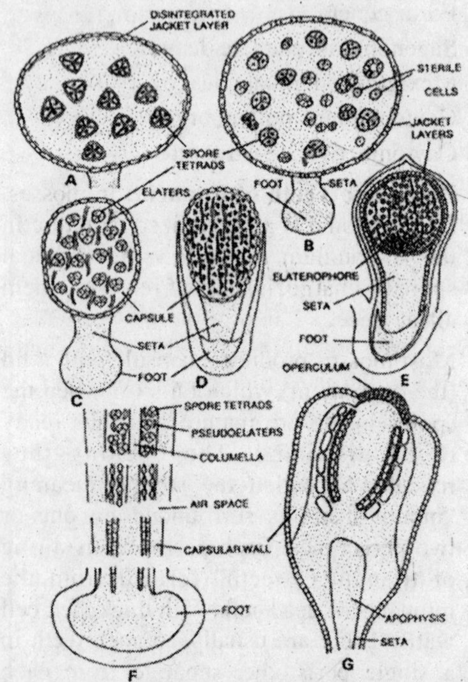

Progressive sterilization of sporogenous tissue in bryophytes; A. sporophyte of Riccir; B. sporophyte of Sphaerocarpos sp; C. sporophyte of targionia Sp.; D. sporophyte of Marchantia sp; E. sporophyte of Pellia sp.; F. sporophyte of Anthoceros; G. sporophyte of Funaria hygrometrica.

In Sphaerocarpos, some cells of the sporogenous tissue become sporocytes which form spores by meiotic division. Other cells of the sporogenous tissue develop into sterile nurse cells which supply food to the spores. Here the sterilization of sporogenous tissue has progressed to some extent.

In Bryopsida the sterilization of the sporogenous tissue reaches to its climax. In Funaria, the sterilization reaches to its highest peak. The sterile tissue in Funaria consists of a foot, a long seta, many-layered wall of the capsule, columella, apophysis, peristome, operculum, etc. Here the sporogenous tissue is very much reduced. For the study of the spore sac and spores the longitudinal section of the capsule may be examined under the low power of the compound microscope.

6. (*b*) Theories of Endemism: Endemism means the confinement of a particular species, genus, or groups of plants and animals to a particular area. Taxa occurring only a single restricted geographical area is known as endemics. Endemism is normally applied only where there is a considerable restriction in the area of distribution. There are two main theories of Endemism. The first theory believes that the last survivors of once flourishing flora which is now declining are the relics or epibiotics which are endemics. However, second theory believes that these are recent and youthful forms in course of gradual extinction. The theory is also known as Age and Area hypothesis. The first theory is supported by the geographers like Sequoia semipenirens of the Central Valley of California and Oregon and S. gigantea of Sierra Nevada which are endemic to their respective native homes, were extensively distributed in Cretaceous and Tertiary periods. The supporters of second theory have the examples of Primula, Impatiens Rhododendron, etc. According to this theory, Area is directly proportional to its age in the scale of evolution. So, a small area of distribution shows relatively young in age, *e.g.*, Coleus is distributed on the summit of the dry Ritigala mountains in Sri Lanka, with two species C. elongatus and C. barbatus. C. elongatus is endemic and C. barbatus is widely distributed in tropical Asia and Africa. Willis believed C. elongatus to be derived from C. barbatus.

6. (*c*) Taxonomic Hierarchy: The study of taxonomy has led to the taxonomic categories – Kingdom, phylum, class, order, family, genus and species. Now let us see how all the organisms are classified into the hierarchy.

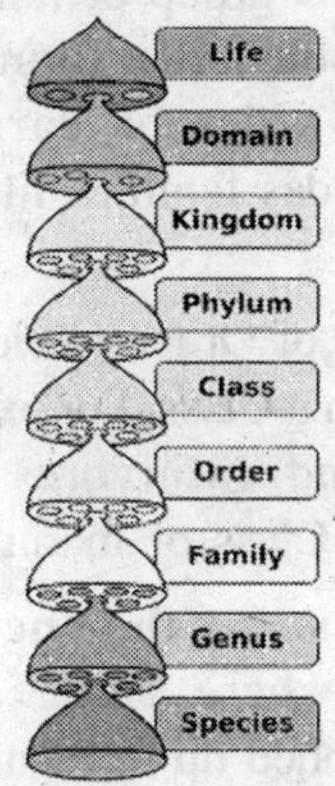

Taxonomic Hierarchy

Species: It is the lowest level of classification and shows the high level of similarities among the organisms. One species can be distinguished from the other closely related species based on distinct differences in morphology. Let us look at an example; Plasmodium vivax and Plasmodium falciparum – both are malaria causing parasites, but have different effects on a patient. Plasmodium is the name of the genus and has a number of species which show distinct morphological characteristics.

Genus: This taxonomic group is composed of multiple species which have similar characteristics but different from that of species from other genus. Considering the same example of Plasmodium, it is a genus with multiple species which are similar to each other, but different from the species of other genus.

Family: This category of taxonomy comprises a number of genus which share some similarity among themselves. However, the number of similarities decreases compared to species and genus. For example, the genus of tiger, leopard, lion, *i.e.*, Panthera and the genus of cats *i.e.*, Felis are grouped together in the family Felidae.

Order: The classification starting from order has less similarities as a result, they are categories based on aggregates of characteristics. A group of families showing somewhat few similarities forms an order. For example, the order of carnivores, *i.e.*, Carnivora includes families like Felidae and Canidae.

Class: A group of Orders which share a few similarities form a Class. For example, Orders of primates and carnivores are grouped together in the Class of mammals.

Phylum: This is the next level of classification where along a number of Classes are clubbed up to form one Phylum. Example – Fishes, reptiles, apes, amphibians and mammals together form the phylum of Vertebrates or Chordata.

Kingdom: This is the highest level of classification. We have Kingdoms like Plantae, Animalia, Fungi, Protista and Monera.

8. (*a*) These are specialized cells of the filament distinguished from others by their thick wall, polar nodule(s) and homogeneous contents. Heterocysts are commonly found in the members of Stigonematales and Nostocales (except Oscillatoriaceae). They grow in the filament either terminally (Gloeotrichia) or intercalary (Nostoc) or both terminal and intercalary (Anabaena desikacharyiensis).

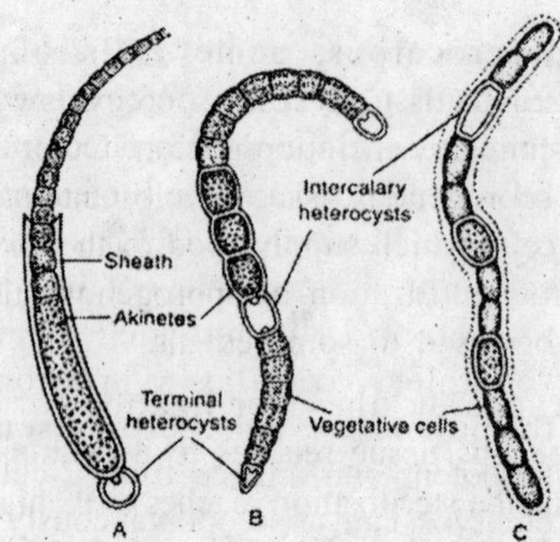

Heterocysts at different position on the plant boyd: A. Terminal (Gloeotrichia), B. Both terminal and intercalary (Anabaena desika charyiensis) and C. Intercalary (Nostoc)

8. (*b*) Floral Diagram of Monandrae Group

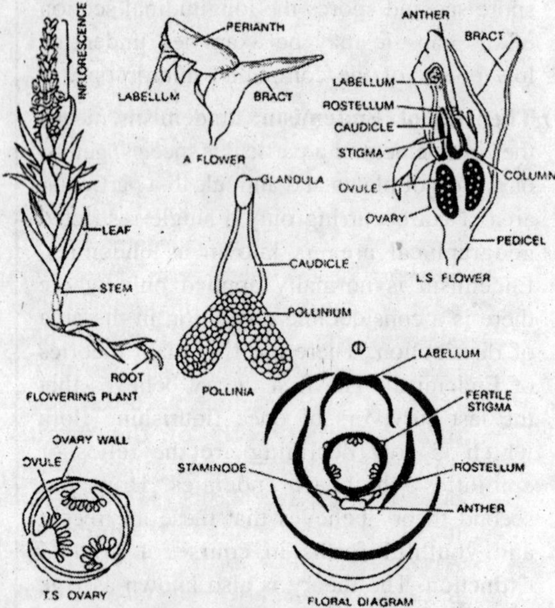

Zeuxine strateuamatica L.

8. (*c*) (*i*) Totipotency: Totipotency is the ability of a single cell to divide and produce all of the differentiated cells in an organism. Spores and zygotes are examples of totipotent cells. In the spectrum of cell potency, totipotency represents the cell with the greatest differentiation potential. Toti comes from the Latin *totus* which means "entirely".

It is possible for a fully differentiated cell to return to a state of totipotency. This conversion to totipotency is complex, not fully understood and the subject of recent research. Research in 2011 has shown that cells may differentiate not into a fully totipotent cell, but instead into a "complex cellular variation" of totipotency. Stem cells resembling totipotent blastomeres from 2-cell stage embryos can arise spontaneously in the embryonic stem cell cultures and also can be induced to arise more frequently in vitro through down-regulation of the chromatin assembly activity of CAF-1.

The human development model is one which can be used to describe how totipotent cells arise. Human development begins when a sperm fertilizes an egg and the resulting fertilized egg creates a single totipotent cell, a zygote. In the first hours after fertilization, this zygote divides into identical totipotent cells, which can later develop into any of the three germ layers of a human (endoderm, mesoderm, or ectoderm), into cells of the cytotrophoblast layer or syncytiotrophoblast layer of the placenta. After reaching a 16-cell stage, the totipotent cells of the morula differentiate into cells that will eventually become either the blastocyst's Inner cell mass or the outer trophoblasts. Approximately four days after fertilization and after several cycles of cell division, these totipotent cells begin to specialize. The inner cell mass, the source of embryonic stem cells, becomes pluripotent.

(*ii*) **Cybrids:** We can define cybrids as plants or cells containing nucleus of one species but cytoplasm from both the parental species. It may be a single cell or a complete growing plant called cybrid plant. For production of a cybrid cell two parental cells can be used but one should be a complete cell (cytoplasm with nucleus) and other should be without nucleus or inactive nucleus. For inactivation of nucleus technologists use gamma rays and X-rays.

Aim of Cybrid Production: Aim of this production is to combine cytoplasm gene of one species to another species which have nucleus with cytoplasm. This is also a way for those species which don't perform sexual reproduction with each other. So this way provides to make a desired species with combination of both species.

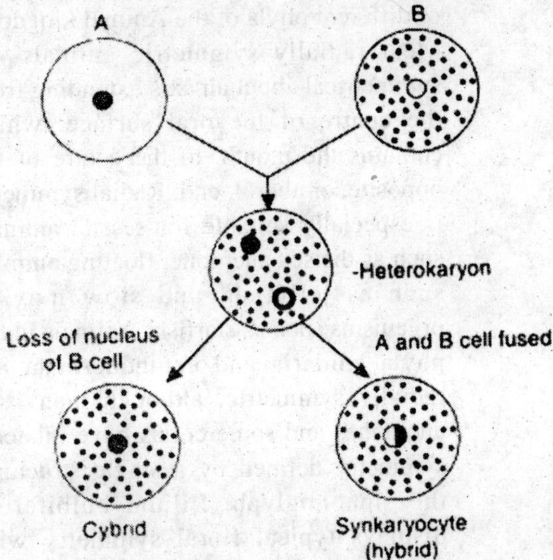

(*iii*) **Symmetry and Differentiation:** Symmetry in biology is the balanced distribution of duplicate body parts or shapes within the body of an organism. In nature and biology, symmetry is always approximate: for example, plant leaves, while considered symmetrical, rarely match up exactly when folded in half. Symmetry creates a class of patterns in nature, where the near-repetition of the pattern element is by reflection or rotation. The body plants of most multicellular organisms exhibit some form of symmetry, whether radial, bilateral, or spherical. A small minority, notably among the sponges, exhibit no symmetry (*i.e.*, are asymmetric).

Radially symmetric organisms resemble a pie where several cutting planes produce roughly identical pieces. Such an organism exhibits no left or right sides. They have a top and a bottom surface only.

Symmetry has been important historically in the taxonomy of animals; animals with radial symmetry were classified in the taxon Radiata, which is now generally accepted to be a polyphyletic assemblage of different phyla of the Animal kingdom. Most radially symmetric animals are symmetrical about an axis extending from the centre of the oral surface, which contains the mouth, to the centre of the opposite, or aboral, end. Radial symmetry is especially suitable for sessile animals such as the sea anemone, floating animals such as jellyfish, and slow moving organisms such as starfish. Animals in the phyla cnidaria and echinodermata are radially symmetric, although many sea anemones and some corals have bilateral symmetry defined by a single structure, the siphonoglyph. Lilium bulbiferum displays typical floral symmetry with repeated parts arranged around the axis of the flower. Many flowers are radially symmetric or actinomorphic. Roughly identical flower parts – petals, sepals, and stamens occur at regular intervals around the axis of the flower, which is often the female part, with the carpel, style and stigma. Many viruses have radial symmetries, their coats being composed of a relatively small number of protein molecules arranged in a regular pattern to form polyhedrons, spheres, or ovoids. Most are icosahedrons. Tetramerism is a variant of radial symmetry found in jellyfish, which has four canals in an otherwise radial body plan.

Apple cut horizontally, showing pentamerism: Pentamerism, another variant of radial symmetry (also called pentaradial and pentagonal symmetry), means the organism is in five parts around a central axis, 72° apart. Among animals, only the echinoderms such as sea stars, sea urchins, and sea lilies are pentamerous as adults, with five arms arranged around the mouth. Being bilaterian animals, however, they initially develop with mirror symmetry as larvae, then gain pentaradial symmetry later.

Flowering plants show fivefold symmetry in many flowers and in various fruits. This is well seen in the arrangement of the five carpels (the botanical fruits containing the seeds) in an apple cut transversely.

Hexamerism is found in the corals and sea anemones (class Anthozoa) which are divided into two groups based on their symmetry. The most common corals in the subclass Hexacorallia have a hexameric body plan; their polyps have sixfold internal symmetry and the number of their tentacles is a multiple of six.

Octamerism is found in corals of the subclass Octocorallia. These have polyps with eight tentacles and octameric radial symmetry. The octopus, however, has bilateral symmetry, despite its eight arms.

Spherical symmetry occurs in an organism if it is able to be cut into two identical halves through any cut that runs through the organism's centre. Organisms which show approximate spherical symmetry include the freshwater green alga Volvox.

In bilateral symmetry (also called plane symmetry), only one plane, called the sagittal plane, divides an organism into roughly mirror image halves. Thus there is approximate reflection symmetry.

Internal organs are however not necessarily symmetric.

Differentiation in plants refers to the processes by which distinct cell types arise from precursor cells and become different from each other. Plants have about a dozen basic cell types that are required for everyday functioning and survival. Additional cell types are required for sexual reproduction. While the basic diversity of plant cell types is low compared to animals, these cells are strikingly different. For example, some cells such as parenchyma cells retain the potential to respond to environmental and/or hormonal signals throughout their life and, under the right conditions, can be transformed into another cell type (transdifferentiation). Other cells such as the water-conducting vessel elements undergo cell death as part of their differentiation pathway and thus can never transdifferentiate to another cell type.

(iv) **Apomixis:** In botany, apomixis was defined by Hans Winkler as replacement of the normal sexual reproduction by asexual reproduction, without fertilization. Its etymology is Greek for "away from" + "mixing". This definition notably does not mention meiosis. Thus "normal asexual reproduction" of plants, such as propagation from cuttings or leaves, has never been considered to be apomixis, but replacement of the seed by a plantlet or replacement of the flower by bulbils are types of apomixis. Apomictically produced offspring are genetically identical to the parent plant.

Some authors included all forms of asexual reproduction within apomixis, but that generalization of the term has since died out.

In flowering plants, the term "apomixis" is commonly used in a restricted sense to mean agamospermy, *i.e.,* clonal reproduction through seeds. Although agamospermy could theoretically occur in gymnosperms, it appears to be absent in that group.

Apogamy is a related term that has had various meanings over time. In plants with independent gametophytes (notably ferns), the term is still used interchangeably with "apomixis", and both refer to the formation of sporophytes by parthenogenesis of gametophyte cells. Male apomixis (paternal apomixis) involves replacement of the genetic material of the egg cell by that from the pollen.

Types of apomixis in flowering plants

Caribbean Agave produces plantlets on the old flower stem.

Maheshwari used the following simple classification of types of apomixis in flowering plants:

Nonrecurrent apomixis: In this type "the megaspore mother cell undergoes the usual meiotic divisions and a haploid embryo sac [megagametophyte] is formed. The new embryo may then arise either from the egg (haploid parthenogenesis) or from some other cell of the gametophyte (haploid apogamy)." The haploid plants have half as many chromosomes as the mother plant, and "the process is not repeated from one generation to another" (which is why it is called nonrecurrent).

Recurrent apomixis, is now more often called gametophytic apomixis: In this type, the megagametophyte has the same number of chromosomes as the mother plant because meiosis was not completed. It generally arises either from an archesporial cell or from some other part of the nucellus.

PAPER-II

1. (*a*) Chloroplasts are organelles present in plant cells and some eukaryotic organisms. Chloroplasts are the most important plastids found in plant cells. It is the structure in a green plant cell in which photosynthesis occurs. Chloroplast is one of the three types of plastids. Chloroplasts take part in the process of photosynthesis and it is of great biological importance. Animal cells do not have chloroplasts. All green plants take part in the process of photosynthesis which converts energy into sugars and the byproduct of the process is oxygen that all animals breathe. This process happens in chloroplasts. The distribution of chloroplasts is homogeneous in the cytoplasm of the cells and in certain cells chloroplasts become concentrated around the nucleus or just beneath the plasma membrane. A typical plant cell might contain about 50 chloroplasts per cell.

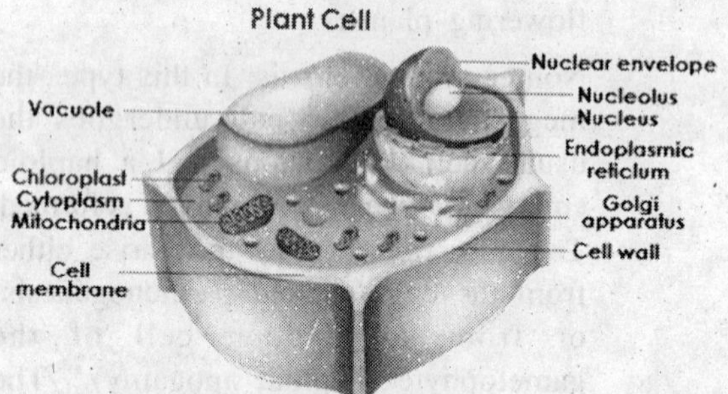

1. (*b*) **Principles of cell signalling:** The principle of cell signalling is hinged on the fact that cellular communication frequently involves converting signals that carry information from one form to another. During cell communication, the signalling cell releases a particular signalling molecule that is then detected by the target cell. Most animal cells send and receive signals and as such act as both signalling and target cells. Animal cells can communicate through direct contact or by secreting local regulators such as growth factors or neurotransmitters.

There are three stages of cell signalling:

Reception – where the target cell detects a signalling molecule present in the exogenous environment.

Transduction – the conversion of the signal to a form that can bring about a specific cellular response.

Response – the specific cellular effect brought about by the signalling molecule.

Reception: A signal molecule (ligand) binds to a receptor protein (receptor), causing it to change shape. The interaction between a ligand and a receptor is highly specific. A conformational change in a receptor is often the initial stage in the transduction of a signal. Receptors are found in two places.

Intracellular proteins are found inside the plasma membrane in the cytoplasm or nucleus. The signalling molecule must cross the plasma membrane and therefore must be hydrophobic (for instance the steroid hormone testosterone), or very small (Nitric Oxide).

Cell-surface proteins are embedded in the plasma membrane, and these receptors bind to water-soluble ligands.

Transduction: Cascades of molecular interactions relay signals from receptors to target molecule in the cell. Signal transduction pathways often involve a phosphorylation cascade. Because the pathway is usually a multistep one, the possibility of greatly amplifying the signal exists. At each step, enzymes called protein kinases phosphorylate and thereby activate many proteins at the next level. This cascade of phosphorylation greatly enhances the signal, allowing for a large cellular response. Not all components of signal transduction pathways are proteins, some are small non-protein water-soluble ions called second messengers, for example, cyclic AMP.

Response: Cell signalling leads to the regulation of transcription or cytoplasmic activities. Many signalling pathways ultimately affect protein synthesis, usually by turning specific genes on or off within the nucleus. Often, the final activated molecule in a signalling pathway functions as a transcription factor. In the cytoplasm, signalling pathways often regulate the activity of proteins rather than their synthesis. For example, the final step in the signalling pathway may affect the activity of enzymes or cause cytoskeleton rearrangement.

1. (*c*) Basis of Molecular Sex Differentiation: The formation of ovules is a key step in the plant life cycle which alternates between a diploid and haploid generation, the sporophyte and the gametophyte. The transitions between the two generations in the female occur in the ovule, the site of meiosis, female gametogenesis and double fertilization. The intimate association of sporophytic and gametophytic tissues in the ovule allows an investigation of their cellular interactions during ovule and seed development. In Arabidopsis, several sporophytically acting loci which primarily affect the morphogenesis of the integuments have been identified. Early acting genes may respond to positional information leading to a region-specific initiation of morphogenesis, whereas later acting genes affect cellular aspects of integument growth. Much less is known about the mechanisms controlling the development of the megagametophyte. Comparative morphology and genetic analyses suggest that regulatory mechanisms ensure a tight coordination of independently controlled cellular processes with cell specification and differentiation.

1. (*d*) Nuclear Pore Complex: Nuclear pores are large protein complexes that cross the nuclear envelope, which is the double membrane surrounding the eukaryotic cell nucleus. There are about an average of 2000 nuclear pore complexes (NPCs), in the nuclear envelope of a vertebrate cell, but it varies depending on cell type and the stage in the life cycle. The proteins that make up the nuclear pore complex are known as nucleoporins. About half of the nucleoporins typically contain solenoid protein domains—either an alpha solenoid or a beta-propeller fold, or in some cases both as separate structural domains. Each NPC contains at least 456 individual protein molecules and is composed of 30 distinct proteins (nucleoporins). The other half shows structural characteristics typical of "natively unfolded" or intrinsically disordered proteins, *i.e.*, they are highly flexible proteins that lack ordered secondary structure. These disordered proteins are the FG nucleoporins, so called because their amino-acid sequence contains many phenylalanine—glycine repeats.

1. (*e*) Cell Cycle Checkpoints Effected During the Cell Cycle

A **checkpoint** is a stage in the eukaryotic cell cycle at which the cell examines internal and external cues and "decides" whether or not to move forward with division.

There are a number of checkpoints, but the three most important ones are:

- The G_11 , 1, checkpoint, at the G_11 , 1, end subscript/S transition.
- The G_22 , 2, checkpoint, at the G_22 , 2, end subscript/M transition.
- The spindle checkpoint, at the transition from metaphase to anaphase.

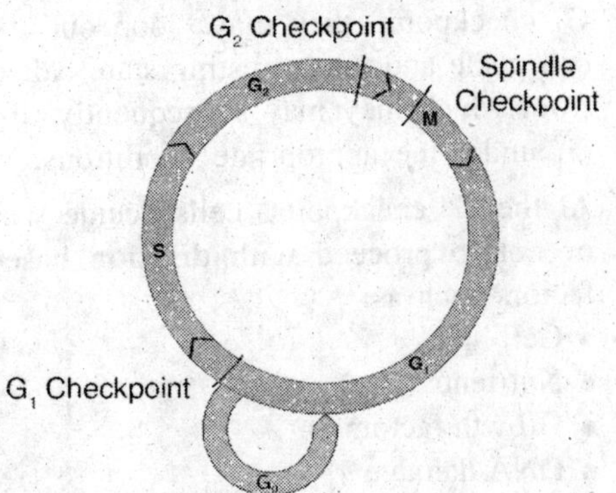

Diagram of cell cycle with checkpoint marked G_1 checkpoint is near the end of G_1 (close to the G_1/S transition). G_2 checkpoint is near the end of G_2 (close to the G_2/M transition). Spindle checkpoint is partway through M phase, and more specifically, at the metaphase/anaphase transition.

The G_11 , 1, checkpoint

The **G_11 , 1, checkpoint** is the main decision point for a cell – that is, the primary point at which it must choose whether or not to divide. Once the cell passes the G__11, 1, checkpoint and enters S phase, it becomes irreversibly committed to division. That is, barring unexpected problems, such as DNA damage or replication errors, a cell that passes the G_11, 1, checkpoint will continue the rest of the way through the cell cycle and produce two daughter cells.

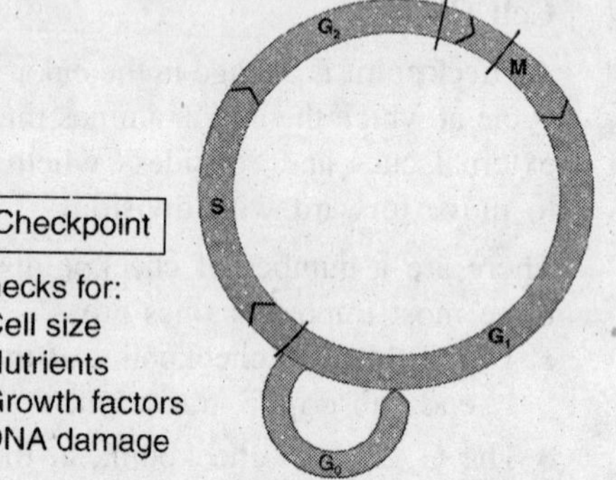

The G_1 checkpoint. The G_1 checkpoint is located at the end of G_1 phase, before the transition to S phase. If cells don't pass the G_1 checkpoint, they may "loop out" of the cell cycle and into a resting state called G_0, from which they may subsequently re-enter G_1 under the appropriate conditions.

At the G_1 checkpoint, cells decide whether or not to proceed with division based on factors such as:

- Cell size
- Nutrients
- Growth factors
- DNA damage

At the G_11, 1, checkpoint, a cell checks whether internal and external conditions are right for division. Here are some of the factors a cell might assess:

- **Size:** Is the cell large enough to divide?
- **Nutrients:** Does the cell have enough energy reserves or available nutrients to divide?
- **Molecular signals:** Is the cell receiving positive cues (such as growth factors) from neighbours?
- **DNA integrity:** Is any of the DNA damaged?

These are not the only factors that can affect progression through the G_11, 1, end subscriptcheckpoint, and which factors are most important depending on the type of cell. For instance, some cells also need mechanical cues (such as being attached to a supportive network called the extracellular matrix) in order to divide^11 start superscript, 1, end superscript.

If a cell doesn't get the go-ahead cues it needs at the G_11, 1, checkpoint, it may leave the cell cycle and enter a resting state called **G_00, 0, phase**. Some cells stay permanently in G_00, 0, end subscript, while others resume dividing if conditions improve.

The G_22, 2, checkpoint

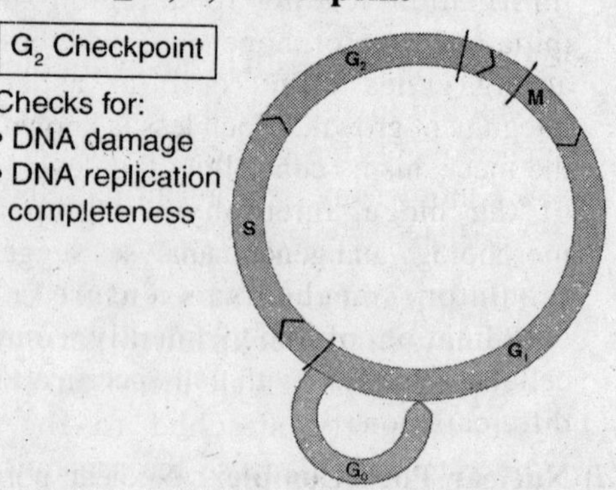

Image of the cell cycle with the G_2 checkpoint marked. At the G_2 checkpoint, the cell checks for:

- DNA damage
- DNA replication completeness

To make sure that cell division goes smoothly (produces healthy daughter cells with complete, undamaged DNA), the cell has an additional checkpoint before M phase, called the **G_22, 2, checkpoint**. At this stage, the cell will check:

- **DNA integrity:** Is any of the DNA damaged?
- **DNA replication:** Was the DNA completely copied during S phase?

If errors or damages are detected, the cell will pause at the G_22, 2, checkpoint to allow for repairs. If the checkpoint mechanisms detect problems with the DNA, the cell cycle is halted, and the cell attempts to either complete DNA replication or repair the damaged DNA.

The spindle checkpoint

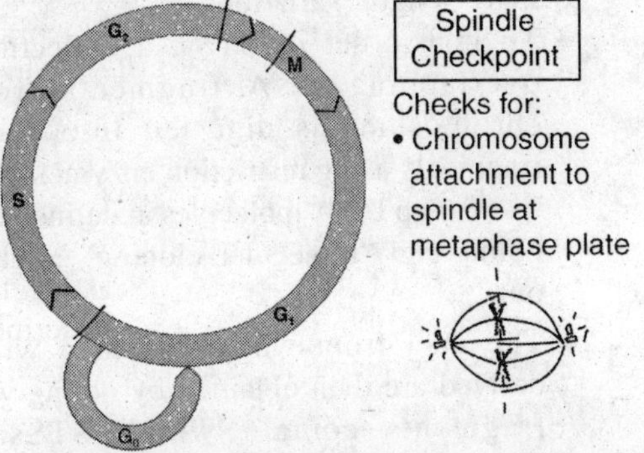

Image of the cell cycle with the spindle checkpoint marked. At the spindle checkpoint, the cell checks for:

- Chromosome attachment to spindle at the metaphase plate

The M checkpoint is also known as the **spindle checkpoint**: here, the cell examines whether all the sister chromatids are correctly attached to the spindle microtubules. Because the separation of the sister chromatids during anaphase is an irreversible step, the cycle will not proceed until all the chromosomes are firmly attached to at least two spindle fibres from opposite poles of the cell.

How does this checkpoint work? It seems that cells don't actually scan the metaphase plate to confirm that all of the chromosomes are there. Instead, they look for "straggler" chromosomes that are in the wrong place (*e.g.*, floating around in the cytoplasm)^33 start superscript, 3, end superscript. If a chromosome is misplaced, the cell will pause mitosis, allowing time for the spindle to capture the stray chromosome.

2. (*a*) Genetic Code Regulates Gene Expression: Have you ever wished that you had an identical twin? Sometimes I'm jealous of people who have twins. I think it would be interesting to see how another me would turn out. I mean, identical twins don't turn out completely identical. Usually, they end up slightly different heights, with slightly different facial features and different personalities. Some identical twins are easy to tell apart even though their genes are exactly the same. But that seems odd, doesn't it? If identical twins have the same exact genes, then why are there noticeable differences at all? Are genes really the only things that define our physical features? Or, do genes get tweaked a little by the rest of our cellular functions?

Let's go back to what a gene really is. It's a section of DNA that codes for, or specifies, a particular protein. The gene is first transcribed into mRNA, then translated into a polypeptide chain. That polypeptide is a component of the proteins that make up your body, including your height, facial features, and everything else. When the codes hidden inside our genes come out to light as physical traits, we call it gene expression.

Gene expression is just what it sounds like. It's the act of genes expressing themselves. How do people express themselves? They show off their emotions, right? They put out actions and words that result from the thoughts and feelings they have inside. When genes express themselves, they put out protein molecules that result from the genetic codes they have inside. Genes express themselves by turning the DNA code into a protein by way of transcription and translation. It's basically another way of talking about the central dogma. Gene expression describes how the genetic makeup of an organism is shown as an organism's physical traits. It's the process by which information flows from genes to proteins.

Genes are the basic physical and functional units of heredity.

"A gene is a specific sequence of nucleotide bases, whose sequences carry the information required for constructing proteins, which provide the structural components of cells and tissues as well as enzymes for essential biochemical reactions".

Molecular mapping can be of following two types.

1. Genetic maps and
2. Physical maps.

Both genetic and physical maps provide the likely order of items along a chromosome. Genetic map, serves to guide a scientist toward a gene, just like an interstate map guides a driver from city to city. Physical maps mark an estimate of the true distance, in measurements called base pairs, therefore, allow a scientist to more easily home in on the location of a gene.

PHYSICAL MAPS

Physical maps can be divided into three general types:

Chromosomal or cytogenetic maps,

Radiation hybrid (RH) maps, and

Sequence maps. The different types of maps vary in their degree of resolution, that is, the ability to measure the separation of elements that are close together.

Sequence Mapping: Sequence tagged site (STS) mapping is another physical mapping technique. An STS is a short DNA sequence that has been shown to be unique. To qualify as an STS, the exact location and order of the bases of the sequence must be known, and this sequence may occur only once in the chromosome being studied or in the genome as a whole if the DNA fragment set covers the entire genome.

Common Sources of STSs: Expressed sequence tags (ESTs) are short sequences obtained by analysis of complementary DNA (cDNA) clones. They represent the sequences of the genes being expressed. An EST can be used as an STS if it comes from a unique gene and not from a member of a gene family in which all of the genes have the same, or similar, sequences.

Simple sequence length polymorphisms (SSLPs) are arrays of repeat sequences that display length variations.

- To map a set of STSs, a collection of overlapping DNA fragments from a chromosome is digested into smaller fragments using restriction enzymes, agents that cut up DNA molecules at defined target points and "molecular cloning" is carried out.
- The data from which the map will be derived are then obtained by noting which fragments contain which STSs. To accomplish this, scientists copy the DNA fragments using a known process.
- Cloning involves the use of a special technology, called recombinant DNA technology, to copy DNA fragments inside a foreign host.
- First, the DNA fragments are united with a carrier, also called a vector. After introduction into a suitable host, the DNA fragments can then be reproduced along with the host cell DNA, providing unlimited material for experimental study.
- An unordered set of cloned DNA fragments is called a library.
- Next, the clones, or copies, are assembled in the order they would be found in the

original chromosome by determining which clones contain overlapping DNA fragments.

2. (*b*) The inheritance of most of the characters of an individual is governed by nuclear genes. But in some cases, the inheritance is governed by cytoplasmic factors or genes. When the transmission of characters from parents to offspring is governed by cytoplasmic genes; it is known as cytoplasmic inheritance or extra nuclear inheritance or extra chromosomal inheritance or non-Mendelian inheritance or organellar inheritance.

The first case of cytoplasmic inheritance was reported by Conens in 1909 in four 'o' clock (Mirabilis jalapa) for leaf colour. Later on, cytoplasmic inheritance was reported by various workers in various organisms.

Cytoplasmic inheritance differs from Mendelian inheritance in several aspects and exhibits some characteristic features.

1. **Reciprocal Differences:** Characters which are governed by cytoplasmic inheritance invariably exhibit marked differences in reciprocal crosses in F1, whereas in case of nuclear inheritance such differences are not observed except in case of sex linked genes.
2. **Maternal Effects:** In case of cytoplasmic inheritance, distinct maternal effects are observed. This is mainly due to more contribution of cytoplasm to the zygote by female parent than male parent. Generally ovum contributes more cytoplasm to the zygote than sperm.
3. **Mappability:** Nuclear genes can be easily mapped on chromosomes, but it is very difficult to map cytoplasmic genes or prepare linkage map for such genes. Now chloroplast genes in Chlamydomonas and maize, and mitochondrial genes in human and yeast have been mapped.
4. **Non-Mendelian Segregation:** The Mendelian inheritance exhibits typical segregation pattern. Such typical segregation is not observed in case of cytoplasmic inheritance. The segregation when occurs, is different from Mendelian segregation.
5. **Somatic Segregation:** Characters which are governed by cytoplasmic genes usually exhibit segregation in somatic tissues such as leaf variegation. Such segregation is very rare for nuclear genes.
6. **Infection-Like Transmission:** Cytoplasmic traits in some organisms exhibit infections like transmission. They are associated with parasites, symbionts or viruses present in the cytoplasm. Such cases do not come under true cytoplasmic inheritance.
7. **Governed by Plasma Genes:** The true cases of cytoplasmic inheritance are governed by chloroplast or mitochondrial DNA. In other words, plasma genes are made of cp-DNA or mt-DNA.

Classes of Cytoplasmic Inheritance: There are three different classes of cytoplasmic inheritance or non-Mendelian inheritance, viz., 1. maternal effects, 2. inheritance due to infective particles, and 3. cytoplasmic inheritance. These are briefly described below with examples.

1. **Maternal Effects:** When the expression of a character is influenced by the genotype of female parent, it is referred to as maternal effect. Such characters exhibit clear-cut differences in F1 for reciprocal crosses. Maternal effects are known both in plants and animals. Some examples of maternal effects are briefly presented below.

(*i*) Coiling Pattern of Shell in Snail:

The effect of maternal genotype on the coiling behaviour in water snail was studied by Sturtevant. There are two types of coiling pattern of shell in snail (Limnaeaperegra), viz., right handed (dextral) and left handed (sinistral).

(*ii*) Pigment in Flour Moth:

The maternal effect for inheritance of pigment in flour moth (Ephestia kuhniella) was reported by Caspari in 1936. In flour moth, production of pigment in the eye and skin is governed by single pair of dominant nuclear genes. Production of pigment is related to a substance known as kynurenine.

The production of kynurenine is controlled by a dominant gene A. This dominant gene results in darkening of the skin both in larvae and adults leading to the development of dark eyes. The recessive allele fails to produce pigment in the skin of larvae resulting in red eyes in the adult.

A cross between recessive female (aa) and heterozygous male (Aa) produced pigmented and un-pigmented larvae in F1 in the ratio of 1 : 1. However, the reciprocal cross, viz., heterozygous female (Aa) x recessive male (aa) produced in F1 all larvae with pigments. But when they became adult half of them had dark eyes and half un-pigmented eyes.

Both the larvae (Aa and aa) are pigmented because they have received cytoplasm from the pigmented female (Aa). When they become adult, the heterozygous larvae (Aa) are able to synthesize pigment due to the presence of one dominant allele and hence have dark eyes. The homozygous recessive larvae (aa) are not able to synthesize kynurenine which produces pigment and hence lose pigment when they become adult.

Parents	Unpigmented Female aa	×	Heterozygous Pigmented male Aa
F_1	1 aa Unpigmented	↓	1 Aa Pigmented
Reciprocal cross			
	Heterozygous Pigmented female Aa	×	Unpigmented Male aa
F_1 (Larval stage)	Aa Pigmented	↓	aa Pigmented
Adult stage	pigmented		unpigmented

Fig.: *Maternal Effect for Pigment in Flour Moth*

2. **Inheritance Involving Infective Particles:** In some cases, cytoplasmic inheritance is associated with infective particles like parasite, symbiont or viruses which are present in the cytoplasm of an organism. However, such cases are not considered as true examples of cytoplasmic inheritance. Some examples of this type are given below:

Kappa Particles in Paramecium:

There are two types of strains in Paramecium. One has kappa particles in its cytoplasm but the other does not have such particles. The presence of kappa particles in the cytoplasm leads to production of a toxin known as paramecin. This toxin can kill the strain of Paramecium which lacks kappa particle. Thus, the strain with kappa particle is known as killer strain and that without kappa particle is known as sensitive strain.

Multiplication of kappa particles in the cytoplasm takes place by fission. However, their multiplication is governed by a dominant nuclear gene (K). They can multiply in the homozygous dominant (KK) or heterozygous (Kk) individuals.

Kappa particles cannot multiply in recessive (kk) individuals. Even if kappa particles are introduced into kk strains, they will gradually disappear due to their inability to multiply and the strain will become sensitive.

3. (*a*) **Methods of gene transfer in plants**

The gene transfer techniques in plant genetic transformation are broadly grouped into two categories:

I. Vector-mediated gene transfer

II. Direct or vector less DNA transfer

The salient features of the commonly used gene (DNA) transfer methods are given in Table

Method	Salien feaures
I. *Vector-mediaed gene transfer*	
Agrobacerium (Ti plasmid)-mediated gene transfer	Very effifient, but limited to a seleced group of plans
Plant viral vecors	Ineffective method, hence not widely used
II. Direct or vectorless DNA transfer	
(A) Physical methods	
Electroporation	Mostly confined o prooplasts that can be regenerated to viable plants. Many cereal crops developed.
Microprojectile (particle bombardment)	Very successful mehod used for a wide range of plants/ tissues. Risk of gene rearrangement high.
Microinjection	Limited use since only one cell can be microinjected at a time. Technical personnel should be highly skilled.
Liposome fusion	Confined to protoplasts that can be regenerated into viable whole plants.
Silicon carbide fibress	Required regenerable cell suspensions. The fibres, however, required careful handling.
(B) Chemical methods	
Polyethylene glycol (PEG-mediated)	Confined to protoplasts. Regeneration of fertile plants is frequently problemattical.
Diethylaminoethyl (DEAE) dextran-mediated	Does not in stable trasformants.

Method # I. Vector-Mediated Gene Transfer: Vector-mediated gene transfer is carried out either by Agrobacterium-mediated transformation or by use of plant viruses as vectors.

Agrobacterium-Mediated Gene Transfer: Agrobacterium tumefaciens is a soil-borne, Gram-negative bacterium. It is rod shaped and motile, and belongs to the bacterial family of Rhizobiaceae. A. tumefaciens is a phytopathogen, and is treated as the nature's most effective plant genetic engineer.

Some workers consider this bacterium as the natural expert of inter-kingdom gene transfer. In fact, the major credit for the development of plant transformation techniques goes to the natural unique capability of A. tumefaciens. Thus, this bacterium is the most beloved by the plant biotechnologists.

There are mainly two species of Agrobacterium:

(*i*) A. tumefaciens that induces crown gall disease.

(*ii*) A. rhizogenes that induces hairy root disease.

Crown Gall Disease and Ti Plasmid: More than 100 years ago (1907), Smith and Townsend postulated that a bacterium was the causative agent of crown gall tumours, although its importance was recognized much later. As A. tumefaciens infects wounded or damaged plant tissues, it induces the formation of a plant tumour called crown gall. The entry of the bacterium into the plant tissues is facilitated by the release of certain phenolic compounds (acetosyringone, hydroxy acetosyringone) by the wounded sites.

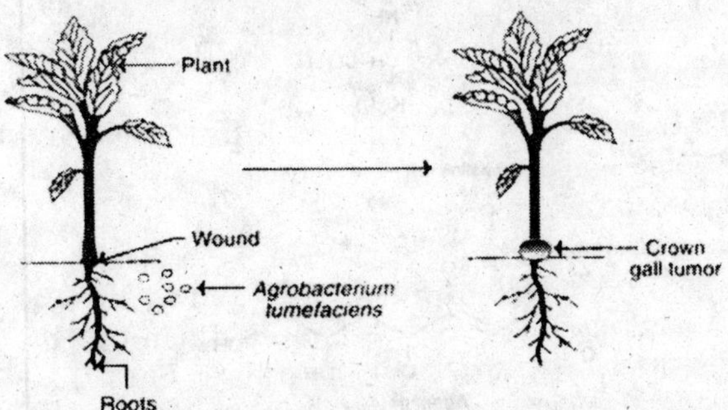

Fig.: *Formation of a crown gall tumour in a plant infected with Agrobacterium tumefaciens.*

Crown gall formation occurs when the bacterium releases its Ti plasmid (tumour-inducing plasmid) into the plant cell cytoplasm. A fragment (segment) of Ti plasmid, referred to as T-DNA, is actually transferred from the bacterium into the host where it gets integrated into the plant cell chromosome (*i.e.*, host genome). Thus, crown gall disease is a naturally evolved genetic engineering process.

The T-DNA carries genes that code for proteins involved in the biosynthesis of growth hormones (auxin and cytokinin) and novel plant metabolites, viz., opines — amino acid derivatives and agropines — sugar derivatives.

The growth hormones cause plant cells to proliferate and form the gall while opines and agropines are utilized by A. tumefaciens as sources of carbon and energy. As such, opines and agropines are not normally part of the plant metabolism (neither produced nor metabolised). Thus, A. tumefaciens genetically transforms plant cells and creates a biosynthetic machinery to produce nutrients for its own use.

NH
‖
H_2N—C—NH—$(CH_2)_3$—CH—COOH
NH
CH-COOH
CH_3
Octopine

NH
H_2N—C—NH—$(CH_2)_3$—CH—COOH
NH
CH-COOH
$(CH_2)_2$
COOH
Nopaline

O O N OH OH OH O
Agropine

Fig.: *Structure of three opines-octopine, nopaline, and agropine*

As the bacteria multiply and continue infection, grown gall develops which is a visible mass of the accumulated bacteria and plant material. Crown gall formation is the consequence of the transfer, integration and expression of genes of T-DNA (or Ti plasmid) of A. tumefaciens in the infected plant.

The genetic transformation leads to the formation of crown gall tumours, which interfere with the normal growth of the plant. Several dicotyledonous plants (dicots) are affected by crown gall disease, *e.g.*, grapes, roses, stone-fruit trees, etc.

Organization of Ti plasmid:

The Ti plasmids (approximate size 200 kb each) exist as independent replicating circular DNA molecules within the Agrobacterium cells. The T-DNA (transferred DNA) is variable in length in the range of 12 to 24 kb, which depends on the bacterial strain from which Ti plasmids come. Nopaline strains of Ti plasmid have one T-DNA with length of 20 kb while octopine strains have two T-DNA regions referred to as TL and TR that are respectively 14 kb and 7 kb in length.

A diagrammatic representation of a Ti plasmid is depicted in the above figure. The Ti plasmid has three important regions.

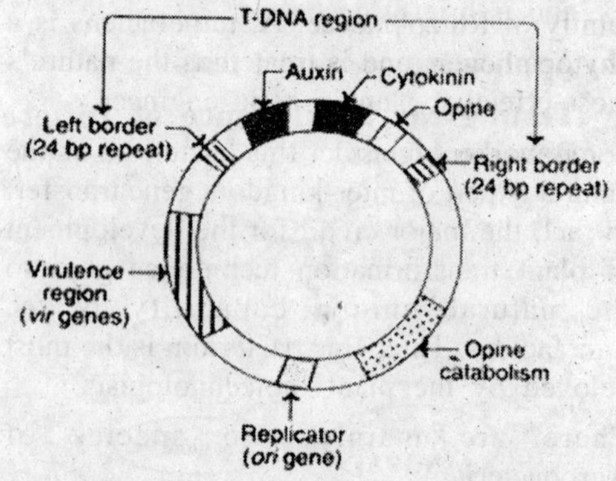

Fig.: *A diagrammatic representation of a Ti plasmid*

1. **T-DNA region:** This region has the genes for the biosynthesis of auxin (aux), cytokinin (cyt) and opine (ocs), and is

flanked by left and right borders. These three genes—aux, cyto and ocs are referred to as oncogenes, as they are the determinants of the tumour phenotype.

T-DNA borders — A set of 24 kb sequences present on either side (right and left) of T-DNA are also transferred to the plant cells. It is now clearly established that the right border is more critical for T-DNA transfer and tumori-genesis.

2. **Virulence region:** The genes responsible for the transfer of T-DNA into the host plant are located outside T-DNA and the region is referred to as vir or virulence region. Vir region codes for proteins involved in T-DNA transfer. At least nine vir-gene operons have been identified. These include vir A, vir G, vir B1, vir C1, vir D1, D2 and D4, and vir E1, and E2.

3. **Opine catabolism region:** This region codes for proteins involved in the uptake and metabolisms of opines. Besides the above three, there is ori region that is responsible for the origin of DNA replication which permits the Ti plasmid to be stably maintained in A. tumefaciens.

T-DNA transfer and integration: The process of T-DNA transfer and its integration into the host plant genome is depicted in the figure and is briefly described.

3. (*b*) Application of *t* and *z* tests

Testing the Significance of Difference Between Means

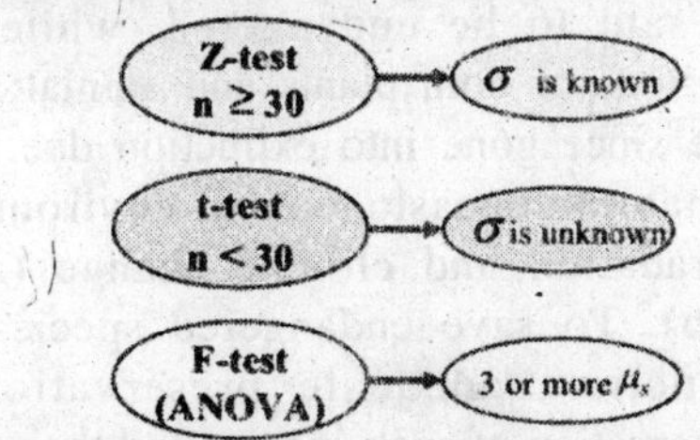

Z-test vs T-test

Normal distribution describes continuous data which have a symmetric distribution, with a characteristic 'bell' shape.

Binomial distribution describes the distribution of binary data from a finite sample. Thus it gives the probability of getting *r* events out of *n* trials.

Poisson distribution describes the distribution of binary data from an infinite sample. Thus it gives the probability of getting *r* events in a population.

The Normal Distribution

It is often the case with medical data that the histogram of a continuous variable obtained from a single measurement on different subjects will have a characteristic 'bell-shaped' distribution known as a Normal distribution. One such example is the histogram of the birth weight (in kilograms) of the 3,226 new born babies shown in Figure.

Distribution of birth weight in 3,226 newborn babies

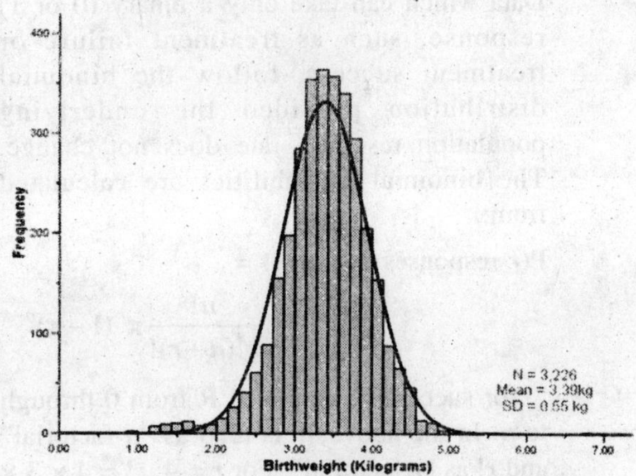

To distinguish the use of the same word in normal range and Normal distribution we have used a lower and upper case convention throughout.

The histogram of the sample data is an estimate of the population distribution of birth weights in new born babies. This population distribution can be estimated by the superimposed smooth 'bell-shaped' curve or 'Normal' distribution shown. We presume that if we were able to look at the entire population of new born babies then the distribution of birth weight would have exactly the Normal shape. We often infer, from a sample whose histogram has the approximate Normal shape, that the population will have exactly, or as near as makes no practical difference, that Normal shape.

Binomial Distribution

If a group of patients is given a new drug for the relief of a particular condition, then the proportion p being successively treated can be regarded as estimating the population treatment success rate π.

The sample proportion p is analogous to the sample mean $\bar{x}$, in the sense that if we score zero for those s patients who fail on treatment, and 1 for those r who succeed, then $p = r/n$, where $n = r + s$ is the total number of patients treated. Thus p also represents a mean.

Data which can take only a binary (0 or 1) response, such as treatment failure or treatment success, follow the binomial distribution provided the underlying population response rate does not change. The binomial probabilities are calculated from:

P(r responses out of n) =

$$\frac{n!}{r!(n-r)!}\pi^r(1-\pi)^{n-r}$$

...for successive values of R from 0 through to n. In the above, $n!$ is read as "n factorial" and $r!$ as "r factorial". For $r = 4$, $r! = 4 \times 3 \times 2 \times 1 = 24$. Both 0! and 1! are taken as equal to 1. The shaded area marked corresponds to the above expression for the binomial distribution calculated for each of $r = 8, 9, ..., 20$ and then added. This area totals 0.1018. So the probability of eight or more responses out of 20 is 0.1018.

5. (*a*) Methods of Conservation of Endangered Species

An endangered species is a population of organisms, which are at high risk of becoming extinct either due to loss of habitat, high death rate or changes in environmental and predation parameters. An organism is termed an endangered species if its population has become small such that free mating and reproduction becomes difficult. Environmental degradation, climate change and changes in prey-predation ratio are some of the factors driving many species to extinction today. Without adequate protection, a preservation or conservation measure, an endangered species finally goes into extinction, that is, permanent disappearance from the earth surface. Such species are never seen alive again in this world except in the form of fossil (remains) only. In this paper, we examined *in situ* and *ex situ* conservation as well as some measures that can be employed in saving some endangered species from extinction. The paper also recommends adequate documentation and publicity of the species for conservation and preservation.

According to the International Union for the Conservation of Nature (IUCN), an endangered species is an organism or a population of organism that faces a high risk of becoming extinct due to loss of its habitat, high death rate or changes in environmental and prey-predator parameters. The death rate of such organism far outweighs its birth rate over a period of time resulting to a decline in its population. Some common examples of endangered animal species include African Elephant, Tiger, Lion and Cheetah. In Nigeria, of the 4,600 plant species, 707 are said to be endangered, while some hundreds of both plants and animal species have since gone into extinction due to loss of habitat occasioned by environmental degradation and climate change (ANFP, 2006). To save endangered species from extinction, adequate preservation and conservation of such species and their habitat is necessary. Two main methods of conserving biodiversity as reported by IUCN , 2009 are considered. These include: ex-situ and in-situ conservation.

EX SITU CONSERVATION

This is the process of protecting or preserving an endangered species of either plants or animal outside of its natural habitat either by removing whole or part of that population from the threatened habitat and placing it in a new environment which may be a wild area or within human control environment. In ex-situ conservation, species whose life is threatened in a particular habitat is removed and placed in a well-protected habitat and taken care of by man.

Corker (2002) listed the oldest and best known methods of ex-situ conservation to include Zoos, Botanical Gardens, and Aquaria. Other modern methods of ex-situ conservation where reproductive parts of an endangered species are stored for future reproduction or propagation include Seed bank, Gene bank, Germplasm bank, and In-vitro Storages (IUCN, 2010).

BOTANICAL GARDEN

These are areas set aside for propagation and preservation of plant species to ensure their continuous existence. An endangered plant species is harvested in the wild and grown in the garden under human care to prevent it from becoming extinct. Barbara (2004), reported that about 354,000 plant species are grown in 1,500 botanical gardens around the world. The Royal Botanical Garden of England (Kew Garden) alone is said to house about 25,000 plant species out of which 2,700 are said to be endangered.

AQUARIA

Aquaria are facilities used for captive breeding of fish and other aquatic animals. In the past, aquaria were only used for display (decoration) of environment. However, due to growing threat to freshwater species they are now being used for captive breeding programs. The World Conservation Union (IUCN) is said to be working on captive breeding programs for conservation of fishes in the Lake Victoria in Africa, the desert fishes of North America and Appalachian stream fishes where aquaria are being designed to depict the natural habitats for conservation of these fishes.

SEEDBANK

The term 'seed bank' refers to a cryogenic laboratory facility in which seeds of certain plant species are preserved for a long time without losing their fertility. It can also refer to a special kind of arboretum where seeds are harvested and the crop is rotated.

IN VITRO STORAGE

Is a storage facility in the form of glass tube or vessel containing nitrogen liquid which keeps the temperature in the vessel at about - 150 degrees Celsius. Hence cuttings, stems or other reproductive parts of plant stored in these strict conditions remain viable for a long time without losing their fertility. Seeds or reproductive parts of endangered plant species stored in seed Bank or in in-vitro tubes can survive for a long time up to hundreds of years making the propagation of such plant species in future possible.

GENE BANK

These are cryogenic facilities used for the storage of living sperm, eggs or embryos for future reproduction.

IN SITU CONSERVATION

This involves the conservation and preservation of species in their natural habitat in places where the species naturally occurs. Under this method the entire ecosystem is protected and maintained so that all the constituent species, both known and unknown are conserved. The main methods of in-situ conservations as stated by Barbara (2004) include:

- Strict Nature Reserve (SNR)
- Games Reserve
- National Park

Strict Nature Reserves: These are plant communities reserved in perpetuity in their natural state for economic, educational, scientific, cultural and aesthetic values. SNR are established in remote areas and given adequate protection.

National Parks: These are areas exclusively set aside for the propagation, protection, conservation and management of flora and fauna as well as the protection of site, landscape or geological formation of a particular place for scientific or aesthetic values for the benefit of the general public. National parks are owned by the Federal Government.

CULTURAL CONSERVATION

Before the advent of modern conservation methods in Nigeria, some cultural beliefs had helped a lot in conservation. To prevent endangered species from going into extinctions, the following measures should be taken.

1. Some cultural practices which favour conservation of natural resources should be encouraged.
2. Government should develop and encourage the use of alternative resources of energy to discourage most Nigerians from using fuel wood as a source of energy which has caused the depletion of forest resources over the years, (forests serve as habitat to many species).
3. Adequate protection of the existing forest reserves and national parks should be carried out to check activities of illegal timber dealers and poachers.
4. Adequate documentation and publicity of the endangered species should be carried out so that the general public can also help in their protection and conservation.
5. Massive aforestation program by both government and private individuals to check the effect of climate change and environmental degradation which is responsible for loss of biodiversity should be encouraged.

5. (*b*) ATPases (EC 3.6.1.3, adenylpyrophosphatase, ATP monophosphatase, triphosphatase, SV40 T-antigen, adenosine 5′-triphosphatase, ATP hydrolase, complex V (mitochondrial electron transport), (Ca^{2+} + Mg^{2+}) – ATPase, HCO3— ATPase, adenosine triphosphatase) are a class of enzymes that catalyze the decomposition of ATP into ADP and a free phosphate ion. This dephosphorylation reaction releases energy, which the enzyme (in most cases) harnesses to drive other chemical reactions that would not otherwise occur. This process is widely used in all known forms of life. Some such enzymes are integral membrane proteins (anchored within biological membranes), and move solutes across the membrane, typically against their concentration gradient. These are called transmembrane ATPases.

Functions of Na+/K+ATPase

Transmembrane ATPases import many of the metabolites necessary for cell metabolism and export toxins, wastes, and solutes that can hinder cellular processes. An important example is the sodium-potassium exchanger (or Na+/K+ATPase) that maintains the cell membrane potential. And another example is the hydrogen potassium ATPase (H+/K+ATPase or gastric proton pump) that acidifies the contents of the stomach.

Besides exchangers, other categories of transmembrane ATPase include co-transporters and pumps (however, some exchangers are also pumps). Some of these, like the Na+/K+ATPase, cause a net flow of charge, but others do not. These are called "electrogenic" and "nonelectrogenic" transporters, respectively.

The coupling between ATP hydrolysis and transport is more or less a strict chemical reaction, in which a fixed number of solute molecules are transported for each ATP molecule that is hydrolyzed; for example, 3 Na+ ions out of the cell and 2 K+ ions inward per ATP hydrolyzed, for the Na+/K+ exchanger.

Transmembrane ATPases harness the chemical potential energy of ATP, because they perform mechanical work: they transport solutes in a direction opposite to their thermodynamically preferred direction of movement—that is, from the side of the membrane where they are in low concentration to the side where they are in high concentration. This process is considered active transport.

For example, the blocking of the vesicular H+-ATPases would increase the pH inside vesicles and decrease the pH of the cytoplasm.

The ATP synthase of mitochondria and chloroplasts is an anabolic enzyme that harnesses the energy of a transmembrane proton gradient as an energy source for adding an inorganic phosphate group to a molecule of adenosine diphosphate (ADP) to form a molecule of adenosine triphosphate (ATP).

This enzyme works when a proton moves down the concentration gradient, giving the enzyme a spinning motion. This unique spinning motion bonds ADP and P together to create ATP.

ATP synthase can also function in reverse, that is, use energy released by ATP hydrolysis to pump protons against their electrochemical gradient.

5. (c) Role of Fe, Mg, Mn and K in Plants

Plant nutrition is the study of the chemical elements and compounds necessary for plant growth, plant metabolism and their external supply. Plants must obtain the following mineral nutrients from their growing medium: the macronutrients: nitrogen (N), phosphorus (P), potassium (K), calcium (Ca), sulfur (S), magnesium (Mg) the micronutrients (or trace minerals): boron (B), chlorine (Cl), manganese (Mn), iron (Fe), zinc (Zn), copper (Cu), molybdenum (Mo), nickel (Ni). and cobalt (Co).

Functions of nutrients

At least 17 elements are known to be essential nutrients for plants. In relatively large amounts, the soil supplies nitrogen, phosphorus, potassium, calcium, magnesium, and sulfur; these are often called the macronutrients. In relatively small amounts, the soil supplies iron, manganese, boron, molybdenum, copper, zinc, chlorine, and cobalt, the so-called micronutrients. Nutrients must be available not only in sufficient amounts but also in appropriate ratios.

I. Iron

Iron is necessary for photosynthesis and is present as an enzyme cofactor in plants. Iron deficiency can result in interveinal chlorosis and necrosis. Iron is not a structural part of chlorophyll but very much essential for its synthesis. Copper deficiency can be responsible for promoting an iron deficiency. It helps in the electron transport of plant.

II. Magnesium

The outstanding role of magnesium in plant nutrition is as a constituent of the chlorophyll molecule. As a carrier, it is also involved in numerous enzyme reactions as an effective activator, in which it is closely associated with energy-supplying phosphorus compounds. Magnesium is very mobile in plants, and, like potassium, when deficient is translocated from older to younger tissues, so that signs of deficiency appear first on the oldest tissues and then spread progressively to younger tissues.

III. Manganese

Manganese is necessary for photosynthesis, including the building of chloroplasts. Manganese deficiency may result in coloration abnormalities, such as discoloured spots on the foliage.

IV. Potassium

Unlike other major elements, potassium does not enter into the composition of any of the important plant constituents involved in metabolism, but it does occur in all parts of plants in substantial amounts. It seems to be of particular importance in leaves and at growing points. Potassium is outstanding among the nutrient elements for its mobility and solubility within plant tissues. Processes involving potassium include the formation of carbohydrates and proteins, the reguiation of internal plant moisture, as a catalyst and condensing agent of complex substances, as an accelerator of enzyme action, and as a contributor to photosynthesis, especially under low light intensity.

Potassium regulates the opening and closing of the stomata by a potassium ion pump. Since stomata are important in water regulation, potassium regulates water loss from the leaves and increases drought tolerance. Potassium deficiency may cause necrosis or interveinal chlorosis. The potassium ion (K^+) is highly mobile and can aid in balancing the anion (negative) charges within the plant. Potassium helps in fruit coloration, shape and also increases its brix. Hence, quality fruits are produced in potassium-rich soils. Potassium serves as an activator of enzymes used in photosynthesis and respiration. Potassium is used to build cellulose and aids in photosynthesis by the formation of a chlorophyll precursor. Potassium deficiency may result in higher risk of pathogens, wilting, chlorosis, brown spotting, and higher chances of damage from frost and heat.

When soil-potassium levels are high, plants take up more potassium than needed for healthy growth. The term 'luxury consumption' has been applied to this. When potassium is moderately deficient, the effects first appear in the older tissues, and from there progress towards the growing points. Acute deficiency severely affects growing points, and die-back commonly occurs. Symptoms of potassium deficiency in white spruce include: browning and death of needles (chlorosis); reduced growth in height and diameter; impaired retention of needles; and reduced needle length. A relationship between potassium nutrition and cold resistance has been found in several tree species, including two species of spruce.

5. (*d*) Did you ever wonder how plants breathe, drink, eat, and grow? They carry out these functions just like us yet in different ways. One category of specialized organelles that plants use in order to survive is plastids. Plastids are double membrane bound organelles found inside plants and some algae, which are primarily responsible for activities related to making and storing food. Many plastids are photosynthetic but some are not.

Some of the most common plastids include: Chloroplasts, Chromoplasts, Gerontoplasts and Leucoplasts.

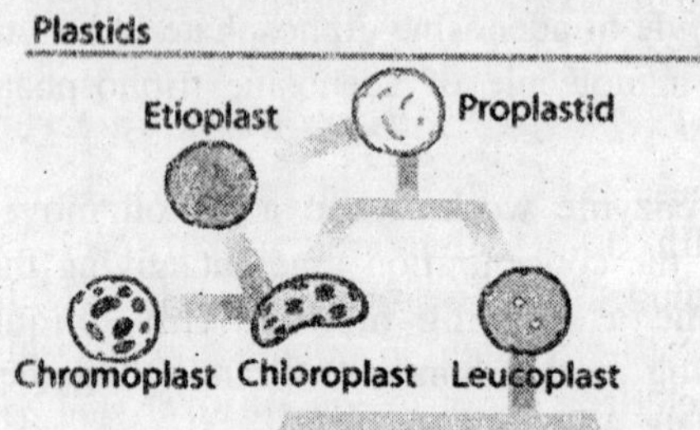

The chloroplasts are probably the most known of the plastids. These are responsible for photosynthesis. The chloroplast is filled with thylakoids, which is where photosynthesis occurs, and chlorophyll.

5. (*e*) Structure of N_2 ase

Nitrogen Fixation: Nitrogen fixation is a natural process where nitrogen gas is converted into ammonium either by microbes or by lightning. This process is vital to life on the planet, as well as food production, as nitrogen is needed for biomass production. Nitrogen fixation would not occur without a special enzyme called nitrogenase, an enzyme found in some types of microbes that allows for the reduction of nitrogen gas to ammonium.

Nitrifying Microbes, There are two main forms of these nitrifying microbes:

1. Symbiotic nitrogen fixing bacteria.

These microbes live on plants and are found around the world. They are most commonly associated with Rhizobia bacteria that live on a class of plants called legumes (which include the pinto beans on your burrito, chickpeas in your hummus, soybeans in your tofu, and green peas in your salad). These bacteria live in nodules on the roots, which look like little pearls, for protection from the outside world: nitrogenase is incapable of functioning when oxygen is present. The plant provides simple sugars to the microbe, and in return, the plant receives the excess nitrogen fixed by the microbe.

2. Free-living nitrogen fixing bacteria:

These bacteria do not require associations with other organisms to survive. These include some cyanobacteria, green sulphur bacteria, and purple sulphur and non-sulphur bacteria. Cyanobacteria fix over half of the nitrogen found in marine ecosystems.

Nitrogenase Structure and Activity

So now we know that nitrogenase is the enzyme responsible for fixing atmospheric nitrogen, and it's found in various microbes that may live alone in the nature or in symbiotic relationships with plants. Now let's discuss its structure. The nitrogenase molecule looks similar to a sandwich. On both ends of the molecule there are two irons containing proteins that are bonded to a molybdenum/iron protein.

6. (*a*) Carbon fixation or carbon assimilation is the conversion process of inorganic carbon (carbon dioxide) to organic compounds by living organisms. The most prominent example is photosynthesis, although chemosynthesis is another form of carbon fixation that can take place in the absence of sunlight. Organisms that grow by fixing carbon are called autotrophs. Autotrophs include photoautotrophs, which synthesize organic compounds using the energy of sunlight, and lithoautotrophs, which synthesize organic compounds using the energy of inorganic oxidation. Heterotrophs are organisms that grow using the carbon fixed by autotrophs. The organic compounds are used by heterotrophs to produce energy and to build body structures. "Fixed carbon", "reduced carbon", and "organic carbon" are equivalent terms for various organic compounds.

It is estimated that approximately 258 billion tons of carbon dioxide are converted by photosynthesis annually. The majority of the fixation occurs in marine environments, especially in the areas of high nutrients. The gross amount of carbon dioxide fixed is much larger since approximately 40% is consumed by respiration following photosynthesis. Given the scale of this process, it is understandable that RuBisCO is the most abundant protein on Earth.

Overview of pathways: Six autotrophic carbon fixation pathways are known as of 2011. The Calvin cycle fixes carbon in the chloroplasts of plants and algae, and in the cyanobacteria. It also fixes carbon in the anoxygenic photosynthetic proteobacteria called purple bacteria, and in some non-phototrophic proteobacteria.

Oxygenic photosynthesis: In photosynthesis, energy from sunlight drives the carbon fixation pathway. Oxygenic photosynthesis is used by the primary producers—plants, algae, and cyanobacteria. They contain the pigment chlorophyll, and use the Calvin cycle to fix carbon autotrophically. The process works like this:

$$2H_2O \rightarrow 4e^- + 4H^+ + O_2$$

$$CO_2 + 4e^- + 4H^+ \rightarrow CH_2O + H_2O$$

In the first step, water is dissociated into electrons, protons, and free oxygen. This allows the use of water, one of the most abundant substances on Earth, as an electron donor—as a source of reducing power. The release of free oxygen is a side-effect of enormous consequence. The first step uses the energy of sunlight to oxidize water to O_2, and, ultimately, to produce ATP

$$ADP + Pi \rightleftharpoons ATP + H_2O$$

and the reductant, NADPH

$$NADP^+ + 2e^- + 2H^+ \rightleftharpoons NADPH + H^+$$

In the second step, called the Calvin cycle, the actual fixation of carbon dioxide is carried out. This process consumes ATP and NADPH. The Calvin cycle in plants accounts for the preponderance of carbon fixation on land. In algae and cyanobacteria, it accounts for the preponderance of carbon fixation in the oceans. The Calvin cycle converts carbon dioxide into sugar, as triose phosphate (TP), which is glyceraldehyde 3-phosphate (GAP) together with dihydroxyacetone phosphate (DHAP):

$$3\ CO_2 + 12e^- + 12H^+ + Pi \rightarrow TP + 4H_2O$$

An alternative perspective accounts for NADPH (source of e^-) and ATP:

$$3CO_2 + 6NADPH + 6H^+ + 9ATP + 5H_2O \rightarrow TP + 6NADP^+ + 9ADP + 8Pi$$

The formula for inorganic phosphate (Pi) is HOPO32⁻ + 2H+. Formulas for triose and TP are $C_2H_3O_2\text{-}CH_2OH$ and $C_2H_3O_2\text{-}CH_2OPO_3^{2-} + 2H^+$

Carbon concentrating mechanisms

Many photosynthetic organisms have not acquired inorganic carbon concentrating mechanisms (CCM), which increase the concentration of carbon dioxide available to the initial carboxylase of the Calvin cycle, the enzyme RuBisCO. The benefits of CCM include increased tolerance to low external concentrations of inorganic carbon, and reduced losses to photorespiration. CCM can make plants more tolerant of heat and water stress.

Carbon concentrating mechanisms use the enzyme carbonic anhydrase (CA), which catalyze both dehydration of bicarbonate to carbon dioxide and hydration of carbon dioxide to bicarbonate

$$HCO^{3-} + H^+ \rightleftharpoons CO_2 + H_2O$$

Lipid membranes are much less permeable to bicarbonate than to carbon dioxide. To capture inorganic carbon more effectively, some plants have adapted the anaplerotic reactions

$$HCO^{3-} + H^+ + PEP \rightarrow OAA + Pi$$

catalyzed by PEP carboxylase (PEPC), to carboxylate phosphoenolpyruvate (PEP) to oxaloacetate (OAA) which is a C4 dicarboxylic acid.

CAM plants

CAM plants that use Crassulacean acid metabolism as an adaptation for arid conditions. CO_2 enters through the stomata during the night and is converted into the 4-carbon compound, malic acid, which releases CO_2 for use in the Calvin cycle during the day, when the stomata are closed. The dung jade plant (Crassula ovata) and cacti are typical of CAM plants. Sixteen thousand species of plants use CAM. These plants have a carbon isotope signature of –20 to –10 ‰.

C4 plants

C4 plants preface the Calvin cycle with reactions that incorporate CO_2 into one of the 4-carbon compounds, malic acid or aspartic acid. C4 plants have a distinctive internal leaf anatomy. Tropical grasses, such as sugarcane and maize are C4 plants, but there are many broadleaf plants that are C4. Overall, 7600 species of terrestrial plants use C4 carbon fixation, representing around 3% of all species. These plants have a carbon isotope signature of –16 to –10 ‰.

C3 plants

The large majority of plants are C3 plants. They are so-called to distinguish them from the CAM and C4 plants, and because the carboxylation products of the Calvin cycle are 3-carbon compounds. They lack C4 dicarboxylic acid cycles, and therefore have higher carbon dioxide compensation points than CAM or C4 plants. C3 plants have a carbon isotope signature of –24 to –33‰.

6. (*b*) Different Processes Involved in the Molecular Basis of Fruit Ripening

Ripening is the process by which fruits attain their desirable flavour, quality, colour, palatable nature and other textural properties. Ripening is associated with change in composition, *i.e.*, conversion of starch to sugar. On the basis of ripening behaviour, fruits are classified as climacteric and non-climacteric fruits.

Climacteric: Climacteric fruits are defined as fruits that enter 'climacteric phase' after harvest, *i.e.*, they continue to ripen. During the ripening process the fruits emit ethylene along with increased rate of respiration. Ripe fruits are soft and delicate and generally cannot withstand rigours of transport and repeated handling. These fruits are harvested hard and green, but fully mature and are ripened near consumption areas. Small dose of ethylene is used to induce ripening process under controlled conditions of temperature and humidity.

Climacteric fruits are: Mango, Guava, Fig, Apricot, Banana, Sapota, Apple, Plum, Papaya, Kiwi, Passion fruit and Pear.

Non-Climacteric: Non-climacteric fruits once harvested do not ripen further. Non-climacteric fruits produce very small amount of ethylene and do not respond to ethylene treatment. There is no characteristic increased rate of respiration or production of carbon dioxide.

Non-climacteric fruits are:

Orange, Mousambi, Kinnow, Grapefruit, Grapes, Pomegranate, Litchi, Watermelon, Cherry, Raspberry, Blackberry, Strawberry, Carambola, Rambutan, Cashew

In order to improve external skin colour and market acceptance, citrus like orange, lemon, mousambi and kinnow can be treated with ethylene, as a de-greening agent. Ethylene treatment breaks down the green chlorophyll pigment in the exterior part of the peel and allows the yellow or orange carotenoid pigments to be expressed.

Technologies for Ripening of Fruits

Lack of easier and rapid methods for uniform ripening poses a major problem in the fruit industry. Almost all methods of ripening, either conventional or the modern chemical methods, come with their own merits and demerits. There are several simple technologies and methods available today for farmers for proper ripening. Normally, the number of days taken for edible ripening varies for different fruits and prevailing climatic conditions. For instance, it takes about 5 to 6 days for mangoes and 6 to 7 days for sapotas to ripen. Under natural conditions, ethylene, a ripening hormone produced by the plant plays a major physiological role in the ripening process.

- A simple technology practised in households to trigger ripening is to keep un-ripened and ripened fruits together inside an air tight container. Since the already ripened fruits release ethylene, ripening will be faster.
- Another method is to place the fruits intended for ripening inside an air tight room and induce ripening through smoking inside smoke chambers. Smoke emanates acetylene gas. Several fruit traders follow this technique to achieve uniform ripening especially in edible fruits like banana and mango. But the major drawback of this method is that the fruits do not attain

uniform colour and flavour. In addition, the persistence of smoke odour on the product impairs its quality.

- Spreading unripe fruits as layers over paddy husk or wheat straw for a week to ripen is an another alternative.
- Another practice is that some farmers dip unripe mature fruits in 0.1 per cent ethrel solution (1 ml of ethrel solution in 1 litre of water) and wipe it dry. The fruits are then spread over a newspaper without touching each other and a thin cotton cloth is covered over this. In this method, the fruits will ripen within two days.
- In one of the simple and harmless techniques, 10 ml of ethrel and 2 gm of sodium hydroxide pellets are mixed in five litres of water taken in a wide mouthed vessel. This vessel is placed inside the ripening chamber near the fruits and the room is sealed air tight. About one third of the room is filled with fruits leaving the remaining area for air circulation. Ripening of fruits takes place in about 12 to 24 hours. In order to reduce the cost of chemical, some ethylene releasing fruits such as papaya and banana can also be kept in the same room.
- Ethylene gas filled in pressurized cans promote fruit ripening in 24-48 hours.

Fruit Ripening using Calcium Carbide

Most climacteric fruits in India are ripened with industrial grade calcium carbide. Industrial-grade calcium carbide usually contains traces of arsenic and phosphorus, and, thus, use of this chemical for this purpose is illegal in most countries. In India too, use of calcium carbide is strictly banned as per PoFA (Prevention of Food Adulteration) Act [Section 44AA]. Calcium carbide, once dissolved in water, produces acetylene which acts as an artificial ripening agent. Acetylene is believed to affect the nervous system by reducing oxygen supply to brain. Arsenic and phosphorus are toxic and exposure may cause severe health hazards.

The only safe and worldwide accepted method is using ethylene, which is a natural hormone for ripening when done under controlled temperature and relative humidity conditions.

Degreening

Controlled degreening sometimes is carried out on citrus grown in tropics. Many citrus cultivars mature before green colour disappears from peel. Breakdown of chlorophyll and production of a rich orange colour require exposure to low temperature during maturation, and this explains why mature citrus frequently is sold green on markets in humid tropics, where even night temperatures may not drop much below 25°C. The ceiling of room is relatively high, allowing boxes to be stacked at least four boxes high. A false ceiling is added to provide for adequate air.

Previous Years' Paper (Solved)

Indian Forest Service

IFS–Botany Main Examination, 2015

PAPER-I

INSTRUCTIONS: *There are EIGHT questions in all, out of which FIVE are to be attempted. Questions no. 1 & 5 are compulsory. Out of the remaining SIX questions, THREE are to be attempted selecting at least ONE question from each of the two Sections A and B. Attempts of questions shall be counted in sequential order. Unless struck off, attempt of a question shall be counted even if attempted partly. Any page or portion of the page left blank in the Question-cum-Answer Booklet must be clearly struck off. All questions carry equal marks. Answer must be written in ENGLISH only. Neat sketches may be drawn, wherever required.*

SECTION—A

1. *Answer the following keeping your answers brief and to the point:*

(*a*) What is plant quarantine?

(*b*) What is the significance of aflatoxins?

(*c*) Describe the role of microbes in production of antibiotics.

(*d*) Comment upon the palmella-stage.

(*e*) Discuss the stages of development of male gemetophyte in *Pinus* before pollination.

(*f*) What is the use of Bordeaux mixture? How is it prepared?

(*g*) What is the importance of VAM?

(*h*) With the help of labelled diagram, describe the reproductive organs of *Chara.*

2. (*a*) Describe the asexual reproduction in *Penicillium.*

(*b*) Explain the structure of TMV.

(*c*) How are the fungal toxins classified according to their source of origin?

(*d*) Draw a well-labelled diagram through median LS of strobilus of *Selaginella* and discuss its main features.

3. (*a*) With the help of suitable diagrams, describe the development of sporophyte in bryophytes.

(*b*) What are the various methods of genetic recombination in bacteria?

(*c*) Compare the morphological characters of male and female strobili in *Gnetum.*

4. (*a*) Draw scientifically accurate diagrams of the following and label the parts:

(*i*) Flower of *Cycadeoidea.*

(*ii*) LS of *Pinus* seed.

(*iii*) TS of leaf of *Cordaites.*

(*b*) Write short notes on the following:

(*i*) Tundu disease of wheat.

(*ii*) Powdery mildew diseases in plants.

(*iii*) Diseases caused by mycoplasma.

(*c*) What is the main basis of classification in algae? Describe the important characters of various classes of algae.

SECTION—B

5. *Write on the following keeping your answers brief and to the point:*

(*a*) Inflorescence in Musaceae.

(*b*) Primitive characters of Magnoliaceae.

(*c*) *Allium* type of embryo sac.

(d) Parthenocarpy.

(e) Kranz anatomy.

(f) Distinguishing features of Orchidaceae.

(g) Plants as source of spices.

(h) Inflorescence of Euphorbiaceae.

6. (a) Write down the botanical names and the uses of the plants of economic importance belonging to the family Cucurbitaceae.

(b) Briefly discuss the technique for raising haploids from microspores.

(c) Comment upon the applied aspects of palynology.

(d) Write a brief and critical note on polyembryony and give its importance.

7. (a) Which plants are being used as a potential source of future energy?

(b) What are the salient features of the family Poaceae?

(c) Write short notes on the following:

(i) Botanical gardens.

(ii) Herbaria.

8. (a) Write short notes on the following:

(i) Protoplast fusion.

(ii) Role of somatic hybrids in crop improvement.

(b) Give the salient features of Engler and Prantl's system of classification and compare it with that of Bentham and Hooker's system of classification.

PAPER-II

INSTRUCTIONS: *There are EIGHT questions in all, out of which FIVE are to be attempted. Questions No. 1 & 5 are compulsory. Out of the remaining SIX questions, THREE are to be attempted selecting at least ONE question from each of the two Sections A and B. Attempts of questions shall be counted in sequential order. Unless struck off, attempt of a question shall be counted even if attempted partly. Any page or portion of the page left blank in the answer book must be clearly struck off. All questions carry equal marks. Answer must be written in ENGLISH only. Neat sketches may be drawn, wherever required.*

SECTION—A

1. Explain each of the following:

(a) Suggest why prions should not be included among viruses.

(b) Discuss the role of central control system in managing surveillance at check points during cell cycle.

(c) Give two popular examples where genetic differences influence induction of mutation.

(d) Is the genetic code universal?

(e) Explain Binomial and Poisson distribution.

2. (a) Describe nuclear pores and their role in nucleocytoplasmic traffic with suitable diagrams.

(b) How will you distinguish cytologically between paracentric inversion and pericentric inversion?

3. (a) $\frac{X}{A}$ ratio is not only a primary sex determining signal but has several major regulatory genes in function. Discuss what role do they play in sex differentiation, with suitable examples.

(b) Describe multigene families with divergent members of globin genes and pseudogenes subject to the difference in expression to the time and space.

4. (a) Why is *Agrobacterium tumefaciens* the most popular and important tool in genetic engineering of plant systems? Describe the various steps used in T-DNA mediated transfer of foreign genes into plants.

(b) What are the merits of pedigree methods? Describe the pedigree-bulk methods developed at CIMMYT, Mexico for wheat breeding.

SECTION—B

5. Write brief notes on each of the following:

(*a*) "Tricarboxylic acid cycle is an amphibolic process." Explain.

(*b*) "Phenolic substances are not mere metabolic waste products." Discuss.

(*c*) What is 'triple response growth'? How is it induced?

(*d*) How does El Niño result in extensive disruption of weather around the world?

(*e*) Describe the phenomenon of 'biomagnification' with special reference to chlorinated hydrocarbons.

6. (*a*) In what way does carbon fixation pathway in malate formers differ from that in aspartate formers?

(*b*) Trace the physiological changes associated with the process of seed germination. How is the process of germination regulated by phytohormones?

7. (*a*) How do seasonal variations in day length conditions influence flowering patterns of plants? Give a comprehensive account of the structure and mode of action of the photoreceptor involved.

(*b*) What are 'carrier proteins'? Describe the ion uptake mechanism in plants mediated by carrier proteins.

8. (*a*) Write an account of 'Joint Forest Management Programme' (JFMP). How does people's participation ensure sustainable forest resource management?

(*b*) Discuss the strategies adopted for phytoremediation. Add a critical note on potentialities and limitations of phytoremediation to clean up heavy metal contaminated sites.

ANSWERS

PAPER-I

1. (*a*) **Plant quarantine** is a technique for ensuring disease- and pest-free plants, whereby a plant is isolated while tests are performed to detect the presence of a problem.

Plant quarantine regulatory measures derive legal sanctity from the Destructive Insects and Pests Act, 1914.

The purpose and intent of this Act is to prevent the introduction of any insect, fungus or pest which is or could be destructive to crops.

Import of agricultural commodities into India is regulated by plant quarantine.

Plant quarantine operations in India are carried out by the Directorate of Plant Protection, Quarantine and Storage, which functions under the aegis of the Ministry of Agriculture.

Objectives of the Scheme

- To prevent the introduction and spread of exotic pests that are destructive to the country by regulating the import of plants and plant products through adequate policy and statutory measures.
- To support India's agricultural exports through credible export certification.
- To facilitate safe global trade in agriculture by assisting producers, exporters and importers and by providing technically comprehensive and credible Phytosanitary certification.

1. (*b*) Aflatoxins are a group of related fungal secondary metabolites primarily produced by the fungi, *Aspergillus flavus* and *Aspergillus parasiticus. Aspergillus flavus* and *Aspergillus parasiticus* colonize a wide variety of food commodities including maize, oilseeds, spices, groundnuts, tree nuts, milk, peanut and dried fruits. However, production of aflatoxin by these fungi depends on drought stress, rainfall, suitability of crop genotype for its climate, insect damage, agricultural practices and post harvest conditions (storage, transportation and food processing). Four major aflatoxins produced naturally are known as aflatoxin B_1, B_2, G_1 and G_2. Aflatoxin is both a food safety and public health issue because of its toxicity. When it is consumed, it can exert toxicity by altering intestinal integrity or modulate the expression of cytokins which can result to stunted growth in children and/or immune suppression. In the liver, aflatoxin may be transformed by certain p450 enzyme to its DNA reactive form Aflatoxin-8-9-epoxide which binds to liver proteins and lead to their failure, resulting in acute aflatoxicosis or it may bind to DNA, contributing to aflatoxin induced hepatocellular carcinoma (liver cancer). In high doses, aflatoxin can lead to acute liver cirrhosis and death in both human and animals. Aflatoxin exposure is linked to increased risk of liver cancer, immunesuppression, increased susceptibility to diseases such as HIV and malaria and possible compromised vaccine efficacy. Aflatoxin accumulation can be managed by primary interventions involving improved irrigation, use of fungicides, pesticides and insecticides, use of cereal strains resistant to fungal colonization, biocontrol by introduction of competitive non-aflatoxigenic strains of *A. flavus* and genetically modified crops that inhibit fungal colonization and improved storage conditions. Intervention strategies also encompass chemoprevention, using compounds that interfere with the absorption or metabolism of aflatoxins once ingested.

1. (*c*) **Antibiotic,** any of a variety of substances, usually obtained from microorganisms, that inhibit the growth of or destroy certain other microorganisms.

Antibiotics are produced industrially by a process of fermentation, where the source microorganism is grown in large containers (100,000-150,000 liters or more) containing a liquid growth medium. Oxygen concentration, temperature, pH and nutrient levels must be optimal, and are closely monitored and adjusted if necessary. As antibiotics are secondary metabolites, the population size must be controlled very carefully to ensure that maximum yield is obtained before the cells die. Once the process is complete, the antibiotic must be extracted and purified to a crystalline product. This is easier to achieve if the antibiotic is soluble in organic solvent. Otherwise it must first be removed by ion exchange, adsorption or chemical precipitation.

Microorganisms used in fermentation are rarely identical to the wild type. This is because species are often genetically modified to yield the maximum amounts of antibiotics. Mutation is often used, and is encouraged by introducing mutagens such as ultraviolet radiation, x-rays or certain chemicals. Selection and further reproduction of the higher yielding strains over many generations can raise yields by 20-fold or more. Another technique used to increase yields is gene amplification, where copies of genes coding for enzymes involved in the antibiotic production can be inserted back into a cell, via vectors such as plasmids. This process must be closely linked with retesting of antibiotic production.

1. (*d*) **Palmella-stage :** At the time of zoospore formation, sometimes the parent cell wall gets gelatinized and the daughter protoplasts are not liberated outside because of some unfavourable conditions. New daughter protoplasts also undergo process of gelatinization of their wall. Because of continuous gelatinization and division of

protoplasts the number of daughter protoplasts increases and so also the size of the entire body. At this stage *Chlamydomonas* resembles with another green alga, *Palmella* (of Tetrasporales), and therefore this stage is called Palmella-stage (See Fig.). On return of the favourable conditions, the daughter protoplasts of Palmella-stage revert to the typical motile condition. So it is a temporary feature in *Chlamydomonas*.

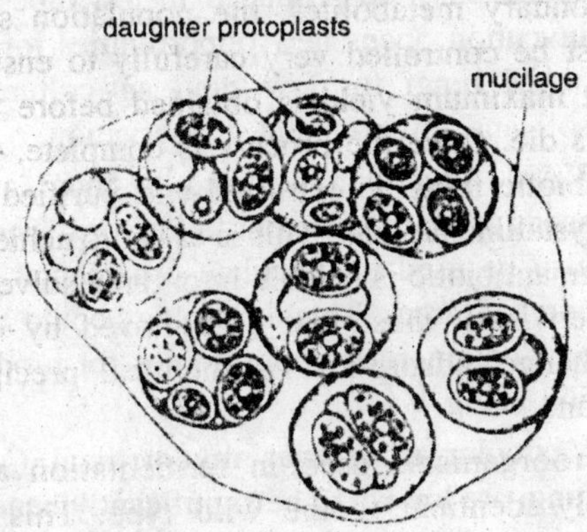

Fig. *Palmella-stage of Chlamydomonas.* (after Fritsch).

Palmella-stage is commonly seen in species like *C. braunii* and *C. kleinii*. Induced Palmella-stages of *Chlamydomonas* have been ultrastructurally studied by Nakamura, *et al.* (1973). According to Chapman and Chapman (1973), Palmella-stage in *C. kleinii* is a dominant phase in the life-cycle, and therefore they regard this species a transition stage between *Chlamydomonas* and *Tetraspora*.

1. (*e*) **Development of male gametophyte within Pinus before pollination:** The microspore divides asymmetrically into a small lenticular cell and a larger cell. The former, known as first prothallial cell, does not divide further. The larger cell, known as apical cell, divides asymmetrically and forms a lenticular second prothallial cell and a large antheridial cell. The second prothallial cell does not divide further and remains attached to the first prothallial cell.

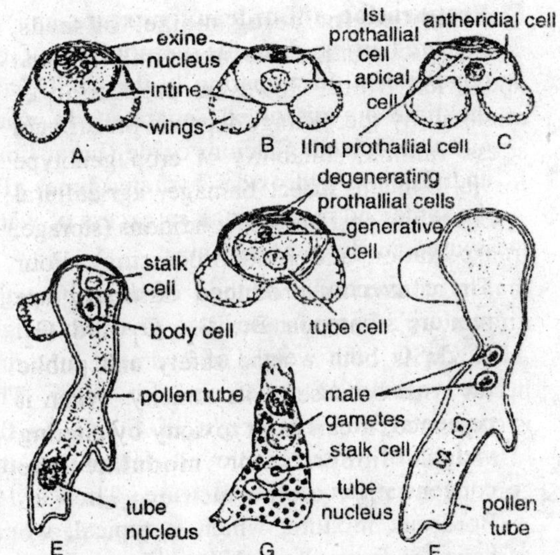

The antheridial cell divides to form a generative cell (adjacent to the second prothallial cell) and a large tube cell. At this stage, the male gametophyte has four cells first and second prothallial cells, a generative cell and a tube cell. The microspores are released from the microsporangium at 4 celled stage. They are disseminated by wind.

1. (*f*) **Bordeaux mixture** is a mixture of copper (II) sulphate ($CuSO_4$) and slaked lime ($Ca(OH)_2$) used as a fungicide. It is used in vineyards, fruit-farms and gardens to prevent infestations of downy mildew, powdery mildew and other fungi. It is sprayed on plants as a preventative; its mode of action is ineffective after a fungus has become established. It was invented in the Bordeaux region of France in the late 19th century. If it is applied in large quantities annually for many years, the copper in the mixture eventually becomes a pollutant.

In addition to its use to control fungal infection on grapevines, the mixture is also widely used to control potato blight, peach leaf curl and apple scab. It is approved for organic use, so is often used by organic gardeners where nonorganic gardeners would prefer other controls.

Preparation : Bordeaux mixture can be prepared using differing proportions of the components. In preparing it, the $CuSO_4$ and the lime are dissolved separately in water and then mixed. Calcium oxide (burnt lime) and Calcium hydroxide (hydrated lime) give the same end result, since an excess of water is used in the preparation.

The conventional method of describing the mixture's composition is to give the weight of $CuSO_4$, the weight of hydrated lime and the volume of water, in that order. The percentage of the weight of $CuSO_4$ to the weight of water employed determines the concentration of the mixture. Thus a 1% Bordeaux mixture, which is typical, would have the formula 1:1:100, with the first "1" representing 1 kg $CuSO_4$ (pentahydrated), the second representing 1 kg hydrated lime, and the 100 representing 100 litres (100 kg) water. As $CuSO_4$ contains 25% copper, the copper content of a 1% Bordeaux mixture would be 0.25%. The quantity of lime used can be lower than that of the $CuSO_4$. One kg of $CuSO_4$ actually requires only 0.225 kg of chemically pure hydrated lime to precipitate all the copper. Good proprietary brands of hydrated lime are now freely available, but, as even these deteriorate on storage (by absorbing carbon dioxide from the air), a ratio of less than 2 : 1 is seldom used, which corresponds to a 1 : 0.5 : 100 mixture.

1. (*g*) Vesicular-arbuscular mycorrhizal (VAM) fungi form a beneficial interaction with a wide range of plants, including horticultural and forage field crops. The fungi promote efficient nutrient absorption and increase plant growth and yield. VAM interactions with the soil play an important role in controlling soil fertility, soil erosion and plant water stress. Overall, using VAM fungi in crop production should reduce fertilizer amounts applied to farmland. The importance of VAM fungi to sustainable agriculture and the ecosystem has led to its commercial development. However, for the past thirty years, progress on VAM cultivation has not been very successful, partly because the research is very difficult and time consuming. ARS researchers have found optimal conditions for propagating the dual culture of root and fungus. Pure and clean VAM fungi can be grown on gel plates in a completely reproducible manner. As a result of this breakthrough, many billions of fungal spores may be produced in test tubes. This invention opens new opportunities for using VAM fungi for low-input agriculture, and soil and environment conservation.

VAM fungi can be used to inoculate the seeds of many different field crops. They can also be used to inoculate ornamental plants and fruit trees. This technology could lead to new commercial opportunities for producing and using VAM.

Vesicular-arbuscular mycorrhizal (VAM) fungi are known to be significantly beneficial to the nutrition of host plants and are ubiquitous in distribution and physiologically unspecialised. Now-a-days serious degradation in the quality of forest and significant reduction in the area of the forest cover. A survey was carried in forty-five tree species growing in Dharwad moist deciduous forest to-study the effect of VAM fungi. Emphasis has been laid on nutrient uptake, host growth response and host-pathogen interactions.

1. (*h*) *Chara* is a genus of green algae in the family Characeae. They are multicellular and superficially resemble land plants because of stem-like and leaf-like structures. They are found in fresh water, particularly in limestone areas throughout the northern temperate zone, where they grow submerged, attached to the muddy bottom. They prefer less oxygenated and hard water and are not found in waters where mosquito larvae are present. They are covered with calcium carbonate deposits. *Cyanobacteria* have been found growing as epiphytes on the surfaces of Chara, where they may be involved in fixing nitrogen, which is important to plant nutrition.

Reproduction : Chara reproduces vegetatively and sexually. Vegetative reproduction takes place by tubers, amylum stars and secondary protonema. The fructifications for sexual reproduction are globule or antheridium (male) and nucule or archegonium (female). The antheridia and archegonia may occur on separate plants (dioecy), together on the same plant (conjoined monoecy) or separately on the same plant (sejoined monoecy). After fertilization, the zygote develops into an oospore.

Sexual reproduction

Sexual reproduction is oogamous in Chara. Sex organs are antheridia and archegonia. They are enclosed by multicellular sheath. This sheath forms male and female fructification. The male fructification is called **globule.** The female fructification is called **nucule.**

The plants are homothallic. Both globule and nucules are borne on the node of the leaves. Nucule borne above the globule. A few species are heterothallic.

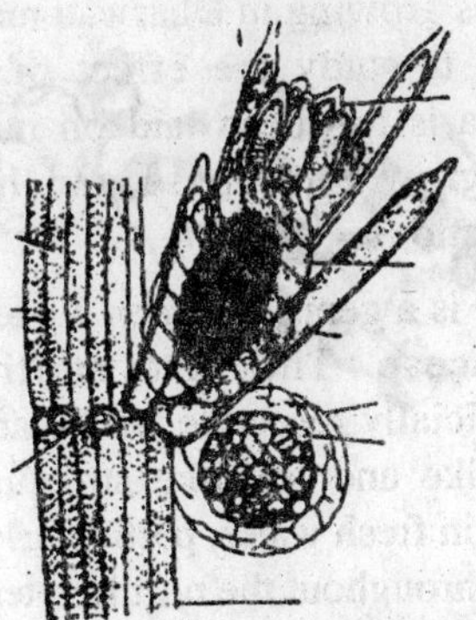

Fig. *Reproductive organs of Chara*

2. (*a*) *Penicillium* species are commonly known as green or blue molds. It includes about 140 species that grow on varied habitats. Most of the species are saprophytes and grow on decaying fruits and vegetables. Some *Penicillium* species are common inhabitants of soil.

Reproduction : *Penicillium* species reproduce by two methods (1) Asexual reproduction; (2) Sexual reproduction. Asexual reproduction is very common and sexual reproduction is rather rare.

Asexual reproduction : It takes place under favourable conditions *i.e.* availability of moisture and abundant food materials. During asexual reproduction non-motile exogenous conidia are produced at the tips of long, erect, special branches called conidiophores.

At the beginning of asexual reproduction, erect tubular aerial branches are produced from any cell of the basal mycelial hyphae. These branches are called conidiophores which are almost similar to vegetative hyphae. These conidiophores are unbranched upto certain height and later produce profuse branches on all sides. These primary branches which directly arise from the conidiophore are called *rami.* The secondary and tertiary branches are produced on the rami are called 'metulae' (Fig. B). Due to the presence of

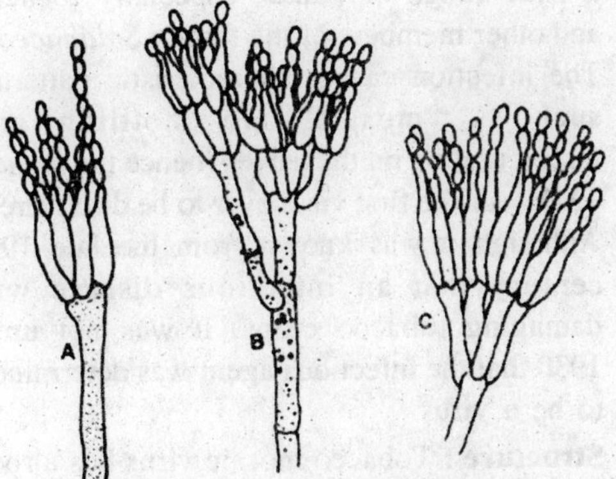

Fig : *Three types of conidiophores of Penicillium.* A. *Penicillium thomit,* B. *Penicillium lanoso-coerulcum;* C. *Penicillium wortmanni.*

primary and secondary branches the entire conidiophore appears like a brush and hence the name *Penicillum* (penicillus = brush; Fig. C). The last branches of the conidiophores bear a tuft of flask shaped structures called 'phialides' or sterigmata. In some *Penicillium* species the condiophores are unbranched and as a result the phialides are produced at the tip of the conidiophore axis. (Fig. A).

The conidia are formed within the narrow tubular tip of the flask shaped phialide. The nucleus of the phialide divides into two, one of which passes into the terminal tube of the phialide. The terminal portion of the latter is then cut off as a short uninucleate cell, the conidium. The second conidium is also cut off in the same manner below the first one. This process continues until a basipetal chain of conidia is formed. Each conidium secretes a wall around it and assumes the shape and size of characteristic of species. Conidia are generally blue or green coloured and possess one or many nuclei. They are easily disseminated by wind and upon falling on a suitable substratum germinate by producing mycelia.

2 (*b*) **Tobacco mosaic virus** (TMV) is a positive-sense single stranded RNA virus that infects a wide range of plants, especially tobacco and other members of the family *Solanaceae.* The infection causes characteristic patterns, such as "mosaic"-like mottling and discolouration on the leaves (hence the name). TMV was the first virus ever to be discovered. Although it was known from the late 19th century that an infectious disease was damaging tobacco crops, it was not until 1930 that the infectious agent was determined to be a virus.

Structure : Tobacco mosaic virus has a rod-like appearance. Its capsid is made from 2130 molecules of coat protein (see Fig.) and one molecule of genomic single strand RNA, 6400 bases long. The coat protein self-assembles into the rod like helical structure (16.3 proteins per helix turn) around the RNA which forms a hairpin loop structure. The protein monomer consists of 158 amino acids which are assembled into four main alpha-helices, which are joined by a prominent loop proximal to the axis of the virion.

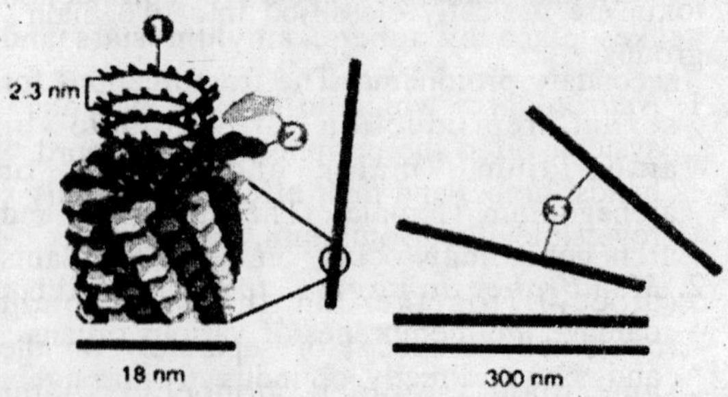

Fig. *Schematic model of TMV:* 1. *nucleic acid (RNA),* 2. *capsomer protein (protomer),* 3. *capsid*

Virions are ~300 nm in length and ~18 nm in diameter. Negatively stained electron microphotographs show a distinct inner channel of ~4 nm. The RNA is located at a radius of ~6 nm and is protected from the action of cellular enzymes by the coat protein. There are three RNA nucleotides per protein monomer. X-ray fiber diffraction structure of the intact virus was studied based on an electron density map at 3.6 Å resolution.

Tobacco mosaic virus coat protein

A monomeric unit of the tobacco mosaic virus coat protein.

Identifiers

Symbol	CP
Entrez	1494073
UniProt	P03579

2. (*c*) The toxins can be classified according to this mechanism of action or according to their source of origins.

According to their mechanism of action, the toxin are basically classified into two main groups:

1. *Neurotoxins:* which affect the nervous system; often the peripheral (spinal cord, hands, limbs) and their effects are usually reversible like Botulinum, saxotoxin.
2. *Membrane damaging toxins:* which damage the membranes of various organs and tissues directly or indirectly through the release of mediators. The membrane damage of toxins is less reversible than the neurotoxic effect. The examples: *Ricin, Mycrocystin,* and *Trichothecene mycotoxins.*

According to their source they are classified into bacterial, plant, Marine, fungal and venoms.

1. *Bacterial toxins:* These are the botulinum toxin, staphylococcal enterotoxins.
2. *Marine toxins:* Like saxitoxin from marine shellfish, clams mussels, tetrodotoxin.
3. *Fugal toxins:* Tricothecyene mycotoxins: (yellow rain of Southwest area) T2.
4. *Plant toxins:* like ricin. These toxins are dangerous from military point of view as they are easy to produce in large numbers in a low, technology environment (Ricin from caster plant *Abris precatorius*).

Venom toxins: which are abundant in snakes (rattle & snakes, cobra) or scorpions and cone snails.

2. (*d*) **A median L.S. of the Strobilus :** In the axils of the sporophylls are stalked spherical sporangia which are of two kinds, *microsporangia,* which contain a large number of *microspores* and the slightly larger *megasporangia* which contain four large megaspores, the microsporangia being more concentrated towards the upper end. The leaves bearing the sporangia are known as *microsporophylls* and *megasporophylls* respectively. As spores of different sizes are produced, the plant is said to be *heterosporous.*

Each microspore gives rise to a microprothallus which bears an antheridium. The megaspore develops into a megaprothallus on which are several archegonia. These sexual organs are similar to those of the fern but the prothallial tissue is more reduced. The megaspore begins to germinate while still in the sporangium.

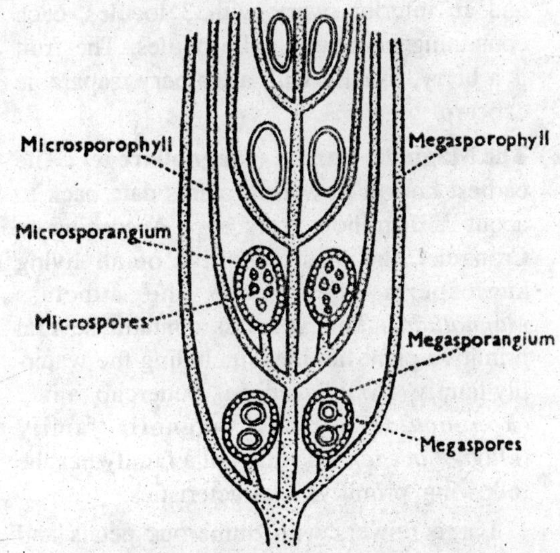

Fig. *Selaginella. L.S. strobilus.*

5. (*a*) The Musaceae are large, often treelike perennial herbs comprising 2 genera and about 45 species. The leaves are alternate and very large, with the proximal concentric, appressed sheathing portions comprising a pseudotrunk from which the individual petioles and blades diverge. The blades are simple with a prominent midrib and numerous penni-parallel lateral veins. Eventually, an inflorescence axis arising from the corm grows upward through the channel formed by the overlapping leaf bases and produces a terminal series of large overlapping bracts, each of which subtends and hides a cymose cluster of flowers. As each cyme reaches anthesis, the subtending bract reflexes to expose the flowers and eventually abscises from the inflorescence axis. The flowers are zygomorphic and functionally unisexual, the proximal ones being female and the distal ones male.

The perianth comprises 2 series of 6 petaloid tepals, 5 of which are connate into a 5-lobed tube leaving one inner segment free. The androecium usually consists of 5 fertile stamens and a staminode that is opposite the free tepal. The gynoecium consists of a single compound pistil of 3 carpels, a single style, and an inferior ovary with 3 locules, each containing numerous axile ovules. The fruit is a berry, usually with a leathery, separable exocarp.

5. (*b*) **The Magnolia Family (Magnoliaceae) :** The earliest known flowering plants date back to about 130 million years ago. According to Cronquist, the most primitive of all living angiosperms belong to the subclass *Magnoliidae.* This subclass contains several primitive plant families, including the water-lily family *(Nymphaeaceae),* buttercup family *(Ranunculaceae)* and magnolia family *(Magnoliaceae).* The magnolia family has the following primitive characteristics:

1. Large flowers with numerous petals and sepals (called tepals because they are similar in size and shape);
2. Numerous spirally arranged stamens at the base of a conelike receptacle bearing numerous spirally arranged carpels. At maturity the carpels develop into a woody, conelike aggregate of seed-bearing follicles. Each seed has a fleshy red outer layer (aril) and hangs from its follicle by a threadlike stalk. Other primitive floral characteristics are radial symmetry or actinomorphic (floral parts similar in size & shape), perfect (with functional androecium and gynoecium), complete (with all 4 floral parts: *calyx, corolla, androecium & gynoecium*), and floral axis (receptacle) elongated. The latter characteristic is clearly visible in the magnolia blossom. With all the woody, spirally arranged carpels (follicles), this axis truly resembles a conelike structure.

Large blossom of the southern magnolia *(Magnolia grandiflora),* a beautiful shade tree native to the southeastern United States. The numerous sepals and petals are called tepals because they are similar in size and shape. The conelike receptacle in the center is composed of numerous spirally arranged carpels above numerous spirally arranged stamens.

Conelike receptacle of *Magnolia grandiflora* bearing numerous follicles. At maturity, each follicle bears a bright red seed. The seeds often hang out of the individual follicles by their long, threadlike stalks.

5. (*c*) **Allium type of embryo sec**

The Themidaceae are not closely allied to Allium, as was believed until quite recently. Thus, the embryological evidence regarding affinity to the Alliaceae agrees with the molecular, morphological, and biochemical data offered by Fay and Chase as their basis for resurrection of Themidaceae and by Pires and Sytsma in their phylogenetic evaluation of the Brodiaea complex.

Alliaceous odor is considered one of the most characteristic qualities of the genus Allium. It is present, also, in most other genera of the Alliaceae. *Alliaceous odor* does not occur in any Themidaceae, nor in any Hyacinthaceae. A statement by Fay and Chase to the effect that Androstephium of the Themidaceae possesses alliaceous chemistry is based on erroneous information given by Greene. *Androstephium breviflorum* does not have an *Alliaceous odor* and neither does, *A. coeruleum* to judge from descriptions in which *Alliaceous odor,* if present, in all probability would have been mentioned.

In characteristics where the Themidaceae and the Alliaceae differ, the character state considered plesiomorphic among monocotyledons occurs in the Themidaceae.

5. (*d*) Parthenocarpy in plants is a relatively unusual condition but it does occur in some of our most common fruit. This circumstance occurs when the ovary of a flower develops into a fruit without fertilization. The result is a seedless fruit.

The word comes from Greek meaning virgin fruit. As a rule, flowers need to be pollinated and fertilized to create fruit. In some species of plants, a different method has developed, requiring either no fertilization or no fertilization and no pollination.

Pollination is done through insects or wind and spread pollen to the stigma of a flower. The resulting action promotes fertilization which allows a plant to develop seeds.

Examples of Parthenocarpy

In cultivated plants, parthenocarpy is introduced with plant hormones such as gibberellic acid. It causes ovaries to mature without fertilization and produces bigger fruits. The process is being introduced to all kinds of crops from squash to cucumber and more.

It is also a natural process as in the case of bananas. Bananas are sterile and develop no viable ovaries. They do not produce seeds, which mean they must propagate vegetatively. Pineapples and figs are also examples of parthenocarpy which occur naturally.

Effects : Parthenocarpy allows the grower to keep insect pests from his crop without chemicals. This is because no pollinating insect is required for fruit formation so the plants can be covered to prevent the bad insects from attacking the crop.

In the world of organic production, this is a significant improvement from the use of even organic pesticides and improves crop yield and health. Fruits and vegetables are bigger, the growth hormones introduced are natural and the results are easier to achieve and more healthful.

5. (*e*) **Kranz anatomy :** A special structure in the leaves of plants that have a C4 pathway of carbon dioxide fixation. The leaves contain a ring of mesophyll cells, containing a few small chloroplasts concerned with the initial fixing of carbon dioxide, surrounding a sheath of parenchyma cells (the bundle sheath) which has large chloroplasts involved in the Calvin cycle.

According to recent works by scientist at Cornell University discovered that certain gene allows some plants to photosynthesize 50% more efficient than most common plants, including crops like wheat or rice.

The gene is responsible for controlling a special leaf structure called the Kranz anatomy, known to render better photosynthesis efficiency—the ability to turn energy from light into chemical energy.

Scarecrow gene is the first gene discovered to control a special leaf structure, known as Kranz anatomy, which leads to more efficient photosynthesis.

C3 photosynthesis is being used by most of the plants for their photosynthesis and some plants like grasses, maize, sorghum and sugarcane will use C4 photosynthesis.

If C4 photosynthesis can be converted into C3 photosynthesis one could expect more yield crops.

5. (*f*) The Orchidaceae is one of the largest and most diverse families of plants, including somewhere between one tenth and one fourteenth of all flowering plant species.

The major distinguishing features of the orchid family are:

1. The stamens are all on one side of the flower, rather than being symmetrically arranged. Most orchids have only one fertile stamen, and only one genus of living orchids has three; but whether one, two, or three, the stamens are always on one side of the flower.

2. The stamen and the pistil are at least partly united. In most orchids, these parts are completely united, so that we speak of a single structure, the column.
3. The seeds are tiny and numerous. Some of the primitive orchids have much larger and more complex seeds than others, but even these must be characterized as tiny and numerous as compared with most other plants.
4. The flower usually has a lip, or labellum. This is really the petal (or inner perianth segment) that is opposite to the fertile stamen, but it is usually so unlike the other two petals that it receives a special name. In some orchids, however, the lip is not very different from the other two petals.
5. The flower usually twists around in the course of development. This process is known as resupination. In the orchid bud the fertile stamen develops on the side away from the stem and the lip develops on the side next to the stem. If the bud merely bent away from the stem, the lip would be uppermost and the fertile stamen would be on the underside of the flower. Some orchid flowers develop in this way and function well in this position, but most buds twist around during their development, so that the lip is on the lower side of the flower when it opens. This is so general that nonresupinate orchid flowers seem to be upside down.
6. Part of the stigma (the rostellum) is usually involved in transferring the pollen from one flower to another. This is one of the major themes of orchid evolution.
7. The pollen is usually bound together in a few large masses (pollinia). One of the most distinctive features of the family, this characteristic, along with the rostellum, is intimately involved in pollination by insects and birds.

5. (g) There are many spices available, many of them grown in warmer climates, such as India and the Far East. Here are some of the more common spices, their scientific names, the parts used, and a few of the possible health benefits follows.

Plant Sources of Spices

Spice (Scientific Name)	***Part(s) Used***	***Possible Health Benefit***
Allspice *(Pimenta dioica)*	Fruit/berries	For indigestion, gas, and nervous exhaustion
Black pepper *(Piper nigrum)*	Fruit	For indigestion and gas
Capsicum *(Capsicum annuum; Capsicum baccatum; Capsicum chinense; Capsicum frutescens)*	Fruit/seed	Stimulates circulation and the digestive tract; increases perspiration; capsaicin is the compound that causes the burn when you eat hot peppers
Cinnamon *(Cinnamomum zeylanicum)*	Inner bark	Ceylon cinnamon, although other cinnamons also work; stimulates circulation; good for gastrointestinal problems; antioxidant properties
Cloves *(Eugenia caryophyllata:* syn. *Syzygium aromaticum)*	Flower buds	For gastrointestinal problems; known to lessen toothaches; antioxidant properties
Ginger *(Zingiber officinal)*	Root (rhizome)	Good for motion sickness, nausea, and indigestion; antioxidant properties

Spice (Scientific Name)	*Part(s) Used*	*Possible Health Benefit*
Mace *(Myristica fragrans)*	Seed (outer)	Outer covering of nutmeg seed, used for gastrointestinal problems
Nutmeg *(Myristica fragrans)*	Seed (inner)	Good for nervous and digestive system problems; often used for insomnia
Saffron *(Crocus sativus)*	Styles	Improves digestion and stimulates circulation, increases perspiration
Turmeric *(Curcuma longa)*	Root (rhizome)	For digestive and skin complaints; antioxidant properties
Vanilla *(Vanilla planifolia)*	Fruit (pods)	Improves digestion

5. *(h)* **Euphorbiaceae :** All flowers in the Euphorbiaceae are unisexual (either male or female only), and they are often very small in size. In *Euphorbia,* the flowers are reduced even more and then aggregated into an inflorescence or cluster of flowers known as a "cyathium" (plural cyathia). This feature is present in every species of the genus but nowhere else in the plant kingdom. Whereas most other large genera of plants differ in features of the flowers themselves, *Euphorbia* varies instead in features of the cyathium, which can show amazing modifications in different groups within the genus.

The main defining feature of the cyathium is the floral envelope or involucre that surrounds each group of flowers. The involucre almost always has one or more special glands attached to it, most often on the upper rim, and these glands and their appendages vary greatly in size and shape. There may be specialized leaves called cyathophylls or cyathial leaves that surround the cyathium and give an overall flower-like appearance to the whole complex inflorescence.

Inside the involucre are the flowers, usually with a number of extremely simplified male flowers consisting of a single anther, filament, and pedicel. Generally there is a single female flower in the center consisting of a pedicel, a three-parted ovary, and no petals or sepals associated with it.

6. *(a)* Cucurbitaceae–Gourd Family characters, Floral formula & species

Diagnostic characters

1. **Habit:** Mostly annual or perennial herbs. They are mostly tendril climbers.
2. **Roots:** Tap root.
3. **Stem:** Herbaceous. Stem is very solid, it has tendrils.
4. **Leaves:** Petiolate; Leaves are alternate; simple; exstipulate; palmately reticulate venation. Sonic leaves bear tendrils in their axils.
5. **Inflorescence:** The flowers are solitary but some have Racemose or cymose clusters.
6. **Flower:** Ebracteate; actinomorphic; regular; complete or incomplete; unisexual or hermaphrodite; plant may be monoecious or dioecious; epigenous.
7. **Calyx: 5** sepals; united; campanulae.
8. **Corolla: 5** petals; united at base or free; yellow or white.
9. **Stamens in male flowers:** 3 to 5 symens; united by various degree; anther are very long. Stamens are borne on calyx tube.
10. **Carpels in female flowers:** 3 fused carp Is; syncarpous; inferior ovary; Parietal placentation.
11. **Fruits:** Fleshy berry
12. **Seed:** Non-endospermic seed.

Economic Importance

1. **Vegetables and fruits:** Many members of this family produce vegetables and fruits. Some of vegetables and fruits are: wax gourd, watermelon, *Citrullus vulgaris,* Maskmelon, vegetable marrow, cucumber, *Momordica charantia.*
2. **Medicinal importance:** Some plants of this family give important drugs. The fruits and seeds of majority of them are laxatives.
3. **Bath sponges:** The vegetable sponge (*Luna*) is dried. Its inner fibrous fruit is removed and used as bath sponge. It is also used for dish washing.
4. **Ornamental plants:** Certain vines of this family are grown as ornamental plants.
5. **Dangerous plants:** Some plants are very dangerous to humans. The juice of *Echo elaterium* (Squirting cucumber).
6. **Weeds:** Some plants of this family act as weeds.

Distribution pattern : This family has 100 genera and 850 species. Most of the plants are tropical and sub-tropical. Some species are temperate.

Common species

1. *Cucurhita pepo* (pumpkin)
2. *Cucumis meta* (melon
3. *Cucumis sans* (cucumber)
4. *Momordica charantia*
5. *Luffli aeuptica.*

6. (*b*) **Haploids from Isolated Microspore or Pollen Culture :** In 1953, Tulecke was able to obtain the callus from isolated pollen cultures of gymnosperms.

This raised the possibility of obtaining haploids from isolated microspores or pollen cultures. The advantage of using this method was soon realised since pollen grains within an anther would constitute a heterogenous population. The first report on the tissue formation from isolated pollen of an angiosperm was from Kameya and Hinata.

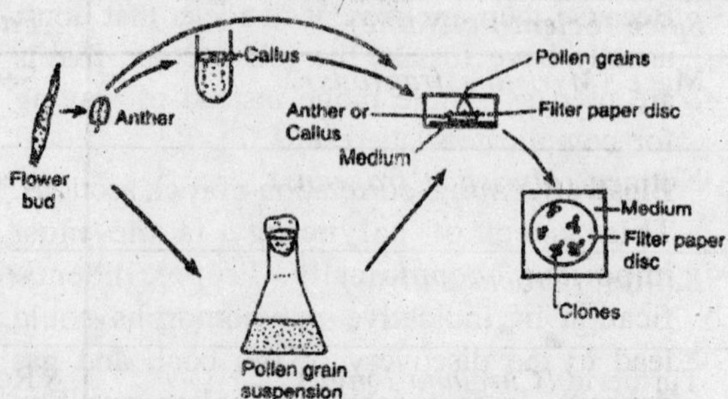

Fig. *Illustration showing the technique of nurse culture for cloning isolated pollen grains.*

They used hanging drops to culture mature pollen about 80 pollen grains per drop isolated from *Brassica oleracea* and the hybrid *B. alboglabra* × *B. oleracea* at low temperature. In the subsequent years workers found the nurse-culture technique (See Fig.) suitable for raising haploid tissue clones from isolated pollen grains.

Intact microspores are mounted on a filter paper disc which, in turn, is placed over an intact anther or callus derived from the floral parts. The extract of cultured anthers has equal nursing effects on the growth and development of microspores, and may be used in place of a nurse callus or anther. A purely synthetic medium developed for raising haploid plants from isolated pollen grains of tobacco and *Datura* may also be suitable for other systems. The crucial ingredients of this medium are glutamine, L-Serine and Inositol.

6. (c) **Applications of Palynology :** There are a few geological fields in which palynology can be applied to, here are the major fields:

- Geochronology
- Biostratigraphy
- Paleoecology
- Quaternary Palynology

Geochronology–dating of rocks. Palynoflora are used to date rocks. Palynomorphs are great indicators of narrow time ranges because of the rapid evolution of the samples.

Because they are present in rocks that don't usually have fossils, the microscopic fossils are used as a time range instead of waiting for complicated lab results.

Biostratigraphy–correlation of rock sections. This aspect of palynology is the most important economically. Proper indentification of indicative palynomorphs could lead to the discovery of oil, coal, and gas deposits. In fact, fossilized pollen was first discovered in a coal thin section. Because pollen and spores have the tendency of being dragged along with migrating petroleum through pourous rocks–they are good indicators that petroleum isn't too far away. The small sizes of palynomorphs are ideal for drill core samples. The colouration and type of palynomorph represents the thermal maturity and hydrocarbon potential of the area.

Paleoecology - past environments. Because palynomorphs are sensitive to any minor fluctuation in their surroundings, they are highly indicative of the environment in which they are deposited. The advantage of palynomorphs over other fossils is their widespread distribution; they can be found in either terrestrial, freshwater, saltwater, and estuary sources of sedimentary rocks.

Quaternary palynology–Although very similar to the purposes of paleoecology, Quaternary deals more with more recent environmental and climate change. This field of study uses quantitive analysis and precise dating for correlating stratigraphic sequences and reconstructing rats of environmental change. Studies show that the most influenced environmental changes have occurred since the appearance of humans.

6. **(*d*)** Polyembryony is the process in which the fertilization of single egg leads to the formation of two or more embryos. Polyembryony has been reported as occurring in a large number of species. Braun in 1860 reported polyembryony as known in twenty-one species, in thirteen genera, and in twelve families. Since that time it has been reported in a number of other species. The causes of this phenomenon are not thoroughly understood and are not always the same. Coulter and Chamberlain give six different methods by which two or more embryos may be produced in a single seed and three forms of pseudo-polyembryony as follows :

True Polyembryony

A. Embryos derived from cells outside the sac, hence sporophytic tissue (vegetative multiplication or budding).

1. Embryos derived from cells of the nucellus.
2. Embryos derived from cells of the integument.

B. Embryos derived from cells within the sac (parthenogenesis and vegetative apogamy); although not in the same morphological category, embryos from the suspensor are also included in the list (vegetative multiplication or budding).

1. Normal occurrence of two eggs.
2. Embryos from synergids.
3. Splitting of embryos derived from egg.
4. Embryos from antipodal cells.
5. Embryos from endosperm cells.
6. Embryos from the suspensor.

Importance : It is important in the formation of identical twins. Formation of embryos by cells of the embryo sac other than the egg. Embryos develop from additional embryo sacs in an ovule.

8. **(*a*)** (*i*) Protoplasts are the cells of which cell walls are removed and cytoplasmic membrane is the outermost layer in such cells. Protoplast can be obtained by specific lytic enzymes to remove cell wall. Protoplast fusion is a physical phenomenon, during fusion two or more protoplasts come in contact and adhere with one another either spontaneously or in presence of fusion inducing agents. By protoplast fusion it is possible to transfer some useful genes such as nitrogen fixation, rapid growth rate, more product formation rate, protein quality, frost hardiness, drought resistance, herbicide resistance, heat and cold resistance from one species to another. Protoplast fusion an important tools in strain improvement for bringing genetic recombinations and developing hybrid strains in filamentous fungi. Protoplast fusion has been used to combine genes from different organisms to create strains with desired properties.

Methods of Protoplasts Fusion

(A) Spontaneous Fusion:

During the enzymatic degradation of cell walls some of the adjacent protoplasts may fuse together to form homocaryons. These plurinucleate cells sometimes contain 2-3 nuclei, a phenomenon attributed to expansion and subsequent coalescence of the plasmodesmatal connections between the cells. The protoplasts once they are freely isolated, do not fuse spontaneously with each other.

Mechanical Fusion: The giant protoplast of Acelabularia have been fused mechanically by pushing together two protoplast. This fusion does not upon the presence of fusion inducing agents. However, in this procedure protoplasts are likely to get injury. Protoplast released from meiocytes in enzyme solutions readily fuse by gentle tapping in depression slide.

(B) Induced Fusion:

Fusion of freely isolated protoplasts from different sources with the help of fusion inducing chemical agents is known as induced fusion. Normally, isolated protoplasts do not fuse with each other because the surface of the isolated protoplasts carries negative charge around the outside of plasma membrane and thus is a strong tendency for protoplasts to repel one another due to their same charges.

(*i*) **$NaNO_3$ Treatment:** Equal densities of protoplasts from two different sources are mixed and then centrifuged at 100 g for 5 minutes to get a dense pellet. This is followed by addition of 4 ml of 5.5% sodium nitrate in 10.2% sucrose solution to Resuspend the protoplast pellet. The suspended protoplasts are kept in water–bath at 35°C for 5 minutes and again centrifuged at 200 g for 5 minutes. The pellet is once again kept in water bath at 30°C for 30 minutes. The fusions of protoplast take place at the time of incubation. Finally, the protoplasts are plated in semisolid culture medium. The frequency of fusion is not very high in this method.

(*ii*) **High pH or Ca++ Treatment:** Kelier and Melchers (1973) developed a method to effectively induce fusion of tobacco protoplasts at a high temperature (37°C) in media containing high concentration of Ca++ ions at a highly alkaline condition (pH 10.5). Equal densities of protoplasts are taken in centrifuge tube and protoplasts are spun at 100 g for 5 minutes. The pellet is suspended in 0.5 ml of medium. A 4 ml of 0.05 M $CaCl_2$, $2H_2O$ in 0.4 M mannitol at pH 10.5 is mixed to the protoplast suspension. The centrifuge tube containing protoplast at high pH or Ca++ is placed in water bath at 30°C for 10 minutes and is spun at 50 g for 3 to 4 minutes. This followed by keeping the tubes in water bath (37°C) for 40-50 minutes. About 20-30% protoplast are involved in this fusion experiment.

(iii) **PEG Treatment:** PEG induces protoplast aggregation and subsequent fusion. But the concentration and molecular weight of PEG are important with respect to fusion. A solution of 37.5% w/v PEG of molecular weight 1500 to 6000 aggregates mesophyll and cultured cell protoplasts during a 45 minutes incubation at room temperature. Fusion of protoplast takes place during slow elusion of PEG with liquid culture medium. Carrot protoplast can be fused by 28% PEG 1500 and fusion can be promoted by Ca++ ion at concentration of 3.5 mM. But higher concentration of Ca++ ion has been considered beneficial. In some studies, high pH/Ca++ and PEG method have been combined. The PEG method has been modified slightly to fuse higher plant protoplast as indicated below:

(*a*) PEG is more effective when it is mixed with 10-15% dimethyl sulphoxide.

(*b*) Addition of concanvalin A to PEG increases protoplast fusion frequency.

(*c*) Sea water has been used alone or in combination with PEG to fuse protoplasts.

(iv) **Electro Fusion:** Recently, mild electrical stimulation is being used to fuse protoplasts. This technique is known as electrofusion of protoplasts. Two glass capillary microelectrode are placed in contact with the protoplasts. An electric field of low strength (10kv m-3) give rise to dielectrophoretic pole generation within the protoplast suspension. This lead to pearl chain arrangement of protoplasts. The number of protoplasts within a pearl chain depends upon the population density of the protoplast and the distance between the electrodes. Subsequent application of high intensity electric impulse (100kv m-3) for some microseconds results in the electric breakdown of membrane and subsequent fusion.

8. (*a*) (*ii*) Somatic hybridization: Improvement of crop plants by conventional breeding is time consuming and, therefore, expensive. Unconventional techniques can shorten the process. One of these is protoplast fusion, developed and successfully used already in past year by Melchers and Labib. Somatic hybridization is especially useful for heterozygotic crops, which possess different ploidy levels, as for example potato. Breeding programs of potato require prebreeding for easier and faster selection at the diploid level. To reach the productive tetraploid level without rearrangement of chromosomes in meiosis, protoplast fusion was utilized successfully. One of the most serious diseases of potato worldwide is caused by *Phytophthora infestans* Bitt. (Oomycete). New sources of resistance against this pathogen have been identified in related wild species of potato. Several of them had so far not been used as they cannot be crossed with the cultivated potato. Protoplast fusion has overcome this incompatibility. Several wild species have been successfully combined with diploid breeding lines and cultivars. The hybrids were identified by RFLPs. Crossing of the somatic hybrids with cultivars of breeding lines lead to populations segregating for resistance to *Ph. infestans.* We are looking for molecular markers related to the resistance and trying to identify the components of resistance. In an EC-INCO project somatic hybrids have been produced and distributed to the cooperators in different institutions in Spain and Latin America. There they have been evaluated for resistance and crossed to locally adapted cultivars. This cooperative effort including agronomic techniques as management of resistance and participation of local farmers will allow sustainable production with lower fungicide application.

Applications of somatic hybridization

1. Novel interspecific and intergeneric crosses which are difficult to produce by conventional methods can be easily obtained.
2. Important characters, such as resistance to diseases, ability to undergo abiotic stress and other quality characters, can be obtained in hybrid plant by the fusion of protoplasts of plant bearing particular character to the other plant which may be susceptible to diseases.
3. Protoplasts of sexually sterile haploid, triploid, aneuploid plants can be fused to obtain fertile diploids and polyploids.
4. Studying cytoplasmic genes may be helpful to carry out plant breeding.
5. Most of the agronomically important traits, such as cytoplasmic male sterility, antibiotic resistance and herbicide resistance, are cytoplasmically encoded, hence can be easily transferred to other plant.
6. Plants in juvenile stage can also be hybridized by means of somatic hybridization.
7. Somatic hybridization can be used as a method for the production of autotetraploids.

Limitations of somatic hybridization

1. Application of protoplast methodology requires efficient plant regeneration system from isolated protoplasts. Protoplasts from two species can be fused, however, production of somatic hybrids is not easy.
2. Lack of a proper selection method for fused products (hybrids) poses a problem.
3. The end product of somatic hybridization are often unbalanced (sterile, misformed and unstable).
4. Somatic hybridization of two diploids leads to formation of amphidiploids which is unfavourable.
5. It is not sure for a character to completely express after somatic hybridization.
6. The regeneration products of somatic hybridization are often variable due to somaclonal variation, chromosome elimination, organelle segregation.
7. All diverse intergeneric somatic hybrids are sterile and, therefore, have limited chances of development of new varieties.
8. To transfer useful genes from wild species to cultivated crop, it is necessary to achieve intergeneric recombination or chromosome substitution between parental genomes.

8. (*b*) Salient Features of Engler and Prantl's system of classification:

- Plant Kingdom has been divided into 13 Divisions
- Divisions 1 to 12 dealing with Bacteria, different types of Algae, Fungi, Bryophytes, and Pteridophytes.
- The 13th Division is named as Embryophyta Siphonogamia which includes all seed producing plants.
- It is divided into 2 sub-divisions:

  (I) Gymnospermae (naked ovules/seeds)

  (II) Angiospermae (enclosed ovules/seeds)
- Gymnospermae has been divided into 7 orders, from Cycadofilicales to Gnetales.
- The sub-division Angiospermae divided into two Classes (*i*) Monocotyledonae (*ii*) Dicotyledonae.

- Monocots divided into 11 Orders and 45 Families, First order is Pandanales which possesses naked, unisexual flowers with Typhaceae as the Starting family.
- The last order is Microspermae with orchidaceae as the last family.
- Dicots are divided into 2 subclass namely: (*i*) Archichlamydeae, and (*ii*) Sympetalae or Metachlamydeae
- In Archichlamydeae, the flowers are achlamydous or mono/dichlamydous, but petals are mostly free (polypetalous condition).
- In sympetalae, the petals are fused (gamopetalous).
- Archichlamydeae has 33 Orders and 206 Families. The first order being Verticillatae and Casuarinaceae as the starting family. The last order being Umbelliflorae with Cornaceae as the last family.
- Sympetalae has 11 Orders with 52 Families. The first Order being Ericales with Clethraceae as the starting family.
- The last order is Campanulales with Asteraceae as the last family.

Outline of Engler & Prantl Classification

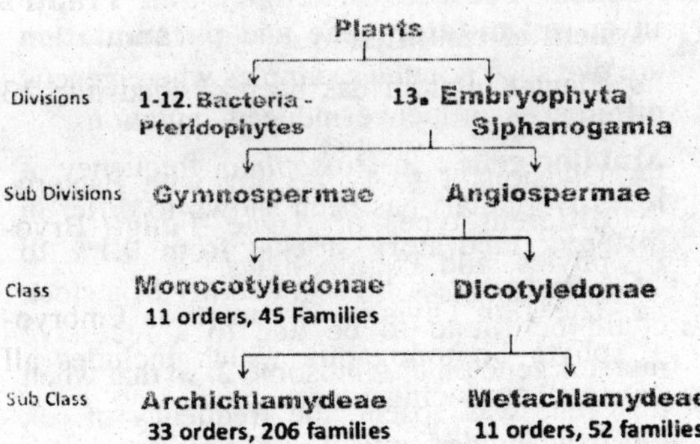

Benthem and Hooker's System *vs* Engler and Prantl System of Classification

Benthem and Hooker's System (1862–1883)

1. It is a natural system
2. Based on de Candolle's system.
3. Phanerogams were classified.
4. Gymnosperms were kept between dicots and monocots.
5. Bennettitalian origin of angiospermic flower is taken.
6. Dicots divided into polypetalae, gamopetalae and monochlamydae.
7. Euphorbiaceae highly advanced in dicots.
8. Gramineae highly advanced in monocots.
9. There are 202 families.
10. Fixity of species was taken into account.

Engler and Prantl System of Classification (1887–1899)

1. It is aphylogenetic system.
2. Based on Eichler's system.
3. Entire plant kingdom was classified.
4. Gymnosperms are more primitive to angiosperms.
5. Unisexual, anemophilous flowers are primitive (like Amentiferae)
6. Dicots divide into Archichlamydae and Metachlamydae.
7. Compositae highly advanced in dicots.
8. Orchidaceae highly advanced into monocots.
9. There are 280 families.
10. Concept of evolution was taken into account.

PAPER-II

1. (*a*) Prions are not a lifeform is because they cannot evolve beyond their structure into a more complex entity. They are more similar to a computer virus that although it might change a bit adapting to different computer antivirus tools it will not be able to occupy a function in the real world. Prions on the other hand, while they are in the real world, they are only replicating through a sort of geometric "bug": they cannot create any ecosystem for themselves which instead a virus could.

Most Biologists would not consider Viruses alive because they do not have certain properties that many other living things do. However the Physicists approach to life defined as an entity with negative entropy would qualify viruses as lifeforms with the caveat that their negative entropy (their ability to create more order) is dependent on other organisms. Prions also appear to qualify the negative entropy criteria for being a lifeform because they cause a cascade in a protein folding error, but given that the error is non functional I think you can argue that the new broken protein is actually more entropic than the correctly folded one. I would need a physicist to confirm but this negative entropic approach would seem to differentiate the two classes.

1. (*b*)

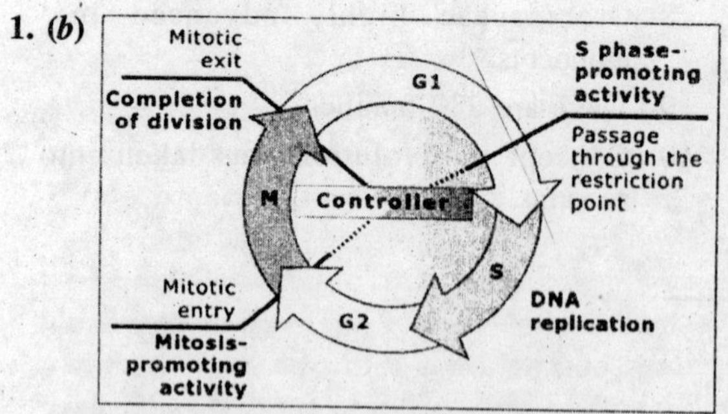

Fig. *Major transitions in the cell cycle are regulated by a cell cycle control system.*

Cell cycle transitions are regulated by a set of proteins that form a central cell cycle control system. This system regulates the machineries that replicate and segregate the DNA and that divide the cell, telling each when to perform its functions. **Checkpoints,** which impinge on the central controller, exist for two critical purposes. One is to ensure a cell cycle event does not start before the previous one is completed successfully. The other is to impose dependence of the initiation of the cell cycle on the cell's surroundings, as was discussed earlier. Fig. shows the major points in the cell cycle regulated by the cell cycle control system and checkpoints.

The central cell cycle control system receives constant feedback throughout the cycle. As long as an event is still in progress, a signal is sent to the central control system that prevents it from moving on to initiate the next event. Only after an event has been completed successfully does the inhibitory signal cease, allowing the central control system to proceed to the next phase.

1. (*c*) In maize **mutator gene** and **paramutation** are two such popular examples where genetic differences influence induced mutations.

Mutator gene : In *Drosophila,* frequency of recessive lethals has been shown to differ in different laboratory stocks, from 0.1% to 1.0%. Sometimes, high mutability of a stock could be found to be due to a recessive mutator gene on chromosome 2, so that when this gene was absent, the frequency of sex linked recessives fell down to 0.07%. Other mutator genes have also been identified both in *Drosophila* and other organisms like *Escherichia coli* and are related with DNA polymerase enzyme involved in DNA replication and repair.

The most popular example of mutator gene known in corn relates to a gene a which is located on chromosome 3 and causes absence of anthocyanin leading to loss of purple colour in corn kernel endosperm and other parts of the plant.

Paramutations : It is usually accepted that the two alleles *A* and *a* present in a heterozygote *(Aa)* remain uncontaminated and that their temporary association does not affect each other. This basic assumption was questioned when **Brink** in 1956 discovered the phenomenon of paramutation in corn. It was shown that at *R* locus for pigment there are different alleles having different phenotypic effects as follows:

R^r = full colour

R^{st} = stippled effect

R^{mb} = marbled effect

Paramutations, though rare, are also found in *Oenothera,* tomato and ferns.

1. (*d*) The genetic code allows an organism to translate the genetic information found in its **chromosomes** into usable **proteins.** Stretches of deoxyribonucleic acid (DNA) are built from four different **nucleotide** bases, while proteins are made from twenty unique subunits called **amino acids.**

	Second Position of Codon				
First Position	T	C	A	G	Third Position
T	TTT Phe [F]	TCT Ser [S]	TAT Tyr [Y]	TGT Gys [C]	T
	TTC Phe [F]	TCC Ser [S]	TAC Tyr [Y]	TGC Gys [C]	C
	TTA Leu [L]	TCA Ser [S]	TAA *Ter* [end]	TGA *Ter* [end]	A
	TTG Leu [L]	TCG Ser [S]	TAG *Ter* [end]	TGG Trp [W]	G
C	CTT Leu [L]	CCT Pro [P]	CAT His [H]	CGT Arg [R]	T
	CTC Leu [L]	CCC Pro [P]	CAC His [H]	CGC Arg [R]	C
	CTA Leu [L]	CCA Pro [P]	CAA Gln [Q]	CGA Arg [R]	A
	CTG Leu [L]	CCG Pro [P]	CAG Gln [Q]	CGG Arg [R]	G
A	ATT Ile [I]	ACT Thr [T]	AAT Asn [N]	AGT Ser [S]	T
	ATC Ile [I]	ACC Thr [T]	AAC Asn [N]	AGC Ser [S]	C
	ATA Ile [I]	ACA Thr [T]	AAA Lys [K]	AGA Arg [R]	A
	ATG Met [M]	ACG Thr [T]	AAG Lys [K]	AGG Arg [R]	G
G	GTT Val [V]	GCT Ala [A]	GAT Asp [D]	GGT Gly [G]	T
	GTC Val [V]	GCC Ala [A]	GAC Asp [D]	GGC Gly [G]	C
	GTA Val [V]	GCA Ala [A]	GAA Glu [E]	GGA Gly [G]	A
	GTG Val [V]	GCG Ala [A]	GAG Glu [E]	GGG Gly [G]	G

the Genetic Code in the table above has been called "The Universal Genetic Code". It is known as "universal", because it is used by all known organisms as a code for DNA, mRNA, and tRNA. The universality of the genetic code encompases animals (including humans), plants, fungi, archaea, bacteria, and viruses. However, all rules have their exceptions, and such is the case with the Genetic Code; small variations in the code exist in mitochondria and certain microbes. Nonetheless, it should be emphasized that these variances represent only a small fraction of known cases, and that the Genetic Code applies quite broadly, certainly to all known nuclear genes.

1. (*e*) **Binomial distributions** are useful to model events that arise in a binomial experiment. Examples include how many coin flips show heads, how many scratch-off lottery tickets are winners, how many of a doctor's patients die during surgery, and how many free throws I make in one hundred attempts. Key ingredients of such an experiment include:

- A fixed number of repeated, identical, independent trials. *n* is usually the parameter chosen to label the number of trials.
- Every trial results in either a success, with probability *p*, or a failure, with probability 1-*p*. These must be the only two outcomes for a trial.
- The random variable of interest is the total number of trials that ended in a success.

The probability mass function for the binomial distribution is given by:

$$p(x) = \binom{n}{x} p^x (1-p)^{n-x} \quad \text{for } x = 0, 1, 2, ..., n$$

Poisson distributions are useful to model events that seem to take place over and over again in a completely haphazard way. For example, how many magnitude 8+ earthquakes will take place in a particular year? Or, how many babies will be born in a large hospital on a particular day? Or, how many hits will a website get in a particular minute? Key assumptions for the Poisson model include:

- The random variable counts the number of events that take place in a given interval (usually of time or space)
- All events take place independently of all other events
- The rate at which events take place is constant usually denoted λ.

The probability mass function is given by:

$$p(x) = \frac{e^{-\lambda t}(\lambda t)^x}{x!} \text{ for } x = 0, 1, 2, ...$$

2. (*a*) **Nuclear pores** are large protein complexes that cross the nuclear envelope, which is the double membrane surrounding the eukaryotic cell nucleus. There are about an average of 2000 nuclear pore complexes (NPCs), in the nuclear envelope of a vertebrate cell, but it varies depending on cell type and the stage in the life cycle. The proteins that make up the nuclear pore complex are known as nucleoporins.

Nuclear pore complexes allow the transport of molecules across the nuclear envelope. This transport includes RNA and ribosomal proteins moving from nucleus to the cytoplasm and proteins (such as DNA polymerase and lamins), carbohydrates, signaling molecules and lipids moving into the nucleus.

Nucleocytoplasmic Transport

A basic necessity of the eukaryotic cell is the ability to transport macromolecules bidirectionally between the nucleus and cytoplasm. The traffic between these two compartments is both heavy and complex with multiple classes of cargo being actively transported in both directions (See Fig.). Nuclear proteins such as transcription factors and histones are, like all proteins, made in the cytoplasm and must cross the nuclear envelope into the nuclear interior to carry out their function. Conversely, ribosomal subunits, transfer RNAs (tRNAs), and messenger RNAs (mRNAs) produced inside the nucleus must cross the nuclear envelope in the opposite direction into the cytoplasm in order to be used for protein translation.

Nucleocytoplasmic traffic is restricted to nuclear pore complexes (NPCs), which are large proteinaceous structures that bridge the double membrane of the nuclear envelope to form aqueous channels linking the cytoplasm and nucleoplasm. The vertebrate NPC is composed of ~30 different proteins, and a HeLa cell contains ~3000 NPCs. At present, all NPCs appear to be functionally identical with the same NPC capable of carrying out both import and export virtually simultaneously. While molecules up to ~50 kDa can diffuse through the NPC, the majority of nuclear proteins (both larger and smaller than 50 kDa) as well as the other classes of transport cargo appear to undergo signal-mediated active transport rather than diffusion.

There are two types of nuclear transport signals, nuclear localization sequences (NLSs) that mediate nuclear import and nuclear export sequences (NESs) that mediate nuclear export. There are multiple types of NLSs and NESs found on different types of cargo, and, in general, each type of signal is recognized by a different nuclear receptor/carrier. Most nuclear carriers are members of the karyopherin-β superfamily and there are over 20 members of this family in human cells.

During nuclear import, a soluble carrier binds the NLS-containing cargo in the cytoplasm, then moves the cargo through the NPC and releases it in the nuclear interior. Nuclear export works essentially the same way in reverse, with an NES-containing cargo being recognized by its specific carrier inside the nucleus, movement of the export complex through the NPC, and disassembly of the complex and release of the cargo upon reaching the cytoplasm.

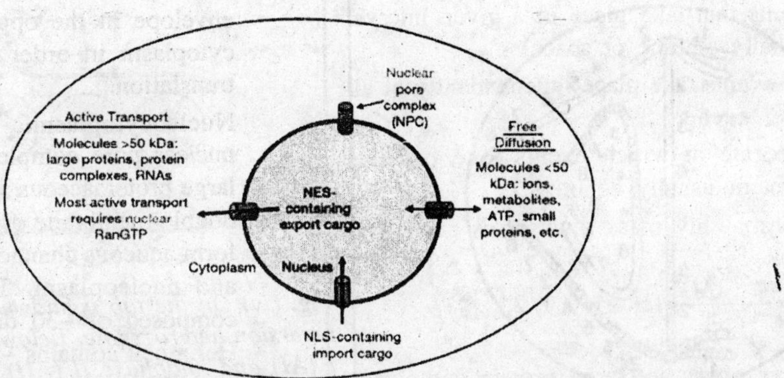

Some NLS-containing import cargo	*Some NES-containing export cargo*
Nuclear proteins	Shuttling proteins
Shuttling proteins	Newly formed ribosomal subunits
	tRNAs
	mRNAs

Fig. *Overview of nucleocytoplasmic transport*

2. (*b*) Cytology of inversions

Due to an inverted segment in one of the two homologous chromosomes, the normal kind of pairing is not possible in an inversion heterozygote. In order to enable pairing of homologous segments, a shape of loop is formed by each of the two chromosomes as shown in Figures (*i*) and (*v*). This kind of configuration will be observed both in paracentric as well as in paracentric inversions. As will be observed, the products of crossing over and the subsequent stages of meiosis will differ in these two kinds of inversions.

1. Paracentric inversion. A single crossing over or an odd number of crossovers in inverted region will result into formation of a dicentric chromosome (having two centromeres) and an acentric chromosome (with no centromere). Of the remaining two chromatids, one will be normal and the other will carry the inversion (Fig. (*i*)). The dicentric chromatid and acentric chromatid will be observed at anaphase I in the form of a bridge and a fragment (Fig (*ii*)). Double crossovers and corssovers within and outside inversion will give various kinds of deficiencies and duplication (Fig. (*iii*)), these will also give rise to a variety of characteristic configurations at anaphase I and anaphase II (Fig. (*iv*)); for details consult author's advanced text book *Cytogenetics*).

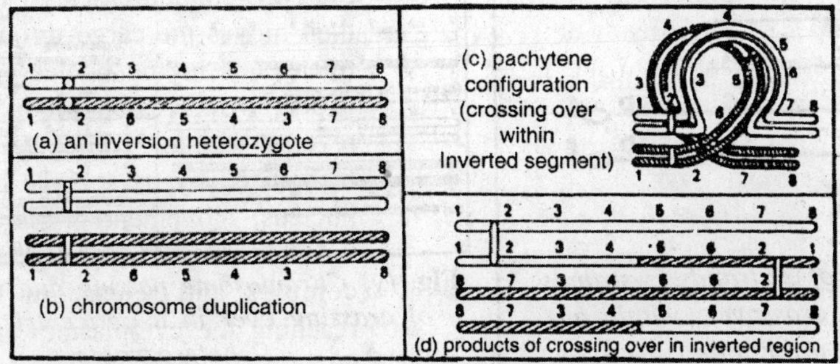

Fig. (*i*) *Chromosome pairing and products of crossing over in a paracentric inversion heterozygote.*

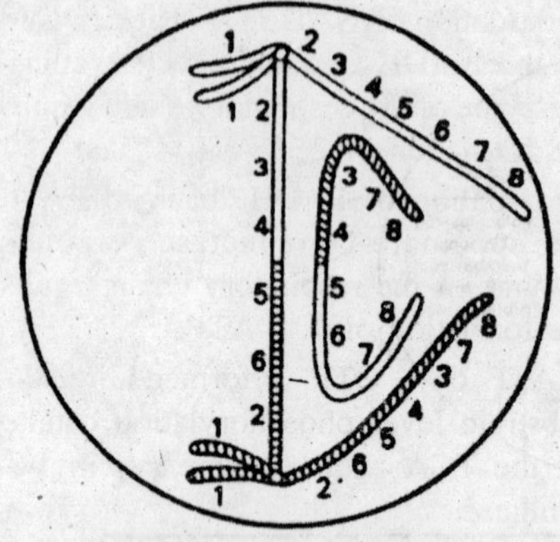

Fig. *(ii) Dicentric bridge and an acentric fragment at anaphase I.*

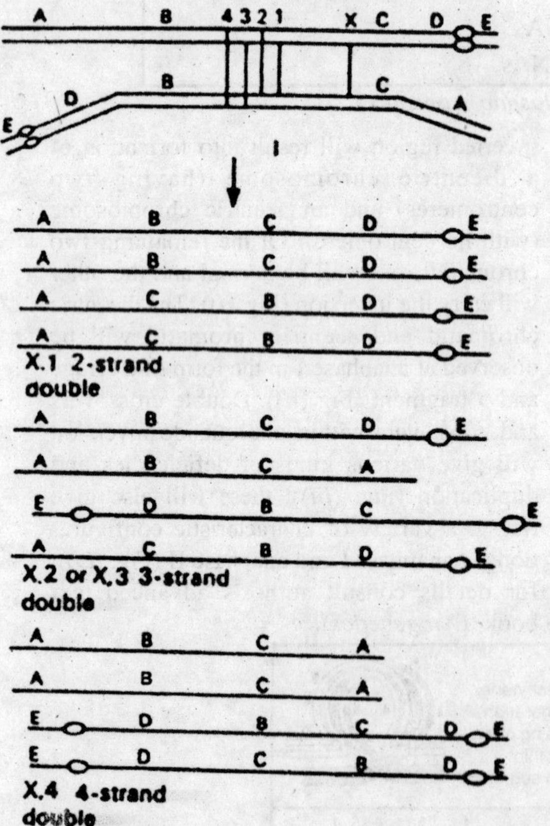

Fig. *(iii) Consequences of 2-strands, 3-strands and 4-strands double crossovers within a paracentric inversion.*

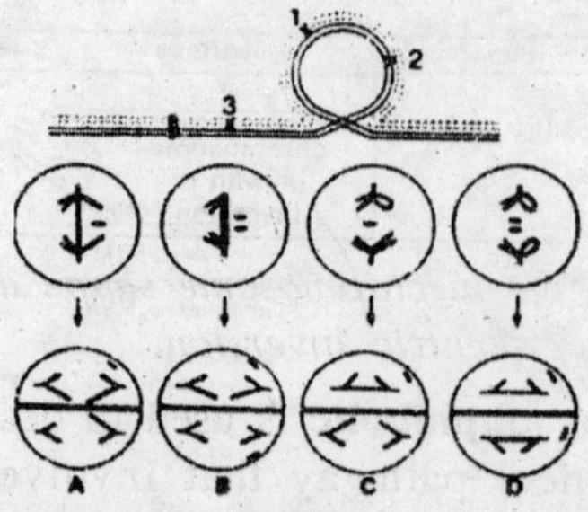

Fig. *(iv) On the top is shown inversion loop in an inversion heterozygote. Below are shown anaphase I (AI) and anaphase II (AII) configurations (A-D) resulting from four different combinations of crossovers within and outside the inversion loop.*

2. Pericentric inversion. In a pericentric inversion (where centromere is present within the inverted segment), the pachytene configuration observed is similar to the one described above for paracentric inversion (Fig. (*i*)). However, the products of crossing over and configurations at subsequent stages of meiosis differ. In this case, two of the four chromatids resulting after meiosis will have deficiencies and duplications. However, unlike paracentric inversion, no dicentric bridge or acentric fragment will be observed (Fig. (*v*)). Consequently, at anaphase I, no bridge or fragment will be seen.

However, in pericentric inversion, if two breaks are not situated equidistant from the centromere, this will result in a change in shape of the chromosome. For instance, a metacentric chromosome (with centromere in the centre) may become submetacentric and *vice versa* (Fig. *vi*).

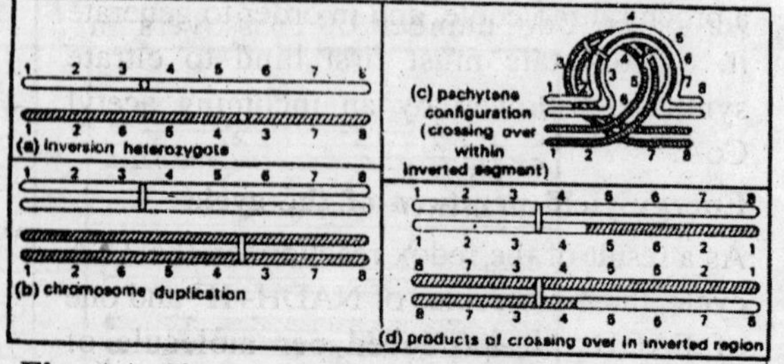

Fig. *(v) Chromosome pairing and the products of crossing over in a pericentric inversion heterozygote.*

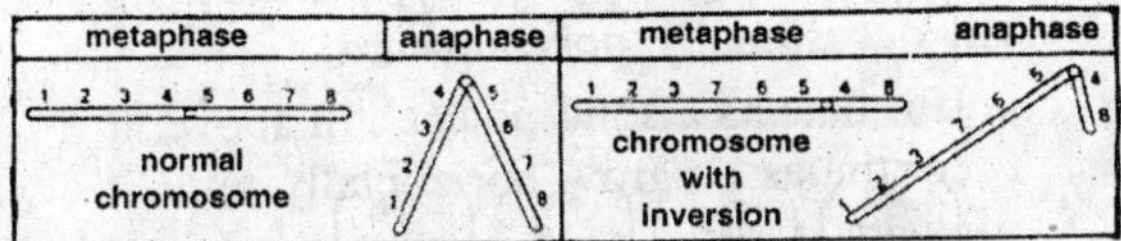

Fig. *(vi) Change in chromosome shape due to pericentric inversion.*

5. *(a)* The term **amphibolic** is used to describe a biochemical pathway that involves both catabolism and anabolism.

The Citric acid cycle (aka Kreb's cycle and Tricarboxylic acid cycle-TCA cycle) is a sequence of reactions, of an amphibolic overall nature (both catabolic and anabolic), occurring in mitochondrial matrix that oxidizes acetyl moieties of acetyl-CoA. It is the final common pathway for oxidation of carbohydrate, protein and lipids as glucose, fatty acids and amino acids are metabolized to acetyl-CoA or intermediates of the cycle. The cycle starts with anabolic condensation of acetyl-CoA (3C) and oxaloacetate (3C), to yield citric acid (6C), the tricarboxylic acid of the cycle. In the subsequent catabolic reactions two molecules of CO_2 are released (in the isocitrate dehydrogenase and a-ketoglutarate dehydrogenase complex steps) and oxaloacetate is regenerated, commencing another cycle. The enzymes of the cycle are located in the mitochondrial matrix either free or bound to the inner mitochondrial membrane where the enzymes of the respiratory chain and oxidative phosphorylation are also found. The molecule citrate is a prochiral molecule, and in order to generate it, oxaloacetate must first bind to citrate synthase, followed by an incoming acetyl CoA.

Energy yield per turn of the cycle

As a result of the redox reactions in the TCA cycle, three molecules of $NADH+H^+$ and one of $FADH_2$ are produced per molecule of acetyl-CoA catabolized in one turn of the cycle. The total energy yield per turn of the TCA cycle is 10 ATP.

- Reoxidation of $NADH+H^+$ back to NAD+ by the NADH-Q oxidoreductase/complex I enzyme of the respiratory chain results in the formation of 2, 5 ATP.
- Reoxidation of $FADH_2$ back to FAD by the succinate-Q reductase/complex II enzyme of the respiratory chain results in the formation of 1, 5 ATP.
- 1 ATP or 1 GTP is formed directly by substrate level phosphorylation catalyzed by the TCA cycle enzyme syccinyl-CoA synthase.

5. *(b)* Phenolics have long been suspected to be involved in a plant's defense against invading phytophathogens. The outer-neck scales of coloured onion bulbs were found to be resistant to infection by *Collectotrichum circinans,* whereas unpigmented varieties lacked resistance. This type of resistance was subsequently correlated with the presence of protocatechuic acid in the scales. Several other reports are available indicating the plant species being more or less resistant to pests or pathogens depending upon their content of natural tannin or other phenols. It has been shown that the general response to attack by pathogens commonly involves the production of high levels of phenols adjacent to the injury and an increase in the activity of phenolase enzymes. It is now commonly believed that quinones and phytomelanin complexes are responsible for disease resistance. Such oxidation products are often more toxic to potential invaders than are the original phenols, and their polymerization helps seal off the injured surface and begin the healing process. In some instances, unusual phenols and other toxic compounds are clearly a part of the normal resistance mechanism of a plant, such as gossypol glands in cottonseed. In other cases, phytoalexins are produced in response to microbial or fungal attack. These compounds specifically inhibit plant pathogens. According to Muller and Berger, phytoalexins are absent in a healthy plant, but

occur whenever a plant is invaded by a fungus, and if produced in high concentrations, are toxic to the invader. Such resistance is not inherited, but appears as a result of infection. However, the sensitivity and subsequent speed of the response of the plant to the invader seem to be genetically controlled.

Phenols appear to be involved in hypersensitive self-toxic reactions within a given plant and in allelopathic competition among plants. These self-toxic reactions include the natural inhibitors of seed germination, such as coumarins, which must be leached or destroyed during the dormancy period before a seed can sprout. High-tannin grain sorghum types resist preharvest germination under adverse climatic conditions. The thick testa layer of the seed has been shown to retard or delay seed germination by retarding the absorption of water. It is quite likely that tannins present in this layer enter into the endosperm with water and retard the metabolic processes by inactivating the hydrolytic enzymes essential for seed germination. These reports indicate that Phenolic substances (tannins) are not metabolic waste products of plants or "accidents of plant metabolism" but these substances have pertinent biological functions.

5. (*c*) Triple Response:

- When there is mechanical stress on the stem of a plant (e.g. pushing against a rock above as it is sprouting) Ethylene is produced.
- Ethylene instigates seedling to perform growth maneuver called Triple Response.
- Triple response allows stem to go around an object above.
- Three parts to it:
  - Slowing of Stem Elongation
  - Thickening of Stem (making it stronger)
  - Curvature that causes stem to start growing horizontally
- When growing horizontally, the stem tip will occasionally poke upward...
  - If it detects a solid object still above, it continues to grow horizontally until it clears it.
  - At that point (when stem tip is clear of an object) the triple response will go away because the plant will stop producing Ethylene and plant grows upright as normal.

Ethylene is what causes the plant to grow sideways, not the force of the rock or object above pushing the stem sideways as it continues to grow up.

Ethylene – Fruit Ripening

- Seed becomes mature when fruit is ripe.
- Boost of Ethylene triggers the ripening.
- Enzymatic breakdown of cell wall components soften fruit, and the conversion of starches and acids to sugars makes fruit sweet.
- Fruits produce new scents and colours so that they are attractive to animals, who eat the fruits and disperse the seeds.
- Ethylene production is a rare positive feed back loop in physiology. Ethylene triggers fruit ripening, and fruit ripening triggers more ethylene production.
- One bad apple does not spoil the lot, we know this because ethylene is a gas and the signal to ripen can spread from ovary to ovary.
- Speed ripening process by putting it in container with boosted ethylene levels.
- Apples are stored in CO_2 to retard the natural ripening process. This makes apples picked in autumn stay fresh until the following summer.
- Genetic engineering involves ethylene because scientists are able to change when different seasonal fruits ripen. Also they have already created ready to ripen fruits such as tomatoes that ripen on demand, just add ethylene.

5. (*d*) El Nino

El Nino and La Nina are triggers for many natural hazards because they produce unusual weather throughout the world. The Earth's oceans and atmosphere are closely connected and hence a change in one produces an immediate or delayed change in the other. El Nino involves the warming of sea surface temperatures in the equatorial Pacific Ocean. This temperature change at the ocean's surface causes the usual positions of the jet streams and pressure cells to shift.

This causes changes in the global weather patterns produces floods, droughts and other hazards, leading to thousands of deaths and property damages. A La Nina event usually occurs the year after the end of an El Nino event and involves abnormal cooling of the same ocean waters. This can also cause changes in atmospheric circulation, thereby altering weather patterns for many locations around the world.

Because El Nino and La Nina produce considerable changes in atmospheric circulation, the effects are noticeable globally. However, certain locations feel the effects of El Nino and La Nina more than others due to a variety of factors. El Nino events usually begin between January and March and peak during the month of December. Not every El Nino event is followed by a La Nina event. When it happens, the effects of La Nina are usually most noticeable between the months of December and January.

5. (*e*) Chlorinated hydrocarbons such as the insecticides DDT, DDD, dieldrin, and methoxychlor, the dielectric fluids known as PCBs, and the chlorinated **dioxin,** TCDD, have a very sparse **solubility** in water. As a result, these chemicals cannot be "diluted" into this ubiquitous solvent, which is so abundant on the surface of **Earth** and in organisms. Therefore, even situations considered to be highly contaminated by chlorinated hydrocarbons have very small concentrations of these chemicals in water, typically less than 1 ppb, and in the case of the dioxin TCDD smaller than 1 ppt (*i.e.,* 0.001 ppb). However, chlorinated hydrocarbons are highly soluble in lipids. Because most lipids within ecosystems occur in biological tissues, the chlorinated hydrocarbons have a strong affinity for living organisms, and they tend to biomagnify by many orders of magnitude from vanishingly small aqueous concentrations. Furthermore, because chlorinated hydrocarbons are persistent in the environment, they accumulate progressively as organisms grow older, and they accumulate into especially large concentrations in top predators, as described previously.

In some cases, older individuals of top-predator animals such as raptorial birds and fish-eating marine mammals have been found to have thousands of ppm of DDT and PCBs in their fatty tissues. The toxicity caused by these animals accumulated exposures to DDT, PCBs, and other chlorinated hydrocarbons is a well-recognized environmental problem.

The biomagnification and food-web accumulation characteristics of DDT are especially well known. Typically, DDT has extremely small concentrations in air and water, and, to a lesser degree in soil. However, concentrations are much larger in organisms, especially in animals at or near the top of their food web, such as humans and predatory birds. The food-web biomagnification of DDT can be illustrated by the case of Lake Kariba, Zimbabwe. Although banned in most industrialized countries since the early 1970s, DDT is still used in many tropical countries for agriculture purposes and to control insect vectors of human diseases. The use of DDT in agriculture was banned in Zimbabwe in 1982, but DDT continues to be used to control mosquitoes and tsetse flies, insects that spread malaria and diseases of livestock. The concentration of DDT in the water of Lake Kariba was less than 0.002 ppb, but concentrations in sediment were 0.4 ppm (because sediment contains a relatively large concentration of organic matter, it contains much more DDT than the overlying water). Planktonic algae contained 2.5 ppm. A filter-feeding mussel had 10 ppm, while two species of plant-eating fish contained 2 ppm, and a bottom-feeding fish contained 6 ppm. A predatory fish and a fish-eating bird, the great cormorant, contained 5-10 ppm. The Nile crocodile is the top predator in Lake Kariba (other than humans), and it had 34 ppm. Therefore, the data for Lake Kariba illustrates a substantial biomagnification of DDT from water, and to a lesser degree from sediment, as well as a marked food-web accumulation from herbivores to top carnivores.

In some species, effects on predatory birds were severe enough to cause large declines in abundance beginning in the early 1950s, and resulting in local or regional losses of populations. Prominent examples of North American birds that suffered population decreases because of exposure to chlorinated hydrocarbons include bald eagle, golden eagle, **peregrine** falcon, osprey, brown pelican, and double-crested cormorant, among others. However, since the banning of the use of DDT in North America in the early 1970s, these birds have increased in abundance. In the case of the peregrine falcon, this increase was enhanced by a captive-breeding and release program over much of its former range in eastern North America.

7. (*a*) Maximizing Seed Production Through Flowering Date

Daylength provides plants with a consistent environmental variable for controlling date of flowering. At a given latitude, photoperiodism ensures that plants will flower near the same day of year every year. It is not surprising that day length-controlled mechanisms have evolved for maximizing seed production and quality to aid survival of plant species. Such consistency in flowering date is important in temperate regions and tropical regions for two different survival strategies. In a temperate climate, seed production must be completed before immature embryos or seeds are killed by autumn frosts. Conversely, premature senescence results in low seed production and also may result in deterioration of seed exposed to long periods of warm moist conditions. Thus, species have survived which optimize their seed production depending on when they emerged as seedlings.

Planting date studies demonstrate this optimization of flowering date very well. Plantings at various dates will often flower on the same or nearly the same date. While low temperatures during early development contribute to the delay in flowering for early plantings in temperate regions, photoperiodism is also important. Floral initiation of long-day plants is delayed until the daylength is sufficiently long.

In order to understand the importance of the sensitivity of short-day plants to daylength, one must look at their regions of origin. Sorghum and maize, both short-day plants, are of tropical origin. Their sensitivity is important for inducing flowering during the most productive season relative to rain, as discussed previously. Breeding programs for producing maize and sorghum cultivars for temperate regions have included reduction or elimination of photoperiod sensitivity. In more northern environments, reduced photoperiod sensitivity, along with reduction of the basic vegetative phase, has provided hybrids that mature in very short growing seasons.

Thus, one concludes that daylength effects play an important role in determining the region of adaptation. However, during the growth cycle, daylength effects are less important than temperature effects.

Photoreceptor proteins are light-sensitive proteins involved in the sensing and response to light in a variety of organisms. Some examples are rhodopsin in the photoreceptor cells of the vertebrate retina, phytochrome in plants, and bacteriorhodopsin and bacteriophytochromes in some bacteria. They mediate light responses as varied as visual perception, phototropism and phototaxis, as well as responses to light-dark cycles such as circadian rhythm and other photoperiodisms including control of flowering times in plants and mating seasons in animals.

Structure

Photoreceptor proteins typically consist of a protein moiety and a non-protein photopigment that reacts to light via photoisomerization or photoreduction, thus initiating a change of the receptor protein which triggers a signal transduction cascade. Pigments found in photoreceptors include retinal (retinylidene proteins, for example *rhodopsin* in animals), *flavin* (*flavoproteins*, for example cryptochrome in plants and animals) and *bilin* (*biliproteins*, for example *phytochrome* in plants).

7. (*b*) **Carrier proteins** are integral/intrinsic membrane proteins; that is they exist within and span the membrane across which they transport substances. The proteins may assist in the movement of substances by facilitated diffusion or active transport.

Plant roots are in contact with soil clay particulates which have colloidal dimensions, Root cells which are living, secrets hydrogen ions which are positively charged. Such ions can easily displace cations like K^+, Na^+ ions that are bound to clay particulates. Thus the cations are made available for the root system to absorb the required ion. But the relative retentive capacity of the clay particles, though not absolutely fixed, is in the order of $H^+ > Ca_2^+ > Ng_2^+ > K^+ > NH_4^+ > Na^+$. But hydrogen ions are capable of replacing any cation found on the clay particles. Nonetheless it appears that hydrogen ions can replace any bound ions to clay particles but there is a preference of ions to be released. As hydrogen ions have greater affinity, they can replace any of the above ions easily.

Both cations and anions have a tendency to get adsorbed on the surfaces of the cell walls, and exchange with ions present in the soil solution. This process of exchange between the adsorbed ions and ions in solution is known as ion exchange.

Negatively charged Cl^- and Br^- are exchanged without disturbing the electrical neutrality; this theory describes the effect of fixed or non-diffusible ions which mostly accumulate on the inner surface of the outer membrane. Process is named after its discoverer F.G. Donnan. If there is a negative non-diffusing charge on one side of a membrane, it will create a potential gradient across the membrane from which ions will diffuse. The result will be an electrochemical equilibrium. The concentration (chemical potential) of ions will not necessarily be the same inside and outside. Thus, as an electrical disequilibrium is maintained because of diffusing charges thus concentration disequilibrium is established.

$$\frac{\text{Positive ions inside}}{\text{Positive ions outside}} = \frac{\text{Negative ions outside}}{\text{Negative ions inside}}$$

Therefore, according to Donnan, Donnan equilibrium is attained if the product of anions and cations in the internal solution becomes equal to the product of anions and cations in the external solution.

8. (*a*) Joint Forest Management (JFM) has become almost synonymous with forest and natural resource management these days. Any approach or strategy for the protection, conservation and development of forest resources and forest ecosystem involves the participation of local people in the entire management process. However, the JFM methodology currently being applied all round the globe is not generating much confidence. Experiences in many places in India have emphasised the need to have a fresh look at the whole approach. It has been

noted that if a village is approached with an entry point activity and an investment package in the name of JFM, people start losing interest in the whole process once that input package is over. This ultimately reflects on the sustainability of the entire programme. If the villagers are themselves not ready for a change then sustainability of any rural development programme or poverty alleviation programme cannot be ensured only by pumping in fluid in the name of development projects or schemes, etc. If people are to develop a genuine interest in the whole development process, the initiative should come from within the village itself. The expectations of the villagers should be kept low. At the same time, they should be encouraged to take decisions themselves for the improvement of the entire village. Also, conscious efforts should be made to introduce accountability as well as transparency in the whole system at each stage. A "village bank" consisting of willing villages should be set up in different areas and the concept of voluntary labour (shramdan) should be given top priority during the entire selection and prioritization process. Such a fresh approach would pave the way for sustainable forest management; which is a must for improving living standards.

Joint Forest Management (JFM) has become the keyword in the present management of forestry sector. People's participation in overall protection of forest has become *sine qua non.* JFM has been recognized as an important tool, nay, strategy for ensuring sustainable development of forest ecosystem. However, a close scrutiny of the progress of JFM activities in India does indicate non-attainment of desired success in this field. Notwithstanding the fact that around 15% of the total forest area of the country has been brought under JFM yet the overall dent of this strategy has not been up to desired level and, this has necessitated to have a fresh look into the whole concept of JPIVL.

Achievements of JFM Cell

The main task of the cell is to effectively monitor the impact of the JFM programme being implemented by various State Governments on protection and development of forests. It has been a handicap to get true and reliable data on JFM programme. Most of the work on the subject, was being done by different agencies to publish case studies to highlight the success stories without having a systematic approach to study the programme. The JFM Cell in a short period of time since its inception has made numerous achievements. The main achievements are as under.

1. **Review of JFM programme:** At the initiative of JFM Cell, a Standing Committee on Joint Forest Management was constituted. The Committee has submitted its interim recommendations to the Government on the issues of
   (*i*) Implementation of microplans in JFM areas
   (*ii*) Extension of JFM on good forest area
   (*iii*) Participation of women in JFM programme.

   These recommendations have been accepted by the Government.
2. **Coordination with State Governments:** To fill the communication gap between Ministry of Environment and Forests, Government of India and various state forest departments and for better coordination and sound policy decisions, the State Governments were asked to appoint JFM Nodal Officers in their states. So far 11 states have appointed JFM Nodal Officers in their states at the initiative of the JFM Cell.
3. **Data Collection:** For the success of any programme and to steer it on the right track, foremost requirement is availability of correct data. The cell took up the issue with various State Governments and has collected and compiled information about the extent of JFM programme in various states of the country.

8. (*b*) Toxic metal pollution of waters and soils is a major environmental problem, and most conventional remediation approaches do not provide acceptable solutions. The use of specially selected and engineered metal-accumulating plants for environmental clean-up is an emerging technology called phytoremediation. Three subsets of this technology are applicable to toxic metal remediation: (1) Phytoextraction–the use of metal-accumulating plants to remove toxic metals from soil; (2) Rhizofiltration–the use of plant roots to remove toxic metals from polluted waters; and (3) Phytostabilization–the use of plants to eliminate the bioavailability of toxic metals in soils. Biological mechanisms of toxic metal uptake, translocation and resistance as well as strategies for improving phytoremediation are also discussed.

Phytoremediation of toxic metals

Soils may become polluted with high concentration of toxic metals and their remediation may often involve excavation and removal of soil to secured landfills, an expensive technology that requires site restoration. Moreover, besides being an expensive and labour intensive effort, cleaning up contaminated sites has been accompanied by secondary environmental and legal problems. The phytoremediation of heavy metal contaminated soil basically involves the extraction or inactivation of these metals in soils. However, some metals such as Pb are largely immobile in soil and their extraction rate is limited by solubility and diffusion to the root surface. Conventional technologies suitable for water and soil remediation used *in situ* and *ex situ* are: pneumatic fracturing, soil flushing, solidification/stabilization, vitrification, chemical reduction/oxidation, soil washing and excavation. All these methods are cost prohibitive and often can generate secondary waste. The use of several chelating agents, such as EDTA (ethylenediaminetetraacetic acid), EGTA (ethylene glycol-O,O'-bis-[2-amino-ethyl]-N,N,N',N',-tetraacetic acid), EDDHA (ethylenediamine di(o-hyroxy-phenylacetic acid) and citric acid, has been developed to chemically enhance phyto-extraction by mobilizing metals and increasing metal accumulation. However, there is a potential risk of leaching of metals to the ground water and there is still a lack of detailed studies regarding the persistence of metal-chelating agent complexes in contaminated soils.

It is also known that some metal contaminated soils are difficult to remediate and such soils are usually excavated and land filled. Sites can also be treated by acid leaching, physical separation of the contaminant or electro-chemical processes. Moreover, the costs associated with soil remediation are variable and depend on the properties of the soil, the contaminants, site conditions and the volume of material to be remediated. Considering these limitations, phytoremediation is one innovative approach that offers more environmental benefits and a cost effective alternative.

In phytoextraction and phytomining, accumulated toxic metals in plant tissues are harvested for metal recovery and reuse. Normally, the plants termed hyperaccumulators are preferably used, since they have the ability to withstand and build up high concentrations of metals, when compared to other plants. These plants can be processed to recover the metals accumulated during the phytoremediation process. Although it is cheaper than the conventional methods, phytoremediation is not an easy technology that consists of simply planting and growing some hyperaccumulating plants in the metal polluted area. It is in fact a highly technical strategy, requiring expert project designers with field experience that choose the proper species and cultivars for particular metals and regions. Research carried out with hyper-accumulator plant species has mainly focused attention on the physiological mechanisms by which the metal is taken up, transported and sequestrated, but little is know regarding the genetic basis of hyperaccumulation when compared with the genetic basis of metal tolerance. There is evidence for a quantitative genetic variation controlling the ability of these plants to hyperaccumulate between and within populations.

Table. *Advantages and limitations of some of the sub-processes of phytoremediation.*

Advantage	Limitation
Phytoextraction	
The plant must be able to produce abundant biomass in short time. E.g. in green house experiments, gold was harvested from plants.	Metal hyperaccumulators are generally slow-growing and bio-productivity is rather small and shallow rcot systems. Phytomass after process must be disposed off property.
Phytostabilization	
It circumvents the removal of soil, low cost and is less disruptive and enhances ecosystem restoration/re-vegetation.	Often requires extensive fertilization or soil modification using amendments, long-term maintenance is needed to prevent leaching.
Phytovolatilization	
Contaminant Pollutant will be transformed in to less-toxic forms. E.g. elemental mercury and dimethyl selenite gas. Atmospheric processes such as photochemical degradation for rapid decontamination/transformation.	The contaminant or a hazardous metabolite might accumulate in vegatation and be passed on in later products such as fruit or lumber. Low levels of metabolites have been found in plant tissue.
Phytofiltration/rhizofiltration	
It can be either in situ (floating rafts on ponds) or *ex situ* (an engineered tank system); terrestrial or aquatic.	pH of the medium to be monitored continually for optimizing uptake of metals; chemical speciation and interactions of all species in the influent need be understood; functions like a bioreactor and intensive maintenance is needed.

Previous Years' Paper (Solved)

IFS Botany Main Examination, 2014

PAPER-I

INSTRUCTIONS: *There are EIGHT questions in all, out of which FIVE are to be attempted. Questions no. 1 & 5 are compulsory. Out of the remaining SIX questions, THREE are to be attempted selecting at least ONE question from each of the two Sections A and B. Attempts of questions shall be counted in chronological order. Unless struck off, attempt of a question shall be counted even if attempted partly. Any page or portion of the page left blank in the Question-cum-Answer Booklet must be clearly struck off. All questions carry equal marks. The number of marks carried by a question/ part is indicated against it. Answer must be written in ENGLISH only. Neat sketches may be drawn, wherever required.*

SECTION—A

1. *Answer the following keeping your answers brief and to the point:* 5 × 8 = 40

(*a*) What are the pigments that are found in red algae?

(*b*) What are the different types of flagella found in fungi?

(*c*) How significant is the parasexuality in *Aspergillus*?

(*d*) Comment on the structure, location and function of transfusion tissue.

(*e*) Comment on the contractile vacuoles in *Euglena*.

(*f*) What is the heterotrichous habit of moss protonema growth?

(*g*) What are the xerophytic and hydrophytic characters found in the rhizome anatomy of *Equisetum?*

(*h*) Differentiate between prokaryote and eukaryote.

2. (*a*) Explain the molecular basis of plant-pathogen interaction. 10

(*b*) Explain variations in male reproductive structures in liverworts. 10

(*c*) Briefly discuss the phylogeny of algae. 10

(*d*) Write notes on the distribution of bryophytes and pteridophytes in deciduous and evergreen forests of India. 10

3. (*a*) What is meant by modelling and how does it help in disease forecasting? 10

(*b*) Giving suitable reasons, discuss inter-alia evolutionary status of *Psilotum, Selaginella* and *Marsilea.* 15

(*c*) Discuss the role of amphibious plants in the evolution of land plants. 15

4. (*a*) Explain to what extent has the technique of micropropagation been successful in achieving our goals. 15

(*b*) Citing suitable examples, explain how laxity in quarantine procedure can have disastrous effects. 15

(*c*) Write a brief note on the advantages of diploid carposporophyte generation in red algae. 10

SECTION—B

5. *Answer the following keeping your answers brief and to the point:* 5 × 8 = 40

(*a*) Differentiate between megasporogenesis and megagametogenesis.

(*b*) Differentiate between Palaeozoic and Coenozoic plants.

(*c*) Differentiate between Isotype and Syntype.

(*d*) Comment on the stratification of pollen grain walls.

(e) Why are gymnosperms called naked-seeded plants?

(f) Comment on *Plumbago* type of embryo sac development.

(g) What are the angiospermic features of *Gnetum?*

(h) What are the unique features of Brassicaceae?

6. Draw scientifically accurate diagrams of the following and label the parts: 10 × 4 = 40

(a) Floral formula and floral diagram of Ranunculaceae and Rosaceae

(b) L.S. of capsule of *Funaria*

(c) Anatomy of *Pinus* needle

(d) Stages depicting the formation of vegetative and generative cells during male gametophyte development in angiosperms

7. (a) "Ethnobotany provides important clues to the discovery of modern drugs." Justify the statement giving suitable examples. 15

(b) "*Gnetum* is a link between seed plants and seedless plants." Justify the statement. 10

(c) Differentiate between normal and abnormal secondary growth in dicot stem. Discuss with diagrams wherever necessary. 15

8. (a) Compare Bentham and Hooker's system of classification with the system of classification of Hutchinson. 15

(b) Give a concise account of Cordaitales and justify why they form an important group. 10

(c) Write the botanical name, family, active constituents and uses of any five medicinal plants of commercial importance in India. 15

PAPER-II

INSTRUCTIONS: *There are EIGHT questions in all, out of which FIVE are to be attempted. Question No. 1 & 5 are compulsory. Out of the remaining SIX questions, THREE are to be attempted selecting at least ONE question from each of the two Sections A and B. Attempts of questions shall be counted in chronological order. Unless struck off, attempt of a question shall be counted even if attempted partly. Any page or portion of the page left blank in the answer book must be clearly struck off. All questions carry equal marks. The number of marks carried by a question/part is indicated against it. Answer must be written in ENGLISH only. Neat sketches may be drawn, wherever required.*

SECTION—A

1. Explain the following in about 150 words each:

(a) Basic chromosome number may be different from haploid number. 8

(b) Can an accessory chromosome become an essential chromosome? 8

(c) Ribosomes are synthesized. 8

(d) Presence of factors for all the seven characters studied by Mendel on a single chromosome would have affected Mendel's work? 8

(e) ISH has helped in better understanding of cell bilogy. 8

2. (a) How is a tertiary trisomic identified? Draw and describe various disjunctional possibilities of the chromosome associations formed during meiosis in a tertiary trisomic. 5 + 20

(b) Which the help of a well established example explain transversions. 15

3. (a) What is achieved through back cross breeding? Describe the procedure and explain what will happen if the original parents are not pure lines? 5 + 15

(b) Describe stepwise how goodness of fit is established for an assumption? 20

4. (a) What is accounted for by Lyon's hypothesis? Cite an example. 5 + 5 (*b*) What is tripartite type of sex determination? Justify your answer with suitable example. 10

(*c*) With the help of U's triangle explain the role of amphiploids in evolution of crop plants. 20

SECTION—B

5. Write brief notes on the following in about 150 words each: $8 \times 5 = 40$

(*a*) Endemism

(*b*) NOD genes

(*c*) Eutrophication

(*d*) Fermentation

(*e*) Allelopathy

6. (*a*) Describe the adverse anthropogenic effects on terrestrial ecosystems. How can these be mitigated? 15 + 5

(*b*) Explain various physiological processes that help in fruit ripening. How can this knowledge help overcome problems likely to be faced because of climate change? 15 + 5

7. (*a*) Describe various structural and chemical defence mechanisms developed by plants. 20

(*b*) Describe the process explained by chemiosmotic theory. 20

8. (*a*) Describe bottom up regulation of plant respiration. 20

(*b*) Describe the differences and importance of afforestation, reforestation and social forestry. 20

ANSWERS

PAPER-I

1. (*a*) Red algaes are, not surprisingly, red, reddish or purplish in colour. There are about 6,000 species of red algae, and they are protists in the phylum Rhodophyta. Red algae species range from simple one-celled organisms to complex, multi-celled, plant-like organisms. Red algae get their energy from photosynthesis. One thing that distinguishes red algae from other algae is that their cells lack flagella.

Red algae contains a variety of pigments, including cholorophyll a, phycobiliproteins, red phycoerythrin, blue phycocyanin, carotenes, lutein, and zeaxanthin. The most important pigment is phycoerythrin, which provides the algae's red pigmentation by reflecting red light and absorbing blue light. Red algae with little of this pigment may appear more green or blue than red due to the other pigments in this algae.

Because red algae contains pigments that absorb blue light waves, it can be found deeper in the ocean than some other algaes.

(*b*) Flagellated fungi include several divisions that are *not* closely related and is used here only as a matter of convenience. Also, while these divisions do have flagellated stages, they are not necessarily restricted to an aquatic environment. Many species, including the well-known Phytophthorainfestans, which causes the Late Blight of Potato, have become adapted to the terrestrial environment.

Flagellated fungi reproduce *asexually* by means of flagellated spores called **zoospores** that are produced in **zoosporangia**. These divisions were once regarded as the most primitive fungi because of their aquatic habitat, when mycelium is produced, it is usually **coenocytic** (nonseptate), **asexual** spores are produced in a sporangium, and they lack a complex spore producing body **(=sporocarp)**.

The two types of flagella are whiplash and tinsel type flagella. The whiplash flagellum is unbranched with an acute bend at the end. As flagellar movement propels the cell, the bent end whips back and forth. Thus, the name whiplash. The tinsel type is branched with many **mastigonemes,** along its axis and resembles the tinsels of an aluminum christmas tree.

(*c*) The parasexual cycle with parameiosis has been characterized by the occurrence of genetic recombination and haploidization inside heterokaryotic hyphae prior to conidial formation. The characteristics of this, through genetic and cytological analyses, an asexual development mutant strain of *A. nidulans* and to use it to obtain parameiotic segregants. Analyses showed the medusa phenotype of the B84 strain, whose mutant allele was mapped in the chromosome I. The heterokaryons B84(med) //G422(med+) and B84(med)//G839(brl) were formed in liquid MM+2% CM and inoculated in the appropriate selective media. Two mitotic segregant groups were obtained: aneuploids and haploid stable recombinants. Mitotic segregants, wild-types, and developmental mutants, which did not produce new visible mitotic sectors in the presence of Benomyl and which showed normal meiotic behaviour during the sexual cycle, were classified as parameiotics.

(*d*)

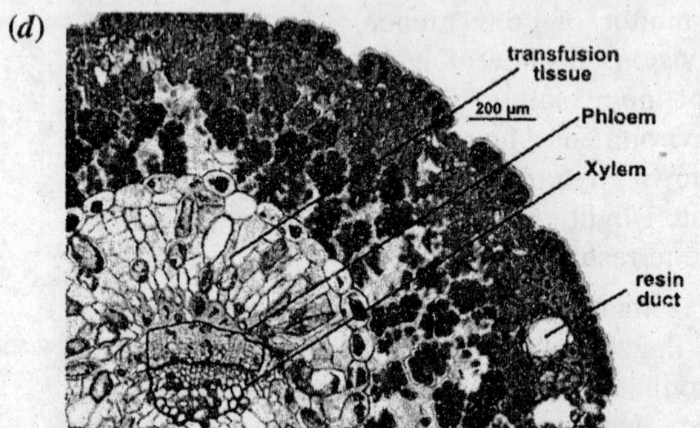

Transfusion tissue: A peculiar type of conducting tissue, which consists largely of short tracheids with thin, cellulose walls and boradered pits or reticulate or scalariform thickening, often accompanies typical vascular tissue in the leaves of the gymnosperms. These cells are trached-like in the character of their pitting and in the absence of a protoplast but otherwise suggest elongate parenchyma cells. They lie adjacent to typical xylem at the sides of the bundle and may partly or even completely surround it. Since these cells seem to serve as conducting tissue, connecting the veins and the mesophyll of the leaves, taking the place of the usual very small branches of the veins, they form together what is called *transfusion tissue.* Though, the function of this tissue is still uncertain, it undoubtedly represents modified vascular tissue.

Arrangements of Tissue: All the tissues of a plant which perform the same general function, regardless of position or continuity in the body, may be considered to form, together, a *tissue system.* In this sense, the term is wholly a physiological one. There are found in physiologically treatments of anatomy such tissue systems as the "mechanical system", the absorbing system," and the "storage system." The vaious parts of most of such systems, however, are bound together only by function; they have little or no structural or morphological unity. Continuity and similarity of nature or of origin may be lacking. From a morphological viewpoint the grouping of tissues into tissue systems is sometimes convenient.

In the morphological sense, a tissue system must be a complex of cells extending continuously throughout the plant body or over a considerable portion thereof. It may be so simple as to consist of only one type of cell or one type of tissue or may consist of two or more types of tissues. Very few systems in any was structurally distinct can be distinguished. The epidermal system has sometimes included a hypodermis and other cortical tissues—even periderm; the fundamental system, the cortex, pericycle, and pith. Recognition of these systems has value in a strictly topographical sense and is especially useful in the interpretation of meristematic tissues.

In young organs, the epidermal system consists of the dermatogen (or protoderm) alone; the vascular system consists of the procambium and the earliest formed xylem and phloem elements; the fundamental system consists of ground meristem—all the remaining tissues, which at this stage show little or no differentiation. In the mature primary body these form, respectively, the epidermis, the vascular tissues, and the cortex, pericycle, pith, and mesophyll. The epidermis and vascular system are tissue systems of such uniformity and continuity of structure and of such constancy of function that they constitute important gross structural features of the plant body. The terms "epidermal system"—if used to cover epidermis only— and "vascular system" are convenient and valuable. "Ground tissues system" covers the heterogeneous remaining parts.

(*e*) A contractile vacuole (CV) is a sub-cellular structure involved in osmoregulation. It is found predominantly in protists and in unicellular algae. It was previously known as pulsatile or pulsating vacuole. Euglena are unicellular organisms classified into the Kingdom Protista, and the Phylum Euglenophyta. All euglena have chloroplasts and can make their own food by photosynthesis. They are not completely autotrophic though, euglena can also absorb food from their environment; euglena usually live in quiet ponds or puddles.

The interior or the cell contains a jelly-like fluid substance called cytoplasm. **Colour the cytoplasm light yellow**. Toward the posterior of the cell is a star-like structure: the contractile vacuole. This organelle helps the cell remove excess water, and without it the euglena could take in some much water due to osmosis that the cell would explode. **Colour the contractile vacuole is orange.**

(*f*) **Growth of Protonema:** It has been known since the early work of Klebs that growth and development of moss protonema is greatly influenced by light level. The significance of different spectral regions of light was recognized by Listowski and Stephan. Pringsheim and Pringsheim observed that in *Funaria* protonemal growth is fairly good in blue light, but in green light the protonema has sparingly branched, pale-green filaments which closely resemble those produced in dark. In *Pohlia nutans* blue and red light have promotory effect on protonemal growth, whereas green light is inhibitory In blue light branching is more profuse than in red light, but in both treatments protonema shows heterotrichous habit. In red light, prominent nutation patterns are observed both in the prostrate and erect filaments. Protonema is very attenuated and yellowish-green as a result of scanty development in green light, and there is no indication of heterotrichous habit. Far-red light has no effect on protonemal growth in *Pohlia nutans.* According to Mitra blue light with red light produces greater protonemal growth than red light alone.

Nebel observed that in *Physcomitrium turbinatum* the growth rate of lateral branches of chloronema is controlled by the quality of light. Growth is maximum in red light and minimum in far-red. According to him, growth and orientation in this species is dependent upon an interaction between the photosynthetic and the phytochrome systems. The physiological activity of phytochrome in photo-orientation of growth does not result from a certain amount of P_{fr} or P_{fr}/P_r ration but rather from the simultaneous excitation and consequent cycling of P_r and P_{fr}. By using polarized red and far-red light, Nebel concluded that the active photoreceptors are dichroic and are coin- or disc-shaped. Synergistic interaction between red and far-red irradiations supports the hypothesis that the photoreceptor is phytochrome and that the growth response is proportional to the total quanta absorbed by the pigment and/or the consequent cycling of the phytochrome between P_r and P_{fr}.

Blue light favours branching and promotes growth of protonema in *Anoectangium thomsonii.* In red light, the protonema is pale-green and sparse. Red light induces the development of lateral outgrowths and additional growth primordia, thereby increasing the amount of cytoplasmic RNA in apical chloronemal cells of *Funaria hygrometrica.* The light spectrum region in which maximum apical cell branching is noticed corresponds to the action spectrum of the phytochrome reaction. Treatment with far-red immediately after red light reduced the promotory effect to the latter. This indicates that phytochrome system is also involved in the induced morphological effect. Red light also causes an increase in the volume of nuclei and nucleoli. Effect of red light on the early stages of the moss ontogeny proved to be associated with its ability to activate RNA and probably protein synthesis as well. Red light stimulates growth and ramification of protonema of *Ceratodon purpureus.* Cove et al. reported that protonemal growth in *Physcomitrella patens* is promoted by red light, and this effect is reversible by far-red, suggesting the phytochrome-mediated control of protonemal growth. In *Didymodon recurvus* red light was more effective than blue light in promoting protonemal growth.

(*g*) The anatomical features of *Equisetum* show both xerophytic and hydrophytic characters. The xerophytic characters of the plant are:

1. Presence of thick coat of cuticle all over the epidermal layer of stem.
2. Photosynthetic stem having chlorenchymatous cortex.
3. Stem behaving as leaves.
4. Presence of small, scale like leaves with limited number of chloroplast.
5. Presence of sunken stomata in groove of stem.
6. Stiff Epidermis and presence of ridges and furrows.
7. Deep seated rhizome.

(*h*) Comparison between Prokaryotic and Eukaryotic Cells

Characteristic	Prokaryotes	Eukaryotes
Size of cell	Typically 0.2-2.0 μm in diameter	Typically 10-100 μm in diameter
Ilucleus	No nuclear membrane or nucleoli (nucleoid)	True nucleus, consisting of nuclear membrane & nucleoli
Membrane-enclosed organelles	Absent	Present; examples include lysosomes, Golgi complex, endoplasmic reticulum, mitochondria & chloroplasts
Flagella	Consist of two protein building blocks	Complex; consist of multiple microtubules
Glycocalyx	Present as a capsule or slime layer	Present in some cells that lack a cell wall
Cell wall	Usually present; chemically complex (typical bacterial cell wall includes peptidoglycan)	When present, chemically simple
Plasma membrane	No carbohydrates and generally lacks sterols	Sterols and carbohydrates that serve as receptors present
Cytoplasm	No cytoskeleton or cytoplasmic streaming	Cytoskeleton; cytoplasmic streaming
Ribosomes	Smaller size (70S)	Larger size (80S); smaller size (70S) in organelles
Chromosome (DNA) arrangement	Single circular chromosome; lacks histones	Multiple linear chromosomes with histones
Cell division	Binary fission	Mitosis
Sexual reproduction	No meiosis; transfer of DNA fragments only (conjugation)	Involves meiosis

2. (*a*) **Molecular Bases of Plant-Pathogen Interactions:** The existence of susceptible and resistant cultivars implies specificity in plant diseases. One explanation for this high specificity is a "recognition" mechanism between pathogen and host. Understanding the molecular bases that determine his specificity in recognition or in the pathogen's ability to alter the host's metabolism should yield new, definitive, and more efficient ways to prevent attacks on crop plants or to mitigate disease symptoms.

Molecular Determinants of Resistance and Susceptibility: It is widely held that some forms of resistance to fungal and bacterial pathogens are the result of a host plant's ability to synthesize chemicals that inhibit the growth and development of the pathogen. During infection by a pathogen, metabolic pathways in the plant are activated, leading to the detectable biosynthesis of the inhibitors. A major class of inhibitors, called phytoalexins, are primarily low-molecular-weight, secondary plant metabolites that possess wide-ranging activity against fungi and, to a lesser extent, bacteria. In the last two decades, more than 100 phytoalexins have been identified. The induction of the biosynthesis of phytoalexins, however, does not follow the specificity that most pathogens have for a specific cultivar. For example, phytoalexin synthesis can be induced by abiotic agents, such as wounding or other stress conditions, in both resistant and susceptible plants. Phytoalexins can be toxic to both virulent and avirulent pathogens. It appears that phytoalexin synthesis might be a general, nonspecific type of active resistance.

An alternate approach, the study of susceptibility, has revealed mechanisms that show a high degree of specificity. Many pathogens possess specific agents for virulence, such as toxins or enzymes, that determine the course of events in susceptible plants. In the last five years, six host-specific or host-selective toxins have been chemically characterized. These toxins affect only susceptible cultivars and are produced only by specific pathogens that can attack these same susceptible cultivars. One well-studied example is the toxin produced by the fungus Helminthosporium maydis, mentioned earlier. The H. maydis toxin disrupts energy generation in susceptible mitochondria that characterize the T cytoplasm of corn. Normal mitochondria are resistant and are unaffected by the toxin because they apparently lack a receptor site for it.

Genetic specificity also exists for resistance and susceptibility to plant viruses, but there is no information on how such genes act. With respect to plant viruses the term resistance is used rather loosely. Quite often only the appearance of disease symptoms is considered. Thus, a plant that supports virus replication but shows no symptoms is considered to be resistant because it superficially appears to be so. More correctly, that plant should be called tolerant.

Recent observations suggest that one type of resistance may involve the ability of viruses to spread from cell to cell in their hosts. The continuum of responses ranges from rapid and complete invasion of the whole plant by the virus to slow invasion to circumstances where the virus is unable to spread from an infected cell, even though it might replicate well there. Accumulating evidence indicates that viruses induce the synthesis of proteins that are necessary for the movement of viruses from cell to cell. The host, however, depending on its genotype, can in some way interfere with this protein. Although the process is poorly understood, it may be, in part, the basis of resistance of plants to viruses.

In a sense, viruses might be thought of as packages of genes; they are composed primarily of RNA or DNA, and they can replicate only in a favourable host cell environment. Studies of the interaction between vital RNA or DNA and genes in the host cell can lead not only to an understanding of how viruses function but also to the development of viruses as gene-carrying vectors for genetic engineering.

An improved understanding of the basic concepts controlling resistance and susceptibility will result from research based on interrelated approaches to the analysis of the genetics of these traits, the gene products, the structure of the genes, and the methods that will permit their transfer between organisms.

Additional basic information is needed about the cellular interactions between host and pathogen during the onset of resistance reactions. For example, the precise mechanisms employed by phytoalexins to exert their effects on pathogens are unknown and need to be actively studied. Metabolic pathways for the biosynthesis of phytoalexins must be clarified, and other compounds associated with resistance need to be identified. The regulation and coordinated synthesis or the enzymes involved in these pathways must be detailed.

In addition, the phenomenon of acquired resistance in plants needs further study. Resistance can be localized or can occur throughout the plant. Systemic resistance, however, may be of more practical value. This phenomenon can appear after a host plant is inoculated with an avirulent strain of the bacterial, fungal, or vital pathogen. This exposure somehow induces resistance properties so that when the plant is subsequently challenged by one or more pathogenic strains, it will resist infection or exhibit only mild disease sysmptoms.

Acquired resistance is most actively being studied using Pseudomonas solanacearum, some strains of which cause wilt and stem rot in tobacco, ginger, potato, tomato, and banana. Other avirulent strains only induce resistance. The experimental approach is to find mutants of the avirulent strains that fail to induce the acquired resistance. A comparison of the gene libraries of the active with the inactive mutants could lead to the identification of the genes and gene products responsible for triggering the acquired resistance.

(*b*) The gametophytes of nonvascular plants have distinct male or female reproductive organs (see Figure below). Male reproductive organs, called antheridia, produce motile sperm with two flagella. Female reproductive organs, called archegonia produce eggs.

Antheridium (plural antheridia): Make sex organ or gametangium, within which male gametes (spermatozoids) are formed in algae, fungi, bryophytes, and ferns. In bryophytes, it is a multicellular globose to broadly cylindric, stalked structure.

Nonvascular plants include mosses, liverworts, and hornworts. They are the only plants with a life cycle in which the gametophyte generation is dominant. Figure below shows the life cycle of moss. The familiar, green, photosynthetic moss plants are gametophytes. The sporophyte generation is very small and dependent on the gametophyte plant.

Fig.: *The reproductive organs of bryophytes like this liverwort are male antheridia and female archegonia.*

In order for fertilization to occur, sperm must swim in a drop of water from an antheridium to an egg in an archegonium. If fertilization takes place, it results in a zygote that develops into a tiny sporophyte on the parent gametophyte plant. The sporophyte produces haploid spores, and these develop into the next generation of gametophyte plants. Then the cycle repeats.

(*c*) Phylogeny, the history of the evolution of a species or group, especially in reference to lines of descent and relationships among broad groups of organisms. The path of evolutionary history of the algae comes from diverse evidence, and the photosynthetic pigments contribute to a small but important part of it.

Algal phylogeny and the photosynthetic pigments: The pigments are just one of a number of properties used in building phylogenetic trees: Structure of flagella, chloroplast, cell walls, and mitochondria; methods of reproduction; type of nuclear and cell division; type and location of food reserves; sequence data of nucleic acids and proteins; and extent of immunological cross-reactivity of bili-proteins and pigment-protein complexes can also be used for this purpose.

Value of the three types of pigment in determining phylogeny

Chlorophylls: Chlorophyll *a* is ubiquitous in algae and is of no value in phylogeny. Chlorophyll *b* delimits the small division, Prochlorophyta, in the Prokaryota, and the Chlorophyta in the Eukaryota. After the two forms of chlorophyll *c* were discovered, the original distribution was thought to be chlorophyll c_2 only in the Cryptophyceae and Dinophyceae, and both c_1 and c_2 in the remainder of the Chromophyta. However, we now know that there is no c_1 in some pennate marine diatoms and no c_2 in the new calss, Synurophyceae. If we regard chlorophyll c_2 as primitive and c_1 as derived, we must decide whether the pennate diatoms without c_1 are primitive, or, as seems more likely, the absence of c_1 is a secondary derived state. In the Synurophyceae, absence of c_2 is certainly a derived state. The value of the distribution of chlorophyll c_3 in phylogeny is uncertain.

Carotenoids

Carotenes: With the exception of the Cryptophyta, β-carotene is ubiquitous and thus of little phylogenetic value. The concentration of α-carotene is relatively high in some Chlorophyceae, and its occasional dominance over β-carotene in some taxa could be of value as a derived state.

Xanthophylls: Liaaen-Jensen and Ragan and Chapman have stressed that the biosynthetic pathways of carotenoid synthesis rather than the individual pigments are of phylogenetic value. The important reactions are the synthesis of the triple bond between C-7 and C-8 or C-7′ and C-8′, allene bond formation at C-7 or C-7′, and synthesis of the C-8 carbonyl and C-19 hydroxyl groups.

Biliproteins: The major biliproteins of the Cyanophyceae and Rhodophyceae are essentially similar, and Ouchterlony tests have shown cross-reaction between the similar pigments in the two classes. The biliproteins of the Cryptophyceae, originally believed not to react with the equivalent pigments from the other two classes, are now known to show some reactivity with them.

(*d*) The Western Ghats of India is one of the 34 hot spots of biodiversity in the world and is encompassed amongst eight of the hottest 'Hot Spots' on the earth. The Western Ghats is the major source of water shade due to the southern monsoon filled with water and soaked by the Ghats; hill ranges. The Deccan plateau of Karnataka state is divided into malnad and maidan regions. The Ghats with evergreen and semi-evergreen forests constitute the core of the malnad. Malnad region of Chikmagalur district includes forests and high altitude grasslands governed by Karnataka state forest department. The forests of malnad region are evergreen not only due to monsoon but also due to the mossy effect of a group of green land plants commonly referred as bryophytes.

Over five million hectares of pristine tropical forests are disturbed and transformed into agricultural land each year and the majority of remaining tropical forests undergo frequent disturbance by human activities, such as timber extraction and agriculture. Continues habitat disturbances such as road constructions, road extensions, cuttings of road side trees etc. cause great loss of plant diversity; is myriad. Eventhough, studies of bryophytes are less and neglected compared to other fauna and flora. As bryophytes are substrate specific, their ecological niche is nothing but a world within a world.

Bryophytes are diverse and a distinct group of primitive plants with about 25,000 species distributed over the world, making in the second largest group of land plants and these bryophytes can be further classified into three main classes viz. Liverworts, Hornworts and Mosses. The most important features of the group are how the embryophytes evolved from these lower plants.

Bryophytes grow on a wide range of substrates. They grow on logs, mud walls, tiled roofs which grow closely packed together in mats or cushions on soil, growing as epiphytes on barks of trees, on leaves, on rocks, on stones, on fallen logs, river banks and road sides are common sights.

The knowledge on the taxonomy and distribution of bryophytes are far from adequate and still relies on the work done during the last 20th and early 21st centuries. So far, 2489 taxa of bryophytes recorded from India, comprising 1786 species in 355 genera of mosses, 675 species in 121 genera of liverworts and 25 species in six genera of hornworts. 340 species as endemic of which 269 species are of mosses, 67 are of liverworts and 4 are of hornworts.

5. (*a*) **Megasporogenesis:** In gymnosperms and flowering plants, the megaspore is produced inside the nucellus of the ovule. During megasporogenesis, a diploid precursor cell, the **megasporocyte** or megaspore mother cell, undergoes meiosis to produce initially four haploid cells (**the megaspores**). Angiosperms exhibit three patterns of megasporogenesis: monosporic, bisporic, and tetrasporic, also known as the Polygonum type, the Alisma type, and the Drusa type, respectively. The monosporic pattern occurs most frequently (>70% of angiosperms) and is found in many economically and biologically important groups such as Brassicaceae (e.g., *Arabidopsis*, *Capsella*, *Brassica*), Gramineae (*e.g.*, maize, rice, wheat), Malvaceae (*e.g.*, cotton), Leguminoseae (*e.g.*, beans, soybean), and Solanaceae (*e.g.*, pepper, tobacco, tomato, potato, petunia).

This pattern is characterized by cell plate formation after meiosis 1 & 2, which results in four one-nucleate megaspores, of which three degenerate. The bisporic pattern is characterized by cell plate formation only after meiosis 1, and results in two two-nucleate megaspores, of which one degenerates. The tetrasporic pattern is characterized by cell plates failing to form after either meiosis 1 or 2, and results in one four-nucleate megaspore. Therefore, each pattern gives rise to a single functional megaspore which contains one, two, or four meiotic nuclei, respectively. The megaspore then undergoes megagametogenesis to give rise to the female gametophyte.

Megagametogenesis: After megasporogenesis, the megaspore develops into the female gametophyte (the embryo sac) in a process called megagametogenesis. The process of megagametogenesis varies depending on which pattern of megasporogenesis occurred. Some species, such as *Tridax trilobata*, *Ehretia laevis*, and *Alectra thomsoni*, can undergo different patterns of megasporogenesis and therefore different patterns of megagametogenesis. If the monosporic pattern occurred, the single nucleus undergoes mitosis three times, producing an eight-nucleate cell. These eight nuclei are arranged into two groups of four. These groups both send a nucleus to the center of the cell; become the polar nuclei. Depending on the species, these nuclei fuse together before or upon fertilization of the central cell. The three nuclei at the end of the cell near the micropylar become the egg apparatus, with an egg cell in the center and two synergids. At the other end of the cell, a cell wall forms around the nuclei and forms the antipodals. Therefore, the resulting embryo sac is a seven-celled structure consisting of one central cell, one egg cell, two synergid cells, and three antipodal cells.

The bisporic and tetrasporic patterns undergo varying processes and result in varying embryo sacs as well. In *Lilium* which has a tetrasporic pattern, the central cell of the embryo sac is 4N. Therefore, upon fertilization the endosperm will be 5N rather than the typical 3N.

(*c*) In botanical nomenclature, a *type* (*typus*, *nomenclatural type*), "is that element to which the name of a taxon is permanently attached." In botany a type is either a specimen or an illustration. A specimen is a real plant (or one or more parts of a plant or a lot of small plants), dead and kept safe, "curated", in a herbarium (or the equivalent for fungi). Examples of where an illustration may serve as a type include:

The ICN provides a listing of the various kinds of type, the most important of which is the holotype. These are:

- Holotype
- Lectotype
- Isotype
- Syntype
- Paratype
- Neotype
- Epitype.

"An *isotype* is any duplicate (part of a single gathering made by a collector at one time) of the holotype; it is always a specimen."

For example, if a new species is based on a single gathering (consisting of three specimens and three herbarium sheets made out of them) having the same field. It will designate one among them as a holotype and the remaining two will be isotypes.

"A *syntype* is any or two or more specimens cited by the author when no holotype was designated, or any one of two or more specimens simultaneously designated as types."

(*d*) In general, the stratification of angiosperm pollen grain walls can be understood in terms of the layers defined in Figure. Variations occur in the relative thickness of the various components; for example, there are some grains where the nexine 2 is enormously thick, and there appear to be others in which it is absent. Subdivisions may occur within the various layers to produce aspects that can be of considerable taxonomic significance. Thus, Larson, Skvarla and Lewis and Skvarla and Turner, extending the earlier work of Stix on composite pollen, showed that the foot layer or nexine 1 may be detached in some species from the bases of the bacula, and that the latter may be connected by a second foot layer or *stutzmembran,* separated from the nexine 1 by a *cavus.* Also exemplified in the Compositae is the development of bacula in more than one layer. An 'internal tectum' may be produced below the level of the tectum proper, and this may form a continuous stratum or be present over only part of the surface of the grain. In still more elaborate examples several layers of tecta may be formed, sometimes in such complexity that the numbers cannot be distinguished.

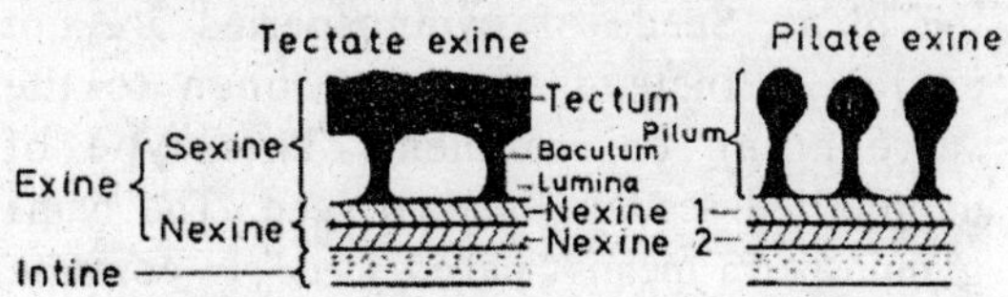

Fig.: *Terminology of pollen wall layers, based upon that of Erdtman.*

Pores and slits form conspicuous features of the pollen wall. These are defined as regions where the full exine stratification is absent or modified, the area of the aperture 'eing covered only by the intine and layers corresponding to the nexine, usually without bacula, or with bacula over only part of the area. Papillae or more distinct elongated processes may arise from the nexine over the aperture region, and not infrequently the central part is found to be thickened somewhat, forming and operculum, lens-shaped in section. In certain pollen grains, as in those of the grasses, the pore region is surrounded by an annulus derived by the thickening of the nexine 2. In other pollen types, the annulus is bordered in turn by a region of modified sexine structure, so that an elaborate 'aperture mechanism' exists.

(*e*) Gymnosperms are one of the two groups of seed plants. The flowering plants (angiosperms), are the other. In going from mosses and ferns to the seed plants, we see a very significant difference in plant life cycles. In mosses and ferns, the propagating units for new individuals are spores. In the seed plants, gymnosperms and angiosperms, the propagating units for new individuals are seeds. Spores are single, haploid cells, and develop into gametophytes. Seeds, in contrast, are complex structures that contain an immature sporophyte, the embryo.

The remainder of this reading is concerned with how a seed is formed. Although seeds of gymnosperms and angiosperms have similarities, this and the reading for angiosperms make several important distinctions between seeds of gymnosperms and angiosperms. A major difference between gymnosperms and angiosperms is how the seeds are attached to the plant. Seeds of gymnosperms are not enclosed; instead, they are open to the surrounding environment. This type of unprotected seed is a **naked seed**. The name gymnosperm means "naked seed." In contrast, seeds of angiosperms are enclosed in a special structure that at maturity is called the fruit.

Gymnosperms are a diverse group of plants, one group of which has cones involved in reproduction. The cone-producers, botanically called **conifers**, are the gymnosperms most commonly seen. Pines, spruces, and firs are conifers. Since you probably are most familiar with pines, we use them for our example of a gymnosperm life cycle.

The **gymnosperms have 'naked seeds'**, i.e. their ovules and seeds (fertilized ovules) are exposed on the surface of sporophylls and analogous structures. The **megagametophyte (female gametophyte, n)** develops from the functional megaspore (n) within the **nucellus (megasporangium, 2n)**. The megagametophyte of the gymnosperms is homologous to the **megaprothallium (n)** of the ferns and is sometimes called primary endosperm (n). The megagametophyte of seed plants is retained and nourished by the parent plant within the ovule. **Ovule** = megagametophyte + megasporangium (nucellus) + integument (seed coat). The megagametophytes of the gymnosperms produce several **archegonia** (n) with egg cells (n). Fertilization by the sperm from the **pollen grain (microgametophyte, male gametophyte, n)** often leads to the development of several **embryos (2n)** within a single ovule. **Polyembryony** of gymnosperm seeds is a known phenomenon. In most cases only one embryo survives and therefore relatively few fully developed gymnosperm seeds contain more than one embryo.

(*f*) The functional megaspore represents the first cell of the female gametophyte. It is mostly chalazal and grows mainly along the micropyle-chalazal axis. As the functional megaspore grows, many small vacuoles appear in its cytoplasm which later join together to form a large vacuole. The nucleus undergoes three mitotic divisions and form eight nuclei.

Types of Embryo Sacs(Female Gametophyte): The following three types of embryo sacs have been recognized on the basis of (i) the number of megaspores taking part in the development of embryo sac. (ii) the number of divisions occurring in the nucleus of the functional megaspore. And (iii) organization of nuclei in the mature embryo sac.

Monosporic
Bisporic
Tetrasporic

Tetrasporic embryo sacs: Sometimes meiotic division of the megaspore mother cell is not accompanied by cytokinesis and hence all the four haploid nuclei lie in a single cell called coeno-megaspore. All the four nuclei of coeno-megaspore participate in the formation of the embryo sac. This type of embryo sac is called as tetrasporic.

Plumbago type: In this type of the four haploid nuclei of the coeno-megaspore one migrates to the micropylar end, one to the chalazal end and two on two lateral sides. Each of these four nuclei divides again, with the result four groups of two nuclei each are formed. One of the nucleus from each group moves to the centre of the cell and these form four polar nuclei.

The remaining nucleus at the micropylar end is cut off by a membrane and forms the egg. There are no synergids. The other three nuclei (i.e. one chalazal and two lateral) usually disappear but occasionally they too may be cut off by membranes and appear as accessory egg cells.

The Plumbago type of embryo sac is thus characterized by the absence of synergids and antipodals.

(*g*) **Resemblances of Gnetum with Angiosperms:** Gnetum resembles angiosperms in many respects; vegetative, anatomical and reproductive features.

1. Gnetun plant appears like an angiospermic dicotyledonous plant with opposite, decussate leaves.
2. The leaves show reticulate venation as in dicotyledonous plant.
3. The presence of vessels in the wood is an angiospermic character, not known in any gymnospermous plant. But the development of vessels in Gnetum is different from that of angiosperms.
4. The shoot apex shows tunica-corpus configuration.
5. Presence of perianth in both the male and female flowers.
6. Tetrasporic type of embryo-sac development.
7. Absence of archegonia. Any nucleus of the female gametophyte can function as an egg.
8. The female gametophyte becomes completely cellular only after the fertilization.
9. The zygote does not undergo any free nuclear divisions.
10. The embryo contains two cotyledons.

In the above features Gnetum approaches angiosperms. These similarities led the authors to think that gnetales and Angiosperms had a common ancestor. Arber and Parkin designated this common stock as 'Hemi angiosperms'. Some others believed that ancestors of angiosperms were like those of Gnetum.

It is concluded that "The Gnetum is a phylogenetic puzzle. It is gymnospermous but possess some strong angiospermic features".

(*h*) *Brassica,* meaning "cabbage" in Latin, is the root for the revised family name. The former name, Cruciferae, refers to the "cruci-form" or crosslike shape formed by the four petals of each flower.

Brassicaceae Icon Features

- Four free petals spreading above four sepals to form a cross or X
- Four long stamens plus two short stamens (sometimes two or four stamens in total)
- Superior ovary often long and thin with a short style

Distinctive Features of Brassicaceae: It has four separate petals in the shape of a cross, with four long stamens and two short ones. There are rare exceptions: a few species have six uniformly sized stamens, or only two or only four, and a few species have no petals. Individual petals are usually in the shape of an L- narrow at the attached end and wider where they spread to form limbs of the cross. Typical colours are yellow, white, deep red, pink, or lavender. Flowers, though often small, are frequently displayed in large, elongated clusters on the ends of shoots and therefore appear quite showy.

The ovary is superior and divided down the middle by a membranous partition, known as the septum, that resembles waxed paper or cellophane.

This is readily visible as fresh fruit is dissected, and often becomes a distinctive feature of dried fruit that has split open. The (usually) many seeds may be see attached to the perimeter rim of the septum as the sides of the drying fruit peel away starting at the stem end. Whole fruits are frequently long and thin, sticking out from the stem like bristles on a bottle brush. Several general have short, rounded or triangular fruits, sometimes notched at the tip. Fruit shape, orientation of the septum with respect to any flattening of the fruit, and arrangement of seeds are important in determining the genus of a specimen.

Members of the Mustard Family are usually annuals, biennials, or perennials, with basal or alternate leaves, or both. A few species are shrubs or subshrubs. Leaves do not have stipules, but may be variously shaped from entire to deeply lobed or compound. Many species are hairy, and individual hairs may be branched in ways that help to identify species.

As the name "mustard" implies, most members of the family contain spicy oils, in a clear astringent sap.

Similar Families: The Caper family (Capparaceae) is closely related to the Mustard family, and may look similar for species that have four free sepals, four free petals, and six stamens. However, Capparaceae species never have four long stamens and two short ones, and they lack a septum partitioning the ovary chamber. In addition, Caper family members generally have an ovary on the end of a stalk, which is rare is mustards. However, two genera of capers found in California's deserts have ovaries with a tiny to nonexistent stalk, and a few mustards have ovaries with a conspicuous stalk, so this characteristic is not utterly reliable. The most common desert genus of Capparaceae, *Cleome,* has flowers with bilateral symmetry, very unlike the characteristic cross of the Brassicaceae. Moreover, of the few species of Capparaceae represented in California deserts, all have leaves with three leaflets, a feature not found in any of our Brassicaceae species.

A few other families have members with four free petals, but they do not also have four long and two short stamens, superior ovaries, or fruits with a septum.

7. (*a*) The term "Ethnobotany" was first used by Harshberger in 1896. He defined it as a study of plants used by primitive and aboriginal people. The term was broadened by Robbins, Harrington and Freire-Marreco, in 1916 and they suggested that the science of ethnobotany should include the investigation and evaluation of the knowledge of all phases of life amongst primitive societies and of the effects of the vegetal environment upon the life customs, beliefs and history of these tribal peoples.

As mentioned above, plants have formed the basis for traditional medicine systems, which have been used for thousand or years in countries such as China and India. The use of plants in traditional medicine systems of many cultures has been extensively documented. These plant-based systems continue to play an essential role in health care and the World Health Organisation estimates that 80% or the world's inhabitants continue to rely mainly on traditional medicines systems for their health care. Plant products also play an important role in health care systems of the remaining 20% of the population, mainly residing in developed countries. Analysis of the data on prescriptions dispensed from community pharmacies in the US from 1959 to 1980, indicates that 25% contained plant extract or active principles derived from higher plants and at least 119 chemical substances, derived from 90 plant species, can be considered as important drugs currently in use in one or more countries.

Of these 119 drugs, 74% were discovered as a result of chemical studies directed at the isolation of the active substances from plants used in traditional medicine. In addition, the use of so-called complementary or alternative herbal products has expanded in recent decades.

The isolation of the anti-malarial drug, quinine from the bark of *Cinchona* species was reported in 1820 by the French pharmacists, Caventou and Pelletier. The bark had long been used by indigenous groups in the Amazon region for the treatment of fevers, and was first introduced into Europe in the early 1600s for the treatment of malaria.

There are four basic ways in which plants that are used by tribal peoples are valuable for modern medicine:

1. Plants from the tropics are sometimes used as sources of direct therapeutic agents (*e.g.* the alkaloid D-tubocurarine is extracted from the South American jungle liana *Chondrodendron tomentosum* is widely used as a muscle relaxant in surgery. Chemists are still unable to produce this drug synthetically in a form that has all the attributes of the natural product and therefore collection from the wild is still relied upon. Surprisingly, harvesting of medicinal plants in often less costly than artificial drug synthesis. Another good example to illustrate this feature is Reserpine, an important hypotensive agent extracted from *Rauwolfia.* The synthesis of this molecule would cost three times as much as opposed to collection).
2. Tropical plants are also used as sources of starting points for the elaboration of semi-synthetic compounds. As example of this would saponin extracts that are chemically altered to produce sapogenins necessary for the manufacture of steroidal drugs. Until relatively recently, 95% of all steroids were obtained from extracts of neo-tropical yams of the genus *Dioscorea.*
3. Flora from the tropics can serve as sources of substances that can be used as models for new synthetic compounds. Cocaine from Coca plants, *Erythroxylum coca,* has served as model for the synthesis of a number of local anaesthetics such as procaine. New and unusual chemical substances found in plants will continue to serve as 'blueprints' for novel synthetic substances and will prove to be increasingly important in the future.
4. Plants can also be used as taxanomic markers for the discovery of new compounds. From a phytochemical standpoint, the Plant Kingdom has been investigated in a haphazard manner; some families have been relatively well-studied while others have been almost completely overlooked. For example, many uses have been documented for the Liliaceae and the family is known to be rich in alkaloids. Little, on the other hand is known on the Orchidaceae. Some plants from the family have been investigated because of their close relationship to the Liliaceae. Research has shown that they are not only rich in alkaloids but that some of the alkaloids are unique and could prove useful in the future.

Value of ethnobotany and ethnopharmacology to the search for new biodynamic compounds or new leads

Ethnobotany and Ethnopharmacology are interdisciplinary fields of research that look specifically at the empirical knowledge of indigenous peoples concerning medicinal substances, their potential health benefits and their health risks associated with such remedies. As can be seen, many of the plant-derived pharmaceuticals and phytomedicines currently in use, were used by native people around the world. Some of this knowledge has been documented and codified or studied scientifically.

Also of the hundreds of thousands of species of living plants, only a fraction has been investigated in the laboratory. This poor understanding of plants is particularly acute in the tropics. Brazil, which has some 55,000 species of plants, has reports on only 0.4% of the flora.

The importance of ethnobotanical inquiry as a cost-effective means of locating new and useful tropical plant compounds cannot be over emphasized. Most of the secondary plant compounds employed in modern medicine were 'first' discovered through ethnobotanical investigation.

Of the 119 pure chemical compounds extracted from higher plants used in medicine throughout the world and 74% of these compounds have the same or related use as the plants from which they were derived.

The Rosy Periwinkle represents a classical example of the importance of plants used by local peoples. This herbaceous plant, native to southeastern Madagascar, is the source of over 75 alkaloids, two of which are used to treat childhood leukaemia and Hodgkin's disease with a very high rate of success. This species was first investigated in the laboratory, mainly because of its use by local people as an oral hypoglycaemic agent. Like the *Catharanthus,* many drugs that are commonly used today came through the use of indigeous medicine that is through the bioscientific investigations of plants used by people throughout the world.

Thus, it can be seen that the investigation of plants used for medicinal purposes by 'unsophisticated' peoples can provide us with new biodynamic compounds that may have important application in our society.

When one considers the importance of medicinal plants in the developing countries, it is not surprising that most of the world's populations depends on traditional medicine for their primary health care needs. In many cases, developing countries simply cannot afford to spend millions of dollars on imported medicines. Several African and Asian nations are now encouraging traditional medicines as an integral component of their public health care programs. Indigenous medicines are relatively inexpensive and locally available and are readily accepted by the local population.

(*b*) ***Gnetum*** is a genus of gymnosperms, the sole genus in the family **Gnetaceae** and order **Gnetales**. They are tropica evergreen trees, shrubs and lianas. Gnetum is a link between seed plants and seedless plants. Unlike other gymnosperms they possess vessel elements in the xylem. Some species have been proposed to have been the first plants to be insect pollinated as their fossils occur in association with the extinct pollinating scorpionflies. Molecular phylogenies based on nuclear and plastid sequences from most of the species indicate hybridization among some of the Southeast Asian species. Fossil-calibrated molecular-clocks suggest that the *Gnetum* lineages now found in Africa, South America, and Southeast Asia are the result of ancient long-distance dispersal across seawater.

Today there are four major lineages of extant gymnosperm seed plants: **Cycadopsida (cycads, "Palmfarne"), Ginkgopsida (ginkgos), Pinopsida/Coniferopsida (conifers, "Nadelbäume"), and Gnetopsida (gnetophytes)**. Extinct gymnosperm groups include the **Lyginopteridopsida (seed ferns, Pteridosperms, "Samenfarne"**, paraphyletic group including Devonian/Carboniferous Lyginopterids and Carboniferous/Permian Medullosans), **Bennettitales (cycadeoids), Gigantopteridales (gigantopterids), Pentoxylales** (*e.g. Pentoxylon*), **Caytoniales** (*e.g. Caytonia*), **Glossopteridales**, **Voltziales** (*e.g. Emporia*), and **Cordaitales**. The evolutionary connections between these gymnosperm groups are uncertain and especially the position of the Gnetales is a matter of controverse debate. Based on molecular (DNA sequences), morphological (including fossil seeds), and biogeochemical evidence (oleanone) the different gymnosperm groups are either monophyletic or paraphyletic, and their evolutionary relationships to the angiosperms are unclear.

Anthophyte hypothesis: Virtually all morphology-based cladistic analyses propose a monophyletic group consisting of angiosperms + Bennettitales + Pentoxylales + Caytoniales + Glossopteridales + Gnetales (= anthophytes). This implies that the Gnetales are sisters of angiosperms and the gymnosperms are paraphyletic. This hypothesis is not supported by molecular data, which place the Gnetales as sister to all remaining seed plants, and in several molecular analyses even within the conifers as sister to Pinaceae. Based on many molecular analyses, the gymnosperms are a monophyletic sister group of angiosperms. Among several other possibilities, the Caytoniales, Pentoxylales, Glossopteridales,

Bennettitales and Gigantopteridales have been proposed as ancestors of the angiosperms. **Gigantopterid hypothesis:** The Bennettitales (cycadoeoids), which are morphologically highly similar to the Cycadopsida (cycads), are a group of gymnosperms that are highly similar to angiosperms.

Oleanane, a triterpene important for insect defense is widespread among angiosperms, has been discovered in fossils of **Cretaceous Bennettittales** (cycadoeoids) and **Permian Gigantopteridales** but not in other gymnosperm groups. The gigantopterid hypothesis claims that the angiosperms derived from seed ferns via cycadoeoid-related gymnosperms. Note that at the present time the issue of seed plant evolution remains unsolved.

(*c*) **Normal Secondary Growth in Dicot Stem**

"Increase in diameter (girth) of the axis due to formation of new tissues as a result of activity of lateral meristems and interfascicular cambium and extra stelar cambium is called normal secondary growth."

In a normal dicot stem, the secondary growth takes place as follows:

(A) Formation of secondary tissue by the stelar cambium

The living cells of cambium ring are of two types:

(*a*) **Fusiform initials:** These are elongated, wedge-shaped, wider tangentially than radially. They form elements such as tracheids, fibres, vessels and sieve tubes.

(*b*) **Ray initials:** These are much shorter than fusiform initials and appear as isiand of small cells. They give rise to parenchyma cells and take part in the formation of vascular rays. Ray initials divide periclinally or tangentially into two cells—meristematic and permanent. If the permanent cells is formed on the outer side it develops into phloem when it develops on the inner side, gives rise to xylem. In this way cambium cells divide to form phloem on outcrside and xylem towards the inner side. Due to newly formed secondary phloem and secondary xylem, the primary phloem and primary xylem get separated.

Secondary Tissues

(*a*) **Secondary phloem**

- It is made up of sieve tubes, companion cells and phloem parenchyma and sometimes bast fibres.

(*b*) **Secondary xylem**

- It is made up of scalariform and pitted vessels, tracheids and sclerenchymatous fibres (wood fibres).
- Primary xylem is pushed towards pith as a result of secondary xylem formation.

(B) Formation of secondary tissues by extra-stelar cambium (cork cambium)

In many wood plants increase in girth takes place by formation of new tissues in extra-stelar regions. These new tissues are better known as periderm. Periderm is made up of three tissues as follows:

(*a*) **Phellogen or cork cambium:** The phellogen, in contrast to the cascular cambium is relatively simple in structure composed of one type of cells. Their protoplasts are vacuolated. Intercellular spaces lacking except in the lenticels. Phellogen is a secondary lateral meristem that may arise from permanent living cells of hypodermis or outer cortex.

(*b*) **Phellem or cork:** Phellem cells are formed as a result of tangential and periclinal divisions of phellogen cells towards the outer face. As they mature there is a gradual loss of living matter and cells get elongated radially, vertically or tangentially. Due to development of fatty substance, the suberin, the cell walls become thick. Cork or phellen provides thermal insulating quantities.

(*c*) **Phelloderm or secondary cortex:** Layers of thin-walled cells cut off towards the inner side of the phellogen form phelloderm or secondary cortex. The phelloderm cells are living with cellulose walls. In some species, they act as photosynthetic tissue and aid in starch storage.

Anomalous or abnormal secondary growth may be caused due to following reasons:

(*i*) The normal cambium behaves peculiarly or irregularly, resulting in abnormal arrangements of vascular tissues.

(*ii*) The normal cambium is situated in an abnormal position hence the tissues cut off are placed abnormally.

(*iii*) The normal cambium does not develop or if present, is replaced by additional or accessory cambial rings.

Abnormal secondary growth in plants may be studies under two headings:

(*i*) Plants in which cambium is of normal type but its activity is abnormal, resulting in abnormal arrangement of vascular tissues.

(*ii*) Plants in which the normal cambium is not formed or if formed, is soon replaced by accessory cambium. This accessory cambium may develop either from the cortex or pericycle region and exhibits abnormal activity.

However, the abnormal secondary growth may be studied as follows:

I. Cambium normal but showing abnormal activity

The cambium ring is formed normally but behaves in abnormal manner. The abnormal activity of the cambium may be categorised into the following types.

1. The cambium form vascular tissues only in the region of vascular bundle. This type of anomaly is found typically in many woody climbers or lianas. The normal cambium ring is formed by the union of fascicular and interfascicular cambium, but the activity is abnormal in the sense that either the fascicular cambium or the interfascicular cambium is active. In case of the stems of *Vitis* and *Clematis,* the interfascicular cambium is active cutting off parenchyma only, whereas in case of Cucurbitae, the fascicular cambium is active cutting of vascular tissue. However, in Aristolochiae, the fascicular cambium cuts off secondary vascular tissue and the interfascicular cambium cuts off parenchyma cells.
2. The cambium forms unusually large proportion of vascular tissues in the vascular region only. The cambium ring is formed normally by the union of the fascicular and interfascicular cambium. However, the cambial ring behaves abnormally, in the sense that it is more active in certain regions and less active or inactive in other regions. This peculiar growth pattern is well exemplied by *Bauhinia, Bignonia, Doxantha, Menispermum, Tinospora* etc.
3. The cambium forms irregular patches of parenchyma in xylem. This type of abnormal activity is seen in *Urtica dioica* stem.

II. Abnormal cambium showing abnormal activity

In a number of dicot families such as Amaranthaceae, Chenopodiaceae, Nyctaginaceae etc. a new cambium ring of accessory cambium arises from the cortex or pericycle after the older, vascular cambium has ceased functioning or when the normal cambium ring does not develop at all. The cambial ring being placed abnormally functions in an abnormal manner, which may be of the following types:

(*i*) Formation of rings of vascular bundles embedded in parenchymatous tissue. This type of secondary growth has been observed in *Amaranthus, Mirabilis, Bougainvillea* etc. and occurs in the following manner:

1. The first ring of cambium arises *de novo* in the pericycle region. Such a type of cambium, arising outside the vascular bundle is known as extra-stelar cambium.
2. The extra-stear cambium behaves abnormally, cutting off xylem patches alternating with parenchymatous patches on the inner side, whereas on the outer side, it cuts off continuous layers of parenchyma initially and later phloem patches over the xylem and parenchyma at the remaining places.

3. After a complete ring of vascular bundle has been formed, the cambial ring becomes passive and ceases to function.
4. A new ring of cambium (accessory cambium) is now formed from the parenchymatous cells cut off externally by the first cambium (extra-stelar).
5. This cambium also behaves abnormally, similar to the previous one and cuts off a ring of vascular bundles separated by parenchyma. It then ceases to function and becomes passive.
6. Similarly, more accessory cambia are formed consecutively which give rise to consecutive rings of vascular bundles.

***(ii)* Formation of rings of vascular bundles embedded in conjunctive tissue.** The cambial ring originates in the extra-stelar region and cuts off secondary xylem and thick-walled conjunctive tissue on the inner side and secondary phloem and conjunctive tissue on the outer side. The vascular bundles appear to be embedded in a mass of conjunctive tissue, *e.g. Bougainvillea, Boerhaavia* etc.

8. (*a*) Comparison of systems of classification

S. No.	Bentham and Hooker	Engler and Pranti	Hutchinson
1.	It is a natural system of classification.	It is a transitional phylogenetic system.	It is phylogenetic system.
2.	It is based on de Candolle's system of classification.	It is based on Eichler's system of classification.	It is based on Bessey's system of classification.
3.	Fixity of species is the main idea behind this system.	Darwinian theory of descent is the main idea behind this system.	Considerable knowledge of phylogeny is the basis of this classification.
4.	Dicots are divided into: (*i*) Polypetalae (*ii*) Gamopetalae (*iii*) Monochlamydae.	Dicots are divided into: (*i*) Archichlamydae (*ii*) Metachlamydae.	Dicots are divided into: (*i*) Lignosae (*ii*) Herbaceae in this system.
5.	Gymnosperms are placed in between dicots and monocots.	Gymnosperms are placed before dicots.	Gymnosperms are placed before dicots.
6.	Monocots are treated after dicots.	Monocots are treated before dicots.	Monocots are treated after dicots.
7.	Orchidaceae and some other advanced families are regarded as primitive, and treated in the beginning.	Orchidaceae are treated as advanced.	Orchidaceae are treated as advanced.
8.	Families with free petals are placed in Polypetalae, with fused petals in Gamopetalae, and without petals in Monochlamydeae.	Polypetalae and Monochlamydeae are placed together under a single group Archichlamydeae. Families with fused petals are placed under Metachlamydeae.	Emphasis is on resemblances in place of differences, and so the Gamopetalae and Monochlamydeae are distributed according to their relationship in Polypetalae.
9.	Monocotyledonous families are arranged in 7 series.	Monocotyledons are arranged in 11 orders.	Monocotyledons are arranged in 29 orders.
10.	All flowering plants are placed in 200 families.	280 families of flowering plants have been recognized.	Number of recognised angiospermic families is 411.
11.	Gramineae is the last family of monocots.	Orchidaceae is the last family of monocots.	Gramineae is the last family of monocots.

(*b*) The Cordaitales are an extinct group of gymnosperms that can be traced from the Mississippian to the Permian. The most complete records of these plants come from central Europe. North America, and China, where they represented a conspicuous portion of the late Paleozoic flora. Paleoecological studies indicate that many forms inhabited low land peat mires where they either formed more or less monotypic stands or were part of mixed vegetation types, growing interspersed among calamites, tree ferns, and lycophytes. Other forms lived in poorly to well-drained mineral soils, forming fire-prone communities on drier sites. A few giant forms grew in upland settings. Some cordaitaleans are suggested as inhabiting marine-influenced coastal mires and thus represented the earliest known mangrove communities, the so-called cordaitalean mangrove hypothesis; however, this hypothesis has more recently been challenged. For example, Falcon-Lang (2005a) described cordaitalean trees from the Lower Pennsylvanian of Joggins, Nova Scotia, which grew in a coastal setting that was flood prone but not permanently submerged. Because the forest layers do not show evidence of marine influence, and several key physiological adaptations to growth in brackish waters are absent in the trees, he concluded that the term "mangrove" for these fossil forests is probably inappropriate.

Several cordaitaleans have been reconstructed as whole plants, including *Pennsylvanioxylon birame, Cordaixylon dumusum Mesoxylon priapi, C. iowensis* and *Shanxioxylon sinense.* The names used to refer to the entire plants are typically the names originally given to the stems (as in *Lepidodendron, Psaronius*, and *Medullosa*), because this part of the plant usually provides the most distinctive characters.

Arborescent Cordaitales consist of monopodial trunks with a distal crown that produces large, strap-shaped leaves. They represent the largest trees in the Pennsylvanian tropical zone, with some forms growing to more than 45 m tall, but the group also includes long-lived, scrambling shrubs, such as *C. dumusum,* and small trees, such as *S. sinense.* Some of the small trees, such as *P. birame,* have aerial roots that form at the base of the stem and probably looked much like the basal portions of some modern mangrove trees. Pollen and seed-producing organs of the cordaites consist of compound cones and are generally borne on distal leaf-bearing branches. Pollen is saccate and the seeds are typically bilaterally symmetrical; some have conspicuous lateral extensions of the integument in the form of wings.

(*c*) **Osmunda regalis L.**

Syn.: *Osmunda hugeliana* Presl.

Family: Osmundaceae

Aquatic fern, rhizome erect. Lamina ovate, bipinnate, secondary pinna alternate, sessile, elliptic oblong. Fertile pinna compressed, cylindrical.

World: Throughout.

India: Himalayas, Khasi hills and Western Ghats.

Trade name: Royal Fern.

Medicinal uses: The roots are mucilaginous, tonic, stimulant and styptic. An aqueous extract of the fern is administered for intestinal gripe and used externally in rheumatism. It is said to have antibacterial action. The fern is also prescribed in dysentery, rickets and muscular debility. Tender twigs are used in balms and healing plasters. The fronds enter into the preparation of diuretic drinks, used in body swellings.

Pancraium zeylanicum L.

Family: Amaryllidaceae

A perennial bulbous herb, bulbs globose. Leaves bifarious, linear-lanceolate. Flowers sessile, white, fragrant.

World: Asia.

India: Throughout.

Medicinal uses: The plant contains an alkaloid, possible lycorine, which acts as an emetic and causes death by paralysis of the central nervous system. It is used in ear troubles. The roots are irritant in action and employed externally in fevers in Java. In Sri Lanka, the bulb is said to be medicinal. The bulb macerated with ghee is applied externally to promote suppuration of boils.

Papaver bubium L.

Family: Papaveraceae

An annual herb, up to 60 cm tall. Leaves sessile, pinnatifid. Flowers red with a dark spot at the base of petals. Fruit an obovoid capsule, seeds numerous.

World: Nepal, Pakistan, Afghanistan and Iran to Europe.

India: Western Himalayas from Kashmir to Garhwal.

Medicinal uses: The plant is reported to be used in Homeopathy. The petals are sudorific.

Chemistry: The ripe capsules contain alkaloids.

Parkia roxburghii G. Don

Syn.: *Parkia javanica* (Lam.) Merr.

Mimosa biglobosa Roxb. non Jacq.

Family: Mimosaceae

A medium sized tree, bark light grey to brown, rough. Leaves large, bipinnate, leaflets numerous. Flowers yellowish in dense heads. Fruit pod, dark drown, seeds many.

World: South East Asia.

India: North East and Central India.

Local name: *Ben.*: Supota; *Hin.*: Khurial, Supota.

Medicinal uses: In Malaya, pods and seeds are valued in Medicine and are used in different ways both externally and internally; for stomach disorders. Bark and the leaves are employed in making lotions for skin diseases and ulcers. Seed serves as carminative, anti-diarrhoea and analgesic.

Paramignya monophylla Wight

Family: Rutaceae

Large scandent thorny shrub with sharp, recurved axillary spines. Leaves simple, gland-dotted, elliptic lanceolate. Flowers white, fragrant, axillary, 1–3 together. Fruit obovoid berry, yellow when ripe.

World: Nepal, Bhutan, Myanmar and Sri Lanka.

India: Eastern Himalayas, Khasi hills, Orissa, Andhra Pradesh.

Local name: *Kan.*: Kadukanji, Kannimbe, Kankanchiballi; *Mar.*: Kurva-Wagutti; *Tam.*: Katillinsecham.

Fl. & Fr.: October–March.

Medicinal uses: The roots are used as alterative and diuretic.

PAPER-II

1. (*a*) Chromosomes are the gathering of genetic material known as DNA or deoxyribonucleic acid. Each chromosome is made of one continuous macro molecule. The DNA that is contained in these are expressed in the organism through phenotype and cellular interactivity. Each group of chromosomes is contained in every cell in an organism other then sporophytes and gametophytes or sperm and eggs. In any cell, the ploidicity or ploidy number of that cell represents how many complete sets of the chromosomes that are meant to be present.

The term **haploid** refers to a single set of all the chromosomes found in normal gametes, sperm or ovum (symbol: 1N). In man, N = 23. The zygote, formed by the fertilisation of an ovum by a sperm, has therefore 23 pairs of chromosomes. This constitutes, in the zygote and all the normal somatic cells derived therefrom, the diploid state (symbol: 2N). A chromosome number which differs by one or more from an exact multiple of the haploid number; e.g., 2N – 1 or 2N + 1, where N is the haploid number of chromosomes, is referred to as aneuploid.

Polyploid means any multiple of the basis haploid chromosome number, other than the diploid; thus 3N, 4N and so on.

(*b*) **Accessory chromosome (B chromosome; supernumerary chromosome):** Any chromosome that is additional to the regular karyotype of a species. Such chromosomes vary in size and composition and may or may not affect the phenotype. In humans, about one person in every 1500 carries an accessory chromosome, and some of these are associated with mental or physical abnormalities. For example, cat-eye syndrome occurs in people who carry an extra chromosome that partly duplicates chromosome 22. It is characterized by enlarged pupils, skin malformations, cardiac and urinary defects, and, sometimes, mental handicap.

(*c*) The **ribosome** is a large and complex molecular machine, found within all living cells, that serves as the site of biological protein synthesis (translation). Ribosomes link amino acids together in the order specified by messenger RNA (mRNA) molecules.

The ribosome is responsible for the synthesis of proteins in cells and is found in all cellular organisms. It serves to convert the instructions found in messenger RNA (mRNA, which itself is made from instructions in DNA) into the chains of amino-acids that make up proteins.

In bacterial cells, ribosomes are synthesized in the cytoplasm through the transcription of multiple ribosome gene operons. In eukaryotes, the process takes place both in the cell cytoplasm and in the nucleolus, which is a region within the cell nucleus. The assembly process involves the coordinated function of over 200 proteins in the synthesis and processing of the four rRNAs, as well as assembly of those rRNAs with the ribosomal proteins.

They are not considered as a membrane bound organelle. Ribosomes are built from 2 subunits. Its only when these subunits are properly placed together that the ribosome becomes functional. The large subunit is composed of 45 proteins and 3 molecules of RNA while the small subunit consists of 33 proteins molecules and 1 RNA. Fully assembled it measures 20-30 nm. Sometime ribosomes work in units called polysomes.

There are 2 types of ribosomes: bound and free. The bound are found attached to the ER, while the free ones float around in the cytosol. The proteins made by the free will usually stay within the cell, while the bound are destined to become part of the membrane system or exported from the cell.

(*d*) **Single Gene Inheritance:** Genetic conditions caused by a mutation in a single gene follow predictable patterns of inheritance within families. Single gene inheritance is also referred to as Mendelian inheritance as they follow transmission patterns he observed in his research on peas. There are four types of Mendelians inheritance patterns:

Autosomal dominant	X-linked recessive
Atuosomal recessive	X-linked dominant

Autosomal: The gene responsible for the phenotype is located on one of the 22 pairs of autosomes (non-sex determining chromosomes).

X-linked: The gene that encodes for the trait is located on the X chromosome.

Dominant: Conditions that are manifest in heterozygotes (individuals with just one copy of the mutant allele).

Recessive: Conditions are only manifest in individuals who have two copies of the mutant allele (are homozygous).

(*e*) *ISH* (*in situ* hybridization) technology, based on ACD's unique, patented probe design strategy which enables simultaneous signal amplification and background noise suppression. RNA scope Technology represents one of the most significant advances in ISH technology in over 40 years.

The value of Quantitative Molecular Detection and Morphological Context (MD & MC) in a single assay

- **Molecular Detection:** RNA scope detects single RNA molecules and provides quantitative analysis of gene expression at the single-cell resolution.
- **Morphological Context:** RNA scope localizes RNA molecules providing spatial

and cell-specific expression while preserving tissue architecture.

- **Quantitative:** RNA scope quantifies *RNA molecules per cell*, giving accurate expression level at the single cell resolution across heterogeneous cell populations.
- **Universal:** RNA scope's patented probe design can be applied to virtually ANY gene in ANY genome in ANY tissue.
- **Scalable:** The assay is robust and easy to implement in basic, translational and clinical research labs. Availability of Manual Assays, Automated Assays and Assay Services provide ultimate flexibility.

RNA scope enables *in situ* detection of RNA biomarkers—filling a long standing gap in *in situ* molecular analysis.

RNA scope can complement IHC when antibodies are unavailable or have insufficient sensitivity or uncertain specificity. RNA scope is ideal for detecting RNAs for secreted proteins and non-coding RNA—a limitation of IHC. Downstream of microarrays and NGS (e.g., RNA-seq), RNA scope is an ideal platform for translating new scientific advances into clinical applications due to the speed of RNA scope assay development and its superior sensitivity and specificity.

4. (*a*) **X-inactivation** (also called **lyonization**) is a process by which one of the two copies of the X chromosome present in female mammals is inactivated. The inactive X chromosome is silenced by its being packaged in such a way that it has a transcriptionally inactive structure called heterochromatin. As nearly all female mammals have two X chromosomes, X-inactivation prevents them from having twice as many X chromosome gene products as males, who only possess a single copy of the X chromosome. The choice of which X chromosome will be in activated is random inplacental mammals such as humans, but once an X chromosome is inactivated it will remain inactive throughout the lifetime of the cell and its descendants in the organism. Unlike the random X-inactivation in placental mammals, inactivation in marsupials applies exclusively to the paternally derived X chromosome.

In 1959 Susumu Ohno showed that the two X-chromosomes of mammals were different: one appeared similar to the autosomes; the other was condensed and heterochromatic. This finding suggested, independently to two groups of investigators, that one of the X-chromosomes underwent inactivation. In 1961, Mary Lyon proposed the random inactivation of one female X chromosome to explain the mottled phenotype of female mice heterozygous for coat colour genes. The Lyon hypothesis also accounted for the findings that one copy of the X chromosome in female cells was highly condensed, and that mice with only one copy of the X chromosome developed as infertile females. This suggested to Ernest Beutler, studying heterozygous females for Glucose-6-phosphate dehydrogenase (G6PD) deficiency, that there were two red cell populations of erythrocytes in such heterozygotes: deficient cells and normal cells, depending on whether the inactivated X chromosome contains the normal or defective G6PD allele.

Expressed genes on the inactive X chromosome: A fraction of the genes along the X chromosome escape inactivation on the Xi. The Xist gene is expressed at high levels on the Xi and is not expressed on the Xa. Many other genes escape inactivation; some are expressed equally from the Xa and Xi, and others, while expressed from both chromosomes, are still predominantly expressed from the Xa. Up to one quarter of genes on the human Xi are capable of escape. Studies in the mouse suggest that in any given cell type, 3% to 15% of genes escape inactivation, and that escaping gene identity varies between tissues.

Many of the genes which escape inactivation are present along regions of the X chromosome which, unlike the majority of the X chromosome, contain genes also present on the Y chromosome. These regions are termed pseudoautosomal regions, as individuals of either sex will receive two copies of every gene in these regions (like an autosome), unlike the majority of genes along the sex chromosomes. Since individuals of either sex will receive two copies of every gene in apseudoautosomal region, no dosage compensation is needed for females, so it is postulated that these regions of DNA have evolved mechanisms to escape X-inactivation. The genes of pseudoautosomal regions of the Xi do not have the typical modifications of the Xi and have little Xist RNA bound.

The existence of genes along the inactive X which are not silenced explains the defects in humans with abnormal numbers of the X chromosome, such as Turner syndrome (X0) or Klinefelter syndrome (XXY). Theoretically, X-inactivation should eliminate the differences in gene dosage between affected individuals and individuals with a normal chromosome complement, but in affected individuals the dosage of these non-silenced genes will differ as they escape X-inactivation.

The precise mechanisms that control escape from X-inactivation are not known, but silenced and escape regions have been shown to have distinct chromatin marks. It has been suggested that escape from X-inactivation might be mediated by expression of long non-coding RNA (lnc RNA) within the escaping chromosomal domains.

Uses in experimental biology: Stanley Michael Gartler used X chromosome inactivation to demonstrate the clonal origin of cancers. Examining normal tissues and tumors from females heterozygous for isoenzymes of the sex-linked G6PD gene demonstrated that tumor cells from such individuals express only one form of G6PD, whereas normal tissues are composed of a nearly equal mixture of cells expressing the two different phenotypes. This pattern suggests that a single cell, and not a population, grows into a cancer. However, this pattern has been proven wrong for many cancer types, suggesting that some cancers may be polyclonal in origin.

Besides, measuring the methylation (inactivation) status of the polymorphic human androgen receptor (HUMARA) located on X-chromosome is considered the most accurate method to assess clonality in female cancer biopsies. A great variety of tumors was tested by this method, some, such as renal cell carcinoma, found monoclonal while others (e.g. mesothelioma) were reported polyclonal.

Researchers have also investigated using X-chromosome inactivation to silence the activity of autosomal chromosomes. For example, Jiang *et al.* inserted a copy of the Xist gene into one copy of chromosome 21 in stem cells derived from an individual with trisomy 21 (Down's syndrome). The inserted Xist gene induces Barr body formation, triggers stable heterochromatin modifications, and silences most of the genes on the extra copy of chromosome 21. In these modified stem cells, the Xist-mediated gene silencing seems to reverse some of the defects associated with Down's syndrome.

(*b*) Hypotheses pertaining to associations between brooding rumination and tripartite factors were tested by multiple latent growth curve analyses (LGM) using Mplus 5.0. In LGM, multiple waves of data on individuals at different time points can be considered simultaneously, permitting the study of initial levels, individual change, average change, and predictors of individual differences in change over time. Full Information Maximum Likelihood (FIML) was used to handle missing data. Parameter estimates from FIML provide less biased information than ad hoc procedures (*e.g.*, listwise and pairwise deletion, imputation of means) and is more robust to non-normal data.

Each of the tripartite growth constructs was comprised of two latent factors or growth parameters. The first latent factor (intercept) represents the initial level (or intercept mean,

Mi) of the outcome of interest and individual differences in the intercept (or intercept variance, *Di*). The intercept factor is defined by fixing all of the factor loadings (or bases) of the three repeated measures to 1 and serves as a constant for each child over time, thus capturing the starting point of the developmental growth trajectory at Time 1. The second latent factor (slope) represents the growth rate (slope mean, *Ms*) and individual differences in rates of change over time. Loadings on the slope factor define the shape of the trajectory over time, which were fixed to identify the model. Specifically, the first loading was fixed at 0, the second loading at 1, and the third loading at 2, indicating that change over time was linear. Error variances and intercept-slope correlations were allowed to be freely estimated. Growth parameters of these three univariate models, which included the intercept mean, slope mean, intercept variance, slope variance, and the covariance between the intercept and slope, were then estimated. Multigroup analysis was conducted separately for each tripartite factor to determine whether sex differences were present in the mean or variance of each growth parameter (*i.e.*, intercept and slope). A univariate latent growth curve model for each tripartite model was fitted simultaneously for boys and girls, allowing each parameter to be estimated freely across sex and thus determining a baseline χ^2 for each tripartite factor. The next step involved setting equality constraints on specific growth parameters (*i.e.*, factor means, factor variances), to determine whether the model that forces boys and girls to have equal estimates of a certain parameter provides a significantly worse fitting model than the model that allows the growth parameters to differ by groups (*i.e.*, unconstrained model).

The three tripartite variables were then examined in the same multivariate latent growth curve model, regressing all six latent growth parameters (*i.e.*, intercepts and slopes for each of the three tripartite factors) on the time invariant predictors of baseline brooding and age, as illustrated in Figure. To determine whether there were sex differences in the associations between brooding rumination and the tripartite factors, we tested for significant χ^2 differences between a model in which the different paths between brooding and the six latent growth curve parameters (*i.e.*, intercepts and slopes for each of the tripartite factors) were constrained to be equal for boys and girls and an alternative model in which these paths were allowed to be freely estimated. Results of the best-fitting model were used to interpret effects of brooding on the tripartite factors. Several fit indices were examined to determine model fit: the χ^2 statistic, Comparative Fit Index (CFI; Bentler, 1990), Tucker-Lewis Index (TLI; Tucker & Lewis, 1973); Root Mean Square Error of Approximation (RMSEA; Steiger, 1990), and the Standardized Root Mean Square Residual (SRMR; Kenny & McCoach, 2003).

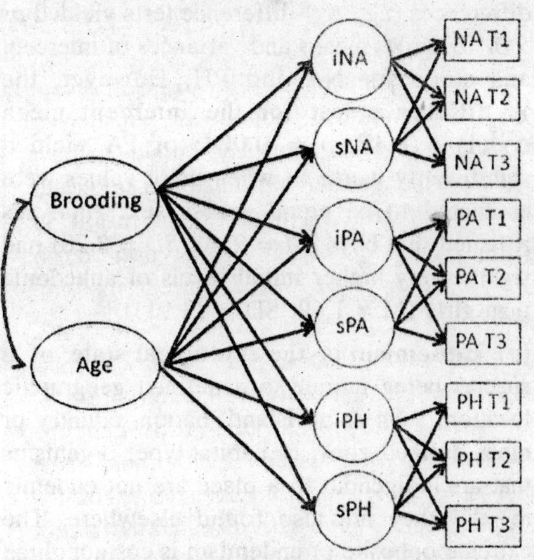

Fig.: *Multivariate Model*

Separate Tripartite Factor Models: Fit indices from the LGMs, run separately for each tripartite factor, indicated good fit to the data—all models: $\chi^2(2) = 0.95 - 1.93$, $ps > 0.10$; CFI = 1.00; TLI = 1.00 – 1.01; RMSEA = 0.00 (90%

C.I. = 0.00–0.10); SRMR = 0.01–0.02. Intercept and slope means were significant for all tripartite factors. Inspection of the slope means across NA, PA, and PH models indicated that all three factors had significant decreases in symptoms over time. In addition, variances for intercept and slope (*i.e.*, random effects) were significant across all models, indicating significant individual differences in initial levels and changes over time in NA, PA, and PH. For the PA model; slope and intercept were not correlated significantly (p = 0.18). However, the NA slope and intercept correlation (r = –0.41, p = 0.03) as well as the PH slope and intercept correlation (r = –0.33, p = 0.001) were significant indicating that children endorsing initially higher levels of NA and/or PH showed steeper declines in NA and/or PH symptoms over time.

We then tested each of the univariate models with two groups: boys and girls. Results of the models demonstrated no significant sex differences (*i.e.*, $\Delta\chi^2$ difference tests yielded *ps* > 0.10) across means and variances of intercept and slope for NA and PH. However, the χ^2 difference test for the intercept mean $\Delta\chi^2(1)$ = 8.47, p = 0.004; of PA yielded significantly worse fit when these values were estimated to be equal across sex. Analyses revealed that boys (M = 2.40, SD = 2.20) had significantly higher initial levels of anhedonia than girls (M = 1.69, SD = 11.91).

5. (***a***) **Endemism** is the ecological state of a species being unique to a defined geographic location, such as an island, nation, country or other defined zone, or habitat type; organisms that are indigenous to a place are not endemic to it if they are also found elsewhere. The extreme opposite of endemism is cosmopolitan distribution. Another term for a species that is endemic is precinctive, which applies to species (and subspecific categories) that are restricted to a defined geographical area. A native species, such as a native plant, is one that is considered to have been endemic for a relatively long period of time.

Physical, climatic, and biological factors can contribute to endemism. The orange-breasted sunbird is exclusively found in the fynbos vegetation zone of southwestern South Africa. The glacier bear is found only in limited places in Southeast Alaska. Political factors can play a part if a species is protected, or actively hunted, in one jurisdiction but not another.

There are two subcategories of endemism – paleoendemism and neoendemism. Paleoendemism refers to species that were formerly widespread but are now restricted to a smaller area. Neoendemism refers to species that have recently arisen such as through divergence and reproductive isolation, or through hybridization and polyploidy in plants.

Endemic types or species are especially likely to develop on geographically and biologically isolated areas such as islands and remote island groups, such as Hawaii, the Galápagos Islands, and Socotra; they can equally develop in biologically isolated areas such as the highlands of Ethiopia, or large bodies of water far from other lakes, like Lake Baikal.

(***b***) **Nod Genes:** Nod genes lie in a cluster in between *nif I*, and *nif B* genes, *Nod A, nod B, nod C* and *nod D* are common to all species of *Rhizobium*. They are found close together in a 8.5 Kb Eco RI segment. They are called common nod genes. Nod A codes for 196 amino acids, nod B'codes for 217 amino acids, nod C codes for 426 amino acids and nod D codes for 311 amino acids.

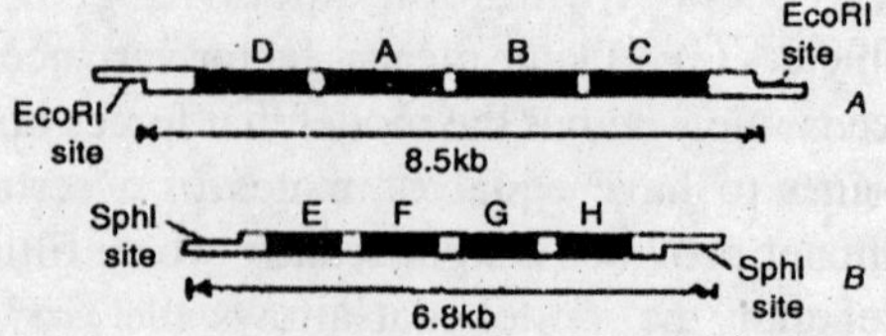

Fig.: *Nod genes of Rhizobium meliloti : A-A 8.5 kb segment of megaplasmid having common nod genes: B-A 6.8kb segment of the same plasmid having hns genes.*

The other nod genes vary between the species. For example, ***Rhizobium leguminosarum*** has nod genes, E.F.I and J along with the common nod genes. A 6.8 kb segment obtained from *R. meliloti* by using Sphl, has nod genes E, F, G and H. These variable nod genes are known as HSN genes.

The nod genes do the following functions:

(*i*) Nod-A, -B and -C code for proteins that cause swelling and curling of root hairs.

(*ii*) *Nod D* codes for a protein that binds with a flavonoid produced by legume and induces the transcription of nod genes.

(*iii*) *Nod-E* and *-F* control host specific nodulation. Nod-E codes for enzyme that elicits the formation of capsular polysaccharide in the bacterium, Nod-F codes for an acyl carrier protein participating in nodulation.

(*iv*) Function *of nod G* is not known.

(*v*) *Nod H codes* for a protein that elicits host specific response with *Rhizobium* infects root hairs.

(*vi*) *Nod I codes* for an ATP carrier protein.

(*vii*) *Nod I codes* for a protein that transfers electrons.

(*c*) **Eutrophication** or more precisely **hypertrophication**, is the ecosystem response to the addition of artificial or natural substances, mainly phosphates, through detergents, fertilizers, or sewage, to an aquatic system.

Eutrophication arises from the oversupply of nutrients, which induces explosive growth of plants and algae which, when such organisms die, consume the oxygen in the body of water, thereby creating the state of hypoxia.

According to Ullmann's Encyclopedia, "the primary limiting factor for eutrophication is phosphate." The availability of phosphorus generally promotes excessive plant growth and decay, favouring simple algae and plankton over other more complicated plants, and causes a severe reduction in water quality. Phosphorus is a necessary nutrient for plants to live, and is the limiting factor for plant growth in many freshwater ecosystems. Phosphate adheres tightly to soil, so it is mainly transported by erosion. Once translocated to lakes, the extraction of phosphate into water is slow, hence the difficulty of reversing the effects of eutrophication.

Eutrophication poses a problem not only to ecosystems, but to humans as well. Reducing eutrophication should be a key concern when considering future policy, and a sustainable solution for everyone, including farmers and ranchers, seems feasible. While eutrophication does pose problems, humans should be aware that natural runoff (which causes algal blooms in the wild) is common in ecosystems and should thus not reverse nutrient concentrations beyond normal levels. Cleanup measures have been mostly, but not completely, successful. Finnish phosphorus removal measures started in the mid-1970s and have targeted rivers and lakes polluted by industrial and municipal discharges. These efforts have had a 90% removal efficiency. Still, some targeted point sources did not show a decrease in runoff despite reduction efforts.

(*d*) Fermentation, a type of anaerobic respiration, an energy-releasing process that takes place in the absence of free (chemically uncombined) oxygen. Fermentation results in the breakdown of carbohydrates and other complex organic substances into simpler substances.

Certain organisms perform fermentation to obtain the energy they need to carry on their life processes. (Most organisms obtain the energy for these processes through aerobic respiration, in the presence of free oxygen.) Various microorganisms, including yeasts and certain molds and bacteria, obtain their energy through fermentation. Many of the fermentation processes result in products that are important in medicine, food preparation, and other fields.

The specific product resulting from fermentation is determined by the type of microorganism carrying on the process and the substance in which the fermentation occurs.

For example, wine is the product of yeast fermentation in fruit juice, while beer is the product of yeast fermentation in grain. Antibiotics (drugs used to fight infectious diseases) are obtained from both bacterial and mold fermentation. Fermentation by various microorganisms is used to produce substances called enzymes, which are used in many medical and industrial processes to speed up chemical reactions. Vinegar and cheese are products of bacterial fermentation. Yeast fermentation is used to make leavened bread.

(*e*) **Allelopathy** is a biological phenomenon by which an organism produces one or more biochemicals that influence the growth, survival, and reproduction of other organisms. These biochemicals are known as **allelochemicals** and can have beneficial (positive allelopathy) or detrimental (negative allelopathy) effects on the target organisms. Allelochemicals are a subset of secondary metabolites, which are not required for metabolism (*i.e.* growth, development and reproduction) of the allelopathic organism. Allelochemicals with negative allelopathic effects are an important part of plant defense against herbivory.

The process by which a plant acquires more of the available resources (such as nutrients, water or light) from the environment without any chemical action on the surrounding plants is called resource competition. This process is not negative allelopathy, although both processes can act together to enhance the survival rate of the plant species.

The possible application of allelopathy in agriculture is the subject of much research. Current research is focused on the effects of weeds on crops, crops on weeds, and crops on crops. This research furthers the possibility of using allelochemicals as growth regulators and natural herbicides, to promote sustainable agriculture. A number of such allelochemicals are commercially available or in the process of large-scale manufacture. For example, Leptospermone is a purported thermochemical in lemon bottlebrush (*Callistemon citrinus*). Although it was found to be too weak as a commercial herbicide, a chemical analog of it, mesotrione (tradename Callisto), was found to be effective. It is sold to control broadleaf weeds in corn but also seems to be an effective control for crabgrass in lawns.

6. (*a*) Adverse human impacts on biodiversity occur in very different ways, such as: habitat-destruction; overharvesting; climatic change; environmental pollution (air pollution, eutrophication, acid rain); commercial trade of (rare) plants and animals; introductions of species; and genetic engineering.

Habitat destruction: Destruction of habitats for all kind of purposes, construction of roads, canals, dams and houses is probably the most important threath to biodiversity.

Illustrative are the side effects of some well-intentioned international development projects. These are sometimes sponsored by international agencies concerned with such affairs and sometimes by the foreign-assistance departments of individual donor nations. Usually, the projects are intended to benefit one segment of the economy of the recipient nation; but, because ecological advice generally is not sought and because of the broad effect of the proposed development on other resources or on the total environment, the side effects of some of these activities often far outweigh any benefits that are derived. An example is the Aswan High Dam of Egypt, where the need to increase the supply of water for irrigation and power was considered as paramount. The environmental side effects, however, have been enormous and include the spread of the disease schistosomiasis by snails that live in the irrigation channels, loss of land in the delta of the Nile River from erosion once the former sediment load of the river was no longer available for land building, and a variety of other consequences. The responsibility of agencies concerned with international development to seek the best environmental advice is now generally accepted, but implementation of this responsibility has been slow. Overharvesting, overcultivation or over-exploitation of natural resources is also a big threat to biodiversity.

Global Climatic Change: Climate change is likely to have considerable impacts on most or all ecosystems. The distribution patterns of many species and communities are determined to a large part by climatic parameters, however, the responses to changes in these parameters are rarely simple.

At the simplest level, changing patterns of climate will change the natural distribution limits for species or communities. In the absence of barriers, it may be possible for species or communities to migrate in response to changing conditions. Vegetation zones may move towards higher latitudes or higher altitudes following shifts in average temperatures. Movements will be more pronounced at higher latitudes where temperatures are expected to rise more than near the equator. In the mid-latitude regions (45 to 60°), for example, present temperature zones could shift by 150–550 km.

In most cases natural or man-made barriers will impact the natural movement of species or communities. Arctic tundra and alpine meadows may become squeezed by the natural configuration of the landscape, while these and many other natural systems may be further confined by human land-use patterns. Many national parks and protected areas are now surrounded by urban and agricultural landscapes which will prevent the simple migration of species beyond their boundaries.

Rainfall and drought will also be of critical importance. Extreme flooding will have implications for large areas, especially riverine and valley ecosystems. Increasing drought and desertification may occur in tropical and sub-tropical zones, and at least one model has predicted a drying out of large parts of the Amazon.

Rates of change will also be important, and these will vary at regional and even local levels. The maximum rates of spread for some sedentary species, including large tree-species may be slower than the predicted rates of change in climatic conditions. In many cases further complications will arise from the complexity of species interactions and differential sensitivities to changing conditions between species. Certain species may rapidly adapt to new conditions and may act in competition with others.

Changes in seasons are already being noticed in many temperate regions. Bird song is being reported earlier and spring flowers are emerging when it was once winter. In agricultural landscapes, changes in the length of growing seasons may improve productivity in mid-latitudes and increase the potential for arable crops at high latitudes.

Negative impacts may include increased ranges of insect pests and diseases, and failure of crops in some regions from drought or flooding. On the relatively narrow habitats of the coastal margins, especially where these are backed by areas of intense human use, rising sea levels may lead to the squeezing out of important coastal habitats. Rising sea temperatures will further affect the distribution and survival of particular marine resources.

In addition to causing a warming effect, increased concentrations of atmospheric carbon dioxide are known increase rates of photosynthesis in many plants, as well as improving water use efficiency. In this way the climate changes may increase growth rates in some natural and agricultural communities.

Environmental pollution: Environmental pollution or pollution is the addition of any substance (nutrients) or form of energy (*e.g.*, heat, sound, radioactivity) to the environment at a rate faster than the environment can accommodate it by dispersion, breakdown, recycling, or storage in some harmless form. A pollutant need not be harmful in itself. Carbon dioxide, for example, is a normal component of the atmosphere and a by-product of respiration that is found in all animal tissues; yet in a concentrated form it can kill animals. Human sewage can be a useful fertilizer, but when concentrated too highly it becomes a serious pollutant, menacing health and causing the depletion of oxygen in bodies of water. By contrast, radioactivity in any quantity is harmful to life, despite the fact that it occurs normally in the environment as so-called background radiation.

Pollution has accompanied mankind ever since groups of people first congregated and remained for a long time in any one place. Primitive human settlements can be recognized by their pollutants—shell mounds and rubble heaps. But pollution was not a serious problem as long as there was enough space available for each individual or group. With the establishment of permanent human settlements by great numbers of people, however, pollution became a problem and has remained one ever since. Cities of ancient times were often noxious places, fouled by human wastes and debris. In the Middle Ages, unsanitary urban conditions favoured the outbreak of population-decimating epidemics. During the 19th century, water and air pollution and the accumulation of solid wastes were largely the problems of only a few large cities. But, with the rise of advanced technology and with the rapid spread of industrialization and the concomitant increase in human populations to unprecedented levels, pollution has become a universal problem.

Of all the pollutants released into the environment every year by human activity, Persistent Organic Pollutants or POPs are among the most dangerous. They are highly toxic, causing an array of adverse effects, notably death, disease, and birth defects, among humans and animals. Specific effects can include cancer, allergies and hypersensitivity, damage to the central and peripheral nervous systems, reproductive disorders, and disruption of the immune system. These highly stable compounds can last for years or decades before breaking down. POPs released in one part of the world can, through a repeated and often seasonal process of evaporation, deposit, be transported through the atmosphere to regions far away from the original source. In addition, POPs concentrate in living organisms through another process called bioaccumulation. Though not soluble in water, POPs are readily absorbed in fatty tissue, where concentrations can become magnified by up to 70,000 times the background levels. Fish, predatory birds, mammals, and humans are high up the food chain and so absorb the greatest concentrations.

Depletion of the Ozone Layer: Scientists also fear that the ozonosphere (or ozone layer of the atmosphere) is being depleted by the chemical action of chlorofluorocarbons emitted from aerosol cans and refrigerators and by pollutants from rockets and supersonic aircraft. Depletion of the ozone layer, which absorbs ultraviolet radiation from the Sun, would have serious effects on living organisms on the Earth's surface, including increasing frequency of skin cancer among humans.

Acid Rain: Another climatic effect of pollution is acid rain. The phenomenon occurs when sulphur dioxide and nitrogen oxides from the burning of fossil fuels combine with water vapour in the atmosphere. The resulting precipitation is damaging to water, forest, and soil resources. It is blamed for the disappearance of fish from many lakes in the Adirondacks, for the widespread death of forests in European mountains, and for damaging tree growth in the United States and Canada. Reports also indicate that it can corroded buildings and be hazardous to human health. Because the contaminants are carried long distances, the sources of acid rain are difficult to pinpoint and hence difficult to control. Acid rain has been reported in areas as far apart as Sweden and Canada. The drifting of pollutants causing acid rain across international boundaries has created disagreements between Canada and the United States and among European countries over the causes and solutions of the precipitation. The international scope of the problem has led to the signing of international agreements on the limitation of sulphur and nitrogen oxide emissions.

Eutrophication and Oligotrophication: Freshwater ecosystems go through eutrophication or oligotrophication. Eutrophication is an aging process in the life cycle of a lake, pond or slow moving stream. When this occurs a lot of dead organic matter settles at the bottom of the water. It all decomposes and forms an evergrowing layer of silt. This can take many thousand years to complete. The other aging process is known as oligotropication. This is a the total opposite of eutrophication, it is nutrient poor.

Lakes face to basic kinds of environmental problems which are: threats to water quality and the deterioration of shoreland. Pollution by industries, shipping and poor agricultural practices have led to poisoning of the water. Also changes in temperature lead to accelerated eutrophication. Eutrophication is an overload of different nutrients in the water which put an excessive demand on the oxygen content of the water, resulting in the chemical-biological death of a lake. Some of the world's major lakes currently suffer from such problems.

The effects of pollution on land (and in water) are to favour small-bodied, rapidly reproducing organisms that do not depend on complex food webs. The process of simplification and impoverishment is now global and affects terrestrial and aquatic communities alike. It is the continuously expanding result of chronic intrusions on natural systems by human influences. The impoverishment threatens all life because it reduces systematically the capacity of the Earth to support plants.

In rivers, the most widespread pollutant in geographic terms is phosphorus, which results in the development of large quantities of seasonal plant growth, leading to other types of impact such as perturbed oxygen and pH cycles, organic pollution and massive growth of toxic algae.

In coastal marine waters, the frequency and geographic extent of eutrophication phenomena are increasing, even in marine areas previously believed to be unaffected.

In terrestrial ecosystems, nutrient impacts appear to be serious because of the uncertainty of recovery of the land-based systems, leading to losses of species and ecosystems.

Commercial trade of plant and animal species: Commercial trade of living animals and plants as well as in the products derived from them is also a severe threat to biodiversity. Demands by wealthy nations for certain animal and plant products create particularly severe problems in less affluent countries. The trade in endangered species of wildlife is illustrative. The demand for furs and skins of rare animal species is artificially created in the fashion centres of the world. Prices paid by wealthy people for these items in affluent countries exceed the lifetime income of most people in the countries from which the leopards, crocodiles, tigers, and other wild species come. Poachers go to great lengths to obtain these animals wherever they can be found, including inside national parks and reserves. Because effective policing is virtually impossible, legal and illegal trade in wildlife begin to overlap, and both become firmly established. Exporters of wild animals and their products are the end links of profitable business chains that include far greater numbers of hunters and trappers in remote areas. Furthermore, for each animal or skin that reaches a foreign market, many more are destroyed in hunting, trapping, and transporting.

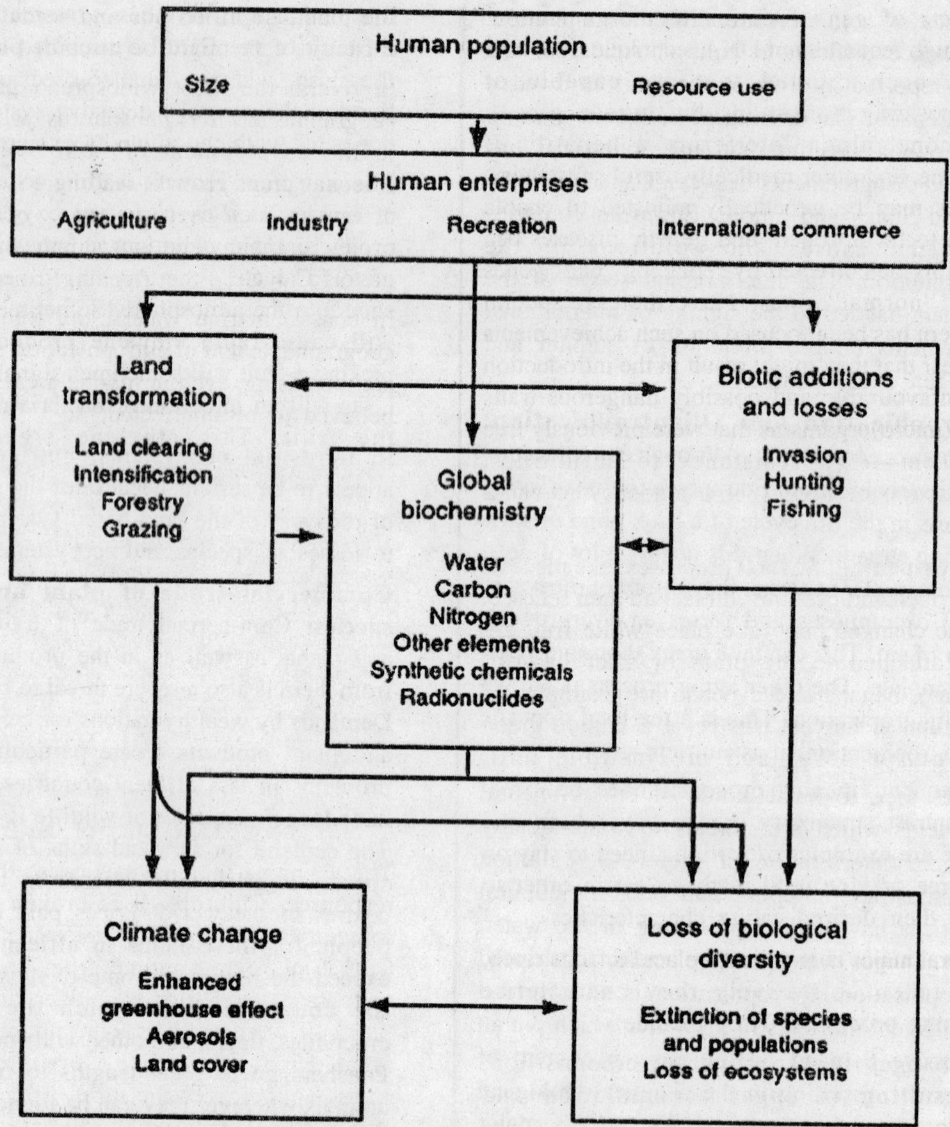

Fig.: Direct and indirect impacts of human activities on Earth's ecosystems.

Genetic engineering: The term genetic engineering initially meant any of a wide range of techniques for the modification or manipulation of organisms through the processes of heredity and reproduction. As such, the term embraced both artificial selection and all the interventions of biomedical techniques, among them artificial insemination, *in vitro* fertilization (e.g., 'test-tube' babies), sperm banks, cloning, and gene manipulation. But the term now denotes the narrower field of recombinant DNA technology, or gene cloning, in which DNA molecules from two or more sources are combined either within cells or *in vitro* and are then inserted into host organisms in which they are able to propagate. Genetic engineering has advanced the understanding of many theoretical and practical aspects of gene function and organization. Through recombinant DNA techniques, bacteria have been created that are capable of synthesizing human insulin, human growth hormone, alpha interferon, a hepatitis B vaccine, and other medically useful substances. Plants may be genetically adjusted to enable them to fix nitrogen, and genetic diseases can possibly be corrected by replacing "bad" genes with "normal" ones. Nevertheless, special concern has been focused on such achievements for fear that they might result in the introduction of unfavourable and possibly dangerous traits into (micro)organisms that were previously free of them—*e.g.*, resistance to antibiotics, production of toxins, or a tendency to cause disease.

(*b*) **Fruit ripening:** Several processes take place as fruit ripen and become edible, and then senesce. These changes may take place while fruit are still attached to the plant or after harvest. Tomato, banana and avocado are examples of fruit that at harvest can be at a mature green but unripe stage and are inedible until subsequent ripening processes have occurred. In contrast, strawberry, orange, boysenberry and grape are examples of fruit that need to stay on the tree or vine until ready to eat in order to have their desired eating characteristics.

Several major changes take place as fruits ripen, and taken collectively they characterise ripening processes. They include:

1. Changes in carbohydrate composition, resulting in sugar accumulation and increased sweetness;
2. Change in colour;
3. Flesh softening and textural change;
4. Formation of aroma volatiles;
5. Accumulation of organic acids with associated development of flavour.

These changes make the ripe fruit attractive to animals, which in eating the fruit will disperse the seeds and enlarge the range and improve the survival chances of the next generation of the plant. Lignified pits and seeds encased in a fibrous core might be discarded after eating the flesh, whereas smaller seeds might pass through the animal's digestive system and be deposited with the animal's excrement.

The way fruits ripen is that there is commonly a ripening signal...a burst of ethylene production. Ethylene is a simple hydrocarbon gas ($H_2C = CH_2$) that ripening fruits make and shed into the atmosphere. Sometimes a wound will cause rapid ethylene production...thus picking a fruit will sometimes signal it to ripen ... as will an infection of bacteria or fungi on the fruit. This ethylene signal causes developmental changes that result in fruit ripening.

New enzymes are made because of the ethylene signal. These include hydrolases to help break down chemicals inside the fruits, amylases to accelerate hydrolysis of starch into sugar, pectinases to catalyze degradation of pectin (the glue between cells), and so on. Ethylene apparently "turns on" the genes that are then transcribed and translated to make these enzymes. The enzymes then catalyze reactions to alter the characteristics of the fruit.

The action of the enzymes cause the ripening responses. Chlorophyll is broken down and sometimes new pigments are made so that the fruit skin changes colour from green to red, yellow, or blue. Acids are broken down so that the fruit changes from sour to neutral. The degradation of starch by amylase produces sugar. This reduces the mealy (floury) quality and increases juiciness (by osmosis, a process we will study later). The breakdown of pectin, thanks to pectinase, between the fruit cells unglues them so they can slip past each other. That results in a softer fruit...at an extreme, pectin losses may make a fruit "pithy". Also enzymes break down large organic molecules into smaller ones that can be volatile (evaporate into the air) and we can detect as an aroma.

Finally, this stimulated ripening process helps explain the old phrase, "one bad apple spoils the bunch." In the olden days, apples were packed into barrels for storage in a root cellar. The cool temperature of the cellar helped keep the apples from ripening until the family wanted to eat them during the winter. However in packing the barrel with apples you had to be careful not to put any wormy or fungus-infected apples with the bunch. Why? Because the wounded, infested apple would produce ethylene inside the barrel. If you came back in a month, all the apples in the barrel would be too-ripe (bruised by weight, soft, mushy, etc.) because they responded to that ethylene!

7. (*a*) Plants are completely resistant to the vast majority of the myriad of potentially pathogenic micro-organisms. Only a handful of microbes are able to overcome the multiple resistance barriers-preformed or induced-that protect a given plant species from pathogen attack. This so-called 'non-host resistance' of plants is often due to preformed resistance factors, which can be structural barriers or preformed chemical resistance factors. Only those microbes capable of breaching this line of non-specific resistance can colonize the plant successfully, *i.e.*, the plant becomes a host species for this pathogen and so-called 'basic compatibility' is achieved. The ensuing selection pressure can lead to coevolution between host and pathogen and to the occurrence of race/cultivar-specific resistance phenomena: some cultivars of the host plant species develop resistance to some races or strains of the pathogen. This race/cultivar-specific resistance is always based on infection-induced active resistance mechanisms which may be structural or chemical in nature.

Clearly then, there are two different structural aspects of defense in plants against microbial pathogens: structural barriers as preformed resistance factors and structural barriers as Induced resistance mechanisms. The former usually act at the level of host recognition or primary penetration of the pathogen, while the latter usually interfere either with primary penetration or with the establishment of a functional host/pathogen-relationship and the spread of the pathogen in the host tissue. A look at the recognition and penetration strategies of fungal and bacterial plant pathogens pinpoints the crucial steps where structural resistance factors or mechanisms may interfere with pathogen ingress and growth.

After having passively reached, or actively found, a suitable host plant, the pathogen has to recognize it, possibly orient itself on the surface, and initiate the penetration process in order to be able to use the plant as a source of nutrients. These processes are all vitally necessary components of infection, and failure of any of these invariably leads to resistance of the plant to the micro-organism.

Except for the rather few cases where the pathogen is motile and, thus, capable of actively searching out a suitable host plant or the inoculation of host plants by mobile vectors, contact with a host plant is accidental. Attachment of a fungal spore to a potential host plant and ensuing germination are usually thought to be rather non-specific processes. Little is known at present concerning the specificity or surface attachment and whether chemical or structural surface properties – such as hydrophobicity – influence the process. Spore germination is usually triggered by the presence of moisture in the form of free water, or at least high humidify. In some cases, germination seems to be stimulated chemically by the presence of nutrients or even more specific host plant metabolites. Recently, surface hydrophobicity has been shown to be a possible structural trigger of spore germination.

In order to penetrate into the host tissue, the emerging germ tube has to breach the host plant's surface (Fig.). Penetration can be *via* natural openings such as stomata or lenticels or *via* self-inflicted wounds (*e.g.*, during the emergence of lateral roots) or after traumatic damage (*e.g.*, by agricultural practices or animal feeding). Alternatively, some pathogens penetrate directly through the outer periclinal epidermal cell wall into an epidermal cell or *via* the middle lamella between anticlinal epidermal cell walls into the underlying intercellular spaces between the mesophyll cells. In most, and possibly all, of these cases, penetration does not occur at random but only after recognition of an appropriate site such as a stoma or an underlying anticlinal cell wall. Recognition most likely occurs at the tip of the growing germ tube, and the triggering signals may be chemical or physical in nature. Looking for possible structural defense factors of plaits against microbial infection, it can be concluded that an inappropriate surface hydrophobicity or topography leading to failure of attachment, germination, or correct recognition may present effective structural defense factors.

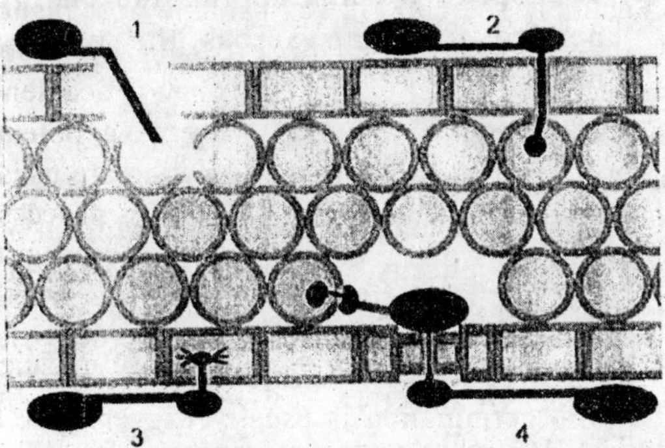

Fig.: *Penetration strategies of microbial plant pathogens*

If the pathogen penetrates *via* the epidermal cell walls, then first the cuticle and later the middle lamella or the intire cell wall must be breached. If the initial penetration allows the pathogen access to the intercellular spaces of the host tissue, a secondary penetration through the cell walls of mesophyll cells, or the dissolution of the host cell walls, is often required in order for the pathogen to reach the intracellular nutrients of its host plant. Both cuticular and cell wall penetration may be either by chemical means (*i.e.*, by the action of hydrolytic enzymes secreted by the pathogen) or by physical means (*i.e.*, by the exertion of a highly localized pressure). Both the chemical and the physical structure of the cell wall, thus determine its resistance to microbial penetration, and resilient cell walls are therefore the major line of structural defense of plants against microbial pathogens.

If the host plant's cell wall in its native, pre-infection state is not completely resistant to penetration, the host cell may attempt to reinforce it during the actual process of penetration. In contrast to the above described preformed or passive structural barriers to resistance, this is an active process induced by the infection of the plant by the pathogen. The process does not necessarily involve the production of new cell wall material. Instead, re-arrangement or cross-linking of pre-existing cell wall components may render them more resistant to enzymatic hydrolysis or physical pressure. Usually, though, the incorporation of new components into the existing wall is concomitantly induced, and these are typically components that are easily cross-linked or polymerized, such as phenolics, offering additional strength to the wall. In many cases, the cell wall is further strengthened by the local apposition of new wall material onto the existing cell wall, forming a so-called 'papilla' which may later also become encrusted with polymerizing molecules. Lastly, the production of new cell walls or even new tissue may be attempted to isolate the infecting pathogenic micro-organism.

In all of the above cases of both preformed structural resistance factors and infection-induced structural defense mechanisms, it is the host plant's cell wall, its chemical composition or its physical form, that represents the crucial structural barrier to microbial attack. We will thus have to look firstly at the highly sophisticated, complex three-dimensional 'extracellular organelle' that is the cell wall. We will then get to know the tools phytopathogenic micro-organisms have developed to overcome the structural barriers of their host plants before we proceed to discuss the defense strategies adopted by the plants to counter the microbial attack. We close the discussion with a few thoughts about how to prove a presumed causal role of anyone structural feature of a plant in resistance against a given pathogen.

(*b*) Mitchell's chemiosmotic theory of ATP production was supported by Andre Jagendorf. According to Jagendorf, an electrochemical gradient establishes first. The electrochemical gradient was established by first soaking isolated chloroplasts in an acid medium and then the pH was abruptly changed to basic. ATP production occurred after ADP and Ⓟ were added. This all occurred in the dark, providing that ATP synthesis is not directly linked to the chloroplasts ETS, which work only in the light.

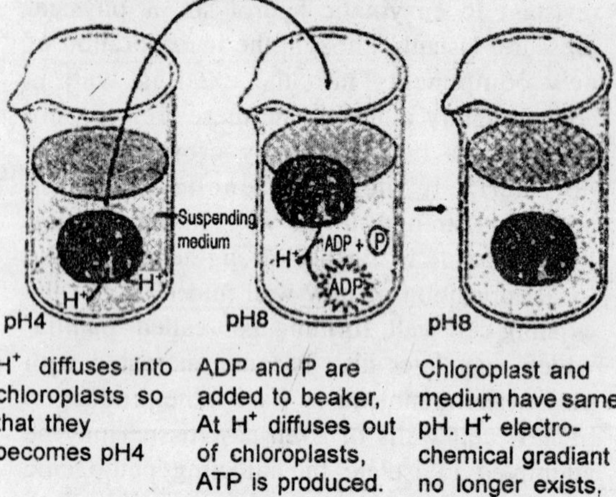

Fig.: *An experiment performed by Andre Jagendorf in supports of the chemiosmotic theory.*

The energy released by ATP breakdown is used by the cell to do various types of work and eventually it becomes nonusable heat. ATP accomplishes most of its work by transferring its terminal (end) phosphate group to another molecule in a process called phosphorylation which energizes the molecules receiving the phosphate group so that they can be used in later reactions.

ATP breakdown is coupled with the reaction that requires energy, *i.e.*, the two reactions take place at the same time and in the same place, and they usually utilize the same enzyme. A phosphate group, during the coupling process, is often transferred to an intermediate compound. For example, during active transport a phosphate group is transferred to a membrane-bound protein. When ATP becomes ADP + Ⓟ, the amount of energy released is just about enough for most biological reactions.

ATP is utilized for the following purposes:

(*i*) **Mechanical work:** Supplies the energy needed to cause cilia and flagella to beat, organelles to move and so forth.

(*ii*) **Chemical work:** Supplies the energy needed to synthesize macromolecules that make up the cell.

(*iii*) **Transport work:** Supplies the energy needed to pump across the plasma membrane.

Key Concepts

- The sun's energy is collected by plants and placed in chemicals that represent a form of potential energy, which is converted to energy of ATP molecules.
- ATP is one of the building blocks of nucleic acids DNA and RNA.
- The ΔG (change in free energy) for ATP formation is positive, which means it requires an input of energy.
- ATP is composed of the nitrogen-containing base adenine, the five-carbon sugar ribose, and three phosphate groups (each group including a phosphorus atom bonded to four oxygen atoms).
- When the endmost phosphate group of an ATP molecule detaches, energy is released and the molecule becomes ADP.
- The covalent bond that join ATP's phosphate groups can break, releasing a large amount of energy.
- When a cell needs energy for an activity, it spends ATP by converting it to ADP, inorganic phosphate (Pi) and energy.

YOUR SPACE

YOUR SPACE

IFS—BOTANY
PAPER-I

CHAPTER–1

MICROBIOLOGY AND PLANT PATHOLOGY

GENERAL ACCOUNT OF INFECTION

Plant viruses enter into host cell at points of injuries upon leaf surfaces or inoculated through Arthropod vectors. Viruses enter into our body by insect biting (e.g. dengue fever is caused by *Aedes* mosquito which also causes yellow fever) genital contact (e.g. AIDS), blood transfusion, food and drinks, skin abrasions, animals bites (rabies), Hypodemic needles (AIDS, Hepatitis B etc.).

Bacteria causes various dangerous diseases like tuberculosis, pneumonia, typhoid fever, cholera, dysentry in man. In plants bacteria causes potato wilt, fire blight of apple and pear, crown gall, canker of citrus, Black rot of cabbage etc.

"Infection is invasion and multiplication of microorganisms in body tissues, especially that causing local cellular injuury due to competitive metabolism, toxins, intracellular replication, or anitigen-antibody response".

Phytoimmunology

Immunity is the condition of being immune *i.e.*, being highly resistant to a disease because of the formation of humoral antibodies cells, or both, or as a result of same other mechanisms, as interferon activities in viral infections. (*Interferons* are proteins made by virus infected cells of vertebrates, which prevents infection by a second kind of virus or it can also be defined as species specific, but virus-unspecific proteins, one of the main defense mechanisms of humans and animals against the numerous viral pathogens). *Immunity* is security against a particular disease, nonsusceptibility to the invasive or pathogenic effects of foreign microorganisms or to the toxic effect of anitgenic substances. *Immunity* can also be said as capacity to distinguish foreign material from self and to neutralize, eliminate or metabolize that which is foreign by the physiologic mechanisms of the immune response.

In case of plants, when they are affected by microorganisms or are wounded or are affected by some kind of stress, there are certain mechanisms to overcome those conditions. Under salinity stress, water stress, or heavy metal toxicity stress, there is enhanced production of certain quaternary ammonium compounds like glycine betaine and levels of some amino acid like proline increases to sustain life of plant. Also the level of some enzyme's activity increases to fight the condition, for example under water and salinity stress conditions activities of catalase, superoxide dismutase, peroxidase and other oxidases increases to scavange the peroxide radicals produced under stressful conditions while activities of metabolic enzymes like malate dehydrogenase and glutamate dehydrogenase in plants decreases under stressful conditions. Some plant harmones also fights against diseases or wounds. Plant hormones *abscisic acid (ABA)* is known to affect a number of physiological processes, such as dormancy, flowering, of plant cells to water and resistance against various stress conditions, for example, in maize ABA induces heat shock protein (hsp 70), which saves plant or makes plant able to fight increased heat. DNA sequences encoding many of these stress proteins and those regulating their expression have been isolated and are presently being characterized. One such gene induced by ABA in response to water stress, encodes a glycine rich protein in maize embryo. Further characterization of the genes should provide a significant insight into role of ABA in stress tolerance in plants. Resistance to most plant diseases is not mediated by single gene and hence is not detectable in culture. However, sometimes the toxic effect of phytotoxin on tissues, cell or protoplast cultures is equivalent to its effect on whole plant (Earle, 1978).

Furthermore, if the phytotoxin is the only reason for pathogenecity, direct selection for disease resistance *in vitro* using the phytotoxin may come to reality. It was Carlson (1973) who extended experimental support to this hypothesis, he reported that plants regenerated from tobacco protoplasts selected for resistance to methionine sulfoximine (MSO) showed enhanced resistance to *Pseudomonas tabaci*. Though methionine sulfoximine has not been analogous to the phytotoxin of *P. tabaci*, this observation opened the door of selecting phytotoxin—resistant cell lines. Similarly, plants produce various proteins (enzymes) for being resistant to herbicides, resistance to amino acids and their analogues e.g.,5-methyltryptophan resistant potato cell line has been used to demonstrate the presence of two possible isoenzymes of anthranilate synthase (Carlson & Widholm, 1978) the first regulatory enzyme unique to tryptophan biosynthesis. Further 5 MT resistant cell lines were isolated by Jacobsen *et. al.* (1975). The cells accumulated free tryptophan and phenylalanine and tyrosine demonstrating the possibility of manupulating the free amino-acid pools of potato cells. Salt tolerant & low temperature tolerant cell lines of *Nicotiana tabacum* and *N. sylvestris* have been isolated. Under certain conditions secondary metabolites likes high amount synthesis of serpentine and ajmalicine by selected cell lines of *Catharanthus roseus* have been reported. Anthraquinone is commercially obtained from the cortical cells and bark cells of the roots of *Morinda citrifolia*. This alkaloid is now being obtained from cell line suspension cultures. If calculated in percentage dry weight, the cell line cultures result in about eight times higher alkaloid content than the whole plant yield. Suspension cultures of *Coleus blumei* have been reported to accumulate rosmarinic acid upto 15% of the dry weight of the cells which stands five times higher than the alkaloid content in the intact plant.

Important Plant Diseases

(i) Caused by Viruses

(*a*) Yellow mosaic of Mung
(*b*) Curlytop of Sugar beet
(*c*) Malformation of Mango
(*d*) Leaf Curl of Tomato
(*e*) Phyllody of Sesam and Sunhemp
(*f*) Bunchytop of Banana
(*g*) Stenosis of Cotton
(*h*) Mosaic, Leaf curl of Papaya
(*i*) Tristeza, Viral Necrosis of citrus
(*j*) Verigated Mosaic of Apple
(*k*) Mosaic of Tobacco
(*l*) Tobacco Necrosis
(*m*) Yellow Vein Mosaic of Bhindi
(*n*) Potato leaf roll

(ii) Caused by Bacteria

Sl. No.	*Disease*	*Name of Crop*	*Causal Organism*
1.	Crown gall of legumes	Leguminous Plants	*Agrobacterium tumefaciens*
2.	Ear-rot of wheat	Wheat	*Corynebacterium tritici*
3.	Ring disease of Potato	Potato	*Aplandobacter sepedanium*
4.	Fire blight of pears and apples	Pears and Apples	*Erwinia amylovora*
5.	Soft rot of carrot and turnips	Carrot and turnips	*Erwinia caratovora*
6.	Wilt disease	Potato	*Pseudomonas solanacaerum*
7.	Citrus Canker	Citrus	*Xanthomonas citri*
8.	Angular leaf spot	Cotton	*Xanthomonas malvacearum*
9.	Blight disease	Rice	*Xanthomonas oryzae*
10.	Red stripe	Sugarcane	*Xanthomonas rubrilineans*
11.	Wilt disease	Maize	*Xanthomonas stewartii*
12.	Blight diesease	Onion	*Xanthomonas striafornians*
13.	Black rot of cabbage	Cabbage	*Xanthomonas campestris*

(iii) Caused by Mycoplasma

1. Yellow dwarf disease of rice
2. Phyllody of Sunhemp
3. Little leaf of brinjal

4. Greening of citrus
5. Grassy shoot of sugarcane

(iv) Caused by Fungi

Sl. No.	Disease	Name of Crop	Causal Organism
1.	Covered smut	Barley	*Ustilago hordei*
2.	Loose smut	Barley	*Ustilago nuda*
3.	Leaf rust	Barley	*Puccinia hordei*
4.	Stem rest (Black rust)	Barley	*Puccinia graminis tritici*
5.	Powdery mildew	Barley	*Erysiphe graminis*
6.	False smut	Rice	*Ustilaginoidea virens*
7.	Stem rust	Wheat	*Puccinia graminis*
8.	Stripe rust	Wheat	*Puccinia glumarum (P. striiformis)*

(v) Caused by Nematodes

Sl. No.	Disease	Name of Crop	Causal organism
1.	Root galls	Various plants	*Hemicycliophora*
2.	Root knot	Tomato, bhindi, brinjal, potato, cucurbits, pulses, crucifers, sugarcane, banana	*Meloidogyne*
3.	Cyst forming	Pulses, maize	*H. cajani* *M. zeae*

Mode of Infection and Dissemination

Plant diseases may be caused by microorganisms including fungi, bacteria, viruses, mycoplasmas, etc. or may be incited by physiological causes including high or low temperature, lack of excess of soil moistures and aeration deficiency or excess of plant nutrients, soil acidity or alkalinity etc.

The micro-organisms obtain their food either by breaking down dead plant and animal remains (saprophytes) or by attacking living plants and animals (parasites). In order to obtain nutrients, the parasitic organisms excrete enzymes or toxins and kills the cells of the tissues of host plant, as a result of which either the whole plant or a part of it is damaged or killed, or considerable disturbance takes place in its normal metabolic processes. Micro-organisms are reproduced and disseminated mainly by spores. Wind, water, seed, diseased plants, cuttings and tubers, animals, men and insects and soil help to disseminate diseases. Viral diseases are spread as a result of direct contact, through seeds, diseased cuttings and grafts, and more commonly by insects and other vectors. Most of the fungi and bacteria errupt or ooze from the surface after the host tissues have been damaged, whereas, the viruses work altogether internally. Therefore, control of the plant diseases usually lies in preventing infection, as it is very difficult to kill the fungi or bacteria or to inactivate the viruses inside the host plants.

However, as the result of recent studies made in the development of systemic fungicides, it appears that in near future the diseased plants may even be cured. The evolvement of disease resistant varieties is another important and cheap method of controlling diseases. However, this method of control has its limitations because of the appearance of new races of the pathogens from time to time.

Seed Borne Diseases : In the case of seed borne diseases, the pathogens are carried either on the surface of the seed or within it. When a pathogen is external, it may be destroyed by treating the seed with a chemical, e.g. Formalin, TMTD, Copper carbonate, Captan, Organo-mercurials, like Agrosan and Ceresan. Except Formalin, all chemicals are available in the dust form. Systemic organic compounds have also been shown to be effective in eradicating both externally and internally seed-borne infections.

Soil-Borne Diseases : In the case of soil-borne diseases which attack the seeds or seedlings, the use of soil disinfectants or sterilizers is helpful in destroying the pathogens. The soil treatment involves the use of chemicals Formaldehyde, Captun, Thiram, Zineb, Organo-mercurials, PCNB, Ethylene dibromide, Vapam etc. They are used to drench the soil or are broadcast on it, or are applied to it in furrows, or are used to fumigate it.

Air Borne Diseases : In the case of diseases caused by air-borne pathogens, the application of chemicals to the foliage is the most effective way of controlling them. Though many fungal and bacterial diseases can be controlled in this way, chemicals have not yet proved very successful in controlling virus diseases. In their case, profective measures have to be aimed at controlling the insect vectors by spraying insecticides on the host plants or by using disease-free material for propagation.

Physiology of parasitism and Control Measures

The association between parasite and host can be divided into *spatial* and *temporal* relationships. In spatial relationship the part of the host's body is exploited by the parasite i.e. endo and ectoparasitism. Temporal relationship means that is the time that the parasite spends in or on its host. Gut parasites are permanent lodgers, certain ectoparasites attach to host while they feed and mosquito and to tsetse fly are examples and are called *occasional visitors*. Parasitism is a close coexistence of two species; beneficial to one partner (the parasite) and at the expense of the other (the host). A facultative parasite (e.g. *Claviceps* can live and grow without a host, and it can be easily cultivated *in vitro*. An obligate parasite (e.g. rickettsias, viruses, rust and smut fungi) cannot survive separately from its host, to which has become adapted by evolution. Parasitism may be regarded as a special form of symbiosis in which the predator, or the parasite, is much smaller than the prey and remains closely associated with it. Parasitism is harmful to the prey organism and beneficial to the parasite. The concept of parasitism seems obvious, but individual instances are often surprisingly difficult to distinguish from predation and from other kinds of symbiosis

Parasites are of two types :

(i) Ectoparasites : Parasites that feed on exterior surface of an organism are external or ectoparasites. e.g. lice, which live on the bodies of vertebrates.

(ii) Endoparasites : Vertebrates are parasitized internally by endoparasities, members of many different phyla of animals and protists. Invetebrates also have many kinds of parasites that live within their bodies. Some parasites live in or, just beneath the skin, others in the gut, others in the tissue fluid between the cells (intercellular parasites), and so on. The most 'endo' of all parasites are those that penetrate individual cells. The malerial parasite and certain parasitic fungi are examples of such 'intracellular parasites'.

Benefits Gained by Parasites : The two main benefits gained by the parasites are shelter and food. For maximum shelter endoparasites are in the best situation they are ensured of a stable environment from which nourishment can be derived with the minimum of effort. In some cases this involves no more than soaking up the host's body fluids. Admittedly gut parasites have a special problem in that they must protect themselves from being digested by the host's digestive enzymes, but this can be achieved by the production of appropriate inhibitors. These inactivate the enzymes in the immediate vicinity of the parasite's body.

Harms Suffered by the Host : In extreme cases, where the parasite feeds on the tissues, much harm, even death, may be suffered as a result of sheer damage to the cells. Such is the case with parasitic fungi such as *Phytophthora infestans*, the cause of potato blight, and *Pythium debaryanum* which causes dumping off in seedings.

Fungi that causes some important plant diseases are as follows :

Name of disease		Fungi
1. White rust of crucifers	→	*Albugo candida* *Cystopus candida* syn
2. Powdery mildew of cereals and grasses	→	*Erysiphe* species
3. Fruit rot of apple	→	*Peronospora sp.*
4. Downy mildew of crucifers	→	-do-
5. Early blight of potato	→	*Alternaria solani*
6. Late blight of potato (cause of severe famine in Ireland (1845) leading to death of 10 lacs of people)	→	*Phytophthora infestens*
7. Stem gall of *Coriandrum*	→	*Protomyces macrosporus*
8. Red rot of sugarcane	→	*Colletotrichum falcatum*

9. Black (stem) rust of wheat → *Puccinia graminis tritici*
10. Loose smut of wheat → *Ustilago nuda tritici*
11. Tikka disease of Groundnut → *Cercospora personata* syn *C. Arachidicola*
12. Wart disease of potato → *Synchytrium* species
13. Damping off → *Phythium debaryanum*
14. Brown leaf spot of rice → *Helminthosporium oryzae* (cause of severe famine in Bengal (1943) leading to death of 20 lakh people.).

Fungal toxins : Poisonous substances that stimulate the formation of antitoxin in the animal body. Several fungi produce toxins. Toxins produced by *Aspergillus niger* are termed *aflatoxins.* These aflatoxins belong to the group mycotoxins. They are natural carcinogens causing liver cancers, and they are 100 times as active as previously known liver carcinogens. They are also produced by *Aspergillus flavus, A. parasiticus* and *A. oryzae* as well as *Penicillium islandicum.* They are coumerin difuran derivatives. In higher plants toxins are less common. Aflatoxins are produced by various fungi while growing on mustrard and groundnut cakes. This substance if eaten by animals cause disease in animals. From *Claviceps* fungus is extracted a substance called LSD (diethylamide tartarate of dilysergic acid of ergot or lysergic acid diethylamide) which is hallucinogenic in man *i.e.,* causes distortion of perception.

Control Measures of Various Diseases : The general methods of control are :

(A) Eradication of alternate and collateral hosts.

(B) Alternation in manuring practices.

(C) Use of chemicals and antibiotics.

(D) Breeding of diseases resistant varieties.

(1) For Rust Control : (Caused by *Puccinia* sp.)

(A) *Eradication of alternate* and *collateral host* is an important method where the rusts penetrate on them. In India the problem is of over summering on stray or self-sown wheat plants and other collateral hosts on the hills. If these sources could be destroyed during the summer months the inoculum for the out break of rusts in the plains during the following winter would get greatly reduced. Also, if only rust resistant varieties could be grown in hills it would greatly solve the rust problem in the plains.

(B) *Alternations in manuring practices* : It has been found that susceptibility to rusts increases with nitrogenous fertilizers and decreases with an application of potash fertilizers so an alternation in the fertilizer pattern is called for the proportion of nitrogen in N-P-K fertilizer ratio should be reduced in order to reduce the incidences of rust in a susceptive variety.

(C) *Chemical Control* : An application of sulphur dust is found to be effective in controlling the incidence of rust, the proportion should be 30 pounds of fine sulphur dust per acre at 4-day intervals during the period when rusts usually occurs on the crop. Others recommended chemicals are nabam and zinc-sulphate, Dithane D-14 or Dithane M-45. Certain sulpha compounds like sodium-salts of sulphadiazine, sulphapyridine have also been found to be effective.

(D) *Breeding of rust resistant varieties* is a very useful method of control. Systematic breeding of such varieties was started in 1935 but it has been a difficult task to find a variety resistant to all the three types of rusts and also the increase in the physiological race flora causes complications.

(2) For Red Rot Control : (caused by *Colletorichum falcatum*)

(A) Field sanitation is one of the important measures to check the building up of the inoculum and thus preventing an epiphytotic infection.

(B) Use of healthy sets for raising a new crop. The sets should be selected from healthy canes (and those showing any reddening of pith should be rejected.

(C) Ratooning should not be permitted specially when the disease is known to be present in the locality.

(D) Rotation of crops should be practicised in order to minimize soil-borne infection. A rotation of 2-3 years has been found effective.

(E) Use of disease resistant varieties is the best method of conrtol.

Fungicides Used for Control Measures : Copper, sulphur, organo-mercury and organo-sulphur compounds and antibiotics are some of the important

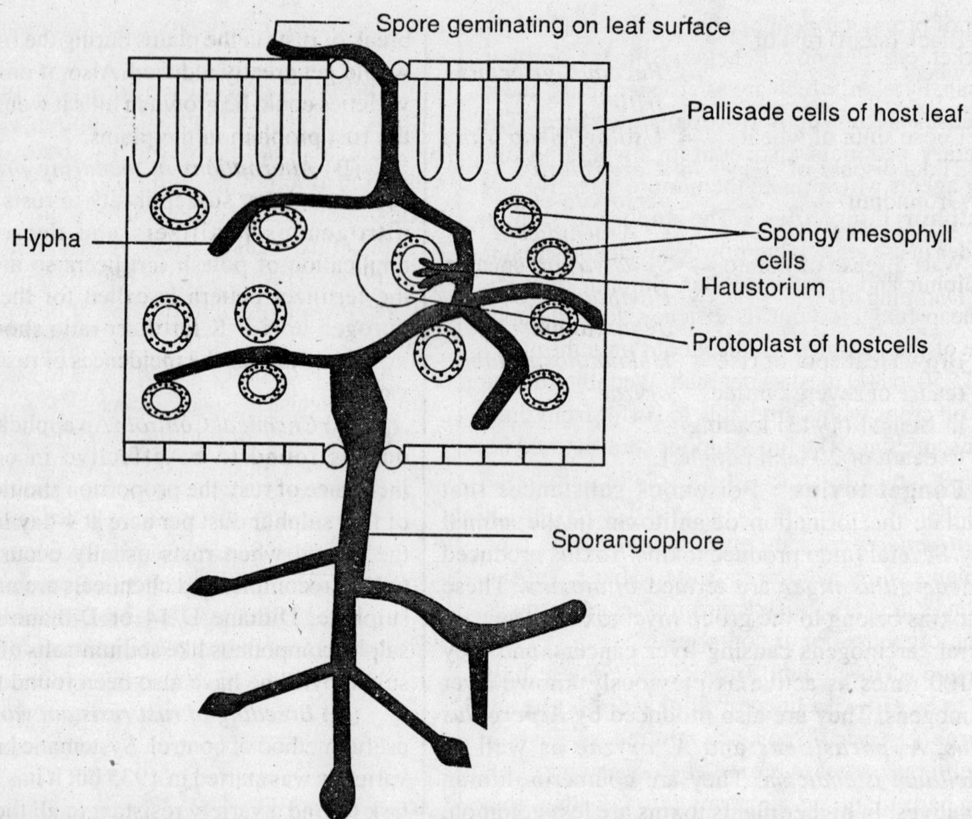

Fig. Parasitic fungi such as *Phytophthora infestans*, the cause of potato blight, are partly intercellular and partly intracellular. A spore landing on the surface of moist leaf sends out a slender filament (hypha) which enters the leaf either through a stroma or by penetrating the epidermis. The fungus consists of an intercellular network (mycelium) of slender filaments (hyphae) which grow through the plant sending short side branches into the cells. The latter represent the intracellular part of the parasite. They penetrate the cellulose walls of the host's cells by secreting cellulase at their tips. Once inside the cell they develop finger-like haustoria which secrete digestive enzymes. The soluble products are absorbed and sent back to the rest of the mycelium. *Phytophthora* reproduces prolifically by means of pear shaped bodies formed at the tips of the branches of tree-like sporangiophores which grow out of the stomata. Light, and therefore readily dispersable by wind, these bodies can reinfect other plants either directly or via motile zoospores.

fungicides. Recently some systemic organic compounds have also been developed. The choice of fungicide depends on the nature of disease and on the suceptibility of crop. They are available as dusts or wettable powders and sometimes in liquid forms. The method of applying them depends on the availability of water, suitable machinery, the nature of the crop to be treated, the area to be covered and the cost of labour.

Copper Fungicides : Bordeaux & Burgandy mixtures are the dispersible forms of cuprous oxide, copper oxychloride and basic carbonates are among the important copper fungicides. For preparing 5 : 5 : 50 *Bordeaux mixture*, 2 kg of copper sulphate and 2 kg of quicklime are dissolved in 225 litres of water. At first the stock solution of the two constituents (½ kg in 4 litres of water) are prepared. Bordeaux mixture deteriorates on standing hence only fresh preparations are used. Addition of 60 g cane-sugar per 225 litre prevents deterioration.

Burgandy mixture is a variation of Brodeaux mixture in which lime in replaced by sodium carbonate (washing soda). The method is same. The usual strength of solution is 4-6¼-50. There are a number of proprietary copper fungicides available in the market. e.g. Perenox, Penelan, Blitox, Cuprokyt, Cuprosan, Fytolan, which are as efficacious as, and in some cases better than Bordeaux mixture. The proprietary products also contain dispersing and wetting agents which make them more effective.

Sulphur Fungicides : The important sulphur fungicides in use are sulphur powder, wettable sulphur, lime sulphur and organo sulphur. Sulphur dust is a very cheap fungicide but its efficacy depends upon the size of the particles which should pass through a sieve of 250 to 300 meshes per inch. Wettable sulphur is used on crops which are liable to suffer from lime-sulphur scorching. The lime sulphur spray should not be used on tender foliage as it is likely to scorch it. A number of organo-sulphur compounds e.g. *thiram* and *dithiocarbamates* are extremely safe to use on most of the plants with tender & sensitive foliage. Tulisan, Zineb, and Ziram are some of the proprietary products, based on organo-sulphur compounds.

Organo-Mercurials Fungicides : These have proved to be effective in controlling weed borne and soil-borne diseases. They are applied as dusts in extremely small doses to the seed before sowing. They have no harmful effect on germination. Rather, they prevent emergence losses caused by soil-borne pathogens and result in a better stand of the crop. e.g. Agrosan GN, Ceresan, Semesan and Perrugen. Great care is taken for handling these. Linseed and some vegetable seeds are non-tolerant to mercury. In the recent years, certain chemicals such as captan, Thiram, Busan-72 and Dithane M-42, and some systemic fungicides have been developed. They may be used for seed treatment instead of the mercurials.

Systemic Fungicides : These can move mainly upwards only within the plant and kill the pathogen away from the point of application. They can be applied as seed or soil treatment, and as sprays. Some of the important systemic fungicides are Oxathin., derivatives (Plantvax & Vitavax), Benlate, Demosan and Bavistin.

Antibiotics : Antibiotics are mainly used against bacterial plant pathogens. Some of the promising antibiotics are streptomycin sulphate, streptomycin, terramycin, agrimycin-100 (a mixture of streptomycin and tetracycline), agrimycin-500 (containing copper) etc.

Cultural Control Measures : Cultural practices such as crop rotation, mixed cropping, adjustment of the date of sowing, depth of sowing and field sanitation through the removal of diseased debris, weeds, alternate and collateral hosts are very effective in controlling plant diseases. A strict enforcement of quarantine, especially in the case of imported plants, helps to prevent the introduction of new diseases into country.

As virus diseases and difficult to control or cure with chemicals, the use of disease free propagating material is very important. For this purpose, it is necessary to establish disease-free nurseries at isolated places.

Examples of Some Diseases and Control Measures

Name of Disease	*Causal organism*	*Control measure*
1. Covered smut of barley	*Ustilago hordei*	Treat with Cerasan or Agrosan GN before sowing, grow resistant varieties, rogue out the smutted plants
2. Stem rust of barley	*Puccinia graminis tritici*	Spray the crop with Zineb 1.70 kg in 1.025 litres of water at fort-nightly intervals, seed treatment with Plantvax (0.25%), grow resistant varieties.
3. Blast of rice	*Piricularia oryzae*	Treat seed with ceresan or Agroson GN before sowing. Grow tolerant varieties.
4. Loose smut of wheat & barley	*Ustilago tritici* & *Ustilago nuda respectively*	Solar-heat or hot-water treatment of seed, grow respectively resistant variety, rogue out the smutted plants, dry seed treatment with carboxin (0.25%)
5. Brown spot	*Physode-rma maydis*	Practice crop rotation & sanitation.

APPLICATIONS OF MICROBIOLOGY

Application of Microbiology in Agriculture, Industry, Medicine, pollution control in air, soil and water :

Uses of Virus : (1) Cyanophages are used in the control of water blooms.

(2) Ganga water is believed not to be spoilt because of the presence of phages in it.

(3) Attenuated viral doses are used in vaccine against specific diseases.

(4) Viruses are useful to geniticists as they bring about transduction and help to establish that DNA is a genetic material.

Economic Importance of Bacteria :

(A) *In Agriculture :* Some bacteria increase soil fertility. The plants take nitrogen in the form of nitrates. In soil nitrates are formed by three process :

(i) By Nitrogen-Fixing Bacteria : Bacteria are found in soil either free, e.g. *Azotobacter* and *Clostridium* or in root nodules of leguminous plants; e.g., *Rhizobium leguminosarum.* These bacteria are capable of converting atmospheric free nitrogen into nitrogenous compounds.

(ii) Nitrifying Bacteria : These bacteria convert nitrogen of ammonia into nitrite (NO_2) e.g., *Nitrosomanas* and convert nitrite compounds into nitrates e.g. *Nitrobacter.*

(iii) Decay of Dead Plants and Animals : Some bacteria attack dead bodies of plants and animals and convert their complex compounds into simpler substances, e.g. carbondioxide (CO_2), water (H_2O), nitrate (NO_3) & sulphate (SO_4).

(B) *In Dairy :* *Bacterium lactici acidi* and *B. acidi lactici* are found in milk. These bacteria ferment lactose sugar found in milk to form lactic acid by which milk becomes sour. If the milk is heated at 62.8°C for 30 minutes and is simultaneously cooled the number of lactic acid bacteria is reduced but all spores and cells of these bacteria are not destroyed and pathogenic spores are destroyed. In this way milk becomes sour but it takes longer time to become sour than ordinary milk. This process is known as **pasteurization.**

Lactic acid bacteria bring together droplets of caesin, a protein found in milk help in the formation of curd.

On churning of curd, butter is derived in the form of fat's rounded droplets & the butter on heating is converted into "ghee". On freezing of caesin of milk protein, it is fermented by bacteria with the result that foamy and soft substances, different in taste is formed.

(C) *Industrial Value :* From industrial point of view, bacteria are most important. Some of the uses of bacteria in industries are as follows :

(i) Vineger Industry : Vineger is manufactured from sugar solution in the presence of *Acetobacter aceti.*

(ii) Alcohol & Acetone : Clostridium acetobutyllcum takes part in the manufacture of butyl alcohol and acetone.

(iii) Fibre Ratting : By this process, fibres of jute, hemp and flax are prepared. In the preparation of flax, hemp and jute; the ratting of stems of *Linum ustiatissimum* (Flax = Hindi : Sunn), *Cannabis sativa* (Hemp = Hindi : Patson) and *Corchorus capsularis* (Jute) respectively is done. In this process the stems are kept under water for some days and when stems begins to decay, fibres are separated from the stem on thrashing. The process of separation of fibres is known as ratting. This process is carried out by *Clostridium butyricum* inhabiting the water.

(iv) In Tobacco Industry : Bacillus megathenium mycococcus is used for its fermentative capacity for developing flavour and taste in tobacco leaves.

(v) In Tea Industry : By fermentative action of *Mycococcus condisans* curing of tea leaves is done. By this process special taste is developed in tea leaves.

(vi) Tanning of Leather : Some bacteria decompose fats which are found in skin of animal with the result that skin and hair are separated from each other and this leather becomes ready for use.

(D) *Medicines :* Some of the antibiotics are manufactured by bacteria actions, e.g. *Bacillus brevis*-antibiotic thyrothricin, *B. subtilis*-antibiotic subtelin. Vitamin B_2 is manufactured by fermentative action of *Clostridium acetobutylicum*. Some of the antibiotics obtained from different species of *Streptomyces* are given below :

Name of Antibiotic	*Bacteria from which derived*
1. Streptomycin	*Streptomyces grisieus*
2. Chloromycin	*S. venezuelae*
3. Aureomycin	*S. aureofaciens*
4. Terramycin	*S. rimosus*
5. Neomycin	*S. fradiae*

Viral Vaccines

When an animal is injected with killed (inactivated) or severely weakened (attenuated) viruses (the substance injected is called 'viral vaccine'), the latter induce the animal's defence system to make antibodies against the proteins of injected viruses. Thesre antibodies tend to protect the animal against infection by the same virus. Viral vaccines are of two types, (*i*) Live vaccines : those which are prepared from live, avirulent or severely weakened (attenuated) viruses and (*ii*) Killed vaccines : those which are prepared from killed inactivated viruses.

(E) ***Pollution Control :*** In the present day world environmental pollution poses a great threat to the lives of living beings and natural environment. Sewage, oil-spills, pesticides, herbicides, chemical effluents and heavy metals are just some of pollution hazards. However, biotechnology gives a hope for controlling the pollution hazards, the biotechnical processes directed towards the control of pollution primarily aim at destruction of specific raw materials of pollution, i.e. the pollutants. This aim can be achieved in the following ways :

(*i*) *Microorganisms can be deployed as voracious scavengers removing all manner of pollutants.* For example : (*a*) various strains of *Pseudomonas* can consume hydrocarbons of oil & petrol, however each individual strain can consume only one or a few of the many different types of hydrocarbons. The genes that code for enzymes which attack hydrocarbons are not found on the main bacterial chromosome but on plasmids. No single strain of *Pseudomonas* can consume all varieties of hydrocarbons constituting oil because the same does not contain all the genes that code the enzymes which attack the hydrocarbons varieties. Anand Chakrabarty (1979), an India born American scientist created a single strain of *Pseudomonas* that would be able to consume all the genes responsible for oil consumption and thus mop up all the types of hydrocarbons in the oil. This unique bacterial strain, the product of genetic engineering is called a SUPERBUG. This superbug was created by introducing plasmids from different strains of *Pseudomanas* into a single cell. Also the use of mixture of strains of bacteria has been successfully used to clear up oil contaminated water from oil spills from ships and clearing up water supplies.

(*b*) *Mixture of bacterial strains are also being used to clear up other pollutions.* An impressive example is the removal of grease deposited on the inside of a holding tank of a ship. The same tank become grease free after four and half month's operation during which 'mixtures' of bacterial strains were added. These bacteria very efficiently prevented the build up of grease on the tank's interior. However, this kind of use of bacterial strains mixtures may prove significant in factories which process meat and poultry where pipes and vessels can become plugged with grease.

(*c*) New chemicals (such as pesticides, herbicides), and the substances which previously appeared on the Earth's surface only in small amounts (such as oil, many metals) tend to persist since few of the common microorganisms in soil or water can use them as food. This has created a growing demand for tailor made packages of microorganisms which can consume such specific forms of pollutants. Several major companies, especially in United States, manufacture mixtures of microorganisms and enzymes designed to clean-up chemical wastes like oil, detergent, waste waters from paper mills and highly toxic materials such as dioxin, the chemical that wreaked havoc on the town of Seveso (Italy).

(*ii*) *The root cause of pollution i.e. the sources of pollution should be attacked.* For example, some bacteria convert organic faecal substances e.g. cow-dung, decaying leaves of plants into manure and humus. Municipal sewage treatment systems which are generally operated in most of the towns and cities carry out various steps involved. These steps are namely, primary (or mechanical) treatment, secondary (or biological) treatment and tertiary (or final) treatment. Secondary or biological treatment is a purely biological treatment of mechanically treated sewage and concerns microbial activity. This treatment accomplishes two important phases, namely *aerobic phase* and *anaerobic phase*. The aerobic phase consists of aerobic digestion of sludge by various filters (e.g. trickling filters), oxidations ponds and activated sludge process, and the anaerobic phase is represented by anaerobic digestion of sludge.

(*a*) *Trickling filters* generally consists of 6-10 feet deep bed of crushed stone, gravel, slag or similar material. The sewage effluent is sprayed over the surface of the bed, the spraying saturates the effluent with oxygen. The bed surface becomes coated with aerobic microbial flora consisting of microalgae, microfungi, bacteria and protozoa. As the effluent seeps over, the aerobic microbes degrade the organic matter.

(*b*) *Oxidation pond sewage treatment is recommended for small communities in rural areas.* Oxidation ponds (also called Lagoons or Stabilization ponds) are generally 2-5 feet deep shallow ponds designated to allow direct wind action and algal growth on the sewage effluent. Oxygen supplied from air and produced as a result of algal photosynthesis fulfils *biochemical oxygen demand (BOD)* of sewage effluent and thus helps in maintaing aerobic condition in sewage effluent. In such condition the aerobic microorganisms grow rapidly and digest organic matter. *Chlorella pyrenoidosa* is a common algal representative grown in oxidation ponds.

(*c*) *In Activated Sludge process* the mechanically treated sewage effluent is pumped into a sedimentation or setting tank wherein the sewage floes and settles out. A portion of sewage floe is returned to activate a new batch of mechanically treated sewage effluent and the rest is pumped to activated sludge digester where air is blown by several jets. Thus in the presence of plentiful oxygen, oxidation of sewage effluent is brought about by aerobic microorganisms which break down organic matter to carbon dioxide and water. Now the effluent is passed through a sedimentation tank and about 10% of organic matter of the effluent in digested via this process.

The sludge collected after primary treatment of sewage is subjected to anaerobic digestion in a separate tank designed specially for the purpose. Since anaerobic conditions prevail in this tank, the anaerobic microorganisms bring about digestion of organic matter by degrading them to soluble substances and gaseous products (methane 60-70%, CO_2 20-30%, and smaller amounts of H_2 & N_2). This gas mixture can be used for operating power of the sewage plant or as a fuel. Recently, the Municipal Corporation of Delhi (India) has started supplying this gas mixture to about 100,000 people for cooking purposes.

(*d*) *Heavy Metal's Pollution Control* : Certain heavy metals like mercury, lead and cadmium are among the most harmful pollutants disposed off in waste-effluents by modern industries. Mercury causes metal poisoning which attacks the nervous system of patients. Though heavy metals are as toxic to most types of micro organisms as they are to animals including humans, there are some algal and bacterial species which avidly extract these metals from their surrounding. Biotechnologists are creating new biotechnological methodologies which could be used to purify metal laden effluents. The biotechnologists are seriously thinking to grow metal-extracting forms of microorganisms, particularly algal forms, in ponds filled with heavy metal containing factory effluents and suitable nutrients. This would allow the microorganisms to extract metals from their surroundings and sequester them inside their cell membrane. Finally, these microorganisms would be filtered from their liquid environment and deposited in special dumps. e.g. *Thiobacillus* bacteria can accumulate silver. A certain amount of silver inevitably appears in waste waters from film factories and other industrial sites. The *Thiobacillus* bacteria could collect this wasted silver and provide it for re use. This way they could reduce the losses of this expensive resource.

(*e*) *Acid rain Pollution Control* : Sulphur-dioxide, an air pollutant is produced when materials containing sulphur, especially coal, are burned. Sulphur dioxide when released into the air, dissolves in water droplets and forms sulphuric acid (acid rain). Its harmful effects are partly attributable to a lowering of pH and partly because it releases soluble aluminium salts into the environment in toxic quantities. However, the acid rain accumulates in lakes scattered generally in a wide area of hundred kilometers from the source of pollution, and kills fish and plants in vast numbers. Several types of bacteria, specially those that inhabit hot water springs have a great appetite for sulphur compounds, from which they derive energy. If such bacteria are put to coal, their activities would separate much of the sulphur from high-sulphur coal. This would result in sulphur free coal.

(*iii*) *Biotechnological production methods, which are intrinsically less polluting, can be employed to replace conventional methods.* By this the hazards of polution can be brought very much under control. For instance, the conventional processes for manufacturing chemicals for the plastic industry use oil based raw material, some of which inevitably escape to pollute the environment. This can be checked by replacing the conventional methods by biotechnological methods in which, however, microbes are fed on innocuous raw materials, e.g. sugars (glucose) in manufacturing chemicals for the plastic industry. Another example is that, at present, the conversion of alkenes to alkene oxide (which are used for polymerization form plastics) is accomplished by purely chemical techniques but use of microbial enzymes for this conversion is on the horizon. A Californian firm, namely, Cetus employs a series of three microbial enzymes. The schematic representation of alkene's conversion to alkene oxide according to this method is given below :

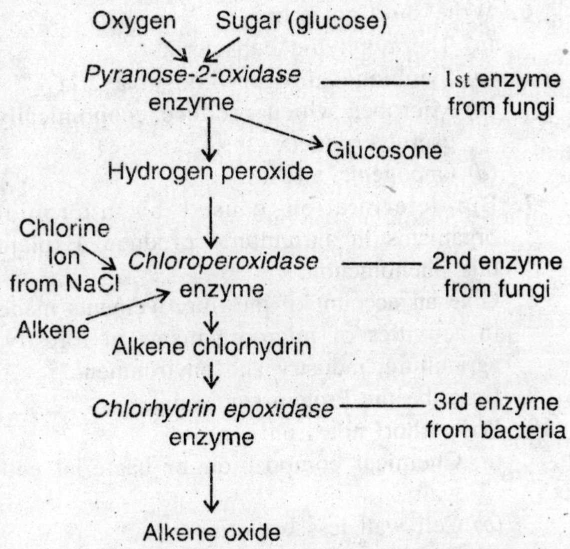

A more promising biotechnological process to convert alkenes to alkene oxides has been patented in 1981 by scientists from the Waswick University (UK). These scientists discovered a bacterium namely *Methylococcus capsulatus* which can add oxygen to alkenes. When this microorganism is supplied with ethylase or propylene gases, it inserts an oxygen atom into each molecule of these gases to produce ethylene oxide or propylene oxide respectively. This is thermophillic bacteria which lives upto 45°C, upto which the oxides are gaseous and it is much simpler to collect product as a gas than as liquid because the latter is mixed in with all the other materials in fermentation apparatus.

QUESTIONS FROM PREVIOUS YEARS' PAPERS

1. Explain the following:
(*a*) Mollicute
(*b*) Viroids
(*c*) Bioleaching
(*d*) Biopesticides
(*e*) Suspension cell culture

2. Distinguish between Macrandrous and Nanandrous.

3. Mention the symptoms, causal organism, mode of infection and control measures of:

(*a*) Stripe disease of barley, and
(*b*) Citrus canker

4. Describe the process of liquid waste treatment by micro-organisms.
5. Describe the role of Phytotoxins in plant pathogenesis.
6. Write short notes on:
(*a*) Thermophyllic eubacteria
(*b*) Symbiotic nitrogen-fixing bacteria
(*c*) Microbes which produce economically useful products
(*d*) Oncogenic viruses
7. Bio-deterioration caused by microbial organisms in agricultural produce. Explain this phenomenon.
8. Give an account of the improvements made in activities of microorganisms in forestry, agriculture, industry and environment.
9. Describe the Protein synthesis.
10. Write short notes on:
(*a*) Chemical composition of bacterial cell wall
(*b*) Cell wall less bacteria
(*c*) Define parasite
(*d*) Red rot of sugarcane
(*e*) Sandal spike
(*f*) Bacterial blight of paddy
11. Give an account of Protoplast culture.
12. Describe the following:
(*a*) Apospory (*b*) Caruncle
(*c*) X-bodies (*d*) NPC system
13. Write short notes on:
(*a*) Types of bacterial culture media
(*b*) Structure of bacteriophage
(*c*) T.M.V. (Tobacco masiac virus)
(*d*) Economic importance of bacteria.
(*e*) Structure of *Polytrichum* capsule.
14. Write an account of the different types of antibiotics, their sources and modes of action.
15. Write short notes on:
(*a*) Flagellation in bacteria
(*b*) Gram negative cell wall
(*c*) Pathogenic *Escherichia coli*
(*d*) Transmission of viruses
(*e*) Ear cockle of wheat
(*f*) Use of micro-organisms of bioremediation.
16. Differentiative between:
(*a*) Zoospore and compound zoospore.
(*b*) Obligate and facultative parasites.
17. Municipal waste treatment by anaerobic and aerobic micro-organisms.
18. Write a note on Control of viral diseases of plants.
19. Write an account of the importance of bacteria in soil fertility.
20. Write an account of drug yielding plants.
21. What makes the bacterial spores highly resistant?
22. Provide brief notes on:
(*a*) Lysozyme
(*b*) Viroids
(*c*) Oogamy
(*d*) Synangium of *Psilotum*
23. Give an account of the causal organism, symptoms and control of red rot of sugarcane.
24. Enumerate the benefits of bacteria.
25. Briefly bring out the molecular basis of infection and disease resistance.
26. Differentiative between:
(*a*) Somatic embryogenesis and caulogenesis.
(*b*) Disease prevention and disease cure.
27. Name several species of pathogenic organisms that may be present in polluted water.
28. Comment upon the importance of Heterospory.
29. Write a note on any two important diseases caused by Nematodes.
30. Why are coloured mushrooms not edible? Give reason(s).
31. Write critical notes on the following:
(*a*) Bacteriophage (*b*) Organ culture
32. Distinguish between:
(*a*) Zoospore and Oospore
(*b*) Virion and Prion
33. How do food infection and food poisoning occur? Explain.
34. What are the major differences between Gram positive and Gram negative bacteria?

CHAPTER–2

CRYPTOGAMS

The first terrestrial plants evolved from an organism that, if it existed today, would be classified as a multicellular green alga. Extensive biochemical and morphological similarities between green algae and plants make this conclusion inescapble green algae and plants share chlorophyll *a* and *b*, and carotenoids, they also have cellulose in their cell walls and starch as their primary food reserve. Moreover, the details of cell division are similar in the two groups. After mitosis is complete, animal cells pinch inward toward the centre, while plant cells from an interior *cell plate*, which grows out from the centre between the two daughter cells. Aside from plants, the only organisms that form a cell plate during cytokinesis are a few groups of green algae. Living plants are grouped into 12 phyla. Members of 9 of the 12 plant phyla are collectively called 'vascular plants' and include among others, the ferns, conifers, and flowering plants. Vascular plants have water-conducting xylem and food conducting phloem strands of cells in their stems, roots, and leaves. Members of the other three phyla either lack such strands or have poorly developed ones. These three phyla are mosses (Phylum : Bryophyta), liverworts (Phylum: Hepaticophyta), and hornworts (Phylum: Antocerotophyta).

The Green Invasion of the Land : Plants and fungi are the only major groups of organisms that are primarily terrestrial. There are some 267,000 known species of living plants. They dominate almost every part of the terrestrial landscape, except for extreme deserts, polar regions, and the tops of the highest mountains. Several other groups, including arthropods, chordates, and mollusk arc also well represented on land. Plants probably came first, their cell-walls helping to protect their propagules during dispersal. Most plants are protected from *desiccation*--the tendency of organisms to lose water to the air by a waxy *cuticle* secreted onto their exposed surfaces. The cuticle is relatively impermeable and provides an effective barrier to water loss.

Special structures in this barrier allow the entry of CO_2, which is necessary for photosynthesis, and the exist of oxygen by diffusion. These tiny slit-like or eye-shaped pores are called *stomata* (singular stoma) and make up about 1% of most leaf and green stem surfaces. Water and gas diffusion into and out of a plant is regulated by the opening and closing of stomata, which typically number into the thousands per square centimeter.

At an early stage of their evolution, plants evidently also developed a special kind of relationship with fungi that has been a key to their successful occupation of terrestrial habitats. *Mycorrhizae* (a symbiotic association of fungi with the plant roots) are found in about 80% of all plants and are frequently seen in fossils of the earliest plants. Mycorrhizae play an important role among today's plants in the assimilation of phosphorus and probably other ions. We can surmise that mycorrhizae also did so in the raw, unrelated soils that existed before the earliest plants. Many other features such as efficient water and food conducting systems, developed and contributed to the success of plants on land. Roots, shoots, and leaves-expanded areas of photosynthetically active tissue—also evolved and diversified in relationship to the varied habitats that existed on land specialization in key reproductive features improved the chances for survival of embryonic tissues within seeds as they were dispersed.

Plants are terrestrial, with life cycles that alternate between haploid and diploid :

- Plants are derived from an aquatic ancestor, a multicellular green algae but the evolution of their conducting tissues, cuticle, stomata, and seeds has made them progressively less dependent on external water for reproduction. The oldest plant fossils date from the Silurian period, some 330 million years ago.

- The evidence that plants are derived from green algae lies in their common photosynthetic pigments (chlorophyll *a* & *b*, carotenoids); chief storage product (starch); cellulose rich cell walls (in some green algae only) and cell division by means of a cell plate (in certain green algae only).
- All plants have a life cycle involving an alternation of generation in whcih haploid gametophyte alternate with diploid sporophyte. The spores that sporophyte forms as a result of meiosis grow into gametophytes, which produce gametes (sperms and eggs) by mitosis.

Nonvascular plants like mosses are relatively unspecialized :

- The three phyla of plants that lack well-developed vascular tissues are the simplest in structure and have been grouped as bryophytes. This grouping does not reflect a common ancestory or close relationship between them.
- Sporophytes of mosses, liverworts and hornworts are usually nutritionally dependent on the gametophytes. They are mostly brown or straw-colored at maturity. The gametophytes which are more conspicuous, are green and nutritionally independent of the sporophytes.

Seedless vascular plants likes ferns have well developed conducting tissues :

- Nine of the 12 plant phyla contain vascular plants, which have two kinds of well defined conducting tissues : xylem for water conduction and dissolved minerals and phloem for conducting food molecules that the plant manufacture.
- In ferns and other seedless vascular plants, the sporophyte generation is dominant. The fern sporophyte has vascular tissues and well-differentiated roots, stems and leaves.

Seed plants like pine trees and roses have protected embryos specialized for dispersal :

- Seeds were an important evolutionary advance. In seed plants, the gametophytes are nutritionally dependent on the sporophytes.
- In gymnosperms, ovules are exposed directly to pollens at the time of pollination, in angiosperms ovules are enclosed within an ovary, and a pollen tube grows from the stigma to the ovule.
- The pollen of gymnosperms is usually disseminated by wind, although some angiosperms are wind-pollinated in many the pollen is transported by insect and other animals. The ripened ovaries of angiosperms develop into fruits. Both flowers & fruits are found only in angiosperms.

The plant kingdom is divided into 4 major kingdoms :

Division 1 → Thallophyta : (*i*) Thallus like plant body with no differentiation into root stem and leaves.

(*ii*) Vascular tissues absent.

(*iii*) Reproductive organs are simple, unicellular & non-jacketed.

(*iv*) Asexual reproduction takes place by spores or zoospores during growing season.

(*v*) No embryo formation after the fusion of gametes.

(*vi*) This major division contains about 1,10,000 species.

Subdivision 1 → Algae : (*i*) Plants containing chlorophyll and thallus like plant body without true roots & leaves.

(*ii*) In many of the algae chlorophyll is marked by brown, red or yellow pigments.

(*iii*) Algae are divided into a number of classes on the basis of pigments and other features.

Class 1 : *Cyanophyceae*—Blue green algae
Class 2 : *Chlorophyceae*—Green algae
Class 3 : *Phaeophyceae*—Brown algae
Class 4 : *Rhodophyceae*—Red algae
Class 5 : *Xanthophyceae*—Yellow green algae.

(*iv*) Algae are microscopic, unicellular to larger multicellular plants.

(*v*) In algae, generally the reproductive organs are unicellular but they may be multicellular is some brown algae.

(*vi*) In multicellular reproductive organs all the cells are fertile and take part in reproduction.

(*vii*) There is no jacket of sterile cells surrounding the reproductive organs.

Range of Vegetative Structure of Alage :

(1) Unicellular Algae : These are of following two types :

(*a*) *Motile :* In these algae movement takes place by flagella e.g. *Chlamydomonas.*

(*b*) *Non-motile :* e.g. *Chlorella.*

(2) Multicellular Algae : These are of following kind :

(*a*) *Colonial :* In these algae, definite number of cells are found and these are motile, e.g. *Volvox.* This type of colony is known as motile colony. But a different kind of colony, *coccoid colony* is also found is multicellular algae. Number of cells in these colonies is indefinite and they are non motile e.g. *Hydrodictyon.*

(*b*) *Aggregation :* In these algae cells are found in the form of indefinite colony. These are of two types :

(*i*) *Palmelloid forms :* Algae cells in these are surrounded by a viscous mucilalginous substance e.g. *Tetraspora.*

(*ii*) *Dendroid colony :* Cells of these forms produce mucilaginous substance and are folded in such a manner that they look like branches of a plant. e.g. *Prasinocladus.*

(*c*) *Filamentous :* These are of following types :

(*i*) Simple unbranched filaments, e.g. *Ulothrix.*

(*ii*) Simple branched filaments, e.g. *Cladophora.*

(*iii*) Heterotrichous—Thallus consists of two parts, i.e. horizontally running main shoot/trichome and a vertical erect trichome/shoot e.g. *Draparnaldiopsis, Coleochaete.*

(*d*) *Pseudoparenchymatous :* These algae are characterized by uniaxial filaments, e.g. *Polysiphonia* and *multiaxial* filaments e.g. *Nemalion.*

(*e*) *Siphonous :* These algae consists of multinucleate tube like cells having no septa, e.g. *Vaucheria.*

(*f*) *Parenchymatous :* In these algae, cell division takes place on different sides with the result that they become parenchymatous, e.g. *Ulva.*

Reproduction in Algae : Reproduction in algae takes place by following methods :

(A) Vegetative

(B) Asexual

(C) Sexual.

(A) Vegetative Reproduction : It is a simple process of reproduction in algae. By this process thallus divides into small fragments and each part later on gives rise to a new plant. This process is termed Fragmentation. In class Myxophyceae it takes place by hormogones.

(B) Asexual Reproduction : In this process some cells or protoplasm of few cells of the plant divides to form a small sized structure, the spore. Each spore is liberated from the mother cell and gives rise to a new plant. It generally takes place by the following method :

(*i*) *By Zoospores :* In this process, under favourable conditions biciliated (e.g. *Ulothrix*), tetraciliate (e.g. *Ulothrix*) or multiciliate (e.g. *Oedogonium*) zoospores are formed and on bursting of mother cells (300 sporangium) come out and give rise to new plant.

(*ii*) *By Aplanospore :* In this case the protoplasm gets separated from cell wall to form one or more thin-walled, nonciliated aplanospores and each aplanospore gives rise to a new plant, e.g. *Chlorella.*

(*iii*) *By Hypnospore :* In this process under unfavourable conditions the protoplasm of the cell separates from the cell wall and collects in the centre. These are non-motile and thick-walled. They give birth to new plant on the commencement of favourable conditions, e.g. *Vaucheria.*

(*iv*) *By Akinete :* In this process, entire cell becomes thick. Akinetes are *formed under unfavourable conditions* and on commencement of favourable conditions each akinete develop into a new plant e.g. *Cladophora.*

(*v*) *Palmella Stage :* On the approach of dry conditions, zoospores or aplanospores do not come outside the mother cell but get surrounded by mucilaginous sheath. The division continues with the result they take the shape of a colony. This is known as palmella stage. Under favourable conditions, they come out. Each zoospore or aplanospore gives rise to a new plant, e.g. *Chlamydomonas.*

(*vi*) *By Endospores :* In most of the members of *Myxophyceae*, development of large number of endospores takes place inside the mother cell. Endospores gives rise to a new plant under favourable conditions.

(*vii*) *By Autospores :* In some algae, the resting spores develop into new plants inside the mother cell, e.g. *Chlorococcus.*

(*viii*) *By Cysts* : In some algae under unfavourable conditions and abundant food supply, the thallus divides into multinucleate and thick walled smaller segments, which are termed *cysts*. In favourable conditions cysts give rise to new plants, e.g. *Vaucheria*.

(C) Sexual Reproduction : Sexual reproduction takes place by fusion of gametes. These gametes develop in gametangia. This is of following types.

(*i*) *Isogamous* : In some algae the gametes are similar in their external morphology and size. In this type (+) and (–) strain gametes fuse together to form zygospore. Isogametes may be motile (zoogametes) e.g. *Chalmydomonas debaryanum* and *Ulothrix* or nonmotile (aplanogametes) e.g. *Spirogyra*.

(*ii*) *Anisogamous* : In some algae the gametes are similar in their external morphology but they differ in behaviour and size. The larger gamete is passive and it is known as *macrogamete*. The smaller gamete is active and is known as *microgamete*. The fusion of these two gives zygote which later on undergoes reduction divisions to form new plants e.g. *Chlamydomonas braunii*.

(*iii*) *Oogamous* : In this type of sexual reproduction, fusion of small, biciliate or multiciliate and active male gamete with large non-ciliated and passive female gamete (which is retained within the oogonium either permanently or upto maturity) takes place and zygote (oospore) in formed, e.g. *Oedogonium* and *Chlamydomonas coccifera*.

Subdivision 2 → Fungi : (*i*) These are plants which lack chlorophyll but have a thallus-like plant body, i.e. they are non-green thallophytes.

(*ii*) These are nonvascular.

(*iii*) Not differentiated into root, shoot, leaves.

(*iv*) They are parasitic or saprophytic and reproduce by spores.

The important classes of fungi are as follows :

Class 1 : *Schizomycetes*
Class 2 : *Myxomycetes*
Class 3 : *Phycomycetes*
Class 4 : *Ascomycetes*
Class 5 : *Basidiomycetes*
Class 6 : *Deuteromycetes*

Structure of Fungi : The structure of plant body of fungi is simple. They range from unicellular, uninucleate forms to thread like structures called mycelium (plural) (singular-hypha) which is usually branched tube like structure, having protoplasm with reserve food and bounded by a wall of chitin. The protoplasm of the hypha may be continuous without cross walls and is called aseptate hypha or with transverse partitions or septa and is known as septate hypha. An aseptate hypha is nothing but a multinucleate tube like structure, called coenocyte. In aseptate hyphae, septa are formed when reproductive structures are produced.

In septate hypha, septa has a central pore and septa are thus perforated or porous. Sometimes pore may be absent in the septa (nonporous septa) or more than one pores may be present.

On the basis of number of nuclei in each cells, septate hyphae may be of 3 kinds, *multinucleate*, *uninucleate* (monokaryotic hyphae), with *binucleate* cells (dikaryotic hyphae) with each nucleus from different parent plant.

The fungus cell-wall is generally composed of a complex substance known as *chitin* which is often impregnated with some *salts* (not structurally identical with animal chitin). Formula of fungus chitin is $(C_{22}H_{54}N_4O_{21})_n$. In some fungi true cellulose has been detected. Sometimes a complex polysaccharide known as *callose* has also been reported.

Inside the cell, endoplasmic reticulum, dictyosomes, mitochondria, vacuoles, centroioles, storage product glycogen, alcohol mannitol and oils have been detected. Many hyphae together form the plant-body of fungi and is called *mycelium*. The mycelium may be *hyaline* or variously coloured. Sometimes the mycelium takes different forms which are as follows :

(1) Plectenchyma : When hyphae of a mycelium grow together and intertwine with one another forming a thick woven tissue, it is called *plectenchyma*. *Plectenchyma* may be of two types :

(*a*) Rather loosely interwoven tissue whose hyphae component lie more or less parallel to each other and are recognizable—is known as *prosenchyma* or *prosoplectenchyma*.

(*b*) Hyphae lying adpressed to one another forming a compactly woven tissue whose hyphae component have lost their identity and appear isodimetric and continuous in section resembling parenchyma of higher plants is known as *pseudoparenchyma* or *paraplectenchyma.*

(2) Sclerotia (Single Sclerotium) : In some fungi, the mycelium may pass into a dormant or resting stage by the formation of hard resting bodies resistant to unfavourable conditions, called *scelerotium.* The scelerotia may germinate upon the return of favourable conditions. Each sclerotium is composed of central prosenchymatous and peripheral pseudoparenchymatous tissue which are again surrounded by a ring of pigmented hyphae.

(3) Rhizomorph : When the fungal hyphae aggregate together, behave as an organized unit to form a root like strand with a thick hard cortex and develop a growing tip somewhat resembling that of a root tip. It mainly serves the function of absorption.

Reproduction in Fungi : Fungi also have 3 type of reproductions :

(A) Vegetative (B) Asexual (C) Sexual

(A) Vegetative Reproduction : Vegetative reproduction in fungi may be of following types :

(*i*) *Fragmentation :* Fragmentation of the vegetative hyphae may be accidental and fragments develop into new plants under favourable conditions.

(*ii*) *Fission :* In this, simple splitting of vegetative cells into two daughter cells takes place by constriction.

(*iii*) *Budding :* Some fungi produce small outgrowths i.e. *buds* from their vegetative body. Such buds receive one daughter nucleus as a result of division of the parent nucleus. Eventually the buds are cut off from parent cell and mature to form new individuals. The buds may remain attached to the parent cell for a long time resultating in the formation of a chain of buds (called pseudomycelium).

(*iv*) *Oidium formation :* In some fungi, the hyphae breakup into numerous small fragments known as *oidia* and give rise to new hyphae.

(*v*) *Chlamydospore :* In some fungi, the hyphae forms under unfavourable conditions, thick walled resting resistant spores which later separate apart from each other. They may be *terminal* or *intercalary.* They may remain viable for several years. On return to favourable conditions they germinate to give rise to new individuals. Thus chlamydospores are organs of perennation.

(B) Asexual Reproduction : This is of the following types :

(*i*) *Zoospore formation :* Zoospores may be uniflagellate, e.g. *Synchitrium* or biflagellate e.g. *Saprolgenia, Phythium* and are thin walled uninucleate structures formed in zoosporangia. They germinate to give rise to new mycelium. Biflagellate zoospores are of two kinds, pearshaped or pyriform with two flagella placed at anterior end (primary zoospore) and kidney shaped or bean shaped, bearing two oppositely directed flagella inserted laterally in a furrow or concave side (secondary zoospores).

(*ii*) *Aplanospore formation :* Aplanospores are thin-walled non-motile spores produced in a sporangium which after liberation give rise to new mycelium, e.g. *Rhizopus, Mucor.*

(*iii*) *Conidia :* Conidia are non-motile thin walled exogenous spores produced on a condiophore. They are arranged in chains upon the conidiophore e.g. *Aspergillus* and *Penicillium.* They may also be produced singly on a conidiophore e.g. *Phythium.*

(C) Sexual Reproduction : Sexual reproduction is reduced in fungi and take place by two fusing gametes. It includes 3 stage, which are as follows :

(*a*) *Plasmogamy :* In this, there is union between two protoplasts which result in bringing the fusing nuclei of different parentage close together.

(*b*) *Karyogamy :* The two haploid nuclei which come together in plasmogamy fuse and thus a diploid zygote is produced.

(*c*) *Meiosis :* In the zygote, reduction takes place, thus reducing the number of chromosomes to half. Sexual reproduction in fungi is of the following types:

(*i*) *Planogametic Copulation :* This is the simplest type of sexual reproduction. In this process, fusion of two gametes of opposite sex or strains takes place. One or both of the fusing gametes are motile. It results in the formation of a diploid zygote. This process is usually of three types.

(1) *Isogamy :* In this process fusing gametes are morphologically similar but physiologically dissimilar. These gametes are produced by different parents, e.g. *Synchytrium.*

(2) *Heterogamy :* When the fusing gametes are morphologically as well as physiologically different, the process is known as *heterogamy.* Heterogamous

reproduction is of two types, *anisogamous* and *oogamous*. *Anisogamy* consists in the fusion of two gametes, the male gamete being more active and small while the female gamete is larger and less active e.g. *Allomyces*. In *oogamy*, the gametes are produced inside the morphologically different gametangia. The male gametangia is smaller and called *antheridium* while the female gametangium is larger and is called *oogonium*. The antheridium bears smaller, active and motile gametes known as sperms while the oogonium bears non-motile, large egg.

(*ii*) *Gametangial Contact :* In this process, two gametangia come in contact with one another. Either a passage is formed by dissolution of common wall at the point of contact or fertilization tube is developed to facilitate the migration of entire contents of male gametangium into the female gametangium. Both the gametangium never fuse together loosing their identity.

(*iii*) *Gametangial Copulation :* In this process, fusion of entire contents of two gametangia is accomplished either by dissolution of their common walls resulting in the formation of a single cell, in which protpolasts of two gametangia fuse or transfer of one entire protoplast of one gametangia into the other takes place through a pore developed in the gametangial wall at the point of contact. (Difference with heterogamy is that here two gametangia originate from two zoospores, whereas in heterogamy, two gametangia develop on somatic hyphae).

(*iv*) *Spermatization :* Some fungi produce many minute, spore like, single celled structure called spermatia (non-motile gametes). These structures are transferred through agencies like water, wind and insects to either special receptive hyphae or trichogyne of ascogonium. The contents migrate into recpetive structure. Thus dikaryotic condition is established.

(*v*) *Somatogamy :* This takes place in fungi where formation of gametes is absent. In such fungi, anastamoses takes place between somatic structures bearings nuclei of different parentage whereby nuclei of one passes into cooresponding somatic cell by dissolving the wall, thus establishing a dikaryotic condition.

Division 2 → Bryophyta : (*i*) Most simple & primitive group of Embryophyta.

(*ii*) It includes 840 genera and 23,500 species.

(*iii*) Plants are very small and cosmopolitan.

(*iv*) Plant body is green thallus like without vascular tissues.

(*v*) Sex organs are multicellular & jacketed.

(*vi*) Asexual reproduction by mitospores is entirely absent.

(*vii*) Presence of distinct embryo stage in the life cycle is seen.

(*viii*) A heterologous type of alternation of generations occurs constantly.

(*ix*) The gametophyte is the conspicuous plant in the life cycle.

(*x*) The male reproductive structure is *antheridium* and female reproductive structure is *archegonium*.

Bryophyta can further be classified into :

Class 1 : *Hepaticae* or Liverworts

Class 2 : *Musci* or Mosses.

Structure of Bryophytes : The main plant is gametophyte. It is green thallus as in *Riccia* and *Marchantia* or it may be differentiated into rhizoids, stem like structure and leaf like structure e.g. *Funaria*. Both the types of gametophyte are attached to substratum with the help of rhizoids which may be unicellular or multicellular and also function for absorption of water and minerals. These plants lack vascular tissues. The length of the plants vary from several mms to several cms. The largest plant of the group is *Dawsonia* which is approximately 40-50 cm long. All cells of gametophyte except rhizoids have chloroplasts due to which they are photoautotrophic. The sporophyte of moss, *Funaria* is divided into foot, seta & capsule.

Capsule is again divided into *Apophysis*—the basal sterile region, theca—the central fertile region and *operculum*—the upper region of capsule is enclosing peristome.

Reproduction in Bryophytes : It is of two types:

(A) Vegetative Reproduction : The gametophyte reproduce by fragmentation, by gemmae, by tubers, by protonema and by bulbils.

(*i*) *Fragmentation of primary protonema :* Protonema formed by germination of spores is called primary protonema. In the protonema, some cells here and there die, due to which small fragments are produced. If a fragment of protonema has a bud of leafy gametophyte, it develops into an adult plant.

(*ii*) *By secondary protonema :* From any portion of adult leafy plant, e.g. 'leaf', 'stem', 'rhizoid', some cells produce a protonema. This is called secondary protonema. Leafy buds arise here and their and are capable of giving rise to new adult plants.

(*iii*) *By Bulbils :* Bulbils are resting buds produced on rhizoids or protonema. They get detached from the parent plant and under favourable conditions give rise to new plants.

(*iv*) *By Gemma :* From the apical region of 'leaves' or axis, small gemma are produced which after being detached from parent give rise to new plant.

(*v*) *Apospory :* Some cells from any part of sporophyte separate from the parent, fall on the soil and form a protonema. Buds of leafy gametophore are produced on protonema and give rise to a gametophyte like plant but the cells have diploid set of chromosome ($2n$). In this way a gametophyte like plant is produced from sporophyte without reduction division.

(B) Sexual Reproduction : Sexual reproduction is oogamous. The biciliate antherozoids are borne in antheridia and oospheres (= eggs) are borne in archegonia, which are flask shaped structures differentiated into stalk, venter and neck.

Water is essential for fertilization. Oospore (zygotes) are produced as a result of fusion of male and female gametes. Oospore gives rise to the sporophytic generations, called *sporogonium*. Sporogonium is completely (as in *Riccia*) or partially (as in *Moss*) dependent upon gametophyte. Sporophyte may be very simple and represented by a spore sac only as in *Riccia* or differentiated into foot, seta and capsule as in *Moss*. In the spore sacs are borne spore mother cells which after reduction division give rise to haploid spores. All bryophytes are homosporous. Usually the spore germinate to produce a protonema which later on develop into an adult gametophyte. All bryophytes show alternation of generation.

Division 3 → Pteridophyta : Pteridophytes are *vascular cryptogams* i.e., plant of this group possess vascular tissues (i.e xylem and pholem) for the conduction of water, minerals and for translocation of foods. They are mostly herbacious and grow in moist and shady places. Some important characteristics of pteridophyte are (*i*) The main plant body is sporophyte, usually differentiated into roots (except Psilophyta), stems and leaves (sometimes leaves absent).

(*ii*) Vascular tissue is differentiated into xylem & phloem.

(*iii*) In xylem, trachea (vessels) are absent and in phloems *companion cells* are absent.

(*iv*) They are flowerless plants.

(*v*) They do not produce seeds.

(*vi*) Spores are borne in sporangia.

(*vii*) Sporangia are produced in groups (sori) on sporophylls.

(*viii*) The gametophytic plant is smaller and less differentiated (i.e. simple).

(*ix*) The gametophyte bears male reproductive structure called antheridium and female reproductive structures called archegonia.

(*x*) The antheridia bears antherozoids and archegonia bears oosphere (egg).

(*xi*) There is no secondary growth.

(*xii*) The zygote produces a distinct embryo stage.

(*xiii*) Distinct alternation of generation is present with the sporophyte as the conspicuous plant in the life cycle.

(*xiv*) The division contains nearly 10,000 species which is further divided into :

Class 1 *Filicineae*
Class 2 *Lycopodineae*
Class 3 *Equisetineae.*

(*xv*) Various kind of stele are seen in Pteridophyta.

Structure of Pteriodophytes : The plant of *Selaginélla* is sporophyte and is evergreen, delicate herb with adventitious roots. The plants are diverse in form. In some species the branching stem is prostrate growing along the surface of the ground or may be suberect or may be scandent. The stem is covered with four rows of small leaves, out of these, two rows are of smaller leaves and two rows are of large leaves. Species with dimorphic leaves such as *S. kraussiana*, *S. heivetica* are grouped in the sub genus *Heterophyllum*. In other species of *Selaginella*, the stem may be erect with a spreading mass of foliage leaves uniform in size, such species like *S. oregana*, *S. spinulosa* are grouped in the sub-genus *Homoeophyllum*. The stem, covered with these green leaves present a moss like appearance, hence the plant is called *little club moss*. The leaves are in pairs and are conspicuously different in size. The small leaf of each pair is inserted on dorsal side of the stem and the larger on the ventral side. Successive pairs of leaves are so arranged that large leaf alternates with a large leaf and small leaf with a small leaf. The leaves are always narrowly triangular and pointed. They are liguate, in that they bear a flap like out-growth at the base called the *ligule* (Latin, ligule = little tongue). The leaves are simple, lanceolate or ovate in form. Usually they are thin and delicate except those of xerophytic species.

At the place of bifurcation of stem, a leafless, colourless, elongated cylindrical structure grows downwards. This was called 'Rhizophore' by Nageli, and is quite different from the root in that it has no root cap. Rhizophores are unknown in *S. cuspidata*. Rhizophores typically develops tufts of adventitious roots at its apex.

The main plant body of *Dryopteris* is also a sporophyte and is differentiated into root, stem and leaves. The stem is a rhizome which grows obliquly under the surface of soil, only the apical portion coming out of the soil surface. The old portion of rhizome is covered by brown hairy structure called rementa. From the upper surface of rhizome arise large number of leaves from 25 cms to 1 metre in length. These leaves are bipinnately compound. There are two rows of pinnae on the rachis, each pinna redivided into pinnules. Rachis is also covered over with ramenta. Leaves show **circinate vernation** (i.e. coiled like a spring) when young. The gametophyte of fern is called prothallus which bears archegonia and antheridia and rhizoids.

Reproduction in Pteridophytes :

(A) Vegetative (B) Sexual.

(A) Vegetative reproduction : It is of rare occurrence and may take place by fragmentation as in *S. rupestris*. The prostrate branches develop roots and break into small fragments each developing into a new plant. Certain species of *Selaginela* propagate by bulbils or by smaller tubur as in *S. chrysocaulos* and *S. chrysorrhizos*. In the former case the tubers are formed at surface of the ground and are called surface tubers. In the latter case they are developed underground hence called underground tubers.

In *Dryopteris* adventitious buds arise in the axil of leaves and are detached from the plant and form new plants.

(B) Sexual Reproduction : The reproductive structure is a compact one is *Selaginella* and develops at the terminal portions of branches. It is called strobilus or spike and is a sessile structure. The strobilus is either erect or horizontal. It tapers towards the apex and the length varies from ¼ of an inch to inches. In some cases the strobili owing to the loose arrangement of sporophylls become, inconspicuous.

A strobilus posseses many-liguate sporophylls arranged in the form of cluster, each bearing on its upper side and near its base a small short stalked sporangium. The sporangia, instead of being all alike, are of two distinct kinds. One type of sporangia contains four large spores and the other contains many small spores. The large spores are megaspores and the sporangium which bears them is the megasporangium borne on a megasporophyll. Similarly the small spores are microspores formed in microsporangium borne on a microsporophyll. Each sporophyll, like the leaf has got a ligule in its axil. The dimorphic condition is known as *heterospory*.

For fertilization, usually the male gametophytes are shed from the microsporangium on the ground at **13-celled stage**. Some of microgametophytes shift down between the sporophylls and may fall into the partly opened microsporangia. Now-lying in the megasporagium, the two kinds of gametophyte complete their development. If sufficient water is present, fertilization takes place. The young embryos develop within the wall of megasporangium and drop out as soon as they develop a root and primary shoot. Later on the openings of the megasporangium becomes wider and the megagametophyte with their developing embryos fall on the ground.

This is specially significant since it introduces in the life cycle a close parallel to the pollination and seed formation habits found in the spermatophytes. Therefore, when the megaspore with its newly formed embryonic sporophite falls to the ground, it is for all practical purposes a seed and hence *Selaginella* approaches the seed habit. The oosphere after fertilization gets surrounded by a wall and becomes oospore. After divisions oospore develops, into embryo or sporophyte. In fern also sexual reproduction takes place through spores which are borne is sporangia. When the leaves are mature they bear groups of sori on the undersurface of fertile pinnae. Such fronds are called sporophylls. The sori are borne in two rows on two sides of median vein of a pinnule in between the margin and the midrib. Each sorus is covered by a kidney shaped indusium covering the sorus. In the centre of the sorus the vein ends in a placental tissue from which a number of sporangia arise without any order of development. Each mature sporangium has a long slender multicellular stalk and number of spores enclosed in the capsule wall may be 64 or less. When capsule is mature and dry, spores are thrown out. All the entire sporangium develops from a single initial cell and the development of sporangium is leptosporangiate type. Spores are homosporus i.e. similar and under suitable conditions gives rise to gametophyte which bears antheridium and archegonia. Antherezoids are produced in antheridium and are large spirally coiled and bears numerous large flagella. Archegonium is flask shaped and contain egg, ventral canal cell and neck cancel cell. Venter encloses egg (oosphere) and ventral canal cell. Neck canal cell has two nuclei in fern. During fertilization, ventral canal cell and neck canal cell along with the tip of neck disintegrate and the neck forms a canal like passage full of mucilage and some chemicals like malic acid. These chemicals attract antherozoids and one of male gametes fuses with the oosphere forming a diploid oosphere. Although there are several archegonia in the prothallus, only one is fertilized. The oospore formed gives rise to embryo or sporophyte and usually one sporophyte is developed out of a gametophyte.

Division 4 → Spermatophyta :

(*i*) These are vascular plants bearing seeds.

(*ii*) Secondary growth is present in most members.

(*iii*) The sporophyte is conspicuous plant in the life cycle.

(*iv*) This division contains subdivisions Angiosperms & Gymnosperms.

Distribution of Cryptogams in India :

Algae : Algae occur in fresh water, hot water streams, sea, on moist land (soil), stems of plants and stones. Some algae are found on mud, e.g. *Chara*. Few algae occur on banks of lakes and ponds, e.g. *Rivularia*. Some algae complete their life cycle while living at 70-80°C temperature in hot water stream. Some blue-green algae survive at 85°C. Some algae are found floating on water, e.g. diatoms and *Volvox*. Some algae are found floating on band of pond, e.g. *Spirogyra*. Some algae are epiphytes i.e. they grow on other plants (algae or branches of trees) e.g. *Oedogonium*. *Protoderma*, an algae grows on back of tortoise and *Cladophora* lives upon snail. In addition some algae live inside the animal bodies e.g. *Zoochlorella* is found in *Hydra*. Sometimes algae are parasitic e.g. *Cephaeleuros* is parasite on leaves of tea and coffee. *Phyllobium sphagnicolum* (a green algae) is parasite on *Sphagnum* (a moss) and *Rhodochytrium spilanthidis* (a green algae) is parasitic on leaves of *Ambrosia*. *Oscillatoria* and *Simonsiella* live as mild parasites in the intestine of man and other animals. Some algae are marine, e.g. *Sargassum* and *Fucus*.

Various kinds of algae grow on damp soil, e.g. *Vaucheria*. Algae are found inside the soil upto one metre depth. Algae, are also found on bark of trees, walls and stones etc. e.g. *Scytonema*. Sometimes snow gives different colours on account of algae occurring in snow, e.g. *Chlamydomonas*. *Nostoc* and *Anabaena* are found in the body of Anthoceros and Azolla plant respectively. *Anabaena* with Azolla is found in rice field in India. Also these algae live in coralloid roots of *cycas*. Some algae live symbiotically with fungi in lichens. *Cladophora* may live in symbiotic relationship with sponge (*Eplydatea fuiritalis*). Some blue green algae live in protozoans and are called cynallele.

Trichodesmium erythrium (myxophyceae) lives in red sea imparting it red shade. In ponds near temples in India where old flowers are thrown, *Spirogyra* is dominantly found.

Spirogyra is fresh water olive green algae. It is known as 'pondscum', 'pond silk' or water silk. It is generally found in stagnant reservoirs, ditches & streams. In India, *S. jogens, S. crassata, S. elongata, S. communis, S. condensata, S. parvula, S. microspora, S. sahnii, S. indica* etc. are used.

Fungi : Fungi are found everywhere. Due to lack of chlorophyll pigments, they are unable to synthesize their food. Therefore, they are either parasites or saprophytes. Some fungi may grow on cow dung (*Coprophilous* fungi) or may occur symbiotically. Parasitic fungi take their food from host plants and with the death of host, is caused the death of parasitic fungi. Such fungi are called *obligate* parasites. Some fungi which are usually parasitic but after the death of host plant, are able to absorb their good from the decaying body of the plant are called *facultative saprophytes*. Those fungi which always take their food from decaying organic matter (decaying leather, food, gems, jellies, bread, fruits etc.) are called *obligate saprophytes* and those fungi which are usually saprophytes but can live parasitically under some conditions are called *facultative parasites*.

Those parasites which grow on the surface of the host cells and absorb their food through haustoria are called ectoparasites (*ecotophytic parasites*) while those parasites which enter into the tissues of the host are called endoparasites or *endophytic* parasites.

Some fungi, e.g. *Dactylella* and *Arthrobotrys* derive their food from protozoans, eelworms and rotifers. Such fungi are called *predaceous* fungi. Some fungi live symbiotically with algae (in *lichens*). Some fungi live in the roots of higher plants, e.g. in the roots of *Pinus*. This type of symbiotic relationship is called mycorrhiza. *Rhizopus* is saprophytic fungus living on dead organic matters. Its mycelium is made up of thin, white hyphae growing on pickles, vegetables neglected shoes, specialy in rains. It may become parasitic under some conditions causing softrot in sweet potato. In laboratory it can be grown within 2-3 days on a moist piece of bread covered by jar. Yeast is a saprophyte fungus found on substratum which is rich in sugars e.g. sugarcane, juice, fruits, milk some species are found on animal excreta.

Penicillium occurs in decaying material

Bryophyta : These plants are terrestrial. They are more advanced than thallophyta and grow in moist and shady places. Bryophytes have been called *amphibians* of plant world. They grow on damp walls, damp soil, damp rocks, damp pieces of wood, on river banks and on banks of pools. Some species e.g. *R. fluitans* are aquatic. *Bauxbaumia aphylla* is a saprophyte. *Riccia* grow mostly in wet, terrestrial habitats. However *R. fluituns* and *R. natans* are free floating or submerged. In India, *Riccia* grows in plains or on foot of hills. Some species may grow at higher altitudes (upto 14000 ft.). Most common Indian species are *R. gangetica, R. fluitans, R. pathankotensis. Funaria* has approximately 117 species occurring throughout the whole world. In India 15 species of *Funaria* have been reported. The common Indian species are *F. hygrometrica* (most common), *F. fascicularis, F. obtusa, F. attenuata* etc. Plants of *Funaria* are found in moist, shady place in patches on damp soil, moist rocks, burnt humid soil, damp walls or on tree trunks.

Pteridophyta : They are mostly herbacious and grow in moist and shady places. *Dryopteris* is found in subtropical and warm temperate regions. *Selaginella* is mostly abundant in tropical rain forests, some also grow in temperate regions. Other species thrive best in relatively moist and shady habitats of the hills. A few particularly adopted to xeric environments living on rocks or in dry sandy soils. During the dry periods the plant rolls up into a compact ball, accompanied with the disorganisation of the root system. Such balls roll away in the wind and may tide over the unfavourable period. During the next rain, the ball absorb moisture, unrolling the stems and growth is resumed, e.g. *S. lepidophylla* and *S. rupestris*. These xerophytic species are called '*resurrection plants*' or 'bird's nest moss' and are often sold as a novelty. *S. oregana* is an epiphytic species which grows on the branches and trunks of moss covered trees.

Concept of Progymnosperms

The first use of the word 'gymnosperm,' is referred to Theophrastus (300 BC) in his book "Inquiry into plants" to embrace the plants with unprotected seeds. Gymnosperms (gymnos : naked, sperma = seed), as evident from their name, are naked seeded plants with their ovules freely exposed on megasporophylls unlike angiosperms which bear them enclosed within closed *megasporophylls* (carpels). They form a distinct subdivision of spermatophyta (seed bearing plants) and behave as replicate to angiosperms. Goebel has rightly described them 'phaneogams without ovary', Geological history speaks of gymnosperms as the most ancient seed plants that originated during the late Paleozoic (265 million years ago), but flourished well during the Mesozoic. The long geological history of the group is full of diverse lines of evolution. Alike present day angiosperms, some of the gymnosperms were dominant during past geological ages as know by their fossil record. Many examples of gymnosperms flourished during long geological past and then became extinct. Certain primitive gymnosperms like *Cycadofilicales* (Pteridospermales), *cycadeoidales* (Bennettitales) and *cordaitales* are now extinct. *Cycadales, Ginkgoales* and *coniferales* represent both fossil and living states, *Gnetales* is a recent group. *Cycadofilicales* appeared during carboniferous era and are an evidence of the origin of gymnosperms from an ancient stock of fern like individuals. These bore primitive seeds and resembled with the ferns so much that the period, during which cycadofilicales flourished, is often called as 'age of ferns.' Cycadeoidales showed striking resemblance with modern Cycads, and flourished well during early Mesozoic. These in having bisporangiate cones, are regarded as possible precursor of angiospermous flower. Botanists consider them giving a way to angiosperms at the end of Mesozoic. Cordaitales were well developed during late Palezoic and early Mesozoic and formed the ancestral stock for modern coniferales and Gnetales.

Gymnosperms constitute a heterogenous plant group with several evolution trends which have been operating since past to the present day. Evolutionary tendencies reveal that gymnosperms form a bridge between pteridophytes and angiosperms.

ECONOMIC IMPORTANCE OF CRYPTOGAMS

Algae : (A) Uses : The algae are useful for human beings as follows :

(1) *Algae as Food :* Carbohydrates, organic compounds and vitamins are abundantly found in algae. Vitamin A, C, and D, E are mostly found in algae. In Japan, *Porphyra* of the class *phycophyceae* is eaten. Chiefly *P. umblicus* and *P. perfbrarata* are used as food in many countries. In Japan and nearly countries, *Alaria, Ulva, Sargassum, Laminaria*, etc. are used as salad (vegetable). Iodine is manufactured from *Laminaria*. *Ulva* is commonly known as sea lettuce. In India, pepole of sea shore states take marine algae as favourite food. In China *Nostoc commune* is used as food. In Scotland, *Rodomenia palmata* is chewed as tobacco.

Now a days, various scientists are doing research to obtain foods from *Chlorella* as it contains proteins and vitamins A and D in abundant quantity. Some algae, e.g. *Gelidium, Gracilaria* etc., produce agar-agar, a jelly like substance employed in the manufacture of icecream.

Sargassum and *Macrocystis* are used as food for marine as well as domestic animals. Some algae are commercially cultivated in fish culture ponds and are used as their food.

(2) *Algae in Industry :* Diatoms develop into diatomaceous earth which is employed as :

(*i*) filter for microorganisms in sugar industry.
(*ii*) in manufacture of glass and porcelin.
(*iii*) insulator in boiler and blast furnace.
(*iv*) abrasive for manufacture of metal paints, varnish, polish, tooth paste.
(*v*) absorbent of liquid nitroglycerine.

Algin is derived from an marine algae and is used in vulcanisation, typewriter roller and in the manufacture of inflammable films. It is also found in manufacture of artificial fibres and to control blood flow during surgery. In Japan *Sargassum* is used in manufacture of artificial wool. A mucilaginous substance, the caroganin obtained from the alga *Charadrus* is used in the manufacture of cosmetics, boot-polish and shampoo.

Agar-Agar is also used for conducting tissue-culture experiments in the laboratory and it is also used as heat and sound proof. This substance is also used in manufacture of artificial fibres, leather, sauce etc. Various algae e.g. *Laminaria, Fucus* etc., are used in the manufacture of iodine, bromine, acetone etc.

(3) *Algae in Agriculture nitrogen fixation :* Myxophycean plants, e.g. *Nostoc, Anabaena*, etc.

convert atmospheric (elemental) nitrogen into nitrogen compounds which are absorbed by higher plants. This process is known as nitrogen fixation. Bacteria also take part in this process. By this action, fertility of soil is increased.

Some algae are used as fertilizer and some blue-green algae are capable of converting clay soil into cultivable land.

(4) *Medicinal Use of Algae :* An antibiotic chlorellin is extracted from *Chlorella*. It is crystalline and is active at 120°C. It antagonises effect of gram-negative bacteria and *Nitella* causes death of mosquitoes in ponds hence it is used in control of malaria.

(5) *Algae in Biological Research :* Recent knowledge about the photosynthetic processes is based on the research carried out in *Chlorella*. *Acetabularia* and *Valonia* are used in research to study nucleocytoplasmic relations.

(B) Harmful effects of Algae : In addition to useful effects of some alage such as *Microcystis*, *Chrococcus*, *Oscillatoria*, *Anabaena* etc. cause water blooms in water reservoirs and on death and decay emit bad smell. Water get contaminated with such things which make it unfit for drinking by animals and fishes as they die upon drinking such water. Sometimes marine algae grow more and more and retard speed of ships. *Cephaleuros* species are parasitic on leaves of tea and causes harm to tea industry.

Fungi : (A) Useful Activities

(1) As *Food Morchella*, *Agaricus* and *Lycoperdon* are most common edible fungi often cooked with rice and vegetables. Yeast cells are good source of various vitamins. Vitamin 'B' is obtained from fresh yeast cells. Some yeasts like *Torulopsis utilis* are rich in proteins.

(2) In Industry (*a*) *In Cheese Production :* A few species of Pencillium like *P. comemberti* and *P. roquefoti* are used in ripening of cheese and also help in imparting them a characteristic flavour. These varieties of cheese are delicious are highly valued.

(*b*) *In baking Industry :* Some yeasts like *Saccharomyces cervevisiae* are very useful to bakers in manufacture of bread.

(*c*) *In Alcohol Industry :* Yeast is used in fermentation of carbohydrates to produce alcohol on commercial scale by its enzymatic activity as follows:

$$C_6H_{12}O_6 \xrightarrow{\text{Zymase}} 2C_2H_5OH + 2CO_2 + \text{Energy}$$

(*d*) In Manufacture of Acid, Enzymes and Fats

(*i*) *Gallic acid :* By *Pencillium glauccum* and *Aspergillus gallomyces*

(*ii*) *Citric acid :* By *Citromyces pfefferiaur* a *mucor*

(*iii*) *Gluconic acid : Aspergillus niger*

(*iv*) *Amylase :* By *Aspergillus aryzae*

(*v*) Invertase : By *Saccharomyces cerevisiae*

(*vi*) Fats : By *Aspergillus nidulans*, *A. fisheri*, *Penicillium piscarum*, *P. javanicus*

(3) *Soil Fertility :* Saprophyte fungi disintegrate the decaying organic matter and thus help in release of minerals which can be again absorbed by plants.

(4) *As medicines :* Several fungi are good sources of antibiotics, drugs, which inhibit the growth of microorganisms.

Some important antibiotics produced from fungi are given below :

Name of Medicine	Name of Fungi
Penicillin	*Penicillium notatum*
Penicillin	*Penicillium chrysogessum*
Ergot	*Claviceps purpurea*
Chaetomin	*Chacfomian coenoides*
Griseofulvin	*P. griseofulvum*

(5) *In nutrition of plants :* Several fungal members associate themselves with the surface of roots, forming micorrhizae which is important for nutrition of certain-trees like *Pinus*, *Zamia* etc.

(6) *Control of insect-pests :* Several fungi like *Aschesosonia aleyroides*, *Isoria ferinosa*, *Empusa spulcharoies* help in controlling the infection of insects on plants.

(7) *In Manufacture of Phytohormones :* Gibberellins which help in promoting growth of the plants are synthesized from a fungus named *Fusarium moniliforme*.

(8) *In Biological Research :* Several fungi like *Neurospora*, yeast, *Ascobolus* have been used for a long time, in research (genetics, cytology and metabolism).

(9) *As test organisms :* Some strains of *Aspergillus niger* are highly sensitive to some trace elements. They can detect trace elements like Cu, Zn and Mo even if they are present in very small quantity in the substrate. These elements when taken up by the fungus may give a particular colour to the conidia.

(B) Harmful Activities

(1) Fungi causing diseases in plants :

	Name of Disease	Causal fungi
(i)	White rust of crucifers	*Cystopus candida* syn *Albugo candida*
(ii)	Powdery mildew of cereals and grasses	*Erysiphe* species
(iii)	Fruit rot of apple	*Peronospora* species
(iv)	Downy mildew of crucifers	*Peronospora* species
(v)	Early blight of potato	*Alternaria solani*
(vi)	Late blight of potato	*Phytophthora infestans*
(vii)	Stem gall of coriandrum	*Protomyces macrosporus*
(viii)	Red rot of sugarcane	*Collectotrichum falcatum*
(ix)	Black (stem) rust of wheat	*Puccinia graminis tritici*
(x)	Loose smut of wheat	*Ustilago nuda tritici*
(xi)	Tikka disease of groundnut	*Cercospora personata* *C. arachidicola*
(xii)	Wart disease of potato	*Synchytrium* species
(xiii)	Damping off	*Pythium defaryanum*
(xiv)	Brown leaf spot of rice	*Helminthosporium oryzae*

(2) Fungi Causing diseases of human beings

	Disease	Causal fungi
(i)	Aspergillosus (a lung disease)	*Aspergillus* niger, *A. flavus*
(ii)	Ringworm	*Trichophyton*, *Microsporum*
(iii)	Infection of nervous system	*Mucor pusillus*
(iv)	Mental disorder	*Lipomyces neoformans*
(v)	Ear infection (otomycoses)	*Aspergillus flavus* *A. nidulans*

(3) *Animal diseases :* Some species of *Saprolegina* are parasitic on eggs and gills of fishes.

(4) *Destruction of timber : Armillaria mellea* causes red rot of apple trees and *Polyporus* causes wood rot in many trees.

(5) *Spoilage of food :* Spores of *Rhizopus, Mucor, Aspergillus* germinate on gems, jellies, pickles, bread and destroy them. *Penicillium, Mucor, Aspergillus* destroy meat.

(6) *Destruction of common goods :* Some fungi e.g. *Alternaria, Pencillium, Trichoderma, Mucor, Chactomium Cephalothecium, Fusaria* destroy leather cloth, rubber, paper and even camera lenses.

(7) *Fungi as Poison :* Some fungi as *Amantia*, which resembles *Agaricus* are eaten in place of *Agaricus* and become fatal to man. *Aspergillus flavus, A. fumigatus, Penicillium islandicum* produce a poisonous substance called *aflatoxin* while growing on mustard and ground nut cakes. The substance if eaten by animals cause disease in animals.

(8) *Hallucinogenic fungi :* From *Claviceps* fungus is extracted a substance called LSD which is hallucinogenic in man i.e. causes distortion of perception.

Bryophyta : They are of less economic importance.

(1) *Sphagnum* has the capacity to retain water for long periods and such is used to cover the plant roots during transportation.

(2) Some mosses which grow in pools settle to bottom on their death and this helps in soil formation.

(3) When they grow on rocks they help in soil formation.

(4) Some Bryophyta also work as soil binders when they grow in aggregations.

(5) Some are used as foddes for herbivorus animals.

(6) Some as *Sphagnum* are used as bed for animals.

(7) *Sphagnum* is also used as fuel.

(8) *Sphagnum* plants are also used to tie grafts.

(9) *Sphagnum* is also used in seed beds because of its water retention capacity.

Pteridophytes : They are mostly used as decoratives in door plants.

QUESTIONS FROM PREVIOUS YEARS' PAPERS

1. Explain the following:
(*a*) Elicitors
(*b*) Rhizophore

2. Describe the following:
(*a*) Economic importance of marine algae
(*b*) Gametophytes in *Selaginella*
(*c*) Pollenia
(*d*) Female inflorescence in *Gnetum*
(*e*) Ovule bearing organs of Cycadofilicales
(*f*) Beta taxonomy
(*g*) Distribution of *Welwitschia*
(*h*) Cytomixis

3. Distinguish between the following:
(*a*) Axile and Parietal placentation
(*b*) Synergid and egg cells

4. Describe different types of Endosperms.

5. Describe the floral characteristics of orchids.

6. Economic importance of Dipterocarpaceae.

7. Discuss the importance of Herbarium.

8. Describe a natural system of classification up to the rank of orders of flowering plants.

9. What are fungicides and how are they applied in standing crops and plants products?

10. Describe the following:
(*a*) Heterocysts
(*b*) Akinetes
(*c*) Water bloom algae
(*d*) Witches' broom
(*e*) Economic importance of blue-green algae.
(*f*) Sporophyte of *Selaginella*.
(*e*) *Equisetum* species are not primitive vascular cryptogams.
(*f*) Anomalous secondary growth.
(*g*) Reproductive structure in *Lycopodium*.
(*h*) External morphology of *Ephedra*.

11. Write a short note on distribution of *Williamsonia*.

12. Write about the reproduction of *Taxus*.

13. Write an account of Takhtajan system of classification of plants.

14. Write a short note on Fungal cell wall.

15. What is a zoospore? Mention its function.

16. Write a note on Heterothallism in Fungi.

17. Write a note on Heterotrichous thallus in Algae.

18. Write short notes on:
(*a*) Types of sexual reproduction in Fungi
(*b*) Palmella stage
(*c*) Telome theory
(*d*) Tracheids

19. Describe the following:
(*a*) Pollen grain in *Pinus*
(*b*) Structure of ovule in *Gnetum*
(*c*) Ovule in Cordaitales
(*d*) Leaf anatomy in *Cycas*

20. Write short notes on:
(*a*) Classification of angiosperms
(*b*) Canada balsam
(*c*) Tapetum
(*d*) Importance of Palynology in Taxonomy
(*e*) Criteria of Phylogenetic classification
(*f*) Taxol
(*g*) Triple fusion

21. Give the phylogenetic considerations of *Gnetum*.

22. Describe the role of Anatomy in Taxonomy.

23. Discuss Takhtajan's principles in evaluating the relative degree of advancement of flowering plants.

24. Write a note on:
(*a*) Modes of nutrition in fungi.
(*b*) L.S. female receptacle of *Marchantia*.
(*c*) Blue-green algae as biofertilizers.

25. Differentiate between Strobillus of *Lycopodium* and *Selaginella*.

26. Write an account of various types of spores found in algae. Give labelled diagrams.

27. Write a short account of the economic importance of algae.

28. Write notes on:
(*a*) Anatomy of *Selaginella* root.
(*b*) Stem anatomy of Equisetum
(*c*) Sporocarp of Marsilea.
(*d*) Lenticels—structure and function
(*e*) Cambium—structure and function
(*f*) Principles of numerical taxonomy

29. Give suitable answer on the following: (Draw labelled diagrams wherever necessary)
(*a*) Monosporic embryo sacs
(*b*) Wood anatomy of *Pinus*
(*c*) Ruminate endosperm
(*d*) Gum arabic and gum ghatti

30. Write what you know on the following:
(*a*) Somatic hybrids and cybrids
(*b*) Asexual reproduction in diatoms
(*c*) Thallus structure in *Vaucheria*
(*d*) Sexual reproduction in *Fucus*

31. Why are bryophytes found only in moist habitats?

32. What are the adaptations for effective dispersal of spores of *Funaria*?

33. Write short notes on:
(*a*) Internodal anatomy in *Equisetum*
(*b*) Phylogenetic affiliations of blue-green algae

34. Draw the basic features of cell structure in prokaryotic and eukaryotic algae, and explain the important differences in the cell organisation.

35. With the help of suitable diagrams, describe the life history of *Albugo*. (No descriptions).

36. Write an illustrated account of the gametophyte and reproductive structures in *Anthoceros*.

37. Write a short account of the different types of stele found in pteriodophytes.

38. Write a short note on Algae of food.

39. Distinguish between Stomata and Lenticels.

40. Write what you know on:
(*a*) Male germ unit.
(*b*) Embryo development in *Paeonia.*
(*c*) Classification of angiosperms by Armen Takhtajan.

41. What are the structural features of guard cells which help in opening and closing of stomata?

42. Write a short note on Interxylary phloem.

43. Differentiate between:
(*a*) Ascospore and auxopsore.
(*b*) Archegonium and carpogonium.

44. Write short notes on:
(*a*) Heterocyst in blue-green algae.
(*b*) Interferon.
(*c*) Thallus of *Penicillium.*
(*d*) Thallus structure of *Saprolegnia.*

45. With the help of labelled diagrams only, show the evolutionary trend in the steles of Pteridophyta.

46. Discuss the morphological nature of rhizophore of *Selaginella.* Draw a neat labelled diagram of T.S. of rhizophore.

47. Mention the important work done by the following botanists:
(*a*) Prof. S.R. Kashyap
(*b*) Prof. F.E. Fritsch
(*c*) Prof. P. Maheshwari
(*d*) Prof. Birbal Sahni

48. Draw labelled diagrams of the following:
(*a*) L.S. of *Pinus* female cone.
(*b*) Stem anatomy of *Gnetum.*
(*c*) T.S. normal root of *Cycas.*
(*d*) T.S. young root of *Ginkgo biloba.*

49. Describe the principles governing the construction of mechanical system in plants.

50. With the help of diagrams differentiate between the following:
(*a*) Cranial canals and vallecular canals.
(*b*) Homoiomerous and heteromerous thalli in lichens.
(*c*) Plectostele and dictyostele.
(*d*) Structure of *Oscillatoria* and *Nostoc.*

51. Critically examine some authors' concept that the rhizophore can be considered as morphologically a root.

52. With the help of labelled diagrams only depicts the major stages and events in the life cycle of *Funaria.*

53. Giving suitable examples, highlight the economic importance of marine algae.

54. Draw the labelled diagram of stages in sexual reproduction of *Penicillium.*

55. Describe the salient features of Bentham and Hooker's system of classification. What are its merits and demerits?

56. Write a short note on vegetative reproduction in bryophytes.

57. In what way does a fungal cell differ from an algal cell.

58. Write briefly about the following:
(*a*) Origin and evolution of sex in algae.
(*b*) Columella in bryophytes.

59. Distinguish between the following:
(*a*) Cleistothecium and Apothecium.
(*b*) Gymnosperms and Pteridophytes.

60. Comment upon the process of progressive sterilization of sporogenous tissue in bryophytes.

61. Describe the process of Ascus development in Ascomycetes.

62. Write notes on the following:
(*a*) Progymnosperms
(*b*) Double fertilization.

61. Draw only the labelled diagrams of the following:
(*a*) L.S. of an embryo sac
(*b*) T.S. of *Drocaena* stem
(*c*) V.S. of *Cycas* ovule
(*d*) Floral diagram of Asclepiadaceae

62. Give an account of the following:
(*a*) Development of a dicot embryo.
(*b*) Differences between cycadales and coniferales.

63. Differentiate between the following:
(*a*) Prokaryote and Eukaryote
(*b*) Coenobium and Colony

64. Write critical notes on the following:
(*a*) Hybrid
(*b*) Herbarium
(*c*) Major types of embryos with examples.
(*d*) Anomocytic stomata
(*e*) Cycas and its importance
(*f*) Penicillin
(*g*) Fungicides

65. Draw the scientifically accurate diagrams of the following and label the parts:
(*a*) Synandrous and syngenesious stamens
(*b*) Marchantia capsule—vertical section
(*c*) Bacterial cell—ultrastructure
(*d*) V.S. of *Gnetum* ovule

66. Compare Bentham and Hooker's system of classification with Hutchinson's system of classification.

67. Discuss the role of Algae in human welfare.

68. Draw a diagram of T.S. of leaf of *Typha.*

69. Differentiate between normal and abnormal secondary growth in dicot stem. Discuss with suitable examples. Draw labelled diagrams wherever necessary.

CHAPTER–3

PHANEROGAMS : GYMNOSPERMS

GENERAL STRUCTURE AND REPRODUCTION OF CYCAS AND PINUS

Cycas

General Morphology : The plant belongs to the sprophytic generation and is differentiated into root, stem and leaves. The adult cycas plant is about 2 meters high. *C. media* is the tallest species. The stem is thick, unbranched (*caudex*, but branches may arise when terminal bud is injured) and bears triangular leaf bases on its surface. The leaves show *circinate vernation* and are loosely arranged. Cycas leaves are of two types (*a*) scale leaves (*b*) green foliage leaves. The number of foliage leaves formed in one year will be constant for any given species. The petiole is *stout* and called *rachis*. Rachis bears leaf lets or pinnules on either side. The lower leaf-lets of rachis are modified into spine. Lateral veins are absent in pinnule. The primary root persists and forms a tap root system. The lateral branches of the root come out of the soil (apo-geotropic) and branch repeatedly to form dwarf dichotomously branched coral like man called *coralloid* roots or *corallrhiza*. Blue green algae *Anabaena* live symbiotically in the coralloid roots. It fixes the nitrogen.

General Anatomy : The vascular bundles in stem are conjoint, collateral open and arranged in a ring. The xylem of the bundles consists of tracheids only. The pholem comprises of sieve tube and phloem parechyma, they lack *companion cells*. The secondary growth in a young stem is normal, but as it becomes older, new rings are formed giving rise concentric rings of secondary vascular tissues (polyxylic condition).

Transfusion tissue is present in the leaves which help in conduction. Tough and leathery texture and other structures such as strongly cutinized thickend hypodermis, *sunken stomata* restricted only to the lower surface, presence of *transfusion* tissue all these point to a xerophytic adaption of *cycas*.

Internal Structure of Pinnule : Show xerophytic nature. Mesophyll is differentiated into palisade and spongy tissue. Vascular bundle of innule is conjoint, collateral, xylem is *diploxylic*, the larger patch is the centripetal xylem and the two lateral patches are centrifugal xylem. Phloem is present below the centrifugal xylem.

Anatomy of Root : Resembles that of a dicot root. Xylem is diarch or triarch. In the coralloid root, the algal zone is in the cortex, which is termed as middle cortex.

Sexual Reproduction :

Male cone : Cycas is dioecious. The male plant has a cone at its apex. Each cone has a thick central axis around which microsporophylls are spirally arranged. Groups of *sporangia* or *sori* are present on the abaxial (lower) side of the sporophyll. Each sorus contains 2-6 sporangia or anthers which are filled up with pollen grains or microspores. Microspore represents the first cell of male gametophyte stage. The upper part of microsporophyll is sterile and pointed called *apophysis*.

Male gametophyte The pollen germinates in pollen chamber of ovule.

Pollen grain → 2 Prothallial cells
Pollen grain → 1 Antheridial cell → 1 tube cell
1 Antheridial cell → 1 generative cell → 1 stalk cell (sterile)
1 generative cell → 1 body cell → 2 multiciliate antherozoids (Top shaped)

Female Cone : There is no true female cone is *cycas*. The megasporophyll arise at the apex of the female plant and are loosely arranged in rosette manner. On either side of the broader part of sporophyll 4-6 red coloured ovules or megasporangia are arranged. *Cycas* ovule has a single, thick *three* layered integument which is hard and inner layers are fleshy and the middle layer is hard and stony. Deep in the nucellus of the mature ovules lies the megaspore mother cell which divides into four megaspores. Only one of the four megaspores is functional and rest three degenerate. By repeated divisions of the functional megaspore, female gametophyte is formed. On the upper surface of the female gametophyte. 2-8 archegonia are formed, each having a ventral cell and an egg.

Fertilization : The pollen grains reach the ovule through the medium of air. The method of fertilization in said to be siphano-zooidiogamy (because of multiciliate antherozoids and tube). In *Cycas* polyembryony is often seen as egg of almost all the archegonia are fertilized and produce embryo. In *Cycas*, alternation of generation in quite prominent.

Vegetative Reproduction : Bulbils (resting adventitious buds) are produced on the stem in the axil of scale leaves. They break up from the parent plant and germinate to give rise to new plant.

PINUS

General Morphology : The *Pinus* tree represents the sporophytic generation. The stem displays the *excurrent habitat.* The main stem is branched. Branches are of two types :

(*a*) *Long branches :* Branches with unlimited growth (grwo by means of apical bud)

(*b*) *Dwarf branches :* Branches with limited growth, arising directly from the trunk.

Leaves are also of two kinds :

(*a*) *Foliage leaves :* These are unusual type being long, narrow, tough, green and are frequently known as *Pinus-spur* or *Pine*-needles. They are borne only on the dwarf shoots in clusters of two (*P. merkusii*), three (*P. roxburghii*) or five (*P. wallichana*).

Branches with foliage leaves are called *spurs.* Spurs could be monofoliar, bifoliar, trifoliar, pentafoliar having 1, 2, 3, 5 foliar leaves.

(*b*) *Scale leaves :* These are brown, membranous and are protective in function. These are borne on both type of branches, but they fall off as the dwarf shoots mature. Scale leaves of dwarf shoots are called *cataphylls.*

Primary root persists and forms a typical elongated straight tap root. Mycorrhizal roots develop like that of *cycas.*

General Anatomy : It is composed of a small pith, a thick vascular cyclinder made up of a ring of separate collateral and open vascular bundles. Well developed resin canals are present in the stem. Primary xylem contains neither true vessels (tracheae) nor wood fibres which characteristic of angiosperms. Mesophyll cells not differentiated into palisade and spongy tissue in the leaves. Resin canals and transfusion tissue are present in the leaves.

Anatomy of Root : Resembles dicots. There are 2, 3 or 4 (diarch, triarch or tetrach) exarch bundles (more or less Y shaped) with alternating xylem and phloem (radical). Pith is generally absent. In the apical root meristem there is no dermatogen.

Sexual Reproduction

Pinus is monoecious, it bears male and female reproductive cones on the same tree but on separate branches.

Male cone : It is shortly stalked and consists of an elongated central axis, bearing a number of small spirally arranged and closely fitted scale—like microsporophylls. Numerous winged microspores are produced from microspore mother cell in the microsporangium.

Male gametophyte : The microspore nucleus divides into a small protallus cell and a large central cell. The nucleus of large central canal cell called the antheridial cell divides into a generative cell and a tube cell.

Tube cell : The tube cell grows out to form a delicate pollen tube which grows into the nucellar tissue upon which it now depends for its nourishment and protection. The pollen tube rests for about a year in this condition because the ovule is not yet ready for fertilization. Hence further growth of microgametophyte is arrested. It rests throughout the late summer and following winter resuming activity in the following April (second year).

The tube becomes active again and it penetrates the nucellar tissue. The generative cell divides to give rise to a barren stalk cell (sterile cell) and a fertile body cell (Spermatogenous cell). The body cell along with protoplasmic contents of the tube and stalk cell, pass down the pollen tube. The body cell divides into two unequal cells, which are the male gametes. The gametes are formed only a week before the fertilization.

Female cone : Arise singly or in a small cluster of two to four, each as a bud in the axial of the scale leaf towards the end of the new shoots of unlimited growth which do not bear the male cones. The female cones are very slow in growth. They take almost a year to be mature enough to receive the pollens. The central axis bears paired scales in a close spiral.

Bract scales or *Carpellary scales* (Each corresponding to a carpel or megasporophyll), lower scale, small, leathery, brownish scales.

Ovuliferous scales : It bears two sessile ovules on its upper surface at the base. Each ovule is *orthotropous*, and consists of a central mass of tissue the nucellus, surrounded by single integuments made of three layers.

Pollination : Takes place in March/April in Eastern Himalayas. The amount of pollens liberated by the pine forests at this time is prolific so that the air gets saturated with them and there is a yellow deposit of pollens on the forest floor. This phenomenon is known as 'sulphur-shower'.

Pollination drop : As the ovule matures for the pollination, the nucellar cells dissolve just below the micropyle. The dissolved tissue becomes mucilagenous and project out through the micropyle in the form of a droplet and is called pollination drop.

Fertilization : The pollen tube on reaching the archegonial neck (which takes place a year after pollination i.e. two years after the female cone first emerged) the pollen tube destroys the neck cell. Just before fertilization, the body cell divides into two nake male cells or gametes.

Simple polyembryony : (A number of embroys from a number of fertilized eggs) is common is some genera of Pinaceae viz. *Larix* & *Picea* but is *Pinus* (also *Cedrus*) the proembryo tires split from one another-into 4-along the 4-cells of each tire giving rise to 4-separate embryos. This is knwon as *cleavage polymebryony*. Usually one of these embryos survive in the seed.

Resemblances of Gymnosperms with Pteridophytes

(1) Both shows marked haterologous alternation of generation. Sporophytic generation is dominant, independent and large at maturity while gametophytic generation shows progressive reduction and dependence.

(2) Both gymnosperms and pteridophytes exhibit gradual increase in the complexity of external and internal characters of sporophytes :

- Sporophytes distinguished into root, stem and leaves.
- Sporophyte possesses a well marked vascular system.
- Absence of vessels in the xylem and companion cells in the phloem (except, *Gnetum*, *Ephedra* and *Welwitschia*).
- In having mesarch vascular bundles in the leaves.
- Pteridophytes like *Isoetes* and *Botrychium* resemble gymnosperms is undergoing secondary growth which although is not much pronounced.
- Presence of dichotomous venation in ferns and Ginkgo.
- Presence of megaphyllous leaves.

(3) Many cycads closely resemble ferns in having large compound leaves and circinate vernation. Ancient gymnosperms, cycadofilicales (Pteridosperms were so much identical with pteridophytes (ferns) that for a long time they were mistaken for ferns and were called 'seeds bearing ferns'.

(4) Many pteridophytes (e.g. *Selaginella*, *Isoetes*, *Marselia*, *Azolla* and *Salvinia*) are heterosporous and possess one megaspore in the megasporangium like the gymnosperms. Germination of spores is precocious.

(5) Both heterosporous pteridophytes and gymnosperms possess endosporic gametophytes.

(6) Male gametes of cycads (e.g. *cycas*) and *Ginkgo* are motile like the pteriodophytes.

(7) Female sex organs are archegonia in both pteridophytes and gymnosperms.

(8) Male gametophytes is heterosporous pteridophytes and majority of gymnosperms are highly reduced and possess only two prothallial cells.

(9) Endosperm (female prothallus) develops before fertilization as a result of free nuclear divisions in the tissue of female gametophyte in both gymnosperms and pteridophytes.

(10) Embryogeny is endoscopic in many pteridophytes and majority of gymnosperms.

Differences between Gymnosperms & Pteridophytes

(1) Gymnosperms are commonly large sized trees, shrubs or climbers and exhibit xeric characters. Pteridophytes on contrary are relatively smaller in size and are more commonly hygroscopic.

(2) Both gymnosperms and pteridophytes differ in external and internal characters of sporophytes :

- Gymnosperms are characterized by the presence of tap roots whereas the roots of pteriodophytes are adventitious.
- Gymnosperms possess aerial stem, where as stem of pteridophytes (ferns) are mostly underground.
- Gymnosperms have eustelic organization, whereas in pteridophytes eustele is not found.
- Excessive secondary growth occurring in higher gymnosperms (conifers) is a distinct anatomical advancement over the pteridophytes.

(3) In gymnosperms, male and female gametophyte are simple, non-green and dependent on the sporophytes. They are very much reduced in comparison to the gametophytes of pteridophytes.

(4) In all living gymnosperms, pollen tube develops as a result of germination of pollen grains. Such a structure does not occur even in the heterosporous pteriodophytes.

(5) In gymnosperms, microspores, that are light and wind dispersed, are shed from the sporophyte soon after their particle development and come to lie on the exuding nucellus from the micropyle. In pteridophytes on the other hand microspores may or may not germinate *in situ* and male cells move in presence of water.

(6) In gymnosperms, megaspores remain in the megasporangium, whereas, in pteridophytes they are shed from the sporangia and develop into independent female prothallus.

(7) Archegonial neck in gymnosperms is very small and lacks neck canal cells and venter canal cell. Archegonia are provided with neck canal cells and venter canal cell in pteridophytes. *Gnetum* lacks archegonia.

(8) Seed formation is not common in pteridophytes (except *Selaginella*), whereas, in gymnosperms seeds are produced.

Important Characteristics of Gymnosperms :

(1) Most plants are perennial and woody

(2) They are xerophytic, with sunken stomata and thick cuticle.

(3) The xylem is without vessels and phloem lacks companion cells.

(4) Reproductive organs are usually in the form of *cones* or *strobili*. The male cones are made up of microsporophylls and female cones are made up megasporophylls.

(5) Microsporophylls bear microsporangia (900-1000 microsporangia in sori in *cycas* and two microsporangia in *Pinus* sps.)

(6) Large number of microspores (pollen grains) are produced in microsporangia, after reduction division, which later form male gametophytes.

(7) Male gametophytes of all gymnosperms produces pollen tubes.

(8) In the nucellus of megasporangia (ovules) one of the cells forms megaspore mother cell which after reduction division forms a linear tetrad of megaspores of which only one is functional.

(9) Functional megaspore forms female gametophyte (also called endosperm). Thus, the endosperm is a pre-fertilization tissue in gymnosperms.

(10) On the micropylar end of female gametophyte are differentiated in two or more archegonia.

(11) All gymnosperms are wind pollinated.

(12) Usually polyembryony is found in seed although ultimately only one embryo survives.

(13) Archegonia lacks neck canal cells.

(14) Embryo bears two as in *Cycas* or more (10-11 in *Pinus*) cotyledons.

(15) All gymnosperms are woody and perennial, some of these are very large live for thousands of years e.g. *Sequoia sempervirens*.

Classification & general account of various classes & subclasses :

Gymnosperms are divided into *Four groups* :

(1) *Ginkgophyta :* Fossils as well as living plant. *Only one* plant is living e.g. *Ginkgo biloba.*

(2) *Gnetophyta :* Small trees or shrubs. All plants are living. Reproductive structures are unisexual, secondary xylem has vessels : e.g. *Gnetum, Ephedra, Welwitschia.*

(3) *Cycadophyta :* Plants are small with unbranched stem. Large compound leaves. In T.S. of stem, pith and cortex are large and vascular tissue less. Manoxylic wood.

Cycadophyta has been divided into following 3 orders.

Order 1 : *Cycadofilicales :* (Pteridosperms) fossils only, Plants showed some characters of ferns and other characters of gymnosperms e.g. *Medullosa.*

Order 2 : *Bennettitales :* (Cycadeoidales) fossils only, Leaf base permanently attached to stem. e.g. *Williamsonia.*

Order 3 : *Cycadales :* Some fossils and some living plants. Palm like plants e.g. *Cycas.* Cycas has approximately 20 species found in Australia, New-Zealand, Japan, China, India, Burma, Indonesia and Pacific Islands. In India, *cycas* species are common in Orissa, Bengal, Assam, Madras, Karnataka and Andmans. Four species are found in India : *Cycas revoluta, C. circinalis, C. rumphi* and *C. beddomei.*

(4) *Coniferophyta :* Large trees with unbranched stem. Simple foliage leaves. T.S. of stem shows small pith and cortex and large vascular tissue. It has Pycnoxylic wood. The plants are evergreen with dense and massive vascular tissue and non-motile gametes. They are monoecious (Both types of cones are present on the same plant). Cones are compact and woody. *Araucaria* (Monkey's puzzle) (A tall conifer of South America, New-Zealand and East Australia) grows in warm weather in plains as well as foot hills. Other conifers form vast and dominant wood lands in mostly north temperate regions of Europe, Asia, North America etc. e.g. *Pinus, Cedrus, Picea, Abies* (Fir), *Thuja, Larix.* Conifers are dominant constituents of north temperate flora due to following reasons :

(*i*) In the temperate areas, conifers have an advantage over angiospermic trees. While the angiosperm trees shed their leaves during autumn winter period, the conifers remain evergreen.

(*ii*) Conifers have a number of xerophytic characteristics which help in conserving water. They are thus able to tide over the winter period when the soil becomes frozen and water availability is very little.

(*iii*) Enzymes of confiers are functional even at –35°C at which temperature they become inactivated in other plants.

Coniferophyta has been divided into following four orders :

Order 1 : *Cordaitales* : Fossils only. Leaves were spirally arranged on the stem with parallel venation. e.g. *Cordaites.*

Order 2 : *Ginkgoales :* Fossils as well as living plant. Only one plant is living e.g. *Ginkgo biloba.*

Order 3 : *Coniferales :* Fossils as well as living plants. Usually dwarf and long branches. Foliage leaves on dwarf branches only e.g. *Pinus.* In India about six species of *Pinus* are common. The plants grow in North-East and North-West Himalayas. In the hills of South India, the plants grow under cultivation. *Pinus gerardiana* (Chilgoza pine) is common in dry valley of North-West Himalayas—Kashmir and quite common in Kinnaur district of Himachal Pradesh. Plants prefer scantly rainfall and Leany snow-fall. Trees may attain a height of 11-20 meters. *Pinus wallichiana* (*P. excelsa*) or *Blue Pine* are commonly called "Kail". They grow in the hills of Kashmir, Himachal Pradesh and Punjab. Trees may attain a height of upto 50 meters. *Pinus roxburghii* or *P. longifolia* (*Chir Pine*) commonly occur in the outer Himalaya regions ranging from Indus to Bhutan. It grows in Kashmir, Punjab, Himachal Pradesh and Uttar Pradesh. Trees may attain a height of about 35 to 53 meters.

Pinus merkusii (Teenasserim pine) commonly grow on hillocks in Burma and East India—Bengal etc. Trees are usually very small reaching a height of hardly 3 meters.

Pinus insularis or *P. khasya* (Khasi Pine) commonly occur in the hill ranges of Assam. It is abundant in Khasia hiils but also occurs in Naga Hills and Chittagong.

P. armandi : (Armand's Pine) plants are very common in Nefa.

In addition to these species, several exotic pines like *P. montana*, *P. laricia* and *P. sylvestris*, have been introduced in India.

Order 4 : *Gnetales :* Small trees or shrubs. All plants living. Reproductive structures are unisexual secondary xylem has vessels e.g. *Gnetum.*

ANGIOSPERMS

Comparative account of various systems of Angiosperm Classification : Taxonomy began with man's purely utilitarian interest in the flora of the earth. It grew with apparent observations of the various types of plants and their relationship which were, of course, based on the studies made by unaided eyes. The word taxonomy was introduced by A.P. de Candolle to designate the theory of plant classification. It has summoned innumerable people of the world since times gone by. It led to the systematic grouping of plants.

Classification is the inclusion of a plant or plants in categories based on a definite system and also according to the rules of International Code of Botanical Nomenclature (ICBN).

Aristotle and Theophrastus may be regarded as the two intellectual giants who infused life in plant taxonomy. The history of classification may be divided into ancient, middle and modern ages.

There are various systems of classification :

(A) Artificial System : According to this system, plants are classified on the basis of one or few convenient characteristics, e.g.

(1) Theophrastus (370 BC-285 BC), Father of Botany, ancient ages) in his book *'Historia Plantarum'* classified about 480 plants into Trees, Shrubs, Undershrubs and Herbs.

(2) *Linnaeus (1707-1778, Middle ages) :* Carlous Linnaeus called *'father of plant taxonomy'* described a sexual system of plant classification, details of which were published in *'Species Plantarum'* (1753). He took into consideration, the nature and number of stamens and carpels. He divided plants into 24 classes, e.g.

(*i*)	Monandria	1 stamen
(*ii*)	Diandria	2 stamens
(*iii*)	Triandria	3 stamens
(*iv*)	Tetrandria	4 stamens
(*v*)	Pentandria	5 stamens
(*vi*)	Hexandria	6 stamens
(*vii*)	Heptandria	7 stamens
(*viii*)	Octandria	8 stamens
(*ix*)	Enneandria	9 stamens
(*x*)	Decandria	10 stamens
(*xi*)	Dodecandria	11-19 stamens
(*xii*)	Polyandria	20 or more stamens on calyx
(*xiii*)	Isosandria	20 or more stamens on receptacle
(*xiv*)	Didynamia	Stamens didynamous (two pairs, different length)
(*xv*)	Tetradynamia	Stamens tetradynamous (4 long & 2 short)
(*xvi*)	Monadelphia	Stamens united in one group
(*xvii*)	Didelphia	Stamens united in two groups
(*xviii*)	Polydelphia	Stamens united in 3 or more groups
(*xix*)	Syngensia	Stamens syngenesious (united by anthers)
(*xx*)	Gynandria	Stamens united to Gynoecium
(*xxi*)	Monoecia	Plants monoecious
(*xxii*)	Dioecia	Plants Dioecious
(*xxiii*)	Polygamia	Plants polygamous
(*xxiv*)	Cryptogamia	Flowerless plants

(B) Natural System (Modern Classification) : According to this system, overall resemblance (all important characters of plants are taken into consideration.

Bentham & Hooker (1862-1883) gave most important system of classification of angiosperms and published in three volumes of *'Genera Plantarum'*. They described 202 families.

Bentham & Hooker divided plant kingdom into two subkingdoms.

Subkingdom 1 : Cryptogamia—it includes non-flowering plants.

Subkingdom 2 : Phanerogamia—it includes flowering plants.

This subkingdom 2 includes :

(1) Class Dicotyledonae

(2) Class Gymnospermae

(3) Class Monocotyledonae

(1) *Class Dicotyledonae :* It is further divided into three subclasses

(*i*) *Subclass Polypetalae* Petals free.

***Series (A) Thalamiflorae* :** Petals & stamens are hypogynous.

Order 1 : *Ranales* : Families 8

(*a*) Rununculaceae (*b*) Dilleniaceae
(*c*) Calycanthaceae (*d*) Menispermaceae
(*e*) Anonaceae (*f*) Magnoliaceae
(*g*) Berberidaceae (*h*) Nymphaceae.

Order 2 : *Perietales* : Families 9

(*a*) Sarraceniaceae (*b*) Papaveraceae
(*c*) Cruciferae (*d*) Capparidaceae
(*e*) Resedaceae (*f*) Cistineae
(*g*) Violaceae (*h*) Canellaceae
(*i*) Bixineae.

Order 3 : *Polygalinae* : Families 4

(*a*) Pittosporeae (*b*) Tremandreae
(*c*) Polyglaeae (*d*) Vochysiaceae.

Order 4 : *Caryophyllineae* : Families 4

(*a*) Frankeniaceae (*b*) Caryophyllaceae
(*c*) Portulaceae (*d*) Tamariscineae.

Order 5 : *Guttiferales* : Families 6

(*a*) Elatineae (*b*) Hypericineae
(*c*) Guttiferae (*d*) Ternstroemiaceae
(*e*) Dipterocarpaceae (*f*) Chlaenaceae.

Order 6 : *Malvales* : Families 3

(*a*) Malvaceae (*b*) Sterculiaceae
(*c*) Tiliaceae.

***Series (B) Disciflorae* :** The sepals are free or fused. These sepals are fused with ovary or free. A fleshy disc is found below ovary. Sometimes this disc is divided into some small glands. Here ovary is superior.

Order 7 : *Geraniales* : Families 10

(*a*) Lineae (*b*) Humiriaceae
(*c*) Malpighiaceae (*d*) Zygophyllaceae
(*e*) Geraniaceae (*f*) Rutaceae
(*g*) Simarubeae (*h*) Ochnaceae
(*i*) Burseraceae (*j*) Meliaceae
(*k*) Chailletiaceae.

Order 8 : *Olacales* : Families 3

(*a*) Olacineae (*b*) Ilicineae
(*c*) Cyrilleae

Order 9 : *Celastrales* ; Families 4

(*a*) Celastrineae (*b*) Rhamnaceae
(*c*) Stackhousieae (*d*) Ampelideaceae.

Order 10 : *Sapindales* : Families 5

(*a*) Sapindaceae (*b*) Sabiaceae
(*c*) Anacardiaceae (*d*) Coriarieae
(*e*) Moringeae.

***Series (C) Calyciflorae* :** Sepals are fused or free (sometimes) They are fused with ovary. Sepals are arranged in one or two whorls. Ovary is usually inferior.

Order 11 : *Rosales* : Families 9

(*a*)Connaraceae (*b*) Leguminosae
(*i*) Papilionaceae
(*ii*) Caesapinioideae
(*iii*) Mimosoideae
(*c*) Rosaceae (*d*) Saxifragaceae
(*e*) Craunulaceae (*f*) Droseraceae
(*g*) Hamamelidaceae (*h*) Bruniaceae
(*i*) Haloragaceae.

Order 12 : *Myrtales* : Families 6

(*a*) Rhizophoraceae (*b*) Combretaceae
(*c*) Myrtaceae (*d*) Melastomaceae
(*e*) Lythraceae (*f*) Onagraceae.

Order 13 : *Passiflorales* : Families 7

(*a*) Samydaceae (*b*) Loaseae
(*c*) Turneraceae (*d*) Passifloraceae
(*e*) Cucurbitaceae (*f*) Begoniaceae
(*g*) Datisceae.

Order 14 : *Ficoidales* : Families 2

(*a*) Cactaceae (*b*) Ficoideae.

Order 15 : *Umbellales* : Families 3

(*a*) Umbelliferae (*b*) Cornaceae
(*c*) Araliaceae.

(*ii*) *Subclass Gamepetalae* : The petals are fused. Stamens are usually epipetalous. Carpel may be syncarpour or apocarpous.

***Series (A) Inferae* :** Overy is inferior and stamen usually equal to petal lobes.

Order 1 : *Rubiales* : Families 2

(*a*) Caprifoliaceae (*b*) Rubiaceae

Order 2 : *Asterales* : Families 4

(*a*) Valerianeae (*b*) Dipsaceae
(*c*) Calycereae (*d*) Compositae.

Order 3 : *Campanales* : Families 3

(*a*) Stylidieae (*b*) Goodenovieae
(*c*) Campanulaceae.

Series (B) Heteromerae :

Order 4 : *Ericales* : Families 6

(*a*) Ericaceae (*b*) Vacciniaceae
(*c*) Monotropeae (*d*) Epacrideae
(*e*) Diapensiaceae (*f*) Lennoaceae.

Order 5 : *Primulales* : Families 3

(*a*) Plumbagineae (*b*) Primulaceae
(*c*) Myrsineae.

Order 6 : *Ebenales* : Families 3

(*a*) Sapotaceae (*b*) Ebenaceae
(*c*) Styraceae.

Series (C) Bicarpellate : Ovary is superior. Stamens are usually equal to corolla lobes or lesser in number. Stamens are alternate to petals. Carpels are usually two, sometimes they may be lesser or more than two.

Order 7 : *Gentianales* : Families 6

(*a*) Oleaceae (*b*) Salvadoraceae
(*c*) Apocynaceae (*d*) Asclepiadaceae
(*e*) Loganiaceae (*f*) Gentianceae.

Order 8 : *Polemonials* : Families 5

(*a*) Polemoniaceae (*b*) Hydrophyllaceae
(*c*) Boragineae (*d*) Convolvulaceae
(*e*) Solanaceae.

Order 9 : *Personales* : Families 8

(*a*) Scrophulariaceae (*b*) Orobanchaceae
(*c*) Lentibulariaceae (*d*) Columelliaceae
(*e*) Gesneraceae (*f*) Bignoniaceae
(*g*) Pedaliaceae (*h*) Acanthaceae.

Order 10 : *Lamiales* : Families 5

(*a*) Myoporineae (*b*) Selagineae
(*c*) Verbenaceae (*d*) Labiatae
(*e*) Plantaginaceae (Anomalous family)

(iii) Subclass Monochlamydae : Incomplete-- In flowers perianth is in one whorl. Sometimes perianth may be absent. This subclass is divided into 8 series.

Series (A) Curvembrayae : Families 6

(*a*) Nyctaginaceae (*b*) Illecebraceae
(*c*) Amaranthaceae (*d*) Chenopodiaceae
(*e*) Phytolaccaceae (*f*) Batideae
(*g*) Polygonaceae.

Series (B) Multiovulate Aquaticae : Family 1

(*a*) Podostemaceae

Series (C) Multiovulate Terrestres : Families 3

(*a*) Nepenthaceae (*b*) Aristolochiaceae
(*c*) Cytinaceae.

Series (D) Microembryeae : Families 4

(*a*) Piperaceae (*b*) Chloranthaceae
(*c*) Myristicaceae (*d*) Monimiaceae.

Series (E) Damphnales : Families 5

(*a*) Laurineae (*b*) Protecaceae
(*c*) Thymelaceae (*d*) Penaeaceae
(*e*) Elaegnaceae.

Series (F) Achlamydosporeae : Families 3

(*a*) Loranthaceae (*b*) Santalaceae
(*c*) Balanophoreae.

Series (G) Unisexuales : Families 9

(*a*) Euphorbiaceae (*b*) Balanopseae
(*c*) Urticaceae (*d*) Platanaceae
(*e*) Leitnerieae (*f*) Juglandaceae
(*g*) Myricaceae (*h*) Casuarinaceae
(*i*) Cupuliferae.

Series (H) Ordines Anomali : Families 4

(*a*) Salicaceae (*b*) Empetraceae
(*c*) Lacitemaceae (*d*) Ceratophyllaceae.

(2) *Class Gymnospermae :* Families 3

(*a*) Gnetaceae (*b*) Coniferaceae
(*c*) Cycadaceae.

(3) *Class Monocotyledonae :*

Series (A) Microspermae : Families 3

(*a*) Hydrocharidaceae (*b*) Burmanniaceae
(*c*) Orchidaceae.

Series (B) Epigynae : Families 7

(*a*) Scitamineae (*b*) Bromeliaceae
(*c*) Halmodoraceae (*d*) Irideae
(*e*) Amaryllidaceae (*f*) Taccaceae
(*g*) Dioscoreaceae

Series (C) Coronaireae : Families 8

(*a*) Roxburgluaceae (*b*) Liliaceae
(*c*) Pontederiaceae (*d*) Philydraceae
(*e*) Xyrideae (*f*) Mayaceae
(*g*) Commelinaceae (*h*) Repateaceae.

Series (D) Calycineae : Families 3

(*a*) Flagellarieae (*b*) Juncaceae
(*c*) Palmae.

Series (E) Nudiflorae : Families 5

(*a*) Pandanceae (*b*) Cyclanthaceae
(*c*) Typhaceae (*d*) Aroideae
(*e*) Lemnaceae.

Series (F) Apocarpae : Families 3

(*a*) Triurideae (*b*) Alismaceae
(*c*) Naiadaceae.

Series (G) Glumaceae : Families 5

(*a*) Eriocauleae (*b*) Centrolepideae
(*c*) Restiaceae (*d*) Cyperaceae
(*e*) Gramineae.

(C) Phylogenetic System : These systems are based on evolutionary and genetical tendancies of plants. Some of the important phylogenetic systems are as follows :

(1) *Engler & Prantl (1884-1930) :* They formulated a detailed classification and published in 23 volumes of *"Die Nuturlichen Pflanzen Families"*. The general plan is as follows :

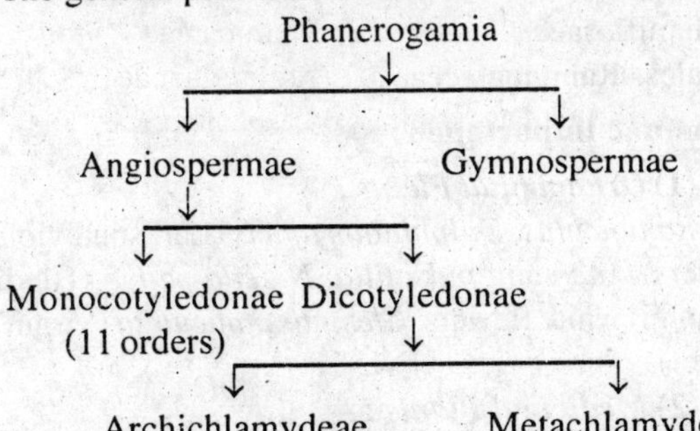

(2) *Hutchinson (1959) :* He published a book *'Families of flowering plants'* in two volumes. (Vol. I. Dicotyledons, Vol. II. Monocotyledons.)

He divided angiosperms into 411families.

(*i*) **Dicotyledonae Groups**
Division 1 : Lignosae-246 families
Division 2 : Herbacae-96 families

(*ii*) **Monocotyledonae Groups**
(*a*) Calyciflorae
(*b*) Corolliflorae
(*c*) Glumiflorae.

(3) *A.L. Takhtajan (1967) :* In his book *"A System of Phylogeny of Flowering Plants"* classified Angiosperms (Magnoliophyta). The outline of his classification is as follows :

Division : Magnoliophyta or Angiospermae
Class : Magnoliatae (or Dicotyledons)
Divided into : 7 subclasses
15 super orders
20 orders.
Class : Liliatae or Monocotyledons
Divided into 4 subclasses
5 super orders
20 orders.

Units of Classification : In the modern classification, plant kingdom is divided in certain phyla. Each phylum is divided into classes. (Here phylum Anthophyta is taken as an example).

Phylum : Whole of plant kindgom is divided into 25 phyla. The suffix of a phylum in either—*ophyta* or *mycoty*. Last phylum in Anthophyta.

Class : Each phylum is divided into classes. Its suffix is usually -ae. The phylum Anthophyta has only a single class Angiospermae.

Subclass : In modern classification, class is further divided into subsclass e.g. class Angiospermae in divided into two subclasses Dicotyledonae & Monocotyledonae.

Series : Subclass is divided into more than one series.

Order : This is the main part of the classification. Its suffix is -ales. In each order one or more families are included on the basis of similarities and dissimilarities in their specific characters.

Family : This is smaller and important unit of taxon, in which plants of one or more than one genera are included. Its suffix is -aceae.

Genus : Each family has one or more than one genera. Generic nomenclature is important.

Species : This is the smallest unit of taxonomical classification. Its first letter is denoted with small letter.

ANGIOSPERMS : STUDY OF FAMILIES

Study of Angiospermic Families :

1. Family Ranunculaceae (Buttercup Family): It is commonly known as buttercup family. They are chiefly found in temperate and arctic regions. *Ranunculus aquatilis* is a halophyte.

Vegetative characters :

Habit : The plants are annual or perennial herbs or a climbing shrubs, *Clematis* (twining petiole), *Narvelia* (terminal leaflet modified into tendril) and rarely trees. They perennate by means of tuberous roots (Aconitum) or rhizomes.

Root : Tap root, adventitious or tuberous (*Ranunculus* spp. and *Aconitum*). The tap root system in the initial stage but sooner or later repeated by the adventitious roots.

Stem : Herbaceous, in some climbing (clematis) or underground rhizome or erect, branched.

Leaves : Generally simple, alternate or opposite (*clematis*), exstipulate, rarely stipulate (*Thalictrum*). Sheathing leaf base. Petiolate rarely sessile (*Delphinium*). In some aquatic species leaves may show dimorphy (Heterophilly) (*Ranunculus aquatilis*), unicostate or multicostate, reticulate venation.

Inflorescence : Solitary terminal (*Anemone*), axillary (*Clematis*), raceme (*Aconitum, Delphinium*) and cymose (*Ranunculus*).

Flower : Pedicellate, ebracteate, rarely bracteate, hermaphrodite, (unisexual in *Thalictrum*). Mostly actinomorphic (Ranunculus), rarely zygomorphic (*Delphinium* and *Aconitum*) hypogynous, complete pentamerous.

Perianth : There is no distinction of calyx and corolla in most of the plants.

Calyx : Sepals 5, caducous, polysepalous, petaloid, inbricate or valvate aestivation.

Corolla : Petals 5, polypetalous, variously coloured, caducous or wanting, nectaries present at the base of petals. Petals are united to form spurin Delphinium.

Androecium : Stamens indefinite, polyandrous, spirally arranged on the thalamus inferior, anthers dithecous, extrose and adnate.

Gynoecium : Multicarpellary (one carpel in *Delphinium* and 3 to 5 in *Aconitum*), apocarpous. Rarely syncarpous (Nigella), ovary superior, marginal placentation as in *Delphinium*, basal as in *Ranunculus* and axile in *Nigella*.

Fruit : Aggregate, etaerio of achienes (Ranunculus), etaerio of follicles (*Aconitum*), follicle (*Delphinium*), Septicidal capsule (*Nigella*) or berry (*Actaea*), etaerio of drupes (*Adonis*). Etaerio of berries (*Hydrastis*) and simple pod (*Xanthorhiza*)

Seed : Small, oily and endospermic.

Floral Formula : ⚥ ⊕ P_{5+5} $A \infty$ $\underline{G} \infty$

Systemic Position :

Engler & Prantle	***Bentham & Hooker***	***Hutchinson***
Phanerogams	Dicotyledons	Angiosperms
Dicotyledonae	Polypetalae	Dicotyledons
Archichlamydeae	Thalmiflorae	Herbacease
Ranals	Ranales	Ranales
Ranunculaceae	Ranunculaceae	Ranunculaceae

or

Phanerogams
Dicotyledonae
Polypetalae
Thalamiflorae
Ranales, Ranunculaceae.

Economic Importance :

(1) *Ornamental Plants :*

Ranunculus, *Dalphinium ajacis* (Larkspur, violet flowers) *Anemone pulsatilla*, *Nigella sativa* (Hindi-Kalaunji) white flowers, *Clematis paniculata* (Virgin's Bower).

(2) *Medicinal Plants :*

(*a*) *Aconitum napillus :* Alkaloid aconite extracted from roots, used for blood pressure.

(*b*) *Anemone pulsatilla :* Yields famous homeopathic medicine pulsatilla. It is used for nerve exhaustion in women and for menstrual troubles.

(*c*) *Ranunculus ficaria :* Used for piles.

(3) *Condiments :*

(*a*) *Nigella sativa* (Hindi-Kalaunji) : Seeds used as condiment.

2. Family Brassicaceae (Cruciferae)

Habit : Usually annual or perennial herb.

Root : Tap root system.

Stem : Herbaceous, branched, erect, solid, cylindrical, nodes and internodes clear.

Leaf : Simple, alternate, radicle or cauline, usually entire, sometimes lobed, petiolate, exstipulate, reticulate venation.

Inflorescence : Raceme or corymbose raceme as in candytuft.

Flower : Ebracteate, pedicellate, usually actinomorphic but sometimes zygomorphic (candytuft), hermaphrodite, hypogynous, complete, regular, dimerous or tetramerous.

Calyx : Sepals 4, polysepalous, arranged in two whorls of two each, imbricate aestivation.

Corolla : Petals 4, arranged in one whorl and alternate with sepals, polypetalous, often with long claws and spread out in the form of Greek cross. This arrangement of the petals which is characteristic of the family is known as the cruciform arrangement and corolla is described as cruciform corolla, valvate aestivation.

Androecium : Stamens 6, polyandrous, arranged in two whorls, tetradynamous, the outer two stamens are short while the four inner ones are long, anther bilobed, basifixed, introse.

Gynoecium : Bicarpellary, syncarpous, ovary superior, unilocular but becomes bilocular due to the anterio-posterior partition (Pseudo septum) which develops by the ingrowth of the placentae i.e. parietal placentation, one or more than one ovule in each locule, style short with two stigmas, sometimes bilobed.

Fruit : Siliqua or silicula.

Floral Formula :

Mustard $\oplus$ ⚥ $K_{2+2}\ C_{\times 4}\ A_{2+4}\ \underline{G_{(2)}}$

Condytuft : % $K_{2+2}\ C_{\times 4}\ A_{2+4}\ \underline{G_{(2)}}$

Economic Importance :

(A) Plants used as Food : *Brassica oleracea.* There are a number of varieties Cabbage (Pattagobhi) is eaten for its leaves. (*B. oleracea* var *capitata*), the cauliflower (*B. oleracea* var *botrytis*) for its inflorescence and knol-knol (*B. oleracea* var *coulorapa*) for its thickened stem or the corm. All these are used as vegetables. *Raphanus sativus*-roots & leaves are used as vegetables. *Brassica campestris* (yellow mustard). The seeds yield oil, the husk of oil seeds after extraction of the oil is used in the form of cakes for cattle. *B. nigra* (Black mustard), *B. alba* (white mustard) and *B. juncea* (rye) are used in spice.

(B) Plants used as Medicine : *Sisymbrium officinale :* Stem and leaves are used for scurvy and scrofula diseases, *Nasturtium indica* seeds are used in asthma. *Eruca satira* oil is used in burns and other injuries. *Lepidium sativum* (garden cress) seeds are used in liver diseases.

(C) Ornamental Plants : *Alyssum, Cherianthus, Ibris amara* (candytuft), *Mathiola.*

Systemic Position :

Engler & Prantle	*Bentham & Hooker*	*Hutchinson*
Phanerogams	Dicotyledons	Angiosperms
Dicotyledoneae	Polypetalae	Dicotyledons
Archichlamydeae	Thalamiflorae	Herbaceae
Rhoeadales	Parietales	Cruciales
Cruciferae	Cruciferae	Cruciferae.

or

Kingdom	Plantae
Subkingdom	Phanerogamia
Division	Angiospermae
Class	Dicotyledonae
Subclass	Polypetalae
Series	Thalamiflorae
Order	Parietales
Family	Cruciferae (= Brassicaceae)

3. Family : Malvaceae

Habit : Annual, biennial, herb, shrub or tree.

Root : Tap root system branched.

Stem : Erect, branched, cylindrical, usually, mucilaginous.

Leaf : Stipulate, alternate, simple, petiolate, entire or lobed, reticulate venation.

Inflorescence : Solitary, axillary or terminal bacemose or helicoid cyme.

Flower : Bracteate or ebractate, hermaphrodite, complete, hypogynous, actinomorphic, pentamerous.

Calyx : Sepals 5, basically connate or polysepalous, valvate aestivation, usually epicalyx present.

Corolla : Petals 5, polypetulous but basically fused with staminal tube, twisted or imbricate aestivation, showy.

Androecium : Numerous stamens, monadelphous, filaments fused to form a staminal tube, adnate to basal part of petals, epipetalous, anther lobes unilocular (monothecous), basifixed.

Gynoecium : $3-\infty$ carpels, syncarpous, multilocular, ovary superior, axile placentation, each locule has $1-\infty$ ovules, style single & simple, stigma multilobed.

Fruit : Dry loculicidal capsule.

Floral formula of Gurhal :

$\oplus$ ⚥ $Ep_{5-7}\ K_{(5)}\ C_5\ A_{(\infty)}\ \underline{G_{(5)}}$

Malva : $\oplus$ ⚥ $Ep_3\ K_{(5)}\ C_5\ A_{(\infty)}\ \underline{G_{(\infty)}}$

Economic Importance

(A) Plants used as food :

(1) *Gossypium sp. :* The oil extracted from its seeds is used in preparing vegetable ghee Residual part of seed is used as cake for cattle.

(2) *Hibiscus esculentus (Bhindi) :* Fruits are used as vegetables..

(B) Plants used in medicine :

(1) *Urena rependa :* Juice extracted from roots and bark is used in hydrophobia.

(2) *Abutilon indicum :* Root, stem, leaves and seeds are used in preparing certain ayurvedic medicines.

(C) Fibre yielding plants :

(1) *Gossypium sp :* Fibres of seed coat are used in textile industry. Important species of cotton are *G. arboreum, G. herbaceum* and *G. barbadense.*

(2) *Hibiscus cannabinus :* Madras hemp, *H. mutabilis* and *H. sabdariffa* are used in rope industry. Firbre obtained from *Urena lobata* is used in preparing bags.

(D) Ornamental plants :

(1) Hibiscus rosa-sinensis (China-rose) Gurhal

(2) Althea rosea.

Systemic Position :

Division	Angiospermae
Class	Dicotyledonae
Subclass	Polypetalae
Series	Thalamiflorae
Order	Malvales
Family	Malvaceae

4. Family Leguminosae

Habit : Annual or biennial, herb, shrub or Tree.

Root : Tap root system

Stem : Erect or creeping, solid or week.

Leaf : Alternate or whorled, stipulate, petiolate, simple or usually compound, reticulate venation.

On the basis of inflorescene and flower characters, this family is divided into 3 sub-families.

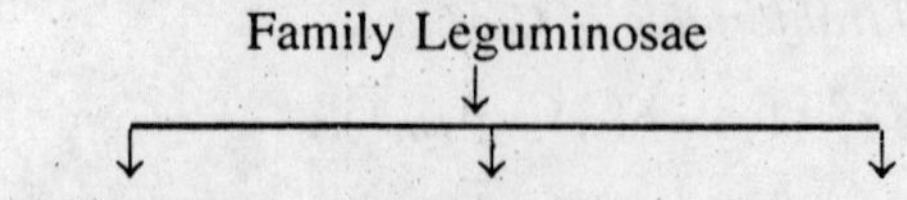

1. Flowers-very zygomorphic	1. Flowers-more or less zygomorphic	1. Flower-actinornorphic
2. Coralla-descending imbricate	2. Coralla ascending imbricate	2. Valvate, petals free or connate
3. Stamens-diadelphous	3. Some staminodes	3. Stamens-usually indefinite.

Sub-family Papilionatae (Fabaceae)

Inflorescence : Racemose or solitary axillary.

Flower : Bracteate, pedicellate, hermaphrodite, complete, zygomorphic, hypogynous.

Calyx : Sepals 5, connate at the base valvate aestivation.

Corolla : Petals 5, polypetalous, papilionaceous, descending imbricate aestivation, one posterior long standard, two lateral short wings, two anterior petals jointed to each other forming keel.

Androecium : 10 stamens, diadelphous, 9 fused with each other on anterior side, one free on posterior side. Anther lobes bilocular, dorsifixed, introse.

Gynoecium : Monocarpellary, unilocular, marginal placentation, ovary superior.

Fruit : Legume

Floral formula :

Br. % ⚥ $K_5\ C_{1+2+(2)}\ A_{1+(9)}\ \underline{G_{(1)}}$

Economic importance

(A) Plants used as food :

(1) *Pulses :* Various kinds of pulses are obtained from the plants of this subfamily, e.g. garden pea = edible peas (*Pisum sativum*) gram (*Cicer arietinum*), Lobia (*Vigna sinensis*), Arhar (*Cajanus cajan*), Masoor (*Lens esculenta*), Urd (*Phaseolus mungo*), Mung (*P. aureus*). Pulses are rich source of protein.

(2) *Sem :* (*Dolichos lablab*), Lobia (*Vigna sinensis*), Pea (*Pisum sativum*) are used as vegetables. Leaves of *Trigonella* are also used as vegetable.

(3) Groundnut (*Archis hypogea*). Its embryo is used is preparation of vegetables ghee. Soyabeen (*Glycine soja*)—from it a special type of milk is extracted which is rich in protein.

(B) Plants used in medicines :

(1) *Clitoria ternatea* : Leaves and flowers are used in snake bite.

(2) *Desmodium gangetium* : Roots are used in diarrhoea, cough, asthma, snake and scorpion bite.

(C) Fibre yielding plants :

(1) *Crotolaria* juncea = Sunn hemp

(D) Ornamental plants :

(1) *Sesbanea grandiflora*

(2) *Butea monosperma*

(3) *Lathyrus odoratus* (sweet pea = wild pea)

(E) Plants used in manufacture of Dyes :

(1) *Indigofera tinctoria*

(2) *Erythrina variegata*

(3) *Pterocarpus santalinus* (red sandal wood)

(F) Timber yielding plants :

(1) Dalbergia sissoo (Shesham)

(G) Spice yielding plants :

(1) *Trigonella Foenum graecum* (methi)

Systemic position :

Division	Angiospemae
Class	Dicotyledonae
Sub-class	Polypetalae
Series	Calyciflorae
Order	Rosales
Family	Leguminosae
Sub-family	Papilionatae

Sub-family Caesalpinoideae

Inflorescence : Raceme, umbel or solitary flower.

Flower : Bracteate or ebracteate, pedicellate, hermaphrodite, complete, zygomorphic, hypogynous.

Calyx : Sepals 5, polysepalous, imbricate aestivation.

Corolla : Petals 5, polypetalous, ascending imbricate aestivation.

Androecium : 10 stamens, or staminodes are found in *cassia*, free filaments of unequal size, anther lobes bilocular, introse, versatile.

Gynoecium : Monocarpellary, unilocular ovary superior, marginal placentation, stigma capitate.

Fruit : Legume

Floral formula :

% ⚥ $K_5C_5A_{5+5}$ (staminodes) or 7 + 3 $\underline{G_1}$

Economic Importance

(A) Plants used in Medicines :

(1) *Cassia occidentalis* : In skin diseases.

(2) *C. glauca* : Bark & leaves are used in diabetes & gonorrhea.

(3) *C. fistula* : Fleshy mass of fruits is used as purgative.

(4) *Tamarindus indica* : Its fruits and leaves are used in digestion.

(B) Plants used as food :

(1) *Bauhinia variegata* (Kachnar) buds are used as vegetables.

(C) Plants used in Dye Manufacture :

(1) *Hematoxylon campechianum*

(2) *Caesalpinea sappam*

(D) Plants used in leather tanning : The bark of some of the species of *Bauhinia* and *Caesalpinia* is used in leather tanning.

(E) Ornamental plants :

(1) *Delonix regia* : Gulmohar.

(2) *Caesalpinia pulcherima* : Peacock flower.

(3) *Saraca indica* : Ashok.

(4) *Cassia fistula* : Amaltas.

Sub-family Mimosoideae

Inflorescence : Head or capitulum or spike. Flowers arranged in acropetal succession.

Flower : Bracteate or ebracteate, sessile, hermaphrodite, complete, actinomorphic hypogynous, pentamerous.

Calyx : Sepals 4-5, gamosepalous, connate at the base, valvate aestivation.

Corolla : Petals 4-5, gamopetalous, or polypetalous, membranous, valvate aestivation.

Androecium : Stamens many, free in many whorls, filaments long, dithecous, introse.

Gynoecium : Monocarpellary, unilocular, ovary superior, style long, cylindrical, stigma single and capitate, marginal placentation.

Fruit : Lomentum.

Floral formula :

Br. or Ebr. ⊕ ⚥ $K_{(5)}C_{(5)}$ or 5 A_∞ $\underline{G_1}$

Economic Importance

(1) *Timber yielding plants* : *Albizia lebbek* (Sires) *Adenanthera pavonina*.

(2) *Fibres yielding plants : Acacia leucophloea.*

(3) *Gum yielding plant : Acacia sps.*

(4) *Perfume yielding plant—Acacia farnesiana :* Its flowers are used to extract perfume.

(5) *Ornamental plants : Neptunia oleracea, Prosopis spicigera, Mimosa pudica, Pitheclobium dulce.*

(6) *Dye yielding plant :* From the heart wood of *Acacia catechu* a dye 'Kathha' is obtained.

5. Family Compositae (= Asteraceae)

Habit : Mostly annual, rarely biennial herbs, shrubs, sometimes trees.

Root : Adventitious stilt roots.

Stem : Erect, herbaceous, branched, angular or cylinderical, node and internodes clear.

Leaf : Simple, alternate or opposite, exstipulate, petiolate, hairy, reticulate venation.

Inflorescence : Head or capitulum which may be terminal or axillary surrounded by bracts, peduncle flat on which florets are attached. Florets are surrounded by involcure.

Flower : Epigynous, usually pentamerous with reduction in certain whorls, hermaphrodite or unisexual, compelete on incomplete, tubular (actinomorphic) or ligulate (zygomorphic), bracteate or ebracteate.

(A) Ray florets : Towards periphery of head, sessile bracteate, pistillate or neutral, zygomorphic, liguate, epigynous.

Calyx : Absent or hairy pappus or scaly, persistant.

Corolla : Petals 5, gamopetalous, ligulate, strap shaped.

Androecium : Absent.

Gynoecium : Bicarpellary, syncarpous, ovary inferior, unilocular, one ovule in each locule, basal placentation, style simple narrow, stigma branched.

(B) Disc florets : In the centre of head, bracteate, bisexual, actinomorphic, tubular, pentamerous, epigynous.

Calyx : Absent or pappus.

Corolla : Petals 5, gamopetalous, tubular.

Androecium : 2 stamens, epipetalous, syngenesious, dithecous, bilobed, introse, filament free.

Gynoecium : Bicarpellary, syncarpous, ovary inferior, unilocular, single ovule in the locule, basal placentation, style single, short, stigma bifid.

(C) Natural florets : Androecium and Gynoecium both are absent. Remaining structures are similar to ray & disc florets.

Fruit Cypsella

Floral formula

Ray florets : Br. % ⚥ K_0 or P $C_{(5)}$ A_0 $\overline{G}_{(2)}$

Disc florets : Br. % or ⊕ ⚥ K_0 or P $C_{(5)}$ $A_{(3)}$ $\overline{G}_{(2)}$

Natural florets : % or ⊕ K_0 $C_{(5)}$ A_0 G_0

Economic Importance

(A) Plants used as food : *Lactuca sativa* (Letuuce = salad), *Elephentopus*—Their leaves are used as vegetable. Flowers of *Cynara scolymus* are used as vegetable. Tubers of *Helianthus tuberosus* are eaten. Its seeds are also used to extract oil.

(B) Plants used in medicine : *Carthamus tinctorius*—its oil is used in injuries. Leaves of *Centipeda orbicularis* and *Xanthium stramonium* are used in teeth pain. Insulin, is extracted from *Cynara scolymus* flowers, which is used in diabetes. Roots of *Saussuarea lappa* are used in gastric troubles and asthama. *Santonin* is prepared from the flowers of *Artemisia obsinthium* which is used in removing the worms from body.

(C) Ornamental Plants : *Helianthus annuus* (sunflower), *Tagetus erectus* (Marigold), *Chrysanthemum, Cosmos, Vernonica cinerea, Zinnia* etc.

(D) Other commercial materials :

Perfume oil is prepared from *Eclipta erecta* and *Malricaria chamonilla*. Anti-insect oil is prepared from *Pyrethrum*.

Systemic Position :

Division	Angiospermae
Class	Dicotyledonae
Subclass	Gamopetalae
Series	Inferae
Order	Asterales
Family	Compositae (Asteraceae)

6. Family Cucurbitaceae

Habit : Climber or prostrate, annual herb.

Stem : Herbaceous, branched, pentangular, fistular, tendrils in axil of leaf or opposite to leaves. The morphological nature of tendrils is of dispute.

Leaf : Exstipulate, petiolate, alternate, simple, palmate, five lobed.

Inflorescence : Axillary solitary or cymose or racemose, peduncle of male flower profusely branched while female solitary.

Flower : Ebracteate, pedicellate, unisexual, incomplete, actinomorphic, pentamerous.

Male Flower

Calyx : Sepals 5, gamosepalous, quincuncial aestivation.

Corolla : Petals 5, gamopetalous, campanulate or rotate, imbricate or valvate aestivation.

Androecium : Stamens 5, polyandrous as in *Fevillea* or (2) + (2) + 1 as in *Momordica*, anthers twisted, alternate to petals, sometimes epipetalous, dehiscence longitudinal.

Gynoecium Absent.

Female Flower

Calyx & Corolla similar to male flower.

Androecium : Absent but sometimes 2, 3, 5 staminodes present.

Gynoecium : Tricarpellary, syncarpous, unilocular, ovary inferior, numerous ovules, parietal placentation but looks as axile placentation, style is simple, stigma 3.

Fruit-Pepo

Floral formula

Male flower : $\oplus$ ♂ $K_{(5)}\ C_{(5)}\ A_{(2)+(2)+1}\ G_0$

Female flower : $\oplus$ ♀ $K_{(5)}\ C_{(5)}\ A_0\ \overline{G}_{(3)}$

Economic Importance

(A) Plants used in food : Fruits of the plants of this family are mainly used as vegetables, e.g. *Cucurbita maxima* (Great Pumpkin = Wilati Kado.), *C. moschata* (Halwa Kado. = Kanshiphal, Mitha Kadoo = Sitaphal) *Legenaria siceraria* (Lauki), *Luffa cylindrica* (Ghia tori), *Lufa acutangula* (Kali tori), *Momordica charantia* (Karela), *Trichosanthes anguina* (Chachinda), *Cucumis sativus* (Kheera), *Cucumis milo* (Kharbooja), *Cucumis utilissimus* (Kakri), *Citrullus vulgaris* (water-melon-Tarbooj) etc.

(B) Plants used in medicines : The roots, fruit and leaf extract of *Coccinia indica* is used in diabetes. Extract of *Ecballium* is used in malaria and hydrophobia.

Systemic Position :

Division	Angiospermae
Class	Dicotyledonae
Sub-class	Polypetalae
Series	Calyciflorae
Order	Passiflorales
Family	Cucurbitaceae

7. Family Solanaceae

Habit : Mostly herbs, shrubs & trees.

Root : Branched tap root system.

Stem : Aerial, erect, climbing (*Solanum jasminoides*) herbaceous or woody, cylindrical branched, solid or hollow, hairy, or glabrous, underground stem in *Solanum tuberosum* (potato).

Leaves : Cauline, ramal, exstipulate, petiolate, or sessile, alternate, sometimes opposite, simple, entire pinnatisect in *Lycopersicum* (tomato) unicostate reticulate venation.

Inflorescence : Solitary axillary, umbellate cyme or helicoid cyme in Solanum nigrum.

Flower : Bracteate or ebracteate, pedicellate, complete, hermaphrodite, actinomorphic, pentamerous, hypogynous.

Calyx : Sepals 5, gamosepalous, tubular or campanulate, valvate or imbricate, persistent, green or coloured, hairy.

Corolla : Petals 5, gamosepalous, tubular or infundibuliform, valvate or imbricate aestivation, scale or hair-like outgrowth may arise from the throat of the corolla tube, coloured.

Androecium : Stamens 5, epipetalous, polyandrous, alternate to petals, filaments inserted deep in the corolla tube, anthers dithecous, usually basifixed or dorsifixed, introse.

Gynoecium : Bicarpellary, syncarpous, ovary superior, bilocular, unilocular in *Henoonia*, axile placentation, placentae swollen, many ovules in each locule, ovary obliquely placed, posterior carpel to the right about 45° from median and the anterior to the left. In some cases nectariferous disc is present, style simple, stigma bifid or capitate.

Fruit : A capsule or berry.

Seed : Endospermic.

Floral formula : Br. $\oplus$ ⚥ . $K_{(5)}\ C_{(5)}\ A_5\ \underline{G}_{(2)}$

Economic Importance

The familly is of great economic importance.

(A) Ornamental plants : These include many species of the genera *Brunfelsia, Browallia, Cestruna, Datura, Lycium, Petunia, Cestrum nocturnum* (the queen of the night) is an extremely fragrant plant. *Hyoscyamus niger* (the Henbane is also cultivated as an ornamental plant).

(B) Food plants :

(*i*) *Solanum tuberosum :* The stem tubers are the potato.

(*ii*) *S. melongena : Brinjal*, the fruit are eaten as vegetables.

(*iii*) *Lycopersicum esculentum :* The tomato fruit eaten raw and cooked as vegetable, other spices such as *L. glandulosum, L. pinpinelligolium, L. pissi* etc. also furnish edible fruits.

(*iv*) *Physalis peruviana :* Cape gooseberry (Raspberry) and other spices of the genus yield edible fruits.

(*v*) *Capsicum annus :* The chillies (Lal mirch) the fruits are used as spices and condiments.

(C) Tobacco : *Nicotiana tabacum* and *N. rustica* are the two species whose leaves after proper curing give the tobacco of commerce. The leaves contain the alkaloid nicotine and are also used as insecticide.

(D) Medicinal plants : Some plants of the family contain strong alkaloids and are of great medicinal value. The important ones are as follows :

(*i*) *Atropa belladona and A. acuminata :* The roots are used in the manufacture of belladona plasters and tinctures, as a sedative stimulant and antispasmodic. The alkaloid atropine is also extracted from this plant.

(*ii*) *Hyoscyamus niger :* The henbane—the leaves yield alkaloid hysocyamine and are used as sedative narcotic and also in the treatment of asthama and whooping cough.

(*iii*) *Withania somnifera* (Ashwangandh) the fruits leaves and roots are used in the treatment of cough. They have narcotic and sporific properties.

Systemic position :

Division	Angiospermae
Class	Dicotyledonae
Sub-class	Gamopetalae
Series	Bicarpellate
Order	Polemoniales
Family	Solanaceae.

8. Family Gramineae (Poaceae)

The family is commonly known as *grass family*. It is one of the largest among the angiospermic families. It consists of 620 genera and 6,000 species. The members are cosmopolitan in distribution. The plants represent all the 3 ecological types i.e. hydrophytes, xerophytes and mesophytes. In India it is represented by 850 species.

Habit : Herbs, annuals or perennials, or shrubs, sometimes tree like (*Bambusa, Dendrocalamus*)

Roots : Adventitious, fibrous, branched, fascid or stilt (*Zea mays*).

Stem : Underground rhizome in all perennial grasses, cylindrical, culm with conspicuous nodes and internodes, internodes hollow, herbaceous or woody, glabrous or glaucous, vegetative shoots arising from the base of aerial stem or from underground stems are called tillers.

Leaves : Alternate, simple, distichous, exstipulate, sessile, ligulate (ligules the portion of leaf sheath which projects above the attachment of lamina) (absent in *Bambusa*), leaf base forming tubular sheath, sheath open, surrounding internode incompletely, ligule is present at the junction of the lamina and sheath, entire, hairy or rough, linear, parallel venation.

Inflorescence : Compound spike which may be sessile or stalked. Each unit of inflorescence is spiklet. The spiklets are arranged in various ways on the main axis. A compound inflorescence may be spike of spikelets (*Triticum*), panicle of spikelets (*Avena*).

The spikelet consists of a short axis called Rachilla, on which one to five sessile or short stalked flowers are borne. The florets may be arranged in alternate or opposite manner on the central axis.

At the base of the rachilla two sterile scale, called *glumes*, are present. The glumes are placed one above the other on the opposite side. The lower one is called first glume and the upper one is called second glume.

Both the glumes are boat shaped and sterile. Above the glumes a series of florets are present. Each floret has an inferior *palea* or *lemma* and above it a *superior palea*. The lemma frequently bears a long stiff hair called awn.

Flower : Bracteate and bracteolate, sessile, incomplete, hermaphrodite or unisexual (*Zea mays*) irregular, zygomorphic, hypogynous, cyclic.

Perianth : Represented by membranous scales called *lodicules*. The lodicules are situated above and opposite the superior palea or may be absent or many (*Ochlandra*) or 2 or 3.

Androecium : Usually stamens 3, rarely 6 (*Oryza, Bambusa*) and one in *Cinna* and various species of *Fistuca*. Filaments long, anthers dithecous, versatile, linear, extrose. Pollen grains dry.

Gynoecium : Monocarpellary, according to some authors, carpels 3 of which 2 are abortive, ovary superior, unilocular with single ovule, basal placentation, style short or absent, stigma two.

Fruit : Caryopsis, a pericarp compeletely united or adherent with the seed coat, or rarely nut (*Dendrocalamus*) or berry (*Bambusa*).

Seed : Endospermic and containing a single cotyledon called *scutellum*, which in *shield shaped* and pressed against the endosperm.

Floral formulae

A. % ♂ P_0 or 2 (Lodicules) A_3 or $_6G_0$

B. % ♀ P_2 (Lodicules) A_0 $\underline{G_1}$ or $\underline{G_{(3)}}$

C. % ⚥ P_2 (Lodicules) A_3 $\underline{G_1}$

Economic Importance

Cereals :

(1) *Triticum aestivum* (Wheat)
(2) *Zea mays* (Maize)
(3) *Oryza sativa* (Rice)
(4) *Avena sativa* (Oat, jai)
(5) *Hordeum vulgare* (Barley = jau)

Millets :

(1) *Sorghum vulgare* (Jawar = Great millet)
(2) *Pennisetum typhoides* (Bajra)

Sugar plant :

(1) *Saccharum officinarum* (Sugarcane)

Grass :

(1) *Cynodon dactylon* (Doob grass)
(2) *Andropogon muricatus* (Khas, oil extracted from root)

Paper grass :

(1) *Themeda gigantia* (Kuproon grass)
(2) *Eucaliopsis binata* (Bhabar grass)

Other use :

(1) *Bambusa species :* Bamboo of commerce used for making poles, chairs, baskets, tables etc.
(2) *Dendrocalumus* species
(3) *Sachharum munja* (Munj)

The fibre called munj is used for making ropes.

Systemic position :

Division	Angiospermae
Class	Monocotyledonae
Series	Glumaceae
Family	Gramineae (Poaceae).

9. Family Liliaceae

Habit : Usually perennial herb as *Polygonatum*, sometimes small shrubs as *Resscus*, climbers as *Smilax*, trees as *Yucca*.

Root : Adventitious, fibrous.

Stem : Erect or climbing as smilax, branched or unbranched, herbaceous, phyllocade as Ruscus. Cladode as Asparagus. *Bulb* as *Allium cepa*.

Leaf : Radicle or cauline, exstipulate, stipulate in *Smilax*, scaly or fleshy or both, alternate or whorled, parallel ventation, but reticulate venation in *Smilax*.

Inflorescence : Raceme, umbel, sometimes solitary.

Flower : Pedicellate, bracteate, hermaphrodite, sometimes unisexual as *Ruscus*, *Smilax*, complete, actinomorphic, trimerous, hypogynous.

Perianth : 6 perianth in two whorls, anthers dithecous, introse, dorsifixed or basifixed or versatile, porous, longitudinal dehiscence.

Gynoecium : Tricarpellary, syncarpous, superior ovary, axile placentation, trilocular, two or more ovules in each locule, style are simple, stigma trilobed.

Fruit : Berry or capsule.

Floral Formula : Br. ⊕ ⚥ P_{3+3} A_{3+3} $\underline{G_{(3)}}$

Economic Importance

(A) Plants used as food : *Allium cepa, A. sativum* and *Asparagus racemosus* are used as vegetables.

(B) Plants used in medicines : Leaves of *Allium cepa* (onion) are used in dental and ear troubles. The leaves of *Allium sativum* (Lahsun) are used in cough and fever. The leaf extract of *Crinum latifolium* (Sukhdarshan) is used in ear pain. Bulb and leaf of *Crinum asiaticum* are used in urinary troubles. Medicine obtained from *Smilax zeylanica* roots is used in arthritis and dysentry.

(C) Ornamental plants : *Dracaena terniflora Yucca* sps. *Lilium candidum, Gloriosa superba* (Glory lily) etc.

(D) Other commercial uses : Colchicine, an alkaloid obtained from *Colchicum autumnale* in used to induce polyploidy in plants. A poison to kill rats, is prepared from bulbs of *Urginea indica* (white squill).

Systemic Position :

Division	Angiospemae
Class	Monocotyledonae
Series	Coronarieae
Family	Liliaceae.

10. Family Rosaceae

Habit : Creeping herbs, scapigenous herbs with creeping stolon, perennial herbs, erect or climbing shrubs and trees.

Root : Tap root system, adventitious roots appear where plants are grown or cultivated by cutting or any other method of vegetative reproduction.

Stem : Herbaceous to woody, erect, or trailing by means of runners or suckers, climbers and underground creeping stem in *Rubus chamaemorus*, cylindrical, sometimes prickly or thorny, branched and solid.

Leaves : Alternate, petiolate, stipulate, stipules adnate (*Rosa*) or *caducous* (*Pyrus*) simple or compound, sometimes simple and compound are found in the same genus margin of the leaf or leaflet is entire or serrate, leaf base conspicuous, unicostate reticulate venation.

Inflorescence : Solitary axillary, raceme, cyme, spike like raceme, corymb, terminal corymb, compound corymb, terminal cyme, terminal panicle, corymbose, sub-umbellat, axillary or terminal corymbose panicle and dense panicle.

Flower : Pedicellate, bracteate, hermaphrodite, rarely unisexual, generally actinormorphic but sometimes zygormorphic, hypogynous, perigynous, or epigynous, complete, tetra or pentamerous.

Calyx : 5 or 4 sepals, gamosepalous, imbricate or valvate aestivation. Sometimes epicalyx is present as in *Fragaria* while in *Rosa* sepals may be foliaceous.

Corolla : Petals 5 or multiples of 5; polypetalous, rosaceous, conspicuous, attractive, imbricate aestivation. In cultivated species petals increase and become indefinite as stamens are said to be converted into petals or petal like structures. Rarely petals may be absent as in *Archimilla.*

Androecium : Stamens many, arranged one or more than one whorl, rarely the stamens may be four as in Archimilla (number varies from 1 to 4), polyandrous usually incurved in bud, anthers are small and filaments are generally long.

Gynoecium : Carpels one to many one in *Prunus*, 2 in *Agremonin*, 2 to 5 in *Pyrus*, 1 to 5 in *Crataegus*, many in *Rosa.* When more than one, condition may be syn or apocurpous, ovary superior or inferior, unilocular when carpel is one or locules as many as the number of carpels, basal to marginal placentation in *Pyrus*, generally two ovules, each *loculus* when placentation is axile.

Fruit : Drupe in *Prunus*, pome in *pyrus*, berry in *Eriobotrya*, etaerio of drupes in *Rubus*, follicle in *Neillia*, etaerio of achenes in *Potentilla*, etario of follicles in *Spiraea.*

Pollination : By insects mostly, by wind in *Poterium.*

Economic importance

Fruit and ornamental plants.

(1) Prunus : Fruits *P. persica* (Peach), *P. armeniaca, P. uddcum, P. communis* (Alucha). Fruit oil *P. amygodalus* (Badam).

(2) Rubus : *R. ellipticus* and *R. lasiocarpus* are important species popularly known as 'Black berry'.

(3) *Fragaria indica* wild variety of strawberry.

(4) *Potentilla supina* herb growing on moist places or near banks.

(5) *Rosa :* Ornamental of various colours like pink, yellow, red, purple black or even green.

(6) *Pyrus* Fruits *P. Communis* (Chinapear, Nashpati) or *P. malus, P. sinensis* (nakh), *Malus sylvestris* (apple).

(7) *Crataegus cramilate* evergreen glabrous shrub.

(8) *Eriobotrya japonica* the loqual tree is cultivated for its fruits.

Systemic Position :

Angiospermae
Dicotyledons
Polypetalae
Calyciflorae
Rosales
Rosaceae.

11. Family Euphorbiaceae

Habit : Herbs, which may be erect, or prostate, shrubs and trees.

Root : Tap root system.

Stem : Herbaceous to woody, erect or prostrate, cylindrical, branched & solid.

Leaves : Generally alternate, sometimes opposite, rarely whorled, petiolate, sub-sessile, usually stiuplate, stipulses may be spiny in fleshy species of *Euphorbia*, occassionally exstipulate, simple with various shapes, margin of the leaf entire or serrate, unicostate, or multicostate reticulate venation.

Inflorescence : Raceme, Dichasial cyme, cyathium in *Euphorbia* in this single female flower in surrounded by many male flowers enclosed in a cup like involucre of bracts, having nectaries to it. Each stamen represent a single male flower, because it has its own jointed stalk and possesses bract at its base.

Flower : Pedicellate or sessile, unisexual, male & female flowers situated on the same plant. In racemose, male flowers are situated above and female flower is below. In *Cyathium* many male flowers surrounded a single female flower, actinomorphic, hypogynous and incomplete.

Perianth : Absent in *Euphorbia*, 5 in *Ricinus communis*, 4 sepaloid in *Acalypha* 6 in two whorls of 3 each in *Phyllanthes*. Aestivation valvate, when perianth is in one whorls, imbricate when in two whorls, sepals petalloid with valvate aestivation and corolla polypetalous with twisted aestivation in *Jatropha*.

Androceium : Stamens one in *Euphorbia*, 3 in *Phyllanthes* 6 to 8 polyandrous in *Acalypha*, 5 branched in *Ricinus*, 10 monadelphous in *Jatropha* and many polyandrous in *Croton*.

Gynoecium : Tricarpellary, syncarpous, ovary superior, tri or hexalocular, axile placentation with one or two ovules in each locule, styles three stigma three or six.

Fruit : Capsule or regma in *Euphorbia*, regma in *Ricinus*, berry in *Bischofia*, drupe in *Bridelia* and *Putranjiva*. Berry or drupe in *Phyllanthus* and *Acalypha*.

Pollination : By insects generally, also anemophyllous as in *Mercurialis* & *Ricinus*.

Economic Importance

Euphorbia : Herbs, shrubs or small trees with white latex, *E. hirta* and *E. prostrata* are common weeds. *E. royleana* is cultivated to make good hedge plant. It is cactus like herb. *E. splendens* is an ornamental pot plant. *E. triucalli* is a leafless ornamental shrub or a small tree.

Breynia forms good hedge and is medicinally useful.

Emblica officinalis (Amla) is an important tree, cultivated for its fruits, which are eaten either as pickle or in the form of jam. It is also medicinally important.

Putranjiva roxburghii is an evergreen ornamental tree.

Ricinus communis : The cast or plant is cultivated because the seeds yield commercially important oil, the castor oil. Besides many uses of this oil it is also medicinally important.

Hevea brasiliensis : The Indian rubber plant is a 60 to 100 feet long tree. The rubber is obtained by tapping the bank and coagulating the latex, later on it is pressed and dried.

Systemic Position :

Angiospermae
Dicotyledons
Monochlamydeae
Euphorbiales
Euphorbiaceae.

12. Family Umbelliferae

Habit : Herbs, occassionally shrubs.

Root : Tap root system.

Stem : Herbaceous, erect or creeping, or climbing, cylindrical, glabrous but sometimes slightly pubescent as in *Hydrocotyle javanica*, branched and green, generally fistular.

Leaves : Alternate, rarely opposite, petiolate, exstipulate, usually compound, sometimes decompound as in *Daucus*, sometimes simple, sheathing leaf base, unicostate reticulate venation, (Heterophylly is noticeable in *Coriandrum sativum* when plant is very old.

Inflorescence : Generally compound umbel, sometimes simple umbel, surrounded by an involucre of bracts.

Flower : Pedicellate, sometimes sessile in Hydrocotyle, bracteate, hermaphrodite, actinomorphic (Flowers become zygomorphic in *Conandrum* when the outer flowers posses unequal corolla), epigynous and complete.

Calyx : 5 sepals, gamosepalous teeth may be present, calyx tube adnate to the ovary wall.

Corolla : 5 petals, polypetalous, reflexed, sometimes inflexed as in *Foeniculum* occasionally lobes are unequal as in coraindrum, imbricate aestivation.

Androecium : Stamens 5, polyandrous, anthers dorsifixed, filaments long.

Gynoecium : Bicarpellary, syncarpous, ovary inferior, bilocular axile placentation, situated anterio-posteriorly with one ovule each loculus, style two, stigma two surrounded by a honey disc called stylopodium.

Fruit : It is a schizocarpic cremocarp, containing two mericarps, joined by a carpophore.

Pollination : The flowers are aggregated in dense inflorescence, possess attractive corolla and also some fragrant odour so the insects are attracted by them. The pollination is therefore entomophilous. The pollination takes place chiefly through flies and bettles.

Economic Importance

Medicinal Plants : Hydrocotyle javanica & H. *asiatica, Apium greveolens* is a biennial herb, where roots and seeds are sometimes eaten. *Carum captiuum* is cultivated for its fruits, which are used as condiments and also medicinally important. *C. carui* has fruits which give an important condiments-the *carraway* (Zeera).

Foeniculum vulgare (Saunf) important condiment.

Peucedanum greveolens glabrous herb with linear pinnate leaves and is based as vegetables (Vernacular-Soya)

Coriandrum sativum (Coriander; Dhania) is cultivateed for its leave which make good sauce and fruits are important condiment for flavouring curries. It is also medicinally important.

Systemic Position :

Angisopermae
Dicotyledons
Polypetalae
Calyciflorae
Umbellales
Umbelliferae.

13. Family Asclepiadaceae

Habit : Perennial herbs, climbing shrubs, or twiners.

Root : Tap root system.

Stem : Herbaceous, woody, erect, twiner, climbers, cylindrical, generally pubescent, branched and solid.

Leaves : Opposite, decussate, exstipulate, shortly petioled, simple, generally pubescent, margin entire, unicostate reticulate venation. Leaves reduced to spines in *Stapelia.*

Inflorescence : Generally cymose and occassionally a raceme, Axillary cyme in *Hemidesmus.* Terminal or axillary cyme in *Periploca*, umellate cyme in *calotropis* and *Gymnema*. Umbellate or corymbose cyme in *Marsdenia.*

Flower : Pedicellate, bracteate, hermaphordite, actinomorphic, hypogynous, complete.

Calyx : Sepals 5, polysepalous, or united near the base, quincuncial aestivation.

Corolla : Petals 5, gamopetalous, aestivation contorted or valvate, corona generally present.

Androecium : Stamens 5, polyandrous, stamens & stigmatic head adhere together to form pentagonal gynostigium. The pollen grains of each half anthers are united together in a structure called pollinium. Each pollinium has a translator by means of which the pollinia of two adjacent anther halves are united. Translator has corpusculum which is gland like and a pair of retinaculi or the connectives.

Gynoecium : Bicarpellary, ovary superior. Apocarpous because the ovaries are invariably separate. Each ovary is unilocular with marginal placentation. Styles two at the base but finally become one. The style finally ends in pentogonal stigmatic head.

Fruit : An aggregate fruit in the form of etaerio of follicles.

Pollination : By insects.

Economic Importance : Asclepias are the most ornamental plants of the family. *Periploca* flowers are eaten. Its stem yields fibre which is used in making ropes. Its latex is also medicinally important. *Gymnema sylvestre* (Gurmar) in a pubsescent climbing shrub. Its leaves contain gymnemic acid and when chewed, temporarily destroy the sense of tasting sweets.

Marsdenia is also a twinning shrub and its stem yields a very strong fibre. *Cryptostegia grandiflora* is a climbing shrub with beautiful rose coloured flowers. It is cultivated for its ornamental value. It is ever green and an extreme xerophyte.

Systemic Position :

Angiospermae
Dicotyledons
Gamopetalae
Bicarpellalae
Gentianales
Asclepiadaceae

14. Family Verbenaceae

Habit : Herb, shrub or a tree. Some plants may be climbers as *Vitex* and *Clerodendron*.

Root : Tap root system.

Stem : Herbaceous or woody, erect or creeping, cylindrical or angular, glabrous, hairy, branched and solid.

Leaves : Opposite, whorled, petiolate, or sub-sessile, exstipulate, generally simple, rarely compound. Leaves have serrate or crenate margin and the leaf blade is pubescent with unicostate reticulate venation.

Inflorescence : Cylindrical spikes, axillary heads, corymbose spike, dichotomous cyme forming terminal panicles in *Tectona*, axillary panicles or corymbs in *vitex*, axillary cymes, terminal raceme in *Duranta* and terminal spike in *Stachytarpheta*.

Flower : Sessile or pedicellate, generally bracteate, hermaphrodite, zygomorphic, hypogynous and complete.

Calyx : Sepals generally 5, gåmosepalous, lobes variable, 2-lipped and ribbed in *Verbessa*.

Corolla : 5 petals, gamopetalous, usually unequal in size, may be tubular, campanulate, bilipped in most of the cases, caducous in *Petrea*, falls of as a calyptra as the fruit ripens in case of Lippia.

Androecium stamens usually 4, polyandrous, didynamous, occassionally all the 5 stamens are present in *Tactona* and *Verbascum*, rarely stamens are only 2 as in *Oxera*.

Gynoecium : Bicarpellary (4, 5 or more carpels in *Duranta*), syncarpous, superior ovary, 2 to 4 locular, ovules variable, attached in axile placentation.

Fruit : Drupe in *Lantana*, *Tectona* and *Clerodendron*. Capsule in *Caryopteris*. Berry in Duranta.

Pollination : Entomophilous generally.

Economic Importance

Verbena, Lantana, Clerodendron, Caryopteris wallichiana, Duranta plumieri, Petrea are all ornamental plants. *Tectona grandis* is the teak tree of high economic value which is cultivated for its extremely fine wood. *Gmelina arborea* is not a common tree but is cultivated in gardens for ornamental purposes. The wood is similar to teak but more soft. It last well under water.

Systemic Position :

Angiospermae
Dicotyledons
Gamopetalae
Bicarpellate
Verbenales
Verbenaceae.

15. Family Rubiaceae

Habit : Herbs, shrubs, and trees.

Root : Tap root system.

Stem : Herbaceous to woody, erect or twining cylindrical with or without spines, branched and solid.

Leaves : Opposite (decussate) or whorled, stipulate, stipules inter-petiolar or intra-petiolar, occassionally foliaceous as in *Galium*, simple, shape variable margin entire or incised, unicostate reticulate venation.

Inflorescence : A dichasial or panicled cyme, terminal cyme in some species of *Mussaenda*, axillary in coffea. The dichasial cyme may be condensed into globose heads as in *Anthocephalus* and *Adina*, occasionally terminal trichotomously branched corymbose cyme as in *Ixora*. Sub-umbellate cyme in *Hamiltonia*.

Flower : Pedicellate or sub-sessile, bracteate, sometimes bracteoles also present, hermaphrodite (rarely unisexual), actinomorphic (rarely zygomorphic as in *Henriquezia*), epigynous, complete, incomplete when the flower is unisexual, tetra or penatamerous.

Calyx : Sepals 4 or 5, gamosepalous, occassionally one sepal enlarges in size and becomes very conspicuous and attractive (*Mussaenda*), sepals may be prominent in the fruit as in *Nematostylis* or after fertilization as in *Albertia*.

Corolla : Petals 4 or 5, gamopetalous, tubular or funnel shaped, aestivation may be valvate, twisted or imbricate (bilabiate corolla in *Henriquezia*).

Androceium : 4 or 5 stamens, epipetalous, filaments long, sometimes united, heterostylly in *Oldenlandia*.

Gynoecium : Bicarpellary, syncarpous, inferior ovary (rarely superior as in *Pogamea*), bilocular (unilocular in *Gardenia* where placentation is parietal), axile placentation, style one, stigma bilobed or simple.

Fruit : Capsule in Anotis, berry in *Mussaenda* and *Coffea*, somewhat schizocarpic in *Galium*.

Pollination : By insects.

Economic Importance : Coffea arabica and *C. liberica* are the evergreen coffea plants. The fruit is a drupe and seed after roasting and grinding yield the coffea of commerce *Cinchona officinalis* is widely cultivated on account of the important alkaloids like quinine and cinchonidina. Which are medicinally very imporant.

Mussaenda glabrata is an ornamental shrub, cultivated in the gardens for its beautiful flowers. Here one sepal becomes enlarged and attractive. *Hamelia patens* is another ornamental garden shrub.

Systemic Position :

Angiospermae
Dicotyledons
Gamopetalae
Inferae
Rubiales
Rubiaceae.

16. Family Palmae

Habit : Trees reaching to a height of 40-50 feet or even more (Phoenix, *Areca catecheu*), short sized garden palm i.e. *Livestonia* and occassionally traling in habit (*Calamus*). *Thrinax* is only a foot in height.

Root : Adeventitious root system.

Stem : Woody, erect, sometimes scandent as in *Calamus* and occassionally underground as in *Nipa*, cylindrical having persistent woody leaf bases or ring like scars, generally unbranched, rarely branched as in *Hyphaene*. The stem is very tall and its girth is also prominent but secondary growth does not take place by the expansion of apical meristem which gives rise to innumberable vascular bundles and ground tissue made up of parenchyma.

Leaves : Alternate and generally crowded in terminal region, petiolate, petiole sheathing, exstipulate, compound, pinnately (*Phoenix*) or palmately (*Borassus*), leaf base woody, many leaves have waxy coating over them while the apex of the leaf or leaflet is pointed.

Inflorescence : Spadix having sessile or pedicellate flowers enclosed within a huge bract called the spathe which may sometimes be hard. The flowers may be single or in panicles. Plants of this family may be monocarpic (fruiting only once during life time e.g. *Corpha*) or polycarpic as most of the plants. The spadix is interfoliar and very much branched in *Nannorrhops*.

Flower : Sessile or shortly pedicellate, bracteate, generally unisexual (*Phoenix*) or hermaphrodite, actinomorphic, hypogynous, complete or incomplete and trimerous. Plants may be monoecious (*Cocos*) or dioecious (*Phoenix*).

Perianth : Tepals 6 in two whorbs of 3 each, polyphyllous or slightly connate, imbricate aestivation, fleshy, coriaceous and persistent.

Androecium : Stamens 6 (in hermaphrodite and male flowers) in two whorls of 3 each, polyandrous, staminodes may be present in the female flowers, sometimes the number of stamens may be reduced to 3 as in *Nipa*.

Gynoecium : Absent or only rudimentary as in male flowers but when present in hermaphrodite and female flowers it is tricarpellary, syncarpous, ovary superior, trilocular, axile placentation, one ovule in each locule.

Fruit : A drupe (*Cocos*) or a berry (*Phoenix, Areca*).

Pollination : By wind.

Economic Importance

(1) *Phoenix :* Date palm, important species are *P. sylvestris, P. dactylifera, P. acaulis, P. humilis*. Berry fruits are eaten.

(2) *Calamus : C. tenuis* is important for making mats & baskets. This species and *C. rotang* yield cane of commerce and its furniture is light and durable.

(3) *Nannorrhops retchieana* used by Pathans for making mats & fans. Its seeds are made into rosaries and are common in Makka & Madina.

(4) *Areca catechu :* The Betlenut palm has one seeded berry cultivated in South for its commercial value. It is of medicinal importance also.

(5) *Borassus :* It is an ornamental tall tree having a crown of leaves at the top which are fan shaped. The leaves are used in thatching, making mats, baskets, fans. The inflorescence is incised and toddy is taken from it.

(6) *Caryota urens :* The toddy palm is tapped and a pitcher is tied near the incision so that the liquid is collected in it. On fermentation, the liquid yield alcohol and the fresh toddy is also taken and supposed to be a good stimulant and to some extent an intoxicant.

(7) *Capernicia cerifera :* It yields a sort of wax which was formerly used for making candles and gramophone records.

(8) *Cocos nucifera :* It is largely cultivated near sea shores and elsewhere for its high economic value. The coconut palm is a fibrous drupe and the edible portion is the endosperm. The oil is extracted from it which is commercially very valuable. Its hard endocarp is made into toys and pipes ("Hyqyua") by villagers.

(9) *Metroxylon rumphii* is a monocarpic genus which yield the sago ("Sabudana") of commerce.

(10) *Nipa fruitcans* is found in *S. India* and Ceylon and its delicate round leaves are used as cigarette paper.

Systemic position :

Angiospermae
Monocotyledones
Calycinae
Palmae.

17. Family Musaceae (Scitamineae)

Habit : Perennial herbs but reaching to a height to 10-15 feet on account of their leaf sheaths which roll into a pseudo-stem (Musa).

Root : Adventitious root system.

Stem : It is an underground rhizome.

Leaves : Petiole and leaf blade very long, mid-rib prominent and formed as a result of continuation of the petiole. Unicostate parallel venation.

Inflorescence : Spadix covered by coloured bracts. The flowers are situated (particularly in case of *Musa*) in 3 rows separated by 5 sapathes. Each row is biseriated. The flowers situated above are male while those situated in the innermost row are female, flowers in the middle row may be hermaphrodite.

Flower : Sessile, bracteate, unisexual, or hermaphrodite, zygomorphic, epigynous, complete or incomplete and trimenous.

Perianth : Tepals 6 in two whorls of 3 each. *Musa* is characterized by having 3 tepals in outer whorls and 2 in the inner whorls to form a tube while the 6th posterior remains free, perianth is coloured and attractive, free or united imbricate aestivation.

Androecium : 6 stamens in two whorls of 3 each, generally only 5 stamens are present, the 6th posterior one of the inner whorls is staminode or completely absent, polyandrous. In *Ravenala* all the 6 stamens are fertile.

Gynoecium : Tricarpellary, syncarpous, ovary, inferior, trilocular with axile placentation, one to many ovules each loculus.

Fruit : Berry in Musa, capsule in *Ravenala*, and a schizocarpic in *Heliconia*.

Pollination : Entomophilous or ornithophilous. The insects or birds visit the flower in search of honey.

Economic Importance

(1) *Musa :* It is one of the most important species of this family and its various species yield banana, the fruit value of which is so well known. *M. paradisiaca* (*M. balbisiana*) & *M. chinensis* or dwarf banana are cultivated in India for fruits. *M. texilis* is also cultivated for its hemp which is obtained from its leaf bases.

Ravenala madagascariesnis : Popularly known as traveller tree, it has a woodly stem and it reaches to a height of 100 feet. It is ornamental and its leaf bases accumulate water which can be used in emergency by puncturing the bases.

Zingiber capitatum and Z. *officinale* are the wild and cultivated ginger plants are cultivated for their valued rhizome.

Systemic Position :

Angiospermae
Monocotyledones
Calyciferae
Zingiberales
Musaceae or Scitamiceae.

18. Family Orchideae

Habit : Terrestrial, Saprophytes, Bulbophyllum is an epiphytic climber.

Root : Adventitious roots which are of three kinds normal roots, tuberous roots and aerial roots. The latter again are of three types—clinging roots which are negatively geotropic and finally aerial roots which are most important, hand downwards and are branched. These possess velamen thickenings which are meant to absorb moisture.

Stem : More or less elongate, solitary composed of discrete pseudobubs, jointed and made up of elongated pseudobubs, leafy, tuber or rhizome, sealy bulb in *Dendrophylax* and very short in *Ornithochilus*. Stem of an epiphytic form is generally a **pseudobulb**. Saprophytic types have no chlorophyll.

Leaf : Foliage leaves are lacking in *Dendrophylax* radical leaves in *Orchis* and *Pogonia*, hair like in *Bulbophyllum*, solitary or in pairs, in *Pholidota*, almost sessile, exstipulate, leaf base sheathing, unicostate parallel venation.

Inflorescence : Usually racemose which may be short lined or perennial.

Flower : Pedicellate or sessile, usually bracteate, hermaphrodite, zygomorphic, epigynous, incomplete, trimerous. Flowers are generally large, showy and quite attractive, in some cases like *Pleurothalis* these may be small and *inconspicuous*.

Perianth : Tepals 6 in two whorls of 3 each. Free or slightly united, 3 outer more or less similar (2 lateral sometimes united forming a short or long sac or spur like base which is also called *mentum*). Three inner tepals dissimilar. (2 lateral similar, one medium is of different shape, variable in colour and is called *lip* or *labellum*). Labellum is bigger than others of the inner whorl. A spur develops partly from lip and partly from axis in *Orchis* where it store honey.

Androecium : Stamens usually one (two in case of *cypripedium*). When it is one it is of the outer whorl and two of the inner whorl are staminodes, free or adnate. Stamens and style united to form a column opposite the labellum. Top of the column sometimes protrudes towards labellum into a beak like process called *rostellum*. Pollen grains coherent in each cell into 1, 2 or 4 pairs of globose waxy or powdery masses called pollinia which may be free or attached by a sterile stalk known as candicle. Stocky gland may be present at the base of candicle which is called *Corpusculum*. The staminodes may be foliaceous (Diuris) or in the form of auricles (*Orchis*).

Gynoecium : Tricarpellary, syncarpous, ovary inferior, unilocular, parietal placentation, stamen, stigma and style united together to form column or gynoecium. The portion of style in column is strong. Stigma lobes three of which only two lateral are fertile (all the three fertile in *Cypripedium*). Third is sterile and modified into rostellum.

Fruit : Is a capsule.

Pollination : By insects.

Economic Importance

Aerides & *Vanda* are epiphytes with leafy stems. Roots of *vanda* are well known to the students for their peculiar anatomy. The special velamen thikening absorb moisture. Tubes of *Eulophia epidendrae* are used as vermifuge. Root stocks of

Geodorum densiflora are used as insecticides. Roots of *Vanda roxburghii* is used for rheumatism and scorpion bite. Leaves of *Calanthe veratriflora* yield blue dye. Ornamental plants of *Papliopedalum* are very costly. Dried pulpy fruits of *Vanilla palfolia* yield *vanilla* scent which is so extensively used in ice creams, chocolates and confectionary.

Systemic Position :

Angiospermae
Monocotyledons
Corolliferae
Orchidales
Orchidaceae.

Development of Male and Female Gametophytes

In the life history of Angiosperms, there is a highly developed sporophyte and highly reduced gametophyte. Which alternate with each other (Alternation of generations). These two generations are clearly distinguishable in their morphological as well as cytological characters and are formed from one another i.e. gametophytic generation gives rise to sporophytic generation and *vice versa*. The sporophytic generation is reported by roots, stems, leaves and flowers (which bears calyx, corolla, androecium and gynoecium). Each cell bears 2n number of chromosomes i.e., the sporophyte is diploid. The gametophytic generation is represented by pollen grains (male gametophyte) and embryo sac (female gametophyte) and each cell bears *n* number of chromosomes i.e. the *gametophyte is haploid*.

Stamen (Microsporophyll) : The fertile portion of stamens is called anther. Each anther is usually made up of two lobes (antherlobes) connected by a connective. In turn, each anther lobe contains two pollen chambers, placed longitudinally. Each pollen chamber represents a microsporangium and is filled with a large number of pollen grains or microspores. Thus a typical anther consists of four microsporangia (pollen chambers). This type of anther is known as *dithechous*. In Malvaceae *monothecous* condition is found i.e. anthers bears only one lobe (theca with 2 microporangia).

Each lobe of the mature anther is an elongated cavity or pollen sac or microsporangium which consists of pollen grains. The outermost layer of the wall of microsporangium is epidermis. The next layer made up of large columnar cells with fibrous thickening arising from inner side is called *endothecium*. The cells of the endothecium opposite the partition between two microsporangia are thin-walled and constitute the *stomium* through which pollen grains are discharged from the anther lobes. Beneath the endothecium are present two to three layers of cells called middle layers. Below the middle layers and outer to the pollen sac the innermost layer of cells known as *tapetum* is present which surrounds the microsporogenous tissue. Its cells divide freely and form a layer of enlarged cubical cells which elongate centripetally as the microsporogenous tissue develops into pollen mother cells. The layer called *tapetum* disappears when the pollen grains become mature and before dehiscence of anthers.

A young anther in a T.S. appears quadrilobed. The development of microsporangia is *eusporangiate* type. Certain cells of hypodermal layer in each lobe begin to enlarge, and protoplasm becomes denser than the neighbouring cells. These are *archesporial initials*. These cells divide periclinally to form *primary parietal layer* towards outside and *primary microsporogenous* cells towards the inner side. The cells of the formen usually undergo further periclinal and anticlinal divisions to form a series of 3 to 5 concentric layers making the wall of the anther. The primary microsporogenous cells separate from one another and give rise to microspore mother cells.

The epidermal cells of the wall of anther become stretched and flattened as the anther enlarges. The parietal layer lying below the epidermis form endothecium. The endothecium is followed by 2-3 middle layers. The cells between middle layer and microsporogenous cells develop into tapetum. Later the tapetal cells becomes loose and nuclei may degenerate. Tapetum plays an important role in pollen development (specially microspore walls). Generally, all the microsporogenous cells are capable of producing the microspores but some of them distintegrate and are absorbed by remaining cells. Microspore mother cells divide to form microspores by reduction divisions. The division may be *successive type* or *simultaneous type*.

In the former, each of the two nuclear divisions are followed by the formation of wall. In *successive* type the cell plate is formed in the center and then extends centrifugally on both sides dividing the cell into similar parts. In simultaneous type, divisions occurs centripetally dividing the cells into four parts with the formation of furrows. Generally successive type occurs in monocotyledons and simultaneous type in dicotyledons. The tetrad produced by successive type is called *isobilateral tetrad* and that produced by *simultaneous* type is called *tetrahedral tetrad*. Other tetrads are *decussate*, *T-shaped* and *linear*.

Most commonly the microspores soon separate from one another but sometimes they adhere in tetrads to form *compound pollen grains* e.g. *Drimys, Anona, Drosera, Elodea, Typha.* In Asclepiadaceae family all microspores of a sporangium cohere in a single mass called *pollinium*. Development of microspores (pollen grains) from archesporial cells is called *microsporogenesis*.

Structure of Microspores and the Development of Male Gametophyte (= germination of Microspores)

The microspore consists of a centrally situated nucleus, dense cytoplasm and two distinct walls, the outer *exine* and inner *intine* usually at 2 or 3 points the exine in absent, these points are called *germpores*. Exine is variously sculptured. Before discharge from the microsporangium, the nucleus divides forming a small cell called *Generative cell* which is adjacent to spore wall. The remaining part of microspore is filled with a cell called *vegetative cell* (= Tube cell = Siphonogenic cell). It is in this two celled stage that pollen grains are usually released from the anther (In some plants, the generative cell may divide into two male gametes before liberation of pollen grains from anther), and reaches the stigma of the carpel.

A typical Gynoecium (= Pistil): The gynoecium (pistil) is the topmost central whorl of the flower and is made up of one or more carpel (megasporophylls). Each gynoecium consists of stigma at the top, an elongated style and the bulbous ovary. Each ovary contains one or more ovules (megasporangia). Ovary is the most important part of gynoecium.

Structure of the ovule (Megasporangium)

The mature ovule is differentiated into the following parts, a centrally located large cell with eight nuclei called *embryo sac* (mature female gametophyte). Surrounding the embryosac is multicellular nucellus (2n). If there are 2 integument the voule is called *bitegmic*, if there is only one integument, the ovule is called *unitegmic*. Sunflower, *Tagetus* have only one integument. Some ovules do not have any integument, e.g. *Lovanthus, Santalum*. The integuments are incomplete at the apex of ovule forming a pore called micropyle. The base of ovule from which integuments arise is called *Chalaza*. The ovule is attached to the placenta by a slender stalk known as *funicle*. The point of attachment of the body of the ovule to its stalk (*funicle*) is known as *hilum*. Sometimes the funicle continues beyond the hilum, along the body of the ovule forming a sort of ridge which is called *raphe*.

Kinds of ovules :

(1) *Orthotropous (Straight) :* The micropyle, chalaza and funicle lie in one straight line. e.g. Family Polygonaceae, Piperaceae.

(2) *Anatropous (Inverted) :* The body of the ovule is completely inverted so that micropyle and hilum come to lie very close to each other. e.g. All plants of gamopetalae.

(3) *Hemitropous :* When nucellus and integuments lie more or less at right angles to the funiculus.

(4) *Campylotropous :* When the ovule is curved, the micropyle is directed toward chalaza. Chalaza is situated at right angle to funicle. e.g. Members of Liguminosae family.

(5) *Amphitropous :* The ovule curvature is more pronounced and embryosac become horse-shaped. e.g. Families, Alismaceae, Butamaceae.

(6) *Circinotropous :* The funicle is exceptionally long and forms a complete circle around the ovules which is free from it except for a small area at the end of funicle. e.g. *Opuntia* and other members of families *Cactaceae* and *Plumbaginaceae*.

Archesporium : Either hypodermal cell at the apex of nucellus functions directly as Megaspore mother cell or hypodermal cell first divides unequally into outer parietal and an inner megaspore mother cell. The parietal cell in this case may from a variable number of wall cells.

Megasporogenesis (Megaspore Formation) : The first meiotic division of megaspore mother cell is always transverse forming a dyad of cells. Second meiotic division is also transverse resulting in a *linear tetrad* of *megaspores*. Linear tetrad of megaspores is most common, but T-shaped, ⊥-shaped or isobilateral tetrads may also occur.

Generally the lowermost megaspore (farthest from micropyle) is functional i.e. develops into-embryosac or female gametophyte. The first division of functional megaspore gives rise to two nuclei, the primary micropylar and primary chalazal nuclei. The second division results in one pair of nuclei at each end, and the third division produces four nuclei at one end and four on the other end (i.e., at opposite poles of the now elongated developing embryosac). Three of the nuclei at the micropylar end become originated to form *egg apparatus* and one nucleus does not participate in the formation of egg apparatus and is called upper polar nucleus. At the opposite (challazal) end of the developing embryosac three nuclei differentiate as *antipodal cells* (or *nuclei*) and the fourth remaining nucleus as lower polar nucleus. The two polar nuclei from opposite ends (micropylar and chalazal) migrate into the centre of the embryosac giving rise to secondary nuclei (= definitive nucleus). This type of development is normal type of *polygonum type*. When the embryosac develops from one megaspore, it is called *monocarpic* embryosac. Many other variations are however found.

Structure of the Mature Embryo sac (Female Gametophyte) (Megagametogenesis)

A typical mature embryosac consists of a large cell with two polar nuclei (which on fusion give rise to secondary nucleus in the centre). At the micropylar end there is an *egg apparatus* (1 egg cell with 2 synergids) and at its chalazal end are found 3 antipodals. The cells of egg apparatus and antipodal cells are uninucleate and haploid but the central cell is first binucleate which fuses later forming a diploid nucleus called secondary nucleus = definitive nucleus.

POLLINATION, FERTILIZATION AND SEED FORMATION

Pollination: Pollination is defined as the process of transfer of pollen grains, "from an anther to the stigma of the same flower or of different flower."If the pollen grains are transferred from an anther to the stigma of the same flower, the process is called self pollination or autogamy. If these are transferred to the stigma of different flower on the same plant or different flower of different plant or the same species or different flower of a different plant of different species, it is called *cross pollination* or *allogamy.*

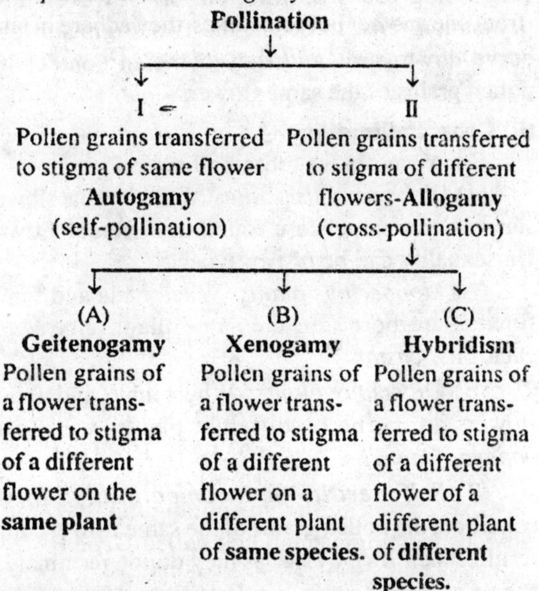

(i) Self Pollination

Contrivances for self pollination

For self pollination, following adaptations are found in plants:

(1) *Bisexuality (Hermaphrodites) :* It is only in bisexual flowers that self pollination can take place.

(2) *Homogamy:* Both sex organs of a flower should mature at the same time.

(3) *Cleistogamy :* In some plants *e.g. Commelina, Viola, Impatiens, Archis, Oxalis,* the anthers mature and burst liberating their pollen grains in a closed flower. Such plants usually have two types of flowers (a) underground closed flowers and (b) aerial flowers which open like normal flowers. Cleistogamous

(closed) flowers are very small, colourless, odourless, and without nectar. Aerial flowers are larger, brightly coloured and scented and in these flowers cross pollination takes place.

In some plants, *e.g. Helianthus,* if cross pollination fails, selfing is sure. The flower is protandrous *i.e.,* anther mature first. Stigma is bilobed which is hidden in tube formed by anthers. At maturity, pollen grains are discharged in the anther tube but self pollination does not occur as the stigma is not mature mid receptive. At maturity, the stigma grows out of the anther tube, both stimatic lobes open, thus facilitating cross pollination. If, however, cross pollination fails, to occur, the two stigmatic lobes. curve downwards and they come in contact with pollen grains of the same flowers.

(ii) Cross Pollination

Contrivances for cross pollination are:

(1) *Dicliny or unisexuality :* In unisexual flowers, stamens and carpels are found in different flowers. Unisexuality can be of two types:

(A) *Monoecious plants:* When male and female flowers are borne on the same plant, *e.g. Maize, cucurbits, castor.*

(B) *Dioecious plants:* When male and female flowers are borne on different plants, *e.g. Casica papaya, Cannalis.*

(2) *Self sterility or incompatibility:* In this condition, the pollen grains of the same flower cannot fertilize their own ovules as they donot germinate on stigma of same flowers. *e.g. Passiflora, Malva, Potato.*

(3) *Dichogamy:* In many hermaphrodite flowers, stamens and carpels of a flower donot mature at the same time. Dichogamy is of two types.

(A) *Protandry :* The anthers of a flower mature earlier than carpels, *e.g. Jasminum, Foeniculum, Tagetus, Sunflower.*

(B) *Protogyny :* The carpels of a flower mature earlier than stamens *e.g. Ficus benghalensis, Polyathea, Anona, Michelia, Rose.*

(4) *Heterostyly :* The flowers may be of two or mpre types with regard to the length of the style and lengths of stamens and pollens from a flower cannot bring about effective pollination in flowers of its own type, *e.g. Oxalis, Lythrum, Primula.*

(5) *Herkogamy :* In some homogamous flowers, there are some adaptations due to which self pollination cannot occur. These adoptations are as follows: In caryophyllaceous flower, the stigma projects beyond the stamens so that pollen donot fall on it. Conversely in *Gloriosa* they dehisce at a distance so that stigma is out of reach to its own pollen.

Modes of Cross Pollination: The agencies which transfer pollen grains from anthers of one flower to the stigma of a different flowers are as follows: WIND (Anemophily), WATER (Hydrophily), INSECTS (Entomophily), BIRDS (Ornithophily)' and BATS (Cheiropterophily).

(1) *Anemophily:* Anemophilous plants produce enormous amount of pollen grains: A single plant of *Mercurialis* annually has been estimated to produce 1,352,000,000 pollen grains. Anemophilous plants bear small and inconspicuous flower. The pollen grains are small, light, smooth and dry. Pollen of some plants are said to be blown to 1,300 km. In some plants as *Pinus*, pollen grains are winged. The flowers are usually unisexual in some plants *e.g.* Mulberry are borne in independent catkins which can sway freely and shake off their pollen in air. The flowers may be borne on long axis (as in grasses) much above the leaves. The anther are versatile so as to oscillate in all directions at the tip of filament. In Urticaceae filaments are very long. Anempohilous flowers have adequate devices to catch the air-borne-pollen grains with utmost efficiency. For this the stigma is usually large and feathery (as in grasses) and brush like as in *Typha.*

(2) *Hydrophily :* It is of two types:

(*a*) *Hypohydrogamy :* Includes plants which are pollinated inside the water, *e.g. Ceratophyllum, Najas.*

(*b*) *Epihydrogamy : Vallisneria spiralis* (ribbon weed) is a submerged dioecious plant. The flowers are borne under water. When mature, the male flower get detached from the parent plant and float on the surface of water. The pistillate flowers also develop under water, at the time of pollination, they are brought to the surface by their long and slender stalks. As it arrives on the surface it forms a cuplike depression. If male flowers floating on water get lodged into the depression, the pollination takes place. After pollination, the stalk of the pistillate flower undergoes spiral torsion bringing the pollinated flower under water once more.

(3) *Entomophily :* Some of the insects which help in pollination are bees, flies, wasps, moths and beetles. Bees, flies and beetles visit flowers which open after sunset. Bees probably carry out 80% of all pollination done by insects. Bee pollinated flowers are coloured, possess special smell and/or produce nectar. Pollen grains are sticky or with spinous exine. Also the stigma is sticky and bees are colour blind for red.

(4) *Ornithophily:* Tiny birds like humming birds and honey thrushes (hardly 1 inch long) feeds on the nectar of flower like *Bignonia, Erythrina* is visited by crows.

(5) *Chiropteriphily : Bauhinia megalandra of Java* and *Anthocephalus* are pollinated by bats.

(6) *Malcophily :* Many aroids which are usually pollinated by *Diptera* are also pollinated by snails.

Prints 3, 4, 5 & 6 given above are included in Zoophily.

Fertilization

Fertilization involves the fusion of male gamete with female gamete. It was first discovered by Strasburger (1884). In angiosperms the female gametophyte is seated deep in the ovarian cavity quite away from stigma. The partially developed male gametophyte (pollen grains) are normally held at stigma. To effect fertilization, the pollen grains germinate on the stigma by putting forth pollen tube which grows through the style and reach the ovules where they discharge the male gametes in the vicinity of egg. The fertilization in angiosperms can be studied under the following headings.

(A) Germination of Pollen Grains and Growth of Pollen Tubes: The pollen grains are. usually monosiphonous (*i.e.,* develop one pollen tube) but some plants are *polysiphonous e.g.* develop more than one pollen tubes. 10 pollen tubes in *Althea rosa* (Malvaceae) and 14 pollen tubes in *Malva neglecta* (Malvaceae) have been reported. Similarly, polysiphonous conditions has been reported in members of cucurbitaceae. On the basis of movement of pollen tube through style, styles are of three types:

(1) *Open Style:* The style is hollow and pollen tubes creep on the canal *e.g.* Papavaraceae and most monocots. Here the canal cells are lined with secretary cells and transmitting tissue is developed.

(2) *Half Closed Style:* Here the canal is surrounded by a rudimentary transmitting tissue *e.g.* Cactaceae.

(3) *Closed Type:* No open channel is present but instead a solid core of elongated cells with rich protoplasm, through which pollen tube moves is presented, *e.g. Datura, Cotton.*

(B) Entry of Pollen Tube into Ovule: The generative cell divides to form two male gametes.

After ariving at the top of ovary, the pollen tube may enter the ovule either through the micropyle or by some other routes. The former is usual condition and is known as *Porogamy.* In some plants, the pollen tube enters the ovule through *Chalaza.* This condition is known as chalazogamy. *e.g. Casuarina, Rhus.* In *Alchemilla* and *Cucurbita* the pollen tube enters the ovule through funiculus or the integument. This is known as mesogamy.

(C) Entry of Pollen Tube into Embryo sac : After entering the ovules the pollen tube passes through the nucellus and reaches the embryo sac. The apex of the pollen tube may either pass between the egg and one synergid or between the embryo sac wall and a synergid or directly into the synergid. As a rule one synergid is destroyed by the impact of the pollen tube and the other remains intact until sometimes afterwards.

(D) Discharge of Male Gametes from Pollen Tube: Male gametes are discharged into embryo sac by one of the following methods:

(*i*) Two subterminal openings are produced, one gamete is discharged through each opening.

(*ii*) The apex of the pollen tube bursts at the apex releasing both male gamets.

(*iii*) The tip of the pollen tube divides into two short branches one of which is directed towards the egg and other towards the secondary nucleus: Later the apical end of each pollen tube bursts releasing the male gametes.

(E) Fusion of Male and Female Gametes (Syngamy) and Fusion of Male Gamete with Secondary Nucleus (Triple Fusion) : After discharge from pollen tube one of the male gametes fuses with the egg and forms the oospore (zygote). This is called true fertilization (also called syngamy = Amphimixis). The oospore is diploid (2*n*). The second male gamete fuses with the secondary nucleus (2*n*) and forms a triploid (3*n*) nucleus called *endosperm mother nucleus*. This is called triple fusion. Thus both the male gamete participate in fertilization, i.e., fertilization takes place twice, this is called *Double fertilization* (double fertilization includes syngamy as well as triple fusion). Zygote produced as a result of syngamy develops into embryo and the triploid nucleus (= Endosperm mother nucleus) develops into the endosperm which is used for nutrition of embryo.

Antipodals and synergids degenerate after fertilization.

Significance of Double Fertilization

Double fertilization was discovered by *Nawaschin* in 1898. As a result of fertilization, the second male gamete fuses with the secondary nucleus to produce endosperm. The endosperm produced as a result of double fertilization, supplies food materials to the developing embryo, due to which embryo is differentiated properly leading to the formation of healthy seeds. According to Brick and Cooper (1940)" the endosperm is a tissue developed to compensate for the extreme reduction of female gametophyte in angisoperms.

Embryo and its Development (Embryogeny)

After syngamy the egg is called oospore (zygote). After some rest period it develops into embryo. Although in the earlier stages of development there is no difference in monocotyledonous and dicotyledonous plants, but in later stages their development is different.

Dicotyledonous Embryo: The first division of oospore is transverse. Of the two cells thus formed the one which lies towards the interior of the embryosac is called terminal cell (embryonal cell) and the other basal cell (suspensor cell). The terminal cell may divide vertically. The suspensor cell divides by several transverse divisions forming a 5-10 celled suspensor. The uppermost cell of this or haustorial cell. The suspensor pushes the developing embryo into food laden endosperm and the upper cell functions as haustorium. The lowermost cell of suspensor is called *hypophysis*. This cell gives rise to the apex of radicle. In the mean time, two cells formed from terminal cell divide by a transverse division forming four embryonal cell (Quadrant stage). These four cells divide by another vertical division forming eight cells (octant stage). Four cells at the apex (epibasal cells) give rise to plumule and cotyledons. Four cells in between the epibasal cells and suspensor (called hypobasal cells) give rise to hypocotyl and most of the radicle.

All cells of octant stage, divide by a periclinal division forming one layered outer (epidermal) cells which after anticlinal divisions form *dermatogen*. The inner (central cells) divides by several transverse and vertical divisions forming plerome in the centre and periblem in between plerome and dermatogen. Dermatogen gives rise to epidermis, periblem to cortex and plerome to vascular tissue. After several more divisions, the embryo becomes *cordate*. Later the cotyledons enlarge and may even get curved. In this way a completely mature embryo with two cotyledons attached to an axis are formed. The portion of axis in between the cotyledons is called plumule and the other part as radicle. The above given description of development of embryo takes place in *Capsella bursa pastoris*, a member of family *Cruciferae*. This type of embryo development is called *Crucifer* type or *Onagrad* type and is considered as typical mode of development of embryo.

Monocotyledonous Embryo: There is no difference between dicotyledons and monocotyledonous embryo upto octant stage. *Luzula forsteri* (Juncaceae) is characteristic of simple type of embryogeny. The zygote divides by a transverse division into a basal cell and a terminal cell. The terminal cell of the two celled proembryo divides by a vertical wall to produce two juxtaposed cells and a little later basal cell divides by a transverse division. Thus a T-shaped proembryo is differentiated. Terminal cell divides by another vertical division to produce four cells. Cell basal forms suspensor and all the remaining cells contribute to the formation of embryo. 6-cells divide further to give rise to a tissue 'I'. The lower half part of this tissue go to form the lower half portion of single cotyledon, hypocotyl, plumule and radicle. From a part of basal cell, terminal part of radicle is formed which forms apical part of root cap and from other portion of basal cell remaining part of root cap is formed.

Polyembryony

Polyembryony is the phenomenon of development of more than one embryos in a seed. It was discovered by Leeuwenhoek in 1719 in orange. It may be of two types:

I. True or II. False

I. True: When embryos arise in the same embryosac in which zygotic embryo has developed.

II. False: When extra embryos are developing in one embryosac other than the one in' which zygotic embryo has developed.

More than one embryo may be developed in the seed by one of the following methods:

(1) *Cleavage Polyembryony:* When more than one embryos are formed by cleavage or splitting of normal zygote. *e.g. Erythronium americanum, Nymphea advena, Nicotiana rustica.*

(2) *Embryo from Synergid :* Synergid is fertilized by sperm *e.g. Saggitaria.*

(3) *Embryo from Antipodal: e.g. Ulmus americana.*

(4) *Embryo from Endosperm: e.g. Balanophora.*

(5) *Adventive Polyembryony :* Embryo formed form cells of nucellus which penetrate into embryo sac. *Eugenia, Mangifera.*

(6) Embryo originating from other embryosac in the ovule: *e.g. Citrus.*

Apomixis: In normal sexual cycle, fertilization (Amphimixis *i.e.,* fusion of male and female gametes), leads to the formation of embryo and later on seed. Seed germinates to produce new plant where male and female gametophyte are formed after meiosis. This normal sexual cycle involves *fertilisation* and *meiosis*.

However, substitution of usual sexual reproduction by a form of reproduction which does not involve meiosis and-syngamy is called apomixis a term introduced by Winkler in 1908. There are two main types of apomixis:

I. *Vegetative Reproduction:* New plant is produced from stem, leaf, buds, etc. (Seed is not required).

II. *Agamospermy:* Seeds are produced and embryo is formed but meiosis and fertilization are eliminated. It may be of three types:

(*a*) *Adventive Embryony:* Embryo formed from cells of nucellus or integuments.

(*b*) *Diplospory:* Megaspore mother cell develops into an unreduced embryosac. The embryo is formed from unfertilized egg (parthenogenesis), or some cell of embryo sac (apogamy).

(*c*) *Apospory:* A somatic cell in the nucellus directly forms an unreduced embryosac and the diploid egg parthenogenetically develops into embryo.

Endosperm

The endosperm is important because it is the main source of food for the embryo. In gymnosperms it is haploid and is formed by the repeated divisions of megaspore nucleus (*i.e.,* female gametophyte and endosperm terms in gymnosperms are the same). In angiosperms on the other hand, it is a new structure formed in most cases as a result of the fusion of the two polar nuclei and one of the male gametes. Since all the three fusing nuclei are usually haploid, the endosperm contains the triploid number of chromosomes.

Endosperm formation is supressed in *Orchidaceae* and *Podostemonanceae*. In these forms, triple fusion is complete but the fusion product either degenerates immediately or undergo only 1 or two divisions.

Types of Endosperm Formation

(1) *Nuclear Type:* The endosperm mother nucleus divides repeatedly without wall formation. In later stages the nuclei may remain free or wall formation follows. This type of endosperms is common in polypetalae. *e.g. Capsella.*

(2) *Cellular Type:* The first and most of the subsequent divisions are accompanied by wall formation so that the embryosac becomes divided into several chambers. This type of endosperm formation is common in gamopetalae *e.g. Villarsia.*

(3) *Helobial Type:* It is intermediate between nuclear and cellular type and is common in order Helobeales. The first division of endosperm mother nucleus is followed by wall formation forming two unequal cells, a very big micropylar and small chalazal. Micropylar cell divides by free nuclear divisions later followed by wall formation. In the

chalazal 1 or 2 divisions may take place and it functions as a small haustorial cell. e.g. *Eremurus.*

Histology of Endosperm : The cells of endosperm are usually isodimetric and store large quantities of food materials whose exact nature and properties vary much more from one plant to another. As a rule, walls are thin, devoid of pits but when hemicellulose is the chief reserve food, they are greatly thickened and pitted. Endosperm is well-known for high degree of polyploidization of its cells during development.

There are no intercellular spaces in cells of endosperm. Endosperm may be starchy (Rice) or oily (castor). In cereals, outermost layer of endosperm constitutes aleurane tissue (protein).

(1) *Endospermic seeds:* In some seeds, the endosperm forms a permanent tissue (*Ricinus, Phoenix, Triticum*) which persists until the germination of seed. Such seeds are called endospermic seeds (= albuminous seed).

(2) *Nonendospermic seeds:* In other seeds (*Cucurbits, Pisum, Arachis*) it is used up by the growing embryo and is no longer seen in mature seed. Such seeds are called 'nonendospermic seeds' (exalbuminous seeds). Of special interest is *Symplocarpus* in which the embryo devours not only the endosperm but also integuments so that the embryo lies naked inside the ovary wall. An even more extreme case is that of *Melocamna bambusiodes* in which embryo dissolves even the ovary wall and is completely naked at maturity.

Patterns of Endosperm development in *Xenia*: Focke (1881) described the phenomenon for the first time. In plants like maize, the influence of male gamete is shown in the development of endosperm. If the male parent has a yellow endosperm and female parent a colourless endosperm: after fertilization the endosperm of new seed becomes yellow. This transference of characters by a male gamete and its influence on endosperm is known as *Xenia.*

Metaxenia : The effect of pollen on the character of the seed coat or pericarp is called metaxenia.

Mosaic endosperm: Occasionally there is lack of uniformity in the tissue of endosperm. The patches of two different colours are observed in *Zea mays* forming a sort of irregular pattern. Some portion of endosperm may be starchy and other part is sugary.

Ruminate Endosperm: Mature endosperm with any degree of irregularity and unevenness in its surface contour is called ruminate endosperm. e.g. *Passiflora, Calarata* and *Cocoloba.*

Morphological Nature of Endosperm: In gymnosperms, endosperm is a gametophyte tissue because it is derived from megaspore nucleus before fertilization. However, the morphological nature of endosperm is debatable and is considered as follows by different workers:

I. *Endosperm is a sporophyte:* Monnier.(1890) Miss Sargent.

II. *Endosperm is a gametophyte :* Strasburger (1900), Coulter & Chamberlain (1911).

III. Endosperm is an entirely new structure *i.e., Tissue sui generis.* According to *Brink & Cooper* (1940) double fertilization is a device to compensate for the extreme reduction of female gametophyte in angiosperms. Due to an extra amount of chromosomes, it is more active in getting food for the embryo the nucellus and the integument.

Formation of Seed and Fruit

Seed: As a result of double fertilization, many changes are brought about in the ovule due to which ovule is converted to seed. The outer integument becomes hard and form testa and the inner integument becomes thin and papery and converted to tegmen. The point of attachment of funicle of ovule is seen as a scar after detachment of seed from fruit wall.

Fruit: Fruit is a ripened ovary enclosing the seeds. The ovary wall develops into fruit wall.

Application of Palynology: Palynology is the study of fossil spores, pollen and similar structures, while polygeny is evolutionary history of organisms of a group.

QUESTIONS FROM PREVIOUS YEARS' PAPERS

1. Distinguish between protostele and siphonostele.
2. Explain the following:
   (*a*) Polarity
   (*b*) Archesporium
3. Descrihe the structure of antheridiophore in *Funaria.*
4. Distinguish between the following:
   (*a*) Perigenous and Mesogenous Stomata.
   (*b*) Phyllospermous and Stachyspermous.
3. Describe the following:
   (*a*) Distribution of cycads in India.
   (*b*) Stamens in Magnoliaceae.
   (*c*) Ovule of *Taxus.*
   (*d*) Male organs of *Williamsonia.*
   (*e*) Stamens in Leguminosae.
   (*f*) Inflorescence in Euphorbiaceae.
   (*g*) Carpels in Ranunculaceae.
   (*h*) Floral formula of Apiaceae
4. Compare the characters of cycadales and Bennettitales.
5. Describe the male "flower" of *Ephedra.*
6. Mention the botanical name, family and die plant parts used of the following:
   (*a*) Rice (*b*) Lentil
   (*c*) Walnut (*d*) Heeng
   (*e*) Clove (*f*) Fennal
   (*g*) Ashwagandh (*h*) Cocaine
   (*i*) Mamla hemp (*j*) Coir
7. Write short notes on:
   (*a*) Diatoms (*b*) Viroids
   (*c*) Mycoplasma (*d*) Proteases
8. Describe the following:
   (*a*) Archegoniphore of *Marchantia.*
   (*b*) Sporophyte of *Marsilea.*
9. Distinguish between the following:
   (*a*) Interxylary and intraxylary phloem.
   (*b*) Latex-tubes and resin canals.
10. Describe the following:
   (*a*) Stamens in Cucurbitaceae.
   (*b*) Translators in Asclepiadaceae.
   (*c*) Cycadofilicales.
   (*d*) Floral diagram in Solanaceae.
   (*e*) Carpels in dicots.
   (*f*) Hydrosere
11. Write an account of the family Rubiaceae and compare it with that of Verbenaceae.
12. Describe the family Cucurbitaceae, giving floral diagrams and floral formulae.
13. Write about the economic importance of the family Asteraceae.
14. Mention the botanical name, family and plant part used of the following:
   (*a*) Teak (*b*) Heeng
   (*c*) Jute (*d*) Turmeric
   (*e*) Sarapgandha (*f*) Cocoa
   (*g*) Cotton (*h*) Bamboo
   (*i*) Opium (*j*) Peppermint
15. Describe the following:
   (*a*) Structure of *Funaria* capsule
   (*b*) Tetrasporophyte
   (*c*) Gemma cups
   (*d*) Types of Protosteles
16. Distinguish the following:
   (*a*) Compare diagnostic features of Orchidaceae and Liliaceae.
   (*b*) Compare Floral structures in Ranunculaceae and Magnoliaceae.
   (*c*) Compare pollination in Fabaceae and Poaceae along with their flower structures.
   (*d*) Compare Floral formulae of *Musa paradisiaca L.* and *Oryza sativa L.*
17. Give the Floral structure in Poaceae.
18. Mention the botanical name, family and plant parts used of the following:
   (*a*) Maize (*b*) Tea
   (*c*) Turmeric (*d*) Marigold
   (*e*) Asafoetida (*f*) Cocoa
   (*g*) Ergot (*h*) Caraway
   (*i*) Sugar palm (*j*) Barley
19. Answer the following:
   (*a*) Gametangium of *Ectocarpus.*
   (*b*) An illustrated account of nucule of *Nitella.*
   (*c*) Flagellate apparatus in *Chlamydomonas.*
   (*d*) Outline diagrams showing various parts of pennate diatoms.
   (*d*) Auxospore formation in diatoms.

(*f*) Strobillus of *Selaginella.*

20. Differentiate between:
(*a*) Oogonium and sporangium
(*b*) Isomorphic and heteromorphic life cycles.
(*c*) Akinete and zygote.

21. With the help of suitable diagrams describe the life history of *Oedogonium.* (No description)

22. Write an illustrated account of sporophytic phase of *Anthoceros.*

23. Make a comparative study of the following families giving flora formula and floral diagram. Give important differentiating morphological features only.
(*a*) Musaceae and Liliaceae
(*b*) Asclepiadaceae and Verbenaceae
(*c*) Euphorbiaceae and Malvaceae
(*d*) Solanaceae and Rubiaceae

24. Draw neat labelled diagrams of the following: (No description)
(*a*) T.S. coralloid roots of *Cycas*
(*b*) L.S. *Ginkgo* seed
(*c*) L.L. *Pinus* ovule
(*d*) T.S. leaf of *Gnetum*

25. Write notes on:
(*a*) Salient features of floral structure of *Magnolia grandiflora.*
(*b*) L.S. of flower of *Rosa* species and floral diagram.
(*c*) L.S. of female flower of *Cucurbita maxima* and its floral formula.
(*d*) Economic importance of the family Orchidaceae.
(*e*) Anatomy of phyllode.
(*f*) Anatomical differences between C_3 and C_4 plants.
(*g*) Medicinal importance of *Catharanthus roseus (=Vinca rosea).*

26. Mention the botanical name, family and the part's of the plant used as shown below:

(*a*) Indian rubber	(*b*) Indigo
(*c*) Sandalwood oil	(*d*) Vanilla
(*e*) Guava	(*f*) Finger millet
(*g*) Cinnamon	(*h*) Agar agar
(*i*) Betel	(*j*) Opium

27. Distinguish between the following:
(*a*) Mature sporophyte of *Riccia* and *Marchantia*
(*b*) Cleistothecia and Apothecia in Ascomycetes.
(*c*) Sexual reproduction in *Chlamydomonas* and *Volvox.*
(*d*) *Oscillatoria* and *Anabaena.*

28. Write a short note on Morphological nature of sporocarp of *Marsilea.*

29. Distinguish between Aril and caruncle.

30. Write what you know on Floral characters of Asclepiadaceae.

31. Describe the following:
(*a*) Distribution of gymnosperms in India
(*b*) Cyathium
(*c*) Bennettitales
(*d*) Orchidaceae in India

32. What are the diagnostic floral features of Brassicaceae?

33. Describe male gemetes of *Ginkgo biloba.*

34. Write a short note on diagnostic features of family Euphorbiaceae.

35. Mention the botanical name, family and the part(s) used for each of the following:

(*a*) Cashew	(*b*) Nutmeg
(*c*) Kenaf	(*d*) Oil palm
(*e*) Vetiver oil	(*f*) Cork
(*g*) Annatto	(*h*) Clove
(*i*) Belladonna	(*j*) Ginger

36. Write short notes on:
(*a*) Plurilocular sporangia in *Ectocarpus.*
(*b*) Hetermorphic life cycle in Phaeophyceae (Give a diagrammatic sketch).
(*c*) Alternation of generations in slime molds (Pictorial presentation of life cycle).
(*d*) Gametophytic phase in *Laminaria.*
(*e*) L.S. of sporocarp of *Marsilea* (Labelled diagram only).
(*f*) T.S. of *Equisetum* stem (Diagram only).
(*g*) Nucule of *Chara.*
(*h*) Cleistothecium in *Erysiphe.*

37. With the help of diagrams, describe the structure of *Marchantia* antheridiophore.

38. Draw neat labelled diagrams of the following:
(*a*) Anatomy of *Equisetum* cone.
(*b*) Cross-section of the gametophytic thallus of *Riccia.*

(c) Life cycle of *Ectocarpus*- (Pictorial presentation only).

(d) Structure of prothallus of *Adiantum*.

39. Give F.F. and F.D. of the following families:

(a) Euphorbiaceae

(b) Asteraceae (Compositae)

(c) Liliaceae

(d) Rubiaceae

40. Write short notes on:

(a) Functions of endosperm.

(b) Experimental induction of polyembryony.

(c) Causes and significance of apomixis.

(d) Draw a neat labelled diagram of a typical organised embryo sac.

(e) T.S. of *Ephedra* leaf.

(f) Economic importance of plants belonging to family Umbelliferae.

41. Describe the type of anomalous secondary growth found in the stems of the following (Draw neat labelled diagrams):

(a) *Aristolochia*

(b) *Bignonia*

(c) *Boerhaavia*

(d) *Dracaena*

42. Mention the botanical name, family and plant parts used in the following:

(a) Henna (b) Penicillin

(c) Ginger (d) Chestnut

(e) Indian bow string hemp

(f) Camphor (g) Clove oil

(h) Sassafras (i) Mulberry

(j) Date Palm

43. Write short notes on:

(a) Dolipore

(b) Pseudoelaters of *Anthoceros*—the structure and function.

(c) Peristomial teeth of *Funaria*.

44. How are the young sporogonia of *Marchantia* protected?

45. Present diagrammatic depictions of different life cycle patterns in *Saccharomyces* spp. What is the trend exhibited.

46. Write short notes on:

(a) Plurilocular sporangia of *Ectocarpus*.

(b) Conceptacles of *Fucus*.

(c) Spores of *Lycopodium* in comparison with those of *Selaginella*.

(d) Sporophyte of *Riccia* at maturity.

47. Draw the labelled diagram of the following:

(a) T.S. of rhizome of *Pteridium*.

(b) Life cycle of *Puccinia graminis*.

(c) Life cycle of *Polysiphonia*.

48. Describe briefly the following:

(a) Egg apparatus in the majority of angiosperms.

(b) Kranz Anatomy and its importance with respect of photosynthesis.

(c) Practical value of polyembryony.

(d) Role of anther tapetum.

49. Give floral formulae and floral diagrams of the following families:

(a) Solanaceae

(b) Apiaceae

(c) Brassicaceae

(d) Liliaceae

50. Draw neat, labelled diagrams of the following:

(a) L.S. mature seed of cycas.

(b) L.S. female cone of *Pinus*.

(c) Pollen grain of *Ginkgo* at the time of shedding.

(d) L.S. female strobilus of *Ephedra*.

51. Mention the botanical name, family and plants part(s) used in the following:

(a) Kapok (b) Rye

(c) Oil palm (d) Cashew

(e) Cassava (f) Turmeric

(g) Saffron (h) Poppy

(i) Vasaka (j) Wormwood

52. Protoplast-to-plant regeneration has been achieved in almost all the important plants. Describe the method of isolation, culture and regeneration of plants from protoplasts isolated from any model plant species.

53. Characteristic features of reproductive organs of Bennettitales.

54. Distinguish between:

(a) Monosporic and bisporic embryo sac.

(b) Androecium of Malvaceae and Asteraceae.

55. Write short notes on the following:

(a) Magnoliaceae

(b) Herbarium

(c) Intraxylary Phloem

(*d*) Androecium of Euphorbiaceae
(*e*) Gynoecium of Solanaceae
(*f*) Botanical names of any five cereal plants.
(*g*) Inflorescence in Asteraceae.
(*h*) Pollen allergy
(*i*) Types of pollination
(*j*) Gynostegium

56. Give botanical name, family and utility of each of the following:
(*a*) Coffee
(*b*) Cardamum
(*c*) Button mushroom
(*d*) Castor
(*e*) Coconut
(*f*) Sago
(*g*) Ashwagandha
(*h*) Periwinkle
(*i*) Jute
(*j*) Pumpkin

57. Describe the following:
(*a*) Asteraceae and Liliaceae
(*b*) Rubiaceae and Verbenaceae

58. Write a short note on anatomical structure of *Rhynia* stem.

CHAPTER–4

PLANT UTILITY AND EXPLOITATION

Origin of Cultivated Plants

Through carbon dating, of human remains and utility items, it has been found that prehistoric humans led a nomadic life of hunter-gatherer. Agriculture originated about 10,000 years ago. However, hunter-gatherer tribes (*e.g.* Kung Bushmen of Kalahari desert) still persist. Early humans preferred plants with multiple uses, *e.g.* Coconut, Date-Palm, Mulberry, *Acacia.* Agriculture originated in river valley areas and well watered highlands like those of *Indus,* Nile, Tigris, Euphrates, Tehuacan valley, Yellow River Valley, etc. Grain and pulses are unpalatable without cooking. They therefore, became part of diet only when fire had been used for cooking and roasting. .

Vavilov's Centres of Origin : *Nikolai Ivanovitch Vavilov* (1926) proposed different centres of origin for various crop plants on two criteria (i) Occurrence & wild relatives. (ii) Occurrence of maximum variations in the crop.

They are 11 in number, which are as follows:

(1) *South-East Asia:* Rice, Pigeon Pea, Banana, Mango, Orange, Brinjal, Black-Pepper, Sugarcane.

(2) *China:* Onion, Tea, Soyabean.

(3) *South-West Asia:* Wheat.

(4) *Asia Minor and Afganistan :* Rye, Lentil, Apple, Pear, Apricot, Pomegranate, Pistachio, Almond.

(5) *Mediterranean:* Oat, Lettuce, Cabbage, Beet.

(6) *Ethiopia:* Barley, Sorghum, Coffee.

(7) *Brazil:* Groundnut, Pineapple, Rubber.

(8) *Peruvian Andes:* Potato, Tomato, Chilli.

(9) *Mexico and Central America:* Maize & cotton.

(10) *USA:* Sunflower.

(11) *European Siberian Region:* Cherry, Cichory, Hops.

Important plants of New World are Maize, Potato, Tomato, Sunflower, Groundnut, Red Pepper (Chilli), Pineapple, Guava, Sapota, Cashew, Cocao & Coca.

Natural Home: It is place of origin of a cultivated crop.

Secondary Home: It is the major centre of production of a crop where wild relatives do not occur and which is far away from the centre of origin or natural home. India is secondary home for groundnut whose natural home are Peru & Brazil.

Plants as Sources: From early times, Angiosperms are meeting the basic necessities of man *i.e.,* food, clothing, and shelter. All the requirements of food are coming from cereals, vegetables, pulses, fruits and roots etc. Fibres derived from plants are used as cloth and other different purposes *i.e.,* ropes, bags, nets etc. Wood obtained from plants are used as structural unit for shelter and also used as furniture, fuel, alçohol and gas etc.

Besides these basic needs angiosperms are also used as spices, drugs, oil etc.

(A) Plants as sources for Food and Fodder:

(*a*) ***Cereals:*** They belong to family Gramineae. There yield grain or single seeded fruit called caryopsis.

(1) Major Cereals include:

(i) Rice (Oryza sativa): It is a Tropical crop now grown in almost all parts of India. In North India it is grown as Kharif crop but in other parts 2-3 crops are raised. It is a staple food of 60% of world population and more than 50% Indians. 90% production in Asia. Grain husk is called *paddy.* Rice is deficient in protein. Rice bran yields oil. Basmati is flavoured rice cultivated in parts of D.P. and Haryana. It contains 90% starch & 8-10% protein.

(ii) Wheat (Triticum aestivum): Temperate crop grown in North India. Staple food in majority of the countries. Its Tonnage output is more than Rice and Maize. Two types of it include:

(1) ***Durum Wheat (Triticum durum)*** which is tetraploid and grows in drier parts, used in macroni and noodles.

(2) Bread Wheat (*Triticum aestivum* = T. vulllgare) is hexaploid and employed in making bread, cakes, chápaties etc.

Wheat contain 60-70% starch' and 10-17% protein.

***(iii)* Maize (corn = *Zea mays*) :** It is the tallest cereal from New World. It cannot tolerate ground frost. Maize grains yield popcorn (*Zea mays var, everta*), flour corn oil, corn starch and protein Zein (for artificial fibre and foamming agent in fire extinguisher).

(2) ***Minor Cereals and Millets:*** Rye (*Secale cereale*), Oat (*Avena sativa*), Barley (*Hordeum vulgare*) and millet are called minor cereals.

Millets

(*i*) *Jowar, Great Millet (Sorghum vulgare or S. bicolor).* It is raw material for malting industry. It is food for poor and also cattle *i.e.,* it is also fodder.

(*ii*) *Bajra* (Pearl/Bulrush Millet or *Pennisetum typhoides = P. americanum*): It is food for poor and is small sized grain.

(*iii*) *Ragi* (Finger Millet) or *Eleusine coracana.*

(*iv*) *Italian/Foxtail Millet* or *Setaria italica.*

(*v*) *Common Millet:* (Prosomillet) or *Panium miliaceum.*

(*vi*) *Little Millet or Panicum miliase.*

(*vii*) *Shama Millet* (Jungle Rice) or *Echinochloa colona.*

(***b***) **Pulses:** (Family Leguminosae, Sub-family Papilionodeae). These are legume seeds. Green pods are also used as vegetables. Pulses are rich in proteins. However, some of them lack amino-acids lysine, tryptophan and methionine. Soyabean is the richest plant food (36.5% protein) which is given to diabetic patients. Higher protein content is due to symbiotic root nodule bacterium of genus *Rhizobium.*

These are

(*i*) *Gram* (Chick pea). *Cicer arietinum.* This is used as besan, bread and also cattle feed.

(*ii*) *Red Gram* (Pigeon Pea, Arhar, Tur) *Cajanus cajan.* It is used as Dal and Cattle feed.

(*iii*) *Black Gram* (Urd) *Vigna or Phaseolus mungo (= P. radiatus).*

(*iv*) *Green Gram* (Mung) *Vigna radiatus = Phaseolus aureus.*

(*v*) *Pea* (Mattar) *Pisum sativum.* It contains 7.2% protein, 15.8% carbohydrate and also some vitamins. It is eaten green or canned or as vegetable.

(*vi*) *Soyabean* (Bhat) *Glycine max.* It is is eaten roasted or as milk which is a refreshing drink. It also yields oil.

(*vii*) *Mat Bean* (Moth) *Vigna aconitifolia = Phaseolus aconitifolius.*

(*viii*) *Lentil* (Masur) *Lens esculentua = L culinaris.*

(*ix*) *Red kidney bean* (Rajmah) *Phaseolus vulgaris.*

(*x*) *Lablab Lablab purpureus = Dolichos lablab.*

(*xi*) *Guar/Claster Bean. Cyamopsis tetragonolobas.*

(*xii*) *Moongphali* (groundnut) *Archis hypogea.* It is rich in protein. Eaten roasted or as vegetable ghee.

(*xiii*) *Cow Pea Lohia Vigna unguiculata (V. sinensis) = Phaseolus lunetus: Lathyrism,* a crippling dissability marked by muscular weakness, tremors and paraplegia is caused by eating seeds of *Lathyrus sativus* (Grass Pea, Chickling vetch, vern, Khesari Dal). The seeds contain *osteotoxin* B-amino Propionitrile (BAPN) and water soluble *neurotoxin* B-N-oxalyl amino alanine (BOAA). Red Kidney Bean and French Bean possess *lectins* which are destroyed only on boiling for sometime. Low temperature cooking or eating raw soaked beans can be dagnerous.

(*c*) Nuts/Dry Fruits:

(1) *Almond (Vern. Badam) : Prunus amygdalus (P. ducis)* Edible part is seed inside drupe (parts outside endocarp peeled off in marketed product).

(2) *Walnut (Vern. Akhroat) : Juglans regia (J. nigra).* Edible part kernel inside nut/drupe (older view).

(3) *Cashewnut(vern. Kaaju) : Anacardium occidentale.* Kaaju is seed of nut. The juiey thalamus of Cashew- Apple is source of cashew-wine.

(4) *Pistachio (Vern. Pista): Pisiacia vera.* Edible part is kernel.

(5) *Pine nut (vern. Chilgoja = Neja) : Pinus gerardiana.* Edible part is kernel.

(d) Edible Oils:

(1) *Mustard (Sarson) Brassica campestris var sarson. = Brassica rapus* var-glauca.

(2) Rape (Toria) *Brassica Campestris var. toria = Brassica napus var-napus.*

(3) *Groundnut (Pea nut) Arachis hypogea.* Fruits are indehisent pods formed underground (geocarpy).

(4) *Sesame or Gingelly (Til) Sesamum indicum.*

(5) *Cotton Gossypium herbaceums = G. arboreum.* Seeds yield cotton fibres from surface.

(6) *Sunflower. Helianthus annus.* Oil is rich in unsaturated fats.

(7) *Coconut: Cocos nucifera.* Copra or dried endosperm yield oil. Coir from mesocarp. Coir industry is concentrated mostly, in Kerala.

(8) *Oil palm. Elaeis guineensis.*

(e) Fruits: Fleshy fruits which are eaten raw because they are palatable & sweet.

(1) *Mango: Mangifera indica.* Fleshy drup with pulpy mesocarp.

(2) *Banana: Musa paradisiaca.* Parthenogenic berries. Most nutritious with 20% sugar, 4.7% proteins, minerals and five vitamins A, B, C, D and E.

(3) *Apple: Malus pumila. Pome.*

(4) *Grape: Vitis vinifera. Berry.*

(5) *Orange: Citrus reticulata.* Special berry called hesperidium. Juicy placental hair. Sweet orange is *Citrus sinensis.*

Remaining citrus fruits include grape fruit *(Citrus paradis)* pomello/shaddock (Chakotra, *Citrus deumana or maxima*) citron (Tarunj, *citrus medica*), hill lemon (Galgal, *Citrus limon*), rough lemon (Khatta, *Citrus jambiri*), lime (Nimbu, *Citrus aurantifolia*), Kama (*Citrus kama*), Kinnow (*Citrus reticulata sinensis*) etc.

(6) **Other fruits include:**

Peach-*Prunus persica*-drupe
Apricot-*Prunus armeniaca*-drupe
Pear-*Pyrus communis*-pome
Loquat-*Eriobotrya japonica*-pome
Jambolan-*Syzgium cumini*-berry
Papaya-*Curica papaya*-berry
Date-*Phoenix dactylifera*-berry also considered drupe.
Musk melon-*Cucumis melo*-pepo
Water melon-*Citrullus vulgaris*-pepo
Snapmelon-*Cucumis melo*-pepo
Pomegranate- *Punica granatum*-balastula
Sapota-*Manilkara achras*
Mangosteen-*Qascinia mangostana*
Phalsa-*Grewia asiatica*-drupe
Emblic-Amla-*Emblica officinalis*-berry rich in Vitamin C.
Litchi-*Litchi chinensis*-Sorosis.
Custard apple-*Annona squamosa*-etaerio of berries.
Pineapple-*Ananas camosus*-Sorosis.
Fig-*Ficus carica*-Syconus.

***(f)* Starchy Tubers:**

(1) *Potato-Solanum tuberosum:* Stem tubers. New World crop cultivated throughout, most abundantly in East Europe.

(2) *Tapioca: Manihot utilissica* roots tubes requiring treatment, New World crop now being cultivated in Kerala.

(*g*) Vegetables: They are eaten for roughage, minerals and vitamins. Vegetables are usually cooked but some are eaten raw.

(1) *Carrot (Daucos carota) :* Root vegetable rich in β-carotene.

(2) *Radish (Raphanus sativus) :* Root and fruit vegetable.

(3) *Turnip (Brassica rapa) :* Root vegetable.

(4) *Okra (Lady's finger): Abeloschus* or *Hibiscus esculentus.* Fruit vegetable.

(5) *Brinjal : Solanum melongena,* Fruit vegetable.

(6) *Pumpkin : Cucurbita pepo.* Fruit vegetable.

(7) *Round Gourd: Citrullus lonatus* var. *Fistulosus.* Fruit vegetable.

(8) *Tomato: Lycopersicon lycopersium* or *L. esculentum.* Fruit vegetable also used in Ketchup.

(9) *Onion: Allium cepa.* Bulb or underground vegetable cum spice.

(10) *Garlic: Allium sativum.* Bulb or underground vegetable cum spice.

(11) *Taro: Colocasia esculenta = C. antiquorum.* Coron or underground vegetable.

(12) *Potato: Solanum tuberosum.* Stem tuber, underground vegetable, annual production of over 300 million tonnes. Researches have been going to reduce its water content (74.7%), increase its carbohydrate content from 23% to 46% and enhance its protein content 1.6% to 15%.

(13) *Cabbage: Brassica oleracea var. capitata.* Vegetative or terminal bud.

(14) *Cauliflower: Brassica oleracea var. botrytis.* unripe fleshy inflorescence.

(15) *Bottle Gourd: Lagenaria siceraria.*

(16) *Sponge Ridged Gourd: Luffa acutangula.*

(17) *Smooth Gourd: Luffa cylindrica.*

(18) *Pointed cucumber: Cucumis sativus.*

(19) *Snake/Long cucumber: Cucumis melo* var *utilissima.*

(20) *Celery: Apium graveolens var dulce* as a salad.

(21) Lettuce: *Lactuca sativa* as salad.

(*h*) Sugar:

(1) *Sugarcane: Saccharum officinarum* Commonly aneuploid. Juice from canes yield sugar. By products are molasses and - Bagasse. Maximum production in U.P. Leading sugarcane producing country is Brazil, almost parallel to India.

(2) *Sugar Beet: Beta vulgaris.* Root (Napiform).

(B) Plants as Sources for Fibres:

(1) *Cotton:* Epidermal hair from seed surface of *Gossypium arboreum, G. herbaceum,* G. hirsutum and other species. Epidermal hair present on the seed surface are of two types, extractable *lint* and nonextractablc *fluffy/frizzed fuzz.* Long stapled (narma) and short stapled (desi cotton). Fibres are made up of cellulose only. They are ideal for textiles, celluloid, cellophane, rayon and paper pulp. Cotton is a widely cultivated kharif crop. India produces 10% of the world output, maximum in Punjab state.

(2) *Jute:* Bast fibres or phloem fibres from stems of *Corchorus capsalaris* and *C. olitorius.* Mostly cultivated in W. Bengal.

(3) *Hemp:* Stemlbast fibres from *Cannabis sativa.*

(4) *Flax:* Stem/bast fibres from *Lilium usitatissimum.* Oil from seeds.

(5) *Sunn Hemp:* Stemlbast fibres from *Crotorlaria juncea.*

(6) *Coir:* Mesocrap (of pericarp) from fruit of *Cocos nucifera* (coconut).

(7) *Rosella:* Stem/bast fibres from *Hibiscus sabdarifa.* Other fibres include Agave/Sisal fibres (leaves of *Agave sislana*) and Abaca/Manila hemp. (leaf stalks of *Musa textilis*).

(8) *Munj :* Lower portion of stem, is used for making chairs, tables, baskets and upper portion of stems and leaves. of *Saccharam munja* are used for cordage, baskets etc.

(C) Plants as Source for Spices & Condiments :

(1) *Chillies:* Red Pepper. *Caisicum annuum, Capsicum frutescens.*

(2) *Black Pepper: Piper nigrum* (dried fruits).

(3) *Cinnamon: Cinnamomum zeylanicum* (inner bark, verno Dalchini).

(4) *Cloves: Syzygiilm aromaticum* (= *Eugenia caryophyllus,* verno Laung, Unopened floral buds) Clove is obtained from them.

(5) *Ginger: Zingiber officinale* (rhizome).

(6) *Cardamom: Elettria cardamomum* verno Choti Elaichi, Dried fruits.

(7) *Bengal Cardamom: Amomum aromaticum,* vern. Bari Elaichi.

(8) *Turmeric: Curcuma longa* (vern. Haldi). Dried, boiled, cleaned and polished rhizome.

(9) *Asafoetida: Ferula asafoetida* (vern. Hing) Gum-resin from roots.

(10) *Saffron: Crocus sativus* (Vern. Kesar, Jaffran) Dried styles and stigmas.

(11) *Nutmey: Myristicafragrans* (vern. Jaiphal) Seed and aril.

(12) *Caraway:* (vern. Jeera) *Carumcarvi.*

(13) *Cassia:* (Tejpat) *Cinnamomum tamula.*

(14) *Coriander:* (Dhania) *Coriandrum sativum.*

(15) *Anise:* (Saonf) *Pimpinella anisum.*

(16) *Fennel:* (Saunf) *Foeniculum vulgare.*

(D) Plants as a source for Beverages:

(*a*) Non-alcoholic:

(1) *Tea.: Thea sinensis = Camellia sinensis.* Young leaves and shoot tips are processed to obtain tea.

(2) *Coffee: Cofea arabica.* Roasted seeds are powdered. Native of Ethiopia.

(3) *Cocoa: Theobroma cacao.* Beans are roasted in iron drums, seeds are ground seeds, possess an alkaloid-theobromine. After curing yield cocoa & chocolate. (It should not be confused with cocaine containing Coca or *Erythroxylon coca.*

(4) *Cola:* It isobtained from seeds of *Cola nitida.* Cola contains caffeine.

(*b*) Alocholic Beverages :

(1) *Beer:* Lightly hopped (Hop is *Humulus lupulus*), fermented malt having 3-6% alcohol. Malt is got from barley (*Hordeum vulgare*) and to lesser extent Pearl/Bulrush Millet/Rice, Maize and Rye. Lager beer is aged beer.

(2) *Wine:* Alcoholic beverage produced from plant juices like Grape, Sugarcane, Palm exudate (also fresh). Alcohol content is 10-20%. Occassionally fortified by addition of alcohol. Champagne is the most popular wine followed by Port wine and Scherry wine. Cider is fermented juice of Apple.

(3) *Gin:* Alcoholic beverage prepared from distilled spirit flavoured with berries of Juniper (*Juniperus communis*).

(4) *Rum:* Alcoholic distillate or mixture of distillates from molasses (sugarcane juice) having 40% alcohol and distilled at less than 87° proof.

(5) *Brandy:* Distillate or mixture of distillates of fermented juices/wines at less than 89°. Alcohol range is 60-70%.

(6) *Whisky:* Distilled fermented grain mashes (Barley, Wheat, Rye, Oat, Corn, Potato). Most famous is *Scotch.*

(7) *Vodka:* Multicolumn distillation from fermented mash of potato at or above 87° proof with 60-80% alcohol.

(8) *Sake:* Alcoholic beverage of Japan from Rice.

(E) Plants Used as a Source forDrugs & Narcotics :

(1) *Sarpgandha : Rauwolfia serpentina.* Root gives reserpine alkaloid which is used for blood pressure, snake bite and mental disorders.

(2) *Opium:* (afeem) *Papaver somniferum.* Fruit (capsule) gives morphine, codine. Which is narcotic, sedative and given in relieving pain.

(3) *Quinine: Cinchona officinalis*, Calisaya. Bark used for malaria. *Coptis teeta* of Arunachal Pradesh and *Artemesia annua* of Uttarakhand also yield antimalarial drugs.

(4) *Belladona : Atropa belladona.* Dried leaves and roots are useful. Leaves have atropine and Hyoscymus alkaloid. It is used as Narcotic, diuretic, antispasmodic, Leaves are stimulant of CNS relieving pain.

(5) *Datura: Datura staramonium.* Fruit juice is important for removing dandruff, for bronchital ailments.

(6) *Amla : Emblica officinalis.* Fruits are diuretic laxative for hoemeorage, used in diarrhea, dysentry.

(7) *Kuchla: Strycnos nux-vomica.* Seed are used as a source for alkaloid strichnum. Used in Paralysis and mental disorder.

(8) *Senna:* Leaves and pods of *Cassica angustifolia* and *C. acutifolia* are purgative and anthelmintic.

(9) *Isabgol :* Seeds husks of Plantago ovata for constipation and gastric ulcers.

(10) *Digitalis:* Leaves *otdigitalis purpurea* and *D. lanara* as cardiac stimulant, relieving dropsy and stimulatlng renal secretions.

(11) *Aconite:* Roots of *Aconitum napellus* (highly poisonous) are used for cholera and leprosy.

(12) *Liquorice:* Root of Glycyrrhiza glabra is used for cough and bronchitis.

(13) *Santonin:* Flowers of Artemesia cina and *A. maritima* yield anthelminthetic drug. *Artemesin* is antimalarial drug obtained from *A. annua.*

(14) *Nux-vomica:* Fruits and seeds of *Strychrous nux-vomica.*

(15) *Dioscorea (Yam) :* Its tubers are edible. The extract diosgenin is starting point of several cortico-steroid drugs and contraceptive. Dioscorea is one of the most over-exploited plant.

(16) *Vasaca :* Leaves of *Adhatoda vasica* yield an expectorant drug against bronchitis.

(17) *Taxol :* Anticancer drug got from *Taxus baccata* (gymnosperm). *Podophyllum hexandrum* also contain anticancer ingredients.

(F) Plants Used as a Source of Timber

Wood suitable for carpentary and building is known as timber. It is of two types, hardwood (most dicots) and soft wood (gymnosperms and some dicots like *Salix; Salmalia* and *Morus*). Heaviest wood is that of *Guaiacum officinale* but in India, Acacia sundra. Some common timber yielding trees are:

(1) *Teak:* (Sagwan) *Tectona grandis.* Most durable wood.

(2) *Sal : Shorea robusta.*

(3) *Sissoo : (Shisham). Dalbergia sisso* (Indian Red wood) *Dalbergia latifolia* is Indian Rose wood.

(4) *Sins: Albizzia lebbeck.*

(5) *Arjun : Terminalia arjuna.*

(6) *Indian Almond: Terminalia catappa.*

(7) *Harir : Terminalia chebuta.*

(8) *Hollock : Terminalia myriocarpa.*

(9) *Deodar: Cedrus deodara.*

(10) *Ironwood: Mesua* ferra (Nagkesar, Nagchampa).

Tree are also planted under social forestry programme on village common land, vacant land along roads and railway embankment. The plants should be fast growing, capable of giving fodder and fuel besides some timber, *e.g. Leucaena, Allanthus, Anogeissus.* Certain woods are used for specific purposes. For example, wood of *Salix alba* and *Salix purpurea* is useful for making cricket bats. Hockey sticks are prepared from wood of *Morus alba.*

(G) Plants Used as a Source of Resin : Alcohol soluble sticky exudation. Pine resin (*Pinus roxburghii* and other species, gymnosperm) yields turpentine and *rosin* Damar is obtained from *Shorea robusta* or Sal.

(H) Plants Used as a Source of Gums: Gums are sticky exudation of bark which are insoluble in alcohol but form colloidal solution in water.

(1) Kuteera gum—*Sterculia urens.*

(2) Bengal Kingo gum—*Butea monosperma.*

(3) Salai—*Boswellia serrata.*

(4) Dhaora—*Anogeissus latifolia.*

(5) Gum Arabic—*Acasia sapota.*

(6) Milky latex of Achras sapota forms chickle gum from which chewing gum is produced.

(I) Plants Used as a Source of Tannins: These are astringent acidic substances used in preparation of dyes, inks and leather. *Acacia nilotica, WalnutJuglans regia, Cesalpinia, Uncania* (leaves and young branches).

(J) Plants Used as a Source of Dyes :

(1) *Cutch (Kattha) :* Heart wood of *Acacia catechu* in betel leaves and colouring textiles.

(2) *Henna (Mehndi) :* Leaves of *Lawsonia inermis.*

(K) Plants Used as a Source for Insecticides: Insecticides kill or repel insects. Natural insecticides include

(1) *Azadirachta indica (Magosa/Neem)*

(2) *Boenighauscnia alhiflora.*

(3) *Peganum harmala.*

(4) *Derris* (rotenone)

(5) *Chrysanthemum* (Pyrethrum).

First commercial bioinsecticide is sporeine developed in Germany. Synthetic insecticides are organochlorines, organophosphates, carbamates, pyrethroids.

Latex, Cellulose, Starch and their products

Latex: Latex is fluid produced in many higher plants and by certain agaric fungi (*Lactariub*). In green plants, it is stored in laticifers and in fungi, it is produced in latex ducts consisting of anastomosing hyphae. Latex consists of various substances like alkaloids, starch grains, sugars, minerals salts etc. Rubber concentration is very high in certain plants.

Product: Milky latex of *Hevea brasiliensis* yield rubber, which is poly terpene made of isoprene units. Other rubber producing plant are *Parthenium argentatum* (Guayule), *Manihot glaziovii* (Ceara Rubber) and *Ficus elastica* (Assam or India rubber).

Cellulose: Cellulose is polysaccharide having subunits of glucose linked by (β-1-4) glycosidic bonds. It is most abundant in cell wall and structural polysaccharide in plants and most probably the most abundant of all compounds found in living organisms. In cell wall, it is present in highly organized form, as microfibrils. It is thought to be synthesized in golgibodies from primary molecules and diphosphate derivatives of gluclose (*e.g.* UDP & GDP glucose) by action of enzymes that are tightly memebrane bound. It is broken down to cellobiose by enzyme cellulase and cellobiae is further hydrolysed to gluclose units by enzyme cellobiose.

Product: Ancient Indians used the treated bark of *Betula utilis* (Bhojpatra) as paper. Egyptians prepared the first paper from *Papyrus reed* (*Cyperus papyrus*). These days paper is prepared from a number of cellulose rich wood like Bamboos (most common in India), gymnospermous wood (*Picea, Pinus, Abies*-most common in western countries), *Boswellia, Eucalyptus,* Grasses, sawmill waste, cotton rags and waste paper. The articles are chopped, cooked in steam and converted into pulp. Pulp is chemically treated to remove lignin. It is then bleeched and passed through rollers to produce paper. Nepanagar has a large newspaper manufacturirig industry.

Starch: (Amylose). Is the most abundant and important polysaccharide in plants formed from glucose, bulk in plant found in storage organs, consists of two structurally different fractions, amylose and amylopectin. The amylose component consists of D-glucose units linked in a linear fraction by α-1- 4 linkages. Amylopectin is a branched polysaccharide, in this molecule shorter chains (of about 30 units) of glucose units linked by α-1-6 linkages (from which isomaltose can be obtained). Shape and relative proportions of these two constituents in starch grain is characteristic feature of species.

Products: (*i*) Used in making of few beverages. (ii) Major source of carbohydrate from various vegetables & fruits as in potato & Topica.

Perfumery: Volatile oils, perfumes, e.g. oil of Vetiver, Otto of Roses, Citronella. Flowers and fruits of *Mesua ferra* (Nagchampa) are used in cosmetics. Fragrant anthers are used in stuffing pillows. Vanilla (flavour) is got from fruits of orchid *Vanilla planifolia*. Certain plants from their various parts yield good smelling perfumes as rose (*Rosa indica*) leaves yield rose water. after proper distillation. Various other flowers gives various kind of perfumes. *Acacia farnesiana* flowers are used to extract perfumes. This belongs to family *Leguminosae*.

Perfume oil is also prepared from *Eclipta erecta* and *Matricaria chamonilla* of family compositae. Anti insect oil is prepared from Pyrethrum of compositae.

QUESTIONS FROM PREVIOUS YEARS' PAPERS

1. Distinguish between the following:
(*a*) Biodegradation and bioremediation
(*b*) Disease and disorder
(*c*) Storied and non-storied wood.

2. Explain the following:
(*a*) Crozier (*b*) NPC-system
(*c*) Fruit of wheat (*d*) Canker
(*e*) Blight (*f*) Galls
(*g*) Masaic (*h*) Paddy blast

3. What is 'koji' fermentation? How is it formed and what are the products produced by it?

4. Give an account of various kinds of biofertilizers.

5. "The rusts of cereals are polymorphic in nature." Explain this statement and draw the life-cycle and control measures.

6. Define Type Specimen and add a not on the importance of Herbarium.

7. Mention the plants as sources with reference to paper, drugs and resins.

8. Discuss in detail about Ethnobotany.

9. Answer the following:
(*a*) Cell structure of *Zygnema.*
(*b*) Importance of diatomaceous earth.

10. Write short notes on the following:
(*a*) Chemical preservatives and dyes used in anatomical studies.
(*b*) Cultivation practice of turmeric in the hilly tracts of India.
(*c*) Seasoning of wood.
(*d*) Plants producing essential cosmetic oil.
(*f*) Three spice yielding plants showing the part's used as the spice. (Give botanical names of these plants).
(*g*) Preparation of Vinegar
(*h*) NPC system.

11. What is the cause of sandal spike? Mention how the disease can be controlled.

12. Describe the following:
(*a*) Conifer wood
(*b*) Polyembryony in *Gnetum*
(*c*) Latex
(*d*) Endothecium
(*e*) Bird-pollinated plants
(*f*) Herbarium Techniques

13. Distinguish between:
(*a*) Nuclear and Cellular endosperm
(*b*) Green and Black tea

14. Why is jute considered a labour-intensive crop?

15. Cultivation of edible mushroom (*Volvariella* sps.) steps leading to sprouting of basidiocarp.

16. Write a short note on Economic importance of Diatomaceous earth.
17. What is unusual about the secondary growth in *Salvadora* and *Bignonia?*
18. What are the applications of palynology?
19. What is somaclonal variation? What is its major application?
20. What are the adaptive features of wind-pollinated plants?
21. "Botanical gardens are more than mere gardens." Substantiate the statement.
22. Describe the following:
   (*a*) Vavilov's centres of origin
   (*b*) Ethnobotany
23. Why is the name 'Botanical Garden' given. Give reason.
24. Do we need Energy plantations? Give reasons? and add a critical note on energy plantations.
25. Discuss the role of microbes in agriculture, industry, medicine and pollution control.
26. Write critical notes on:
   (*a*) Molecular methods to create disease resistance in plants.
   (*b*) Physiology of parasitism.
   (*c*) Plants as source for fibres and spices.
   (*d*) Plasmid structure and reproduction.

CHAPTER-5

MORPHOGENESIS

It is the capacity exhibited by certain types of isolated, differentiated plant cells to regenerate whole plant. The phenomenon is thought to be evidence supporting the theory that all nucleated plant cells essentially have some complement of genes which are necessary for formation of a complete plant and inhibition of many genes causes differentiation.

Cellular Totipotemy : Steward and his co-workers succeeded in demonstrating that even mature, fully differentiated tissues have the capability to grow in an organized fashion when excised from parent plant and grown *in vitro*. This capacity of plant cells is termed as *cellular totipotency*.

Steward excised-small pieces of tissues from the phloem region which were grown in special flasks containing liquid medium. This liquid nutrient medium was also containing coconut milk. These special flasks containing liquid medium and excised tissues of carrot were gently shaken by artificial automatic shaker. Due to shaking of culture, cells and clumps of cells became separated and remained flaoted into the liquid medium. Some of the cells clusters developed roots. When these rooted clumps were transferred to a semi-solid medium in glass tubes, they formed shoots. These plantlets developed into whole plant that flowered and produced seeds. It was also found that phloem tissues excised from roots of these plants could be used to repeat the experiment.

Muir and co-workers (1958) performed a successful experiment to grow single cell in total isolation to demonstrate the cellular totipotency. Normally, single cell does not grow in isolation. They took a single cell from tobacco callus and placed it on a filter paper below which callus of tobacco was growing. This technique though physically separated the single cell from rest of the callus, called *nurse tissue*, but provided the chance to pass necessary factor(s) from nurse tissue to the single cell. This single cell divided and formed a lump of tissue which on being transferred to the medium from the filter showed further growth. 1965, Vasil Hildebrondt also succeeded in growing whole plants of tobacco from a single cell of pith tissue callus. They took a small piece of tissue explanted from pith of tobacco plant. From this pith tissue, a callus was raised in a test tube containing semi -solid nutrient medium. A small piece of this callus was then transferred to flasks containing liquid medium and by shaking. By mechanical shaking of these flasks single cells and clumps of these cells were obtained in the liquid medium. Callus tissue was dissociated into single cell and clumps of cells. Now, they transferred a single cell to a drop of liquid medium placed on a glass slide and a small bridge was raised around the cell by putting three coverslips. This single cell when grown into small mass of cells by repeated division, was transferred to semi-solid medium where it differentiated into plantlet consisting of roots, stem and leaf. These plantlets, when grown on soil developed into mature plants with flowers, fruits and seeds.

On the basis of above said work of Steward, Muir, Vasil and Hildebrandt, one can infer that every living cell of plant is totipotent, irrespective of location and age. Scientists have succeeded to grow whole plants from single cell *in vitro* culture at least in case of carrot, tobacco and several other plants. In spite of totipotency of a single cell, it cannot be compared with the single celled zygote. As zygote undergoes a series of cell divisions and directly give rise to bipolar embryo (with plumule and radicle) in a predetermined manner while the isolated single cell in *vitro* culture first develops into irregular callus and then differentiate into roots and shoot buds.

Polarity: Condition that results from establishment of definite orientation during differentiation as in cell, tissue or organ, evident in early growth of plants as is shown by separate development of root and shoot system from initially formed dipolar embryo.

The embryo lies dormant in the seed, but when the latter is supplied with moisture and the other necessary conditions it becomes active and tends to grow and develop into a small seedling. Germination may be defined as the process by which the dormant embryo wakes up, grows out of the seed coat and establishes itself as a seedling. For its growth the embryo utilizes the food stored up in the cotyledons or in the endosperm if that is present.

CELL, TISSUE, ORGAN AND PROTOPLAST CULTURE

Cell culture : It was Haberlandt in 1890s who put forth the pioneering attempt to culture mechanically isolated mesophyll cells. He succeeded in maintaining these cells alive for about 10 days in culture but cells did not divide. He failed to achieve division of isolated cells. Since then, the progress in the field of isolating and culturing individual cells has been so spectacular that it has become possible not only to culture isolated single cells but also to induce divisions in such cells in complete isolation and, finally, to regenerate whole plants from them. The most important aspect that deserves attention in isolated single cell culture technology is the initation of division and proliferation of isolated single cells which starts only when they are placed into "conditioned medium" (medium in which the tissue has been grown for some time). Isolated single plant-cells resemble with animal cells in this respect. However, a conditioned medium is prepared by culturing high densities of cells of the same or different species in fresh medium for a few days and then the cultured cells are removed by filter-sterlization making the medium free of them. This medium now contains essential amino acids such as glutamine and serine as well as growth regulators such as cytokinins. When the isolated single cell are placed into the conditioned medium in exactly the same way as microorganisms, they initiate division and, instead of developing a colony as do the microorganisms, they proliferate to result in a callus. The latter is induced to regenerate plants.

Isolation of Single Cells

(*a*) *From Intact Plant Organs :*

(*i*) *Mechanical Isolation :* Leaf tissue is considered the most suitable material for single cell isolation. The widely used mechanical method for the isolation of mesophyll cells is the gentle grinding of leaves followed by cleaning the cells by filteration and centrifugation. Another device for the large scale mechanical isolation of leaf cells have been developed by Rossini (1969). In this method the leaves are first surface sterlized by rapid immersion in 95% ethanol followed by rinsing for 15 minutes in filter-sterilized 7% solution of calcium hypochlorite. The leaves are now washed in sterile distilled water and cut into small pieces which are homogenized with culture medium (1.5 g of leaf material with 10 ml of culture medium). The homogenate is filtered, the filterate is subjected to slow speed centrifugation which sediments the isolated cells. The supernatant is removed and the cells are transferred to suittable medium. Mechanical isolation of cells is considered advantageous atleast in two aspects, over the enzymatic method. First, it eliminates the exposure of cells to the harmful effects of enzymes, second, the cells need not be plasmolysed.

Composition of media recommended for the culture of isolated mesophyll cells (after Bhojwani and Rajdan, 1983)

Constituents	*Amounts (mg/litre)*	
	Rossini (1972)	*Joshi & Ball (1968)*
KNO_3	950	
KCl	—	750
NH_4NO_3	725	—
$NaNO_3$	—	600
$MgSO_4.7H_2O$	187	250
$CaCl_2$	169	—
$CaCl_2.6H_2O$	—	112
KH_2PO_4	69	—
$NaH_2PO_4.2H_2O$	—	141
NH_4Cl	—	5.35
$MnSO_4.4H_2O$	12.5	—
$MnCl_2.4H_2O$	—	0.036
H_3BO_3	5	0.056

$ZnSO_4.4H_2O$	5	—
$ZnCl_2$	—	0.15
$NaMoO_4.2H_2O$	0.125	0.025
$CuSO_4.5H_2O$	0.0125	0.05
$CuCl_2.2H_2O$	—	0.054
$COCl_2$	—	0.02
$FeSO_4.7H_2O$	13.9	—
$FeCl_3.6H_2O$	—	0.5
Na.EDTA		
Disodium salt of ethylene	18.6	—
Dinitrilotetraacetic acid	—	0.8
Glycine	2	—
Nicotinic acid	5	—
Pyridoxine HCl	0.5	—
Thiamine HCl	0.5	—
Biotin	0.05	—
Folic acid	0.5	—
Casein hydrolysate (acid hydrolysate acid and vitamin free)	—	400
m-Inositol	100	—
BAP	0.1	—
Kinetin	—	0.1
2, 4-D	1	1
Sucrose	10000	20000
pH	5.0	—

(ii) Enzymatic Isolation : Enzymatic isolation of plant cells is generally undertaken by plant physiologists and biochemists. In this metthod, the fully expanded leaves are taken from 60 to 80 day old plants. They are surface sterilized in 70% ethanol and rinsed in 3% sodium hypochlorite solution contain 0.05% Teepol or Cetavelon. The leaves are now washed with sterile distilled water and their lower epidermis is peeled off with the help of fine forceps. A piece of peeled area is excised and transferred to enzyme solution. The enzyme, however, is infiltrated into the leaf-tissue with the aid of vacuum pump. The material is incubated at 25°C on a reciprocating shaker with a stroke of 4-5 cm at the rate of 120 cycles/min. The enzyme solution is changed every half an hour. The solution collected after the first 30 minutes is discarded. The solution collected after the second 30 minutes contains largely spongy parenchyma cells, and those after the third and fourth 30 minutes contains predominantly palisade cells. These isolated cells are washed twice with culture medium, and finally cultured.

(iii) Isolation from Cultured Tissue : Traditionally, the single cell systems used in basic and applied researches are isolated from cultured tissue because this approach is convenient and widely applicable. Cultures are initiated by simply placing explants from surface-sterlized plant parts (e.g. leaves) on a nutrient medium containing phytohormones, viz. auxins and cytokinins. The explant develops a callus which is separated and transferred to a liquid medium. The callus is agitated in the liquid medium. As a result, it breaks up in the medium and gives a suspension of isolated cells, small clusters of cells and much larger aggregates. When the isolatted single cells are separated from the suspension culture and placed onto a suitable medium, they initiatte dividing and proliferate to give a callus.

Culture Techniques

Though a number of techniques have been developed to culture isolated single plant cells, the following are those which are used frequently.

(a) Bergmann's Cell Plating Technique : This is the most popular technique of single cell culture. The density of the isolated single cells in suspension culture is balanced to twice the finally desired plating cell density. Melted agar (0.6-1%) containing medium of otherwise the same composition as the suspension culture medium is cooled and maintained at 35°C in a water bath. Equal volumes of the two media are mixed and rapidly spread out in petri-dishes in such a manner that the cells are evenly distributed and fixed in a thin layer of the medium after it has cooled and solidified. The petri-dishes are sealed with paraffin. Suspension cultures which carry cell aggregates in addition to isolated single cells should be filtered through a seive which allows only single cells or small cell aggregates to pass through. The large cell aggregates are discarded and only the fine suspension is plated. The petri dishes are observed under the microscope in inverted position and the single cells are marked on the outside of the dish by a fine marker to ensure the isolation of pure single cell-clones. The culture containing petridishes are incubated in the dark at 25°C.

Suspension Culture : When the pieces of calli are transferred to liquid medium and the medium is continuously agitated to obain isolated single cells, the culture is called 'suspension culture'. Basically there are two types of suspension cultures, viz., batch culture and continuous culture.

(*i*) *Batch culture* when cultures are continuously propagated by routinely taking a small aliquot of the suspension and transferring it to a fresh medium, the suspension culture is called 'Batch culture '.

(*ii*) *Continuous culture* when cultures are grown in culture vessels under steady state for prolonged periods by adding fresh medium and draining out the used medium, the suspension culture is called 'continuous culture'.

(*b*) *The Filter Paper Raft-Nurse Technique :* This technique has been developed by Muir *et al* (1954). It involves culturing isolated single cells on the top of an actively growing callus separated by a piece of filter paper. What is done actually is that the single cells are isolated from suspension cultures with the aid of a micropipette. Several days earlier to this isolation, sterile 8 mm × 8 mm squares of filter paper are placed under aseptic conditions on the top of the established callus, called "nurse tissue", of the same or different species. The filter paper is wetted by liquid and nutrients from the nurse tissue. The isolated single cell is now placed on the wet filter paper raft. When a microscopic colony proliferates from the cell, it is transferred to suitable agar-medium for further growth and development of cell alone.

(*c*) *The Microchamber Technique :* This technique has been developed by Jones *et al* in 1960. A drop of the nutrient medium carrying a single cell is taken out by micropipette from the suspension culture, is transferred on a sterile microscopic slide. A drop of sterile mineral oil is placed on either side of the medium-drop and a coverglass placed on each mineral oil drop. A third coverglass in now taken and placed on the medium drop bridging the two coverglasses and forming a microchamber to enclose the single cell aseptically within the mineral oil. The latter does not allow any loss of water from the microchamber but allows exchange of gases. The whole slide in then placed in a petri-dish and incubated. When a microscopic colony develops from the cell, the coverglass is removed and the colony is transferred to fresh suitable medium for further growth and development of cell alone.

Applications

(*a*) *Crop Improvement :* It has been found that when plants are regenerated by growing somatic explants (other than those of apical meristems and auxillary bud tissue) *in vitro*, they usually show genetic variations (called 'somaclonal variations'). The high degree of their variations is being exploited in mutant (variant) selection in relation to crop improvement. Two approaches have been followed to recover such variant plants : first, plants are regenerated from somatic explants cultured for different periods and screened for the desired traits, second for a number of somalclonal variations, the screening is required to be done at single cell level. The merit of screening of plant variants at single cell level is that it permits screening millions of cells with a comparatively small input of effort and resources.

Steps Involved in Variant—Selection Through Single Cell Cultures

Isolation of real variants through single cell cultures requires a series of step-wise investigations (Umiel, 1978). These are as follows :

(*i*) Characterization of isolated variant cell lives.
(*ii*) Phenotypic expression of the trait in tissue culture.
(*iii*) Production of plants from the variant cells.
(*iv*) Test in tissue culture for the transmission of the variation through plant regeneration.
(*v*) Production of seeds and progenies.
(*vi*) Tests in tissue cultures for the transmission of the variation through seeds.
(*vii*) Tests for the expression of the variation at the plant level in plants derived from seeds.
(*viii*) Genetic studies and the establishment of seed stock for the variant lines.
(*ix*) Studies on the nature of the variations.

(*b*) *Resistance to Diseases :* Sections of cell lines resistant to diseases may be of direct practical values. Resistance to most plant diseases is not mediated by single gene and hence is not detectable in culture. However, sometimes the toxic effect of a phytotoxin on tissue, cell or protoplast cultures is equivalent to its effect on the whole plant. Furthermore, if the phytotoxin is the only reason for pathogenecity direct selection for disease resistance *in vitro* using the phytotoxin may come to reality. It was Carlson (1973) who extended experimental support to this hypothesis, he reported that plants regenerated from tobacco protoplasts selected for resistance to methionine sulfoximine (MSO) showed enhanced resistance to *Pseudomonas tabaci*. Though methionine sulfoximine has not been analogous to the phytotoxin of *P. tabaci*, this observation opened the door of selecting phytotoxin-resistant cell lines.

(c) *Resistance to Herbicides :* Similar to the disease resistance, selection of cell lines resistance to herbicides may also be of direct practical value. In the recent past fertile plants resistant to herbicides such as amitrol, 2, 4-D, sodium chlorate, picloram, chlorsulfuron and sulfometuron methyl have been selected from cultivated cells of *Nicotiana*. However, further research on the metabolism of herbicide action on cells and plants is required if the potential for isolating herbicide-resistant phenotypes using tissue/single cell techniques is to be exploited fully.

(d) *Resistance to Amino Acids and their Analogues :* Selection of cell lines resistant to amino acids or their analogoues has been stimulated by the prospect of improving nutritional quality of plants. A potato cell line resistant to 5-methyl-tryptophan (5MT) has been used to demonstrate the presence of two possible isoenzymes of anthranilate synthase the first regulatory enzyme unique to tryptophan biosynthesis. Further 5 MT resistant cell lines were isolated by Jacobsen *et al* (1985). The cells accumulated free tryptophan and phenylalanine and tyrosine demonstrating the possiblity of manupulating the free amino acid pools of potato cells.

(e) *Tolerance to Environmental Stress :* High salt levels in the soil and the low temperatures are the main environmental stress on the distribution of sites where a particular crop can be grown. Scientists are busy in isolating stress-tolerant cells-lines and demonstrating this characteristics in plants regenerated from such cell-lines. For instance, salt tolerant cell lines of *Nicotiana tabacum* and *N. sylvestric* have been isolated. Salt tolerance in *N. tabacum* is transmitted sexually although at low frequency, but no plants were regenerated from salt tolerant *N. sylvestris* cells lines. Similarly, low temeprature (cold) tolerant cell lines of *N. Sylvestris* have been isolated but the characteristic is yet not transmitted sexually.

(f) *Secondary Metabolite Production :* A few but well established examples of secondary metabolites production in high amounts by selected cell lines are known. Following table indicates the increased yields so far achieved with products in selected cell-line suspension cultures.

Chemical	*Plant*	*Cell Culture Yield (% dry wt)*	*Whole (Field grown) Plant Yield (% dry wt)*	*Ratio Cell Culture/ Whole Plant*
Glutathione	*Nicotiana-tabacum*	1.0	0.1	10
Nicotine	-do-	5.0	2.1	2
Anthra-quinones	*Merinda citrifolia*	18.0	2.2	8
Rosmarinic acid	*Coleus blumei*	15.0	3.0	5
Ajmalicine	*Catharanthus roseus*	2.2	0.3	7
Serpentine	-do-	1.8	0.5	3
Diosgenin	*Dioscorea deltoidea*	3.3	2.0	2

Table : Examples of enhancement in natural product yield in selected cell lines, compared with parent plant material (after Fowler, 1983).

Anthraquinone is commercially obtained from the cortical cells and bark cells of the roots of *Morinda citrifolia*. This alkaloid is now being obtained from cell line suspension cultures. If calculated, in percentage dry weight, the cell line cultures result in about eight times higher alkaloid content than the whole plant yield.

High amount synthesis of serpentine and ajmalicine by selected cell lines of *Catharanthus roseus* have been reported. The total content of these two alkaloids in the roots of *C. roseus* is generally less than 0.5% of their dry weight. The selected cell lines of some strains of this species, however, show an alkaloid content as high as 2%.

Suspension cultures of *Coleus blumei* have been reported to accumulate rosmarine acid upto 15% of dry weight of the cells which stands five times higher than the alkaloid content in the intact plant.

The suspension culture of *Glycoyrrhiza glabra* can produce glycoyrrhizin in a fair amount of atleast 3-4% of dry weight.

(g) *Biotransformation :* Biotransformation of particular substrates to more useful compounds by plant cell is now considered to be one of the most promising area in the biotechnological application of plant cell culture. The projected potentials of the biotransformation lie in the conversion of less expensive and bulk product to value added high cost and low volume products. It is expected that specific modifications of chemical structures of certain compounds may be performed more easily by cultured plant cells than by microorganisms or by chemical synthesis. The biotransformation of 'digitoxin' or 'β-methyldigitoxin' to 'digoxin'or 'B-methyldigoxin' by specific hydroxylation of suspension cultures of '*Digitalis lantana* can carry out biotransformation at 15% conversion in 24 hours and 70% in 7 days. Digoxin is used in cardiac treatment. Cultured cells of Datura posses a remarkably high capability for glycosylation of hydroquinone to form 'arbutin' which finds its use as a diuretic and urinary antiseptic. The diterpenoid stevioside is widely used as natural sweetener (it is 100 times sweeter than cane sugar) but not its aglycone steviol. The cell cultures of *Stevia rebaudiana* and *Digitalis purpurea* can biotransform the Steviol to *steviolbiocide* and *stevioside.*

(*h*) *Plant Cell Culture and Cotton :* Cotton plants are no longer the only source of cotton. Biotechnologists at Texas University Lubbock (USA) have successfully explored a technique to convert isolated cotton plant cells of any type into fibre cells and to grow cotton fibres in solution. The resulting cotton is a microorganism free fibre of controllable length, thickness and quality for specific uses. Individual cotton plant cells have been *teased* apart from plant parts in water solutions. These isolated cells have been cultured in nutrient solutions containing the hormones auxins, cytokinins and gibberellins. There has been found a balance of these hormones that caused cells to lose differentiation. Further, changes in the hormonal balance caused undifferentiated cells to become fibre cells. Thousands of such cells on cotton seed surfaces normally grow into individual cotton fibres.

Plant Tissue Culture : Tissue culture is a technique whereby small pieces of viable tissue (called 'explants') are isolated from parent plants and grown in a defined nutritional and controlled environment for prolonged period under aseptic conditions. For successful plant tissue culture it is best to proceed with an explant rich in undermined cells, e.g. those from the cortex or meristem, because such cells are capable of rapid proliferation. The explants to proceed with tissue culture technique in plants are usually taken from leaves, buds, root apex, shoot-spex, nodal segments or germinating seeds. These explants are transferred onto the suitable culture media under specific conditions where they grow into an undifferentiated mass of cells called 'callus'. To develop a callus from the explant it is essential that the nutrient medium used contains phytohormones such as auxins (e.g. IAA), cytokinins. These hormones vary for different tissue explants from different parts of the same plant and for the same explant from different genera of plants. Thus there is no 'ideal' medium, but, however, the typical medium used in plant tissue culture technology is Murashige-Scoog (MS) medium.

(A) Technique : There are four main stages involved in plant tissue culture technology. These are:

(*a*) *Initiation of Culture :* The most important factor in tissue culture technology is the maintenance of aseptic conditions. To meet this condition, the plant material which usually contains bacterial or fungal spores has first to be surface sterilized by the use of chlorine water or mercuric chloride or some other surface-sterilizing agents to eliminate micro-organisms. This is necessary because the culture medium on which these tissue pieces are inoculated contains mineral salts, vitamins, sugars, phytohor-mones and other growth regulators on which microbial contaminants would grow at a faster rate than plant tissue. After inoculation, the cultures are incubated under controlled conditions at 25°C in light.

(*b*) *Multiplication or Sub-Culture Stage :* After 2-3 weeks, the explants show visible growth by forming either callus or differentiated organs like shoots, roots, or complete plant depending upon the composition of the medium. If one desires to obtain large number of plantlets from the callus, he sub-cultures the callus. What is done is that the callus produced from the explant is taken out, cut into small pieces, and each piece is transferred to fresh medium in a separate tube where the callus pieces grow into big mass of callus. This is called sub-culture stage. Sub-culturing may be repeated if required.

(*c*) *Development and Differentiation of Sub-Culture :* The sub-cultured callus is now induced to proceed for further development and, finally, differentiation. If the concentration of phytohormones in the medium are altered then the callus can be induced to differentiate. A very high auxin to cytokinin ratio induces root formation and a high cytokinin-to-auxin ration induces shoot formation. This is referred to as *'organogenesis'*. Alternatively, a structure called *embryoid* may develop if media concentration is so altered, this process is called *'somatic embryogenesis'*. If the hormonal conditions are correctly balanced then an entire plantlet can be induced to grow on culture medium, this process is called *'regeneration'*.

(*d*) *From Test-Tubes to Field :* In the last stage, which is followed only when full-grown plants are to be obtained, the test-tube rooted plantlets are first subjected to *"aclamatization"* so that they can adjust later in the field conditions, and then transferred to the field. The plantlet is takes out from the rooting medium, is washed slowly with running water for an hour or more to ensure that no piece of agar is left on the surface of the plantlet. If agar remains their it would invite microbes to grow and destroy the plantlet. Now the plantlet is put to low minimal salt medium (LMSM) for 24-48 hours and then transferred to a pot that contains autoclave—sterilized mixture of clay-soil, core sand leaf moults in 1 : 1 : 1 proportion. The plantlet—containing pot is covered generally with transparent polythene (beakers may also be used) to maintain the humidity. This condition is maintained for about 15-30 days. At this stage the plantlet is fully aclamatized and is able to withstand open environment conditions. The plantlet then is transferred to soil and the techniques employed are similar to normal agricultural practices.

(B) Applications :

(*a*) *Improvement of crops and ornamentals :* Plant tissue culture technology bears tremendous potential for the improvement of crops and ornamentals. Some major areas of this application are :

(*i*) *Large Scale Plant Regeneration : Clonal Propagation (Micropropagation) :* One of the most important aspects of plant tissue culture technology is its use in clonal propagation of selected species of crops and ornamentals. The clonal propagation via tissue culture technique (i.e. *in vitro* clonal propagation) is popularly called *"micropropagation"*. In most cases, *in vitro* clonal propagation has been achieved using shoot apex tissue or axillary bud tissues. The apical shoot tip or axillary bud is surface sterilized and placed onto a culture medium that promotes formation of additional shoot (the medium is called shooting medium). Subsequently, multiple shoots are separated and transferred onto such a medium that induces root formation (the medium is called *rooting medium*). Plantlets are then aclamatized and transferred to the green-house or field.

Interest in *in vitro* clonal propagation of plants originated from the success of G. Morel (1960) with orchids. At present, however, *in vitro* clonal propagation is the only commercially viable method of propagation of orchids and almost all economically important orchids are clonable *in vitro*. Certain species of ornamentals or parental breeding lines are often difficult or time consuming to propagate using conventional sexual methods. In either case, mass clonal propagation using tissue culture technique could be commercially useful. Shoot apex clonal propagation has already been used to commercially propagate a large number of marketable ornamentals. For instance, ornamental plants such as *Gerbera, Cordyline, Dracaena, Hemerocallis* are now commercially propagated via cloning.

[*Clonal propagation*, which is popularly called 'micropropagation' represents the technique in which vegetative tissue are used to produce plants that are genetically identical to their parents. A *clone* is however, the genetically alike progeny of plant derived from its vegetative tissue.]

Clonal propagation is, however, being used commercially for large-scale plant propagation in certain crop species (e.g. potato) by the production of *minitubers*. When the axillary shoot cultures of potato are cultivated in the presence of appropriate levels of phytohormones such as cytokinin and gibberellin, they result in large number of small tubers called 'minitubers'. The later are transferred directly to the field and generate normal plants. One can see from the following table that the method of minituber-oriented plant propagation is advantageous.

Traditional	*Micropropagation*
Year I	
100 g tuber	100 g tuber
↓	↓
1 mature plant	1 preconditioned plant
↓	↓
1600 g tuber	10 nodal cultures
	↓
	Shoot multiplication
	↓
	Dormant 650000 minitubers
Year II	**Ist season**
16 mature plants	617500 plants
↓	↓
16 × 600 g tubers = 25.6 kg.	617500 × 500 g tubers = 308750 kg.

Chart : Comparison of traditional and tissue culture method for propagating potato tubers. The reduced number of plants obtained from the minitubers is an allowance for 5% loss on establishment in soil.

The significant advantages offered by *in vitro* clonal propagation over the conventional methods of clonal propgation (methods of vegetative propagation) *in vivo* are :

(1) Over a million plants can be regenerated from a small even microscopic, piece of plant tissue within a year. Contrary to it, none of the *in vivo* methods of clonal propagation can result in such a prolific rate of multiplication.

(2) *In vitro* clonal propagation can continue throughout the year irrespective of the season.

(3) An enhanced rate of *in vitro* clonal propagation reduces considerably the period between the selection and the release of a new culture.

(4) *In vitro* clonal propagation provides reliable and economic methods of maintaining pathogen free plants in a state that can achieve rapid multiplication when needed, irrespective of the time of the year.

(ii) Non-Clonal Production : Contrary to the shoot apex propagation which faithfully produces clones, there are sizable number of evidences which suggest that the regeneration of plants from callus, leaf explants, protoplasts does not result in production of clones, the regenerated plants bear genetic variability. Regeneration of plants from long-term callus culture is associated with *in vitro* chromosome instability and recovery of aneuploid plants. Regeneration of plants directly from leaf explants has resulted in morphological variation. It has been reported that the regenerates of potato and sugarcane varied in response to diseases. Plants regenerated from callus of sugarcane were examined in detail and have been found resistant to eye-spot diseases. Fiji disease and downy mildew for which the parent was susceptible. These regenerate-lines are being incorporated into a conventional breeding programme. In this way the large scale plant regeneration using callus, leaf explants etc. may lead to the production of genetically variable crop species which may prove novel agriculturally. However, no new crop varieties have yet been produced using the culture induced genetic variability although this method will probably produced new varieties shortly.

(b) Production of Virus Free Plants : Virus infection has been a major problem of crop and ornamental plants. Such infections greatly reduce the yield, vigour and quality of plants and their products. For instance, virus infection of ornamental plants reduces the size and number of blooms produced and infection of fruit crops reduce yield by upto 90%. The traditional method of virus elimination is by heat-treatment, but, only a few viruses can be eliminated by this method. It has been observed in a large number of species, however, that the concentration of infective virus is low in the apical

meristems of a plant. It is so because the lack of vacular differentiation in the meristem prevents intercellular movement of viruses and the active metabolism of mitotic cells precludes viral infection. It is considered, therefore, that if a small enough piece of apical meristem is exised and cultured, it is often possible to obtain virus-free plant regenerates. Genetic stability as measured by phenotypic and chromosomal stability is usually preserved in plant regenerates recovered from apical meristem cultures.

G. Morel and C. Martin (1952) succeeded for the first time in obtaining virus-free *Dahlia* plants by culturing apical meristem from infected plants. Since then virus have been eliminated using shoot-apex culture from a number of economical species. These species include the elimination of mottle virus from strawberry, potato Virus-X from potato, mosaic virus from cassava, and cauliflower mosaic virus from cauliflower. Virus-free plants regenerated from shoot-apex cultures have resulted in significant increase in yield when compared to virus infected plants. Result have been particularly favourable in potato where yield of virus-free potatoes is 60% higher than that of infected plants.

Besides apical meristems, callus from tissue explants is also used to regenerate virus free plants. callus is considered similar to apical meristems as mitosis occurs rapidly and the vascular differentiation is incomplete. In callus, viral infection may be completely eliminated via repeated sub-culture. Virus free plants have been regenerated from callus in tobacco, germanium, gladiolus, potatoes, Although plants regenerated from callus are virus-free, it has been found that the chromosomal abnormalities occurs frequently among callus derived plant regenerates. Simultaneously, it has also been demonstrated that the populations of callus-derived regenerates are not as uniform as apical meristem-derived regenerates.

Plants regenerated from viral infection-free leaf tissue explants have also been found virus-free. Murakishi and Carlson (1976) regenerated tobacco plants from dark green uninfected explants of a TMV-infected leaf. They observed that approximately half of the regenerated plants were virus-free. Similarly, Shepard (1977) reported that 7.5% of plants regenerated from potato virus-X infected tobacco leaves were free of viruses.

(*c*) *Forestry :* One of the most important aspects of tissue culture technology is rapid regeneration of forest plants. This have been successfully demonstrated in case of orchids, herbaceous plants, and some fruit tree species. However, realization of the importance of tissue culture in accelerating improvement programmes for forest tree spp. is a recent origin. A number of reports on methods of producing plants by tissue culture of a whole range of forest tree belonging to angiosperms such as teak, eucalyptus, sandalwood, populus, birch, tamarind, rubber, oil palm, and gymnosperms such as *Picea abies*, *Pinus radiata*, *Sequoia sempervirens*, *Thuja plicata* have recently been published.

In India, the scientists of National Chemical Laboratory, Pune have developed tissue culture methods by which hundreds of plants of teak (*Tectona grandis*) and *Eucalyptus citriodora* could be obtained from a single bud in a year. Over 600 plants of teak produced by this method have been supplied to Forest Development Corporation, Maharashtra for field trials. National Botanical Research Institute (NBRI), Lucknow has perfected a method for the mass propagation of *Dioscorea floribunda* by tissue culture technique.

(*d*) *Production of Secondary Metabolities :* Plant tissues cultured *in vitro* produce some or all of the primary and secondary metabolites produced by mature plants. The primary metabolities consists of proteins, carbohydrates, fats, vitamins etc. which are essential for growth, while secondary metabolities like alkaloids, steroids, phenolics, flavonoids may be produced as defence mechanisms by the plant. Secondary metabolities have a wide range of applications in the pharmaceuticals, chemical and food industries. Commercial production of these high cost secondary metabolities by plant tissue cultures is attracting greater attention now than before. This is evident from the large number of commercial companies taking keen interest to exploit the potential. Till recnetly, only a few groups in W. Germany, Japan and Canada were actively involved in the production of metabolities from tissue culture, but now, many companies have actively entered this area of biotechnology which offers great promise for the days to come.

Commercial Production at Present : Though there are still some problems of growth and productivity which are to be overcome to make commercial products cheeper, there are already some secondary metabolite products commercially, obtained mainly by Japanese, Americans, W. Germans. Mitusui Pharmaceutical Industries of Japan have started producing 'Shikonin' from *Lithospermum erythrorhizon*. Shikonin, a red pigment is an anti-bacterial and anti-inflammmatory compound used widely in Japanese pharmacopea. Since it is also a safe red dye, it is now being marketed as *'bio-lipstics'*. Bethesda Rsearch Laboratory, Maryland, U.S.A. is marketing 'Phosphodiesterase' obtained from tobacco tissue cultures. The production of 'berberin' used against stomach distress, by '*Coptis japonica*' is likely to be industrialzed. The production of two or more products from one culture is being explored, for instance, tobacco cells cultured in 20,000 litre fermentors are being used for producing *ubiquinone* (used against heart ailments), biotin, and *low tar tobacco* for cigarettes.

Future Prospects of Commercial Production : B. Kaul and E.T. Staba of College of Pharmacy, University of Minneseta (U.S.A.) have reported that 'diosgenin', a major raw material for manufacture of cortricosteroids and steroid contraceptives, can be obtained from '*Dioscrea deltoidea* (Yam) using tissue culture technique. The tissue culture of valuable Chinese drug 'Ginseng' can result in ginsenosides in large amounts (more than 20% of dry weight as crude saponins) in Japan.

Plant tissue culture can produce certain types of quinone. The callus culture of *Cassia tora* (Fetid cassia) contain more than ten times as much as quinones as anthraquinones. Similar results have been reported using suspension cultures of *Morinda citrifolia* (Indian Mulberry) and *Cassia angustigolia* (Indian Senna). Ubiquinone-10, used us a remedy for congestive heart failure has been produced by *Nicotiana* (Tobacco) cell/tissue suspension cultures at a rate of 360 kg/hectare dry weight which is higher than that by microbes.

Similarly, the content of napthaquinone pigments used for the treatment of skin diseases, burns and haemorrhoids, has been successfully increased in callus culture of *Lithospermum erythrorhizon* (Gromwell). The increase in the amount of napthaquinones through callus culture is important especially because of the decreasing availability and unsuccessful cultivation of the plant.

Screening of various tissue cultures by bioassays for definite pharmaceutical activities may be an effective method for exploiting active substances produced by cultured tissues. For instance, some of callus tissues isolated from *Emblica officinalis* (Amla) and *Isodan Japonicus* produce proteinase inhibitor showing a marked antiplasmin activity. Similarly, dried callus of *vinca rosea* (Peri winkle) is a cure for coccidium disease of chicks and a powerful prophylactic against pathogenic protozoa.

Table : A list of suggested plant products of industrial potential, which can be obtained using plant tissue culture system is given :

Product	*Plant*	*Source*
(1) Pharmaceuticals Ajmalicine, Vincristine, Serpentine, Vinblastine	*Cathasanthus roseus*	Root
Atropine, Hyoscyamine	*Atropa belladona*	
Codeine, Morphine, Thebaine	*Papaver somniferum* and *P. bracteatum*	Capsule, Seedlings
Anthraquinones	*Cassia tora, Morinda citrifolia*	Fruit
Berberine	*Coptis japonica*	Rhizome
Digitoxin-Digoxin	*Digitalis purpurea*	Leaves
Reserpine	*Digitalis lanata*	Leaves
Visnagin	*Rauwelfia serpentina, Ammi visnaga*	Roots
(2) Chemicals		
Diosgenin	*Disocorea deltoidea*	Tubers
Essential oils	*Mentha* Spp.	Leaves

(3) Flavours

Angelica	*Angelica sylvestric*	Roots
Capsicum	*Capsicum annum*	Fruit
Celery	*Apium graveolens*	Leaves
Garlic	*Alium sativum*	Bulbs
Ginger oil	*Zingiber officinale*	Roots
Hops	*Humulus lupulus*	Flowers
Onion	*Alium cepa*	Bulbs

(4) Insecticides

Pyrethrins	*Chrysanthemum Cineraria folium*	Flowers

(5) Colourants

Anthocyanin, Carotenoids	*Dacus carota*	Roots
Betanine	*Beta vulgaris*	Roots

(6) Non-Nutritive *Sweeteners*

Thaumatin	*Thamatococcus danielli*	Fruits
Stevioside	*Stevia rebaudiana.*	

Representative Indian Institutions

High cost secondary metabolitic production via plant tissue culture technique have attracted the Indian Scientist's attention and the work is in progress in various instititutions. Following are some representative institutions which are actively engaged in such activities :

Institutions	Metabolities
Bhaba Atomic Research Centre, Bombay	Fermentative production of Ajmalicine, Vinblastin, Vincristine
Central Food Technological Research Institute, Mysore	Capsaicin (pungent spice), Pyrethrines, (bioinsecticide for grain storage), Saffron (flavour & colour) Garlic (flavour) and Carum (spice)
Central Institute of Medicinal and Aromatic plants, Lucknow	Artemesin, Essential oils
M.S. University of Baroda	Atropine, Nicotine, Phenolics, Solasodine, Phytoecdysones
Regional Research Laboratory, Jammu-Tawi	Diosgenin, Indole Alkaloids, Morphine alkaloids, Scopoletin and Visnagin
University of Rajasthan, Jaipur	Atropine, Berberine, Diosgenin, Opium alkaloids, Hyoscyamine, precursor biotransformation
University of Jodhpur, Jodhpur	Ephedrine, Indole alkaloids

Plant Organ Culture :

(A) Anther Culture : Though *in vitro* culture of anthers was first undertaken by Shimakura (1934), it were Guha & Maheshwari (1964) of Delhi University who first successfully obtained numerous embryo-like structures called *embryoids* and subsequently the plantlets from mature anthers of *Datura innoxia.* These two workers observed the embryoids developed from the inside of the anthers at that time but in 1966 they confirmed that the origin of embryoids has been the regeneration of plants from anthers (androgenesis) as well as from excised pollen grains has been of much interest. The intact anthers containing the developing pollen have been cultured in numerous laboratories of the world and this has resulted in the development of embryoids directly from pollen grains. These embryoids have been induced to develop into whole plants which are true haploids (with reference to higher plants, haploids represents the gametic chromosomes constitution). (N.B. seeds of most flowering plants are diploids). It is evident from a recent review that most species capable of haploid production proceed via *anther culture or androgenesis.*

There is a long list of species in which haploids have been produced by anther culture technique. Some of these are *Datura metal, Nicotiana tabacum, N. sylvestris, N. alata, N. rustica, N. glutinosa, Solanum nigrum, Lycopersicon esculentum, Petunia hybrida* and *Capsicum annum.*

As it is apparent, the solanaceous plants respond well to anther culture technique probably because of the fact that they have long-sized anthers and the latter flourish well in almost every culture medium. However, the following are crop species capable of haploid plant production from anther culture : rapseed, tobacco, rice, rye, potato, corn, asparagus, pepper, strawberry, rubber, barley, sweet potato, wheat, grapes and clover.

(*a*) *Technique :* For successful anther and excised pollen culture, it is essential to excise the flower buds at the correct time, the correct time is the stage of the first mitotic division of the uninucleate microspores tetrad. Buds are surface sterilized with alcohol, chlorine-water, sodium hypochloride or ethyl mercuric chloride. Now, the anthers are excised and transferred onto nutrient medium. Different nutrient media used for anther culture are Murashige-Scoog media, Nitsch medium and certain other modifications-1% agar is added to the medium to provide solid base. The transferred anthers, in the beginning, show slight swelling followed by initiation of cell division inside the massive connective tissue. This latter show initiations of light green crumbled callus. Simultaneously, the pollen sac swells up and raptures along its upper margin lengthwise exhibiting a mass of pale-green pollen-callus. The callus arising from pollen shows slow growth as compared to connective callus. Now, the nutrient medium is supplemented with high concentration of kinetin for multiplication of callus, keeping the auxin concentration quite low. However, when formation of root and shoot is desired, the ratio of kinetin and auxin concentration is reserved in the medium.

(*b*) *Applications :* (*i*) Contrary to the fact that mutations are difficult to detect in higher plant because they are usually recessive and do not express themselves in the presence of their dominant alleles on the homologous chromosomes, the mutations induced in haploids can be easily detected because they have only a single set of genes and, consequently there is no interference by their dominant alleles.

(*ii*) Haploids provide a source of haploid tissue. Suspension of haploid cells can be obtained from haploid tissue. These haploid cells can be used to carry out new genetic researches on higher plants by applying the techniques used for microorganisms.

(*iii*) Haploids can be easily treated with colchicine to obtain homozygous diploids in a single generation. It is much advantageous to the traditional plant breeding methods because it involves selfing for many generations in many years to obtain homozygous diploids when conventional method of plant breeding is applied.

(B) Ovary Culture :

(*a*) *Technique* LaRue (1942) was probably the first who successfully obtained *in vitro* rooting of the pedicel and a limited growth of ovaries. Nitsch (1951) developed this technique by growing excised ovaries of some plants (e.g. *Cucumis anguria, Nicotiana tabacum, Lycopersicon esculentum, Phaseolus vulgaris*) *in vitro* under aspetic conditions, the excised ovaries from pollinated flowers of *Cucumis anguria* and *Lycopersicon esculentum* viable seeds. But, however, the fruits so developed were comparatively smaller than those naturally developed. Maheshwari and Lal (1958) excised the ovaries from flowers of *Iberris amara* one day after pollination, grew them on a simple midium containing mineral salts and sugar supplemented with B-Vitamins and obtained normal healthy fruits matching the naturally developed ones.

(*i*) *Fruits developments :* The knowledge of fruit physiology is valuable in improving the quality of fruits. The technique of excised ovary culture may allow one to study the effect of chemicals directly on ovaries. Contrary to it, when the entire plant is employed with chemicals to study their effects on ovaries, it remains questionable whether the chemical used act in its original form or its originality is somewhat altered in the plant system before it reaches the ovary.

(*ii*) *Parthenogenetic Haploid Production :* Hess and Wagner ((1974) successfully obtained parthenogenetic haploids of *Mimulus luteus cv. tigrirus grandiflorus* by pollinating their exposed ovaries in *in vitro* ovary culture studies. Similar results of producing parthenogenetic haploids have been obtained in the cultures of unfertilized ovaries of *Hordeum vulgare*, *Nicotiana tabacum* and *Triticum aestivum*.

(C) Nucellus Culture :

(*a*) *Technique :* Nucellar tissue excised from post pollinated carpels, when the adventive embryos (the embryos arising from the maternal sporophytic tissue, outside the embryosac, are called *adventive embryos*), are already in torpedo-shaped stage, and cultured on case in hydrolysate supplemented with White's medium, proliferate and result in the development of callus. Numerous outgrowths, referred to as pseudobulbils, differentiate from the callus. The pseudobulbils develop into embryoids which germinate and finally, give rise to seedlings. It has been found for the first-time by Button and Bormann (1971) that the excised nucellar tissue from unfertilized ovule (i.e. the case where there are no adventive embryos present), when grown *in vitro* under suitable conditions, develop embryoids. When the embryoids are excised and planted individually on a medium supplemented with GA_3 they sometime form plantlets. These plantlets have been successfully transplanted to soil by Button and Borman.

(*b*) *Applications :* The nucellar tissue culture may prove of great significance in horticulture. The seedlings obtained from embryoids are of parental type, as obtained through vegetative propagation by cuttings. However, nucellar seedings of *Citrus* furnish better clones of orchard stock than cuttings as a result of the following reasons :

(*i*) The nucellar seedlings, have a tap root, and, therefore develop a better root system than do the cuttings. The latter have only a small lateral root system.

(*ii*) The nucellar seedlings generally restore the vigour which is lost after repeated propagation by cuttings.

(*iii*) The nucellar embryos prove to be disease free. The nucellar polyembryony has been used as a significant practical approach to develop virus-free clones of polyembryonate *Citrus* varieties.

Protoplast Culture

Protoplasts (Torrey and Landgren, 1977, have defined higher plant protoplast as "cells with their walls stopped off and removed from the proximity of their neighbouring cells) represent the plant cells minus their cell wall (*i.e.*, the naked cells) which are removed by either a mechanical or an enzymatic device. They are unusual because of being limited only by plasma membrane which is fully exposed and is the only barrier between external environment and the interior of the living cell.

Protoplasts represents the finest single cell sytem and offer exciting possibilities in the fields of somatic cell genetics and crop improvements. Since the isolated protoplasts grown in culture often perform better than single whole cells, they may serve as an excellent starting material for cell cloning and development of mutant lines. Besides being useful for somatic hybridization technique, higher plant protoplasts can introduce in them foreign DNA, cell organelles, bacteria, or virus particles through their exposed plasma membrane. These unique properties of protoplasts, combined with the totipotent nature of plant cells, have opened up an entirely new area of fundamental and applied research in experimental biology and somatic cell genetics.

The use of protoplasts for the introduction of foreign germplasm, somatic hybridization, and for studies of hormone action, membrane structure and function, and cell wall synthesis are well documented for model plant systems. These aspects of protoplast applications are described in application section.

Most of the early works on protoplast technology were confined to spongy and palisade mesophyll cells obtained from mature leaves of *Nicotiana* and *Petunia*. However, at present, the protoplasts can be obtained either indirectly from *in vitro* cultured tissues, e.g. suspension cultures or callus tissues, or directly from the intact tissues of the plants such as pollen, fruits, tumors, leaves etc. The mesophyll cells of leaves are most commonly used. This is because it is easy to disrupt leaves into single cells and because leaf cells have a high regeneration potential allowing mature plants to be derived from protoplsats.

(A) Isolation and Purification of Protoplasts : Isolation of protoplasts from higher plants can be traced back to Klerker (1892), involving plasmolysing the cells and subsequent cutting of walls to release protoplasts during deplasmolysis. However, the protoplasts are isolated either by mechanical distruption or preferably by enzymatic dissolution of the cell walls.

(*a*) *Mechanical Disruption :* The mechanical disruption of cell wall to obtain isolated protoplasts involves cutting a plasmolysed tissue with a sharp razor. This enables release of protoplasts through the cut ends of cell walls. In practice, this technique is difficult and the yield of viable protoplasts is meager. One advantage, however, is that the complex and often deleterious effects of wall degrading enzymes on the metabolism of the protoplasts are eliminated. Protoplast isolation by this technique was first achieved almost a century ago, but this technique has limited applications because of small yield of protoplasts.

(*b*) *Enzymatic Dissolution :* The isolation of protoplasts by enzymatic dissolution technique has been in use since 1960 when Cocking demonstrated the possibility of enzymatic isolation of a large number of protoplasts from cells of higher plants. Earlier, there was no satisfactory method of removing cell wall without injuring the cell. But, later it was realized that fungi which grow on wood must be endowed with all the enzymes necesary to digest the plant cell wall. And indeed today most of the enzymes which are employed for protoplast isolation are extracted from fungi, while a few are isolated from intestinal juice of the Roman Snail (*Helix pomatia*) and from bacteria. Following table gives an idea of the fungal source of some common enzymes.

Enzyme		**Source**
Pectinases :		
Macerozyme-R-10	→	*Rhizopus* sp.
Pectinase	→	*Aspergillus niger*
Cellulases		
Cellulase-R-10	→	*Trichoderma viride*
Driselase	→	*Irpex* sp.
Rhyzome HP-150	→	*Myrothesium* sp.
Hemicellulose-H-2125	→	*Rhizopus* sp.

The common enzymes used in the process are pectinases, hemicellulases, cellulases. These enzymes attack the chemical constituents of the primary wall and middle lamella. Pectinases are necessary to breakup cell aggregates into individual cells (i.e., losses the cells) while hemicellulases and cellulases do break down the cell wall. However, by using enzymes one can obtain a high yield (2.5×10^6 protoplasts/g leaf tissue) of uniform protoplasts that can be cleaned of cellular debris.

There have been two approaches to the use of these enzymes, *sequential procedure* and *mixed-enzyme procedure.* Naguta and Takebe (1971) introduced sequential procedure, a two step process, to isolate protoplasts, this procedure involves treatment of sample with pectinase to loosen the cell followed by cellulase to breakdown the walls. Simultaneously, Cocking and Power suggested a single step process, called *mixed-enzymes procedure,* in which they used a mixture of pectinase and cellulase enzymes to the sample. The enzyme mixture macreates the cells and simultaneously destroys their walls. Although both procedures have certain advantages and disadvantages, the mixed enzymes procedure is preferably used at present.

Technique of Enzymatic Dissolution : The basic technique of protoplast isolation (from an excised leaf, for instance) by enzymatic process and its purification consists of following steps :

— Surface sterilization of the leaf sample
— Rinsing in a suitable plasmolyticum
— Peeling off the lower epidermis or slicing the tissue
— Enzyme treatment
— Purification of the isolated protoplasts.

Surface Sterilization of the Leaf Sample : Mature healthy leaves are removed from the plants and they are surface sterilized using suitable sterilizant such as calcium or sodium hypochlorite solution. If the leaves are waxy or have surface appendages a few cubic centimetres of Teepol (1% v/v) should be added as a wetting agent.

Rinsing in a Suitable Plasmolyticum : The surface sterilized leaves are rinsed at least three times to remove all traces of hypochlorite solution. Although the leaves may be rinsed in sterile distilled water

(Sterile DDH_2O), it is preferable to rinse them in a culture medium adjusted to the osmolality and pH of the enzyme solution to be used : generally mannitol (13% w/v) plus agar (2% w/v) medium is used.

Peeling off the Lower Epidermis or Slicing the Tissue : When the leaves are in the final rinsing solution, a sharp forcep is inserted below the junction of the lateral vein and midrib and the epidermis is peeled away towards the margin thus exposing the mesophyll. This facilitates enzyme-penetration. If the leaves can not be peeled immediately, then they should be allowed to wilt before another attempt is made. If the leaves can not be successfully peeled, then the lower epidermis is scored several times with a scalpel to aid the penetration of the enzymes.

Enzyme Treatment : The preplasmolysed excised leaf portions are transferred to petridishes containing enzyme solution, preferably, for mixed-enzyme treatment. The enzyme solution consists of Macerozyme (0.5% w/v) plus Onozulea Cellulase (2.0% w/v) dissolved in mannitol (13% w/v) at pH 5.4. The petridishes are sealed with paraffin and wrapped with aluminium foil. Usually the petridishes are incubated overnight (12-18 hrs) at 25°C. The leaf portions are then teared gently with forcep so that the protoplasts are released.

Purification of the Isolated Protoplasts : The isolated protoplasts are purified by a combination of filtration, centrifugation and warming. First the enzyme solution containing isolated protoplasm is filtered through a nylon mesh (45 μ pore size) to remove undigested tissue, cell clumps and cell wall debris. Second, the filtrate is transferred to a centrifuge tube and is centrifuges for 5 minutes at 75 × g, the protoplasts form a pellet at the base of the tube while the remaining debris suspends in the supernatant.The supernatant is carefully removed with a pasteur pipette. The pellet at the base containing protoplast is resuspended in 10 ml of Murashige Scoog (MS) medium plus mannitol (13.1% w/v) and the process is repeated three times. The resuspension of the protoplast must be carried out carefully in order to avoid injury, for convenience, wide-mouthed pipette (10 cms) should be used. Now the isolated protoplasts are considered purified. Before the purified isolated protoplasts are transferred to suitable culture medium, it is necesary to examine them for density and viability.

After the protoplast have been examined for density and viability, they are ready for culture and are transferred to suitable culture medium.

(B) Culture Technique : The isolated and purified protoplasts are transferred to suitable culture medium after testing their density and viability.

Method of Culture : Protoplasts have been cultured using different methodologies, for instance, on a liquid medium employing handig drop culture technique, in microculture chamber, and in a soft agar matrix. The soft agar matrix technique is one of the better methodologies as it ensures supports for the protoplasts and permits observation of their development. Five cubic centimetres of the purified protoplasts is added to a petridish (100 × 15 mm) and to this dish is then added 5 cm^3 of the complete Murasighe-Scoog (MS) medium plus 13% (w/v) mannitol, this latter solution also contains warm agar 2.0% (w/v) in the sol state at 40°C. Care is taken that the temperature does not exceed 45°C. The two aliquots are mixed by swirling the dish, and the final result is 10 cm^3 of a medium containing 5×10^4 protoplasts/cm^3. The culture of embedded protoplasts is incubated at 25°C in the presence of a low density white light.

Regeneration of Cell Wall : The isolated protoplast when placed on culture medium are spherical due to the absence of rigid cell wall. Once a suitable culture medium is made available the protoplasts starts to regenerate new cell wall quickly. However, a significant role is played by the nucleus in the wall formation process. It is considered that there is a direct relationship between wall formation and cell division, protoplasts which are not able to regenerate a proper wall, fail to undergo normal mitosis. Generally, the wall formation has been observed between the adjacent plasma membranes and the initial events of wall formation can be seen microscopically by using calcofluor White ST (0.1% w/v). This white dye binds to wall material and exhibits fluorescence or irradication with blue light.

Formation of Plants from the Protoplast : Once the protoplast have regenerated their cell wall, they undergo cell division and form a callus. This callus can be subcultured onto plates or flasks containing a freshly prepared medium that lacks mannitol and auxin. The medium lacking mannitol and auxin induces embryogenesis (i.e. the formation of embryoids) on the callus after about 3-4 weeks. The formation of these embryoids have been reported by Kameya and Uchimiya (1972) and Lorz *et al* (1979). The embryoid when provided proper care and attention, can be made to develop into seedlings and eventually result in mature plants.

(C) Applications of Isolated Protoplasts : The protoplasts have considerably attracted biotechnologists attension despite several technical difficulties and are now either being utilized in several areas of academic as well as applied interests or thought to be used in different aspects in future. Some of the most important applications of isolated protoplasts, for instance are as follows :

Plant Regeneration : The first report of plant regeneration from isolated protoplast in *Nicotiana tabacum* was published in 1971by Takeba *et al.* Since then, scientists throughout the globe are engaged in regenerating new plants directly from isolated protoplasts. Successful plant regeneration have been achieved for a wide range of cultivars and breeding lines of potato of US and European origin. In addition, plants have also regenerated from several other species of *Solanum.* The latter include *S. brevidens, S. phureja, S. etuberosu* and *S. penelliti.*

Two reports of plant regeneration from proloplasts of temperate fruit trees are encouraging. First, Ochatt and Cane (1986) have regenerated plants from mesophyll protoplast of wild pear, *Pyrus communis* var *pyraster* C. and second Ochatt *et al* (1987) have successfully regenerated whole plant from mesophyll protoplast of the cold cherry (*Prunus* sp). This marks the first report of plant regeneration from protoplast of a temperate fruit tree of significant commercial value.

Improvement of cereals by protoplast culture technique still waits development of reproducible methods of plant regeneration because, at present, the culture of cereal protoplasts faces extreme difficulties. However, true regeneration, from a cereal protoplast culture has been reported in *Pennisetum americanum.* Protoplast from an embryo-derived suspension culture were able to proceed all the way to an intact plant. But, it is not yet confirmed whether this phenomenon will turn out to be generally for all cereals.

Cell Wall Biosynthesis : The cultured protoplasts rapidly regenerate new cell wall, and thus they offer a novel system for the study of wall biosynthesis and deposition.

Protoplasts in Plant Physiology : When growth promoters like indole acetic acid (IAA) are applied to plants, they act directly on plasma membrane of the cell and increase the permeability of the membrane to water thus enabling the cell to elongate. This phenomenon can be established using protoplasts *in vitro* when IAA is applied to the plasmolyticum containing protoplasts, the latter expands rapidly and finally burst due to too much vacuolation. Further, it can be verified by applying antiauxins, that suppress this bursting, indicating that the site of action of IAA is the plasmamembrane of the plant cell. Similarly, the action-site of 'Paraquat' can also be established. This herbicide disrupts plasmamembrane and enables protoplast bursting.

Introduction of "Foreign " Material : The protoplasts, because of being wallless, show high pinocytic activity and can ingest biologically active 'foreign' materials such as macromolecules like ferritin and polystyrene latex particles, nuclei, chloroplasts, mitochondria, DNA, plasmids, bacteria, viruses etc. in their cytoplasm by a process similar to endocytosis as described for certain animal cells and protozoans. Carlson claimed to have achieved uptake of chloroplasts by protoplast, uptake of isolated nuclei of *Petunia* by mesophyll protoplasts of *Petuma,* tobacco and maize was reported by Potrykus and Hoffmann (1973) Davey and Cocking (1972) and Davey (1977) demonstrated that isolated mesophyll protoplasts of leguminous plants could take up the cells of *Rhizobium.*

However, the ingestion of "foreign" materials results in modified cells after cell wall regeneration. These procedures may be more advantageous to a plant breeder in getting more efficient crop varieties in near future.

Plant Virus Interrelationships : The plant virus interrelationships in the part were not clearly known due to lack of suitable experimental systems. This problem has come to an end as a result of the innovation of protoplast isolation and its culture. Protoplasts can directly be inoculated with pathogenic virus and their effects can be studied extensively with relative care.

Use of Protoplast-Populations as Single Cellular Systems : One of the exciting and potential properties of protoplasts that each isolated protoplast is entirely separated from another and thus corresponds to microorganisms. In this way, a population of protoplasts provides the best possible approach to a single isolated cell system and can be used to study the selection of mutant cell lines, cloning of cell populations, and the synchronous infection of protoplasts by virus.

Protoplast and Biochemical Studies : Isolated plant protoplasts have opened vistas for certain biochemical studies.

QUESTIONS FROM PREVIOUS YEARS' PAPERS

1. Explain the following:
   (*a*) Cybrids
   (*b*) Oncogenesis
   (*c*) Totipotency of plants cells
   (*d*) Adventitive embryogenesis
2. Discuss the molecular basis of host-parasite interaction.
3. Write a short account of host specific toxins.
4. Distinguish between free central placentation and parietal placentation.
5. Describe the following:
   (*a*) Kranz Syndrome (*b*) Paraphyses
   (*c*) Trabeculae (*d*) Totipotency
   (*e*) Somatic hybrids
6. Give an account of sporocarp in *Marsilea* and add a note on leaf modification into sporocarp.
7. Discuss about heterospory and seed habit citing suitable examples.
8. Write a note on Cleavage polyembryony.
9. Answer the following:
   (*a*) Polyembroyony.
   (*b*) What is the role of plasmids in drugs resistance?
   (*c*) Kranz anatomy
   (*d*) Role of synergids in double fertilization.
   (*e*) Preservation of plant specimens.
   (*f*) Application of protoplast culture.
10. Explain Tunica-corpus theory relating to structural development and differentiation of shoot apex.
11. Write short notes on the following:
    (*a*) F-factor
    (*b*) Embryo development in *Paeonia.*
    (*c*) Energy plantations.
    (*d*) Cycadeoidean 'flower'
    (*e*) Totipotency
12. Distinguish between:
    (*a*) Gametophytic and sporophytic apomixis.
    (*b*) Somatic hybrids and cybrids
    (*c*) Diacytic type and Anisocytic type of stomata
    (*d*) Nutmeg and mace
13. Explain principles of cell, tissue, organ and protoplast cultures. Examine the significance of each for future of mankind.
14. Write short note on concept of totipotency in plants.
15. What is morphogenesis? Why do we need cell culture? Give an account of cell culture and its importance.

IFS–BOTANY PAPER-II

CHAPTER-1

Cell Biology

CELL

Cell is a unit of biological activity made of an organised mass of protoplasm surrounded by a protective and selectively permeable covering.

Living beings or organisms are made of one or more cells. Cell is a basic unit of structure and function of organisms. It was discovered by Robert Hooke (1665). He wrote a book 'Micrographia' and coined the term *cell*. Leeuwenhoek (1672) was the first to see *free cells*. He observed bacteria, protozoa, red blood cells, sperms etc. under his microscope. In 1809, Lamarck came to the conclusion that all living beings are formed of cells. Dutrochet (1824) believed in individuality of cells. Living substances was first observed by Corti (1772) and was named *sarcode* by Dujardin (1836). Robert Brown (1831) discovered nucleus while Von Mohl (1838, 1846) & Purkinje (1839) named the jelly-like living substance or sarcode of the cell as *protoplasm*.

Cell Theory : In 1838, Schleiden found that all plant cells have essentially similar structure. Schwann (1838) working independently observed that animal cells do not have cell wall but are otherwise similar amongst themselves. He put forward cell hypothesis bodies of animals and plants are made up of cells and their products. Schleiden and Schwann (1839) compared their findings and formulated *cell theory* which states that :

(*i*) Living beings are made of one or more cells
(*ii*) A cell is a mass of protoplasm having a nucleus.
(*iii*) Cells are similar in basic structure and metabolism.
(*iv*) The functions of an organism are due to activities and interactions of its cells.

However, there are several **short comings** in Cell Theory :

(*a*) Viruses do not have cellular structure
(*b*) Monerans and protistans are not divisible into cells. They are *acellular.*
(*c*) Certain organisms are multinucleate.
(*d*) A typical nucleus is absent in procaryotes
(*e*) Connective tissues have a lot of non-living material as compared to living matter.
(*f*) Certain cells lose their nuclei in the mature state, e.g. RBC, sieve tube elements.

Cell theory was first modified in the light of Virchow's findings (1855, 1858) that cells develop from pre-existing cell-*Omnis cellula-e-cellula.* It is known as law of other modifications were carried out in the cell theory. The modern cell theory is called 'cell principle'.

Protoplasm Theory : It was proposed by Max Schultze (1861) which states that living matter of an organism in protoplasm and the cell is simply an accumulation of protoplasm limited by an outer membrane and containing a nucleus.

Organismal Theory : Sachs (1874) proposed that the whole organism functions as a single entity which is made of a continuous mass of protoplasm incompletely divided into cells.

Cellular Autonomy and Multicellularity : Cells are autonomous or self contained units because

(*i*) They obtain or manufacture food
(*ii*) All cells require energy for overcoming entropy, performing body activities and biosynthesis. For this they oxidise food materials in respiration.
(*iii*) Cells convert nonliving materials into components of living protoplasm.
(*iv*) Worn out parts are replaced by news ones.
(*v*) There is exchange of gases.
(*vi*) Cells discard waste materials.
(*vii*) They are able to regulate their activities through flow of energy and information.
(*viii*) Cells maintain their own internal physico-chemical environment

(ix) They may divide and form daughter cells.

(x) There is a definite life span. Cells of unicellular organisms lead independent existence with no dependent on others for any function, material or information. They depend upon their own intrinsic information. Irritability is, of course present. Cells of multicellular organisms possess autonomy but show various interactions and specialities.

Multicellularity is more advantageous then unicellularity because it

(i) Increases survival
(ii) Induces specialisation
(iii) Ensure uninterrupted activity
(iv) Provides for division of labour
(v) Outer cells became specialised to protect internal cells.
(vi) Internal cells develop their own environment
(vii) Keeps the cells small except where they take part in conduction and support.
(viii) Death of a few cells or reproduction does not kill the organisms. Rather some dead cells are functionally important, e.g. tracheary elements.
(ix) Differentiated cells may take over the function of division through the process of *dedifferentiation* e.g. plant cells.
(x) In some cases differentiation leads to loss of some basic activities like :
  (a) RBCs do not have aerobic respiration, DNA replication and RNA synthesis since nucleus is lost towards maturity.
  (b) Sieve tube cells become enucleate
  (c) Nerve cells posses nuclei but are unable to differentiate.
  (d) Liver and muscle cells do not divide normally but retain the ability to do so.

Cellular Totipotency and Survival : Somatic nucleated cells are totipotent or able to produce a complete organism. This is especially so in case of plant cells. It was first suggested by Haberlandt (1902) and proved by Steward *et al* in 1957, through tissue or cell culture experiments. For its survival and proper functioning, a cell always requires :

(i) *Flow of Energy* for overcoming entropy (tendency for disorderliness) and performing various life activities.

(ii) *Flow of Information* which is of two types, *intrinsic* or genetic and *extrinsic* through nerves and hormones. Intrinsic or genetic information is contained in DNA. Specific triggers activate DNA segments to transcribe m RNAs which then help synthesise specific polypeptides/proteins/enzymes, etc. Stimulated nerves secrete chemicals to activate certain cells. Hormones are recognised by either membrane receptors or intracellular receptors. The complexes allow particular activities.

Surface Volume Ratio : Metabolically active cells are small since small cells have higher nucleo-cytoplasmic ratio for better control and higher surface-volume ratio for quicker exchange of materials. Larger cells can be efficient only if they are elongated, branched or possess membrane extensions like microvilli. Large sized animals do not possess large sized cells but more numerous small cells.

Size & Shape of Cells : The diameter of most of the cells ranges from 0.5 μ to 20 μ (1 μ = 0.001 mm). The largest known cell is the egg of an Ostrich which can be as long as 170 mm. The smallest cell is perhaps yet to be discovered. The shape also is varied and depends upon the environmental conditions; surroundings, function and need of the organism. Simple bacteria can be rod shaped, spiral, oval, round etc. The shapes of desmids and diatoms are varied. Amoeba keeps on changing its shape. The body of unicellular marine alga, *Acetabularia* is differentiated into a rhizoid like base, a long and slender stalk and an umbrella like cap. The RBCs of human beings are round, whereas, the muscle cells are long and with pointed ends. Animals cells are capable of changing their shapes; but the shape of plant cell is fixed due to the presence of cellulose cell-wall.

Cell Type	*Cell Size*
Smallest Virus (no cellular structure)	7.0×10^{-7} μm^3
Smallest Bacterium	2.0×10^{-2} μm^3
Human Sperm	1.7×10^{1} μm^3

Cell Type	Cell Size
Hen Egg (60 × 45 mm)	5.0×10^{13} μm^3
Mycoplasma	1.0×10^{-3} μm^3
Largest Bacterium	7.0×10^{0} μm^3
Human Egg	(diameter 100 μm)
Ostrich Egg	(170 × 150 mm)
RBC	7 μ
E. coli	1.5 × 0.7 μ
Influenza Virus	100 μm
TMV	300 × 15 μm
T_3 Bacteriophage	45 mμ

Nerve cells are the longest cells of the human body, reaching 90 cm. Certain plant fibres are similarly very long, e.g. Jute (30-90 cm); Ramie (55 cm), Hemp (1m).

Prokaryotic and Eukaryotic Cells : Basically cells are of two types, procaryotic and eucaryotic.

A **procaryotic** cell has one envelope system with no membrane lined internal organelles, except thylakoids, if present. A nucleus is absent, instead, a nucleoid made of naked and folded DNA lies freely in cytoplasm. Internal compartments are absent. Respiratory enzymes are located on the cell membrane. Cytoplasm does not show streaming. Sap vacuoles are absent. Gas vacuoles may occur-Cell wall, if present, contains peptidoglycan or mucopeptide. Flagella, if present are single stranded and made of flagellin.

An **eucaryotic** cell has internal compartments and double envelope system, that is, besides cell membrane, the cell organelles are also covered by membranes. Mitosis and meiosis occurs in the life cycle. Cytoplasm show streaming, sap vacuoles occur. Flagella if present are double-stranded and made of tubulin.

Comparison of Cell Organisation in Prokaryotic and Eukaryotic cells

Cellular Component	Prokaryotic Cells	Eukaryotic cells
1. Nuclear Envelope	Absent	Present
2. DNA	naked	combined with proteins
3. Chromosome	Single	Multiple
4. Division	amitosis	mitosis or meiosis
5. Ribosomes	70 s (50 s + 30 s)	80 s (60 s + 40 s)
6. Endomembranes	Absent	Present
7. Mitochondria	Absent, Respiratory & photosynthetic enzymes in the plasma membrane	Present
8. Chloroplast	Absent	Present in plant cells
9. Cell wall	non-cellulosic	Cellulosic, only in plants.
10. Exo & Endocytosis	Absent	Present
11. Locomotion	Single fibril flagellum	Cilia and flagella
12. Examples	Bacteria, blue green algae mycoplasma (PPLO)	Protozoa, other algae, metaphyta & metazoa.

General Organization of the Eukaryotic Cell

Main Component or components	Subcomponent or subcomponents	Main Function
1. Cell Membrane	Cell wall Cell coat	Protection cell-cell interaction
	Plasma membrane	permeability, endocytosis, exocytosis
2. Nucleus	Chromatin & chromosomes	Genetic information system
	Nucleolus	Synthesis of Nucleoplasm, Ribosomes
3. Cytoplasm matrix, cytosol, cytoskeleton	Soluble Enzymes	Glycolysis,
	Microfilaments	Cell motility,
	Microtubules	Cell shape & Motility,
	Ribosomes	Protein Synthesis.

Main Component or components	*Subcomponent or subcomponents*	*Main Function*
4. Endomembrane System	Nuclear Envelope	Nuclear permeability,
	Endoplasmic reticulum, rough & smooth	Synthesis and transport of materials, Secretion
	Golgi complex	Secretion
5. Membrane organelles	Mitochondria	Cell respiration
	Chloroplast	Photosynthesis
	Lysosomes	Digestion
	Peroxisomes	Peroxidation
6. Microtubular organelles	centroioles & spindle	Cell division
	basal bodies, cilia and flagella	Cell motility

Plant and Animal Cells : Both plant and animals posses eucaryotic cells. A plant cell is characterised by a cell wall, central vacuole, plastids and anastral spindle (centrioles are generally absent). Golgi apparatus consists of separate units called dictyosomes. Lysosomes are rare. Glyoxysomes and crystals may occur.

Animal cells are bathed by tissue fluid. They are covered by cell membranes only. Vacuoles are small. Plastids are absent. Spindle is amphiastral (centrioles present). Due to absence of wall, animal cells will burst if placed in hypotonic solution, Glyoxysomes and crystal are absent. Lysosomes are present.

A typical plant cell consists of cell wall and protoplast. Cell wall is absent in animal cells. Protoplast (Hanstein, 1880) is made of a plasmalemma, cytoplasm, nucleus and vacuoles.

Cell-wall : It is the outer rigid protective covering of plant cells and some procaryotes. Cell wall has a matrix of hemicellulose, pectin, glycoprotein and water in which are embedded microfibrils. Microfibrils are made up of cellulose in plant cells, chitin or fungus cellulose in fungi and peptidoglycan (mucopeptide) in bacteria. Plant cell wall may have lignin for strength (e.g. woody tissue), silica for stiffness and protection (e.g. epidermal cells), *cutin* for preventing loss of water (e.g. epidermal cells), suberin for impermeability (e.g. cork cells, endodermal cells), etc.

The cell wall gives a definite shape and provides protection to the protoplasm. It is nonliving in nature and is permeable. Adjacent cells in the plant body remain interconnected by plasmodesmata. A cell wall may have upto three parts-middle lamella, primary wall, secondary wall.

(*i*) *Middle lamella :* It is the outermost region which functions as a cementing layer between two cells. It is absent on the outer free surface. It ruptures to create intercellular spaces. It is formed of calcium and magnesium pectate. Pectic acid is long polygalacturonic acid compound in which α-D-galacturonic acid units are joined together by glycosidic linkages in (1 : 4). It is hydrophilic in nature.

(*ii*) *Primary wall :* It is thin (0.1 - 3.0 μm), elastic, first wall layer. It contains microfibrils oriented variously, commonly forming a loose network. Cellulose content (5% dry weight basis), hemicellulose (50% dry weight basis), lipid content (5-10% dry basis) are high. An association of about 100 cellulose chains is termed as a micelle, 20 micelles constitutes a microfibril while an aggregation of 250 microfibrils is called fibril. Lignin, hemicellulose, some pectic substances and proteins present altogether form **amorphous matrix**.

(*iii*) *Secondary wall :* It is laid inner to primary wall. It is less hydrated i.e. less hydrophilic in nature (30-40%) as compared to primary wall. Cellulose content is high with long closely arranged straight and parallel microfibrils. Hemicellulose content is 25%. Protein is very little while lipid is nearly absent. Lignin deposit is quite common. Secondary wall is often made of three layers—S_1, S_2, & S_3. In each layers, microfibrils lie straight, parallel to one another but at an angle to longitudinal axis. Orientation is different in different layers. It is more pronounced in dead cells such as tracheids and sclerenchyma.

In gymnosperms tension wood, the innermost

layer contains xylan and is called 'tertiary wall'. Filler substance of wall matrix is *pectin*. It has methylated and polymerised galacturans, glucouronic acid and neutral sugars.

Hemicellulose is made of polymerised arabino-galactans, xylans, mannans, etc. It binds microfibrils with matrix.

Lignin is formed from coniferyl and coumaryl alcohols and aldehydes through dehydrogenation and polymerisation. Lignin reduces hydration and increases hardness of wall.

Cell wall possesses minute cytoplasmic bridges between adjacent cells. They are called 'plasmodesmata' (Strassburger, 1901). Plasmodesmata produce a continuum of living material called *symplasm* cell walls and intercellular spaces constitute a nonliving component of plant body known as *apoplasm.* Certain thick cell walls possess unthickened areas called *pits*.

In some animal cells, a *cell coat* is present outside the cell membrane, made up of 'glycocalyx' alongwith deposition of silica & calcium salts.

Comparison of Primary and Secondary wall

Primary wall	*Secondary wall*
1. Extensible layer	Non-extensible layer
2. Dispersed texture of microfibril	Parallel texture of microfibrils (to long axis)
3. Smallest cellulosic unit micelle or microfibril	Smallest cellulose unit microfibril or fibril
4. Cellulose 5.2%	Cellulose 50-94%
5. Lipid contents 5-10%	Normally no lipid
6. Protein 5%	Normally very little
7. Hemicellulose 50%	Hemicellulose 25%

Cell Membranes : (Biomembranes, e.g. Plasmalemma) Cell membranes or biomembranes are quasifluid film like partitions of about 75 A° thickness. They are selectively permeable. Plasmalemma or plasma membrane lies on the outside of protoplast and separates it from external environment. *Tonoplast* occurs around vaculoles. Most of the eucaryotic cell organells have their own membrane coverings. Under electron microscope, a cell membrane appears *trilaminar* or *tripartite* with a middle electron transport layer and electrons dense layer on either side. Chemically, it has proteins (60-70%), lipids (20-40%) and carbohydrates (1-5%). Proteins are both structural and enzymatic. Lipids are generally phospholipids with polar hydrophilic heads and nonpolar hydrophilic tails (amphipathic or amphiatic).

Overton (1900) : He was the first scientist to propose that cell membranes are made of lipids.

Deniell & Davson Model (1935) : States that a double phospholipid layer is surrounded on either side by a layer of hydrated globular proteins or P-L-L-P. The hydrophobic or nonpolar tails of the two lipid layers are towards the centre.

Robertson Model (1959) : States that a lipid bilayer is surrounded on either side by extended or β-protein with a difference in their type for outer and inner side. Robertson also gave UNIT MEMBRANE CONCEPT, which proposed that all biomembranes have a trilaminar structure with an electron transparent lipid bilayer (35 A°) lying sandwitched between electrons dense protein layers (20 A° each).

Both the above given models are lamellar models.

Fluid Mosaic Model : (Singer & Nicolson, 1972). Cell membranes are quasifluid with viscous lipid bilayer having proteins at places (mosaic) both on the surface and inside. Singer & Nicolson have described cell membranes as protein icebergs in sea of lipids. External proteins are called EXTRINSIC or PERIPHERAL (30% of total) while internal proteins are named INTRINSIC or INTEGRAL (70% of total). Membrane proteins may function as enzymes, permeases, carriers, receptors etc. Proteins extending from outside to inside are called 'tunnel proteins' or 'transmembrane proteins'. They function as channels. At places the external proteins and lipid molecules bear oligosaccharides forming glycoproteins and glycolipids for recognition; attachment and antigenic properties. They make the cell membrane asymmetric.

Lipid nature of the cell membrane can be destroyed with benzene. Benzene treated beet roots leak out anthocyanin pigment while the pigment is retained in untreated roots. Fluidity of cell membranes can be tested by mixing two types of animal cells treated with green and red fluorescent dyes in the presence of polyethylene glycol. They will initially show half green and half red surface. The cells kept at

0°C do not show further mixing while the lot kept at 37°C exhibits complete mixing.

According to Selby (1959) plasma membrane often exhibits certain specialised structures which are as follows :

(i) *Microvilli.* The plasma membrane at its surface, has certain narrow elongated projections called *microvilli.* The function of microvilli is to increase its absorptive surface.

(ii) *Plasmodesmata :* There are fine strands of cytoplasm through which the adjacent cells remain inter-connected in the plant body. The plasmodesmata were first of all observed by Tangel (1879) and finally by Strasburger (1882).

(iii) *Caveolae :* These are the hair like invaginations of plasma membrane. It was first reported by Yamada (1955). The function of caveolae is to increase the absorptive area of the cell.

(iv) *Desmosomes :* In certain cells, the plasma membrane of adjacent cells become thicker in certain regions and from these thickened areas arises many fine filaments known as 'tonofibrils'. Such thickened areas of the plasma membrane are called **desmosomes.** The intercellular space between desmosomes contain a coating material which provides cellular adhesion to the cell.

Plasmalemma : It is the outer membrane covering of the protoplast which was called cell membrane by Nageli and Crames (1855). It was given the present name by Plowe (1931). Plasmalemma is both protective and selectively permeable. Antigenic, recognition, attaching and receptor sites occur over it. The membrane may show *microvilli* (0.6 - 0.8 μm long and 0.1 μm diameter). Plasma infoldings occur in bacteria and fungi. They are called *mesosomes* in bacteria (Fitz. Jammes, 1960) and *lomasomes* is fungi (Moore and McLean).

In animals the plasmalemmae of adjacent cells may show tight junctions, desmosomes, gap junction, interdigitations or intercellular bridges.

(i) *Desmosomes* (Macular Adherantes; singular Macula Adherans). Adjacent membranes are thickened with disc shaped adhesive material in between and *tonofibrils* radiating out from the adhesive regions, e.g., epithelia subjected to disruption. In *hemidesmosome*, the thickening is present on one membrane. *septate desmosomes* possesses parallel septa in between the two membrances.

(ii) *Tight Junction* (Zonulae Occludentes). Plasmalemmae of two cells fused to form impermeable or occluding junctions e.g. epithelial cells of capillaries and brain cells.

(iii) *Terminal Bars* (Zonulae Adherantes). Both plasmalemma and adjacent cytoplasm are thickened.

(iv) *Gap Junctions.* They have intercellular gaps and allow movement of substances in betweeen two cells. Hence, communicating junctions. Very common.

(v) *Interdigitations :* They are intercellular bridges formed by membrane infoldings and contacts for rapid conduction of stimuli.

Cytoplasm : (Strasburger, 1882). It is the bulk of protoplasm excluding nucleus. Cytoplasm is differentiated into cytoplasmic matrix, cell organelles and cell inclusions. Cytoplasmic matrix, or cytosol is jelly-like semifluid that exist in both sol and gel states. Cytoplasmic matrix is often differentiated into outer gel part called 'ectoplast' (plasmagel) and inner sol part called 'endoplast' (plasmasol). Endoplast is usually in perpetual motion called **cyclosis,** cytoplasmic or protoplsamic streaming (Amici, 1818). In **rotation** type of cyclosis, cytoplasmic matrix continuously flows in one direction. (e.g. young cells of *Hydrilla* leaf). In *Circulation* type of cyclosis, matrix flow in different directions in the same cell (e.g. cell of staminal hair of Tradescantia = Rhoea).

Endoplasmic Reticulum (ER) : (Ergastoplasm of Garnier, 1897). E.R or EPR was discovered by Porter *et al* (1945). It was given the present name by Porter (1953). According to Dallmer (1966) E.R. originats from the plasma membrane by invagination. According to De Roberties (1970), ER originates from the nuclear envelope. E.R. is a system of membrane lined channels found in all eucaryotic cells except ova, embryonic cells and mature erythrocytes. It constitutes more than 50% of total cell membranes. In muscle cells it is called SARCOPLASMIC RETICULUM. *Mycloid bodies* (granulls at base of retinal pigment cells) and *Nissl granules* are believed to be formed from E.R. It is less developed in meristematic cells. It is made of a few tubules in adipose tissue, few vesicles in spermatocytes but is best developed in cells of liver, pancreas and fibroblast. Endoplasmic reticulum has three parts

(*i*) Cisternae (parallel interconnected flattened sacs)

(*ii*) Tubules (often branched network)

(*iii*) Vesicles (round or oval)

Membranes of E.R. may bear ribosomes when E.R. is called granular/rough endoplasmic reticulum or R.E.R. Attachment between ribosome and endoplasmic reticulum is through glycoprotein called ribophorin. The union is actually between 60 s ribosome subunit and E.R. by means of two types of glycoproteins : ribophorin I (mol. wt.-65000) and ribophorin II (mol. wt. 64000). R.E.R. often contains minute pores below ribosomes to pass synthesied polypetide into its lumen for transport. E.R. without attached ribosomes is called agranular/smooth endoplasmic reticulum or S.E.R. It takes part in synthesis of glycogen, fats and sterols, and detoxification. S.E.R., therefore, occurs in adipose cells, muscle cells, liver cells, steroid synthesising cells, etc. R.E.R. is abundant in cells engaged in production and excretion of protein, e.g. plasma cells, goblet cells, pancreatic cells, certain liver cells. Broken pieces of endoplasmic reticulum appear as microsomes (Claude, 1941). Transitional E.R. is R.E.R. without ribosomes. Glycosylation of newly synthesized proteins occurs within the cisternae through activity of glycosyl transferase located in the E.R. membrane.

Function of ER :

(*i*) The endoplasmic reticulum divides the cell into separate compartments, making it possible for the cells different chemical products and activities to be segregated from each other.

(*ii*) Many of the enzymes that carry out there activity from a part of the lipoprotien structure of the membrane forming the endoplasmic reticulum.

(*iii*) According to Sjostrand (1964), the tubules and vesicles have surfaces which may play role in enzymic reactions.

(*iv*) In addition to site of protein synthesis, it is also thought to function as a transport and storage system.

(*v*) E.R. also plays important role in lipid metabolism and glycogen synthesis.

Ribosomes (Protein Factories, Palade Granules) : They are submicroscopic polypeptide manufacturing naked nucleoprotein organelles which were discovered by Robinson and Brown (1953) in plant cells and palade (1955) in animal cells. Palade (1955) also gave them the present name, ribosomes. Ribosomes are of two types, cytoplasmic & organelle. **Organelle ribosomes** are 70 s (Svedberg or sedimentation units). They occur inside mitochondria and plastids. Organelle ribosomes do not occur in procaryotes. Instead, their cytoplasmic ribosomes are 70 s. **Cytoplasmic ribosomes** of eucaryotes are 80 s. They may occur freely or attached to E.R. Ribosomes are subspherical in outline with a diameter of 150-250 A° and are not bounded by any membrane. Each ribosome has two parts, smaller avoid or cap like and larger dome-shaped. The smaller subunit has a platform, cleft, head and base. The larger subunit has a protuberance, a ridge and a stalk. On the basis of sedimentation coefficient, the larger and smaller subunits are respectively 60 s and 40 s (50 s & 30 s in 70 s ribosomes). The larger subunit has 28 s, 5.8 s and 5 s r RNA (23 s and 5 s in 70 s ribosomes). While the smaller subunit has 18 s r RNA (16 s r RNA is 70 s ribosome's smaller unit). Besides r RNA, ribosomes has a number of protein molecules like core and split proteins, structural and enzymatic proteins. As compared to r RNA, protein content is higher in 80 s ribosomes (40 : 60) while reverse is true is 70 s ribosomes (60 : 40). A groove is present in between the two ribosomes subunits for m RNA. The larger subunit also has a channel for the passage of synthesized polypeptide. Magnesium ion is essential for binding the ribosome subunits. Smaller subunit has peptidyl transferase, binding site for t RNA and A-site. P-site is jointly formed by the two subunits. Ribosomes may occurs in helical or rosette group linked by m RNA. Such a group is called *polyribo-*

some (Rich, 1963) or *polysome*. It is useful in producing a number of copies of the same polypeptide. The ribosomes remain attached with the membrane of endoplasmic reticulum by 60 s subunits. The 40 s subunit occurs on the larger subunit and forms cap-like structure. Peterman (1964) reported several kinds of RNA from ribosomes on the basis of analysis of purine and pyrimidine bases.

Ribosomes are not attached to membranes in prokaryotes, chloroplasts and mitrochondria but are commonly membrane bound is eukaryotic cells (specially actively secreting ones), forming rough endoplasmic reticulum, as well as being attached to outer surface of outer nuclear membrane. The origin of r RNA is the nucleolus.

Golgi Apparatus (Golgi Complex) : It is complex organelle made of membrane lined stack of cisternae, network of tubules, vesicles and vacuoles which was first seen by George (1867) but studied by Camillo Golgi in 1898 in nerve cells of Barn Wol and cat through metallic impregnation technique (osmium chloride + silver salts). Due to metallic impregnation artefacts, the apparatus was once called internal reticular apparatus/canalicular system/*apparato reticolare*. The concept changed after observation of the apparatus under electron microscope by Dalton and Felix (1954). Golgi apparatus is presented in all eucaryotic cells except RBC and sieve tube elements. It is also absent in procaryotes and sperm cells of seedless embroyphytes. A unit of Golgi apparatus is called *Golgisome*. In palnt cells, Golgi apparatus consists of a number of isolated units called *dictyosomes* while in animal cells it occurs as single compact or loose complex. The number of Golgi bodies/dictyosomes in generally 9-10 in a plant cell but is very high in cells engaged in secretory activity (e.g. root cap cells) and rapid division. Golgi apparatus has a central stack of 3-10 curved but parallel membrane-lined narrow sacs called *cisternae*, cisternae are interconnected. Unicisternal dictyosomes occur in fungi. Golgi apparatus has two faces, maturing and forming (Mollenhauer and Whaley, 1963). The convex *forming face* (cis-face) receives materials from endoplasmic reticulum (GER = Golgi associated E.R.) and cytosol while concave *maturing face* (trans-face, normally towards plasma membrane) gives out large Golgian vacuoles and small vesicles having transformed materials. Vesicles develop from the tubules as well. They are of two types, smooth and coated. Golgi apparatus produces materials for secretion, takes parts in transformation of membranes, formation of number of products like glycoproteins (e.g. mucin from goblet cells), complex hetero-polysaccharides (e.g. mucilage from root cap cells), hormones, melanin, matrix of connective tissue, middle lamella, acrosome and lysosome.

Animal cells usualy contain one. In granular cells, the golgi bodies are usually situated close to the nucleus and has according to Grasse (1957), definite polarity. There are also known as *Lyphochondria*. The membrane of G.C. or apparatus are of lipoproteins and are supposed to be originated from the membranes of endoplasmic reticulums. In plant cells, scales, both organic and inorganic, are formed in the G.C. before being transported to the periphery. In diatoms, the golgi body gives rise to translucent vesicles which collect beneath the plasmalemma where they fuse to form a *silicalemma* in which the siliceous cell wall forms. Two types of vesicles are budded from the golgi body :

Coated vesicles (about-50 nm diameter) and the larger **secretory vesicles** (about 100 nm diameter), which tend to leave from the trans-surfaces. It has a system of outer flattened cisternae which appear as roughly parallel membranes enclosing a space 60-90 A° with a distance of about 200 A° between them. Cisternae and vesciles are associated with the inner cisternae particularly in glandular cells. It is also considered as the source of primary lysosomes membrane bounded particles containing hydrolytic enzymes and also functions as packing centre of the cell.

Lysosomes (Suicide bags, Disposal Units) : These are small vesicles (0.2 - 0.8 μm) containing hydrolysing enzymes and surrounded by single membrane. They were discovered by Christian de Duve in 1955 but were named and observed under electron microscopes by Novikoff (1956). They are formed by golgi apparatus and contain some 40 types of *acid hydrolases* for digestion of various materials (e.g. nucleases, proteases, phosphatases, sulphatases). Therefore, they can hydrolyse almost all types of organic substances except cellulose. Lysosomes are most abundant in phagocytic cells (WBC) and osteoclasts. Lysosomes show polymorphism: primary lysosomes, secondary lysosomes (digestive vacuoles = heterophagosomes, primary lysosomes + phagosome); residual (lysosomes having undigested materials, undergo ephagy) and *autophagic* vacuoles (performing autophagy or autolysis of degenerate and useless parts). In many plant cells the function of lysosome is performed by spherosomes and vacuoles. Lysosome membrane is strengthened by cortisome, cortisol, antihistamise, heparin, chloroquine and a type of cholesterol. It becomes fragile in the absence of oxygen or presence of excess vitamin A, vitamin E, progesterone, testosterone, bile salts and high energy radiations. Failure of exocytosis or absence of some hydrolytic enzymes causes accumulation of residual bodies in the cells producing various diseases like hapatitis, polynephritis, Hurler's disease (deformed bones due to accumulation of mucopoly saccharide glucosaminoglycan as its hydrolytic enzyme is absent). Fruit rotting can be however, checked by slowing down the action of rotting enzyme *polygalactouronase*.

Mitochondria (Power Houses) : Mitochondria were disccovered by Kolliker (1880) in striated muscles of insects and given the present name by Benda (1897). Mitochondria were called *sacromeres* by Kolliker (1880), *flia* by Flemming (1882) and *bioblasts* by Altman (1890). Other names are *chondriosomes, chondriomites* and *plastochondria. Chondriome* includes all the mitochondria of a cell. They can be stained by Janus Green. Mitochondria are absent from anaerobic cells and RBCs. A single mitochondrion occurs in *Microsterias, Trypanosoma* and *chlorella*. The number is 5,00,000 per cell in flight muscles. They are 1-10 μm long and 0.5 - 1.0 μm broad with spherical to cylindrical shape. Each mitochondrion is covered by a double membrane envelope. Intermembrane shape of outer chamber is present in between the two membranes. Innner memberane is thrown into various types of folds called *cristae* (cristae mitochondriale, Palade, 1952). The inner membrane bears oxysomes (10^4-10^5) and Electron Transport Chains (flavoprotein, *cyt.b, cyt. c, cyt. a, cyt. a_3). Oxysomes take part in ATP synthesis (oxidative phosphorylation). They are, therefore, functional units of mitochondria. Each oxysome (= elementary particle = EP = $F_0 - F_1$ or Fernandes Moran particle, Fernandes-Moran, 1961) has a flat base of F_0 subunit, a stalk and a head of F_1 subunit.

The inner chamber or matrix of a mitochondria contains DNA (Nass and Afzelius, 1965), RNA, ribosomes (70 s), lipids, granules and enzymes of Kreb's cycle. DNA can be circular and linear. It is naked or without association with histones. Mitochondria are semi-autonomous. They multiply by division (Luck & Rich, 1964). As mitochondria are centres of Kreb's cycle or respiration, they liberate the maximum amount of energy. They are, therefore, called 'power houses' of the cell (Seeckevitz). In prokaryotes, where mitochondria are absent, the site for oxidative phosphorylation and electron transport including dehydrogenases is plasma membrane.

Ordinarily mitochondria are evenly distiributed in the cytoplasm. In columnar or prismatic cells, mitochondria are oriented parallel to the long axis of the cell. Mitochondria may move freely in some cells, carrying ATP wherever required, or may be localized in a particular region. Movement is less in animals than in plants. Often movements are rhythmical.

In one respect the mitochondrion is a part of the eucaryotic cell, in another, it is an independent organism. Mitochondrial genetic code differs from both 'nuclear' and bacterial codes in that the triplet UGA codes for tryptophan and is not a stop codon. Other codons may also have different meanings; even between mitochondria from different organisms Mitochondria of most C_3 plants of temperate latitudes do not engage in aerobic respiration during daylight, this being restricted to the hours of darkness. Instead these plants engage in the seemingly wasteful process of photorespiration,which is greatly reduced or absent is C_4 plants of tropical region.

Plastids : Plastids (Haeckel, 1866) are semiautonomous cell organelles which are surrounded by double membrane envelope, take part in storage and synthesis of organic compounds which occur in plants and some protistans. Plastids develop from colourless precussors called 'proplastids'. Plastids are

* cyt = cytochrome).

of three main types (Schimper, 1883). Leucoplasts, chromoplasts, chloroplasts.

(*i*) *Leucoplasts :* They are colourless plastids of various shapes. These are found in storage organs where light is not available, e.g. underground stem and roots. They are found in parenchymatous cells, embryonic cells, sex cells and meristernatic cells. These get specialised into :

(*a*) *Amyloplasts :* Large plastids containing starch.

(*b*) *Elaioplasts* (oleosomes). They store fats and are found in seeds.

(*c*) *Proteinoplast* or *Aleuroplasts*. They store protein and are found in seeds.

(*ii*) *Chromoplasts :* These plastids are coloured other than green due to presence of carotenoids but lack chlorophylls, e.g. red chillies, tomatoes. Chromoplasts attract animals and insect to flowers and fruit for performing pollination and fruit dispersal. They are responsible for the bright colours of not only fruits & flowers but also leaves and vegetables.

They are also of various types including :

(*a*) *Phaeoplasts :* These plastids are present is Brown algae, Diatoms and Dino-flagellates. Brown coloured pigment Fucoxanthium is the main pigment along with chlorophyll. However chlorophyll b is replaced by chlorophyll c.

(*b*) *Rhodoplasts :* These are found in Red algae. The red pigment R-phycoerythrin and R-phycocyanin, are present alongwith chlorophyll a, however chlorophyll b is replaced by chlorophyll d.

(*c*) *Chromatophores of blue green algae :* These are found in blue green algae (BGA). They have C-phycocyanin, C-phycoerythrin and chlorophyll a.

(*d*) *Chromatophores of photosynthetic bacteria:* These are found in purple and non-purple photosynthetic bacteria. These bacteria have purple red carotenoid pigments. Special type of chlorophylls bacteriochlorophyll and bacterioviridin are also found in these bacteria.

(*iii*) *Chloroplasts*. (Autoplasts of Meyer, 1883) They are green plastids which take part in photosynthesis and temporary or permanent storage of starch. In green algae, chloroplasts are of various shapes and sizes but chloroplasts of higher plants are disc-shaped with diameter of 4 - 6 μm and thickness of 2 - 4 μm . The number is small in algae but numerous in higher plants. Each chloroplast is surrounded by a double membrane envelope. Internally it contains matrix or stroma and thylakoids. Thylakoids (Menlee, 1961) or baggy trousers are *structural elements* of chloroplasts. They are membrane lined flattened sacs. At places they form stacks called **grana**. A chloroplasts may have 40-60 grana with each granum having 10-100 thylakoids. Thus there is differentiation of granal and stromal (intergranal) thylakoids. Space present in a granal thylakoid is called *loculus* while that of stromal thylakoid is termed as *Fret channel*. Photosynthetic pigments are located in the membranes of thylakoids in specific areas (according to Park and Biggins, 1963) called *quantasomes* (20 × 10 nm). Photosynthetic pigments of higher plants include *chl a, *chl b, carotenes and xanthophylls. A quantasome is believed to have 230 chlorophyll (160 a + 70 b) and 50 carotenoid molecules. The matrix or **stroma** contains naked DNA (Ris & Plant, circular as well as linear), RNA, ribosomes (70 s), plastoglobuli (lipid/fat globuli) and enzymes of carbon assimilation.

Unlike isolated plant cells, isolated cell organelles like chloroplasts and mitochondria cannot be kept in distilled water as they would burst. They can be maintained only in solutions of specific concentrations e.g. 0.25% sucrose. Each quantasome contains 250 molecules of chlorophyll. The evolutionary origin of chloroplasts is currently explained in terms of 'Endosymbiosis'.

Spherosomes : (Perner, 1953). Spherosomes or sphaerosomes are single membrane covered small spherical organelles (10.5 - 1.0 μm) which synthesise and store fats.

Microbodies : They are single membrane

* chl = chlorophyll

covered small cell organelles which take part in oxidation reactions other than those of respiration. Microbodies often posses a crystalline core and granular matrix. They are two types—peroxisomes & glyoxisomes/glyoxysomes.

(*i*) *Peroxisome* : (Rhodin, 1954). The microbodies have enzymes for peroxide biosynthesis. They include (*a*) Peroxide, producing oxidative enzymes like peroxidase, urate oxidase (hence uricosome), amino acid oxidase and (*b*) peroxide destroying enzymes like catalase. In mesophyll cells, peroxisomes interact with chloroplasts and mitochondria to take part in 'photorespiration' (Tolbert *et at*, 1969). For this they have glycolate oxidase for metabolism of glycolate. Their number can be 70-100 per mesophyll cell. Other enzymes found in dense granular matrix of peroxisome of both plant and animal cells are D-amino acid oxidase and α-hydroxy acid oxidase. Peroxisome is involved in purine metabolism and in the conversion of fat to carbohydrate.

(*ii*) *Glyoxysomes* : (Briedenbach, 1967, Beevers, 1963). The microbodies occur only in fat rich plant cells where they take part in β-oxidation of fats and perform glyoxylate cycle. Glyoxysomes possess catalase.

Cytoskeletal Structures : They are fibrous or fine tubular structure which constitute the supportive structures of the cell. Cytoskelatal structures are of three types—

(*i*) microtubuls.
(*ii*) microfilaments.
(*iii*) intermediate fibres.

(*i*) ***Microtubules :*** (Robertis & Franchi, 1953). They are unbranched tubules of indefinite length, 25 nm of thickness with 15 nm core and formed of 13 helically arranged *protofilaments* of α and β, tubulins. Lateral projections occur for establishing cross-bridges. Microtubules grow from nucleating regions. Their tips can grow and shorten quickly. They are basic structures of spindle apparatus, centrioles, basal bodies, cilia and flagella. They play important role in cell division, and transport of ions, water and small organic and inorganic molecules.

(*b*) ***Microfilaments :*** (Paleviz *et al*, 1974). They are cylindrical rods or filaments of actin-like material with a diameter of 5-6 nm and that of indefinite length. Microfilaments can form hexagonal bundles and three dimensional microtrabecular lattice, take part in cytoplasmic streaming, membrane undulations, microvilli cleavage.

(*c*) ***Intermediate Fibres :*** They are solid, unbranched protein fibrils of about 10 nm thikness which are made up of noncontractile protein like keratin, desmin, vimetin etc.

Centrioles : They are minute, submicroscopic subcylindrical structures of 0.3 - 0.5 µm length and 0.15 µm diameter which usually occur in pair (diplosome) inside a specialised cytoplasm called centrosphere or kinplasm. The complex is called *centrosome* (Boveri, 1888) or central apparatus. Each centriole has whorl of **nine triplet fibrils** of tubulin with interconnections amongst adjacent triplets (C-A linkers) as well as with a central *hub* through spokes. Centrioles are surrounded by *massules* or pericentriolar satellites for formation of new centrioles in G_1 phase. (Typical replication is absent). ATPase activity is present. Centrioles are required to form basal bodies, cilia, flagella and astral spindle poles. They occur in most animal cells except some protozoan protists. Amongst others they are found in flagellate forms or forms having flagellate stages (e.g. many green algae, bryophytes, pteridophytes and cycads). Many visual receptor cells and retinal rod cells are originated from centrioles and cilia like bodies. Centrioles in some way can initiate and control the formation of fibrous protein structures.

Basal granules or kinetosomes : The plant or animal cells which are having locomotary organelles such as the cilia and flagella, contain spherical bodies called basal granules at the base of cilia and flagella. These are found embedded in the ectoplasm below plasmalemma and are composed of nine fibrils. Each fibril consists of, three microtubules, out of which two enter in the cilia or flagella. The basal granules may contain both DNA and RNA.

Cilia and Flagella : They are vibratile hair-like narrow protoplasmic processes which are made of four parts—basal body, rootlets, basal plate and shaft. Shaft consists of an external membrane (extension of plasmalemma), a semifluid matrix and an axoneme. Axoneme has nine peripheral doublet fibrils and two central singlet fibrils. Adjacent peripheral doublet fibrils are interconnected (B-A linkers of protein *nexin*). They also give out nexin spokes which bear transition junctions near the central proteinanceous sheath around the central fibrils. Subfibre A of each doublet has two bent arms, the outer one with a hook. The central fibrils and side arms of subfibre A are made of *dynein* protein with ATP-ase activity. Cilia are shorter (5 - 10 μm as compared to 150 μm for flagella), more numerous (number of flagella 1-4) have, sweeping or pendular movements (flagella have undulatory motion) and beat in a coordinated rhythmic movement (flagella show independent movements). In both cilia & flagella, the entire assembly is sheathed by a unit membrane which is simply a part of the plasma membrane.

Many animals have cells, the cilia of which serve simply to move materials part the cells.

Vacuoles : They are noncytoplasmic sacs which are separated from cytoplasm by a membrane or tonoplast*. In young cells the vacuole is absent. Mature cells may have a large central vacuole. The vacuoles are filled with a watery solution of many inorganic and organic substances and gases and is known as cell-sap. The cell-sap is responsible for maintaining osmotic relations of the cell. Colours of vast majority flowers are chiefly due to the presence of anthocyanin pigments dissolved in the cell sap which determines the particular colour in fruits and vegetables. Vacuoles are absent from cells of bacteria and blue green algae.

(*i*) *Sap vacuoles :* They enclose sap or water with dissolved inorganic and organic substances. A sap vacuole is surrounded by TONOPLAST. Plant cells have usually a single large central vacuole. Animal cells have numerous smal sap vacuoles. Sap vacuoles maintain osmotic pressure for turgidity and osmosis. They also store useful as well as waste substances.

(*ii*) *Contractile vacuoles :* They occur in some simple fresh water forms (e.g. *Amoeba, Paramecium, Chlamydomonas*. Contractile vacuoles are surrounded by a few feeding canals. They pick up water from surrounding cytoplasm, expand (diastole) and collapse (systole) to throw water to the outside. Contractile vacuoles perform osmoregulation and excretion.

(*iii*) *Food vacuoles :* It is a complex of lysosomes & phagosome. Digestion occurs inside them.

(*iv*) *Gas Vacuoles :* (Pseudovacuoles). They occur in some procaryotes. Each gas vacuole is made of a large number of submicroscopic hexagonal gas vesicles. A gas vesicle is surrounded by a thin protein membrane. Gas vacuoles store metabolic gases and take part in buoyancy regulation.

Cell Inclusions (Ergastic/Deutoplasmic, Paraplasmic Substances) : They are non-living substances of four categories: reserve, excretory, pigment and mineral. Due to their presence, a cell may become different from other surrounding cells. It is then called IDIOBLAST.

(*i*) *Reserve Food :* It can be starch (plant cells) glycogen (animal cells, fungi & bacteria), fat droplets and aleurone grains. Aleurone grains are storage proteins developed inside aleuroplasts. They can be amorphous, with crystalloid alone (aleurone grains of Maize, Wheat), with globloid alone and with both crystalloid and globloid (e.g. castor seed). Crystalloid is protein carbohydrate while globloid has lipid and phytin.

(*ii*) *Excretory/secretory products :* They include mucus, gums, tannins, resins, alkaloids, latex, glucosides, essential oils, nectar etc.

(*iii*) *Pigments :* The major pigments dissolved in

* **Tonoplast :** It forms the inner most boundary of the cytoplasm and surrounds the vacuoles and hence also known as vacuolar membrane. Tonoplast is selectively permeable and Lipo-Protein in nature. It acts as barrier between cytoplasm and vacuole.

cell sap are anthocyanins (bluish or reddish depending upon pH) and anthoxanthins (yellowish).

(*iv*) *Mineral Crystals :* Calcium carbonate occurs as a mass of crystals around a cellulose core to form CYSTOLITH (leaf hypodermis of Banyan, epidermis of *Momordica*). Cystolith is like a bunch of grapes but is worn like in *Justicia*. Calcium oxalate forms needle-shaped *raphides* (e.g. *Lemna, Eichhornia*), prismatic crystals (e.g. scales of Onion), star shaped sphaeraphide or druse (e.g. *Colocasia, Chenopodium*) or powdery mass named *crystal sand* (e.g. *Atropa*).

Nucleus : (Discovered by Robert Brown, 1831). It is a double membrane covered protoplasmic body that contains hereditary information. With the help of grafting experiments on *Acetabularia*, Hammerling, (1913) proved that nucleus is a store-house of hereditary information. A cell usually contains a single nucleus. However, binucleate (e.g. *Paramecium*) and multinucleate forms also occur. Multinucleate forms is called *Plasmodium* in slime moulds. It is *syncytium* in animal cells (also by fusion of cells) and *coenocytic* in plant cells. Nucleus is commonly rounded but can be oval, disc shaped, lobed or irregularly branched. A typical nucleus is 5-25 μm in diameter. It is the largest amongst cell components. Nucleus has four parts—nuclear envelope, nucleoplasm, chromatin and nucleolus.

(*i*) *Nuclear Envelope* (Karyotheca). It is made up of two membranes, separated by 10-70 nm perinuclear space. The outer membrane may have ribosomes and interconnections with E.R. Nuclear envelope has a large number (1000-10000) of pores with diameter of 200-800 A° (100-1000 A°). Nuclear pores may have diaphragms, septa, annuli, blebs or micropores with a central micropore surrounded by peripheral micropores. The central micropore or channel has *nucleoplasmin* for movement of substances.

(*ii*) *Nucleoplasm* (Nuclear Sap). It is a colloidal complex that fills the nucleus. Its outer part is firm with fibrous protein network. It is called *fibrous lamina*. Nucleoplasm contain raw materials for synthesis of DNA and RNA.

(*iii*) *Chromatin* (Discovered by Flemming, 1879). It is a fibrous hereditary material formed by DNA-historic complex. Chromatin fibres are of two types, narrow, elongated lightly stained *euchromatin* and broader darkly stained granular *heterochromatin* (Heitz). Chromatin is actually folded nucleosome (DNA + histone) containing DNA chains. During nuclear division, chromatin fibres fold variously to produce chromosomes.

(*iv*) *Nucleolus :* It was originally discovered by Fontana (1781) and given the present name by Bowman (1840). It is *naked* (without covering membrane), roughly rounded, darkly stained structure that is attached to chromatin at specific spot called NUCLEOLAR ORGANISER REGION or NOR. It is the area of synthesis of r RNA. It contains four parts, *amorphous, fibrillar, granular* and *chromatin*. Both fibrillar and granular parts are formed of RNA and protein. Nucleolus is the site for elaboration of r RNA and synthesis of ribosomes. Ribosomal protein is synthesised in the cytoplasm.

(Nucleus carries the hereditary information and regulates the ongoing activities of the cell, ensuring the complex molecules the cell requires are synthesized in the number and of the kind needed which are involved in various activities and also in forming organelles & other structures).

Nucleoid : In prokaryotes, DNA is circular and folded variously to form a nearly compact structure called *nucleoid* or genophore. There is no membrane, no nucleolus and no nucleoplasm. The anionic charges present on internucleotide phosphate are balanced by polyamines. Histone are absent. DNA is, therefore, naked.

Mechanism of Cell Division (mitosis & meiosis): Cell division was first studied by Prevost and Dumas (1824) when they described cleavage in fertilized egg of Frog. Rudolf Virchow (1855, 1859) *gave cell lineage theory* that new cells arise by division of pre-existing one—*omnis cellulae cellula*. Strasburger (1873) found that new nuclei develop from pre existing ones. The details were worked out by Strasburger (1875) and Flemming (1879). The term of *mistosis* was coined by Flemming (1882). Meiosis was studied by Sutton (1900) and to some extent by Strasburger (1888) and Winiwater (1900). The term meiosis was coind by Farmer and Moore (1705). The agents which stimulate cell division are called mitogens e.g. cytokinins and some steroids. There are some agents which inhibits cell division. They are called *mitotic poisons*, e.g. *azides, cyanides, colchicine etc.*

(*i*) *Cell Cycle :* Cell cycle is a series of cyclic changes through which a cell passes during its growth and divisions. Time interval between two successive divisions is called *generation time*. Cell cycle has two parts: long nondividing I-phase and short dividing M-phase.

INTERPHASE (I-phase) : It is complex of changes that occur in newly formed cell before it is able to divide. Interphase has three stages

(*a*) *G_1-Phase*. In this, first growth or post mitotic gap phase, the cell and its nucleus grow in size. RNA and protein (including histone) synthesis occurs.

(*b*) *S-Phase*. Chromosomes replicate. Therefore it is called invisible stage of M-phase.

(*c*) *G_2-Phase.* It is the second growth or pre-mitotic gap phase where macro-molecules including protein tubulin are synthesised for cell division. A new centriole pair is formed.

M-Phase. It is the phase of cell division. Cell division consists of nuclear division of *karyokinesis* and protoplast division or *cytokinesis*. Cell division or M-phase is of three types-amitosis, mitosis, meiosis.

(*ii*) *Amitosis :* (Direct Division, Robert Remark, 1841). During amitosis, nucleus elongates, constricts in the middle divides directly into two daughter nuclei. This is followed by division of cytoplasm through constriction, e.g. cartilage cells, degenerate cells.

(*iii*) *Mitosis :* It is also called somatic division, because it occurs during formation/of somatic or body cells. Mitosis is studied in plants in the regions of meristems, e.g. stem tip, root tip (onion $2n = 16$). In animals it is studied in bone marrow, skin, base of nails etc. Mitosis is equatiorial division in which a parent cell divides into two identical daughter cells; each of which contains the same number and kind of chromosomes as are present in the parent cell. Mitosis occurs in two steps, karyokinesis & cytokinesis.

(A) ***Karyokinesis :*** It is the stage of nuclear division (indirect nuclear division) which is continuous but is divided into four stages for the sake of convenience—prophase, metaphase, anaphase and telophase.

(*a*) *Prophase :* In early prophase, the chromatin fibres condense to form elongated chromosomes. The nucleus appears as ball of wool. Centrosome has already divided. The daughter centrosome begin to move away from each other. In *mid prophase*, chromosomes shorten and become distinct with each having two chromatids attached to narrow point called CENTROMERE. The centrosomes develop astral rays and migrate farther. In *late prophase*, the centrosome reach the poles, form asters and begins to develop spindle fibres. Nucleolus degenerates and nuclear envelope starts breaking. In plant cells, centrosomes are absent, spindle fibres develop without them.

(*b*) *Metaphase :* A bipolar spindle is produced. It is anastral (without asters) in plants and *amphiaster* in animals. Spindle is observable with the help of polarising microscope. Spindle has three types of fibres (I) Continuous (pole to pole) (II) Discontinuous (come out of one pole but do not reach the other pole, (III) Chromosome Fibre (Fibres that attach chromosomes to spindle poles. Each spindle fibre is made of 4-20 microtubules. The middle part of spindle having the maximum diameter is called *equator*. Chromosomes move to the equatorial plane and form equatorialor *metaphasic plate* with their centrosomes attached to both the poles by chromosomal fibres. *Colchicine arrests cell division at metaphase stage. Metaphase is the best time to see chromosomes.*

(*c*) *Anaphase :* The centromere of each chromosome divides. This converts the two chromatids into daughter chromosomes each being attached to the spindle pole of its side by independent chromosomal fibre. The chromosomes move towards the spindle poles. The two pole-ward moving chromosomes of each type remain attached to each other by *interzonal fibres.* Ultimately, two groups of chromosomes come to lie at the spindle poles. The spindle fibres shorten one third to one fifth of the original length.

(*d*) *Telophase :* Chromosome again unfold, elongate forming chromatin fibres. Nucleolus, nucleoplasm and nuclear envelope appear form ER so that two daughter nuclei are formed.

Dinomitosis is the type of nuclear division found is dinoflagellates in which the nuclear envelope persists. Microtubular spindle is not formed. Chromosome move while attached to inner membrane of nuclear envelope.

Karyochorisis : Intranuclear spindle is formed with spindle pole bodies (SPBs) developing at the two ends.

(B) *Cytokinesis :* It is the process of separation of the cytoplasm. In animal cells, there is constriction at the equator that finally results in the separation of the daughter cells. It is of two types.

(*a*) *Cleavage Cytokinesis :* The cell membrane constricts and develops a centripetal furrow or cleavage in the middle. The furrow deepens and divides the parent protoplast into two uninucleate protoplasts or cells. Cleavage is the usual method of cytokinesis in animal. It also occurs in some lower plants where wall material is deposited in the furrow between the two daughter protoplasts.

(*b*) *Cell Plate Cytokinesis :* It occurs in plants vesicles having pectic compounds and other wall materials appear in the middle of persisting spindle called 'Phragmoplast'. They fuse and form a film or *cell plate* with membrane on either side. This divides the parent binucleate cell into two daughter uninucleate cells. Cell plate grows centrifugally and functions as middle lamella. Primary wall is deposited on its either side by the two daughter protoplasts.

(*iv*) *Meiosis :* Meiosis is a special type of cell division present in germ cells of sexually reproducing organisms. Sexual reproduction occurs by way of sexual cells or gametes (eggs & sperms), which after fertilization constitute the Zygote. Meiosis consists of a single duplication divisions. In animals and lower plants, meiosis is *terminal* or *gametic* (i.e., it occurs before the formation of the gametes). In the male, four haploid sperms are produced, in female, one ovum and three polar bodies are produced. In most plants, meiosis is *intermediary* or *sporic* i.e. it occurs sometime between fertilization and the formation of gametes). Cells in meiosis are called *Meiocytes.*

Meiosis is divided into division I and II. In division I, there is a long prophase of which the stages are preleptonema and leptonema, zygonema, pachynema, diplonema and diakinesis.

(A) Meiosis I : Meiosis I is the actual reduction division which is also called heterotypic division (the two chromatids of a chromosome often become different due to crossing over.)

(*a*) *Prophase I :* It is longest phase which is complex and divisible into five stages-leptotene, zygotene,pachytene, diplotene and diakinesis.

(*i*) *Leptotene :* (Leptonema). Chromatin fibres condense and form chromosomes. The chromosomes often show chromomeres. They may also develop baset like arrangement called *bouquet* stage (diverging from a common point lying near centrosome). Chromosome number is diploid where there are two chromosomes of each type called 'homologous chromosomes'. Their chromatids are not clear because of the development of nucleoprotein core between them.

(*ii*) *Zygotene :* (Zygonema). Homologous chromosomes join laterally in the process of synapsis (Montgomery, 1901)/*syndesis* to form bivalents. The two chromosomes of a bivalent are held together by nucleoprotein core. The whole structure is called 'Synaptonemal Complex' (Moses, 1956). SC is composed of two lateral arms (which appear in each homologous at the end of leptonema) and a medial element. At the time of paring the packing of DNA is 300/1 and there is only 0.3% matching between homologous DNA. Pairing starts at random, but telomeres are generally inserted at the nuclear envelope. The 0.2 μm space between homologous chromosomes is occupied by the SC. This may have the appearance of a ladder, with bridges crossing the medial element. The main component of this complex is protein. The macromolecular organization of meiotic chromosomes is similar to that of mitotic ones with a 20-30 nm chromatin fiber composed of nucleosomes. In early prophase, the fibres make discrete loops that coalesce in dense foci, where the lateral arms of SC are deposited. The packing of there loops increases throughout meiotic prophase, and some RNA transcription may be seen in certain loops corresponding to active nucleolar genes.

(*iii*) *Pachytene (Pachynema)* : The nonsister chromatids of a bivalent may exchange segments in the process of crossing over. However, individual chromatids are not clear. In this pairing is complete and chromosomes become shorter & thicker. The number of chromosomes have been halved (i.e. bivalents or tetrads). Each tetrad has four kinetochores (two homologous and two sister). During pachynema, two homologous chromatids exchange segments at a molecular level (recombination). The SC appears to stabilise the pairing thus enabling the interchange. At pachynema the SC may show the recombination nodules or bars, which may be actual sites of crossing over.

(*iv*) *Diplotene :* (Diplonema). During diplotene the paired chromosomes begin to separate, but they are held together at the *chiasmata* (points of interchange or crossing over). Chiasmata (first seen by Johanssen, 1909) or nucleoprotein attaching points occur at places between the homologous chromosomes. There is at least one chiasma per bivalent chromosome. At diplonema, the SC is shed from the bivalents. At each chiasma, there is a piece of SC that ultimately disappears and is replaced by a chromatin bridge. Diplonema may last for months or years. In this the chromatids become clear. Each bivalent now appear as tetrad.

(*v*) *Diakinesis :* Chiasmata shift towards the chromosome ends (terminalisation). Nucleolus degenerates. Nuclear envelope breaks at places. A spindle begins to develop with centrioles in animals & without centrioles. There is reduction in the number of chiasmata and further contraction. This is followed by prometaphae, metaphase I, anaphase I, telophase I.

(*b*) *Metaphase I :* A bipolar fibrous spindle appears in the area of nucleus. It has asters at the two poles in animal cells (amphiaster) while the same are absent in plant cells (anastral). The chromosome pairs shift to the equator of spindle forming two or double metaphasic plate with the help of their centromeres. Each chromosome gets attached to spindle pole of its side by a chromosome fibre.

(*c*) *Anaphase I :* Chiasmata disappear completely and the homologous chromosomes separate. The process in called *disjunction*. The separated chromosomes (univalents) show divergent chromatids and are called *dyads*. They move towards the spindle poles and ultimately form two groups of haploid chromosomes.

(*d*) *Telophase I :* Chromosomes elongate. Nucleolus, nucleoplasm and nuclear envelope appear over each chromosome group forming nuclei.

During the interphase between the two meiotic divisions there is no replication of the chromosomes, and division II is very similar to mitosis, by the end of which each nucleus has a haploid number of chromosomes composed of single chromatids.

The fact that in meiotic division I there is separation of homologous kinetochores (and chromatids) and in division II the sister kinetochores (and chromatids) are separated, can be explained by the orientation of kinetochores, which determines nucleation and preferential polarization of microtubules.

(B) ***Meiosis II :*** It is homotypic or equational division which is meant for maintaining the haploid number and separating the two chromatids of a chromosome which have become different due to crossing over. DNA replication is absent.

(*a*) *Prophase II :* The chromatin fibres shorten to

form chromosomes. Nucleolus and nuclear envelop break down. Spindle in formed in the area of each nucleus. Both telophase I and prophase II are omitted in some organisms where anaphase I directly leads to metaphase II; e.g. Trillium.

(*b*) *Metaphase II :* Chromosomes come to lie at the equator of the spindle forming a single metaphasic plate. The centromere of each chromosome gets attached by both its surfaces to the spindle poles of their sides by distinct chromosome fibres.

(*c*) *Anaphase II :* Centromere of each chromosome divides into two. This separates the two chromatids of a chromosome into two independent daughter chromosomes. Each daughter chromosome is attached to spindle pole of its side by a chromosome fibre. Chromosomes move towards the spindle poles forming two groups. Since there were two spindle, a total of four groups are formed.

(*d*) *Telophase II :* The four groups of chromosomes organise themselves into four haploid nuclei.

(C) *Cytokinesis :* Cytokinesis may occur after each division (successive type) or simultaneously at the end of meiosis. It is generally through cleavage. In case of plants, wall material is deposited in the furrows. Cytokinesis give rise to four haploid cells.

(D) *Significance of Meiosis :* In all organisms 'Meiosis' takes place at the time of gamete formation. 4 haploid cells are produced as a result of meiosis in a diploid cell. The product of meiosis gives rise to gametes after metamorphosis, some of them may be viable or nonviable.

The object of reduction division is as follows:

(*a*) To keep the chromosome number same in daughter cells.

(*b*) To keep the parental characters in daughter cells.

(*c*) This division enables the cells to pass from one generation to another.

(*d*) In the sporophytic generation, the number of chromosome is $2x$ i.e. diploid and passes into gametophytic generation, reduction in number of chromosomes take place so that each of the gametophytic generation has got only x number of chromosomes. So this phenomenon is most essential for completing a life history of a plant.

(*e*) Fertilization duplicates the chromosome number but meiosis halves it to maintain the chromosomal balance in all organisms.

(*f*) At the time of chiasmata formation, the exchange of chromatid material causes a combination of new characters. Thus meiosis helps in bringing about variation in population.

Meiosis may last for 50 years in human female as the number of oocyte in a new born female is about one million. By the age of 07 years, there are some 300,000 oocytes left while only 400 reach maturity between 12 & 50 years. Thus meiosis may last upto 50 years. This may explain the increase in incidence of chromosonal aberrations with the increasing age of mother. While in human male, meiosis starts after puberty.

The essential differences between mitosis and meiosis are as follow :

(*a*) Mitosis occurs in all somatic cells while meiosis is limited to germinal cells only.

(*b*) In mitosis, one replication cycle of DNA is followed by one division, resulting in diploid cells. In Meiosis, one replication of DNA is followed by two divisions, resulting in haploid cells.

(*c*) In mitosis DNA replication occurs in the 'S' phase, which is followed by G_2. In meiosis there is a premeiotic DNA synthesis, which is very long and followed immediately by meiosis.

(*d*) In mitosis, each chromosome behaves independently, while in meiosis there is pairing of homologous chromosomes.

(*e*) Mitosis last 1 to 2 hours and meiosis lasts longer; in the male it may last 24 days and in the female, several years.

(*f*) In mitosis, the genetic material remains constant, and in meiosis there is genetic variability.

The essential processes of meiosis are

(*a*) pairing of homologous chromosomes;

(*b*) Formation of chiasmata with underlying genetic recombination;

(*c*) Segregation of the homologous chromosomes.

Cell differentiation : Cell differentiation is the process by which stable differences arise between cells. All higher organisms develop from a single cell, the fertilized ovum, which gives rise to various tissues and organ. Cell differentiation leads to distinguishable cell types whose character and properties are determined by their pattern of gene activity and the *proteins* they produce. Transplantation of nuclei from differentiated animal cells into fertilized eggs and cell fusion studies show that the pattern of gene expression in the nucleus of a differentiated cell can often be reversed, implying that it is determined by factors supplied by the cytoplasm and that no genetic material has been lost. Although the differentiated state of an animal cell *in vivo* is usually extremely stable, some causes of differentiation are reversible. Transdifferentiation of one differentiated cell type into another type has been shown to occur during regeneration and in cells in tissue culture. In many cases, the pattern of gene activity is under continuous control. Maintenance and inheritance of a pattern of gene activity may involve several mechanisms, including the continued action of gene regulatory proteins; changes in the packing state of chromatin, and chemical modifications to the DNA.

(A) *Cytoplasmic determinants :* Nuclear transplantation experiments in frog have shown that the genome remains constant during cell differentiation. Cytoplasm contains substances called 'determinants' that become unequally distributed among embryonic cells and cause them to follow a particular differentiation pathway.

The best example of cytoplasmic determinants is provided by the granules present in germ cells. When they are centrifuged or transplanted into different positions, they will induce the formation of germ cells in a different position.

In early embryos, rate of cell division is very fast and during this period there is no RNA synthesis, but when the 4000-cell stage (called-mid-blastula transition) is reached, synthesis of most types of RNA starts simultaneously.

(B) *Molecular Differentiation :* How is a gene expressed in certain tissues and not in others? It seems that not one but multiple mechanisms are used. Activation of *transcription* is probably the most common one, used in many protein-coding genes, e.g. globin in red blood cells, ovalbumin in oviduct & silk fibroin in the silk gland. Exactly how this is achieved is not known. Chromatin structure and DNA methylation have been explored as possible mechanisms. *Translational* control is known to occur is some eggs that have "marked" m RNAs that are translated only after fertilization. The best example of translational control is provided by the heat shock m RNA of *Xenopus* oocytes, which are stored but not translated unless the temperature is raised.

In *gene amplification* specific genes are

Differentiation establishes a pattern of gene activity

⇓

Pattern of gene activity is passed onto daughter cells by various mechanisms.

⇓	⇓	⇓
Positive feddback control of gene expression and interaction with other gene	DNA methylation	Changes in chromatin state (e.g. in inactivated X-chromosome)

Pattern of gene activity is reversible

Transfer of nucleus of differentiated cell to egg support embryonic development	Transdifferentiation e.g. lens retinal pigment cells.

selectively replicated to attain a higher level of expression. Gene amplification happens with r DNA in some oocytes, the DNA puffs of *Rhynocosciara*, and with the chorion (egg shell) genes of *Drosophila*. It is a rare event, and in all cases the amplified DNA is not passed on to future cell generations.

Transposition of genes form a 'silent' site in the chromosome into an 'expression site', where they are actively transcribed, occurs in the yeast mating type switch and in trypanosomes that change periodically their surface antigens as a defense against the host's immune system. Transposition is known not to occur for globin, ovalbumin and many other genes.

The production of antibodies by B- lymphocytes is the best example of how intricate the control of cell differentiation might be. Initially, variable region DNA is brought close to a constant region by a DNA deletion. A membrane-bound antibody molecule is initially produced but upon stimulation with antigen, the cell starts secreting antibody by a mechanism controlled at the RNA processing level. Finally another DNA deletion might bring the same variable region closer to a new type of constant heavy chain, producing different types of immunoglobulins (IgG, Ig E, Ig A).

It is possible in adult tissue mechanisms similar to those of cytoplasmic determinants in embroyes might operate. For example, when cytoplasmic components become unequally distributed among daughter cells, one cell may become differentiated while the other remains as a *stem cell*.

The differentiation of the various lineages seems to depend on external signals, although there is evidence for autonomous diversification, and external factors are essential for survival and proliferation of specific cell types. Similar processes also occur in the diversification of neural crest. Before migration, single crest cells have a broad developmental potential, and environmental signals can both direct the pathways of neural crest differentiation and promote survival of particular cell types. Programmed cell death is common fate for cells, especially during development and there is evidence that positively acting signals are generally required to prevent programmed cell death and allow cells to continue to survive.

Cell-Cell Interaction :

(A) ***Differentiation of the Cell Membrane :*** The cell membrane may present regional differentiations that are related to specialized functions such as absorption, fluid transport, electrical coupling. Microvilli are found at the apical surface of the intestinal epithelium and form the brush border of the kidney tubules. They increase the absorption surface and are covered by a coat of glycoproteins.

Intercellular attachments comprise tight junctions, belt desmosomes, and spot desmosomes. **Tight junctions** serve to seal the intercellular spaces and to maintain the intercellular environment. They form a network of sealing strands below the apical regions of the cells. **Belt desmosomes** have a system of action and intermediate filaments and are situated below the zone of tight junctions. These belt desmosomes represent the terminal bars or intermediary junctions of the old literature. **Spot desmosomes** are localized circular areas of mechanical attachment having two dense plaques with keratin tonofilaments. The number of spot desmosomes is correlated with the degree of mechanical stress that the tissue has to support e.g. epithelium of vagina is rich is spot desmosomes.

Hemidesmosomes are found at the base of certain epithelia. Therefore similar to desmosomes in fine structure, but represent only half of them, the outer side frequently substituted with collagen fibrils.

Tight junctions are also known as *zonula occludens,* belt desmosomes as *zonula adherens* & spot desmosomes as *macula adherenes.*

(B) ***Gap Junctions & Intercellular Communications :*** Cellular interactions are essential for the coordination of activities, and furthermore, the propagation between cells of signals for growth and differentiation is indispensable for development. It is now known that most cells in an organized tissue are interconnected by *junctional channels* and that they share a common pool of many small metabolities and ions that pass freely from one cell to another. Their individuality, however, is maintained by macromolecules that are not exchanged between cell.

The so called *gap junctions* (nexus) are essential in intercellular communications. They represent regions in which there are junctional channels through which ions and molecules can pass from one cell to another. Cells having gap junction are electrically coupled i.e. there is a free flow of electrical current carried by ions. At the gap junction the membranes are separated by a space of only 2 to 4 nm, and there is a hexagonal array of 8 to 9 nm particles. At the centre of each particle there is a channel 1.5 to 2 nm in diameter. The macromolecular unit of the gap junction is called the **connexon**, which appears as annulus of six subunits surrounding the channel. It is thought that the sliding of the subunits causes the channel to open & close.

Gap junction provides direct intercellular communication by allowing the passage of molecules upto a limiting weight of 1300 to 1900 daltons (in chironomous salivary glands). The permeability is regulated by Ca^{++} , if the intracellular Ca^{++} level increases, the permeability is reduced or abolished. Through the gap junction, metabolities (i.e., labeled nucleotides) can pass from one cell to another. In several strains of cancer cells, there is no coupling as seen in normal cultured cells. Coupling is genetically determined, and probably genes linked to one chromosome can correct the cancerous growth and the channel defect. Junctional communication may convey electrical signals between certain neurons (i.e. electrical synapses) and between cardiac cells, however, most neurons and skeletal muscle lack electrical coupling. Gap junctions are also used in the transfer of substances that control growth and differentiation in cells.

(C) *Cell Coats and Cell Recognition :* Most cell membranes have a coat, sometimes referred to as *glycocalyx*, made of glycoproteins or polysaccharides. The cell coat is negatively charged and may bind Na^{+} and Ca^{++}. Several cytochemical techniques are used to reveal the cell coats (e.g. PAS & ruthenium red). The oligosaccharides may be visualised by the use of *lectins*. The cell-coat is a kind of secretion product that undergoes an active turnover.

Extracellular materials lie outside the cell coat proper and the fuzzy layer of certain cells. In these extracellular materials collagens and glycosaminoglycans are the main components. There are polysaccharides, such as *hyaluronic acid* and *chondroitin sulfate*, in which there is a repeating disaccharide unit. These acidic molecules are associated with proteins forming proteoglycans.

Many functions are attributed to the cell coat, like filtration, diffusion, protection of membrane. The cell coat makes a kind of microenvironment for the cell. It contains enzymes involved in the digestion of carbohydrates and proteins.

Molecular recognition between cells may depend on a molecular code made up of the individual monosaccharides such as galactose, hexosamine, mannose, fucose and sialic acid. The classical ABO blood groups are based on specific antigens of the red cell coat, which are specified by their terminal carbohydrates. Several other antigens are found on the cell-coat. Molecular recognition reaches maximum expression in the nervous tissue. Cell adhesion and cell dissociation and reassociation are dependent on cell coat. Cells are able to recognize similar cells in a tissue. In all cell recognition phenomena, the presence of specific carbohydrates at the membrane is essential. From embryonic and adult animal tissues, low molecular weight proteins that act as plant lectins have been isolated. These animal lectins recognize saccharides on the cell surface and cause a β-galactoside hemoagglutination. Cells can also interact through diffusible substances acting at a distance. One such example is the life cycle of *Dictyostelium discoideum*, a slime mold in which the single amoeba may aggregate by the long range action of c AMP.

(D) *Cell Surface in Cancer Cells :* Cancer cells are characterized by uncontrolled growth, invasion and dissemination (metastasis). In a tumor all cancer cells are monoclonal. They may show changes in karyotype, increased glycolysis, and disorganization of cytoskeleton.

In cancer cells, there are many changes in the cell membrane and cell coat, such as the disappearance of gap junctions, loss of coupling, changes in glycolipids and glycoproteins and a reduction in gangliosides. There is also more mobility of surface receptors, increased transport of sugars, and growth of new antigens.

While in normal cells, the transport of iron and trace metal ions involves transferrin and transferrin receptors, in transformed cells there is an alternative mechanism. Transformed cells secrete siderophore like growth factors (chelating agents that trap the metal ions), which compete with transferrin and transport the iron inside the cell.

In the cell coat, **fibronectin,** a large glycoprotein found in "footprints" of moving cultured cells is reduced in cancer cells. A major characteristic of cancer cells is the combined loss of contact inhibition, motility and growth control, which is characteristics of normal cells in culture. Cancer cells are "immortal" and tend to pile up, while normale cells die after a number of divisions and tend to form monolayers.

A normal cell can be converted into a cancerous cell by a number of transforming agents, all of which affect the DNA and cause mutations. Different DNA and RNA viruses can produce transformation. Among the DNA viruses, polyoma and SV 40 are extensively used in experiments. Adeno and Herpes virus (DNA) may also be involved. The RNA retroviruses are natural agents in animal tumors and can be transmitted to the offspring through the mother's milk. In all these cases the viral genome becomes, integrated in certain regions of the host's genome and is expressed in cancerous cells.

QUESTIONS FROM PREVIOUS YEARS' PAPERS

1. Write short notes on the following:
   (*a*) Ultrastructural in details of an eukaryotic cell (Draw neat labelled diagrams).
   (*b*) Structure and functions of ribosomes.
   (*c*) Ultrastructure of plama membrane.
   (*d*) Sex Chromosomes
   (*e*) E.R.
2. Describe the structure and function of mitochondria.
3. How the mitochondrial function is controlled?
4. Write short notes on:
   (*a*) Cell fractionation.
   (*b*) Nucleolus
   (*c*) Nucleosome
5. Describe briefly various structural changes in Chromosomes.
7. Explain the different types of aneuploidy.
8. With suitable classical experiments on sex-linked inheritance, prove that genes are carried on the chromosomes.
5. Write short notes on the following:
   (*a*) Stages of cell cycle.
   (*b*) Y-chromosome
   (*c*) Lysosomes
   (*d*) Cytoskeleton
6. With suitable sketches, distinguish between the major types of cell surface receptors.
7. Explain in detail the structure of G protein and its role in signal transduction.
8. With suitable diagrams, explain the structure of chromatin found in interphase nucleus.
9. Explain the significance of the condensation/decondensation cycle of chromatin.
10. Give a detail account of prokaryotic protein synthesis.
11. Discuss critically structure and functions of cell membranes.
12. Describe different types of polyploidy giving suitable examples.
13. Describe the process of meiosis sequentially with suitable diagrams contrast in with mitosis.
14. What is the balance concept of sex determination and how was this established?

CHAPTER–2

GENETICS, MOLECULAR BIOLOGY & EVOLUTION

Development of genetics :

Initial Ideas on Heredity

(A) *Ideas of Hippocrates and Aristotle :* Earliest writings on the subject of heredity are those of Hippocrates (400 BC) and Aristotle (350 BC). Hippocrates believed that characters are inherited from parents because reporudctive material is handed over from all parts of the body of an individual.

Aristotle could not agree with Hippocrates, because this could not explain inheritance of characters like nails, hair, voice, grey hairs etc. because most of these are dead tissues and could not have contributed to reproductive tissue. Aristotle also pointed out cases where children may resemble their grandparents rather than their parents. He believed that reproductive material was not derived from different parts but from nutrient substances meant for different parts and diverted to reproductive path. These nutrient substances would differ depending upto different parts for which they are meant. He also believed that female sex contributed the material and the male sex contributed something to define the form of the embryo. Both of them believed in direct inheritance of traits, which are handed over from parents to offsprings, through reproductive material. This is the simplest theory of inheritance, which do not hold good today.

(B) *Preformation and epigenesis :* In 1679, J. Swammerdam studied development of insects and suggested that development of an organism is simple enlargement of a minute but preformed individual, which was called "homunculus" and could be present in sperm or in the ovum. But it could not be accepted. K.F. Wolff (1738-1794), proposed that neither egg nor sperm had a homunculus like structure but that the gametes contained undifferentiated living substances capable of forming the organized body after fertilization. Such an idea was called the theory of "epigenesis".

(C) *Pangenes & Acquired Characters :* J.B. Lamarck (1744-1829). Characters which are acquired during the lifetime of an individual are inherited. This concept is known as *Lamarckism* or "The Theory of Inheritance of Acquired Characters". This theory was very popular in the eighteenth century to explain evolution and heredity. However *Lamarck* did not point out the physical basis of this theory. Charles Darwin (1809-1882) tried to suggest that every part of the body produced very small invisible bodies called "gemmules" or "pangenes", which are transported through the blood stream to the sex organs and are assembbed into gamates. During fertilization, gemmules from both parents are broguht together for redistribution to different organs during development, thus determining different charcters. This theory is almost a copy of Lamarck's theory except that it suggested a physical basis.

(D) *Experiments of Knight & Goss on Pea :* Knight (1799) and Goss (1824) had conducted experiments on edible pea (*Pisum sativum*), much before Mendel, but failed to formulate the law of inheritance, only because they could not give a mathematical treatment of their results. They were more concerned for improvement of peas rather than their concern for understanding the mechanism.

(E) *Germplasm Theory and the Genotype Phenotype Concept :* A. Weismann (1834-1914) demonstrated that "Pangenesis" could not be verified. His popular experiments consisted of cutting the tails of mice and then studying the inheritance. Repeating such a treatment for 22 generations, he found that complete tail structure was still inhibited. There experiments of mutilation may appear now rather crude, but results can definitely be used as argument against "pangenesis" because one the tail was removed, the 'pangenes' or 'gemmules' for the tail will not be available and therefore this structure should not develop in the next generation if pangenesis holds good.

Weismann also proposed his own *germplasm theory* to account for heredity. According to this theory, the body of an individual can be divided into "germplasm" and "somatoplasm". The somatoplasm was not able to enter the sex cells, consequently the variations present in the somatoplasm will not be transmitted to next generation. The germplasm on the other hand, was meant for the reproductive purpose only, so that any change occurring in germplasm will influence the progeny. This was very significant advancement in understanding of heredity.

In order to make definite distinction between hereditary and environmental variations, Johannsen, 1909, formulated the *genotype–phenotype concept*. According to him, the genotype of an individual represents sum total of heredity.

On the other hand, phenotype represents features which are produced by interaction between genotype and environment.

A genotype can thus exhibit different phenotype under different conditions. This is referred to as individidual's "norm of reaction" to the environment. Therefore similar genotypes may not have the same phenotype. Conversely, similar phenotypes do not necessarily mean some genotype.

(F) *Gregor Mendel (1822-1884)* is appropriately called **"father of genetics"**. Mendel (1865) discovered the laws of heredity by studying crosses between peas having pair of *contrasting* characters (i.e. allelic). In a cross between parents with yellow seeds and parents with green seeds, he found that in F_1 generation, all the hybrid had yellow seeds (dominant gene). In the F_2 generation 75% of the plant had yellow seeds and 25% had green seeds (recessive gene). Mendel postulated that the genes are transmitted without mixing (*law of segregation*). He demonstrated that in F_2 there are 1 dominant homozygous, 2 heterozygous and 1 ressive homozygous offsprings. The 'genotypic' segregation is 1 : 2 : 1 although the "phenotypic" proportion is 3 : 1. The law of segregation can be explained in terms of the behaviour of chromosomes during meiosis. At times there is *incomplete dominance* (i.e. intermediary heredity).

The behaviour of two or more pairs of allelic genes follow the *"law of independent assortment"*. Genes that lie in different chromsomes are independently distributed during meiosis. For the two pairs of alleles, the phenotypic proportion is 9:3:3:.

Mendel was not the first to perform hybridization experiments, but he was the first to consider the results in terms of single traits. Sageret, (1826) had studied the inheritance of contrasting traits. Others of Mendel's predecessors had considered whole organism, which incorporate a nebulous complex of traits, thus, they could observe only that similarity and differences occured among parents and progeny. They missed the significance of individual differences. Employing the scientific method, Mendel designed the necessary experiments, counted and classified the peas resulting from his crosses, compared the proportions with mathematical models, and formulated a hypothesis for there differences. Although Mendel devised a precite mathematical pattern for the transmission of hereditary units, he had no concept of the biological mechanisms involved. Nevertheless, on the basis of his preliminary experiments and hypotheses, he predicted and subsequently verified his predictions with the results of later crosses.

In 1990, Mendel's paper was discovered simultaneously by three botanists :

(*i*) Hugo de Vries in Holland—Known for his *mutation theory* and studies on the evening primrose and maize.

(*ii*) Carl Correns in Germany—who investigated maize, peas, beans.

(*iii*) Eric von Tschermak-Seysenegy in Austria—who worked with several plants, including garden pea.

Each of there investigators obtained evidence for Mendel's principles from his own independent studies. They all found Mendel's report while searching the literature for related work and cited it in their own publications.

(G) *William Bateson*, an Englishman, gave this developing science the name "GENETICS" is 1905. He coined the term from a Greek word meaning "to generate".

(H) *Concept of the Gene :*

(*a*) Bateson actively promoted Mendel's view of paired genes. He used the word **"Allelomorph",** shortened to *allele* to identify members of pairs that control different alternative traits.

(*b*) During early 1800s, a Frenchman, Lucien Cuenot, showed that genes controlled fur colour in the mouse.

(*c*) An American, W.E. Castle related genes to sex and to fur colour and pattern is mammals.

(*d*) A Dane and W.L. Johannsen, studied the influence of heredity and environment in plants. He began using the word *gene* from the last syllable of Darwin's term "pangene".

The gene concept, however had been implict in Mendel's visualization of a physical element or **factor** that acts as the foundation for development of a trait. These men and their peers were able to build on the basic principles of cytology, which were established between 1865 (when Mendel's work was completed) and 1900 (when it was discovered).

(I) Chromosome Theory :

(*a*) **Wilhelm Roux** has postulated as early as 1883 that chromosomes within the nucleus of the cell were the bearers of hereditary factors. The only model he was able to devise that would account for his observed genetic result was a row of lined-up objects duplicated exactly. To explain the mechanics of gene transmission from cell to cell he, therefore, suggested that nuclei must have invisible structures held in rows or chains that duplicated themselves when the cell divided. Constituents of the nuclei that seemed best designed to carry genes and fill there requirements were chromosomes.

(*b*) In 1900, **Von Winiwarter,** discovered that in the ovary of a half day old rabbit (*Oryctolagus cuniculus*) chromosomes had associated in pairs side by side for a part of their length. This association appeared at what are now call zygotene stage of meiosis, which was very common in rabbits ovary 1½ & 2½ days old.

(*c*) **Montgomery** (1901), after a study of meiosis in 42 species of insects came to conclusion that each association of chromosomes in pairs at zygotene involves one paternal & one maternal chromosome.

(*d*) **Sutton** (1902) extended Montgomery's observation while studying meiosis in grasshopper. The male grasshopper has 23 chromosomes in somatic cells, and their chromosomes differed very much in size, so that the largest chromosome was 5-6 times as long as the smallest. Sutton observed that apart from one X-chromosome, 11-paired associations were present in each nucleus and showed same size differences as at mitosis. It was also shown that although due to degree of contraction, absolute lengths of paired chromosomes differed at different stages of meiosis, but their relative lengths were constant. This confirmed Montgomery's conclusion that association were brought about only between paternal and maternal chromosomes.

(*e*) **T. Boveri** (1902) : Who demonstrated in sea urchin, that different chromosomes of a set possess different qualities and also showed presence of a complete set of chromosomes was important for survival. This observation derives support now from the fact that a **hypodiploid** (chromosome no. < 2) does not survive while a haploid individual may survive. It is also proved by the fact that trisomics involving different chromosomes differed morphologically as in case of *Detura* and many other plant species and also in Human.

(*f*) Experiments of **T. Boveri & W.S. Sutton** in 1902 brought confirming evidence that a gene is part of a chromosome. The theory of the **gene as a discrete unit of a chromosome** was developed by T.H. Morgan and his associates from studies on the fruit fly, *Drosophila melanogaster*.

(*g*) **H.J. Muller** later promoted the merger of the two sciences that had contributed most to the chromosome theory-cytology (the study of cells) and genetics as **CYTOGENETICS.**

(J) *Formulation of Chromosome Theory :* On the basis of findings of Montgomeny and Boveri and on the basis of his own studies, W.S. Sutton for the first time in 1903 formulated **chromosome theory of Mendelian inheritance** in clear terms. He drew attention to following features which suggested that Mendelian factors should be located on chromosomes:

(*i*) There is a resemblance between separation of homologus chromosomes during anaphase I of meiosis and the postulated separation of character differences at the time of gamete formation.

(*ii*) If each pair of homologous chromosome is so oriented at metaphase I, so that in a pair the orientation of maternal and paternal chromosomes, towards specific poles is independent of the orientation of these chromosomes in the other pair, we expect that 2^n combinations are possible (n = haploid chromosomes number). This is true of Mendelian factors also. This will further suggest that in Sea Urchin with $n = 18$, $n^{18} = 262,144$ possible combinations of maternal and paternal chromosomes will be available. Therefore, there is a parallelism between presumed independent assortment of homologous chromosomes at meiosis and Mendel's prinsiple of independent assortment. Confirmation of random orientation of different chromosome pairs came by use of sex chromosomes.

(K) Sex Chromosome and Chromosome Theory :

(*a*) The first definite evidence for chromosome theory came from sex-determination. **C.E. Mc Clung** in 1902 reported two types of sperms in grasshoppers, one containing an X-chromosome and the other lacking it. Since this was the only difference in sperms and since all eggs were similars with respect to X-chromosome it was concluded that x-chromosome must be responsible for determination of sex.

(*b*) Proof of parallelism between chromosomes and mendelian factors with respect to independent assortment came from **E.E. Carothers** in 1913. She used a particular grasshopper of three pairs of chromosome could be morphologically distinguished. If these three pairs are designated as AA', BB' & CC', the possible arrangements at metaphase I can be shown as in following figure:

AA'	A'A	AA'	AA'
BB'	BB'	B'B	BB'
CC'	CC'	CC'	C'C
A'A	A'A	AA'	A'A
B'B	BB'	B'B	B'B
CC'	C'C	C'C	C'C

Eight types of combinations in gametes would then be possible in equal proportions from arrangements shown in the above figure. When crosses of thus marked grasshoppers were made with normal grasshoppers, all eight combinations could be identified morphologically through cytological preparations, suggesting an assortment just like that for mendelian factors in a trihybrid cross.

Mendel had fortunately selected those characters which were located on separate chromosomes. Had he selected two chracters located on the same chromosome, independent assortment would not be observed, since chromosomes and not part thereof, will exhibit independent assortment. A very strong cytological evidence for chromosome theory of inheritance came from **C. Stern's** experiment on crossing over & **C.B. Bridge's** experiment on the non-disjunction of X-chromosomes.

Principles of Mendelian *Inheritance* (Mendelism)

(A) ***Principle of Unit Characters :*** An individual is made up a large number of characters, each of which behaves as a unit.

(B) ***Principle of Paired Factors :*** A trait or character is represented genetially in an individual by two factors present on the some locus in the two homologous chromosomes. The two factors may represent the same expression of the trait. (TT for tallness, *tt* for dwarfness) or both expressions as in hybrid (T*t* for heigh/tallness) though only one is evident externally. Factors representing the different expressions of a trait are known as *alleles/ allelomorphs/allelomorphic* pair. These days, the two similar factors of a trait/gene are also called *alleles.*

(C) ***Principle of Dominance :*** In a hybrid, where both the contrasting alleles are present, only one factor/allele called *dominant* is able to express its effect while the other factor/allele called recessive remains suppressed. In a cross between pure/true breeding red flowered (RR) Pea plant and white flowered (*rr*) Peal plant, the F_1 generation is red flowered though it has received both the factors (R & *r*). It is because of the dominant nature of factor for red flower colour and recessive nature of the factor for white flower colour. On self breeding, the recessive trait reappears in the F_2 generation showing that it is suppressed in F_1 generation and not lost.

(D) ***Law of Segregation (Principle of Purity of Gametes/First Law of Mendelism) :*** Mendelian factors or alleles of a trait are particulate entities which keep their identity in the hybrid, separate out at the time of gametogenesis randomly passing to different gametes for random pairing during passage to offspring.

In a monohybrid cross, say between a pure tall pea plant and dwarf pea plant, F_1 or hybrids are all tall. On self breeding them, both tall and dwarf appear in the ratio 3 : 1 (787 tall to 273) dwarf in Mendel's experiment). Further self breeding shows that dwarf plants breed true. Amongst tall, one third are true while two third (one half of total progeny) behave as hybrids. This shows that phenotypic monohybrid ratio of 3 : 1 is genotypically 1 pure tall : 2 hybrid talls : 1 dwarf. Therefore, F_1 plants or hybrids carry both the factors or alleles which separate out in gemetes, one half from each parent having the factor for tallness and the second half the factor for dwarfness.

Male Gametes (♂)		*Female Gametes* (♀)		*Offsprings*	
1/2 T	×	1/2 T	=	1/4 TT	
1/2 T	×	1/2 *t*	=	1/4 T*t*	1/2 T*t*
1/2 *t*	×	1/2 T	=	1/4 T*t*	
1/2 *t*	×	1/2 *t*	=	1/4 *tt*	

Since gametes carry only one factor of a trait, the principle of segregation is also called *principle of purity of gametes*. It can be proved by taking those expamples in which the gametophytes or pollen grains carry specific genetic traits, e.g. starchy and waxy (= glutinous, lacking starch), pollen in maize and rice. When true breeding starchy pollen bearing variety is crossed with true breeding waxy pollen bearing plant, the offspring or F_1 plants (diploid) produce pollen (haploid) through meiosis of both the types, starchy and waxy in the ratio 1 : 1 indicating that the two mendelian factor segregate in the ratio of 1 : 1 at the time of sporogenesis/gametogenesis and that a gamete/gametophyte contains single factor of a trait so that 50% of them contain one factor while the other 50% possess the second factor.

(E) *Law of Independent Assortment (Second Law of Mendelism)* : The two factors of each trait assort at random and independent of the factor of other traits at the time of meiosis (gametogenesis / sporogenesis) and get randomly as well as independently rearranged in the offspring. In monohybrid cross, the F_1 organisms produce two types of male and two types of female gametes, so that there is possibility of four types of gamete combinations.

In a dihybrid cross, if the gene/factors are to assort independently, F_1 organism will produce four types of male (2 × 2, e.g. RY, R*y*, *r*Y and *ry*) and four types of female gametes with 16 types of gametic recombinations (4 × 4). Mendel crossed genetically pure yellow round seeded (YYRR) pea plant with green wrinkled seeded (*yyrr*) pea plant. F_1 plants were all yellow and round seeded. In F_2 generation, four types of plants appeared—315/556 or 9/16 yellow rounded, 101/556 or 3/16 yellow and wrinkled, 108/556 or 31/6 yellow rounded and 32/556 or 1/16 green wrinkled. The ratio of seed colour (416/556 or 3/4 yellow : 140/556 or 1/4 green) and seed texture (423/556 or 3/4 rounded : 133/556 or 1/4 wrinkled) or individual traits is 3 : 1 showing that the factors for each trait behave independent of the factors of the other trait.

Law of Independent assortment is applicable to only those factors or genes which are present on different chromosomes. Chromosomes have hundreds of genes which show linked inheritance or linkage. Mendel himself found linkage between flower and seed colour (white flower and white seed, red flower and grey seed) in pea.

- **Post Mendelian Discoveries are**

(*a*) Gene Interaction
(*b*) Incomplete Dominance
(*c*) Overdominance (super dominance)
(*d*) Codominance
(*e*) Multiple Alleles
(*f*) Blood group Inheritance
(*g*) Isoalleles
(*h*) Pseudoalleles
(*i*) Lethal genes
(*j*) Suppressor/Inhibitor Gene
(*k*) Epistasis
(*l*) Complementary genes
(*m*) Supplementary genes
(*n*) Duplicate genes
(*o*) Polymeric/Additive Genes
(*p*) Multiple factors
(*q*) Pleiotropic genes
(*r*) Qualitative Inheritance
(*s*) Quantitative/Poly Inheritance
(*t*) Pedigree Analysis

Chemical Nature of Gene

In the 1930s, G.W. Beadle, B. Ephrussi, E.L. Tatum, J.B.S. Haldane and others provided a basis for understanding the functional properties of genes and suggested functional extensions of the **classical gene concept**. The gene was at first characterized as an indivisible unit of structure, unit of mutation and unit of function. A.E. Garrod, had indicated in 1902 that genes in humans function through 'enzymes'.

Early triumphs were the identification of maromolecules carrying genetic information in a bacterium by O.T. Avery and associates and in a virus by A. Hershey and M. Chase. The Avery *et al* experiments showed that a chemical, deoxyribo-nucleic acid (DNA) could bring about genetic change **(transformation)** in a *Peumococcus* bacterium; **Hershey and Chase** demonstrated that the nucleic acid component (DNA) and not the protein is the genetic material carried by the bacteriophage. **H. Fraenket Conrat & B. Singer** showed that ribonucleic acid (RNA) is the genetic material in tobacco mosaic virus. Thus, RNA performs the function in some viruses that DNA performs in other organisms.

J.D. Watson and **F.H.C. Crick** worked out the double helix structure of the chemical DNA. The central problem of genetics was thus resolved with the discovery that **DNA is the genetic material**. Genetic mechanisms could now be forumlated in biochemical terms. Also, it became clear how do units (genes) of DNA control specific traits in organisms and how do assemblages of DNA units carried in fertilized eggs provide 'blueprints' for development of entire organisms.

(A) *Functional Perspective :* Genes accomplish their function (*a*) through **replication** that results in more units like themselves & (*b*) through **transcription** and **translation**, whereby, proteins that function as determiners in the metabolism of the cell are synthesized. Although genes are usually stable, they are susceptible to occasional change or **mutation,** which provides altered forms of genes (alleles). Mendel first postulated the existence of genes from their end effects, as expressed in altered characteristics. Now genes have been defined chemically and are know for what they do in directing the formation of traits through the specificity of protein enzymes. Thus, DNA carries the specifications for growth, differentiation & functioning of cells in the organism.

Gene *versus* Allele Concepts (Pseudoalleles)

Gene : "Hereditary unit specifying the production of a distinct protein (e.g. an enzyme) or RNA." In modern sense, an inherited factor that determines a biological character of an organism is called a gene. This is a functional unit of hereditary material. In the part, gene was believed to be unit of structure also, but recent knowledge has shown that it is no longer a unit of structure.

Alleles (Allelomorphs) : Alleles, the abbreviated form of the term "allelomorphs" (meaning one form or the other) indicates alternative forms of the same gene. i.e. "One of two genes for a given trait that occurs in a specific position on each homologous chromosome". For instance, 'D' & '*t*' are two alleles of the gene for plant height. In pure tall or pure dwarf plants, same allele is duplicated (DD or *dd*), while in hybrid tall both the alleles will be present (D*d*). An individual having only one allele or in other words, two identical genes, is known as **homozygous** (DD or *dd*). Similarly, an individual, having two different alleles will be called **heterzygous** or **hybrid** (D*d*). In the present usage the term gene and the allele are interchangable, but while gene can be used for any factor, allele is used with reference to another allele. For instance, while 'D' & '*d*' are alleles to each other, they cannot be allelic to any other gene.

Pseudoalleles : Pseudogenes are partial duplicates of structural genes that have incorporated sufficient changes, that they are not biologically active and are usually not transcribed. Pseudogenes are turning out to be quite common in eukoryotes. There are **inactive but stable component** of a genome resembling a gene, apparently derived from active genes by mutation. The pseudogenes, which are relatively frequent in the mammalian genome, can be identified because they have undergone mutations that render them unable to produce functional *m* RNA e.g., a pseudogene might contain premature chain termination codons, (insertions or deletions) that cause the message to be read out of frame. Most frequently the promoters of pseudogenes are inactive. Because there is no selective pressure to maintain a functional gene product, in due course, pseudogenes accumulate multiple mutations and eventually become random sequence DNA.

Quantitative Genetics and Multiple Factors

Soon after rediscovery of Mendel's experiments, two main groups of geneticists emerged :

(*i*) *"Mendelians" :* Who believed that all evolutionary important heritable differences are qualitative and discontinuous.

(*ii*) *"Biometricians" :* Who proposed that heritable variation is basically quantitative and continuous and that genes did not exist as separate units.

To prove that both "mendelian" and "biometricians" were only partly correct, **Johannsen (1903)** used the character of seed weight in beans and analysed its breeding behaviour. In a commercial seed lot of a variety, seed weight ranged from 1 cg (cg = centigram) to 90 cg. In the progeny of seed of every weight group, great-variation was observed, and by successive self pollinations for several generations, it was possible to isolate 19 pure lines. Each pure line had a distinct average seed weight, which was maintained in the progeny, although variation did exist in each pure line and was attributed to environmental effect.

Thus by Johannsen's experiment, it could be shown that continuous variation can be heritable, a belief opposed by 'mendelians'. However since differences between 19 different pure lines isolated by **Johannsen (1903)** could not be ascribed to specific genes, genetic basis of quantitative traits still remained disputed and it could not be proved that like qualitative traits, quantitative traits exhibiting continuous variation are also controlled by individual genes comparable to Mendelian factors.

Subsequently, it was **Yule (1906)**, who suggested that quantitative variation may be controlled by large number of individual genes, each having a small effect. Soon after Yule's proposal, **H. Nitsson-Ehle (1908)** and **East (1910)**, demonstrated segregation and assortment of genes controlling quantitative traits, kernel colour in wheat and corolla length in tobacco. Such genes were later called **polygenic systems** and inheritance due to such a system was explained in the form of **"multiple factor hypothesis."**

Alleles that had small but *cumulative effect* with semidominance rather than complete dominance were postulated to behave in a Mendelian fashion. Several to many nonallelic genes were postulated to have cumulative effects on particular traits. An explanation for continuous variation thus emerged in the form of the **'multiple-gene-hypothesis'.** Experimental results and interpretations substantiating this hypothesis were obtained from the classical investigations of H. Nilsson Ehle in Sweden & E.M. East in the United States during the period 1910-1913.

Numerical and structural variations in chromosomes and their significance

Changes in the number and structure of the chromosomes may occur spontaneously or experimentally by the action of radiation or chemicals. The number of chromosomes is generally constant for plant and animal species. 'Chromosomal change' in number are of two main kinds : (1) *Euploids :* a change in the number of chromosome sets, the set being kept balanced (2) *Aneuploids :* there is a loss or gain of one or more chromosomes. In exceptional cases there are *haploid* organisms. In plants, *polyploids* (triploid, tetraploid) are rather common. They originate by **reduplication without cytokinesis**. In animals, polyploids are scarce, because sex is frequently determined by a pair of different chromosomes (XY). **Polyploidy** can be induced by colchicine, this substance in used in agriculture to improve certain plant species. *Allopolyploidy* consists of the formation of a hybrid with different sets of chromosomes. Sometimes a diploid gamete fertilizes a normal haploid gamete, producing a new species with a triploid number. Thus there are two main kinds of change in the number of chromosomes. In *euploids* the change is in the haploid number but the entire set of chromosome is kept balanced, whereas, in *aneuploids* there is a loss or gain of one or more chromosome(s) causing the set to become unbalanced. In humans aneuploidy may cause severe alterations of the phenotype. Polyploidy and allopolyploidy are expamples of euploidy.

Among the aneuploid organisms there are the *trisomic* (i.e. with three similar chromosomes instead of a normal pair) and the *monosomic* (missing one member of a pair of homologous chromosomes) conditions. There two conditions are important in humans and may arise by **nondisjunctional** division.

Chromosomal aberrations

Also called **'structural alterations'** involve a change in the molecular organization of the chromosome. One or two breaks are produced at the level of the chromatin fiber, and the effect depends on whether it occurs in the G_1 phase (one chromatid) or in the G_2 (two chromatids). Chromosomal aberration should be differentiated from *gene* or *point mutations*, which occur at molecular level. Ionizing radiations X-rays, γ-rays, β-rays, fast neutrons, slow neutrons and ultraviolet light can produce point mutations or chromosomal aberrations. The number of mutations increases proportionally with the dose of X-radiation. The effect of radiation is cumulative. An exposure of culture cells to 2DR (roentgen units) is sufficient to produce one chromosome break per cell. In contrast to mutations which increase proportionally with the dose, chromosomal aberrations increase exponentially with the dose. Breakage can be followed by "healing" of the broken end (the breaks may be at the chromosome or the chromatid level). Chromatid breaks are produced in cells irradiated after the S-phase. If two breaks are produced, **translocation, inversions,** and **large deletions** may be induced. **Dicentric chromosomes** may be produced, which form a bridge at anaphase. In the human, heavy medical radiation, nuclear accidents or radioactive substances may produce chromosomal aberrations. In the production of new antibiotics and plants, irradiation is being used to economic advantage. *Somatic mutations* are not transmitted from one generation to another, whereas, germ cell mutations may be passed to the offsprings.

Some of the main chromosomal aberrations are

(1) *Deficiency or deletion*, in which a part (either interstitial or terminal) of the chromosome is missing. The parts of the chromosome lacking the kinetochore are generally lost. Deficiency may be 'heterogygous' (one chromosome normal) or 'homozygous' (both chromosome are deficient). The latter generally does not survive.

(2) *Duplication*, in which a chromosome segment is represent two or more times (tandem duplication).

(3) *Translocation* in which there is an exchange of segments between non-homologous chromosomes (reciprocal type) or between different parts of the same chromosome (simple type). Sometime *centric* fusion occurs when the two chromosomes are broken near the kinetochore and form a metacentric (v-shaped) chromosome.

(4) *Inversion*, in which there is breakage of a segment, followed by its fusion in a reverse position. It is **'pericentric'** if the kinetochore is outside. Isochromosomes may arise from a break at kinetochore, resulting in two chromosomes with identical arms.

Sister chromatid's exchange consists of the interchange of DNA segments between sister chromatids in a chromosome. First described in studies using ^{3}H-thymidine, it was interpreted as the result of radiation from ^{3}H. This aberration can be studied with bromodeoxyuridine (BrdU), which is incorporated instead of thymidine and which produces changes in fluorescence or in the **Giemsa stain.** This technique permits the detection of diseases, characterized by chromosome fragility and enables the study of the action of mutagenic drugs which increase the number of breaks.

Significance

Cytogenetic studies have provided excellent methods for establishing taxonomic interrelationships and have, thereby, contributed to studies of *evolution* and systematics. One of the most frequent causes of evolution is a change in the order of genes as a result of chromosomal aberrations. In plants, aneuploids and polyploidy are frequent sources of variations, where as in mammals and birds, speciation depends more on chromosomal rearrangement and point mutations.

In the study of evolution, the number of chromosomes, the characteristics of the karyotype, the total chromosomal area, and the content of DNA are investigated. The presence of metacentric chromosomes may, in some cases, result from fusion of two aerocentric chromosomes. The contrasting phenomenon (i.e. dissociation) may lead to an increase in chromosome number. The problem of *evolution* is very complex. Knowledge of cytogenetics is most fundamental to the understanding of this problem of evolution. One example of importance of cytogenetics in evolution is given in a comparison of the chromosome pairs of the primates and humans. Primates have 48 chromosomes (24 pairs) while human have 23 pairs instead of 24 pairs of primates. There comparative studies have demonstrated that

(*i*) 13 pairs of chromosome in humans are identical with 13 pairs in the chimpanzee.

(*ii*) Chromosome number 2 in humans has resulted from centric fusion (or **Robertsonion translocation**) of two chromosomes present in hominoid apes.

(*iii*) The other chromosomes differ in the occurrence of nine pericentric inversions and two additions of chromatin material.

Study of Structure, behaviour and significance of Polytene, Lampbrush and B-Chromosomes

Polytene Chromosome : Polytene chromosomes provided the first evidence that eukaryotic gene activity is regulated at the level of RNA synthesis. When ***dipteran*** chromosomes become polytenic, the DNA replicates by ***endomitosis***; and the resulting daughter chromatids remain aligned side by side. There chromatids are visible during interphase and have a characteristic morphology of dark bands and alternating interbands. Within these chromosomes it is possible to osberve the genetic activity of specific loci at local enlargements called **puffs**, which represent DNA undergoining intense gene transcription. Puff distribution varies from one tissue to another and can be induced experimentally, indicating the cell specialization results from variable gene transcription.

Polytene chromosomes constitute a valuable material for the study of gene regulation because their gene transcription can be visualized directly in the microscope.

Some cells of dipteran (flies, mosquitoes, midges) larvae become very large and have a high DNA content. The most prominent ones are located in the salivary gland, but other cells from the gut, fat body, and malpighian tubules of the larva also become 'polytenic'. (Polyteny differs from polyploidy, in which there is also excess DNA per nucleus, but in which the new chromosomes are separate from each other).

A polytene chromosome of *Drosophila* salivary glands has about 1000 DNA molecules arranged side by side which arise from 10 rounds of DNA replication ($2^{10} = 1024$). Other dipteran species have even more DNA molecules per polytene chromosome, for example, *chironomus* has 16,000.

In polytene cells, the chromosomes are visible during interphase, and the *chromomeres* (regions in which the chromatin is more tighly coiled) alternate with regions where the DNA fibres are folded more loosely. The alignment of many chromosomes gives polytene chromosomes their characteristic morphology, in which a series of dark bands alternates with clear zones called *interbands*. There are about 5000 bands in the *Drosophilla* genome. They have characteristic morphology and positions, which permit detailed chromosome mapping.

An additional characteristic of polytene chromosomes is that the maternal and paternal homologue remain associated side by side, in what is called *'somatic pairing'*. This permits the identification of deletions, inversions, duplications as regions looped out of the chromosomes. The pericentromeric heterochromatin of all the *Drosophila* chromosomes coalesces in a chromocenter, where the chromosomes are joined together. The satellite DNAs of the chromocenter are underreplicated with respect to the rest of the chromosome. (i.e. they undergo fewer rounds of replication). Polytene cells are unable to undergo mitosis and are destined to die. Not all the cells in a dipteran larva have polytene chromosomes. Those destined to produce the adult structures after metamorphosis (***imaginal discs***) remains diploid.

Polytene chromosomes have become even more important with the advent of recombinant DNA techniques because they make it possible to map any DNA segment to specific chromosomal loci by *in situ* hybridization. Polytene chromosomes are very suitable for *in situ* hybridization because their 1000 DNA molecules are aligned side by side, thereby greatly facilitating the detection of single copy genes.

The bands have greatly helped in the mapping of chromosomes in cytogenetics studies. The bands occasionally form reversible "puffs" known as *"chromosome puffs"* or *"Balbiani rings"* which are associated with differential gene activation. A puff can be considered a band in which the DNA unfolds into open loops as a consequence of intense gene transcription. i.e. "puffs are sites of intense gene transcription".

In salivary glands, the appearance of some puffs has been correlated with the production of specific proteins which are secreted in large amounts in the larval saliva. e.g. *Chironomous* has at the base of the salivary glands four specialized cells that contain cytoplasmic granules of a special secretory protein. The gene for this protein is located in a distinct puff that appears only in the four specialized cells. These results show that cell specialization results from variable gene transcription.

Puffing is a cyclic and reversible phenomenon. The steroid hormone **'ecdysone'**, which induces molting in insects, will induce the formation of specific puffs when injected into larvae or when added to salivary glands in culture by temperature shock. When *Drosophila* larvae normally grown at 25°C, are exposed to a temperature of 37°C, a series of specific genes is activated while most other genes are represed. Five minutes after the heat shock, nine new puffs are seen on the giant chromosome of the salivary glands. There puffs are active in RNA synthesis as can be demonstrated by ^{3}H-uridine labeling and radioautography. These new RNAs are accumulated in cytoplasm after being released from the puffs and give rise to eight specific heat shock proteins, so the induction of specific proteins is due to an increased transcription of individual genes RNA polymerase II accumulates in the heat shock puffs, while it disappears from other regions of chromosomes.

In D. *melanogaster* the giant chromosomes are found in the form of five long and one short strands radiating from a single more or less amorphous mass known as *chromocentre*. One long strand corresponds to the X-chromosome and the remaining four long strands are the arms of IInd and IIIrd chromosomes. The short strand which is small dot like is IVth chromosome. The centromeres of all there chromosomes fuse to form chromocentre. In the male files, the Y chromosome is also found fused within the chromocentre and is therefore not seen as a separate strand.

Lampbrush Chromosomes : Special kind of chromosomes known as lampbrush chromosomes are found during the prolonged diplotene stage of first meiotic division and in spermatocyte nuclei of *Drosophila*. They are characterized by a remarkable change in structure. The change in structure includes an enormous increase in length. These chromosomes may sometimes become even larger than polytenic giant salivary gland chromosomes. The largest chromosome having a length up to 1 mm have been observed in *urodele* amphibian. The chromosomes seem to have a chromomeric pattern with loops projecting in pairs from a single chromomere. The size of loops varies from an average of 9.5 μ in frog to upto 200 μ in newt. The chromomeres are connected by inter-chromomeric fibres. These pair of loops in these chromosomes give them the characteristic lampbrush appearance. Frequently there loops exhibit a thin axis (which probably consists of one DNA double helix) from which fibres project which are covered with a loop matrix consisting of RNA and protein. The number of pairs of loops gradually increases in meiosis till it reaches maximum in diplotene. As meiosis proceeds further, number of loops gradually decreases and the loops ultimately disappear due to disintegration rather then reabsorption back into the chromomere. (H. Ris., had though that the loops were integral parts of chromonemata which are extended in the form of major coils.) It is also believed that the loops represent the modified chromosome structures at the loci of active genes. It has been observed that, if the activity of there genes is checked by actinomycin D, the loops will collapse. Numerous small nucleoli are commonly formed from the lampbrush chromosomes due to the rings detached from the loops at specific loci.

Lampbrush chromosomes occur at the diplotene stage of meiotic prophase of all animal species. Highly condensed chromomeres form the chromosome axis, from which loops of DNA extend laterally as a result of intense RNA synthesis. Each loop has an axis formed by a single DNA molecule which is covered by a matrix of nascent RNA with hn RNA-binding proteins attached to it. Transcriptional units in oocyte may be extremely long-upto 100 μ. Some experiments suggest that the long transcriptional units of lampbrush chromosomes may be due to a failure of transcriptional termination.

Lampbrush chromosomes were first observed by Flemming in 1882 and were described in detail in shark oocyte by Ruckert in 1892. He coined the name because the chromosomes look like the brushes used in those times to clean the chimneys of oil lamps.

Lampbrush chromosomes occur at the diplotene stage of meiotic prophase in oocytes of all animal species, in spermatocytes of several species, and even in the giant nucleus of the unicellular alga *'Acetabularia'*. They are visualized best in *Salamander* oocytes because they have a high DNA content and therefore very large chromosomes.

Because Lampbrush chromosomes are found in meiotic prophase, they are present in the form of 'bivalents' in which the maternal and paternal chromosomes are held together by chiasmata at those sites where crossing over has previously occurred. Each bivalent has four chromatids, two in each nomologue. The axis of each homologue consists of a row of granules or chromomeres from which lateral loops extend. The loops are always symmetrical, each chromosome having two ot them, one for each chromatid (two additional symmetrical loops will be found on the homologue because cells in prophase of meiosis have a 4C DNA content—equivalent to a tetraploid cell.

The loops can be distinguished by size, thickness, and other morphologic characteristics. Each loop appears at a constant position in the chromosome, and detailed chromosome maps can be drawn. There are about 10,000 loops per chromosome set. Each loop has an axis formed by a single DNA molecule that is unfolded from the chromosome as a result of intense RNA synthesis. About 5 to 10% of the DNA is in the lateral loops; the rest being tightly condensed in the chromomeres of the chromosome axis, which are transcriptionally inactive.

Lampbrush chromosomes are very good material for *in situ* hybridization of cloned DNA to RNA because the thousands of nascent RNA molecules aligned side by side along the loop greatly amplify the hybridization signal. Studies with there techniques have shown that in some loops simple sequence satellite DNAs are transcribed; which is unusual because satellite DNA are normally not expressed.

The hybrization results are due to initiation of transcription at a histone gene promoter that then foils to terminate normally. Enormous transcripts are produced which result from read through into the satellite DNA. Eventually transcription stops when the next transcriptional unit is reached. This failure of termination may be generalized throughout the lampbrush chromosome and may explain the long loops.

TABLE : Size of the Lampbrush Lateral Loops Increases with the Genome Size

	C-value (pg of DNA)	*C-value Increase*	*Lampbrush Loop Size*
Xenopus laevis (South African clawed frog)	3.1	1	5-10μm
Triturus cristatus (Common European newt)	23	7.4	30-50μm
Neiturus maculosus (American "Mudpuppy" Salamander)	78	25.1	>100μm

Bacterial Chromosome : Bacterial and blue green algae are designated as the *akaryobionta* as against the *karyobionta* having better differentiated nuclei. However, feulgen positive bodies are seen in bacteria and blue-green algae, a reaction meant for the nucleus of chromosomes. There bodies can be clearly observed with the help of electron microscope. It has also been demonstrated that there bodies consist of a network of fine thread. Further work by a number of workers demonstrated that the network of threads consists of a single chromosome in the form of a ring. However, the exact three dimensional arrangement by which 1100 μ - 1400 μ long DNA chain is packed in a nucleoid is not very clear. The cross sections showed 500-900 strands indicating that a single DNA strand is folded back and forth several hundred times. It is also known that large part of the DNA in bacterial nucleoid is not combined with proteins. It has also been shown that the nucleoid is not combined with proteins. It has also been shown that the nucleoid of *Escherichia coli*, one of the most extensively studied bacterium often has a point of contact with the plasma membrane. This is perhaps the point at which the replication of DNA strand is initiated.

MOLECULAR BIOLOGY

Gene : The term gene was coined by Johanssen (1909) for mendelian *factor* or particulate elementary unit of inheritance which takes part in expression of a trait. Morgan (1911) called gene as the smallest segment of a chromosome which determines a trait as well as undergo crossing over. Beadle & Tatum (1948) proposed *one gene-one enzyme* hypothesis.

Yanofsky *et al* (1965) proposed *one gene/cistron one polypeptide* hypothesis. Berzer, distinguished three structural units of DNA—*cistron* (unit of function, determines synthesis of polypeptide), *recon* (unit of recombination or crossing over) and *muton* (unit of DNA that can undergo mutation). A *muton* can be as small as a nitrogen base. Cistron is commonly used as a synonym of gene. A gene can be structural or regulatory in nature. *Regulatory gene* is the one which controls the functioning of structural genes, e.g. regulator genes are repressor, promoter & operator types. *Structural gene* in the one which produces a biochemical molecule required for cellular machinery—*t* RNA, *r* RNA, *m* RNA. *m* RNA is involved in synthesis of structural proteins, enzymes, transport proteins, proteinaceous hormones, toxins, antigens etc. A structural gene normally codes for only a single polypeptide but a few produce POLYPROTEINS which are later broken to produce individual proteins. There is colinearity in the arrangement of nitrogen bases (in triplets) of a structural gene and amino acid sequence of polypeptide synthesized by it. A change in even a single nitrogen base may change the amino acid specified by its triplet. Eucaryotes possess split genes where the coding bases are not continuous but are interrupted by non-coding sequences. The two are respectively called *exons* and *introns*. Intron portions are also called *spacer* DNA or intervening sequences (IVS). Functional eucaryotic *m* RNA is formed by SPLICING—removal of intron portions and fusion of coding parts or exon portions. Split genes are also known from prokaryotes, e.g. thymidylate synthetase gene, ribonucleotide reductase gene of T_4. A few eucaryotic genes are without introns. They are called *exonic genes* (= nonsplit genes), e.g. histone genes and interferon genes. Certain eucaryotic exonic gens are called **processed genes.** Processed genes lack both introns and promoters. They are, therefore, nonfunctional. Processed genes are believed to have been formed by reverse transcription. In some viruses, the genetic material has *overlapping functions* with a segment of genetic material participating in two or more genes **(overlapping genes)**, e.g. D within E and B within A in ϕ 174.

In a cell, hardly 10% of the genes are active, (90% being inactive). Different genes are active in different types of tissues/cells. *Constitutive* or *house keeping* genes are those genes which are always in action because their products are always in action because their products are always required for cellular activities, e.g. ATPase, enzymes of glycolysis. *Nonconstitutive genes* are those genes which can be switched on or off as per requirements. They are of two kinds, *inducible* (remain repressed but are switched on in the presence of an inducer chemical) and *repressible* (remain active till switched off by a chemical).

60-70% of functional genes are a *single copy genes* as they are represented only once in the whole genome. The genes having more than one copy in the same genome are called *repeated genes,* e.g. histone gene, *t* RNA genes, *r* RNA genes, actin genes. *Multigenes* or multiple gene family is a group of nearly similar products, e.g. globin gene family *Pseudogenes* are nonfunctional genes. They are unable to produce functional products due to inactivation of promotoer region, presence of intervening nonsense codons, insertions or deletions, e.g. several sn RNA genes.

Transposons or **jumping genes** are those DNA segments which can pass from one place to another in the genome. At their ends, transposons have similar or inverted repetitive DNA sequences. The sequences can be cleaved by an enzyme **'transposase'.** Most common human transposon is Alu-family (so called as has a site for restriction endonuclease Alu-I). Transposons may take strong promoters to new sites or cause reshuffling of gene segments which lead to change in gene expression, e.g. protooncogene → oncogene.

Gene Expression in Viruses

The shape of viruses can be **cylindrical/helical** (e.g. TMV), **polyhedral/cuboidal** (e.g. Adeno-Virus, Herpes Virus, Mumps Virus) and binal with polyhedral head and **helical coil** (e.g. T_2, T_4). Holmes (1948) has differentiated viruses into 'phytophagineae' (plant viruses), 'Zoophagineae' (animal viruses) and 'phagineae' (microbe viruses). Phagineae includes **'bacteriophages'** (bacterial viruses, e.g. T_2, T_4, Lambda Phage) and **cyanophages** (Blue Green Algae Viruses, e.g. LPP-1, SM-1).

Viral Components : A virus is made of two parts—nucleoid and capsid. Additionally, it may have an envelope. Enzymes are rare.

1. *Nucleoid/Viral Chromosome :* It is made up of a single molecule of either DNA (Deoxyviruses or RNA (Riboviruses). DNA is generally double stranded (e.g. T_2, T_4) and rarely single stranded (e.g. coliphage *fd*, ϕ 174). RNA of riboviruses is commonly single stranded (e.g. TMV, Polio Virus, Influenza Virus) while rarely double stranded (Reovirus, Rous Sarcoma Virus). It may be even fragmented (e.g. Influenza Virus). Depending upon the mode of replication of RNA genome, riboviruses are of two types, RNA-RNA (negative strand RNA) and RNA-DNA (positive strand RNA). Nucleoid contains a few genes, e.g. 100 in T_4. Nucleic acid is coiled by means of polyamines. Some viruses possess enzyme lysozyme (e.g. T_2) and transcriptase (Retroviruses).

2. *Capsid :* It is a protein covering around nucleoid and other parts.

3. *Envelope :* It is a loose membranous covering in some zoophagineae (e.g. HIV). Envelope often possesses surface spikes.

Cryptogram : It is symbolic representation of various traits of viruses which was proposed by Gibbs *et al* (1966) and adopted by ICNV. A cryptogram has four parts:

(*i*) Nucleic acid type, (D or R) and number of strands (1 or 2).

(*ii*) Molecular weight of nucleic acid in millions/ percentage of nucleic acid of total particle.

(*iii*) Outline of particles like S or E or X (complex)/outline of nucleocapsid like S.

(*iv*) Host/vector like seed plant (S), invertebrate (I), vertebrate (V), bacterium (B), fungus (Fu) dipera (Di), Coleoptera (Cl), aphid (Af), nil (Zero or 0), unknown*.

Based on cryptogramic representation, below are given few examples of description of viruses.

1. Influenza Virus (*Myxovirus influenzae*)
   R/1, 2-3/10, S/E, V/O
2. Pox Virus (Poxvirus variolae)
   D/2, 160/5-7-5, X/*, V/O
3. T_4, D/2, 130/40, X/X, B/O
4. Polio Virus (Poliovirus primus)
   R/1, 2.5/30, S/S, V/O

Viral Reproduction

(A) *Lytic cycle :* T_4 bacteriophage is binal virus which attaches to the surface of bacterium *E. coli* by its tail fibres. Lysozyme creates a hole in the host cell wall. The tail sheath contracts and ejects the viral chromocome/DNA into the bacterium. Viral DNA controls the metabolic machinery of the host cell. It produces nucleases. Nuclease degrade DNA and *m* RNAs of the host. Viral DNA is not affected as its cytosine bases are methylated (huydroxy methylated cytosine or HMC). A number of copies of viral DNA are produced followed by synthesis of capsid proteins, polyamines and lysozyme. The components assemble and form phage particles or viruses. The hose cell ruptures or releases.

(B) **Lysogenic Cycle :** Lambda phage (λ) attaches to the surface of *E. coli* by means of tail, which produces a hole in host cell wall and injects the phage DNA. Phage DNA produces a repressor (CI), becomes nonvirulent or temperate and attaches to bacterial chromosome at a specific site (e.g. galctose locus in λ phage) by means of enzyme **intergrase**. The viral genome is now called **prophage/provirus**. It multiplies alongwith bacterial genome and is passed on to the progeny. The phenomenon of existence of nonvirulent prophage in the host is called *Lysogeny*. The host cell is called *Lysogenic* cell. Occasionally the synthesis of repressor is stopped. The temperate/nonvirulent phage is now changed to lytic/virulent phage.

The single strand DNA of $\phi \times 174$ or coliphage *fd* is known as *'plus strand'*. It forms its complementary or *'negative strand'*. The double strand or 'replicative' DNA takes over the metabolic machinery of host of synthesise plus strand DNAs and proteins for assembly of new phages.

(C) *Pinocytic Reproduction :* The whole virus enters the host cell except the envelope. It is quite common in RNA viruses which are of two types :

(*a*) **RNA-RNA Viruses :** DNA has no role in their multiplication. After entering the host cell, the viruses produce enzyme *replicase* which helps in producing more genetic RNA genome. The latter also produces *m* RNAs for synthesis of viral proteins.

(*b*) **RNA-DNA Viruses :** They are also called *retroviruses* (Temin, 1970) e.g. Tumour/Cancer Viruses, HIV. The viruses possess enzyme *reverse transcriptase* (Temin & Baltimore, 1972, in Rous Sarcoma Virus or RSV of Mouse). The enzyme builds DNA over RNA genome. The phenomenon is called reverse transcription or *teminism.* The *copy DNA (c DNA)* builds its complementary strand. The double strand copy DNA attaches to host DNA/chromosome and is now called *provirus.* It produces chemicals which disturb cellular machinery. The cell with provirus may dedifferentiate and start dividing leading to cancer (uncontrolled growth forming tumour which sends branches/roots to invade different parts). Some **20 viral oncogenes** (genes that trigger cancer) have been recorded. However, no virus has been definitely proved to cause cancer in humans. Humans have some proto-oncogenes (similar to viral oncogenes) which take part in growth but under certain circumstances they get changed to *cellular oncogenes.* Jumping genes/transposons can also cause cancer. There are a number of chemicals, physical factors and some viruses (i.e., Hepatitis B, Herpes, Papiloma, Epstein-Barr Virus) which promote Cancer. HIV (Human Immunodeficiency Virus) destroys immune system of the body and causes AIDS. The provirus ultimately dissociates, transcribes viral RNA genomes, produces reverse transcripture and viral proteins. Different parts assemble to form retroviruses. The latter come out through exocytosis or pass out to other cells through protoplasmic connections.

Gene Expression in Procaryotes

Bacterial Chromosome : A circular double strand or duplex DNA is folded variously with the help of RNA and polyamines to form bacterial chromosome, nucleoid, or genophore. It has 1/1000 DNA content of a eucaryotic genome. DNA of *E. coli* has a length of 1100 μm with some 2500 genes. Nucleoid is connected by γ-shaped forks to a membranous body/mesosome that develops over the plasmalemma.

Plasmids : A bacterial cell contains one to several circular extrachromosomal DNA segments called *plasmids* (Hoyes and Lederberg, 1952). They are capable of replication like nucleoid. At times the plasmid integrates with bacterial chromosome. It is then called *episome.* A plasmid carries a few genes, e.g. fertility factor (F^+), R-factors (resistance factors against common antibiotics like chloroamphenicol, tetracycline, streptomycin, sulphonamide), *Nif* (Nitrogen fixation) or colicinogenic factors (for synthesis of bacteriocidal and bacteriostatic chemicals).

Genome Replication : Bacteria multiply by binary fission. Generation time is 20 minutes in *E. coli* to 15-20 hours in *Myxobacterium tuberculosis.* Nucleoid replicates while attached to mesosome. It behaves like a single replicon (Cairns, 1963). Mesosome divides alongwith replication of nucleoid so that each daughter nucleoid is attached to its own mesosome.

Gene Recombination in Bacteria

Sexual reproduction and **haploid-diploid alternation** are absent in bacteria. However, one way gene reschuffling or recombination **(mesomixis)** can occur by three methods-conjugation, transformation & transduction.

(1) *Conjugation :* It was discovered by Lederberg and Tatum (1946) in *E. coli.* They found that mixing of two different double (Bio^-, Met^-) and triple (Thr^-, Leu^-, Thi^-) auxotrophs over minimal medium produced occassional prototrophs. Cell contact was required. Anderson (1957) observed conjugation sare dimorphic, male donor having fertility factor (F^+) and *sex pili* while female or recipient is without both fertility factor (F^-) and sex pili. Contact between the two types cause development of 'conjugation tube' by means of a pilus of donor.

Meromixis occurs by two methods.

(*a*) **Sterile Male Method :** No gene of the male chromosome is transferred to the recipient cell. Fertility factor replicates. One plasmid passes into recipient/female cell through the conjugation tube to make it donor as well. The phenomenon is called *sexduction*.

(*b*) **Fertile Male Method :** The plasmid of fertility factor gets integrated to bacterial chromosome and is called *episome*. The donor F^+ cell with episome is called Ffr (High frequency of recombination) or **super male** as recombination frequency increases to some 1000 times. The integrated F^+ factor breaks bacterial chromosome at the end of its attachment. The freed chromosome end (zero end) becomes linear and passes into recipient cell. The whole male chromosome is rarely transferred (it takes some two hours). The fertility factor is the last to migrate. Conjugation is generally interrupted any time. A few to several genes of male/donor are transferred to female/recipient cell. The latters is now called *merozygote* or *partial zygote*. The donor cell generally dies after conjugation. Some donor genes get integrated to recipient genome while others degenerate.

(2) Transformation : It is the picking up of genes from DNA of the dead relatives. Transformation was discovered by Griffith (1928) in *Diplococcus pneumoniae* (transfer of gene for virulence from dead bacteria to nonvirulent bacteria). Avery *et al* (1944) found transferring material to be segment of DNA. Transformation is quite common as DNA is released into the medium after death of cells. *Competence* or ability to pick up foreign DNA is present for a brief period towards the end of active growth. Additionally calcium chloride in required by *E. coli*. A competent cell has many receptor sites for attachment of foreign DNAs but only a specific DNA segment gains entry. It attaches to fork of mesosome and gets integrated to host DNA during its replication. The competent recipient cell now becomes recombinant.

(3) Transduction : Transfer of genes from one organism to another with the help of a virus/vector is known as transduction. It was discovered by Zinder & Lederberg (1952) in case of *Salmonella typhimurium* (typhoid in mice). Later it was reported in a number of other bacteria. Bacteriophages have two types of multiplication, **lysogenic** and **lytic**. In lysogenic/nonvirulent/temperate phase, the virus genome is integrated to bacterial genome and called **prophage**. At times the prophage dissociates from the bacterial genome, becomes virulent and performs lytic cycle. However, the bacterial DNA is not destroyed completely so that some of the phage particles come to have segments of bacterial genome. They are called 'transducting phages' as they transfer some genes of the previous host to the new host. (the new host is not harmed as the phage becomes deficient in some of its own genes). Transduction is of two types, 'generalised' (genes not fixed) and 'restricted' (same gens, e.g. *lac* or *bio* gene in case of lambda phage in *E. coli* K-12, because the phage genome attaches between the two). Donor gene may integrated between the two. Donor gene may integrate with genome of recipient (becomes recombinant, hence complete transduction) or fails to get associated with recipient DNA and degenerate (*abortive* transduction.)

Operon Concept

Operons are segments of genetic material which function as regulatory units or units or units that can be switched on and off. Operon concept was given by two French scientists, working at Pasteur Institute, Francois Jacob and Jacques Monod (1961). While studying lactose utilisation in mutants of *E. coli*. An operon consists of one to several structural genes (three in lac operon and five in tryptophan operon of *E. coli*, nine in histidine or operon of *Salmonella typhimurium*), one operator gene, a promoter gene, a regulator gene, a repressor and inducer/or corepressor. Operons are of two types, inducible and repressible.

Inducible Operon System/Lac Operon System: An inducible operon system is that regulated genetic material which remains regulated genetic material which remains switched off normally but becomes operational in the presence of an inducer. It occurs in *catabolic pathways*. The components are :

(1) *Structural Genes* : They are genes which produce *m* RNAs for forming polypeptide/proteins/enzymes. Lac operon of *E. coli* has three structural genes-Z (produces enzyme β-galactosidase for splitting lactose/galactoside into glucose and galactose), Y (produces enzymes galactoside permease required in entry of lactose/galactoside) and A (produces enzyme galactoside acetylase/ transacetylase without any function in *E. coli*). The three structural genes of *lac operon* produce a single polycistronic *m* RNA. The three enzymes are, however, produced in different concentrations.

2. *Operator Gene :* It gives passage to RNA polymerase when the structural genes are to express themselves. Normally it is covered by a repressor. Operator gene of the *lac operon* is small, made up only of 27 base pairs.

3. *Promoter Gene :* It is recoginition centre/ initiation point for RNA polymerase of the operon.

4. *Regulator Gene (i Gene) :* It produces a repressor that binds to operator gene for keeping it nonfunctional to pass from promoter to structural genes).

5. *Repressor :* It is a small protein formed by regulator gene which binds to operator gene and blocks passage of RNA-polymerase towards structural enzymes. Repressor has two allosteric sites, one for attaching to operator gene and second for binding to inducer. Repressor to *lac operon* has a molecular weight of 160,000 and 4 subunits of 40,000 each.

4. *Inducer :* It is a chemical which attaches to repressor, changes the shape of operator binding site so that repressor no more remains attached to operator. Lactose/galactose is inducer of *lac operon*. As soon as the operator gene becomes free, RNA polymerase is recognised by promoter gene. This process requires c AMP. RNA polymerase passes over the operator gene and then reaches the area of structural genes. Here it catalyses transcription of *m* RNAs.

Repressible Operon System/Tryptophan Operon System : A repressible operon system is that regulates genetic material which normally remains active/operational and enzymes formed by its structural genes present in the cell till the operon is switched off when concentration of an end product crosses a threshold value. Repressible operon system usually occurs in *anabolic pathways*, e.g., *tryptophan operon, arginine operon*. Each has the following parts:

(1) *Structural Genes :* They are genes which take part in synthesis of polypeptide/proteins/enzymes through the formation of specific *m* RNAs. **Tryptophan operon** has five structural genes-E, D, C, B and A.

(2) *Operator Gene :* It provides passage to RNA polymerase moving from promoter to structural genes. Operator gene of repressible operon is normally kept swtiched on as **aporepressor** formed by regulator gene is unable to block the gene.

(3) *Promoter Gene :* It is initiation/recognition point for RNA polymerase.

(4) *Regulator Gene :* The gene produces an apropressor.

(5) *Aporepressor :* It is a proteinaceous substance formed through the activity of regulator gene. It is able to block operator gene only when a corepressor is also available.

(6) *Corepressor :* The nonproteinaceous component of repressor which can be end product (feed back inhibition/repression) of the reaction mediated through enzyme synthesized by structural genes. Corepressor of tryptophan operon is tryptophan. It combines with apropressor, forms repressor which then blocks the operator gene to swtich off operon.

Multigene Families

Multigene family is a group of similar or nearly similar genes that help in forming multiple copies either for meeting higher demand or time/tissue specific products. The former are called repeated genes. Globin gene family is an example of time/ tissue specific multigene family.

Repeated Genes : There are genes occurring in multiple copies or having variant repetition are called repeated genes, e.g., histone genes, *t* RNA genes, Ss RNA genes, actin genes, Sn RNA genes, heat shock protein genes.

Globin Gene Family in Humans : In early embryo, haemoglobin consists of $\zeta_2 \epsilon_2, \zeta_2 \gamma_2$ and $\alpha_2 \epsilon_2$ claim. In foetal stage haemoglobin is $\alpha_2 \gamma_2$. In adult, 97% of haemoglobin in $\alpha_2 \beta_2$, 2% $\alpha_2 \delta_2$ and 1% $\alpha_2 \gamma_2$ (foetal form). ϵ, δ, β and γ genes are located on chromosome 11 while ζ and α genes occur on chromosome 16.

Sn RNA : Small nuclear RNA. Uridine rich, seven types, named U_1 to U_7. They are stable and ubiquitous. Each Sn RNA combines with 7-8 molecules of molecules of protein to form ribonucleoprotein or Sn RNP. Sn RNPs are involved in splicing (U_1 and U_2), *r* RNA processing (U_3) and *m* RNA processing.

MUTATIONS

Mutations : (Biochemical & Molecular Basis)

There are sudden inheritable/transmissible discontinuous variations which appear in organisms due to permanent change in their genotypes. They are also known as *sports* or *saltations*. The term mutation was coined by Hugo de Vries (1901) who also proposed *mutation theory of evolution*. He observed 834 mutations in a population of 54343 plants of *Oenothera lamarckiana* (Evening Primrose). Most of the mutations observed by de Vries were due to changes in chromosome number and chromosomal aberrations. Genotype can change due to changes in chromosome numbers, chromosome structure and gene mutations.

Changes in Chromosome Number/Genomatic Mutations

They are of two types, *euploidy* and *eneuploidy*. Euploidy is the condition in which chromosome number is exact multiple of a genome, e.g. monoploidy, diploidy, polyploidy.

Polyploidy : It is the phenomenon of having more than two genomes or sets of chromosomes, e.g. 3n (triploid), 4n (tetraploid), 5n (pentaploid), etc. Polyploids with odd number of genomes are sexually sterile e.g. Banana, Pineapple. They are propagated vegetatively. Other polyploids also become genetically distinct because they do not cross-breed freely with diploids. Polyploidy can develop due to:

(*i*) Failure of spindle development
(*ii*) Failure of meiosis I
(*iii*) Fusion between unreduced gametes, unreduced and normal gametes, one egg with more than one sperm, etc.

Polyploidy is induced by :

(*i*) Decaptiation
(*ii*) High or low temperatures
(*iii*) Mechanical injury
(*iv*) Infection
(*v*) Irradiation
(*vi*) Chemicals like colchicine, granosan, sulphanilamide, veratrine sulphate etc.

Colchicine ($C_{22}H_{25}O_6N$) is an alkaloid obtained from Autumn Crocus (*Colchicum autumnale*). It is a mitotic poison (Blakeslee, 1937) which inhibits spindle formation without affecting replication of chromosomes.

Polyploidy is of three types-

1. Autopolyploidy
2. Allopolyploidy
3. Autoallopolyploidy.

There is a *gigas effect* with larger size and often higher yield (due to polyploidies).

1. Autopolyploidy : It is the increase in number of same genome e.g. AAA, AAAA-Rice, Gram, Lablab, Maize, Guava, Potato, Groundnut, Coffee, etc. (Banana is autotriploid). Seedless autotriploid variety of water melon has been evolved. Triploid sugarbeet has more sugar content. Colchicine induces autotetraploidy.

2. Allopolyploidy : It is the increase in number of chromosome set due to coming together of genomes of two or more species—hence *interspecific polyploidy*, e.g. AABB, AABBDD. Allotetraploids like AABB are also called *amphidiploids*. Allopolyploidy has occurred in nature due to hybridisation between two species followed by doubling of chromosomes e.g. wheat (Durum AABB, Bread wheat, AABBDD), American cotton, and *Nicotiana tabacum*. *Raphanobrassica* was the first man made allopolyploid developed by Karpechenko (1928) after crossing Radish (*Raphanus sativus*, $2n = 18$) and cabbage (*Brassica oleracea*, $2n = 18$) followed by doubling of chromosome (AABB, 36).

Triticale was formed by Muntzing by crossing Rye (*Secale* cereale, $2n = 14$) and wheat (*Durum*, $4n = 28$, Bread wheat, $6n = 42$) followed by doubling of chromosome so that it can be hexaploid or octaploid. *Brassica juncea* (Rai) is an allopolyploid between *Brassica compestris* (Yellow mustards, $2n = 18$) and *Brassica nigra* (Black mustard $2n = 16$) produced through hybridisation followed by chromosome doubling (AABB = 34).

3. *Autoallopolyploidy* : It is the increase in chromosome sets due to coming together of different genomes and the occurrence of one genome in more than diploid state, e.g. AAABB (*Helianthus tuberosus*).

Aneuploidy/Heteroploidy : It is the deletion or addition of one or more chromosomes from the original genomes. Aneuploidy develops due to nondisjunction of homologous chromsomes at the time of meiosis so that abnormal gametes develop which are either deficient in chromosomes (e.g. $n-1$, $n-1-1$) or surplus in chromosomes (e.g. $n+1$, $n+1+1$). **Hypoploidy** is **aneuploidy** with loss of chromosomes while **hyperploidy** is **aneuploidy** with addition of chromosomes. *Double aneuploidy* is change in number of two homologous chromosome pairs (e.g., $2n-1-1$) while 'triple aneuploidy' is changed chromosome number for three homologous chromosome pairs (e.g. $2n+1+1+1$). Organisms having aneuploidy are called **aneuploids**. They are provided with a name corresponding to number of affected chromosomes appended with suffix-*somic*, e.g. monosomic, nullisomic, trisomic, tetrasomic, pentasomic. Aneuploidy is corresponding trisomy, tetrasomy, pentasomy, etc.

Monosomic : It is an aneuploid in which a chromosome is deficient of its homologue causing genetic imbalance resulting in weaker than a normal man. Monosomic is formed by the union of deficient gamete ($n-1$) and normal gamete. A sex chromosome monosomic in human beings is TURNER's SYNDROM (44 + X). In double monosomic, two different chromosomes are deficient of their homologues ($2n-1-1$).

Nullisomic : It is an aneuploid in which a pair of homologous chromosomes is deficient ($2n-2$) resulting in absence of certain genes. Nullisomy is lethal in diploid organisms but can survive in polyploidy. It is produced by the union of two gametes deficient in the same chromosome $(n-1)\times(n-1)$.

Trisomic : Trisomic is an aneuploid or heteroploid which has one chromosome represented in triplicate ($2n+1$). It is followed by the union of a normal gamete (n) with a gamete having an extra chromosome ($n+1$). Trisomics show gigas effect for certain genes and abnormality for others. **'Down's syndrome'** of human beings is due to trisomy of chromsome 21 while **Klinefelter's Syndrome'** is due to additional X-chromosome in otherwise male individual (XY). All the possible trisomics have been studied in *Datura*.

Tetrasomic : It is an aneuploid in which one chromosome is represented in quadraplicate. Tetrasomic is formed by union of two gametes each having the similar extra chromosome, $(n+1)\times(n+1)$. Two chromosomes are represented in quadruplicate in *double tetrasomic* ($2n+2+2$) and three in *triple tetrasomic* ($2n+2+2+2$). Tetrasomic super females (44 + XXXX) are infertile and have mental abnormality. Otherwise, tetrasomics are most stable of all the aneuploids showing gigas effect of many genes.

Pentasomic : An aneuploid with one chromosome represented five times ($2n+3$) e.g. a rare super female in human beings (44 + XXXXX).

Mixed Aneuploid : It is an aneuploid with both hypoploidy (deficiency) and hyperploidy (addition), e.g. $2n+1A-1B$.

Chromosome Aberrations : They are changes involving chromosome morphology which result in changes in number and sequence of genes without altering ploidy or gene structure. Chromosome aberrations involve breaking of chromosome segments, their loss or union with same (intrachromosomal aberration) or different chromosomes (interchromosomal aberration). The important types are as follows :

(A) *Deficiency :* It is the loss of chromosome segment. The lost segment may be *terminal* (deficiency or terminal deficiency) or *intercalary* (intercalary deficiency or deletion). The terms deficiency and deletions are also used interchangeably. Terminal deficiency involves a single break near the chromosome end. In intercalary/intrestitial deficiency or deletion, there are two breaks (double breaks), loss of separated segment and the union in the region of breaks. In **heterozygous deficiency** (deficiency in one out of two chromosomes of a homologous pair) the synapsed chromosomes would show difference in length at one end (terminal deficiency) or loop (intercalary deficiency/deletion). **Homozygous deficiency** may be lethal if some vital gene is involved (e.g. sex-linked notch wing deletion in *Drosophila*). Notch wing heterozygous deficiency produces notched wings margins in female *Drosophila*. Even a recessive gene may express if corresponding gene on the other homologous chromosome has become deficient. The phenomenon is called **pseudodominance.**

(B) *Duplication :* It is the phenomenon of having one or more genes in excess of the normal complement segment :

(*i*) **Tandem/Repeat Duplication :** The duplicating segment gets incorporated next to normal corresponding segment, e.g. ABCDEFGHGH.

(*ii*) **Reverse Tandem Duplication :** The duplicating segment is incorporated next to normal corresponding segment but the order is reversed, e.g. ABCDEFGHHG.

(*iii*) **Displaced Duplication :** The duplicating segment is incorporated away from the correponding segment on the same chromosome.

(*iv*) **Transposed Duplication :** The duplicating segment is incorporated in a nonhomologous segment. Duplication increases the number of genes which increases genetic redundancy, allows development of variations and hence evolution. However, some duplications are harmful, e.g. development of bar eye in *Drosophila*. Presence of single B gene on X-chromosome (both chromosomes in female) produces normal eye with 780 facets. An extra B gene due to duplication produces smaller and narrow *bar eye* with 350 facets in heterozygous state and 200 facets in homozygous state. If, by chance, there is shifting of one B gene from one chromosome to its homologue, it results in 3 B genes on one and one B gene on second. This produces *double bar eye* which is very small. The change in phenotypic expression when genes are reallocated without altering their number is called **'position effect'**.

(C) *Inversion :* A chromosome segment having one or more genes gets separated and reinserted in its position but after inversion or rotation by 180° so that the order of genes is reversed. Inversion may include centromere **(pericentric)** or occur beyond centromere **(paracentric).** Chromosomes remain unsynapsed in the region of inversion with crossing over resulting in development of deficiencies, duplications, and bridge formation so that cross-over products are sterile. Therefore, inversion suppresses genetic recombinations. This is helpful in maintaining heterozygosity and balanced lethal systems.

(D) *Translocation :* It is an aberration in which a chromosome segment separates and gets attached to a non-homologous chrmosome.

(*i*) *Reciprocal Translocation :* Mutual exchange segments between two non-homologous chromosomes.

(*ii*) *Simple Translocation :* One sided translocation. If a chromosome segment gets inserted in interstitial position of a non-homologous chromosome, it is known as '*shift translocation*'. Reciprocal translocation develops multivalents instead of bivalents at synapsis. During anaphase it breaks chromosomes, develops new linkages, produces a large number of sterile gametes, causes position effect (e.g. recessive hairiness to dominant hairiness in *Drosophila*) but is useful in maintaining heterozygosity and balanced lethal sysetem.

(*iii*) *Whole-arm translocation* or *centric fusion* reduces the number of chromosomes. Human chromosome number 2 has been produced by centric fusion of two chromosomes of ape-like ancestors.

Gene Mutations : They are sudden stable changes in the structure of gene or cistron due to change in nucleotide type and/or nucleotide sequence. Most of gene mutations involve a change in single nucleotide. They are called **'point mutations'.** *Ancon Sheep* was the first recorded mutation (Seth Wright, 1791) followed by Hornless (Polled) Cattle (1889). Scientific study of mutations started with the noticing of white eye colour in *Drosophila* (Morgan, 1910). A mutation from wild to a new type is called **'forward mutation'.** The reversal of mutated gene back to its original/wild form is called **reverse/back mutation**. Mutations affecting vegetative cells are called *somatic mutations.* They are not inheritable, and disappear with the death of the individual. Somatic mutations occur in some of the cells from *chimeras*, patches or mosaics, e.g. **variegation.** In plants, somatic mutations can be preserved and passed on to future generations through vegetative propagation & tissue culture. *Germinal mutations* occur in the sex cells and are inheritable. Depending upon the effect, mutations may be *dominant* or *recessive*. The recessive mutations show their effect after a few generations when they become homozygous. A single mutation affecting more than one character is called *pleotropic mutation*. Mutations have helped in development of new varieties of plants and animals, e.g. *Sharbati Sonora* from Sonora-64.

Spontaneous Mutations : They are mutations which develop at random naturally, automatically or spontaneously in an organism due to internal reasons without any relation to any external/environmental factor. The frequency of spontaneous mutations is different for different organisms and their different genes, e.g., 1 in one million in *Drosophila*, 1 in 10 million cell generations in bacteria & 1 in 50,000 in human beings. The genes which mutate frequently are called MUTABLE GENES, e.g. R-gene of colour in maize (1 in 2000 gametes). *Stable genes* do not mutate even once in several million gametes. ***Mutator*** genes increase frequency of spontaneous mutations, while ***antimutator*** genes prevent spontaneous mutations. Spontaneous mutations may be due to (*i*) Errors in replication (*ii*) Failure of proof reading machinery (*iii*) Presence of tautomeric form of nitrogen bases e.g. imino tautomer instead of amino group (e.g. cytosine, adenine) or enol group instead of keto-group (e.g. thymine, guanine). (*iv*) Slow spontaneous deamination of cytosine to uracil. (*v*) Back ground radiations.

Induced Mutations : They are mutations that are produced in response to specific external factors or chemicals. Muller (1927) was the first scientist to produce induced mutations in *Drosophila* with the help of X-rays (upto 150 times the spontaneous sex-lined lethal mutations). He got nobel prize in 1946.

Mutagens : There are physical and chemical factors which bring about new mutations and increase the frequency of spontaneous mutations.

Physical Mutagens : They are physical factors which induce mutations. Physical mutagens are of three types-temperature, ultra-violet radiations and ionising radiations.

(*i*) *Temperature :* Increase in temperature increases the frequency of mutations. Q_{10} being 5 for Rice. Very low temperature is also mutagenic.

(*ii*) *UV Radiations :* (Muller and Altenberg, 1932). They induce hydrolysis of cytosine and formation of thymine dimers. Thymine dimers cause bending and misreplication of DNA. Organisms overcome damage from UV radiations present in normal sunlight by photorepair (photoreactivation), excision repair and post replication repair.

(*iii*) *Ionising Radiation :* They include X-rays (man-made, Roentgen, 1895), cosmic ray (proton and helium nuclei present in space), α-particles (helium nuclei), β-particles (electrons), gamma rays (massless radiations). The latter three are emitted from radioactive elements and radio-isotopes. P-32 is radio-isotope which gets incorporated in DNA but starts decaying and changed to sulphur. DNA develops breaks in there regions. Ionising radiations produce electrically charged particles which ionise biomolecules and bring about several changes in DNA. There is deamination and dehydration of nitrogen bases, formation of peroxides and oxidation of deoxyribose.

Chemical Mutagens : They are chemicals which induce mutations. Most of the mutagens are also carcinogens.

(A) *Nitrous acid :* It deaminates cytosine to uracil, guanine to reanthin and adenine to hypoxanthin. This results in replacement of A-T with H-C, C-G with U-A and C-X. Nitrous acid is a common insustrial chemical and preservative of meat products.

(B) *Alkylating agents :* They bring about methylation and ethylation of nitrogen bases, e.g. methyl guanine, ethyl gaunine. The alkylated base may slip out of DNA duplex or cause change of base pair, e.g. C-G to A-T. Alkylating agents include ethyl ethane sulphonate (EES), ethyl methane sylphonate (EMS), diethyl sulphate (DES), dimethyl nitrosamine dibromide, griseofulvin, endrin, etc. Ethyl dibromide (EDB) is used in food preservation, Griseofulvin is common antifungal medicine while endrin is an insecticide.

(C) *Base Analogous :* e.g., (*i*) 5-bromouracil (Bu), (*ii*) 5-iodouracil (Iu), (*iii*) 5-chlorouracil (Cu), (*iv*) 5-Flurouracil (Fu)

All these replace thymine and pair with guanine. 2-aminopurine is incorporated in place of adenine with its tautomes pairing with cytosine. Thymine in its enol state pairs with guanine.

(D) *Acridines :* Proflavin, acriflavin, euflavin and acridine orange are intercalated in between base pairs leading to their insertion and deletion so as to cause **frame-shift** or **gibberish** mutations.

MOLECULAR BASIS OF GENE MUTATION :

(*i*) *Inversion :* Base sequence of a segment is reversed.

(*ii*) *Transition Substitution :* One nitrogen base is replaced by another of similar type, e.g A $\rightleftharpoons$ G, C $\rightleftharpoons$ T. It is induced by **tautomerisation** (alternate state due to rearrangement of hydrogen atoms, – NH_2 into –NH or – CO, into – COH), deamination, base analogue and ionisation.

(*iii*) *Transversion Substitution :* One nitrogen base is replaced by another of different type, e.g. C $\rightleftharpoons$ G, A $\rightleftharpoons$ T.

(*iv*) *Insertion Frameshift :* Addition of a nucleotide changes the reading of codons.

(*v*) *Deletion Frameshift :* Deletion of a nucleotide changes the reading of codons. Gene mutations often change them into inactive, recessive or lethal state.

Same Sense, Mis-Sense and Non-Sense Mutations

Due to **wobble** position, a change in one neucleotide of a codon does not change amino-acid specificity. This is called *same sense* (or silent) mutation, e.g. AGA = AGG = AGC. When a nucleotide change in one codon causes the change of one amino acid of a polypeptide, it is called *mis-sense mutation.* If a mutation causes early termination of polypeptide synthesis, it is termed as *non-sense mutation.*

Hardy Weinberg Genetic Equilibrium

A Mendelian population is an interbreeding group of organisms sharing a common *gene pool.* A gene pool is the total genetic information possessed by reproductive members in a population of sexually reproducing organisms. Alleles in the pool have *dynamic relations* with other alleles and with the environment in which the organism reside. Environmental factors that collectively provide selection tend to alter allele frequencies and thus to cause evolutionary changes in local populations.

In 1908, an English mathematician, G.H. Hardy and a German physician, W.Weinberg, independently discovered, the principle concerned with the frequency of alleles in a population, called the ***Hardy-Weinberg equilibrium principles.*** It states that at equilibrium, both allele and genotype frequencies remain constant from generation to generation. This occurs among diploid, sexually reproducing organisms with nonoverlapping generations in which mating is random and no selection or other factors are present for changing the allele frequencies or as long as the following assumptions are met :

1. The population size is very large
2. Random mating is occurring
3. No mutation takes place
4. No genes are input from other sources
5. (No migration takes place)
6. No selections occurs.

Dominant alleles thus do not, in fact, replace recessive ones, Because their proportions do not change, the genotypes are said to be in *Hardy-Weinberg Equilibrium.*

In algebric terms, the H.W. equilibrium principle is written as an equation. Its form is what is known as *bionomial expansion.* For a gene with two alternative alleles, which one will call B and *b*, the equation looks like,

$(p+q)^2 =$ p^2	+ $2pq$	+ q^2
(Individuals homozygous for allele B)	(Individuals heterozygous with alleles B + *b*)	Individuals homozygous for allele *b*)

In *statistics, frequency is defined as the proportion of individuals falling within a certain category in relation to the total number of individuals under consideration.* Thus, in a population of 100 cats, with 84 black and 16 white cats, the respective frequencies would be 0.84 (or 84%) and 0.16 (or 16%). In the algebric terms of this equation, the letter p designates the frequency of one allele, the letter q designates frequency of alternative allele. By convention, the more common of the two alleles is designated p and rarer q. Because there are only two alleles, p plus q must always equal 1.

If we assume that the white cats are homozygous recessive for a gene designated *b*, and the black cats are, therefore, either homozygous dominant BB or heterozygous B*b*, we can calculate the *allele frequencies* of the two alleles in the population from the proportion of black and white individuals. If $q^2 = 0.16$ (the frequency of white cats), then $q = 0.4$. Therefore, p, the frequency allele B, would by 0.6 $(1.0 - 0.4 = 0.6)$. We can now easily calculate the genotype frequencies, there are $p^2 = (0.6)^2 \times 100$ (the number of individuals in the total population), or 36 homozygous dominant BB individuals. The heterozygous individuals have the Bb genotype, and there would be $2pq$, or $(2 \times 0.6 \times 0.4) \times 100$, or 48 heterozygous B*b* individuals.

Phenotype	*Black*		*White*
Genotype	BB	B*b*	*bb*
Frequency of genotype in population	0.36	0.48	0.16
Frequency of gametes	0.36 + 0.24 = 0.6 B		0.24 + 0.16 = 0.4b

In the absence of factors that alter them, the frequency of gametes, genotypes and phenotypes remain constant genertion after generation.

Using the Hardy-Weinberg Equation

The H.W. equation is a simple extension of the Punnett squares with two alleles assigned frequencies p and q. From the table given above, one can trace genetic reassortment during sexual reproduction and sea how it affects the frequencies of the B and *b* alleles during the next generation. In this table, it is assumed that the union of sperm and egg in these cats is random, so that all combinations of *b* and B alleles are equally likely. For this reason, the alleles are mixed randomly and represented in the next generation. Each individual in each generation has a 0.6 chance of receiving a B allele ($p = 0.6$) and a 0.4 chance of receiving a *b* allele ($q = 0.4$).

In the next generation therefore, the chance of combining two alleles is p^2, or 0.36 (that is, 0.6×0.6), and approximately 36% of the individuals in the population will continue to have the BB genotype. The frequency of *bb* individuals is q^2 (0.4×0.4) and so will continue to be about 16%, and the frequency of B*b* individuals will be $2pq$ $(2 \times 0.6 \times 0.4)$, or approximately 48%. Phenotypically, 84 black individuals (with either BB or B*b* genotypes), and 16 white individuals (with *bb* genotype) in the population are seen. The simple relationship has proved extraordinarily useful in assessing actual situations. Consider the recessive allele responsible for the serious human disease *cystic fibrosis*. This allele is present in North Americans of Caucasian descent at a frequency q of about 22 per 1000 individuals, or 0.022. What proportion of North American Caucasians, therefore, is expected of express this trait? The frequency of double recessive individuals (q^2) is expected to be 0.022×0.022, or 1 in every 2000 individuals. What proportion is expected to be heterozygous carriers? If the frequency of the recessive allele q is 0.022, then the frequency of the dominant allele p must be $1 - 0.022$, or 0.978. The frequency of heterozygous individuals ($2pq$) is thus expected to be $2 \times 0.978 \times 0.022$, or 43 in every 1000 individuals.

Most human populations are large and effectively random-mating and are, therefore, similar to the "ideal" population envisioned by Hardy and Weinberg. For some genes, the calculated predictions do not match the actual values. The reasons they do not tell us a great deal about evolution.

Why Do Allelle Frequencies Change : According to the Hardy-Weinberg principle, both the allele and genotype frequencies in a large, random-mating population will remain constant from generation to generation if no mutation, no migration, and no selection occurs. The stipulations tacked onto the end of the statement are important. In fact, they are the key to the importance of the Hardy-Weinberg principle, because individual allele frequencies *are* changing all the time in natural populations, with some alleles becoming more common than others. The Hardy Weinberg principle establishes a convenient baseline against which to measure such changes. By looking at how various factors alter the proportions of homozygous and heterozygous in populations (usually expressed as the HETEROZYGOSITY, the likelihood that a randomly selected individual will be heterozygous at the gene locus), one can identify the factors affecting particular situation.

Many factors can alter allele frequencies. Only five, however, alter enough the proportions of homozygous and heterozygous to produce significant deviations froim the proportions predicted by H.W. principle : **mutation, migration** (both immigration into and emigration out of a given population); **genetic drift** (random loss of alleles, which is more likely in small populations), **nonrandom mating,** and **selection** (see table below). Of there only selection produces adaptive evolutionary change because only in selection does the result depend upon the nature of the environment. The other factors operate relatively independently of the environment, so the changes they produce are not shaped by environmental demands.

Agents of Evolutionary Change

Factor	*Description*
1. Mutation	The ultimate source of variation. Individual mutations occurs so rarely that mutation alone does change allele frequency much.
2. Migration	A very potent agent of change. Populations exchange members.
3. Nonrandom mating	Inbreeding is the most common form. It does not alter allele frequency but decreases the proportion of heterozygotes.
4. Genetic drift	Statistical accidents. Usually occurs only is very in very small populations. Genetic drift can result in the permanent loss of alleles from a population.
5. Selection	The only form that produces adaptive evolutionary changes. Only rapid for allele frequencies greater than 0.01.

EVOLUTION

Organic Evolution, Evidences, Mechanism and Theories

Theory of Special Creation : Life was created by God. According to Genesis of Bible, God created the world in six days in the following order:

(*i*) Heaven & Earth
(*ii*) Sky & water
(*iii*) Land and land plants
(*iv*) Sun, moon & stars
(*v*) Birds and fishes
(*vi*) Land Animals and Humans

The first man was Adam and the first woman Eve (takes out from ribs of Adam). Hindu mythology believes that the word was created by Brahma-gods, demons and humans from his head, birds from breast, goats from mouth, herbs, fruits & roots from hair. Hindu mythology also believes that there was a first man named Manu and the first woman named Sharadha. No scientific basis nor any evidences.

Theory of Spontaneous Generation/Abiogenesis (=Autobiogenesis)

It orginated in Egyptian civilisation. Greek philosophers believed in it. Anaximander (611-547 BC) thought life to arise from mud warmed by sun. Aristotle (384-322 BC) believed plants to develop from soil while worms and snails to be product pertrefaction. Van Helmont (1577-1644) had claimed origin of mice of both sexes from human sweat and wheat bran kept in dark for 21 days.

Biogenesis : Theory of spontaneous generation was disapproved through that finding, the "life comes from pre-existing life (*omme vivum evivo*). *Fransesco*

Redi (1668) placed thoroughly cooked meat in three jars:

(*i*) uncovered

(*ii*) covered with parchment

(*iii*) covered with muslin.

Maggots developed only in the uncovered jar. No maggot developed in jar covered by parchment. Flies visited the third jar and laid eggs on the muslin. Eggs fallen in the jar produced maggots. Spallanzani (1965) boiled nutrition broth in glass flasks, sealed the flasks and kept them. The broth remained clear indefinitely with no signs of living beings. *Pasteur* (1860, 1862, 1864) took broth in flasks having swan (bent S-shaped) necks, boiled and allowed the broth to cool. No germs developed in the broth through it can was connected with the atmosphere through curved necks of the flasks. The dirt pastides could not reach the broth because they got trapped in the bend of the neck. When the swan necks were broken, broth developed colonies of microorganisms showing that the same have come from air. The theory of biogenesis is, however, not applicable to origin of life.

Cosmozoic/Interplanatery Theory (Theory of Panspermia)

Primitive life or 'Panspermia' came to earth in the form of germs and spores from other heavenly bodies through meteorites (Richter, 1865, Arrhenius, 1908). Some of the meteorites are found to contain organic compounds, e.g. Orgenel meteorite in Paris, Murray meteorite in U.S.A. Murchison meteorite in Australia. The latter has many left handed amino-acids. Possibility of living structures coming from other planets is remote became of high temperature and lethal radiations in the interstellar space.

Oparin-Haldane Theory/(Biochemical Origin of Life)

It is also called theory of 'protobiogenesis' (Fox and Dose, 1972). The theory was proposed by Russian scientist Alexander Ivanovich Oparin (Origin of Life, 1923), and British turned Indian Scientist J.B.S. Haldane (1928).

Chemical Evolution

(A) ***Earliest Atmosphere on Earth :*** Earth development around 4.6 billion years back by condensation of ylem or cloud of consmic dust and gases. It was made of radioactive elements which decayed and generated heat. Condensation and cooling resulted in startfication with heavier elements (e.g. Nickel, Iron). Passing to the core, intermediate to middle (e.g. silicon, Aluminium) while the lighter ones remained on the surface and the atmosphere. Since the surface was very hot, the lighter elements occurred only in their atomic state. They included hydrogen, carbon, nitrogen and oxygen.

(B) ***Formation of Early Molecules :*** With slight lowering of the surface temperature of the earth, the lighter elements interacted to form water (H_2O), methane (CH_4), ammonia (NH_3), carbon monooxide (CO), carbondioxide (CO_2) and hydrogen cyanide (HCN). Metal carbides, nitrides and oxides also formed on the surface. Free oxygen disappeared and the environment became *reducing*. Intially water existed as superheated steam. On cooling, it came down as hot water rain but evaporated again. This continued for several centuries till the surface of earth came to have hot water oceans and lakes with large number of dissolved salts coming from atmosphere, bottom, shore-line and volcanoes.

(C) ***Formation of Simple Organic Molecules :*** Surface of earth had a temperature of 50°-60°. It was constantly receiving UV radiations and cosmic rays. Lightning was frequent. This helped methane, ammonia, water and other molecules to form a whole array of simple organic substances like aldehydes, alcohols, organic acids, amino acids, purines, pyrimidines, pentose, hexose and other sugars, fatty acids, glycerol etc. Water bodies changed into a broth/ primordial soup/prebiotic soup.

Experimental Proof : Stanley Cloyed Miller (1953, Miller and Urey, 1953) took ammonia, water, methane and hydrogen in a sterilised apparatus having provisions for heating , cooling, circulation and electrical discharges. The materials and conditions resemble those present on early earth. The experiment was continued for one week after which the contents of the apparatus were analysed. A number of simple organic compounds were present—amino acids (glycine, alanine, aspartic acid, glutamic acid), organic acids (formic, acetic, propionic, lactic acid, succinic), purines, pyrimidines and sugars.

(D) *Formation of Larger Organic Molecules :* In the priomordial/prebiotic hot, sterile soup, the simple organic molecules reacted amongst themselves to form newer and larger molecules. The environment was oxygen free. Radiations, lightning and volcanic eruptions were abundant. Simple sugars condensed to form polysaccharides, fatty acids and glycerol reacted to produce fats while amino acids condensed into peptides, polypeptides and proteins. All these reactions occurred without the agency of enzymes, DNA and ribosomes. S.W. Fox (1957) obtained polypeptides by heating a mixture of amino acids for long period. Nucleotides developed due to condensation of nitrogen bases (purines, pyrimidines), phosphoric acid and pentose sugar.

(E) *Formation of Complex Biomolecules :* Some of the nucleotides came to have more phosphates and functional as energy suppliers. Nucleotides also underwent polymerisation to form nucleic acids, DNA and RNA. DNA has the ability of replication and transcription. Enzymes and coenzymes came into existence. ATP prophyrin and other biomolecules have been synthesized under hot,oxygen free, iradiated environment stimulating the one present on early earth (Fox, 1964).

Biological Evolution

(F) *Formation of Coacervates/Pre-cells/Pre-bionts :* On the shores, organic molecules tended to aggregate due to wave action and partial drying up. Some of these molecular aggregates formed Coacervates. Coacervates developed the ability to grow and divide giving rise to *microspheres* that were separated from their environment by lipid membrane. Microspheres could grow by absorbing material from outside. They could also increase in number by budding. Close association of biomolecules evolved into an organisation based on interactions and development of enzymes for the same.

(G) *Formation of Protocells/Eobionts/ Protobionts :* Some of the microspheres having DNA and RNAs evolved further. They developed lipoprotein membrane and enzyme mediated reactions. They are called protocells, *eobionts* or *protobionts*. The latter developed their own internal environment distinct from outside. Nucleic acids could replicate and help in multiplication of eobionts. It is probable that viruses developed simultaneously with the evolution of protocells. They could effect assembly of their parts by controlling reaction in the premordia/or prebiotic soup.

(H) *First Cells/Living Beings :* Protocells evolved into cells and living beings. They were procaryotic unicells which had naked DNA, protein manufacturing machinery, mode of energy liberation and its utilisation. The first procaryotes were *anaerobes* and *chemoautotrophs*. They absorbed organic molecules from outside for body building and energy.

(I) *Development of Chemoautotrophs :* Drop in temperature stopped synthesis of organic molecules in the water bodies. Organic content of primordial soup decreased due to continuous withdrawl by chemoautotrophs. Some of the early procaryotes got converted into chemoautotrophs. They developed the ability to synthesise organic materials from inorganic raw materials with the help of energy obtained from reducing inorganic substances of the medium. Some present day chemoautotrophs are iron bacteria, nitrifying bacteria, sulphate reducing bacteria.

(J) *Development of Phototrophs/Pigments evolved* which could trap solar energy. The absorbed energy could be used in various reactions. Certain prokaryotes developed bacteriochlorophyll and later chlorophyll. The pigment could trap solar energy which could be used in synthesis of organic material from inorganic substances. The process is called 'photosynthesis'. The first photoautotrophs were anaerobic and performed '*anoxygenic photosynthesis*', Hydrogen was obtained from sources other than water. All present day photoautotrophic bacteria are anoxygenic e.g. *Chlorobium*, *Rhodoseudomonas*. Aerobic photoautotrophs developed around 3300-3500 million years ago in the form of cyanobacteria or blue-green algae. They performed 'oxygenic photosynthesis' using water as hydrogen donor and liberating oxygen. Fossils of there cyanobacteria or blue-green algae have been found in rocks as old as 2-9 billion years old, e.g. *Archaeophoroides barhertonensis*. In India 3.2 billion years old fossils of photosynthetic blue green algae have been found from Kashia region in Orissa. Oxygen accumulated in the atmosphere. The latter became oxidising. Methane and ammonia disappeared because they react with oxygen to form CO_2 and N_2 respectively. High energy radiations in the upper layers of atmosphere changed some of the oxygen into ozone. Ozone formed a shield that protects the livnig beings from UV radiations.

(K) ***Development of Eukaryotes :*** Eukaryotes evolved around 1600 million years back. They came into existence due to (*i*) Evolution from prokaryotes through mutations (Raff and Maller, 1972) (*ii*) Symbiotic association of different types of prokaryotes (Marguilis, 1970).

Types of Organic Evolution

Organic evolution in the formation of newer types of organisms from the pre-existing ones through modification. Evolution, is therefore, often called 'descent with modification' (Darwin, 1859). Evolution is of several kinds as given below :

(*i*) *Progressive Evolution :* Formation of more complex, elaborate and specialized structures from simpler ones

(*ii*) *Retrogressive Evolution :* Development of simpler and less elaborate forms from complex ones.

(*iii*) *Microevolution :* Development of minute changes due to gene mutations and recombinations. The changes occur below the level of species.

(*iv*) *Macroevolution :* Development of large changes like formation of new species and genra due to mutation causing large scale changes in chromosomes.

(*v*) *Megaevolution :* Large changes giving rise to new families, orders, classes etc.

(*vi*) *Parallel Evolution :* Independent formation of similar traits by related groups of organisms.

(*vii*) *Convergent Evolution :* Formation of similar traits by unrelated groups of organisms as wings in insects bird and bats.

(*viii*) *Divergent Evolution :* (Adaptive Radiation). Formation of different structures from a common ancestral form e.g. fore limbs in horse, bat and human beings.

Evidences of Organic Evolution :

Evidences from Palaeontology : Palaeontology is the study of 'fossils' or remains traces and impressions of past organisms found in the rocks of different ages. It has two main branches

(*i*) *Palaeozoology :* Study of animals fossils

(*ii*) *Palaeobotany :* Study of plant fossils.

Types of Rocks :

(*a*) **Sedimentary Rocks :** They are formed through sedimentation and hardening of mud at the bottom of water bodies and exposed due to upheavals in earth's crust. e.g. limestone, sandstone.

(*b*) **Metamorphic Rocks :** Sedimentary rocks changed due to heat, pressure or gases. e.g. marble from limestone, slate from clay.

Age of Rock/Fossil : 1/7600 gm out of 1 million gm of uranium is changed to (Pb^{206}) in one year or 1% of uranium decays to lead-206 (Pb^{206}) in 66 million years. Decay of radioactive Potassium to Argon-40 has a half life of 1300 million years. Age of rock and fossil contained in it is calculated by ratio of Uranium to Lead or radioactive Potassium to Argon.

Types of Fossils :

(*a*) *Actual Remains :* Animals, plants and humans got embedded in permafrost of arctic/alpine snow remains preserved in actual state.

(*b*) *Petrification :* They are fossils in which organic materials are replaced by mineral matter. In some petrified fossils even cellular details are found.

(*c*) *Compressions :* Internal structure is absent but a thin carbon film indicates the outline of external features.

(*d*) *Incrustation :* They are external moulds formed around organic remains which later degenerate.

(*e*) *Moulds :* They are hardened encasements formed in the outer parts of extinct organic remains which later decay leaving cavities.

(*f*) *Casts :* They are hardened pieces of mineral matter deposited in the cavities of moulds.

(*g*) *Impressions/Imprints :* They are external features of organisms or their parts left in hardening rocky matter before complete decay.

Pseudofossils are patterns developped in rocky matter during crystallisation of mineral substances.

(*h*) *Polynofossils/Microfossils :* They are fossil spores, pollen and microscopic organisms. Some of these help locate fossil fuels.

Formation of Fossils : Dead bodies of plants and animals (aquatic directly and terrestrial by water currents) settle down at the bottom of a big lake or sea along with mud and sand. Mineral matter may penetrate and replace different parts. Slow decay may leave only hard parts or form impressions, moulds, casts etc. with the hardening of mud and sand. The sediment is converted into rock which may come to the surface due to upheavals in earth's crust.

Amber, lava, bogs, snow, earthquakes also help in fossilisation.

Extinct Forms : A number of animals and plants are found only in fossil state e.g. pteridosperms, dinosaurs, toothed birds etc.

Missing Links : They are fossil forms transitional between two present day groups of organisms, e.g., pteridosperms (between pteridophytes and gymnosperms).

Evidences from Biogeography : Biogeography in the study of patterns and factors controlling the distribution of plants and animals in different parts of Earth.

Restricted Distribution : Double coconut occurs only in Seychles Island.

Evidences from Comparative Morphology & Anatomy

(*a*) *Homologous Organs :* They are organs which have similar internal structure and similar origin. Homologous organs may appear different externally and functionally in different organisms. e.g.

- *Leaves* may be simple, compound, reduced to scales or modified into spines and tendrils.
- *Stems* may be modified into tendrils (*Passiflora*), thorn (*Bongainvillea*, *Duranta*), cladode (*Ruscus*) phylloclade (*Opuntia*).

Differences in homologous organs are examples of *divergent* evolution/adaptive radiation. Occurrence of similar types of biomolecules in various groups of organisms is called 'Molecular homology', e.g. RUBISCO in plants.

(*b*) *Analogous Organs :* They are structurally different organs which get modified to perform similar function. Analogous organs having similar external appearance are called 'homoplastic'. e.g. photosynthesis in wild pea (stipules), Australian Acacia (petiole), and Ruscus (cladodes).

(*c*) *Vestigial Organs :* They are imperfectly developed nonfunctional organs which are fully developed and functional in related and ancestral forms. The vestigial organs are not required by organisms due to alternate development. e.g. Leaves are reduced to scales in *Ruscus* and *Asparagus*. Pistil is reduced in ray florets of sunflower.

(*d*) *Atavism :* It is reappearance of an ancestral trait which is presently absent or vestigial.

(*e*) *Connecting Link :* They are intermediate forms between two groups and show the possible path of evolution.

Evidences from Embryology

(*a*) Australian *Acacia* shows transitional stages between bipinnate leaves and phyllodes in the seeding state.

(*b*) Juvenile protonema state resembling filamentous algae occurs in mosses.

(*c*) Presence of ciliated sperms in Cycads and Ginkgo though they are carried by pollen tubes indicating resemblance with bryophytes/pteridophytes where ciliated sperms swim in external water to reach female sex organs.

Recapitualation Theory/Biogenetic law

Earnst Haeckel (1868, 1874) formulated biogenetic law or recapitualation theory which states that ontogeny (developmental history of an individual) repeats phylogeny (developmental history of the race). The occurrence of ancestral traits in the embryo in called *palaeogenesis.*

Evidences from Physiology/Biochemistry

Living beings possess similar types of biochemicals, biochemical reactions and body function. e.g., aerobic organisms perform Krebs' cycle having similar types of enzymes from *Clamydomonas*, *Amoeba* to human beings and Peepal tree. Hormones of vertebrate are similar in structure and function. Chlorophyll 'a' is universal in eukaryotic autotrophs as well as blue green algae.

Evidences from Genetics

Accumulation of mutations produce new varieties and races e.g. Porto santo rabbits, ancon sheep, dwarf wheat, red sunflowers etc. Hybridisation and induction of polyploidy hars given rise to new plants like *Triticale*, *Raphanobrassica*.

Evidences from Taxonomy

Depending upon their resemblances and differences, living beings are divided into groups e.g. Monera, Protista, Fungi, Plantae and Animalia. Kingdom Plantae has four divisions while Animalia has a number of phyla. The common characters present in a species, genus, family, order, class or phylum indicate a common ancestry while the difference amongst them indicate evolution or modifications.

Theories of Evolution

∗ Lamarckism

It is the first theory of evolution proposed by Jean Baptiste de Lamarck (1744-1829) in 1801 and 1809 (in book *Philosophic Zoologique*) which proposes that organisms undergo changes for adapting themselves to environment and the characters thus acquired are passed on to the next generation. Lamarckism is popularly called *'theory of inheritance of acquired characters'*.

∗ Neo-Lamarckism

It is an attempted revival of Lamarckism by modifying it and finding evidences for direct effect of environment on germ cells and the effect of somatic cells on germ cells.

∗ Theory of Germplasm

The theory of germplasm (Weismann, 1892) states that inheritance of characters from parents to offspring is mediated through germplasm which continues generation after generation-hence "THEORY OF CONTINUITY OF GERMPLASM". The theory is not completely true because somatoplasm can give rise to germplasm as during regeneration and culture experiments because all cells contain the same sets of chromosomes/genes whether they are somatic or germinal.

∗ Darwinism/Theory of Natural Selection

Darwinism or theory of natural selection is a theory of organic evolution which states that new species evolve over a long period of time through accumulation of small variations which provide the organisms with structural and functional speriority over other in their survival and differential reproduction.

Neo-Darwinism

It is a refinement of original theory of natural selection of remove objections.

Mutation Theory

It was given by Hugo de Vries in 1902 in his book *Species and Varieties* their origin by mutation. He studied the inheritance for seven generations, in Evening Primose (*Oenothera lamarckiana*). He found that most of the offspring resembled parents but a few variants were not connected with the normal characters by any intermediate form. The modifications were, therefore, called DISCONTINUOUS variations or *sports* or *mutations*. They were inherited. The variants, therefore, produced variants and not normal plants. Rather a few variants also developed more variations.

Mutation theory successfully explains progressive and retrogressive evolution, continuation of vestigial and overspecialized organs, struggle for existence and survival of the fittest alongwith inheritance of useful mutations and formation of new species. A number of mutations have produced new varities, subspecies and even species.

e.g.
- Ancon Sheep (1791)
- Hornless or Polled Cattle (1889)
- Delicious Apple
- Navel Orange
- Red Sunflower
- Hairless Cat
- Double Toed Cat
- *Cicer gigas* etc.

Mutations are mostly retrogressive or negative and rate is also very low as compared to requirement of evolutions. It cannot explain origin of certain phenomenon like symbiosis and mimicry.

Genetic Drift

It is the change in number and frequency of genes in small isolated population due to intensive inbreeding causing permanent fixation of some alleles, disappearance of a number of alleles and change in frequency of others.

Isolations

It is prevention of mating between, otherwise interbreeding groups due to physical and biotic barriers. The barriers allow isolated groups to evolve into distinct populations/varieties/subspecies/ species.

RNA—Role in Origin and Evolution

RNA is a single stranded polynucleotide and simpler than DNA. It is proved that viruses evolved prior to complex organisms and most of viruses contain RNA as gentic material.

The RNA molecules synthesized in mammalian cells are often very different from those made in prokaryotic organisms, particularly the *m* RNA encoding transcripts. Prokaryotic *m* RNA can be translated as it is being synthesized, whereas, in mammalian cells, most RNAs are made as precursor molecules that have to be processed into mature, active RNA. Erroneous processing and splicing of *m* RNA transcripts are a cause of disease.

The process of synthesizing RNA from a DNA template has been characterized best in prokaryotes. Although in mammalian cells the regulation of RNA synthesis and the processing of the RNA transcripts are different from that in prokaryotes, the process of RNA synthesis *per se* is quite similar in these two classes of organisms. Therefore, the description of RNA synthesis in prokaryotes is applicable to eukaryotes even though the enzymes involved and the regulatory signals are different.

Bacterial DNA dependent RNA polymerase is a multisubunit enzyme which in mammals are of various types and these polymerases are much more complex than prokaryotic RNA polymerases. They all have two large subunits and a number of smaller subunits (as a many as 14 in the case of RNA pol II). The eukaryotic RNA polymerases have extensive amino acid homologies with prokaryotic RNA polymerases. Bacterial promoters are relatively simple and eukaryotic promoters are more complex.

In prokaryotic organisms, the primary transcripts of *m* RNA-encoding genes begin to serve as translation templates even before their transcription has been completed. This is presumably because the site of transcription is not compartmentalized into a nucleus as it is in eukaryotic organisms. Thus, transcription and translation are coupled in prokaryotic cells. Consequently, prokaryotic *m* RNAs are subjected to little processing prior to carrying out their intended function in protein synthesis. Prokaryotic *r* RNA and *t* RNA molecules are transcribed in units considerably longer than the ultimate molecule. In fact, many of the *t* RNA transcription units contain more than one molecule. Thus, in prokaryotes the processing of these *r* RNA and *t* RNA precursor molecules in required for the generation of mature functional molecules.

Nearby all eukaryotic RNA primary transcripts undergo extensive processing between the time they are synthesized and time at which they serve their ultimate function, whether it is *m* RNA or *r* RNA. The process includes nucleolytic cleavage to smaller molecules and coupled nucleolytic and ligation reactions (splicing of exons).

In addition to the catalytic action served by the sn RNA in the formation of *m* RNA, several other enzymatic functions have been attributed to RNA. *Ribozymes* are RNA molecules with catalytic activity. They are generally involved transesterification reactions and most are concerned with RNA metabolism (splicing and endoribonuclease). Recently, a ribosomal RNA component was noted to hydrolyze an aminoacyl ester and, thus, to play a central role in peptide bond function. There observations made in organelles from plants, yeasts, viruses and higher eukaryotic cells, show that RNA can act as an enzyme. This has revolutionized thinking about enzyme action and the origin of life itself.

QUESTIONS FROM PREVIOUS YEARS' PAPERS

1. Write a short note on cytoplasmic inheritance. (Give suitable examples).
2. Give an illustrated account of linkage and crossing-over.
3. Write a brief account of evidences of organic evolution.
4. What is meant by coefficient of variation? Calcualte the coefficients of variation in the

following example:
Number of leaves per plant
Set I: 10, 14, 18, 16, 15, 18, 17, 12.
Set II: 12, 20, 11 , 21, 18, 22, 10, 23.
Draw a conclusion on the basic of the basic of the c.v. of the 2 sets.

5. Write a short note on correlation and regression.

6. Describe the process of Meiosis sequentially with suitable diagrams. Contrast it with Mitosis.

7. "Ontogeny repeats Phytogeny." Discuss.

8. Write short notes on the following:
(*a*) Evolution
(*b*) Correlation and regression
(*c*) Pseudoallelism

9. Describe in detail the synthesis of nucleic acids and proteins.

10. Enumerate various techniques used for gene mapping.

11. 'Recombination and independent assortment are dependent on the positions that the genes occupy.' Justify this statement.

12. What are transgenics and how do they differ from recombinants?

13. What was the impact of the discovery of sex chromosomes on genetics?

14. Write short notes on:
(*a*) Peroxisomes
(*b*) Amphidiploid
(*c*) Polygenic inheritance
(*d*) B-Chromosomes
(*e*) Tests of significance

15. Give a concise amount of cytoplasmic inheritance.

16. Explain the biochemical and molecular basis of mutation.

17. Write short notes on;
(*a*) Trisomics
(*b*) One-gene, one-enzyme concept.
(*c*) Non-green plastids
(*d*) Darwinism

18. Explain the various methods of transfer of genes.

19. Explain the regulatory mechanism of gene action, in microbes.

20. Discuss the principles of the double-helix structure of DNA proposed by Watson and Crick, and compare with that of 'Z-DNA'.

21. Explain different types of DNA replication in prokaryotes.

22. Write short notes on the following:
(*a*) Multiple factor inheritance
(*b*) Two component regulatory system
(*c*) Cytoplasmic inheritance
(*d*) Transgenic plants
(*e*) DNA Transcription

23. Enumerate the salient feature of genetic code. How is it related to evolution?

24. What is heterosis? Explain the genetic basis of heterosis and inbreeding depression.

25. How one can produce hybrids of maize and cotton?

26. 'Knowledge of genetic engineering can be utilized to improve crop plants', Justify.

CHAPTER–3

PLANT BREEDING, BIOTECHNOLOGY AND BIOSTATICS

BREEDING IN PLANTS

INTRODUCTION

Reproduction : Process of producing offspring and a mean of self-perpetuation.

Asexual reproduction (vegetative reproduction or vegetative propagation) : Plant reproduce without fusion of gametes.

Apomixis : Formation of new individuals through asexual reproduction without involving the formation and fusion of gametes.

Amphimixis : Formation of new individuals through the normal process of sexual reproduction by meiotic formation of gametes and their subsequent fusion during fertilization.

Apomixis takes place by three methods :

1. Agamospermy
2. Spore formation
3. Vegetative propagation

1. Agamospermy

Formation of new individuals by asexual reproduction without involving fusion and formation of gametes. Three types.

(*a*) **Adventive embryony** : One or few extra embryos are formed from a diploid cell of nucellus or integument but never from egg *e.g., Opuntia, Citrus.*

(*b*) **Recurrent apomixis** : Diploid egg grows parthenogenetically into diploid embryo *e.g., Poa, Allium.*

(*c*) **Non-recurrent agamospermy** : Development of embryo from haploid female gamete without fertilization.

- **Parthenogamy** : Union of two incompatible gametes *e.g.,* fusion of two female gametes.
- **Parthenospore or azygospore** : A spore formed directly from a gamete.
- **Parthenoapogamy** : Fusion of vegetative nuclei.
- **Apospory** : Involves development of gametophyte from sporophyte directly may be **somatic apospory** (embryo sac from somatic cell) or **generative apospory** (embryosac from archesporium).
- **Apogamy** : Development of sporophyte from gametophyte without the fusion of gametes.
- **Diplospory** : Diploid embryosac can develop directly from diploid megaspore mother cell.
- **Parthenogenesis** : Development of seed/embryo from a female gamete without fertilization.

2. Spore formation

Spores which take part in asexual reproduction are called **accessory spores** or **mitospores** (produced by mitotic division of a parent cell) *e.g.,* conidia, sporangiospores, aplanospores, akinetes, zoospores etc. They are quite common in algae, fungi, bacteria and protistans.

3. Vegetative reproduction

Occurs naturally in a number of wild and domesticated plants. Two types:

(A) Natural, and (B) Artificial methods.

(A) Natural methods

(*a*) **By stems** : Runners (*Cynodon*, *Oxalis*), stolons (*Vallisneria*), offsets (*Pistia*), bulbs (Onion, Garlic), corms (*Colocasia*, Banana), rhizomes (*Typha*, Ginger), suckers (Mint, *Chrysanthemum*), tubers (Potato) etc.

(*b*) **By roots** : Adventitious buds (*Dalbergia*, Guava), tuberous roots (Topoïoca, *Dahlia*) etc.

(*c*) **By leaves** : Adventitious buds (*Bryophyllum*, *Begonia*), buds on the tip of leaves (*Adiantum*).

(*d*) **By bulbils** : *e.g.*, *Oxalis*, *Agave*, *Allium* etc.

(*e*) **By turions** : *e.g.*, aquatic plants (*Utricularia*, *Potamogeton*) etc.

(B) Artificial methods

(*a*) **Cutting** *e.g.*, Sugarcane, rose, cocoa, bougainvillea etc.

(*b*) **Layering** : May be **mound layering** (*e.g.*, Grape vine, strawberry etc.) or **air layering** or **gootee** (*e.g.*, Litchi, orange etc.).

(*c*) **Grafting** : Especially in dicotyledonous plants having vascular cambia *e.g.*, mango, rose, apple, peach, *Citrus*. etc.

(*d*) **Bud grafting or Budding** *e.g.*, Rose, Apple, Peach etc.

(*e*) **Micropropagation** (Propagation by plant tissue culture) *e.g.*, Chrysanthemum, gladiolus, orchids, carnation, ornamental plants etc.

Significance

Quicker, easier, cheaper method of multiplying the plants which have either poor viability or prolonged seed dormancy.

- Helps is removing common infections from the parent plant.
- Grafting helps in getting an economically important plant having useful characters of two different individuals in a short time.

Sexual reproduction

- The sexual reproductive organs are present in the flowers of angiosperms.
- Stamens and carpels represent the male and female sex organs, respectively.
- **Perfect or bisexual or hermaphrodite** : Flower which possesses both the essential organs *i.e.*, stamens and carpels.
- **Male or staminate flower** : Unisexual flower, carpels absent.
- **Female or pistillate flower** : Unisexual flower, stamens absent.
- **Monoecious** : Plant with both male and female flowers *e.g.*, Maize, Castor etc.
- **Dioecious** : Male and female flowers present on the different plants *e.g.*, Papaya, Mulberry etc.

Development of the male gametophyte

- Each stamen consists of a cylindrical, massive thread like **filament** and a broad terminal bilobed **anther.**
- Typical anther is **tetrasporangiate** with four microsporangia **(dithecous)** but sometimes with only two microsporangia **(monothecus)** *e.g.*, Malvaceae.
- In dithecous anther, the two lobes are separated in the anterior side by a deep groove and attached on back side by the **connective.**
- There is a single vascular bundle in the connective.
- In the anther wall of a mature anther, the outer most layer is **epidermis** followed by a single layer of **endothecium,** then one to three middle layers and innermost is single layered **tapetum.**
- Endothecium (radially elongated, fibrous thickening of cellulose) attains its maximum development when the anther is ready to dehisce. The **hydroscopic** nature of endothecial cells help in the dehiscence of the anthers by the means of **slits.**
- **Pollen grain** (haploid) represents the first stage of male gametophyte and may be referred to as **male gametophyte** or **partially developed male gametophyte** or **male gamete.**
- A pollen grain has two layered wall :

  (*i*) An **outer exine** (tough, cuticularised and with spinous out growth) and

  (*ii*) an inner **intine** (thin and made up of cellulose). Exine is made up of **sporopollenin.** Exine possess one or more weak spots known as **germ pores** (usually 3 in dicots and 1 in monocots).
- Development of male gametophyte starts in pollen grain. Microspore undergoes only two

mitotic divisions and produces bigger **vegetative cell** (tube cell) and a smaller **generative cell.** At this stage, dehiscence of the anther takes place and the two celled pollen grains are released.

- After falling of pollen grains on stigma, pollen grains absorb water and nutrients of the stigmatic secretion through its germ pores.
- The intine grows out through a germ pore into a slender pollen tube. The generative nucleus divides to form two male nuclei. Usually generative cell comes down into pollen tubes and then divides to form the male gametes. The male gametophyte in angiosperms is highly reduced.

Development of female gametophyte

- The ovule is technically a **megasporangium** having nucellus (parenchymatous tissue), integuments (one or two covering) and a short stalk-like structure **(funicle)** by which it is attached to the **placenta** and the integuments enclose-an opening *i.e.,* **micropyle.**
- In young ovule, a hypodermal **archesporial** cell is differentiated which forms the **archesporium** of the ovule. Archesporial cell divides by a periclinal division and forms :
  (*i*) an **outer primary parietal cell** (forms nucellus) and
  (*ii*) **inner primary sporogenous cell** (differentiates as **megaspore mother cell).**
- The **megaspore mother cell** (megasporophyte) divides by meiosis and a linear tetrad of four megaspores is produced. The upper three towards micropyle degenerate and the lowermost towards chalaza is functional.
- The fuctional megaspore is the first cell of the female gametophyte. It divides by three mitotic divisions so that eight nuclei are formed : 4 towards the micropyle and 4 towards the chalaza. Out of four nuclei at each pole, one nucleus **(polar nucleus)** moves towards the centre. The two polar nuclei fuse together just at the time and fertilization of form a diploid **secondary** or **definitive** nucleus. Three nuclei towards micropyle form **egg apparatus** (one **egg cell** and **two synergids**) : all haploid. The three nuclei towards chalaza form antipodal cells (haploid and vestigeal). So, the mature or organized embryo sac at the time of fertilization is **7-celled and 8 nucleate.**
- 7-celled, 8 nucleate and monosporic embryo sac is known as **Polygonum** type of **embryo sac** because it was discovered for the first time in **Polygonum** by **Strasburger.**
- In an embryo sac, all the cells are haploid except the secondary nucleus (2n).
- **P. Maheshwari** (1950) classified the female gametophyte into monosporic, bisporic and tetrasporic embryo sac, depending upon the number of megaspore nuclei taking part is the development.

POLLINATION

Transfer of pollen grains from anthers to the stigma.

(A) **Self-pollination** (Autogamy) : Transfer of pollen grains within the same flower *e.g.,* pea, wheat and rice.

(B) **Cross-pollinaion** (Allogamy) : Transfer of pollen grains from one flower to another.

(1) **Xenogamy** : Transfer of pollen grains from one plant to another of the same species.

(2) **Gietnogamy** : Transfer of pollen grains from one flower to another on the same plant. Also called **genetically self pollination.**

(3) **Hybridism** : Transfer of pollen grains from one plant to another related allied species.

Advantages of cross pollination

Heal their progeny of offsprings, better adaptability, production of new varieties, more number of viable seeds etc.

Advantages for self-pollination

(A) Homogamy : Anthers and stigmas of a flower mature at the same time *e.g.,* in *Brassica* and *Gardenia florida.*

(B) Cleistogamy : Flowers remain closed. They never open throughout their life span *e.g.,* in *Arachis hypogea* (ground nut) and *Commelina bengalensis.*

(C) Geitonogamy : Transfer of pollen grain from one flower to another on the same plant *e.g., Triticum aestivum.*

Advantages of cross-pollination

(A) **Dicliny** (unisexuality) : *e.g.*, pumpkin, palm, cucumber.

(B) **Self sterility** : *e.g.*, Tea, *Malva*, Orchids.

(C) **Dichogamy** : Anther and stigma of a flower mature at different times.

(*i*) **Protandry** : Anthers mature earlier than the stigmas of the same flower *e.g.*, Cotton.

(*ii*) **Protogyny** : Stigma matures earlier than the anthers of the same flower *e.g.*, *Ficus*.

(D) **Heterostyly** : Stamens, style and stigma are of different heights.

(E) **Herkogamy** : A natural barrier develops between anthers and stigma to check self pollination *e.g.*, *Calotropis*.

Anemophily : Pollination by **wind ;** Flowers are colourless ; pollen grains are produced in**large amount ;** style and stigma are hairy *e.g.*, *Bambusa*, *Saccharum*, grasses, wheat, maize, rice, barley and palms.

Entomophily : Pollination by **insects ;** rough and sticky pollen grains ; insects are attracted by necter/scent/colour. Example of insects are bees, butterflies and moths. The flowers of Asteraceae and Labiatae families are generally pollinated by the bees and butterflies.

Hydrophily : Pollination by **water currents ;** pollen grains are sticky *e.g.*, *Vallisneria*, *Hydrilla*, *Ceratophyllum*, *Zostera* etc.

Zoophily : Pollination by **animals** *e.g.*, in *Bombax* (silk cotton) by *birds* **(Ornithophily)**, in *Anthocephalous*, *Adamsonia* and *Kigelia* by **bats (Cheiropterophily) ;** in *Arisaema* by **snakes (Ophiophily)**, in *Colocasia* by **snails (Malacophily)**.

POLLEN GERMINATION AND FERTILIZATION

Pollen tube enters the ovule through micropyle **(porogamy)**, sometimes it enters through chalaza **(chalazogamy)** or through the base of ovule or through funicle or integuments **(mesogamy)**.

Pollen tube produce enzymes which digest the tissues of the stigma and the style. After entering into the embryo sac, pollen tube liberates the male gametes and disintegrates.

Syngamy : One of the male gamete fuses with the egg resulting in the production of zygote (diploid).

Triple fusion : Second male gamete fuses with the secondary diploid nucleus, producing a triploid primary endosperm nucleus.

The process of fertilization was discovered by **Strasburger** (1884).

Double fertilisation

Takes place in angiosperms only ; discovered by **Nawaschin** (1898) in *Frittilaria* and *Lilium* and later by **Guignard** (1899). It is the fusion of :

(*i*) One male gamete with the egg cell **(real fertilization** or **syngamy)** and

(*ii*) Another male gamete with the **secondary** or **definitive nucleus** or **polar nuclei.**

In double fertilization, above all **five nuclei** are involved.

ENDOSPERM AND EMBRYO DEVELOPMENT

- Endosperm (triploid, nutritive tissue) develops after fertilization from secondary nucleus.
- 3 types of endosperm, depending on the development.

(A) **Free Nuclear** : Most common ; the first division and many subsequent divisions of primary endosperm nucleus are not followed by wall formation *e.g.*, cotton, maize, wheat, rice, sunflower etc.

(B) **Cellular** : Every nuclear division is followed by cytokinesis, making it cellular from the beginning.

(C) **Helobial** (Intermediate type)--First division of primary endosperm nucleus results in the formation of a **large micropylar chamber** and a small chalazal chamber. Rest of the divisions are free nuclear.

- **Perisperm** : Remnant of nucellus or persistent nucellus surrounding the embryo.
- **Chalazosperm** : Perisperm like tissue in chalazal region ; subtitute for endosperm.
- In dicots like pea, bean etc. reserves in the endosperm are consumed by the developing embryo and visible only as few cell layers in the mature seed.

- In many other plants *e.g.*, cereals, coconut etc. endosperm enlarges considerably by cell division and is much bigger than the embryo on seed maturation.
- The **first division** of the zygote is **transverse** and a **basal** (hypobasal) cell towards the micropyle and a **terminal** (epibasal) cell is formed towards the chalaza.
- The epibasal cell divides repeatedly to produce a row of 4-8 cells.
- The terminal cell divides in various planes to produce a cluster of cells, called **proembryo.**
- The hypobasal and the remaining cells constitute the **suspensor** which pushes the proembryo into the endosperm to enable the developing embryo to receive nutrition.
- A few cells of the proembryo nearest to suspensor develop into hypocotyl and radicle. The other cells give rise to epicotyl, plumule and cotyledons (two in dicots and one in monocots).
- As the embryo and endosperm develop and mature, the integument of the ovule become hard (seed coat) and lead to the formation of seed.
- **Post-fertilization changes : Ovary** (carpel) : fruit; **Ovule** (megasporangium):seed ; **Nucellus** : perisperm ; **Egg cell** : embryo ; **Secondary nucleus** : endosperm ; **Outer integument** : outer seed coat (testa) ; **Inner integument** : inner seed coat (tegmen) and **Micropyle** : an opening in seeds (micropyle).

INCOMPATIBILITY (INTRASPECIFIC OR SELF-STERILITY OR SELF-INCOMPATIBILITY)

- Inability of certain otherwise viable gametes from the genetically specific individuals to fuse with each other.
- Reported in 66 families of angiosperms.
- Can be morphological or physiological.
  (1) **Morphological self-incompatibility** : Two or three mating types viz. distyly (*e.g., Primula*), tristyly (*e.g., Lyhrum*).
  (2) **Physiological self-incompatibility** : Due to physiology. Morphological differences absent. May be :
  (A) **Gametophytic self-incompatibility** (GSI) : Due to the genotype of the pollen *e.g., in* Poaceae, Solanaceae, Liliaceae.
  (B) **Sporophytic self-incompatibility** (SSI) : Due to the genotype of the sporophytic/stigmatic tissues *e.g.*, Asteraceae, Brassicaceae.
  - it prevent pollen germination, retardation of growth, deorientation of pollen tube or even failure of nuclear fusion.
  - This incompatibility is due to a single multiallelic gene (S-allele). Usually, in develops with the maturation of stigma.

SPECIAL MODES OF REPRODUCTION

- Cases where propagation without the act of fertilization.
- **Apomixis** : The term opomixis was given by Winkler in 1908. Development without fertilization of fusion of gametes *e.g.*, Citrus.
- **Agamospermy** : Formation of seeds without fertilization.
- **Parthenogenesis** : Formation of embryo from an unfertilized egg.
- **Parthenocarpy** (coined by F. Nou, 1902) : Development of fruit without pollination and fertilizaton. *e.g.*, Pineapple, grapes, apple, pear and banana.
- **Sporophytic budding** : Sometimes takes place in the nucellus and integuments, resulting in the development of an embryo. *e.g.*, orange, opuntia, mango and onion.
- **Polyembryony** : Development of more than one embryos in the same seed ; discovered by Leeuwenhoeck (1719) in citrus; quite common in *Citrus* and *Pinus*.

SOME IMPORTANT FACTS

- **Allergenic** : Pollen grains of many plants including *Parthenium*, *Chenopodium*, *Prosopis*, *Sorghum*, *Amaranthus* are allergenic.
- **Palynology** : Study of pollen grains.

- **Myrmacophily** : Pollination by ants *e.g.*, many members of family Rubiaceae.
- **Hay fever** : Due to allergic reaction due to the presence of pollen in air.
- **Lever mechanism** or **Turn pipe mechanism :** Pollination in the members of family Labiatae *e.g.*, *Salvia* (sage flower).
- **Flytrap mechanism** : *Aristolochia.*
- **Trap door mechanism** : Present in hypanthodium inflorescence of *Ficus* species which receives Blastophaga for laying eggs and pollination. This is an example of mutualism.
- **Largest pollen tube** : *Zea mays.*
- *In Calotropis* and orchids pollen is packed in **pollinia** (massulae).
- **Absence of endosperm (double fertilization in angiosperms)** : 3 families *e.g.*, Orchidaceae, Podostemonaceae and Trapaceae.
- **Size of pollen-Longest** : *Zostera* (filamentous without exine) = 2500 μm.
  - **Biggest**—*Mirabilis* diameter 250 mm
  - **Smallest**—*Myosotis*, 2.5-3.5 μm
- **Panmictic** : Plant reproducting asexually.
- **Apomictic** : Plant multiplying parthenogenetically.
- **Amphimictic** : Plant reproducing sexually.
- *Erythrina* : Pollinated by crows as well as squirrels.
- **P. Maheswari** : Great plant embryologist of India, wrote a book "An Introduction to the Embryology of Angiosperms".
- **G.B. Amici** (1824) : First to observe pollen tube in *Portulaca.*
- **Hanstein** (1868, 1870) : First to study early development of embryo.
- **S. Miller** : Reported importance of **coconut milk** in tissue culture.
- **Guha and Maheswari** : Obtained pollen and anther culture embryos from family Solanaceae.
- **Piston mechanism of pollination** : White **Centaurea.**
- **Edible pollen** : *Rosa, Magnolia, Clematis.*
- **Translator type pollinia** : Family Asclepiadaceae.
- **Sporopollenin** : Present in exine of pollen and preserved during fossilization as it is resistant to decomposition.
- **Prepotency** : In many plants the pollen grains form a flower when present on the stigma of another genetically different flower germinate more quickly as compared to the pollen grains of the same flower so, help in cross pollination *e.g.*, Grape, pear and apple.
- **Primrose** : Two type of flowers based on the length of styles.
- **Pollinium** : In *Calotropis* and orchids, the pollen of each anther lobe form a sac likemass called **pollinium.** Each of which is provided with a stalk called **caudicle** and a sticky base called **disc** or **corpusculum.**
- **Biotransformation/culture products** : Plant product can be more easily obtained from tissue culture *e.g.*, Shikonin (*Lithospermum erythrorhizon*), taxol (*Taxus brevifolia*), digoxin (*Digitalis lanata*), ajmnalicin (*Catharanthus roseus*).
- **Wetraore and Wardlaw** : Successfully cultured shoot tips of pteridophytes *e.g.*, *Selaginella, Equisetum* and ferns.
- **Embryo sac** : Monosporic is *Polygonum* ; bisporic in *Allium* and tetrasporic in *Peperomia.*
- **Heteromorphism** : A single species with flowers of different forms. The length of stamen and style varies in these flowers *e.g.*, *Linum ussitatissimum* and *Primula.*
- **Cleavage polyembryony** : Cleavage of the zygote or proembryo *e.g.*, in Orchidaceae family.
- **Adventive embryony** : Formation of several embryos due to the 'budding' or proliferation of the cells of the nucellus or integuments.
- **In** *Bryophyllum*, plantlets develop along the margin of intact leaves.
- **Gynogenic haploids** : Possible from unpollinated ovules.
- **Rudolph Camerarius** (1694) : First to describe sexual reproduction in plants.

APPLICATION OF IMMUNOLOGICAL PRINCIPLES (VACCINES, DIAGNOSTICS), TISSUE AND CELL CULTURE METHODS FOR PLANTS AND ANIMALS

INTRODUCTION

The technique of growing plant cells, tissues, organs in an artificial prepared nutrient medium static or liquid under septic conditions.

- **Haberlandt** (1898) successfully cultured somatic cells of higher plants in simple nutrient solution.
- Plant tissue cultures are generally classified according to the type of *in vitro* growth viz. **callus and suspension cultures** or the **explant** used for culture initiation *e.g.*, embryo culture, anther culture etc.
- **Explant**—The plant part which is excised from the original and is used for initiating a culture. Explant is disinfected with antimicrobial chemicals in procedure called **surface sterilisation.** Common disinfectants are dilute hypochlorite, methiolate or clorox water.
- **Sterilisation**—The vessels, media and instruments are also suitably treated with steam, dry heat or alcohol, or subjected to filtration to make them free from microbes.
- **Culture medium**—It is required for the desired growth and development of the explants. It contains inorganic salts, certain vitamins, sucrose and the desired growth regulators (*e.g.*, **auxins** like 2, 4-D and **cytokinins** like BAP). The cultures are generally kept in a culture room at about 24°C with some illumination.

CALLUS AND SUSPENSION CULTURES

Callus culture

Callus is an unorganised mass of loosely arranged parenchymatous cells which develop from parent tissue due to proliferation of cells. Darkness and solid medium gelled by agar stimulates callus formation. The medium generally possess auxin 2, 4-D (2, 4-dichlorophenoxy acetic acid) and often a cytokinin like BAP (benzyl aminopurine). A callus mass is generally obtained in 2-3 weeks.

Suspension culture

Consists of single cells and small groups of cells suspended in a liquid medium. Generally medium possessess the auxin (2, 4-D). Suspension culture must be constantly agitated at 100 – 250 rpm. Agitation helps in aeration of culture, mixing of the medium and breakage of cell aggregates into smaller cell groups. This culture grows much faster than callus culture.

- With the passage of time, cell or tissue dry matter (biomass) increases, the level of nutrients in the medium decreases and medium volume declines due to evaporation.
- **Subculturing**—Cultures are regularly divided and transferred to containers having fresh medium. During subculture, only apart of the culture from a vessel is transferred in the new culture vessel.
- The callus and suspension cultures can be used to achieve cell biomass production, regeneration of plantlets, production of transgenic plants and isolation of protoplasts.

Regeneration of plantlets

Plantlets can be obtained from cultured cells by two different routes :

(*a*) **Short regeneraton** followed by roots of the shoots

(*b*) **Regeneration of somatic embryos** followed by their germination.

Regeneration

Formation of organised structures like shoot, root. somatic embryo (embryoid) or plantlet from callus/ suspension and other forms of tissue culture. Regeneration is possible because plant cells are totipotent.

1. **Shoot Regeneration—**Shoot regeneration is promoted by a **cytokinin** (*e.g.*, BAP) while root regeneration is promoted by an auxin like NAA (napthalene acetic acid). Callus culture first kept on a BAP containing medium, differentiates into shoots. When the shoot become 2-3 cm

long they are excised and transferred to an auxin containing medium. Roots develop at the lower ends to shoot to form plantlets.

2. **Somatic embryo regeneration**—It is induced by a relatively high concentration of an auxin *e.g.*, 2, 4-D. These young embryo develop into mature embryos either on the same medium or on another medium. Mature somatic embryos germinate to yield complete plantlets.

Establishment in the field

Plantlets are transferred to small earthern pots in a green house under reduced light and high humidity for 3-4 weeks. It brings about hardening, which helps the plantlets to develop root system and leaf structure capable of withstanding field conditions. These hardened plants are then established in the field.

Applications

1. **Rapid clonal propagation**—All the cells in a callus or suspension culture are derived from a single explant by mitotic division so all plantlets regenerated from a callus/suspension culture generally have the same genotype and constitute a clone. The technique used is rapid propagation of superior and rare lines *e.g.*, oil palm.
2. **Somaclonal variation**—There are genetic variation present among plant cells of a culture. This variation have been incorporated in plant breeding programmes. *e.g.*, rust resistance and high temperature tolerance in wheat, resistance to Tongo virus and leaf hopper in rice etc.
3. **Transgenic plants**—Transgene is a gene that is transferred into an organism by genetic engineering. **Transgenic organism** are such organism which contains and expresses a transgene. **Transgenics** are cells or organisms with transgenes. Transgenic cells are multiplied in tissue culture. Plantlets and plant are then regenerated from them.
4. **Resistance to weedicides**—Weedicides are added to obtain desired level of resistance in culture. The developed resistant cells are then regenerated to form plantlets and plants.
5. **Induction and selection of mutations**—Mutagens are added to single cell liquid cultures for induction of mutations. Useful mutants are selected for further breeding.

MERISTEM CULTURE

Usually **shoot tips** and **nodal segments** (3rd and 4th nodes) are used as explants. Cytokinins (*e.g.*, BAP) are used in culture medium to promote the formation of axillary branches by overcoming the phenomenon of apical dominance. Therefore, they support multiple shoot development from each explant. The technique also called as **multiple shoot culture.** Such shoots develop more easily over nodal segments. For developing multiple shoots from shoot tips, salt and NAA are often added to culture medium. Shoots of 2-3 cm are excised and transferred to medium rich in auxin for induction of rooting. The plantlets thus obtained are subjected to hardening and ultimately established in the field.

Meristem culture are used for rapid clonal multiplication, for production of virus free plants, for germplasm conservation and for production of transgenic plants.

EMBRYO CULTURE

Excision of young embryos from developing seeds and their development on culture medium is called **embryo culture.** The embryo culture allows the young embryos to complete development and ultimately give rise to seedlings. Applications are—

1. **Embryo rescue**—*i.e.*, taking out the fragile embryos from fertilised ovules of interspecific crosses before their abortion and culturing them to form viable hybrid seedlings. *e.g.*, Tomato (*Lycopersicon peruvianum* × *L. lycopersicum*), Bean (*Phaseolus vulgaris* × *P. angustissimus*) etc.
2. **Orchids**—Orchids lack stored food. Empbryo culture allows seedling development from most of the embryos. This method in orchids also used for rapid clonal propagation.
3. **Dormant seeds**—Seeds in some species may remain dormant due to presence of inhibitors in the endosperm or seed coat. Embryo culture allows the embryo to develop into seedlings

by eliminating the inhibitors and the dormancy.

4. **Rare plants**—Embryo culture is useful in multiplication of some rare plants *e.g.*, Makapuno nut.

ANTHER CULTURE AND HAPLOID PRODUCTION

Anther culture represents the production of haploid plants from pollen grains. Embryo like structure called embryoid were formed from anther culture of *Datura innoxia* by **Guha** and **Maheswari** (1964). It is highly useful for immediate expression of mutations and quick formation of pure lines.

- Anthers are introduced over culture medium within 4-6 weeks each anther gives rise to either a number of haploid embryoids from its haploid pollen or a haploid callus from which shoot regenerate. In many plant species, haploids can also be produced by culturing unfertilized ovaries or ovules.
- **Gynogenic haploids** are produced by using unfertilised ovules.
- Haploids are completely sterile and of no direct value. They are useful as that homozygous inbred lines can be rapidly and readily achieved through them. There are helpful in detection of mutations in haploids because of presence of single set of chromosomes.
- Haploid culture method is useful in reshufling of alleles. For this two pure breeding plants (*e.g.*, AA and aa) are allowed to hybridise and the anthers of hybrid are used to develop haploids which are converted into homozygous diploids by colchicine treatment. Superior lines are selected for further breeding.

PROTOPLAST CULTURE AND SOMATIC HYBRIDISATION

Somatic Hybridisation or **Parasexual hybridization** is the technique of production of hybrids through the fusion of protoplasts from different genetic backgrounds. It takes place by the removal of cell wall by digestion with a combination of **pectinase and cellulase.** The plant cells lacking cells wall are called **protoplasts.** The fusion between protoplasts of the selected parents is induced by a solution of polyethylene glycol (PEG) or by a very brief voltage electric current. When the protoplasts are cultured on a suitable medium, they regenerate cell walls and begin to divide to ultimately produce plantlets.

Somatic hybridisation is useful in the production of hybrids between lines and species that cannot be produced normally by means of sexual hybridisation. *e.g.*, somatic hybrid between a non-flowering clone of potato and a flowering potato clone produced fertile flowers. Somatic hybrid has also been produced between monocot rice and dicot carrot. This technique may be used for gene transfer, transfer of cytoplasm and production of useful allopolyploids. **Pomato** is a somatic hybrid of potato and Tomato while **Bomato** is formed between Brinjal and Tomato.

Cytoplasmic hybrids (Cybrids or heteroplast)

Plant or cell which is a cytoplasmic hybrid produced by fusion of a protoplast and cytoplast. They can be formed by removal of one of the nuclei after the formation of heterokaryon or fusion between a normal protoplast with a protoplast having a non-viable nucleus or selective loss of genome of one of the nuclei.

BIOTECHNOLOGY

It is the controlled use of biological agents, such as micro-organisms or cellular components for beneficial use.

Microorganisms were first used to produce some organic compounds like citric acid, following the first World War. Subsequently a variety of products, including antibiotics. In addition, animal and plant cells cultured *in vitro* are used to obtain several valuable products. In some cases, genetic improvements have enhanced the levels of production *e.g.*, Penicillin yield has been improved by a factor of about 1000. However, there has been no change in the type of product. These activities are called as **old biotechnology.**

Modern biotechnology

Use of genetic engineering/recombinant technology to enhance productivity and obtain new products from microorganisms, plant and animai cells.

Recombinant protein

The protein produced by transgenes (expressed in transgenic cells or organisms). These proteins can not be naturally produced by the concerned cells/ organisms.

The first useful commercial product of transgenic microorganisms was the synthesis of human insulin by bacterium *Escherichia coli* with the help of newly inserted human insulin gene.

Application of biotechnology

The products of biotechnology are food (bread, sauce, dosa etc.) dairy products (yoghurt, butter etc.) alcoholic beverages (beer, wine etc.), nonalcoholic beverages (coffee beans, tea leaves etc.), sewage treatment, Biogas (Gobar gas), biofertilizers, organic acids (lactic acid, acetic acid etc.), enzymes, antibiotics, vitamins, hormones/ insulin, growth hormone etc.), tissue culture, vaccines, monoclonal antibodies, transplants, (test tube babies, embryo transplant etc.), genetic engineering (recombinant DNA technology etc.), steroids etc.

GENETICALLY MODIFIED CROPS OR GM CROPS

Such crops are transgenic crops which possess and express one or more useful foreign genes or transgenes. **Two unique advantages are:** (*a*) Any gene from any organism or a gene synthesised chemically can be used for transfer and (*b*) Change in genotype is precisely controlled.

This technology is advantageous to breeding programmes because in the breeding activities only the already present genes are reshuffled and that changes would occur in all traits for which the parents are different.

The transgene can perform following functions.

1. **Production of a desired proteins—Hirudin** protein is present in leech which prevents blood clotting. Its gene was chemically synthesised and introduced in *Brassica napus*. The seeds of the *Brassica* come to have hirudin which could be extracted, purified and used as medicine.
2. **Production of a desired phenotype**—Soil bacterium *Bacillus thuringiensis* produces a crystal (cry) protein which is toxic to larvae of certain species. There cry proteins are of various types. Each of which is toxic to a different group of insects. **Cry** gene (gene encoding cry protein) have been isolated and transferred into several crops (*e.g.*, cotton). This Bt cotton is not attacked by boll worm and other insects.
3. **Modify an existing biosynthetic pathway—** Transgenic Golden rice and transgenic potato produce, respectively higher content of vitamin A and protein.
4. **Mask expression of a native gene**—*e.g.*, Tomato variety "Flavr Savr" in which production of polygalacturonase was blocked. This enzyme degrades the pectin and promote the fruit softening. In the absence of enzyme, pectin degradation is stopped and fruit remains fresh for long with a superior taste and increased total soluble solids.

Caution is required in the development of GM crops without proper safe guards because (*i*) Gene transfer from GM crops to weeds would make them more virulent (*ii*) Transgenic crops may become persistent weeds (*iii*) Pollen of transgenic crops may carrying the transgenes to wild relatives (*iv*) Transgenic crops would disturb the balance of nature and damage the ecosystem.

BIORESOURCE AND USES OF BIODIVERSITY

GENETICALLY MODIFIED FOOD OR GM FOOD

The genetically modified food is the produce of genetically modified (transgenic) crops. Technology used during production of transgenic crops involves the use of antibiotic and antibiotic resistance genes. Their persistence is GM food in frought with danger :

(1) GM foods possess transgenic proteins and related metabolites which may cause toxicity and allergies.

(2) Enzyme for antibiotic resistance would cause altergen reactions.

(3) The bacteria present in the alimentary canal of the humans could take up the antibiotic resistance gene that is present in the GM food.

It will make the disease resistant to many antibiotics. So these bacteria could become difficult to manage.

SUSTAINABLE AGRICULTURE

Successful management of resources for the purpose of agriculture to satisfy the changing human needs along with maintenance and enhancement of the quality of environment and conservation of natural resources.

Sustainable agriculture would primarily use renewable resources, would cause the minimum pollution and maintain the optimum yield level. Biotechnology is advantageous to sustainable agriculture in following ways—

1. Biofertilizers

Microorganisms which bring about nutrient enrichment of soil enhancing the availability of such nutrients *e.g.*, nitrogen (N) and phosphorus (P).

- Biofertilizers are low cost input, renewable, reduced dependence on chemical fertilizers and donot pollute the environment. Some examples are :
  (*a*) **Free living nitrogen fixing bateria**—*e.g., Clostridium, Chromatium, Azotobacter* etc.
  (*b*) **Free living nitrogen fixing cyanobacteria**—*e.g., Anabaena, Nostoc, Tolypothrix* etc.
  (*c*) **Symbiotic nitrogen fixing bacteria**—*e.g., Rhizobium* in root nodules of legumes.
  (*d*) **Symbiotic nitrogen fixing cyanobacteria**—*e.g., Anabaena azollae* in small aquatic fan *Azolla pinnata* often inoculated in rice fields.
  (*e*) **Phosphate bacteria**—*e.g., Bacillus megatherium* var. *phosphaticum.*
  (*f*) **Phyllosere** and **Rhizosphere nitrogen fixing bacteria**—*e.g., Azospirillum, Beijerinckia.*
  (*g*) **Mycorrhiza**—Symbiotic association of fungus and plant roots. These are of irregular shapes often coralloid with wooly covering and absence of root hair and root cap. These fungi solubilise phosphorus, produce plant growth promoting substances and protect host plant from soil pathogens.

Biofertilizers donot produce quick and spectacular results but are slow and take time to become effective.

2. Biopesticides

- The biological agents that are used to control weeds, insects and pathogens are called **biopesticides.**
- The biological agents which are used as biopesticides are viruses, bacteria, fungi, protozoa and mites.
- Insect pest can be overcome by the use of **azadirachtin** (from Neem) due to its antifeedant characteristic, predators (*e.g.,* Preying mantis, lady bird beetle), parasites, parasitoids, pathogens of insects, pyrethrin, thurioside etc.
- Weeds are controlled by the use of predator herbivore, smoother crops and mycoherbicides.
- Fungus *Trichoderma* is used in biocontrol of fungal pathogens by its ability to secrete chitinase.
- **Sporeine** was the first bioinsecticide.
- The first bioherbicide was mycoherbicide (based on the fungus *Phytophthora palmivora*) and was developed in 1981. It is used to control the growth of milk weed in citrus orchards.
- The bacterium, *Bacillus thuringiensis* produces protein toxins. One of these, **thurioside** is active against different groups of insects. The toxins accumulate as crystals inside the bacteria during sporulation. On being ingested by insects, these are converted into active form and kill them by inhibiting ion transport in the midgut.
- Due to use of biopesticides, the application of chemicals to control the diseases, insect pest and weeds is reduced which are the source of widespread pollution.

3. Disease and Insect-Resistant Varieties

Genetic engineering has enabled the development of crop varieties resistant to certain insects and diseases. The disease resistant genes are isolated and transferred to high yielding susceptible plants to produce pathogen-free plants. Several disease resistant somaclones have been identified for resistance to early blight of potato caused by *Alternaria solani*. Progress in engineering insect resistance in transgenic plants has been made through the expression of insect toxin gene of *Bacillus thuringiensis* in plants by transferring the viral genes of coat proteins. The technique has been used to produce a virus-resistant variety of squash.

Development of disease and insect resistant varieties would minimise the use of pesticides, prevent pollution, reduces yield losses due to insects and diseases and enhance agricultural production.

4. Single cell protein (SCP)

Microorganisms (*e.g.*, Algae, filamentous fungi, bacteria, yeast etc.) which can be cultured on a commercial scale in a fermenter, treated in various ways dried and used as food source or as animal feed are called **single cell protein** (SCP). In SCP, biomass is obtained not only from unicellular organisms but also from multicellular organisms. CO_2 produced from industry effluents and materials like saw dust and paddy straw are being used for production of many types of single cell proteins. SCP contain very high amount of proteins with little quantity of fats. Some microorganisms which lend themselves to biotechnological processing belong to—Algae (*e.g.*, *Chlorella, Scenedesmus*); Filamentous fungi (*e.g.*, *Fusarium gramineranum, Chaetomium cellulolyticum*); bacteria (*e.g.*, *Methylopphilus methylatrophus, Brevibacterium* sp. etc.); cyanobacteria (*e.g.*, *Spirulina* sp.) ; yeasts (*e.g.*, *Saccharomyces cerevisiae, Candida utilis* etc.) Processing is required to remove contaminants and excess nucleic acids. Besides providing the much needed proteins, single cell protein is beneficial in reducing environmental pollution by managing industrial and agricultural wastes.

BIOREMEDIATION AND PHYTOREMEDIATION

BIOPATENT

A **patent** is the right granted by a government to an inventor to prevent other from commercial use of his invention. A patent is granted for (*a*) an invention, (*b*) an improvement in an earlier invention, (*c*) the process of generating a product, (*d*) a concept or design.

Biopatent is the patent granted for biological entities and for products derived from them. Biopatents are awarded for (*i*) strains of microorganisms (*ii*) cell lines (*iii*) genetically modified strains of plants and animals (*iv*) DNA sequences, (*v*) the proteins encoded by DNA sequences (*vi*) various biotechnological procedures, (*vii*) production processes (*viii*) products and (*ix*) product applications.

Many biopatents are very broad in their coverage *i.e.*, one patent covers all transgenic plants of *Brassica* family. Such broad patents are considered morally unacceptable and fundamentally inequitable, since these would enable financially powerful corporation to acquire monopoly control over biotechnological processes.

BIOPIRACY

It is the exploitation of **bioresources** of a country by organisations and multinationals for commercial exploitation with or without patent but without any **Access and Benefit sharing agreement** (ABA).

Biological resources or bioresources include all those organisms that can be used to derive commercial benefits.

Traditional knowledge related to bioresources is the knowledge developed by various communities over long period of history, regarding the utilization of the bioresources *e.g.*, use of herbs etc as drugs. Traditional knowledge helps in saving time, effort and expenditure indeveloping refined product for commercialisaton.

Based on the traditional knowledge, institution and companies of industralized nations are collecting and exploiting bioresources of other nations by getting them patented.

1. A patent granted in USA covers the entire 'basmati' rice germplasm indigenous to our country.
2. The bioresources are being analysed for identification of valuable biomolecules (compound produced by a living organism). The useful biomolecules are got patented.
3. Useful genes from the bioresources are isolated, patented and commercialised.

4. Traditional knowledge is used to get a bioresource patented.

Bioresources of the developing world have always been commercially exploited by the industrialized nations without an adequate compensation to the developing world. Some nations are developing comprehensive laws to prevent unauthorised exploitation of their bioresources and traditional knowledge.

BIOWAR OR BIOLOGICAL WARFARE

It is the international conflict in which viruses, bacteria and other biological agents noxious to or destructive of life are used against enemies.

Bioweapon or biological weapon is a device that carries and delivers to the target organisms a pathological biological agent or a toxin derived from it.

Bioweapon agent

The biological agent or toxin which is kept in a suitable container so that it remains active and virulent during delivery, which in delivered in various ways, including missiles and aircraft. Potential pathogens for bioweapons are *Bacillus anthracis, Vibrio cholerae,* small pox virus, *Pasteurella/Yersinia pestis,* botulinum toxin etc.

Bioweapons are—(*i*) low cost weapons, (*ii*) almost invisible, (*iii*) cause for more casualities than chemical or conventional weapons.

The possible defences against bioweapons include the use of respirator or gas mask, vaccination, administration on of appropriate antibiotics, decontamination and sensitive detection systems.

BIOETHICS

It is a set of perceptions, standards and principles which regulate our activities in relation to exploitation of biological world particularly in view of the latest break through in biotechnology.

The major bioethical concerns related to biotechnology are :

(1) Animals are used for producing pharmaceutical proteins are virtually functioning as factory for human beings.

(2) Use of animals in biotechnology causes great suffering to them.

(3) Transfer of human genes into animals (and vice-versa) dilutes the 'concept of humanness'.

(4) Biotechnology by manipulating genes is producing new genotypes, some of which may be dangerous to the living world.

(5) Transgenics are likely to damage environment.

(6) It would change the crop-weed interaction by the transfer of new genes to weeds and other plants.

(7) It violates integrity of species.

Biotechnologies do these things on a much larger scale and at a much faster rate.

SOME IMPORTANT FACTS

- **Golden rice :** Genetically altered rice with yellow coloured grains, rich in vitamin A.
- **Terminator seeds :** Produced by genetic engineering are in fact seeds that develop into fertile plants which produce nongerminable seeds.
- **Plasticulture :** Use of plastic in agriculture. This technology in being considered as an important tool for evergreen revolution.
- Citizens of Delhi contains the highest level of pesticides is their body fat in the world.
- **Therapeutic cloning :** Used to repair damaged tissues and diseased organs.
- **Reproductive Cloning :** Used to create babies identical in genetic makeup to a given genome. Helps to seek immortality, bypass infertility, triumph over death by recreating a loved one etc.
- **Bioenergy** the energy obtained from biological sources *i.e.*, animal energy and biofuels.
- A transgenic cow has been produced that bears a gene for the production of human lactoferin in cow milk.
- **Bioreactor :** The fermentation tank where fermentation is caried out in the presence of micro-organisms.
- **Hybridomas :** The hybrid cells of same clone.
- **PNA (Peptide Nucleic Acid) :** Nucleotide bases attached to back bone of small peptides stick to RNAs of food poisoning bacteria. The latter fail to produce proteins and die after some time.

- **Biological weapons** convention and Treaty-1972.
- **Broad spectrum antibiotics :** The antibiotics which have the ability to act on several pathogenic species differing from each other in structure and composition of cell wall.
- Department of Biotechnology (DBT)—India.
- Information Centre for Genetic Engineering and Biotechnology (ICGEB) : New Delhi and Italy.
- Central Food and Training Research Institute (CFTRI) : Mysore.
- Central Drug Research Institute (CDRI) : Lucknow.
- Central Institute of Medicinal and Aromatic Plants (CIMAP) : Lucknow.
- Animal energy is available in two forms :

  HMP (Human Muscle Power) and **DAP** (Draught Animal Power).
- **Shikonin :** A red dye used for manufacturing cosmetics.
- **Second generation vaccines :** Those produced by genetic engineering for Hepatitis B and Herpes Virus.
- **Third generation vaccines :** Synthetic vaccines.
- **TPA** (Tissue Plasminogen Activator) enzyme is used to dissolve blood clots particularly in case of heart attacks.
- **Gene bank :** is an institution where valuable genetic material is stored either in the form of seeds or as vegetative material.
- **Germplasm :** The genetic material especially that contained within the reproductive cells.
- **G. Haberlandt** (1854 – 1945) : Father of plant tissue culture, first to have cultured cells which were fully differentiated (on Knop's salt solution + sucrose).
- **Somatic embryogenesis :** Represents the embryo like structures derived from sporophytic or somatic cells of the plant.
- **IPRs :** Intellectual Property Rights (Patents).
- **Humulin :** first genetically engineered human insulin produced by the American firm Eli Lilly.
- **Cellular totipotency :** The ability of somatic cells of a plant to produce a new complete plant.

TRANSGENIC ANIMALS AND PLATNS, MOLECULAR APPROACHES TO DIAGNOSIS AND STRAIN IDENTIFICATION

INTRODUCTION

Domestication

The process of bringing certain plants and animals under human management. Presently, the field of agriculture is the result of continuous and progressive researches in various branches of agricultural sciences.

Genotype

Genotype is the genetic set up of an organism. It is responsible for performance of an organism. The degree of genotype expression depends upon the environment.

Phenotype

Morphology and performance of a crop or domesticated animal is called phenotype which depends upon two factors *i.e.*, genotype/heredity and environment.

The **environment** includes all living and non-living factors with which an individual or the variety interacts. The environmental factors include climatic, edaphic, topographical and biotic factors.

Maximisation of food production would involve the improvement in crop or animal genotypes, as well as the environments under which the crops and animals are raised.

Improved management practices

These practices are undertaken to modify the environment for maximising the yield of crops and animals.

(*a*) **Improved management practices for crops :** *i.e.*, preparation of soil (through ploughing, levelling, manuring etc.), good quality of certified seeds (may be treated with fungicide to check seed borne or soil borne infection), sowing (at proper depth place and time), nutrients (manure, compost, fertilisers etc.), irrigation, weeding, crop protection (from pests and pathogens), multiple cropping, crop rotation etc.

(*b*) **Improved management practices for domesticated animals :** Shelter (well lighted, ventilated and spacious), feed (optimum quality and quantity), drinking water (clean fresh water), washing and grooming (periodically), disinfection (periodically), vaccination, sick animals (should be separated and treated) etc.

IMPROVEMENT IN GENOTYPE

Improvement in genotype is mainly done by improving the genetic potentialities in plants and animals.

- **Trait or Character** : any morpholgical, anatomical, behavioural and biochemical feature of an organism *e.g.*, plant maturity, fruit size, shattering and non-shattering nature, yield, quality.
- **Selection** : the process that leads to different rates of reproduction by different genotypes present in a population.
- **Breeding** : When genotype of an organism is modified to make that organism more useful to humans, the process is called breeding.
- **Plant breeding** : The science of producing improved varieties of crop plants by changing their heredity for one or more traits like higher yield, better quality, shorter duration, suitability to particular environment and resistance to common diseases.
- **Animal breeding** : aims at genetic improvement of domesticated animal species.

IMPROVED VARIETIES

- **Variety** : A variety consists of a group of plants which have the same genotype or similar genotypes and it differs for one or more characters from other varieties of the same crop.
- **Improved Variety** : the race/strain/breed of a species which is superior to all other existing varieties in one or more traits. It is recognized as such by a variety release committee based on its detailed evaluation for yield and other characters.

DEVELOPMENT OF NEW VARIETIES

Consists of the following main steps.

(*i*) Creation of genetic variation,

(*ii*) Selection,

(*iii*) Evaluation and release as a variety and

(*iv*) Seed multiplication and distribution to farmers.

(i) Creation of genetic variation

Two most important steps in plant breeding are to create genetic variation and selection.

Variation means differences among individuals of a population or species for a specific character.

Genetic variation

It is the source of raw material for selection. These are heritable due to genotype and are transmitted from one generation to other. Such variations are useful in selection.

- Success of a breeding programme usually depends on creation of the desired genetic variation. It can be done in following ways *i.e.*, domestication, germplasm collection, plant introduction, hybridisation, polyploidy, mutation and genetic engineering.
- **Hybridisation** : The crossing of two plants differing from each other genotypically in one or more traits.
- **Line** : A group of individuals having a common lineage and similar genotype.
- **Parents** : The individials or lines used in hybridisation.
- **Emasculation** : The removal of male parts or anthers from the future female parent plants in the young state so as to avoid chances of contamination from their pollen. It is essential in bisexual flowers to prevent self-pollination. By doing emasculation, the plant breeder makes a female flower which can be artificially pollinated by the desired pollen grains. This is generally done by hand, through suction pressure, hot or cold water treatment, alcohol treatment or by the use of chemical gametocides.
- **Hybrid or F_1 Seeds** : Seeds produced by emasculated flowers of the female parent are hybrid or F_1 seeds. There will be segregation, independent assortment and recombination in the F_2 and later generations obtained from these F_1 seeds.

- **Single cross :** When a hybridisation is performed between the two plants.
- **Multiple cross :** When a hybridisation is performed between more than two plants.
- **Hybridisation may be**
  (*i*) **Intravarietal** : Between the two plants belonging to same variety.
  (*ii*) **Intervarietal or intraspecific** : Between the two varieties of the same species.
  (*iii*) **Interspecific** : Between the different species of the same genus. *e.g.*, all the sugarcane varieties being cultivated today are interspecific hybrids.
  (*iv*) **Intergeneric** : Between two different genera.

(ii) Selection

During selection, the individual plants or groups of plants having the desired characters are picked up from a population eliminating the undesirable ones. These selected plants are allowed to reproduce for setting their seeds. The seeds are collected and again a new crop is developed. Selection acts on the genetic variation present in a population and produces a new population with improved characters.

- **Selection in self-pollinated crops** : In self-pollinated crops, the amount of cross-pollination is less than 5 per cent. Self-pollination causes a rapid increase in **homozygosity.** Self-pollinated crops gradually becomes **homozygous.** Best homozygous individuals can be easily isolated in such crops. By selection, **pure lines** are produced. Which have identical genotype. Due to self-pollination seeds of such crops can be used year after year.
- **Selection in cross-pollinated crops** : Cross-pollinated crops are **heterozygous** and contains mixture of many genotypes. A cross-pollinated population contains plants of several different genotypes. Some of there genotypes are superior, but many are inferior. Selection in such crops targets at enhancing the frequency of superior genotypes with reducing the heterozygosity.

(iii) Evaluation and release of varieties

A newly developed variety is evaluated for its yield, quality, disease and insect resistance before it is released to farmers. Indian council of Agricultural Research (ICAR) carries out the evaluations in India. In every agro-climatic zone, every crop is evaluated for minimum three years. A new pure line, population or hybrid that is superior to the existing varieties, as well as to other new material may be released as a new variety. Variety release committee recommends the release of improved variety under new name with permission of Government.

(iv) Multiplication of improved seed

Seed means any plant part which is used to grow a crop like grains in wheat, tubers of potato, stems of sugarcane etc. Grains used as food cannot be termed as seed whereas, those used for raising a crop are called **seeds.**

Improved seed : Seed of a varietiy with superior traits which must be of high purity, and have a high germination percentage. These seeds must also be free from weed seeds and diseases.

The quality of seed is often certified by an agency. Such seed is called **certified seed.** National seed corporation (NSC) was established to streamline seed production in India.

GERMPLASM COLLECTION AND CONSERVATION

Germplasm

The sum total of all the alleles of the genes present in a crop and its related species.

Germplasm Materials

(*i*) Cultivated and non-cultivated improved varieties.

(*ii*) Old local/*desi* varieties of different places.

(*iii*) Lines produced by plant breeders, and

(*iv*) Wild species/relatives of the crop plant.

The **first germplasm centre** of the world was established by Vavilov in Leningrad.

International Board of Plant Genetic Resources was established in 1971.

International Crops Research Institute for Semi Arid Tropics (ICRISAT) is located in Hyderabad, which is responsible for conserving germplasm of groundnut, pigeonpea, chick pea, pearl millet and sorghum.

Germplasm is maintained in **gene/germplasm banks.** They are institutes that maintain stocks of viable seeds (seed banks), live growing plants (orchards), tissue culture and frozen germplasm (Cryopreservation).

Orthodox seeds

Partially dehydrated and stored at low temperature of – 10° to – 20°C under anaerobic conditions for long periods *e.g.,* cereals, legumes.

Recalcitrant Seeds

Kept at room temperature under partially humid aerobic conditions for shorter duration *e.g.,* tea, cocoa, jackfruit, coconut etc. All the varieties of trees and plants with recalcitrant seeds are maintained in orchards.

Plant introduction

Shifting of a variety, line or population of a plant species to a new area, where it was not grown earlier. Improved varieties like **"Sonora-64"** of wheat and **"Taichung Native-1"** of rice are examples of plant introduction. These dwarf varieties provided the starting material for "green revolution" in India.

Quarantine

Checking of incoming plants, seeds, fruits, tissues and other organism for any harmful effect the same can cause to the local flora, fauna and humans. Plant quarantine is meant for preventing introduction of exotic pests, weeds and diseases into the country under Destructive Insects and Pests (DIP) Act, 1914. It is applicable to other types of introductions as well like animals and sometimes human beings to reduce the chances of pathogen/pest entry in a country. *Argemone mexicana*, a weed entered India with introduction.

HETEROSIS AND INBREEDING DEPRESSION

Heterosis or Hybrid vigour

Term **Heterosis** was coined by Shull (1914) and in ordinary use hybrid vigour and heterosis are practically synonymous.

Hybrid vigour

The superiority of the hybrid over either parent in one or more traits. When two unrelated individuals or lines are crossed, the performance of F_1 hybrid is often superior to both its parents. Almost all species exhibit heterosis. It is essentially the reverse of inbreeding depression.

Inbreeding Depression

Loss of vigour and appearence of a number of defective traits associated with inbreeding is called **inbreeding depression.** Many cross-pollinated crops and all animals species exhibit inbreeding depression. On the other hand, the self-pollinated crops do not exhibit ill effects of inbreeding because cross-pollination makes the plants highly heterozygous.

Inbreeding is the mating of two individuals of a species which are related to descent.

MUTATION BREEDING

- **Mutation** : Sudden, stable discontinuous and inheritable variations which appear in organism due to permanent change in their genotype.
- **Spontaneous mutation** : Mutations which occur naturally, *i.e.,* both germinal and somatic.
- **Induced mutations** : Mutations produced in response to a treatment with a mutagen. They

were first produced by Muller (1927) with the help of X-rays on *Drosophila* and by Stadler in maize.

- **Mutagens** : Rate of mutations is increased by means of certain factors and chemicals called **mutagens.** 2 types :
  (*i*) **Chemical mutagens** : A variety of chemicals like ethylmethane sulphonate (EMS) and sodium azide which induce mutations.
  (*ii*) **Physical mutagens** : Various kinds of radiations *e.g.*, X-rays, gamma rays, ultraviolet rays etc.
- Mutation can arise due to a change in any of the following :
  (*i*) Chromosome structure
  (*ii*) Chromosome number
  (*iii*) Base sequence of the concerned gene.

Mutation breeding

The use of induced mutations in plant breeding to develop improved varieties. In such breeding usually seeds are treated with a suitable mutagen. The treated seeds are grown in the field and self-pollinated. Progeny from these plants are grown during the next crop season. These plants are carefully observed to identify and select mutations of interest. In the end, a desirable mutant line may be obtained which may be good enough to be released as a new variety. Over 200 varieties have been produced from mutation breeding in India.

POLYPLOIDY IN CROP IMPROVEMENT OR POLYPLOID BREEDING

- **Polyploid** : An organism which possesses more than two sets of chromosomes.
- **Polypoidy** : Phenomenon of having one or more genomes in addition to the normal number for the species.
- A polyploid on the basis of number of chromosome set present may be triploid (3N), tetraploid (4N), pentaploid (5N), hexaploid (6N), septaploid (7N), octaploid (8N) etc. The polyploid species are of two types :
  (*i*) **Autopolyploid species/individual** : Contains more than two copies of a single genome.
  (*ii*) **Allopolyploid species/individual** : Contains two or more genomes and each genome is ordinarily present in two copies.

Autopolyploidy

The polyploidy which takes place within a species and results due to multiplication of the same set of chromosomes. It can be induced artificially by the use of a chemical called **colchicine** which arrests and breaks the spindle so that nuclear division is not followed by wall formation. All autopolyploids exhibit **gigas effect** *i.e.*, larger size, more juice, more sugar, more grains etc. Triploids are sexually sterile which are propagated vegetatively *e.g.*, many banana varieties, seedless water melon, triploid sugar beet with more sugar and larger roots, some apple and pear varieties with large sized and more juicy fruits. An autotriploid (three copies of a single genome) variety of tea has also been developed in India.

Alloployploidy

The polyploids which arise as a result of chromosome doubling following hybridisation of two distinctly different species are called allopolyploids. It is also called **interspecific polyploidy** because increase in number of genomes or chromosome sets is due to pooling from individuals of two or more species caused by hybridisaion followed by chromosome doubling *e.g.*, AABB, AABBCC.

Among artificially produced allopolyploidy *Triticale* is the first man made crop derived by crossing wheat (*Triticum*) and rye (*Secale*). The chromosome number of the resulting F_1 was doubled to produce triticale.

Haploidy

The haploid bears only one set of chromosomes *i.e.*, only one copy of each chromosome. Haploids of higher plants are sterile and generally do not survive. However, they are highly useful in producing pure homozygous lines for breeding programmes. Such plants are developed through a culture technique developed by Guha and Maheshwari (1964). It is called **androgenic haploid culture.** Gynogenic haploids are also developed by using unfertilised ovules.

BREEDING FOR NUTRITIONAL QUALITY

Quality : an important aspect for plant breeders because it determines the suitability of plant produce for various uses. **Qualitative characters** differ from crop to crop and also vary with the use of plant produce *e.g.*, size, shape, colour, milling, baking, malting and cooking in food grains, size, colour, taste, flavour and nutrition in fruits etc.

Nutritional quality of a fruit/crop/vegetable etc. is its value in human/animal nutrition as to number of calories, amount and presence of essential amino acids and fatty acids, vitamins, minerals, roughage and absence of antinutritional factors.

Antinutritional factors are those compounds which badly affect the human/animal growth and development *e.g.*, Glucosinolates in oils and cakes of rapeseed and mustard ; Neurotoxin found in seeds of *Lathyrus sativus* etc.

Protein Quality : The quality of essential amino acids in proteins relative to contents required in human diet represents the **protein quality.** Pulses lack methionine and cysteine (sulphur containing amino acids) Cereals and millets do not possess amino acids lysine and tryptophan. A combination of pulses and cereals are able to provide all essential amino acids.

"Shakti", "Rattan"and "Protina" are the newly developed varieties of maize which are rich in amino acids lysine.

Oil Quality is determined by the presence and relative amounts of saturated and unsaturated fatty acids. Saturated long chain fatty acids like **erucic acid** (22-carbon fatty acid) are not good for health. In contrast polysaturated fatty acids are beneficial to human health. Therefore, oil seed varieties with higher polyunsaturated fatty acid contents are being developed.

BREEDING FOR DISEASE RESISTANCE

There are various physical, chemical and biological methods for disease control but the cheapest and the most convenient method is to produce resistant varieties.

- **Pathogen** : an organism that causes disease in another organism (*i.e.*, host).
- Development of disease in plant depends on (*i*) host genotype, (*ii*) pathogen genotype and (*iii*) the environment.
- **Disease resistance :** the ability of host to inhibit the growth of pathogen so that no or little harm is done to it. It can be mechanical/anatomical feature, protective reaction, antibiosis and non-supply of nutrition by the host which checks pathogen to enter and flourish in the host's body.
- **Susceptible Host :** Term is used for those lines which are not resistant to the pathogen but are attacked and harmed by the pathogen.
- A successful breeding for disease resistance depends mainly on :

  (*a*) good source of resistance, and (*b*) dependable disease test.
- **Disease test :** Is carried out by growing various varieties in an area under conditions in which the susceptible plants would develop the disease.
- Disease resistant varieties provide the cheapest and a hazard-free means of controlling diseases. Is any case, such varieties are very important component of any package designed for disease control. Almost all modern day varieties incorporate in them resistance for important diseases of the crop.

BIOSTATISTICS

Key Topics

- Principles and Practice of Statistical Methods in Biological Research
- Samples and Populations
- Basic Statistics Average, Statistics of Dispersion
- Coefficient of Variation; Standard Error
- Probability Distributions, (Binomial, Poisson and Normal)
- Tests of Statistical Significance
- Simple Correlation of Regression
- Analysis of Variance

STATISTICAL METHODS IN BIOLOGICAL RESEARCH

Sample and Populations

Research Methodology: Any type of research, especially in biological fields involves collection of data related to the problem of study. This data is then compiled, sorted and finally analyzed before arising at a conclusion or result. For the accurate analysis of the data, various statistical methods are employed. These include classification, tubulation, comparison, correlation and interpretation. The quantitative application of statistical methods to biological facts/ data is known *as biometry.*

Methods of Collecting Data

There are two methods by which data can be collected, namely census method and sample method.

(i) *Census Method:* In this method, information regarding each member of the population is collected. This method is preferred only when very accurate results are needed. This method is not feasible in certain cases such as quality control, where analysis of each item would render the product useless.

(ii) *Sampling Method :* In this method, only a part or fraction of the total population is considered for the actual experiments and data collected from them. The sample is considered as the representative of the total population and conclusions and inferences are drawn on that basis.

Methods of Sampling : Sample may be selected in two ways-deliberate selection or random sampling.

(i) *Deliberate Selection :* In this method, the investigator chooses a few samples from the population, which he thinks are the best representatives of that population. The demerit of this method is that the degree of accuracy is not reliable.

(ii) *Random Samplin :* This technique is based on the theory of probability according to which each item of the population has an equal chance of being included in the sample. This method is economical and saves time.

Classification of Data

Biological data are usually classified in either of the following ways:

(i) Classification according to attribute

(ii) Classification according to class intervals.

(i) ***Classification according to Attribute:*** This is qualitative grouping where the data are classified on the basis of some attributes which are possessed by the population like intelligence, colour of hair, etc. This type of classification may be two types:

(a) *Simple Classification :* Usually only one parameter is considered, *e.g.*, gender, mantal status, literacy status.

(b) *Manifold Classification :* Here more than one type of attributes are considered simultaneously, *e.g.*, the students in a class can be divided on the basis of the gender. Also they can be grouped based on their intelligence quotient.

(i) ***Classification according to Class Interval:*** This type of classification is known as quantitative classification or frequency distribution. Here classification is based on some measurable quantity.

This method can be used in studies related to height, weight, productivity, etc. When a large number of observations varying over a wide range are available, these are classified according to the size of the values. Each of these groups is defined by an interval called class interval or class. Frequency distribution table can be overlapping or non-overlapping.

Example : In a routine medical examination the pulse rates of 35 girls were recorded as:

61, 56, 72, 65, 70, 59, 68, 82, 60, 66, 52, 59, 73, 78, 66, 61, 51, 59, 84, 68, 79, 75, 68, 58, 71, 62, 57, 53, 74, 70, 66, 60, 71, 54, 72.

Construct over lapping and non-overlapping frequency table with the data.

Overlapping Frequency Table		***Non-overlapping Table***	
Class Interval	***Frequency***	***Class Interval***	***Frequency***
50-55	4	51-55	4
55-60	6	56-60	8
60-65	5	61-65	4
65-70	7	66-70	9
70-75	8	71-75	7
75-80	3	76-80	2
80-85	2	81-85	1
Total	35	Total	35

In biological experiments, usually the data is expressed in % frequency.

Class Interval	***Frequency***	***Cumulative Frequency***	***Relative Frequency***	***% Frequency***
51-55	4	4	0.04	4%
56-60	8	12	0.12	12%
61-65	4	16	0.16	16%
66-70	9	25	0.25	25%
71-75	7	32	0.32	32%
76-80	2	34	0.34	34%
81-85	1	35	0.35	35%

Tabulation

The classified data then presented in tables. Tabulation is the process of arranging the data in columns and rows. A tabular arrangement of data facilitates quick comparison and also makes the errors easily detectable. There are two broad categories of table – simple and complex.

(i) ***Simple Tables*** **:** In this type only one characteristic is studied. For instance, in the above example, only one characteristic namely the pulse rate was studied.

(ii) ***Complex Tables*** **:** In this type two or more characteristics are studied together, *e.g.*, for the study of various blood parameters like HDL, LDL, total cholesterol, total sugar of control mice and diabetes induced mice, the following complex table can be constructed.

S. No.	***Blood Parameter***	***Mice***	
		Normal	***Diabetic***
1.	HDL	a_1	x_1
2.	LDL	a_2	x_2
3.	VLDL	a_3	x_3
4.	Cholesterol	a_4	x_4
5.	Glucose	a_5	x_5

Usually a table has the following parts:

(i) ***Table Number:*** Given at the top of the table.

(ii) ***Title:*** A suitable title should be given at the top of table.

(iii) ***Captions:*** The heading of column is caption and it is placed at the top centre of each column along with the respective units.

(iv) ***Stubs:*** The designations of the horizontal rows in the table are called stub items. These are placed on the left-side of the rows.

(v) ***Body:*** The body represents the data presented in the table.

(vi) ***Footnotes:*** These are used to explain the data and is placed at the bottom of the table.

Graphical Representation of Data

A more useful method of presenting data is by graphical representation. There are many different ways like histogram, frequency polygon, frequency curve, relative frequency map, cumulative frequency curve or ogive and scatter or dot diagram.

Histogram: This type of graph is used for continuous frequency distribution. The width of the class interval are marked along the X-axis. On these lengths rectangles of aras proportional to the frequencies of the respective class intervals are erected.

Example: The age and frequency of cancer patients recorded in a hospital are:

Age	40-49	50-59	60-69	70-79	80-89
No. of Patients	2	3	15	21	18

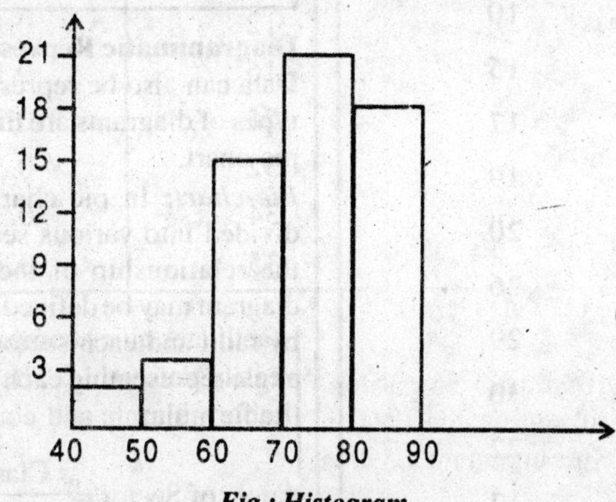

Fig : Histogram

Frequency Polygon : A frequency polygon is a curve representing a frequency distribution. It is constructed from a histogram by joining the mid-points of the tops of the different rectangles with straight lines.

In the above example, frequency polygon can be drawn as:

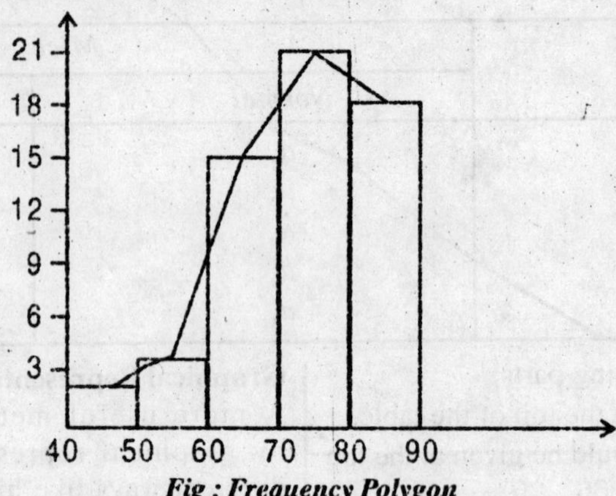

Fig : Frequency Polygon

Cumulative Frequency Curve: The graphical representation of cumulative frequency distribution is called cumulative frequency curve or ogive. There are two methods to contruct an ogive.

(i) ***'Less than' Method:*** The upper limit of each class is plotted along the X-axis and cumulative frequencies along the Y-axis. The plotted points are joined by a smooth curve and the resulting curve is the ogive.

(ii) ***'More than' Method:*** Here the upper limit of each class is taken along X-axis.

Example:

Height (in cm)	*Frequency*
160-162	10
162-164	15
164-166	17
166-168	19
168-170	20
170-172	26
172-174	29
174-176	30
176-178	22
178-180	12

Cumulative frequency distribution table:

Height (in cm)	*Frequency Class Frequency*
160-162	10
162-164	15
164-166	17
166-168	19
168-170	20
170-172	26
172-174	29
174-176	30
176-178	22
178-180	12

Diagrammatic Representation of Data

Data can also be represented by diagrams. Different types of diagrams are linke diagram, bar diagram and pie-chart.

Pie-chart: In pie-chart or pie-diagram a circle is divided into various sectors and the diagram shows the relationship of the parts to the whole. A pie-diagram may be defined as a circle divided into sectors by radii and each sector represents a frequency. The angle representing each sector can be calculated from the formula:

$$\text{Angle of Sector} = \frac{\text{Class Frequency}}{\text{Total Observation}} \times 360°$$

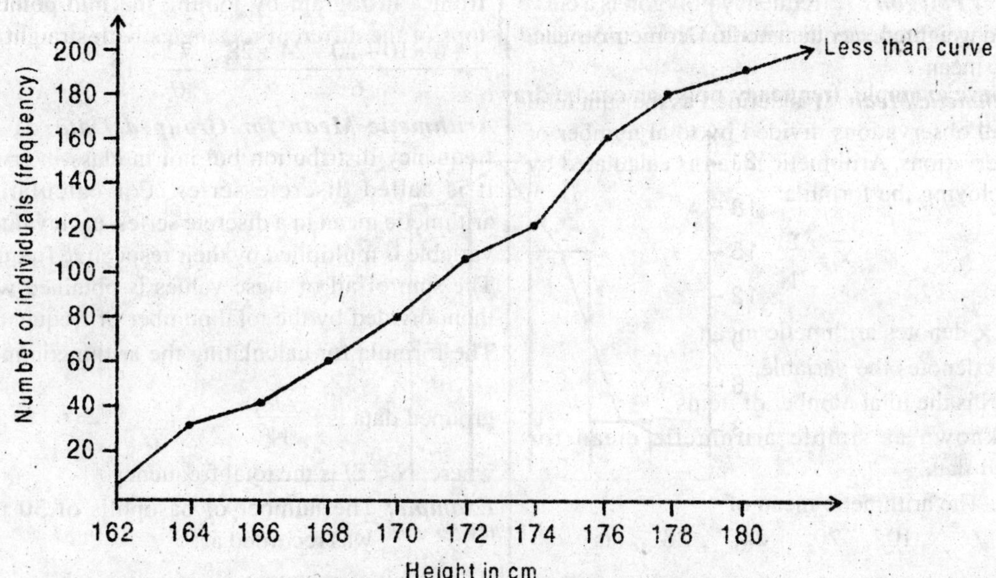

Fig : Cumulative Frequency Curve:

Example : The various types of lipids of plasma membrane was found to be:

Cholesterol	Lecithin	Cephalin	Phosphatidyl Serine	Sphingomyelin	Glycolipid
20	19	12	7	12	10

	Percentage	*Degrees*
Cholesterol	25%	90.0
Lecithin	23.75%	85.5%
Cephalin	15%	54.0
Phosphatidyl Serine	8.75%	31.5
Sphingomyelin	15%	54.0
Glycolipid	12.5%	45.0

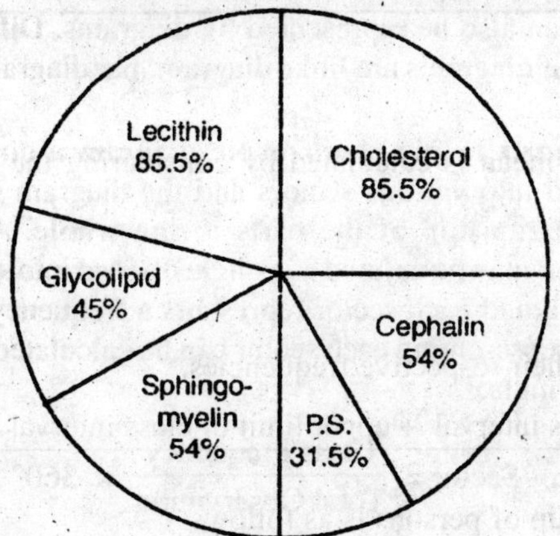

Analysis and Interpretation of Data

The size of the data may be too large even after classification and tabulation. To make the analysis of data easter, ratio, percentages, averages dispersion, etc. can be used.

Measures of Central Tendency

In a statistical data, it is found that the values of the variables tend to concentrate around some central value which can be considered as a representative for the whole data. Such values or measures are referred to as measures of central tendency or averages. Averages are of different types : Arithmetic mean—

simple and weighted, median, mode, Geometric mean. Harmonic mean.

(1) ***Arithmetic Mean:*** It is defined as the sum total of all observations divided by total number of observations. Arithmetic mean is calculated by employing the formula

$$\overline{X} = \frac{\Sigma x}{N}$$

where, $\overline{X}$ denotes arithmetic mean,
x denotes the variable,
N is the total number of items.

This is known as simple arithmetic mean for ungrouped data.

Example: The arithmetic mean of 4, 6, 10, 20, 24, 28 is

$$\frac{4+6+10+20-24+28}{6} = \frac{72}{6} = 12$$

Arithmetic Mean for Grouped Data: If data is frequency distribution but not in class interval then it is called discrete series. For calculating the arithmetic mean in a discrete series, each value of the variable is multiplied by their respective frequencies. The sum of all of these values is obtained which is them divided by the total number of frequencies. The formula for calculating the arithmetic mean for grouped data is : $\frac{\Sigma fx}{N}$

where, N = Σf is the total frequency.

Example: The number of basophils of 30 patients was recorded as:

No. of Basophils	11	14	17	19	22
Frequencies	5	6	8	7	4

Calculate the arithmetic mean

$$\overline{X} = \frac{\Sigma fx}{\Sigma f}$$

Variable (x)	*Frequency (f)*	*fx*
11	5	55
14	6	84
17	8	136
19	7	133
22	4	88
	$\Sigma f = 30$	$\Sigma fx = 496$

$$\overline{X} = \frac{496}{30} = 16.53$$

Continuous Series: In grouped continuous series, arithmetic mean is calculated by considering the mid-points of various classes. The formula used is

$$\overline{X} = \frac{\Sigma f.m}{\Sigma f}$$

where, $\Sigma f.m$ is the sum of values of mid-points multiplied by their respective frequencies.

$$\text{mid-point } m = \frac{\text{lower limit of class interval} + \text{upper limit of class interval}}{2}$$

Example: The frequency distribution according to the age group of persons is as follows:

Calculate the arithmetic mean of their ages:

Groups	5-15	15-25	25-35	35-45	45-55	55-65
No. of Persons	4	7	12	9	5	3

Class Interval C.I.	*Mid-value (m)*	*Frequency (f)*	$m \times f$
5-15	10	4	40
15-25	20	7	140,
25-35	30	12	360
35-45	40	9	360
45-55	50	5	250
55-65	60	3	180
		$\Sigma f = 40$	$\Sigma mxf = 1330$

$$\overline{X} = \frac{1330}{40} = 33.25$$

(2) ***Median:*** This is also a measure of central tendency. Median can be defined as the value of the variable which divides the distribution so that exactly half of the distribution has the same or larger values of exactly half has the same or lower values. For finding the median, the variables are arranged either in ascending or descending order, and then the middle value is chosen. The middle value is chosen by applying the formula:

$$\text{median} = \text{size of } \frac{N+1}{2} \text{ th item}$$

Example: From the following data of the weight of 7 women, determine the median weight.

Weight (in kg) 50 60 62.5 65 70 75 80

No. of Items	*Weight (in ascending order)*
1	50
2	60
3	62.5
4	65
5	70
6	75
7	80

$$\text{median} = \left(\frac{N+1}{2}\right) \text{th item}$$

$$= \frac{7+1}{2} = 4\text{th item.}$$

Hence, median = 65 kg

Calculation of Median when N is Even: Here, median is given by arithmetic mean of the two middle values $\left(\frac{N}{2}\right)^{th}$ and $\left(\frac{N+1}{2}\right)^{th}$ items.

(1) ***Discrete Series:*** Here cumulative frequency is calculated and applied to the formula

$$\text{median} = \left(\frac{N+1}{2}\right)^{th} \text{item}$$

where,

Example: Weight is *g* of 50 grasshoppers and their frequency was recorded as:

Weight (in g)	21	22	23	24	25	26	27	28	29	30
Frequency	4	2	6	4	9	9	7	5	1	3
Cumulative Frequency	4	6	12	16	25	34	41	46	47	50

$$\text{median} = \left(\frac{N+1}{2}\right)^{th}$$

$$= \frac{50+1}{2} = 25.5\text{th item}$$

$$\text{median} = 26$$

(Since items from 25 to 34 have weight 26 as shown by C.F.)

(ii) ***Continuous Series:*** In this method, the position of the median item is first located by calculating $\frac{n+1}{2}$.

$$\text{median} = L_1 + \frac{N/2 - C}{fm} \times h$$

where, L_1 is the lower limit of the class in which median lies,

N is the total frequency Σf

C is the cumulative frequency of the class preceding the median class.

h is the width of the class interval

fm is the frequency of the class in which median lies.

Example : Calculate the median from the following data:

Variable	*Frequency*
20–40	6
40–60	9
60–80	11
80–100	14
100–120	20
120–140	15
140–160	10
160–180	8
180–200	7

Class Interval	*Frequency*	*C.F*
20–40	6	6
40–60	9	15
60–80	11	26
80–100	14	40
100–120	20	60
120–140	15	75
140–160	10	85
160–180	8	93
180–200	7	100

$$\frac{n+1}{2} = 50.5$$

$$\text{median} = L_1 + \frac{N/2 - C}{fm} \times h$$

$$= 100 + \frac{50-40}{20} \times 20$$

$$= 100 + 10 = 110$$

(3) ***Mode :*** It is the value which occurs most frequently in a set of observations and around with other items of the set cluster densely.

Example : Find the Value of mode from the following data:

100, 120, 100, 120, 130, 120, 120, 130, 120, 100.

We find that the value 120 occurs the maximum number of times, hence the value of mode is 120. If two or more values occur the same number of times, the mode is then calculated by using the formula:

$$\text{median} = 3\text{ median} - 2\text{ mean}$$

(4) ***Geometric Mean :*** Geometric mean of *n* items is defined is the *n*th root of the product of *n* items of series. If $X_1, X_2, X_3 \ldots\ldots X_n$ are the number of the data then their geometric mean

$$\text{Gm} = \sqrt[n]{X_1, X_2, X_3 \ldots\ldots X_n} \quad \text{(or)}$$

$$\text{Gm} = (X_1, X_2, X_3 \ldots\ldots X_n)^{1/n}$$

If *n* is very large number, logarithms are used for calculating geometric mean.

$$\text{Gm} = \text{antilog} \frac{\log X_1 + \log X_2 + \log X_3 \ldots\ldots \log X_n}{N}$$

$$\text{Gm} = \text{antilog} \frac{\log X}{N}$$

Example : The number of Basophils of 30 patients was recorded in frequencies. Calculate the Gm.

No. of Basophils	11	14	17	19	22
Frequencies	5	6	8	7	4

Variable (x)	*Frequency (f)*	*log x*	*Freq. log x*
11	5	1.0414	5.2070
14	6	1.1461	6.8766
17	8	1.2304	9.8432
19	7	1.2788	8.9516
22	4	1.3424	0.3696
	$\Sigma f = 30$		$\Sigma f.\log x = 36.24$

$$\text{Gm} = \text{antilog } (\Sigma f.\log x/\Sigma f)$$
$$= \text{antilog } (36.2480/30)$$
$$= 16.15$$

Statistics of Dispersion

Dispersion can be defined as the degree to which the mdividual values of the variate scatter away from the average of the central value. There are four measures of dispersion which can be either absolute or relative. These are :

(i) Range
(ii) Quartile Deviation
(iii) Mean Deviation or Average Deviation
(iv) Standard Deviation

(i) ***Ranger*** : It is defined as the difference between the smallest and the largest figure in the data.

Example: If the values of a data are 7.4, 12.0, 8.5, the rage is

$$\text{Range} = 12.0 - 5.8$$
$$= 6.2$$

Range is an absolute measure of dispersion. It connot be used for purposes of comparison. Hence the coefficient of range is calculated using the formula.

$$\text{Coefficient of Range} = \frac{\text{L} - \text{S}}{\text{L} + \text{S}}$$

In a grouped frequency distribution, range is calculated by taking the difference between the upper limit of the largest class and the lower limit of the lowest class.

Example : Calculate the range and coefficient of range from the following data number of clusters per plant in blackgram.

No. of Clusters	11–20	21–30	31–40	41–50	51–60	61–70	71–80
No. of Plants	6	10	12	15	11	7	4

$$\text{Range} = \text{L} - \text{S} = 80 - 11 = 69$$

$$\text{Coefficient of Range} = \frac{\text{L} - \text{S}}{\text{L} + \text{S}} = \frac{80 - 11}{80 + 11}$$

$$= \frac{69}{91} = 0.758$$

(ii) ***Quartile Deviation*** : It is a measure of dispersion based on the upper quartile Q_3 and the lower quartile Q_1.

$$\text{Inter-Quartile Range} = Q_3 - Q_1$$

Quartile deviation is obtained by dividing interquartile range by 2 and hence is also known as semi interquartile range. Quartile deviation gives the average amount by which the two quartiles differ from a median.

$$\text{Quartile Deviation} = \frac{Q_3 - Q_3}{2}$$

Quartile deviation is an absolute measure of dispersion and hence, cannot be used for comparative studies. Hence coefficient of Q.D. is computed as

$$\text{Coefficient of Q.D.} = \frac{Q_3 - Q_{1/2}}{Q_3 + Q_{1/2}} = \frac{Q_3 - Q_1}{Q_3 + Q_1}$$

Example : Length of earthworms in cm and their frequency was studied, Find the quartile deviation.

Length	16–20	21–25	26–30	31–35	36–40	41–45	46–50	51–55	56–60	61–65
Frequency	4	3	8	9	14	3	3	2	2	2
Cum. Freq.	4	7	15	24	38	41	44	46	48	50

Here $N = 50 \therefore \frac{N}{4} = 12.5; \frac{3N}{4} = 37.5$

Hence, Q_1 will occur in the 3rd C. In *i.e.* 26–30 and Q_3 will be in 5th C.I. *i.e.* 36–40.

$$Q_1 = L + \frac{(N/4 - F)}{fq} \times i = 25.5 + \frac{(12.5 - 7)}{8} \times 5$$

$Q_1 = 28.93$

$$Q_3 = L + \frac{(3/4\,N - F)}{fq} \times i = 36.5 + \frac{(37.5 - 24)}{14} \times 5.$$

$Q_3 = 40.32$

$$Q = \frac{Q_3 - Q_3}{2} = \frac{40.32 - 28.93}{2} = 5.69$$

(iii) ***Mean Deviation*** **:** It is the average of the deviation of the items from some measure of central tendency *i.e.*, mean, mode or median. Mean deviation is also known as average deviation. The results are more appropriate when eviations are taken from the median.

Example : Length of 50 butterflies of a species and their frequency obtained from a survey is given below. Calculate the mean deviation from median.

Length	2	2.5	2.7	2.9	3	3.1	3.3	3.7	3.9	4	4.6	4.8	4.9	5	5.5	5.9	6	6.1	6.7	6.9
Frequencey	2	1	1	2	3	1	3	2	4	3	2	3	3	3	2	3	3	3	3	3

Variable X	*Frequency* f	fX	*Deviation* x	fx
2	2	4	–2.62	5.24
2.5	1	2.5	–2.12	2.12
2.7	1	2.7	–1.92	1.92
2.9	2	5.8	–1.72	3.44
3	3	9.0	–1.62	4.86
3.1	1	3.1	–1.52	1.52
3.3	3	9.9	–1.62	3.96
3.7	2	7.4	–0.92	1.84
3.9	4	15.6	–0.72	2.88
4	3	12.0	–0.62	1.86
4.6	2	9.2	–0.02	0.04
4.8	3	14.4	0.18	0.54
4.9	3	14.7	0.28	0.84
5	3	15.0	0.38	1.14
5.5	2	11.0	0.88	1.76
5.9	3	17.7	1.28	3.84
6	3	18.0	1.38	4.14
6.1	3	18.3	1.48	4.44
6.7	3	20.1	2.08	6.24
6.9	3	20.7	2.28	6.84
	$\Sigma f = 50$	$\Sigma fX = 231.1$		$\Sigma fx = 59.46$

Mean $\bar{X} = \frac{231.1}{50} = 4.62$

Mean Deviation $\delta = \frac{\Sigma |fx|}{\Sigma f}$

$\delta = \frac{59.46}{50} = 1.18$

(iv) ***Standard Deviation :*** It is defined as the positive square root of the arithmetic mean of the squares of deviations of the given data from their arithmetic mean. If $X_1, X_2, \ldots\ldots, X_n$ is a set of n observations, then its standard deviation is given by

$$\sigma = \sqrt{\frac{1}{n}\Sigma(X-\bar{X})^2}$$

where, $\bar{X} = \frac{1}{n}\Sigma X$, is the arithmetic mean of the given values.

In case of frequency distribution.

$$\sigma = \sqrt{\frac{1}{N}\Sigma f(X-\bar{X})^2}$$

where, X is the value of the variable or mid-value of the class.

Here arithmetic mean, $\bar{X} = \frac{1}{N}\Sigma fX$.

Example : Ovary weight of 50 fishes and their frequency is given. Find the standard deviation.

Wt of Ovary	2–2.9	3–3.9	4–4.9	5–5.9	6–6.9
Frequency	6	13	11	8	12

Class Interval	*Mid-point* m	*Frequency* f	*f.m*	*Deviation* $X-\bar{X}=x$	x^2	fx^2
2–2.9	2.45	6	14.7	–2.14	4.579	27.47
3–3.9	3.45	13	44.85	–1.14	1.299	16.88
4–4.9	4.45	11	48.95	–0.14	0.019	0.21
5–5.9	5.45	8	43.64	+0.86	0.739	5.91
6–6.9	6.45	12	77.4	+1.86	3.459	41.5
		$\Sigma f = 50$	$\Sigma fm = 229.5$		$\Sigma x^2 = 10.088$	$\Sigma fx^2 = 91.97$

$$\bar{X} = \frac{\Sigma f.m}{\Sigma f} = \frac{229.5}{50} = 4.59$$

$$\text{S.D } \sigma = \sqrt{\frac{\Sigma fx^2}{\Sigma f}} = \sqrt{\frac{91.97}{50}} = 1.35$$

The standard deviation is an absolute measure of dispersion. The corresponding relative measure is known as the coefficient of variance. This is used when comparision are made between variabilities of to or more series. Coefficient of variation is usually expressed as percentage and is calculated using the formula:

$$\text{C.V.} = S\sqrt{x} \times 100$$

Example : Following are the weights of two rate in 10 months. Both were fed normal diet. Calculate which one maintains consistency.

Rat X	50	45	55	40	47	50	45	40	48	50	$\Sigma X = 470$
Rat Y	55	46	51	45	52	45	50	45	40	47	$\Sigma Y = 476$

	X	$X - \bar{X} =$ $X - 47 = x$	x^2	Y $X - \bar{X} = x$	$Y - \bar{Y} =$ $Y - 47.6 = y$	y^2
1	50	+3	9	55	+7.4	54.79
2	45	−2	4	46	−1.6	2.56
3	55	+8	64	51	+3.4	11.56
4	40	−7	49	45	−2.6	6.76
5	47	0	0	52	+4.4	19.36
6	50	+3	9	45	−2.6	6.76
7	45	−2	4	50	+2.4	5.76
8	40	−7	49	45	−2.5	6.76
9	48	+1	1	40	−7.6	57.76
10	50	+3	9	47	−0.6	0.36
N = 10	$\Sigma x = 470$	$\Sigma x = 0$	$\Sigma x^2 = 198$	$\Sigma y = 476$	$\Sigma y = 0.6$	$\Sigma y^2 = 172.40$

Co-efficient of variance for X.

$$\bar{X} = \frac{\Sigma x}{N} = \frac{470}{10} = 47$$

$$\text{S.D.} = \sqrt{\frac{\Sigma x^2}{N}} = \sqrt{\frac{198}{10}} = 4.44$$

$$\text{C.V.} = \frac{\text{S.D.}}{\bar{X}} \times 100 = \frac{4.44}{47} \times 100 = 9.44$$

Co-efficient of variance of Y.

$$\bar{Y} = \frac{\Sigma y}{N} = \frac{476}{10} = 47.6$$

$$\text{S.D.} = \sqrt{\frac{\Sigma y^2}{N}} = \sqrt{\frac{172.40}{10}} = 4.15$$

$$\text{C.V.} = \frac{\text{S.D.}}{\bar{Y}} \times 100 = \frac{4.15}{47.6} \times 100 = 8.71$$

Since co-efficient of variation of rat Y (8.71) is less than that of rat X (9.44). Rat Y is more consistent.

Analysis of Correlation

Correlation can be defined as the relationship between two related variables in such a way that a change in value of one variable results in a corresponding change in the other variable also.

Simple Correlation: When only two variables are studied, it is known as simple correlation, whereas in partial and multiple correlation, three or more variables are studied simultaneously.

Types of Correlation

(i) ***Positive Correlation:*** When the values of the two variables deviate together, then the correlation is positive, *e.g.*, relation between height and weight of an individual. Usually weight of the body increases with increase in height. Entropy increases when temperature is increased.

(ii) ***Negative Correlation:*** If the values of the two variables deviate in the opposite direction, then it is negative correlation, here the relationship is inversely proportional, *e.g.*, volume and pressure of a perfect gas according to Boyle's law. This is an example of negative correlation because when pressure of a gas is increased, its volume decreases.

(iii) ***Zero Correlation:*** When the variation in one variable produces no change in the other variable, it is known as zero correlation, *e.g.*, life span and intelligence of a person; heamoglobin content and rate of clotting.

Methods of Studying Correlation

Three methods are usually employed to study correlation.

(i) ***Scatter Diagram Method:*** This method provides a simple way of finding the correlation between two variables. Consider there are n pairs of values (x_1, y_1), (x_2, y_2), ...(x_n, y_n) of two variables x, y. If X and Y represent the height and weight respectively, then the pairs (x_1, y_1), (x_2, y_2), ... and (x_n, y_n) represent the heights and weights of n individuals. These n points may be plotted as dots on the x axis and y axis. Usually the dependent variable is plotted along the y axis and independent variable along the x axis. The diagram of dots so obtained is known as scatter diagram. The scatter diagram gives a rough idea about the relationship between the two variables. From the scatter diagram it can be interpreted that,

(a) if the points are lying close to each other, then there is a good amount of correlation between the two variables.

(b) if the pattern of dots show a linear path diagonally across the graph paper from the bottom left hand corner to the top right, the correlation will be positive *i.e.*, $r = +1$. If the points lie on a straight line, the correlation is said to be perfect positive.

(c) if the pattern of dots show a downward trend, from the upper left hand corner to the bottom right, the correlation will negative $r = -1$.

Example : Following are the heights and weights of 10 students of class. Interpret from the scatter diagram whether the correlation is positive or negative.

Height X:	62	72	68	58	65	70	66	63	60	72
Weight Y:	50	65	63	50	54	60	61	55	54	65

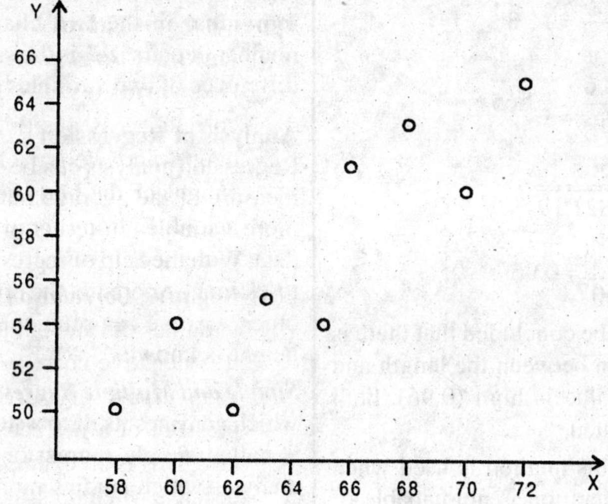

Since the points are close to each other, and the trend shows a rise from far left hand corner towards the upper right hand corner, the correlations is found to be positive.

(ii) ***Co-efficient of Correlation (Covariance Method):*** This is most widely used method proposed by Karl Pearson. Co-efficient of correlation is a numerical measure of linear relationship between the two variables and is defined as the ratio of the covariance between x and y, written as Cov (x, y) to the product of the standard deviations of x and y, Co-efficient of correlation r is given by

$$r_{x,y} = \frac{\Sigma xy}{\sqrt{\Sigma x^2 \cdot \Sigma y^2}}$$

where, r is the correlation co-efficient,

x is the deviations of X variable

y is the deviations of Y variable.

Example : The length and weight of 7 groups of fishes of a species is given below. Find the correlation co-efficient of the two variables.

Lenght	11.7	13.9	15.5	17.8	18.5	19.2	21
Weight	7.10	12.42	15.35	23.20	28.45	32.25	39.84

	Lenght X	*Weight* Y	x	y	x^2	y^2	$x.y$
1	11.7	7.10	−5.1	−15.55	26.01	241.8	79.3
2	13.9	12.42	−2.9	−10.23	8.41	104.6	23.36
3	15.5	15.35	−1.3	−7.3	1.69	53.12	9.49
4	17.8	23.20	+1	0.55	1.0	0.30	0.55
5	18.5	28.45	+1.7	+5.8	2.89	33.64	9.86
6	19.2	32.25	+3	+9.6	9.0	92.16	28.8
7	21.0	39.84	+4.2	+17.19	17.64	295.49	72.2
N=7	$\Sigma X = 117.6$	$\Sigma Y = 158.6$			$\Sigma x^2 = 66.64$	$\Sigma y^2 = 821.19$	$\Sigma x.y = 223.56$

$$N = 7 \Sigma X = 117.6$$

$$\overline{X} = \frac{\Sigma X}{N} = \frac{117.6}{7} = 16.8$$

$$\overline{Y} = \frac{\Sigma Y}{N} = \frac{158.6}{7} = 22.65$$

$$r = \frac{223.56}{\sqrt{66.64 \times 821.19}}$$

$$= \frac{223.56}{\sqrt{54724.10}} = 0.96$$

Thus, from the result it can be concluded that there is a strong positive correlation between the length and weight of body. Since r value is high (0.96), both variables are highly correlated.

(iii) ***Rank Correlation:*** This method is used when the data under consideration is not capable of quantitative measurement, but can be arranged in serial order.

Example : Qualitative characters such as colour, intelligence, stress, tolerance, etc. The individuals are arranged serially and are then ranked. Rank correlation coefficient can be calculated by the formula.

$$\rho = 1 - \frac{6\Sigma d^2}{n(n^2 - 1)}$$

where, ρ is the rank difference of X and Y variables, d is the difference between the pair of the same individual in the two characteristics and n is the number of pairs. Σd^2 is the summation of square of the difference of two variables rank I and II.

Analysis of Regression

Regression analysis can be defined as a mathematical measure of the average relationship between two or more variables in terms of the original units of the data. With the help of regression analysis it is possible to estimate or predict the effect of one variable on the other, *e.g.*, we can predict the weight of a man if his height is known.

Simple and Multiple Regression: The regression study which confines itself to a study of only two variables is called simple regression whereas, the regression analysis which studies more than two variables at a time is called multiple regression.

Dependent and Independent Variables: In studying the relation between yield of paddy and the amount of fertilizer added to the crop, yield would constitute the dependent variable or regressed variable, and the fertilizer is the independent variable or regressen.

Thus, regression also helps in studying the relationship between two variable but differs from correlation analysis, in that regression considers one variable as a cause and the dependent as its effect.

Regression Equation: The estimation or predicion of the average value of one variable for a specified value of the other variable is obtained by Regression Equation and its graphical representation is known as Regreesion Curve. Regression equation of X on Y is

$$\bar{X} - \bar{Y} = bxy\,(Y - \bar{Y}) = \frac{r.\delta x(Y - \bar{Y})}{\delta y}$$

where, X is the value of X,

$\bar{X}$ is the mean of X

δx is the standard deviation of X series.

r is the correlation coefficient,

b is slope or coefficient of regression,

Y value of Y,

$\bar{Y}$ is mean of Y,

δy is the standard deviation of Y series,

Regression equation of Y on X is

$$Y - \bar{Y} = byx\ X - \bar{X}$$

$$= \frac{r.\delta y(X - \bar{X})}{\delta x}$$

If a bivariate data are plotted as points on a graph paper, it will be found that the concentration points follow a certain pattern showing the relationship between the variables. When the trend points are found to be linear, the best fitting straight line is determined by least square method. Such straight lines which are used to obtain best estimates of one variable for given values of the other are called regression lines. If two variables are linearly related then that relation can be expressed as Y = $bx + a$

where, b is the slope of the line relating Y to X and a is the Y intercept of that line.

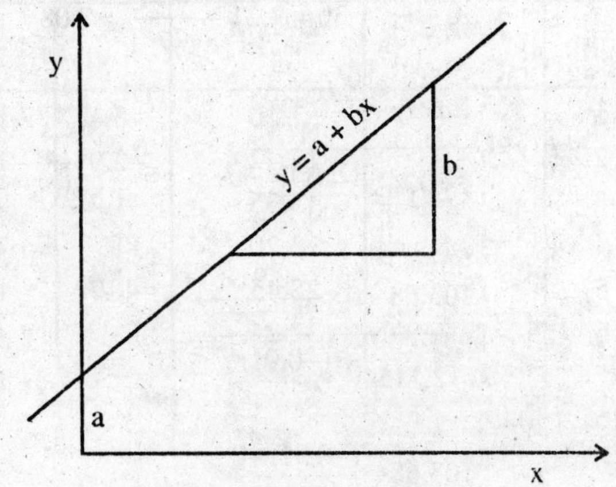

Regression coefficient of Y on X is

$$= byx = \frac{r.\delta y}{\delta x}$$

Example : Obtain the equation of the regression line of weight of body and length of a insect.

Length	12	18	24	30	36	42	48
Weight	5.27	5.68	6.25	7.21	8.02	8.71	8.42

Estimate the most probable weight of insect for 40 cm length of that species of insect.

x	dx $(x - 30)$	dx^2	y	dy $(y - 7.21)$	dy^2	$dxdy$
12	−18	324	5.27	−1.94	3.7636	34.92
18	−12	144	5.68	−1.53	3.06	18.36
24	−6	36	6.25	−0.96	0.9216	5.76
30	0	0	7.21	0	0	0
36	6	36	8.02	1.81	0.6561	4.85
42	12	144	8.71	1.50	2.25	18.00
48	18	324	8.42	1.21	1.4641	21.78
	$\Sigma dx = 0$	$\Sigma dx^2 = 1008$		$\Sigma dy = -0.91$	$\Sigma dy^2 = 12.1154$	$\Sigma dxdy = 103.68$

Assume that mean of X, A_x = 30 and mean of Y, $A_x = 7.21$

$$\bar{X} = A_x + \frac{\Sigma dx}{N} \quad \bar{Y} = A_y + \frac{\Sigma dy}{N}$$

$$= 30 + \frac{0}{7} = 30 = 7.21 - \frac{0.91}{7} = 7.08$$

$$bxy = \frac{\Sigma dxdy - \frac{\Sigma dx\, \Sigma dy}{N}}{\Sigma dy^2 - \frac{(\Sigma dy)^2}{N}}$$

$$= \frac{103.68 - 0 \times \frac{(-0.91)^2}{7}}{12.1154 - \frac{(-0.91)^2}{7}}$$

$$= \frac{103.68 - \frac{(-0.91) \times 0}{7}}{1008 - \frac{(0)^2}{7}}$$

$$= \frac{103.68}{11.9971}$$

$$= \frac{103.68}{1008}$$

$$= 8.64 = 0.103$$

Regression equation of X on Y:

$$(Y - \bar{Y}) = byx(X - \bar{X})$$

$$(Y - 7.08) = 0.103\,(X - 30)$$

$$= 0.103\,X - 3.09 + 7.08$$

$$= 0.103\,X + 3.99$$

Putting X = 40cm, we get

$$Y = 0.103 \times 40 + 3.99$$

$$= 8.11 \text{ g}$$

Distribution Patterns

The statistical measures like averages, dispersion, correlation, etc, for the sample frequency distributions give us the nature and form of the sample data and also helps in formulating certain. A more scientific way of drawing inferences about the population characteristics is through the study of theoretical distributions. In the population, the values of the variable may be distributed according to some probaility law which can be expressed mathematically and the corresponding probability distribution is known as theoretical probability distribution. These distributions are based on expectations on the basis of previous experience. Theoretical distributions also enable us to fit a mathematical model or a function of the form $y = p(x)$ to the given data.

Theoretical probability distribution is of three types: Binomial distribution. Poisson distribution and Normal distribution. The first two types are discrete probability distributions and the third is a continuous probability distribution.

(1) ***Binomial Distribution:*** Binomial distribution also known as Bernoulli distribution was first explained. James Bernoulli. Binomial distribution can be used under the following situations:

(a) *n.* the number of trials in finite

(b) there are only two outcomes for every trial, namely success and failure.

(c) trials are independent *i.e.,* the result of one trial doesn't affect the result of either the preceding or succeeding trials.

(d) the probability for success *p*, is constant for each trial. Hence, $q = 1 - p$ is the probability constant for failure.

For Example : Consider the birth of a child. Here there are only two possible hapeenings either male or female child. The chances of occurrence of male *i.e.,* $p = ½$ and female *i.e.,* $q = ½$. Thus, $p + q = 1$ and binomial is $(p + q)^n$.

If delivery of two women occurs simultaneously, there are four possible outcomes. Here binomial expansion is

$$(p + q)^2 = p^2 + 2pq + q^2$$

Thus, the probability is getting two males (p^2) or two females (q^2) or 1 male and 1 female ($2pq$).

Similarly, in case of three simultaneous births, it is $(p + q)^3 = p^3 + q^3 + 3p^2q + 3q^2p$, and hence the probability in 3 males, 3 females, 2 males + 1 female or 2 females + 1 male.

It has been observed that in large number of births, chances of male births may be 51% and female births 49%. Hence, $p = .51$ and $q = 1 - .51 = 49$.

By substituting these values in the equation, $p^2 + 2pq + q^2$, we get

$$(0.51)^2 + 2\,(0.51 \times 0.49) + (0.49)^2$$
$$= 0.2601 + 0.4998 + 0.2401$$

Thus, probability of getting two boys are 26.01%, two girls is 24.01% and one boy one girl is 49.98%.

(2) ***Poisson Distribution :*** Poisson distribution was derived by Simeon D. Poisson for a discrete probability distribution. Poisson distribution may be obtained as a limiting case of binomial probability distribution under the following conditions:

(a) n, the number of trials is indefinitely large *i.e.*, $n \to \infty$

(b) p, the constant for success of each trial is infinitely small

(c) $np = m$ is finite

Thus, Poisson distribution is made use of in situations where event occurred (p) is very small.

Probability of r sucess

$$p(r) = \frac{e^{-m} m^r}{r!}$$

where, $r = 0, 1, 2, 3, \ldots\ldots, n$ successes and $e = 2.7183$ is a constant.

Poisson distribution can be used to explain the behaviour of discrete random variables where the probability of occurrence of the event is very small and the total number of possible cases is large. There are a large number of situations in biological field where Poission distribution is applied, *e.g.*, it is used to count the number of bacteria per field, the number of RBCs per field, number of deaths reported in a hospital due to some disease.

(3) ***Normal Distribution :*** In a population many characteristics such as mass, height, colour show a continuous gradation from one extreme to the other without any break. If measures of distribution are arranged in linear fashion and vary continuously on both the sides from the central value then the distribution is called normal distribution. The normal distribution is concerned with both complete and fractional numbers. In normal distribution measures are concentrated closely around the centre and taper off towards the sides.

Normal Distribution Curve : The normal distribution curve is a bell shaped curve also known as Gaussian curve. The Gaussian curve is continuous for continuous variables.

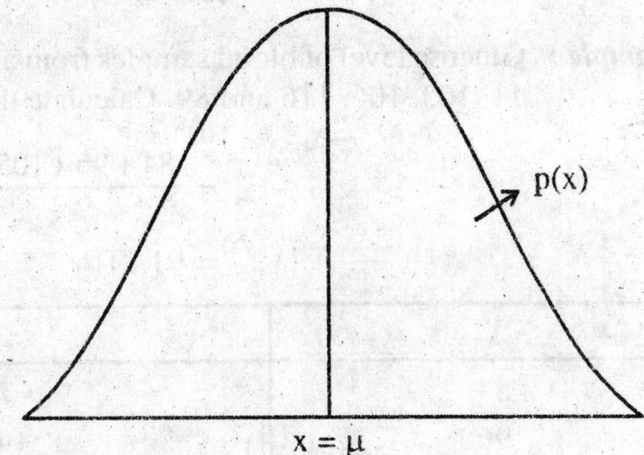

The top of the bell is directly above them can μ.

Since the distribution is symmetrical, mean, median and mode are the same. Most of the variables are clustered around the mean and there are very few observations at the extremes. The variables having lower values lie on the left side of the mean while those variables having higher values lie at the right side of the mean on horizontal line.

Test of Significance : Test of significance is used to determine whether observed differences between two samples are actually due to chance or wheter they are really significant. This is applied for comparing a characteristic of two samples like comparing the yield of two crop varieties, fat content in two varieties of oil seeds; comparing the haemoglobin percentage in men and women.

Standard Error : Error is the difference between the true value and the estimated value. Thus, error is defined as the difference between the true value of a population parameter and its estimate provided by an appropriate sample statistic computed by some standard statistical device. It differs from mistakes or inaccuracies which may be committed during the course of observing the data. Standard error of a statistics provides a measure of the accuracy of that statistics. Standard error is the index number and theoretically the difference between statistics and parameter should be zero. But in biological experiments this is never zero. Standard error of mean is computed using the formula:

$$SE\bar{X} = \frac{SD}{\sqrt{N}} \text{ or } \frac{\sigma}{\sqrt{N}}$$

Thus, standard error of mean is the standard deviation of the sample divided by the square root of the number of observations in the sample.

Example : Glucose level of blood samples from a human population is measured as 84, 96, 105, 96, 98, 106, 11, 103, 106, 116 and 89. Calculate the standard deviation andstandard error of mean.

$$\bar{X} = \frac{84+96+105+96+98+106+11+103+106+116+89}{11}$$

$$= 91.81$$

X	*x*	x^2
84	−7.81	60.996
96	+4.19	17.556
105	+13.19	173.976
96	+4.19	17.556
98	+6.19	38.316
106	+14.19	201.356
11	−80.81	6530.256
103	+11.19	125.216
106	+14.19	201.356
116	+24.19	345.156
89	−2.81	7.896
		$\Sigma x^2 = 7719.636$

$$SD\,\sigma = \sqrt{\frac{\Sigma x^2}{N}} = \sqrt{\frac{7719.636}{11}}$$

$$= 26.46$$

$$SE_m = \frac{\sigma}{\sqrt{N}} = \frac{26.46}{\sqrt{11}} = 8.003$$

Standard Error of Standard Deviation : Standard deviation also varies from one sample to the other of the same population. Standard error of standard deviation can be calculated by using the formula.

$$SE_\sigma = \frac{\sigma}{\sqrt{2N}}$$

Example : Weight of 50 grasshoppers and their frequencies were found to be as follows. Calculate SE of SD.

Weight	2	2.5	2.7	2.9	3	3.1	3.3	3.7	3.9	4	4.6	4.8	4.9	5	5.5	5.9	6	6.1	6.76
Frequency	2	1	1	2	3	1	3	2	4	3	2	3	3	2	3	3	3	3	3

C.I.	*Frequency*	*Mid Point X*	*Freq. X*	$X - \bar{X} = x$	x^2	fx^2
2–2.9	6	2.45	14.7	–2.14	4.5796	27.47
3–3.9	13	3.45	44.85	–1.14	1.2996	16.89
4–4.9	11	4.45	48.95	–0.14	0.0196	0.21
5–5.9	8	5.45	43.6	+0.86	0.7396	5.91
6–6.9	12	6.45	77.4	+1.86	3.4596	41.57
	$\Sigma f = 50$		$\Sigma fm = 229.5$		$\Sigma x^2 = 10.088$	$\Sigma fx^2 = 92.02$

Actual Mean

$$\bar{X} = \frac{\Sigma f \cdot X}{\Sigma f} = \frac{229.5}{50} = 4.59$$

$$SD = \sqrt{\frac{\Sigma fx^2}{\Sigma f}} = \sqrt{\frac{92.02}{50}} = 1.35$$

$$SE_\sigma = \frac{\sigma}{\sqrt{2f}} = \frac{1.35}{\sqrt{2 \times 50}} = \frac{1.35}{10} = 0.14$$

Hence, standard error of deviation is 0.14.

Signigicance Test : If the observed difference between the two means is greater than 1.96 times SE $(\bar{X}_1 - \bar{X}_2)$, it is significant at 5% level of significance.

If the observed level difference is greater than 3 times the SE, its real variability is more than 99% cases.

In the above example, standard deviation (1.35) is repeated 95 times out of 100 times. Thus (± 1.96 × 0.14) = ± 0.27 unit may deviate from standard deviation of population. Thus, the standard deviation is reliable.

Student's Test: Student's 't' test is an estimate of the extent by which values in a small set of data deviate from the mean. It is used to determine the variation within a set of data and to compare two sets of data. The probability of occurrence of any calculated value of 't'is determined by comparing it with the value given in the 't' table corresponding to the combined degree of freedom, derived from the number of observations in the samples under study. If the calculated value of 't' is less than the value given in the table, it is not significant.

Degree of Freedom: The quantity in the denominator which is one less than the independent number of observations in a sample is called degree of freedom. In unpaired 't' test, $df = N - 1$. In paired 't' test $df = N_1 + N_2 - 2$ where N_1 and N_2 are the number of observations in each of the two series.

Unpaired 't' test is applied to unpaired data of independent observations made on individuals of two different or separate groups or samples drawn from two populations. The list of significance of difference is calculated by using the formula

$$t = \frac{\bar{X}_1 - \bar{X}_2}{\sqrt{\frac{\sigma_1^2}{N_1} + \frac{\sigma_2^2}{N_2}}}$$

Example : The ESR values of 15 males and 10 females are given below. Calculate the significance of the difference in the means.

Males	65	60	115	82	43	103	125	118	83	75	90	95	128	65	84
Females	63	85	90	100	90	105	98	93	100	125					

$$\Sigma X_1 = 1331, \ \Sigma X_2 = 949$$

$$\bar{X}_1 = \frac{\Sigma X_1}{N_1} = \frac{1331}{15}, \ \bar{X}_2 = \frac{\Sigma X_2}{N_2} = \frac{949}{10}$$

$$= 88.73 = 94.9$$

X_1	$X_1 - X_1 = x_1$	x_1^2	X_2	$X_2 - \bar{X}_2 = x_2$	x_2^2
65	−23.73	563.11	63	−31.9	1017.61
60	−28.73	825.41	85	−9.9	98.01
115	+26.27	690.11	90	−4.9	24.01
82	−6.73	45.29	100	5.1	26.01
43	−45.73	2091.23	90	−4.9	24.01
103	14.23	203.63	105	10.1	102.01
125	36.27	1315.51	98	3.1	9.61
118	29.27	856.73	93	−1.9	3.61
83	−5.73	32.83	100	5.1	26.01
75	−13.73	188.57	125	30.1	906.01
90	1.27	1.61			
95	6.27	39.31			
128	39.27	1542.13			
65	23.73	563.11			
84	4.73	22.31			
		$\Sigma x_1^2 = 8980.86$			$\Sigma x_2^2 = 2236.9$

$$\sigma_1 = \sqrt{\frac{\Sigma x_1^2}{N_1}} = \sqrt{\frac{8980}{15}} = 24.46$$

$$\sigma_2 = \sqrt{\frac{\Sigma x_2^2}{N_2}} = \sqrt{\frac{2236.9}{10}} = 14.95$$

$$\text{Combined SD}^2 = \frac{\Sigma(X_1 + \bar{X}_2)^2 + \Sigma(X_2 + \bar{X}_2)^2}{N_1 + N_2 - 2}$$

$$= \frac{8980.86 + 2236.9}{25 - 2}$$

$$= \frac{11217.76}{23} = 487.73$$

$$\therefore \quad \text{Combined SD} = \sqrt{487.73} = 22.08$$

$$\text{SE}\,\sigma = \sigma\sqrt{\frac{1}{N_1} + \frac{1}{N_2}}$$

$$= 22.08\sqrt{\frac{1}{15} + \frac{1}{10}} = 9.010$$

$$t = \frac{\bar{X}_1 - \bar{X}_2}{\text{SE}_D(1-2)}$$

$$= \frac{88.73 - 94.9}{9.01} = -0.68$$

From the 't' table it was found that at degree of freedom 23, the probability of occurrence of calculated value by chance is greater than 0.4. This leads to a rejection of null hypothesis. Hence the observed difference between the mean weight of two groups of male and female ESR is insignificant.

Paired 't' Test: It is applied to paired data of independent observation from one sample only when each individual gives a pair of observation, *e.g.*, to compare the effect of two drugs like effect of adrenaline and noradrenaline on pulse rate in same individuals.

't' value is computed as:

$$t = \frac{\bar{x} - 0}{\frac{S}{\sqrt{N}}} = \frac{\bar{X}}{\text{SE}_d}$$

It is assumed that there is no real difference between the means of before and after observations.

Example : Oxygen consumption of ten fishes of a species was observed. Thyroxine was administered and then rate of O_2 consumption was studied. From the values, find out whether fishes were influenced by T_4 injection.

Weight	40	36	38	44	34	40	38	32	42	38
Frequency	44	38	34	36	42	46	38	40	44	40

Control	*Test*	$X = A - B$	$X - \bar{X}$	$(X - \bar{X})^2$
40	44	4	2	4
36	38	4	0	0
38	34	–4	–6	36
44	36	–8	–10	100
34	42	8	6	36
40	46	6	4	16
38	38	0	–2	4
32	40	8	6	36
42	44	2	0	0
38	40	2	0	0
		$\Sigma X = 20$		$\Sigma (X - \bar{X})^2 = 232$

$$\bar{X} = \frac{20}{10} = 2$$

$$SD = \sqrt{\frac{\Sigma(X - \bar{X})^2}{N_1 - 1}}$$

$$= \sqrt{\frac{232}{10 - 1}} = 5.08$$

$$t = \frac{\bar{X} \cdot \sqrt{N}}{SD} = \frac{2 \times \sqrt{10}}{5.08} = 1.25$$

Degree of freedom = 10 – 1 = 9

'*t*' table shows at *df* 9 *t* value is 2.262. The calculated value (1.25) is lesser which indicates that mean on X is significant. Thus, it can be said that the injection of T_A do not enhance the rate of respiration.

Analysis of Variance: Analysis of variance or Anova is the technique used to compare the mean of more than two samples, *e.g.*, a farmer may be interested in comparing the average yield of same crop using five different fertilizers.

Analysis of variance is carried out in two ways:

(i) One way classification

(ii) Two way classification.

One Way Classification : In this method the influence of any one factor on different sample groups is considered.

Two way classification: here effect of two different factors are studied together, *e.g.*, effect of two drugs on different types of animals.

QUESTIONS FROM PREVIOUS YEARS' PAPERS

1. Write short notes on the following:
   (*a*) Hybrid vigour and its importance in agriculture.
   (*b*) Null hypothesis
   (*c*) Degrees of freedom
2. Write an account of genetic code and regulation of gene expression.
3. Give an account of structural, biochemical

and metabolic changes associated with senescence of flowers and ornamentals.

4. Write short notes on the following:
(*a*) Heterosis
(*b*) TRIPS
(*c*) Haze
(*d*) Gametophytic apomixis
(*e*) Mass selection
(*f*) Hybridization
5. How do tetraploidy and aneuploidy originate. What are their roles in Plants Breeding?
6. Enumerate the secondary plant products with emphasis on the roles of pigments.
7. What is micropropagation? Describe the generalized technique of micropropagation.
8. Discuss the advantages of micropropagation.
9. List of various *Rhizobium* species and their host legumes.
10. Write a short notes on importance of apomixis in plant breeding.
11. What is Bt cotton?
12. Discuss the *pros* and *cons* of the use of transgenic crops.
13. Draw a well-labelled diagram of a chloroplast as seen under an electron microscope.
14. What is heterosis? Explain the various theories of heterosis.
15. Explain hydridization as a method of plant breeding.
16. Write short notes on the following:
(*a*) Male sterility (*b*) Chi-square test
(*c*) Hydroponics (*d*) Nitrogenase
(*e*) Dormancy (*f*) Endemism
(*g*) Xerosere (*h*) Prion
(*i*) Standard deviation
17. What is recombinant DNA technology? How is it employed in genetic engineering?
18. What is genetic code? Explain the mechanism of genetic code in the transfer of information from DNA to amino acids.
19. Evaluate the different gene transfer techniques for the production of transgenic plants.
20. Discuss the Biotechnology and Agriculture.
21. Enumerate the types of selectable marker genes employed in developing transgenic plants.
22. Write brief notes on different strategies for the improvement of self-pollinated crops.
23. Critically discuss the significance of light in flowering.
24. Explain the mechanism of flower induction in crop plants by vernalization.
25. Explain aspects and importance of gene mapping in crop improvement.
26. What is the nature of genetic code? Examine methods to decipher the genetic code.
27. Discuss methods to measure plant growth. Suggest suitable growth indices to the breeders to screen better plant types.
28. Describe the morphological and biochemical changes accompanying seed germination.

CHAPTER–4

PHYSIOLOGY AND BIOCHEMISTRY

SOLUTE TRANSPORT AND PHOTOASSIMILATE TRANSLOCATION

WATER

- Most important constituent of the protoplasm.
- 80 - 90% of the fresh weight of most herbaceous plants and over 50% of the fresh weight of woody plants.
- Acts as solvent, reactant or reagent and maintains turgidity.

WATER POTENTIAL (Ψ, PSI)

Difference between the free energy of water in a system and free energy of pure water at atmospheric pressure.

- The measurement unit of water potential is pascal (Pa).
- 1 mega pascal, MPa = 10 bars.
- Water potential is influenced by 3 factors - concentration, pressure and gravity.

  Water potential $\psi W = \psi s + \psi p + \psi g$

  where,

  ψs = Solute potential or osmotic potential (the amount by which the water potential is reduced as a result of the presence of solutes).

  ψp = Pressure potential or hydrostatic pressure (is positive in contrast to negative value of water potential and solute potential and operates in plant cell in the form of wall pressure).

  ψg = Gravity potential (the component of water potential influenced by the effect of gravity on water potential). The gravity potential depends on the height of water above the reference state of water, the density of water and the acceleration due to gravity. When vertical length is less than 5 metres, value of ψg is negligible and the modified equation is–

$$\psi w = \psi s + \psi p$$

- Theoretically ψw of the pure water = **zero**, so ψW inside plant cells is negative.

ABSORPTION AND MOVEMENT OF WATER

- Water is mainly absorbed through the roots, especially **at the tips in the region of the root hairs.**
- **Pathways of water movement in root**

  (1) **Apoplast pathway:** Water moves exclusively through the cell wall without crossing any membranes. Apoplast or outer space is a non-living continuous system made up of water-filled **cellulosic cell wall** and **inter cellular spaces** from epidermis to xylem.

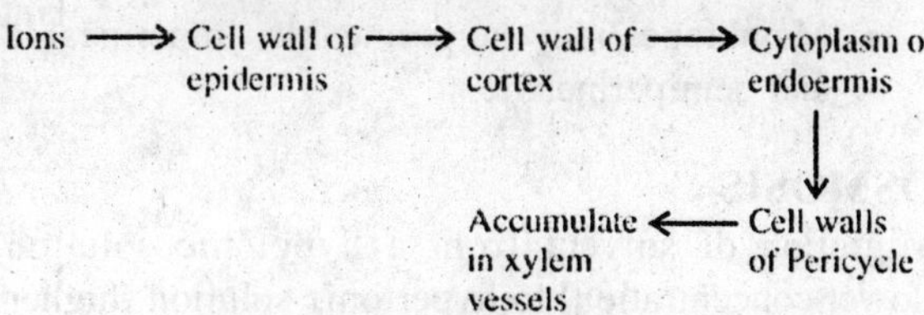

  (2) **Symplast pathway:** Water moves from one cell to another cell through **plasmodesmata**. Symplast or inner space is a living continuous system formed by cytoplasm and plasmodesmata from epidermis to xylem parenchyma.

Ion ⟶ Cytoplasm of epidermis ⟶ Cytoplasm, cortex endodermis, pericycle through plasmodesmata ⟶ Xylem vessel

(3) **Transmembrane pathway :** Water after passing through cortex is blocked by casarian strips (deposition of wax like substance **suberin**) present on endodermis. Water crosses at least two membranes from each cell in its path. These two plasma membranes are found on entering and exiting of water. Here, water may also enter through tonoplast surrounding the vacuole *i.e.*, also known as **vacuolar pathway**.

DIFFUSION

The net movement of molecules or ions of a given substance from a region of higher concentration to lower one by virtue of their kinetic energy. The rate of diffusion of molecules is affected by temperature, density of diffusing molecules, medium in which diffusion takes place and concentration gradient.

- **Diffusion pressure:** The potential ability of a substance to diffuse from an area of its greater concentration to an area of lesser concentration is called diffusion pressure.

PERMEABILITY

The degree of diffusion of gases, liquids and dissolved substances through a membrane. It depends on the membrane composition, as well as the chemical nature of thesolute.

- It can be measured readily by determining the rate at which solute passes through a membrane under a specific set of conditions.
- Membranes may be permeable, impermeable and semipermeable.

OSMOSIS

Migration of solvent from a hypotonic solution (lower concentration) to hypertonic solution (higher concentration) through a semi-permeable membrane to keep the concentration equal.

- **Exosmosis :** Water moves out of the cell due to hypertonic solution (of higher concentration).
- **Endosmosis :** Water enters the cell due to hypotonic solution (of lower concentration).
- **Osmotic pressure :** The pressure needed to prevent the passage of pure water into an aqueous solution through a differentially permeable membrane thereby preventing an increase in the volume of the solution.
- Osmotic pressure depends upon **concentration** of solute particle, **ionisation** of solute particles, hydration of solute particles and temperature.
- **Reverse osmosis :** By applying additional pressure, water can be made to move out of solution from thistle funnel into water. This process can be used for removing salts from saline waters.
- **Osmosis is driven by two factors :** Concentration of dissolved solutes in a solution and pressure difference.
- **Osmotic potential or solute potential (ψs) :** Negative of osmotic pressure, since they are equal but opposite forces

$$\psi s = -\pi$$

e.g., Osmotic pressure of a plant is 200.5 atms but an osmotic potential of –200.5 atms.

PLASMOLYSIS

The phenomenon of shrinkage of protoplasm from the cell wall under the influence of some hypertonic solution is called as plasmolysis. As plasmolysis begins (incipient plasmolysis) the protoplasm is no more pressed against the cell wall, and the cell wall is said to be in a flaccid condition. However, further loss of water results in more shrikage of protoplasm and the cell is called **plasmolysed.**

- Continuous loss of water from plant cells results in wilting and drooping of leaves and stems.
- Plasmolysis is helpful in killing weeds from 'tennis courts', preservation of meat, jelly etc., to determine the osmotic pressure of cell, to know the living nature of cell, explains the phenomenon of osmosis etc.

IMBIBITION

A physical process by which solvent is adsorbed by certain substances making them swell. The solid particles which adsorb water or any other liquid are called imbibants and the liquid which is imbibed is known as **imbibate**.

- **Imbibition pressure (matrix potential) :** The potential maximum pressure that an imbibant will develop if it is submerged in pure water.
- Inbibition depends upon the affinity between imbibant and imbibed (*e.g.,* Rubber does not imbibe water, but imbibes kerosene oil and swells) and the water potential gradient between the surface of the adsorbant and the liquid imbibed.
- Dry seeds have a highly negative water potential.
- Both living and dead plant cells possess large amounts of **carbohydrates, proteins** and **polypeptides** etc. which are **hydrophilic colloids** and therefore, have very strong affinity for water.

TURGIDITY AND TURGOR PRESSURE

If a plant cell is placed in a **hypotonic solution** or pure water, water starts moving into the cell by osmosis. As the volume of the protoplast increases, it begins to exert pressure against the cell wall and stretches it. The pressure exerted by the protoplast against the cell wall is called turgor pressure (TP).

- **Wall pressure (WP) :** The cell wall being rigid, exerts an equal and opposite pressure on the protoplast which is called wall pressure.
- The two pressures are equal and opposite in direction.
- As a result of this interplay of forces, the plant cell under these conditions is said to be **turgid**.

DPD, OP AND TP

- DPD (diffusion pressure deficit) or SP (suction pressure) is the amount by which diffusion pressure of a solution is lower than that of its pure solvent. DPD was coined by B.S. Meyer (1938).
- The greater the concentration of a solution, the greater is its DPD.
- When a flaccid cell was placed in pure water, the suction pressure or DPD is roughly equal to the osmotic pressure of cell.

$$\text{SP or DPD} = \text{OP}$$

But when the cell became turgid, the turgor pressure resisted the entry of water into the cell and in that condition

$$\text{SP or DPD} = \text{OP} - \text{TP}$$

- Cell to cell movement of water depends upon the DPD and not on osmotic pressure and turgor pressure.

THEORIES OF WATER TRANSLOCATION

- The upward movement of water through stem is called ascent of sap (water with dissolved minerals).
- Goldlewski proposed **relay pump theory** and J.C. Bose proposed pulsation theory to explain the vitalistic view of ascent of sap.
- The three most prominent theories are-

(1) Root pressure theory

Stocking (1956) defined the root pressure "a pressure developed in the tracheary elements of xylem as a result of metabolic activities of the root.

- The development of root pressure is an active process which depends upon active secretion of salts or other solutes into the xylem sap, thereby lowering its osmotic potential.
- This theory can not account for water movement up the xylem in tall trees.

(2) Capillarity

In capillarity, water moves upward in narrow tubes due to the force of surface tension in small sized plants.

Boehm (1809) proposed that xylem vessels are narrow and ascent of sap occurs through capillarity further supported by atmospheric pressure.

- According to this theory, water is first taken in due to the force of adhesion between water and the wall of thin xylem vessels. As the water flows upwards along the wall, strong cohesive forces between water molecules come into play to pull the water upward. This continues until the forces of adhesion and cohesion are balanced by the downward force of gravity.

(3) Cohesion theory

Given by Henry Dixon in 1914. This depends upon the force of cohesion between water molecules. The important points are:

(i) **Cohesion force :** Water molecules are held together by strong cohesion force (due to hydrogen bonds). Another force of adhesion holds water to the walls of xylem channels.

(ii) **Continuous water column :** Present in the xylem channels of plant.

(iii) **Transpiration pull :** Transpiration from aerial parts causes a suction pressure in the water column of the plant. It is known as transpiration pull which lifts the water upwardly.

- Water column is continuous and cannot be pulled away from xylem walls due to cohesive and adhesive properties.
- The value of cohesive force for plant sap has been calculated to be 47 – 207 atm. by Dixon and Jolly.
- Cohesive force is also called as **tensile strength**.

TRANSPIRATION

The loss of water in the form of vapours trom the living tissues of aerial parts of the plant is called transpiration.

- About 98% of water absorbed by land plant is transpired.

Types of transpiration

(1) Cuticular : Cuticle provides a relatively impermeable covering. If cutilcle is thin and green, about 20% of the total transpiration takes place through it, but if its thickness is increased, the extent of water vapour loss is significantly reduced.

(2) Lenticular : Lenticels are small regions on bark etc. and possess small loosely arranged cells called as complementary cells.

According to Huber, this loss through lenticels is only 1.0 per cent of the total transpiration.

(3) Stomatal : Stomata are tiny pores present on the epidermal surface of leaves, young stems and in certain truits. Nearly 97 per cent of the total transpiration takes place through these stomata.

STOMATA

Help in aseous exchange at the time of respiration and photosynthesis.

- There are two kidney shaped guard cells which bound a minute elliptical pore in a stoma. Guard cells are modified epidermal cells. The wall of guard cells near the pore is thick. The outer wall is thin, elastic and semipermeable.
- Loftfield classified stomata on the basis of their daily movement into four main types-

  (a) **Alfalfa type :** Open throughout the day and closed all night *e.g.,* radish, mustard, turnip, apple, pea.

  (b) **Potato type :** Open throughout the day and night except few hours following sunset *e.g.,* cabbage, pumpkin, onion.

  (c) **Barley type :** Open only for a few hours in day *e.g.,* barley, maize, oat, wheat.

  (d) **Equisetum type :** Always open throughout day and night *e.g., Equisetum.*

Distribution of stomata on the leaves

1. **Apple or mulberry type :** On the under surface of leaves only *e.g. apple.*
2. **Potato type :** More on under surface than upperside. *e.g. Potato, brinjal.*
3. **Oat type:** Equally distributed on both the surfaces. *e.g. rice, wheat.*
4. **Water lily type :** Only on the upper surface. *e.g. water lily.*
5. **Potamogeton type :** Either absent or if present, they are functionless, present mostly in submerged aquatic plants. *e.g. Potamogeton.*

Significance of transpiration

- Removal of water in the form of vapours has a cooling effect on the leaves. So it does not allow the leaf temperature to rise to detrimental levels.
- It helps in movement of xylem sap which simultaneously increases the absorption of mineral nutrients by the roots from the soil. It enhances extensive development of root system that supports the heavy aerial growth against wind.
- Curtis (1926) called transpiration as necessary evil.

FACTORS AFFECTING TRANSPIRATION

(A) External factors

1. **Atmospheric humidity :** If atmosphere is humid, it reduces the rate of transpiration. When the air is dry, the rate of transpiration increases.
2. **Wind :** A high wind speed or a dry breeze will greatly increase transpiration.
3. **Atmospheric pressure :** Low atmospheric pressure increases the rate of transpiration.
4. **Soil temperature :** Plants growing in warm regions exhibit less transpiration at a temperature lower than 5 - 8°C.
5. **Air temperature :** The rate of evaporation doubles with every rise in temperature by 10°C. High temperature affects the closure of stomata, reduces transpiration.
6. **Water :** Less amount of soil water decreases the rate of transpiration. If the rate of transpiration exceeds the rate of absorption, the stomata get closed and plant wilts.

(B) Internal Factors

1. **Leaf structure :** Presence of thick cuticle and sunken stomata reduces the rate of transpiration.
2. **Leaf orientation :** Transpiration is low in north-south orientation as compared to other orientation.
3. **Leaf area :** Directly proportional to the transpiration rate.
4. **Plant age :** Germinating seeds exhibit a slow rate of transpiration. It becomes maximum at maturity and decreases at senescence stage.
5. **Root shoot ratio :** The increase in ratio of root and shoot enhances the rate of transpiration.
6. **Water contents of the leaves :** Directly proportional to the rate of transpiration.

STOMATAL OPENING AND CLOSING

Opening and closing of stomata takes place due to turgor changes in guard cells. Solutes are taken in by the guard cells from the neighbouring epidernal and mesophyll cells so both osmotic potential and water potential of the guard cells are lowered. This create a water potential gradient between the guard cells and the neighbouring cells and make the water move into the guard cells. The guard cells become turgid and swell in size, resulting in stomatal opening.

- With a decline in guard cells solutes, water moves out of the guard cells, making them flaccid to stomata close.
- Levitt (1974) proposed active potassium theory. He observed that proton (H^+) uptake by guard cells. chloroplasts takes place with the help of ATP. This leads to increase in value of pH in guard cells. Rise in pH converts starch into organic acid (like malic acid).

Starch ⟶ Phosphoglyceric acid —Carboxylase⟶ Phosphoenol pyruvic acid + CO_2
↓
Malic acid ⟵ Oxaloacetic acid

Malic acid further dissociates to form H^+ and malate anion.

- The uptake of K^+ ion in balanced by one of the following: uptake of Cl^-, transport of H^- ion from organic acid or by negative changes of organic acid when they lose H^+ ions. Thus all these factors lead to the opening of stomata.
- The stomata closure is due to excretion of K^+ from guard cells surrounding epidermal and subsidiary cells.

Factors affecting stomatal movement

1. **Light :** Stomata open in the presence of light and close in darkness. Light intensity required to open the stomata is very low, as compared to the intensity required for photosynthesis. In CAM (Crassulacean Acid Metabolism) plants, stomata open during dark and remain closed during the day. Even moonlight is sufficient to keep the stomata open in some plant species.

2. **Temperature :** Rise in temperature induces stomatal opening while fall in temperature causes closure. At 38°–40°C, stomata open even in darkness. In some plant species. stomata remain closed even under continuous light at 0°C.
3. **Carbon dioxide :** Low CO_2 concentration induces stomatal opening and vice versa. In closed stomata, external CO_2 concentration has no effect.
4. **Oxygen :** Essential for stomatal opening.
5. **Water availability :** Water stressed (less water available to plant and high transpiration rate) plants induces stomatal closure, due to formation of ABA and lowering of water potential in epidermal cells.
6. **Potassium :** Influx of K^+ causes opening of stomata while efflux of K^+ from guard cells causes closure of stomata.
7. **Mechanical shock :** Causes stomatal closure.
8. **Hormones :** Abscisic acid brings about closure of stomata. Cytokinins are required for keeping the stomata open.

GUTTATION

The loss of water in the form of liquid is called guttation. It generally occurs from tips and margins of leaves during night or early morning when there is high atmospheric humidity as during wet seasons.

- **Hydathodes** or **water pores** are special pores on the leaves in the region of guttation which are permanently open pores as their guard cells are immobile.
- Gutted water possess minute quantities of both inorganic and organic substances.

SOME IMPORTANT FACTS

- DPD can become zero (fully turgid cell). TP can also become zero (flaccid cell) but O.P. of a cell can never be zero.
- **Cryoscopic osmometer :** Measures osmotic potential of solution by measuring its freezing point.
- **Tensiometer :** Instrument for measuring soil water tension.
- **Psychorometer :** To mearene relative humidity as well as transpiration.
- **Manometer :** To measure pressure like root pressure.
- **Barometer :** To measure atmospheric pressure.
- **Porometer (F. Dawin, 1912) :** To measure the size of stomata.
- **Potometer :** To measure the rate of transpiration.
- **Atmometer :** To measure pull caused by evaporation of water from a porous pot.
- Term **guttation** was coined by Bergerstein (1887).
- **$CoCl_2$ Paper Method** (Hygrometric method, Stahl, 1894)-Used to compare the rates of transpiration.
- **Blue light** of visible light promotes stomatal opening.
- Plants growing at high altitudes exhibit xeromorphy *i.e.*, adaptation to minimise transpiration.
- **Transpiration ratio :** The amount of water lost per unit of dry matter produced during the growing season of a plant.
- **Stomatal frequency :** Number of stomata per unit area of leaf Its value is 1000 - 60,000/cm^2 or 10 - 600/mm^2.
- **Permanent wilting coefficient (PWP or PWC):** Amount of soil water at which the plants growing in it show first signs of permanent wilting.
- **Antitranspirants :** Chemicals which have been found to reduce the rate of transpiration without affecting CO_2 uptake. They may be **metabolic inhibitors** (*e.g.*, ABA-Abscissic acid, PMA - Phenyl mercuric acetate and Aspirin) **or film forming anti-transpirants** (*e.g.*, silicon emulsions and some low viscosity waxes).
- **Selectively or differentially permeable membrane :** Membrane which is normally semipermeable but allows selective transport of certain solutes.
- **SPAC (Soil Plant Atmosphere Continuum) :** Plants function as living connecing system between soil water and atmospheric water.

- **Stephen Hales (1676 -1761)**-Father of Plant Physiology, coined the term **root pressure.**
- **Yon Mohl :** Gave diagrammatic representiation of size of stoma at different times of the day.
- **Transpiration flux:** The quantity of water transpired by a unit area of leaf surface in a unit time.
- **Pfeffer :** Proposed term **'osmotic pressure'. Nollet :** Coined term **"osmosis"**.
- TP = 0 in plasmolysed cell.
- **Deplasmolysis :** A plasmolysed cell regains normal condition if placed in a hypotonic solution.
- **Slatyer and Taylor :** Proposed concept of water potential.
- Cohesive force of attraction between water molecules is upto **300 bars.**
- In *Saxifraga-Rate* of guttation is high during flowering.
- Active hydathode lack cuticle over specialized cells.
- *Lactuca scariola* and *Sylphium laciniatum* are called **compass plants** as their leaves lie vertically in north-south direction.
- In *Colocasia antiquorum,* guttation is a normal process.
- Transpiration is old stems and fruits takes place through lenticels.
- Osmotic pressure can be calculated by following relationship OP = cRT (where c = molar concentration of solution, R is gas constant and T is absolute temperature –273°C).
- Root pressure is absent in Gymnosperms.
- When the transpiration pull is exerted, a negative pressure or tension is generated in the xylem.
- **Isotonic solution :** Solution which has concentraton similar to that of cell sap.
- **Steward (1964) :** Proposed starch sugar hypothesis.

NITROGEN METABOLISM

INTRODUCITON

- **Mineral Nutrition :** The study of source, mode of absorption, distribution and metabolism of various inorganic substances or minerals by plants for their growth, development, structure, physiology and reproduction.
- **Autotrophs :** Organisms which use inorganic source of carbon *i.e.,* CO_2, Two types:
  (a) **Photoautotrophs (photosynthetic) :** Use light energy *e.g.,* all green plants, blue green algae, green and purple sulphur bacteria.
  (b) **Chemoautotrophs (chemosynthetic) :** Use chemical energy *e.g., Nitrosomonas, Nitrosococcus* and some other nitrogen cycle bacteria.
- **Heterotrophs :** Organisms which depend upon organic sources of carbon. Two types-
  (a) **Photohetrotrophs :** Use light energy *e.g.,* some purple nonsulphur bacteria.
  (b) **Chemoheterotrophs :** Use chemical energy *e.g.,* all animals, fungi, most bacteria and some flowering plants.

ESSENTIAL MINERAL ELEMENTS

- Such elements without which the plant cannot complete its life cycle.
- Arnon and Stout (1939) proposed criteria of essentiality of an element *i.e.,* the element must be directly involved in the nutrition of plant, must be absoiutely necessary for supporting nornlal growth and reproduction and the requirement must be specific and not replaceable by another element.
- Based on the quantity in which they are required by plants:
  (a) **Macro nutrients (major elements):** Required by plants in quantity of more than 1 milligram/gram dry matter. Total 9 in number-C, H, O, N, P, K, S, Mg and Ca.
  (b) **Micro nutrients (Micro or minor or rare or trace elements):** Required by plants in quantity less than 1 milligram/gram of dry matter. Total 8 in number-Fe, Mn, Zn, Cu, Mo, B, Cl and Ni.

Sources of essential elements for plants

- **Carbon:** As atmospheric carbon dioxide
- **Hydrogen:** Mainly in the form of water.

- **Oxygen:** From the air or water or in the form of inorganic ions.
- **Nitrogen:** Absorbed by plants is the form of nitrate from the soil. Nitrogen fixers (organisms) convert nitrogen gas (N_2) to anionic forms such as nitrate (NO_3^-) or nitrite (NO_2^-) or a reduced cationic form such as ammonium (NH_4^+). These compounds enter plants through the root and are assimilated as organic nitrogen.
- **Other elements:** Absorbed from the soil e.g., phosphorus as phosphates and sulphur as sulphate etc.

ROLE OF MACRO-AND MICRO-NUTRIENTS

Element	Obtained in the form of	Specific role in Plants	Deficiency symptoms
1. Nitrogen	NO_2^-, NO_3^- or NH/	Consituent of proteins, vitamins, hormones, nucleic acids, coenzymes, ATP, chlorophyll etc.	Stunted growth, chlorosis, development of anthocyanin
2. Phosphorus	HPO_4^-	Constituent of nucleic acids, phospholipids, coenzymes, nucleotides, NAD^+, $NADP^+$ etc.	Poor growth, leaves dull green, premature fall of leaf and flower buds and delayed seed germination.
3. Potassium	K^+	Involved in protein synthesis in opening and closing of stomata, activates enzymes and helps in maintenance of turgidity of cells.	Yellow edges of leaves, inward curving of leaves, premature death.
4. Calcium	Ca^{2+}	As calcium pectate in the middle lamella of the cell wall, activates certain enzymes involved in selective permeability of cell membranes.	Stunted growth, disintegration of apical meristems and chlorosis.
5. Magnesium	Mg^{2+}	Constituent of chlorophyll, maintains ribosome structure, activates enzymes in phosphate metabolism	Interveinal chlorosis
6. Sulphur	SO_4^{2-}	Constituent of amino acids (methionine, cysteine and cystine), vitamins, ferredoxin etc.	Chlorosis, rolling oftips and leaf margins.
7. Iron	Fe^{3+}	Constituent of ferredoxin, cytochromes, activates catalase, required for synthesis of chlorophyll	Chlorosis
8. Manganese (trace)	Mn^{2+}	Activates some enzymes necessary for O_2 evolution in photosynthesis.	Chlorosis, grey spots on leaves
9. Molybdenum (trace)	Mo^{3+} or Mo^{4+} or MoO_2^{2+}	Activates certain enzymes in nitrogen metabolism ascorbic acid synthesis.	Slight retardation of growth, whiptail in crucifers, loosening of cauliflower head.
10. Boron (trace)	BO_3^{3-} or or $B_4O_7^{2-}$	Calcium metabolism, pollen germination, cell differentiation, carbohydrate translocation	Suppression of flower formation, leaves becomes coppery in texture, heart rot or brown heart of Sugar beet and Turnip.
11. Copper (trace)	Cu^{2+}	Constituent of several oxidising enzymes, plastocyanin, cytochrome oxidase	Dieback, brown heart disease, blackening of potato tuber, reclamation of leguminosae
12. Zinc (trace)	Zn^{2+}	Activates various enzymes especially carboxylases, part of carbonic anhydrase and various dehydrogenases involved in synthesis of growth hormone auxin (IAA).	Little leaf disease, mottle leaf disease of apple and citrus, white bud, stunted growth, interveinal chlorosis.
13. Chlorine (trace)	Cl^-	Photolysis of water, with Na^+ and K^+ helps in maintaining solute concentration and anion-cation balance in cells, activator of amylase.	Wilting, stunting of roots and swollen root tips, flower abscission, reduced fruiting bronze coloured leaves.

MECHANISM OF ABSORPTION OF ELEMENTS

- **Flux :** Movement of ions
- **Influx :** Movement into the cell
- **Efflux :** The outward movement

Two ways:

1. Passive absorption

Movement of mineral ions into root cells as a result of diffusion. Three theories:

(a) **Donann's equilibrium (Donann, 1911) :** Entry of ions into the cell across the plasma membrane to maintain equilibrium is called **Donann's equilibrium.**

(b) **Ion exchange theory (Jenny and Overstreet, 1938) :** Exchange of anions and cations absorbed to the root surface with similarly charged ions of soil solution is called as ion exchange.

(c) **Mass flow/Bulk flow theory Hylmo (1955) :** Movement of ions takes place through root alongwith the stream of water under the influence of transpiration.

2. Active absorption

Uptake of mineral ions against concentration gradient. Metabolic energy is utilized for this. This energy is derived from respiration and is supplied through ATP.

- **Carrier concept (Van den Honert, 1937) :** Some organic substances (carriers) transfer ions from outer surface to the inner surface of plasma membrane by forming **carrier-ion complexes.**
- **Cytochrome pump hypothesis** (Lundegardh, 1954) explains the absorption of anions only.

ION TRAFFIC INTO THE ROOT

1. **Apoplastic pathway :** Occurs due to diffusion and bulk flow of water from cell to cell through spaces between cell wall polysaccharides.

Ions → Cell wall of epidermis → Cell wall of cortex → Cytoplasm of endodermis → Cell walls of pericycle → Xylem Vessels

2. **Symplastic pathway :** Active transport of mineral nutrients.

Ions → Cytoplasm of epidermis → Cytoplasm → Cortex → Endodermis of pericycle through plasmodesmata → Xylem vessels

TRANSLOCATION OF SOLUTES

- Stout and Hoagland (1939) proved that mineral salts are translocated through xylem.
- The rates at which inorganic solutes are translocated through the xylem vessels, correspond closely with the rates of translocation of water.
- Some of the minerals are transferred radially from xylem to the phloem mainly through parenchymatous cells.

NITROGEN METABOLISM

- **Nitrogen Cycle :** Regular circulation of nitrogen amongst living organisms, reservoir pool in the atmosphere (78% of atmosphere is N_2) and cycling pool in lithosphere. Plants obtain nitrogen from soil as nitrate, ammonium nitrite and urea.
- The atmospheric nitrogen is fixed into oganic combinations such as amino acids, protenis, nucleic acids etc. in living organisms via inorganic forms such as NH_4^+.
- **Ammonification :** The dead remains of animals and plants are decomposed through microbial activities to produce ammonia.
- **Nitrification :** Ammonia is rapidly converted first to nitrites and then to nitrates by the process of nitrification.

$$\text{Ammonia} \xrightarrow{\textit{Nitrosomonas}} \text{Nitrite} \xrightarrow{\textit{Nitrobacter}} \text{Nitrate}$$

- **Denitritication :** Nitrate is converted to nitrogen gas by the micro-organisms *e.g., Pseudomonas.*
- **Biological nitrogen fixation:** Nitrogen gas fixed in the form of NH_4^+ by both free living and symbiotic bacteria.
- Freeliving nitrogen fixing bacteria includes cyanobacteria, *Azotobacter* and *Clostridium.*
- **Symbiotic N_2 fixation :** Symbiotic bacteria are found in the root nodules of the members of family Leguminosae, they have the ability

to take up atmospheric N_2 through a process called **Symbiotic N_2 fixation**. *Rhizobium (e.g., R. leguminosarum, R. meliotii)* present root nodules of fabaceae *e.g., Cajanus, Cicer, Glycine, Lens, Phaseolus, Vigna, Pisum* etc.

- Root hair of legume secrete flavonoids and betaines which attract bacteria of *Rhizobium* species *(e.g., R. leguminosarum, R. melilotii)*.
- Bacteria release nod factors that cause curling of root hair, degeneration of cell wall, passage into root hair where infection thread carrying bacteria is formed.
- Finer branehes of infection thread pass into cells where bacteria stop dividing and form irregular, polyhedral bodies called bacteroids. These bacteroids present in groups or vesicles surrounded by host membrane.
- A pinkish pigment *i.e.,* **leg haemoglobin** (Lb) develops around each vesicle which is related to blood pigment haemoglobin. In root nodules, it found as **oxygen scavenger**, protecting enzyme nitrogenase from oxygen.
- Symbiotic nitrogen fixation requires **Nod** genes of legume, **nod**, **fix** and **nif** gene clusters of bacteria.
- Nitrogen fixation requires an enzyme **nitrogenase**, ATP, a source of hydrogen (NADPH, FMNH) and organic acids to trap ammonia produced through nitrogen fixation.

$$N_2 + 2H \xrightarrow[\text{Nitrogenase}]{\text{ATP}} N_2 + H_2 \xrightarrow[\text{Nitrogenase}]{\text{+4H, ATP}} 2NH_3$$

$$NH_3 + \alpha - \text{ketoglutarate} + NAD(P)H \xrightarrow{\text{dehydrogenase}} \text{Glutamate} + NAD(P)^+ + H_2O$$

From this other amino acids and nitrogenous substances of different types are formed.

- Amino acids are translocated to other parts of the plant, which act as building blocks for the synthesis of various types of proteins.

SYNTHESIS OF AMINO ACIDS

- Amino acids are the main building blocks of proteins and in plants they act a number of additional functions in regulation of metabolism and the transport and storage of nitrogen.
- Amino acids are the initial products of nitrogen assimilation.

1. Reductive amination

$$\alpha - \text{ketoglutaric acid} + \underset{\text{ammonium}}{NH_4^+} + NAD(P)H \xrightarrow[\text{Dehydrogenare}]{\text{Glutamate}} \text{Glutamate} + H_2O + NAD(P)$$

2. Transamination : Involves transfer of amino group from one amino acid to the keto group of keto acid. From glutamic acid other 17 amino acids are formed through transamination in the presence of enzyme **transaminase**.

- **Amides :** Amino acids, glutamic acid and aspartic acid takes part in the formation of amides **asparagine** and **glutamine**. The hydroxyl part of the acid is replaced' by any other NH_2 radical and this takes place in the presence of enzyme **glutamine synthetase or asparagine synthetase.**
- **Protein synthesis :** Proteins are nitrogenous compounds containing C, H, O and N. Sometimes P and S are also associated with protein. The amino group of one amino acid attaches to the carboxyl group of its neighbour amino acid. In this process a molecule of water is eliminated and peptide bond (NH–CO–) is formed.
- Proteins consist of one or more chains called **polypeptide chains** each of which consists of hundreds of amino acids.

HETEROTROPHIC NUTRITION

Some plants are incapable of photosynthesizing and obtain water, mineral and certain organic compounds from other autotrophs are called heterotrophs and the nutrition is called heterotrophic nutrition.

1. Parasitic nutrition

Parasites obtains their nutrition from living plants or animals which are called hosts. Parasites may be obligate (total parasite) or partial (semi-parasites).

(A) Obligate parasites : Without chlorophyll, take whole of their nutrition from host.

- Total stem *parasite-Cuscuta*
- Total root *parasite-Orobanche, Balanophora, Raffesia.*

(B) Partial parasites : Green, manufacture their own food but depend upon other plants for minerals and water.

- Partial stem *parasite-Viscum album, Loranthus*
- Partial root *parasite-Santalum, Thesium, Striga.*

2. Saprophytic nutrition

Saprophytes obtain their nutrition from dead and rotting organic matter *e.g.,* Many bacteria, fungi mosses, some pteridophytes etc.

- *Neothia* (Bird's nest orchid) : Grows on **humus rich soil.** Roots are associated with ectotrophic mycorrhiza.
- *Monotropa* (Indian Pipe) : Grown on humus rich soil of pine forests, under ground part is associated with endotrophic mycorrhiza.

3. Symbionts

Symbiosis is an association of dissimilar organisms to their mutual advantage *e.g.,* Lichen (association of algae and fungi), a coralloid root of *Cycas,* Mycorrhiza etc.

- **Mycorrhiza :** An association between a fungus and roots of higher plants. Fungus supplies the water and salts to the higher plants and in return obtain the prepared food from the green plants. Such association may be endotrophic or ecto-trophic.

4. Insectivorous plants

Such green plants which obtain their nourishment partly from soil and atmosphere and partly by catching and digesting small insects, the decomposition products of which are rich in nitrogen. The leaves of such plants are modified in various ways for capturing insects. *e.g., Drosera. (sundew), Utricularia* (bladder wort), *Dionaea* (venusfly trap), *Pinguicula* (butterwort), *Nepenthes* (pitcher plant), *Aldrovanda* (water flea trap) etc.

SOME IMPORTANT FACTS

- **Most abundant element :** Oxygen on fresh weight basis and Carbon on dry weight basis.
- **Frame work elements :** Constitute the carbohyrates which form the cell wall *i.e.,* C, H and O.
- **Balancing elements :** Ca, Mg, K -Counteract the toxic effect of other minerals by ion balancing.
- **Protoplasmic elements :** Form part of protoplasm alongwith C, H, O. These are N, and S.
- **Functional elements :** Occur in the range of micro nutrients. These are cobalt, vanadium and aluminium.
- Micronutrients are as important as macro nutrients in plant nutrition.
- Pungent smell of onion and garlic is due to sulphur compounds.
- Deficiency of Mo causes : Whiptail of *Brassica,* scald of beans, water core in turnip.
- Deficiency of Zn causes : Exanthema of fruit trees, mottle leaf of *Citrus,* white bud of maize, sickles leaf or cocoa.
- Deficiency of S causes : Tea yellows.
- Deficiency of Bo Causes : Heart rot of sugarbeet, Corky Core of apple, Water core in turnip, Celery stem crack, Top sickness of tobacco.
- Deficiency of Mn causes : Speckled yellows of beet, marsh spots of peas, gray specks of oats.
- Some plants require other essential elements *e.g.,* silica (grasses and diatoms), sodium (Halophytes and plants rith Cu pathway) **Cobalt** (algae and microbes), Aluminium (ferns and *Lycopodium*) and Iodine (marine algae).
- **Hydroponics :** Solless growth or tank farming or water or solution cutlures. Various scientists suggested suitable media for hydroponics are Sach (1860), Knop (1865), Pfeffer (1900) and Crone (1902). The pH of medium should be 5 - 6. This helps in knowing the essentiality of mineral element, dificiency symptoms developed due to nonavailability of particular nutrient, toxicity to plant when element is present in excess,. role of essential element is the metabolism of plant etc.

- **Aeroponics :** Grouping plants in stands provided with five mist of solution having all the required inorganic nutrients.
- **Liebig's Law of minimum** (Liebig, 1840, father of Biochemistry). Productivity of soil depends upon the proportionate amount of that essential element which is deficient in that soil.
- Deficiency symptoms are also known as **hunger signs**.
- *Aulosirafertilissima : Most* active nitrogen fixer in rice fields.
- **Vanadium** is essential for alga *Scenedesmus.*
- **Rubedium** has chemical properties similar to potassium.
- **Selenium :** Absorbed and accumulated in relatively high concentration by *Astragalus* species.
- **Nickel :** Essential part of enzyme **Urease** which catalyzes hydrolysis or urea to CO_2 to NH_4.
- Most mobile element-**Potassium**.
  Most immobile element-**Iron**.
- **Phytotran :** Place or laboratory where plants can be maintained and studied under a wide range of controlled conditions.
- **Molybdenum :** Required by plant in least quantity.
- **Gold :** Reported to occur in stem *of Equisetum.*
- **Plant ash :** The ash which is left on heating a dry plant or plant part at 600°C in a crucible which contain oxides and carbonates of elements.
- **Holophytic nutrition :** Photoautotrophic nutrition.
- **Phyllosphere association :** Ruiner (1954-61) observed considerable variety of micro-organisms occurring abundantly on the surface of the leaves of many trees and strubs under humid tropical conditions and suggested that these organisms might fix nitrogen. The environment provided by the wet leaf surface for microbial development was termed by her as **phyllosphere**.
- *Rafflesia : Plant* grows as total root parasite on the roots of figs. Flowers are red in colour, unisexual, borne singly and the largest flowers is plant kingdom (measuring 3 feet in diameter, with 3/4" thickness and 5lb weight.

PHOTOSYNTHESIS

- Synthesis of organic compounds (carbohydrates) from inorganic raw materials (CO_2 and Hydrogen donor) by green plants in the presence of light (solar energy)

$$CO_2 + 2H_2O \xrightarrow[\text{Green plants}]{\text{Light energy}} (CH_2O)_n + H_2O + O_2$$

  This equation was given by **C.B. Van Niel** for photosynthesis.
- Only 0.2% of the light energy falling on earth is utilised by photosynthetic organisms.
- **Cyanobacteria:** Where photosynthesis was first appeared.

HISTORY

1. **Aristotle (320 BC) :** Plants get their food only from the soil.
2. **Von Helmont (1648) :** All the substance of the plant was produced from water and none from the soil.
3. **Stephen Hales (1727) :** Air and light are important for nourishment of plants.
4. **Joseph Priestley (1772) :** Plants have ability to take up CO_2 from the atmosphere and release O_2.
5. **Jan Ingenhousz (1779) :** Recognize importance of sunlight and chlorophyll.
6. **Senebier (1782) :** Rate of purification of air depends upon concentration of foul air.
7. **Theodore de Saussure (1804) :** Water also participate in photosynthesis.
8. **Pelletier and Caventou (1818) :** Discovered chlorophyll due to which leaves are green in colour.
9. **Von Mayer (1845) :** Solar energy is changed into chemical energy.
10. **Sachs (1862) :** Starch is formed as a reserve product of photosynthesis.
11. **Engelman (1888) :** Plotted the action spectrum of photosynthesis.
12. **Blackman (1905) :** Proposed law of limiting factors and possibility of two phases of photosynthesis.

13. **Emerson and Arnold (1932) :** Light reaction consists of two distinct photochemical reactions.
14. **Robert Hill (1937) :** Evolution of oxygen does not require carbon dioxide; photolysis of water; light produces assimilatory power.
15. **Ruben, Hassid and Kamen (1941) :** Oxygen evolved in photosynthesis comes from water by using heavy isotope of oxygen *i.e.*, $H_2{}^{18}O$.
16. **Calvin (1954) :** Calvin cycle/C_3 cycle/Calvin Benson cycle with the help Of $^{14}CO_2$ discovered cycle involved in carbon assimilation.
17. **Arnon, Allen and Whatley (1954) :** Demonstrated fixation of CO_2 by chloroplast using $^{14}CO_2$, discovered photophosphorylation.
18. **Emerson *et.al.* (1957) :** Emerson effect, proposed two photosystems.
19. **Hatch and Slack (1965) :** C_4 cycle for CO_2 fixation.
20. **Huber *et.al.* (1985) :** Crystallised photosynthetic reaction centre of bacterium *Rhodobacter* and got Nobel Prize in 1988.

SITE FOR PHOTOSYNTHESIS

- Mainly leaves, though all green parts containing chloroplasts have the potential to carry on photosynthesis.
- Chlorophyll (green pigment) is present in chloroplasts *i.e.*, localised.

PHOTOSYNTHETIC PIGMENTS: 3 TYPES

(1) Chlorophyll

- Total 9 types; **chlorophyll 'a'** and **chlorophyll 'b'** are important types of chlorophyll.
- **Chlorophyll :** Molecule consist of a porphyrin ring (hydrophilic) and a **phytol** tail (lipophilic).
- **Porphyrin ring :** Flat, square structure having smaller **pyrrole** rings with a magnessium atom at the centre. Chiorophyll *a* ($C_{55}H_{72}O_5N_4Mg$) possess a **CH_3 (methyl)** group and chlorophyll *b* ($C_{55}H_{70}O_6N_4Mg$) possess a **- CHO (aldehyde)** group. The head is joined to a long' hydrocarbon tail *i.e.*, **Phytol.**
- **Chlorophyll *a* :** most abundant, only pigment in all photosynthetic plants.
- Chlorophyll absorbs light near both ends of the visible spectrum *i.e.*, blue and red light and transmit or reflect green light *i.e.*, why looks green in colour.
- Chlorophyll synthesis in flowering plants require **light** and **iron.**
- Algae, bryophytes, pteridophytes and gymnosperms develop chlorophyll even in absence of light.
- Raw materials for chlorophyll synthesis are glycine (amino acid) and succinyl co-A.
- **Fluorescence :** isolated chlorophyll a in pure form emits red colour. It is known as fluorescence.
- **Phosphorescence :** The delayed emission of long wave radiation from an activated molecule is called phosphorescence.

(2) Carotenoids

- Yellow to orange pigments, absorb light strongly in the blue-violet range.
- Called shield pigments because protect chlorophyll from photo oxidation by light of high intensity and also from oxygen produced during photosynthesis.
- Absorb light and transfer' it to chlorophyll for use in photosynthesis.
- Two types: ***(a)* Carotenes :** (Orange coloured) - hydrocarbons (tetrapenes)
  ***(b)* Xanthophylls :** (Yellow) - contain oxygen

(3) Phycobilin

- Water soluble, open tetrapyrrole pigments found in red algae and blue green algae.
- Found in phycobilisomes attached to thylakoids and transform light energy to chlorophyll. 3 types *i.e.*, **Phycocyanin** (blue), Allophycocyanin (blue) and Phycoerythrin (red).

Quantasome

- Present as small units on the membranes of thylakoids.
- This term coined by **Park** and **Biggins** (1964) for a group of pigment molecules required for carrying out a photochemical reaction.

- Each quantasome consists of about **250-300 chlorophyll** molecules, carotenoids, quinone compounds, sulpholipids, phospholipids, proteins etc.

ABSORPTION AND ACTION SPECTRA

- **Action Spectra :** Graph exhibiting the rate of photosynthesis at different wavelengths of light.
- **Absorption Spectra :** Graph depicting amount of light of different wavelengths absorbed by a pigment.
- Close similarity between action spectrum of photosynthesis and absorption spectrum of chlorophyll exhibits that chlorophylls are responsible for absorption of light in photosynthesis.

MECHANISM OF PHOTOSYNTHESIS

Two-phases *i.e.*, light reaction and dark reaction.

(A) Photochemical phase (light reaction or Hill reaction)

- Takes place in thylakoids of grana.
- Solar energy is trapped by chlorophyll and is stored in form of chemical energy (ATP) and as reducing power (NADPH)
- **Photosystems :** Groupings of photosynthetic units which possess photocentres and are surrounded by specific light harvesting pigment molecules. 2 types.
  - *(a)* **Photosystem-I (PS I) :** Present in stroma thylakoid and non-appressed parts of granal thylakoid.
- Photocentre P_{700} along with accessory pigments which absorb at or below 700 nm constitute the PS-I.
  - *(b)* **Photosystem-II (PS II) :** Present in appressed part of granal thylakoids.
- Possess chlorophyll ***a***, chlorophyll ***b*** and carotenoids.
- The cluster of pigment molecules which transfer their energy to P_{680} absorb light at or below the wavelegnth of 680 nm.
- **Light reaction :** in which light energy is transformed by photophosphorylation into chemical energy in the form of the energy source ATP and $NADPH_2$ which is used to reduce CO_2. Takes place in following steps.
  1. Excitation of pigments by light so that excited pigments lose electrons and become oxidised.

$$\text{Chlorophyll} \xrightarrow{\text{Light energy}} \underset{\text{oxidised}}{\text{Chlorophyll}^{+}} + \underset{\text{electron}}{e^{-}}$$

  2. The electron is captured by an electron acceptor. This represent the conversion of light energy into chemical energy.

  Depending upon whether the electron lost by chlorophyll molecule is returned to it or not, the further events may be cyclic or non-cyclic.

Non-cyclic photophosphorylation (Hill and Bendall proposed Z-scheme for electron transport)

- Light energised ATP synthesis in which the electron expelled by excited photocentres does not return to them.
- Both PS I and PS II are involved.
- Coordinate their activities to produce assimilatory power (ATP and NADPH).
- Oxygen is released during photolysis of water.
- Takes place at one place only.

Cyclic photophosphorylation

- Light energised ATP synthesis in which the electron expelled by excited photo centre is returned to it after passing over a chain of electron carriers.
- It is related to photo act I (PS I) only.
- Electron released from chlorophyll return back.
- There is no photolysis of water and release of oxygen.
- NADP is not oxidised.
- Takes place at two places.
- It occurs under low light conditions, wavelength longer than 680 nm and when CO_2 fixation is being inhabited.

(B) Biosynthetic phase (Dark phase or Blackman's reaction)

- Independent of light and studied by **Blackman** in following steps:
  - *(a)* **Carboxylation** *i.e.*, acceptance of CO_2 by

RuBP - CO_2 receptor, carboxylation of RuBP is catalysed by the enzyme **RuBP carboxylase** or **Rubisco** (most abundant protein on earth).

(b) **Glycolytic reversal :** The 6 molecules of PGA (3 phosphoglyceric acid) utilises 6 ATP molecules to form 6 molecules of 1,3-diphosphoglyceric acid. These, in turn, utilizes 6 NADPH supplied by the light reactions and get converted to a 3-C glyceraldehyde phosphate.

(c) **Regeneration of RuBP :** RuBP is regenerated through the formation of 4-C, 5-C and 7-C intermediates. Five molecules of triose phosphate (TP) and three molecules of ATP are involved in the regeneration of RuBP.

- Dark reaction takes place in stroma. It comprises a series of reactions controlled by enzymes. The sequence of these reactions was determined in *Chlorella* and *Scendesmus* by **Calvin, Benson** and **Bassham** using radioactive carbon ^{14}C and techniques like chromatography and autoradiography. This is also known as **Calvin Cycle** or **Calvin-Benson Cycle** or **C_3 Cycle or Reductive Pentose Pathway or Photosynthetic Carbon Reduction or PCR.**

PHOTORESPIRATION (DICKER AND TIO, 1959)

- Respiration which is initiated in chloroplasts and takes place in light only is called **Photo respiration.**
- The enzyme Rubisco catalyses the carboxylation reaction where CO_2 combines with RuBP, called **oxygenation.**
- Also called **Photosynthetic Carbon Oxidation Cycle** and involves an interaction of three organelles *i.e.,* **chloroplast, peroxisome** and **mitochondria.**
- The function of photorespiration is to recover some of the carbon from the excess glycolate. However, there is a **wasteful loss of carbon** as **CO_2** and **loss of energy.**
- It is stimulated by high light intensity, high temperature, ageing of leaf and high oxygen concentration.
- Two molecules of phosphoglycolate (2C) produced by oxygenation of RuBP are changed into one molecule of phosphoglycerate (3C) and one molecule of CO_2.
- 75% of carbon lost to oxygenation is recovered by PCO cycle.

HATCH-SLACK PATHWAY OR C_4-PATHWAY OR DICARBOXYLIC ACID PATHWAY

- C_4 plants possess a characteristic leaf anatomy (**Kranz anatomy**). In which vascular bundles are surrounded by two rings of cells *i.e.* **inner ring (bundle sheath cells** having starch-rich chloroplasts lacking grana) and **outer ring (mesophyll cells).**
- It C_4 plants CO_2 is picked up by phosphoenol pyruvate (PEP - 3 Compound) in the **cytoplasm of mesophyll cells** and form **oxaloacetate** (4C) which is converted to malic acid or aspartic acid (4–C) for transport to bundle sheath cells.
- In bundle sheath cells, CO_2 is released and is assimilated through Calvin cycle. Pyruvate is released which passes back into mesophyll cells where PEP is regenerated.
- The C_4 Pathway is more efficient than the C_3 pathway due to the absence of photorespiration.

CRASSULACEAN ACID METABOLISM (CAM)

- Takes place in succulents *(e.g.,* Cactus, *Bryophyllum, Kalanchoe, Sedum* etc.) and other plants that normally grow in dry conditions. Such plants have a photosynthetic pathway similar to C_4 plants.
- CO_2 taken up by the leaves on green stems through open stomata during night and fixed as malic acid with the help of **phosphoenol pyruvate.**
- Calvin cycle takes place during the day when stomata are closed. Fomation of malic acid

during dark is called acidification (Phase I) and the release of CO_2 for actual photosynthesis during day is called deacidification (Phase II).

- CAM is a type of adaptation that allows certain plants *(e.g.,* pineapple) to carry out photosynthesis without much loss of water which is inevitable in plants with C_3 and C_4 mechanisms.

FACTORS AFFECTING PHOTOSYNTHESIS

Blackman (1905) Proposed Law of limiting factors which states that "When a biological process is conditioned as to its rapidity by a number of separate factors, the rate of the process is limited by the pace of the slowest factor".

1. Light

Provides energy for photosynthesis.

(i) **Light quality:** Photosynthesis successfully takes place only in the visible light (3800 Å - 7600 Å wave length). Rate of photosynthesis is maximum in red light, average in blue light and minimum in green light.

(ii) **Light intensity :** It has a direct relationship with the rate of photosynthesis. As the intensity of light (μ mol. $m^{-2}s^{-1}$) increases, the rate of photosynthesis increases. At higher light intensities, the rate of photosynthesis decreases.

(iii) **Light duration:** Long continuous periods of light increase the rate of photosynthesis.

2. Carbon dioxide

As the CO_2 concentration increases upto 0.9%, the rate of photosynthesis also increases. At the same time very high concentration of CO_2 becomes toxic to plants and inhibit photosynthesis.

3. Temperature

Generally, the rate of photosynthesis increases by increase in temperature upto 40°C. High temperature results into the deactivation of enzymes and so, the dark reaction is affected. The effect of temperature varies from plant to plant. C_4 plants have higher optimum temperature than C_3 plants. 25-30°C is the optimum temperature for photosynthesis.

4. Water

It rarely act as a limiting factor because less than 1 % of the water absorbed by a plant is used in photosynthesis. Electrons in the photochemical phase are supplied by the water but its availability for photosynthesis depends upon the closure of stomata. However, lowering of photosynthesis has been observed if the plants are inadequately supplied with water.

5. Nutrient supply

Nitrogen has a direct relationship with photosynthesis since it is a basic part of chlorophyll and all enzymes involved in carbon reactions, so any reduction in nitrogen supply leads an adverse effect on photosynthesis. Deficiency of mineral elements *(e.g.,* Mg, Fe, Cl, Cu, Mn, P etc.) ultimately reduces photosynthesis.

6. Chlorophyll

Emerson (1929) found the direct relationship between the chlorophyll content and the rate of photosynthesis.

Willstatter studied **assimilatory number** *i.e.,* **Photosynthesis/chlorophyll unit** in leaves of different ages of plants and the effect of amount of chlorophyll on the rate of photosynthesis. Assimilatory number decreases with the age of the leaf.

7. Leaf Factors

i.e., leaf age, leaf angle and leaf orientation etc. have effect on photosynthesis. Leaf age has the most prominent effect on photosynthesis. Rate of photosynthesis is maximum in just matured leaves but declines with age. In a senescence leaf there is deactivation of enzymes and degeneration of chlorophyll.

TRANSLOCATION OF PHOTOSYNTHATES

- The transport of photosynthates or photoassimilates (energy rich carbon compounds) formed during photosynthesis from the production centres (leaves) to the consumption centres (non-photosynthetic organs *i.e.,* apices, roots, tubers, fruits etc.)

through phloem is called translocation of organic solutes or long distance transport.

- Translocation may be upward, downward and radial in directions from the source to the sink *i.e.*, fruits, tubers, roots, apices etc.) through phloem.
- Photosynthates provides energy to the non-photosynthetic tissues through respiration.

SIGNIFICANCE OF PHOTOSYNTHESIS

- Helps in conversion of solar energy into organic matter.
- Consumes atmospheric carbon dioxide and yields carbohydrates and molecular oxygen.
- Evolves molecular oxygen for use by other living organisms and maintains the level of atmospheric oxygen which is continuously consumed by plants and animals during respiration.
- Produces carbohydrates and used by plants and animals to synthesize organic acids, proteins, fats, nucleic acids, pigments, hormones, vitamins, alkaloids and other metabolites.

CHEMOSYNTHESIS

Such reactions in which reduction of carbon dioxide to carbohydrates does not require light and takes place in presence of energy obtained from oxidations of inorganic substances is called **chemosynthesis** *e.g.*, **Nitrifying bacteria** *(Nitrosomonas, Nitrosococcus)* obtain energy by oxidising ammonia to nitrites), sulphur bacteria *(e.g., Beggiatoa* convert H_2S to sulphur), Carbon monooxide bacteria *(e.g., Carboxydomonas* convert CO to CO_2), **methane bacteria** *(e.g., Methanococcus* oxidise methane into CO_2 and HzO) etc.

SOME IMPORTANT FACTS

- **Compensation point :** The light intensity at which rate of photosynthesis is equal to the rate of respiration *i.e.*, in morning, in evening.
- **Photosynthesis :** Anabolic, endergonic, oxidation - reduction process.
- **NADP :** Acts as hydrogen acceptor during photosynthesis in plant cells.
- **Rubisco :** RuBP carboxylase enzyme, is a large protein molecule and constitute about 16% of the chloroplast protein and is the most abundant protein on the earth.
- Grass Alloteropsis semi-alata possess both C_3 and C_4 ecotypes.
- **Fret membranes:** Membranes of thylakoids.
- Plastidome: Plastid complex of a cell.
- **Keilin (1925) :** Coined the term cytochrome.
- Electrons accepted from reaction centres by the acceptors are passed down hill through the electron transport chain.
- The reaction centre of PS II is P_{680} (or chlorophyll a_{680}) and that of PS I is P_{700} (or chlorophyll a_{700}).
- **Assimilatory power :** NADPH + H^+ produced in light reaction constitute assimilatory power *i.e.*, reducing power.
- **Redox potential :** The tendency of an atom/ molecule to give or take up electrons. Electrons move from substances having low redox potentials to those having high redox potentials.
- In C_3 plants, more CO_2 is released in light than in dark (due to photorespiration).
- **Solarisation :** Destruction of chlorophyll due to high light intensity.
- **Carbon dioxide :** Most common limiting factor for photosynthesis.
- Only 0.2% of the light energy falling on the earth is utilised by photosynthetic organisms.
- The reaction centre in bacteria is B-890.
- The size of quantosome is about 180 × 155 × 100 Å.
- DCMU (Dichlorophenyl dimethyl Urea) – a herbicide which inhibits PS II and oxygen release in light phase.
- Calvin cycle is exhibited by *A triplex rose us* whereas Hatch-Slack cycle is exhibited by *A. hastata*
- In bacteria only one ATP molecule is generated during cyclic or non-cyclic electron transport.
- **K^+ ions :** Helps in the translocation of solutes.
- Annually, about 75 × 1012 kg of carbon (in the form of CO) is fixed through

photosynthesis, producing about 1700 million tonnes of dry matter. About 90% of it is carried out in the oceans (mostly by the phytoplanktons and algae).

- **Photosynthetic material :** 264 g of CO_2 and 216 g of water give rise to 108 g of water, 192 g of O_2 and 180 g of glucose.
- **PEP or Phosphoenol pyruvate :** Primary CO_2 acceptor in C_4 and CAM plants. Combination of CO_2 and PEP is called **initial fixation.** It takes place in me ophyll cells and the enzyme is pepco.
- **RuBP or ribulose biphosphate :** Secondary/ final, CO_2 acceptor in C_4 and CAM plants. The phenomenon is called final fixation. It takes place in bundle sheath chloroplasts of C_4 plants and mesophyll cells in CAM plants and the enzyme is **rubisco.**
- **C.G. Strokes (1864) :** first to separate pure fractions of Chlorophyll ***a*** and Chlorophyll ***b***.
- Protochlorophyllide *a* is reduced to chlorophyllide a in presence of light and then esterified with phytol group to form chlorophyll.
- Orange wavelength (586-647 nm) are least absorbed and also least effective.
- T.W. Englemann (1880) determined the approximate action spectrum of photosynthesis.

RESPIRATION AND PHOTORESPIRATION

INTRODUCTION

Respiration

It is an energy liberating enzymatically controlled multistep catabolic process of stepwise breakdown of organic substances inside the living cells.

Respiratory Substrates

The organic substances which can be catabolised to liberate energy inside the living cells *e.g.*, carbohydrates, fats and proteins.

Type of respiration

1. **Aerobic :** Takes place inside the mitochondria in the presence of molecular oxygen in most of plants and animals called aerobes. Divided into 4 phases-Glycolysis, oxidative decarboxylation, Krebs or TCA cycle and Electron Transport system.
2. **Anaerobic (Fermentation) :** Involves the production of energy from the food nutrients in the absence of oxygen.

Respiratory Ratio or quotient (RQ)

The ratio of the volume of carbon dioxide released to the volume of oxygen taken in respiration in the given period of time at standard temperature and pressure.

$$RQ = \frac{\text{Moles of } CO_2 \text{ produced}}{\text{Moles of } O_2 \text{ absorbed}}$$

It provides the nature of the substrate being respired by a particular tissue.

(1) Carbohydrate RQ = 1 or unity
(2) Fats RQ = 0.7 *i.e.,* less than one
(3) Proteins RQ = less than unity (usually 0.5 to 0.9)
(4) Fermentation RQ = ∞ or infinity
(5) Succulents RQ = 0 or zero
(6) Maturing fatty seeds RQ = more than one
(7) Organic acids RQ = more than one
(8) Germinating fatty seeds RQ = less than one

MECHANISM OF RESPIRATION

- Glycolysis (splitting of sugar) results in the break down of glucose molecules into pyruvic acid.
- Completed in the **cytoplasm** of the living cells.
- Also known as **Embden-Meyerhof-Parnas** (EMP) pathway.
- 3 steps.
  1. **Phosphorylation of Glucose :** Initial, 6-carbon sugar is transformed into 6-carbon sugar diphosphate. This addition of phosphate groups is called phosphorylation, it activates the sugar and preventing it from getting out of the cell.
  2. **Splitting of fructose-I, 6-diphosphate :** Fructose-l, 6-diphosphate is broken down into two molecules of 3-carbon sugar phosphates *i.e.,* dihydroxy acetone

phosphate and glyceraldehyde-3-phosphate (undergoes further glycolysis). Both the molecules are interconvertible.

3. Formation of Pyruvic acid-3-phosphoglyceraldehyde in combination with one inorganic phosphate and coenzyme NAD is converted into 1, 3-diphosphoglyceric acid which is dephosphorylated to 3-phosphoglyceric acid and further changed to 2-phosphoglyceric acid. On dehydration 2-phosphoglyceric acid forms phosphoenol pyruvate or PEP which transformed to pyruvic acid.

- In glycolysis, a molecule of glucose is broken down to two molecules of pyruvic acid. There is gain of 2NADH and 2ATP or equivalent to 8 ATP.

Fate of pyruvic acid during aerobic respiration

Each pyruvic acid molecule enters a **mitochondrion** where its oxidation is completed. Pyruvic acid molecule undergoes oxidative decarboxylation *i.e.,* removal of CO_2 from pyruvic acid and oxidation of pyruvic acid by dehydrogenation. The 2-carbon fragment combines (7.64) with coenzyme **A** and form Acetyl coenzyme **A**. During this process, two molecules of NADH are produced and results in a net gain of6ATP molecules.

Fate of pyruvic acid during anaerobic respiration

- When oxygen is limiting, NADH and pyruvic acid begin to accumulate.
- Under anaerobic conditon plants carry out **fermentation** and leading to the formation of CO_2 and either ethanol or lactic acid.
- Pyruvic acid releases one molecule of CO_2 to produce acetaldehyde which reoxideses NADH and itself reduced to ethanol.
- These reaction are catalysed by **pyruvic acid decarboxylase and alcohol dehydrogenase enzymes.**
- Net yield of ATP in anaerobic respiration is of only 2 molecules of ATP that too during glycolysis is anaerobic respiration.

CITRIC ACID CYCLE

(Tricarboxylic acid or TCA cycle or Kreb's cycle).

- Sir Hans Krebs (1937) discovered the second phase in the aerobic oxidation of pyruvic acid. Got Nobel prize in 1953 (Fig. 1).

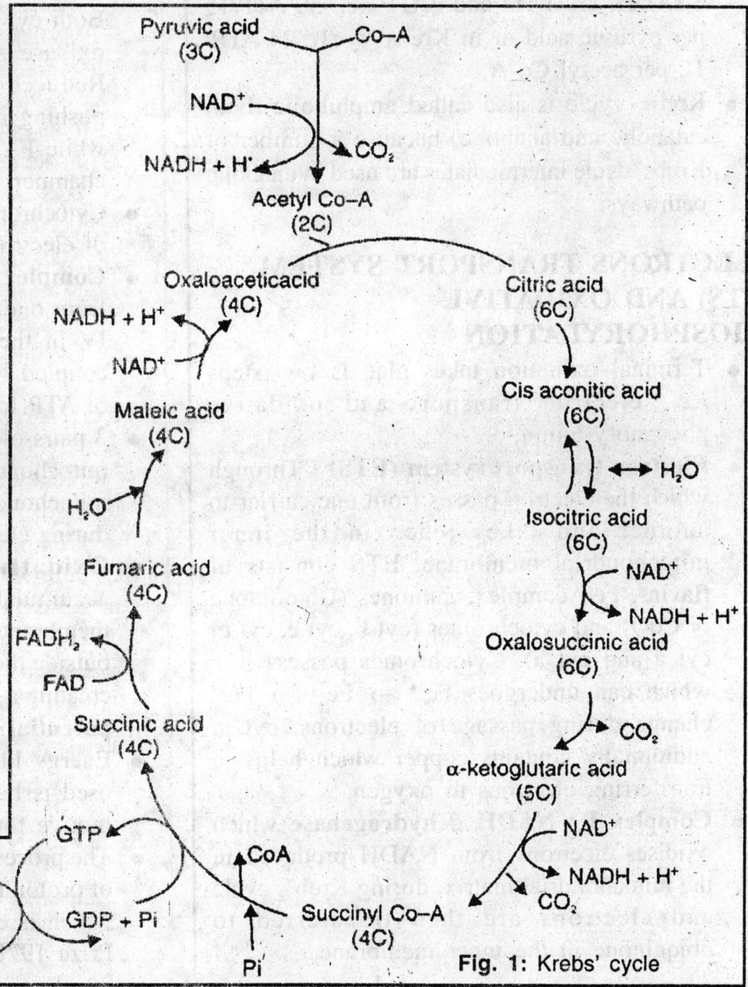

Fig. 1: Krebs' cycle

- It takes place in the matrix of mitochondria.
- Acetyl Co-A is a common intermediate of carbohydrate and fat metabolism, it is a substrate entrant of Kreb's cycle or connecting link between glycolysis and Krebs' cycle.
- Acetyl CoA produced not only from pyruvic acid but also that produced as a result of β-oxidation of fatty acids undergoes TCA cycle.
- Enzymes required for cycle are present in the-matrix of mitochondria.
- In total there are five oxidations and three decarboxylations (one decarboxylation and one oxidation outside Kreb's cycle)
- The net products from two pyruvates are 8NADH, 2FADH2 and 2ATP *i.e.,* 30 ATP/15 per pyruvic acid or in Krebs' cycle 24 ATP/ 12 per acetyl Co-A.
- Krebs' cycle is also called amphibolic (both catabolic and anabolic) because a number of Krebs' cycle intermediates are used in anabolic pathways.

ELECTRONS TRANSPORT SYSTEM (ETS) AND OXIDATIVE PHOSPHORYLATION

- Terminal oxidation takes plae is two steps *i.e.,* electron transport and oxidative phosphory-lation.
- **Electron transport system (ETS) :** Through which the electron passes from one carrier to another and takes place in the inner mitochondrial membrane. ETS consists of flavins, FeS complex, quinones (Ubiquinone or CoQ) and cytochromes (cyt b, cyt c, cyt c] cyt a and cyt a). Cytochromes possess iron which can undergoes $Fe^{2+} \rightarrow Fe^{3+} \rightarrow Fe^{2+}$ change during passage of electrons. cyt a_3 additionally contains copper which helps in transferring electrons to oxygen.
- **Complex I : NADH dehydrogenase** which oxidises electrons from NADH produced in the mitochondrial matrix, during Kreb's cycle and electrons are then transferred to ubiquinone in the inner membrane.
- **Complex II : Succinate dehydrogenase** Ubiquinone receives electrons from NADH and also by reducing equivalents via $FADH_2$ which is generated during oxidation of succinate, through the activity of the enzyme succinate dehydrogenase.
- **Complex III : Dihydroubiquinone, cytochrome** oxidoreductase and two forms of **cytochrome b and cytochrome c_1** The reduced ubiquinone (ubiquinol) is oxidised with the transfer of electrons to cytochrome c via this complex.
- **Complex IV : Cytochrome c, Cytochrome oxidase, cytochrme a, cytochrome a_3 and two copper centres :** Electrons are handed over to cyt C_1 → cyt c → cyt a → cyt a_3. Both cyt a and cyt a_3 fuction as cytochrome oxidase and handover electrons to oxygen. Reduced coenzyme NADH + H^+ helps is pushing out 3 pairs of H^+ to outer chamber while $FADH_2$ sends two pairs of H^+ to outer chamber.
- Cytochrome c acts as mobile carrier for transfer of electrons between complex III and IV.
- **Complex V : ATP synthase**–Electrons pass from one carrier to another via complex I to IV in the electron transport chain, they are coupled to ATP synthase for the production of ATP from ADP and inorganic phosphate.
- 3 pairs of protons ($6H^+$) are transported from mitochondrial matrix to outer side of the inner mitochondrial membrane. The energy released during electron transfer is used for this work.
- **Oxidative phosphorylation:** The accumulation of protons outside the inner membrane results in their higher concentration outside the inner membrane than in the matrix creating a **proton gradient** (Δ.pH) and **electric potential** (Δ.ψ) across the membrane.
- Energy liberated during electron transport in used is building a proton gradient or proton motive force (PMF) in the outer membrane.
- The process of synthesis of ATP at the expense of proton motive force is called chemiosmosis which is explained by Mitchell (1961, Nobel Prize 1978).

- Protons can not diffuse back into the matrix across the membrane but can enter the membrane via a proton channel established by the membrane bound **adenosine triphosphatase** (ATPase).
- ATPase is a multienzyme complex containing two parts F_0 and F_1.F_1 (acting as ATP sythethase) catalyses the synthesis of ATP from ADP. For each pair of protons flowing back into the matrix, one molecule ofATP is synthesized.
- F_0 is an integral membrane protein complex that forms the channel through which protons cross the inner membrane.
- $FADH_2$ donates its electrons to CoQ and not to FMN, only 4 protons are transported outside the membrane. Therefore, the back flow of these 4 protons through $F_0 - F_1$ complex results in the formation of only 2 ATP molecules.
- Total 38 ATP molecules are yielded during aerobic respiration of glucose. In most eukaryotic cells, 2 ATP molecules are expended in transporting the NADH produced in glycolysis into the mitochondrion for further oxidation in such cells, the net gain of **36 ATP** molecules instead of 38.

Pentose pathway (Pentose phosphate pathway (PPP) or Hexose monophosphate (HMP) shunt or Warburg Dickens pathway

- Takes place mainly in liver, lactating mammary glands, adipose tissues, adrenal cortex, gonads and erythrocytes.
- Takes place in the cytoplasm like glycolysis.
- This starts with a 6-carbon sugar, **glucose 6-phosphate** formed by phosphorylation of simple glucose with the help of hexokinase and ATP, and produces **5-carbon sugar, ribose 5-phosphate.**
- Six molecules of glucose produce via HMP shunt as much energy as produced by one glucose molecule via glycolysis and Kreb's cycle.
- Ribulose 5-phosphate formed in this pathway is of major importance in reaction involved in photosynthesis.

COMPENSATION POINT

- At given low concentration of CO_2 and non-limiting light intensity, the photosynthetic rate of a given plant will be equal to the total amount of respiration.
- **CO_2 compensation point :** The atmospheric concentration of CO_2 at which photosynthesis just compensates for respiration
- CO_2 compensation point is reached when the amount of CO_2 uptake is equal to that generated through respiration at a non limiting light intensity.
- The CO_2 compensation point is usually much higher in C_3 plants (25-100 $\mu l.l^{-1}$) as compared to C_4 plants (less than 5 $\mu l.l^{-1}$).

FACTORS AFFECTING RESPIRATION

1. **Temperature :** Affecting the activity of enzymes. Q_{10} = 2 or 3. Optimum temperature is 20 – 30°C. At high temperature the rate of respiration declines with time and at very low temperature, the respiration rate is insignificant.
2. **CO_2 :** Increase in CO_2 concentration and absence of O_2 adversely affect the rate of aerobic respiration.
3. **Light :** Control respiration by raising the temperature of an organism.
4. **O_2-Extinction point :** *i.e.,* minimum oxygen concentration at which aerobic respiration takes place which is 3 - 10% of oxygen. In some cases a direct relation between the respiration rate and oxygen concentration has been reported.
5. **Water :** Very low water content in dry seeds and stored tubers is responsible for very feeble rate of respiration. In wilted tissues the stored starch converted into sugars which increase the rate of respiration while in well hydrated plants the rate of respiration is not likely to be affected much by slight changes in the water content.
6. **Respiratory substrates :** Higher availability of respiratory substrates increases the rate of respiration upto a certain limit.

7. **Stimulation :** Mechanical disturbance, injury or infection increases respiration. Hopkins (1927) found that in wounded plant tissue the sugar content is suddenly increased which is responsible for temporary increase in the respiration rate.
8. **Climacteric fruits :** Such fruits have high rate of respiration during their ripening *e.g.*, Banana, Apple.
9. **Inhibitors :** A number of chemicals inhibit respiration *e.g.*, azide, cyanide, malonate, carbon monoxide etc.
10. **Protoplasmic factor :** Young growing cells exhibit high rate of respiration as compared to mature cells.

SOME IMPORTANT FACTS

- **Floating respiration :** Carbohydrates and fats are used as respiratory substrates.
- **Protoplasmic respiration (Blackman) :** Proteins are used as respiratory substrates.
- The energy present in one granl of different respiratory substrates is-
  Carbohydrates: 4.4 kcal or 18.4 kJ.
  Fats: 9.8 kcal or41 kJ.
  Proteins: 4.8 kcal or 20 kJ.
- **Lohmann** discovered ATP in 1929 and coined it in 1931.
- **Lipmann (1941) :** discovered ATP cycle.
- **Gaylussac :** To measure rate of respiration.
- Viruses do not exhibit respiration.
- **Pasteur effect (Louis Pasteur) :** A sudden change from anaerobic to aerobic respiration due to availability of oxygen.
- **α-Ketoglutaric acid :** An organic acid, undergoes both dehydrogenation and decarboxylation and is first dicarboxylic acid formed during Kreb's cycle.
- **Mercury (Hg) :** Used in anaerobic respiration experiments because it does not react with CO_2.
- **Oligomycin :** Inhibits oxidative phosphorylation *i.e.*, energy transfer inhibitor.
- **Meldrum :** Wrote book **"Cellular Respiration"**.
- **Glyoxylate cycle :** Takes place in seeds that contains tissues rich in fat and enable stored fat to be converted into carbohydrates. Enzymes for the cycle are present in glyoxysomes.
- Cyanide resistant respiration is characteristic of plants and very useful for **climacteric action** *(i.e.,* helpful in fruit ripening.)
- **Red or dark muscles :** Store myoglobin and hence oxygen for meeting the gap between supply and consumption during continuous activity.
- **White or pale muscles :** Do not store much myoglobin.
- **Lactic acid fermentation :** In muscles, pyruvic acid is reduced by NADH to form lactic acid which is catalysed by enzyme lactic dehydrogenase. Net gain is 2 ATP molecules per glucose molecule.
- **Zymase :** Enzyme complex present in yeast which helps in fermentation (zymosis)
- Some of the energy liberated during respiration is wasted as heat.
- **Proton motive force :** Proton gradient + electric potential.
- **Dinitrophenol (DNP) :** Inhibits ATP synthesis *i.e.*, uncoupling of oxidative phosphorylation.
- Mammalian RBCs are usually without mitochondria, so these show glycolytic pathway.
- **Cardiac muscles :** Fatigueless because have enzyme which can convert lactic acid into pyruvic acid to bel used in aerobic respiraton.
- **Robinson's ester :** Glucose - 6 - P.
- **Newber's ester :** Fructose- 6 - P.
- **Harden and Young ester :** Fructose - I, 6-DiP.
- **Fermentation :** 2 types *i.e.*, **Homofermentative** (when only one end-product) and **Heterofermentive** (when two or more than two types of end-products).
- **Kostychev (1902) :** gave term anaerobic respiration.
- Respiration is regulated by : Regulatory enzymes of cell respiration (phospho fructokinase) ; inhibited by ATP build up. while activated by excess of ADP ; Allosteric inhibition or negative feed back by

accumulation of $NADH_2$ and decreased in dark and by high sugar solution (osmotic effect).

- Cut surfaces of apple becomes dark as tannins are oxidised to polyphenols in the presence of iron of knife. which is prevented by ascorbic acid (vitamin C) as it acts as anti-oxidant.
- In bacteria, mesosomes are sites of ATP synthesis.

SENSORY PHOTOBIOLOGY

INTRODUCTION

- **Plant growth** : A vital process which brings about a slow, permanent and irreversible increase in size or volume or mass accompanied by an increase in dry weight.
- **Development** : A process in which there is sequence of qualitative changes, towards a higher or more complex state. Plants exhibit a regular sequence of seed germination, growth, differentiation, maturation, seed formation and senescence.
- The growth of a multicellular organism can be divided into 3 phases *i.e.,* cell division, cell expansion and cell differentiation.

DORMANCY AND SEED GERMINATION

- Internal inhibition of germination of an otherwise viable seed even when it is placed in most favourable external conditions is called as **dormancy.**
- The suspension of growth of a viable seed may be due to exogenous control such as a change in environmental conditions and is called as **quiescence.**
- **Dormancy of seed** may be due to : Tough seed coats (*e.g., Capsella, Lepidium*), rudimentary embryos (*Eranthis hiemalis*), impermeable seed coat (*Chenopodium, Brassica, Xanthium*), mechanically resistant seed coats, excess salts (*Atriplex*), after ripening (Oat, Barley, Wheat/and even by the presence of germination inhibitors *e.g.,* abscisic acid, phenolic acids, short-chain fatty acids and coumarin).
- **Natural breaking of seed dormancy** : Leaching of inhibitors and salts ; development and after-ripening of embryo ; development of growth hormones ; destruction of inhibitors by heat, cold, light and oxidation ; weakening of impermeable and tough seed coats by mechanical abrasions, microbial activity and digestive eyzymes of the alimentary canal of animals.
- **Artificial breaking of seed dormancy** : By mechanical scarification (machine threshing, chipping or filing), chemical scarification (hot water, fat solvents, mineral acid etc.), vigrous shaking, pressure (about 2000 kg for 5-20 min), chilling treatment, light (red light breaks domancy and induces seed germination in Lettuce and Tobacco), counter acting inhibitors (soaking seeds in KNO_3, thiourea, ethylene chlorohydrin, gibberellin etc.).
- **Seed germination** : This is the first step towards plant growth. After seed dormancy and necessary conditions for growth are present, the dormant embryo resumes metabolic activities and growth. This process is called **seed germination.**
- **Water, oxygen and temperature** are the essential condition for seed germination. **Red region** of visible spectrum is most effective for the onset of seed germination.
- **Internal factors** for seed germination are completion of after-ripening, completion of seed-dormancy, maturity of embryo, presence of sufficient food and viability.
- **Vivipary** : Phenomenon of producing young ones in advanced state of development. Seed germinate inside the fruit, while still attached to the parent plant. It is found in mangrove plants *e.g., Rhizophora, Sonneratia* and *Heritiera*, such plants grow in marshy land. The seedling of such plant is heavy and falls down into salt rich marshy water with plumule remaining outside.

CHARACTERISTICS OF GROWTH

- **Primary growth** : Formation of primary permanent tissues and organs which is caused by activity of apical and intercalary meristems.
- **Secondary growth** : Initiated by cambium, which are essentially lateral meristem (vascular cambium and cork cambium) *i.e.,* increase in girth.

- **Limited growth** : Growth which stops after some time *e.g.*; leaves, flowers, fruits.
- **Unlimited growth** : Growth that continues throughout life as in case of root and stem.
- **Efficiency index** : is the rate of growth which can be measured by an increase in size or area of an organ of the plant, like leaf, flower and fruit in a unit time.
- The supply of nutrients, water, oxygen, suitable temperature and light are necessary for proper growth.
- The force of gravity and light determines the direction of root and shoot growth.
- Salt, mineral deficiencies and stress factors also influence the rate of growth.

PHASES OF GROWTH

- In plants, the growth in length is due to enlargement and elongation of cells at the apical regions and in thickness due to the activity of lateral and intercalary meristems.
- In unicellular organisms growth consists of a single step while in higher plants, growth involves three steps or phases *i.e.*, **phase of cell division** (formative phase), **phase of cell enlargement** (elongation phase) and **phase of cell maturation** (maturation phase). The phases are also known as **regions.**
- **Grand period of growth** : time internal from the formative phase to maturation phase.
- **Growth curve** : The mathematical curve which represents the variation in growth rate, it is somewhat flattened S-shaped curve (sigmoid growth curve). It is differentiated into three phases :

  (A) Lag phase (slow phase)

  (B) Logphase (exponential phase)

  (C) Stationary phase (steady state)

MEASUREMENT OF GROWTH

- **Horizontal microscope** : Used to measure growth in length of a potted plant and herb/seedling.
- **Auxanometer** : Devised to measure the growth in length of a plant.
- Growth in plants can be measured in terms of
  - (*i*) Increase in the length of girth (in case of stem and root).
  - (*ii*) Increase in fresh or dry weight.
  - (*iii*) Increase in area or volume (in case of fruits and leaves) or
  - (*iv*) Increase in number of cells produced.
- **Growth regulators** : In all plant, minute quantities of some chemical substances (plant growth regulators or phytohormones) are present which regulate growth and differentiation. These are organic compounds and are capable of influencing physiological activities leading to promotion, inhibition and modification of growth.

Major types of Growth substances

1. Auxins : related to cell enlargement and differentiation.
2. Gibberellins : related to cell enlargement and differentiation.
3. Cytokinins : related to cell division.
4. Ethylene : related with senescence.
5. Abscisic acid : related to resting states like lateral buds.

Other related growth regulators are Jasmenic acid, Salicylic acid and Brassinosteroids.

PLANT HORMONES

AUXIN

- Weak organic acids with the acidic group.
- Indole-3-acetic acid (IAA) and other natural or synthetic growth regulating substances having structures and functions similar to IAA are called **auxins.**
- **First plant growth hormone** to be discovered.
- First indication of their existence came from the work of **Darwin** (1880).
- **F.W. Went** (1928) proved that the coleoptile tips contained a substance **auxin** and found that the degree of curvature of coleoptile is proportional to the amount of active substance in the agar blocks. This test is known as **avena curvature test.**

- Maximum concentration of auxins are found in the growing tips of the plant. From tip, it is transported **towards the base.**
- Same concentration of auxin exhibit different responses in different parts of the plant.

Functions

Cell elongation (stimulate the cell walls to stretch in more than one directions) ; **cell division** (in the vascular cambium that results in secondary growth) ; **phototropism ; geotropism** (high concentrations of auxins are stimulatory for stem *i.e.*, negatively geotropic, on the other hand, higher concentrations of auxins are inhibitory for roots *i.e.*, positively geotropic) ; **apical dominance** (auxins in apical bud inhibit the development of lateral buds) ; **prevention of abscission layer** (leaves and fruits have to produce auxin continuously to prevent the formation of abscission layer) and **root initiation** (very low concentration of auxins promote the growth of root).

Uses of Some Synthetic Auxins

Type of Auxin	Examples	Uses
Indoles and Napthyls	NAA (Naphthalene acetic acid)	1. Flower initiation in litchi and pineapple 2. Root initiation in cuttings. 3. Help in natural fruit setting. 4. Methyl ester of NAA is used to prevent sprouting of potatoes.
	IBA (Indole butyric acid)	1. Induces rooting of cuttings.
	IPA (Indole propionic acid)	1. Induces rooting of cuttings. 2. Help in natural fruit setting.
Phenoxyacetic acids	2, 4–D (2, 4-dichlorophenoxyacetic acid)	1. Flower initiation in litchi and pineapple 2. Prevents fruit drop (abscission) 3. Selective weed killer *i.e.*, kills broad leaved plant (dicots) but does not affect mature monocots
Benzoic acids	2, 3, 6-trichlorobenzoic acid 2, 4, 6-trichlorobenzoic acid	Powerful weed killers

- Auxin treated plants have been found to develop fruits even in the absence of pollination and seeds.
- Auxins stimulate the activity of enzymes. They exhibit inhibitory effect on isoenzymes like peroxidase in tobacco.
- **Auxin precursors** : Compounds which can be converted into auxins.
- **Anti-auxins** : Compounds which inhibit the actions of auxins.
- **Free-auxins** : Auxins which can easily be extracted. Active form.
- **Bound-auxins** : Auxins which are hard to extract and need the use of organic solvents. Inactive in growth.
- **Auxin bioassays** : The *Avena* curvature test and root growth inhibition test are the bioassays for examining auxin activity.

GIBBERELLINS (GA)

- The discovery of gibberellin (GA) was based upon the observations made in Japan in early 1800s on the **bakane** or **foolish seedling disease of rice.**
- Widely distributed in nature particularly in angiosperms.
- Chemically, all GA are **terpenes** and weak acids.
- Found in abundance in young, expanding organs; being synthesised especially in embryos, young apical leaves, buds seeds and root tips.

Functions

Overcoming genetic dwarfism (help in stem elongation) ; **bolting (elongation of intermodes to floweing in hosette plants) and flowering** (*e.g.*, Cabbage) ; **breaking of dormancy and germination of seeds** (after imbibition of water, the embryo secretes gibberellin which diffuses to the aleurone layer, stimulating the synthesis of several enzymes including amylase, proteases, lipases) ; **breaking of bud dormancy ; control of flowering** (promote flowering in some long days plants even under short day conditions, **control of fruit growth; promoting growth** (in both stems and leaves) ; **overcoming vernalisation; stimulate maleness** (*e.g.*, cucurbits and *Cannabis*) ; **increases fruit yield** etc.

- Gibberellin bioassay is performed through **dwarf maize/pea test** and **cereal endosperm test.**
- **Yabuta** (1935) coined the term gibberellin.
- About 100 different types of gibberellins have been isolated. They are denoted as GA_1, GA_2, GA_3 and so on.
- Antigibberellins like **maleic hydrazide, phosphon D** and **chorocholins chloride** (CCC) are also called **antiretardants.**

CYTOKININS

- **Skoog** (1954 – 1956) found that coconut milk contained a substance which stimulated cell division in **tobacco pith cultures.**
- Miller and his colleagues isolated and purified the substance in crystalline form from **herring sperm DNA.** This substance was identified as **6-furfuryl aminopurine.** They named this compound **kinetin** because of its property to activate cell division (cytokinesis).
- First naturally occurring cytokinin to be chemically identified was from young maize (*Zea mays*) grains in 1963, and was called **zeatin.**
- Cytokinins are quite abundant wherever rapid cell division occurs, especially in growing tissues such as embryos, developing fruits and roots. In mature plants, these are frequently synthesized in the **roots** and move to the shoots through xylem.
- **Functions : Cell division and differentiation** (in the presence of auxins, cytokinin promote cell division even in non-meristematic tissues) ; **control of apical dominance** (cytokinin stimulate the growth of lateral buds) ; **delaying senescence** (by controlling protein synthesis and mobilisation of resources) ; **induce flowering ; breaking the dormancy of seeds** and **initiation of interfascicular cambium.**
- The common bioassays for cytokinins include promotion of cell division in tobacco pith culture, expansion of excised radish cotyledons, delay in senescence etc.

ETHYLENE

- Crocker *et. al.* (1935) identified ethylene as natural plant hormone.
- Ethylene is formed from amino acid **methionine.**
- **Auxin IAA** is known to stimulate ethylene formation.
- **Only gaseous** natural plant growth regulator.
- It does not generally move through the air spaces in the plants. Rather, it escapes from the plants surface.

Functions

Apical dominance (in pea seedlings and suppresses the growth of apical buds) ; **stem swelling** (transverse expansion of stem) ; **leaf abscission** (formation of abscission zone is leaves, flowers and fruits) ; **epinasty** (leaf bending) ; **fruit growth and ripening** (a rise in the rate of respiration) ; **accelerates flowering ; sex expression** (increases the number of female flowers and fruits in cucumber plants) and **graviperception** (reduces sensitivity to gravity, seeddlings develop tight epicotyl hook).

- Commercial compound **"Ethaphone** (2-chloroethyl phosphoric acid) breaks down to release ethylene in plants.

ABSCISIC ACID (ABA)

- Fredericle Addicott (1963) and P.F. Wareing (1964) discovered this hormone.
- Liu and Crans (1961) isolated ABA from mature cotton fruit.

- It is slso called stress hormone or dormin because the production of hormone is stimulated by drought, water logging and other adverse environmental condition.
- Chemically, ABA is a **Terpenoid**.
- ABA synthesized in the leaves, stems, fruits and seeds and distributed through the vascular system especially phloem.
- Isolated chloroplasts can synthesize it either from mevalonic acid or xanthophyll like violoxanthin.

Functions

Growth inhibitor (antagonistic to all the three growth promoters) ; **bud dormancy** (by inhibiting growth processes) ; **senescence** (of leaves) ; **abscission** (of leaves, flowers and fruits in plants) ; **stomatal closure** ; **hardiness** (promotes cold hardiness and inhibits growth of pathogens) ; **promotes flowering** (in some short day plants) etc.

- It is a **stress hormone** *i.e.*, helps the plants to cope with adverse environmental conditions.
- ABA is sprayed on tree crops to regulate fruit drop at the end of the season.

VITAMINS

- Heterogenous group of organic compounds, needed in very small quantities for different metabolic processes.
- Plant store the vitamins in different plant organs.
- Most of the vitamins function as coenzymes and prosthetic groups of various enzymes connected with protein, fat and carbohydrate metabolism.
- Some important examples of vitamins are : vitamins A, B, C, D, E and K.
- Some vitamins are essential in maintaining cell membranes and acting as antioxidants.

PHOTOPERIODISM

- The response of plants to the relative lengths and alternations of light and dark periods with regard to the initiation of flowering is called photoperiodism.
- The effect of photoperiods on flowering was discovered by **Garner** and **Allard** (1920) in case of Maryland Mammoth variety of Tobacco (an SDP).
- On the basis of length of photoperoid requirements of plants, the plants have been classified into :

  (A) **Short-day plants (SDP)** : Plants requiring light for a shorter period than their critical period *e.g., Xanthium, Glycine max*, Rice, Potato, Tobacco etc.

  (B) **Long-day plants (LDP)** : Plants requiring longer exposure to light than their critical period *e.g,* Lettuce, Radish, Sugarbeet, Oat, Wheat etc.

  (C) **Day-neutral or intermediate day plants (DNP)** : Plants which would flower irrespective of the photoperiod, once they are mature *e.g.,* Cucumber, Tomato, Maize, Cotton etc.

  (C) **Short-long day plants (SLDP)** : Plants requiring first short days and then long days *e.g., Trifolium repens, Campanula medium* etc.

  (E) **Long-short day plants (LSDP)** : Long photoperiods for initiation of flowering and short photoperiods for blossoming *e.g., Bryophyllum, Cestrum* etc.

- **Critical dark period** : It is actually the length of dark period which is critical.
- **Critical day length** : Continuous duration of light which must always be exceeded in long day plants and must not be exceeded in short-day plants.
- **Short-night plants (SNP)** : Long day plants do not require any continuous dark period.
- **Long-night plants (LNP)** : Short-day plants and any interruption of critical dark period even by a flash of light prevents flowering. The reaction is called **light break reaction.**
- **Photoperiodic induction** : Phenomenon of perceiving approriate light periods and obtaining the stimulus of flowering.

- **Flowering hormone** : Chailakhyan (1937) proposed the view that flower hormone namely **florigen** in synthesized in the leaves under favourable photoperiodic conditions. This hormone is transmitted to the growing point where the flowering takes place.

VERNALIZATION

- Term **Vernalization** was coined by **Lysenko** (1928) to refer to the method of accelerating the flowering ability of biennials or winter annuals, by exposing their soaked seeds to low temperature for a few weeks.
- The various requirements of vernalization are:
  (*i*) Actively dividing cells
  (*ii*) Proper nourishment
  (*iii*) Proper hydration
  (*iv*) Continuous low temperature for a few days
  (*v*) Aerobic respiration.
- The site of vernalization is believed to be **shoot apical meristem.**
- Vernalisation effect is reversible and the reverse process is called **devernalization.**
- The vernalisation stimulus can be transmitted between plants by grafting hence the stimulus is believed to be a hormone called **vernalin.**
- **A. Lang** discovered that during vernalization, the levels of gibberellins increase and also that the application of gibberellins to unvernalised plants can substitute for vernalization.

SENESCENCE

- The sum of deteriorative processes which naturally terminate that functional life of an organism.
- Ageing is a sum total of changes in the total plant or its constituents while senescence represents degenerative and irreversible changes in a plant.
- Senescence may be **whole plant senescence** (*e.g.*, monocarpic plants) ; **shoot senescence** (some perrennials *e.g.*, banana, gladiolus) ; **sequential** or **progressive senescence** (perrennials *e.g.*, mango, *Eucalyptus*) and **simultaneous** or **synchronous leaf senescence** (perrennial polycarpic deciduous plants *e.g.*, maple, elm, poplar etc.).
- Senescense can be delayed by removing flowers from the plants.

ABSCISSION

- Shedding of leaves, foliage branches, floral parts, fruits etc. without causing any injury is called abscission.
- It generally occurs due to change in the hormonal balance.
- Abscission zone is usually located at the base of petiole which is made up of two distinct layers *i.e.*,
  (*i*) The **abscission** (or separation) **layer** where breakdown of cells takes place and
  (*ii*) **The protective layer,** which develops next to abscission layer to protect the exposed surface.
- Abscisic acid is known to play an important role in abscission.

PLANT MOVEMENT

- Plant movement is change in position and these are not as much apparent as in case of animals.

SOME IMPORTANT FACTS

- **Hitchcock** and **Zimmerman** exhibited that flowering in *Nicotiana* can be enhanced by auxins.
- **Auxins** are synthesised mainly in apices and exhibit **polar transport.**
- **Crescograph** : Used for recording plant growth in seconds.
- Plants having **deliquescent** stem **have poor apical dominance** while plants having **excurrent** habit (palms, conifers, polyalthia) have **greater apical dominance.**
- **IPA** (Isopentenyl adenine) : Most widely occurrinng cytokinin, isolated from *Pseudomonas tumefaciens.*
- **IAA** : Promotes the liberation of a water soluble **xyloglucan** from the cell wall.
- **Mowing of grass** : removes apical bud,

Plant Movements

Vital
(Shown by living cells)
Movements of locomotion
(movements in whole plant body cell or cytoplasm

(A) Autonomic
(not induced by external stimuli)

1. **Ciliary/ flagellar movement**
e.g. *Chlamydomonas. Paramecium, Volvox,* zoospores etc.
2. **Amoeboid movements**
e.g., Protistans, slime molds etc.
3. **Cyclosis movements**
e.g., leaf calls of Hydrilla, staminal hair of Tradescantia, chara, moss etc

(B) Paratonic (Tactic)
(induced by external stimuli)

1. **Phototactic**
(in response to direction and intensity of light)
e.g., zoospores of algae
2. **Chemotactic**
(in response to chemical)
e.g., antherozoids.
3. **Thermotactic**
(in response to temperature)
e.g., *Chlamydomonas*

Hygroscopic
(Shown by dead plant parts)
Movements of curvature
(bending in some plant parts)

(A) Autonomic
- **Variation movement**
(temporary bending)
e.g., Telegraph plant
- **Paratonic movement** of curvature

(B) Paratonic
- **Growth movement**
(permanent bending)

1. **Hyponastic**
(greater growth on abaxial side) *e.g.*, closing of Cycas and ferns.
2. **Epinastic**
(greater growth on adaxia side)*e.g.*, opening of flowers, fem leaves when mature
3. **Nutation**
(autonomic side ways movements of shot apex and tendril) *e.g.*, trailers and creepers
4. **Circumnutation**
(spiral movement or bending in all direction)
e.g., stem tips of twiners.

Tropic
Growth movements
(due to differential growth)

1. **Geotropic** (in response to gravity stimulus)
(a) Positive geotropism (roots)
(b) Negative geotropism (stem)
(c) Diageotropic (rhizomes of certain grasses)
(d) Plageotropic (leaves, lateral shoots etc.)
(e) Ageotropic
2. Phototropic (in response to external unilateral light)
(a) Positively phototropic (stem tips)
(b) Negatively phototropic (roots)
3. **Thigmotropic** (in response to touch) *e.g.*, tendrils in the members of family cucurbitaceae
4. **Hydrotropic** (in response to water)
e.g., roots are positively hydrotropic
5. **Chemotropic** (in response to chemicals)
e.g., fungal hyphae and movement of pollen tube
6. **Thermotropic** (in response to temperature)
e.g., seedlings curve towards warm side.

Nastic
Variation movement
(due to turgor changes, not necessarily directed towards or away from stimulus)

1. **Photonastic** (due to changes in intensity of light)
e.g., Flowers of Oxalis open in morning and close at night
2. **Nyctinastic** (due to alternation of day and night)
e.g., flowers of *Gerbera. Portulaca*
3. **Thermonastic** (due to variation in temperature)
e.g., flowers of *Oxalis* open quickly when temperature rises
4. **Seismonastic** (due to mechanical stimuli *e.g.*, touch etc.)
e.g., *Mimosa pudica* (sensitive plant, touch me- not).

stimulates axillary buds and intercalary meristem.

- **Double sigmoid curve** : Growth curve present in some fruits *e.g.*, Grape, Plum etc.
- **Agent orange** : A mixture of 2, 4-D and 2, 4, 5-T (Trichlorophenoxyacetic acid) was used in Vietnam war by U.S. to defoliate the forests under the name 'Agent orange'.
- **HDT** : Hormone directed transport. It is believed that cytokinin promotes movement of nutrients towards apical bud. So, lateral buds do not sprout near it.
- **Morphactins** (Zeigler, 1970) : Synthetic growth regulator having a skeleton of 9-hydroxy-fluorine 9-carboxylic acid. It reduce cell division, shorten internodes, cause

dwarfism, inhibit seed germination and seedling growth, overcome apical dominance, break bud dormancy, reduce leaf growth and curvature movements, stimulate growth of primary root but inhibit growth of lateral roots. They affect flowering, fruiting and sex expression.

- **Ephemeral movements** : Once in life *e.g.*, expansion of leaf.
- **Clinostat/Klinostat** : Instrument which can eliminate the effect of gravity and allow a plant to grow horizontaly by slowly rotating it.
- **Perceptive region** : The area of perception of stimulus.
- **Responsive region** : The area of response.
- **Presentation time** : The minimum time required for a stimulus to become effective.
- **Reaction time** : The period required for a stimulus to exhibit response.
- **Relaxation time** : Time required for the effect of a response to disappear.
- **Weber-Fechner law :**
  (*i*) Within limits, the equal relative differences between two stimuli of the same type are equally perceptible.
  (*ii*) There is a tendency of the intensity of sensation to vary as logarithm of the stimulus.
- **Richmond-Lang effect** : Cytokinin prevent chlorophyll degradation, hence ageing.
- **Sleep disease** (in rolling of petals in opened flowers) is caused by ethylene. Even 1 ppm of ethylene prevents the opening of flower buds.
- **Tromatropism** : Movement induced by injury.
- **Photomorphogenesis** : The control of development of form (*i.e.*, morphogenesis) by light.
- **Phytochrome** : Proteinaceous pigment. The sensitivity of seeds to the effect of red and far-red wavelengths of light is due to the presence of phytochrome. It is a regulatory pigment which regulates several light-dependent developmental processes in plants.
- **ABA** : Inducing synthesis of carotenoids and turns green organges into yellow.
- **Automatic or Pfeffer's auxanometer** : Register total growth, rate of growth at specific time and overall pattern of growth. An improved auxanometer over the arc auxanometer.
- **Phenology** : The different aspects or appearences of plants in different seasons of a year.
- **IAA destruction** : Takes place due to photo-oxidation by blue light and dark oxidation by IAA oxidase.
- **IAA-aspartic acid, IBA-alanine** : More effective in bound state.
- **Human Urine** : Also natural source of auxins.
- **DCMU** (Dichlorophenyl dimethyl urea) : Strong inhibitor of photosystem II.
- **Impaction** : Treatment given to seeds when they are shaken vigorously.
- **Antiauxins** : Compounds which compete with the auxins for the reactive site *e.g.*, TIBA, 4-chlorophenoxy isobutyric acid, 2, 6-dichlorophenoxy acetic acid, 2, 4-dichloroanisole.
- *Gibberella fujikuroi* : A fungus, causes **"Foolish seedling"** disease in rice plant in Japan. Gibberellin (a growth hormone) was first extracted from this fungus.

QUESTIONS FROM PREVIOUS YEARS' PAPERS

1. Write short notes on Cyclic photophosphorylation.
2. Write a short note on Krebs' cycle or citric acid cycle.
3. What is meant by Plant Succession? Discuss the phenomenon in relation to a drying pond giving different successional stages.
4. Discuss photoperiodism and flowering.
5. Write short notes on the following:
   (*a*) Colchicine and EMS.
   (*b*) β-oxidation.
6. Distinguish between growth movements and stomatal movements.
7. Classify and characterise phytohormones.

8. Explain Biogeochemical Cycles. Describe the hydrological cycle in detail.

9. Write short notes on the following:
(*a*) Growth regulators
(*b*) Photoperiodism
(*c*) Controlled storage of seeds

10. What is mineral deficiency?

11. What are the deficiency symptoms of the following minerals:
(*a*) Nitrogen (*b*) Zinc
(*c*) Calcium (*d*) Iron

12. Discuss the mechanism of nitrogen fixation by the leguminous plants. How the nitrogen fixation is measured?

13. Write short notes on:
(*a*) MPF (*b*) Coenzymes
(*c*) Fermentation (*d*) Vernalization

14. Describe the importance of studying stress physiology of plants growing under adverse conditions.

15. Describe the molecular basis of fruit ripening. How has our understanding of this process helped in fruit marketing.

16. Write short notes on:
(*a*) Water potential (*b*) Senescence
(*c*) Endemism (*d*) Acid rain
(*e*) Testing for seed viability

17. Explain C_4 photosynthetic carbon pathway.

18. Explain the biochemical changes that occur in photysystem I and photosystem II of photosynthesis.

19. What are Auxins? Explain the physiological effects of Auxins.

20. Explain the uses of plant growth substances in Agriculture and Horticulture.

21. Write short notes on:
(*a*) CAM Pathway (*b*) Phytochrome
(*c*) Gibberellins

22. Explain the molecular basis of fruit ripening and show how fruit ripening is manipulated.

23. Explain the physiology of nitrogen metabolism.

24. Explain the mechanism of photorespiration in plants.

25. Describe the biochemical process by which two molecules of ATP are produced from one molecule of glucose. Mention the names of the participating enzymes.

26. Discuss the role of mitochondrion for pyruvic acid oxidation.

27. What are the physiological changes associated with plant senescence? Add a note on senescence-retarding hormones.

28. Enumerate the ethylene-induced responses in plants. What are the commercial uses of ethylene?

29. Write short notes on:
(*a*) Antitranspirants
(*b*) Chemiosmotic theory
(*c*) Plant succession
(*d*) Photorespiration
(*e*) Photophosphorylation

30. Trace the path of carbon in C_3 plants during photosynthesis.

31. Explain how Hatch and Slack pathway in C_4 plants in integrated with Calvin cycle.

32. Discuss various physiological changes occurring in plants due to water stress.

33. Examine the role of plant growth hormones in floral induction.

34. Illustrate different pathways in fixation of dinitrogen by microorganisms.

35. Describe step-wise various reactions involved in the process of photosynthesis.

CHAPTER–5

ECOLOGY AND PLANT GEOGRAPHY

Ecological Factors : Ecology is the study of plants in reciprocal relationship with their environment. The two aspects of ecology are :

(*i*) Autoecology : Ecology of individuals.

(*ii*) Synecology : It is the study of interaction between all the living organisms in a natural community.

Ecosystem : It is a system of interacting organisms and non-living substances. Ecosystem may be large or small, complex or simple.

The common ecological factors are

(A) Physical Factors

(B) Chemical Factors.

(A) *Physical Factors :* They include temperature, light, wind, gravity, soil conditions, pressure and presence or absence of natural barriers. Most organisms have an optimum temperature for their living and minimum and maximum temperature beyond which they cannot survive.

Adaptations such as aestivation, hibernation and diapause help the organisms to overcome adverse temperatures. Light also plays a major role in life of plants and animals. The organisms active during the day are **diurnal** and those active in the night are **nocturnal**.

Wind, rather the velocity and direction of wind affects the usual course of animals.

(B) *Chemical Factors :* They include quality of soil and water, oxygen, carbon dioxide, obnoxious gases and the quality and quantity of usuable foods.

Limiting Factors and their Operation

Limiting factors are often classified in two categories : (a) Density Dependent and (b) Density Independent.

The effect of the former on a population increases as the population increases in density. It is essentially a stabilizing influence on growth and causes a population to level off at carrying capacity. A density-independent factor, coversely, affects many or few individuals without reference to the population level.

Food supply is generally density dependent. The more there are to eat it, the less there is for each individual and the greater the effect of food scarcity. By contrast, a flood is density independent, since it may wipe out an entire population of a species, whether there are few or many. The more important limiting factors are as follows :

(*a*) Climatic and Atmospheric Factors : These operate in a variety of ways to affect species populations. To begin with, any species has limits of tolerance and some optimum range of tolerance for such factors as sunlight, temperature, humidity, rainfall or wind. If a food climate normally exceeds the limits of tolerance for a species, then the species will not occur in that area, if it exceeds the optimum limits, the species will not thrive there. If the local climate only rarely exceeds the limits of tolerance, then a species may temporarily occupy that area, but will be eliminated in those years when the climate becomes extreme.

Assuming that the climate is favourable to the establishment of a species, then a number of climatic factors may influence population growth. Changes in temperature—years that are warmer or colder than normal—may permit a species to thrive and increase, or they may cause a decrease and permit its survival only in the most favourable sites. Changes in rainfall and humidity, dry years (or cycles) and wet years (or cycles), have major effects. Fluctuations in temperature and rainfall tend to be most severe in areas where temperature or moisture is already near the limits of lowlands where rainfall and temperature are high and near the optimum for the growth of the greatest fluctuation in either factor. In the dry tropics fluctuations in rainfall from year to year may be extreme. In northern temperate regions where winter is cold and the duration of low temperatures restrict the growing season for plants, one finds the greatest variation between temperatures in one year and another.

Climatic and atmospheric factors tend to have their most severe effects upon those introduced populations of plants and animals which man attempts to grow or produce in areas that have climate more extreme than the optimal climate for the species concerned. Native species are adapted to the range of climate in the area they occupy, and although they may be affected by climatic extremes, these effects are usually much less limiting than for a domesticated species introduced outside its normal climatic range. In the African savannas, a drought will be more likely to wipe out a high percentage of the cattle than of the native antelopes. Climatic and atmospheric factors also have more effect of species that are at. or approaching, the level of subsistence density. Well-situated animals or plants, with adequate nutrients, water and other essentials are less likely to be affected by drought than populations which have increased and expanded into marginal areas and are already in poor condition because of nutritional limitations. Certain factors of weather and climate may have catastrophic effects on all populations in an area-hurricanes, torandoes, unusually severe floods or droughts, but usually there are less significant than the more normally occurring changes, except in the case of those species which are highly limited in distribution. With most species, normal fluctuations in climate have their greatest effect when animal population densities are excessive, or when plants are established in sub-optimum environments.

(*i*) **Temperature :**

Stenothermal : Organisms living at nearly constant temperature cannot tolerate variations.

Eurythermal : Organisms which can tolerate wide variations in temperature.

Megatherm : Living at high temperature.

Mesotherm : High summer temperature and low winter temperature.

Microtherm : Moderate warmth in summer, low temperature in winter.

Hekistotherm : Living with brief summer below 10°C and winter prolonged with very low temperature.

Temperature ranges have created different life zones—tropical, subtropical, temperate, arctic/alpine.

Poikilothermal (= Ectothermal = Cold Blooded). Temperature varies with the surroundings.

Homoisothermal : (= Endothermal, Warm Blooded) : Temperature constant due to internal regulation. Excessive subcutaneous fat (blubber) protects whale, seal and polar bear from low temperature. Shivering is a mechanism to increase body temperature. 'Persipration' and 'panthing' reduce body temperature.

Hibernation (= Winter Sleep), aestivation (= Summer Sleep), periodic activity and winter/summer eggs/seeds are adaptations of poikilothermics to avoid unfavourable temperatures. Thick cuticle, corky bark, hair, thick leaves, high solute content, mucilage and tannins are protective mechanisms in plants to tolerate high (55°-73°C) or low (– 20° to – 35°C) temperatures. Generally seeds, spores and cysts tolerate temperature extremes better due to low water content and thick covering.

Thermoperiodicity controls phenology in several cases.

● **Bergmann's Rule** states that avian and mammalian forms are generally of larger size in colder regions as compared to warmer/hotter regions.

(*ii*) **Light :** It controls photosynthesis, tissue differentiation, growth, pigmentation, plant movements, period of activity, reproduction in plants and animals. Depending upon the period of activity, animals are *diurnal* (active during day, e.g. Sparrow, Pigeon, Butterfly), *nocturnal* (active and dusk) and *crepuscular* (active at dawn/dusk, e.g. Rabbit) Depending upon period of breeding, animals and plants are called long day (e.g. Turkey, Ferret, Radish), shortday (e.g. Sheep, Deer, Xantheium, Dahlia) or day neutral (e.g. Guinea Pis, Tomato).

(*iii*) **Wind :** (Air Current). It determines cloud formation, pollination and dispersal in many organisms. Wind restricts flight animals, nest formation and height in plants. It enhances soil erosion, transpiration and develops flag trees.

(*iv*) **Humidy/Precipitation :** *Epiphytes* can be found only in humid areas. Arid areas do not have them. Transpiration in inversely proportional to atmospheric humidity. Low atmospheric humidity produces aridity and xerophytism. Periodicity and amount of precipitation determine type of vegetation—evergreen, deciduous, chapparal, savannah, grassland, desert etc.

(*b*) **Soils :** Here the limiting factors operate directly on plants, and through plants, upon animal populations (other than those of the soil fauna itself, which is often directly limited by soil conditions). The requirements of plants and animals, however, are not identical.

An abundant growth of vegetation does not necessarily mean there will be an abundant food supply for animals, nor that the food supply will have high nutritional value. Certain plants may produce abundant vegetative growth and high amounts of carbohydrates under conditions where certain soil chemicals are in short supply, however, they may produce relatively small amounts of the proteins and vitamins needed to support an abundance of animal life. Thus, a shortage of a trace elements, such as cobalt, in the soil may have little effect on plant growth. However, cattle feeding on there plants may do poorly or do not survive. Addition of a cobalt top-dressing to the soil, which is then taken up by the plants can open up a rangeland to livestock use. For another example, a dense forest may produce an abundance of vegetation, but will support very few ground-dwelling grazing or browsing animals. There is no lack of food for them, but plants growing on a forest floor under dense tree cover are commonly lacking in protein.

Animals grazing of browsing them can receive adequate carbohydrates but not enough protein to thrive or reproduce. Thus, in many areas of dense forest, grazing and browsing animals will only be common around natural or man-made clearings.

The abundance of natural vegetation in an area often has little relation to the inharent fertility of a soil. Thus, the *ferasols* and *acrisols* of the humid tropics are notoriously infertile, yet they support the most luxuriant vegetation to be found on earth. Examination of this situation reveals, however, that virtually all the nutritional elements required for the support of life are tied up in the vegetation and animal life of the area, and recirculate quickly from the dead plant or animal back into a new, living individual. Below the organic surface layer the soil contains few of the elements needed for plant or animal nutrition, and if the vegetation is scraped away with a bulldozer, the soil that remains is often highly infertile. By contrast, some desert soil that support little plant life, because of lack of water, may have a rich supply of soluble mineral elements needed for the support of life. When water can be made available, they will support high levels of productivity, although there may be new ill effects such as salinization, water logging and water borne diseases.

(*c*) **Water :** Water is an obvious limiting factor for plants and animals. Plants are classified in relation to their tolerance for dry medium or wet conditions as *xerophytes, mesophytes* and *hydrophytes*. Most land plants are in the intermediate, mesophytic range, desert plants are usually, but not always xerophytes, hydrophytes grown in water or require an abundance of water in the soil. All plants require water to support their active growth and metabolism. Some plants cannot tolerate even brief periods of moisture deficiency and that will wilt and die when the soil dries out.

Xerophytes have special adaptations that permit them to survive under prolonged drought, but must have some moisture in order to grows and reproduce.

Where present in abundance, water limits the occurrence of terrestrial organisms and provides a habitant for aquatic forms of life. The latter will relate in their diversity and abundance to the quality of the water, its ability of supply oxygen, its salinity, temperature, velocity and other factors. All of these are capable of being affected, usually adversely, by pollution or siltation.

In relation to terrestrial vegetation, an abundance of water or in the soil limits the plant growth primarily by restricting the availability of oxygen. Those plants growing in wet soil or flooded areas have the ability to derive oxygen through special structures, such as PENUMATOPHORES of mangrooves, or the so-called 'Knees' of balt cypresses are good examples. Continuously moist or flooded soils inhibit the bacterial fungal action that would otherwise bring about decay of organic debris and litter—Organic remains will usually accumulate on such soils in the form of organic mucks or peat. Animals, like plants, require moisture for their continued existence, but vary greatly in their ability to endure drought. Apart from purely aquatic animals, amphibious animals such as the crocodile and hippopotamus cannot long survive away from water. Most land animals must drink water regularly in order to continue to live. However, some desert species can exist indefinitely in the absence of free water as long as the food which is eaten contains sufficient moisture and they can find enough shelter to hold the loss of water from their body surfaces to a minimum. A severe drought, bringing an absolute shortage of water to an extensive area, can be fatal to all animals that require water for drinking. Nevertheless, much of the mortality attributed to drought results not from a shortage of water, but from a shortage of food within reach of water.

(*d*) **Biotic Factors :** The greatest number of limiting factors influencing plant or animal growth, abundance and distribution are biotic in nature.

Food supply for animals is one of these, and in the most common factor limiting the growth of animal populations, either directly, through being short of requirements, or indirectly, through behavioural responses to food shortage. The number of plant-eating animals in any area is ultimately limited by the abundance of the plants of which the animals feed. Furthermore, since the plants must survive and reproduce, there must always be a greater abundance of plants than what is actually needed to provide food to the animals. Most plants produce a surplus of vegetative growth and of seed, part of which can be used by animals. However, each plant, in order to survive, must maintain a metabolic reserve—a minimum amount of leaf age to permit it to store food for its own survival, or set seed for its own reproduction.

Plant growth may be limited by competition from other plants of the same or different species, each drawing on the same reserves of soil and water, or shading one another from essential sunlight. Some plants secrete substances which inhibit the growth or establishment of other plants. A variety of organisms may prey upon plants, from the seed stage through the life cycle to the mature plant. It is obvious that the number of carnivores or meat-eating animals in any area is limited by the availability of the prey upon which they feed. Also there must be enough prey animals to enable the prey species to survive and reproduce, the predator cannot eat all of prey, or both would become extinct. Most prey animals have developed behaviour patterns in relation to their habitat conditions that permit some of them to escape predators. Predators seek the most valnerable and available prey, and usually do not hunt down and capture the more elusive individuals. Often the individuals thus captures are either very young and very old or the most diseased or genetically least vigorous stock, therefore, natural predation tends to have overall beneficial effects on the population of a prey species.

The relationship of the abundance of predators and prey is sometimes illustrated in the form of a **biotic pyramid.** Green plants occupy the base of the pyramid and must always have a greater total volume (biomass) than the plant-eaters that feed upon them. The latter, the herbivores, form the second step be wider and represent a greater biomass than the third step, representing the carnivores that eat other carnivores they must be fewer in number and contain less biomass than their prey.

Each succeeding level in the biotic pyramid also represents a consistent loss of energy from green plants of herbivores to predators, since at each transfer of energy is necessarily lost. Far more calories are available at the lowest level of the pyramid than at any higher level.

The sequence of plants and animals feeding upon one another is called **'food chain'**. Food chains are interconnected, since more than one herbivore may feed on a plant and more than one kind of carnivore may eat a herbivore. These interconnected chains form a **'food web'**.

As elements pass from soil (or atmosphere) to plants, and are then eatern by herbivores and in turn by carnivores, they are often concentrated in varying degrees by a process known as **'biological magnification'**.

Thus, the element iodine may be present in the soil in small quantities and taken up by plants as it goes into solution and reaches plant roots. It has little direct function in plants, but is essential to plant eating mammals. They must obtain enough iodine from the plants they eat and concentrate it in their thyroid glands for there glands to function properly. Therefore, the level of iodine in an animal's thyroid is far greater, than in either the plants or the soil.

Although the number of herbivores is limited by the supply of plants, and the number carnivores is determined by the number of their prey, the reverse is also true in varying degrees. The abundance and distribution of plant can be limited by the presence of herbivores. If a plant is introduced into an area where there are no species that feed upon it, can spread rapidly and become transformed into a weed or pest. Similarily, the abundance and distribution of plant-eating insects and other animals is often controlled by a wide variety of diseases, insects or other predators that feed upon them. If the predators are destroyed, their plant eating prey can increase suddenly and explosively, since its reproductive rate in nature is adjusted to the need for survival under constant predation. Sudden increases in number of rodents or other plant-eating mammals have often been related to extermination of the predators that formerly held them in check.

Populations of many animals species are limited by the effects of interactions among individuals within a species. The species concerned are described as *territorial* and comprise a proportion of individuals which persistently or seasonally occupy a particular area to the exclusion of other individuals of the same species. Commonly, territorial animals will tolerate or encourage the presence of certain other members of their species a mate or mates, their juvenile offspring, and sometimes the members of a larger social group, a herd, troop, flock, or pack. However, they will drive off or otherwise exclude animals that do not belong to the tolerated category. Territorialism tends to limit the number of animals of any one species that occupy an area and to reserve for the territorial individual or group an adequate habitat and food supply, however, there are many kinds and degrees of territorial behaviour, and not all of them serve directly to limit population increase. Plants might also be considered to compete for 'territories' the well-established individual holds its ground against competitors. Their territorial defence mechanisms include the shading out of competitiors and the secretion of chemical which prevent rival from germinating or growing.

Numerous studies have now been made of the effect of overcrowding on a variety of animal species under condition where food supply is abundant, and all other essentials (except space) are present is adequate supply. All of these studies show adverse effect upon individuals in a population where numbers exceed a certain level. These adverse effects are caused by social interactions, and vary from mild behavioural disturbances to serious forms of beahvioural pathology, leading to increased mortality and a decline in birth rate.

(*e*) **Interaction of Factors :** Virtually all limiting factors interact and either reinforce or diminish their mutual effects. Thus, the effects of animal overcrowding may be seen in the limitations imposed by diminished food supply, increased predation, greater mortality from disease and various behavioural disturbances. Similarly among plants, factors of soil, water, air, nutrients, the presence or absence of intense sunlight, all interact to influence the germination or growth of a plant.

Simple solutions to biological problems are, therefore, seldom likely to produce permanent, positive results. Modifying the impact of one limiting factor may simply increase the operation of others. For example, in an area of scarce water supply, it may seem sensible to make additional water in order to permit animal populations to increase. Yet doing so has, in many observed instances, quickly led to major dies-offs from malnutrition resulting from an insufficient food-supply for the increased population. Similarly, destruction of predators may cause protected herbivores to die in an epidemic and the elimination of a disease may cause a crash die-off from starvation. It is, therefore, always necessary in management planning to look at the operation of the total ecosystem and consider how all the factors interact.

Failure to recognize these principles has caused many economic developments activities to fail and much money to be wasted.

Other abiotic components are pH, gases and minerals which determine the types of plants and animals found in an area.

Topography : Surface behaviour of earth determines environement including wind, rainfall, light and temperature.

Background : Most animals have the colour of their background—muddy in case of elephant and rhino, sandy in cammel and lion, green in praying mantis.

Concept and Dynamics of Community—Plant Succession

A community, or *biocenose*, is an aggregate of organisms which form a distinct ecological unit. Such a unit may be defined in terms of flora, fauna, or both. Community units may be very small like the community of invertebrates and fungi in a decaying log. The extent of a community is limited only by the requirement of a more or less uniform species composition.

A different community occurs in each different habitat and environmental unit of larger size, and in fact the composition and character of the community is an excellent indicator of the type of environment that is present. Since plants and animals, bacteria and fungi, all occur together in the same habitat and have many interrelations, they can scarcely be considered independently of each other. Together they make up the **biotic community.**

Communities may be distinguished as major or minor. Major communities are those which, together with their habitats, form more or less complete and self sustaining units or ecosystems, except for the indispensable input of solar energy. Minor communities, often called **societies**, are secondary aggregations within a major community and are not, therefore, completely independent units as far as circulation of energy is concerned.

The biotic community along with its habitat is called an ecosystem. The term "ecosystem" has been loosely applied to units of various sizes and characteristics but had best he limited to distinctive combinations of air, soil, water conditions with vegetative, animal and microbic life that possess functional unity. In short one can say that biotic community is a grouping of different but interacting populations of different species which live harmoniously in a given locality, e.g. pond community, lawn community may further be split into animal community, plant community and microbe community. Plants provide food, shelter and oxygen to animals. The latter provide CO_2, plough the soil, help in pollination and dispersal. Microbes take part in decomposition of dead bodies and release of minerals.

(A) Interactions : They may be neutral, positive or negative. Various kinds of interactions are as follows :

(*i*) *Scavenging :* Feeding on dead bodies. Animals feeding on flesh of dead animals are called 'scavengers' e.g. Vulture, Jackal, Hyena (eat left over from lion/tiger's kill), Crow (actually omnivorous) Ant (actually omnivorous). Scavenging keeps the earth clean.

(*ii*) *Commensalism :* One is benefitted without the other being harmed e.g. *E. coli* in human intestine and epiphytes perched on other plants for space only.

(*iii*) *Mutalism :* It is a mutually beneficial relationship/interaction between individuals of two different species.

Mutualism and symbiosis are synonyms though symbiosis was formerly considered to be any interaction between two different organisms. e.g. (*i*) Association between fungus (protection, fixation and absorption of water) and alga (food manufacture) in lichen. (*ii*) *Rhizobium* (nitrogen fixation) and root (shelter, food) in nodulated legumes etc.

(*iv*) *Protocooperation :* It is non-obligatory beneficial relationship that develops when two different organisms get associated. Cattle Egret feeds on lice and ticks of cattle.

(*v*) *Amensalism :* Without deriving much benefits, one inhibits the other by secreting allochemics, e.g. *Pencillium* on *staphylococus* (Flemming, 1928) by *Penicillin*. *Juglans* (walnut) on other nearby plants by *Juglone*, *Tagetes* on soil nematodes. *Chlorella vulgaris* against diatom *Nitzschia frustrulum*.

(*vi*) *Competition :* It is rivalry for obtaining the same resource. Intraspecific competition reduces the size of population. Interspecific competition causes one to be eliminated (*Gause hypothesis/principle of competitive exclusion*) or undergo different adaptations (e.g. 14 species of Finches in Galapagos

Islands or 20 species of Antelopes in Serngeti plains, roots of different depths).

(*vii*) *Mimicry :* Mimicry is the resembling to another organism, structure or surroundings (camoulflage).

(*a*) *Protective :* Concealing type provides protection from predators, e.g. Stick Insect, Leaf Insect, Dead leaf Butterfly. In warming type, the mimic resembles a ferocious/poisonous/distasteful organism, e.g. Vicerory Butterfly mimics Monarch Butterfly.

(*b*) *Aggressive :* In *concealing type*, a predator resembles the surroundings, e.g. *Praying Mantis.* In *alluring type*, the predator has resemblance with a favoured article, e.g. mouth of African Lizard resembles a flower. Flower of *Ophyrs* resemble female wasp (Colpa) and are pollinated by male wasp.

(*vii*) *Parasitism :* One organism called parasite obtains nourishment from another organism called host.

(*a*) Non pathogenic (e.g. *Entamoeba coli*) and pathogenic (e.g. *Entamoeba histolytica*).

(*b*) Temporary/Intermittent (e.g. female mosquito) and permanent (e.g. *Ascaris*).

(*c*) Ectoparasite (e.g. Aphids, Lice) and endoparasite (e.g. intracellular *Plasmodium*, tissue parasite *Trichinella*).

(*d*) Holoparasite (complete parasite, e.g. animal parasites) or hemiparasite (semiparasite e.g. *Lovanthus*).

(*e*) Stem parasite (e.g. Cuscuta, stem borer) root parasite (e.g. *Rafflesia,* rootnematodes).

(*f*) *Hyperparasite :* Parasite over parasite e.g. *Cicinnobolus cesatii* on powdery mildew.

At times the parasite spread in *epidemic* form and causes large scale misery.

(*ix*) *Predation :* One organism called predator captures, kills and eath another organisms called prey. Predators are carnivorous but some herbivores which destroy whole plants/seeds are also called predators. A predator may become prey for another.

(*x*) *Negative Human Interactions :* They include primitive shifting agriculture (jhoom), felling of trees, hunting, overgrazing, scarping and litter removal, introduction of weeds, forest clearing and human induced forest fires.

(B) Biotic Stability : It is the absence of major fluctuations and the ability of a biotic community to undergo homeostasis or achieving equilibrium after a disturbance. It depends upon species diversity, presence of biological control, population density and carrying capacity of environment, biogeochemical cycling, seeding growth, degree of disturbance, climax/seral community, etc. The larger the number of species present in a biotic community, the more stable it is.

Maintenance of almost same number of different types of organisms within an ecosystem or biotic community is called 'balance of nature.'

(C) Biotic/Ecological Succession : It is the successive development of different biotic communities at the same site till a climax community develops there.

Even when the climate of an area remains stable year after year, ecosystems have a tendency to change from simple to complex in a process known as *succession.* This process is familiar to anyone who has seen a vacant lot or cleared woods slowly become occupied by an increasing number of plants, or a pond become dry land as it is filled with vegetation encroaching from the sides.

(*i*) *Primary Succession :* Primary succession occurs on base, lifeless substrate, such as rocks, or in open water, where organisms gradually move into an area and change its nature. Primary succession occurs in lakes left behind after the retereat of glaciers, on volcanic islands that rise above the sea, and on land exposed by retreating glaciers. Primary succession that occurs on land in called *XERARCH* succession, to distinguish it from the *hydrarch* primary succession that occurs in open water. Primary succession on glacial moraines provides an example. On bare, mineral-poor soils, lichens grow first, forming small pockets of soil. Acidic secretions from the lichens help to break down the substrate and add to the accumulation of soil. Mossess then colonize there pockets of soil, eventually building to take hold. Over a hundred years, the alders build up the soil nitrogen levels until spruce are able to thrive, eventually crowding out the older and forming a dense spruce forest.

In a similar example involving *Hydrach*

succession, an *oligotrophic* lake (poor in nutrients)—may gradually, by the accumulation of organic matter, become *eutrophic*—(rich in nutrients).

Primary succession in different habitats may over the long term arrive at the same kinds of vegetation—vegetation characteristic of the region as a whole. This relationship led American ecologist F.E. Clements, at about the turn of the century, to propose the concept of a final *climax vegetation* (and the related term 'climax community'). With an increasing realization that (1) the climate keeps changing, (2) The process of succession is often very slow, and (3) the nature of a region's vegetation is being determined to an increasing extent by human activities, ecologists do not consider the concept of 'climax vegetation' to be as useful as they once did.

(*ii*) *Secondary Succession :* If a wooded area is cleared and left alone, plants will slowly reclaim the area. Eventually, traces of the clearing will disappear and the area will again be woods. This kind of succession, which occurs in area where an existing community has been disturbed, is called *secondary succession.* Humans are often responsible for initiating secondary succession, but it may also take place when a fire has berned off an area, or in abandoned agricultural fields.

Why Succession Happens

"Communities evolve to have greater total biomass and species richness in a process called succession." In other words, succession happens because species alter the habitat and the resources available in it, often in ways that favour other species. There dynamic concepts are of critical importance in the process : tolerance, inhibition and facilitation.

(A) Tolerance : Early successioal stages are characterized by weedy-γ-selected species that do not complete well in established communities but are tolerant of the harsh, abiotic conditions in barren areas.

(B) Facilitation : The weedy early successional stages introduce local changes in the habitat that favour other, less weedy species. Thus, the mosses in the Glacier Bay succession fix nitrogen that allows alders to invade. The alders in turn lower soil pH as their fallen leaves decompose, and spruce and hemlock, which require acidic soil, are able to invade.

(C) Inhibition : Sometimes the changes in the habitat caused by one species, while favouring other species, inhibit the growth of the species that caused them. Alders, for example, do not grow as well in acidic soil as the spruce and hemlock that replace them.

As ecosystem mature, and more K-selected species replace γ-selected one, species richness and total biomass increase but net productivity decreases. Because earlier successional stages are more productive than later ones, agricultural systems are internationally maintained in early successional stage to keep net productivity high.

Primary succession takes long time of 1000 years or more while secondary succession takes 50-100 years for grass and 100-200 years for forest. *Ferns* are generally the first to grow after forest fire because of their underground rhizomes. Secondary succession is not completed if invaded by weeds e.g. *Sphagnum*, *Eichhornia*, *Lantana*, *Eupatorium*.

Pioneer Community : It is the first biotic community on a base area.

Seral Community : Transitional community appearing in an area during biotic succession.

Climax Community : Stable, self-perpetuating and final community appearing in an area and at the end of biotic succession which is in perfect harmony with climate of the area-hence *climate climax community*.

Dominant Species : It is the most numerous and generally the largest of the species present in a seral/climax community which exerts the maximum influence.

Sere : It is the sequence of developmental stages from pioneer to climax communities, e.g. Lithosere (on rock), psammosere (on sand), hydrosere (in water). *Xerarch/Hydrarch* : series of developmental stages in an area/water body. Biotic succession involves changes to long-lived plants, greater species diversity, niche specialisation, increase in biomass, higher soil humus, food webs, stable biotic community and mesic conditions.

So one can say that causes of succession are as follow :

(*i*) Baring of an area

(*ii*) Changes brought about by pioneer and seral

communities not favourable to them but favourable to next ones.

Lithosere-Xerosere (Succession on Bare Rocks) :

(A) Lichen Stage : Bare rock is invaded first by *crustose* lichens (e.g. *Graphis, Rhizocarpon*). They corrode the rock at places causing *foliose lichens* (e.g. *Parmelia, Dermatocarpon*) to invade, eliminate crustose lichens and creating conditions for invasion by mosses. In tropics, blue green algae are pioneers instead of lichens.

(B) Moss Stage : Mosses capable of tolerating drough invade the human rich holes created by foliose lichens, e.g. *Tortula, Grimmia, Polytrichum*. They create more humus and shade to eliminate lichens.

(C) Annual Grass Stage : Annual grasses are slowly replaced by perennial grasses with runners and rhizomes, e.g. *Heteropogon, Cymbopogon*. Several small animals begin to reside. Herbivorous animals visit the site.

(D) Shrub Stage : Shrubs begin to grow in area occupied by perennial grasses. They increases soil and humus contents besides moisture, e.g. *Rubus, Rhus, Capparis, Zyzyphus*.

(E) Climax Community : Initially hardy, light demanding small trees invade the area. They make the habitat shadier and move moist. Ultimately, trees shrubs and herbs representing the climax community begin to grow in the area.

Hydrosere :

(A) Plankton Stage : Phytoplanktons (diatoms, flagellates, blue green algae and green algae) are the pioneers in a freshly formed water body. They are almost immediately followed by zooplanktons that feed on phytoplanktons. Plakton growth produces organic matter which gets mixed with bottom silt for growth of next stage.

(B) Submerged Stage : *Hydrilla, Potamogeton* and *Najas* form dense growth at bottom enriched with organic matter.

(C) Floating Stage : In the shallower regions appear plants with tuberous rhizomatous and creeping stems and leaves floating on the surface of water, e.g. *Nymphaea, Nelumbo*. at places, free floating plants also appear (e.g. *Azolla, Wolffia, Lemna*) to cover to the water surface. Humus rich bottom begins to rise making water shallower.

(D) Red Swamp Stage : In shallower water, amphibian plants (with emergent leaves begin to grow (e.g. *Sagittaria, Typha, Phragmites*). They add more silt and humus at the bottom so that shoves built up.

(E) Sedge/Marsh Meadow Stage : On newly built up shores, *Larese* (Sedge), Juncus, Cyperus, some grasses and herbs (Themeda,Caltha, Polygonum) grow rapidly and lower the water table.

(F) Woodland Stage : Rhizome bearing shrubs and small trees capable of tolerating excessive light and water logged conditions appear on the edges of sedge/marsh meadow, e.g. *Cormus, Cephalanthus, Populus, Alnus*.

(G) Climax Stage : New trees, shrubs and herbs appear which are in perfect harmony with the climate of the area.

Concept of Biosphere

Biosphere/ecosphere is the living mantle or biologically inhabited part of earth (soil, water and air from depth of oceans to tops of mountains) alongwith its abiotic physico-chemical compound. Biosphere extends to some 22.5 km. Life is most abundant at the interfaces of sea, air and earth. Foundation/maintenance of life is based on (*i*) Flow of energy (*ii*) Circulation of nutrients or biogeochemical cycles.

Subdivisions of Biosphere : Biosphere consists three interacting subdivisions, viz., atmosphere, lithosphere and hydrosphere.

(*i*) **Atmosphere :** It is the transparent gaseous mantle surrounding the earth which extends to several kilometers and in differentiated into troposphere (10-18 km), stratosphere (18-50 km), mesophere (50-85 km), thermosphere (85-500 km) and exosphere (500 km to about 1600 km). Troposphere shows lowering of temperature with height (15°C to – 55°C), cloud formation and manifestation of weather conditions. Dust particles are restricted to its lower part. Stratophere contains an *ozonosphere* or ozone layer (for filtering ultraviolet rays) at a height of about 25 km. Ozone (O_3) is produced by action of ultraviolet and other high energy radiations on oxygen, resulting in splitting and interaction of oxygen molecules ($3O_2 \rightarrow 2O_3$). *Ionosphere* is a region of thermosphere which is protective and radioreflective.

(*ii*) **Lithosphere :** It is outer solid crust of earth. The exposed part or soil supports terrestrial life. It possesses minerals, moisture and organic matter.

(*iii*) **Hydrosphere :** Hydrosphere is liquid mantle of earth. It is differentiated into fresh water sea water. Both air and water are essential for supporting life.

Closed and Open System : Earth is an open system of energy. It is continuously receiving solar energy. A fraction of it is trapped by autotrophs. Rest is emitted back as heat waves. Earth is closed system for materials, neither receiving (except for occasional meteorites) nor giving out anyway. There is recycling of materials/matter between biotic and abiotic components of biosphere. Energy flows through the biosphere to consumers, consumers to consumers organisms to microbes, as also dissipating as heat.

Ecosystems and their Conservation

Ecosystem or biocenosis is a segments of nature/ biosphere consisting of a community of living beings and the abiotic/physical environment both interacting and exchanging materials between them. Ecosystem can be temporary (e.g. rain water pond) or permanent, natural or man-made (e.g. aquarium, agriculture), small or large.

Biotic Components : They include all living beings present in an ecosystem producers, consumers and decomposers. The component are connected through food, its contained energy and a web of interrelationships.

(A) Producers : They are autotrophs that manufacture organic compounds from inorganic raw materials with the help of solar energy. Producers are also called *transducers* as they convert solar radiations into chemical energy. Besides food, producers give out oxygen and take in carbon dioxide.

(B) Consumers : They are heterotrophs, mostly animals which feed on other organisms. Consumers are also called *phagotrophes* as they ingest food. *Herbivores/First Order Consumers.* They feed on producers. Also called key industry animals (Elton, 1927), e.g. Deer, Rabbit, Cattle, Goat/Sheep, Grasshopper, protozoans, molluscs, many crustaceans. *Primary Carnivores/second orders consumers.* Feed on primary carnivores, e.g. Owl, Peacock. *Top Carnivores.* Carnivores which are not preyed upon. e.g Lion.

(C) Decomposers : They are saprotrophs which decompose the organic remains by secreting extracellular digestive enzymes. Due to degradation of organic remains, decomposers are also called *reducers*. They are also known as mineralisers as they release minerals trapped in organic remains. *Detrivores* are decomposers, as well as scavengers. Scavangers are consumers of dead bodies, e.g. Vulture, Carrion Beetle. Parasites are consumers that feed on small part of a living being.

Abiotic Components : (*a*) Temperature (*b*) Light (*c*) Wind/Air current (*d*) Humidity/Precipitution (*e*) Water (*f*) Topography (*g*) Back ground.

Trophic Levels

They are steps or divisions of food chain characterised by specific method of obtaining food. Producers belong to T_1 or first trophic level, herbivores/primary consumers T_2, primary carnivores/ secondary consumers T_3, secondary carnivores T_4 etc. Parasites do not have any fixed trophic level. Decomposers constitute the last or deteritus trophic level. *Guild* is the group of species belonging to the same trophic level and exploiting the same resource.

(A) Food Chain : It is the sequence of populations/organisms through which food and its contained energy pass in an ecosystem with members at one step becoming food of later step of the sequence. Common food chains are predator food chains.

Detritus food chain is the *shortest*. Parasitic food chain is the third type.

(*a*) *Aquatic Food Chain :*

Phytoplankton → Zooplankton → Small Crustaceans → Water Insects → Small Fish → Larger Fish → King Fishes.

(*b*) *Land Food Chain :*

- Grass → Grasshopper → Frog → Snake → Peacock → Falcon → Eagle.
- Herbs → Rabbit → Fox → Wolf → Tiger

(B) Food Web : It is a network of food chains which are interconnected at different trophic levels so as to form a number of feeding connections amongst members of a biotic community. e.g. Rabbits preyed upon by Wild dog, Fox, Wild cat and Jackal. These carnivores can also prey upon mice, shrews, and squarrels. Wolf preys upon Jackal, Fox, Wild cat and Sheep/goat. It is eaten by Tiger. Tiger preys upon Deer, Antelope and a number of other animals. In Sunderbans, Tiger does not have its natural preys. It feeds there on fish and crabs.

Flow of Energy

Ecosystem is continuously obtaining solar energy which is trapped by producers—1.15% in grasslands, 0.9% in Savannah, 0.81% in mixed forest, 5% in crops and 10-12% in sugarcane. The rest is dissipated as heat. A part of energy stored in food is released during respiration. Some of the released energy is used in carrying out body activities while the rest is dissipated. Herbivores feed on producers. Part of the food energy is wasted in digestion and assimilation. Some of the assimilated food is broken down to release energy for performing body activities.

Some of the energy is lost as heat. A very small portion becomes part of the body of herbivore. Herbivores are eaten by primary carnivores, the latter by secondary carnivores and so on. At every step, a lot of energy is wasted. Flow of energy in an ecosystem is unidirectional.

Ecological Pyramids/Eltonian Pyramids (Elton, 1927)

Ecological pyramid is the graphic representation of an ecological parameter (number, biomass, energy) sequence-wise in various trophic levels of a food chain. It can be upright, inverted or spindle-shaped.

(*a*) *Pyramid of Numbers :* It is an ecological/ eltorian pyramid which employs the numbers of individuals per unit area at various trophic levels sequence-wise with producers at the base and various consumers at successively higher levels. It is generally *upright* as maximum number of individuals occur at the producer level, followed by smaller number of herbivores, fewer primary carnivores and still fewer higher levels of carnivores. However, a single large-sized tree can provide food to several herbivores (e.g. birds, squirrels) which support a few carnivores. Such a pyramid of number is *spindle shaped.* When the herbivores support a large number. of ecotoparasites, which are further parasitised by still larger number of hyperparasites, the pyramid of numbers is *inverted.*

(*b*) *Pyramid of Biomass : Biomass :* It is the amount of living matter present in the individual/ population/community/trophic level/ecosystem. Biomass is measured on both fresh and dry weight basis. It is ecological/electronian pyramid which represents the biomass in various trophic levels. It is more real than the numbers at various trophic levels. Only 10-20% biomass is transferred from one trophic level to the next – 10% law. 1000 kg (one tonne) vegetation shall form only 100 kg of herbivore, 10 kg of primary carnivore, 1 kg of secondary carnivore and only 0.1 kg of tertiary carnivore. Therefore, with increasing dependence on animal diet (nonvegetarian), the human population will require higher amount of farm produces—total nonvegetarian 10 times, 50% non vegetarian 5 times, vegetarian with milk 1.5 times. Pyramid of biomass is upright, exception equatic food chain involving short lived plankton (biomass at one time will be less than consumers at higher levels.

(c) *Pyramid of Energy :* It is ecological/eltorian pyramid that gives graphic representation of amount of energy trapped by different traphic levels per unit area. It is always upright because during transfer of energy from one trophic level to the next, a lot of wastage occurs in feeding, digestion, assimilation and respiration.

Homoestasis/Biological Equilibrium

It is the maintenance of a functional dynamic balance or state of equilibrium amongst various components of an ecosystem. Homeostasis is maintained through a number of controls/cybernetics/ limitations like :

(*i*) Carrying Capacity : It is the maximum number of individuals the environment can support. Near it, the rate of population growth begins to decline. Beyond it, the population decreases rapidly.

(*ii*) Recycling of Wastes : It controls the availability of raw materials and space.

(*iii*) Self regulation : Mortality decreases and natility increases in case of small population while reverse is true in case of larger population.

(*iv*) Feedback System : It is of two types, positive and negative. In *positive feedback* the increased availability of a resource increase number of utilisers.

For example, predator population will increase with the increase in population of prey. In *negative feedback*, the increase in number of members of a higher trophic level will decrease the number of individuals at the lower level which in turn shall reduce their number as well.

Habitat : It is a specific place/locality delimited by a combination of factors and barriers where an individual/population/community resides, e.g. pond, desert, river, bark of tree, burrow, intestine.

Microhabitat : It is part of the habitat having a specific property, e.g. forest floor, tree canopy, tree trunk, edge of a pond.

Niche/Ecological Niche : It is specific/part of habitat occupied by individuals of a species which is circumscribed by its range of tolerance, range of movement, microclimate, type of food and its availability, shelter, type of predator, timing of activity. Tadpole and adult frog occupy different ecological niches as the former is herbivorous aquatic while the latter is carnivorous amphibian. Water Bug and water Boatman live in shallow edges of ponds but occupy different niches as the former is predator while the latter scavenger. Both owl and cat feed on shrews and mice. They occupy the same niche because of being *ecological equivalents* though their habitats are different.

Life Forms

Raunkiarer (1934) has distinguished plants into five forms on the basis of size, shape, branching, crown, life span and perennation.

(*i*) *Therophytes :* Annual plants which perennate in the form of seeds.

(*ii*) *Cryptophytes :* Perennial plants with underground storage parts,

(*a*) *Geophytes :* Subterranean perennating structures (root, root tuber, bulb, stem tuber, rhizome, corm).

(*b*) *Helophytes :* (Marshy plants). Perennating structures are embedded in mud.

(*c*) *Hydrophytes :* Aquatic plants.

(*iii*) *Hemicryptophytes :* Peremating structures occur at ground level. Aerial shoots die on the onset of winter, e.g. rosette plants.

(*iv*) *Chemaephytes :* Small plants of cold areas where perennating buds or shoot apices lie at or above the ground level.

(*v*) *Phanerophytes :* Pernnial herbs, shrubs, and trees, epiphytes, succulenty lianas etc. where perennating buds occur at 10 cm or more heigh above ground level.

Biomes/Major Ecosystems

Biomes are major ecosystems delimited by particular climates or geographical areas, e.g. Marsh, Desert, Tundra, Pond, Sea.

Ecotone : It is transitional or overlapping zone between two biomes where plants/animals of both the biomes are found.

Major Biomes : They are of two types, terrestrial and aquatic. The terrestrial biomes include tundra, taiga, deciduous forest, tropical rain forest, chapparal tropical savannah, grassland and desert. Aquatic biomes include ocean lake, pond, marsh and stream.

(A) Tundra/Arctic Tundra : It lies north of 60° N in North America. Europe and Asia. Precipitation is 25 cm/yr, mostly as snow. Winter temperature is – 30° to – 40°C. Summer is for 45-75 days with highest temperature of 10°C. Ponds, pools, marshes, bogs occur during summer. Lower part of soil is under permafrost. Tundra is *arctic desert* with *mosses* (e.g. *Sphagnum*) lichens (*Cladonia*), grasses, sidges, dwarf willow (*Salix*), dwarf birch (*Betula*) and a few shrubs. Amphibians and reptiles are absent. Arthoropods and worms appear during summer. Common animals are lemmings, Snow Grouse, Snow Owl, Arctic Fox, Polar Bear, Arctic Hare, Caribou, Reindeer. Polar Bear, *hibernates* during winter while Reindeer and caribou migrate to less cold areas.

(*a*) **Alpine/Alpine Tundra :** It is treeless area on high mountains (above 3500 m) which has snow for long months. It is well drained and sloppy. Plants include lichens, mosses, grasses, herbs, small shrubs (e.g. *Artemesia, Primula*) and dwarf trees (*Juniperus*). Animals are Snow Leopond , Snow Bear, Mountain Goat, and migratory birds.

(B) Taiga/North Coniferous Forest : Taiga occurs is temperate areas (mostly Northern Hamisphere, parts of New Zealand) with precipitation both as snow and rain (variable). Winters are chilly while summers are pleased. Marches have cotton grass and *Sphagnum*. Vegetation consists of evergreen conifers—Deodar (*cectrus*), Larch, Juniper, Spruce, Fir, Pine, Hemlock, Yew. They are adapted to severe cold winters. The needle like leaves lose very little in transpiration. Being green, they continue to manufacture food, Broad-Leaved Birch, Mple, Poplar and Aspen occur at places. Lichens, mosses, ferns and herbs are abundant. Ground has thick covering of fallen needles us the latter decay slowly. Fauna includes Wolf, Deer, Rabbit, Hare, Weasel, Elk, Beaver, Pumas, Squirrels, RAven, Muskrat, Porcupine, Lynx, Grouse and Jay. Migration from Tundra (Reindeer, Caribou) and from here to warmer places is quite common.

(C) Temperate Deciduous Forests : The areas have warm summer and moderately cool winter. Rainfall is 75-150 cm. Dominant trees are Oak, Elm, Birch, Maple Ash, Chestnut, Hickory, Beech, Poplar and Magnolia. Conifers occur at places. Shrubs, herbs, ferns, mosses, lichens, grasses vines and epiphytes are abundant. Most trees shed their leaves during autumn or fall making the soil brown. A mixed coniferous-broad leaved forest occurs in Indian hills between 1500-3500 m. Trees height can reach 30-40 m. Fauna consists of Deer, Fox, Beaves, Wild Cat, Racoon, Opossum, Squirrel, Rabbit, Hare, Snakes, Lizards, Salamanders, Thrushes, Owls, Sparrows, Song birds.

(D) Tropical Deciduous Forests : Climate is warm with alternate wet and dry periods. Rainfall is 100-200 cm. Vegetation includes broad leaved trees which shed their leaves during dry season, e.g. Butea, *Bonbax*,*Shorea*, *Dalbergia*. Famous Sal (*Shorea*), Teak (*Tectona*) and Samdal (*Santalum*) forests of India belong to their category. Animal population is similar to evergreen tropical forests.

(E) Tropical Evergreen/Rain Forests : The biome occurs over equatorial/subequatorial regions with abundant warmth and rainfall (200-1000 cm/yr) almost throughout the year. The forest are impenetrable (= jungle) with maximum *diversity*, 200 types of trees in one hectare, 70-80% of all insects and 80-85% of all birds. *Productivity* is also maximum 12,000 K cal/m^2/yr as compared to 2000 K cal/m^2/yr for taiga. The forests occurs in famous congo basin of Africa and Amazon basin in South America. In India they occur in Western Ghats, Assam and Andamans Vegetation shows *stratification* (layering), emergent tree layer (50 m or more), understorey tree layer, shrub layer and ground layer. Epiphytes, climbers, mosses, ferns and orchids are abundant. Trees include Cinnamon, Mahogony, Ebony, Rosewood, Rubber Tree, Nutmeg, Artacarpus, Fig etc. Palms, plantains and bamboos occur here and there. Fauna consists of Deer, Goat, Antelope, Tapir, Elephant, Leopard, Jaguar, Snakes, Lizards, monkeys, lemurs, bats, sloths, parakeets, Toucan, Birds of Paradise and several others.

Chapparal : It is a broad-leaved scrub-forest (sclerophyllous or thick leaved shrubs and small trees) found in Mediterranean and pacific coast of several countries with winter rain and dry summer. Bush fires are common. Several plants are fire resistant including *Sage*, *Arctostaphylos*, *Adenostemma* and *Coenothus*. Trees of Oak and *Eucalyptus*, (in Australia) occur at places. Fauna consists of rabbits, chipmunks, deer, tiger, rats, snakes, lizards and birds.

(F) Tropical Savannah : It is a warm climate plain with coarse grasses, scattered shrubs and trees, seasoned rain (wet and dry periods) and frequent fire. Savannah is named after dominant tree like *Acacia*, *Phoenix*, *Eucalyptus*. Hoofed herbivores are quite common. Animals include Antelope, Zebra, Giraffe, Goat, Gazelle, Rhino, Elephand, Fox, Wolf, Lion. Tiger, Kangaroo (in Australia).

(G) Grassland : Grases are dominant with nongraminaceous herbs, scattered bushes and occasional tree, e.g. prairies of USA/Canada, pampas of South America, Steppes of Eurasia, tussocks of New Zealand and Veldts of South Africa. There is hot summer, cold winter, seasonal 25-75 cm rainfall. Grasses can be short or long. Fauna consists of Deer, Elk, Bison, Wolf, Prairie Dog, Bear, Bighorn Sheep, Rabbit, Mice, Budges, Coyote, Burrowing owl.

(H) Desert : It occupies about 1/5 of land. It lacks rain (less than 25 cm) due to either being present in rain shadow (area beyond high mountains which cut of clouds, e.g. Tibet), lack of cloud intercrepting mountains (e.g. Thar) or leging away from cloud seeding regions, e.g.

Death Valley (Great Western Deserts) of USA, Shara (Africa), Gobi, Arabian and Thar of Asia.

Rajasthan lies in the Thar desert. Deserts can be cold (e.g. Tibet, Gobi) and hot (e.g. Thar, Sahara). Ground is sandy or rocky. Vegetation is sparse consisting of Cacti, euphorbia (succulents) *Acacia, Phoenix, Tamarix, Echinops, Aerua* etc. Animals are Kangaroo Desert Rat, Hare, Fox Jackal, Cat, Rattle Snake, Coral Snake, lizards (Gila, Monster, Horned Lizard), spiders, scorpions, locusts, ants, wasps and a number of birds like Swifts, Swallows, Quails, Doves, etc. Camel is adapted to desert conditions as it can protect its eyes and nostrils from dust, has insulated spreading feet, and is capable of tolerating dehydration upto 40% with highly reduced urine output.

(I) Oceanic Biome : Oceans occupy 75% of earth's surface with salinity of 3.5% (0.5% in Red Sea and 1% Baltic Sea), temperature of 28°C on surface in equatorial region (colder below) and 0°C near poles (warmer below). Continental shelf is gradually sloping (0%) sea shore upto 160 km and depth of 8-200 m. It passes into continental slope (3°-6°) which leads to *ocean floor* at a depth of 6 km-10 km. There littoral zone in continental shelf and a neritic zone above the same. The open seal pelagic part is differentiated into *photic zone* (upto 200 m depth, light penetrates the zone), *aphotic zone* (200-2000 m depth, little light) and *abyssal zone* (dark zone), *epipelagic* (photic zone), *mesopelagic* (alphotic zone), *bathy belagic* (2000 m to near ocean floor) and *abyssopelagic* (ocean floor).

(J) Open Ocean : Productivity is 1000 K cal/m^2/yr. The surface has phytoplankton (diatoms, dinoflagellates, other unicellular and multicellular algae, some luminescent flagellates), 300 plankton (protozoans larvae, crustacens) and *neuston* (photosynthetic like *Sargassum*, phagotrophic like some crabs, gustropods, jelly dishes, *physallia*). The surface as well as lower part has necton/nekton or swimming animals like turtles, snakes, squids, fishes, marine birds, etc. producers are absent in deep water. The abyssal zone contains only carnivores/predators. Some of them have luminescent organs (e.g. Devil Fish, Hatchet Fish), baits (e.g. Angles Fish), large heads (Granadier Fish, Gulper Eel). The benthonic region has scavengers and decomposes.

(K) Coastal Region : Productivity is 2000-6000 K cal/m^2/yr.. The important producers of intesdial regions are *Dictyota*, Ulva, *Fucus*, *Polysiphoria*, *Enteromorpha*, *Cladophora*, *Zostena* (the only seed plant) besides phytoplankton. Consumers include Zooplankton, biralves, snails, crabs, barnades, sponges, bryozoans, *Nereis*, Star Fish, Sea Urchin, tunicates etc. In littoral zone there are strong waves. Attached algae include *Laminaria*, *Macrocystis*, *Neroecystis*, *Alaria*, *Gelidium*, & *Corallian*.

Lithothamnion, consumer of the area are sponges, corals, polychaetes, tunicates and sea anemones. Nekton of the neritic zone also visit the area. *Neritic zone* (constant water, pelagic) has plankton, neuston and necton. *Coral reef* is the area of maximum productivity and diversity.

(L) Estuary : Tidal mout of river/coastal bay where there is mixing of fresh and sea water. Highly productive due to turbulence. There are fluctuations in temperature and salinity. Species found are phytoplankton (blue-green algae, green algae, diatoms, dinoflagellates), zooplankton (protozoans, crustaceans, rotifers), necton (fishes and some crustaceans) and benthon (attached algae, snails, clams, prawns etc.)

(M) Pond/Lake Biome : Ponds and lakes are stationary fresh waters. Deep lakes and brackish lakes are oligotrohic with sparse biota due to little circulation of nutrients. Shallow lakes and ox-bow (from main stream of river) lakes are *eutrophic* with rich biota and quick circulation of nutrients. Ponds are generally shallower with depth less than 2 m. Producers includes phytoplankton (e.g. diatoms, desmids, *Chlorella*, *Chlamydomonas*, *Spirogyra*, *Oedogmium*, *Zygnema*, free floating macrophytes (e.g. Lemna, Pistia, Azolla, suspended macrophytes (e.g. Utricularia, Ceratophyllum, Hydrilla), submerged, anchored plants (e.g. Scirpus, Sagittaria, Phragmites).

Consumers comprise zooplankton (ciliates, flagellates, rotifers, small crustaceans like *cyclops* and *Daphnia*, larvae), necton (e.g. Water Boatman, Water Spider, Diving Beetle, amphilians, burtles, fishes) and benthon (e.g. snails, clams, mussels, crabs, prawns). A number of decomposers also occur on the bottom. Water birds include Duck, Heron, Crane and Kingfisher.

(N) Marsh Biome : It is turbid muddy biome with little planktons. Flora includes emergent hydrophytes (e.g. *Typha, Phragmites*), *Sphagnum* and *Eichhornia*. Fauna consists of snails, mosquito larvae, some insects and frogs.

(O) Lotic/River Biome : It has high speed and low temperature in upper reaches. Water becomes muddy during rains. Detritus form land constitutes important component of food. Produces grow along shallow banks with very slow moving water. They include attached algae, encrusting diatoms, aquatic mosses (e.g. *Fontinalis*) submerged seed plants, reeds, water grasses etc. Consumers are more abundant including flatworms nymphs, larvae, snails, fishes, otter, mink, muskrat, crocodile etc.

(P) Man-Made/Artificial Ecosystem : They include aquaria, dams, parks, gardens, orchards, plantations, human settlements and agriculture. Artificial or man-made ecosystems have little diversity (generally monocultures), little recycling of nutrients and no self regulatory mechanisms. Agriculture (crop raising, animal husbandry) has created an agroecosystem which differs from place to place depending upon climate, latitude, topographic and edaphic factors. *Agroecology* is the study of relationships between agricultural crops and there surrounding animate as well as inanimate environment. Biotic community is rich when crop is in the field-crop, weeds, pests, birds, polinators, nematodes, earth worms, insects, rodents, birds and decomposers. Since there is little circulation of nutrients, agroecosystem is artifically irrigated, provided wil biogenetic nutrients, protected from weeds, pests and pathogens. There is little accumulation of biomass. Manure is, therefore added. Technology is being increasingly used in creating new varieties, sowing and reaping.

Conservation of Ecosystem

Some of the man's activities like hunting of various animals, disrupts the food chains in which there animals normally take parts. The shortening of food chains due to man's activities leads to an imbalance in the functioning of an ecosystem and ultimately in the functioning of the whole biosphere. Modern argicultural activities use a large number of toxic chemicals like pesticides, weedicides and rodenticides, to protect the crop plants from pests and diseases. Some of these poisonous chemicals mix-up with soil and water and are absorbed by the plants from the soil along with water other minerals. In this way, the poisonous chemical substances enter the food chain right from the producer level. When man and other animals eat these plants or their products, the poisonous chemical substances are transformed to their bodies. During the process of food transfer through trophic levels, there harmful chemicals get concentrated at each successive level. The increase in concentration of harmful chemical substances like perticides in the body of living organisms at each trophic level of a food chain is called *biological magnification*. To consume ecosystem, such activities should be minimised.

QUESTIONS FROM PREVIOUS YEARS' PAPERS

1. Write short notes on the following:
   (*a*) Carbon cycle in an ecosystem (Give diagrammatic representation).
   (*b*) Acid rain and its impact on vegetation and human habitation.
   (*c*) Community dynamics.
   (*d*) Conservation of endangered plant species.
   (*e*) Water Pollution
2. What is meant by smog? How does somg affect vegetation and human health?
3. Give a brief account of various factors responsible for water pollution. Suggest methods to control water pollution of important rivers of India.
4. Write short notes on the following;
   (*a*) Ecosystem
   (*b*) Kranz Syndrome
   (*c*) Social Forestry
   (*d*) Air pollution
   (*e*) Global warming
5. Where are the National Botanical Gardens and Lloyd Botanical Gardens? How are the herbaria in botanical gardens arranged.
6. Define and distinguish any *four* major ecosystems of India.

7. What do you understand by ecosystem?
8. How would you maintain an ecosystem?
9. Discuss the causes and consequences of water pollution.
10. What is meant by biodiversity and how can it be conserved?
11. Enumerate various forest types of India.
12. Explain the concepts and dynamics of Community.
13. Describe the characteristics of different categories of Aquatic ecosystem.
14. Write short notes on the following:
    (*a*) Bioindicators
    (*b*) Red Data Books
    (*c*) Intellectual Property Rights
15. Explain the characteristics of various forest types of India.
16. Explain forests as renewable resources.
17. What is the significance of ozone layer? What are the contributing factors for its depletion and what can be the possible consequences?
18. Illustrate the energy flow in an aquatic ecosystem.
19. Give a comparative account on the biogeochemical cycle of nitrogen and phosphorus.
20. Describe any two biogeochemical cycles studied by you.
21. Examine various aspects of global warming and suggests suitable measures to control the same.

YOUR SPACE

YOUR SPACE

YOUR SPACE